EDGAR ALLAN POE

EDGAR ALLAN POE

ESSAYS AND REVIEWS
Theory of Poetry
Reviews of British and Continental Authors
Reviews of American Authors and American Literature
Magazines and Criticism
The Literary and Social Scene
Articles and Marginalia

THE LIBRARY OF AMERICA

Distributed to the trade in the United States
by Penguin Books USA Inc
and in Canada by Penguin Books Canada Ltd.

The paper used in this publication meets the
minimum requirements of the American National Standard
for Information Sciences—Permanence of Paper for
Printed Library Materials, ANSI Z39.48–1984.

Library of Congress Catalog Card Number: 83-19923
For cataloging information, see end of *Notes* section.
ISBN 0-940450-19-4

Fifth Printing
The Library of America—20

Manufactured in the United States of America

G. R. THOMPSON
WROTE THE NOTES AND SELECTED
THE CONTENTS FOR THIS VOLUME

Contents

Each section has its own table of contents.

THEORY OF POETRY

Contents

Letter to B——*

IT HAS BEEN SAID that a good critique on a poem may be written by one who is no poet himself. This, according to *your* idea and *mine* of poetry, I feel to be false—the less poetical the critic, the less just the critique, and the converse. On this account, and because there are but few B——'s in the world, I would be as much ashamed of the world's good opinion as proud of your own. Another than yourself might here observe, "Shakspeare is in possession of the world's good opinion, and yet Shakspeare is the greatest of poets. It appears then that the world judge correctly, why should you be ashamed of their favorable judgment?" The difficulty lies in the interpretation of the word "judgment" or "opinion." The opinion is the world's, truly, but it may be called theirs as a man would call a book his, having bought it; he did not write the book, but it is his; they did not originate the opinion, but it is theirs. A fool, for example, thinks Shakspeare a great poet—yet the fool has never read Shakspeare. But the fool's neighbor, who is a step higher on the Andes of the mind, whose head (that is to say his more exalted thought) is too far above the fool to be seen or understood, but whose feet (by which I mean his every-day actions) are sufficiently near to be discerned, and by means of which that superiority is ascertained, which *but* for them would never have been discovered—this neighbor asserts that Shakspeare is a great poet—the fool believes him, and it is henceforward his *opinion*. This neighbor's own opinion has, in like manner, been adopted from one above *him*, and so, ascendingly, to a few gifted individuals, who kneel around the summit, beholding, face to face, the master spirit who stands upon the pinnacle.   *   *   *   *

You are aware of the great barrier in the path of an American writer. He is read, if at all, in preference to the combined and established wit of the world. I say established; for it is

*These detached passages form part of the preface to a small volume printed some years ago for private circulation. They have vigor and much originality—but of course we shall not be called upon to endorse all the writer's opinions.—*Ed.*

with literature as with law or empire—an established name is an estate in tenure, or a throne in possession. Besides, one might suppose that books, like their authors, improve by travel—their having crossed the sea is, with us, so great a distinction. Our antiquaries abandon time for distance; our very fops glance from the binding to the bottom of the title-page, where the mystic characters which spell London, Paris, or Genoa, are precisely so many letters of recommendation.

*   *   *

I mentioned just now a vulgar error as regards criticism. I think the notion that no poet can form a correct estimate of his own writings is another. I remarked before, that in proportion to the poetical talent, would be the justice of a critique upon poetry. Therefore, a bad poet would, I grant, make a false critique, and his self-love would infallibly bias his little judgment in his favor; but a poet, who is indeed a poet, could not, I think, fail of making a just critique. Whatever should be deducted on the score of self-love, might be replaced on account of his intimate acquaintance with the subject; in short, we have more instances of false criticism than of just, where one's own writings are the test, simply because we have more bad poets than good. There are of course many objections to what I say: Milton is a great example of the contrary; but his opinion with respect to the Paradise Regained, is by no means fairly ascertained. By what trivial circumstances men are often led to assert what they do not really believe! Perhaps an inadvertent word has descended to posterity. But, in fact, the Paradise Regained is little, if at all, inferior to the Paradise Lost, and is only supposed so to be, because men do not like epics, whatever they may say to the contrary, and reading those of Milton in their natural order, are too much wearied with the first to derive any pleasure from the second.

I dare say Milton preferred Comus to either—if so—justly.   *   *   *   *   *   *   *   *   *

As I am speaking of poetry, it will not be amiss to touch slightly upon the most singular heresy in its modern history—the heresy of what is called very foolishly, the Lake

School. Some years ago I might have been induced, by an occasion like the present, to attempt a formal refutation of their doctrine; at present it would be a work of supererogation. The wise must bow to the wisdom of such men as Coleridge and Southey, but being wise, have laughed at poetical theories so prosaically exemplified.

Aristotle, with singular assurance, has declared poetry the most philosophical of all writing*—but it required a Wordsworth to pronounce it the most metaphysical. He seems to think that the end of poetry is, or should be, instruction—yet it is a truism that the end of our existence is happiness; if so, the end of every separate part of our existence—every thing connected with our existence should be still happiness. Therefore the end of instruction should be happiness; and happiness is another name for pleasure;—therefore the end of instruction should be pleasure: yet we see the above mentioned opinion implies precisely the reverse.

To proceed: ceteris paribus, he who pleases, is of more importance to his fellow men than he who instructs, since utility is happiness, and pleasure is the end already obtained which instruction is merely the means of obtaining.

I see no reason, then, why our metaphysical poets should plume themselves so much on the utility of their works, unless indeed they refer to instruction with eternity in view; in which case, sincere respect for their piety would not allow me to express my contempt for their judgment; contempt which it would be difficult to conceal, since their writings are professedly to be understood by the few, and it is the many who stand in need of salvation. In such case I should no doubt be tempted to think of the devil in Melmoth, who labors indefatigably through three octavo volumes, to accomplish the destruction of one or two souls, while any common devil would have demolished one or two thousand.

*   *   *

Against the subtleties which would make poetry a study—not a passion—it becomes the metaphysician to reason—

*Spoudiotaton kai philosophikotaton genos.

but the poet to protest. Yet Wordsworth and Coleridge are men in years; the one imbued in contemplation from his child-hood, the other a giant in intellect and learning. The diffidence, then, with which I venture to dispute their authority, would be over-whelming, did I not feel, from the bottom of my heart, that learning has little to do with the imagination—intellect with the passions—or age with poetry.   *   *   *   *   *   *   *   *   *

"Trifles, like straws, upon the surface flow,
    He who would search for pearls must dive below,"

are lines which have done much mischief. As regards the greater truths, men oftener err by seeking them at the bottom than at the top; the depth lies in the huge abysses where wisdom is sought—not in the palpable palaces where she is found. The ancients were not always right in hiding the goddess in a well: witness the light which Bacon has thrown upon philosophy; witness the principles of our divine faith—that moral mechanism by which the simplicity of a child may overbalance the wisdom of a man.

We see an instance of Coleridge's liability to err, in his Biographia Literaria—professedly his literary life and opinions, but, in fact, a treatise *de omni scibili et quibusdam aliis*. He goes wrong by reason of his very profundity, and of his error we have a natural type in the contemplation of a star. He who regards it directly and intensely sees, it is true, the star, but it is the star without a ray—while he who surveys it less inquisitively is conscious of all for which the star is useful to us below—its brilliancy and its beauty.

*   *   *

As to Wordsworth, I have no faith in him. That he had, in youth, the feelings of a poet I believe—for there are glimpses of extreme delicacy in his writings—(and delicacy is the poet's own kingdom—his *El Dorado*)—but they have the appearance of a better day recollected; and glimpses, at best, are little evidence of present poetic fire—we know that a few straggling flowers spring up daily in the crevices of the glacier.

He was to blame in wearing away his youth in contemplation with the end of poetizing in his manhood. With the increase of his judgment the light which should make it apparent has faded away. His judgment consequently is too correct. This may not be understood,—but the old Goths of Germany would have understood it, who used to debate matters of importance to their State twice, once when drunk, and once when sober—sober that they might not be deficient in formality—drunk lest they should be destitute of vigor.

The long wordy discussions by which he tries to reason us into admiration of his poetry, speak very little in his favor: they are full of such assertions as this—(I have opened one of his volumes at random) "Of genius the only proof is the act of doing well what is worthy to be done, and what was never done before"—indeed! then it follows that in doing what is *un*worthy to be done, or what *has* been done before, no genius can be evinced: yet the picking of pockets is an unworthy act, pockets have been picked time immemorial, and Barrington, the pick-pocket, in point of genius, would have thought hard of a comparison with William Wordsworth, the poet.

Again—in estimating the merit of certain poems, whether they be Ossian's or M'Pherson's, can surely be of little consequence, yet, in order to prove their worthlessness, Mr. W. has expended many pages in the controversy. *Tantæne animis?* Can great minds descend to such absurdity? But worse still: that he may bear down every argument in favor of these poems, he triumphantly drags forward a passage, in his abomination of which he expects the reader to sympathize. It is the beginning of the epic poem *"Temora."* "The blue waves of Ullin roll in light; the green hills are covered with day; trees shake their dusky heads in the breeze." And this—this gorgeous, yet simple imagery—where all is alive and panting with immortality—this—William Wordsworth, the author of Peter Bell, has *selected* for his contempt. We shall see what better he, in his own person, has to offer. Imprimis:

> "And now she's at the pony's head,
> And now she's at the pony's tail,
> On that side now, and now on this,
> And almost stifled her with bliss—
> A few sad tears does Betty shed,

> She pats the pony where or when
> She knows not: happy Betty Foy!
> O Johnny! never mind the Doctor!"

Secondly:

> "The dew was falling fast, the—stars began to blink,
> I heard a voice, it said——drink, pretty creature, drink;
> And looking o'er the hedge, be—fore me I espied
> A snow-white mountain lamb with a—maiden at its side,
> No other sheep were near, the lamb was all alone,
> And by a slender cord was—tether'd to a stone."

Now we have no doubt this is all true; we *will* believe it, indeed we will, Mr. W. Is it sympathy for the sheep you wish to excite? I love a sheep from the bottom of my heart.

*   *   *

But there *are* occasions, dear B——, there are occasions when even Wordsworth is reasonable. Even Stamboul, it is said, shall have an end, and the most unlucky blunders must come to a conclusion. Here is an extract from his preface—

"Those who have been accustomed to the phraseology of modern writers, if they persist in reading this book to a conclusion (*impossible!*) will, no doubt, have to struggle with feelings of awkwardness; (ha! ha! ha!) they will look round for poetry (ha! ha! ha! ha!) and will be induced to inquire by what species of courtesy these attempts have been permitted to assume that title." Ha! ha! ha! ha! ha!

Yet let not Mr. W. despair; he has given immortality to a wagon, and the bee Sophocles has transmitted to eternity a sore toe, and dignified a tragedy with a chorus of turkeys.

*   *   *

Of Coleridge I cannot speak but with reverence. His towering intellect! his gigantic power! He is one more evidence of the fact "que la plupart des sectes ont raison dans une bonne partie de ce qu'elles avancent, mais non pas en ce qu'elles nient." He has imprisoned his own conceptions by the barrier he has erected against those of others. It is lamentable to think that such a mind should be buried in meta-physics, and, like the Nyctanthes, waste its perfume upon the night alone. In reading his poetry I tremble—like one who stands upon a volcano, conscious, from the very darkness bursting from the crater, of the fire and the light that are weltering below.

*   *   *

What is Poetry?—Poetry! that Proteus-like idea, with as many appellations as the nine-titled Corcyra! Give me, I de-manded of a scholar some time ago, give me a definition of poetry? "Tres-volontiers,"—and he proceeded to his library, brought me a Dr. Johnson, and overwhelmed me with a def-inition. Shade of the immortal Shakspeare! I imagined to my-self the scowl of your spiritual eye upon the profanity of that scurrilous Ursa Major. Think of poetry, dear B——, think of poetry, and then think of—Dr. Samuel Johnson! Think of all that is airy and fairy-like, and then of all that is hideous and unwieldy; think of his huge bulk, the Elephant! and then—and then think of the Tempest—the Midsummer Night's Dream—Prospero—Oberon—and Titania!

*   *   *

A poem, in my opinion, is opposed to a work of science by having, for its *immediate* object, pleasure, not truth; to ro-mance, by having for its object an *indefinite* instead of a *defi-nite* pleasure, being a poem only so far as this object is attained; romance presenting perceptible images with definite, poetry with *in*definite sensations, to which end music is an *essential*, since the comprehension of sweet sound is our most indefinite conception. Music, when combined with a pleasur-able idea, is poetry; music without the idea is simply music; the idea without the music is prose from its very definitive-ness.

What was meant by the invective against him who had no music in his soul?

*   *   *

To sum up this long rigmarole, I have, dear B——, what you no doubt perceive, for the metaphysical poets, *as* poets,

the most sovereign contempt. That they have followers
proves nothing—

> No Indian prince has to his palace
> More followers than a thief to the gallows.

Southern Literary Messenger, July 1836

The Philosophy of Composition

CHARLES DICKENS, in a note now lying before me, alluding to an examination I once made of the mechanism of "Barnaby Rudge," says—"By the way, are you aware that Godwin wrote his 'Caleb Williams' backwards? He first involved his hero in a web of difficulties, forming the second volume, and then, for the first, cast about him for some mode of accounting for what had been done."

I cannot think this the *precise* mode of procedure on the part of Godwin—and indeed what he himself acknowledges, is not altogether in accordance with Mr. Dickens' idea—but the author of "Caleb Williams" was too good an artist not to perceive the advantage derivable from at least a somewhat similar process. Nothing is more clear than that every plot, worth the name, must be elaborated to its *dénouement* before any thing be attempted with the pen. It is only with the *dénouement* constantly in view that we can give a plot its indispensable air of consequence, or causation, by making the incidents, and especially the tone at all points, tend to the development of the intention.

There is a radical error, I think, in the usual mode of constructing a story. Either history affords a thesis—or one is suggested by an incident of the day—or, at best, the author sets himself to work in the combination of striking events to form merely the basis of his narrative—designing, generally, to fill in with description, dialogue, or autorial comment, whatever crevices of fact, or action, may, from page to page, render themselves apparent.

I prefer commencing with the consideration of an *effect*. Keeping originality *always* in view—for he is false to himself who ventures to dispense with so obvious and so easily attainable a source of interest—I say to myself, in the first place, "Of the innumerable effects, or impressions, of which the heart, the intellect, or (more generally) the soul is susceptible, what one shall I, on the present occasion, select?" Having chosen a novel, first, and secondly a vivid effect, I consider whether it can best be wrought by incident or tone—whether by ordinary incidents and peculiar tone, or the converse, or by peculiarity both of incident and tone—afterward looking about me (or rather within) for such combinations of event, or tone, as shall best aid me in the construction of the effect.

I have often thought how interesting a magazine paper might be written by any author who would—that is to say, who could—detail, step by step, the processes by which any one of his compositions attained its ultimate point of completion. Why such a paper has never been given to the world, I am much at a loss to say—but, perhaps, the autorial vanity has had more to do with the omission than any one other cause. Most writers—poets in especial—prefer having it understood that they compose by a species of fine frenzy—an ecstatic intuition—and would positively shudder at letting the public take a peep behind the scenes, at the elaborate and vacillating crudities of thought—at the true purposes seized only at the last moment—at the innumerable glimpses of idea that arrived not at the maturity of full view—at the fully matured fancies discarded in despair as unmanageable—at the cautious selections and rejections—at the painful erasures and interpolations—in a word, at the wheels and pinions—the tackle for scene-shifting—the step-ladders and demon-traps—the cock's feathers, the red paint and the black patches, which, in ninety-nine cases out of the hundred, constitute the properties of the literary *histrio*.

I am aware, on the other hand, that the case is by no means common, in which an author is at all in condition to retrace the steps by which his conclusions have been attained. In general, suggestions, having arisen pell-mell, are pursued and forgotten in a similar manner.

For my own part, I have neither sympathy with the repugnance alluded to, nor, at any time, the least difficulty in recalling to mind the progressive steps of any of my compositions; and, since the interest of an analysis, or reconstruction, such as I have considered a *desideratum*, is quite independent of any real or fancied interest in the thing analyzed, it will not be regarded as a breach of decorum on my part to show the *modus operandi* by which some one of my own works was put together. I select "The Raven," as the most generally known. It is my design to render it manifest that no one point in its composition is referrible either to accident or intuition—that the work proceeded, step by step, to its completion with the precision and rigid consequence of a mathematical problem.

Let us dismiss, as irrelevant to the poem *per se*, the circumstance—or say the necessity—which, in the first place, gave rise to the intention of composing a poem that should suit at once the popular and the critical taste.

We commence, then, with this intention.

The initial consideration was that of extent. If any literary work is too long to be read at one sitting, we must be content to dispense with the immensely important effect derivable from unity of impression—for, if two sittings be required, the affairs of the world interfere, and every thing like totality is at once destroyed. But since, *ceteris paribus*, no poet can afford to dispense with *any thing* that may advance his design, it but remains to be seen whether there is, in extent, any advantage to counterbalance the loss of unity which attends it. Here I say no, at once. What we term a long poem is, in fact, merely a succession of brief ones—that is to say, of brief poetical effects. It is needless to demonstrate that a poem is such, only inasmuch as it intensely excites, by elevating, the soul; and all intense excitements are, through a psychal necessity, brief. For this reason, at least one half of the "Paradise Lost" is essentially prose—a succession of poetical excitements interspersed, *inevitably*, with corresponding depressions—the whole being deprived, through the extremeness of its length, of the vastly important artistic element, totality, or unity, of effect.

It appears evident, then, that there is a distinct limit, as regards length, to all works of literary art—the limit of a single sitting—and that, although in certain classes of prose composition, such as "Robinson Crusoe," (demanding no unity,) this limit may be advantageously overpassed, it can never properly be overpassed in a poem. Within this limit, the extent of a poem may be made to bear mathematical relation to its merit—in other words, to the excitement or elevation—again in other words, to the degree of the true poetical effect which it is capable of inducing; for it is clear that the brevity must be in direct ratio of the intensity of the intended effect:—this, with one proviso—that a certain degree of duration is absolutely requisite for the production of any effect at all.

Holding in view these considerations, as well as that degree of excitement which I deemed not above the popular, while not below the critical, taste, I reached at once what I conceived the proper *length* for my intended poem—a length of about one hundred lines. It is, in fact, a hundred and eight.

My next thought concerned the choice of an impression, or effect, to be conveyed: and here I may as well observe that, throughout the construction, I kept steadily in view the design of rendering the work *universally* appreciable. I should be carried too far out of my immediate topic were I to demonstrate a point upon which I have repeatedly insisted, and which, with the poetical, stands not in the slightest need of demonstration—the point, I mean, that Beauty is the sole legitimate province of the poem. A few words, however, in elucidation of my real meaning, which some of my friends have evinced a disposition to misrepresent. That pleasure which is at once the most intense, the most elevating, and the most pure, is, I believe, found in the contemplation of the beautiful. When, indeed, men speak of Beauty, they mean, precisely, not a quality, as is supposed, but an effect—they refer, in short, just to that intense and pure elevation of *soul*—*not* of intellect, or of heart—upon which I have commented, and which is experienced in consequence of contemplating "the beautiful." Now I designate Beauty as the province of the poem, merely because it is an obvious rule of Art that effects should be made to spring from direct causes—that objects should be attained through means best adapted for their attainment—no one as yet having been weak enough to deny that the peculiar elevation alluded to, is *most readily* attained in the poem. Now the object, Truth, or the satisfaction of the intellect, and the object Passion, or the excitement of the heart, are, although attainable, to a certain extent, in poetry, far more readily attainable in prose. Truth, in fact, demands a precision, and Passion, a *homeliness* (the truly passionate will comprehend me) which are absolutely antagonistic to that Beauty which, I maintain, is the excitement, or pleasurable elevation, of the soul. It by no means follows from any thing here said, that passion, or even truth, may not be introduced, and even profitably introduced, into a poem—for they may serve in elucidation, or aid the general effect, as do discords in music, by contrast—but the true artist will always contrive, first, to tone them into proper subservience to the predominant aim, and, secondly, to enveil them, as far as possible, in that Beauty which is the atmosphere and the essence of the poem.

Regarding, then, Beauty as my province, my next question referred to the *tone* of its highest manifestation—and all experience has shown that this tone is one of *sadness*. Beauty of whatever kind, in its supreme development, invariably excites the sensitive soul to tears. Melancholy is thus the most legitimate of all the poetical tones.

The length, the province, and the tone, being thus determined, I betook myself to ordinary induction, with the view of obtaining some artistic piquancy which might serve me as a key-note in the construction of the poem—some pivot upon which the whole structure might turn. In carefully thinking over all the usual artistic effects—or more properly *points*, in the theatrical sense—I did not fail to perceive immediately that no one had been so universally employed as that of the *refrain*. The universality of its employment sufficed to assure me of its intrinsic value, and spared me the necessity of submitting it to analysis. I considered it, however, with regard to its susceptibility of improvement, and soon saw it to be in a primitive condition. As commonly used, the *refrain*, or burden, not only is limited to lyric verse, but depends for its impression upon the force of monotone—both in sound and thought. The pleasure is deduced solely from the sense of identity—of repetition. I resolved to diversify, and so vastly heighten, the effect, by adhering, in general, to the monotone of sound, while I continually varied that of thought: that is to say, I determined to produce continuously novel effects, by the variation *of the application* of the *refrain*—the *refrain* itself remaining, for the most part, unvaried.

These points being settled, I next bethought me of the *nature* of my *refrain*. Since its application was to be repeatedly varied, it was clear that the *refrain* itself must be brief, for there would have been an insurmountable difficulty in frequent variations of application in any sentence of length. In proportion to the brevity of the sentence, would, of course, be the facility of the variation. This led me at once to a single word as the best *refrain*.

The question now arose as to the *character* of the word. Having made up my mind to a *refrain*, the division of the poem into stanzas was, of course, a corollary: the *refrain* forming the close to each stanza. That such a close, to have force, must be sonorous and susceptible of protracted emphasis, admitted no doubt: and these considerations inevitably led me to the long *o* as the most sonorous vowel, in connection with *r* as the most producible consonant.

The sound of the *refrain* being thus determined, it became necessary to select a word embodying this sound, and at the same time in the fullest possible keeping with that melancholy which I had predetermined as the tone of the poem. In such a search it would have been absolutely impossible to overlook the word "Nevermore." In fact, it was the very first which presented itself.

The next *desideratum* was a pretext for the continuous use of the one word "nevermore." In observing the difficulty which I at once found in inventing a sufficiently plausible reason for its continuous repetition, I did not fail to perceive that this difficulty arose solely from the pre-assumption that the word was to be so continuously or monotonously spoken by *a human* being—I did not fail to perceive, in short, that the difficulty lay in the reconciliation of this monotony with the exercise of reason on the part of the creature repeating the word. Here, then, immediately arose the idea of a *non*-reasoning creature capable of speech; and, very naturally, a parrot, in the first instance, suggested itself, but was superseded forthwith by a Raven, as equally capable of speech, and infinitely more in keeping with the intended *tone*.

I had now gone so far as the conception of a Raven—the bird of ill omen—monotonously repeating the one word, "Nevermore," at the conclusion of each stanza, in a poem of melancholy tone, and in length about one hundred lines. Now, never losing sight of the object *supremeness*, or perfection, at all points, I asked myself—"Of all melancholy topics, what, according to the *universal* understanding of mankind, is the *most* melancholy?" Death—was the obvious reply. "And when," I said, "is this most melancholy of topics most poetical?" From what I have already explained at some length, the answer, here also, is obvious—"When it most closely allies itself to *Beauty*: the death, then, of a beautiful woman is, unquestionably, the most poetical topic in the world—and equally is it beyond doubt that the lips best suited for such topic are those of a bereaved lover."

I had now to combine the two ideas, of a lover lamenting his deceased mistress and a Raven continuously repeating the word "Nevermore"—I had to combine these, bearing in mind my design of varying, at every turn, the *application* of the word repeated; but the only intelligible mode of such combination is that of imagining the Raven employing the word in answer to the queries of the lover. And here it was that I saw at once the opportunity afforded for the effect on which I had been depending—that is to say, the effect of the *variation of application*. I saw that I could make the first query propounded by the lover—the first query to which the Raven should reply "Nevermore"—that I could make this first query a commonplace one—the second less so—the third still less, and so on—until at length the lover, startled from his original *nonchalance* by the melancholy character of the word itself—by its frequent repetition—and by a consideration of the ominous reputation of the fowl that uttered it—is at length excited to superstition, and wildly propounds queries of a far different character—queries whose solution he has passionately at heart—propounds them half in superstition and half in that species of despair which delights in self-torture—propounds them not altogether because he believes in the prophetic or demoniac character of the bird (which, reason assures him, is merely repeating a lesson learned by rote) but because he experiences a phrenzied pleasure in so modeling his questions as to receive from the *expected* "Nevermore" the most delicious because the most intolerable of sorrow. Perceiving the opportunity thus afforded me—or, more strictly, thus forced upon me in the progress of the construction—I first established in mind the climax, or concluding query—that to which "Nevermore" should be in the last place an answer—that in reply to which this word "Nevermore" should involve the utmost conceivable amount of sorrow and despair.

Here then the poem may be said to have its beginning—at the end, where all works of art should begin—for it was here, at this point of my preconsiderations, that I first put pen to paper in the composition of the stanza:

"Prophet," said I, "thing of evil! prophet still if bird or
    devil!
By that heaven that bends above us—by that God we both
    adore,
Tell this soul with sorrow laden, if within the distant
    Aidenn,
It shall clasp a sainted maiden whom the angels name
    Lenore—
Clasp a rare and radiant maiden whom the angels name
    Lenore."
            Quoth the raven "Nevermore."

I composed this stanza, at this point, first that, by establishing the climax, I might the better vary and graduate, as regards seriousness and importance, the preceding queries of the lover—and, secondly, that I might definitely settle the rhythm, the metre, and the length and general arrangement of the stanza—as well as graduate the stanzas which were to precede, so that none of them might surpass this in rhythmical effect. Had I been able, in the subsequent composition, to construct more vigorous stanzas, I should, without scruple, have purposely enfeebled them, so as not to interfere with the climacteric effect.

And here I may as well say a few words of the versification. My first object (as usual) was originality. The extent to which this has been neglected, in versification, is one of the most unaccountable things in the world. Admitting that there is little possibility of variety in mere *rhythm*, it is still clear that the possible varieties of metre and stanza are absolutely infinite—and yet, *for centuries, no man, in verse, has ever done, or ever seemed to think of doing, an original thing*. The fact is, originality (unless in minds of very unusual force) is by no means a matter, as some suppose, of impulse or intuition. In general, to be found, it must be elaborately sought, and although a positive merit of the highest class, demands in its attainment less of invention than negation.

Of course, I pretend to no originality in either the rhythm or metre of the "Raven." The former is trochaic—the latter is octameter acatalectic, alternating with heptameter catalectic repeated in the *refrain* of the fifth verse, and terminating with tetrameter catalectic. Less pedantically—the feet employed throughout (trochees) consist of a long syllable followed by a short: the first line of the stanza consists of eight of these feet—the second of seven and a half (in effect two-thirds)—the third of eight—the fourth of seven and a half—the fifth the same—the sixth three and a half. Now, each of these lines, taken individually, has been employed before, and what originality the "Raven" has, is in their *combination into stanza*; nothing even remotely approaching this combination has ever been attempted. The effect of this originality of combination is aided by other unusual, and some altogether novel effects, arising from an extension of the application of the principles of rhyme and alliteration.

The next point to be considered was the mode of bringing together the lover and the Raven—and the first branch of this consideration was the *locale*. For this the most natural suggestion might seem to be a forest, or the fields—but it has always appeared to me that a close *circumscription of space* is absolutely necessary to the effect of insulated incident:—it has the force of a frame to a picture. It has an indisputable moral power in keeping concentrated the attention, and, of course, must not be confounded with mere unity of place.

I determined, then, to place the lover in his chamber—in a chamber rendered sacred to him by memories of her who had frequented it. The room is represented as richly furnished—this in mere pursuance of the ideas I have already explained on the subject of Beauty, as the sole true poetical thesis.

The *locale* being thus determined, I had now to introduce the bird—and the thought of introducing him through the window, was inevitable. The idea of making the lover suppose, in the first instance, that the flapping of the wings of the bird against the shutter, is a "tapping" at the door, originated in a wish to increase, by prolonging, the reader's curiosity, and in a desire to admit the incidental effect arising from the lover's throwing open the door, finding all dark, and thence adopting the half-fancy that it was the spirit of his mistress that knocked.

I made the night tempestuous, first, to account for the Raven's seeking admission, and secondly, for the effect of contrast with the (physical) serenity within the chamber.

I made the bird alight on the bust of Pallas, also for the effect of contrast between the marble and the plumage—it being understood that the bust was absolutely *suggested* by the bird—the bust of *Pallas* being chosen, first, as most in keeping with the scholarship of the lover, and, secondly, for the sonorousness of the word, Pallas, itself.

About the middle of the poem, also, I have availed myself of the force of contrast, with a view of deepening the ultimate impression. For example, an air of the fantastic—approaching as nearly to the ludicrous as was admissible—is given to the Raven's entrance. He comes in " with many a flirt and flutter."

Not the *least obeisance made he*—not a moment stopped or
  stayed he,
But with mien of lord or lady, perched above my chamber
  door.

In the two stanzas which follow, the design is more obviously carried out:—

Then this ebony bird beguiling my sad fancy into smiling
By the *grave and stern decorum of the countenance it wore*,
"Though thy *crest be shorn and shaven* thou," I said, "art
  sure no craven,
Ghastly grim and ancient Raven wandering from the
  nightly shore—
Tell me what thy lordly name is on the Night's Plutonian
  shore!"
        Quoth the Raven "Nevermore."

Much I marvelled *this ungainly fowl* to hear discourse so
  plainly,
Though its answer little meaning—little relevancy bore;
For we cannot help agreeing that no living human being
Ever yet was blessed with seeing bird above his chamber door—
Bird or beast upon the sculptured bust above his chamber door,
  With such name as "Nevermore."

———

The effect of the *dénouement* being thus provided for, I
immediately drop the fantastic for a tone of the most profound seriousness:—this tone commencing in the stanza directly following the one last quoted, with the line,

But the Raven, sitting lonely on that placid bust, spoke
  only, etc.

From this epoch the lover no longer jests—no longer sees
any thing even of the fantastic in the Raven's demeanor. He
speaks of him as a "grim, ungainly, ghastly, gaunt, and ominous bird of yore," and feels the "fiery eyes" burning into his
"bosom's core." This revolution of thought, or fancy, on the
lover's part, is intended to induce a similar one on the part of
the reader—to bring the mind into a proper frame for the
dénouement—which is now brought about as rapidly and as
directly as possible.

With the *dénouement* proper—with the Raven's reply,
"Nevermore," to the lover's final demand if he shall meet his
mistress in another world—the poem, in its obvious phase,
that of a simple narrative, may be said to have its completion.
So far, every thing is within the limits of the accountable—
of the real. A raven, having learned by rote the single word
"Nevermore," and having escaped from the custody of its
owner, is driven, at midnight, through the violence of a
storm, to seek admission at a window from which a light
still gleams—the chamber-window of a student, occupied
half in poring over a volume, half in dreaming of a beloved
mistress deceased. The casement being thrown open at the
fluttering of the bird's wings, the bird itself perches on the
most convenient seat out of the immediate reach of the stu-

dent, who, amused by the incident and the oddity of the visiter's demeanor, demands of it, in jest and without looking for a reply, its name. The raven addressed, answers with its customary word, "Nevermore"—a word which finds immediate echo in the melancholy heart of the student, who, giving utterance aloud to certain thoughts suggested by the occasion, is again startled by the fowl's repetition of "Nevermore." The student now guesses the state of the case, but is impelled, as I have before explained, by the human thirst for self-torture, and in part by superstition, to propound such queries to the bird as will bring him, the lover, the most of the luxury of sorrow, through the anticipated answer "Nevermore." With the indulgence, to the utmost extreme, of this self-torture, the narration, in what I have termed its first or obvious phase, has a natural termination, and so far there has been no overstepping of the limits of the real.

But in subjects so handled, however skilfully, or with however vivid an array of incident, there is always a certain hardness or nakedness, which repels the artistical eye. Two things are invariably required—first, some amount of complexity, or more properly, adaptation; and, secondly, some amount of suggestiveness—some under current, however indefinite of meaning. It is this latter, in especial, which imparts to a work of art so much of that *richness* (to borrow from colloquy a forcible term) which we are too fond of confounding with *the ideal*. It is the *excess* of the suggested meaning—it is the rendering this the upper instead of the under current of the theme—which turns into prose (and that of the very flattest kind) the so called poetry of the so called transcendentalists.

Holding these opinions, I added the two concluding stanzas of the poem—their suggestiveness being thus made to pervade all the narrative which has preceded them. The under current of meaning is rendered first apparent in the lines—

"Take thy beak from out *my heart*, and take thy form from
    off my door!"
            Quoth the Raven "Nevermore!"

It will be observed that the words, "from out my heart," involve the first metaphorical expression in the poem. They, with the answer, "Nevermore," dispose the mind to seek a moral in all that has been previously narrated. The reader begins now to regard the Raven as emblematical—but it is not until the very last line of the very last stanza, that the intention of making him emblematical of *Mournful and Never-ending Remembrance* is permitted distinctly to be seen:

And the Raven, never flitting, still is sitting, still is sitting,
On the pallid bust of Pallas just above my chamber door;
And his eyes have all the seeming of a demon's that is
    dreaming,
And the lamplight o'er him streaming throws his shadow
    on the floor;
And my soul *from out that shadow* that lies floating on the
    floor
                Shall be lifted—nevermore.

Graham's Magazine, April 1846

The Rationale of Verse*

T HE WORD "Verse" is here used not in its strict or primitive sense, but as the term most convenient for expressing generally and without pedantry all that is involved in the consideration of rhythm, rhyme, metre, and versification.

There is, perhaps, no topic in polite literature which has been more pertinaciously discussed, and there is certainly not one about which so much inaccuracy, confusion, misconception, misrepresentation, mystification, and downright ignorance on all sides, can be fairly said to exist. Were the topic really difficult, or did it lie, even, in the cloud-land of metaphysics, where the doubt-vapors may be made to assume any and every shape at the will or at the fancy of the gazer, we should have less reason to wonder at all this contradiction and perplexity; but in fact the subject is exceedingly simple; one tenth of it, possibly, may be called ethical; nine tenths, however, appertain to the mathematics; and the whole is included within the limits of the commonest common sense.

"But, if this is the case, how," it will be asked, "can so much misunderstanding have arisen? Is it conceivable that a thousand profound scholars, investigating so very simple a matter for centuries, have not been able to place it in the fullest light, at least, of which it is susceptible?" These queries, I confess, are not easily answered:—at all events a satisfactory reply to them might cost more trouble than would, if properly considered, the whole *vexata quæstio* to which they have reference. Nevertheless, there is little difficulty or danger in suggesting that the "thousand profound scholars" *may* have failed, first because they were scholars, secondly because they were profound, and thirdly because they were a thousand— the impotency of the scholarship and profundity having been thus multiplied a thousand fold. I am serious in these suggestions; for, first again, there is something in "scholarship" which seduces us into blind worship of Bacon's Idol of the Theatre—into irrational deference to antiquity; secondly, the

*Some few passages of this article appeared, about four years ago, in "The Pioneer," a monthly Magazine published by J. R. Lowell and R. Carter. Although an excellent work it had a *very* limited circulation.

proper "profundity" is rarely profound—it is the nature of Truth in general, as of some ores in particular, to be richest when most superficial; thirdly, the clearest subject may be overclouded by mere superabundance of talk. In chemistry, the best way of separating two bodies is to add a third; in speculation, fact often agrees with fact and argument with argument, until an additional well-meaning fact or argument sets every thing by the ears. In one case out of a hundred a point is excessively discussed because it is obscure; in the ninety-nine remaining it is obscure because excessively discussed. When a topic is thus circumstanced, the readiest mode of investigating it is to forget that any previous investigation has been attempted.

But, in fact, while much has been written on the Greek and Latin rhythms, and even on the Hebrew, little effort has been made at examining that of any of the modern tongues. As regards the English, comparatively nothing has been done. It may be said, indeed, that we are without a treatise on our own verse. In our ordinary grammars and in our works on rhetoric or prosody in general, may be found occasional chapters, it is true, which have the heading, "Versification," but these are, in all instances, exceedingly meagre. They pretend to no analysis; they propose nothing like system; they make no attempt at even rule; every thing depends upon "authority." They are confined, in fact, to mere exemplification of the supposed varieties of English feet and English lines;—although in no work with which I am acquainted are these feet correctly given or these lines detailed in anything like their full extent. Yet what has been mentioned is all—if we except the occasional introduction of some pedagogue-ism, such as this, borrowed from the Greek Prosodies:—"When a syllable is wanting, the verse is said to be catalectic; when the measure is exact, the line is acatalectic; when there is a redundant syllable it forms hypermeter." Now whether a line be termed catalectic or acatalectic is, perhaps, a point of no vital importance;—it is even possible that the student may be able to decide, promptly, when the *a* should be employed and when omitted, yet be incognizant, at the same time, of *all* that is worth knowing in regard to the structure of verse.

A leading defect in each of our treatises, (if treatises they can be called,) is the confining the subject to mere *Versification*, while Verse in general, with the understanding given to the term in the heading of this paper, is the real question at issue. Nor am I aware of even one of our Grammars which so much as properly defines the word versification itself. "Versification," says a work now before me, of which the accuracy is far more than usual—the "English Grammar" of Goold Brown—"Versification is the art of arranging words into lines of correspondent length, so as to produce harmony by the regular alternation of syllables differing in quantity." The commencement of this definition might apply, indeed, to the *art* of versification, but not to versification itself. Versification is not the art of arranging &c., but the actual arranging—a distinction too obvious to need comment. The error here is identical with one which has been too long permitted to disgrace the initial page of every one of our school grammars. I allude to the definitions of English Grammar itself. "English Grammar," it is said, "is the art of speaking and writing the English language correctly." This phraseology, or something essentially similar, is employed, I believe, by Bacon, Miller, Fisk, Greenleaf, Ingersoll, Kirkland, Cooper, Flint, Pue, Comly, and many others. These gentlemen, it is presumed, adopted it without examination from Murray, who derived it from Lily, (whose work was *"quam solam Regia Majestas in omnibus scholis docendam præcipit,"*) and who appropriated it without acknowledgment, but with some unimportant modification, from the Latin Grammar of Leonicenus. It may be shown, however, that this definition, so complacently received, is not, and cannot be, a proper definition of English Grammar. A definition is that which so describes its object as to distinguish it from all others:—it is no definition of any one thing if its terms are applicable to any one other. But if it be asked—"What is the design—the end—the aim of English Grammar?" our obvious answer is, "The art of speaking and writing the English language correctly:"—that is to say, we must use the precise words employed as the definition of English Grammar itself. But the object to be obtained by any means is, assuredly, not the means. English Grammar and the end contemplated by English Grammar, are two matters

sufficiently distinct; nor can the one be more reasonably regarded as the other than a fishing-hook as a fish. The definition, therefore, which is applicable in the latter instance, *cannot*, in the former, be true. Grammar in general is the analysis
of language; English Grammar of the English.

But to return to Versification as defined in our extract
above. "It is the art," says this extract, "of arranging words
into lines *of correspondent length*." Not so:—a correspondence
in the length of lines is by no means essential. Pindaric odes
are, surely, instances of versification, yet these compositions
are noted for extreme diversity in the length of their lines.

The arrangement is moreover said to be for the purpose of
producing "*harmony* by the regular alternation," &c. But *harmony* is not the sole aim—not even the principal one. In the
construction of verse, *melody* should never be left out of view;
yet this is a point which all our Prosodies have most unaccountably forborne to touch. Reasoned rules on this topic
should form a portion of all systems of rhythm.

"So as to produce harmony," says the definition, "by the
regular alternation," &c. A *regular* alternation, as described,
forms no part of any principle of versification. The arrangement of spondees and dactyls, for example, in the Greek hexameter, is an arrangement which may be termed *at random*.
At least it is arbitrary. Without interference with the line as a
whole, a dactyl may be substituted for a spondee, or the converse, at any point other than the ultimate and penultimate
feet, of which the former is always a spondee, the latter nearly
always a dactyl. Here, it is clear, we have no "*regular* alternation of syllables differing in quantity."

"So as to produce harmony," proceeds the definition, "by
the regular alternation of *syllables differing in quantity*,"—in
other words by the alternation of long and short syllables; for
in rhythm all syllables are necessarily either short or long. But
not only do I deny the necessity of any *regularity* in the
succession of feet and, by consequence, of syllables, but dispute the essentiality of any *alternation*, regular or irregular, of
syllables long and short. Our author, observe, is now engaged
in a definition of versification in general, not of English versification in particular. But the Greek and Latin metres
abound in the spondee and pyrrhic—the former consisting of

two long syllables; the latter of two short; and there are innumerable instances of the immediate succession of many spondees and many pyrrhics.

Here is a passage from Silius Italicus:

> Fallis te mensas inter quod credis inermem
> Tot bellis quæsita viro, tot cædibus armat
> Majestas eterna ducem: si admoveris ora
> Cannas et Trebium ante oculos Trasymenaque busta,
> Et Pauli stare ingentem miraberis umbram.

Making the elisions demanded by the classic Prosodies, we should scan these Hexameters thus:

> Fāllīs | tē mēn | sās īn | tēr qūod | crēdĭs ĭn | ērmēm |
> Tŏt bēl | līs qūæ | sītă vĭ | rŏ tŏt | cædĭbŭs | ārmāt |
> Mājēs | tās ē | tērnă dŭ | cēm s'ād | mōvĕrĭs | ōrā |
> Cānnās | ēt Trĕbĭ' | ānt'ŏcŭ | lōs Trăsy | mēnăqŭe | būstā
> ēt Pāu | lī stā | r'ĭngēn | tēm mī | rābĕrĭs | ūmbrām |

It will be seen that, in the first and last of these lines, we have only two short syllables in thirteen, with an uninterrupted succession of no less than *nine* long syllables. But how are we to reconcile all this with a definition of versification which describes it as "the art of arranging words into lines of correspondent length so as to produce harmony by the *regular alternation of syllables differing in quantity?*"

It may be urged, however, that our prosodist's *intention* was to speak of the English metres alone, and that, by omitting all mention of the spondee and pyrrhic, he has virtually avowed their exclusion from our rhythms. A grammarian is never excusable on the ground of good intentions. We demand from him, if from any one, rigorous precision of style. But grant the design. Let us admit that our author, following the example of all authors on English Prosody, has, in defining versification at large, intended a definition merely of the English. All these prosodists, we will say, reject the spondee and pyrrhic. Still all admit the iambus, which consists of a short syllable followed by a long; the trochee, which is the converse of the iambus; the dactyl, formed of one long sylla-

ble followed by two short; and the anapæst—two short succeeded by a long. The spondee is improperly rejected, as I
shall presently show. The pyrrhic is rightfully dismissed. Its
existence in either ancient or modern rhythm is purely chimerical, and the insisting on so perplexing a nonentity as a
foot of *two short* syllables, affords, perhaps, the best evidence
of the gross irrationality and subservience to authority which
characterize our Prosody. In the meantime the acknowledged
dactyl and anapæst are enough to sustain my proposition
about the "alternation," &c., without reference to feet which
are assumed to exist in the Greek and Latin metres alone: for
an anapæst and a dactyl may meet in the same line; when of
course we shall have an uninterrupted succession of four short
syllables. The meeting of these two feet, to be sure, is an accident not contemplated in the definition now discussed; for
this definition, in demanding a "regular alternation of syllables differing in quantity," insists on a regular succession of
similar *feet*. But here is an example:

Sīng tŏ mĕ | Isăbēlle.

This is the opening line of a little ballad now before me,
which proceeds in the same rhythm—a peculiarly beautiful
one. More than all this:—English lines are often well composed, entirely, of a regular succession of syllables *all of the
same quantity*:—the first lines, for instance, of the following
quatrain by Arthur C. Coxe:

> *March! march! march!*
>   Making sounds as they tread,
> Ho! ho! how they step,
>   Going down to the dead!

The line italicized is formed of three cæsuras. The cæsura,
of which I have much to say hereafter, is rejected by the English Prosodies and grossly misrepresented in the classic. It is
a perfect foot—the most important in all verse—and consists
of a single *long* syllable; *but the length of this syllable varies.*
    It has thus been made evident that there is *not one* point of
the definition in question which does not involve an error.

And for anything more satisfactory or more intelligible we shall look in vain to any published treatise on the topic.

So general and so total a failure can be referred only to radical misconception. In fact the English Prosodists have blindly followed the pedants. These latter, like *les moutons de Panurge*, have been occupied in incessant tumbling into ditches, for the excellent reason that their leaders have so tumbled before. The Iliad, being taken as a starting point, was made to stand in stead of Nature and common sense. Upon this poem, in place of facts and deduction from fact, or from natural law, were built systems of feet, metres, rhythms, rules,—rules that contradict each other every five minutes, and for nearly all of which there may be found twice as many exceptions as examples. If any one has a fancy to be thoroughly confounded—to see how far the infatuation of what is termed "classical scholarship" can lead a book-worm in the manufacture of darkness out of sunshine, let him turn over, for a few moments, any one of the German Greek Prosodies. The only thing clearly made out in them is a very magnificent contempt for Liebnitz's principle of "a sufficient reason."

To divert attention from the real matter in hand by any farther reference to these works, is unnecessary, and would be weak. I cannot call to mind, at this moment, one essential particular of information that is to be gleaned from them; and I will drop them here with merely this one observation: that, employing from among the numerous *"ancient"* feet the spondee, the trochee, the iambus, the anapæst, the dactyl, and the cæsura alone, I will engage to scan *correctly* any of the Horatian rhythms, or any true rhythm that human ingenuity can conceive. And this excess of chimerical feet is, perhaps, the very least of the scholastic supererogations. *Ex uno disce omnia*. The fact is that *Quantity* is a point in whose investigation the lumber of mere learning may be dispensed with, if ever in any. Its appreciation is universal. It appertains to no region, nor race, nor æra in especial. To melody and to harmony the Greeks hearkened with ears precisely similar to those which we employ for similar purposes at present; and I should not be condemned for heresy in asserting that a pendulum at Athens would have vibrated much after the same fashion as does a pendulum in the city of Penn.

Verse originates in the human enjoyment of equality, fitness. To this enjoyment, also, all the moods of verse—rhythm, metre, stanza, rhyme, alliteration, the *refrain*, and other analogous effects—are to be referred. As there are some readers who habitually confound rhythm and metre, it may be as well here to say that the former concerns the *character* of feet (that is, the arrangements of syllables) while the latter has to do with the *number* of these feet. Thus by "a dactylic *rhythm*" we express a sequence of dactyls. By "a dactylic hexa*meter*" we imply a line or measure consisting of six of these dactyls.

To return to *equality*. Its idea embraces those of similarity, proportion, identity, repetition, and adaptation or fitness. It might not be very difficult to go even behind the idea of equality, and show both how and why it is that the human nature takes pleasure in it, but such an investigation would, for any purpose now in view, be supererogatory. It is sufficient that the *fact* is undeniable—the fact that man derives enjoyment from his perception of equality. Let us examine a crystal. We are at once interested by the equality between the sides and between the angles of one of its faces: the equality of the sides pleases us; that of the angles doubles the pleasure. On bringing to view a second face in all respects similar to the first, this pleasure seems to be squared; on bringing to view a third it appears to be cubed, and so on. I have no doubt, indeed, that the delight experienced, if measurable, would be found to have exact mathematical relations such as I suggest; that is to say, as far as a certain point, beyond which there would be a decrease in similar relations.

The perception of pleasure in the equality of *sounds* is the principle of *Music*. Unpractised ears can appreciate only simple equalities, such as are found in ballad airs. While comparing one simple sound with another they are too much occupied to be capable of comparing the equality subsisting between these two simple sounds, taken conjointly, and two other similar simple sounds taken conjointly. Practised ears, on the other hand, appreciate both equalities at the same instant—although it is absurd to suppose that both are *heard* at the same instant. One is heard and appreciated from itself: the other is heard by the memory; and the instant glides into and is confounded with the secondary, appreciation. Highly cultivated musical taste in this manner enjoys not only these double equalities, all appreciated at once, but takes pleasurable cognizance, through memory, of equalities the members of which occur at intervals so great that the uncultivated taste loses them altogether. That this latter can properly estimate or decide on the merits of what is called scientific music, is of course impossible. But scientific music has no claim to intrinsic excellence—it is fit for scientific ears alone. In its excess it is the triumph of the *physique* over the *morale* of music. The sentiment is overwhelmed by the sense. On the whole, the advocates of the simpler melody and harmony have infinitely the best of the argument;—although there has been very little of real argument on the subject.

In *verse*, which cannot be better designated than as an inferior or less capable Music, there is, happily, little chance for complexity. Its rigidly simple character not even Science—not even Pedantry can greatly pervert.

The rudiment of verse may, possibly, be found in the *spondee*. The very germ of a thought seeking satisfaction in equality of sound, would result in the construction of words of two syllables, equally accented. In corroboration of this idea we find that spondees most abound in the most ancient tongues. The second step we can easily suppose to be the comparison, that is to say, the collocation, of two spondees—of two words composed each of a spondee. The third step would be the juxta-position of three of these words. By this time the perception of monotone would induce farther consideration: and thus arises what Leigh Hunt so flounders in discussing under the title of "The *Principle* of Variety in Uniformity." Of course there is no principle in the case—nor in maintaining it. The "Uniformity" is the principle:—the "Variety" is but the principle's natural safeguard from self-destruction by excess of self. "Uniformity," besides, is the very worst word that could have been chosen for the expression of the *general* idea at which it aims.

The perception of monotone having given rise to an attempt at its relief, the first thought in this new direction would be that of collating two or more words formed each of two syllables differently accented (that is to say, short and long) but having the same order in each word:—in other terms, of collating two or more iambuses, or two or more trochees. And here let me pause to assert that more pitiable nonsense has been written on the topic of *long* and *short* syllables than on any other subject under the sun. In general, a syllable is long or short, just as it is difficult or easy of enunciation. The *natural* long syllables are those encumbered—the *natural* short ones are those *un*encumbered, with consonants; all the rest is mere artificiality and jargon. The Latin Prosodies have a rule that "a vowel before two consonants is long." This rule is deduced from "authority"—that is, from the observation that vowels so circumstanced, in the ancient poems, are always in syllables long by the laws of scansion. The philosophy of the rule is untouched, and lies simply in the physical difficulty of giving voice to such syllables—of performing the lingual evolutions necessary for their utterance. Of course, it is not the *vowel* that is long (although the rule says so) but the syllable of which the vowel is a part. It will be seen that the length of a syllable, depending on the facility or difficulty of its enunciation, must have great variation in various syllables; but for the purposes of verse we suppose a long syllable equal to two short ones:—and the natural deviation from this relativeness we correct in perusal. The more closely our long syllables approach this relation with our short ones, the better, *ceteris paribus*, will be our verse: but if the relation does not exist of itself, we force it by emphasis, which can, of course, make any syllable as long as desired;—or, by an effort we can pronounce with unnatural brevity a syllable that is naturally too long. *Accented* syllables are of course always long—but, where *un*encumbered with consonants, must be classed among the *unnaturally* long. Mere custom has declared that we shall accent them—that is to say, dwell upon them; but no inevitable lingual difficulty forces us to do so. In fine, every long syllable must of its own accord occupy in its utterance, or must be *made* to occupy, precisely the time demanded for two short ones. The only exception to this rule is found in the cæsura—of which more anon.

The success of the experiment with the trochees or iambuses (the one would have suggested the other) must have led to a trial of dactyls or anapæsts—natural dactyls or anapæsts—dactylic or anapæstic *words*. And now some degree of complexity has been attained. There is an appreciation, first, of the equality between the several dactyls, or anapæsts, and, secondly, of that between the long syllable and the two short conjointly. But here it may be said that step after step would have been taken, in continuation of this routine, until all the feet of the Greek Prosodies became exhausted. Not so:—these remaining feet have no existence except in the brains of the scholiasts. It is needless to imagine men inventing these things, and folly to explain how and why they invented them, until it shall be first shown that they are actually invented. All other "feet" than those which I have specified, are, if not impossible at first view, merely combinations of the specified; and, although this assertion is rigidly true, I will, to avoid misunderstanding, put it in a somewhat different shape. I will say, then, that at present I am aware of no *rhythm*— nor do I believe that any one can be constructed—which, in its last analysis, will not be found to consist altogether of the feet I have mentioned, either existing in their individual and obvious condition, or interwoven with each other in accordance with simple natural laws which I will endeavor to point out hereafter.

We have now gone so far as to suppose men constructing indefinite sequences of spondaic, iambic, trochaic, dactylic, or anapæstic words. In *extending* these sequences, they would be again arrested by the sense of monotone. A succession of spondees would *immediately* have displeased; one of iambuses or of trochees, on account of the variety included within the foot itself, would have taken longer to displease; one of dactyls or anapæsts still longer: but even the last if extended very far, must have become wearisome. The idea, first, of curtailing, and, secondly, of defining the length of a sequence, would thus at once have arisen. Here then is the *line*, or verse proper.* The principle of equality being constantly

---

*Verse, from the Latin *vertere*, to turn, is so called on account of the turning or recommencement of the series of feet. Thus a verse, strictly speaking, is a line. In this sense, however, I have preferred using the latter word alone; employing the former in the general acceptation given it in the heading of this paper.

at the bottom of the whole process, lines would naturally be made, in the first instance, equal in the number of their feet; in the second instance there would be variation in the mere number; one line would be twice as long as another; then one would be some less obvious multiple of another; then still less obvious proportions would be adopted:— nevertheless there would be *proportion*, that is to say a phase of equality, still.

Lines being once introduced, the necessity of distinctly de- fining these lines *to the ear*, (as yet written verse does not exist,) would lead to a scrutiny of their capabilities *at their terminations*:—and now would spring up the idea of equality in sound between the final syllables—in other words, of *rhyme*. First, it would be used only in the iambic, anapæstic, and spondaic rhythms, (granting that the latter had not been thrown aside, long since, on account of its tameness;) because in these rhythms the concluding syllable, being long, could best sustain the necessary protraction of the voice. No great while could elapse, however, before the effect, found pleasant as well as useful, would be applied to the two remaining rhythms. But as the chief force of rhyme must lie in the ac- cented syllable, the attempt to create rhyme at all in these two remaining rhythms, the trochaic and dactylic, would necessar- ily result in double and triple rhymes, such as *beauty* with *duty* (trochaic) and *beautiful* with *dutiful* (dactylic.)

It must be observed that in suggesting these processes I assign them no date; nor do I even insist upon their order. Rhyme is supposed to be of modern origin, and were this proved, my positions remain untouched. I may say, however, in passing, that several instances of rhyme occur in the "Clouds" of Aristophanes, and that the Roman poets occa- sionally employ it. There is an effective species of ancient rhyming which has never descended to the moderns; that in which the ultimate and penultimate syllables rhyme with each other. For example:

Parturiunt montes et nascitur ridicu*lus mus*.

and again—

Litoreis ingens inventa sub ilici*bus sus*.

The terminations of Hebrew verse, (as far as understood,) show no signs of rhyme; but what thinking person can doubt that it did actually exist? That men have so obstinately and blindly insisted, *in general*, even up to the present day, in confining rhyme to the *ends* of lines, when its effect is even better applicable elsewhere, intimates, in my opinion, the sense of some *necessity* in the connexion of the end with the rhyme—hints that the origin of rhyme lay in a necessity which connected it with the end—shows that neither mere accident nor mere fancy gave rise to the connexion—points, in a word, at the very necessity which I have suggested, (that of some mode of defining lines *to the ear*,) as the true origin of rhyme. Admit this and we throw the origin far back in the night of Time—beyond the origin of written verse.

But to resume. The amount of complexity I have now supposed to be attained is very considerable. Various systems of equalization are appreciated at once (or nearly so) in their respective values and in the value of each system with reference to all the others. As our present *ultimatum* of complexity we have arrived at triple-rhymed, natural-dactylic lines, existing proportionally as well as equally with regard to other triple-rhymed, natural-dactylic lines. For example:

> Virginal Lilian, rigidly, humblily dutiful;
>   Saintlily, lowlily,
>   Thrillingly, holily
> Beautiful!

Here we appreciate, first, the absolute equality between the long syllable of each dactyl and the two short conjointly; secondly, the absolute equality between each dactyl and any other dactyl—in other words, among all the dactyls; thirdly, the absolute equality between the two middle lines; fourthly, the absolute equality between the first line and all the others taken conjointly; fifthly, the absolute equality between the two last syllables of the respective words "dutiful" and "beautiful;" sixthly, the absolute equality between the two last syllables of the respective words "lowlily" and "holily;" seventhly, the proximate equality between the first syllable of "dutiful" and the first syllable of "beautiful;" eighthly, the

proximate equality between the first syllable of "lowlily" and
that of "holily;" ninthly, the proportional equality, (that of
five to one,) between the first line and each of its members,
the dactyls; tenthly, the proportional equality, (that of two to
one,) between each of the middle lines and its members, the
dactyls; eleventhly, the proportional equality between the first
line and each of the two middle—that of five to two;
twelfthly, the proportional equality between the first line and
the last—that of five to one; thirteenthly, the proportional
equality between each of the middle lines and the last—that
of two to one; lastly, the proportional equality, as concerns
number, between all the lines, taken collectively, and any individual line—that of four to one.

The consideration of this last equality would give birth immediately to the idea of *stanza*—that is to say, the insula-
tion of lines into equal or obviously proportional masses. In
its primitive, (which was also its best,) form, the stanza would
most probably have had absolute unity. In other words, the
removal of any one of its lines would have rendered it imperfect; as in the case above, where if the last line, for example,
be taken away, there is left no rhyme to the "dutiful" of the
first. Modern stanza is excessively loose, and where so, ineffective as a matter of course.

Now, although in the deliberate written statement which I
have here given of these various systems of equalities, there
seems to be an infinity of complexity—so much that it is hard
to conceive the mind taking cognizance of them all in the
brief period occupied by the perusal or recital of the stanza—
yet the difficulty is in fact apparent only when we will it to
become so. Any one fond of mental experiment may satisfy
himself, by trial, that, in listening to the lines, he does actually, (although with a seeming unconsciousness, on account
of the rapid evolutions of sensation,) recognize and instantaneously appreciate, (more or less intensely as his ear is cultivated,) each and all of the equalizations detailed. The pleasure
received, or receivable, has very much such progressive increase, and in very nearly such mathematical relations, as
those which I have suggested in the case of the crystal.

*A stanza is often vulgarly, and with gross impropriety, called a *verse*.

It will be observed that I speak of merely a proximate equality between the first syllable of "dutiful" and that of "beautiful;" and it may be asked why we cannot imagine the earliest rhymes to have had absolute instead of proximate equality of sound. But absolute equality would have involved the use of identical words; and it is the duplicate sameness or monotony—that of sense as well as that of sound—which would have caused these rhymes to be rejected in the very first instance.

The narrowness of the limits within which verse composed of natural feet alone, must necessarily have been confined, would have led, after a *very* brief interval, to the trial and immediate adoption of artificial feet—that is to say of feet *not* constituted each of a single word, but two or even three words; or of parts of words. These feet would be intermingled with natural ones. For example:

ă brēath | căn māke | thĕm ās | ă breāth | hăs māde.

This is an iambic line in which each iambus is formed of two words. Again:

Thĕ ūn | ĭmā | gĭnā | blĕ mīght | ŏf Jōve. |

This is an iambic line in which the first foot is formed of a word and a part of a word; the second and third of parts taken from the body or interior of a word; the fourth of a part and a whole; the fifth of two complete words. There are no *natural* feet in either lines. Again:

Cān ĭt bĕ | făncĭĕd thăt | Dēīty | ēvĕr vĭn | dīctĭvely |
Māde ĭn hĭs | īmagĕ ă | mānnĭkĭn | mĕrely tŏ | māddĕn ĭt? |

These are two dactylic lines in which we find natural feet, ("Deity," "mannikin;") feet composed of two words ("fancied that," "image a," "merely to," "madden it;") feet composed of three words ("can it be," "made in his;") a foot composed of a part of a word ("dictively;") and a foot composed of a word and a part of a word ("ever vin.")

And now, in our supposititious progress, we have gone so

far as to exhaust all the *essentialities* of verse. What follows may, strictly speaking, be recorded as embellishment merely —but even in this embellishment, the rudimental sense of *equality* would have been the never-ceasing impulse. It would, for example, be simply in seeking farther administration to this sense that men would come, in time, to think of the *refrain*, or burden, where, at the closes of the several stanzas of a poem, one word or phrase is *repeated*; and of alliteration, in whose simplest form a consonant is *repeated* in the commencements of various words. This effect would be extended so as to embrace repetitions both of vowels and of consonants, in the bodies as well as in the beginnings of words; and, at a later period, would be made to infringe on the province of rhyme, by the introduction of general similarity of sound between whole feet occurring in the body of a line:—all of which modifications I have exemplified in the line above,

Made in his image a *mannikin* merely to *madden it*.

Farther cultivation would improve also the *refrain* by relieving its monotone in slightly varying the phrase at each repetition, or, (as I have attempted to do in "The Raven,") in retaining the phrase and varying its application—although this latter point is not strictly a rhythmical effect *alone*. Finally, poets when fairly wearied with following precedent— following it the more closely the less they perceived it in company with Reason—would adventure so far as to indulge in positive rhyme at other points than the ends of lines. First, they would put it in the middle of the line; then at some point where the multiple would be less obvious; then alarmed at their own audacity, they would undo all their work by cutting these lines in two. And here is the fruitful source of the infinity of "short metre," by which modern poetry, if not distinguished, is at least disgraced. It would require a high degree, indeed, both of cultivation and of courage, on the part of any versifier, to enable him to place his rhymes—and let them remain—at unquestionably their best position, that of unusual and *unanticipated* intervals.

On account of the stupidity of some people, or, (if talent

be a more respectable word,) on account of their talent for
misconception—I think it necessary to add here, first, that I
believe the "processes" above detailed to be nearly if not accurately those which *did* occur in the gradual creation of what
we now call verse; secondly, that, although I so believe, I yet
urge neither the assumed fact nor my belief in it, as a part of
the true proposition of this paper; thirdly, that in regard to
the aim of this paper, it is of no consequence whether these
processes did occur either in the order I have assigned them,
or at all; my design being simply, in presenting a general type
of what such processes *might* have been and *must* have resembled, to help *them*, the "some people," to an easy understanding of what I have farther to say on the topic of Verse.

There is one point which, in my summary of the processes,
I have purposely forborne to touch; because this point, being
the most important of all, on account of the immensity
of error usually involved in its consideration, would have led
me into a series of detail inconsistent with the object of a
summary.

Every reader of verse must have observed how seldom it
happens that even any one line proceeds uniformly with a
succession, such as I have supposed, of absolutely equal feet;
that is to say, with a succession of iambuses only, or of trochees only, or of dactyls only, or of anapæsts only, or of spondees only. Even in the most musical lines we find the
succession interrupted. The iambic pentameters of Pope, for
example, will be found on examination, frequently varied by
trochees in the beginning, or by (what seem to be) anapæsts
in the body, of the line.

> ŏh thōu | whătē | vĕr tī | tlĕ pleāse | thĭne eār |
> Dĕan Drā | piĕr Bīck | ĕrstāff | ŏr Gūl | ĭvēr |
> Whēthĕr | thŏu choōse | Cĕrvān | tĕs' sē | rĭoŭs ăir |
> ŏr laūgh | ănd shāke | ĭn Rāb | ĕlaĭs' eā | sy chaĭr. |

Were any one weak enough to refer to the Prosodies for a
solution of the difficulty here, he would find it *solved* as usual
by a *rule*, stating the fact, (or what it, the rule, supposes to
be the fact,) but without the slightest attempt at the *rationale*.
"By a *synæresis* of the two short syllables," say the books, "an

anapæst may sometimes be employed for an iambus, or a dactyl for a trochee. . . . In the beginning of a line a trochee is often used for an iambus."

Blending is the plain English for *synæresis*—but there should be *no* blending; neither is an anapæst *ever* employed for an iambus, or a dactyl for a trochee. These feet differ in time; and *no* feet so differing can ever be legitimately used in the same line. An anapæst is equal to four short syllables—an iambus only to three. Dactyls and trochees hold the same relation. The principle of *equality*, in verse, admits, it is true, of variation at certain points, for the relief of monotone, as I have already shown, but the point of *time* is that point which, being the rudimental one, must never be tampered with at all.

To explain:—In farther efforts for the relief of monotone than those to which I have alluded in the summary, men soon came to see that there was no absolute necessity for adhering to the precise number of syllables, provided the time required for the whole foot was preserved inviolate. They saw, for instance, that in such a line as

ŏr lāugh | ănd shāke | ĭn Rāb | ĕlăĭs ēa | sy chāir, |

the equalization of the three syllables *elais ea* with the two syllables composing any of the other feet, could be readily effected by pronouncing the two syllable *elais* in double quick time. By pronouncing each of the syllables *e* and *lais* twice as rapidly as the syllable *sy*, or the syllable *in*, or any other short syllable, they could bring the two of them, taken together, to the length, that is to say to the time, of any one short syllable. This consideration enabled them to effect the agreeable variation of three syllables in place of the uniform two. And variation was the object—variation to the ear. What sense is there, then, in supposing this object rendered null by the *blending* of the two syllables so as to render them, in absolute effect, one? Of course, there must be *no* blending. Each syllable must be pronounced as distinctly as possible, (or the variation is lost,) but with twice the rapidity in which the ordinary short syllable is enunciated. That the syllables *elais ea* do not compose an *anapæst* is evident, and the signs (˘ ˘ ¯) of their

accentuation are erroneous. The foot might be written thus
(⌐⌐) the inverted crescents expressing double quick time; and
might be called a bastard iambus.

Here is a trochaic line:

See thĕ | dēlĭcăte | fōotĕd | rēin-deĕr. |

The prosodies—that is to say the most considerate of them—
would here decide that *"delicate"* is a dactyl used in place of a
trochee, and would refer to what they call their "rule," for
justification. Others, varying the stupidity, would insist upon
a Procrustean adjustment thus (del'cate)—an adjustment recommended to all such words as *silvery, murmuring*, etc.,
which, it is said, should be not only pronounced, but written
silv'ry, murm'ring, and so on, whenever they find themselves
in trochaic predicament. I have only to say that "delicate,"
when circumstanced as above, is neither a dactyl nor a dactyl's
equivalent; that I would suggest for it this (⌐⌐) accentuation;
that I think it as well to call it a bastard trochee; and that all
words, at all events, should be written and pronounced *in
full*, and as nearly as possible as nature intended them.

About eleven years ago, there appeared in "The American
Monthly Magazine," (then edited, I believe, by Mess. Hoffman and Benjamin,) a review of Mr. Willis' Poems; the critic
putting forth his strength, or his weakness, in an endeavor to
show that the poet was either absurdly affected, or grossly
ignorant of the laws of verse; the accusation being based altogether on the fact that Mr. W. made occasional use of this
very word "delicate," and other similar words, in "the Heroic
measure which every one knew consisted of feet of two syllables." Mr. W. has often, for example, such lines as

> That binds him to a woman's *delicate* love—
> In the gay sunshine, *reverent* in the storm—
> With its *invisible* fingers my loose hair.

Here, of course, the feet *licate love, verent in*, and *sible fin*, are
bastard iambuses; are *not* anapæsts; and are *not* improperly
used. Their employment, on the contrary, by Mr. Willis is but
one of the innumerable instances he has given of keen sensi-

bility in all those matters of taste which may be classed under the general head of *fanciful embellishment*.

It is also about eleven years ago, if I am not mistaken, since Mr. Horne, (of England,) the author of "Orion," one of the noblest epics in any language, thought it necessary to preface his "Chaucer Modernized" by a very long and evidently a very elaborate essay, of which the greater portion was occupied in a discussion of the seemingly anomalous foot of which we have been speaking. Mr. Horne upholds Chaucer in its frequent use; maintains his superiority, *on account* of his so frequently using it, over all English versifiers; and, indignantly repelling the common idea of those who make verse on their fingers—that the superfluous syllable is a roughness and an error—very chivalrously makes battle for it as "a grace." That a grace it *is*, there can be no doubt; and what I complain of is, that the author of the most happily versified long poem in existence, should have been under the necessity of discussing this grace merely *as* a grace, through forty or fifty vague pages, solely because of his inability to show *how* and *why* it is a grace—by which showing the question would have been settled in an instant.

About the trochee used for an iambus, as we see it in the beginning of the line,

> Whēthĕr thou choose Cervantes' serious air,

there is little that need be said. It brings me to the general proposition that, in all rhythms, the prevalent or distinctive feet may be varied at will, and nearly at random, by the *occasional* introduction of equivalent feet—that is to say, feet the sum of whose syllabic times is equal to the sum of the syllabic times of the distinctive feet. Thus the trochee, *whēthĕr*, is equal, in the sum of the times of its syllables, to the iambus, *thŏu choōse*, in the sum of the times of *its* syllables; each foot being, in time, equal to three short syllables. Good versifiers who happen to be, also, good poets, contrive to relieve the monotone of a series of feet, by the use of equivalent feet only at rare intervals, and at such points of their subject as seem in accordance with the *startling* character of the variation. Nothing of this care is seen in the line quoted above—although

Pope has some fine instances of the duplicate effect. Where vehemence is to be strongly expressed, I am not sure that we should be wrong in venturing on *two consecutive* equivalent feet—although I cannot say that I have ever known the adventure made, except in the following passage, which occurs in "Al Aaraaf," a boyish poem, written by myself when a boy. I am referring to the sudden and rapid advent of a star:

> Dim was its little disk, and angel eyes
> Alone could see the phantom in the skies,
> Whĕn first thĕ phāntŏm's cōurse wăs fōund tŏ bē
> *Hēadlŏng hĭthĕr*ward o'er the starry sea.

In the "general proposition" above, I speak of the *occasional* introduction of equivalent feet. It sometimes happens that unskilful versifiers, without knowing what they do, or why they do it, introduce so many "variations" as to exceed in number the "distinctive" feet; when the ear becomes at once baulked by the *bouleversement* of the rhythm. Too many trochees, for example, inserted in an iambic rhythm, would convert the latter to a trochaic. I may note here, that, in all cases, the rhythm designed should be commenced and continued, *without* variation, until the ear has had full time to comprehend what *is* the rhythm. In violation of a rule so obviously founded in common sense, many even of our best poets, do not scruple to begin an iambic rhythm with a trochee, or the converse; or a dactylic with an anapæst, or the converse; and so on.

A somewhat less objectionable error, although still a decided one, is that of commencing a rhythm, not with a different equivalent foot, but with a "bastard" foot of the rhythm intended. For example:

> Māny ă | thoūght wĭll | cōme tŏ | mēmŏry. |

Here *many a* is what I have explained to be a bastard trochee, and to be understood should be accented with inverted crescents. It is objectionable solely on account of its position as the *opening* foot of a trochaic rhythm. *Memory*, similarly ac-

cented, is also a bastard trochee, but *un*objectionable, although by no means demanded.

The farther illustration of this point will enable me to take
an important step.

One of our finest poets, Mr. Christopher Pease Cranch, begins a very beautiful poem thus:

> Many are the thoughts that come to me
>   In my lonely musing;
> And they drift so strange and swift
>   There's no time for choosing
> Which to follow; for to leave
>   Any, seems a losing.

"A losing" to Mr. Cranch, of course—but this *en passant*. It
will be seen here that the intention is trochaic;—although we
do *not* see this intention by the opening foot, as we should
do—or even by the opening line. Reading the whole stanza,
however, we perceive the trochaic rhythm as the general design, and so, after some reflection, we divide the first line
thus:

> Many are the | thōughts thăt | cōme tō | me. |

Thus scanned, the line will seem musical. It *is*—highly so.
And it is because there is no end to instances of just such
lines of apparently incomprehensible music, that Coleridge
thought proper to invent his nonsensical *system* of what he
calls "scanning by accents"—as if "scanning by accents" were
anything more than a phrase. Whenever "Christabel" is really
not rough, it can be as readily scanned by the true *laws* (not
the supposititious *rules*) of verse, as can the simplest pentameter of Pope; and where it *is* rough (*passim*) these same
laws will enable any one of common sense to show *why* it is
rough and to point out, instantaneously, the remedy for the
roughness.

A reads and re-reads a certain line, and pronounces it false
in rhythm—unmusical. *B*, however, reads it *to A*, and *A* is
at once struck with the perfection of the rhythm, and wonders at his dulness in not "catching" it before. Henceforward

he admits the line to be musical. *B*, triumphant, asserts that, to be sure, the line is musical—for it is the work of Coleridge—and that it is *A* who is *not*; the fault being in *A*'s false reading. Now here *A* is right and *B* wrong. *That* rhythm is erroneous, (at some point or other more or less obvious,) which *any* ordinary reader *can*, without design, read improperly. It is the business of the poet so to construct his line that the intention *must* be caught *at once*. Even when men have precisely the same understanding of a sentence, they differ and often widely, in their modes of enunciating it. Any one who has taken the trouble to examine the topic of emphasis, (by which I here mean not *accent* of particular syllables, but the dwelling on entire words,) must have seen that men emphasize in the most singularly arbitrary manner. There are certain large classes of people, for example, who persist in emphasizing their monosyllables. Little uniformity of emphasis prevails; because the thing itself—the idea, emphasis,—is referable to no natural—at least to no well comprehended and therefore uniform law. Beyond a very narrow and vague limit, the whole matter is conventionality. And if we differ in emphasis even when we agree in comprehension, how much more so in the former when in the latter too! Apart, however, from the consideration of natural disagreement, is it not clear that, by tripping here and mouthing there, any sequence of words may be twisted into any species of rhythm? But are we thence to deduce that all sequences of words are rhythmical in a rational understanding of the term?—for this is the deduction, precisely to which the *reductio ad absurdum* will, in the end, bring all the propositions of Coleridge. Out of a hundred readers of "Christabel," fifty will be able to make nothing of its rhythm, while forty-nine of the remaining fifty will, with some ado, fancy they comprehend it, after the fourth or fifth perusal. The one out of the whole hundred who shall both comprehend and admire it at first sight—must be an unaccountably clever person—and I am by far too modest to assume, for a moment, that that very clever person is myself.

In illustration of what is here advanced I cannot do better than quote a poem:

> Pease porridge hot—pease porridge cold—
> Pease porridge in the pot—nine days old.

Now those of my readers who have never *heard* this poem pronounced according to the nursery conventionality, will find its rhythm as obscure as an explanatory note; while those who *have* heard it, will divide it thus, declare it musical, and wonder how there can be any doubt about it.

> Pease | porridge | hot | pease | porridge | cold |
> Pease | porridge | in the | pot | nine | days | old. |

The chief thing in the way of this species of rhythm, is the necessity which it imposes upon the poet of travelling in constant company with his compositions, so as to be ready at a moment's notice, to avail himself of a well understood poetical license—that of reading aloud one's own doggrel.

In Mr. Cranch's line,

> Many are the | thoughts that | come to | me, |

the general error of which I speak is, of course, very partially exemplified, and the purpose for which, chiefly, I cite it, lies yet further on in our topic.

The two divisions (*thoughts that*) and (*come to*) are ordinary trochees. Of the last division (*me*) we will talk hereafter. The first division (many are the) would be thus accented by the Greek Prosodies (mānỹ ăre thĕ) and would be called by them αστρολογος. The Latin books would style the foot *Pæon Primus*, and both Greek and Latin would swear that it was composed of a trochee and what they term a pyrrhic—that is to say a foot of two *short* syllables—a thing that *cannot be*, as I shall presently show.

But now, there is an obvious difficulty. The *astrologos*, according to the Prosodies' own showing, is equal to *five* short syllables, and the trochee to *three*—yet, in the line quoted, these two feet are equal. They occupy *precisely* the same time. In fact, the whole music of the line depends upon their being *made* to occupy the same time. The Prosodies then, have demonstrated what all mathematicians have stupidly failed in demonstrating—that three and five are one and the same thing.

After what I have already said, however, about the bastard trochee and the bastard iambus, no one can have any trouble in understanding that *many are the* is of similar character. It is merely a bolder variation than usual from the routine of trochees, and introduces to the bastard trochee one additional syllable. But this syllable is not *short*. That is, it is not short in the sense of *"short"* as applied to the final syllable of the ordinary trochee, where the word means merely *the half of long*.

In this case (that of the additional syllable) "short," if used at all, must be used in the sense of *the sixth of long*. And all the three final syllables can be called *short* only with the same understanding of the term. The three together are equal only to the one short syllable (whose place they supply) of the ordinary trochee. It follows that there is no sense in thus (˘) accenting these syllables. We must devise for them some new character which shall denote the sixth of long. Let it be (‹)—the crescent placed with the curve to the left. The whole foot (mānÿ aré thé) might be called a *quick trochee*.

We come now to the final division (*me*) of Mr. Cranch's line. It is clear that this foot, short as it appears, is fully equal in time to each of the preceding. It is in fact the cæsura—the foot which, in the beginning of this paper, I called the most important in all verse. Its chief office is that of pause or termination; and here—at the end of a line—its use is easy, because there is no danger of misapprehending its value. We pause on it, by a seeming necessity, just so long as it has taken us to pronounce the preceding feet, whether iambus, trochees, dactyls or anapæsts. It is thus a *variable foot*, and, with some care, may be well introduced into the body of a line, as in a little poem of great beauty by Mrs. Welby:

I have | a lit | tle step | sŏ̃n | of on | ly three | years old. |

Here we dwell on the cæsura, *son*, just as long as it requires us to pronounce either of the preceding or succeeding iam-busses. Its value, therefore, in this line, is that of three short syllables. In the following dactylic line its value is that of four short syllables.

Pale as a | lily was | Emily | G͞ray.

I have accented the cæsura with a (͞ᴧᴧ) by way of expressing this variability of value.

I observed, just now, that there could be no such foot as one of two short syllables. What we start from in the very beginning of all idea on the topic of verse, is quantity, *length*. Thus when we enunciate an independent syllable it is long, as a matter of course. If we enunciate two, dwelling on both equally, we express equality in the enumeration, or length, and have a right to call them two long syllables. If we dwell on one more than the other, we have also a right to call one short, because it is short in relation to the other. But if we dwell on both equally and with a tripping voice, saying to ourselves here are two short syllables, the query might well be asked of us—"in relation to what are they short?" Shortness is but the negation of length. To say, then, that two syllables, placed independently of any other syllable, are short, is merely to say that they have no positive length, or enunciation—in other words that they are no syllables—that they do not exist at all. And if, persisting, we add anything about their equality, we are merely floundering in the idea of an identical equation, where, x being equal to x, nothing is shown to be equal to zero. In a word we can form no conception of a pyrrhic as of an independent foot. It is a mere chimera bred in the mad fancy of a pedant.

From what I have said about the equalization of the several feet of a *line*, it must not be deduced that any *necessity* for equality in time exists between the rhythm of *several* lines. A poem, or even a stanza, may begin with iambuses, in the first line, and proceed with anapæsts in the second, or even with the less accordant dactyls, as in the opening of quite a pretty specimen of verse by Miss Mary A. S. Aldrich:

The wa | ter li | ly sleeps | in pride | ᨈ
Dōwn ĭn thĕ | dēpths ŏf thĕ | āzūre | lăke. |

Here *azure* is a spondee, equivalent to a dactyl; *lake* a cæsura.

I shall now best proceed in quoting the initial lines of Byron's "Bride of Abydos:"

Know ye the land where the cypress and myrtle
   Are emblems of deeds that are done in their clime—
Where the rage of the vulture, the love of the turtle
   Now melt into softness, now madden to crime?
Know ye the land of the cedar and vine,
Where the flowers ever blossom, the beams ever shine,
And the light wings of Zephyr, oppressed with perfume,
Wax faint o'er the gardens of Gul in their bloom?
Where the citron and olive are fairest of fruit
And the voice of the nightingale never is mute—
Where the virgins are soft as the roses they twine,
And all save the spirit of man is divine?
'Tis the land of the East—'tis the land of the Sun—
Can he smile on such deeds as his children have done?
Oh, wild as the accents of lovers' farewell
Are the hearts that they bear and the tales that they tell.

Now the flow of these lines, (as times go,) is very sweet and musical. They have been often admired, and justly—as times go—that is to say, it is a rare thing to find better versification of its kind. And where verse is pleasant to the ear, it is silly to find fault with it because it refuses to be scanned. Yet I have heard men, professing to be scholars, who made no scruple of abusing these lines of Byron's on the ground that they were musical in spite of *all law*. Other gentlemen, *not* scholars, abused "all law" for the same reason:—and it occurred neither to the one party nor to the other that the law about which they were disputing might possibly be no law at all—an ass of a law in the skin of a lion.

The Grammars said something about dactylic lines, and it was easily seen that *these* lines were at least meant for dactylic. The first one was, therefore, thus divided:

Knōw yĕ thĕ | lānd whĕre thĕ | cyprĕss ănd | myrtle. |

The concluding foot was a mystery; but the Prosodies said something about the dactylic "measure" calling now and then for a double rhyme; and the court of enquiry were content to rest in the double rhyme, without exactly perceiving what a double rhyme had to do with the question of an irregular foot. Quitting the first line, the second was thus scanned:

Arē ĕmblĕms | ōf deĕds thăt | āre dŏne ĭn | thēir clīme. |

It was immediately seen, however, that *this* would not do:— it was at war with the whole emphasis of the reading. It could not be supposed that Byron, or any one in his senses, intended to place stress upon such monosyllables as "are," "of," and "their," nor could "their clime," collated with "to crime," in the corresponding line below, be fairly twisted into anything like a "double rhyme," so as to bring everything within the category of the Grammars. But farther these Grammars spoke not. The inquirers, therefore, in spite of their sense of harmony in the lines, when considered without reference to scansion, fell back upon the idea that the "Are" was a blunder—an excess for which the poet should be sent to Coventry—and, striking it out, they scanned the remainder of the line as follows:

——ēmblĕms ŏf | deēds thăt ăre | dōne ĭn thēir | clīme. |

This answered pretty well; but the Grammars admitted no such foot as a foot of one syllable; and besides the rhythm was dactylic. In despair, the books are well searched, however, and at last the investigators are gratified by a full solution of the riddle in the profound "Observation" quoted in the beginning of this article:—"When a syllable is wanting, the verse is said to be catalectic; when the measure is exact, the line is acatalectic; when there is a redundant syllable it forms hypermeter." This is enough. The anomalous line is pronounced to be catalectic at the head and to form hypermeter at the tail:—and so on, and so on; it being soon dis-

covered that nearly all the remaining lines are in a similar predicament, and that what flows so smoothly to the ear, although so roughly to the eye, is, after all, a mere jumble of
catalecticism, acatalecticism, and hypermeter—not to say
worse.

Now, had this court of inquiry been in possession of even
the shadow of the *philosophy* of Verse, they would have had
no trouble in reconciling this oil and water of the eye and ear,
by merely scanning the passage without reference to lines,
and, continuously, thus:

> Know ye the | land where the | cypress and | myrtle Are |
> emblems of | deeds that are | done in their | clime Where
> the | rage of the | vulture the | love of the | turtle Now |
> melt into | softness now | madden to | *crime* | Know ye
> the | land of the | cedar and | vine Where the | flowers ever
> | blossom the | beams ever | shine Where the | light wings
> of | Zephyr op | pressed by per | *fume Wax* | faint o'er the
> | gardens of | Gul in their | bloom Where the | citron and
> | olive are | fairest of | fruit And the | voice of the | night-
> ingale | never is | mute Where the | virgins are | soft as the
> | roses they | *twine And* | all save the | spirit of | man is di
> | vine 'Tis the | land of the | East 'tis the | clime of the |
> Sun Can he | smile on such | deeds as his | children have |
> *done Oh* | wild as the | accents of | lovers' fare | well Are
> the | hearts that they | bear and the | tales that they | *tell*.

Here "crime" and "tell" (italicized) are cæsuras, each having
the value of a dactyl, four short syllables; while "fume Wax,"
"twine and," and "done Oh," are spondees which, of course,
being composed of two long syllables, are also equal to four
short, and are the dactyl's natural equivalent. The nicety of
Byron's ear has led him into a succession of feet which, with
two trivial exceptions as regards melody, are absolutely accurate—a very rare occurrence this in dactylic or anapæstic
rhythms. The exceptions are found in the spondee *"twine
And"* and the dactyl, *"smile on such."* Both feet are false in
point of melody. In *"twine And,"* to make out the rhythm, we
must force *"And"* into a length which it will not naturally
bear. We are called on to sacrifice either the proper length of

the syllable as demanded by its position as a member of a spondee, or the customary accentuation of the word in conversation. There is no hesitation, and should be none. We at once give up the sound for the sense; and the rhythm is imperfect. In this instance it is *very* slightly so;—not one person in ten thousand could, by ear, detect the inaccuracy. But the *perfection* of verse, as regards melody, consists in its *never* demanding any such sacrifice as is here demanded. The rhythmical must agree, *thoroughly*, with the reading flow. This perfection has in no instance been attained—but is unquestionably attainable. *"Smile on such,"* the dactyl, is incorrect, because *"such,"* from the character of the two consonants *ch*, cannot *easily* be enunciated in the ordinary time of a short syllable, which its position declares that it is. Almost every reader will be able to appreciate the slight difficulty here; and yet the error is by no means so important as that of the *"And"* in the spondee. By dexterity we *may* pronounce *"such"* in the true time; but the attempt to remedy the rhythmical deficiency of the *And* by drawing it out, merely aggravates the offence against natural enunciation, by directing attention to the offence.

My main object, however, in quoting these lines, is to show that, in spite of the Prosodies, the length of a line is entirely an arbitrary matter. We might divide the commencement of Byron's poem thus:

Know ye the | land where the. |

or thus:

Know ye the | land where the | cypress and. |

or thus:

Know ye the | land where the | cypress and | myrtle are. |

or thus:

Know ye the | land where the | cypress and | myrtle are |
emblems of. |

In short we may give it any division we please, and the lines will
be good—provided we have at least *two* feet in a line. As in
mathematics two units are required to form number, so rhythm,
(from the Greek αριθμος, number,) demands for its formation
at least two feet. Beyond doubt, we often see such lines as

> Know ye the—
> Land where the—

lines of one foot; and our Prosodies admit such; but with
impropriety; for common sense would dictate that every so
obvious division of a poem as is made by a line, should include within itself all that is necessary for its own comprehension; but in a line of one foot we can have no appreciation of
rhythm, which depends upon the equality between *two* or
more pulsations. The false lines, consisting sometimes of a
single cæsura, which are seen in mock Pindaric odes, are of
course "rhythmical" only in connection with some other line;
and it is this want of independent rhythm which adapts them
to the purposes of burlesque alone. Their effect is that of incongruity (the principle of mirth;) for they intrude the blankness of prose amid the harmony of verse.

My second object in quoting Byron's lines, was that of showing how absurd it often is to cite a single line from amid the
body of a poem, for the purpose of instancing the perfection
or imperfection of the line's rhythm. Were we to see by itself

> Know ye the land where the cypress and myrtle,

we might justly condemn it as defective in the final foot,
which is equal to only three, instead of being equal to four,
short syllables.

In the foot (*flowers ever*) we shall find a further exemplification of the principle in the bastard iambus, bastard trochee,
and quick trochee, as I have been at some pains in describing
these feet above. All the Prosodies on English verse would
insist upon making an elision in "flowers," thus (flow'rs,) but
this is nonsense. In the quick trochee (mānÿ are the) occurring in Mr. Cranch's *trochaic* line, we had to equalize the time
of the three syllables (*ny, are, the,*) to that of the one *short*

syllable whose position they usurp. Accordingly each of these syllables is equal to the third of a short syllable, that is to say, the *sixth of a long*. But in Byron's *dactylic* rhythm, we have to equalize the time of the three syllables (*ers, ev, er,*) to that of the one *long* syllable whose position they usurp or, (which is the same thing,) of the *two short*. Therefore the value of each of the syllables (*ers, ev,* and *er*) is the *third of a long*. We enunciate them with only half the rapidity we employ in enunciating the three final syllables of the quick trochee— which latter is a rare foot. The *"flowers ever,"* on the contrary, is as common in the dactylic rhythm as is the *bastard* trochee in the trochaic, or the bastard iambus in the iambic. We may as well accent it with the curve of the crescent to the right, and call it a *bastard dactyl*. A *bastard anapæst*, whose nature I now need be at no trouble in explaining, will of course occur, now and then, in an anapæstic rhythm.

In order to avoid any chance of that confusion which is apt to be introduced in an essay of this kind by too sudden and radical an alteration of the conventionalities to which the reader has been accustomed, I have thought it right to suggest for the accent marks of the bastard trochee, bastard iambus, etc., etc., certain characters which, in merely varying the direction of the ordinary short accent (˘) should imply, what is the fact, that the feet themselves are not *new* feet, in any proper sense, but simply modifications of the feet, respectively, from which they derive their names. Thus a bastard iambus is, in its essentiality, that is to say, in its time, an iambus. The variation lies only in the *distribution* of this time. The time, for example, occupied by the one short (or *half of long*) syllable, in the ordinary iambus, is, in the bastard, spread equally over two syllables, which are accordingly the *fourth of long*.

But this fact—the fact of the essentiality, or whole time, of the foot being unchanged, is now so fully before the reader, that I may venture to propose, finally, an accentuation which shall answer the real purpose—that is to say what should be the real purpose of all accentuation—the purpose of expressing to the eye the exact relative value of every syllable employed in Verse.

I have already shown that enunciation, or *length*, is the point from which we start. In other words, we begin with *a*

long syllable. This then is our unit; and there will be no need
of accenting it at all. An unaccented syllable, in a system of
accentuation, is to be regarded always as a long syllable. Thus
a spondee would be without accent. In an iambus, the first
syllable being "short," or the *half* of long, should be accented
with a small 2, placed *beneath* the syllable; the last syllable,
being long, should be unaccented;—the whole would be thus
(control.) In a trochee, these accents would be merely conversed, thus (manly.) In a dactyl, each of the two final syllables, being the half of long, should, also, be accented with a
small 2 beneath the syllable; and the first syllable left unaccented, the whole would be thus (happiness.) In an anapæst
we should converse the dactyl thus, (in the land.) In the bastard dactyl, each of the three concluding syllables being the
third of long, should be accented with a small 3 beneath the
syllable, and the whole foot would stand thus, (flowers ever.)
In the bastard anapæst we should converse the bastard dactyl
thus, (in the rebound.) In the bastard iambus, each of the two
initial syllables, being the fourth of long, should be accented,
below, with a small 4; the whole foot would be thus, (in the
rain.) In the bastard trochee, we should converse the bastard
iambus thus, (many a.) In the quick trochee, each of the three
concluding syllables, being the *sixth* of long, should be accented, below, with a small 6; the whole foot would be thus,
(many are the.) The quick iambus is not yet created, and most
probably never will be; for it would be excessively useless,
awkward, and liable to misconception—as I have already
shown that even the quick trochee is:—but, should it appear,
we must accent it by conversing the quick trochee. The
cæsura, being variable in length, but always *longer than*
"long," should be accented, *above*, with a number expressing
the length, or value, of the distinctive foot of the rhythm in
which it occurs. Thus a cæsura, occurring in a spondaic
rhythm, would be accented with a small 2 above the syllable,

or, rather, foot. Occurring in a dactylic or anapæstic rhythm, we also accent it with the 2, above the foot. Occurring in an iambic rhythm, however, it must be accented, above, with 1½; for this is the relative value of the iambus. Occurring in the trochaic rhythm, we give it, of course, the same accentuation. For the complex 1½, however, it would be advisable to substitute the simpler expression $\frac{3}{2}$ which amounts to the same thing.

In this system of accentuation Mr. Cranch's lines, quoted above, would thus be written:

$$\frac{3}{2}$$
Many are the | thoughts that | come to | me
    6   6   6   2   2
  In my | lonely | musing, |
    2   2   2

$$\frac{3}{2}$$
And they | drift so | strange and | swift
  2   2   2
  There's no | time for | choosing |
    2   2   2

$$\frac{3}{2}$$
Which to | follow, | for to | leave
    2   2   2
  Any, | seems a | losing. |
  2   2   2

In the ordinary system the accentuation would be thus:

Mānў arĕ thĕ | thōughts thăt | cōme tŏ | mē |
  In my | lōnely | mūsing, |
ānd thĕy | drīft sŏ | strānge ănd | swīft |
  Therē's nŏ | timē fŏr | choōsing|
Whīch tŏ | fōllŏw, | fōr tŏ | lēave
āny, | seēms ă | lōsing. |

It must first be observed, here, that I do not grant this to be the "ordinary" *scansion*. On the contrary, I never yet met the man who had the faintest comprehension of the true scanning of these lines, or of such as these. But granting this to be the mode in which our Prosodies would divide the feet, they would accentuate the syllables as just above.

Now, let any reasonable person compare the two modes.

The first advantage seen in my mode is that of simplicity—of time, labor, and ink saved. Counting the fractions as *two* accents, even, there will be found only *twenty-six* accents to the stanza. In the common accentuation there are *forty-one*. But admit that all this is a trifle, which it is *not*, and let us proceed to points of importance. Does the common accentuation express the truth, in particular, in general, or in any regard? Is it consistent with itself? Does it convey either to the ignorant or to the scholar a just conception of the rhythm of the lines? Each of these questions must be answered in the negative. The crescents, being precisely similar, must be understood as expressing, all of them, one and the same thing; and so all prosodies have always understood them and wished them to be understood. They express, indeed, "short"—but this word has all kinds of meanings. It serves to represent (the reader is left to guess *when*) sometimes the half, sometimes the third, sometimes the fourth, and sometimes the sixth, of "long"— while "long" itself, in the books, is left undefined and undescribed. On the other hand, the horizontal accent, it may be said, expresses sufficiently well, and unvaryingly, the syllables which are meant to be long. It does nothing of the kind. This horizontal accent is placed over the cæsura (wherever, as in the Latin Prosodies, the cæsura is recognized) as well as over the ordinary long syllable, and implies anything and everything, just as the crescent. But grant that it does express the ordinary long syllables, (leaving the cæsura out of question,) have I not given the identical expression, by not employing any expression at all? In a word, while the Prosodies, with a certain number of accents, express *precisely nothing whatever*, I, with scarcely half the number, have expressed everything which, in a system of accentuation, demands expression. In glancing at my mode in the lines of Mr. Cranch, it will be seen that it conveys not only the exact relation of the syllables and feet, among themselves, in those particular lines, but their precise value in relation to any other existing or conceivable feet or syllables, in any existing or conceivable system of rhythm.

The object of what we call *scansion* is the distinct making of the rhythmical flow. Scansion without accents or perpendicular lines between the feet—that is to say scansion *by* the voice only—is scansion *to* the ear only; and all very good in its way. The written scansion addresses the ear through the eye. In either case the object is the distinct making of the rhythmical, musical, or reading flow. There *can* be no other object and there is none. Of course, then, the scansion and the reading flow should go hand in hand. The former must agree with the latter. The former represents and expresses the latter; and is good or bad as it truly or falsely represents and expresses it. If by the written scansion of a line we are not enabled to perceive any rhythm or music in the line, then either the line is unrhythmical or the scansion false. Apply all this to the English lines which we have quoted, at various points, in the course of this article. It will be found that the scansion exactly conveys the rhythm, and thus thoroughly fulfils the only purpose for which scansion is required.

But let the scansion *of the schools* be applied to the Greek and Latin verse, and what result do we find?—that the verse is one thing and the scansion quite another. The ancient verse, *read* aloud, is in general musical, and occasionally *very* musical. *Scanned* by the Prosodial rules we can, for the most part, make nothing of it whatever. In the case of the English verse, the more emphatically we dwell on the divisions between the feet, the more distinct is our perception of the kind of rhythm intended. In the case of the Greek and Latin, the more we dwell the *less* distinct is this perception. To make this clear by an example:

> Mæcenas, atavis edite regibus,
> O, et præsidium et dulce decus meum,
> Sunt quos curriculo pulverem Olympicum
> Collegisse juvat, metaque fervidis
> Evitata rotis, palmaque nobilis
> Terrarum dominos evehit ad Deos.

Now in *reading* these lines, there is scarcely one person in a thousand who, if even ignorant of Latin, will not immediately feel and appreciate their flow—their music. A prosodist, however, informs the public that the *scansion* runs thus:

Mæce | nas ata | vis | edite | regibus |
O, et | præsidi' | et | dulce de | cus meum |
Sunt quos | curricu | lo | pulver' O | lympicum |
Colle | gisse ju | vat | metaque | fervidis |
Evi | tata ro | tis | palmaque | nobilis |
Terra | rum domi | nos | evehit | ad Deos. |

Now I do not deny that we get a *certain sort* of music from the lines if we read them according to this scansion, but I wish to call attention to the fact that this scansion and the certain sort of music which grows out of it, are entirely at war not only with the reading flow which any ordinary person would naturally give the lines, but with the reading flow universally given them, and never denied them, by even the most obstinate and stolid of scholars.

And now these questions are forced upon us—"Why exists this discrepancy between the modern verse with its scansion, and the ancient verse with its scansion?"—"Why, in the former case, are there agreement and representation, while in the latter there is neither the one nor the other?" or, to come to the point,—"How are we to reconcile the ancient verse with the scholastic scansion of it?" This absolutely necessary conciliation—shall we bring it about by supposing the scholastic scansion wrong because the ancient verse is right, or by maintaining that the ancient verse is wrong because the scholastic scansion is not to be gainsaid?

Were we to adopt the latter mode of arranging the difficulty, we might, in some measure, at least simplify the expression of the arrangement by putting it thus—Because the pedants have no eyes, therefore the old poets had no ears.

"But," say the gentlemen without the eyes, "the scholastic scansion, although certainly not handed down to us in form from the old poets themselves (the gentlemen without the ears,) is nevertheless deduced, Baconially, from certain facts which are supplied us by careful observation of the old poems."

And let us illustrate this strong position by an example from an American poet—who must be a poet of some eminence, or he will not answer the purpose. Let us take Mr. Alfred B. Street. I remember these two lines of his:

>His sinuous path, by blazes, wound
>Among trunks grouped in myriads round.

With the *sense* of these lines I have nothing to do. When a poet is in a "fine phrensy" he may as well imagine a large forest as a small one—and "by blazes!" is *not* intended for an oath. My concern is with the rhythm, which is iambic.

Now let us suppose that, a thousand years hence, when the "American language" is dead, a learned prosodist should be deducing from "careful observation" of our best poets, a system of scansion for our poetry. And let us suppose that this prosodist had so little dependence in the generality and immutability of the laws of Nature, as to assume in the outset, that, because we lived a thousand years before his time and made use of steam-engines instead of mesmeric balloons, we must therefore have had a *very* singular fashion of mouthing our vowels, and altogether of hudsonizing our verse. And let us suppose that with these and other fundamental propositions carefully put away in his brain, he should arrive at the line,

>Among | trunks grouped | in my | riads round.

Finding it in an obviously iambic rhythm, he would divide it as above, and observing that "trunks" made the first member of an iambus, he would call it short, as Mr. Street intended it to be. Now farther:—if instead of admitting the possibility that Mr. Street, (who by that time would be called Street simply, just as we say Homer)—that Mr. Street might have been in the habit of writing carelessly, as the poets of the prosodist's own era did, and as all poets will do (on account of being geniuses)—instead of admitting this, suppose the learned scholar should make a "rule" and put it in a book, to the effect that, in the American verse, the vowel *u*, *when found embedded among nine consonants*, was *short*. What, under such circumstances, would the sensible people of the scholar's day have a right not only to think, but to say of that scholar?—why, that he was "a fool,—by blazes!"

I have put an extreme case, but it strikes at the root of the error. The "rules" are grounded in "authority"—and this "authority"—can any one tell us what it means? or can any one

suggest anything that it may *not* mean? Is it not clear that the
"scholar" above referred to, might as readily have deduced
from authority a totally false system as a partially true one?
To deduce from authority a consistent prosody of the ancient
metres would indeed have been within the limits of the barest
possibility; and the task has *not* been accomplished, for the
reason that it demands a species of ratiocination altogether
out of keeping with the brain of a bookworm. A rigid scrutiny will show that the very few "rules" which have not as
many exceptions as examples, are those which have, by accident, their true bases not in authority, but in the omnipreva-
lent laws of syllabification; such, for example, as the rule
which declares a vowel before two consonants to be long.

   In a word, the gross confusion and antagonism of the scholastic prosody, as well as its marked inapplicability to the reading flow of the rhythms it pretends to illustrate, are attributable, first to the utter absence of natural principle as a guide
in the investigations which have been undertaken by inadequate
men; and secondly to the neglect of the obvious consideration
that the ancient poems, which have been the *criteria* throughout, were the work of men who must have written as loosely,
and with as little definitive system, as ourselves.

   Were Horace alive to day, he would divide for us his first
Ode thus, and "make great eyes" when assured by the prosodists that he had no business to make any such division:

> Mæcenas | atavis | edite | regibus |
>   2 2   2 2   2 2   2 2
> O et præ | sidium et | dulce de | cus meum |
>   2 2   3 3 3   2 2   2 2
> Sunt quos cur | riculo | pulverem O | lympicum |
>   2 2   2 2   3 3 3   2 2
> Collegisse | juvat | metaque | fervidis |
>   3 3 3   2   2   2 2
> Evitata | rotis | palmaque | nobilis |
>   3 3 3   2 2   2 2
> Terrarum | dominos | evehit | ad Deos. |
>   2 2   2 2   2 2   2 2

Read by this scansion, the flow is preserved; and the more we
dwell on the divisions, the more the intended rhythm becomes apparent. Moreover, the feet have all the same time;
while, in the scholastic scansion, trochees—admitted tro-

chees—are absurdly employed as equivalents to spondees and dactyls. The books declare, for instance, that *Colle*, which begins the fourth line, is a trochee, and seem to be gloriously unconscious that to put a trochee in apposition with a longer foot, is to violate the inviolable principle of all music, *time*.

It will be said, however, by "some people" that I have no business to make a dactyl out of such obviously long syllables as *sunt*, *quos*, *cur*. Certainly I have no business to do so. I *never* do so. And Horace should not have done so. But he did. Mr. Bryant and Mr. Longfellow do the same thing every day. And merely because these gentlemen, now and then, forget themselves in this way, it would be hard if some future prosodist should insist upon twisting the "Thanatopsis," or the "Spanish Student," into a jumble of trochees, spondees, and dactyls.

It may be said, also, by some other people that in the word *decus*, I have succeeded no better than the books, in making the scansional agree with the reading flow; and that *decus* was not pronounced de *cus*. I reply that there can be no doubt of the word having been pronounced, in this case, de *cus*. It must be observed that the Latin *case*, or variation of a noun in its terminating syllables, caused the Romans— *must* have caused them to pay greater attention to the termination of a noun than to its commencement, or than we do to the terminations of our nouns. The end of the Latin word established that relation of the word with other words, which we establish by prepositions. Therefore, it would seem infinitely less odd to them than it does to us, to dwell at any time, for any slight purpose, abnormally, on a terminating syllable. In verse this license, scarcely a license, would be frequently admitted. These ideas unlock the secret of such lines as the

Litoreis ingens inventa sub ilici *bus sus*,

and the

Parturiunt montes nascetur ridicu *lus mus*,

which I quoted, some time ago, while speaking of rhyme.

As regards the prosodial elisions, such as that of *rem* before O, in *pulverem Olympicum*, it is really difficult to understand how so dismally silly a notion could have entered the brain even of a pedant. Were it demanded of me why the books cut off one *vowel* before another, I might say—it is, perhaps, because the books think that, since a bad reader is so apt to slide the one vowel into the other at any rate, it is just as well to print them *ready-slided*. But in the case of the terminating *m*, which is the most readily pronounced of all consonants, (as the infantile *mama* will testify,) and the most impossible to cheat the ear of by any system of sliding—in the case of the *m*, I should be driven to reply that, to the best of my belief, the prosodists did the thing, because they had a fancy for doing it, and wished to see how funny it would look after it was done. The thinking reader will perceive that, from the great facility with which *em* may be enunciated, it is admirably suited to form one of the rapid short syllables in the bastard dactyl (pulverem O)—but because the books had no conception of a bastard dactyl, they knocked it in the head at once—by cutting off its tail.

Let me now give a specimen of the true scansion of another Horatian measure; embodying an instance of proper elision.

> Integer | vitæ | scelerisque | purus |
> Non eget | Mauri | jaculis ne | que arcu |
> Nec vene | natis | gravida sa | gittis,
> Fusce, pha | retra.

Here the regular recurrence of the bastard iambus, gives great animation to the rhythm. The *e* before the *a* in *que arcu* is, almost of sheer necessity, cut off—that is to say, run into the *a* so as to preserve the spondee. But even this license it would have been better not to take.

Had I space, nothing would afford me greater pleasure than to proceed with the scansion of *all* the ancient rhythms, and to show how easily, by the help of common sense, the intended music of each and all can be rendered instantaneously apparent. But I have already overstepped my limits, and must bring this paper to an end.

It will never do, however, to omit all mention of the heroic hexameter.

I began the "processes" by a suggestion of the spondee as the first step towards verse. But the innate monotony of the spondee has caused its disappearance, as the basis of rhythm, from all modern poetry. We *may* say, indeed, that the French heroic—the most wretchedly monotonous verse in existence—is, to all intents and purposes, spondaic. But it is not designedly spondaic—and if the French were ever to examine it at all, they would no doubt pronounce it iambic. It must be observed that the French language is strangely peculiar in this point—*that it is without accentuation and consequently without verse*. The genius of the people, rather than the structure of the tongue, declares that their words are, for the most part, enunciated with an uniform dwelling on each syllable. For example, *we* say "syl*labifica*tion." A Frenchman would say syl-la-bi-fi-ca-ti-on; dwelling on no one of the syllables with any noticeable particularity. Here again I put an extreme case, in order to be well understood; but the general fact is as I give it—that comparatively, the French have *no* accentuation. And there can be nothing worth the name of verse, without. Therefore, the French have no verse worth the name—which is the fact, put in sufficiently plain terms. Their iambic rhythm so superabounds in absolute spondees as to warrant me in calling its basis spondaic; but French is the *only* modern tongue which has any rhythm with such basis; and even in the French, it is, as I have said, unintentional.

Admitting, however, the validity of my suggestion that the spondee was the first approach to verse, we should expect to find, first, natural spondees, (words each forming just a spondee,) most abundant in the most ancient languages, and, secondly, we should expect to find spondees forming the basis of the most ancient rhythms. These expectations are in both cases confirmed.

Of the Greek hexameter, the intentional basis is spondaic. The dactyls are the *variation* of the theme. It will be observed that there is no absolute certainty about *their* points of interposition. The penultimate foot, it is true, is usually a dactyl; but not uniformly so; while the ultimate, on which the ear *lingers* is always a spondee. Even that the penultimate is usu-

ally a dactyl may be clearly referred to the necessity of winding up with the *distinctive* spondee. In corroboration of this
idea, again, we should look to find the penultimate spondee
most usual in the most ancient verse; and, accordingly, we
find it more frequent in the Greek than in the Latin hexameter.

But besides all this, spondees are not only more prevalent
in the heroic hexameter than dactyls, but occur to such an
extent as is even unpleasant to modern ears, on account of
monotony. What the modern chiefly appreciates and admires
in the Greek hexameter is the *melody of the abundant vowel
sounds*. The Latin hexameters *really* please very few moderns—although so many pretend to fall into ecstasies about
them. In the hexameters quoted, several pages ago, from
Silius Italicus, the preponderance of the spondee is strikingly
manifest. Besides the natural spondees of the Greek and
Latin, numerous artificial ones arise in the verse of these
tongues on account of the tendency which *case* has to throw
full accentuation on terminal syllables; and the preponderance
of the spondee is farther ensured by the comparative infrequency of the small prepositions which *we* have to serve us
instead of case, and also the absence of the diminutive auxiliary verbs with which *we* have to eke out the expression of
our primary ones. These are the monosyllables whose abundance serve to stamp the poetic genius of a language as tripping or dactylic.

Now paying no attention to these facts, Sir Philip Sidney,
Professor Longfellow, and innumerable other persons more
or less modern, have busied themselves in constructing what
they supposed to be "English hexameters on the model of the
Greek." The only difficulty was that (even leaving out of
question the melodious masses of vowel,) these gentlemen
never could get their English hexameters to *sound* Greek. Did
they *look* Greek?—that should have been the query; and the
reply might have led to a solution of the riddle. In placing a
copy of ancient hexameters side by side with a copy (in similar type) of such hexameters as Professor Longfellow, or Professor Felton, or the Frogpondian Professors collectively, are
in the shameful practice of composing "on the model of the
Greek," it will be seen that the latter (hexameters, not profes-

sors) are about one third longer *to the eye*, on an average, than the former. The more abundant dactyls make the difference. And it is the greater number of spondees in the Greek than in the English—in the ancient than in the modern tongue— which has caused it to fall out that while these eminent scholars were groping about in the dark for a Greek hexameter, which is a spondaic rhythm varied now and then by dactyls, they merely stumbled, to the lasting scandal of scholarship, over something which, on account of its long-leggedness, we may as well term a Feltonian hexameter, and which is a dactylic rhythm, interrupted, rarely, by artificial spondees which are no spondees at all, and which are curiously thrown in by the heels at all kinds of improper and impertinent points.

Here is a specimen of the Longfellownian hexameter.

Also the | church with | in was a | dorned for | this was the | season |
In which the | young their | parents' | hope and the | loved ones of | Heaven |
Should at the | foot of the | altar re | new the | vows of their | baptism |
Therefore each | nook and | corner was | swept and | cleaned and the | dust was |
Blown from the | walls and | ceiling and | from the | oil-painted benches. |

Mr. Longfellow is a man of imagination—but *can* he imagine that any individual, with a proper understanding of the danger of lock-jaw, would make the attempt of twisting his mouth into the shape necessary for the emission of such spondees as "par*ents*," or such dactyls as "cleaned and the" and "loved ones of?" "Baptism" is by no means a bad spondee— perhaps because it happens to be a dactyl;—of all the rest, however, I am dreadfully ashamed.

But these feet—dactyls and spondees, all together,— should thus be put at once into their proper position:

"Also, the church within was adorned; for this was the season in which the young, their parents' hope, and the loved ones of Heaven, should, at the feet of the altar, renew the

vows of their baptism. Therefore, each nook and corner
was swept and cleaned; and the dust was blown from the
walls and ceiling, and from the oil-painted benches."

There!—that is respectable prose; and it will incur no danger of ever getting its character ruined by any body's mistaking it for verse.

But even when we let these modern hexameters go, as
Greek, and merely hold them fast in their proper character of
Longfellownian, or Feltonian, or Frogpondian, we must still
condemn them as having been committed in a radical misconception of the philosophy of verse. The spondee, as I observed, is the *theme* of the Greek line. Most of the ancient
hexameters *begin* with spondees, for the reason that the spondee *is* the theme; and the ear is filled with it as with a burden.
Now the Feltonian dactylics have, in the same way, dactyls
for the theme, and most of them begin with dactyls—which
is all very proper if not very Greek— but, unhappily, the one
point at which they *are* very Greek is that point, precisely, at
which they should be nothing but Feltonian. They always
close with what is meant for a spondee. To be consistently
silly, they should die off in a dactyl.

That a truly Greek hexameter *cannot*, however, be readily
composed in English, is a proposition which I am by no
means inclined to admit. I think I could manage the point
myself. For example:

Do tell! | when may we | hope to make | men of sense | out
    of the | Pundits |
Born and brought | up with their | snouts deep | down in
    the | mud of the | Frog-pond?
Why ask? | who ever | yet saw | money made | out of a | fat
    old—
Jew, or | downright | upright | nutmegs | out of a | pine-
    knot? |

The proper spondee predominance is here preserved. Some of
the dactyls are not so good as I could wish—but, upon the
whole, the rhythm is very decent—to say nothing of its excellent sense.

The Poetic Principle

IN SPEAKING of the Poetic Principle, I have no design to be either thorough or profound. While discussing, very much at random, the essentiality of what we call Poetry, my principal purpose will be to cite for consideration, some few of those minor English or American poems which best suit my own taste, or which, upon my own fancy, have left the most definite impression. By "minor poems" I mean, of course, poems of little length. And here, in the beginning, permit me to say a few words in regard to a somewhat peculiar principle, which, whether rightfully or wrongfully, has always had its influence in my own critical estimate of the poem. I hold that a long poem does not exist. I maintain that the phrase, "a long poem," is simply a flat contradiction in terms.

I need scarcely observe that a poem deserves its title only inasmuch as it excites, by elevating the soul. The value of the poem is in the ratio of this elevating excitement. But all excitements are, through a psychal necessity, transient. That degree of excitement which would entitle a poem to be so called at all, cannot be sustained throughout a composition of any great length. After the lapse of half an hour, at the very utmost, it flags—fails—a revulsion ensues—and then the poem is, in effect, and in fact, no longer such.

There are, no doubt, many who have found difficulty in reconciling the critical dictum that the "Paradise Lost" is to be devoutly admired throughout, with the absolute impossibility of maintaining for it, during perusal, the amount of enthusiasm which that critical dictum would demand. This great work, in fact, is to be regarded as poetical, only when, losing sight of that vital requisite in all works of Art, Unity, we view it merely as a series of minor poems. If, to preserve its Unity—its totality of effect or impression—we read it (as would be necessary) at a single sitting, the result is but a constant alternation of excitement and depression. After a passage of what we feel to be true poetry, there follows, inevitably, a passage of platitude which no critical pre-judgment can force us to admire; but if, upon completing the work, we read it again, omitting the first book—that is to say, commencing

71

with the second—we shall be surprised at now finding that admirable which we before condemned—that damnable which we had previously so much admired. It follows from all this that the ultimate, aggregate, or absolute effect of even the best epic under the sun, is a nullity:—and this is precisely the fact.

In regard to the Iliad, we have, if not positive proof, at least very good reason for believing it intended as a series of lyrics; but, granting the epic intention, I can say only that the work is based in an imperfect sense of art. The modern epic is, of the supposititious ancient model, but an inconsiderate and blindfold imitation. But the day of these artistic anomalies is over. If, at any time, any very long poem *were* popular in reality, which I doubt, it is at least clear that no very long poem will ever be popular again.

That the extent of a poetical work is, *cæteris paribus*, the measure of its merit, seems undoubtedly, when we thus state it, a proposition sufficiently absurd—yet we are indebted for it to the Quarterly Reviews. Surely there can be nothing in mere *size*, abstractly considered—there can be nothing in mere *bulk*, so far as a volume is concerned, which has so continuously elicited admiration from these saturnine pamphlets! A mountain, to be sure, by the mere sentiment of physical magnitude which it conveys, *does* impress us with a sense of the sublime—but no man is impressed after *this* fashion by the material grandeur of even "The Columbiad." Even the Quarterlies have not instructed us to be so impressed by it. *As yet*, they have not *insisted* on our estimating Lamartine by the cubic foot, or Pollock by the pound—but what else are we to *infer* from their continual prating about "sustained effort?" If, by "sustained effort," any little gentleman has accomplished an epic, let us frankly commend him for the effort—if this indeed be a thing commendable—but let us forbear praising the epic on the effort's account. It is to be hoped that common sense, in the time to come, will prefer deciding upon a work of art, rather by the impression it makes, by the effect it produces, than by the time it took to impress the effect, or by the amount of "sustained effort" which had been found necessary in effecting the impression. The fact is, that perseverance is one thing, and genius quite another; nor can all the Quarterlies in Christendom confound them. By and by, this proposition, with many which I have been just urging, will be received as self-evident. In the mean time, by being generally condemned as falsities, they will not be essentially damaged as truths.

On the other hand, it is clear that a poem may be improperly brief. Undue brevity degenerates into mere epigrammatism. A *very* short poem, while now and then producing a brilliant or vivid, never produces a profound or enduring effect. There must be the steady pressing down of the stamp upon the wax. De Béranger has wrought innumerable things, pungent and spirit-stirring; but, in general, they have been too imponderous to stamp themselves deeply into the public attention; and thus, as so many feathers of fancy, have been blown aloft only to be whistled down the wind.

A remarkable instance of the effect of undue brevity in depressing a poem—in keeping it out of the popular view—is afforded by the following exquisite little Serenade.

> I arise from dreams of thee,
>   In the first sweet sleep of night,
> When the winds are breathing low,
>   And the stars are shining bright.
> I arise from dreams of thee,
>   And a spirit in my feet
> Has led me—who knows how?—
>   To thy chamber-window, sweet!
>
> The wandering airs they faint
>   On the dark, the silent stream—
> The champak odours fail
>   Like sweet thoughts in a dream;
> The nightingale's complaint,
>   It dies upon her heart
> As I must die on thine,
>   O, beloved as thou art!
>
> O, lift me from the grass!
>   I die, I faint, I fail!
> Let thy love in kisses rain

On my lips and eyelids pale.
My cheek is cold and white, alas!
My heart beats loud and fast:
Oh! press it close to thine again,
Where it will break at last!

Very few, perhaps, are familiar with these lines—yet no less
a poet than Shelley is their author. Their warm, yet delicate
and ethereal imagination will be appreciated by all—but by
none so thoroughly as by him who has himself arisen from
sweet dreams of one beloved, to bathe in the aromatic air of
a southern mid-summer night.

One of the finest poems by Willis—the very best, in my
opinion, which he has ever written—has, no doubt, through
this same defect of undue brevity, been kept back from its
proper position, not less in the critical than in the popular view.

The shadows lay along Broadway,
  'Twas near the twilight-tide—
And slowly there a lady fair
  Was walking in her pride.
Alone walked she; but, viewlessly,
  Walked spirits at her side.

Peace charmed the street beneath her feet,
  And Honour charmed the air;
And all astir looked kind on her,
  And called her good as fair—
For all God ever gave to her
  She kept with chary care.

She kept with care her beauties rare
  From lovers warm and true—
For her heart was cold to all but gold,
  And the rich came not to woo—
But honoured well are charms to sell
  If priests the selling do.

Now walking there was one more fair—
  A slight girl, lily-pale;

And she had unseen company
    To make the spirit quail—
'Twixt Want and Scorn she walked forlorn,
    And nothing could avail.

No mercy now can clear her brow
    For this world's peace to pray;
For, as love's wild prayer dissolved in air,
    Her woman's heart gave way!—
But the sin forgiven by Christ in Heaven
    By man is cursed alway!

In this composition we find it difficult to recognise the Willis who has written so many mere "verses of society." The lines are not only richly ideal, but full of energy; while they breathe an earnestness—an evident sincerity of sentiment—for which we look in vain throughout all the other works of this author.

While the epic mania—while the idea that, to merit in poetry, prolixity is indispensable—has, for some years past, been gradually dying out of the public mind, by mere dint of its own absurdity—we find it succeeded by a heresy too palpably false to be long tolerated, but one which, in the brief period it has already endured, may be said to have accomplished more in the corruption of our Poetical Literature than all its other enemies combined. I allude to the heresy of *The Didactic*. It has been assumed, tacitly and avowedly, directly and indirectly, that the ultimate object of all Poetry is Truth. Every poem, it is said, should inculcate a moral; and by this moral is the poetical merit of the work to be adjudged. We Americans, especially, have patronised this happy idea; and we Bostonians, very especially, have developed it in full. We have taken it into our heads that to write a poem simply for the poem's sake, and to acknowledge such to have been our design, would be to confess ourselves radically wanting in the true Poetic dignity and force:—but the simple fact is, that, would we but permit ourselves to look into our own souls, we should immediately there discover that under the sun there neither exists nor *can* exist any work more thoroughly dignified—more supremely noble than this very poem—this poem *per se*—this poem which is a poem and nothing more—this poem written solely for the poem's sake.

With as deep a reverence for the True as ever inspired the bosom of man, I would, nevertheless, limit, in some measure, its modes of inculcation. I would limit to enforce them. I would not enfeeble them by dissipation. The demands of Truth are severe. She has no sympathy with the myrtles. All *that* which is so indispensable in Song, is precisely all *that* with which *she* has nothing whatever to do. It is but making her a flaunting paradox, to wreathe her in gems and flowers. In enforcing a truth, we need severity rather than efflorescence of language. We must be simple, precise, terse. We must be cool, calm, unimpassioned. In a word, we must be in that mood which, as nearly as possible, is the exact converse of the poetical. *He* must be blind, indeed, who does not perceive the radical and chasmal differences between the truthful and the poetical modes of inculcation. He must be theory-mad beyond redemption who, in spite of these differences, shall still persist in attempting to reconcile the obstinate oils and waters of Poetry and Truth.

Dividing the world of mind into its three most immediately obvious distinctions, we have the Pure Intellect, Taste, and the Moral Sense. I place Taste in the middle, because it is just this position, which, in the mind, it occupies. It holds intimate relations with either extreme; but from the Moral Sense is separated by so faint a difference that Aristotle has not hesitated to place some of its operations among the virtues themselves. Nevertheless, we find the *offices* of the trio marked with a sufficient distinction. Just as the Intellect concerns itself with Truth, so Taste informs us of the Beautiful while the Moral Sense is regardful of Duty. Of this latter, while Conscience teaches the obligation, and Reason the expediency, Taste contents herself with displaying the charms:—waging war upon Vice solely on the ground of her deformity—her disproportion—her animosity to the fitting, to the appropriate, to the harmonious—in a word, to Beauty.

An immortal instinct, deep within the spirit of man, is thus, plainly, a sense of the Beautiful. This it is which administers to his delight in the manifold forms, and sounds, and odours, and sentiments amid which he exists. And just as the lily is repeated in the lake, or the eyes of Amaryllis in the mirror, so is the mere oral or written repetition of these forms, and sounds, and colours, and odours, and sentiments, a duplicate source of delight. But this mere repetition is not poetry. He who shall simply sing, with however glowing enthusiasm, or with however vivid a truth of description, of the sights, and sounds, and odours, and colours, and sentiments, which greet *him* in common with all mankind—he, I say, has yet failed to prove his divine title. There is still a something in the distance which he has been unable to attain. We have still a thirst unquenchable, to allay which he has not shown us the crystal springs. This thirst belongs to the immortality of Man. It is at once a consequence and an indication of his perennial existence. It is the desire of the moth for the star. It is no mere appreciation of the Beauty before us—but a wild effort to reach the Beauty above. Inspired by an ecstatic prescience of the glories beyond the grave, we struggle, by multiform combinations among the things and thoughts of Time, to attain a portion of that Loveliness whose very elements, perhaps, appertain to eternity alone. And thus when by Poetry—or when by Music, the most entrancing of the Poetic moods—we find ourselves melted into tears—we weep then—not as the Abbaté Gravina supposes—through excess of pleasure, but through a certain, petulant, impatient sorrow at our inability to grasp *now*, wholly, here on earth, at once and for ever, those divine and rapturous joys, of which *through* the poem, or *through* the music, we attain to but brief and indeterminate glimpses.

The struggle to apprehend the supernal Loveliness—this struggle, on the part of souls fittingly constituted—has given to the world all *that* which it (the world) has ever been enabled at once to understand and *to feel* as poetic.

The Poetic Sentiment, of course, may develope itself in various modes—in Painting, in Sculpture, in Architecture, in the Dance—very especially in Music—and very peculiarly, and with a wide field, in the composition of the Landscape Garden. Our present theme, however, has regard only to its manifestation in words. And here let me speak briefly on the topic of rhythm. Contenting myself with the certainty that Music, in its various modes of metre, rhythm, and rhyme, is of so

vast a moment in Poetry as never to be wisely rejected—is so
vitally important an adjunct, that he is simply silly who declines its assistance, I will not now pause to maintain its absolute essentiality. It is in Music, perhaps, that the soul most
nearly attains the great end for which, when inspired with the
Poetic Sentiment, it struggles—the creation of supernal
Beauty. It *may* be, indeed, that here this sublime end is, now
and then, attained *in fact*. We are often made to feel, with a
shivering delight, that from an earthly harp are stricken notes
which *cannot* have been unfamiliar to the angels. And thus
there can be little doubt that in the union of Poetry with
Music in its popular sense, we shall find the widest field for
the Poetic development. The old Bards and Minnesingers had
advantages which we do not possess—and Thomas Moore,
singing his own songs, was, in the most legitimate manner,
perfecting them as poems.

To recapitulate, then:—I would define, in brief, the Poetry
of words as *The Rhythmical Creation of Beauty*. Its sole arbiter
is Taste. With the Intellect or with the Conscience, it has only
collateral relations. Unless incidentally, it has no concern
whatever either with Duty or with Truth.

A few words, however, in explanation. *That* pleasure which
is at once the most pure, the most elevating, and the most
intense, is derived, I maintain, from the contemplation of the
Beautiful. In the contemplation of Beauty we alone find it
possible to attain that pleasurable elevation, or excitement, *of
the soul*, which we recognise as the Poetic Sentiment, and
which is so easily distinguished from Truth, which is the satisfaction of the Reason, or from Passion, which is the excitement of the heart. I make Beauty, therefore—using the word
as inclusive of the sublime—I make Beauty the province of
the poem, simply because it is an obvious rule of Art that
effects should be made to spring as directly as possible from
their causes:—no one as yet having been weak enough to
deny that the peculiar elevation in question is at least *most
readily* attainable in the poem. It by no means follows, however, that the incitements of Passion, or the precepts of Duty,
or even the lessons of Truth, may not be introduced into a
poem, and with advantage; for they may subserve, incidentally, in various ways, the general purposes of the work:—

but the true artist will always contrive to tone them down in
proper subjection to that *Beauty* which is the atmosphere and
the real essence of the poem.

I cannot better introduce the few poems which I shall present for your consideration, than by the citation of the Pröem
to Mr. Longfellow's "Waif:"

> The day is done, and the darkness
>   Falls from the wings of Night,
> As a feather is wafted downward
>   From an Eagle in his flight.
>
> I see the lights of the village
>   Gleam through the rain and the mist,
> And a feeling of sadness comes o'er me,
>   That my soul cannot resist;
>
> A feeling of sadness and longing,
>   That is not akin to pain,
> And resembles sorrow only
>   As the mist resembles the rain.
>
> Come, read to me some poem,
>   Some simple and heartfelt lay,
> That shall soothe this restless feeling,
>   And banish the thoughts of day.
>
> Not from the grand old masters,
>   Not from the bards sublime,
> Whose distant footsteps echo
>   Through the corridors of time.
>
> For, like strains of martial music,
>   Their mighty thoughts suggest
> Life's endless toil and endeavour;
>   And to-night I long for rest.
>
> Read from some humbler poet,
>   Whose songs gushed from his heart,
> As showers from the clouds of summer,
>   Or tears from the eyelids start;

Who through long days of labour,
   And nights devoid of ease,
Still heard in his soul the music
   Of wonderful melodies.

Such songs have power to quiet
   The restless pulse of care,
And come like the benediction
   That follows after prayer.

Then read from the treasured volume
   The poem of thy choice,
And lend to the rhyme of the poet
   The beauty of thy voice.

And the night shall be filled with music,
   And the cares that infest the day,
Shall fold their tents, like the Arabs,
   As they silently steal away.

With no great range of imagination, these lines have been justly admired for their delicacy of expression. Some of the images are very effective. Nothing can be better than—

——The bards sublime,
Whose distant footsteps echo
Down the corridors of Time.

The idea of the last quatrain is also very effective. The poem, on the whole, however, is chiefly to be admired for the graceful *insouciance* of its metre, so well in accordance with the character of the sentiments, and especially for the *ease* of the general manner. This "ease," or naturalness, in a literary style, it has long been the fashion to regard as ease in appearance alone—as a point of really difficult attainment. But not so:— a natural manner is difficult only to him who should never meddle with it—to the unnatural. It is but the result of writing with the understanding, or with the instinct, that *the tone*, in composition, should always be that which the mass of mankind would adopt—and must perpetually vary, of course, with the occasion. The author who, after the fashion of "The North American Review," should be, upon *all* occasions, merely "quiet," must necessarily upon *many* occasions, be simply silly, or stupid; and has no more right to be considered "easy," or "natural," than the Cockney exquisite, or than the sleeping Beauty in the wax-works.

Among the minor poems of Bryant, none has so much impressed me as the one which he entitles "June." I quote only a portion of it:

> There through the long, long summer hours,
>   The golden light should lie,
> And thick young herbs and groups of flowers
>   Stand in their beauty by.
> The oriole should build and tell
> His love-tale, close beside my cell;
>   The idle butterfly
> Should rest him there, and there be heard
> The housewife-bee and humming bird.
>
> And what, if cheerful shouts at noon,
>   Come, from the village sent,
> Or songs of maids, beneath the moon,
>   With fairy laughter blent?
> And what, if in the evening light,
> Betrothed lovers walk in sight
>   Of my low monument?
> I would the lovely scene around
> Might know no sadder sight nor sound.
>
> I know, I know I should not see
>   The season's glorious show,
> Nor would its brightness shine for me,
>   Nor its wild music flow;
> But if, around my place of sleep,
> The friends I love should come to weep,
>   They might not haste to go.
> Soft airs, and song, and light, and bloom
> Should keep them lingering by my tomb.

> These to their softened hearts should bear
>   The thought of what has been,
> And speak of one who cannot share
>   The gladness of the scene;
> Whose part in all the pomp that fills
> The circuit of the summer hills,
>   Is—that his grave is green;
> And deeply would their hearts rejoice
> To hear again his living voice.

The rhythmical flow, here, is even voluptuous—nothing could be more melodious. The poem has always affected me in a remarkable manner. The intense melancholy which seems to well up, perforce, to the surface of all the poet's cheerful sayings about his grave, we find thrilling us to the soul—while there is the truest poetic elevation in the thrill. The impression left is one of a pleasurable sadness.

And if, in the remaining compositions which I shall introduce to you, there be more or less of a similar tone always apparent, let me remind you that (how or why we know not) this certain tint of sadness is inseparably connected with all the higher manifestations of true Beauty. It is, nevertheless,

> A feeling of sadness and longing
>   That is not akin to pain,
> And resembles sorrow only
>   As the mist resembles the rain.

The taint of which I speak is clearly perceptible even in a poem so full of brilliancy and spirit as the "Health" of Edward Coote Pinkney:

> I fill this cup to one made up
>   Of loveliness alone,
> A woman, of her gentle sex
>   The seeming paragon;
> To whom the better elements
>   And kindly stars have given
> A form so fair, that, like the air,
>   'Tis less of earth than heaven.

Her every tone is music's own,
  Like those of morning birds,
And something more than melody
  Dwells ever in her words;
The coinage of her heart are they,
  And from her lips each flows
As one may see the burdened bee
  Forth issue from the rose.

Affections are as thoughts to her,
  The measures of her hours;
Her feelings have the fragrancy,
  The freshness of young flowers;
And lovely passions, changing oft,
  So fill her, she appears
The image of themselves by turns,—
  The idol of past years!

Of her bright face one glance will trace
  A picture on the brain,
And of her voice in echoing hearts
  A sound must long remain;
But memory, such as mine of her,
  So very much endears,
When death is nigh, my latest sigh
  Will not be life's but hers.

I filled this cup to one made up
  Of loveliness alone,
A woman, of her gentle sex
  The seeming paragon—
Her health! and would on earth they stood
  Some more of such a frame,
That life might be all poetry,
  And weariness a name.

It was the misfortune of Mr. Pinkney to have been born too far south. Had he been a New Englander, it is probable that he would have been ranked as the first of American lyrists, by that magnanimous cabal which has so long controlled the destinies of American Letters, in conducting the thing called "The North American Review." The poem just cited is especially beautiful; but the poetic elevation which it induces, we must refer chiefly to our sympathy in the poet's enthusiasm. We pardon his hyperboles for the evident earnestness with which they are uttered.

It was by no means my design, however, to expatiate upon the *merits* of what I should read you. These will necessarily speak for themselves. Boccalini, in his "Advertisements from Parnassus," tells us that Zoilus once presented Apollo a very caustic criticism upon a very admirable book:—whereupon the god asked him for the beauties of the work. He replied that he only busied himself about the errors. On hearing this, Apollo, handing him a sack of unwinnowed wheat, bade him pick out *all the chaff* for his reward.

Now this fable answers very well as a hit at the critics— but I am by no means sure that the god was in the right. I am by no means certain that the true limits of the critical duty are not grossly misunderstood. Excellence, in a poem especially, may be considered in the light of an axiom, which need only be properly *put*, to become self-evident. It is *not* excellence if it require to be demonstrated as such:—and thus, to point out too particularly the merits of a work of Art, is to admit that they are *not* merits altogether.

Among the "Melodies" of Thomas Moore, is one whose distinguished character as a poem proper, seems to have been singularly left out of view. I allude to his lines beginning— "Come, rest in this bosom." The intense energy of their expression is not surpassed by anything in Byron. There are two of the lines in which a sentiment is conveyed that embodies the *all in all* of the divine passion of love—a sentiment which, perhaps, has found its echo in more, and in more passionate, human hearts than any other single sentiment ever embodied in words:

Come, rest in this bosom, my own stricken deer,
Though the herd have fled from thee, thy home is still here;
Here still is the smile that no cloud can o'ercast,
And a heart and a hand all thy own to the last.

Oh! what was love made for, if 'tis not the same
Through joy and through torment, through glory and
    shame?
I know not, I ask not, if guilt's in that heart,
I but know that I love thee, whatever thou art.

Thou hast called me thy angel in moments of bliss,
And thy angel I'll be, 'mid the horrors of this,—
Through the furnace, unshrinking, thy steps to pursue,
And shield thee, and save thee,—or perish there too!

It has been the fashion, of late days, to deny Moore imagination, while granting him fancy—a distinction originating
with Coleridge, than whom no man more fully comprehended
the great powers of Moore. The fact is, that the fancy of this
poet so far predominates over all his other faculties, and over
the fancy of all other men, as to have induced, very naturally,
the idea that he is fanciful *only*. But never was there a greater
mistake. Never was a grosser wrong done the fame of a true
poet. In the compass of the English language I can call to
mind no poem more profoundly—more wierdly *imaginative*,
in the best sense, than the lines commencing—"I would I
were by that dim lake,"—which are the composition of
Thomas Moore. I regret that I am unable to remember them.

One of the noblest—and, speaking of fancy, one of the
most singularly fanciful of modern poets, was Thomas Hood.
His "Fair Ines" had always, for me, an inexpressible charm.

O saw ye not fair Ines?
    She's gone into the West,
To dazzle when the sun is down,
    And rob the world of rest;
She took our daylight with her,
    The smiles that we love best,
With morning blushes on her cheek,
    And pearls upon her breast.

O turn again, fair Ines,
    Before the fall of night,
For fear the moon should shine alone,
    And stars unrivalled bright;

And blessed will the lover be
    That walks beneath their light,
And breathes the love against thy cheek
    I dare not even write!

Would I had been, fair Ines,
    That gallant cavalier,
Who rode so gaily by thy side,
    And whispered thee so near!
Were there no bonny dames at home,
    Or no true lovers here,
That he should cross the seas to win
    The dearest of the dear?

I saw thee, lovely Ines,
    Descend along the shore,
With bands of noble gentlemen,
    And banners waved before;
And gentle youth and maidens gay,
    And snowy plumes they wore;
It would have been a beauteous dream,
    —If it had been no more!

Alas, alas, fair Ines,
    She went away with song,
With music waiting on her steps,
    And shoutings of the throng;
But some were sad and felt no mirth,
    But only Music's wrong,
In sounds that sang farewell, farewell,
    To her you've loved so long.

Farewell, farewell, fair Ines;
    That vessel never bore
So fair a lady on its deck,
    Nor danced so light before,—
Alas, for pleasure on the sea,
    And sorrow on the shore!
The smile that blest one lover's heart
    Has broken many more?

"The Haunted House," by the same author, is one of the truest poems ever written—one of the *truest*—one of the most unexceptionable—one of the most thoroughly artistic, both in its theme and in its execution. It is, moreover, powerfully ideal—imaginative. I regret that its length renders it unsuitable for the purposes of this Lecture. In place of it, permit me to offer the universally appreciated "Bridge of Sighs."

> One more Unfortunate,
> Weary of breath,
> Rashly Importunate,
> Gone to her death!
>
> Take her up tenderly,
> Lift her with care;—
> Fashioned so slenderly,
> Young, and so fair!
>
> Look at her garments
> Clinging like cerements;
> Whilst the wave constantly
> Drips from her clothing;
> Take her up instantly,
> Loving, not loathing.—
>
> Touch her not scornfully;
> Think of her mournfully,
> Gently and humanly;
> Not of the stains of her,
> All that remains of her
> Now, is pure womanly.
>
> Make no deep scrutiny
> Into her mutiny
> Rash and undutiful;
> Past all dishonour,
> Death has left on her
> Only the beautiful.

Still, for all slips of hers,
One of Eve's family—
Wipe those poor lips of hers
Oozing so clammily.

Loop up her tresses
Escaped from the comb,
Her fair auburn tresses;
Whilst wonderment guesses
Where was her home?

Who was her father?
Who was her mother?
Had she a sister?
Had she a brother?
Or was there a dearer one
Still, and a nearer one
Yet, than all other?

Alas! for the rarity
Of Christian charity
Under the sun!
Oh! it was pitiful!
Near a whole city full,
Home she had none.

Sisterly, brotherly,
Fatherly, motherly,
Feelings had changed;
Love, by harsh evidence,
Thrown from its eminence;
Even God's providence
Seeming estranged.

Where the lamps quiver
So far in the river,
With many a light
From window and casement,

From garret to basement,
She stood, with amazement,
Houseless by night.

The bleak wind of March
Made her tremble and shiver;
But not the dark arch,
Or the black flowing river:

Mad from life's history,
Glad to death's mystery,
Swift to be hurled—
Anywhere, anywhere
Out of the world!

In she plunged boldly,
No matter how coldly
The rough river ran,—
Over the brink of it,
Picture it,—think of it,
Dissolute Man!
Lave in it, drink of it
Then, if you can!

Take her up tenderly,
Lift her with care;
Fashioned so slenderly,
Young, and so fair!
Ere her limbs frigidly
Stiffen too rigidly,
Decently,—kindly,—
Smooth, and compose them;
And her eyes, close them,
Staring so blindly!

Dreadfully staring
Through muddy impurity,
As when with the daring
Last look of despairing
Fixed on futurity.

> Perishing gloomily,
> Spurred by contumely,
> Cold inhumanity,
> Burning insanity,
> Into her rest,—
> Cross her hands humbly,
> As if praying dumbly,
> Over her breast!
> Owning her weakness,
> Her evil behaviour,
> And leaving, with meekness,
> Her sins to her Saviour!

The vigour of this poem is no less remarkable than its pathos. The versification, although carrying the fanciful to the very verge of the fantastic, is nevertheless admirably adapted to the wild insanity which is the thesis of the poem.

Among the minor poems of Lord Byron, is one which has never received from the critics the praise which it undoubtedly deserves:

> Though the day of my destiny's over,
>   And the star of my fate hath declined,
> Thy soft heart refused to discover
>   The faults which so many could find;
> Though thy soul with my grief was acquainted,
>   It shrunk not to share it with me,
> And the love which my spirit hath painted
>   It never hath found but in *thee*.
>
> Then when nature around me is smiling,
>   The last smile which answers to mine,
> I do not believe it beguiling,
>   Because it reminds me of thine;
> And when winds are at war with the ocean,
>   As the breasts I believed in with me,
> If their billows excite an emotion,
>   It is that they bear me from *thee*.
>
> Though the rock of my last hope is shivered,
>   And its fragments are sunk in the wave,

Though I feel that my soul is delivered
    To pain—it shall not be its slave.
There is many a pang to pursue me:
    They may crush, but they shall not contemn—
They may torture, but shall not subdue me—
    'Tis of *thee* that I think—not of them.

Though human, thou didst not deceive me,
    Though woman, thou didst not forsake,
Though loved, thou forborest to grieve me,
    Though slandered, thou never couldst shake,—
Though trusted, thou didst not disclaim me,
    Though parted, it was not to fly,
Though watchful, 'twas not to defame me,
    Nor mute, that the world might belie.

Yet I blame not the world, nor despise it,
    Nor the war of the many with one—
If my soul was not fitted to prize it,
    'Twas folly not sooner to shun:
And if dearly that error hath cost me,
    And more than I once could foresee,
I have found that whatever it lost me,
    It could not deprive me of *thee*.

From the wreck of the past, which hath perished,
    Thus much I at least may recall,
It hath taught me that which I most cherished
    Deserved to be dearest of all:
In the desert a fountain is springing,
    In the wide waste there still is a tree,
And a bird in the solitude singing,
    Which speaks to my spirit of *thee*.

Although the rhythm, here, is one of the most difficult, the versification could scarcely be improved. No nobler *theme* ever engaged the pen of poet. It is the soul-elevating idea, that no man can consider himself entitled to complain of Fate while, in his adversity, he still retains the unwavering love of woman.

From Alfred Tennyson—although in perfect sincerity I regard him as the noblest poet that ever lived—I have left myself time to cite only a very brief specimen. I call him, and *think* him the noblest of poets—*not* because the impressions he produces are, at *all* times, the most profound—*not* because the poetical excitement which he induces is, at *all* times, the most intense—but because it *is*, at all times, the most ethereal—in other words, the most elevating and the most pure. No poet is so little of the earth, earthy. What I am about to read is from his last long poem, "The Princess:"

> Tears, idle tears, I know not what they mean,
> Tears from the depth of some divine despair
> Rise in the heart, and gather to the eyes,
> In looking on the happy Autumn-fields,
> And thinking of the days that are no more.
>
> Fresh as the first beam glittering on a sail,
> That brings our friends up from the underworld,
> Sad as the last which reddens over one
> That sinks with all we love below the verge;
> So sad, so fresh, the days that are no more.
>
> Ah, sad and strange as in dark summer dawns
> The earliest pipe of half-awakened birds
> To dying ears, when unto dying eyes
> The casement slowly grows a glimmering square;
> So sad, so strange, the days that are no more.
>
> Dear as remembered kisses after death,
> And sweet as those by hopeless fancy feigned
> On lips that are for others; deep as love,
> Deep as first love, and wild with all regret;
> O Death in Life, the days that are no more.

Thus, although in a very cursory and imperfect manner, I have endeavoured to convey to you my conception of the Poetic Principle. It has been my purpose to suggest that, while this Principle itself is, strictly and simply, the Human Aspiration for Supernal Beauty, the manifestation of the Principle is

always found in *an elevating excitement of the Soul*—quite independent of that passion which is the intoxication of the
Heart—or of that Truth which is the satisfaction of the Reason. For, in regard to Passion, alas! its tendency is to degrade,
rather than to elevate the Soul. Love, on the contrary—
Love—the true, the divine Eros—the Uranian, as distinguished from the Dionæan Venus—is unquestionably the
purest and truest of all poetical themes. And in regard to
Truth—if, to be sure, through the attainment of a truth, we
are led to perceive a harmony where none was apparent before, we experience, at once, the true poetical effect—but this
effect is referable to the harmony alone, and not in the least
degree to the truth which merely served to render the harmony manifest.

We shall reach, however, more immediately a distinct conception of what the true Poetry is, by mere reference to a few
of the simple elements which induce in the Poet himself the
true poetical effect. He recognises the ambrosia which nour-
ishes his soul, in the bright orbs that shine in Heaven—in
the volutes of the flower—in the clustering of low shrub-
beries—in the waving of the grain-fields—in the slanting of
tall, Eastern trees—in the blue distance of mountains—in
the grouping of clouds—in the twinkling of half-hidden
brooks—in the gleaming of silver rivers—in the repose of
sequestered lakes—in the star-mirroring depths of lonely
wells. He perceives it in the songs of birds—in the harp of
Æolus—in the sighing of the night-wind—in the repining
voice of the forest—in the surf that complains to the shore—
in the fresh breath of the woods—in the scent of the violet—
in the voluptuous perfume of the hyacinth—in the suggestive
odour that comes to him, at eventide, from far-distant, undiscovered islands, over dim oceans, illimitable and unexplored.
He owns it in all noble thoughts—in all unworldly motives—in all holy impulses—in all chivalrous, generous, and
self-sacrificing deeds. He feels it in the beauty of woman—in
the grace of her step—in the lustre of her eye—in the melody of her voice—in her soft laughter—in her sigh—in the
harmony of the rustling of her robes. He deeply feels it in her
winning endearments—in her burning enthusiasms—in her
gentle charities—in her meek and devotional endurances—

but above all—ah, far above all—he kneels to it—he wor-
ships it in the faith, in the purity, in the strength, in the altogether divine majesty—of her *love*.

Let me conclude—by the recitation of yet another brief
poem—one very different in character from any that I have
before quoted. It is by Motherwell, and is called "The Song
of the Cavalier." With our modern and altogether rational
ideas of the absurdity and impiety of warfare, we are not precisely in that frame of mind best adapted to sympathize with
the sentiments, and thus to appreciate the real excellence of
the poem. To do this fully, we must identify ourselves, in
fancy, with the soul of the old cavalier.

> Then mounte! then mounte, brave gallants, all,
>   And don your helmes amaine:
> Deathe's couriers, Fame and Honour, call
>   Us to the field againe.
>
> No shrewish teares shall fill our eye
>   When the sword-hilt is in our hand,—
> Heart-whole we'll part, and no whit sighe
>   For the fayrest of the land;
> Let piping swaine, and craven wight,
>   Thus weepe and puling crye,
> Our business is like men to fight,
>   And hero-like to die!

Sartain's Union Magazine, October 1850

REVIEWS OF BRITISH AND
CONTINENTAL AUTHORS

Contents

William Harrison Ainsworth

Guy Fawkes; or The Gunpowder Treason. An Historical Romance. By William Harrison Ainsworth, Author of "The Tower of London," "Jack Sheppard," &c. Philadelphia. Lea and Blanchard.

WHAT Mr. William Harrison Ainsworth had been doing before he wrote "Rookwood" is uncertain; but it seems to us that he made his literary *début* with that work. It was generally commended; but we found no opportunity of perusing it. "Crichton" followed, and this we read; for our curiosity was much excited in regard to it by certain discrepancies of critical opinion. In one or two instances it was unequivocally condemned as "flat, stale and unprofitable," although, to be sure, the critics, in these one or two instances, were men of little note. The more prevalent idea appeared to be that the book was a miracle of wit and wisdom, and that Ainsworth who wrote "Crichton," was in fact Crichton *redivivus*. We have now before us a number of a Philadelphia Magazine for the month of April, 1840, in which the learned editor thus speaks of the work in question—"Mr. Ainsworth is a powerful writer; his 'Crichton' *stands at the head of the long list of English novels—unapproachable and alone. . . .* This great glory is fairly Mr. Ainsworth's due, and in our humble opinion, *the fact is incontrovertible*." Upon a perusal of the novel so belauded, we found it a somewhat ingenious admixture of pedantry, bombast, and rigmarole. No man ever read "Crichton" through twice. From beginning to end it is one continued abortive effort at effect. The writer keeps us in a perpetual state of preparation for something magnificent; but the something magnificent never arrives. He is always saying to the reader, directly or indirectly, "*now*, in a *very* brief time, you shall see what you shall see!" The reader turns over the page in expectation, and meets with nothing beyond the same everlasting assurance:—another page and the same result—another and still the same—and so on to the end of the performance. One cannot help fancying the novelist in some perplexing dream—one of those frequently recurring visions, half night-mare half asphyxia, in which the sufferer, although making the most strenuous efforts to *run*, finds a walk or a crawl the *ne plus ultra* of his success in locomotion.

The plot is monstrously improbable, and yet not so much improbable as inconsequential. A German critic would say that the whole is excessively *ill-motivert*. No one action follows necessarily upon any one other. There is, at all times, the greatest parade of *measures*, but measures that have no comprehensible result. The author works busily for a chapter or two with a view of bringing matters in train for a certain end; and then suffers this end to be either omitted—unaccomplished—or brought to pass by accidental and irrelevant circumstances. The reader of taste very soon perceives this defect in the conduct of the story, and, ceasing to feel any interest in marches and countermarches that promise no furtherance of any object, abandons himself to the investigation of the page only which is immediately before him. Despairing of all amusement from the *construction* of the book, he falls back upon its immediate descriptions. But, alas, what is there here to excite any emotion in the bosom of a well-read man, beyond that of contempt? If an occasional interest is aroused, he feels it due, not to the novelist, but to the historical reminiscences which even that novelist's inanity cannot render altogether insipid. The turgid pretension of the style annoys, and the elaborately-interwoven pedantry irritates, insults, and disgusts. He must be blind, indeed, who cannot understand the great pains taken by Mr. Ainsworth to interlard the book in question with second-hand bits of classical and miscellaneous erudition; and he must be equally blind who cannot perceive that *this* is the chicanery which has so impressed the judgment, and dazzled the imagination of such critics as he of the aforesaid Magazine. We know nothing at all of Mr. Ainsworth's scholarship. There are some very equivocal blunders in "Crichton," to be sure; but *Ainsworth* is a classical name, and we must make *very* great allowances for the usual errors of press. We say, however, that, from all that appears in the novel in question, he may be as really ignorant as a bear. True erudition—by which term we here mean only to imply much diversified reading—is certainly discoverable—is positively indicated only in its ultimate and total *results*. We have observed elsewhere, that the mere grouping together of fine things from the greatest multiplicity of the rarest works, or even the apparently natural inweaving into any composition of the sentiments and manner of these works, is an attainment within the reach of every moderately-informed, ingenious, and not indolent man, having access to any ordinary collection of good books. Of all vanities the vanity of the unlettered pedant is the most sickening, and the most transparent.

Mr. Ainsworth having thus earned for himself the kind of renown which "Crichton" could establish with the rabble, made his next appearance before that rabble with "Jack Sheppard." Seeing what we have just seen, we should by no means think it wonderful that this romance threw into the greatest astonishment the little critics who so belauded the one preceding. They could not understand it at all. They would not believe that the same author had written both. Thus they condemned it in loud terms. The Magazine before alluded to, styles it, in round terms, "the most corrupt, flat, and vulgar fabrication in the English language . . . a disgrace to the literature of the day." Corrupt and vulgar it undoubtedly is, but it is by no means so *flat* (if we understand the critic's idea of the term) as the "Crichton" to which it is considered so terribly inferior. By *"flat"* we presume "uninteresting" is intended. To us, at least, no novel was less *interesting* than "Crichton," and the only interest which it *could* have had for any reader must have arisen from admiration excited by the apparently miraculous *learning* of the plagiarist, and from the air of owlish profundity which he contrives to throw over the work. The interest, if any, must have had regard to the author and not to his book. Viewed as a work of art, and without reference to any supposed moral or immoral tendencies, (things with which the critic has nothing to do) "Jack Sheppard" is by no means the *very* wretched composition which some gentlemen would have us believe. Its condemnation has been brought about by the revulsion consequent upon the exaggerated estimate of "Crichton." It is altogether a much better book than "Crichton." Although its incidents are improbable—(the frequent miraculous escapes of the hero, for instance, without competent means) still they are not, as in "Crichton," at the same time inconsequential. Admitting the facts, these facts hang together sufficiently well. Nor is there any bombast of style; this negative merit, to be sure, being no merit of the author's, but an enforced one resulting from the subject. The chief defect of the work is a radical one, the nature and effect of which we were at some pains to point out in a late notice of Captain Marryatt's "Poacher." The story being, no doubt, written to order, for Magazine purposes, and in a violent hurry, has been scrambled through by means of *incident* solely. It is totally wanting in the *autorial comment*. The writer never pauses to speak, in his own person, of what is going on. It is possible to have too much of this comment; but it is far easier to have too little. The most tedious books, *ceteris paribus*, are those which have none at all. "Sir Charles Grandison," "Clarissa Harlowe," and the "Ernest Maltravers" of Bulwer embody instances of its superabundance. The genius of the author of "Pelham" is in nothing more evident than in the interest which he has infused into some of his late works *in spite* of their ultra-didacticism. The "Poacher" just mentioned, and "The Arabian Nights" are examples of deficiency in the commenting principle, and are both intolerably tedious *in spite* of their rich variety of incident. The *juste milieu* was never more admirably attained than in De Foe's "Robinson Crusoe" and in the "Caleb Williams" of Godwin. This latter work, from the character of its incidents, affords a fine opportunity of contrast with "Jack Sheppard." In both novels the hero escapes repeatedly from prison. In the work of Ainsworth the escapes are merely narrated. In that of Godwin they are *discussed*. With the latter we become at once absorbed in those details which so manifestly absorb his own soul. We read with the most breathless attention. We close the book with a real regret. The former puts us out of all patience. His marvels have a nakedness which repels. Nothing he relates seems either probable or possible, or of the slightest interest, whether the one or the other. His hero impresses us as a mere chimæra with whom we have no earthly concern, and when he makes his final escape and comes to the gallows, we would feel a very sensible relief, but for the impracticability of hanging up Mr. Ainsworth in his stead. But if "Jack Sheppard" is a miserably inartistical book, still it is by no means so utterly contemptible and silly as the tawdry stuff which has been pronounced *"the best of English novels, standing at the head of the long list unapproachable and alone!"*

Of "The Tower of London" we have read only some detached passages—enough to assure us, however, that the
"work," like Yankee razors, has been manufactured merely "to
sell." "Guy Fawkes," the book now lying before us, and the
last completed production of its author, is positively beneath
criticism and beneath contempt. The design of Mr. Ainsworth has been to fill, for a certain sum of money, a stipulated
number of pages. There existed a necessity of *engaging* the
readers whom especially he now addresses—that is to say the
lowest order of the lettered mob—a necessity of enticing
them into the commencement of a perusal. For this end the
title "Guy Fawkes or The Gunpowder Plot" was all sufficient,
at least within the regions of Cockaigne. As for fulfilling any
reasonable expectations, derived either from the *ad captandum* title, or from his own notoriety (we dare not say
reputation) as a novelist—as for exerting himself for the
permanent or continuous amusement of the poor flies whom
he had inveigled into his trap—all this, with him, has been a
consideration of no moment. He had a *task* to perform, and
not a duty. What were his readers to Mr. Ainsworth?—
"What Hecuba to him, or he to Hecuba?" The result of such
a state of affairs is self-evident. With his *best* exertions, in his
earliest efforts, with all the goadings of a sickening vanity
which stood him well instead of nobler ambition—with all
this, he *could* do—he *has done*—but little; and without them
he has now accomplished exactly nothing at all. If ever, indeed, a novel were *less* than nothing, then that novel is "Guy
Fawkes." To say a word about it in the way of serious criticism, would be to prove ourselves as great a blockhead as its
author. *Macte virtute*, my dear sir—proceed and flourish. In
the meantime we bid you a final farewell. Your next volume,
which will have some such appellation as "The Ghost of
Cock-Lane," we shall take the liberty of throwing unopened
out of the window. Our pigs are not all of the description
called learned, but they will have more leisure for its examination than we.

Graham's Magazine, November 1841

Eaton Stannard Barrett

The Heroine: or Adventures of Cherubina. By Eaton Stannard Barrett, Esq. New Edition. Richmond: Published by P. D. Bernard.

CHERUBINA! Who has not heard of Cherubina? Who has not heard of that most spiritual, that most ill-treated, that most accomplished of women—of that most consummate, most sublimated, most fantastic, most unappreciated, and most inappreciable of heroines? Exquisite and delicate creation of a mind overflowing with fun, frolic, farce, wit, humor, song, sentiment, and sense, what mortal is there so dead to every thing graceful and glorious as not to have devoured thy adventures? Who is there so unfortunate as not to have taken thee by the hand?—who so lost as not to have cultivated thy acquaintance?—who so stupid, as not to have enjoyed thy companionship?—who so much of a log, as not to have laughed until he has wept for very laughter in the perusal of thine incomparable, inimitable, and inestimable eccentricities? But we are becoming pathetic to no purpose, and supererogatively oratorical. *Every body* has read Cherubina. There is no one so superlatively unhappy as not to have done this thing. But if such there be—if by any possibility such person should exist, we have only a few words to say to him. Go, silly man, and purchase forthwith "The Heroine: or Adventures of Cherubina."

The Heroine was first published many years ago, (we believe shortly after the appearance of Childe Harold;) but although it has run through editions innumerable, and has been universally read and admired by all possessing talent or taste, it has never, in our opinion, attracted half that notice on the part of the critical press, which is undoubtedly its due. There are few books written with more tact, spirit, *naïveté*, or grace, few which take hold more irresistibly upon the attention of the reader, and none more fairly entitled to rank among the classics of English literature than the Heroine of Eaton Stannard Barrett. When we say all this of a book possessing not even the remotest claim to originality, either in conception or execution, it may reasonably be supposed, that we have discovered in its matter, or manner, some rare qualities, inducing us to hazard an assertion of so bold a nature. This is actually the case. Never was any thing so charmingly written: the mere style is positively inimitable. Imagination, too, of the most etherial kind, sparkles and blazes, now sportively like the Will O' the Wisp, now dazzlingly like the Aurora Borealis, over every page—over every sentence in the book. It is absolutely radiant with fancy, and that of a nature the most captivating, although, at the same time, the most airy, the most capricious, and the most intangible. Yet the Heroine must be considered a mere burlesque; and, being a copy from Don Quixotte, is to that immortal work of Cervantes what *The School for Scandal* is to *The Merry Wives of Windsor*. The Plot is briefly as follows.

Gregory Wilkinson, an English farmer worth 50,000 pounds, has a pretty daughter called Cherry, whose head is somewhat disordered from romance reading. Her governess is but little more rational than herself, and is one day turned out of the house for allowing certain undue liberties on the part of the butler. In revenge she commences a correspondence with Miss Cherry, in which she persuades that young lady that Wilkinson is not her real father—that she is a child of mystery, &c.—in short that she is actually and *bona fide* a heroine. In the meantime, Miss Cherry, in rummaging among her father's papers, comes across an antique parchment—a lease of lives—on which the following words are alone legible.

> This Indenture
> For and in consideration of
> Doth grant, bargain, release
> Possession, and to his heirs and assigns
> Lands of Sylvan Lodge, in the
> Trees, stones, quarries, &c.
> Reasonable amends and satisfaction
> This demise
> Molestation of him the said Gregory Wilkinson.
> The natural life of
> Cherry Wilkinson only daughter of
> De Willoughby eldest son of Thomas
> Lady Gwyn of Gwyn Castle.

This "excruciating MS." brings matters to a crisis—for Miss Cherry has no difficulty in filling up the blanks.

"It is a written covenant," says this interesting young lady in a letter to her Governess, "between this Gregory Wilkinson, and the miscreant (whom my being an heiress had prevented from enjoying the title and estate that would devolve to him at my death) stipulating to give Wilkinson 'Sylvan Lodge,' together with 'trees, stones, &c.' as 'reasonable amends and satisfaction' for being the instrument of my 'demise,' and declaring that there shall be 'no molestation of him the said Gregory Wilkinson' for taking away the 'natural life of Cherry Wilkinson, only daughter of' —— somebody 'De Willoughby eldest son of Thomas.' Then follows 'Lady Gwyn of Gwyn Castle.' So that it is evident I am a De Willoughby, and related to Lady Gwyn! What perfectly confirms me in the latter supposition, is an old portrait which I found soon after, among Wilkinson's papers, representing a young and beautiful female superbly dressed; and underneath, in large letters, the name of 'Nell Gwyn.' "

Fired with this idea, Miss Cherry gets up a scene, rushes with hair dishevelled into the presence of the good man Wilkinson, and accuses him to his teeth of plotting against her life, and of sundry other mal-practices and misdemeanors. The worthy old gentleman is astonished, as well he may be; but is somewhat consoled upon receiving a letter from his nephew, Robert Stuart, announcing his intention of paying the family a visit immediately. Wilkinson is in hopes that a lover may change the current of his daughter's ideas; but in that he is mistaken. Stuart has the misfortune of being merely a rich man, a handsome man, an honest man, and a fashionable man—he is no hero. This is not to be borne: and Miss Cherry, having assumed the name of the Lady Cherubina De Willoughby, makes a precipitate retreat from the house, and commences a journey on foot to London. Her adventures here properly begin, and are laughable in the extreme. But we must not be too minute. They are modelled very much after those of Don Quixotte, and are related in a series of letters from the young lady herself to her governess. The principal characters who figure in the Memoirs are Betterton, an old *debauché* who endeavors to entangle the Lady Cherubina in his toils—Jerry Sullivan, an Irish simpleton, who is ready to lose his life at any moment for her ladyship, whose story he implicitly believes, without exactly comprehending it—Higginson, a grown baby, and a mad poet—Lady Gwyn, whom Cherubina believes to be her mortal enemy, and the usurper of her rights, and who encourages the delusion for the purpose of entertaining her guests—Mary and William, two peasants betrothed, but whom Cherry sets by the ears for the sake of an interesting episode—Abraham Grundy, a tenth rate performer at Covent Garden, who having been mistaken by Cherry for an earl, supports the character *à merveille* with the hope of eventually marrying her, and thus securing 10,000 pounds, a sum which it appears the lady possesses in her own right. He calls himself the Lord Altamont Mortimer Montmorenci. Stuart, her cousin, whom we have mentioned before, finally rescues her from the toils of Betterton and Grundy, and restores her to reason, and to her friends. Of course he is rewarded with her hand.

We repeat that Cherubina is a book which should be upon the shelves of every well-appointed library. No one can read it without entertaining a high opinion of the varied and brilliant talents of its author. No one can read it without laughter. Its wit, especially, and its humor, are indisputable—not frittered and refined away into that insipid compound which we occasionally meet with, half giggle and half sentiment—but racy, dashing, and palpable. Some of the songs with which the work is interspersed have attained a most extensive popularity, while many persons, to whom they are as familiar as household things, are not aware of the very existence of the Heroine. All our readers must remember the following.

> Dear Sensibility, O la!
> I heard a little lamb cry ba!
> Says I, so you have lost mamma!
> > Ah!
> The little lamb as I said so,

Frisking about the fields did go,
And frisking trod upon my toe.

Oh!

And this also.

TO DOROTHY PULVERTAFT.

If Black-sea, White-sea, Red-sea ran
One tide of ink to Ispahan;
If all the geese in Lincoln fens
Produced spontaneous well-made pens;
If Holland old or Holland new,
One wondrous sheet of paper grew;
Could I, by stenographic power,
Write twenty libraries an hour;
And should I sing but half the grace
Of half a freckle on thy face;
Each syllable I wrote should reach
From Inverness to Bognor's beach;
Each hair-stroke be a river Rhine,
Each verse an equinoctial line.

We have already exceeded our limits, but cannot refrain
from extracting Chapter XXV. It will convey some idea of the
character of the Heroine. She is now at the mansion of Lady
Gwyn, who, for the purpose of amusing her friends, has
dressed up her nephew to represent the supposed mother of
the Lady Cherubina.

CHAPTER XXV.

This morning I awoke almost well, and towards evening
was able to appear below. Lady Gwyn had invited several
of her friends; so that I passed a delightful afternoon; the
charm, admiration, and astonishment of all.

When I retired to rest, I found this note on my toilette.

To the Lady Cherubina.

Your mother lives! and is confined in a subterranean vault
of the villa. At midnight two men will tap at your door,
and conduct you to her. Be silent, courageous, and circum-
spect.

What a flood of new feelings gushed upon my soul, as I laid down the billet, and lifted my filial eyes to Heaven! Mother—endearing name! I pictured that unfortunate lady stretched on a mattress of straw, her eyes sunken in their sockets, yet retaining a portion of their youthful fire; her frame emaciated, her voice feeble, her hand damp and chill. Fondly did I depict our meeting—our embrace; she gently pushing me from her, and baring my forehead, to gaze on the lineaments of my countenance. All, all is convincing; and she calls me the softened image of my noble father!

Two tedious hours I waited in extreme anxiety. At length the clock struck twelve; my heart beat responsive, and immediately the promised signal was made. I unbolted the door, and beheld two men masked and cloaked. They blindfolded me, and each taking an arm, led me along. Not a word passed. We traversed apartments, ascended, descended stairs; now went this way, now that; obliquely, circularly, angularly; till I began to imagine we were all the time in one spot.

At length my conductors stopped.

'Unlock the postern gate,' whispered one, ' while I light a torch.'

'We are betrayed!' said the other, 'for this is the wrong key.'

'Then thou beest the traitor,' cried the first.

'Thou liest, dost lie, and art lying!' cried the second.

'Take that!' exclaimed the first. A groan followed, and the wretch tumbled to the ground.

'You have killed him!' cried I, sickening with horror.

'I have only hamstrung him, my Lady,' said the fellow. 'He will be lame while ever he lives; but by St. Cripplegate, that won't be long; for our captain has given him four ducats to murder himself in a month.'

He then burst open the gate; a sudden current of wind met us, and we hurried forward with incredible speed, while moans and smothered shrieks were heard at either side.

'Gracious goodness, where are we?' cried I.

'In the cavern of death!' said my conductor; 'but never

fear, Signora mia illustrissima, for the bravo Abellino is your povero devotissimo.'

On a sudden innumerable footsteps sounded behind us. We ran swifter.

'Fire!' cried a ferocious accent, almost at my ear; and there came a discharge of arms.

I stopped, unable to move, breathe, or speak.

'I am wounded all over, right and left, fore and aft, long ways and cross ways, Death and the Devil!' cried the bravo.

'Am I bleeding?' said I, feeling myself with my hands.

'No, blessed St. Fidget be praised!' answered he; 'and now all is safe, for the banditti have turned into the wrong passage.'

He then stopped, and unlocked a door.

'Enter,' said he, 'and behold your mother!'

He led me forward, tore the bandage from my eyes, and retiring, locked the door after him.

Agitated by the terrors of my dangerous expedition, I felt additional horror in finding myself within a dismal cell, lighted with a lantern; where, at a small table, sat a woman suffering under a corpulency unparalleled in the memoirs of human monsters. Her dress was a patchwork of blankets and satins, and her gray tresses were like horses' tails. Hundreds of frogs leaped about the floor; a piece of mouldy bread, and a mug of water, lay on the table; some straw, strewn with dead snakes and sculls, occupied one corner, and the distant end of the cell was concealed behind a black curtain.

I stood at the door, doubtful, and afraid to advance; while the prodigious prisoner sat examining me all over.

At last I summoned courage to say, 'I fear, madam, I am an intruder here. I have certainly been shown into the wrong room.'

'It is, it is my own, my only daughter, my Cherubina!' cried she, with a tremendous voice. 'Come to my maternal arms, thou living picture of the departed Theodore!'

'Why, ma'am,' said I, 'I would with great pleasure, but I am afraid—Oh, madam, indeed, indeed, I am quite sure you cannot be my mother!'

'Why not, thou unnatural girl?' cried she.

'Because, madam,' answered I, 'my mother was of a thin habit; as her portrait proves.'

'And so I was once,' said she. 'This deplorable plumpness is owing to want of exercise. But I thank the Gods I am as pale as ever.'

'Heavens! no,' cried I. 'Your face, pardon me, is a rich scarlet.'

'And is this our tender meeting?' cried she. 'To disown me, to throw my fat in my teeth, to violate the lilies of my skin with a dash of scarlet? Hey diddle diddle, the cat and the fiddle! Tell me, girl, will you embrace me, or will you not?'

'Indeed, madam,' answered I, 'I will presently.'

'Presently!'

'Yes, depend upon it I will. Only let me get over the first shock.'

'Shock!'

Dreading her violence, and feeling myself bound to do the duties of a daughter, I kneeled at her feet, and said:

'Ever respected, ever venerable author of my being, I beg thy maternal blessing!'

My mother raised me from the ground, and hugged me to her heart, with such cruel vigor, that, almost crushed, I cried out stoutly, and struggled for release.

'And now,' said she, relaxing her grasp, 'let me tell you of my sufferings. Ten long years I have eaten nothing but bread. Oh, ye favorite pullets, oh, ye inimitable tit-bits, shall I never, never taste you more? It was but last night, that maddened by hunger, methought I beheld the Genius of Dinner in my dreams. His mantle was laced with silver eels, and his locks were dropping with soups. He had a crown of golden fishes upon his head, and pheasants' wings at his shoulders. A flight of little tartlets fluttered about him, and the sky rained down comfits. As I gazed on him, he vanished in a sigh, that was impregnated with the fumes of brandy. Hey diddle diddle, the cat and the fiddle.'

I stood shuddering, and hating her more and more every moment.

'Pretty companion of my confinement!' cried she, apostrophizing an enormous toad which she pulled out of her bosom, 'dear, spotted fondling, thou, next to my Cherubina, art worthy of my love. Embrace each other, my friends.' And she put the hideous pet into my hand. I screamed and dropped it.

'Oh!' cried I, in a passion of despair, ' what madness possessed me to undertake this execrable enterprise!' and I began beating with my hand against the door.

'Do you want to leave your poor mother?' said she in a whimpering tone.

'Oh! I am so frightened!' cried I.

'You will spend the night here, however,' said she; 'and your whole life too; for the ruffian who brought you hither was employed by Lady Gwyn to entrap you.'

When I heard this terrible sentence, my blood ran cold, and I began crying bitterly.

'Come, my love!' said my mother, 'and let me clasp thee to my heart once more!'

'For goodness sake!' cried I, 'spare me!'

'What!' exclaimed she, 'do you spurn my proffered embrace again?'

'Dear, no, madam,' answered I. 'But—but indeed now, you squeeze one so!'

My mother made a huge stride towards me; then stood groaning and rolling her eyes.

'Help!' cried I, half frantic, 'help! help!'

I was stopped by a suppressed titter of infernal laughter, as if from many demons; and on looking towards the black curtain, whence the sound came, I saw it agitated; while about twenty terrific faces appeared peeping through slits in it, and making grins of a most diabolical nature. I hid my face with my hands.

' 'Tis the banditti!' cried my mother.

As she spoke, the door opened, a bandage was flung over my eyes, and I was borne away half senseless, in some one's arms; till at length, I found myself alone in my own chamber.

Such was the detestable adventure of to-night. Oh, that I should live to meet this mother of mine! How different from the mothers that other heroines rummage out in northern turrets and ruined chapels! I am out of all patience. Liberate her I must, of course, and make a suitable provision for her too, when I get my property; but positively, never will I sleep under the same roof with—(ye powers of filial love forgive me!) such a living mountain of human horror. Adieu.

Southern Literary Messenger, December 1835

Elizabeth Barrett Browning

The Drama of Exile, and other Poems. By Elizabeth Barrett Barrett, Author of "The Seraphim," and other Poems. New York: Henry G. Langley.

A WELL-BRED *man*," says Sir James Puckle, in his "Gray Cap for a Green Head," "will never give himself the liberty to speak ill of women." We emphasize the "man." Setting aside, for the present, certain rare commentators and compilers of the species G—, —creatures neither precisely men, women, nor Mary Wollstonecraft's—setting these aside as unclassifiable, we may observe that the race of critics are masculine—men. With the exception, perhaps, of Mrs. Anne Royal, we can call to mind no female who has occupied, even temporarily, the Zoilus throne. And this, the Salic law, is an evil; for the inherent chivalry of the critical *man* renders it not only an unpleasant task to him "to speak ill of a woman," (and a woman and her book are identical,) but an almost impossible task not to laud her *ad nauseam*. In general, therefore, it is the unhappy lot of the authoress to be subjected, time after time, to the downright degradation of mere puffery. On her own side of the Atlantic, Miss Barrett has indeed, in one instance at least, escaped the infliction of this lamentable contumely and wrong; but if she had been really solicitous of its infliction in America, she could not have adopted a more effectual plan than that of saying a few words about "the great American people," in an American edition of her work, published under the superintendence of an American author.* Of the innumerable "native" notices of "The Drama of Exile," which have come under our observation, we can call to mind *not one* in which there is any thing more remarkable than the critic's dogged determination to find *nothing*

---

*We are sorry to notice, in the American edition, a multitude of typographical errors, many of which affect the sense, and should therefore be corrected in a second impression, if called for. How far they are chargeable to the London copy, we are not prepared to say. "Froze," for instance, is printed "frore." "Foregone," throughout, is printed "forgone." "Wordless" is printed "worldless"—"worldly,""wordly"—"spilt,""split,"etc.,etc.,—while transpositions, false accents, and mis-punctuations abound. We indicate a few pages on which such inadvertences are to be discovered. Vol. 1—23, 26, 37, 45, 53, 56, 80, 166, 174, 180, 185, 251. Vol. 2—109, 114, 240, 247, 253, 272.

barren, from Beersheba to Dan. Another in the "Democratic Review" has proceeded so far, it is true, as to venture a *very* delicate insinuation to the effect that the poetess " will not fail to speak her mind *though it bring upon her a bad rhyme*;" beyond this, nobody has proceeded: and as for the elaborate paper in the new Whig Monthly, all that any body can say or think, and all that Miss Barrett can *feel* respecting it is, that it is an eulogy as well written as it is an insult well intended. Now of all the friends of the fair author, we doubt whether one exists, with more profound—with more enthusiastic reverence and admiration of her genius, than the writer of these words. And it is for this very reason, beyond all others, that he intends to speak of her *the truth*. Our chief regret is, nevertheless, that the limits of this "Journal" will preclude the possibility of our speaking this truth so fully, and so much in detail, as we could wish. By far the most valuable criticism that we, or that any one could give, of the volumes now lying before us, would be the quotation of three fourths of their contents. But we have this advantage—that the work has been long published, and almost universally read—and thus, in some measure, we may proceed, concisely, as if the text of our context, were an understood thing.

In her preface to this, the "American edition" of her late poems, Miss Barrett, speaking of the Drama of Exile, says: — "I decided on publishing it, after considerable hesitation and doubt. Its subject rather fastened on me than was chosen; and the form, approaching the model of the Greek tragedy, shaped itself under my hand rather by force of pleasure than of design. But when the compositional excitement had subsided, I felt afraid of my position. My own object was the new and strange experiment of the fallen Humanity, as it went forth from Paradise into the Wilderness, with a peculiar reference to Eve's allotted grief, which, considering that self-sacrifice belonged to her womanhood, and the consciousness of being the organ of the Fall to her offence, appeared to me imperfectly apprehended hitherto, and more expressible by a woman than by a man." In this abstract announcement of the theme, it is difficult to understand the ground of the poet's hesitation to publish; for the theme in itself seems admirably adapted to the purposes of the closet drama. The poet, nevertheless, is, very properly, conscious of failure—a failure which occurs not in the general, but in the particular conception, and which must be placed to the account of "the model of the Greek tragedies." The Greek tragedies *had* and even *have* high merits; but we act wisely in now substituting for the external and typified human sympathy of the antique Chorus, a direct, internal, living and moving sympathy itself; and although Æschylus might have done service as "a model," to either Euripides or Sophocles, yet were Sophocles and Euripides in London to-day, they would, perhaps, while granting a certain formless and shadowy grandeur, indulge a quiet smile at the shallowness and uncouthness of that Art, which, in the old amphitheatres, had beguiled them into applause of the Œdipus at Colonos.

It would have been better for Miss Barrett if, throwing herself independently upon her own very extraordinary resources, and forgetting that a Greek had ever lived, she had involved her Eve in a series of adventures merely natural, or if not this, of adventures preternatural within the limits of at least a conceivable relation—a relation of matter to spirit and spirit to matter, that should have left room for something like palpable action and comprehensible emotion—that should not have utterly precluded the development of that womanly character which is admitted as the principal object of the poem. As the case actually stands, it is only in a few snatches of verbal intercommunication with Adam and Lucifer, that we behold her as a woman at all. For the rest, she is a mystical something or nothing, enwrapped in a fog of rhapsody about Transfiguration, and the Seed, and the Bruising of the Heel, and other talk of a nature that no man ever pretended to understand in plain prose, and which, when solar-microscoped into poetry "upon the model of the Greek drama," is about as convincing as the Egyptian Lectures of Mr. Silk Buckingham—about as much to any purpose under the sun as the *hi presto!* conjurations of Signor Blitz. What are we to make, for example, of dramatic colloquy such as this?—the words are those of a Chorus of Invisible Angels addressing Adam:

> Live, work on, O Earthy!
> By the Actual's tension

Speed the arrow worthy
   Of a pure ascension.
From the low earth round you
   Reach the heights above you;
From the stripes that wound you
   Seek the loves that love you!
God's divinest burneth plain
Through the crystal diaphane
   Of our loves that love you.

Now we do not mean to assert that, by excessive "tension" of the intellect, a reader accustomed to the cant of the transcendentalists (or of those who degrade an ennobling philosophy by styling themselves such) may not succeed in ferretting from the passage quoted, and indeed from each of the thousand similar ones throughout the book, something that shall bear the aspect of an absolute idea—but we do mean to say first, that, in nine cases out of ten, the thought when dug out will be found very poorly to repay the labor of the digging;—for it is the nature of thought in general, as it is the nature of some ores in particular, to be richest when most superficial. And we do mean to say, secondly, that, in nineteen cases out of twenty, the reader will suffer the most valuable ore to remain unmined to all eternity, before he will be put to the trouble of digging for it one inch. And we do mean to assert, thirdly, that no reader is to be condemned for *not* putting himself to the trouble of digging even the one inch; for no writer has the right to impose any such necessity upon him. What is worth thinking is distinctly thought: what is distinctly thought, can and should be distinctly expressed, or should not be expressed at all. Nevertheless, there is no more appropriate opportunity than the present for admitting and maintaining, at once, what has never before been either maintained or admitted—that there is a justifiable exception to the rule for which we contend. It is where the design is to convey the fantastic—not the obscure. To give the idea of the latter we need, as in general, the most precise and definitive terms, and those who employ other terms but confound obscurity of expression with the expression of obscurity. The fantastic in itself, however,—phantasm—may be materially

furthered in its development by the *quaint* in phraseology:—
a proposition which any moralist may examine at his leisure
for himself.

The "Drama of Exile" opens with a very palpable *bull*:—
"Scene, the outer side of the gate of Eden, shut fast with
clouds"—[a scene out of sight!]—"from the depth of which
revolves the sword of fire, self-moved. A watch of innumerable angels rank above rank, slopes up from around it to the
zenith: and the glare cast from their brightness and from the
sword, extends many miles into the wilderness. Adam and
Eve are seen in the distance, flying along the glare. The angel
Gabriel and Lucifer are beside the gate."—These are the
"stage directions" which greet us on the threshold of the
book. We complain first of the bull: secondly, of the blue-fire
melo-dramatic aspect of the revolving sword; thirdly, of the
duplicate nature of the sword, which, if steel, and sufficiently
enflamed to do service in burning, would, perhaps, have been
in no temper to cut; and on the other hand, if sufficiently cool
to have an edge, would have accomplished little in the way of
scorching a personage so well accustomed to fire and brimstone and all that, as we have very good reason to believe
Lucifer was. We cannot help objecting, too, to the "innumerable angels," as a force altogether disproportioned to the one
enemy to be kept out:—either the self-moving sword itself, we
think, or the angel Gabriel alone, or five or six of the "innumerable" angels, would have sufficed to keep the devil (or
is it Adam?) outside of the gate—which, after all, he might
not have been able to discover, on account of the clouds.

Far be it from us, however, to dwell irreverently on matters
which have venerability in the faith or in the fancy of Miss
Barrett. We allude to these *niäiseries* at all—found here in the
very first paragraph of her poem,—simply by way of putting
in the clearest light the mass of inconsistency and antagonism
in which her *subject* has inextricably involved her. She has
made allusion to Milton, and no doubt felt secure in her
theme (as a theme merely) when she considered his "Paradise
Lost." But even in Milton's own day, when men had the habit
of believing all things, the more nonsensical the more readily,
and of worshipping, in blind acquiescence, the most preposterous of impossibilities—even *then*, there were not wanting

individuals who would have read the great epic with more zest, could it have been explained to their satisfaction, how and why it was, not only that a snake quoted Aristotle's ethics, and behaved otherwise pretty much as he pleased, but that bloody battles were continually being fought between bloodless "innumerable angels," that found no inconvenience in losing a wing one minute and a head the next, and if pounded up into puff-paste late in the afternoon, were as good "innumerable angels" as new the next morning, in time to be at *reveillé* roll-call: And now—at the present epoch—there are few people who do not occasionally *think*. This is emphatically the thinking age;—indeed it may very well be questioned whether mankind ever substantially thought before. The fact is, if the "Paradise Lost" were written to-day (assuming that it had never been written when it was), not even its eminent, although over-estimated merits, would counterbalance, either in the public view, or in the opinion of any critic at once intelligent and honest, the multitudinous incongruities which are part and parcel of its plot.

But in the plot of the drama of Miss Barrett it is something even worse than incongruity which affronts:—a continuous mystical strain of ill-fitting and exaggerated allegory—if, indeed, allegory is not much too respectable a term for it. We are called upon, for example, to sympathise in the whimsical woes of two Spirits, who, upspringing from the bowels of the earth, set immediately to bewailing their miseries in jargon such as this:

> I am the spirit of the harmless earth;
>   God spake me softly out among the stars,
> As softly as a blessing of much worth—
> And then his smile did follow unawares,
> That all things, fashioned, so, for use and duty,
> Might shine anointed with his chrism of beauty—
>   Yet I wail!
> I drave on with the worlds exultingly,
>   Obliquely down the Godlight's gradual fall—
> Individual aspect and complexity
>   Of gyratory orb and interval,
> Lost in the fluent motion of delight

Toward the high ends of Being, beyond Sight—
Yet I wail!

Innumerable other spirits discourse successively after the same fashion, each ending every stanza of his lamentation with the "yet I wail!" When at length they have fairly made an end, Eve touches Adam upon the elbow, and hazards, also, the profound and pathetic observation—"Lo, Adam, they wail!"—which is nothing more than the simple truth—for they *do*—and God deliver us from any such wailing again!

It is not our purpose, however, to demonstrate what every reader of these volumes will have readily seen self-demonstrated—the utter indefensibility of "The Drama of Exile," considered uniquely, as a work of art. We have none of us to be told that a medley of metaphysical recitatives sung out of tune, at Adam and Eve, by all manner of inconceivable abstractions, is not exactly the best material for a poem. Still it may very well happen that among this material there shall be individual passages of great beauty. But should any one doubt the possibility, let him be satisfied by a single extract such as follows:

On a mountain peak
Half sheathed in primal woods and glittering
In *spasms of awful sunshine*, at that hour
A lion couched,—part raised upon his paws,
With his calm massive face turned full on thine,
And his mane listening. When the ended curse
Left silence in the world, right suddenly
He sprang up rampant, and stood straight and stiff,
As if the new reality of death
Were dashed against his eyes,—and roared so fierce,
(*Such thick carnivorous passion in his throat*
Tearing a passage through the wrath and fear)—
And roared so wild, and smote from all the hills
Such *fast keen echoes crumbling down the vales*
To distant silence,—that the forest beasts,
One after one, did mutter a response
In savage and in sorrowful complaint
Which trailed along the gorges.

There is an Homeric force here—a vivid picturesqueness which all men will appreciate and admire. It is, however, the longest quotable passage in the drama, not disfigured with blemishes of importance;—although there are many—very many passages of a far loftier order of excellence, so disfigured, and which, therefore, it would not suit our immediate purpose to extract. The truth is,—and it may be as well mentioned at this point as elsewhere—that we are not to look in Miss Barrett's works for any examples of what has been occasionally termed "sustained effort;" for neither are there, in any of her poems, any long commendable paragraphs, nor are there any individual compositions which will bear the slightest examination as consistent Art-products. Her wild and magnificent genius seems to have contented itself with points—to have exhausted itself in flashes;—but it is the profusion—the unparalleled number and close propinquity of these points and flashes which render her book *one flame*, and justify us in calling her, unhesitatingly, the greatest—the most glorious of her sex.

The "Drama of Exile" calls for little more, in the way of comment, than what we have generally said. Its finest particular feature is, perhaps, the rapture of Eve—rapture bursting through despair—upon discovering that she still possesses, in the unwavering love of Adam, an undreamed-of and priceless treasure. The poem ends, as it commences, with a bull. The last sentence gives us to understand that "there is a sound through the silence, as of the falling tears of an angel." How there can be sound during silence, and how an audience are to distinguish, by such sound, angel tears from any other species of tears, it may be as well, perhaps, not too particularly to inquire.

Next, in length, to the Drama, is "The Vision of Poets." We object to the didacticism of its design, which the poetess thus states: "I have attempted to express here my view of the mission of the veritable poet—of the self-abnegation implied in it, of the uses of sorrow suffered in it, of the great work accomplished in it through suffering, and of the duty and glory of what Balzac has beautifully and truly called '*la patience angelique du génie.*'" This "view" may be correct, but neither its correctness nor its falsity has anything to do with a poem. If a thesis is to be demonstrated, we need *prose* for its demonstration. In this instance, so far as the allegorical instruction and argumentation are lost sight of, in the upper current—so far as the main admitted intention of the work is kept out of view—so far only is the work a poem, and so far only is the poem worth notice, or worthy of its author. Apart from its poetical character, the composition is thoughtful, vivid, epigrammatic, and abundant in just observation—although the critical opinions introduced are not always our own. A reviewer in "Blackwood's Magazine," quoting many of these critical portraits, takes occasion to find fault with the grammar of this tristich:

> Here Æschylus—the women swooned
> To see so awful when he frowned
> As the Gods did—he standeth crowned.

"What on earth," says the critic, "are we to make of the words 'the women swooned to see so awful'? . . . . The syntax will punish future commentators as much as some of his own corrupt choruses." In general, we are happy to agree with this reviewer, whose decisions respecting the book are, upon the whole, so nearly coincident with ours, that we hesitated, through fear of repetition, to undertake a *critique* at all, until we considered that we might say a very great deal in simply supplying his omissions; but he frequently errs through mere hurry, and never did he err more singularly than at the point now in question. He evidently supposes that "awful" has been misused as an adverb and made referrible to " women." But not so; and although the construction of the passage is unjustifiably involute, its grammar is intact. Disentangling the construction, we make this evident at once: "Here Æschylus (he) standeth crowned, (whom) the women swooned to see so awful, when he frowned as the Gods did." The "he" is excessive, and the " whom" is understood. Respecting the lines,

> Euripides, with close and mild
> Scholastic lips, that could be wild,
> And laugh or sob out like a child
> Right in the classes,

the critic observes:—" 'Right in the classes' throws our intellect completely upon its beam-ends." But, if so, the fault possibly lies in the crankness of the intellect; for the words themselves mean merely that Sophocles laughed or cried like a school-boy—like a child right (or just) in his classes—one who had not yet left school. The phrase is affected, we grant, but quite intelligible. A still more remarkable misapprehension occurs in regard to the triplet,

> And Goethe, with that reaching eye
> His soul reached out from, far and high,
> And fell from inner entity.

The reviewer's remarks upon this are too preposterous not to be quoted in full;—we doubt if any commentator of equal dignity ever so egregiously committed himself before. "Goethe," he says, "is a perfect enigma, what does the word 'fell' mean? δεινος we suppose—that is, 'not to be trifled with.' But surely it sounds very strange, although it may be true enough, to say that his 'fellness' is occasioned by 'inner entity.' But perhaps the line has some deeper meaning which we are unable to fathom." Perhaps it has: and this is the criticism—the British criticism—the Blackwood criticism—to which we have so long implicitly bowed down! As before, Miss Barrett's verses are needlessly involved, but their meaning requires no Œdipus. Their construction is thus intended:—"And Goethe, with that reaching eye from which his soul reached out, far and high, and (in so reaching) fell from inner entity." The plain prose is this:—Goethe, (the poet would say), in involving himself too far and too profoundly in external speculations—speculations concerning the world without him—neglected, or made miscalculations concerning his inner entity, or being,—concerning the world within. This idea is involved in the metaphor of a person leaning from a window so far that finally he falls from it—the person being the soul, the window the eye.

Of the twenty-eight "Sonnets," which immediately succeed the "Drama of Exile," and which receive the especial commendation of Blackwood, we have no very enthusiastic opinion. The *best* sonnet is objectionable from its extreme artificiality; and, to be effective, this species of composition, requires a minute management—a well-controlled dexterity of touch—compatible neither with Miss Barrett's deficient constructiveness, nor with the fervid rush and whirl of her genius. Of the particular instances here given, we prefer "the Prisoner," of which the conclusion is particularly beautiful. In general, the themes are obtrusively metaphysical, or didactic.

"The Romaunt of the Page," an imitation of the old English ballad, is neither very original in subject, nor very skilfully put together. We speak comparatively, of course:—It is not very good—for Miss Barrett:—and what we have said of this poem will apply equally to a very similar production, "The Rhyme of the Dutchess May." The "Poet and the Bird"—"A Child Asleep"—"Crowned and Wedded"—"Crowned and Buried"—"To Flush my Dog"—"The Fourfold Aspect"—"A Flower in a Letter"—"A Lay of the early Rose"—"That Day"—"L. E. L's Last Questio"—"Catarina to Camoens"—"Wine of Cyprus"—"The Dead Pan"—"Sleeping and Watching"—"A Portrait"—"The Mournful Mother"—and "A Valediction"—although all burning with divine fire, manifested only in scintillations, have nothing in them idiosyncratic. "The House of Clouds" and "The Last Bower" are superlatively lovely, and show the vast powers of the poet in the field best adapted to their legitimate display:—the *themes*, here, could not be improved. The former poem is purely imaginative; the latter is unobjectionably because unobtrusively suggestive of a moral, and is, perhaps, upon the whole, the most admirable composition in the two volumes:—or, if it is not, then "The Lay of the Brown Rosarie" *is*. In this last the ballad-character is elevated—etherealized—and thus made to afford scope for an ideality at once the richest and most vigorous in the world. The peculiar foibles of the author are here too, dropped bodily, as a mantle, in the tumultuous movement and excitement of the narrative.

Miss Barrett has need only of *real* self-interest in her subjects, to do justice to her subjects and to herself. On the other hand, "A Rhapsody of Life's Progress," although

gleaming with cold corruscations, is the least meritorious, because the most philosophical, effusion of the whole:—this,
we say, in flat contradiction of the *"spoudiotaton kai philosophikotaton genos"* of Aristotle. "The Cry of the Human" is singularly effective, not more from the vigour and ghastly
passion of its thought, than from the artistically-conceived *ar-
abesquerie* of its rhythm. "The Cry of the Children," similar,
although superior in tone and handling, is full of a nervous
unflinching energy—a horror sublime in its simplicity—of
which a far greater than Dante might have been proud. "Ber-
tha in the Lane," a rich ballad, very singularly excepted from
the wholesale commendation of the "Democratic Review," as
"perhaps not one of the best," and designated by Blackwood,
on the contrary, as "decidedly the finest poem of the collection," is *not* the *very* best, we think, only because mere pathos, however exquisite, cannot be ranked with the loftiest
exhibitions of the ideal. Of "Lady Geraldine's Courtship," the
magazine last quoted observes that "some pith is put forth in
its passionate parts." We will not pause to examine the delicacy or lucidity of the metaphor embraced in the *"putting
forth of some pith;"* but unless by "some pith" itself, is intended the utmost conceivable intensity and vigour, then the
critic is merely damning with faint praise. With the exception
of Tennyson's "Locksley Hall," we have never perused a poem
combining so much of the fiercest passion with so much of
the most ethereal fancy, as the "Lady Geraldine's Courtship,"
of Miss Barrett. We are forced to admit, however, that the
latter work *is* a very palpable imitation of the former, which
it surpasses in plot or rather in thesis, as much as it falls below
it in artistical management, and a certain calm energy—lustrous and indomitable—such as we might imagine in a broad
river of molten gold.

It is in the "Lady Geraldine" that the critic of Blackwood
is again put at fault in the comprehension of a couple of passages. He confesses his inability "to make out the construction of the words, 'all that spirits pure and ardent are cast out
of love and reverence, because chancing not to hold.' " There
are comparatively few American school-boys who could not
parse it. The prosaic construction would run thus:—"all *that*
(wealth understood) because chancing not to hold *which*, (or

on account of not holding which) all pure and ardent spirits
are cast out of love and reverence." The "which" is involved
in the relative pronoun "that"—the second word of the sentence. *All that we know is, that Miss Barrett is right:*—here is
a parallel phrase, meaning—"all that (which) we know," etc.
The fact is, that the accusation of imperfect grammar would
have been more safely, if more generally, urged: in descending to particular exceptions, the reviewer has been doing little
more than exposing himself at all points.

Turning aside, however, from grammar, he declares his incapacity to fathom the meaning of

> She has halls and she has castles, and the resonant steam-
>   eagles
> *Follow far on the directing of her floating dove-like hand—*
> With a thunderous vapour trailing underneath the starry
>   vigils,
> So to mark upon the blasted heaven the measure of her
>   land.

Now it must be understood that he is profoundly serious
in his declaration—he really *does not* apprehend the thought
designed—and he is even more than profoundly serious, too,
in intending these his own comments upon his own stolidity,
for wit:—"We thought that steam-coaches generally followed
the directing of no hand except the stoker's, but *it*, certainly,
is always much *liker* a raven than a dove." After this, who
shall question the infallibility of Christopher North? We presume there are very few of *our* readers who will not easily
appreciate the richly imaginative conception of the poetess:—
The Lady Geraldine is supposed to be standing in her own
door, (positively *not* on the top of an engine), and thence
pointing, "with her floating dove-like hand," to the lines of
vapour, from the "resonant steam-eagles," that designate
upon the "blasted heaven," the remote boundaries of her domain.—But, perhaps, we are guilty of a very gross absurdity
ourselves, in commenting *at all* upon the whimsicalities of a
reviewer who can deliberately *select* for special animadversion
the second of the four verses we here copy:

"Eyes, he said, now throbbing through me! are ye eyes that
    did undo me?

Shining eyes like antique jewels set in Parian statue-stone!
Underneath that calm white forehead are ye ever burning
  torrid
O'er the desolate sand desert of my heart and life undone?"

The ghost of the Great Frederic might, to be sure, quote at us, in his own Latin, his favorite adage, "De gustibus non est disputand*us*;"—but, when we take into consideration the moral designed, the weirdness of effect intended, and the historical adaptation of the fact alluded to, in the line italicized, (a fact of which it is by no means impossible that the critic is ignorant), we cannot refrain from expressing our conviction—and we here *express it* in the teeth of the whole horde of the Ambrosianians—that from the entire range of poetical literature there shall not, in a century, be produced a more sonorous—a more vigorous verse—a juster—a nobler—a more ideal—a more magnificent image—than this very image, in this very verse, which the most noted magazine of Europe has so especially and so contemptuously condemned.

"The Lady Geraldine" is, we think, the only poem of its author which is not deficient, considered as an artistical whole. Her constructive ability, as we have already suggested, is either not very remarkable, or has never been properly brought into play:—in truth, her genius is too impetuous for the minuter technicalities of that elaborate *Art* so needful in the building up of pyramids for immortality. This deficiency, then—if there be any such—is her chief weakness. Her other foibles, although some of them are, in fact, glaring, glare, nevertheless, to no very material ill purpose. There are none which she will not readily dismiss in her future works. She retains them now, perhaps, because unaware of their existence.

Her affectations are unquestionably many, and generally inexcusable. We may, perhaps, tolerate such words as "blé," "chrysm," "nympholeptic," "œnomel," and "chrysopras"— they have at least the merit either of distinct meaning, or of terse and sonorous expression;—but what can be well said in defence of the unnecessary nonsense of " 'ware" for "aware"—of " 'bide," for "abide"—of " 'gins," for "begins"—of " 'las," for "alas"—of "oftly," "ofter," and "oftest," for "often," "more often," and "most often"—or of "erelong"

in the sense of "long ago"? That there is *authority* for the
mere words proves nothing; those who employed them in
their day would not employ them if writing *now*. Although
we grant, too, that the poetess is very usually Homeric in her
compounds, there is no intelligibility of construction, and
therefore no force of meaning in "dew-pallid," "pale-pas-
sioned," and "silver-solemn." Neither have we any partiality
for "drave" or "*su*preme," or "*la*ment"; and while upon this
topic, we may as well observe that there are few readers who
do anything but laugh or stare, at such phrases as "L. E. L.'s
Last Questio"—"The Cry of the Human"—"Leaning from
my Human"—"Heaven assist the human"—"the full sense of
your mortal"—"a grave for your divine"—"falling off from
our created"—"he sends this gage for thy pity's counting"—
"they could not press their futures on the present of her courtesy"—or "could another fairer lack to thee, lack to thee?"
There are few, at the same time, who do not feel disposed to
weep outright, when they hear of such things as "Hope with-
drawing her peradventure"—"spirits dealing in pathos of
antithesis"—"angels in antagonism to God and his reflex
beatitudes"—"songs of glories ruffling down doorways"—
"God's possibles"—and "rules of Mandom."

We have already said, however, that mere *quaintness* within
reasonable limit, is not only *not* to be regarded as affectation,
but has its proper artistic uses in aiding a fantastic effect. We
quote, from the lines "To my dog Flush," a passage in exemplification:

> Leap! thy broad tail waves a light!
> Leap! thy slender feet are bright,
>   Canopied in fringes!
> Leap! those tasselled ears of thine
> Flicker strangely, fair and fine,
>   *Down their golden inches!*

And again—from the song of a tree-spirit, in the "Drama
of Exile:"

> The Divine impulsion cleaves
> In dim movements to the leaves

Dropt and lifted, dropt and lifted,
In the sun-light greenly sifted,—
In the sun-light and the moon-light
Greenly sifted through the trees.
Ever wave the Eden trees,
In the night-light and the noon-light,
With a ruffling of green branches,
Shaded off to resonances,
Never stirred by rain or breeze.

The thoughts, here, belong to the highest order of poetry, but they could not have been wrought into effective expression, without the instrumentality of those repetitions—those unusual phrases—in a word, those *quaintnesses*, which it has been too long the fashion to censure, indiscriminately, under the one general head of "affectation." No true poet will fail to be enraptured with the two extracts above quoted—but we believe there are few who would not find a difficulty in reconciling the psychal impossibility of refraining from admiration, with the too-hastily attained mental conviction that, critically, there is nothing to admire.

Occasionally, we meet in Miss Barrett's poems a certain *far-fetchedness* of imagery, which is reprehensible in the extreme. What, for example, are we to think of

Now he hears the angel voices
Folding silence in the room?—

undoubtedly, that it is nonsense, and no more; or of

How the silence round you shivers
While our voices through it go?—

again, unquestionably, that it is nonsense, and nothing beyond.

Sometimes we are startled by knotty paradoxes; and it is not acquitting their perpetrator of all blame on their account to admit that, in some instances, they are susceptible of solution. It is really difficult to discover anything for approbation, in enigmas such as

> That bright impassive, passive angel-hood,

or—

> The silence of my heart is full of sound.

At long intervals, we are annoyed by specimens of repulsive imagery, as where the children cry:

> How long, O cruel nation,
> Will you stand, to move the world, *on a child's heart*—
> *Stifle down with a mailed heel its palpitation?* etc.

Now and then, too, we are confounded by a pure platitude, as when Eve exclaims:

> Leave us not
> In agony beyond what we can bear,
> And in abasement *below thunder mark!*

or, when the Saviour is made to say:

> So, at last,
> He shall look round on you *with lids too straight*
> *To hold the grateful tears.*

"Strait" was, no doubt, intended, but does not materially elevate, although it slightly elucidates, the thought. A very remarkable passage is that, also, wherein Eve bids the infant voices

> Hear the steep generations, how they fall
> Adown the visionary stairs of Time,
> Like supernatural thunders—far yet near,
> Sowing their fiery echoes through the hills!

Here, saying nothing of the affectation in "adown;" not alluding to the insoluble paradox of "far yet near;" not mentioning the inconsistent metaphor involved in the "sowing of *fiery* echoes;" adverting but slightly to the misusage of "like," in place of "as," and to the impropriety of making any thing fall like *thunder*, which has never been known to fall at all; merely hinting, too, at the misapplication of "steep," to the "generations," instead of to the "stairs"—a perversion in no degree to be justified by the fact that so preposterous a figure as *synecdoche* exists in the school books;—letting these things pass, for the present, we shall still find it difficult to understand how Miss Barrett should have been led to think the principal idea itself—the abstract idea—the idea of *tumbling down stairs* in any shape, or under any circumstances,—either a poetical or a decorous conception. And yet we have seen this very passage quoted as "sublime," by a critic who seems to take it for granted, as a general rule, that Nat-Leeism is the loftiest order of literary merit. That the lines very *narrowly missed* sublimity, we grant; that they came within a step of it, we admit;—but, unhappily, the step is that *one* step which, time out of mind, has intervened between the sublime and the ridiculous. So true is this, that any person—that even *we*—with a very partial modification of the imagery—a modification that shall not interfere with its richly spiritual *tone*—may elevate the quotation into unexceptionability. For example: and we offer it with profound deference—

> Hear the far generations—how they crash,
> From crag to crag, down the precipitous Time,
> In multitudinous thunders that upstartle,
> Aghast, the echoes from their cavernous lairs
> In the visionary hills!

We have no doubt that our version has its faults—but it has, at least, the merit of consistency. Not only is a mountain more poetical than a pair of stairs; but echoes are more appropriately typified as wild beasts than as seeds; and echoes and wild beasts agree better with a mountain than does a pair of stairs with the *sowing* of seeds—even admitting that these seeds be seeds of fire, and be sown broadcast "among the hills," by a steep generation while in the act of tumbling down the stairs—that is to say, of coming down the stairs in too violent a hurry to be capable of sowing the seeds as accurately as all seeds should be sown; nor is the matter rendered any better for Miss Barrett, even if the construction of her sentence is to be understood as implying that the fiery seeds were sown, not immediately by the steep generations that tumbled down the stairs, but mediately, through the intervention of the "supernatural thunders" that were *occasioned* by the "steep generations" that tumbled down the stairs.

The poetess is not unfrequently guilty of repeating herself. The "thunder cloud veined by lightning" appears, for instance, on pages 34 of the first, and 228 of the second volume. The "silver clash of wings" is heard at pages 53 of the first, and 269 of the second; and angel tears are discovered to be falling as well at page 27, as at the conclusion of "The Drama of Exile." Steam, too, in the shape of Death's White Horse, comes upon the ground, both at page 244 of the first and 179 of the second volume—and there are multitudinous other repetitions both of phrase and idea—but it is the excessive reiteration of pet *words* which is, perhaps, the most obtrusive of the minor errors of the poet. "Chrystalline," "Apocalypse," "foregone," "evangel," " 'ware," "throb," "level," "loss," and the musical term "minor," are forever upon her lips. The chief favorites, however, are "down" and "leaning," which are echoed and re-echoed not only *ad infinitum*, but in every whimsical variation of import. As Miss Barrett certainly cannot be aware of the extent of this mannerism, we will venture to call her attention to a few—comparatively a *very* few examples.

> Pealing *down* the depths of Godhead—
> And smiling *down* the stars—
> Smiling *down*, as Venus *down* the waves—
> Smiling *down* the steep world very purely—
> *Down* the purple of this chamber—
> Moving *down* the hidden depths of loving—
> Cold the sun shines *down* the door—
> Which brought angels *down* our talk—
> Let your souls behind you *lean* gently moved—
> But angels *leaning* from the golden seats—
> And melancholy *leaning* out of heaven—
> And I know the heavens are *leaning* down—
> Then over the casement she *leaneth*—
> Forbear that dream, too near to heaven it *leaned*—

> I would *lean* my spirit o'er you—
> Thou, O sapient angel, *leanest o'er*—
> Shapes of brightness over*lean* thee—
> They are *leaning* their young heads—
> Out of heaven shall o'er you *lean*—
> While my spirit *leans* and reaches—
> *Leaning* from my human—
> When it *leans* out on the air—
> etc. etc. etc.

In the matter of grammar, upon which the Edinburgh critic insists so pertinaciously, the author of "The Drama of Exile" seems to us even peculiarly without fault. The nature of her studies has, no doubt, imbued her with a very delicate instinct of constructive accuracy. The occasional use of phrases so questionable as "from whence" and the far-fetchedness and involution of which we have already spoken, are the only noticeable blemishes of an exceedingly chaste, vigorous and comprehensive style.

In her inattention to rhythm, Mrs. Barrett is guilty of an error that might have been fatal to her fame—that *would* have been fatal to any reputation less solidly founded than her own. We do not allude, so particularly, to her multiplicity of inadmissible rhymes. We would wish, to be sure, that she had not thought proper to couple Eden and succeeding—glories and floorwise—burning and morning—thither and æther—enclose me and across me—misdoers and flowers—centre and winter—guerdon and pardon—conquer and anchor—desert and unmeasured—atoms and fathoms—opal and people—glory and doorway—trumpet and accompted—taming and overcame him—coming and woman—is and trees—off and sun-proof—eagles and vigils—nature and satire—poems and interflowings—certes and virtues—pardon and burden—threat and great—children and bewildering—mortal and turtle—moonshine and sunshine. It would have been better, we say, if such apologies for rhymes as these had been rejected. But deficiencies of *rhythm* are more serious. In some cases it is nearly impossible to determine what metre is intended. "The Cry of the Children" cannot be scanned: we *never saw* so poor a specimen of verse. In imitating the rhythm of "Locksley Hall," the poetess has preserved with accuracy (so far as mere syllables are concerned) the forcible line of seven trochees with a final cæsura. The "double rhymes" have only the force of a single long syllable—a cæsura; but the natural rhythmical division, occurring at the close of the fourth trochee, should never be forced to occur, as Miss Barrett constantly forces it, in the middle of a word, or of an indivisible phrase. If it do so occur, we must sacrifice, in perusal, either the sense or the rhythm. If she will consider, too, that this line of seven trochees and a cæsura, is nothing more than two lines written in one—a line of four trochees, succeeded by one of three trochees and a cæsura—she will at once see how unwise she has been in composing her poem in quatrains of the long line with alternate rhymes, instead of immediate ones, as in the case of "Locksley Hall." The result is, that the ear, expecting the rhymes before they occur, does not appreciate them when they do. These points, however, will be best exemplified by transcribing one of the quatrains in its *natural* arrangement. That actually employed is addressed only to the eye.

> Oh, she fluttered like a tame bird
>   In among its forest brothers
> Far too strong for it, then, drooping,
>   Bowed her face upon her hands—
> And I spake out wildly, fiercely,
>   Brutal truths of her and others!
> I, she planted in the desert,
>   Swathed her 'wind-like, with my sands.

Here it will be seen that there is a paucity of rhyme, and that it is expected at closes where it does not occur. In fact, if we consider the eight lines as two independent quatrains, (which they are), then we find them *entirely rhymeless*. Now so unhappy are these metrical defects—of so much importance do we take them to be, that we do not hesitate in declaring the general inferiority of the poem to its prototype to be altogether chargeable to *them*. With equal rhythm "Lady Geraldine" had been far—very far the superior poem. Inefficient rhythm is inefficient poetical expression; and expression, in poetry,—what is it?—what is it not? No one living can better answer these queries than Miss Barrett.

We conclude our comments upon her versification, by quoting (we will not say whence—from what one of her poems)—a few verses without the linear division as it appears in the book. There are many readers who would never suspect the passage to be intended for metre at all.—"Ay!—and sometimes, on the hill-side, while we sat down on the gowans, with the forest green behind us, and its shadow cast before, and the river running under, and, across it from the rowens a partridge whirring near us till we felt the air it bore—there, obedient to her praying, did I read aloud the poems made by Tuscan flutes, or instruments more various of our own—read the pastoral parts of Spenser—or the subtle interflowings found in Petrarch's sonnets;—here's the book!—the leaf is folded down!"

With this extract we make an end of our fault-finding—and *now*, shall we speak, equally in detail, of the *beauties* of this book? Alas! here, indeed, do we feel the impotence of the pen. We have already said that the supreme excellence of the poetess whose works we review, is made up of the multitudinous sums of a world of lofty merits. It is the multiplicity—it is the *aggregation*—which excites our most profound enthusiasm, and enforces our most earnest respect. But unless we had space to extract three fourths of the volumes, how could we convey this aggregation by specimens? We might quote, to be sure, an example of keen insight into our psychal nature, such as this:

> I fell flooded with a Dark,
>   In the silence of a swoon—
> When I rose, still cold and stark,
>   There was night,—I saw the moon:
> And the stars, each in its place,
> And the May-blooms on the grass,
> Seemed to wonder what I was.
> And I walked as if apart
>   From myself when I could stand—
> And I pitied my own heart,
>   As if I held it in my hand

> Somewhat coldly,—with a sense
> Of fulfilled benevolence.

Or we might copy an instance of the purest and most radiant imagination, such as this:

> So, young muser, I sat listening
> To my Fancy's wildest word—
> On a sudden, through the glistening
> Leaves around, a little stirred,
> Came a sound, a sense of music, which was rather felt
>   than heard.
> Softly, finely, it inwound me—
> From the world it shut me in—
> Like a fountain falling round me
> Which with silver waters thin,
> Holds a little marble Naiad sitting smilingly within.

Or, again, we might extract a specimen of wild Dantesque vigor, such as this—in combination with a pathos never excelled:

> Ay! be silent—let them hear each other breathing
>   For a moment, mouth to mouth—
> Let them touch each others' hands in a fresh wreathing
>   Of their tender human youth!
> Let them feel that this cold metallic motion
>   Is not all the life God fashions or reveals—
> Let them prove their inward souls against the notion
>   That they live in you, or under you, O wheels!

Or, still again, we might give a passage embodying the most elevated sentiment, most tersely and musically thus expressed:

> And since, Prince Albert, men have called thy spirit high
>   and rare,
> And true to truth, and brave for truth, as some at
>   Augsburg were—
> We charge thee by thy lofty thoughts and by thy poet-
>   mind,

Which not by glory or degree takes measure of mankind,
Esteem that wedded hand less dear for sceptre than for
    ring,
And hold her uncrowned womanhood to be the royal
    thing!

These passages, we say, and a hundred similar ones, exemplifying particular excellences, might be displayed, and we should still fail, as lamentably as the *skolastikos* with his brick, in conveying an idea of the vast *totality*. By no individual stars can we present the constellatory radiance of the book.—*To the book*, then, with implicit confidence we appeal.

That Miss Barrett has done more, in poetry, than any woman, living or dead, will scarcely be questioned:—that she has surpassed all her poetical contemporaries of either sex (with a single exception) is our deliberate opinion—not idly entertained, we think, nor founded on any visionary basis. It may not be uninteresting, therefore, in closing this examination of her claims, to determine in what manner she holds poetical relation with these contemporaries, or with her immediate predecessors, and especially with the great exception to which we have alluded,—if at all.

If ever mortal "wreaked his thoughts upon expression" it was Shelley. If ever poet sang (as a bird sings)—impulsively—earnestly—with utter abandonment—to himself solely—and for the mere joy of his own song—that poet was the author of the Sensitive Plant. Of Art—beyond that which is the inalienable instinct of Genius—he either had little or disdained all. He *really* disdained that Rule which is the emanation from Law, because his own soul was law in itself. His rhapsodies are but the rough notes—the stenographic memoranda of poems—memoranda which, because they were all-sufficient for his own intelligence, he cared not to be at the trouble of transcribing in full for mankind. In his whole life he wrought not thoroughly out a single conception. For this reason it is that he is the most fatiguing of poets. Yet he wearies in having done too little, rather than too much; what seems in him the diffuseness of one idea, is the conglomerate concision of many;—and this concision it is which renders him obscure. With such a man, to imitate was out of the question; it would have answered no purpose—for he spoke to his own spirit alone, which would have comprehended no alien tongue;—he was, therefore, profoundly original. His quaintness arose from intuitive perception of that truth to which Lord Verulam alone has given distinct voice:—"There is no exquisite beauty which has not some strangeness in its proportion." But whether obscure, original, or quaint, he was at all times sincere. He had no *affectations*.

From the ruins of Shelley there sprang into existence, affronting the Heavens, a tottering and fantastic pagoda, in which the salient angles, tipped with mad jangling bells, were the idiosyncratic *faults* of the great original—faults which cannot be called such in view of his purposes, but which are monstrous when we regard his works as addressed to mankind. A "school" arose—if that absurd term must still be employed—a school—a system of rules—upon the basis of the Shelley who had none. Young men innumerable, dazzled with the glare and bewildered with the *bizarrerie* of the divine lightning that flickered through the clouds of the Prometheus, had no trouble whatever in heaping up imitative vapors, but, for the lightning, were content, perforce, with its *spectrum*, in which the *bizarrerie* appeared without the fire. Nor were great and mature minds unimpressed by the contemplation of a greater and more mature; and thus gradually were interwoven into this school of all Lawlessness—of obscurity, quaintness, exaggeration—the misplaced didacticism of Wordsworth, and the even more preposterously anomalous metaphysicianism of Coleridge. Matters were now fast verging to their worst, and at length, in Tennyson, poetic inconsistency attained its extreme. But it was precisely this extreme (for the greatest error and the greatest truth are scarcely two points in a circle)—it was this extreme which, following the law of all extremes, wrought in him—in Tennyson—a natural and inevitable revulsion, leading him first to contemn and secondly to investigate his early manner, and, finally, to winnow from its magnificent elements the truest and purest of all poetical styles. But not even yet is the process complete; and for this reason in part, but chiefly on account of the mere fortuitousness of that mental and moral combination which shall unite in one person (if *ever* it shall) the Shelleyan *aban-*

don, the Tennysonian poetic sense, the most profound instinct of Art, and the sternest Will properly to blend and vigorously to control all;—chiefly, we say, because such combination of antagonisms must be purely fortuitous, has the world never yet seen the noblest of the poems of which it is *possible* that it may be put in possession.

And yet Miss Barrett has narrowly missed the fulfilment of these conditions. Her poetic inspiration is the highest—we can conceive nothing more august. Her sense of Art is pure in itself, but has been contaminated by pedantic study of false models—a study which has the more easily led her astray, because she placed an undue value upon it as rare—as alien to her character of woman. The accident of having been long secluded by ill health from the world has effected, moreover, in her behalf, what an innate recklessness did for Shelley— has imparted to her, if not precisely that *abandon* to which I have referred, at least a something that stands well in its stead—a comparative independence of men and opinions with which she did not come personally in contact—a happy audacity of thought and expression never before known in one of her sex. It is, however, this same accident of ill health, perhaps, which has invalidated her original Will—diverted her from proper individuality of purpose—and seduced her into the sin of imitation. Thus, what she might have done we cannot altogether determine. What she has actually accomplished is before us. With Tennyson's works beside her, and a keen appreciation of them in her soul—appreciation too keen to be discriminative;—with an imagination even more vigorous than his, although somewhat less ethereally delicate; with inferior art and more feeble volition; she has written poems such as he *could not write*, but such as he, under *her* conditions of ill health and seclusion, *would have written* during the epoch of his pupildom in that school which arose out of Shelley, and from which, over a disgustful gulf of utter incongruity and absurdity, lit only by miasmatic flashes, into the broad open meadows of Natural Art and Divine Genius, he—Tennyson—is at once the bridge and the transition.

Broadway Journal, January 4 and 11, 1845

Edward Lytton Bulwer

Rienzi, The Last of the Tribunes. By the Author of "Eugene Aram," "Last Days of Pompeii," &c. &c. Two Volumes in one. Philadelphia: Republished by E. L. Carey and A. Hart.

WE HAVE LONG LEARNED to reverence the fine intellect of Bulwer. We take up any production of his pen with a positive certainty that, in reading it, the wildest passions of our nature, the most profound of our thoughts, the brightest visions of our fancy, and the most ennobling and lofty of our aspirations will, in due turn, be enkindled within us. We feel sure of rising from the perusal a wiser if not a better man. In no instance are we deceived. From the brief Tale—from the "Monos and Daimonos" of the author—to his most ponderous and labored novels—all is richly, and glowingly intellectual—all is energetic, or astute, or brilliant, or profound. There *may* be men now living who possess the power of Bulwer—but it is quite evident that very few have made that power so palpably manifest. Indeed we know of *none*. Viewing him as a novelist—a point of view exceedingly unfavorable (if we hold to the common acceptation of "the novel") for a proper contemplation of his genius—he is unsurpassed by any writer living or dead. Why should we hesitate to say this, feeling, as we do, thoroughly persuaded of its truth. Scott has excelled him in *many* points, and "The Bride of Lammormuir" is a better book than any individual work by the author of Pelham—"Ivanhoe" is, perhaps, equal to any. Descending to particulars, D'Israeli has a more brilliant, a more lofty, and a more delicate (we do not say a *wilder*) imagination. Lady Dacre has written Ellen Wareham, a more forcible tale of Passion. In some species of wit Theodore Hook rivals, and in broad humor our own Paulding surpasses him. The writer of "Godolphin" equals him in energy. Banim is a better sketcher of character. Hope is a richer colorist. Captain Trelawney is as original—Moore is as fanciful, and Horace Smith is as learned. But who is there uniting in one person the imagination, the passion, the humor, the energy, the knowledge of the heart, the artist-like eye, the originality, the fancy and the learning of Edward Lytton Bulwer? In a vivid wit—in profundity and a Gothic massiveness of thought—in style—in a calm certainty and definitiveness of purpose—in industry—and above all in the power of controlling and regulating by volition his illimitable faculties of mind, he is unequalled—he is unapproached.

As Rienzi is the last, so it is the best novel of Bulwer. In the Preface we are informed that the work was commenced two years ago at Rome, but abandoned upon the author's removing to Naples, for the "Last days of Pompeii"—a subject requiring, more than Rienzi, the advantage of a personal residence within reach of the scenes described. The idea of the present work, however, was never dismissed from the writer's mind, and soon after the publication of "Pompeii" he resumed his original undertaking. We are told that having had occasion to look into the original authorities whence are derived all the accounts of modern historians touching Rienzi, Mr. B. was induced to believe that no just picture of the Life or Times of that most remarkable man was at present in the hands of the people. Under this impression the novelist had at first meditated a work of History rather than of Fiction. We doubt, however, whether the spirit of the author's intention is not better fulfilled as it is. He has adhered with scrupulous fidelity to all the main events in the *public* life of his hero; and by means of the relief afforded through the personages of pure romance which form the filling in of the picture, he has been enabled more fully to develop the *private* character of the noble Roman. The reader may indeed be startled at the vast difference between the Rienzi of Mr. Bulwer, and the Rienzi of Sismondi, of Gibbon, and of Miss Mitford. But by neither of the two latter are we disposed to swear—and of Sismondi's impartiality we can at no moment be certain. Mr. B., moreover, very justly observes that as, in the work before us, all the *acts* are given from which is derived his interpretation of the principal agent, the public, having sufficient data for its own judgment, may fashion an opinion for itself.

Generally, the true chronology of Rienzi's life is preserved. In regard to the story—or that chain of fictitious incident usually binding up together the constituent parts of a Romance—there is very little of it in the book. This follows necessarily from the character of the composition—which is essentially Epic rather than Dramatic. The author's apology seems to us therefore supererogative when he says that a work which takes for its subject the crimes and errors of a nation and which ventures to seek the actual and the real in the highest stage of action or passion can rarely adopt with advantage the melo-dramatic effects produced by a vulgar mystery. In his pictures of the Roman populace, and in those of the Roman nobles of the fourteenth century— pictures full at all times of an enthralling interest—Mr. B. professes to have followed literally the descriptions left to us.

Miss Mitford's Rienzi will of course be remembered in reading that of Bulwer. There is however but one point of coincidence—a love-intrigue between a relative of the hero and one of the party of the nobles. This, it will be recollected, forms the basis of the plot of Miss M. In the Rienzi of Bulwer, it is an Episode not affecting in any manner either the story itself, or the destinies of the Tribune.

It is by no means our intention to give an analysis of the volume before us. Every person who reads at all will read Rienzi, and indeed the book is already in the hands of many millions of people. Any thing, therefore, like our usual custom of a digest of the narrative would be superfluous. The principal characters who figure in the novel are Rienzi himself—his brother, whose slaughter by a noble at the commencement of the story, is the immediate cause of Rienzi's change of temper and consequent exaltation—Adrian di Castelle, a young noble of the family of Colonna but attached to the cause of the people—Martino di Porto the chief of the house of the Orsini—Stephen Colonna, the chief of the house of the Colonna—Walter de Montreal, a gentleman of Provence, a knight of St. John, and one of the formidable freebooters who at the head of large "Companies" invaded states and pillaged towns at the period of Rienzi's Revolution—Pandulfo di Guido a student, whom, under the appellation of Pandolficcio di Guido, Gibbon styles "the most virtuous citizen of Rome"—Cecco del Vecchio a smith— Giles D'Albornoz of the royal race of Arragon—Petrarch the poet, and the friend of Rienzi—Angelo Villani—Irene, the

sister of the Tribune and betrothed to Adrian di Castello—
Nina, Rienzi's wife—and Adeline, the mistress of Walter de
Montreal.

But as was said before, we should err radically if we regard
Rienzi altogether in the light of Romance. Undoubtedly as
such—as a fiction, and coming under the title of a novel, it
is a glorious, a wonderful conception, and not the less wonderfully and gloriously carried out. What else could we say of
a book over which the mind so delightedly lingers in perusal?
In its delineations of passion and character—in the fine
blending and contrasting of its incidents—in the rich and
brilliant tints of its feudal paintings—in a pervading air of
chivalry, and grace, and sentiment—in all that can throw a
charm over the pages of Romance, the last novel of Bulwer is
equal, if not superior, to any of his former productions. Still
we should look at the work in a different point of view. It is
History. We hesitate not to say that it is History in its
truest—in its only true, proper, and philosophical garb. Sismondi's works—were not. There is no greater error than dig-
nifying with the name of History a tissue of dates and details,
though the dates be ordinarily correct, and the details indisputably true. Not even with the aid of acute comment will
such a tissue satisfy our individual notions of History. To the
effect let us look—to the impression rather than to the seal.
And how very seldom is any definite impression left upon the
mind of the historical reader! How few bear away—even
from the pages of Gibbon—Rome and the Romans. Vastly
different was the genius of Niebuhr—than whom no man
possessed a more discriminative understanding of the uses
and the purposes of the pen of the historiographer. But we
digress. Bearing in mind that "to contemplate"—ιστορειν*—
should and must be allowed a more noble and a more expansive acceptation than has been usually given it, we shall often
discover in Fiction the essential spirit and vitality of Historic
Truth—while Truth itself, in many a dull and lumbering Ar-
chive, shall be found guilty of all the inefficiency of Fiction.

*History, from ιστορειν, to contemplate, seems, among the Greeks, to
have embraced not only the knowledge of past events, but also Mythology,
Esopian, and Milesian fables, *Romance*, Tragedy and Comedy. But our business is with things, not words.

Rienzi, then, is History. But there are other aspects in which it may be regarded with advantage. Let us survey it as a profound and lucid exposition of the *morale* of Government—of the Philosophies of Rule and Misrule—of the absolute incompatibility of Freedom and Ignorance—Tyranny in the few and Virtue in the many. Let us consider it as something akin to direct evidence that a people is not a mob, nor a mob a people, nor a mob's idol the idol of a people—that in a nation's self is the only security for a nation—and that it is absolutely necessary to model upon the *character* of the governed, the machinery, whether simple or complex, of the governmental legislation.

It is proper—we are persuaded—that Rienzi should be held up in these many different points of view, if we desire fully to appreciate its own merits and the talents of Mr. Bulwer. But regard it as we will, it is an extra-ordinary work—and one which leaves nothing farther to accomplish in its own particular region. It is vastly superior to the "Last Days of Pompeii"—more rich—more glowing, and more vigorous. With all and more than all the distinguishing merits of its noble predecessor, it has none of its *chilliness*—none of that platitude which (it would not be difficult to say why) is the inevitable result of every attempt at infusing warmth among the marble wildernesses, and vitality into the statue-like existences, of the too-distantly antique.

Southern Literary Messenger, February 1836

Night and Morning. A Novel. By the author of *Pelham, Rienzi, Eugene Aram,* &c. 2 vols. Re-published by Harper & Brothers, New York.

THE RIGHT HON. Charles Leopold Beaufort, of Beaufort Court, England, a proud and misanthropical old bachelor, with a rental of twenty thousand pounds, has two nephews, Philip and Robert Beaufort. The former, who is the elder of the two, and heir-apparent to the uncle's estate, is thoughtless and generous, with unsteady principles. The latter is a crafty man-of-the-world, whose only honesty consists in appearing honest—a scrupulous decorist. Philip, in love with

Catharine Morton, the daughter of a tradesman, and in fear of his aristocratic uncle's displeasure, is married clandestinely, in a remote village of Wales, by a quondam college friend, to whom he had presented a living—the Rev. Caleb Price. The better to keep the secret, a very old Welshman, certain soon to die, and William Smith, Philip's servant, are the sole witnesses of the ceremony. This performed, Smith is hired to bury himself in Australia until called for, while the deaf man dies as expected. Some time having elapsed, Philip, dreading accident to the register, writes to Caleb for an attested copy of the record. Caleb is too ill to make it, but employs a neighboring curate, Morgan Jones, to make and attest it, and despatches it, just before dying, to Philip, who, fearing his wife's impatience of the concealment required, deposits the document, without her knowledge, in a secret drawer of a bureau. The register itself is afterwards accidentally destroyed. Catharine has soon two children—first Philip, the hero of the novel, and then Sydney. For their sakes she bravely endures the stigma upon her character. She continues to live openly with her husband as his mistress, bearing her maiden name of Morton; and the uncle, whose nerves would have been shocked at a mis-alliance, and who would have disinherited its perpetrator, winks at what he considers the venial vice. The old gentleman lives on for sixteen years, and yet no disclosure is made. At last he dies, bequeathing his property to his eldest nephew, as was anticipated. The latter prepares forthwith to own Catharine as his wife; relates to his brother the facts of the clandestine marriage; speaks of the secreted document, without designating the place of deposit; is disbelieved by that person entirely; mounts his horse to make arrangements for a second wedding, and for proving the first; is thrown, breaks his neck, and expires without uttering a word. Catharine, ignorant of the secret drawer (although aware that a record had been secreted), failing to find William Smith, and trusting her cause to an unskilful lawyer, is unable to prove her marriage, but in the effort to do so makes an enemy of Robert Beaufort, who takes possession of the estate as heir at law. Thus the strict precautions taken by the father to preserve his secret during the uncle's life, frustrate the wife in her attempts to develope it after his death, and the sons are

still considered illegitimate. This is the pivot of the story. Its
incidents are made up of the struggles of the young men with
their fate, but chiefly of the endeavors of the elder, Philip, to
demonstrate the marriage and redeem the good name of his
mother. This he finally accomplishes, (after her death, and
after a host of vicissitudes experienced in his own person) by
the accidental return of William Smith, and by the discovery
of an additional witness in Morgan Jones, who made the extract from the register, and to whom the rightful heir is
guided by this long-sought document itself, obtained from
the hands of Robert Beaufort, (who had found it in the bureau,) through the instrumentality of one Fanny, the heroine,
and in the end the wife of the hero.

We do not give this as the plot of "Night and Morning,"
but as the ground-work of the plot; which latter, woven from
the incidents above mentioned, is in itself exceedingly complex. The ground work, as will be seen, is of no very original
character—it is even absurdly common-place. We are not asserting too much when we say that every second novel since
the flood has turned upon some series of hopeless efforts, either to establish legitimacy, or to prove a will, or to get possession of a great sum of money most unjustly withheld, or
to find out a ragamuffin of a father, who had been much better left unfound. But, saying nothing of the basis upon which
this story has been erected, the story itself is, in many respects, worthy its contriver.

The word "plot," as commonly accepted, conveys but an
indefinite meaning. Most persons think of it as of simple *complexity*; and into this error even so fine a critic as Augustus
William Schlegel has obviously fallen, when he confounds its
idea with that of the mere *intrigue* in which the Spanish dramas of Cervantes and Calderon abound. But the greatest involution of incident will not result in plot; which, properly
defined, is *that in which no part can be displaced without ruin
to the whole*. It may be described as a building so dependently
constructed, that to change the position of a single brick is to
overthrow the entire fabric. In this definition and description,
we of course refer only to that infinite perfection which the
true artist bears ever in mind—that unattainable goal to
which his eyes are always directed, but of the possibility of

attaining which he still endeavors, if wise, to cheat himself
into the belief. The reading world, however, is satisfied with
a less rigid construction of the term. It is content to think
that plot a good one, in which none of the *leading* incidents
can be *removed* without *detriment* to the mass. Here indeed is
a material difference; and in this view of the case the plot of
"Night and Morning" is decidedly excellent. Speaking comparatively, and in regard to stories similarly composed, it is
one of the best. This the author has evidently designed to
make it. For this purpose he has taxed his powers to the utmost. Every page bears marks of excessive elaboration, all
tending to one point—a perfect adaptation of the very numerous atoms of a very unusually involute story. The better
to attain his object he has resorted to the expedient of writing
his book backwards. This is a simple thing in itself, but may
not be generally understood. An example will best convey the
idea. Drawing near the *dénouement* of his tale, our novelist
had proceeded so far as to render it necessary that means
should be devised for the discovery of the missing marriage
record. This record is in the old bureau—this bureau is at
Fernside, originally the seat of Philip's father, but now in possession of one Lord Lilburne, a member of Robert Beaufort's
family. Two things now strike the writer—first, that the re-
trieval of the hero's fortune should be brought about by no
less a personage than the heroine—by some lady who should
in the end be his bride—and, secondly, that this lady must
procure access to Fernside. Up to this period in the narrative,
it had been the design to make Camilla Beaufort, Philip's
cousin, the heroine; but in such case, the cousin and Lord
Lilburne being friends, the document must have been obtained by fair means; whereas foul means are the most dramatic. There would have been no *difficulties* to overcome in
introducing Camilla into the house in question. She would
have merely rung the bell and walked in. Moreover, in getting
the paper, she would have had no chance of getting up a
scene. This lady is therefore dropped as the heroine; Mr. Bulwer retraces his steps, creates Fanny, brings Philip to love her,
and employs Lilburne, (a courtly villain, invented for all the
high dirty work, as De Burgh Smith for all the *low* dirty work
of the story,) employs Lilburne to abduct her to Fernside,

where the capture of the document is at length (more dramatically than naturally) contrived. In short, these latter incidents were emendations, and their really episodical character is easily traced by the critic. What appears first in the published book, was last in the original MS. Many of the most striking portions of the novel were *interleaved* in the same manner—thus giving to after-thought that air of premeditation which is so pleasing. Effect seems to follow cause in the most natural and in the most provident manner, but, in the true construction, the cause (and here we commit no bull) is absolutely brought about by the effect. The many brief, and seemingly insulated chapters met with in the course of the narrative, are the interposed after-thoughts in question.

So careful has been our author in this working-up of his story—in this nice dovetailing of its constituent parts—that it is difficult to detect a blemish in any portion. What he has intended to do he has done well; and his main intention, as we have before hinted, was *perfection of plot*. A few defects, indeed, we note; and note them chiefly to show the skill with which that narrative is wrought, where such blemishes are the sole ones.

In the first place, there are some descriptive passages such as the love adventures of Caleb Price, the account of Gawtrey's early life, prefaced by that of his grandfather, and the dinner-scene at Love's, which scarcely come within the category of matters tending to develop the main events. These things, in short, might have been omitted with advantage (because without detriment) to the whole.

At page 254, vol. 2, we perceive the first indications of slovenliness, (arising no doubt from the writer's anxiety to conclude his task) in an incident utterly without aim, and composed at random. We mean the relapse of Philip into a second illness when nursed by Fanny through the first, at the house of old Gawtrey.

At page 21, vol. 1, we are told that Caleb Price, having received from his friend Beaufort a certain letter (whose contents would have been important in the subsequent attempts to establish Catharine's claim) held it over the flame of the candle, and that "as the paper dropped on the carpetless floor,

Mr. Jones prudently set thereon the broad sole of his boot, and the maid servant brushed it into the grate."

"Ah, trample it out; hurry it among the ashes. The last as the rest," said Caleb, hoarsely. "Friendship, fortune, hope, love, life—a little flame—and then—and then—"

"Do n't be uneasy— it 's quite out," said Mr. Jones.

Now this is related with much emphasis; and, upon reading it, we resolved to hold in memory that this important paper, although torn, was still unburned, and that its fragments had been thrown into a vacant grate. In fact, it was the design of the novelist to re-produce these fragments in the *dénouement*—a design which he has forgotten to carry out.

We have defined the word "plot," in a definition of our own to be sure, but in one which we do not the less consider substantially correct; and we have said that it has been a main point with Mr. Bulwer in this his last novel, "Night and Morning," to work up his plot as near perfection as possible. We have asserted, too, that his design is well accomplished; but we do not the less assert that it has been conceived and executed in error.

The interest of plot, referring, as it does, to cultivated thought in the reader, and appealing to considerations analogous with those which are the essence of sculptural taste, is by no means a popular interest; although it has the peculiarity of being appreciated in its atoms by all, while in its totality of beauty it is comprehended but by the few. The pleasure which the many derive from it is disjointed, ineffective, and evanescent; and even in the case of the critical reader it is a pleasure which may be purchased too dearly. A good tale may be written without it. Some of the finest fictions in the world have neglected it altogether. We see nothing of it in Gil Blas, in the Pilgrim's Progress, or in Robinson Crusoe. Thus it is not an essential in story-telling at all; although, well-managed, within proper limits, it is a thing to be desired. At best it is but a secondary and rigidly artistical merit, for which no merit of a higher class—no merit founded in nature—should be sacrificed. But in the book before us *much* is sacrificed for its sake, and every thing is rendered subservient to its purposes. So excessive is, here, the involution of circumstances, that it has been found impossible to dwell for more than a brief period upon any particular one. The writer seems in a perpetual flurry to accomplish what, in autorical parlance, is called "bringing up one's time." He flounders in the vain attempt to keep all his multitudinous incidents at one and the same moment before the eye. His ability has been sadly taxed in the effort—but more sadly the time and temper of the reader. No sooner do we begin to take some slight degree of interest in some cursorily-sketched event, than we are hurried off to some other, for which a new feeling is to be built up, only to be tumbled down, forthwith, as before. And thus, since there is no sufficiently continuous scene in the whole novel, it results that there is not a strongly effective one. Time not being given us in which to become absorbed, we are only permitted to admire, while we are not the less chilled, tantalised, wearied, and displeased. Nature, with natural interest, has been given up a bond-maiden to an elaborate, but still to a misconceived, perverted, and most unsatisfactory Art.

Very little reflection might have sufficed to convince Mr. Bulwer that narratives, even one fourth so long as the one now lying upon our table, are *essentially* inadapted to that nice and complex adjustment of incident at which he has made this desperate attempt. In the wire-drawn romances which have been so long fashionable, (God only knows how or why) the pleasure we derive (if any) is a composite one, and made up of the respective sums of the various pleasurable sentiments experienced in perusal. Without excessive and fatiguing exertion, inconsistent with legitimate interest, the mind cannot comprehend at one time, and in one survey, the numerous individual items which go to establish the whole. Thus the high ideal sense of the *unique* is sure to be wanting:—for, however absolute in itself be the unity of the novel, it must inevitably fail of appreciation. We speak now of that species of unity which is alone worth the attention of the critic—the unity or totality *of effect*.

But we could never bring ourselves to attach any idea of merit to mere *length* in the abstract. A long story does not appear to us necessarily twice as good as one only half so long. The ordinary talk about "continuous and sustained effort" is pure twaddle and nothing more. Perseverance is one thing and genius is another—whatever Buffon or Hogarth may assert to the contrary—and notwithstanding that, in many passages of the dogmatical literature of old Rome, such phrases as *"diligentia maxima," "diligentia mirabilis,"* can be construed only as "great talent" or "wonderful ability." Now if the author of "Ernest Maltravers," implicitly following authority like *les moutons de Panurge*, will persist in writing long romances because long romances have been written before— if, in short, he cannot be satisfied with the brief tale (a species of composition which admits of the highest development of artistical power in alliance with the wildest vigor of imagination)—he must then content himself, perforce, with a more simply and more rigidly narrative form.

And here, could he see these comments upon a work which, (estimating it, as is the wont of all artists of his calibre, by the labor which it has cost him,) he considers his *chef d'œuvre*, he would assure us, with a smile, that it is precisely because the book is *not* narrative, and *is* dramatic, that he holds it in so lofty an esteem. Now in regard to its being dramatic, we should reply that, so far as the radical and ineradicable *deficiencies* of the drama go—it is. This continual and vexatious shifting of scene, with a view of bringing up events to the time being, originated at a period when books were not; and in fact, had the drama not preceded books, it might never have succeeded them—we might, and probably should, never have had a drama at all. By the frequent "bringing up" of his events the dramatist strove to supply, as well as he could, the want of the combining, arranging, and especially of the *commenting* power, now in possession of the narrative author. No doubt it was a deep but vague sense of this want which brought into birth the Greek chorus—a thing altogether apart from the drama itself—*never* upon the stage—and representing, or personifying, the expression of the sympathy of the audience in the matters transacted.

In brief, while the drama of colloquy, vivacious and breathing of life, is well adopted into narration, the drama of action and passion will always prove, when employed beyond due limits, a source of embarrassment to the narrator, and it can afford him, at best, nothing which he does not already possess in full force. We have spoken upon this head much at length;

for we remember that, in some preface to one of his previous novels, (some preface in which he endeavored to pre-reason and pre-coax us into admiration of what was to follow—a bad practice,) Mr. Bulwer was at great pains to insist upon the peculiar merits of what he even then termed the dramatic conduct of his story. The simple truth was that, then as now, he had merely concentrated into his book all the *necessary evils* of the stage.

Giving up his attention to the one point upon which we have commented, our novelist has failed to do himself justice in others. The overstrained effort at perfection of plot has seduced him into absurd sacrifices of verisimilitude, as regards the connexion of his *dramatis personæ* each with each, and each with the main events. However incidental be the appearance of any personage upon the stage, this personage is sure to be linked in, will I nill I, with the matters in hand. Philip, on the stage-coach, for example, converses with but one individual, William Gawtrey; yet this man's fate (not subsequently but previously) is interwoven into that of Philip himself, through the latter's relationship to Lilburne. The hero goes to his mother's grave, and there comes in contact with this Gawtrey's father. He meets Fanny, and Fanny happens to be also involved in his *destiny* (a pet word, conveying a pet idea of the author's) through *her* relationship to Lilburne. The witness in the case of his mother's marriage is missing, and this individual turns up at last in the brother of that very Charles De Burgh Smith with whom so perfectly accidental an intimacy has already been established. The wronged heir proceeds at random to look for a lawyer, and stumbles at once upon the precise one who had figured before in the story, and who knows all about previous investigations. Setting out in search of Liancourt, the first person he sees is that gentleman himself. Entering a horse-bazaar in a remote portion of the country, the steed up for sale at the exact moment of his entrance is recognised as the pet of his better days. Now our quarrel with these coincidences is not that they sometimes, but that they everlastingly occur, and that nothing occurs besides. We find no fault with Philip for chancing, at the identically proper moment, upon the identical men, women, and horses necessary for his own ends and the ends of the story—but we do think it excessively hard that he should *never happen upon anything else.*

In delineation of character, our artist has done little worth notice. His highest merit in this respect is, with a solitary exception, the negative one of not having subjected himself to dispraise. Catharine and Camilla are—pretty well in their way. Philip is very much like all other heroes—perhaps a little more stiff, a little more obstinate, and a little more desperately unlucky than the generality of his class. Sydney is drawn with truth. Plaskwith, Plimmins, and the Mortons, just sufficiently caricatured, are very good outline copies from the shaded originals of Dickens. Of Gawtrey—father and son,—of De Burgh Smith, of Robert Beaufort and of Lilburne, what is it possible to say, except that they belong to that extensive firm of Gawtrey, Smith, Beaufort, Lilburne and company, which has figured in every novel since the days of Charles Grandison, and which is doomed to the same eternal con-figuration till romance-writing shall be no more?

For Fanny the author distinctly avows a partiality; and he does not err in his preference. We have observed, in some previous review, that *original* characters, so called, can only be critically praised as such, either when presenting qualities known in real life, but never before depicted (a combination nearly impossible) or when presenting qualities which, although unknown, or even known to be hypothetical, are so skilfully adapted to the circumstances around them, that our sense of fitness is not offended, and we find ourselves seeking a reason why those things *might not have been* which we are still satisfied *are not*. Fanny appertains to this latter class of originality—which in itself belongs to the loftier regions of *the Ideal*. Her first movements in the story, before her conception (which we have already characterized as an after-thought) had assumed distinct shape in the brain of the author, are altogether ineffective and frivolous. They consist of the unmeaning affectation and rhodomontade with which it is customary to invest the lunatic in common-place fiction. But the subsequent effects of love upon her mental develop-ment are finely imagined and richly painted; and, although reason teaches us their impossibility, yet it is sufficient for the purposes of the artist that fancy delights in believing them possible.

Mr. Bulwer has been often and justly charged with defects of *style*; but the charges have been sadly deficient in specification, and for the most part have confounded the idea of mere language with that of style itself, although the former is no more the latter, than an oak is a forest, or than a word is a thought. Without pausing to define what a little reflection will enable any reader to define for himself, we may say that the chief constituent of a good style (a constituent which, in the case of Washington Irving, has been mistaken for the thing constituted) is what artists have agreed to denominate *tone*. The writer who, varying this as occasion may require, well adapts it to the fluctuations of his narrative, accomplishes an important object in style. Mr. Bulwer's tone is always correct; and so great is the virtue of this quality that he can scarcely be termed, upon the whole, a bad stylist.

His mere English is grossly defective—turgid, involved, and ungrammatical. There is scarcely a page of "Night and Morning" upon which a school-boy could not detect at least half a dozen instances of faulty construction. Sentences such as this are continually occurring—"And at last silenced, if not convinced, his eyes closed, and the tears yet wet upon their lashes, fell asleep." Here, strictly speaking, it is the eyes which "fell asleep," and which were "silent if not convinced." The pronoun, "he," is wanting for the verb "fell." The whole would read better thus—"And at last, silent, if not convinced, he closed his eyes, and fell asleep with the tears yet on the lashes." It will be seen that, besides other modifications, we have changed "upon" into "on," and omitted " wet" as superfluous when applied to tear; who ever heard of a dry one? The sentence in question, which occurs at page 83, vol. 1, was the first which arrested our attention on opening the book at random; but its errors are sufficiently illustrative of the *character* of those faults of phraseology in which the work abounds, and which have arisen, not so much through carelessness, as from a peculiar bias in the mind of the writer, leading him, per force, into *involution*, whether here in style, or elsewhere in plot. The beauty of simplicity is not that which can be appreciated by Mr. Bulwer; and whatever may be the true merits of his intelligence, the merit of luminous and precise thought is evidently not one of the number.

At page 194, vol. 1, we have this—"I am not what you seem to suppose—exactly a swindler, certainly not a robber." Here, to make himself intelligible, the speaker should have repeated the words "I am not," before "exactly." As it stands, the sentence does not imply that "I am not exactly a swindler, &c." but (if anything) that the person addressed, imagined me to be certainly not a robber but exactly a swindler—an implication which it was not intended to convey. Such awkwardness in a practised writer would be inconceivable, did we not refer in memory to that moral bias of which we have just spoken. Our readers will of course examine the English of "Night and Morning" for themselves. From the evidence of one or two sentences we cannot expect them to form a judgment in the premises. Dreading indeed the suspicion of unfairness, we had pencilled item after item for comment—but we have abandoned the task in despair. It would be an endless labor to proceed with examples. In fact it is folly to particularize where the blunders would be the rule, and the grammar the exception.

Sir Lytton has one desperate mannerism of which we would be glad to see him well rid—a fashion of beginning short sentences, after very long ones, with the phrase "So there," or something equivalent, and this too, when there is no sequence in the matter to warrant the use of the word "So." Thus, at page 136, vol. 1,—"So there they sat on the cold stone, these two orphans;" at page 179,—"So there by the calm banks of the placid lake, the youngest born of Catharine passed his tranquil days,"—and just below, on the same page,—"So thus was he severed from both his protectors, Arthur and Philip;" and at page 241, vol. 11,—"So there sat the old man," &c. &c.—and in innumerable other instances throughout the work.

Among the *niäiseries* of his style we may mention the coxcombical use of little French sentences, without the shadow of an excuse for their employment. At page 22, vol. 2, in the scene at the counterfeiter's cellar, what can be more nonsensical than Gawtrey's *"C'est juste; buvez donc, cher ami,"*—*"C'est* *juste; buvez donc, vieux rénard,"*—and *"Ce n'est pas vrai; buvez donc Monsieur Favart?"* Why should these platitudes be alone given in French, when it is obvious that the entire conversation was carried on in that tongue? And, again, when, at page 49, Fanny exclaims—*"Méchant*, every one dies to Fanny!"*— why could not this heroine have as well confined herself to one language? At page 38, the climax of absurdity, in this respect, is fairly capped; and it is difficult to keep one's countenance, when we read of a Parisian cobler breathing his last in a garret, and screaming out *"Je m'étouffe—*Air!"

Whenever a startling incident is recorded, our novelist seems to make it a point of conscience that somebody should "fall insensible." Thus at page 172, vol. 1,—" 'My brother, my brother, they have taken thee from me,' cried Philip, and he fell insensible,"—and at page 38, vol. 2, " 'I was unkind to him at the last,' and with these words she fell upon the corpse insensible," &c. &c. There is a great deal too much of this. An occasional swoon is a thing of no consequence, but "even Stamboul must have an end," and Mr. Bulwer should make an end of his syncopes.

Again. That gentlemen and ladies, when called upon to give alms, or to defray some trifling incidental expense, are in the invariable habit of giving the whole contents of their purses without examination, and, moreover, of "throwing" the purse into the bargain, is an idea most erroneously entertained. At page 55, vol. 1, we are told that Philip, "as he spoke, *slid* his purse into the woman's hand." At page 110, "a hint for money restored Beaufort to his recollection, and he *flung* his purse into the nearest hand outstretched to receive it." At page 87, "Lilburne *tossed* his purse into the hands of his valet, whose face seems to lose its anxious embarrassment at the touch of the gold." It is true that the "anxious embarrassment" of any valet out of a novel, would have been rather increased than diminished by having a purse of gold tossed at his head—but what we wish our readers to observe, is that magnificent contempt of filthy lucre with which the characters of Sir Edward Lytton Bulwer "fling," "slide," "toss," and tumble whole purses of money about!

But the predominant and most important failing of the author of "Devereux," in point of style, is an absolute mania for metaphor—metaphor always running into allegory. Pure allegory is at all times an abomination—a remnant of antique barbarism—appealing only to our faculties of comparison, without even a remote interest for our reason, or for our fancy. Metaphor, its softened image, has indisputable force when sparingly and skilfully employed. Vigorous writers use it rarely indeed. Mr. Bulwer is all metaphor or all allegory— mixed metaphor and unsustained allegory—and nothing if neither. He cannot express a dozen consecutive sentences in an honest and manly manner. He is the king-coxcomb of figures-of-speech. His rage for personification is really ludicrous. The simplest noun becomes animate in his hands. Never, by any accident, does he write even so ordinary a word as time, or temper, or talent, without the capital T. Seldom, indeed, is he content with the dignity and mysticism thus imposed;— for the most part it is TIME, TEMPER and TALENT. Nor does the common-place character of anything which he wishes to personify exclude it from the prosopopeia. At page 256, volume 1, we have some profound rigmarole, seriously urged, about piemen crying "all hot! all hot!" "in the ear of Infant and Ragged Hunger," thus written; and, at page 207, there is something positively transcendental all about LAW—a very little thing in itself, in some cases—but which Mr. Bulwer, in his book, has thought proper to make quite as big as we have printed it above. Who cannot fancy him, in the former instance, saying to himself, as he gnaws the top of his quill, "that is a fine thought!" and exclaiming in the latter, as he puts his finger to the side of his nose, "ah, how *very* fine an idea that is!"

This absurdity, indeed, is chiefly observable in those philosophical discussions with which he is in the wicked habit of interspersing his fictions, and springs only from a rabid anxiety to look wise—to appear profound—even when wisdom is quite out of place, and profundity the quintessence of folly. A "still small voice" has whispered in his ear that, as to the real matter of fact, *he is shallow*—a whisper which he does not intend to believe, and which, by dint of loud talking in parables, he hopes to prevent from reaching the ears of the public. Now, in truth, the public, great-gander as it is, is content to swallow his romance without much examination, but cannot help turning up its nose at his logic.

"The men of sense," says Helvetius, "those idols of the unthinking, are very inferior to the men of passions. It is the strong passions which, rescuing us from Sloth, can alone impart to us that continuous and earnest attention necessary to great intellectual efforts"—Understanding the word "efforts" in its legitimate force, and not confounding it altogether with achievements, we may well apply to Mr. Bulwer the philosopher's remark, thence deducing the secret of his success as a novelist. He is emphatically the man "of passions." With an intellect rather well balanced than lofty, he has not full claim to the title of a man of genius. Urged by the burning desire of doing much, he has certainly done something. Elaborate even to fault, he will never write a bad book, and has once or twice been upon the point of concocting a good one. It is the custom to call him a fine writer, but in doing so we should judge him less by an artistical standard of excellence, than by comparison with the drivellers who surround him. To Scott he is altogether inferior, except in that mock and tawdry philosophy which the Caledonian had the discretion to avoid, and the courage to contemn. In pathos, humour, and verisimilitude he is unequal to Dickens; surpassing him only in general knowledge, and in the sentiment of Art. Of James he is more than the equal at all points. While he could never fall as low as D'Israeli has occasionally fallen, neither himself, nor any of those whom we have mentioned, have ever risen nearly so high as that very gifted and very extraordinary man.

In regard to "Night and Morning" we cannot agree with that critical opinion which considers it the best novel of its author. It is only not his worst. It is not as good as Eugene Aram, nor as Rienzi—and is not at all comparable with Ernest Maltravers. Upon the whole it is a good book. Its merits beyond doubt overbalance its defects, and if we have not dwelt upon the former with as much unction as upon the latter, it is because the Bulwerian beauties are precisely of that secondary character which never fails of the fullest public appreciation.

Graham's Magazine, April 1841

The Critical and Miscellaneous Writings of Sir Edward Lytton Bulwer, author of "Pelham," &c. 2 vols. Lea and Blanchard: Philadelphia.

WE HAVE READ these volumes with the highest pleasure. They embrace all of the known minor writings of Bulwer, with the exception of his shorter fictions; and we recognize in the collection several very excellent articles which had arrested our attention and excited our curiosity while their authorship was undivulged.

Mr. Bulwer is *never* lucid, and seldom profound. His intellect seems to be rather well balanced than lofty—rather comprehensive than penetrative. His taste is exquisite. His style, in its involution and obscurity, partakes of the involution of his thoughts. Apart from his mere intellect, however,—or rather as a portion of that intellect—we recognize in his every written word the keenest appreciation of the right, the beautiful, and the true. Thus he is a man worthy of all reverence, and we do not hesitate to say that we look upon the charges of immoral tendency which have been so pertinaciously adduced against his fictions, as absurdly *little* and untenable, in the mass.

The volumes now before us are plain evidence of the noble spirit which has constantly actuated him. The papers here published were written at various epochs of his life. We look through them in vain for anything false, as a whole, or unchivalrous, or impure, or weak, or tasteless, or ignoble. Were we addicted *jurare in verba magistri*, there lives no man upon whose faith we would more confidently rely than upon that of Bulwer—no man whose opinion upon any point involving a question of truth, or justice, or taste, we would be more willing to adopt unexamined.

We have been especially pleased with an article (in the volumes now before us) entitled "Literature Considered as a Profession," and with another "Upon the Spirit of True Criticism." Some remarks in the latter paper are quite as applicable to our own country as to Great Britain.

" 'To say this is good and that is bad,' says La Bruyère, 'is not morality.' Very true, neither is it criticism. There is no criticism in this country—considering that word as the name of a science. A book comes out—it is capital, says one—it is detestable, says another. Its characters are unnatural—its characters are nature itself. On both sides there is affirmation, on neither proof. In fact no science requires such elaborate study as criticism. It is the most analytical of our mental operations—to pause—to examine—to say *why* that passage is a sin against nature, or that plot a violation of art—to bring deep knowledge of life in all its guises—of the heart in all its mysteries to bear upon a sentence of approval or disapprobation—to have cultivated the feeling of beauty until its sense of harmony has grown as fine as the ear of a musician— equally sensitive to discord—or alive to new combinations:— these are no light qualities, and these are not qualities, it may be answered, to be lightly lavished away. Every new book, it may be said, does not deserve that we should so honor it. We need not invoke the Past, and summon all Nature to hear us praise a butterfly, or crush a bug. We may on slight works arrogate the censor—yes, but we must first have been chosen the censor, by the acumen we have testified on great ones. Now, when an author who has risen into eminence, who begins to produce an effect upon his age, whose faults it becomes necessary to indicate as a warning, whose beauties we should illustrate as an example—when such a man produces a new work, what is the cant cry of the critics? 'The peculiar merits and failings of Mr. So and So are too well known for us at this time of day to repeat them. The present work has all the characteristics of the last—if it does not increase, it will not diminish the well-earned reputation of the author.' Then come the extracts, and a word or two at the end as precise and lucid as those at the beginning, and ——there's THE CRITICISM!

"For my part, I please myself sometimes with drawing the ideal picture of a good critic, as Bolingbroke drew that of a patriot king. What a crowd of accomplishments, not easily seen by the superficial, belong to that character! Literature and morality are so entwined that you rarely find the real critic unless he is also the moralist. The union is almost necessary. In Quinctilian how beautifully the deduction closes the dogma! and even in Johnson the habit of moralizing gives dignity to his criticisms. In both sciences the study of mankind, of the metaphysical nature within us, alone insures a sound judgment: in both, without a delicate yet profound perception of the harmonious, the beautiful, the august, no commanding excellency is obtained. The goodness of a man and the goodness of a book are not such different qualities as people suppose. A person, however, *may* be, though he is not often, a good moralist without being a good man: to preach and practice are faculties not inseparable. But I doubt if a man can be a great critic who has not, at least, the elementary qualities of a good man. I consider that he must keep the intellectual sight clear from envy, and malice, and personal dislikes. He must examine the work above and remote from all the petty considerations that attach to the man. He must be on the alert for genius, ready to encourage even a rival to himself. Where this largeness of mind is not visible, there is always something petty and crippled in the mind of the professional critic. He may make one great criticism, but he cannot criticise with greatness habitually. Perhaps he reviews some dead author—for the dead interfere not with the living; or he wastes a world of generosity, like Southey, in praising some rhymester of the pantry, who is little enough while he attracts honor to the praiser to plunge into forgetfulness the praise. The good critic—that rare ideal, must have in him courage to blame boldly, magnanimity to eschew envy, benevolence to search for obscure merit. He must have genius to appreciate, and learning to compare: he must have an eye for beauty, an ear for music, a heart for feeling, a mind for reason. 'We are conscious of excellency,' says some author, 'in proportion to the excellence within ourselves.' "

We wish also to call attention to a very excellent article on the subject of "International Copyright." The only paper in the collection which we could have wished omitted is one entitled "A Letter to the Quarterly Review,"—an attempt at vindictive retaliation upon Lockhart. We admire this gentleman quite as little as Mr. Bulwer can possibly do, but we grieve to see an attack which has neither vigor nor wit, and which proves nothing beyond the writer's wrath and utter incapacity for satire.

Graham's Magazine, November 1841

Henry F. Chorley

Conti the Discarded: with Other Tales and Fancies. By Henry F. Chorley. 2 vols. New York: Published by Harper and Brothers.

MR. CHORLEY has hitherto written nothing of any great length. His name, however, is familiar to all readers of English Annuals, and in whatever we have seen from his pen, evidences of a rare genius have been perceptible. In Conti, and in the "Other Tales and Fancies" which accompany it, these evidences are more distinct, more brilliant, and more openly developed. Neither are these pieces wanting in a noble, and, to us, a most thrillingly interesting *purpose*. In saying that our whole heart is with the author—that the deepest, and we trust, the purest emotions are enkindled within us by his chivalric and magnanimous *design*—we present but a feeble picture of our individual feelings as influenced by the perusal of Conti. We repeat it—our whole heart is with the author. When *shall* the artist assume his proper situation in society—in a society of thinking beings? How long shall he be enslaved? How long shall mind succumb to the grossest materiality? How long shall the veriest vermin of the Earth, who crawl around the altar of Mammon, be more esteemed of men than they, the gifted ministers to those exalted emotions which link us with the mysteries of Heaven? To our own query we may venture a reply. Not long. Not long will such rank injustice be committed or permitted. A spirit is already abroad at war with it. And in every billow of the unceasing sea of Change—and in every breath, however gentle, of the wide atmosphere of Revolution encircling us, is that spirit steadily yet irresistibly at work.

"Who has not looked," says Mr. Chorley in his Preface, " with painful interest on the unreckoned-up account of misunderstanding and suspicion which exists between the World and the Artist? Who has not grieved to see the former willing to degrade Art into a mere plaything—to be enjoyed without respect, and then cast aside—instead of receiving her high works as among the most humanizing blessings ever vouchsafed to man by a beneficent Creator? Who has not suffered shame in observing the Artist bring his own calling into contempt by coarsely regarding it as a mere engine of money getting, or holding it up to reproach by making it the excuse for such eccentricities or grave errors as separate him from the rest of society?"

That genius should not and indeed cannot be bound down to the vulgar common-places of existence, is a maxim which, however true, has been too often repeated; and there have appeared on earth enough spirits of the loftiest and most brilliant order who have worthily taken their part in life as useful citizens, affectionate husbands, faithful friends, to deprive of their excuse all such as hold, that to despise and alienate the world is the inevitable and painfully glorious destiny of the highly gifted.

Very few of our readers, it may be, are acquainted with a particular class of works which has long exercised a very powerful influence on the private habits and character, as well as on the literature of the Germans. We speak of the *Art Novels*—the Kunstromanen—books written not so much in immediate defence, or in illustration, as in personification of individual portions of the Fine Arts—books which, in the guise of Romance, labor to the sole end of reasoning men into admiration and study of the beautiful, by a tissue of *bizarre* fiction, partly allegorical, and partly metaphysical. In Germany alone could so mad—or perhaps so profound—an idea have originated. From the statement of Mr. Chorley, we find that his original intention was to attempt something in the style of the *Kunstromanen*, with such modifications as might seem called for by the peculiar spirit of the British national tastes and literature. "It occurred to me, however," says he, "that the very speculations and reveries which appeared to myself so delicious and significant, might be rejected by the rest of the world as fantastic and over-strained." Mr. C. could never have persevered in a scheme so radically erroneous for more than a dozen pages; and neither the world nor himself will have cause to regret that he thought proper to abandon the *Art Novels*, and embody his fine powers and lofty design in so stirring and so efficient a series of paintings as may be found in the present volumes.

A single passage near the commencement of Conti, will afford to all those who feel and think, direct evidence of the extraordinary abilities of Mr. Chorley. Madame Zerlini is an Italian *prima donna*, who becoming enamored of Colonel Hardwycke, an Englishman, accompanies him to England as his mistress, and after living with him for twelve years, and bearing him a son, Julius, dies suddenly upon hearing of his intention to marry.

"A strange scene greeted his eyes (those of Julius) as he entered the spacious hall, which, as its windows fronted the east, was already beginning to be dusky with the shadows of twilight. On the lowest step of the stairs lay, in violent hysterics, one of the women servants—she was raving and weeping, half supported by two others, themselves trembling so as to be almost powerless.

" 'And here's Master Julius, too!' exclaimed one of the group which obstructed his passage, 'and my master gone away—no one knows for how long. Lord have mercy upon us!—what are we to do, I wonder?'

" 'Don't go up stairs!' shrieked the other, leaving her charge, and endeavoring to stop him. 'Don't go up stairs—it is all over!'

"But the boy, whose mind was full of other matters, and who, having wandered away in the morning, before the delirium became so violent, had no idea of his mother's imminent danger, broke from them without catching the meaning of their words, and forced his way up stairs, towards the great drawing room, the folding doors of which were swinging open.

"He went in. Madame Zerlini was there—flung down upon a sofa, in an attitude which, in life, it would have been impossible for her to maintain for many moments. Her head was cast back over one of the pillows, so far, that her long hair, which had been imperfectly fastened, had disengaged itself by its own weight, and was now sweeping heavily downward, with a crushed wreath of passion flowers and myrtles half buried among it. Every thing about her told how fiercely the spirit had passed. Her robe of scarlet muslin was entirely torn off on one shoulder, and disclosed its exquisitely rounded proportions. Her glittering *negligé* was unclasped, and one end of it clenched firmly in the small left hand, which there was now hardly any possibility of unclosing. Her glazed eyes were wide open—her mouth set in an unnatural, yet fascinating smile; her cheek still flushed with a more delicate, yet intense red than belongs to health; and the excited boy, who was rushing hastily into the room, with the rapid inquiry, 'Where is Father Vanezzi?' stood as fixed on the threshhold, with sudden and conscious horror, as if he had been a thing of marble."

It is not our intention to analyze, or even to give a compend of the Tale of Conti. Such are not the means by which any idea of its singular power can be afforded. We will content ourselves with saying that, in its prevailing tone, it bears no little resemblance to that purest, and most enthralling of fictions, the Bride of Lammermuir; and we have once before expressed our opinion of this, the master novel of Scott. It is not too much to say that no modern composition, and perhaps no composition whatever, with the single exception of Cervantes' Destruction of Numantia, approaches so nearly to the proper character of the dramas of Æschylus, as the magic tale of which Ravenswood is the hero. We are not aware of being sustained by any authority in this opinion—yet we do not believe it the less intrinsically correct.

The other pieces in the volumes of Mr. Chorley are, *Margaret Sterne*, or *The Organist's Journey*—an *Essay on the Popular Love of Music*—*Rossini's Otello*—*The Imaginative Instrumental Writers, Haydn, Beethoven, &c.*—*The Village Beauty's Wedding*—*Handel's Messiah*—and *A few words upon National Music*—all of which papers evince literary powers of a high order, an intimate acquaintance with the science of music, and a lofty and passionate devotion to its interests.

Southern Literary Messenger, February 1836

Memorials of Mrs. Hemans, with Illustrations of her Literary Character from her Private Correspondence. By Henry F. Chorley. New York: Saunders and Otley.

MR. CHORLEY is well known to American readers as a contributor to the chief of the London Annuals, and still better as the author of the stirring volumes entitled "Conti, the Discarded, with Other Tales and Fancies." We have long regarded him as one of the most brilliant among the literary stars of England, as a writer of great natural and cultivated taste, and of a refined yet vigorous and lofty imagination. As a musical connoisseur, or rather as profoundly versed in the only true philosophy of the science, he may be considered as unrivalled. There are, moreover, few persons now living upon whose appreciation of a poetical character we would look with a higher respect, and we had consequently promised ourselves no ordinary gratification in his "Memorials of Mrs. Hemans." Nor have we been disappointed.

About fourteen months ago Mr. Chorley collected and published in the London Athenæum some deeply interesting reminiscences of Mrs. H. of which the volumes now before us are an extension. A variety of materials, afforded him by friends, has enabled him to continue his notices beyond the period of his own personal acquaintance, and, by linking correspondence and anecdote, to trace out, with great facility and beauty, the entire progress of the mind of the poetess. He has exclusively confined himself, however, to this one object, and refrained from touching upon such occurrences in her private life as were not actually necessary in the illustrations of her mental and literary existence. The "Memorials" therefore, it is right to state, lay no claim to the entire fulness of Biography. The following brief personal notice is to be found in the opening pages:

Felicia Dorothea Browne—the second daughter and the fourth child of a family of three sons and three daughters—was born in Duke-street, Liverpool, on the 25th of September, 1794. Her father was a native of Ireland, belonging to a branch of the Sligo family; her mother, a Miss Wagner, was a descendant of a Venetian house, whose old name, Veniero, had in the course of time been corrupted into this German form. Among its members were numbered three who rose to the dignity of Doge, and one who bore the honorable rank of commander at the battle of Lepanto. In the waning days of the Republic, Miss Brown's grandfather held the humble situation of Venetian consul in Liverpool. The maiden name

of his wife was Haddock, a good and ancient one among the
yeomanry of Lancashire; three of the issue of this union are
still surviving. To these few genealogical notices it may be
added that Felicia Dorothea was the fifth bearing that christian name in her mother's family, that her elder sister, Eliza,
of whom affectionate mention is made in her earliest poems,
died of a decline at the age of eighteen; and that her brother
Claude, who reached manhood, died in America several years
ago. Two brothers older than herself, and one sister, her junior, are therefore all that now survive.

It must not be supposed from what we say that Mr.
Chorley has given us nothing of personal history. The volumes abound delightfully in such anecdotes of the poetess
as go to illustrate her literary peculiarities and career. These
indeed form the staple of the book, and, in the truly exquisite narration of Mr. Chorley, are moulded into something
far more impressive than we can imagine any legitimate biography. We cannot refrain from turning over one by one
the pages as we write, and presenting our readers with
some mere outlines of the many reminiscences which the
author has so beautifully filled up. We shall intersperse them
with some of Mr. C's. observations, and occasionally with
our own.

The "stately names of her maternal ancestors" seem to have
made an early and strong impression upon the poetess, ting-
ing her mind at once with the spirit of romance. To this fact
she would often allude half playfully, half proudly. She was
accustomed to say that although the years of childhood are
usually happy, her own were too visionary not to form an
exception. At the epoch of her death she was meditating a
work to be called "Recollections of a Poet's Childhood."——
When a child she was exceedingly beautiful: so much so as to
attract universal attention. Her complexion was brilliant, her
hair long and curling, and of a bright golden color. In her
latter years it deepened into brown, but remained silken, profuse, and wavy to the last.—A lady once remarked in her
hearing, "That child is not made for happiness I know; her
color comes and goes too fast." This remark our poetess never
forgot, and she spoke of it as causing her much pain at the

moment.—She took great delight, when young, in reciting aloud poems and fragments of plays. "Douglas" was an especial favorite. The scene of her rehearsals was generally an old, large, and dimly-lighted room, an old nursery, looking upon the sea. Her memory is said to have been almost supernatural.—When she was little more than five years old, her father removed his family from Liverpool to North Wales. This circumstance had great influence upon her imagination. The mansion removed to was old, solitary, and spacious, lying close to the sea shore, and shut in, in front, by a chain of rocky hills. In her last illness she frequently alluded to the atmosphere of romance which invested her here. The house bore the reputation of being haunted. On one occasion, having heard a rumor concerning a "fiery grey hound which kept watch at the end of an avenue," she sallied forth at midnight anxious to encounter the goblin. Speaking of this period, she observed, that could she have been then able to foresee the height of reputation to which she subsequently attained, she would have experienced a far higher happiness than the reality ever occasioned. Few in similar circumstances but have thought thus without expressing it.—She was early a reader of Shakspeare, and was soon possessed with a desire of personifying his creations. Imogen and Beatrice were her favorites, neither of which characters, Mr. Chorley remarks, is "without strong points of resemblance to herself."—A freak usual with her was to arise at night, when the whole family were asleep, and making her way to the sea shore, to indulge in a stolen bath.—She was *never at school*. "Had she been sent to one," observes Mr. Chorley, "she would more probably have run away." The only things she was ever regularly taught were English Grammar, French, and the rudiments of Latin. Her Latin teacher used to deplore "that she was not a man to have borne away the highest honors at college."—Her attention was first attracted to the literature and chivalry of Spain by the circumstance of a near relation being engaged in the Peninsular war. She shrunk with more than ordinary feminine timidity from bodily pain, refusing even to have her ears pierced for rings, and yet delighted in records of martial glory. One of her favorite ornaments was the Cross of the Legion of Honor, taken on some Spanish battle-field. Campbell's Odes were her delight; the lines, especially,

> Now joy, old England! rise
> In the triumph of they might!

Yet she had little taste for mere pageantry.—An unkind review to which her earliest poems gave occasion so preyed upon her mind as to confine her for several days to bed.— During the latter part of her life a gentleman called upon her and thanked her with great earnestness for the serious benefit he had derived from "the Sceptic," which he stated to have been instrumental in rescuing him from gross infidelity.— The first noted literary character with whom she became intimately acquainted, was Bishop Heber, to whom she was introduced in her twenty-fifth year. She confided her literary plans to him, and always spoke of him with affection. It was at his instigation she first attempted dramatic composition. He was her adviser in the "Vespers of Palermo." This play was brought forward at Covent Garden in December 1823, the principal characters being taken by Young, Charles Kemble, Yates, Mrs. Bartley, and Miss Kelly. It was not well received, but the authoress bore her disappointment cheerfully. The drama was afterwards produced with much greater success in Edinburgh. Sir Walter Scott wrote an epilogue for it, and from this circumstance arose the subsequent acquaintance between the "Great Unknown" and Mrs. H——. Of Kean, she said that "seeing him act was like reading Shakspeare by flashes of lightning."—She possessed a fine feeling for music as well as for drawing.—Of the "Trials of Margaret Lindsay" she thus expresses a just critical opinion: "The book is certainly full of deep feeling and beautiful language, but there are many passages which, I think, would have been better omitted; and although I can bear as much fictitious woe as other people, I really began to feel it an infliction at last."— She compliments Captain Basil Hall's "temperate style of writing."—Speaking of the short descriptive *recitative* which so frequently introduces a lyrical burst of feeling in the minor pieces of our poetess, Mr. Chorley observes: "This form of composition became so especially popular in America, that hardly a poet has arisen since the influence of Mrs. Hemans' genius made itself felt on the other side of the Atlantic, who has not attempted something of a similar subject and construction."—Among the last strangers who visited her in her illness, were a Jewish gentleman and lady, who entreated admittance to "the author of the 'Hebrew Mother.' "—"There shall be no more snow," in the "Tyrolese Evening Hymn," seems to have been suggested by Schiller's lines in the *"Nadowessiche Todtenklage:"*

> Wohl ihm er ist hingegangen
> Wo kein schnee mehr ist!—

The "Lays of Many Lands," which appeared chiefly in the New Monthly Magazine, were suggested, as she herself owned, by Herder's *"Stimmen der Völker in Liedern."* She spoke of the German language as "rich and affectionate, in which I take much delight."—She considered "The Forest Sanctuary" as the best of her works: the subject was suggested by a passage in one of the letters of Don Leucadio Doblado, and the poem was written for the most part in—a laundry. These verses are pointed out by Chorley as beautiful, which assuredly they are.

> And if she mingled with the festive train
> It was but as some melancholy star
> Beholds the dance of shepherds on the plain,
> In its bright stillness present though afar.

He praises also with great justice the entire episode of "Queen-like Teresa—radient Inez!"—She was so much excited by the composition of "Mozart's Requiem," that her physician forbade her to write for weeks afterwards.—She regarded Professor Norton, who undertook the publication of her works (or rather its superintendence) in this country, as one of her firmest friends. A packet with a letter from this gentleman to the poetess containing offers of service, and a self-introduction was lost upon the Ulverstone sands. They were afterwards discovered drying at an inn fire, and forwarded to their address. With Dr. Channing she frequently corresponded. An offer of a certain and liberal income was made her in the hope of tempting her to take up her residence in Boston and conduct a periodical.—Mr. Chorley draws a fine distinction between Mrs. Hemans and Miss Jewsbury. "The former," he says, "came through Thought to Poetry, the latter through Poetry to Thought." He cites a passage in the "Three Histories" of Miss Jewsbury, as descriptive of the personal appearance of Mrs. H. at the period of his first acquaintance with her. It is the portrait of Egeria, and will be remembered by most of our readers. It ends thus: "She was a muse, a grace, a variable child, a dependent woman—the Italy of human beings."—Retzsch and Flaxman were Mrs. H.'s favorites among modern artists. She was especially pleased with the group in the Outlines to Hamlet—of Laertes and Hamlet struggling over the corpse of Ophelia.—In 1828 she finally established herself at Wavertree. "Her house here," says our author, " was too small to deserve the name; the third of a cluster or row close to a dusty road, and yet too townish in its appearance and situation to be called a cottage. It was set in a small court, and within doors was gloomy and comfortless, for its two parlors (one with a tiny book-room opening from it) were hardly larger than closets; but with her harp and her books, and the flowers with which she loved to fill her little rooms, they presently assumed a habitable, almost an elegant appearance."—Some odd examples are given of the ridiculous and hyperbolical compliments paid the poetess, e.g. "I have heard her requested to read aloud that 'the visitor might carry away an impression of the sweetness of her tones.' " "I have been present when another eccentric guest, upon her characterizing some favorite poem as happily as was her wont, clapped her hands as at a theatre, and exclaimed, 'O Mrs. Hemans! do say that again, that I may put it down and remember it.' "—Among Spanish authors Mrs. H. admired Herrera, and Luis Ponce de Leon. The lyrics in Gil Polo's Diana were favorites with her. Burger's *Leonore* (concerning which and Sir Walter Scott see an anecdote in our notice, this month, of *Schloss Hainfeld*) she was never tired of hearing, "for the sake of its wonderful rhythm and energy." In the power of producing awe, however, she gave the preference to the *Auncient Mariner*. She liked the writings of

Novalis and Tieck. Possibly she did not love Goethe so well as Schiller. She delighted in Herder's translation of the Cid Romances, and took pleasure in some of the poems of A. W. Schlegel. Grillpazzer and Oehlenschluger were favorites among the minor German tragedians. Shelley's "Ode to the West Wind" pleased her. In her copy of *Corinne* the following passage was underscored, and the words "C'est moi!" written in the margin. "De toutes mes facultés la plus puissante est la faculté de souffrir. Je suis née pour le bonheur. Mon caractére est confiant, mon imagination est animée; mais la peine excite en moi Je ne sais quelle impetuosité qui peut troubler ma raison, ou me donner de la mort. Je vous le repéte encore, menagez-moi; la gaité, la mobilité ne me servent qu'en apparence: mais il y a dans mon ame des abymes de tristesse dont Je ne pouvais me defendre qu'en me preservant de l'amour."—In the summer of 1829 Mrs. H. visited Scotland, and became acquainted with Sir Walter Scott. One anecdote told by her of the novelist is highly piquant and characteristic of both. "Well—we had reached a rustic seat in the wood, and were to rest there—but I, out of pure perverseness, chose to establish myself comfortably on a grass bank. 'Would it not be more prudent for you, Mrs. Hemans,' said Sir Walter, 'to take the seat?' 'I have no doubt that it would, Sir Walter, but, somehow or other, I always prefer the grass.' 'And so do I,' replied the dear old gentleman, coming to sit there beside me, 'and I really believe that I do it chiefly out of a wicked wilfulness, because all my *good advisers* say it will give me the rheumatism.' "—Speaking of Martin's picture of *Nineveh* Mrs. H. says: "It seems to me that something more of gloomy grandeur might have been thrown about the funeral pyre; that it should have looked more like a thing apart, almost suggesting of itself the idea of an awful sacrifice." She agrees with Wordsworth, that Burns' "Scots wha hae wi Wallace bled" is "wretched stuff." She justly despised all allegorical personifications. Among the books which she chiefly admired in her later days, are the Discourses of Bishop Hall, Bishop Leighton, and Jeremy Taylor; the "Natural History of Enthusiasm;" Mrs. Austin's Translations and Criticisms; Mrs. Jameson's "Characteristics of Women;" Bulwer's "Last Days of Pompeii;" Miss Edgeworth's "Helen," and Miss Mitford's

Sketches. The Scriptures were her daily study.—Wordsworth was then her favorite poet. Of Miss Kemble's "Francis" she thus speaks. "Have you not been disappointed in Miss Kemble's Tragedy? To me there seems a *coarseness* of idea and expression in many parts, which from a woman is absolutely startling. I can scarcely think it has sustaining power to bear itself up at its present height of popularity."

We take from Volume I, the following passage in regard to Schiller's "Don Carlos," a comparison of which drama with the "Filippo" of Alfieri, will be found in this number of the Messenger. The words we copy are those of Mrs. Hemans.

The interview between Philip the Second and Posa, is certainly very powerful, but to me its interest is always destroyed by a sense of utter *impossibility* which haunts me throughout. Not even Schiller's mighty spells can, I think, win the most "unquestioning spirit" to suppose that such a voice of truth and freedom *could* have been lifted up, and endured, in the presence of the cold, stern, Philip the Second—that he would, even for a moment, have listened to the language thus fearlessly bursting from a noble heart. Three of the most impressive scenes towards the close of the play, might, I think, be linked together, leaving out the intervening ones, with much effect—the one in which Carlos, standing by the body of his friend, forces his father to the contemplation of the dead; the one in which the king comes forward, with his fearful dreamy remorse, alone amidst his court,

Gieb diesen Todten mir heraus, &c.

and the subsequent interview between Philip and the Grand Inquisitor, in which the whole spirit of those fanatic days seems embodied.

In perusing these volumes the reader will not fail to be struck with the evidence they contain of a more than ordinary *joyousness* of temperament in Mrs. Hemans. He will be astonished also in finding himself able to say that he has at length seen a book, dealing much in strictly personal memoirs, wherein no shadow of vanity or affectation could be discerned in either the Memorialist or his subject. In concluding this notice we must not forget to impress upon our friends that we have been speaking altogether of the work issued by Saunders and Otley, publishers of the highest respectability, who have come among us as strangers, and who, as such, have an undeniable claim upon our courtesy. Their edition is embellished with two fine engravings, one of the poetess's favorite residence in Wales, the other of the poetess herself. We shall beg our friends also to remember that this edition, and this exclusively, is printed for the benefit of the children of Mrs. Hemans. To Southerners, at least, we feel that nothing farther need be said.

Southern Literary Messenger, October 1836

Henry Cockton

Stanley Thorn. By Henry Cockton, Esq., Author of "Valentine Vox, the Ventriloquist," etc., with Numerous Illustrations, designed by Cruikshank, Leech, etc., and engraved by Yeager. Lea and Blanchard: Philadelphia.

"CHARLES O'MALLEY," "Harry Lorrequer," "Valentine Vox," "Stanley Thorn," and some other effusions now "in course of publication," are novels depending for effect upon what gave popularity to "Peregrine Pickle"—we mean *practical joke*. To men whose animal spirits are high, whatever may be their mental ability, such works are always acceptable. To the uneducated, to those who read little, to the obtuse in intellect (and these three classes constitute the mass) these books are not only acceptable, but are the only ones which can be called so. We here make two divisions—that of the men who *can* think but who dislike thinking; and that of the men who either have not been presented with the materials for thought, or who have no brains with which to "work up" the material. With these classes of people "Stanley Thorn" is a favorite. It not only demands no reflection, but repels it, or dissipates it—much as a silver rattle the wrath of a child. It is not in the least degree *suggestive*. Its readers arise from its perusal with the identical ideas in possession at sitting down. Yet, *during* perusal, there has been a tingling physico-mental exhilaration, somewhat like that induced by a cold bath, or a flesh-brush, or a gallop on horseback—a very delightful and very healthful matter in its way. But these things are not *letters*. "Valentine Vox" and "Charles O'Malley" are no more "*literature*" than cat-gut is music. The visible and tangible tricks of a baboon belong not less to the *belles-lettres* than does "Harry Lorrequer." When this gentleman adorns his countenance with lamp-black, knocks over an apple-woman, or brings about a rent in his pantaloons, we laugh at him when bound up in a volume, just as we would laugh at his adventures if happening before our eyes in the street. But mere incidents, whether serious or comic, whether occurring or described—*mere incidents* are not books. Neither are they the basis of books—of which the idiosyncrasy is *thought* in contradistinction from *deed*. A book without action cannot be; but a book is only such, to the extent of its thought, independently of its deed. Thus of Algebra; which is, or should be, defined as "a mode of computing with symbols by means of signs." With numbers, as Algebra, it has nothing to do; and although no algebraic computation can proceed without numbers, yet Algebra is only such to the extent of its analysis, independently of its Arithmetic.

We do not mean to *find fault* with the class of performances of which "Stanley Thorn" is one. Whatever tends to the amusement of man tends to his benefit. Aristotle, with singular assurance, has declared poetry the most philosophical of all writing, (*spoudiotaton kai philosophikotaton genos*) defending it principally upon that score. He seems to think,—and many following him, have thought—that the end of all literature should be instruction—a favorite dogma of the school of Wordsworth. But it is a truism that the end of our existence is happiness. If so, the end of every separate aim of our existence—of every thing connected with our existence, should be still—happiness. Therefore, the end of instruction should be happiness—and happiness, what is it but the extent or duration of pleasure?—therefore, the end of instruction should be pleasure. But the cant of the Lakists would establish the exact converse, and make the end of all pleasure instruction. In fact, *ceteris paribus*, he who pleases is of more importance to his fellow man than he who instructs, since the *dulce* is alone the *utile*, and pleasure is the end already attained, which instruction is merely the means of attaining. It will be said that Wordsworth, with Aristotle, has reference to instruction with eternity in view; but either such cannot be the tendency of his argument, or he is laboring at a sad disadvantage; for his works—or at least those of his school— are professedly to be understood by the few, and it is the many who stand in need of salvation. Thus the moralist's parade of measures would be as completely thrown away as are those of the devil in "Melmoth," who plots and counterplots through three octavo volumes for the entrapment of one or two souls, while any common devil would have demolished one or two thousand.

When, therefore, we assert that these practical-joke publications are not "literature," because not "thoughtful" in any degree, we must not be understood as objecting to the thing in itself, but to its claim upon our attention as critic. Dr.—what is his name?—strings together a number of facts or fancies which, when printed, answer the laudable purpose of amusing a very large, if not a very respectable number of people. To this proceeding upon the part of the Doctor—or on the part of his imitator, Mr. Jeremy Stockton, the author of "Valentine Vox," we *can* have no objection whatever. His *books* do not please *us*. We will not read them. Still less shall we speak of them seriously as *books*. Being in no respect works of art, they neither deserve, nor are amenable to criticism.

"Stanley Thorn" may be described, in brief, as a collection, rather than as a series, of practical haps and mishaps, befalling a young man very badly brought up by his mother. He flogs his father with a codfish, and does other similar things. We have no fault to find with him whatever except that, in the end, he *does not* come to the gallows.

We have no great fault to find with *him*, but with Mr. Bockton, his father, much. He is a consummate plagiarist; and, in our opinion, nothing more despicable exists. There is not a *good* incident in his book (?) of which we cannot point out the paternity with at least a sufficient precision. The opening adventures are all *in the style* of "Cyril Thornton." Bob, following Amelia in disguise, is borrowed from one of the Smollet or Fielding novels—there are many of our readers who will be able to say *which*. The cab driven over the Crescent *trottoir*, is from Pierce Egan. The swindling tricks of Colonel Somebody, at the commencement of the novel, and of Captain Filcher afterwards, are from "Pickwick Abroad." The doings at Madame Pompour's (or some such name) with the description of Isabelle, are from "Ecarté, or the Salons of Paris"—a *rich* book. The Sons-of-Glory scene (or its *wraith*) we have seen—*somewhere*; while (not to be tedious) the whole account of Stanley's election, from his first conception of the design, through the entire canvass, the purchasing of the "Independents," the row at the hustings, the chairing, the feast, and the petition, is so obviously *stolen* from "Ten Thousand a-Year" as to be disgusting. Bob and the "old venerable"—what are they but feeble reflections of young and old

Weller? The *tone* of the narration throughout is an absurd *echo* of Boz. For example—" 'We've come agin about them there little accounts of ourn—question is do you mean to settle 'em or don't you?' His colleagues, by whom he was backed, highly approved of this question, and winked and nodded with the view of intimating to each other that in their judgment that was the point." Who so dull as to give Mr. Bogton any more credit for these things than we give the buffoon for the *rôle* which he has committed to memory?

That the work will prove amusing to *many* readers, we do not pretend to deny. The claims of Mr. Frogton, and not of his narrative, are what we especially discuss.

The edition before us is clearly printed on good paper. The designs are by Cruikshank and Leech; and it is observable that those of the latter are more effective in every respect than those of the former and far more celebrated artist.

Graham's Magazine, January 1842

Samuel Taylor Coleridge

Letters, Conversations and Recollections of S. T. Coleridge. New York: Harper and Brothers.

WE FEEL EVEN a deeper interest in this book than in the late Table-Talk. But with us (we are not ashamed to confess it) the most trivial memorial of Coleridge is a treasure of inestimable price. He was indeed a "myriad-minded man," and ah, how little understood, and how pitifully villified! How merely nominal was the difference (and this too in his own land) between what he himself calls the "broad, pre-determined abuse" of the Edinburgh Review, and the cold and brief compliments with the warm *regrets* of the Quarterly. If there be any one thing more than another which stirs within us a deep spirit of indignation and disgust, it is that damnation of faint praise which so many of the Narcissi of critical literature have had the infinite presumption to breathe against the majesty of Coleridge—of Coleridge—the man to whose gigantic mind the proudest intellects of Europe found it impossible not to succumb. And as no man was more richly-gifted with all the elements of mental renown, so none was more fully worthy of the love and veneration of every truly good man. Even through the exertion of his great powers he sought no immediate worldly advantages. To use his own words, he not only sacrificed all present prospects of wealth and advancement, but, in his inmost soul, stood aloof from temporary reputation. In the volume now before us, we behold the heart, as in his own works we have beheld the mind, of the man. And surely nothing can be more elevating, nothing more cheering than this contemplation, to one who has faith in the possible virtue, and pride in the possible dignity of mankind. The book is written, we believe, by one of the poet's most intimate friends—one too in whom we recognize a familiarity with the thoughts, and sympathy with the feelings of his subject. It consists of letters, conversations, and fragmentary recollections, interspersed with comment by the compiler, and dedicated to "Elizabeth and Robin, the Fairy Prattler, and still Meek Boy of the Letters." The letters are by far the most valuable part of the compilation—although all is truly so. A portion of one of them we copy as affording a picture, never surpassed, of great mental power conscious of its greatness, and tranquilly submitting to the indignities of the world.

But enough of these generals. It was my purpose to open myself out to you in detail. My health, I have reason to believe, is so intimately connected with the state of my spirits, and these again so dependant on my thoughts, prospective and retrospective, that I should not doubt the being favored with a sufficiency for my noblest undertaking, had I the ease of heart requisite for the necessary abstraction of the thoughts, and such a reprieve from the goading of the immediate exigencies as might make tranquillity possible. But, alas! I know by experience (and the knowledge is not the less because the regret is not unmixed with self-blame, and the consciousness of want of exertion and fortitude,) that my health will continue to decline as long as the pain from reviewing the barrenness of the past is great in an inverse proportion to any rational anticipations of the future. As I now am, however, from five to six hours devoted to actual writing and composition in the day is the utmost that my strength, not to speak of my nervous system, will permit; and the invasions on this portion of my time from applications, often of the most senseless kind, are such and so many as to be almost as ludicrous even to myself as they are vexatious. In less than a week I have not seldom received half a dozen packets or parcels of works, printed or manuscript, urgently requesting my candid *judgment*, or my correcting hand. Add to these, letters from lords and ladies, urging me to write reviews or puffs of heaven-born geniuses, whose whole merit consists in being ploughmen or shoemakers. Ditto from actors; entreaties for money, or recommendations to publishers, from ushers out of place, &c. &c.; and to *me*, who have neither interest, influence, nor money, and, what is still more *àpropos*, can neither bring myself to tell smooth falsehoods nor harsh truths, and, in the struggle, too often do both in the anxiety to do neither. I have already the *written* materials and contents, requiring only to be put together, from the loose papers and commonplace or memorandum books, and needing no other change, whether of omission, addition, or correction, than the mere act of arranging, and the opportunity of seeing the whole collectively bring with them of course, —I. Characteristics of Shakspeare's Dramatic Works, with a Critical Review of each Play; together with a relative and comparative Critique on the kind and degree of the Merits and Demerits of the Dramatic Works of Ben Johnson, Beaumont and Fletcher, and Massinger. The History of the English Drama; the accidental advantages it afforded to Shakspeare, without in the least detracting from the perfect originality or proper creation of the Shakspearian Drama; the contradistinction of the latter from the Greek Drama, and its still remaining *uniqueness*, with the causes of this, from the combined influences of Shakspeare himself, as man, poet, philosopher, and finally, by conjunction of all these, dramatic poet; and of the age, events, manners, and state of the English language. This work, with every art of compression, amounts to three volumes of about five hundred pages each.—II. Philosophical Analysis of the Genius and Works of Dante, Spenser, Milton, Cervantes, and Calderon, with similar, but more compressed, Criticisms on Chaucer, Ariosto, Donne, Rabelais, and others, during the predominance of the Romantic Poetry. In one large volume. These two works will, I flatter myself, form a complete code of the principles of judgment and feeling applied to Works of Taste; and not of *Poetry* only, but of Poesy in all its forms, Painting, Statuary, Music, &c. &c.—III. The History of Philosophy considered as a Tendency of the Human Mind to exhibit the Powers of the Human Reason, to discover by its own Strength the Origin and Laws of Man and the World, from Pythagoras to Locke and Condillac. Two volumes.—IV. Letters on the Old and New Testaments, and on the Doctrine and Principles held in common by the Fathers and Founders of the Reformation, addressed to a Candidate for Holy Orders; including Advice on the Plan and Subjects of Preaching, proper to a Minister of the Established Church.

To the completion of these four works I have literally nothing more to do than *to transcribe*: but as I before hinted, from so many scraps and *Sibylline* leaves, including margins of books and blank pages, that, unfortunately, I must be my own scribe, and not done by myself, they will be all but lost;

or perhaps (as has been too often the case already) furnish feathers for the caps of others; some for this purpose, and some to plume the arrows of detraction, to be let fly against the luckless bird from whom they had been plucked or moulted.

In addition to these—of my GREAT WORK, to the preparation of which more than twenty years of my life have been devoted, and on which my hopes of extensive and permanent utility, of fame, in the noblest sense of the word, mainly rest—that, by which I might,

> "As now by thee, by all the good be known,
>   When this weak frame lies moulder'd in the grave,
> Which self-surviving I might call my own,
>   Which Folly cannot mar, nor Hate deprave—
> The incense of those powers, which, risen in flame,
> Might make me dear to Him from whom they came."

Of this work, to which all my other writings (unless I except my poems, and these I can exclude in part only) are introductory and preparative; and the result of which (if the premises be, as I, with the most tranquil assurance, am convinced they are—insubvertible, the deductions legitimate, and the conclusions commensurate, and only commensurate, with both,) must finally be a revolution of all that has been called *Philosophy* or Metaphysics in England and France since the era of the commencing predominance of the mechanical system at the restoration of our second Charles, and with this the present fashionable views, not only of religion, morals, and politics, but even of the modern physics and physiology. You will not blame the earnestness of my expressions, nor the high importance which I attach to this work; for how, with less noble objects, and less faith in their attainment, could I stand acquitted of folly and abuse of time, talents, and learning, in a labor of three fourths of my *intellectual* life? Of this work, something more than a volume has been dictated by me, so as to exist fit for the press, to my friend and enlightened pupil, Mr. Green; and more than as much again would have been evolved and delivered to paper, but that, for the last six or eight months, I have been compelled to break off our weekly meeting, from the necessity of writing (alas! alas! of *attempting* to write) for purposes, and on the subjects of the passing day. Of my poetic works, I would fain finish the Christabel. Alas! for the proud time when I planned, when I had present to my mind the materials, as well as the scheme of the hymns entitled, Spirit, Sun, Earth, Air, Water, Fire, and Man; and the epic poem on—what still appears to me the one only fit subject remaining for an epic poem—Jerusalem besieged and destroyed by Titus.

And here comes my dear friend; here comes my sorrow and my weakness, my grievance and my confession. Anxious to perform the duties of the day arising out of the wants of the day, these wants, too, presenting themselves in the most painful of all forms,—that of a debt owing to those who will not exact it, and yet need its payment, and the delay, the long (not live-long but *death*-long) behindhand of my accounts to friends, whose utmost care and frugality on the one side, and industry on the other, the wife's management and the husband's assiduity are put in requisition to make both ends meet,—I am at once forbidden to attempt, and too perplexed earnestly to pursue, the *accomplishment* of the works worthy of me, those I mean above enumerated,—even if, savagely as I have been injured by one of the two influensive Reviews, and with more effective enmity undermined by the utter silence or occasional detractive compliments of the other,* I had the probable chance of disposing of them to the booksellers, so as even to liquidate my mere boarding accounts during the time expended in the transcription, arrangement, and proof correction. And yet, on the other hand, my heart and mind are for ever recurring to them. Yes, my conscience forces me to plead guilty. I have only by fits and starts even prayed. I have not prevailed on myself to pray to God in sincerity and entireness for the fortitude that might enable me to resign myself to the abandonment of all my life's best hopes, to say boldly to myself,—"Gifted with powers confessedly above mediocrity, aided by an education, of which, no less from almost unexampled hardships and sufferings than

*Neither my Literary Life, (2 vols.) nor Sibylline Leaves, (1 vol.) nor Friend, (3 vols.) nor Lay Sermons, nor Zapolya, nor Christabel, have ever been noticed by the Quarterly Review, of which Southey is yet the main support.

from manifold and peculiar advantages, I have never yet found a parallel, I have devoted myself to a life of unintermitted reading, thinking, meditating, and observing. I have not only sacrificed all worldly prospects of wealth and advancement, but have in my inmost soul stood aloof from temporary reputation. In consequence of these toils and this self-dedication, I possess a calm and clear consciousness, that in many and most important departments of truth and beauty I have outstrode my contemporaries, those at least of highest name; that the number of my printed works bears witness that I have not been idle, and the seldom acknowledged, but strictly *proveable*, effects of my labors appropriated to the immediate welfare of my age in the Morning Post before and during the peace of Amiens, in the Courier afterward, and in the series and various subjects of my lectures at Bristol and at the Royal and Surrey Institutions, in Fetter Lane, at Willis's Rooms, and at the Crown and Anchor (add to which the unlimited freedom of my communications in colloquial life), may surely be allowed as evidence that I have not been useless in my generation. But, from circumstances, the *main* portion of my harvest is still on the ground, ripe indeed, and only waiting, a few for the sickle, but a large part only for the *sheaving*, and carting, and housing, but from all this I must turn away, must let them rot as they lie, and be as though they never had been, for I must go and gather blackberries and earth-nuts, or pick mushrooms and gild oak-apples for the palates and fancies of chance customers. I must abrogate the name of philosopher and poet, and scribble as fast as I can, and with as little thought as I can, for Blackwood's Magazine, or, as I have been employed for the last days, in writing MS. sermons for lazy clergymen, who stipulate that the composition must not be more than respectable, for fear they should be desired to publish the visitation sermon!" This I have not yet had courage to do. My soul sickens and my heart sinks; and thus, oscillating between both, I do neither, neither as it ought to be done, or to any profitable end. If I were to detail only the various, I might say capricious, interruptions that have prevented the finishing of this very scrawl, begun on the very day I received your last kind letter, you would need no other illustrations.

Now I see but one possible plan of rescuing my permanent utility. It is briefly this, and plainly. For what we struggle with inwardly, we find at least easiest to *bolt out*, namely,—that of engaging from the circle of those who think respectfully and hope highly of my powers and attainments a yearly sum, for three or four years, adequate to my actual support, with such comforts and decencies of appearance as my health and habits have made necessaries, so that my mind may be unanxious as far as the present time is concerned; that thus I should stand both enabled and pledged to begin with some one work of these above mentioned, and for two thirds of my whole time to devote myself to this exclusively till finished, to take the chance of its success by the best mode of publication that would involve me in no risk, then to proceed with the next, and so on till the works above mentioned as already in full material existence should be reduced into formal and actual beings while in the remaining third of my time I might go on maturing and completing my great work (for if but easy in mind I have no doubt either of the reawakening power or of the kindling inclination,) and my Christabel, and what else the happier hour might inspire—and without inspiration a barrel-organ may be played right deftly; but

> "All otherwise the state of *poet* stands:
> For lordly want is such a tyrant fell,
> That where he rules all power he doth expel.
> The vaunted verse a vacant head demands,
> Ne wont with crabbed Care the muses dwell:
> *Unwisely weaves who takes two webs in hand!*"

Now Mr. Green has offered to contribute from 30*l*. to 40*l*. yearly, for three or four years; my young friend and pupil, the son of one of my dearest old friends, 50*l*; and I think that from 10*l*. to 20*l*. I could rely upon from another. The sum required would be about 200*l*., to be repaid, of course, should the disposal or sale, and as far as the disposal and sale of my writings produced the means.

I have thus placed before you at large, wanderingly as well as diffusely, the statement which I am inclined to send in a compressed form to a few of those of whose kind dispositions towards me I have received assurances,—and to their interest and influence I must leave it—anxious, however, before I do this, to learn from you your very, very inmost feeling and judgment as to the previous questions. Am I entitled, have I earned a *right* to do this? Can I do it without moral degradation? and, lastly, can it be done without loss of character in the eyes of my acquaintance, and of my friends' acquaintance, who may have been informed of the circumstances? That, if attempted at all, it will be attempted in such a way, and that such persons only will be spoken to, as will not expose me to indelicate rebuffs to be afterward matter of gossip, I know those to whom I shall entrust the statement, too well to be much alarmed about.

Pray let me either see or hear from you as soon as possible; for, indeed and indeed, it is no inconsiderable accession to the pleasure I anticipate from disembarrassment, that *you* would have to contemplate in a more gracious form, and in a more ebullient play of the inward fountain, the mind and manners of,

My dear friend,

Your obliged and very affectionate friend,

S. T. COLERIDGE.

It has always been a matter of wonder to us that the *Biographia Literaria* here mentioned in the foot note has never been republished in America. It is, perhaps, the most deeply interesting of the prose writings of Coleridge, and affords a clearer view into his mental constitution than any other of his works. Why cannot some of our publishers undertake it? They would be rendering an important service to the cause of psychological science in America, by introducing a work of great scope and power in itself, and well calculated to do away with the generally received impression here entertained of the *mysticism* of the writer.

Southern Literary Messenger, June 1836

J. F. Dalton

Peter Snook, a Tale of the City; Follow your Nose; and other Strange Tales. By the Author of 'Chartley,' the 'Invisible Gentleman,' &c. &c. Philadelphia: Republished by Carey, Lea and Blanchard.

THE 'INVISIBLE GENTLEMAN' was exceedingly popular—and is. It belongs to a class of works which every one takes a pleasure in reading, and yet which every one thinks it his duty to condemn. Its author is one of the best of the English Magazinists—possessing a large share of Imagination, and a wonderful fertility of Fancy or Invention. With the exception of Boz, of the London Morning Chronicle, and, perhaps a couple of the writers in Blackwood, he has no rivals in his particular line. We confess ourselves somewhat in doubt, however, whether Boz and the author of 'Chartley' are not one and the same—or have not some intimate connection. In the volume now before us, the two admirable Tales, 'Peter Snook' and 'The Lodging-House Bewitched,' might very well have been written by the author of 'Watkins Tottle,' of which they possess all the whimsical peculiarities, and nearly all the singular fidelity and vigor. The remaining papers, however, 'Follow your Nose,' and the 'Old Maiden's Talisman,' are more particularly characteristic of the author of the 'Invisible Gentleman.'

The first of the series is also the best, and presents so many striking points for the consideration of the Magazine writer—(by which we mean merely to designate the writer of the brief and piquant article, slightly exaggerated in all its proportions) that we feel inclined to speak of it more fully than is our usual custom in regard to reprints of English light literature.

Peter Snook, the hero, and the beau ideal of a Cockney, is a retail linen-draper in Bishopgate Street. He is of course a stupid and conceited, though at bottom a very good little fellow, and "always looks as if he was frightened." Matters go on very thrivingly with him, until he becomes acquainted with Miss Clarinda Bodkin, "a young lady owning to almost thirty, and withal a great proficient in the mysteries of millinery and mantua-making." Love and ambition, however, set the little gentleman somewhat beside himself. "If Miss Clarinda would but have me," says he, " we might divide the shop, and have a linen-drapery side, and a haberdashery and millinery side, and one would help the other. There'd be only one rent to pay, and a double business—and it would be so comfortable too!" Thinking thus, Peter commences a desperate flirtation, to which Miss Clarinda but doubtfully responds. He escorts the lady to White Conduit House, Bagnigge Wells, and other "genteel" places of public resort— and finally is so rash as to accede to the proposition on her part of a trip to Margate. At this epoch of the narrative the writer takes occasion to observe that the subsequent proceedings of the hero are gathered from accounts rendered by himself, when called upon afterwards for certain explanations.

It is agreed that Miss Clarinda shall set out alone for Margate, and Mr. Snook follows after some indispensable arrangements. These occupy him until the middle of July, at which period, taking passage in the "Rose in June," he safely reaches his destination. But various misfortunes here await him—misfortunes admirably adapted to the meridian of Cockney feeling, and the capacity of Cockney endurance. His umbrella, for example, and a large brown paper parcel containing a new pea-green coat, and flower-patterned embroidered silk waistcoat, are tumbled into the water at the landing place, and Miss Bodkin forbids him her presence in his old clothes. By a tumble of his own too, the skin is rubbed off both his shins for several inches, and his surgeon, having no regard to the lover's cotillon engagements with Miss Clarinda, enjoins upon him a total abstinence from dancing. A cock-chafer, moreover, is at the trouble of flying into one of his eyes, and, worse than all, a tall military-looking shoemaker, Mr. Last, has taken advantage of his delay in reaching Margate, to ingratiate himself with his mistress. Finally, he is "cut" by Last and rejected by the lady, and has nothing left for it but to secure a homeward passage in the "Rose in June." In the evening of the second day after his departure, the vessel drops anchor off Greenwich. Most of the passengers go ashore with the view of taking the stage to the city. Peter, however, who considers that he has already spent money enough to no purpose, prefers remaining on board. "We shall get to Billingsgate," says he, " while I am sleeping, and I shall have plenty of time to go home and dress and go into the city and borrow the trifle I may want for Pester and Company's bill, that comes due the day after to-morrow." This determination is a source of much trouble to our hero, as will be seen in the sequel. Some shopmen who remain with him in the packet, tempt him to unusual indulgences in the way, first of brown stout, and secondly of positive French brandy. The consequence is, that Mr. Peter Snook falls, thirdly, asleep, and, fourthly, overboard.

About dawn, on the morning after this event, Ephraim Hobson, the confidential clerk and fac-totum of Mr. Peter Snook, is disturbed from a sound nap by the sudden appearance of his master. That gentleman seems to be quite in a bustle, and delights Ephraim with an account of a " whacking wholesale order for exportation" just received. "Not a word to *any* body about the matter," exclaims Peter, with unusual emphasis; "it's such an opportunity as don't come often in a man's life time. There's a captain of a ship, he's the owner of her too; but never mind, there an't time to enter into particulars now, but you'll know all by and bye; all you have to do is to do as I tell you, so come along." Setting Ephraim to work, with directions to pack up immediately all the goods in the shop, with the exception of a few trifling articles, the master avows his intention of going into the city "to borrow enough money to make up Pester's bill for to-morrow." "I don't think you'll want much, sir," returned Hobson, with a self-complacent air. "I've been looking up the long winded 'uns, you see, since you've been gone, and have got Shy's money and Slack's account, which we'd pretty well given up for a bad job, and one or two more. There, there's the list, and there's the key to the strong-box, where you'll find the money, besides what I've took at the counter." Peter seems well pleased at this, and shortly afterwards goes out, saying he cannot tell when he will be back, and giving directions that whatever goods may be sent in during his absence shall be left untouched until his return.

It appears that after leaving his shop, Mr. Snook proceeded to that of Messieurs Job, Flashbill & Co. (one of whose clerks, on board the Rose in June, had been very liberal in supplying our hero with brandy on the night of his ducking,) looked over a large quantity of ducks and other goods, and finally made purchase of "a choice assortment" to be delivered the same day. His next visit was to Mr. Bluff, the managing partner in the banking house where he usually kept his cash. His business now was to request permission to overdraw a hundred pounds for a few days.

"Humph," said Mr. Bluff, "money is very scarce but—— Bless me!—yes—it's he! Excuse me a minute, Mr. Snook, there's a gentleman at the front counter whom I want partic-ularly to speak to—I'll be back with you directly." As he ut-tered these words, he rushed out, and, in passing one of the clerks on his way forward, he whispered—"Tell Scribe to look at Snook's account, and let me know directly." He then went to the front counter, where several people were waiting to pay and receive money. "Fine weather this, Mr. Butt. What! you're not out of town like the rest of them?"

"No," replied Mr. Butt, who kept a thriving gin-shop, "no, I sticks to my business—make hay while the sun shines —that's my maxim. Wife up at night—I up early in the morning."

The banker chatted and listened with great apparent inter-est, till the closing of a huge book on which he kept his eye, told him that his whispered order had been attended to. He then took a gracious leave of Mr. Butt, and returned back to the counting-house with a slip of paper, adroitly put in his hand while passing, on which was written, "Peter Snook, Linen Draper, Bishopgate Street—old account—increas-ing gradually—balance 153*l.* 15*s.* 6*d.*—*very* regular." "Sorry to keep you waiting, Mr. Snook," said he, "but we must catch people when we can. Well, what is it you were saying you wanted us to do?"

"I should like to be able to overdraw just for a few days," replied Peter.

"How much?"

"A hundred."

"Won't fifty do?"

"No, not quite sir."

"Well, you're an honest fellow, and don't come bothering us often, so I suppose we must not be too particular with you for this once."

Leaving Bluff, Mr. Snook hurries to overtake Mr. Butt, the dealer in spirits, who had just left the banking house before himself, and to give that gentleman an order for a hogshead of the best gin. As he is personally unknown to Mr. Butt he hands him a card on which is written "Peter Snook, linen and muslin warehouse, No.—, Bishopgate street within, &c. &c." and takes occasion to mention that he purchases at the recommendation of Mr. Bluff. The gin is to be at Queenhithe the same evening. The spirit-dealer, as soon as his new customer has taken leave, revolves in his mind the oddity of a linen-draper's buying a hogshead of gin, and determines to satisfy himself of Mr. Snook's responsibility by a personal application to Mr. Bluff. Upon reaching the bank, however, he is told by the clerks that Mr. Bluff, being in attendance upon a committee of the House of Commons, will not be home in any reasonable time—but also that Peter Snook is a perfectly safe man. The gin is accordingly sent; and several other large orders for different goods, upon other houses, are all promptly fulfilled in the same manner. Meantime Ephraim is busily engaged at home in receiving and inspecting the invoices of the various purchases as they arrive, at which employment he is occupied until dusk, when his master makes his appearance in unusually high spirits. We must here be pardoned for copying about a page.

"Well, Ephraim," he exclaimed, "this looks something like business! You hav'nt had such a job this many a day! Shop looks well now, eh?"

"You know best, sir," replied Hobson. "But hang me if I a'nt frightened. When we shall sell all these goods I'm sure I can't think. You talked of having a haberdashery side to the shop; but if we go on at this rate, we shall want another side for ourselves; I'm sure I don't know where Miss Bodkin is to be put."

"She go to Jericho!" said Peter, contemptuously. "As for the goods, my boy, they'll all be gone before to-morrow morning. All you and I have got to do is to pack 'em up; so let us turn to and strap at it."

Packing was Ephraim's favorite employment, but on the present occasion he set to work with a heavy heart. His master, on the contrary, appeared full of life and spirits, and corded boxes, sewed up trusses, and packed huge paper parcels with a celerity and an adroitness truly wonderful.

"Why, you don't get on, Hobson," he exclaimed; "see what I've done! Where's the ink-pot?—oh, here it is!" and he proceeded to mark his packages with his initials and the letter G below. "There," he resumed, "P. S. G.; that's for me at Gravesend. I'm to meet the Captain and owner there; show the goods—if there's any he don't like shall bring 'em back with me; get bills—bankers' acceptances for the rest; see 'em safe on board *then*—but *not before*, mind that Master Ephraim! No, no, keep my weather eye open as the men say on board the Rose in June. By the bye, I hav'nt told you yet about my falling overboard whap into the river."

"Falling overboard!" exclaimed the astonished shopman, quitting his occupation to stand erect and listen.

"Ay, ay," continued Peter—"see it won't do to tell you long stories *now*. There—mark that truss, will you? Know all about it some day. Lucky job though—tell you that; got this thundering order by it. Had one tumble, first going off, at Margate. Spoilt my peagreen—never mind—that was a lucky tumble too. Hadn't been for that, shouldn't so soon have found out the game a certain person was playing with me. She go to Jericho?"

But for the frequent repetition of this favorite expression, Ephraim Hobson has since declared he should have doubted his master's identity during the whole of that evening, as there was something very singular about him; and his strength and activity in moving the bales, boxes, and trusses, were such as he had never previously exhibited. The phrase condemning this, that, or the other thing or person to "go to Jericho," was the only expression that he uttered, as the shopman said, "naturally," and Peter repeated that whimsical anathema as often as usual.

The goods being all packed up, carts arrive to carry them away; and, by half past ten o'clock, the shop is entirely cleared, with the exception of a few trifling articles, to make show on the shelves and counters. Two hackney coaches are called. Mr. Peter Snook gets into one with a variety of loose articles which would require too much time to pack, and his shopman into another with some more. Arriving at Queen-hithe, they find all the goods previously sent already embarked in the hold of a long decked barge which lies near the shore. Mr. Snook now insists upon Ephraim's going on board and taking supper and some hot rum and water. This advice he follows to so good purpose that he is at length completely bewildered, when his master, taking him up in his arms, carries him on shore, and there setting him down, leaves him to make the best of his way home as he can.

About eight next morning, Ephraim awaking, of course in a sad condition both of body and mind, sets himself immediately about arranging the appearance of the shop "so as to secure the credit of the concern." In spite of all his ingenuity, however, it maintains a poverty-stricken appearance—which circumstance excites some most unreasonable suspicions in the mind of Mr. Bluff's clerk, upon his calling at ten with Pester and Co.'s bill, (three hundred and sixteen pounds seventeen shillings) and receiving, by way of payment, a check upon his own banking house for the amount—Mr. Snook having written this check before his departure with the goods, and left it with Ephraim. Upon reaching the bank therefore, the clerk inquires if Peter Snook's check is good for three hundred and sixteen pounds odd, and is told that it is not worth a farthing, Mr. S. having overdrawn already for a hundred. While Mr. Bluff and his assistants are conversing upon this subject, Butt, the gin-dealer, calls to thank the banker for having recommended him a customer—which the banker denies having done. An explanation ensues and "stop thief!" is the cry. Ephraim is sent for, and reluctantly made to tell all he knows of his master's proceedings on the day before—by which means a knowledge is obtained of the other houses who (it is supposed) have been swindled. Getting a description of the barge which conveyed the goods from Queenhithe, the whole party of creditors now set off in pursuit.

About dawn the next morning they overtake the barge a little below Gravesend—when four men are observed leaving her upon sight of the pursuers and rowing to the shore in a skiff. Peter Snook is found sitting quietly in the cabin, and although apparently a little surprised at seeing Mr. Pester, betrays nothing like embarrassment or fear.

"Ah, Mr. Pester, is it you? Glad to see you, sir! So you've been taking a trip out o' town, and are going back with us? We shall get to Billingsgate between eight and nine, they say; and I hope it won't be later, as I've a bill of yours comes due to-day, and I want to be at home in time to write a check for it."

The goods are also found on board, together with three men in the hold, gagged and tied hand and foot. They give a strange account of themselves. Being in the employ of Mr. Heaviside a lighterman, they were put in charge of "The Flitter," when she was hired by Peter Snook for a trip to Gravesend. According to their orders they took the barge in the first instance to a wharf near Queenhithe, and helped to load her with some goods brought down in carts. Mr. Snook afterwards came on board bringing with him two fierce looking men and "a little man with a hooked nose," (Ephraim.) Mr. S. and the little man then "had a sort of a jollification" in the cabin, till the latter got drunk and was carried ashore. They then proceeded down the river, nothing particular occuring till they had passed Greenwich Hospital, when Mr. S. ordered them to lay the barge alongside a large black sided ship. No sooner was the order obeyed than they were boarded by a number of men from said ship, who seized them, bound them hand and foot, gagged them and put them down into the hold.

The immediate consequence of this information is, that our poor friend Peter is bound hand and foot, gagged, and put down into the hold in the same manner, by way of retaliation, and for safe-keeping on his way back to the city. On the arrival of the party a meeting of the creditors is called. Peter appears before them in a great rage and with the air of an injured man. Indeed, his behavior is so mal-a-propos to his situation, as entirely to puzzle his interrogators. He accuses the whole party of a conspiracy.

"Peter Snook," said Mr. Pester solemnly, from the chair, "that look does not become you after what has passed. Let

me advise you to conduct yourself with propriety. You will
find that the best policy, depend on't."

"A pretty thing for you, for to come to talk of propriety!"
exclaimed Peter; "you that seed me laid hold on by a set of
ruffins, and never said a word, nor given information a'ter-
wards! And here have I been kept away from business I don't
know how long, and shut up like a dog in a kennel; but I
look upon't you were at the bottom of it all—you and that
fellow with the plum-pudding face, as blowed me up about a
cask of gin! What you both mean by it I can't think; but if
there's any law in the land, I'll make you remember it, both
of you—that's what I will!"

Mr. Snook swears that he never saw Mr. Jobb in his life
except on the occasion of his capture in "The Flitter," and
positively denies having looked out any parcel of goods at the
house of Jobb, Flashbill & Co. With the banker, Mr. Bluff,
he acknowledges an acquaintance—but not having drawn for
the two hundred and seventy pounds odd, or having ever
overdrawn for a shilling in his life. Moreover he is clearly of
opinion that the banker has still in his hands more than a
hundred and fifty pounds of his (Mr. Snook's) money. He
also designates several gentlemen as being no creditors of his,
although they were of the number of those from whom large
purchases had been made for the " whacking" shipping order,
and although their goods were found in "The Flitter."
Ephraim is summoned, and testifies to all the particulars of
his master's return, and the subsequent packing, cart-loading
and embarkation as already told—accounting for the extravagances of Mr. Snook as being "all along of *that* Miss
Bodkin."

"Lor', master, hi's glad to see you agin," exclaimed
Ephraim. "Who'd ha' thought as 'twould come to this?"

"Come to what?" cried Peter. "I'll make 'em repent of it,
every man Jack of 'em, before I've done, if there's law to be
had for love or money!"

"Ah, sir," said Ephraim, " we'd better have stuck to the retail. I was afraid that shipping consarn would'nt answer, and
tell'd you so, if you recollect, but you would'nt harken to
me."

"What shipping concern?" inquired Peter, with a look of amazement.

"La! master," exclaimed Ephraim, "it aint of any use to pretend to keep it a secret now, when every body knows it. I did'nt tell Mr. Pester, though, till the last, when all the goods was gone out of the shop, and the sheriff's officers had come to take possession of the house."

"Sheriff's officers in possession of my house!" roared Peter. "All the goods gone out of the shop! What do you mean by that, you rascal? What have you been doing in my absence?" And he sprang forward furiously, and seized the trembling shopman by the collar with a degree of violence which rendered it difficult for the two officers in attendance to disengage him from his hold.

Hereupon, Mr. Snap, the attorney retained by the creditors, harangues the company at some length, and intimates that Mr. Snook is either mad, or acting the madman for the purpose of evading punishment. A practitioner from Bedlam is sent for, and some artifices resorted to—but to no purpose. It is found impossible to decide upon the question of sanity. The medical gentleman in his report to the creditors confesses himself utterly perplexed, and, without giving a decision, details the particulars of a singular story told him by Mr. Snook himself concerning the mode of his escape from drowning after he fell overboard from the "Rose in June." "It is a strange unlikely tale to be sure," says the physician, "and if his general conversation was of that wild imaginative flighty kind which I have so often witnessed, I should say it was purely ideal; but he appears such a plain-spoken, simple sort of a person, that it is difficult to conceive how he could invent such a fiction." Mr. Snook's narration is then told, not in his very words, but in the author's own way, with all the particulars obtained from Peter's various recitations. This narration is singular enough but we shall give it only *in petto*.

Upon tumbling overboard, Mr. Snook (at least according to his own story) swam courageously as long as he could. He was upon the point of sinking, however, when an oar was thrust under his arm, and he found himself lifted in a boat by a "dozen dark looking men." He is taken on board a large ship, and the captain, who is a droll genius, and talks in rhyme somewhat after the fashion of Frazer's Magazine, entertains him with great cordiality, dresses him in a suit of his own clothes, makes him drink in the first place a brimmer of "something hot," and afterwards plies him with wines and liqueurs of all kinds, at a supper of the most magnificent description. Warmed in body and mind by this excellent cheer, Peter reveals his inmost secrets to his host and talks freely and minutely of a thousand things; of his man Ephraim and his oddities; of his bank account; of his great credit; of his adventures with Miss Bodkin, his prospects in trade, and especially the names, residences, et cetera, et cetera, of the wholesale houses with which he is in the habit of dealing. Presently, being somewhat overcome with wine, he goes to bed at the suggestion of the captain, who promises to call him in season for a boat in the morning which will convey him to Billingsgate in full time for Pester and Co.'s note. How long he slept is uncertain—but when he awoke a great change was observable in the captain's manner, who was somewhat brusque, and handed him over the ship's side into the barge where he was discovered by the creditors in pursuit, and which he was assured would convey him to Billingsgate.

This relation we have given in brief, and consequently it implies little or nothing. The result, however, to which the reader is ingeniously led by the author, is that the real Peter Snook has been duped, and that the Peter Snook who made the various purchases about town, and who appeared to Ephraim only during the morning and evening twilight of the eventful day, was, in fact, no other person than the captain of "the strange, black-sided ship." We are to believe that, taking advantage of Peter's communicativeness, and a certain degree of personal resemblance to himself, he assumed our hero's clothes while he slept, and made a bold and nearly successful attempt at wholesale peculation.

The incidents of this story are forcibly conceived, and even in the hands of an ordinary writer would scarcely fail of effect. But in the present instance so unusual a tact is developed in the narration, that we are inclined to rank "Peter Snook" among the few tales which, each in their own way, are absolutely faultless. Such things, however, insignificant in themselves or their subjects, satisfy the mind of the literary critic precisely as we have known a few rude, and apparently unmeaning touches of the brush, fill with unalloyed pleasure the eye of the artist. But no—in the latter case effect is produced chiefly by arrangement, and a proper preponderance of objects. "Peter Snook" is rather a Flemish *home-piece*, and entitled to the very species of praise which should be awarded to the best of such pieces. The merit lies in the *chiaro 'scuro*—in that blending of light and shadow where nothing is *too distinct*, yet where the idea is fully conveyed—in the absence of all rigid outlines and all miniature painting—in the not undue warmth of the coloring—and in the slight tone of exaggeration prevalent, yet not amounting to caricature. We will venture to assert that no painter, who deserves to be called so, will read "Peter Snook" without assenting to what we say, and without a perfect consciousness that the principal rules of the plastic arts, founded as they surely are in a true perception of the beautiful, will apply in their fullest force to every species of literary composition.

Southern Literary Messenger, October 1836

Daniel Defoe

The Life and Surprising Adventures of Robinson Crusoe, of York, Mariner: with a Biograph-ical Account of Defoe. Illustrated with Fifty Characteristic Cuts, from Drawings, by Wil-liam Harvey, Esq. and engraved by Adams. New York: Published by Harper and Brothers.

THIS PUBLICATION is worthy of the Harpers. It is an honor to the country—not more in the fine taste dis-played in its getting up, than as evincing a just appreciation of an invaluable work. How fondly do we recur, in memory, to those enchanted days of our boyhood when we first learned to grow serious over Robinson Crusoe!—when we first found the spirit of wild adventure enkindling within us, as, by the dim fire light, we labored out, line by line, the marvellous import of those pages, and hung breathless and trembling with eagerness over their absorbing—over their enchaining interest! Alas! the days of desolate islands are no more! "Nothing farther," as Vapid says, "can be done in that line." Wo, henceforward, to the Defoe who shall prate to us of "undiscovered bournes." There is positively not a square inch of new ground for any future Selkirk. Neither in the Indian, in the Pacific, nor in the Atlantic, has he a shadow of hope. The Southern Ocean has been incontinently ransacked, and in the North—Scoresby, Franklin, Parry, Ross, Ross & Co. have been little better than so many salt water Paul Prys.

While Defoe would have been fairly entitled to immortality had he never written Robinson Crusoe, yet his many other very excellent writings have nearly faded from our attention, in the superior lustre of the Adventures of the Mariner of York. What better possible species of reputation could the au-thor have desired for that book than the species which it has so long enjoyed? It has become a household thing in nearly every family in Christendom! Yet never was admiration of any work—universal admiration—more indiscriminately or more inappropriately bestowed. Not one person in ten—nay, not one person in five hundred, has, during the perusal of Rob-inson Crusoe, the most remote conception that any particle of genius, or even of common talent, has been employed in its creation! Men do not look upon it in the light of a literary performance. Defoe has none of their thoughts—Robinson all. The powers which have wrought the wonder have been thrown into obscurity by the very stupendousness of the wonder they have wrought! We read, and become perfect abstractions in the intensity of our interest—we close the book, and are quite satisfied that we could have written as well ourselves! All this is effected by the potent magic of verisimilitude. Indeed the author of Crusoe must have possessed, above all other faculties, what has been termed the faculty of *identification*—that dominion exercised by volition over imagination which enables the mind to lose its own, in a fictitious, individuality. This includes, in a very great degree, the power of abstraction; and with these keys we may partially unlock the mystery of that spell which has so long invested the volume before us. But a complete analysis of our interest in it cannot be thus afforded. Defoe is largely indebted to his subject. The idea of man in a state of perfect isolation, although often entertained, was never before so comprehensively carried out. Indeed the frequency of its occurrence to the thoughts of mankind argued the extent of its influence on their sympathies, while the fact of no attempt having been made to give an embodied form to the conception, went to prove the difficulty of the undertaking. But the true narrative of Selkirk in 1711, with the powerful impression it then made upon the public mind, sufficed to inspire Defoe with both the necessary courage for his work, and entire confidence in its success. How wonderful has been the result!

Besides *Robinson Crusoe*, Defoe wrote no less than *two hundred and eight* works. The chief of these are the *Speculum Crape-Gownorum*, a reply to Roger L'Estrange, and characterized principally by intemperate abuse—a *Treatise against the Turks*, written for the purpose of showing England "that if it was the interest of Protestantism not to increase the influence of a Catholic power, it was infinitely more so to oppose a Mohammedan one"—an *Essay on Projects*, displaying great ingenuity, and mentioned in terms of high approbation by our own Franklin—the *Poor Man's Plea*, a satire levelled against the extravagances of the upper ranks of British society—the *Trueborn Englishman*, composed with a view of defending the king from the abuse heaped upon him as a foreigner—the *Shortest Way with the Dissenters*, a work which created strong excitement, and for which the author suffered in the pillory—the *Reformation of Manners*, a satirical poem, containing passages of uncommon force, that is to say, uncommon for Defoe, who was no poet—*More Reformation*, a continuation of the above—*Giving Alms no Charity*, an excellent treatise—a *Preface to a translation of Drelincourt on Death*, in which is contained the "true narrative" of Mrs. Veal's apparition—the *History of the Union*, a publication of much celebrity in the days of its author, and even now justly considered as placing him among the "soundest historians of his time"—the *Family Instructor*, "one of the most valuable systems of practical morality in the language"—the *History of Moll Flanders*, including some striking but coarsely executed paintings of low life—the *Life of Colonel Jaque*, in which an account is given of the hero's residence in Virginia—the *Memoirs of a Cavalier*, a book belonging more properly to History than to Fictitious Biography, and which has been often mistaken for a true narrative of the civil wars in England and Germany—the *History of the Plague*, which Dr. Mead considered an authentic record—and *Religious Courtship*, which acquired an extensive popularity, and ran through innumerable editions. In the multiplicity of his other publications, and amid a life of perpetual activity, Defoe found time, likewise, to edit his *Review*, which existed for more than nine years, commencing in February 1704, and ending in May 1713. This periodical is justly entitled to be considered the original of the Tatlers and Spectators, which were afterwards so fashionable. Political intelligence, however, constituted the greater portion of its *materiel*.

The Edition of *Robinson Crusoe* now before us is worthy of all praise. We have seldom seen a more beautiful book. It is an octavo of 470 pages. The fifty wood cuts with which it is ornamented are, for the most part, admirable. We may instance, as particularly good, those on pages 6, 27, 39, 49, 87, 88, 92, 137, 146, 256, and 396. The design on the title page is superlative. In regard to the paper, typography, and binding of the work, that taste must be fastidious indeed which can find any fault with either.

Southern Literary Messenger, January 1836

Charles Dickens

Watkins Tottle, and other Sketches, illustrative of every-day Life, and every-day People. By Boz. Philadelphia: Carey, Lea and Blanchard.

THIS BOOK IS a re-publication from the English original, and many of its sketches are with us old and highly esteemed acquaintances. In regard to their author we know nothing more than that he is a far more pungent, more witty, and better disciplined writer of sly articles, than nine-tenths of the Magazine writers in Great Britain—which is saying much, it must be allowed, when we consider the great variety of genuine talent, and earnest application brought to bear upon the periodical literature of the mother country.

The very first passage in the volumes before us, will convince any of our friends who are knowing in the requisites of "a good thing," that we are doing our friend Boz no more than the simplest species of justice. Hearken to what he says of Matrimony and of Mr. Watkins Tottle.

Matrimony is proverbially a serious undertaking. Like an overweening predilection for brandy and water, it is a misfortune into which a man easily falls, and from which he finds it remarkably difficult to extricate himself. It is no use telling a man who is timorous on these points, that it is but one plunge and all is over. They say the same thing at the Old Bailey, and the unfortunate victims derive about as much comfort from the assurance in the one case as in the other.

Mr. Watkins Tottle was a rather uncommon compound of strong uxorious inclinations, and an unparalleled degree of anti-connubial timidity. He was about fifty years of age; stood four feet six inches and three quarters in his socks— for he never stood in stockings at all—plump, clean and rosy. He looked something like a vignette to one of Richardson's novels, and had a clean cravatish formality of manner, and kitchen-pokerness of carriage, which Sir Charles Grandison himself might have envied. He lived on an annuity, which was well adapted to the individual who received it in one respect—it was rather small. He received it in periodical payments on every alternate Monday; but he ran himself out about a day after the expiration of the first week, as regularly as an eight-day clock, and then, to make the comparison complete, his landlady wound him up, and he went on with a regular tick.

It is not every one who can put "a good thing" properly together, although, perhaps, when thus properly put together, every tenth person you meet with may be capable of both conceiving and appreciating it. We cannot bring ourselves to believe that less actual ability is required in the composition of a really good "brief article," than in a fashionable novel of the usual dimensions. The novel certainly requires what is denominated a sustained effort—but this is a matter of mere perseverance, and has but a collateral relation to talent. On the other hand—unity of effect, a quality not easily appreciated or indeed comprehended by an ordinary mind, and a *desideratum* difficult of attainment, even by those who can conceive it—is indispensable in the "brief article," and not so in the common novel. The latter, if admired at all, is admired for its detached passages, without reference to the work as a whole—or without reference to any general design—which, if it even exist in some measure, will be found to have occupied but little of the writer's attention, and cannot, from the length of the narrative, be taken in at one view, by the reader.

The Sketches by Boz are all exceedingly well managed, and never fail to *tell* as the author intended. They are entitled, Passage in the Life of Mr. Watkins Tottle—The Black Veil—Shabby Genteel People—Horatio Sparkins—The Pawnbroker's Shop—The Dancing Academy—Early Coaches—The River—Private Theatres—The Great Winglebury Duel—Omnibuses—Mrs. Joseph Porter—The Steam Excursion—Sentiment—The Parish—Miss Evans and the Eagle—Shops and their Tenants—Thoughts about People—A Visit to Newgate—London Recreations—The Boarding-House—Hackney-Coach Stands—Brokers and Marine Store-Shops—The Bloomsbury Christening—Gin Shops—Public Dinners—Astley's—Greenwich Fair—The Prisoner's Van—and A Christmas Dinner. The reader who has been so fortunate as to have perused any one of these pieces, will be fully aware of how great a fund of racy entertainment is included in the Bill of Fare we have given. There are here some as well conceived and well written papers as can be found in any other collection of the kind—many of them we would especially recommend, as a study, to those who turn their attention to Magazine writing—a department in which, generally, the English as far excel us as Hyperion a Satyr.

The *Black Veil*, in the present series, is distinct in character from all the rest—an act of stirring tragedy, and evincing lofty powers in the writer. Broad humor is, however, the prevailing feature of the volumes. *The Dancing Academy* is a vivid sketch of Cockney low life, which may probably be considered as somewhat too *outré* by those who have no experience in the matter. *Watkins Tottle* is excellent. We should like very much to copy the whole of the article entitled *Pawnbroker's Shop*, with a view of contrasting its matter and manner with the insipidity of the passage we have just quoted on the same subject from the *"Ups and Downs"* of Colonel Stone, and by way of illustrating our remarks on the *unity of effect*—but this would, perhaps, be giving too much of a good thing. It will be seen by those who peruse both these articles, that in that of the American, two or three anecdotes are told which have merely a relation—a very shadowy relation, to pawn-broking —in short, they are barely elicited by this theme, have no necessary dependence upon it, and might be introduced equally well in connection with any one of a million other subjects. In the sketch of the Englishman we have no anecdotes at all—the *Pawnbroker's Shop* engages and enchains our attention—we are enveloped in its atmosphere of wretchedness and extortion—we pause at every sentence, not to dwell upon the sentence, but to obtain a fuller view of the gradually perfecting picture—which is never at any moment any other matter than the *Pawnbroker's Shop*. To the illustration of this one end all the *groupings* and *fillings in* of the painting are rendered subservient—and when our eyes are taken from the canvass, we remember the personages of the sketch not at all as independent existences, but as essentials of the one subject we have witnessed—as a part and portion of the *Pawnbroker's*

Shop. So perfect, and never-to-be-forgotten a picture cannot be brought about by any such trumpery exertion, or still more trumpery talent, as we find employed in the ineffective daubing of Colonel Stone. The scratchings of a schoolboy with a slate-pencil on a slate might as well be compared to the groupings of Buonarotti.

We conclude by strongly recommending the Sketches of Boz to the attention of American readers, and by copying the whole of his article on Gin Shops.

*　　　*　　　*　　　*　　　*

Southern Literary Messenger, June 1836

The Posthumous Papers of the Pickwick Club: Containing a Faithful Record of the Perambulations, Perils, Travels, Adventures, and Sporting Transactions of the Corresponding Members. Edited by "Boz." Philadelphia: Republished by Carey, Lea and Blanchard.

IN OUR JUNE "Messenger," we spoke at some length of the "Watkins Tottle and other Papers," by "Boz." We then expressed a high opinion of the comic power, and of the rich imaginative conception of Mr. Dickens—an opinion which "The Pickwick Club" has fully sustained. The author possesses nearly every desirable quality in a writer of fiction, and has withal a thousand negative virtues. In his delineation of Cockney life he is rivalled only by the author of "Peter Snook," while in efforts of a far loftier and more difficult nature, he has greatly surpassed the best of the brief tragic pieces of Bulwer, or of Warren. Just now, however, we can only express our opinion that his general powers as a prose writer are equalled by few. The work is to be continued, and hereafter we may give at some length the considerations which have led us to this belief. From the volume before us we quote the concluding portion of a vigorous sketch, entitled "A Madman's MS." The writer is supposed to be an hereditary madman, and to have labored under the disease for many years, but to have been conscious of his condition, and thus, by a strong effort of the will, to have preserved his secret from the eye of even his most intimate friends.

*　　　*　　　*　　　*　　　*

Southern Literary Messenger, November 1836

The Old Curiosity Shop, and other Tales. By Charles Dickens. With Numerous Illustrations
by Cattermole and Browne. Philadelphia: Lea & Blanchard.
Master Humphrey's Clock. By Charles Dickens. (Boz.) With Ninety-one Illustrations by
George Cattermole and Hablot Browne. Philadelphia: Lea & Blanchard.

WHAT WE HERE GIVE in Italics is the duplicate title, on
two separate title-pages, of an octavo volume of three
hundred and sixty two pages. Why this method of nomenclature should have been adopted is more than we can understand—although it arises, *perhaps*, from a certain confusion
and hesitation observable in the whole structure of the book
itself. Publishers have an idea, however, (and no doubt they
are the best judges in such matters) that a complete work
obtains a readier sale than one "to be continued;" and we see
plainly that it is with the design of intimating the *entireness*
of the volume now before us, that *"The Old Curiosity Shop
and other Tales,"* has been made not only the primary and
main title, but the name of the whole publication as indicated
by the back. This may be quite fair in trade, but is morally
wrong not the less. The volume is only one of a series—only
part of a whole; and the title has no right to *insinuate otherwise.* So obvious is this intention to misguide, that it has led
to the absurdity of putting the inclusive, or general, title of
the series, as a secondary instead of a primary one. Anybody
may see that if the wish had been fairly to represent the plan
and extent of the volume, something like this would have
been given on a single page—

*"Master Humphrey's Clock. By Charles Dickens. Part I. Con-
taining The Old Curiosity Shop, and other Tales, with Numerous
Illustrations, &c. &c."*

This would have been better for all parties, a good deal
more honest, and a vast deal more easily understood. In fact,
there is sufficient uncertainty of purpose in the book itself,
without resort to mystification in the matter of title. We do
not think it altogether impossible that the rumors in respect
to the sanity of Mr. Dickens which were so prevalent during
the publication of the first numbers of the work, had some
slight—some very slight foundation in truth. By this, we
mean merely to say that the mind of the author, at the time,
might possibly have been struggling with some of those manifold and multiform *aberrations* by which the nobler order of

genius is so frequently beset—but which are still so very far removed from disease.

There are some facts in the physical world which have a really wonderful analogy with others in the world of thought, and seem thus to give some color of truth to the (false) rhetorical dogma, that metaphor or simile may be made to strengthen an argument, as well as to embellish a description. The principle of the *vis inertiæ*, for example, with the amount of *momentum* proportionate with it and consequent upon it, seems to be identical in physics and metaphysics. It is not more true, in the former, that a large body is with more difficulty set in motion than a smaller one, and that its subsequent impetus is commensurate with this difficulty, than it is, in the latter, that intellects of the vaster capacity, while more forcible, more constant, and more extensive in their movements than those of inferior grade, are yet the less readily moved, and are more embarrassed and more full of hesitation in the first few steps of their progress. While, therefore, it is not impossible, as we have just said, that some slight mental aberration might have given rise to the hesitancy and indefinitiveness of purpose which are so very perceptible in the first pages of the volume before us, we are still the more willing to believe these defects the result of the moral fact just stated, since we find the work itself of an unusual order of excellence, even when regarded as the production of the author of "Nicholas Nickleby." That the evils we complain of are not, and were not, fully perceived by Mr. Dickens himself, cannot be supposed for a moment. Had his book been published in the old way, we should have seen no traces of them whatever.

The design of the general work, "Humphrey's Clock," is simply the common-place one of putting various tales into the mouths of a social party. The meetings are held at the house of Master Humphrey—an antique building in London, where an old-fashioned clock-case is the place of deposit for the M.S.S. Why such designs have become common is obvious. One half the pleasure experienced at a theatre arises from the spectator's sympathy with the rest of the audience, and, especially, from his belief in their sympathy with him. The eccentric gentleman who not long ago, at the Park, found himself the solitary occupant of box, pit, and gallery, would have derived but little enjoyment from his visit, had he been suffered to remain. It was an act of mercy to turn him out. The present absurd rage for lecturing is founded in the feeling in question. Essays which we would not be hired to read— so trite is their subject—so feeble is their execution—so much easier is it to get better information on similar themes out of any Encyclopædia in Christendom—we are brought to tolerate, and alas, even to applaud in their tenth and twentieth repetition, through the sole force of our sympathy with the throng. In the same way we listen to a story with greater zest when there are others present at its narration beside ourselves. Aware of this, authors without due reflection have repeatedly attempted, by supposing a circle of listeners, to imbue their narratives with the interest of sympathy. At a cursory glance the idea seems plausible enough. But, in the one case, there is an actual, personal, and palpable sympathy, conveyed in looks, gestures and brief comments—a sympathy of real individuals, all with the matters discussed to be sure, but then especially, *each with each*. In the other instance, we, alone in our closet, are required to sympathise *with* the sympathy of fictitious listeners, who, so far from being present in body, are often studiously kept out of sight and out of mind for two or three hundred pages at a time. This is sympathy double-diluted—the shadow of a shade. It is unnecessary to say that the design invariably fails of its effect.

In his preface to the present volume, Mr. Dickens seems to feel the necessity for an apology in regard to certain portions of his commencement, without seeing clearly what apology he should make, or for what precise thing he should apologise. He makes an effort to get over the difficulty, by saying something about its never being "his intention to have the members of 'Master Humphrey's Clock' active agents in the stories they relate," and about his "picturing to himself the various sensations of his hearers—thinking how Jack Redburn might incline to poor Kit—how the deaf gentleman would have his favorite, and Mr. Miles his," &c. &c.—but we are quite sure that all this is as pure a fiction as "The Curiosity Shop" itself. Our author is deceived. Occupied with little Nell and her grandfather, he had forgotten the very existence of his interlocutors until he found himself, at the end of his book, under the disagreeable necessity of saying a word or two concerning them, by way of winding them up. The simple truth is that, either for one of the two reasons at which we have already hinted, or else because the work was begun in a hurry, Mr. Dickens did not precisely know his own plans when he penned the five or six first chapters of the "Clock."

The wish to preserve a certain degree of unity between various narratives naturally unconnected, is a more obvious and a better reason for employing interlocutors. But such unity as may be thus had is scarcely worth having. It may, in some feeble measure, satisfy the judgment by a sense of completeness; but it seldom produces a pleasant effect; and if the speakers are made to take part in their own stories (as has been the case here) they become injurious by creating confusion. Thus, in "The Curiosity Shop," we feel displeased to find Master Humphrey commencing the tale in the first person, dropping this for the third, and concluding by introducing himself as the "single gentleman" who figures in the story. In spite of all the subsequent explanation we are forced to look upon him as two. All is confusion, and what makes it worse, is that Master Humphrey is painted as a lean and sober personage, while his second self is a fat, bluff and boisterous old bachelor.

Yet the species of connexion in question, besides preserving the unity desired, *may* be made, if well managed, a source of consistent and agreeable interest. It has been so made by Thomas Moore—the most skilful literary artist of his day—perhaps of any day—a man who stands in the singular and really wonderful predicament of being undervalued on account of the profusion with which he has scattered about him his good things. The brilliancies on any one page of Lalla Rookh would have sufficed to establish that very reputation which has been in a great measure self-dimmed by the galaxied lustre of the entire book. It seems that the horrid laws of political economy cannot be evaded even by the inspired, and that a perfect versification, a vigorous style, and a never-tiring fancy, may, like the water we drink and die without, yet despise, be so plentifully set forth as to be absolutely of no value at all.

By far the greater portion of the volume now published, is

occupied with the tale of "The Curiosity Shop," narrated by Master Humphrey himself. The other stories are brief. The "Giant Chronicles" is the title of what appears to be meant for a series within a series, and we think this design doubly objectionable. The narrative of "The Bowyer," as well as of "John Podgers," is not altogether worthy of Mr. Dickens. They were probably sent to press to supply a demand for copy, while he was occupied with the "Curiosity Shop." But the "Confession Found in a Prison in the Time of Charles the Second" is a paper of remarkable power, truly original in conception, and worked out with great ability.

The story of "The Curiosity Shop" is very simple. Two brothers of England, warmly attached to each other, love the same lady, without each other's knowledge. The younger at length discovers the elder's secret, and, sacrificing himself to fraternal affection, quits the country and resides for many years in a foreign land, where he amasses great wealth. Meantime his brother marries the lady, who soon dies, leaving an infant daughter—her perfect resemblance. In the widower's heart the mother lives again through the child. This latter grows up, marries unhappily, has a son and a daughter, loses her husband, and dies herself shortly afterward. The grandfather takes the orphans to his home. The boy spurns his protection, falls into bad courses, and becomes an outcast. The girl—in whom a third time lives the object of the old man's early choice—dwells with him alone, and is loved by him with a most doting affection. He has now become poor, and at length is reduced to keeping a shop for antiquities and curiosities. Finally, through his dread of involving the child in want, his mind becomes weakened. He thinks to redeem his fortune by gambling, borrows money for this purpose of a dwarf, who, at length, discovering the true state of the old man's affairs, seizes his furniture and turns him out of doors. The girl and himself set out, without farther object than to relieve themselves of the sight of the hated city, upon a weary pilgrimage, whose events form the basis or body of the tale. In fine, just as a peaceful retirement is secured for them, the child, wasted with fatigue and anxiety, dies. The grandfather, through grief, immediately follows her to the tomb. The younger brother, meantime, has received information of the old man's poverty, hastens to England, and arrives only in time to be at the closing scene of the tragedy.

This plot is the best which could have been constructed for the main object of the narrative. This object is the depicting of a fervent and dreamy love for the child on the part of the grandfather—such a love as would induce devotion to himself on the part of the orphan. We have thus the conception of a childhood, educated in utter ignorance of the world, filled with an affection which has been, through its brief existence, the sole source of its pleasures, and which has no part in the passion of a more mature youth for an object of its own age—we have the idea of this childhood, full of ardent hopes, leading by the hand, forth from the heated and wearying city, into the green fields, to seek for bread, the decrepid imbecillity of a doting and confiding old age, whose stern knowledge of man, and of the world it leaves behind, is now merged in the sole consciousness of receiving love and protection from that weakness it has loved and protected.

This conception is indeed most beautiful. It is simply and severely grand. The more fully we survey it, the more thoroughly are we convinced of the lofty character of that genius which gave it birth. That in its present simplicity of form, however, it was first entertained by Mr. Dickens, may well be doubted. That it was *not*, we are assured by the title which the tale bears. When in its commencement he called it "The Old Curiosity Shop," his design was far different from what we see it in its completion. It is evident that had he now to name the story he would not so term it; for the shop itself is a thing of an altogether collateral interest, and is spoken of merely in the beginning. This is only one among a hundred instances of the disadvantage under which the periodical novelist labors. When his work is done, he never fails to observe a thousand defects which he might have remedied, and a thousand alterations, in regard to the book as a whole, which might be made to its manifest improvement.

But if the conception of this story deserves praise, its execution is beyond all—and here the subject naturally leads us from the generalisation which is the proper province of the critic, into details among which it is scarcely fitting that he should venture.

The Art of Mr. Dickens, although elaborate and great, seems only a happy modification of Nature. In this respect he differs remarkably from the author of "Night and Morning." The latter, by excessive care and by patient reflection, aided by much rhetorical knowledge, and general information, has arrived at the capability of producing books which might be mistaken by ninety-nine readers out of a hundred for the genuine inspirations of genius. The former, by the promptings of the truest genius itself, has been brought to compose, and evidently without effort, works which have effected a long-sought consummation—which have rendered him the idol of the people, while defying and enchanting the critics. Mr. Bulwer, through art, has almost created a genius. Mr. Dickens, through genius, has perfected a standard from which Art itself will derive its essence, in rules.

When we speak in this manner of the "Old Curiosity Shop," we speak with entire deliberation, and know quite well what it is we assert. We do not mean to say that it is perfect, as a whole—this could not well have been the case under the circumstances of its composition. But we know that, in all the higher elements which go to make up literary greatness, it is supremely excellent. We think, for instance, that the introduction of Nelly's brother (and here we address those who have read the work) is supererogatory—that the character of Quilp would have been more in keeping had he been confined to petty and grotesque acts of malice—that his death should have been made the *immediate* consequence of his attempt at revenge upon Kit; and that after matters had been put fairly in train for this poetical justice, he should not have perished by an accident inconsequential upon his villany. We think, too, that there is an air of *ultra*-accident in the finally discovered relationship between Kit's master and the bachelor of the old church—that the sneering politeness put into the mouth of Quilp, with his manner of commencing a question which he wishes answered in the affirmative, with an affirmative interrogatory, instead of the ordinary negative one—are fashions borrowed from the author's own Fagin—that he has repeated himself in many other instances—that the practical tricks and love of mischief of the dwarf's boy are too nearly consonant with the traits of the master—that so much of the propensities of Swiveller as relate to his inapposite appropriation of odds and ends of verse, is stolen from the generic loafer of our fellow-townsman, Neal—and that the writer has suffered the overflowing kindness of his own bosom to mislead him in a very important point of art, when he endows so many of his *dramatis personæ* with a warmth of feeling so very rare in reality. Above all, we acknowledge that the death of Nelly is excessively painful—that it leaves a most distressing oppression of spirit upon the reader—and should, therefore, have been avoided.

But when we come to speak of the excellences of the tale these defects appear really insignificant. It embodies more *originality* in every point, but in character especially, than any single work within our knowledge. There is the grand-father—a truly profound conception; the gentle and lovely Nelly—we have discoursed of her before; Quilp, with mouth like that of the panting dog—(a bold idea which the engraver has neglected to embody) with his hilarious antics, his cowardice, and his very petty and spoilt-child-like malevolence; Dick Swiveller, that prince of good-hearted, good-for-nothing, lazy, luxurious, poetical, brave, romantically generous, gallant, affectionate, and not over-and-above honest, "glorious Apollos;" the marchioness, his bride; Tom Codlin and his partner; Miss Sally Brass, that "fine fellow;" the pony that had an opinion of its own; the boy that stood upon his head; the sexton; the man at the forge; not forgetting the dancing dogs and baby Nubbles. There are other admirably drawn characters—but we note these for their remarkable originality, as well as for their wonderful keeping, and the glowing colors in which they are painted. We have heard some of them called caricatures—but the charge is grossly ill-founded. No critical principle is more firmly based in reason than that a certain amount of exaggeration is essential to the proper depicting of truth itself. We do not paint an object to be true, but to appear true to the beholder. Were we to copy nature with accuracy the object copied would seem unnatural. The columns of the Greek temples, which convey the idea of absolute proportion, are very considerably thicker just beneath the capital than at the base. We regret that we have not left ourselves space in which to examine this whole question as it deserves. We must content ourselves with saying that caricature seldom exists (unless in so gross a form as to disgust at once) where the component parts are *in keeping*; and that the laugh excited by it, in any case, is radically distinct from that induced by a properly artistical *incongruity*—the source of all mirth. Were these creations of Mr. Dickens' really caricatures they would not live in public estimation beyond the hour of their first survey. We regard them as *creations*—(that is to say as original combinations of character) only not all of the highest order, because the elements employed are not always of the highest. In the instances of Nelly, the grandfather, the Sexton, and the man of the furnace, the force of the creative intellect could scarcely have been engaged with nobler material, and the result is that these personages belong to the most august regions of the *Ideal*.

In truth, the great feature of the "Curiosity Shop" is its chaste, vigorous, and glorious *imagination*. This is the one charm, all potent, which alone would suffice to compensate for a world more of error than Mr. Dickens ever committed. It is not only seen in the conception, and general handling of the story, or in the invention of character; but it pervades every sentence of the book. We recognise its prodigious influence in every inspired word. It is this which induces the reader who is at all ideal, to pause frequently, to re-read the occasionally quaint phrases, to muse in uncontrollable delight over thoughts which, while he wonders he has never hit upon them before, he yet admits that he never has encountered. In fact it is the wand of the enchanter.

Had we room to particularise, we would mention as points evincing most distinctly the ideality of the "Curiosity Shop"—the picture of the shop itself—the newly-born desire of the worldly old man for the peace of green fields—his whole character and conduct, in short—the schoolmaster, with his desolate fortunes, seeking affection in little children—the haunts of Quilp among the wharf-rats—the tinkering of the Punch-men among the tombs—the glorious scene where the man of the forge sits poring, at deep midnight, into that dread fire—again the whole conception of this character; and, last and greatest, the stealthy approach of Nell to her death—her gradual sinking away on the journey to the village, so skilfully indicated rather than described—her pensive and prescient meditation—the fit of strange musing which came over her when the house *in which she was to die* first broke upon her sight—the description of this house, of the old church, and of the church-yard—every thing in rigid consonance with the one impression to be conveyed—that deep meaningless well—the comments of the Sexton upon death, and upon his own secure life—this whole world of mournful yet peaceful idea merging, at length, into the decease of the child Nelly, and the uncomprehending despair of the grandfather. These concluding scenes are so drawn that human language, urged by human thought, could go no farther in the excitement of human feelings. And the pathos is of that best order which is relieved, in great measure, by ideality. Here the book has never been equalled,—never approached except in one instance, and that is in the case of the "Undine" of De La Motte Fouqué. The imagination is perhaps as great in this latter work, but the pathos, although truly beautiful and deep, fails of much of its effect through the material from which it is wrought. The chief character, being endowed with purely fanciful attributes, cannot command our full sympathies, as can a simple denizen of earth. In saying, a page or so above, that the death of the child left too painful an impression, and should therefore have been avoided, we must, of course, be understood as referring to the work as a whole, and in respect to its general appreciation and popularity. The death, as recorded, is, we repeat, of the highest order of literary excellence—yet while none can deny this fact, there are few who will be willing to read the concluding passages a second time.

Upon the whole we think the "Curiosity Shop" very much the best of the works of Mr. Dickens. It is scarcely possible to speak of it too well. It is in all respects a tale which will secure for its author the enthusiastic admiration of every man of genius.

The edition before us is handsomely printed, on excellent paper. The designs by Cattermole and Browne are many of them excellent—some of them outrageously bad. Of course it is difficult for us to say how far the American engraver is in fault. In conclusion, we must enter our solemn protest against the final page full of little angels in smock frocks, or dimity chemises.

Graham's Magazine, May 1841

Barnaby Rudge. By "Boz." Author of "Nicholas Nickleby," "Oliver Twist," &c. With Illustrations by G. Cattermole and H. K. Browne. Nos. 1, 2 and 3. Philadelphia: Lea & Blanchard.

WE PRESUME our readers all know that "Barnaby Rudge," now "in course of publication" periodically, is a story supposed to be narrated by one of the members of Master Humphrey's society; and is in fact a continuation of the "Clock," although complete within itself. From the concluding words of "The Curiosity Shop"—or rather of the volume which contained that tale—we gather that the present narrative will be occupied with matters tending to develope the spirit, or, in the language of Mr. Dickens himself, the *"heart"* of the mighty London, toward the conclusion of the eighteenth century. This thesis affords the most ample scope for the great powers of the writer. His opening chapters assure us that he has at length discovered the secret of his true strength, and that "Barnaby Rudge" will appeal principally to the *imagination*. Of this faculty we have many striking instances in the few numbers already issued. We see it where the belfry man in the lonely church at midnight, about to toll the "passing-bell," is struck with horror at hearing the solitary note of another, and awaits, aghast, a repetition of the sound. We recognise it more fully where this single note is discovered, in the morning, to have been that of an alarm pulled by the hand of one in the death-struggle with a murderer:—also in the expression of countenance which is so strikingly attributed to Mrs. Rudge—"the capacity for expressing terror"—something only dimly seen, but never absent for a moment—"the shadow of some look to which an instant of intense and most unutterable horror only could have given rise." This is a conception admirably adapted to whet curiosity in respect to the character of that event which is hinted at as forming the ground-work of the novel; and so far is well suited to the purposes of a periodical story. But this observation should not fail to be made—that the anticipation must surpass the reality; that no matter how terrific be the circumstances which, in the *dénouement*, shall appear to have occasioned the expression of countenance worn habitually by Mrs. Rudge, still they will not be able to satisfy the mind of the reader. He will surely be disappointed. The skilful intimation of horror held out by the artist produces an effect which will deprive his conclusion, of all. These intimations—these dark hints of some uncertain evil—are often rhetorically praised as effective—but are only justly so praised where there is *no dénouement* whatever—where the reader's imagination is left to clear up the mystery for itself—and this, we suppose, is not the design of Mr. Dickens.

But the chief points in which the ideality of this story is apparent are the creation of the hero Barnaby Rudge, and the commingling with his character, as accessory, that of the human-looking raven. Barnaby we regard as an original idea altogether, so far as novel-writing is concerned. He is peculiar, inasmuch as he is an idiot endowed with the fantastic qualities of the madman, and has been born possessed with a maniacal horror of blood—the result of some terrible spectacle seen by his mother during pregnancy. The design of Mr. Dickens is here two-fold—first that of increasing our anticipation in regard to the deed committed—exaggerating our impression of its atrocity—and, secondly, that of causing this horror of blood on the part of the idiot, to bring about, in consistence with poetical justice, the condemnation of the murderer:—for it is a murder that has been committed. We say in accordance with poetical justice—and, in fact, it will be seen hereafter that Barnaby, the idiot, is the murderer's own son. The horror of blood which he feels is the mediate result of the atrocity, since this atrocity it was which impressed the imagination of the pregnant mother; and poetical justice will therefore be well fulfilled when this horror shall urge on the son to the conviction of the father in the perpetrator of the deed. That Barnaby is the son of the murderer may not appear evident to our readers—but we will explain. The person murdered is Mr. Reuben Haredale. He was found assassinated in his bed-chamber. His steward, (Mr. Rudge, senior,) and his gardener (name not mentioned) are missing. At first both are suspected. "Some months afterward," here, we use the words of the story—"the steward's body, scarcely to be recognised but by his clothes, and the watch and ring he wore—was found at the bottom of a piece of water in the grounds, with a deep gash in the breast where he had been stabbed by a knife. He was only partly dressed; and all people agreed that he had been sitting up reading in his own room, where there were many traces of blood, and was suddenly fallen upon and killed, before his master."

Now, be it observed, it is not the author himself who asserts that *the steward's body was found*; he has put the words in the mouth of one of his characters. His design is to make it appear, in the *dénouement*, that the steward, Rudge, first murdered the gardener, then went to his master's chamber, murdered *him*, was interrupted by his (Rudge's) wife, whom he seized and held *by the wrist*, to prevent her giving the alarm—that he then, after possessing himself of the booty desired, returned to the gardener's room, exchanged clothes with him, put upon the corpse his own watch and rings, and secreted it where it was afterwards discovered at so late a period that the features could not be identified. It will appear that Rudge himself, through his wife, gave indication to the police, after due time had elapsed, of the proper spot to be searched—so that when the decomposed body was found, it might be regarded as his own. We say that Rudge, in perpetrating the murder, seized his wife *by the wrist*; and we draw this inference from the fact that Barnaby is said to have upon his wrist the appearance of a smear of blood.

The ruffian who, at the Maypole, listens so attentively to the story told by Solomon Daisy, and who subsequently forces himself into Mrs. Rudge's house, holding with her so mysterious a connexion,—this ruffian is Rudge himself, the murderer. Twenty-two years having elapsed, he has ventured to return. To bring about the conviction of the assassin, after the lapse of so very long a time, through his son's mysterious *awe of blood—an awe created in the unborn by the assassination itself*—is most probably, we repeat, the design of Mr. Dickens, and is, no doubt, one of the finest possible embodiments

of the idea we are accustomed to attach to "poetical justice."
Joe, John Willet's son, who has received a blow from Rudge,
will be made to supply in the idiot, the want of precision of
thought—a precision without which there would be some
difficulty in working out the catastrophe: but the main agency
in the conviction will be that of the hero, Barnaby Rudge.

The elder Rudge himself has probably been only a tool in
the hands of Geoffrey Haredale, the brother of the murdered
man, and the present incumbent of the Warren estate, which
he has inherited upon Reuben's decease. This idea is corrob-
orated by the fact that, the families of Chester and Haredale
being at variance, an attempt is made by Rudge upon the life
of young Chester, who is in love with Miss Haredale, the
daughter of Reuben. She resides at the Warren; is no doubt
the ward of her uncle; her fortune is in his possession, and
that he may not have to part with it, especially to the son of
his enemy, he is anxious to get the young man out of the way.

We may as well here observe that the reader should note
carefully the ravings of Barnaby, which are not put into his
mouth at random, as might be supposed, but are intended to
convey indistinct glimmerings of the events to be evolved,—
and in this evident design of Mr. Dickens' his ideality is
strongly evinced. It would be difficult to impress upon the
mind of a merely general reader how vast a degree of interest
may be given to the story by such means; for in truth that
interest, great as it may be made, will not be, strictly speaking, of a popular cast.

But an example will be necessary to convey our meaning
fully upon this head, and one may be found at page 54, where
the idiot draws Mr. Chester to the window, and directs his
attention to the clothes hanging upon the lines in the yard.

"Look down," he said softly; "do you mark how they whisper in each other's ears, then dance and leap to make believe
they are in sport? Do you see how they stop for a moment,
when they think there is no one looking, and mutter among
themselves again; and then how they roll and gambol, delighted with the mischief they've been plotting? Look at 'em
now! See how they whirl and plunge. And now they stop
again, and whisper cautiously together—little thinking,
mind, how often I have laid upon the ground and watched

them. I say—what is it that they plot and hatch? Do you know?"

Now these incoherences are regarded by Mr. Chester simply as such, and no attention is paid them; but they have reference, *indistinctly*, to the counsellings together of Rudge and Geoffrey Haredale, upon the topic of the bloody deeds committed; which counsellings have been watched by the idiot. In the same manner almost every word spoken by him will be found to have an under current of meaning, by paying strict attention to which the enjoyment of the imaginative reader will be infinitely heightened.

A confirmation of our idea in regard to the perpetrators of the murder, will be seen in the words of Mrs. Rudge addressed to the locksmith, when the latter attempted to prevent the egress of the ruffian from her house. "Come back, come back!" she exclaimed—"do not touch him on your life. I charge you come back. He carries other lives besides his own!"—meaning that, if arrested and recognised, Rudge would involve in his fate not only Geoffrey Haredale, but herself, as an accessary after the fact.

The young Chester, it will be remembered, when found lying wounded in the road by the locksmith and Barnaby, was taken, as if by accident, to the house of Mrs. Rudge. Upon this circumstance will be made to turn some of the most exciting incidents of the story. Many difficulties, we apprehend, will occur before the sick man makes his escape from this house—in which, for several reasons, we are inclined to think that much of the main action of the drama is to come to pass. These reasons are, that it is the home of the murderer Rudge, of Mrs. Rudge so emphatically described, and especially of Barnaby, the hero, and of his raven, whose croakings are to be frequently, appropriately, and prophetically heard in the coarse of the narrative, and whose whole character will perform, in regard to that of the idiot, much the same part as does, in music, the accompaniment in respect to the air. Each is distinct. Each differs remarkably from the other. Yet between them there is a strong analogical resemblance; and, although each may exist apart, they form together a whole which would be imperfect, wanting either. This is clearly the design of Mr. Dickens—although he himself may not at present perceive it. In fact, beautiful as it is, and strikingly original with him, it cannot be questioned that he has been led to it less by artistical knowledge and reflection, than by that intuitive feeling for the forcible and the true, which is the *sixth sense* of the man of genius.

Of the other characters introduced we must be content to speak *in petto*. The locksmith, and his wife, are drawn with that boldness and vigor in which our author is never deficient; but, as far as we yet comprehend them, have nothing distinctive. Miss Miggs, Simon Tappertit, and his society of 'Prentice Knights, cannot be properly called caricatures—for there is a well-sustained exaggeration of all their traits, which has the effect of *keeping*—but they are obviously burlesques. For this reason, we feel sure that they will have no very active agency in the plot. They will form an amusing by-play— much as Swiveller and the Marchioness do in "The Curiosity Shop." Hugh, on the contrary, who is carefully, and truthfully drawn, with no very decided peculiarities as yet appearing—Hugh will be a main instrument in the action. Of Joe Willet we have already spoken. John is an attempt at character for its own sake solely. He is an original, in the sense that, while really existing in nature, he has never as yet been depicted—and such originals are very rare indeed. The features of the ruffian, Rudge, are not yet developed; neither are those of the young Chester, nor of the locksmith's daughter. The manner in which the portraiture of the very gentlemanly and self-composed elder Chester is elaborated, assures us that here we are to look for one of the best efforts of the author.

The *designs* are, for the most part, utterly unworthy the narrative, and, very often, are not even in accordance with it. The thoughts of the writer are sometimes not conveyed at all. The hostelry upon the first page, for instance, is far from Mr. Dickens' conception, and gives the idea of a portion of a street, rather than of an insulated and sequestered inn. In the interior of the tap-room, the figures are all crowded into close juxta-position, while the text places Rudge and the young Chester in situations secluded from the rest of the company. The third design, where Rudge strikes Joe Willet, is well enough executed, but has no force of subject in itself—and we can only regard it as good, when we take a prospective view, and consider that the blow given will have important results. In the fourth plate, where the young Chester is found wounded, there is great vigor of conception. The *abandon* of the prostrate figure is richly ideal; and the author's intention in Barnaby Rudge fully made out. Plate fourth is good—Tappertit, the locksmith and his daughter, are all finely portrayed. Plate the fifth, introducing Tappertit solus, and plate the sixth, where Barnaby plays at thread-puzzles in the sick room, are also sufficiently well done; although, in the latter, the form and character of the locksmith undergo an inexcusable alteration. The tail-piece at the end of the second number, (with the exception of the countenance of the dreaming Barnaby,) is extravagant and ineffective—fully embodying our notion of the *false ideal*. The meeting of the 'Prentice Knights is unworthy of notice. Miss Miggs *sola* is fine, and the expression of her countenance, as described in the text, (a mixture of mischief, cunning, malice, triumph, and patient expectation,) is singularly well embodied. Mr. Chester, Senior, seated by the fire in the large room of the inn, forms the subject of a forcibly conceived picture. The figure of Hugh, in the concluding design of the third number, is true to the description of the author, except in the matter of position. In the plate he sits nearly erect; in the text he reclines. Upon the whole, it is much to be lamented that competent artists cannot be found for the embellishment of a work so rich in material as is "Barnaby Rudge." At all events it is much to be regretted that books such as those of Mr. Dickens—books which have formed an era in the reading of every man of genius—should be thought less worthy of adequate illustration than the wofully inferior compositions which are so popular under the titles of "Confessions of Harry Lorrequer," and "Adventures of Charles O'Malley."

Saturday Evening Post, May 1, 1841

Barnaby Rudge; By Charles Dickens, (Boz) Author of "The Old Curiosity-Shop," "Pickwick," "Oliver Twist," etc. etc. With numerous Illustrations, by Cattermole, Browne & Sibson. Lea & Blanchard: Philadelphia.

WE OFTEN HEAR IT SAID, of this or of that proposition, that it may be good in theory, but will not answer in practice; and in such assertions we find the substance of all the sneers at Critical Art which so gracefully curl the upper lips of a tribe which is beneath it. We mean the small geniuses—the literary Titmice—animalculae which judge of merit solely by *result*, and boast of the solidity, tangibility and infallibility of the test which they employ. The worth of a work is most accurately estimated, they assure us, by the number of those who peruse it; and "does a book sell?" is a query embodying, in their opinion, all that need be said or sung on the topic of its fitness for sale. We should as soon think of maintaining, in the presence of these creatures, the *dictum* of Anaxagoras, that snow is black, as of disputing, for example, the profundity of that genius which, in a run of five hundred nights, has rendered itself evident in "London Assurance." "What," cry they, "are critical precepts to us, or to anybody? Were we to observe all the critical rules in creation we should still be unable to write a good book"—a point, by the way, which we shall not now pause to deny. "Give us *results*," they vociferate, "for we are plain men of common sense. We contend for fact instead of fancy—for practice in opposition to theory."

The mistake into which the Titmice have been innocently led, however, is precisely that of dividing the practice which they would uphold, from the theory to which they would object. They should have been told in infancy, and thus prevented from exposing themselves in old age, that theory and practice are in so much *one*, that the former implies or includes the latter. A theory is only good as such, in proportion to its reducibility to practice. If the practice fail, it is because the theory is imperfect. To say what they are in the daily habit of saying—that such or such a matter may be good in theory but is false in practice,—is to perpetrate a bull—to commit a paradox—to state a contradiction in terms—in plain words, to tell a lie *which is a lie at sight* to the understanding of anything bigger than a Titmouse.

But we have no idea, just now, of persecuting the Tittlebats by too close a scrutiny into their little opinions. It is not our purpose, for example, to press them with so grave a weapon as the *argumentum ad absurdum*, or to ask them why, if the popularity of a book be in fact the measure of its worth, we should not be at once in condition to admit the inferiority of

"Newton's Principia" to "Hoyle's Games;" of "Ernest Maltravers" to "Jack-the-Giant-Killer," or "Jack Sheppard," or
"Jack Brag;" and of "Dick's Christian Philosopher" to "Charlotte Temple," or the "Memoirs of de Grammont," or to one
or two dozen other works which must be nameless. Our present design is but to speak, at some length, of a book which
in so much concerns the Titmice, that it affords them the very
kind of demonstration which they chiefly affect—*practical*
demonstration—of the fallacy of one of their favorite dogmas; we mean the dogma that no work of fiction can fully
suit, at the same time, the critical and the popular taste; in
fact, that the disregarding or contravening of Critical Rule is
absolutely essential to success, beyond a certain and very limited extent, with the public at large. And if, in the course of
our random observations—for we have no space for systematic review—it should appear, incidentally, that the vast
popularity of "Barnaby Rudge" must be regarded less as the
measure of its value, than as the legitimate and inevitable result of certain well-understood critical propositions reduced
by genius into practice, there will appear nothing more than
what has before become apparent in the "Vicar of Wakefield"
of Goldsmith, or in the "Robinson Crusoe" of De Foe—
nothing more, in fact, than what is a truism to all but the
Titmice.

Those who know us will not, from what is here premised,
suppose it our intention, to enter into any wholesale *laudation* of "Barnaby Rudge." In truth, our design may appear, at
a cursory glance, to be very different indeed. Boccalini, in his
"Advertisements from Parnassus," tells us that a critic once
presented Apollo with a severe censure upon an excellent
poem. The God asked him for the beauties of the work. He
replied that he only troubled himself about the errors. Apollo
presented him with a sack of unwinnowed wheat, and bade
him pick out all the chaff for his pains. Now we have not
fully made up our minds that the God was in the right. We
are not sure that the limit of critical duty is not very generally
misapprehended. *Excellence* may be considered an axiom, or a
proposition which becomes self-evident just in proportion to
the clearness or precision with which it is *put*. If it fairly exists, in this sense, it requires no farther elucidation. It is not

excellence if it need to be demonstrated as such. To point out too particularly the beauties of a work, is to admit, tacitly, that these beauties are not wholly admirable. Regarding, then, excellence as that which is capable of self-manifestation, it but remains for the critic to show when, where, and how it fails in becoming manifest; and, in this showing, it will be the fault of the book itself if what of beauty it contains be not, at least, placed in the fairest light. In a word, we may assume, notwithstanding a vast deal of pitiable cant upon this topic, that in pointing out frankly the errors of a work, we do nearly all that is critically necessary in displaying its merits. In teaching what perfection *is*, how, in fact, shall we more rationally proceed than in specifying what it *is not*?

The plot of "Barnaby Rudge" runs thus: About a hundred years ago, Geoffrey Haredale and John Chester were school-mates in England—the former being the scape-goat and drudge of the latter. Leaving school, the boys become friends, with much of the old understanding. Haredale loves; Chester deprives him of his mistress. The one cherishes the most deadly hatred; the other merely contemns and avoids. By routes widely different both attain mature age. Haredale, re-membering his old love, and still cherishing his old hatred, remains a bachelor and is poor. Chester, among other crimes, is guilty of the seduction and heartless abandonment of a gypsy-girl, who, after the desertion of her lover, gives birth to a son, and, falling into evil courses, is finally hung at Ty-burn. The son is received and taken charge of, at an inn called the Maypole, upon the borders of Epping forest, and about twelve miles from London. This inn is kept by one John Wil-let, a burley-headed and very obtuse little man, who has a son, Joe, and who employs his *protégé*, under the single name of Hugh, as perpetual hostler at the inn. Hugh's father mar-ries, in the meantime, a rich *parvenue*, who soon dies, but not before having presented Mr. Chester with a boy, Edward. The father, (a thoroughly selfish man-of-the-world, whose model is Chesterfield,) educates this son at a distance, seeing him rarely, and calling him to the paternal residence, at Lon-don, only when he has attained the age of twenty-four or five. He, the father, has, long ere this time, spent the fortune brought him by his wife, having been living upon his wits

and a small annuity for some eighteen years. The son is recalled chiefly that by marrying an heiress, on the strength of
his own personal merit and the reputed wealth of old Chester,
he may enable the latter to continue his gayeties in old age.
But of this design, as well as of his poverty, Edward is kept
in ignorance for some three or four years after his recall;
when the father's discovery of what he considers an inexpedient love-entanglement on the part of the son, induces him
to disclose the true state of his affairs, as well as the real tenor
of his intentions.

Now the love-entanglement of which we speak, is considered inexpedient by Mr. Chester for two reasons—the first of
which is, that the lady beloved is the orphan niece of his old
enemy, Haredale, and the second is, that Haredale (although
in circumstances which have been much and very unexpectedly improved during the preceding twenty-two years) is still
insufficiently wealthy to meet the views of Mr. Chester.

We say that, about twenty-two years before the period in
question, there came an unlooked-for change in the worldly
circumstances of Haredale. This gentleman has an elder
brother, Reuben, who has long possessed the family inheritance of the Haredales, residing at a mansion called "The
Warren," not far from the Maypole-Inn, which is itself a portion of the estate. Reuben *is a widower*, with one child, a
daughter, Emma. Besides this daughter, there are living with
him a gardener, a steward (whose name is Rudge) and *two*
women servants, one of whom is the wife of Rudge. On the
night of the nineteenth of March, 1733, Rudge murders his
master for the sake of a large sum of money which he is
known to have in possession. During the struggle, Mr. Haredale grasps the cord of an alarm-bell which hangs within his
reach, but succeeds in sounding it only once or twice, when
it is severed by the knife of the ruffian, who then, completing
his bloody business, and securing the money, proceeds to quit
the chamber. While doing this, however, he is disconcerted
by meeting the gardener, whose pallid countenance evinces
suspicion of the deed committed. The murderer is thus forced
to kill his fellow servant. Having done so, the idea strikes him
of transferring the burden of the crime from himself. He
dresses the corpse of the gardener in his own clothes, puts

upon its finger his own ring and in its pocket his own watch—then drags it to a pond in the grounds, and throws it in. He now returns to the house, and, disclosing all to his wife, requests her to become a partner in his flight. Horror-stricken, she falls to the ground. He attempts to raise her. She seizes his wrist, *staining her hand with blood in the attempt.* She renounces him forever, yet promises to conceal the crime. Alone, he flees the country. The next morning, Mr. Haredale being found murdered, and the steward and gardener being both missing, both are suspected. Mrs. Rudge leaves The Warren, and retires to an obscure lodging in London (where she lives upon an annuity allowed her by Haredale) having given birth, *on the very day after the murder*, to a son, Barnaby Rudge, who proves an idiot, who bears upon his wrist a red mark, and who is born possessed with a maniacal horror of blood.

Some months since the assassination having elapsed, what appears to be the corpse of Rudge is discovered, and the outrage is attributed to the gardener. Yet not universally:—for, as Geoffrey Haredale comes into possession of the estate, there are not wanting suspicions (fomented by Chester) of his own participation in the deed. This taint of suspicion, acting upon his hereditary gloom, together with the natural grief and horror of the atrocity, embitters the whole life of Haredale. He secludes himself at The Warren, and acquires a monomaniac acerbity of temper relieved only by love of his beautiful niece.

Time wears away. Twenty-two years pass by. The niece has ripened into womanhood, and loves young Chester without the knowledge of her uncle or the youth's father. Hugh has grown a stalwart man—the type of man *the animal*, as his father is of man the ultra-civilized. Rudge, the murderer, returns, urged to his undoing by Fate. He appears at the Maypole and inquires stealthily of the circumstances which have occurred at The Warren in his absence. He proceeds to London, discovers the dwelling of his wife, threatens her with the betrayal of her idiot son into vice and extorts from her the bounty of Haredale. Revolting at such appropriation of such means, the widow, with Barnaby, again seeks The Warren, renounces the annuity, and, refusing to assign any reason for her conduct, states her intention of quitting London forever, and of burying herself in some obscure retreat—a retreat which she begs Haredale not to attempt discovering. When he seeks her in London the next day, she is gone; and there are no tidings, either of herself or of Barnaby, *until the expiration of five years*—which bring the time up to that of the celebrated "No Popery" Riots of Lord George Gordon.

In the meanwhile, and immediately subsequent to the reappearance of Rudge; Haredale and the elder Chester, each heartily desirous of preventing the union of Edward and Emma, have entered into a covenant, the result of which is that, by means of treachery on the part of Chester, permitted on that of Haredale, the lovers misunderstand each other and are estranged. Joe, also, the son of the innkeeper, Willet, having been coquetted with, to too great an extent, by Dolly Varden, (the pretty daughter of one Gabriel Varden, a locksmith of Clerkenwell, London) and having been otherwise mal-treated at home, enlists in his Majesty's army and is carried beyond seas, to America; not returning until towards the close of the riots. Just before their commencement, Rudge, in a midnight prowl about the scene of his atrocity, is encountered by an individual who had been familiar with him in earlier life, while living at The Warren. This individual, terrified at what he supposes, very naturally, to be the ghost of the murdered Rudge, relates his adventure to his companions at the Maypole, and John Willet conveys the intelligence, forthwith, to Mr. Haredale. Connecting the apparition, in his own mind, with the peculiar conduct of Mrs. Rudge, this gentleman imbibes a suspicion, at once, of the true state of affairs. This suspicion (which he mentions to no one) is, moreover, very strongly confirmed by an occurrence happening to Varden, the locksmith, who, visiting the woman late one night, finds her in communion of a nature apparently most confidential, with a ruffian whom the locksmith knows to be such, without knowing the man himself. Upon an attempt, on the part of Varden, to seize this ruffian, he is thwarted by Mrs. R.; and upon Haredale's inquiring minutely into the personal appearance of the man, he is found to accord with Rudge. We have already shown that the ruffian was in fact Rudge himself. Acting upon the suspicion thus aroused, Haredale watches, by night, alone, in the deserted house formerly occupied by Mrs. R. in hope of here coming upon the murderer, and makes other exertions with the view of arresting him; but all in vain.

It is, also, at the conclusion *of the five years*, that the hitherto uninvaded retreat of Mrs. Rudge is disturbed by a message from her husband, demanding money. He has discovered her abode by accident. Giving him what she has at the time, she afterwards eludes him, and hastens, with Barnaby, to bury herself in the crowd of London, until she can find opportunity again to seek retreat in some more distant region of England. But the riots have now begun. The idiot is beguiled into joining the mob, and, becoming separated from his mother (who, growing ill through grief, is borne to a hospital) meets with his old playmate Hugh, and becomes with him a ringleader in the rebellion.

The riots proceed. A conspicuous part is borne in them by one Simon Tappertit, a fantastic and conceited little apprentice of Varden's, and a sworn enemy to Joe Willet, who has rivalled him in the affection of Dolly. A hangman, Dennis, is also very busy amid the mob. Lord George Gordon, and his secretary, Gashford, with John Grueby, his servant, appear, of course, upon the scene. Old Chester, who, during the five years, has become Sir John, instigates Gashford, who has received personal insult from Haredale, (a catholic and consequently obnoxious to the mob) instigates Gashford to procure the burning of The Warren, and to abduct Emma during the excitement ensuing. The mansion is burned, (Hugh, who also fancies himself wronged by Haredale, being chief actor in the outrage) and Miss H. carried off, in company with Dolly, who had long lived with her, and whom Tappertit abducts upon his own responsibility. Rudge, in the meantime, finding the eye of Haredale upon him, (since he has become aware of the watch kept nightly at his wife's,) goaded by the dread of solitude, and fancying that his sole chance of safety lies in joining the rioters, hurries upon their track to the doomed Warren. He arrives too late—the mob have departed. Skulking about the ruins, he is discovered by Haredale, and finally captured, without a struggle, within the glowing walls of the very chamber in which the deed was committed. He is conveyed to prison, where he meets and recognises Barnaby, who had been captured as a rioter. The mob assail and burn the jail. The father and son escape. Betrayed by Dennis, both are again retaken, and Hugh shares their fate. In Newgate, Dennis, through accident, discovers the parentage of Hugh, and an effort is made in vain to interest Chester in behalf of his son. Finally, Varden procures the pardon of Barnaby; but Hugh, Rudge and Dennis are hung. At the eleventh hour, Joe returns from abroad with one arm. In company with Edward Chester, he performs prodigies of valor (during the last riots) on behalf of the government. The two, with Haredale and Varden, rescue Emma and Dolly. A double marriage, of course, takes place; for Dolly has repented her fine airs, and the prejudices of Haredale are overcome. Having killed Chester in a duel, he quits England forever, and ends his days in the seclusion of an Italian convent. Thus, after summary disposal of the understrappers, ends the drama of "Barnaby Rudge."

We have given, as may well be supposed, but a very meagre outline of the story, and we have given it in the simple or natural sequence. That is to say, we have related the events, as nearly as might be, in the order of their occurrence. But this order would by no means have suited the purpose of the novelist, whose design has been to maintain the secret of the murder, and the consequent mystery which encircles Rudge, and the actions of his wife, until the catastrophe of his discovery by Haredale. The *thesis* of the novel may thus be regarded as based upon curiosity. Every point is so arranged as to perplex the reader, and whet his desire for elucidation:— for example, the first appearance of Rudge at the Maypole; his questions; his persecution of Mrs. R.; the ghost seen by the frequenter of the Maypole; and Haredale's impressive conduct in consequence. What *we* have told, in the very beginning of our digest, in regard to the shifting of the gardener's dress, is sedulously kept from the reader's knowledge until he learns it from Rudge's own confession in jail. We say sedulously; for, *the intention once known*, the *traces* of the design can be found upon every page. There is an amusing and exceedingly ingenious instance at page 145, where Solomon Daisy describes his adventure with the ghost.

"It was a ghost—a spirit," cried Daisy.

"Whose?" they all three asked together.

In the excess of his emotion (for he fell back trembling in his chair and waved his hand as if entreating them to question him no farther) *his answer was lost upon all* but old John Willet, who happened to be seated close beside him.

"Who!" cried Parkes and Tom Cobb—"Who was it?"

"Gentlemen," said Mr. Willet, after a long pause, "you needn't ask. The likeness of a murdered man. This is the nineteenth of March."

A profound silence ensued.

The impression here skilfully conveyed is, that the ghost seen is that of Reuben Haredale; and the mind of the not-too-acute reader is at once averted from the true state of the case—from the murderer, Rudge, living in the body.

Now there can be no question that, by such means as these, many points which are comparatively insipid in the natural sequence of our digest, and which would have been comparatively insipid even if given in full detail in a natural sequence, are endued with the interest of mystery; but neither can it be denied that a vast many more points are at the same time deprived of all effect, and become null, through the impossibility of comprehending them without the key. The author, who, cognizant of his plot, writes with this cognizance continually operating upon him, and thus *writes to himself* in spite of himself, does not, of course, feel that much of what is effective to his own informed perception, must necessarily be lost upon his uninformed readers; and he himself is never in condition, as regards his own work, to bring the matter to test. But the reader may easily satisfy himself of the validity of our objection. Let him *re-peruse* "Barnaby Rudge," and, with a pre-comprehension of the mystery, these points of which we speak break out in all directions like stars, and throw quadruple brilliance over the narrative—a brilliance which a correct taste will at once declare unprofitably sacrificed at the shrine of the keenest interest of mere mystery.

The design of *mystery*, however, being once determined upon by an author, it becomes imperative, first, that no undue or inartistical means be employed to conceal the secret of the plot; and, secondly, that the secret be well kept. Now, when, at page 16, we read that "the body of *poor Mr. Rudge, the steward, was found*" months after the outrage, &c. we see that Mr. Dickens has been guilty of no misdemeanor against Art in stating what was not the fact; since the falsehood is put into the mouth of Solomon Daisy, and given merely as the impression of this individual and of the public. The writer has not asserted it in his own person, but ingeniously conveyed an idea (false in itself, yet a belief in which is necessary for the effect of the tale) by the mouth of one of his characters. The case is different, however, when Mrs. Rudge is repeatedly denominated "the widow." It is the author who, himself, frequently so terms her. This is disingenuous and inartistical: accidentally so, of course. We speak of the matter merely by way of illustrating our point, and as an oversight on the part of Mr. Dickens.

That the secret be well kept is obviously necessary. A failure to preserve it until the proper moment of *dénouement*, throws all into confusion, so far as regards the *effect* intended. If the mystery leak out, against the author's will, his purposes are immediately at odds and ends; for he proceeds upon the supposition that certain impressions *do* exist, which do *not* exist, in the mind of his readers. We are not prepared to say, so positively as we could wish, whether, by the public at large, the whole *mystery* of the murder committed by Rudge, with the identity of the Maypole ruffian with Rudge himself, was fathomed at any period previous to the period intended, or, if so, whether at a period so early as materially to interfere with the interest designed; but we are forced, through sheer modesty, to suppose this the case; since, by ourselves individually, the secret was distinctly understood immediately upon the perusal of the story of Solomon Daisy, which occurs at the seventh page of this volume of three hundred and twenty-three. In the number of the "Philadelphia Saturday Evening Post," for May the 1st, 1841, (the tale having then only begun) will be found a *prospective notice* of some length, in which we made use of the following words—

That Barnaby is the son of the murderer may not appear evident to our readers—but we will explain. The person mur-

dered is Mr. Reuben Haredale. He was found assassinated in
his bed-chamber. His steward (Mr. Rudge, senior,) and his
gardener (name not mentioned) are missing. At first both are
suspected. 'Some months afterward,' here we use the words
of the story—'the steward's body, scarcely to be recognised
but by his clothes, and the watch and ring he wore—was
found at the bottom of a piece of water in the grounds, with
a deep gash in the breast where he had been stabbed by a
knife. He was only partly dressed; and all people agreed that
he had been sitting up reading in his own room, where there
were many traces of blood, and was suddenly fallen upon and
killed, before his master.'

Now, be it observed, it is not the author himself who asserts that *the steward's body was found*; he has put the words
in the mouth of one of his characters. His design is to make
it appear, in the *dénouement*, that the steward, Rudge, first
murdered the gardener, then went to his master's chamber,
murdered *him*, was interrupted by his (Rudge's) wife, whom
he seized and held *by the wrist*, to prevent her giving the
alarm—that he then, after possessing himself of the booty
desired, returned to the gardener's room, exchanged clothes
with him, put upon the corpse his own watch and ring, and
secreted it where it was afterwards discovered at so late a period that the features could not be identified.

The differences between our pre-conceived ideas, as here
stated, and the actual facts of the story, will be found immaterial. The gardener was murdered not before but after his
master; and that Rudge's wife seized *him* by the wrist, instead
of his seizing *her*, has so much the air of a mistake on the
part of Mr. Dickens, that we can scarcely speak of our own
version as erroneous. The grasp of a murderer's bloody hand
on the wrist of a woman *enceinte*, would have been more
likely to produce the effect described (and this every one will
allow) than the grasp of the hand of the woman upon the
wrist of the assassin. We may therefore say of our supposition
as Talleyrand said of some cockney's bad French— *que s'il ne
soit pas Francais, assurément donc il le doit être*—that if we did
not rightly prophesy, yet, at least, our prophecy *should have
been* right.

We are informed in the Preface to "Barnaby Rudge" that "no account of the Gordon Riots having been introduced into any work of fiction, and the subject presenting very extraordinary and remarkable features," our author " was led to project this tale." But for this distinct announcement (for Mr. Dickens can scarcely have deceived himself) we should have looked upon the Riots as altogether an afterthought. It is evident that they have no necessary connection with the story. In our digest, which carefully includes all *essentials* of the plot, we have dismissed the doings of the mob in a paragraph. The whole event of the drama would have proceeded as well without as with them. They have even the appearance of being *forcibly* introduced. In our compendium above, it will be seen that we emphasised several allusions to an interval of *five years*. The action is brought up to a certain point. The train of events is, so far, uninterrupted—nor is there any apparent need of interruption—yet all the characters are now thrown forward for a period of *five years*. And why? We ask in vain. It is not to bestow upon the lovers a more decorous maturity of age—for this is the only possible idea which suggests itself—Edward Chester is already eight-and-twenty, and Emma Haredale would, in America at least, be upon the list of old maids. No—there is no such reason; nor does there appear to be any one more plausible than that, as it is now the year of our Lord 1775, an advance of five years will bring the *dramatis personae* up to a very remarkable period, affording an admirable opportunity for their display—the period, in short, of the "No Popery" riots. This was the idea with which we were forcibly impressed in perusal, and which nothing less than Mr. Dickens' positive assurance to the contrary would have been sufficient to eradicate.

It is, perhaps, but one of a thousand instances of the disadvantages, both to the author and the public, of the present absurd fashion of periodical novel-writing, that our author had not sufficiently considered or determined upon *any* particular plot when he began the story now under review. In fact, we see, or fancy that we see, numerous traces of indecision—traces which a dexterous supervision of the complete work might have enabled him to erase. We have already spoken of the intermission of a lustrum. The opening speeches of old Chester are by far too *truly* gentlemanly for his subsequent character. The wife of Varden, also, is too wholesale a shrew to be converted into the quiet wife—the original design was to punish her. At page 16, we read thus—Solomon Daisy is telling his story:

"I put as good a face upon it as I could, and, muffling myself up, started out with a lighted lantern in one hand and the key of the church in the other"—at this point of the narrative, the dress of the strange man rustled as if he had turned to hear more distinctly.

Here the design is to call the reader's attention to a *point* in the tale; but no subsequent explanation is made. Again, a few lines below—

"The houses were all shut up, and the folks in doors, and perhaps there is only one man in the world who knows how dark it really was."

Here the intention is still more evident, but there is no result. Again, at page 54, the idiot draws Mr. Chester to the window, and directs his attention to the clothes hanging upon the lines in the yard—

"Look down," he said softly; "do you mark how they whisper in each other's ears, then dance and leap to make believe they are in sport? Do you see how they stop for a moment, when they think there is no one looking, and mutter among themselves again; and then how they roll and gambol, delighted with the mischief they've been plotting? Look at 'em now! See how they whirl and plunge. And now they stop again, and whisper cautiously together—little thinking, mind, how often I have lain upon the ground and watched them. I say—what is it that they plot and hatch? Do you know?"

Upon perusal of these ravings we, at once, supposed them to have allusion to some *real* plotting; and even now we cannot force ourselves to believe them not so intended. They suggested the opinion that Haredale himself would be implicated in the murder, and that the counsellings alluded to might be those of that gentleman with Rudge. It is by no means impossible that some such conception wavered in the mind of the author. At page 32 we have a confirmation of our idea, when Varden endeavors to arrest the murderer in the house of his wife—

"Come back—come back!" exclaimed the woman, wrestling with and clasping him. "Do not touch him on your life. *He carries other lives beside his own.*"

The *dénouement* fails to account for this exclamation.

In the beginning of the story much emphasis is placed upon the *two* female servants of Haredale, and upon his journey to and from London, as well as upon his wife. We have merely said, in our digest, that he was a widower, italicizing the remark. All these other points are, in fact, singularly irrelevant, in the supposition that the original design has not undergone modification.

Again, at page 57, when Haredale talks of "his dismantled and beggared hearth," we cannot help fancying that the author had in view some different wrong, or series of wrongs, perpetrated by Chester, than any which appear in the end. This gentleman, too, takes extreme and frequent pains to acquire dominion over the rough Hugh—this matter is particularly insisted upon by the novelist—we look, of course, for some important result—but the filching of a letter is nearly all that is accomplished. That Barnaby's delight in the desperate scenes of the rebellion, is inconsistent with his horror of blood, will strike every reader; and this inconsistency seems to be the consequence of the *afterthought* upon which we have already commented. In fact the title of the work, the elaborate and pointed manner of the commencement, the impressive description of The Warren, and especially of Mrs. Rudge, go far to show that Mr. Dickens has really deceived himself—that the soul of the plot, as originally conceived, was the murder of Haredale with the subsequent discovery of the murderer in Rudge—but that this idea was afterwards abandoned, or rather suffered to be merged in that of the Popish Riots. The result has been most unfavorable. That which, of itself, would have proved highly effective, has been rendered nearly null by its situation. In the multitudinous outrage and horror of the Rebellion, the *one* atrocity is utterly whelmed and extinguished.

The reasons of this deflection from the first purpose appear to us self-evident. One of them we have already mentioned. The other is that our author discovered, when too late, that *he had anticipated, and thus rendered valueless, his chief effect.* This will be readily understood. The particulars of the assassination being withheld, the strength of the narrator is put forth, in the beginning of the story, to *whet curiosity* in respect to these particulars; and, so far, he is but in proper pursuance of his main design. But from this intention he unwittingly passes into the error of *exaggerating anticipation.* And error though it be, it is an error wrought with consummate skill. What, for example, could more vividly enhance our impression of the unknown horror enacted, than the deep and enduring gloom of Haredale—than the idiot's inborn awe of blood—or, especially, than the expression of countenance so imaginatively attributed to Mrs. Rudge—"the capacity for expressing terror—something only dimly seen, but never absent for a moment—the shadow of some look to which an instant of intense and most unutterable horror only could have given rise?" But it is a condition of the human fancy that the promises of such words are irredeemable. In the notice before mentioned we thus spoke upon this topic—

This is a conception admirably adapted to whet curiosity in respect to the character of that event which is hinted at as forming the basis of the story. But this observation should not fail to be made—that the anticipation must surpass the reality; that no matter how terrific be the circumstances which, in the *dénouement*, shall appear to have occasioned the expression of countenance worn habitually by Mrs. Rudge, still they will not be able to satisfy the mind of the reader. He will surely be disappointed. The skilful intimation of horror held out by the artist, produces an effect which will deprive his conclusion of all. These intimations—these dark hints of some uncertain evil—are often rhetorically praised as effective—but are only justly so praised where there is *no dénouement* whatever—where the reader's imagination is left to clear up the mystery for itself—and this is not the design of Mr. Dickens.

And, in fact, our author was not long in seeing his precipitancy. He had placed himself in a dilemma from which even his high genius could not extricate him. He at once shifts the main interest—and in truth we do not see what better he could have done. The reader's attention becomes absorbed in the riots, and he fails to observe that what should have been the true catastrophe of the novel, is exceedingly feeble and ineffective.

A few cursory remarks:—Mr. Dickens fails peculiarly in *pure* narration. See, for example, page 296, where the connection of Hugh and Chester is detailed by Varden. See also in "The Curiosity-Shop," where, when the result is fully known, so many words are occupied in explaining the relationship of the brothers.

The effect of the present narrative might have been materially increased by confining the action within the limits of London. The "Nôtre Dame" of Hugo affords a fine example of the force which can be gained by concentration, or unity of place. The unity of time is also sadly neglected, to no purpose, in "Barnaby Rudge."

That Rudge should so long and so deeply feel the sting of conscience is inconsistent with his brutality.

On page 15 the interval elapsing between the murder and Rudge's return, is variously stated at twenty-two and twenty-four years.

It may be asked why the inmates of The Warren failed to hear the alarm-bell which was heard by Solomon Daisy.

The idea of persecution by being tracked, as by bloodhounds, from one spot of quietude to another is a favorite one with Mr. Dickens. Its effect cannot be denied.

The stain upon Barnaby's wrist, caused by fright in the mother at so late a period of gestation as one day before mature parturition, is shockingly at war with all medical experience.

When Rudge, escaped from prison, unshackled, with money at command, is in agony at his wife's refusal to perjure herself for his salvation—is it not *queer* that he should demand any other salvation than lay in his heels?

Some of the conclusions of chapters—see pages 40 and

100—seem to have been written for the mere purpose of illustrating tail-pieces.

The leading idiosyncrasy of Mr. Dickens' remarkable humor, is to be found in his *translating the language of gesture,
or action, or tone*. For example—

"The cronies nodded to each other, and Mr. Parkes remarked in an under tone, shaking his head meanwhile, *as who
should say 'let no man contradict me, for I won't believe him,'*
that Willet was in amazing force to-night."

The riots form a series of vivid pictures never surpassed.

At page 17, the road between London and the Maypole is
described as a horribly rough and dangerous, and at page 97,
as an uncommonly smooth and convenient one.

At page 116, how comes Chester in possession of the key of
Mrs. Rudge's vacated house?

Mr. Dickens' English is usually pure. His most remarkable
error is that of employing the adverb "directly" in the sense
of "as soon as." For example—"Directly he arrived, Rudge
said, &c." Bulwer is uniformly guilty of the same blunder.

It is observable that so original a stylist as our author
should occasionally lapse into a gross imitation of what, itself,
is a gross imitation. We mean the manner of Lamb—a manner based in the Latin construction. For example—

In summer time its pumps suggest to thirsty idlers springs
cooler and more sparkling and deeper than other wells; and
as they trace the spillings of full pitchers on the heated
ground, they snuff the freshness, and, sighing, cast sad looks
towards the Thames, and think of baths and boats, and saun-
ter on, despondent.

The wood-cut *designs* which accompany the edition before
us are occasionally good. The copper engravings are pitiably
ill-conceived and ill-drawn; and not only this, but are in
broad contradiction of the wood-designs and text.

There are many *coincidences* wrought into the narrative—
those, for example, which relate to the nineteenth of March;

when his father is actually in the house; and the dream of
Haredale previous to his final meeting with Chester. These
things are meant to *insinuate* a fatality which, very properly,
is not expressed in plain terms—but it is questionable
whether the story derives more, in ideality, from their introduction, than it might have gained of verisimilitude from
their omission.

The *dramatis personae* sustain the high fame of Mr. Dickens
as a delineator of character. Miggs, the disconsolate handmaiden of Varden; Tappertit, his chivalrous apprentice; Mrs.
Varden, herself; and Dennis, a hangman—may be regarded
as original caricatures, of the highest merit as such. Their
traits are founded in acute observation of nature, but are exaggerated to the utmost admissible extent. Miss Haredale and
Edward Chester are common-places—no effort has been
made in their behalf. Joe Willet is a naturally drawn country
youth. Stagg is a mere make-weight. Gashford and Gordon
are truthfully copied. Dolly Varden is truth itself. Haredale,
Rudge and Mrs. Rudge are impressive only through the circumstances which surround them. Sir John Chester is, of
course, not original, but is a vast improvement upon all his
predecessors—his heartlessness is rendered somewhat too
amusing, and his end too much that of a man of honor.
Hugh is a noble conception. His fierce exultation in his animal powers; his subserviency to the smooth Chester; his
mirthful contempt and patronage of Tappertit, and his *brutal*
yet firm courage in the hour of death—form a picture to be
set in diamonds. Old Willet is not surpassed by any character
even among those of Dickens. He is nature itself—yet a step
farther would have placed him in the class of caricatures. His
combined conceit and obtusity are indescribably droll, and his
peculiar misdirected energy when aroused, is one of the most
exquisite touches in all humorous painting. We shall never
forget how heartily we laughed at his shaking Solomon Daisy
and threatening to put him behind the fire, because the unfortunate little man was too much frightened to articulate.
Varden is one of those free, jovial, honest fellows at charity
with all mankind, whom our author is so fond of depicting.
And lastly, Barnaby, the hero of the tale—in him we have
been somewhat disappointed. We have already said that his

delight in the atrocities of the Rebellion is at variance with his horror of blood. But this horror of blood is *inconsequential*; and of this we complain. Strongly insisted upon in the beginning of the narrative, it produces no adequate result. And here how fine an opportunity has Mr. Dickens missed! The conviction of the assassin, after the lapse of twenty-two years, might easily have been brought about through his son's mysterious awe of blood— *an awe created in the unborn by the assassination itself*—and this would have been one of the finest possible embodiments of the idea which we are accustomed to attach to "poetical justice." The raven, too, intensely amusing as it is, might have been made, more than we now see it, a portion of the conception of the fantastic Barnaby. Its croakings might have been *prophetically* heard in the course of the drama. Its character might have performed, in regard to that of the idiot, much the same part as does, in music, the accompaniment in respect to the air. Each might have been distinct. Each might have differed remarkably from the other. Yet between them there might have been wrought an analogical resemblance, and, although each might have existed apart, they might have formed together a whole which would have been imperfect in the absence of either.

From what we have here said—and, perhaps, said without due deliberation—(for alas! the hurried duties of the journalist preclude it) there will not be wanting those who will accuse us of a mad design to detract from the pure fame of the novelist. But to such we merely say in the language of heraldry "ye should wear a plain point sanguine in your arms." If this be understood, well; if not, well again. There lives no man feeling a deeper reverence for genius than ourself. If we have not dwelt so especially upon the high merits as upon the trivial defects of "Barnaby Rudge" we have already given our reasons for the omission, and these reasons will be sufficiently understood by all whom we care to understand them. The work before us is not, we think, equal to the tale which immediately preceded it; but there are few—very few others to which we consider it inferior. Our chief objection has not, perhaps, been so distinctly stated as we could wish. That this fiction, or indeed that any fiction written by Mr. Dickens, should be based in the excitement and maintenance of curiosity we look upon as a misconception, on the part of the writer, of his own very great yet very peculiar powers. He has done this thing well, to be sure—he would do anything well in comparison with the herd of his contemporaries—but he has not done it so thoroughly well as his high and just reputation would demand. We think that the whole book has been an effort to him—solely through the nature of its design. He has been smitten with an untimely desire for a novel path. The idiosyncrasy of his intellect would lead him, naturally, into the most fluent and simple style of narration. In tales of ordinary sequence he may and will long reign triumphant. He has a *talent* for all things, but no positive *genius* for *adaptation*, and still less for that metaphysical art in which the souls of all *mysteries* lie. "Caleb Williams" is a far less noble work than "The Old Curiosity-Shop;" but Mr. Dickens could no more have constructed the one than Mr. Godwin could have dreamed of the other.

Graham's Magazine, February 1842

Henry Duncan

Sacred Philosophy of the Seasons; Illustrating the Perfections of God in the Phenomena of the Year. By the Rev. Henry Duncan, D. D., Ruthwell, Scotland. With Important Additions, and some Modifications to adapt it to American readers. By F. W. P. Greenwood. In four volumes. Marsh, Capen, Lyon and Webb, Boston.

IN OUR LAST NUMBER we had barely room to acknowledge the reception of this valuable work, and to speak of it in general terms of commendation. A careful perusal has since assured us that we did not err in our opinion. The book will recommend itself wherever seen, as a well-arranged and well-digested compendium, embracing a vast amount of information upon the various topics of physical science, and especially well adapted to those educational purposes for which the volumes are designed.

We are not aware of the precise period at which the American edition was actually passed through the press: and one or two apparent inaccuracies which have arrested our attention may have been understood as truths at the time of Mr. Greenwood's supervision.

It is questionable whether there be not something of a philosophy *un peu passé* in a passage where a certain argument is spoken of as not proving the absolute permanency of our solar system "because we know from the more sure word of prophecy that it is not destined to last forever." We believe there are few intelligent men of the present day—few, either laymen or divines—who are still willing to think that the prophecies here referred to have any further allusion than to the orb of the earth—or, more strictly, to the crust of this orb alone. The entire system never was meant to be included. Upon this topic we refer the reader, in perfect confidence, to the excellent observations of Dr. Dick, in his "Christian Philosopher."

At page 297, of the fourth volume, and subsequently, there are some passages which strongly insist upon the literal fulfilment of the biblical prophecies in regard to the city of Petra, in Idumea, the ancient Edom: and, in connection with this subject, the work of Dr. Keith on the Prophecies is greatly extolled. "This singular place," (Petra) says Dr. Duncan, "has only lately been minutely surveyed, and indeed little was known of it till after the commencement of the present century, when it was visited first by Dr. Burckhardt, and afterwards by captains Irby and Mangles." To this the American editor adds in a foot-note, "Yet more recently, these wonderful ruins have been visited by our countryman, Mr. Stevens." (Stephens.)

There is, we confess, something here of which we do not altogether approve. Dr. Duncan is perfectly justifiable in avowing that implicit confidence which *he* no doubt feels, in the accuracy of the statements of Dr. Keith, and in the force of the arguments supporting his favorite doctrine—the literal fulfilment of prophecy; but we think Mr. Greenwood should have observed, by way of offsett, that the work in question has been more than once thoroughly refuted; and once, especially, in an unanswerable argument in the pages of the London Quarterly Review. Moreover, as the book of Mr. Stephens *was* alluded to, it would have been as well to say that this book itself affords a very singular, and certainly a very positive refutation, not only of the general argument of Dr. Keith, but of the very portion of it now in question.

It is said in Isaiah, respecting Idumea, that "none shall pass through thee for ever and ever." Dr. K. insists upon understanding this in its most strictly literal sense. He attempts to prove that neither Burckhardt nor Irby passed *through* the country—merely penetrating to Petra, and returning. But then, Mr. Stephens entered Idumea with a full and deliberate design of putting the question of this prophecy to test; he determined to see whether it was meant that Idumea should not be passed through, and he accordingly *passed through it from one end to the other*. The truth is that a palpable mistranslation exists in the passage of Isaiah referred to: a passage which Dr. Keith should have examined critically in the original before basing so long an argument upon it. This mistranslation, and several others upon the same topic, we pointed out ourselves, not very long ago, in an article in the New York Review. The words in question are found in Isaiah 34, 10, and run thus: *Lenetsach netsachim ein over bah*. (We have not the Hebrew Type.) The sentence, word for word, is as follows: *Lenetsach*, for an eternity; *netsachim*, of eternities; *ein*, not; *over*, moving about; *bah*, in it; that is to say, "for an eternity of eternities, (there shall) not (be any one) moving about *in it*," not through it. The participle *over* refers to one moving to and fro, or up and down; and is the same term which is rendered "current" as an epithet of money, in Genesis 23, 16. The prophet simply means that there shall be no mark of life in the land; no living being there; no one moving up and down in it. He merely refers to its general abandonment and desolation.

In the same way we have received an erroneous idea of the meaning of Ezekiel 35, 7, where the same region is mentioned. The common version runs—"Thus will I make Mount Seir most desolate, and cut off from it him that passeth out and him that returneth"—a sentence which Dr. Keith views as he does the one mentioned above—that is to say, he supposes it to forbid any travelling in Idumea under penalty of death, instancing Burckhardt's death shortly after his return, as confirming his opinion, on the ground that he died in consequence of his rash attempt. Now the words which have been construed by "him that passeth out and him that returneth" are *"over vasal,"* and mean strictly "him that passeth and re-passeth." Here, as before, the inhabitants are referred to. Our version is sanctioned by Gesenius, and there is something very analogous in the Hebrew-Greek phrase in Acts 9, 28— Κἀὶ ην μετ' αὐτῶν εἰσπορευδμενος καὶ εκπορευόμενος ἐν Ἰερουσαλημ, "and he was with them in Jerusalem, coming in and going out." The latin *versatus est* hits it off exactly. The meaning is, that Saul, the new comer, was on intimate terms with the true believers in Jerusalem, moving about among them, to and fro, or in and out.

But we have been led off from our immediate purpose; which was chiefly to dissent, in general terms, from the views of Dr. Keith, and to express a regret that a gentleman so well qualified to speak upon this subject as Mr. Greenwood, should not have appended some observations to the remarks of Dr. Duncan. The "Philosophy of the Seasons" is a book of which every one must think well. Its great comprehensiveness, its general accuracy, its ingenious and luminous arrangement, render it, in every respect, a valuable work. Its mechanical execution is exceedingly good, and does high credit to the taste of the publishers, Messrs. Marsh, Capen, Lyon and Webb.

Euripides

The Classical Family Library. Numbers XV, XVI, and XVII. Euripides translated by the Reverend R. Potter, Prebendary of Norwich. Harper & Brothers, New York.

THESE THREE volumes embrace the whole of Euripides— Æschylus and Sophocles having already been published in the Library. A hasty glance at the work will not enable us to speak positively in regard to the value of these translations. The name of Potter, however, is one of high authority, and we have no reason to suspect that he has not executed his task as well as any man living could have done it. But that these, or that any poetic versions can convey to the mind of the merely general reader the most remote conception of either the manner, the spirit, or the meaning of the Greek dramatists, is what Mr. Potter does not intend us to believe, and what we certainly should not believe if he did. At all events, it must be a subject of general congratulation, that in the present day, for a sum little exceeding three dollars, any lover of the classics may possess himself of complete versions of the three greatest among the ancient Greek writers of tragedy.

Ardent admirers of Hellenic Literature, we have still no passion for Euripides. Truly great when compared with many of the moderns, he falls immeasurably below his immediate predecessors. "He is admirable," says a German critic, " where the object calls chiefly for emotion, and requires the display of no higher qualities; and he is still more so where pathos and moral beauty are united. Few of his pieces are without particular passages of the most overpowering beauty. It is by no means my intention to deny him the possession of the most astonishing talents: I have only stated that these talents were not united with a mind in which the austerity of moral principle, and the sanctity of religious feelings were held in the highest honor."

The life, essence, and characteristic qualities of the ancient Greek drama may be found in three things. First, in the ruling idea of Destiny or Fate. Secondly, in the Chorus. Thirdly, in Ideality. But in Euripides we behold only the decline and fall of that drama, and the three prevailing features we have mentioned are in him barely distinguishable, or to be seen only in their perversion. What, for example is, with Sophocles, and still more especially with Æschylus, the obscure and terrible spirit of predestination, sometimes mellowed down towards the catastrophe of their dramas into the unseen, yet not unfelt hand of a kind Providence, or overruling God, becomes in the handling of Euripides the mere blindness of accident, or the capriciousness of chance. He thus loses innumerable opportunities—opportunities which his great rivals have used to so good an effect—of giving a preternatural and ideal elevation to moral fortitude in the person of his heroes, by means of opposing them in a perpetual warfare with the arbitrations and terrors of Destiny.

Again; the Chorus, which appears never to have been thoroughly understood by the moderns—the Chorus of Euripides is not, alas! the Chorus of his predecessors. That this singular, or at least apparently singular feature, in the Greek drama, was intended for the mere purpose of preventing the stage from being, at any moment entirely empty, has been an opinion very generally, and very unaccountably received. *The Chorus was not, at any time, upon the stage.* Its general station was in the orchestra, in which it also performed the solemn dances, and walked to and fro during the choral songs. And when it did not sing, its proper station was upon the *thymele*, an elevation somewhat like an altar, but with steps, in front of the orchestra, raised as high as the stage, and opposite to the scene—being also in the very centre of the entire theatre, and serving as a point around which the semi-circle of the amphitheatre was described. Most critics, however, have merely laughed at the Chorus as something superfluous and absurd, urging the folly of enacting passages supposed to be performed in secret in the presence of an assembled crowd, and believing that as it originated in the infancy of the art, it was continued merely through caprice or accident. Sophocles, however, wrote a treatise on the Chorus, and assigned his reasons for persisting in the practice. Aristotle says little about it, and that little affords no clew to its actual meaning or purpose. Horace considers it "a general expression of moral participation, instruction, and admonition;" and this opinion, which is evidently just, has been adopted and commented upon, at some length, by Schlegel. Publicity among the

Greeks, with their republican habits and modes of thinking, was considered absolutely essential to all actions of dignity or importance. Their dramatic poetry imbibed the sentiment, and was thus made to display a spirit of conscious independence. The Chorus served to give verisimilitude to the dramatic action, and was, in a word, *the ideal spectator*. It stood in lieu of the national spirit, and represented the general participation of the human race, in the events going forward upon the stage. This was its most extended, and most proper object; but it had others of a less elevated nature, and more nearly in accordance with the spirit of our own melo-drama.

But the Chorus of Euripides was not the true and unadulterated Chorus of the purer Greek tragedy. It is even more than probable that he did never rightly appreciate its full excellence and power, or give it any portion of his serious attention. He made no scruple of admitting the *parabasis* into his tragedies*—a license which although well suited to the spirit of comedy, was entirely out of place, and must have had a ludicrous effect in a serious drama. In some instances also, among which we may mention the Danaidæ, a female Chorus is permitted by him to make use of grammatical inflexions proper only for males.

In respect to the Ideality of the Greek drama, a few words will be sufficient. It was the Ideality of conception, and the Ideality of representation. Character and manners were never the character and manners of every day existence, but a certain, and very marked elevation above them. Dignity and grandeur enveloped each personage of the stage—but such dignity as comported with his particular station, and such grandeur as was never at *outrance* with his allotted part. And this was the Ideality of conception. The cothurnus, the mask, the mass of drapery, all so constructed and arranged as to give an increase of bodily size, the scenic illusions of a nature very different, and much more extensive than our own, inasmuch as actual realities were called in to the aid of art, were on the other hand the Ideality of representation. But although in Sophocles, and more especially in Æschylus, character and expression were made subservient and secondary to this ideal

*The *parabasis* was the privilege granted the Chorus of addressing the spectators in its own person.

and lofty elevation—in Euripides the reverse is always found to be the case. His heroes are introduced familiarly to the spectators, and so far from raising his men to the elevation of Divinities, his Divinities are very generally lowered to the most degrading and filthy common-places of an earthly existence. But we may sum up our opinion of Euripides far better in the words of Augustus William Schlegel, than in any farther observations of our own.

"This poet has at the same time destroyed the internal essence of tragedy, and sinned against the laws of beauty and proportion in its external structure. He generally sacrifices the whole to the effect of particular parts, and in these he is also more ambitious of foreign attractions, than of genuine poetical beauty."

Southern Literary Messenger, September 1835

Baron de la Motte Fouqué

Undine: A Miniature Romance; from the German of Baron de la Motte Fouqué. Colman's Library of Romance, Edited by Grenville Mellen. Samuel Colman, New York.

THE RE-PUBLICATION of such a work as "Undine," in the very teeth of our anti-romantic national character, is an experiment well adapted to excite interest, and in the crisis caused by this experiment—for a crisis it is—it becomes the duty of every lover of literature for its own sake and spiritual uses, to speak out, and speak boldly, against the untenable prejudices which have so long and so unopposedly enthralled us. It becomes, we say, his plain duty to show, with what ability he may possess, the full value and capacity of that species of writing generally, which, as a people, we are too prone to discredit. It is incumbent upon him to make head, by all admissible means in his power, against that evil genius of mere matter-of-fact, whose grovelling and degrading assumptions are so happily set forth in the pert little query of Monsieur Casimir Perier—*"A quoi un pöete est-il bon?"* The high claims of Undine, and its extensive foreign reputation, render it especially desirable that he should make use of a careful analysis of the work itself—not less than of the traits of its class—with a view of impressing upon the public mind, at least his individual sense of its most exalted and extraordinary character. Feeling thus, we are grieved that our limits, as well as the late hour in which we take up the book, will scarcely permit us to speak of it otherwise than at random. The story runs very nearly in this manner.

Sir Huldbrand of Ringstetten, a knight of high descent, young, rich, valorous, and handsome, becomes slightly enamored, at a tournament, of a lady Bertalda, the adopted daughter of a German Duke. She, being entreated by the knight for one of her gloves, promises it upon condition of his exploring the recesses of a certain haunted forest. He consents, and is beset with a crowd of illusory and fantastic terrors, which, in the end, compel him to an extremity of the wood, where a long grassy peninsula, of great loveliness, juts out into the bosom of a vast lake. Of this peninsula, the sole inhabitants are an old fisherman and his wife, with their adopted daughter, Undine, a beautiful and fairy-like creature of eighteen, and of an extravagantly wild and perverse, yet amiable and artless temperament. The old couple had rejoiced, some years before, in a child of their own—who playing, one day, by the water's edge, fell in suddenly, and at once disappeared. In the depth of their grief for her loss, they were astonished and delighted, one summer's evening, with the appearance in their hut of the little Undine, who was dripping with water, and who could give no very distinct account of herself—her language being of a singular nature, and her discourse turning upon such subjects as "golden castles" and "chrystal domes." She had remained with the fisherman and his wife ever since, and they had come to look upon her as their own.

By these good people Sir Huldbrand is hospitably entertained. In the meantime, a brook, swollen by rains, renders the peninsula an island, and thoroughly cuts off his retreat. In the strict intercourse which ensues, the young man and maiden become lovers, and are finally wedded by a priest, who is opportunely cast away upon the coast. After the marriage, a new character seems to pervade Undine; and she at length explains to her husband, (who is alarmed at some hints which she lets fall,) the true history of her nature, and of her advent upon the island.

She is one of the race of water-spirits—a race who differ, personally, from mankind, only in a greater beauty, and in the circumstance of possessing no soul. The words of Undine, here divulging her secret to Huldbrand, will speak as briefly as we could do, and far more eloquently—"Both we, and the beings I have mentioned as inhabiting the other elements, vanish into air at death, and go out of existence, spirit and body, so that no vestige of us remains; and when you hereafter awake to a purer state of being, we shall remain where sand, and sparks, and wind and waves remain. We of course have no souls. The element moves us, and, again, is obedient to our will, while we live, though it scatters us like dust when we die; and as we have nothing to trouble us, we are as merry as nightingales, little gold-fishes, and other pretty children of nature. But all beings aspire to rise in the scale of existence higher than they are. It was therefore the wish of my father, who is a powerful water-prince in the Mediterranean Sea, that his only daughter should become possessed of a soul; although she should have to endure many of the sufferings of those who share that gift. Now the race to which I belong have no other means of obtaining a soul, than by forming, with an individual of your own, the most intimate union of love."

Undine has an uncle, Kuhleborn, who is the spirit of a brook, the brook which had cut off the retreat of the knight. It was this uncle who had stolen the fisherman's daughter; who had brought Undine to the island, and who had, by machination in the haunted forest, forced Huldbrand upon the peninsula. The wedding having been accomplished, the brook is dried up; and the married pair, attended by the priest, make their way to the city where the tournament had been held, and where Bertalda and her friends were much alarmed at the long absence of the knight. This lady, who had loved him, and who is, in fact, the lost daughter of the fisherman (having been carried safely to a distant shore by Kuhleborn, and found and adopted by a Duke) this lady is sadly grieved at the marriage of the knight, but feels an unaccountable prepossession in favor of the bride, becomes her most intimate friend, and at length goes to live with her at the castle of Ringstetten—much in opposition to the wishes of the priest and of Kuhleborn. The disasters of the drama now commence. Huldbrand insensibly forgets his love for Undine, and recalls his passion for Bertalda. He is even petulant to his bride; who is aware of all, but utters no reproach. She entreats him, however, to be careful not to reproach her when they are crossing a brook, or in any excursion upon the water; as, in such case, her friends the water-spirits, who resent his behaviour, would have power to bear her away entirely, and for ever. In a passage down the Danube, however, with Undine and Bertalda, he forgets the caution, and upon a trifling occasion bitterly reproves his gentle bride—for whom he still feels a lingering affection. She is thus forced to leave him, and melts into the waters of the river.

Huldbrand returns with Bertalda to castle Ringstetten. His grief, at first violent, settles down at length into a tender melancholy, and finally is merged, although not altogether, in a growing passion for the fisherman's daughter. He sends for the priest; who obeys the summons in haste, but refuses to perform the marriage ceremony. He represents that for many nights previous, Undine had appeared to him in a dream, imploring him with deep sighs, and saying—"Ah prevent him, dear father! I am still living! Ah! save his life! Ah! save his soul!" Huldbrand, however, rejects the advice of the priest, and sends to a neighboring monastery for a monk, who promises to do his bidding in a few days.

Meantime, the knight is borne, in a dream, as if on swans' wings, to a certain spot in the Mediterranean Sea. Here he is held hovering over the water, which becomes perfectly transparent. He sees Undine weeping bitterly and in conversation with Kuhleborn. This conversation gives Huldbrand to know that Undine still lives, and still retains her soul, although separated for ever from her husband—and that, if he should again marry, it will be her fate and her duty to cause his death, in obedience to a law of the water-spirits. Kuhleborn is insisting upon this necessity. He tells Undine that the knight is about to wed—and reminds her of what she must do.

"I have not the power," returned Undine with a smile. "Do you not remember? I have sealed up the fountain securely, not only against myself, but all of the same race." [This is a fountain in the court-yard of Castle Ringstetten, which Undine had caused to be covered up, while she lived upon earth, on account of its affording Kuhleborn and other water-spirits who were ill disposed to the knight, the means of access to the castle.]

"Still, should he leave his castle," said Kuhleborn, "or should he once allow the fountain to be uncovered, what then? for doubtless he thinks there is no great murder in such trifles?"

"For that very reason," said Undine, still smiling amid her tears, "for that very reason he is this moment hovering in spirit over the Mediterranean Sea, and dreaming of this voice of warning which our conversation affords him. It is for this that I have been studious in disposing the whole vision."

Notwithstanding all this, however, Huldbrand weds Bertalda. She in the gaiety of her spirit, upon the night of the wedding, causes the fountain to be uncovered without the knowledge of the knight, who has never revealed his dream to her. She does this, partly on account of a fancied virtue in the wa-

ter, and partly through an arrogant pleasure in undoing what
the first wife had commanded to be done. Undine immediately
ascends and accomplishes the destruction of the knight.

This is an exceedingly meagre outline of the leading events
of the story; which, although brief, is crowded with incident.
Beneath all, there runs a mystic or under-current of meaning,
of the simplest and most easily intelligible, yet of the most
richly philosophical character. From internal evidence afforded by the book itself, we gather that the author has
deeply suffered from the ills of an ill-assorted marriage—and
to the bitter reflections induced by these ills, we owe the conception and peculiar execution of "Undine."

In the contrast between the artless, thoughtless, and careless character of Undine before possessing a soul, and her serious, enwrapped, and anxious, yet happy condition after
possessing it—a condition which, with all its multiform cares
and disquietudes, she still feels to be preferable to her original
fate—M. Fouqué has beautifully painted the difference between the heart unused to love, and the heart which has received its inspiration.

The jealousies which follow the marriage, arising from the
conduct of Bertalda, are the natural troubles of love—but the
persecutions of Kuhleborn and the other water-spirits, who
take umbrage at Huldbrand's treatment of his wife, are meant
to picture certain difficulties from the interference of relations
in conjugal matters—difficulties which the author has himself
experienced. The warning of Undine to Huldbrand—"reproach
me not upon the waters, or we part for ever"—is meant to
embody the truth that quarrels between man and wife, are seldom or never irremediable unless when taking place in the
presence of third parties. The second wedding of the knight,
with his gradual forgetfulness of Undine and Undine's intense grief beneath the waters—are dwelt upon so pathetically
and so passionately—that there can be no doubt of the personal opinions of the author on the subject of such marriages—
no doubt of his deep personal interest in the question.
How thrillingly are these few and simple words made to convey his belief that the *mere death* of a beloved wife does
not imply a final separation so complete as to justify an union
with another—"The fisherman had loved Undine with ex-

ceeding tenderness, and it was a doubtful conclusion to his mind, that the mere disappearance of his beloved child could be properly viewed as her death!" This is where the old man is endeavoring to dissuade the knight from wedding Bertalda.

We have no hesitation in saying that this portion of the design of the romance—the portion which conveys an undercurrent of meaning—does not afford the fairest field to the romanticist—does not appertain to the higher regions of ideality. Although, in this case, the plan is essentially distinct from Allegory, yet it has too close an affinity to that most indefensible species of writing—a species whose gross demerits we cannot now pause to examine. That M. Fouqué was well aware of the disadvantage under which he labored—that he well knew the field he traversed not to be the fairest—and that a personal object alone induced him to choose it—we cannot and shall not doubt. For the hand of the master is visible in every line of his beautiful fable. "Undine" is a model of models, in regard to the high artistical talent which it evinces. We could write volumes in a detailed commentary upon its various beauties in this respect. Its unity is absolute—its keeping unbroken. Yet every minute point of the picture fills and satisfies the eye. Every thing is attended to, and nothing is out of time or out of place.

We say that some private and personal design to be fulfilled has thrown M. Fouqué upon that objectionable under-current of meaning which he has so elaborately managed. Yet his high genius has nearly succeeded in turning the blemish into a beauty. At all events he has succeeded, in spite of a radical defect, in producing what we advisedly consider the finest romance in existence. We say this with a bitter kind of half-consciousness that only a very few will fully agree with us—yet these few are our all in such matters. They will stand by us in a just opinion.

Were we to pick out *points* for admiration in Undine, we should pick out the greater portion of the story. We cannot say whether the novelty of its conception, or the loftiness of its ideality, or its intense pathos, or its rigorous simplicity, or that high artistical talent with which all are combined, is the particular to be chiefly admired. Addressing those who have read the book, we may call attention to the delicacy and grace of transition from subject to subject—a point which never fails to test the power of the writer—as, for example, at page 128, when, for the purposes of the story, it becomes necessary that the knight, with Undine and Bertalda, shall proceed down the Danube. An ordinary novelist would have here tormented both himself and his readers, in his search for a sufficient *motive* for the voyage. But, in connexion with a fable such as Undine, how all-sufficient seems the simple motive assigned by Fouqué!—"In this grateful union of friendship and affection winter came and passed away; and spring, with its foliage of tender green, and its heaven of softest blue, succeeded to gladden the hearts of the three inmates of the castle. The season was in harmony with their minds, and their minds imparted their own hues to the season. *What wonder, then, that its storks and swallows inspired them also with a disposition to travel!*"

Again, we might dwell upon the exquisite *management of imagination*, which is so visible in the passages where the brooks are water-spirits, and the water-spirits brooks—neither distinctly either. What can be more ethereally ideal than the frequent indeterminate glimpses caught of Kuhleborn—or than his singular and wild lapses into shower and foam?—or than the evanishing of the white wagoner and his white horses into the shrieking and devouring flood?—or than the gentle melting of the passionately-weeping bride into the chrystal waters of the Danube? What can be more divine than the character of the soul-less Undine?—what more august than her transition into the soul-possessing wife? What can be more intensely beautiful than the whole book? We calmly think—yet cannot help asserting with enthusiasm—that the whole wide range of fictitious literature embraces nothing comparable in loftiness of conception, or in felicity of execution, to those final passages of the volume before us which embody the uplifting of the stone from the fount by the order of Bertalda, the sorrowful and silent re-advent of Undine, and the rapturous death of Sir Huldbrand in the embraces of his spiritual wife.

Burton's Gentleman's Magazine, September 1839

William Godwin

Lives of the Necromancers: or an Account of the Most Eminent Persons in Successive Ages, who have claimed for themselves, or to whom has been imputed by others, the Exercise of Magical Power. By William Godwin, Author of "Caleb Williams," &c. New York: Published by Harper & Brothers.

THE NAME of the author of Caleb Williams, and of St. Leon, is, with us, a word of weight, and one which we consider a guarantee for the excellence of any composition to which it may be affixed. There is about all the writings of Godwin, one peculiarity which we are not sure that we have ever seen pointed out for observation, but which, nevertheless, is his chief idiosyncrasy—setting him peculiarly apart from all other *literati* of the day. We allude to an air of mature thought—of deliberate premeditation pervading, in a remarkable degree, even his most common-place observations. He never uses a hurried expression, or hazards either an ambiguous phrase, or a premature opinion. His style therefore is highly artificial; but the extreme finish and proportion always observable about it, render this artificiality, which in less able hands would be wearisome, in him a grace inestimable. We are never tired of his terse, nervous, and sonorous periods— for their terseness, their energy, and even their melody, are made, in all cases, subservient to the sense with which they are invariably fraught. No English writer, with whom we have any acquaintance, with the single exception of Coleridge, has a fuller appreciation of the value of *words*; and none is more nicely discriminative between closely-approximating meanings.

The avowed purpose of the volume now before us is to exhibit a wide view of human credulity. "To know"—says Mr. Godwin—"the things that are not, and cannot be, but have been imagined and believed, is the most curious chapter in the annals of man." *In extenso* we differ with him.

> There are more things in Heaven and Earth, Horatio,
> Than are dreamt of in thy philosophy.

There are many things, too, in the great circle of human experience, more curious than even the records of human credulity—but that they form *one* of the most curious chapters, we were at all times ready to believe, and had we been in any degree skeptical, the *Lives of the Necromancers* would have convinced us.

Unlike the work of Brewster, the Necromancy of Mr. Godwin is not a Treatise on Natural Magic. It does not pretend to show the *manner* in which delusion acts upon mankind—at all events, this is not the *object* of the book. The design, if we understand it, is to display in their widest extent, the great range and wild extravagancy of the imagination of man. It is almost superfluous to say that in this he has fully succeeded. His compilation is an invaluable work, evincing much labor and research, and full of absorbing interest. The only drawback to the great pleasure which its perusal has afforded us, is found in the author's unwelcome announcement in the Preface, that for the present he winds up his literary labors with the production of this book. The pen which wrote Caleb Williams, should never for a moment be idle.

Were we to specify any article, in the Necromancy, as more particularly interesting than another, it would be the one entitled 'Faustus.' The prevalent idea that Fust the printer, and Faustus the magician, were identical, is here very properly contradicted.

Southern Literary Messenger, December 1835

S. C. Hall

The Book of Gems. The Poets and Artists of Great Britain. Edited by S. C. Hall. London and New York: Saunders and Otley.

THIS WORK combines the rich embellishments of the very best of the race of Annuals, with a far higher claim to notice than any of them in its strictly literary department. If we regard this volume as the only one to appear, the title will convey no idea of the design—but we are promised a continuation. The whole, if we comprehend, will contain specimens of *all* the principal poets and artists of Great Britain. In the present instance we have the poets as far as Prior, including a period of about four hundred years, with extracts from Chaucer, Lydgate, James I, Hawes, Carew, Quarles, Shirley, Habington, Lovelace, Wyatt, Surrey, Sackville, Vere, Gascoigne, Raleigh, Spenser, Sidney, Brooke, Southwell, Daniel, Drayton, Shakspeare, Walton, Davies, Donne, Jonson, Corbet, Phineas Fletcher, Giles Fletcher, Drummond, Wither, Carew, Browne, Herrick, Quarles, Herbert, Davenant, Waller, Milton, Suckling, Butler, Crashaw, Denham, Cowley, Marvell, Dryden, Roscommon, Dorset, Sedley, Rochester, Sheffield, and Prior. Of these, all the autographs have been obtained and are published collectively at the end of the book, with the exception of the nine first mentioned. The work is illustrated by fifty-three engravings, each by different artists. A sea-side group by Harding, and L'Allegro and Il Penseroso by Parris, are particularly good—but all are excellent.

We had prepared some observations in regard to the book itself, (over which we have been poring for many days with intense delight) and in regard more especially to the character and justice of that deep feeling with which most men, having claim to taste, are wont to look, even through a veil of exceedingly troublesome obscurity and antiquity, upon the writings of the elder poets and dramatists of Great Britain. But we have been so nearly anticipated in our design by a paper in the American Monthly Magazine for July, that what we should now say, and say *con amore*, would be looked upon as little better than a *rifacimento* of the article we mention. At the same time it would be an ill deed to remodel our thoughts, and proceed to think falsely, for the mere purpose of proving that we can think originally. In this dilemma then, we will merely express our general accordance in the opinions of the Northern Magazine, copy, of its *critique*, a portion which seems to embody, in little compass, much of what we have said less forcibly and more diffusely, and add some few additional observations which have lately suggested themselves.

"Among the early English poets, so called," says the American Monthly, "there is combined with marked individuality, a sort of general resemblance, not easily defined, but readily perceived by a discriminating reader. They lived in an age of invention, and wrote from a pleasurable impulse which they could not resist. They did not borrow from one another, or from those who had gone before them, nor pass their time in pouring from one vessel into another. Thus, however different their styles, however various their subjects, whether the flight of their genius be high or low, there is the same aspect of truth and naturalness in the poetry of them all; as we can trace a common likeness in all faces which have an open, ingenuous expression, however little resemblance there may be in the several features. Most of them were well acquainted with books, and many of them were deeply learned; and an air of ripe scholarship sometimes degenerating into pedantry, pervades every thing they wrote. As a class too, they are remarkable for a healthy, intellectual tone, defaced neither by moody misanthropy, nor mawkish sentimentality. The manly Saxon character beams out from every line; and that vigorous good sense, so characteristic of the English stock, every where leaves its impress. Another trait which, with a few exceptions, honorably distinguishes them, is the purity of their sentiments, and their high moral feeling, especially in all that touches the relation of the sexes. We shall find many coarse expressions, such as a man would not read aloud to his family; but very rarely any thing bordering upon heartless profligacy, or studied licentiousness, or any intimation of a want of respect for the great principles of the moral law. Due reverence is always shown for those high personal qualities which constitute the best security for the greatness and prosperity of a people. Homage is always paid to honor in man, and chastity in woman. The passion of love, in its multitudinous forms and aspects, supplies a large proportion of their themes, and it is treated with equal delicacy and beauty. In the amatory strains of the old English poets, we perceive a romantic self-forgetfulness, an idealization of the beloved object, a tenderness and respectfulness of feeling, in which the passion is almost wholly swallowed up in the sentiment, and a wooing with the best treasures of the intellect as well as the heart, such as can be found in no other class of poets."

Notwithstanding the direct truth of what has been here so well advanced, it cannot, we think, be a matter of doubt with any reflecting mind, that at least one-third of the *reverence*, or of the *affection*, with which we regard the elder poets of Great Britain, should be credited to what is, in itself, a thing apart from poetry—we mean to the simple love of the antique—and that again a third of even the proper *poetic sentiment* inspired by these writings should be ascribed to a fact which, while it has a strict connection with poetry in the abstract, and also with the particular poems in question, must not be looked upon as a merit appertaining to the writers of the poems. Almost every devout reader of the old English bards, if demanded his opinion of their productions, would mention vaguely, yet with perfect sincerity, a sense of dreamy, wild, indefinite, and he would perhaps say, undefinable delight. Upon being required to point out the source of this so shadowy pleasure, he would be apt to speak of the quaint in phraseology and of the grotesque in rhythm. And this quaintness and grotesqueness are, as we have elsewhere endeavored to show, very powerful, and if well managed, very admissible adjuncts to Ideality. But in the present instance they arise independently of the author's will, and are matters altogether apart from his intention. The *American Monthly* has forcibly painted the general character of the old English Muse. She was a maid, frank, guileless, and perfectly sincere, and although very learned at times, still very learned without art. No general error evinces a more thorough confusion of ideas than the error of supposing Donne and Cowley metaphysical in the sense wherein Wordsworth and Coleridge are so. With the two former ethics were the end—with the two latter the means. The poet of the *Creation* wished, by highly artificial verse, to inculcate what he considered moral truth—he of the *Auncient Mariner* to infuse the *Poetic Sentiment* through channels suggested by mental analysis. The one finished by complete failure what he commenced in the grossest misconception—the other, by a path which could not possibly lead him astray, arrived at a certainty and intensity of triumph which is not the less brilliant and glorious because concentrated among the very few who have the power to perceive it. It will now be seen that even the "metaphysical verse" of Cowley is no more than evidence of the straight-forward simplicity and single-heartedness of the man. And he was in all this but a type of his *school*—for we may as well designate in this way the entire class of writers whose poems are bound up in the volume before us, and throughout all of whom runs a very perceptible general character. They used but little art in composition. Their writings sprang immediately from the soul—and partook intensely of the nature of that soul. It is not difficult to perceive the tendency of this glorious *abandon*. To elevate immeasurably all the energies of mind—but again—so to mingle the greatest possible fire, force, delicacy, and all good things, with the lowest possible bathos, baldness, and utter imbecility, as to render it not a matter of doubt, but of certainty, that the average results of mind in such a *school*, will be found inferior to those results in one (ceteris paribus) more artificial. Such, we think, is the view of the older English Poetry, in which a very calm examination will bear us out. The quaintness in manner of which we were just speaking, is an adventitious advantage. It formed no portion of the poet's intention. Words and their rhythm have varied. Verses which affect us to day with a vivid delight, and which delight in some instances, may be traced to this one source of grotesqueness and to none other, must have worn in the days of their construction an air of a very commonplace nature. This is no argument, it will be said, against the poems *now*. Certainly not—we mean it for the poets *then*. The notion of *power*, of excessive *power*, in the English antique writers should be put in its proper light. This is all we desire to see done.

We cannot bring ourselves to believe that the selections

made use of in the *Book of Gems*, are such as will impart to a poetical reader the highest possible idea of the beauty of the *school*. Better extracts might be made. Yet if the intention were merely to show the *character* of the school the attempt is entirely successful. There are long passages now before us of the most utterly despicable trash, with no merit whatever beyond their simple antiquity. And it is almost needless to say that there are many passages too of a glorious strength—a radiant loveliness, making the blood tingle in our veins as we peruse them. The criticisms of the Editor do not please us in a great degree. He seems to have fallen into the common cant in such cases. In one instance the American Monthly accords with him in an unjust opinion touching some verses by Sir Henry Wotton, on the Queen of Bohemia, daughter of James I, and about which it is said that "there are few finer things in our language." Our readers will agree with us, we believe, that this praise is exaggerated. We quote the lines in full.

> You meaner beauties of the night
> That poorly satisfy our eyes,
> More by your number than your light,
> You common people of the skies
>   What are you when the sun shall rise?
>
> You curious chaunters of the wood
> That warble forth dame Nature's lays,
> Thinking your passions understood
> By your weak accents; what's your praise
>   When Philomel her voice shall raise?
>
> You violets, that first appear
> By your pure purple mantles known,
> Like the proud virgins of the year
> As if the spring were all your own,
>   What are you when the rose is blown?
>
> So, when my mistress shall be seen
> In sweetness of her looks and mind,
> By virtue first, then choice a queen,
> Tell me if she were not designed
>   Th' eclipse and glory of her kind?

In such lines we can perceive *not one* of those higher attributes of the Muse which belong to her under all circumstances and throughout all time. Here every thing is art—
naked or but awkwardly concealed. No prepossession for the
mere antique (for in this case we can imagine no other prepossession) should induce us to dignify with the sacred name
of Poesy, a series such as this, of elaborate and threadbare
compliments, (threadbare even at the time of their composition) stitched apparently together, without fancy, without
plausibility, without adaptation of parts—and it is needless
to add, without a jot of imagination.

We have been much delighted with the *Shepherd's Hunting*,
by Wither—a poem partaking, in a strange degree, of the
peculiarities of the Penseroso. Speaking of Poesy he says—

> By the murmur of a spring
> Or the least boughs rusteling,
> By a daisy whose leaves spread
> Shut when Tytan goes to bed,
> Or a shady bush or tree
> She could more infuse in me
> Than all Nature's beauties can
> In some other wiser man.
> By her help I also now
> Make this churlish place allow
> Something that may sweeten gladness
> In the very gall of sadness—
> The dull loneness, the black shade
> That these hanging vaults have made,
> The strange music of the waves
> Beating on these hollow caves,
> This black den which rocks emboss
> Overgrown with eldest moss,
> The rude portals that give light
> More to terror than delight,
> This my chamber of neglect
> Walled about with disrespect—
> From all these and this dull air
> A fit object for despair,
> She hath taught me by her might
> To draw comfort and delight.

But these verses, however good, do not bear with them much of the general character of the English antique. Something more of this will be found in the following lines by Corbet—besides a rich vein of humor and sarcasm.

> Farewell rewards and fairies!
>   Good housewives now you may say,
> For now foul sluts in dairies
>   Do fare as well as they:
> And though they sweep their hearths no less
>   Than maids were wont to do,
> Yet who of late for cleanliness
>   Finds sixpence in her shoe?
>
> Lament, lament, old Abbies,
>   The fairies' lost command,
> They did but change priests' babies,
>   But some have changed your land;
> And all your children stolen from thence
>   Are now grown Puritanes,
> Who live as changelings ever since
>   For love of your demaines.
>
> At morning and at evening both
>   You merry were and glad,
> So little care of sleep and sloth
>   These pretty ladies had:
> When Tom came home from labor
>   Or Ciss to milking rose,
> Then merrily went their tabor
>   And nimbly went their toes.
>
> Witness those rings and roundelays
>   Of theirs which yet remain,
> Were footed in Queen Mary's days
>   On many a grassy plain;
> But since of late Elizabeth
>   And later James came in,
> They never danced on any heath
>   As when the time hath bin.

By which we note the fairies
   Were of the old profession,
Their songs were Ave Marys,
   Their dances were procession;
But now alas they all are dead
   Or gone beyond the seas,
Or farther for religion fled—
   Or else they take their ease.

A tell-tale in their company
   They never could endure,
And whoso kept not secretly
   Their mirth was punished sure;
It was a just and christian deed
   To pinch such black and blue—
O how the commonwealth doth need
   Such justices as you!

Now they have left our quarters
   A register they have,
Who can preserve their charters—
   A man both wise and grave.
An hundred of their merry pranks
   By one that I could name
Are kept in store; con twenty thanks
   To William for the same.

To William Churne of Staffordshire
   Give land and praises due,
Who every meal can mend your cheer
   With tales both old and true.
To William all give audience
   And pray you for his noddle,
For all the fairies evidence
   Were lost if it were addle.

The *Maiden lamenting for her Fawn*, by Marvell, is, we are pleased to see, a favorite with our friends of the American Monthly. Such portion of it as we now copy, we prefer not only as a specimen of the elder poets, but, in itself, as a beautiful poem, abounding in the sweetest pathos, in soft and gentle images, in the most exquisitely delicate imagination, and in *truth*—to any thing of its species.

It is a wondrous thing how fleet
'Twas on those little silver feet,
With what a pretty skipping grace
It oft would challenge me the race,
And when 't had left me far away
'Twould stay and run again and stay;
For it was nimbler much than hinds,
And trod as if on the four winds.
I have a garden of my own,
But so with roses overgrown,
And lilies that you would it guess
To be a little wilderness,
And all the spring-time of the year
It only loved to be there.
Among the beds of lilies I
Have sought it oft where it should lie,
Yet could not till itself would rise
Find it although before mine eyes.
For in the flaxen lilies shade,
It like a bank of lilies laid,
Upon the roses it would feed
Until its lips even seemed to bleed,
And then to me 'twould boldly trip,
And print those roses on my lip,
But all its chief delight was still
On roses thus itself to fill,
And its pure virgin limbs to fold
In whitest sheets of lilies cold.
Had it lived long it would have been
Lilies without, roses within.

How truthful an air of deep lamentation hangs here upon every gentle syllable! It pervades all. It comes over the sweet melody of the words, over the gentleness and grace which we fancy in the little maiden herself, even over the half-playful, half-petulant air with which she lingers on the beauties and good qualities of her favorite—like the cool shadow of a summer cloud over a bed of lilies and violets, and "all sweet flowers."

The whole thing is redolent with poetry of the *very loftiest order*. It is positively crowded with *nature* and with *pathos*. Every line is an idea—conveying either the beauty and playfulness of the fawn, or the artlessness of the maiden, or the love of the maiden, or her admiration, or her grief, or the fragrance and sweet warmth, and perfect *appropriateness* of the little nest-like bed of lilies and roses, which the fawn devoured as it lay upon them, and could scarcely be distinguished from them by the once happy little damsel who went to seek her pet with an arch and rosy smile upon her face. Consider the great variety of *truth* and delicate thought in the few lines we have quoted—the *wonder* of the maiden at the fleetness of her favorite—the *"little silver feet"*—the fawn challenging his mistress to the race, " with a pretty skipping grace," running on before, and then, with head turned back, awaiting her approach only to fly from it again—can we not distinctly perceive all these things? The exceeding vigor, too, and beauty of the line

> *And trod as if on the four winds,*

which are vividly apparent when we regard the artless nature of the speaker, and the *four feet* of the favorite— *one for each wind*. Then the garden of *"my own,"* so overgrown—entangled—with lilies and roses as to be "a little wilderness"—the fawn loving to be there and there *"only"*—the maiden seeking it " where it *should* lie," and not being able to distinguish it from the flowers until "itself would rise"—the lying among the lilies "like a bank of lilies"—the loving to *"fill"* itself with roses,

> And its pure virgin limbs to fold
> In whitest sheets of lilies cold,

and these things being its *"chief"* delights—and then the preeminent beauty and naturalness of the concluding lines—whose very outrageous hyperbole and absurdity only render them the more true to nature and to propriety, when we consider the innocence, the artlessness, the enthusiasm, the passionate grief, and more passionate admiration of the bereaved child.

Had it lived long it would have been
Lilies without—roses within.

Southern Literary Messenger, August 1836

William Hazlitt

Wiley and Putnam's Library of Choice Reading. No. XVII. *The Characters of Shakspeare.* By William Hazlitt.

THIS IS ONE of the most interesting numbers of "The Library" yet issued. If anything *could* induce us to read anything more in the way of commentary on Shakspeare, it would be the name of Hazlitt prefixed. With his hackneyed theme he has done wonders, and those wonders well. He is emphatically a critic, brilliant, epigrammatic, startling, paradoxical, and suggestive, rather than accurate, luminous, or profound. For purposes of mere amusement, he is the best commentator who ever wrote in English. At all points, except perhaps in fancy, he is superior to Leigh Hunt, whom nevertheless he remarkably resembles. It is folly to compare him with Macaulay, for there is scarcely a single point of approximation, and Macaulay is by much the greater man. The author of "The Lays of Ancient Rome" has an intellect so well balanced and so thoroughly proportioned, as to appear, in the eyes of the multitude, much smaller than it really is. He needs a few foibles to purchase him *éclat*. Now, take away the innumerable foibles of Hunt and Hazlitt, and we should have the anomaly of finding them more diminutive than we fancy them while the foibles remain. Nevertheless, they are men of genius still.

In all commentating upon Shakspeare, there has been a radical error, never yet mentioned. It is the error of attempting to expound his characters—to account for their actions—to reconcile his inconsistencies—not as if they were the coinage of a human brain, but as if they had been actual existences upon earth. We talk of Hamlet the man, instead of Hamlet the *dramatis persona*—of Hamlet that God, in place of Hamlet that Shakspeare created. If Hamlet had really lived, and if the tragedy were an accurate record of his deeds, from this record (with some trouble) we might, it is true, reconcile his inconsistences and settle to our satisfaction his true character. But the task becomes the purest absurdity when we deal only with a phantom. It is not (then) the inconsistencies of the acting man which we have as a subject of discussion—

(although we proceed as if it were, and thus *inevitably* err,) but the whims and vacillations—the conflicting energies and indolences of the poet. It seems to us little less than a miracle, that this obvious point should have been overlooked.

While on this topic, we may as well offer an ill-considered opinion of our own as to the *intention of the poet* in the delineation of the Dane. It must have been well known to Shakspeare, that a leading feature in certain more intense classes of intoxication, (from whatever cause,) is an almost irresistible impulse to counterfeit a farther degree of excitement than actually exists. Analogy would lead any thoughtful person to suspect the same impulse in madness—where beyond doubt, it is manifest. This, Shakspeare *felt*—not thought. He felt it through his marvellous power of *identification* with humanity at large—the ultimate source of his magical influence upon mankind. He wrote of Hamlet as if Hamlet he were; and having, in the first instance, imagined his hero excited to partial insanity by the disclosures of the ghost—he (the poet) *felt* that it was natural he should be impelled to exaggerate the insanity.

Broadway Journal, August 16, 1845

Thomas Hood

Wiley and Putnam's Library of Choice Reading. No. XVI. *Prose and Verse*. By Thomas Hood. Part I. New-York: Wiley and Putnam.

OF THIS number of the Library we said a few words last week—but Hood was far too remarkable a man to be passed over in so cursory a manner.

"Frequently since his recent death," says the American editor, "he has been called a great author, a phrase used not inconsiderately or in vain." Yet, if we adopt the conventional idea of "a great author," there has lived, perhaps, no writer of the last half century who, with equal notoriety, was *less* entitled than Hood to the term. In fact, he was a literary merchant whose principal stock in trade was littleness—for during the larger portion of his life he seemed to breathe only for the purpose of perpetrating puns—things of such despicable platitude, that the man who is capable of habitually committing them, is very seldom capable of anything else. In especial, whatever merit *may* accidentally be discovered in a pun, arises altogether from *unexpectedness*. This is its element, and is twofold. First, we demand that the combination of the pun be unexpected, and secondly, we demand the most entire unexpectedness in the pun *per se*. A rare pun, rarely appearing, is, to a certain extent, a pleasurable effect—but to no mind, however debased in taste, is a continuous effort at punning otherwise than unendurable. The man who maintains that he derives gratification from any such chapters of punnage as Hood was in the daily habit of putting to paper, has no claim to be believed upon his oath. What, for example, is any rational being to make of such jargon as this, which we copy from the very first page of the volume before us?

COURTEOUS READER!

Presuming that you have known something of the Comic Annual from its Child-Hood, when it was first put into half binding and began to run alone, I make bold to consider you as an old friend of the family, and shall accordingly treat you with all the freedom and confidence that pertain to such ripe connexions.

How many years is it, think you, "since we were first ac-
quent?"

"By the deep *nine!*" sings out the old bald *Count Fathom*
with the lead-line: no great lapse in the world's chronology,
but a space of infinite importance in individual history. For
instance, it has wrought a serious change on the body, if not
on the mind, of your very humble servant;—it is not, however, to bespeak your sympathy, or to indulge in what Lord
Byron calls "the gloomy vanity of drawing from self," that I
allude to my personal experience. The Scot and lot character
of the dispensation forbids me to think that the world in general can be particularly interested in the state of my Household Sufferage, or that the public ear will be as open to my
Maladies as to my Melodies.

Here is something better from page five—but still we look
upon the whole thing as a nuisance:

A rope is a bad Cordon Sanitaire. Let not anxiety have thee
on the hyp. Consider your health as your best friend, and
think as well of it, in spite of all its foibles as you can. For
instance, never dream, though you may have a "clever hack,"
of galloping consumption, or indulge in the Meltonian belief
that you are going the pace. Never fancy every time you
cough, that you are going to coughypot. Hold up, as the
shooter says, over the heaviest ground. Despondency in a nice
case is the over-weight that may make you kick the beam and
the bucket both at once. In short, as with other cases, never
meet trouble half-way, but let him have the whole walk for
his pains; though it should be a Scotch mile and a bittock. I
have even known him to give up his visit in sight of the
house. Besides, the best fence against care is a ha! ha!—where-
fore take care to have one all around you wherever you can.
Let your "lungs crow like Chanticleer," and as like a Game
cock as possible. It expands the chest, enlarges the heart,
quickens the circulation, and "like a trumpet makes the spirit
dance."

The continuous and premeditated puns of Hood, however,
are to be regarded as the weak points of the man. Indepen-

dently of their ill effect, in a literary view, as mere puns, they leave upon us a painful impression; for too evidently they are the hypochondriac's struggles at mirth—they are the grinnings of the death's-head. No one can read his Literary Reminiscences without being convinced of his habitual despondency—and the species of pseudo wit in question, is precisely of that character which would be adopted by an author of Hood's temperament and cast of intellect, when compelled to write, at an emergency. That his heart had no interest in these *niaiseries*, is clear. We allude, of course, to his *mere* puns for the pun's sake—a class of letters by which he attained his most extensive renown. That he did *more* in this way than in any other, would follow as a corollary from what we have already said—for, generally, he was unhappy, and, almost continually, he was obliged to write, *invitâ Minerva*. But his true element was a very rare and ethereal class of *humor*, in which the *mere* pun was left altogether out of sight, or took the character of the richest *grotesquerie*, impressing the imaginative reader with very remarkable force, as if by a new phase of the ideal. It is in this species of brilliant *grotesquerie*, uttered with a rushing *abandon* which wonderfully aided its effect, that Hood's marked originality of manner consisted; and it is this which fairly entitles him, at times, to the epithet "great;"—we say fairly so entitles him; for *that* undeniably may be considered *great*—(of whatever seeming littleness in itself) which has the capability of producing intense emotion in the minds of those who are themselves undeniably great.

When we said, however, that Hood wrought profound impressions upon imaginative men, we spoke only of what is imagination in the popular acceptance of the term. His true province—that is to say the field in which he is distinctive—is a kind of border land between the Fancy and the Fantasy—but in this region he reigns supreme. That we may be the more clearly understood on this head, we will venture to quote a few passages of definition which were used by ourselves on a former occasion—while commenting on the prose style of Mr. Willis:—it is indeed too much the custom to employ at absolute random such words as Wit, Humor, Fantasy, the Fancy, and the Imagination.

In the style of Mr. Willis we easily detect this idiosyncrasy. We have no trouble in tracing it home—and when we reach it and look it fairly in the face, we recognize it on the instant.—It is Fancy.

To be sure there is quite a tribe of Fancies—although one half of them never suspected themselves to be such until so told by the metaphysicians—but the one of which we speak has never yet been accredited among men, and we beg pardon of Mr. Willis for the liberty we take in employing the topic of his *style*, as the best possible vehicle and opportunity for the introduction of this, our *protégé*, to the consideration of the literary world.

"Fancy," says the author of "Aids to Reflection" (who aided Reflection to much better purpose in his "Genevieve")—"Fancy combines—Imagination creates." This was intended, and has been received, as a distinction; but it is a distinction without a difference—without even a difference of degree. The Fancy as nearly creates as the imagination, and neither at all. Novel conceptions are merely unusual combinations. The mind of man can imagine nothing which does not exist:—if it could, it would create not only ideally, but substantially—as do the thoughts of God. It may be said—"We imagine a griffin, yet a griffin does not exist." Not the griffin certainly, but its component parts. It is no more than a collation of known limbs—features—qualities. Thus with all which claims to be new—which appears to be a *creation* of the intellect:—it is re-soluble into the old. The wildest effort of the mind cannot stand the test of the analysis.

We might make a distinction of *degree* between the fancy and the imagination, in calling the latter the former loftily employed. But experience would prove this distinction to be unsatisfactory. What we *feel* to be fancy, will be found still fanciful, whatever be the theme which engages it. No *subject* exalts it into imagination. When Moore is termed a fanciful poet, the epithet is precisely applied; he *is*. He is fanciful in "Lalla Rookh," and had he written the "Inferno," there he would have been fanciful still: for not only is he essentially fanciful, but he has no ability to be any thing more, unless at rare intervals—by snatches—and with effort. What we say of him at this point, moreover, is equally true of all little frisky men, personally considered.

The fact seems to be that Imagination, Fancy, Fantasy, and Humor, have in common the elements, Combination, and Novelty. The Imagination is the artist of the four. From novel arrangements of old forms which present themselves to it, it selects only such as are harmonious:—the result, of course, is *beauty* itself—using the term in its most extended sense, and as inclusive of the sublime. The pure imagination chooses, *from either beauty or deformity*, only the most combinable things hitherto uncombined;—the compound, as a general rule, partaking (in character) of sublimity or beauty, in the ratio of the respective sublimity or beauty of the things combined—which are themselves still to be considered as atomic—that is to say, as previous combinations. But, as often analogously happens in physical chemistry, so not unfrequently does it occur in this chemistry of the intellect, that the admixture of two elements will result in a something that shall have nothing of the quality of one of them—or even nothing of the qualities of either. The range of Imagination is therefore, unlimited. Its materials extend throughout the Universe. Even out of deformities it fabricates that *beauty* which is at once its sole object and its inevitable test. But, in general, the richness or force of the matters combined—the facility of discovering combinable novelties worth combining—and the absolute "chemical combination" and proportion of the completed mass—are the particulars to be regarded in our estimate of Imagination. It is this thorough harmony of an imaginative work which so often causes it to be under-valued by the undiscriminating, through the character of *obviousness* which is super-induced. We are apt to find ourselves asking "*why is it* that these combinations have never been imagined before?"

Now, when this question *does not occur*—when the harmony of the combination is comparatively neglected, and when in addition to the element of novelty, there is introduced the sub-element of *unexpectedness*—when, for example, matters are brought into combination which not only have never been combined but whose combination strikes us *as a difficulty happily overcome*—the result then appertains to the

FANCY—and is, to the majority of mankind more grate-ful than the purely harmonious one—although, absolutely, it is less beautiful (or grand) for the reason that *it is* less harmonious.

Carrying its errors into excess—for, however enticing, they *are* errors still, or Nature lies,—Fancy is at length found im-pinging upon the province of *Fantasy.* The votaries of this latter delight not only in novelty and unexpectedness of com-bination, but in the *avoidance* of proportion. The result is therefore abnormal, and to a healthy mind affords less of plea-sure through its novelty, than of pain through its incoher-ence. When, proceeding a step farther, however, Fantasy seeks not merely disproportionate but incongruous or antag-onistical elements, the effect is rendered more pleasurable from its greater positiveness;—there is a merry effort of Truth to shake from her that which is no property of hers;—and we laugh outright in recognizing *Humor.*

The four faculties in question appear to me all of their class;—but when either Fancy or Humor is expressed to gain an end—is pointed at a purpose—whenever either becomes objective in place of subjective—then it becomes, also, pure Wit or Sarcasm, just as the purpose is well-intentioned or malevolent.

These, we grant, are entirely new views, but we do not consider them as the less surely deduced. At all events their admission for the present will enable us to be lucid on the topic of Hood. When we speak of his province as a border ground between Fantasy and Fancy, of course we do not mean rigorously to confine him to this province. He has made very successful and frequent incursions into the dominions of Humor (in general he has been too benevolent to be witty), and there have been one or two occasions—(those, for in-stance, of his "Eugene Aram" and "Bridge of Sighs,") in which he has stepped boldly, yet vacillatingly, into the realm of Imagination herself. We mean to say, however, that he is never truly imaginative for more than a paragraph at a time.

In a word, the genius of Hood is the result of vivid Fancy impelled, or controlled,—certainly tinctured, at all points, by hypochondriasis. In his wild "Ode to Melancholy," which

forms the closing poem of the volume now reviewed, we perceive this result in the very clearest of manifestations. Few
things have ever more deeply affected us than the passages
which follow:

> "O clasp me, sweet, whilst thou art mine,
>   And do not take my tears amiss;
>   For tears must flow to wash away
>   A thought that shows so stern as this:
>   Forgive, if somewhile I forget,
>   In wo to come, the present bliss.
>   As frighted Proserpine let fall
>   Her flowers at the sight of Dis,
>   Ev'n so the dark and bright will kiss.
>   The sunniest things throw sternest shade,
>   And there is ev'n a happiness
>   That makes the heart afraid!
>
>   All things are touched with Melancholy,
>   Born of the secret soul's mistrust,
>   To feel her fair ethereal wings
>   Weigh'd down with vile degraded dust;
>   Even the bright extremes of joy
>   Bring on conclusions of disgust,
>   Like the sweet blossoms of the May,
>   Whose fragrance ends in must.
>   Oh give her, then, her tribute just,
>   Her sighs and tears, and musings holy!
>   There is no music in the life
>   That sounds with idiot laughter solely;
>   There's not a string attuned to mirth,
>   But has its chords of Melancholy."

In "The Pugsley Papers," with which the volume opens, we
have the correspondence of a Cockney family of shoemakers,
who, receiving a rich legacy, retire at once to the *otium cum
dignitate* of a country mansion. The mishaps and mismanage-
ments of the party are told in the broadest extravaganza admissible or conceivable—very much in the Ramsbottom
way—although the tone of Hood's *jeu d'esprit* is the better of
the two. It is not so much humorous in itself, as productive

of the usual humorous effect. We laugh not altogether at the incongruities of the narrative, but at the incongruity of Hood's supposing that we will laugh at anything so absurd;—and it must be confessed, that it all amounts to pretty much the same thing in the end.

"Black, White and Brown," is an Abolition tale—or rather a squib against Abolition. Its *finale* has some point—but, on the whole, the story has the air of an effort, and is quite unworthy of Hood.

"The Portrait," "The Apology," and "The Literary Reminiscences" (which form one subject,) have, we think, exceedingly little interest. The author himself acknowledges that he has no capacity for Boswellism—and we agree with him altogether.

"An Undertaker" is a mere string of puns—giving no idea of the true spirit of the author.

The rest of the book is verse—and much of it very remarkable verse indeed.

"The Dream of Eugene Aram," is too well known in America to need comment from us. It has (as we observed just now,) more of true imagination than any composition of its author;—but even when engaged on so serious a subject, he found great difficulty in keeping aloof from the grotesque—the result (we say) of warm Fancy impelled by Hypochondriasis. The opening stanza affords an example:

" 'Twas in the prime of summer time,
    An evening calm and cool,
  When four-and-twenty happy boys
    Came bounding out of school;
  There were some that ran, *and some that leapt,*
    Like troutlets in a pool."

Stanza the twenty-fourth approaches more nearly the imaginative spirit than any passage in the poem—but the taint of the fantastical is over it still:

"And peace went with them one and all,
    And each calm pillow spread;
  But Guilt was my grim chamberlain
    That lighted me to bed.

And drew my midnight curtains round,
With fingers bloody red!"

"The Lost Heir" is possibly aimed at a well-known novel of the same title. The effect depends upon the principle to which we referred when speaking of "The Pugsley Papers." We laugh chiefly (although not altogether) at the *author's* absurdity. The lines belong to the class *helter-skelter*—that is to say, they are the flattest of all possible prose—intentionally so, of course. The story (if story it can be called) embodies the lamentations of a poor Irish woman who has lost her son.

"Autumn" and "A Song," (occupying each one page) have nothing about them especially remarkable. "Fair Ines" is so beautiful that we shall purloin it in full—although we have no doubt that it is familiar to our readers:

I.

O saw ye not fair Ines?
    She's gone into the West,
To dazzle when the sun is down,
    And rob the world of rest;
She took our daylight with her,
    The smiles that we love best,
With morning blushes on her cheek,
    And pearls upon her breast.

II.

O turn again, fair Ines,
    Before the fall of night,
For fear the moon should shine alone,
    And stars unrivalled bright;
And blessed will the lover be
    That walks beneath their light,
And breathes the love against thy cheek
    I dare not even write!

III.

Would I had been, fair Ines,
    That gallant cavalier,

Who rode so gaily by thy side,
    And whispered thee so near!
Were there no bonny dames at home,
    Or no true lovers here,
That he should cross the seas to win
    The dearest of the dear?

IV.

I saw thee, lovely Ines,
    Descend along the shore,
With bands of noble gentlemen,
    And banners waved before;
And gentle youth and maidens gay,
    And snowy plumes they wore;
It would have been a beauteous dream,
    —If it had been no more!

V.

Alas, alas, fair Ines,
    She went away with song,
With Music waiting on her steps,
    And shoutings of the throng;
But some were sad and felt no mirth,
But only Music's wrong,
In sounds that sang Farewell, Farewell,
    To her you've loved so long.

VI.

Farewell, farewell, fair Ines,
    That vessel never bore
So fair a lady on its deck,
    Nor danced so light before,—
Alas, for pleasure on the sea,
    And sorrow on the shore!
    The smile that blest one lover's heart
    Has broken many more!

The only article which remains to be noticed, is "Miss Kill-mansegg and Her Precious Leg"—and it is, perhaps, more thoroughly characteristic of Hood's genius than any single thing which he has written. It is quite a long poem—comprising nearly 3000 lines—and its author has evidently laboured it much. Its chief defect is in its versification; and for this Hood had no ear—of its principles he knew nothing at all. Not that his verses, individually, are very lame, but they have no capacity for running together. The reader is continually getting baulked—not because the lines are unreadable, but because the lapse from one rhythm to another is so inartistically managed.

The story concerns a very rich heiress who is excessively pampered by her parents, and who at length gets thrown from a horse and so injures a leg as to render amputation inevitable. To supply the place of the true limb, she insists upon a leg of solid gold—a leg of the exact proportions of the original. She puts up with its inconvenience for the sake of the admiration it excites. Its attractions, however, excite the cupidity of a *chevalier d'industrie*, who cajoles her into wedlock, dissipates her fortune, and, finally, purloining her golden leg, dashes out her brains with it, elopes, and puts an end to the story.

It is wonderfully well told, and abounds in the most brilliant points—embracing something of each of the elementary faculties which we have been discussing—but most especially rich in that which we have termed *Fantasy*. We quote at random some brief passages, which will serve to exemplify our meaning:

> A Lord of Land, on his own estate,
> He lived at a lively rate,
>   But his income would bear carousing;
> Such acres he had of pasture and heath,
> With herbage so rich from the ore beneath,
> *The very ewe's and lambkin's teeth*
>   *Were turn'd into gold by browsing.*
>
> He gave, without any extra thrift,
> A flock of sheep for a birthday gift
>   To each son of his loins, or daughter:
> And his debts—if debts he had—at will
> *He liquidated by giving each bill*
>   *A dip in Pactolian water.*

'Twas said that even *his pigs of lead,*
By crossing with some by Midas bred,
  Made a perfect mine of his piggery.
And as for cattle, one yearling bull
Was worth all Smithfield-market full
  Of the Golden Bulls of Pope Gregory.

The high-bred horses within his stud,
Like human creatures of birth and blood,
  Had their Golden Cups and flagons:
And as for the common husbandry nags,
Their noses were tied in money-bags,
  When they stopp'd with the carts and wagons.

Into this world we come like ships,
Launched from the docks and stocks and slips,
  For fortune fair or fatal;
And one little craft *is cast away*
In its very first trip to Babbicome Bay,
  While another rides safe at Port Natal.

Whilst Margaret, charm'd by the Bulbul rare,
  In a garden of Gul reposes—
Poor Peggy hawks nosegays from street to street,
Till—think of that, who find life so sweet!—
  She hates the smell of roses!

To paint the maternal Kilmansegg
The pen of an Eastern Poet would beg,
  And need an elaborate sonnet;
How she sparkled with gems whenever she stirred,
And her head niddle-nodded at every word,
And seem'd so happy, a Paradise bird
  Had nidificated upon it.

And Sir Jacob the Father strutted and bow'd,
And smiled to himself, and laugh'd aloud,
  To think of his heiress and daughter—
And then in his pockets he made a grope,

And then in the fulness of joy and hope,
Seem'd washing himself with invisible soap,
   In imperceptible water.

Gold! and gold! and besides the gold
The very robe of the infant told
A tale of wealth in every fold,
   It lapp'd her like a vapor!
So fine! so thin! the mind at a loss
Could compare it to nothing *except a cross*
   Of cobweb with bank-note paper.

They praised—how they praised—her very small talk,
   As if it fell from a Solon;
Or the girl who at each pretty phrase let drop
A ruby comma, or a pearl full stop,
   Or an emerald semi-colon.

Plays she perused—but she liked the best
These comedy gentlefolks always possess'd
   Of fortunes so truly romantic—
Of money so ready that right or wrong
It is always ready to go for a song,
Throwing it, going it, pitching it strong—
They ought to have *purses as green and long*
   As the cucumber called the Gigantic.

A load of treasure?—alas! alas!
Had her horse been fed upon English grass,
   And sheltered in Yorkshire Spinneys,
Had he scour'd the sand with the Desert Ass,
   Or where the American whinnies—
But a hunter from Erin's Turf and gorse,
A regular thorough bred *Irish horse,*
Why, he ran away, as a matter of course,
   With a girl worth her weight in guineas!

"Batter her! shatter her!
 Throw her and scatter her!"
 Shouts each stony-hearted clatterer—

"Dash at the heavy Dover!
Spill her! kill her! tear her and tatter her!
Smash her! crash her!" (the stones did'nt flatter her!)
"Kick her brains out! let her blood spatter her!
    Roll on her over and over!"
For so she gather'd *the awful sense*
Of the street in its past unmacadamised tense,
    As the wild horse overran it, —
His four heels making the clatter of six,
Like a Devil's tattoo, played with iron sticks
    On a kettle-drum of granite!

A Breakfast—no unsubstantial mess,
But one in the style of good Queen Bess,
    Who,— *hearty as hippocampus,* —
Broke her fast with ale and beef,
Instead of toast and the Chinese leaf,
    And in lieu of anchovy—grampus!

In they went, and hunted about,
Open-mouth'd, like chub and trout,
And some with the upper lip thrust out,
    Like that fish for routing, a barbel—
While Sir Jacob stood to welcome the crowd,
And rubb'd his hands, and smiled aloud,
And bow'd, and bow'd, and bow'd, and bow'd,
    Like a man who is sawing marble.

But a child—that bids the world good night
In downright earnest and cuts it quite—
    A Cherub no art can copy, —
'Tis a perfect picture to see him lie
As if he had supped on dormouse pie,
(An ancient classical dish by the by)
        With a sauce of syrup of poppy.

So still without,—so still within;—
    It had been a sin
    To drop a pin—
So intense is silence after a din,

It seem'd like Death's rehearsal!
To stir the air no eddy came;
And the taper burnt with as still a flame,
As to flicker had been a burning shame,
In a calm so universal.

And oh! when the blessed diurnal light
Is quench'd by the providential night,
　To render our slumber more certain,
Pity, pity the wretches that weep,
For they must be wretched that cannot sleep
　When God himself draws the Curtain!

Broadway Journal, August 9, 1845

R. H. Horne

Orion: an Epic Poem in Three Books. By R. H. Horne. Fourth Edition. London: Published by J. Miller.

IN THE JANUARY NUMBER of this magazine, the receipt of this work was mentioned, and it was hinted that, at some future period, it should be made the subject of review. We proceed now to fulfill that promise.

And first a word or two of gossip and personality.

Mr. R. H. Horne, the author of "Orion," has, of late years, acquired a high and extensive *home* reputation, although, as yet, he is only partially known in America. He will be remembered, however, as the author of a very well-written Introduction to Black's Translation of Schlegel's "Lectures on Dramatic Art and Literature," and as a contributor with Wordsworth, Hunt, Miss Barrett, and others, to "Chaucer Modernized." He is the author, also, of "Cosmo de Medici," of "The Death of Marlowe," and, especially, of "Gregory the Seventh," a fine tragedy, prefaced with an "Essay on Tragic Influence." "Orion" was originally advertised to be sold for *a farthing*; and, at this price, three large editions were actually sold. The fourth edition, (a specimen of which now lies before us) was issued at a shilling, and also *sold*. A fifth is promised at half a crown; this likewise, with even a sixth at a crown, may be disposed of—partly through the intrinsic merit of the work itself—but, chiefly, through the ingenious novelty of the original price.

We have been among the earliest readers of Mr. Horne—among the most earnest admirers of his high genius;—for a man of high, of the highest genius, he unquestionably is. With an eager wish to do justice to his "Gregory the Seventh," we have never yet found exactly that opportunity we desired. Meantime, we looked, with curiosity, for what the British critics would say of a work which, in the boldness of its conception, and in the fresh originality of its management, would necessarily fall beyond the *routine* of their customary verbiage. We saw nothing, however, that either could or should be understood—nothing, certainly, that was worth understanding. The tragedy itself was, unhappily, not devoid of the ruling cant of the day, and its critics (that cant incarnate) took their cue from some of its infected passages, and proceeded forthwith to rhapsody and æsthetics, by way of giving a common-sense public an intelligible idea of the book. By the "cant of the day" we mean the disgusting practice of putting on the airs of an owl, and endeavoring to look miraculously wise;—the affectation of second sight—of a species of ecstatic prescience—of an intensely bathetic penetration into all sorts of mysteries, psychological ones in especial;—an Orphic—an ostrich affectation, which buries its head in balderdash, and, seeing nothing itself, fancies, therefore, that its preposterous carcass is not a visible object of derision for the world at large.

Of "Orion" itself, we have, as yet, seen few notices in the British periodicals, and these few are merely repetitions of the old jargon. All that has been said, for example, might be summed up in some such paragraph as this:

" 'Orion' is the *earnest* outpouring of the oneness of the psychological MAN. It has the individuality of the true SIN-GLENESS. It is not to be regarded as a Poem, but as a WORK—as a multiple THEOGONY—as a manifestation of the WORKS and the DAYS. It is a pinion in the PROGRESS—a wheel in the MOVEMENT that moveth ever and goeth alway—a mirror of SELF-INSPECTION, held up by the SEER of the Age essential—of the Age *in esse*—for the SEERS of the Ages possible—*in posse*. We hail a brother in the work."

Of the mere opinions of the donkeys who bray thus—of their mere dogmas and doctrines, literary, æsthetical, or what not—we know little, and, upon our honor, we wish to know less. Occupied, Laputically, in their great work of a progress that never progresses, we take it for granted, also, that they care as little about ours. But whatever the opinions of these people may be—however portentous the "IDEA" which they have been so long threatening to "evolve"—we still think it clear that they take a very roundabout way of evolving it. The use of Language is in the promulgation of Thought. If a man—if an Orphicist—or a SEER—or whatever else he may choose to call himself, while the rest of the world calls him an ass—if this gentleman have an idea which he does not understand himself, the best thing he can do is to say nothing about it; for, of course, he can entertain no hope that what he, the SEER, cannot comprehend, should be comprehended by the mass of common humanity; but if he have an idea which is actually intelligible to himself, and if he sincerely wish to render it intelligible to others, we then hold it as indisputable that he should employ those forms of speech which are the best adapted to further his object. He should speak to the people in that people's ordinary tongue. He should arrange words, such as are habitually employed for the several preliminary and introductory ideas to be conveyed— he should arrange them in collocations such as those in which we are accustomed to see those words arranged.

But to all this the Orphicist thus replies: "I am a SEER. My IDEA—the idea which by Providence I am especially commissioned to evolve—is one so vast—so novel—that ordinary words, in ordinary collocations, will be insufficient for its comfortable evolution." Very true. We grant the vastness of the IDEA—it is manifested in the sucking of the thumb—but, then, if *ordinary* language be insufficient—the ordinary language which men understand— *à fortiori* will be insufficient that inordinate language which no man has *ever* understood, and which any well-educated baboon would blush in being accused of understanding. The "SEER," therefore, has no resource but to oblige mankind by holding his tongue, and suffering his IDEA to remain quietly "unevolved," until some Mesmeric mode of intercommunication shall be invented, whereby the antipodal brains of the SEER and of the man of Common Sense shall be brought into the necessary *rapport*. Meantime we earnestly ask if *bread-and-butter* be the vast IDEA in question—if *bread-and-butter* be any portion of this vast IDEA; for we have often observed that when a SEER has to speak of even so usual a thing as bread-and-butter, he can never be induced to mention it outright. He will, if you choose, say any thing and every thing *but* bread-and-butter. He will consent to hint at buckwheat cake. He may even accommodate you so far as to insinuate oatmeal porridge—but, if bread-and-butter be really the matter intended, we never yet met the Orphicist who could get out the three individual words "bread-and-butter."

We have already said that "Gregory the Seventh" was, unhappily, infected with the customary cant of the day—the cant of the muddle-pates who dishonor a profound and ennobling philosophy by styling themselves transcendentalists. In fact, there are few highly sensitive or imaginative intellects for which the vortex of *mysticism*, in any shape, has not an almost irresistible influence, on account of the shadowy confines which separate the Unknown from the Sublime. Mr. Horne, then, is, in some measure, infected. The success of his previous works had led him to attempt, zealously, the production of a poem which should be worthy his high powers. We have no doubt that he revolved carefully in mind a variety of august conceptions, and from these thoughtfully selected what his judgment, rather than what his impulses, designated as the noblest and the best. In a word, he has weakly yielded his own poetic sentiment of the poetic—yielded it, in some degree, to the pertinacious opinion, and *talk*, of a certain junto by which he is surrounded—a junto of dreamers whose absolute intellect may, perhaps, compare with his own very much after the fashion of an ant-hill with the Andes. By this talk—by its continuity rather than by any other quality it possessed—he has been badgered into the attempt at commingling the obstinate oils and waters of Poetry and of Truth. He has been so far blinded as to permit himself to imagine that a maudlin philosophy (granting it to be worth enforcing) could be enforced by poetic imagery, and illustrated by the jingling of rhythm; or, more unpardonably, he has been induced to believe that a poem, whose single object is the creation of Beauty—the novel collocation of old forms of the Beautiful and of the Sublime—could be advanced by the abstractions of a maudlin philosophy.

But the question is not even this. It is not whether it be not possible to introduce didacticism, with effect, into a poem, or possible to introduce poetical images and measures, with effect, into a didactic essay. To do either the one or the other, would be merely to surmount a difficulty—would be simply a feat of literary sleight of hand. But the true question is, whether the author who shall attempt either feat, will not be laboring at a disadvantage—will not be guilty of a fruitless and wasteful expenditure of energy. In minor poetical efforts, we may not so imperatively demand an adherence to the true poetical thesis. We permit *trifling* to some extent, in a work which we consider a trifle at best. Although we agree, for example, with Coleridge, that poetry and *passion* are discordant, yet we are willing to permit Tennyson to bring, to the intense *passion* which prompted his "Locksley Hall," the aid of that terseness and pungency which are derivable from rhythm and from rhyme. The effect he produces, however, is a purely passionate, and not, unless in detached passages of this magnificent philippic, a properly poetic effect. His "Œnone," on the other hand, exalts the soul not into passion, but into a conception of pure *beauty*, which in its elevation— its calm and intense rapture—has in it a foreshadowing of the future and spiritual life, and as far transcends earthly passion as the holy radiance of the sun does the glimmering and feeble phosphorescence of the glow-worm. His "Morte D'Arthur" is in the same majestic vein. The "Sensitive Plant" of Shelley is in the same sublime spirit. Nor, if the passionate poems of Byron excite more intensely a greater number of readers than either the "Œnone" or the "Sensitive Plant"— does this indisputable fact prove any thing more than that the majority of mankind are more susceptible of the impulses of passion than of the impressions of beauty. Readers do exist, however, and always will exist, who, to hearts of maddening fervor, unite, in perfection, the sentiment of the beautiful— that divine sixth sense which is yet so faintly understood— that sense which phrenology has attempted to embody in its organ of *ideality*—that sense which is the basis of all Fourier's dreams—that sense which speaks of GOD through his purest, if not his *sole* attribute—which proves, and which alone proves his existence.

To readers such as these—and only to such as these—must be left the decision of what the true Poesy is. And these— with *no* hesitation—will decide that the origin of Poetry lies in a thirst for a wilder Beauty than Earth supplies—that Poetry itself is the imperfect effort to quench this immortal thirst by novel combinations of beautiful forms (collocations of forms) physical or spiritual, and that this thirst when even partially allayed—this sentiment when even feebly meeting response—produces emotion to which all other human emotions are vapid and insignificant.

We shall now be fully understood. If, with Coleridge, who, however erring at times, was precisely the mind fitted to decide a question such as this—if, with him, we reject *passion* from the true—from the pure poetry—if we reject even passion—if we discard as feeble, as unworthy the high spirituality of the theme, (which has its origin in a sense of the Godhead) if we dismiss even the nearly divine emotion of human *love*—that emotion which, merely to name, *now* causes the pen to tremble—with how much greater reason shall we dismiss all else? And yet there are men who would mingle with the august theme the merest questions of expediency—the cant topics of the day—the doggerel æsthetics of the time—who would trammel the soul in its flight to an ideal Helusion, by the quirks and quibbles of chopped logic. There are men who do this— lately there are a set of men who make a practice of doing this—and who defend it on the score of the advancement of what they suppose to be *truth*. Truth is, in its own essence, sublime—but her loftiest sublimity, as derived from man's clouded and erratic reason, is valueless—is pulseless—is utterly ineffective when brought into comparison with the unerring *sense* of which we speak; yet grant this *truth* to be all which its seekers and worshipers pretend—they forget that it is not truth, *per se*, which is made their thesis, but an *argumentation*, often maudlin and pedantic, always shallow and unsatisfactory (as from the mere inadaptation of the vehicle it *must* be) by which this *truth*, in casual and indeterminate glimpses, is— *or is not*—rendered manifest.

We have said that, in minor poetical efforts, we may tolerate some deflection from the true poetical thesis; but when a man of the highest powers sets himself seriously to the task of constructing what shall be most worthy those powers, we expect that he shall so choose his theme as to render it certain that he labor not at disadvantage. We regret to see any trivial or partial imperfection of detail; but we grieve deeply when we detect any radical error of conception.

In setting about "Orion," Mr. Horne proposed to himself, (in accordance with the views of his junto) to "elaborate a morality"—he ostensibly proposed this to himself—for, in the depths of his heart, we *know* that he wished all juntos and all moralities in Erebus. In accordance with the notions of his *set*, however, he felt a species of shame-facedness in not making the enforcement of some certain dogmas or doctrines (questionable or unquestionable) about PROGRESS, the obvious or apparent object of his poem. This shame-facedness is the cue to the concluding sentence of the Preface. "Mean time, the design of this poem of 'Orion' is far from being intended as a mere echo or reflection of the past, and is, in itself, and in other respects, a novel experiment upon the mind of a nation." Mr. Horne conceived, in fact, that to compose a poem merely for that poem's sake—and to acknowledge such to be his purpose—would be to subject himself to the charge of imbecility—of triviality—of deficiency in the true dignity and force; but, had he listened to the dictates of his own soul, he could not have failed to perceive, at once, that under the sun there exists no work more intrinsically noble, than this very poem *written solely for the poem's sake*.

But let us regard "Orion" as it is. It has an under and an upper current of meaning; in other words, it is an allegory. But the poet's sense of fitness (which, under no circumstances of mere conventional opinion, could be more than half subdued) has so far softened this allegory as to keep it, generally, well subject to the ostensible narrative. The purport of the moral conveyed is by no means clear—showing conclusively that the heart of the poet was not with it. It vacillates. At one time a certain set of opinions predominate—then another. We may generalize the subject, however, by calling it a homily against supineness or apathy in the cause of human PROGRESS, and in favor of energetic action for the good of the race. This is precisely *the* IDEA of the present school of canters. How feebly the case is made out in the poem—how insufficient has been all Mr. Horne's poetical rhetoric in convincing even himself—may be gleaned from the unusual bombast, rigmarole, and mystification of the concluding paragraph, in which he has thought it necessary to say something *very* profound, by way of putting the sting to his epigram,— the point to his moral. The words put us much in mind of the "nonsense verses" of Du Bartas.

> And thus, in the end, each soul may to itself,
> With truth before it as its polar guide,

> Become both Time and Nature, whose fixt paths
> Are spiral, and when lost will find new stars,
> And in the universal MOVEMENT join.

The upper current of the theme is based upon the various Greek fables about Orion. The author, in his brief preface, speaks about " writing from an old Greek fable"—but his story is, more properly, a very judicious selection and modification of a great variety of Greek and Roman fables concerning Orion and other personages with whom these fables bring Orion in collision. And here we have only to object that the really magnificent abilities of Mr. Horne might have been better employed in an entirely original conception. The story he tells is beautiful indeed,—and *nil tetigit*, certainly, *quod non ornavit*—but our memories—our classic recollections are continually at war with his claims to regard, and we too often find ourselves rather speculating upon what he might have done, than admiring what he has really accomplished.

The narrative, as our poet has arranged it, runs nearly thus: Orion, hunting on foot amid the mountains of Chios, encounters Artemis (Diana) with her train. The goddess, at first indignant at the giant's intrusion upon her grounds, becomes, in the second place, enamored. Her pure love spiritualizes the merely animal nature of Orion, but does not render him happy. He is filled with vague aspirations and desires. He buries himself in sensual pleasures. In the mad dreams of intoxication, he beholds a vision of Merope, the daughter of Œnopion, king of Chios. She is the type of physical beauty. She cries in his ear, "Depart from Artemis! She loves thee not—thou art too full of earth." Awaking, he seeks the love of Merope. It is returned. Œnopion, dreading the giant and his brethren, yet scorning his pretensions, temporizes. He consents to bestow upon Orion the hand of Merope, on condition of the island being cleared, within six days, of its savage beasts and serpents. Orion, seeking the aid of his brethren, accomplishes the task. Œnopion again hesitates. Enraged, the giants make war upon him, and carry off the princess. In a remote grove Orion lives, in bliss, with his earthly love. From this delirium of happiness, he is aroused by the vengeance of Œnopion, who causes him to be surprised while asleep, and deprived of sight. The princess, being retaken, immediately forgets and deserts her lover, who, in his wretchedness, seeks, at the suggestion of a shepherd, the aid of Eos (Aurora) who, also becoming enamored of him, restores his sight. The love of Eos, less earthly than that of Merope, less cold than that of Artemis, fully satisfies his soul. He is at length happy. But the jealousy of Artemis destroys him. She pierces him with her arrows while in the very act of gratefully renovating her temple at Delos. In despair, Eos flies to Artemis, reproves her, represents to her the bareness of her jealousy and revenge, softens her, and obtains her consent to unite with herself—with Eos—in a prayer to Zeus (Jupiter) for the restoration of the giant to life. The prayer is heard. Orion is not only restored to life, but rendered immortal, and placed among the constellations, where he enjoys forever the pure affection of Eos, and becomes extinguished, each morning, in her rays.

In ancient mythology, the giants are meant to typify various energies of Nature. Pursuing, we suppose, this idea, Mr. Horne has made his own giants represent certain principles of human action or passion. Thus Orion himself is the Worker or Builder, and is the type of Action or Movement itself—but, in various portions of the poem, this allegorical character is left out of sight, and that of speculative philosophy takes its place; a mere consequence of the general uncertainty of purpose, which is the chief defect of the work. Sometimes we even find Orion a Destroyer in place of a Builder up—as, for example, when he destroys the grove about the temple of Artemis, at Delos. Here he usurps the proper allegorical attribute of Rhexergon, (the second of the seven giants named) who is the Breaker-down, typifying the Revolutionary Principle. Autarces, the third, represents the Mob, or, more strictly, Waywardness—Capricious Action. Harpax, the fourth, serves for Rapine—Briastor, the fifth, for Brute Force—Encolyon, the sixth, the "Chainer of the Wheel," for Conservatism—and Akinetos, the seventh, and most elaborated, for Apathy. He is termed "The Great Unmoved," and in his mouth is put all the "worldly wisdom," or selfishness, of the tale. The philosophy of Akinetos is, that no merely human exertion has any appreciable effect upon the *Movement*; and it is amusing to perceive how this great *Truth* (for most sincerely do we hold it to be such) speaks out from the real heart of the poet, through his Akinetos, in spite of all endeavor to overthrow it by the example of the brighter fate of Orion.

The death of Akinetos is a singularly forcible and poetic conception, and will serve to show how the giants are made to perish, generally, during the story, in agreement with their allegorical natures. The "Great Unmoved" quietly seats himself in a cave after the death of all his brethren, except Orion.

> Thus Akinetos sat from day to day,
> Absorbed in indolent sublimity,
> Reviewing thoughts and knowledge o'er and o'er;
> And now he spake, now sang unto himself,
> Now sank to brooding silence. From above,
> While passing, Time the rock touch'd, and it oozed
> Petrific drops—gently at first and slow.
> Reclining lonely in his fixed repose,
> The Great Unmoved unconsciously became
> Attached to that he pressed; and soon a part
> Of the rock. *There clung th' excrescence, till strong hands,*
> *Descended from Orion, made large roads,*
> *And built steep walls, squaring down rocks for use.*

The italicized conclusion of this fine passage affords an instance, however, of a very blameable concision, too much affected throughout the poem.

In the deaths of Autarces, Harpax, and Encolyon, we recognize the same exceeding vigor of conception. These giants conspire against Orion, who seeks the aid of Artemis, who, in her turn, seeks the assistance of Phoibos (Phœbus.) The conspirators are in a cave, with Orion.

> Now Phoibos thro' the cave
> Sent a broad ray! and lo! the solar beam
> Filled the great cave with radiance equable
> And not a cranny held one speck of shade.
> A moony halo round Orion came,
> As of some pure protecting influence,
> While with intense light glared the walls and roof,

The heat increasing. The three giants stood
With glazing eyes, fixed. Terribly the light
Beat on the dazzled stone, and the cave hummed
With reddening heat, till the red hair and beard
Of Harpax showed no difference from the rest,
Which once were iron-black. The sullen walls
Then smouldered down to steady oven heat,
Like that with care attain'd when bread has ceased
Its steaming and displays an angry tan.
The appalled faces of the giants showed
Full consciousness of their immediate doom.
And soon the cave a potter's furnace glow'd
Or kiln for largest bricks, and thus remained
The while Orion, in his halo clasped
By some invisible power, beheld the clay
Of these his early friends change. Life was gone.
Now sank the heat—the cave-walls lost their glare,
The red lights faded, and the halo pale
Around him, into chilly air expanded.
There stood the three great images, in hue
Of chalky white and red, like those strange shapes
In Egypt's ancient tombs; but presently
Each visage and each form with cracks and flaws
Was seamed, and the lost countenance brake up,
As, with brief toppling, forward prone they fell.

The deaths of Rhexergon and Biastor seem to discard (and this we regret not) the allegorical meaning altogether, but are related with even more exquisite richness and delicacy of imagination, than even those of the other giants. Upon this occasion it is the *jealousy* of Artemis which destroys.

> ———But with the eve
Fatigue o'ercame the giants, and they slept.
Dense were the rolling clouds, starless the glooms;
But o'er a narrow rift, once drawn apart,
Showing a field remote of violet hue,
The high Moon floated, and her downward gleam
Shone on the upturned giant faces. Rigid
Each upper feature, loose the nether jaw;
Their arms cast wide with open palms; their chests

Heaving like some large engine. Near them lay
Their bloody clubs, with dust and hair begrimed,
Their spears and girdles, and the long-noosed thongs.
Artemis vanished; all again was dark.
With day's first streak Orion rose, and loudly
To his companions called. But still they slept.
Again he shouted; yet no limb they stirr'd,
Tho' scarcely seven strides distant. He approached,
And found the spot, so sweet with clover flower
When they had cast them down, was now arrayed
With many-headed poppies, like a crowd
Of dusky Ethiops in a magic cirque
Which had sprung up beneath them in the night.
And all entranced the air.

There are several minor defects in "Orion," and we may as
well mention them here. We sometimes meet with an instance
of bad taste in a revolting picture or image; for example, at
page 59, of this edition:

Naught fearing, swift, brimfull of raging life,
Stiff'ning they lay in pools of jellied gore.

Sometimes—indeed very often—we encounter an altogether purposeless oddness or foreignness of speech. For example, at page 78:

As in Dodona once, ere driven thence
By Zeus *for that* Rhexergon burnt some oaks.

Mr. Horne will find it impossible to assign a good reason
for not here using "because."

Pure *vaguenesses* of speech abound. For example, page 89:

——one central heart wherein
Time beats twin pulses with Humanity.

Now and then sentences are rendered needlessly obscure
through mere involution—as at page 103:

Star-rays that first played o'er my blinded orbs,
E'en as they glance above the lids of sleep,
Who else had never known surprise, nor hope,
Nor useful action.

Here the "who" has no grammatical antecedent, and would naturally be referred to sleep; whereas it is intended for "me," understood, or involved, in the pronoun "my;" as if the sentence were written thus—"rays that first played o'er the blinded orbs of me, who &c." It is useless to dwell upon so pure an affectation.

The versification throughout is, generally, of a very remarkable excellence. At times, however, it is rough, to no purpose; as at page 44:

> And ever tended to some central point
> *In some place—nought more could I understand.*

And here, at page 81:

> The shadow of a stag stoops to the stream
> *Swift rolling toward the cataract and drinks deeply.*

The above is an unintentional and false Alexandrine—including a foot too much, and that a trochee in place of an iambus. But here, at page 106, we have the utterly unjustifiable anomaly of half a foot too little:

> *And Eos ever rises circling*
> The varied regions of Mankind, &c.

All these are mere inadvertences, of course; for the general handling of the rhythm shows the profound metrical sense of the poet. He is, perhaps, somewhat too fond of "making the sound an echo to the sense." "Orion" embodies some of the most remarkable instances of this on record; but if smoothness—if the true rhythm of a verse be sacrificed, the sacrifice is an error. The effect is only a beauty, we think, where *no* sacrifice is made in its behalf. It will be found possible to reconcile *all* the objects in view. Nothing can justify such lines as this, at page 69:

> As snake-songs midst stone hollows thus has taught me.

We might urge, as another minor objection, that all the giants are made to speak in the same manner—with the same phraseology. Their characters are broadly distinctive, while their words are identical in spirit. There is sufficient individuality of sentiment, but little, or none, of language.

We *must* object, too, to the personal and political allusions—to the Corn-Law question, for example—to Wellington's statue, &c. These things, *of course*, have no business in a poem.

We will conclude our fault-finding with the remark that, as a consequence of the one radical error of conception upon which we have commented at length, the reader's attention, throughout, is painfully *diverted*. He is always pausing, amid poetical beauties, in the expectation of detecting among them some philosophical, allegorical moral. Of course, he does not fully, because he cannot uniquely, appreciate the beauties. The absolute necessity of re-perusing the poem, in order thoroughly to comprehend it, is also, most surely, to be regretted, and arises, likewise, from the one radical sin.

But of the *beauties* of this most remarkable poem, what shall we say? And here we find it a difficult task to be calm. And yet we have never been accused of enthusiastic encomium. It is our deliberate opinion that, in all that regards the loftiest and holiest attributes of the true Poetry, "Orion" has *never* been excelled. Indeed we feel strongly inclined to say that it has never been *equaled*. Its imagination—that quality which is all in all—is of the most refined—the most elevating—the most august character. And here we deeply regret that the necessary limits of this review will prevent us from entering, at length, into specification. In reading the poem, we marked passage after passage for extract—but, in the end, we found that we had marked nearly every passage in the book. We can now do nothing more than select a few. This, from page 3, introduces Orion himself, and we quote it, not only as an instance of refined and picturesque imagination, but as evincing the high artistical skill with which a scholar in spirit can paint an elaborate picture by a few brief touches.

> The scene in front two sloping mountains' sides
> Display'd; in shadow one and one in light.
> The loftiest on its summit now sustained
> The sun-beams, raying like a mighty wheel
> Half seen, which left the forward surface dark
> In its full breadth of shade; the coming sun
> Hidden as yet behind: the other mount,

Slanting transverse, swept with an eastward face
Catching the golden light. Now while the peal
Of the ascending chase told that the rout
Still midway rent the thickets, suddenly
Along the broad and sunny slope appeared
The shadow of a stag that fled across
Followed by a giant's shadow with a spear.

These shadows are those of the coming Orion and his
game. But who can fail to appreciate the intense beauty of the
heralding shadows? Nor is this all. This "Hunter of shadows,
he himself a shade," is made symbolical, or suggestive,
throughout the poem, of the speculative character of Orion;
and occasionally, of his pursuit of visionary happiness. For
example, at page 81, Orion, possessed of Merope, dwells with
her in a remote and dense grove of cedars. Instead of directly
describing his attained happiness—his perfected bliss—the
poet, with an exalted sense of Art, *for which we look utterly in*
vain in any other poem, merely introduces the image of the
tamed or subdued *shadow-stag*, quietly browsing and drinking
beneath the cedars.

There, underneath the boughs, mark where the gleam
Of sun-rise thro' the roofing's chasm is thrown
Upon a grassy plot below, whereon
The shadow of a stag stoops to the stream,
Swift rolling toward the cataract, and drinks.
Throughout the day unceasingly it drinks,
While ever and anon the nightingale,
Not waiting for the evening, swells his hymn—
His one sustained and heaven aspiring tone—
And when the sun hath vanished utterly,
Arm over arm the cedars spread their shade,
With arching wrist and long extended hands,
And grave-ward fingers lengthening in the moon,
Above that shadowy stag whose antlers still
Hung o'er the stream.

There is nothing more richly—more weirdly—more
chastely—more sublimely imaginative—in the wide realm of

poetical literature. It will be seen that we *have* enthusiasm—but we reserve it for pictures such as this.

At page 62, Orion, his brethren dead, is engaged alone in extirpating the beasts from Chios. In the passages we quote, observe, in the beginning, the singular *lucidness* of detail; the arrangement of the barriers, &c., by which the hunter accomplishes his purpose, is given in a dozen lines of verse, with far more perspicuity than ordinary writers could give it in as many pages of prose. In this species of narration Mr. Horne is approached only by Moore in his "Alciphron." In the latter portions of our extract, observe the vivid picturesqueness of the description.

> Four days remain. Fresh trees he felled and wove
> More barriers and fences; inaccessible
> To fiercest charge of droves, and to o'erleap
> Impossible. These walls he so arranged
> That to a common centre each should force
> The flight of those pursued; and from that centre
> Diverged three outlets. One, the wide expanse
> Which from the rocks and inland forests led;
> One was the clear-skied windy gap above
> A precipice; the third, a long ravine
> Which through steep slopes, down to the seashore ran
> Winding, and then direct into the sea.
>
> Two days remain. Orion, in each hand
> Waving a torch, his course at night began,
> Through wildest haunts and lairs of savage beasts.
> With long-drawn howl, before him trooped the wolves—
> The panthers, terror-stricken, and the bears
> With wonder and gruff rage; from desolate crags,
> Leering hyenas, griffin, hippogrif,
> Skulked, or sprang madly, as the tossing brands
> Flashed through the midnight nooks and hollows cold,
> Sudden as fire from flint; o'er crashing thickets,
> *With crouched head and curled fangs dashed the wild boar,*
> Gnashing forth on with reckless impulses,
> While the clear-purposed fox crept closely down
> Into the underwood, to let the storm,

Whate'er its cause, pass over. Through dark fens,
Marshes, green rushy swamps, and margins reedy,
Orion held his way—and rolling shapes
Of serpent and of dragon moved before him
With high-reared crests, swan-like yet terrible,
And often looking back with gem-like eyes.

All night Orion urged his rapid course
In the vex'd rear of the swift-droving din,
And when the dawn had peered, the monsters all
Were hemmed in barriers. These he now o'erheaped
With fuel through the day, and when again
Night darkened, and the sea a gulf-like voice
Sent forth, the barriers at all points he fired,
Mid prayers to Hephæstos and his Ocean-Sire.
Soon as the flames had eaten out a gap
In the great barrier fronting the ravine
That ran down to the sea, Orion grasped
Two blazing boughs; one high in air he raised,
The other, *with its roaring foliage trailed*
Behind him as he sped. Onward the droves
Of frantic creatures with one impulse rolled
Before this night-devouring thing of flames,
With multitudinous voice and downward sweep
Into the sea, which now first knew a tide,
And, ere they made one effort to regain
The shore, had caught them in its flowing arms,
And bore them past all hope. The living mass,
Dark heaving o'er the waves resistlessly,
At length, in distance, seemed a circle small,
Midst which one creature in the centre rose,
Conspicuous in the long, red quivering gleams
That from the dying brands streamed o'er the waves.
It was the oldest dragon of the fens,
Whose forky flag-wings and horn-crested head
O'er crags and marshes regal sway had held;
And now he rose up like an embodied curse,
From all the doomed, fast sinking—some just sunk—
Looked landward o'er the sea, and flapped his vans,
Until Poseidon drew them swirling down.

Poseidon (Neptune) is Orion's father, and lends him his aid. The first line italized is an example of sound made echo to sense. The rest we have merely emphasized as peculiarly imaginative.

At page 9, Orion thus describes a palace built by him for Hephæstos (Vulcan.)

> But, ere a shadow-hunter I became—
> A dreamer of strange dreams by day and night—
> For him I built a palace underground,
> Of iron, black and rough as his own hands.
> Deep in the groaning disemboweled earth,
> The tower-broad pillars and huge stanchions,
> And slant supporting wedges I set up,
> Aided by the Cyclops who obeyed my voice,
> *Which through the metal fabric rang and pealed*
> *In orders echoing far, like thunder-dreams.*
> With arches, galleries and domes all carved—
> *So that great figures started from the roof*
> *And lofty coignes, or sat and downward gazed*
> *On those who strode below and gazed above—*
> I filled it; in the centre framed a hall:
> Central in that, a throne; *and for the light,*
> *Forged mighty hammers that should rise and fall*
> *On slanted rocks of granite and of flint,*
> *Worked by a torrent, for whose passage down*
> *A chasm I hewed. And here the god could take,*
> *Midst showery sparks and swathes of broad gold fire*
> *His lone repose, lulled by the sounds he loved;*
> *Or, casting back the hammer-heads till they choked*
> *The water's course, enjoy, if so he wished,*
> *Midnight tremendous, silence, and iron sleep.*

The description of the Hell in "Paradise Lost" is *altogether inferior* in graphic effect, in originality, in expression, in the true imagination—to these magnificent—to these unparalleled passages. For this assertion there are tens of thousands who will condemn us as heretical; but there are a "chosen few" who will feel, in their inmost souls, the simple truth of the assertion. The former class would at least be silent, could they form even a remote conception of *that* contempt with which we hearken to their conventional jargon.

We have room for no farther extracts of length; but we refer the reader who shall be so fortunate as to procure a copy of "Orion," to a passage at page 22, commencing

> One day at noontide, when the chase was done.

It is descriptive of a group of lolling hounds, intermingled with sylvans, fawns, nymphs and oceanides. We refer him also to page 25, where Orion, enamored of the naked beauty of Artemis, is repulsed and *frozen* by her dignity. These lines end thus:

> And ere the last collected shape he saw
> Of Artemis, dispersing fast amid
> Dense vapory clouds, the aching wintriness
> Had risen to his teeth, and fixed his eyes,
> Like glistening stones in the congealing air.

We refer, especially, too, to the description of *Love*, at page 29; to that of a Bacchanalian orgie, at page 34; to that of drought succeeded by rain, at page 70; and to that of the palace of Eos, at page 104.

Mr. Horne has a very peculiar and very delightful faculty of enforcing, or giving vitality to a picture, by some one vivid and intensely characteristic point or touch. He seizes the most salient feature of his theme, and makes this feature convey the whole. The combined *näiveté* and picturesqueness of some of the passages thus enforced, cannot be sufficiently admired. For example:

> The arches soon
> *With bow-arm forward thrust*, on all sides twanged
> Around, above, below.

Now, it is this thrusting forward of the bow-arm which is the idiosyncrasy of the action of a mass of archers. Again: Rhexergon and his friends endeavor to persuade Akinetos to be king. Observe the silent refusal of Akinetos—the peculiar *passiveness* of his action—if we may be permitted the paradox.

"Rise, therefore, Akinetos, thou art king."
So saying, in his hand he placed a spear.
As though against a wall 't were set aslant,
Flatly the long spear fell upon the ground.

Here again: Merope departs from Chios in a ship.

And, as it sped along, she closely pressed
The rich globes of her bosom on the side
O'er which she bent with those black eyes, and gazed
Into the sea *that fled beneath her face.*

The fleeing of the sea beneath the face of one who gazes into it from a ship's side, is the idiosyncrasy of the action— of the subject. It is that which chiefly impresses the gazer.

We conclude with some brief quotations at random, which we shall not pause to classify. Their merits need no demonstration. They *gleam* with the purest imagination. They abound in picturesqueness—force—happily chosen epithets, each in itself a picture. They are redolent of all for which a poet will value a poem.

—her silver sandals glanced i' the rays,
As doth a lizard playing on a hill,
And on the spot where she that instant stood
Naught but the bent and quivering grass was seen.

———

Above the Isle of Chios, night by night,
The clear moon lingered ever on her course,
Covering the forest foliage, where it swept
In its unbroken breadth along the slopes,
With placid silver; edging leaf and trunk
Where gloom clung deep around; but chiefly sought
With melancholy splendor to illume
The dark-mouthed caverns where Orion lay,
Dreaming among his kinsmen.

———

The ocean realm below, and all its caves
And bristling vegetation, plant and flower,
And forests in their dense petrific shade
Where the tides moan for sleep that never comes.

———

A fawn, who on a quiet green knoll sat
Somewhat apart, sang a melodious ode,
Made rich by harmonies of hidden strings.

Autarces seized a satyr, with intent,
Despite his writhing freaks and furious face,
To dash him on a gong, but that amidst
The struggling mass Encolyon thrust a pine,
Heavy and black as Charon's ferrying pole,
O'er which they, *like a bursting billow*, fell.

——then round the blaze,
Their shadows brandishing afar and athwart,
Over the level space and up the hills,
Six giants held portentous dance.

——his safe return
To corporal sense, by shaking off these nets
Of moonbeams from his soul.

——old memories
Slumbrously hung above the purple line
Of distance, to the East, while odorously
Glistened the tear-drops of a new-fall'n shower.

                                        Sing on!
Sing on, great tempest! in the darkness sing!
Thy madness is a music that brings calm
Into my central soul; and from its waves,
That now with joy begin to heave and gush,
The burning image of all life's desire,
Like an absorbing, fire-breathed, phantom god,
Rises and floats! here touching on the foam,
There hovering over it; *ascending swift
Starward, then swooping down the hemisphere
Upon the lengthening javelins of the blast!*

            Now a sound we heard,
Like to some well-known voice in prayer; and next
An iron clang *that* seemed to break great bonds
Beneath the earth, shook us to conscious life.

It is Oblivion! In his hand—though naught
Knows he of this—a dusky purple flower
Droops over its tall stem. Again! ah see!
He wanders into mist and now is lost!—
Within his brain what lovely realms of death
Are pictured, *and what knowledge through the doors*
Of his forgetfulness of all the earth
A path may gain?

But we are positively forced to conclude. It was our design to give "Orion" a careful and methodical analysis—thus to bring clearly forth its multitudinous beauties to the eye of the American public. Our limits have constrained us to treat it in an imperfect and cursory manner. We have had to content ourselves chiefly with assertion, where our original purpose was to demonstrate. We have left unsaid a hundred things which a well-grounded enthusiasm would have prompted us to say. One thing, however, we must and will say, in conclusion. "Orion" will be admitted, by every man of genius, to be one of the noblest, if not the very noblest poetical work of the age. Its defects are trivial and conventional—its beauties intrinsic and *supreme*.

Graham's Magazine, March 1844

Charles James Lever

Charles O'Malley, The Irish Dragoon. By Harry Lorrequer. With Forty Illustrations by Phiz. Complete in One Volume. Carey & Hart: Philadelphia.

THE FIRST POINT to be observed in the consideration of "Charles O'Malley" is the great *popularity* of the work. We believe that in this respect it has surpassed even the inimitable compositions of Mr. Dickens. At all events it has met with a most extensive sale; and, although the graver journals have avoided its discussion, the ephemeral press has been nearly if not quite unanimous in its praise. To be sure, the commendation, although unqualified, cannot be said to have abounded in specification, or to have been, in any regard, of a satisfactory character to one seeking precise ideas on the topic of the book's particular merit. It appears to us, in fact, that the cabalistical words "fun" "rollicking" and "devil-may-care," if indeed words they be, have been made to stand in good stead of all critical comment in the case of the work now under review. We first saw these dexterous expressions in a fly-leaf of "Opinions of the Press" appended to the renowned "Harry Lorrequer" by his publisher in Dublin. Thence transmitted, with complacent echo, from critic to critic, through daily, weekly and monthly journals without number, they have come at length to form a pendant and a portion of our author's celebrity—have come to be regarded as sufficient response to the few ignoramuses who, obstinate as ignorant, and fool-hardy as obstinate, venture to propound a question or two about the true claims of "Harry Lorrequer" or the justice of the pretensions of "Charles O'Malley."

We shall not insult our readers by supposing any one of them unaware of the fact, that a book may be even exceedingly *popular* without *any* legitimate literary merit. This fact can be proven by numerous examples which, now and here, it will be unnecessary and perhaps indecorous to mention. The dogma, then, is absurdly false, that the popularity of a work is *primâ facie* evidence of its excellence in some respects; that is to say, the dogma is false if we confine the meaning of excellence (as here of course it must be confined) to excellence in a literary sense. The truth is, that the popularity of a book is *primâ facie* evidence of just the converse of the proposition—it is evidence of the book's *demerit*, inasmuch as it shows a "stooping to conquer"—inasmuch as it shows that the author has dealt largely, if not altogether, in matters which are susceptible of appreciation by the mass of mankind—by uneducated thought, by uncultivated taste, by unrefined and unguided passion. So long as the world retains its present point of civilization, so long will it be almost an axiom that no extensively *popular* book, in the right application of the term, can be a work of high merit, *as regards those particulars of the work which are popular*. A book may be readily sold, may be universally read, for the sake of some half or two-thirds of its matter, which half or two-thirds may be susceptible of popular appreciation, while the one-half or one-third remaining may be the delight of the highest intellect and genius, and absolute *caviare* to the rabble. And just as

Omne tulit punctum qui miscuit utile dulci,

so will the writer of fiction, who looks most sagaciously to his own *interest*, combine all votes by intermingling with his loftier efforts such amount of less ethereal matter as will give general currency to his composition. And here we shall be pardoned for quoting some observations of the English artist, H. Howard. Speaking of *imitation*, he says:

The pleasure which results from it, even when employed upon the most ordinary materials, will always render that property of our art the most attractive with the majority, because it may be enjoyed with the least mental exertion. *All* men are in some degree judges of it. The cobbler in his own line may criticise Apelles; and popular opinions are never to be wholly disregarded concerning that which is addressed to the public—who, to a certain extent, are generally right; although as the language of the refined can never be intelligible to the uneducated, so the higher styles of art can never be acceptable to the multitude. In proportion as a work rises in the scale of intellect, it must necessarily become limited in the number of its admirers. For this reason the judicious artist, even in his loftiest efforts, will endeavor to introduce some of those qualities which are interesting to all, as a passport for those of a more intellectual character.

And these remarks upon painting—remarks which are mere truisms in themselves—embody nearly the whole *rationale* of the topic now under discussion. It may be added, however, that the *skill* with which the author addresses the lower taste of the populace, is often a source of pleasure, because of admiration, to a taste higher and more refined, and may be made a point of comment and of commendation by the critic.

In our review, last month, of "Barnaby Rudge," we were prevented, through want of space, from showing how Mr. Dickens had so well succeeded in uniting all suffrages. What we have just said, however, will suffice upon this point. While he has appealed, in innumerable regards, to the most exalted intellect, he has meanwhile invariably touched a certain string whose vibrations are omni-prevalent. We allude to his powers of *imitation*—that species of imitation to which Mr. Howard has reference—the *faithful* depicting of what is called still-life, and particularly of *character* in humble condition. It is his close observation and imitation of nature here which have rendered him popular, while his higher qualities, with the ingenuity evinced in addressing the general taste, have secured him the good word of the informed and intellectual.

But this is an important point upon which we desire to be distinctly understood. We wish here to record our positive dissent (be that dissent worth what it may) from a very usual opinion—the opinion that Mr. Dickens has done justice to his own genius—that any man ever failed to do grievous wrong to his own genius—in appealing to the popular judgment *at all*. As a matter of pecuniary policy alone, is any such appeal defensible. But we speak, of course, in relation to fame—in regard to that

> ——spur which the true spirit doth raise
> To scorn delight and live laborious days.

That a perfume should be found by any "true spirit" in the incense of mere popular applause, is, to our own apprehension at least, a thing inconceivable, inappreciable,—a paradox which gives the lie unto itself—a mystery more profound

than the well of Democritus. Mr. Dickens has no more business with the rabble than a seraph with a *chapeau de bras*.
What's Hecuba to him or he to Hecuba? What is he to
Jacques Bonhomme* or Jacques Bonhomme to him? The
higher genius is a rare gift and divine. Ω 'πολλων ου παντι
φαεινεται, ος μιν ιδη, μεγας ουτος—not to all men Apollo
shows himself; *he* is *alone great* who beholds him.† And his
greatness has its office God-assigned. But that office is not a
low communion with low, or even with ordinary intellect.
The holy—the electric spark of genius is the medium of intercourse between the noble and more noble mind. For lesser
purposes there are humbler agents. There are puppets
enough, able enough, willing enough, to perform in literature
the little things to which we have had reference. For one Fouqué there are fifty Molières. For one Angelo there are five
hundred Jan Steens. For one Dickens there are five million
Smolletts, Fieldings, Marryatts, Arthurs, Cocktons, Bogtons
and Frogtons.

It is, in brief, the duty of all whom circumstances have led
into criticism—it is, at least, a duty from which *we* individually shall never shrink—to uphold the true dignity of genius,
to combat its degradation, to plead for the exercise of its
powers in those bright fields which are its legitimate and peculiar province, and which for it alone lie gloriously out-
spread.

But to return to "Charles O'Malley," and its popularity. We
have endeavored to show that this latter must not be considered in any degree as the measure of its merit, but should
rather be understood as indicating a deficiency in this respect,
when we bear in mind, as we should do, the highest aims of
intellect in fiction. A slight examination of the work, (for in
truth it is worth no more,) will sustain us in what we have
said. The plot is exceedingly meagre. Charles O'Malley, the
hero, is a young orphan Irishman, living in Galway county,
Ireland, in the house of his uncle, Godfrey, to whose sadly
encumbered estates the youth is heir apparent and presump-
tive. He becomes enamoured, while on a visit to a neighbor,
of Miss Lucy Dashwood, and finds a rival in a Captain Ham-

*Nickname for the populace in the middle ages.
†Callimachus—*Hymn to Apollo*.

mersley. Some words carelessly spoken by Lucy, inspire him with a desire for military renown. After sojourning, therefore, for a brief period, at Dublin University, he obtains a commission and proceeds to the Peninsula, with the British army under Wellington. Here he distinguishes himself; is promoted; and meets frequently with Miss Dashwood, whom obstinately, and in spite of the lady's own acknowledgment of love for himself, he supposes in love with Hammersley. Upon the storming of Ciudad Rodrigo he returns home; finds his uncle, of course, *just* dead; and sells his commission to disencumber the estate. Presently Napoleon escapes from Elba, and our hero, obtaining a staff appointment under Picton, returns to the Peninsula, is present at Waterloo, (where Hammersley is killed) saves the life of Lucy's father, for the second time, as he has already twice saved that of Lucy herself; is rewarded by the hand of the latter; and, making his way back to O'Malley Castle, "lives happily all the rest of his days."

In and about this plot (if such it may be called) there are more absurdities than we have patience to enumerate. The author, or narrator, for example, is supposed to be Harry Lorrequer as far as the end of the preface, which by the way, is one of the best portions of the book. O'Malley then tells his own story. But the publishing office of the "Dublin University Magazine" (in which the narrative originally appeared) having been burned down, there ensues a sad confusion of identity between O'Malley and Lorrequer, so that it is difficult, for the nonce, to say which is which. In the want of copy consequent upon the disaster, James, the novelist, comes in to the relief of Lorrequer, or perhaps of O'Malley, with one of the flattest and most irrelevant of love-tales. Meantime, in the story proper are repetitions without end. We have already said that the hero *saves the life of his mistress twice, and of her father twice.* But not content with this, he has *two* mistresses, and *saves the life of both, at different periods, in precisely the same manner*—that is to say, by causing his horse, in each instance, to perform a Munchausen side-leap, at the moment when a spring forward would have impelled him upon his beloved. And then we have one unending, undeviating succession of junketings, in which "devilled kidneys" are never by any accident found wanting. The unction and pertinacity with which the author discusses what he chooses to denominate "devilled kidneys" are indeed edifying, to say no more. The truth is, that drinking wine, telling anecdotes, and devouring "devilled kidneys" may be considered as the sum total, as the *thesis* of the book. Never in the whole course of his eventful life, does Mr. O'Malley get "two or three assembled together" without seducing them forthwith to a table, and placing before them a dozen of wine and a dish of "devilled kidneys." This accomplished, the parties begin what seems to be the business of the author's existence—the narration of unusually *broad tales*—like those of the Southdown mutton. And here, in fact, we have the *plan* of that whole work of which the "United Service Gazette" has been pleased to vow it " would rather be the author than of all the 'Pickwicks' and 'Nicklebys' in the world"—a sentiment which we really blush to say has been echoed by many respectable members of our own press. The general plot or narrative is a mere thread upon which after-dinner anecdotes, some good, some bad, some utterly worthless, and *not one truly original*, are strung with about as much method, and about half as much dexterity, as we see ragged urchins employ in stringing the kernels of nuts.

It would, indeed, be difficult to convey to one who has not examined this production for himself, any idea of the exceedingly rough, clumsy, and inartistical manner in which even this bald conception is carried out. The stories are absolutely dragged in by the ears. So far from finding them result naturally or plausibly from the conversation of the interlocutors, even the blindest reader may perceive the author's struggling and blundering effort to introduce them. It is rendered quite evident that they were originally "on hand," and that "O'Malley" has been concocted for their introduction. Among other *niaiseries* we observe the silly trick of whetting appetite by delay. The conversation over the "kidneys" is brought, for example, to such a pass that one of the speakers is called upon for a story, which he forthwith declines for any reason, or for none. At a subsequent "broil" he is again pressed, and again refuses, and it is not until the reader's patience is fairly exhausted, and he has consigned both the story and its author to Hades, that the gentleman in question is prevailed upon to discourse. The only conceivable result of this *fanfarronade* is the ruin of the tale when told, through exaggerating anticipation respecting it.

The anecdotes thus narrated being the staple of the book, and the awkward manner of their interlocution having been pointed out, it but remains to be seen what the anecdotes are, in themselves, and what is the merit of their narration. And here, let it not be supposed that we have any design to deprive the devil of his due. There are several very excellent anecdotes in "Charles O'Malley" very cleverly and pungently told. Many of the scenes in which Monsoon figures are rich—less, however, from the scenes themselves than from the piquant, but by no means original character of Monsoon—a drunken, maudlin, dishonest old Major, given to communicativeness and mock morality over his cups, and not over careful in detailing adventures which tell against himself. One or two of the college pictures are unquestionably good—but might have been better. In general, the reader is made to feel that fine subjects have fallen into unskilful hands. By way of instancing this assertion, and at the same time of conveying an idea of the tone and character of the stories, we will quote one of the shortest, and assuredly one of the best.

"Ah, by-the-by, how's the Major?"

"Charmingly: only a little bit in a scrape just now. Sir Arthur—Lord Wellington, I mean—had him up for his fellows being caught pillaging, and gave him a devil of a rowing a few days ago.

" 'Very disorderly corps yours, Major O'Shaugnessy,' said the general; 'more men up for punishment than any regiment in the service.'

"Shaugh muttered something, but his voice was lost in a loud cock-a-doo-doo-doo, that some bold chanticleer set up at the moment.

" 'If the officers do their duty Major O'Shaugnessy, these acts of insubordination do not occur.'

"Cock-a-doo-doo-doo, was the reply. Some of the staff found it hard not to laugh; but the general went on—

" 'If, therefore, the practice does not cease, I'll draft the men into West India regiments.'

" 'Cock-a-doo-doo-doo!'

" 'And if any articles pillaged from the inhabitants are detected in the quarters, or about the persons of the troops—'

" 'Cock-a-doo-doo-*doo*!' screamed louder here than ever.

" 'Damn that cock—where is it?'

"There was a general look around on all sides, which seemed in vain; when a tremendous repetition of the cry resounded from O'Shaughnessy's coat-pocket: thus detecting the valiant Major himself in the very practice of his corps. There was no standing this: every one burst out into a peal of laughter; and Lord Wellington himself could not resist, but turned away, muttering to himself as he went—'Damned robbers every man of them,' while a final war-note from the Major's pocket closed the interview."

Now this is an anecdote at which every one will laugh; but its effect might have been vastly heightened by putting a few words of grave morality and reprobation of the conduct of his troops, into the mouth of O'Shaughnessy, upon whose character they would have told well. The cock, in interrupting the thread of his discourse, would thus have afforded an excellent context. We have scarcely a reader, moreover, who will fail to perceive the want of *tact* shown in dwelling upon the *mirth* which the anecdote occasioned. The error here is precisely like that of a man's laughing at his own spoken jokes. Our author is uniformly guilty of this mistake. He has an absurd fashion, also, of informing the reader, at the conclusion of each of his anecdotes, that, however good the anecdote might be, he (the reader) cannot enjoy it to the full extent in default of the *manner* in which it was orally narrated. He has no business to say anything of this kind. It is his duty to convey the manner not less than the matter of his narratives.

But we may say of these latter that, in general, they have the air of being *remembered* rather than invented. No man who has seen much of the rough life of the camp will fail to recognize among them many very old acquaintances. Some of them are as ancient as the hills, and have been, time out of mind, the common property of the bivouac. They have been narrated orally all the world over. The chief merit of the writer is, that he has been the first to collect and to print them. It is observable, in fact, that the second volume of the work is very far inferior to the first. The author seems to have exhausted his whole hoarded store in the beginning. His conclusion is barren indeed, and but for the historical details (for which he has no claim to merit) would be especially prosy and dull. *Now the true invention never exhausts itself.* It is mere cant and ignorance to talk of the possibility of the really imaginative man's " writing himself out." His soul but derives nourishment from the streams that flow therefrom. As well prate about the aridity of the eternal ocean εξ ουπερ παντες ποταμοι. So long as the universe of thought shall furnish matter for novel combinations, so long will the spirit of true genius be original, be exhaustless—be itself.

A few cursory observations. The book is filled to overflowing with songs of very doubtful excellence, the most of which are put into the mouth of one Micky Free, an amusing Irish servant of O'Malley's, and are given as his impromptu effusions. The subject of the improvisos is always the matter in hand at the moment of composition. The author evidently prides himself upon his poetical powers, about which the less we say the better; but if anything were wanting to assure us of his absurd ignorance and inappreciation of Art, we should find the fullest assurance in the mode in which these doggrel verses are introduced.

The occasional sentiment with which the volumes are interspersed there is an absolute necessity for skipping.

Can anybody tell us what is meant by the affectation of the word *L'envoy* which is made the heading of two prefaces?

That portion of the account of the battle of Waterloo which gives O'Malley's experiences while a prisoner, and in close juxta-position to Napoleon, bears evident traces of having been translated, and very literally too, from a French manuscript.

The English of the work is sometimes even amusing. We have continually, for example, *eat*, the present, for *ate*, the perfect—see page 17. At page 16, we have this delightful sentence—"Captain Hammersley, however, *never* took further notice of me, but continued to recount, for the amusement of those *about*, several excellent stories of his military career, which I confess were heard with every *test* of delight by all save me." At page 357 we have some sage talk about "the entire of the army;" and at page 368, the accomplished O'Malley speaks of "*drawing* a last look upon his sweetheart." These things arrest our attention as we open the book at random. It abounds in them, and in vulgarisms even much worse than they.

But why speak of vulgarisms of language? There is a disgusting vulgarism of thought which pervades and contaminates this whole production, and from which a delicate or lofty mind will shrink as from a pestilence. Not the least repulsive manifestation of this leprosy is to be found in the author's blind and grovelling worship of mere rank. Of the Prince Regent, that filthy compound of all that is bestial— that lazar-house of all moral corruption—he scruples not to speak in terms of the grossest adulation—sneering at Edmund Burke in the same villanous breath in which he extols the talents, the graces and *the virtues* of George the Fourth! That any man, to-day, can be found so degraded in heart as to style this reprobate, "one who, in every feeling of his nature, and in every feature of his deportment was every inch a prince"—is matter for grave reflection and sorrowful debate. The American, at least, who shall peruse the concluding pages of the book now under review, and not turn in disgust from the base sycophancy which infects them, is unworthy of his country and his name. But the truth is, that a gross and contracted soul renders itself unquestionably manifest in almost every line of the composition.

And this—*this* is the *work*, in respect to which its author, aping the airs of intellect, prates about his "haggard cheek," his "sunken eye," his "aching and tired head," his "nights of toil" and (Good Heavens!) his "days of *thought*!" That the thing is popular we grant—while that we cannot deny the fact, we grieve. But the career of true taste is onward—and now more vigorously onward than ever—and the period, perhaps, is not hopelessly distant, when, in decrying the mere balderdash of such matters as "Charles O'Malley," we shall do less violence to the feelings and judgment even of the populace, than, we much fear, has been done to-day.

Graham's Magazine, March 1842

Thomas Babington Macaulay

Critical and Miscellaneous Essays. By T. Babington Macaulay. Vol. 3d. Carey & Hart: Philadelphia.

MACAULAY HAS OBTAINED a reputation which, although deservedly great, is yet in a remarkable measure undeserved. The few who regard him merely as a terse, forcible and logical writer, full of thought, and abounding in original views often sagacious and never otherwise than admirably expressed—appear to us precisely in the right. The many who look upon him as not only all this, but as a comprehensive and profound thinker, little prone to error, err essentially themselves. The source of the general mistake lies in a very singular consideration—yet in one upon which we do not remember ever to have heard a word of comment. We allude to a tendency in the public mind towards logic for logic's sake—a liability to confound the vehicle with the conveyed—an aptitude to be so dazzled by the luminousness with which an idea is set forth, as to mistake it for the luminousness of the idea itself. The error is one exactly analogous with that which leads the immature poet to think himself sublime wherever he is obscure, because obscurity is a source of the sublime—thus confounding obscurity of expression with the expression of obscurity. In the case of Macaulay—and we may say, *en passant*, of our own Channing—we assent to what he says, too often because we so very clearly understand what it is that he intends to say. Comprehending vividly the points and the sequence of his argument, we fancy that we are concurring in the argument itself. It is not every mind which is at once able to analyze the satisfaction it receives from such Essays as we see here. If it were merely *beauty* of style for which they were distinguished—if they were remarkable only for rhetorical flourishes—we would not be apt to estimate these flourishes at more than their due value. We would not agree with the doctrines of the essayist on account of the elegance with which they were urged. On the contrary, we would be inclined to disbelief. But when all ornament save that of simplicity is disclaimed—when we are attacked by precision of language, by perfect accuracy of expression, by directness and singleness of thought, and above all by a logic the most rigorously close and consequential—it is hardly a matter for wonder that nine of us out of ten are content to rest in the gratification thus received as in the gratification of absolute truth.

Of the terseness and simple vigor of Macaulay's style it is unnecessary to point out instances. Every one will acknowledge his merits on this score. His exceeding *closeness* of logic, however, is more especially remarkable. With this he suffers nothing to interfere. Here, for example, is a sentence in which, to preserve entire the chain of his argument—*to leave no minute gap which the reader might have to fill up with thought*—he runs into most unusual tautology.

"The books and traditions of a sect may contain, mingled with propositions strictly theological, other propositions, purporting to rest on the same authority, which relate to physics. If new discoveries should throw discredit on the physical propositions, the theological propositions, unless they can be separated from the physical propositions, will share in their discredit."

These things are very well in their way; but it is indeed questionable whether they do not appertain rather to the trickery of thought's vehicle, than to thought itself—rather to reason's shadow than to reason. Truth, for truth's sake, is seldom so enforced. It is scarcely too much to say that the style of the profound thinker is never closely logical. Here we might instance George Combe—than whom a more candid reasoner never, perhaps, wrote or spoke—than whom a more complete antipodes to Babington Macaulay there certainly never existed. The former *reasons* to discover the true. The latter *argues* to convince the world, and, in arguing, not unfrequently surprises himself into conviction. What Combe appears to Macaulay it would be a difficult thing to say. What Macaulay is thought of by Combe we can understand very well. The man who looks at an argument in its details alone, will not fail to be misled by the one; while he who keeps steadily in view the *generality* of a thesis will always at least approximate the truth under guidance of the other.

Macaulay's tendency—and the tendency of mere logic in

general—to concentrate force upon minutiæ, at the expense of a subject as a whole, is well instanced in an article (in the volume now before us) on Ranke's History of the Popes. This article is called a review—possibly because it is anything else—as *lucus* is *lucus a non lucendo*. In fact it is nothing more than a beautifully written treatise on the main theme of Ranke himself; the whole matter of the treatise being deduced from the History. In the way of criticism there is nothing worth the name. The strength of the essayist is put forth to account for the progress of Romanism by maintaining that divinity is not a progressive science. The enigmas, says he in substance, which perplex the natural theologian are the same in all ages, while the Bible, where alone we are to seek revealed truth, has always been what it is.

The manner in which these two propositions are set forth, is a model for the logician and for the student of *belles lettres*—yet the error into which the essayist has rushed headlong, is egregious. He attempts to deceive his readers, or has deceived himself, by confounding the nature of that proof from which we reason of the concerns of earth, considered as man's habitation, and the nature of that evidence from which we reason of the same earth regarded as a unit of that vast whole, the universe. In the former case the *data* being palpable, the proof is direct: in the latter it is purely *analogical*. Were the indications we derive from science, of the nature and designs of Deity, and thence, by inference, of man's destiny—were these indications proof direct, no advance in science would strengthen them—for, as our author truly observes, "nothing could be added to the force of the argument which the mind finds in every beast, bird, or flower"—but as these indications are rigidly analogical, every step in human knowledge—every astronomical discovery, for instance—throws additional light upon the august subject, *by extending the range of analogy*. That we know no more to-day of the nature of Deity—of its purposes—and thus of man himself—than we did even a dozen years ago—is a proposition disgracefully absurd; and of this any astronomer could assure Mr. Macaulay. Indeed, to our own mind, the *only* irrefutable argument in support of the soul's immortality—or, rather, the only conclusive proof of man's alternate dissolution and re-juvenescence *ad infinitum*—is to be found in analogies deduced from the modern established theory of the nebular cosmogony.* Mr. Macaulay, in short, has forgotten what he frequently forgets, or neglects,—the very gist of his subject. He has forgotten that analogical evidence cannot, at all times, be discoursed of as if identical with proof direct. Throughout the whole of his treatise he has made no distinction whatever.

This third volume completes, we believe, the miscellaneous writings of its author.

---

*This cosmogony *demonstrates* that all existing bodies in the universe are formed of a nebular matter, a rare ethereal medium, pervading space—shows the mode and laws of formation—and *proves* that all things are in a perpetual state of progress—that nothing in nature is *perfected*.

Graham's Magazine, June 1841

Frederick Marryatt

Joseph Rushbrook, or the Poacher. By Captain Marryatt, Author of Peter Simple, Jacob Faithful, etc. etc. Two Volumes. Philadelphia: Carey and Hart.

IT HAS BEEN well said that "the success of certain works may be traced to sympathy between the author's mediocrity of ideas, and mediocrity of ideas on the part of the public." In commenting on this passage, Mrs. Gore, herself a shrewd philosopher, observes that, whether as regards men or books, there exists an excellence too excellent for general favor. To "make a hit"—to captivate the public eye, ear, or understanding without a certain degree of merit—is impossible; but the "hardest hit" is seldom made, indeed we may say *never* made, by the highest merit. When we wrote the word *seldom* we were thinking of Dickens and the "Curiosity Shop," a work unquestionably of "the highest merit," and which at a first glance appears to have made the most unequivocal of "hits"— but we suddenly remembered that the compositions called "Harry Lorrequer" and "Charles O'Malley" had borne the palm from "The Curiosity Shop" in point of what is properly termed *popularity*.

There can be no question, we think, that the philosophy of all this *is* to be found in the apothegm with which we began. Marryatt is a singular instance of its truth. He has always been a very *popular* writer in the most rigorous sense of the word. His books are essentially "mediocre." His ideas are the common property of the mob, and have been their common property time out of mind. We look throughout his writings in vain for the slightest indication of originality—for the faintest incentive to thought. His plots, his language, his opinions are neither adapted nor intended for scrutiny. We must be contented with them as sentiments, rather than as ideas; and properly to estimate them, even in this view, we must bring ourselves into a sort of identification with the sentiment of the mass. Works composed in this spirit are sometimes purposely so composed by men of superior intelligence, and here we call to mind the *Chansons* of Béranger. But usually they are the natural exponent of the vulgar thought in the person of a vulgar thinker. In either case they claim for themselves *that* which, for want of a more definite expression, has been called by critics *nationality*. Whether this nationality in letters is a fit object for high-minded ambition, we cannot here pause to inquire. If it is, then Captain Marryatt occupies a more desirable position than, in our heart, we are willing to award him.

"Joseph Rushbrook" is not a book with which the critic should occupy many paragraphs. It is not very dissimilar to "Poor Jack," which latter is, perhaps, the best specimen of its author's cast of thought, and *national* manner, although inferior in interest to "Peter Simple."

The plot can only please those who swallow the probabilities of "Sinbad the Sailor," or "Jack and the Bean-Stalk"—or we should have said, more strictly, the incidents; for, of plot, properly speaking, there is none at all.

Joseph Rushbrook is an English soldier who, having long served his country and received a wound in the head, is pensioned and discharged. He becomes a poacher, and educates his son (the hero of the tale and also named Joseph) to the same profession. A pedler, called Byres, is about to betray the father, who avenges himself by shooting him. The son takes the burden of the crime upon himself, and flees the country. A reward is offered for his apprehension—a reward which one Furness, a schoolmaster, is very anxious to obtain. This Furness dogs the footsteps of our hero, much as Fagin, the Jew, dogs those of Oliver Twist, forcing him to quit place after place, just as he begins to get comfortably settled. In thus roaming about, little Joseph meets with all kinds of outrageously improbable adventures; and not only this, but the reader is bored to death with the outrageously improbable adventures of every one with whom little Joseph comes in contact. Good fortune absolutely besets him. Money falls at his feet wherever he goes, and he has only to stoop and pick it up. At length he arrives at the height of prosperity, and thinks he is entirely rid of Furness, when Furness re-appears. That Joseph should, in the end, be brought to trial for the pedler's murder is so clearly the author's design, that he who runs may read it, and we naturally suppose that his persecutor, Furness, is to be the instrument of this evil. We suppose also, of course, that in bringing this misfortune upon our hero, the schoolmaster will involve himself in ruin, in accordance with the common ideas of poetical justice. But no;— Furness, being found in the way, is killed off, accidentally, having lived and plotted to no ostensible purpose, through the better half of the book. Circumstances that have nothing to do with the story involve Joseph in his trial. He refuses to divulge the real secret of the murder, and is sentenced to transportation. The elder Rushbrook, in the meantime, has avoided suspicion and fallen heir to a great property. Just as his son is about to be sent across the water, some of Joe's friends discover the true state of affairs, and obtain from the father, who is now conveniently upon his death-bed, a confession of his guilt. Thus all ends well—if the word *well* can be applied in any sense to trash so ineffable—the father dies, the son is released, inherits the estate, marries his lady-love, and prospers in every possible and impossible way.

We have mentioned the imitation of Fagin. A second plagiarism is feebly attempted in the character of one Nancy, a trull, who is based upon the Nancy of Oliver Twist—for Marryatt is not often at the trouble of diversifying his thefts. This Nancy changes her name three or four times, and so in fact do each and all of the *dramatis personæ*. This changing of name is one of the bright ideas with which the author of "Peter Simple" is most pertinaciously afflicted. We would not be bound to say how many aliases are borne by the hero in this instance—some dozen perhaps.

The novels of Marryatt—his later ones at least—are evidently written to order, for certain considerations, and have to be delivered within certain periods. He thus finds it his interest to *push on*. Now, for this mode of progress, *incident* is the sole thing which answers. One incident begets another, and so on *ad infinitum*. There is never the slightest necessity for pausing; especially where no plot is to be cared for. *Comment*, in the author's own person, upon what is transacting, is left entirely out of question. There is thus none of that *binding* power perceptible, which often gives a species of unity (the unity of the writer's individual thought) to the most random narrations. All works composed as we have stated Marryatt's to be composed, will be run on, *incidentally*, in the manner described; and, notwithstanding that it would seem at first sight to be otherwise, yet it is true that no works are so insufferably tedious. These are the novels which we read with a hurry exactly consonant and proportionate with that in which they were indited. We seldom leave them unfinished, yet we labor through to the end, and reach it with unalloyed pleasure.

The *commenting* force can never be safely disregarded. It is far better to have a dearth of incident, with skilful observations upon it, than the utmost variety of event, without. In some previous review we have observed (and our observation is borne out by analysis), that it was the deep sense of the want of this binding and commenting power, in the old Greek drama, which gave rise to the chorus. The chorus came at length to supply, in some measure, a deficiency which is inseparable from dramatic action, and represented the expression of *the public* interest or sympathy in the matters transacted. The successful novelist must, in the same manner, be careful to bring into view his *private* interest, sympathy, and opinion, in regard to his own creations.

We have spoken of "The Poacher" at greater length than we intended; for it deserves little more than an announcement. It has the merit of a homely and not unnatural simplicity of style, and is not destitute of pathos; but this is all. Its English is excessively slovenly. Its events are monstrously improbable. There is no adaptation of parts about it. The truth is, it is a pitiable production. There are twenty young men of our acquaintance who make no pretension to literary ability, yet who could produce a better book *in a week*.

Graham's Magazine, September 1841

Mrs. L. Miles

Phrenology, and the Moral Influence of Phrenology: Arranged for General Study, and the Purposes of Education, from the first published works of Gall and Spurzheim, to the latest discoveries of the present period. By Mrs. L. Miles. Philadelphia: Carey, Lea, and Blanchard.

PHRENOLOGY IS NO LONGER to be laughed at. It *is* no longer laughed at by men of common understanding. It has assumed the majesty of a science; and, as a science, ranks among the most important which can engage the attention of thinking beings—this too, whether we consider it merely as an object of speculative inquiry, or as involving consequences of the highest practical magnitude. As a study it is very extensively accredited in Germany, in France, in Scotland, and in both Americas. Some of its earliest and most violent opposers have been converted to its doctrines. We may instance George Combe who wrote the "Phrenology." Nearly all Edinburgh has been brought over to belief—in spite of the Review and its ill sustained opinions. Yet these latter were considered of so great weight that Dr. Spurzheim was induced to visit Scotland for the purpose of refuting them. There, with the Edinburgh Review in one hand, and a brain in the other, he delivered a lecture before a numerous assembly, among whom was the author of the most virulent attack which perhaps the science has ever received. At this single lecture he is said to have gained five hundred converts to Phrenology, and the Northern Athens is now the strong hold of the faith.

In regard to the uses of Phrenology—its most direct, and, perhaps, most salutary, is that of *self-examination and self-knowledge*. It is contended that, with proper caution, and well-directed inquiry, individuals may obtain, through the science, a perfectly accurate estimate of their own moral capabilities—and, thus instructed, will be the better fitted for decision in regard to a choice of offices and duties in life. But there are other and scarcely less important uses too numerous to mention—at least here.

The beautiful little work now before us was originally printed in London in a manner sufficiently quaint. The publication consisted of forty cards contained in a box resembling a small pocket volume. An embossed head accompanied the

cards, giving at a glance the relative situations and proportions of each organ, and superseding altogether the necessity
of a bust. This head served as an Index to the explanations of
the system. The whole formed a lucid, compact, and portable
compend of Phrenology. The present edition of the work,
however, is preferable in many respects, and is indeed exceedingly neat and convenient—we presume that it pretends to
be nothing more.

The Faculties are divided into *Instinctive Propensities and
Sentiments* and *Intellectual Faculties*. The Instinctive Propensities and Sentiments are subdivided into *Domestic Affections*,
embracing Amativeness, Philoprogenitiveness, Inhabitiveness,
and Attachment—*Preservative Faculties*, embracing Combat-
iveness, Destructiveness, and Gustativeness—*Prudential
Sentiments*, embracing Acquisitiveness, Secretiveness, and
Cautionness—*Regulating Powers*, including Self-Esteem,
Love of Approbation, Conscientiousness, and Firmness—
Imaginative Faculties, containing Hope, Ideality, and Marvel-
lousness—and *Moral Sentiments*, under which head come
Benevolence, Veneration, and Imitation. The *Intellectual
Faculties* are divided into *Observing Faculties*, viz: Individuality, Form, Size, Weight, Color, Order, and Number—*Scien-
tific Faculties*, viz: Constructiveness, Locality, Time, and
Tune—*Reflecting Faculties*, viz: Eventuality, Comparison,
Casuality and Wit—and lastly, the *Subservient Faculty*, which
is Language. This classification is arranged with sufficient
clearness, but it would require no great degree of acumen to
show that to mere perspicuity points of vital importance to
the science have been sacrificed.

At page 17 is a brief chapter entitled a *Survey of Contour*,
well conceived and well adapted to its purpose which is—to
convey by a casual or superficial view of any head, an idea of
what propensities, sentiments, or faculties, most distinguish
the individual. It is here remarked that "any faculty may be
possessed in perfection without showing itself in a prominence or bump," (a fact not often attended to) "it is only
where *one* organ predominates above those nearest to it, that
it becomes singly perceptible. Where a number of contiguous
organs are large, there will be a general fulness of that part of
the head."

Some passages in Mrs. Miles' little book have a very peculiar interest. At page 26 we find what follows.

"The cerebral organs are double, and inhabit both sides of the head, from the root of the nose to the middle of the neck at the nape. They act in unison, and produce a single impression, as from the double organs of sight and hearing. The loss of one eye does not destroy vision. The deafness of one ear does not wholly deprive us of hearing. In the same manner Tiedman reports the case of a madman, whose disease was confined to one side of his head, the patient having the power to perceive his own malady, with the unimpaired faculties of the other side. It is no uncommon thing to find persons acute on all subjects save *one*—thus proving the possibility of a partial injury of the brain, or the hypothesis of a plurality of organs."

In the chapter on *Combativeness*, we meet with the very sensible and necessary observation that we must not consider the possession of particular and instinctive propensities, as acquitting us of responsibility in the indulgence of culpable actions. On the contrary it is the perversion of our faculties which causes the greatest misery we endure, and for which (having the free exercise of *reason*) we are accountable to God.

The following is quoted from *Edinensis, vol. iv.*

"All the faculties are considered capable of producing actions which are good, and it is not to be admitted that any one of them is essentially, and in itself *evil*—but if given way to beyond a certain degree, all of them (with the sole exception of *Conscientiousness*) may lead to results which are improper, injurious, or culpable."

The words annexed occur at page 102.

"Anatomy decides that the brain, notwithstanding the softness of its consistence, *gives shape to the cranium*, as the crustaceous tenement of the crab is adjusted to the animal that inhabits it. An exception is made to this rule when disease or ill-treatment injure the skull."

And again at page 159.

"By appealing to Nature herself, it can scarcely be doubted that certain forms of the head denote particular talents or dispositions; and anatomists find that *the surface of the brain* presents the same appearance in shape which the skull exhibits during life. Idiocy is invariably the consequence of the brain being too small, while in such heads the animal propensities are generally very full."

To this may be added the opinion of Gall, that a skull which is large, which is elevated or high above the ears, and in which the head is well developed and thrown forward, so as to be nearly perpendicular with its base, may be presumed to lodge a brain of greater power (whatever may be its propensities) than a skull deficient in such proportion.

Southern Literary Messenger, March 1836

Thomas Moore

Alciphron, a Poem. By Thomas Moore, Esq., author of Lalla Rookh, etc., etc. Carey and Hart, Philadelphia.

AMID THE VAGUE mythology of Egypt, the voluptuous scenery of her Nile, and the gigantic mysteries of her pyramids, Anacreon Moore has found all of that striking *materiel*
which he so much delights in working up, and which he has
embodied in the poem before us. The design of the story (for
plot it has none) has been a less consideration than its facilities, and is made subservient to its execution. The subject is
comprised in five epistles. In the first, Alciphron, the head of
the Epicurean sect at Athens, writes, from Alexandria, to his
friend Cleon, in the former city. He tells him (assigning a
reason for quitting Athens and her pleasures) that, having
fallen asleep one night after protracted festivity, he beholds,
in a dream, a spectre, who tells him that, beside the sacred
Nile, he, the Epicurean, shall find that Eternal Life for which
he had so long been sighing. In the second, from the same to
the same, the traveller speaks, at large, and in rapturous
terms, of the scenery of Egypt; of the beauty of her maidens;
of an approaching Festival of the Moon; and of a wild hope
entertained that amid the subterranean chambers of some
huge pyramid lies the secret which he covets, the secret of
Life Eternal. In the third letter, he relates a love adventure at
the Festival. Fascinated by the charms of one of the nymphs
of a procession, he is first in despair at losing sight of her,
then overjoyed at again seeing her in Necropolis, and finally
traces her steps until they are lost near one of the smaller
pyramids. In epistle the fourth, (still from the same to the
same,) he enters and explores the pyramid, and, passing
through a complete series of Eleusinian mysteries, is at length
successfully initiated into the secrets of Memphian priestcraft;
we learning this latter point from letter the fifth, which concludes the poem, and is addressed by Orcus, high priest of
Memphis, to Decius, a prætorian prefect.

A new poem from Moore calls to mind that critical opinion
respecting him which had its origin, we believe, in the dogmatism of Coleridge—we mean the opinion that he is essen-

tially the poet of *fancy*—the term being employed in contradistinction to *imagination*. "The fancy," says the author of the "Auncient Mariner," in his *Biographia Literaria*, "the fancy combines, the imagination creates." And this was intended, and has been received, as a distinction. If so at all, it is one without a difference; without even a difference of *degree*. The fancy as nearly creates as the imagination; and neither creates in any respect. All novel conceptions are merely unusual combinations. The mind of man can *imagine* nothing which has not really existed; and this point is susceptible of the most positive demonstration—see the Baron de Bielfeld, in his *Premiers Traits de L'Erudition Universelle*, 1767. It will be said, perhaps, that we can imagine a *griffin*, and that a griffin does not exist. Not the griffin certainly, but its component parts. It is a mere compendium of known limbs and features—of known qualities. Thus with all which seems to be *new*—which appears to be a *creation* of intellect. It is resoluble into the old. The wildest and most vigorous effort of mind cannot stand the test of this analysis.

We might make a distinction, *of degree*, between the fancy and the imagination, in saying that the latter is the former *loftily employed*. But experience proves this distinction to be unsatisfactory. What we *feel* and *know* to be fancy, will be found still only *fanciful*, whatever be the theme which engages it. It retains its idiosyncrasy under all circumstances. No *subject* exalts it into the ideal. We might exemplify this by reference to the writings of one whom our patriotism, rather than our judgment, has elevated to a niche in the Poetic Temple which he does not becomingly fill, and which he cannot long uninterruptedly hold. We allude to the late Dr. Rodman Drake, whose puerile abortion, "The Culprit Fay," we examined, at some length, in a *critique* elsewhere; proving it, we think, beyond all question, to belong to that class of the pseudo-ideal, in dealing with which we find ourselves embarrassed between a kind of half-consciousness that we ought to admire, and the certainty that we do not. Dr. Drake was employed upon a good subject—at least it is a subject precisely identical with those which Shakspeare was wont so happily to treat, and in which, especially, the author of "Lilian" has so wonderfully succeeded. But the American has brought to his task a mere *fancy*, and has grossly failed in doing what many suppose him to have done—in writing an ideal or imaginative poem. There is not one particle of the true ποίησις about "The Culprit Fay." We say that the subject, even at its best points, did not aid Dr. Drake in the slightest degree. He was never more than *fanciful*. The passage, for example, chiefly cited by his admirers, is the account of the "Sylphid Queen;" and to show the difference between the false and true ideal, we collated, in the review just alluded to, this, the most admired passage, with one upon a similar topic by Shelley. We shall be pardoned for repeating here, as nearly as we remember them, some words of what we then said.

The description of the Sylphid Queen runs thus:

> But oh, how fair the shape that lay
>   Beneath a rainbow bending bright;
> She seemed to the entranced Fay,
>   The loveliest of the forms of light;
> Her mantle was the purple rolled
>   At twilight in the west afar;
> 'Twas tied with threads of dawning gold,
>   And buttoned with a sparkling star.
> Her face was like the lily roon
>   That veils the vestal planet's hue;
> Her eyes two beamlets from the moon
>   Set floating in the welkin blue.
> Her hair is like the sunny beam,
> And the diamond gems which round it gleam
> Are the pure drops of dewy even
> That ne'er have left their native heaven.

In the *Queen Mab* of Shelley, a Fairy is thus introduced:

> Those who had looked upon the sight,
>   Passing all human glory,
> Saw not the yellow moon,
> Saw not the mortal scene,
> Heard not the night-wind's rush,
> Heard not an earthly sound,
> Saw but the fairy pageant,

> Heard but the heavenly strains
> That filled the lonely dwelling—

And thus described—

> The Fairy's frame was slight; yon fibrous cloud
> That catches but the palest tinge of even,
> And which the straining eye can hardly seize
> When melting into eastern twilight's shadow,
> Where scarce so thin, so slight; but the fair star
> That gems the glittering coronet of morn,
> *Sheds not a light so mild, so powerful,*
> *As that which, bursting from the Fairy's form,*
> *Spread a purpureal halo round the scene,*
>   *Yet with an undulating motion,*
>   *Swayed to her outline gracefully.*

In these exquisite lines the faculty of mere comparison is but little exercised—that of ideality in a wonderful degree. It is probable that in a similar case Dr. Drake would have formed the face of the fairy of the "fibrous cloud," her arms of the "pale tinge of even," her eyes of the "fair stars," and her body of the "twilight shadow." Having so done, his admirers would have congratulated him upon his *imagination*, not taking the trouble to think that they themselves could at any moment *imagine* a fairy of materials equally as good, and conveying an equally distinct idea. Their mistake would be precisely analogous to that of many a schoolboy who admires the imagination displayed in Jack the Giant-Killer, and is finally rejoiced at discovering his own imagination to surpass that of the author, since the monsters destroyed by Jack are only about forty feet in height, and he himself has no trouble in imagining some of one hundred and forty. It will be seen that the fairy of Shelley is not a mere compound of incongruous natural objects, inartificially put together, and unaccompanied by any *moral* sentiment—but a being, in the illustration of whose nature some physical elements are used collaterally as adjuncts, while the main conception springs immediately, *or thus apparently springs*, from the brain of the poet, enveloped in the moral sentiments of grace, of color, of motion—of the beautiful, of the *mystical*, of the august—in short, of the ideal.

The truth is that the just distinction between the fancy and the imagination (and which is still but a distinction *of degree*) is involved in the consideration of the *mystic*. We give this as an idea of our own, altogether. We have no authority for our opinion—but do not the less firmly hold it. The term *mystic* is here employed in the sense of Augustus William Schlegel, and of most other German critics. It is applied by them to that class of composition in which there lies beneath the transparent upper current of meaning, an under or *suggestive* one. What we vaguely term the *moral* of any sentiment is its mystic or secondary expression. It has the vast force of an accompaniment in music. This vivifies the air; that spiritual-izes the *fanciful* conception, and lifts it into the *ideal*.

This theory will bear, we think, the most rigorous tests which can be made applicable to it, and will be acknowledged as tenable by all who are themselves imaginative. If we care-fully examine those poems, or portions of poems, or those prose romances, which mankind have been accustomed to designate as *imaginative*, (for an instinctive feeling leads us to employ properly the term whose full import we have still never been able to define,) it will be seen that all so desig-nated are remarkable for the *suggestive* character which we have discussed. They are strongly *mystic*—in the proper sense of the word. We will here only call to the reader's mind, the *Prometheus Vinctus* of Æschylus; the *Inferno* of Dante; the *Destruction of Numantia* by Cervantes; the *Comus* of Milton; the *Auncient Mariner*, the *Christabel*, and the *Kubla Khan*, of Coleridge; the *Nightingale* of Keats; and, most especially, the *Sensitive Plant* of Shelley, and the *Undine* of De La Motte Fouqué. These two latter poems (for we call them both such) are the finest possible examples of the purely *ideal*. There is little of fancy here, and every thing of imagination. With each note of the lyre is heard a ghostly, and not always a distinct, but an august and soul-exalting *echo*. In every glimpse of beauty presented, we catch, through long and wild vistas, dim bewildering visions of a far more ethereal beauty *beyond*. But not so in poems which the world has always persisted in terming *fanciful*. Here the upper current is often exceedingly brilliant and beautiful; but then men *feel* that this upper current *is all*. No Naiad voice addresses them *from below*. The notes of the air of the song do not tremble with the according tones of the accompaniment.

It is the failure to perceive these truths which has occasioned that embarrassment which our critics experience while discussing the topic of Moore's station in the poetic world—that hesitation with which we are obliged to refuse him the loftiest rank among the most noble. The popular voice, and the popular heart, have denied him that happiest quality, imagination—and here the popular voice (*because* for once it has gone with the popular heart) is right—but yet only relatively so. Imagination is not the leading feature of the poetry of Moore; but he possesses it in no little degree.

We will quote a few instances from the poem now before us—instances which will serve to exemplify the distinctive feature which we have attributed to ideality.

It is the *suggestive* force which exalts and etherealizes the passages we copy.

> Or is it that there lurks, indeed,
> Some truth in man's prevailing creed,
> And that our guardians from on high,
>   Come, in that pause from toil and sin,
> To put the senses' curtain by,
>   And on the wakeful soul look in!

Again—

> The eternal pyramids of Memphis burst
> Awfully on my sight—standing sublime
> 'Twixt earth and heaven, the watch-towers of time,
> From whose lone summit, when his reign hath past,
> From earth for ever, he will look his last.

And again—

> Is there for man no hope—but this which dooms
> His only lasting trophies to be tombs!
> But 'tis not so—earth, heaven, all nature shows

He *may* become immortal, *may* unclose
The wings within him wrapt, and proudly rise
Redeemed from earth a creature of the skies!

And here—

The pyramid shadows, stretching from the light,
Look like the first colossal steps of night,
Stalking across the valley to invade
The distant hills of porphyry with their shade!

And once more—

There Silence, thoughtful God, who loves
The neighborhood of Death, in groves
Of asphodel lies hid, and weaves
His hushing spell among the leaves.

Such lines as these, we must admit, however, are not of
frequent occurrence in the poem—the sum of whose great
beauty is composed of the several sums of a world of minor
excellences.

Moore has always been renowned for the number and appositeness, as well as novelty, of his similes; and the renown
thus acquired is strongly indicial of his deficiency in that
nobler merit—the noblest of them all. No poet thus distinguished was ever richly ideal. Pope and Cowper are
remarkable instances in point. Similes (so much insisted upon
by the critics of the reign of Queen Anne) are never, in our
opinion, strictly in good taste, whatever may be said to the
contrary, and certainly can never be made to accord with
other high qualities, except when naturally arising from the
subject in the way of illustration—and, when thus arising,
they have seldom the merit of novelty. To be novel, they must
fail in essential particulars. The higher minds will avoid their
frequent use. They form no portion of the ideal, and appertain to the fancy alone.

We proceed with a few random observations upon Alciphron. The poem is distinguished throughout by a very
happy facility which has never been mentioned in connection

with its author, but which has much to do with the reputation he has obtained. We allude to the facility with which he
recounts a poetical story in a *prosaic* way. By this is meant
that he preserves the tone and method of arrangement of a
prose relation, and thus obtains great advantages over his
more stilted compeers. His is no poetical *style*, (such, for example, as the French have—a distinct style for a distinct purpose,) but an easy and ordinary prose manner, *ornamented
into poetry*. By means of this he is enabled to enter, with ease,
into details which would baffle any other versifier of the age,
and at which La Martine would stand aghast. For any thing
that we see to the contrary, Moore might solve a cubic equation in verse, or go through with the three several demonstra-
tions of the binomial theorem, one after the other, or indeed
all at the same time. His facility in this respect is truly admirable, and is, no doubt, the result of long practice after mature deliberation. We refer the reader to page 50, of the
pamphlet now reviewed; where the minute and conflicting
incidents of the descent into the pyramid are detailed with
absolutely *more* precision than we have ever known a similar
relation detailed with in prose.

In general dexterity and melody of versification the author
of Lalla Rookh is unrivalled; but he is by no means at all
times accurate, falling occasionally into the common foible of
throwing accent upon syllables too unimportant to sustain it.
Thus, in the lines which follow, where we have italicized the
weak syllables:

> And mark 'tis nigh; already *the* sun bids—

> While hark from all the temples *a* rich swell

> I rushed in*to* the cool night air—

He also too frequently draws out the word Heaven into
two syllables—a protraction which it *never* will support.

His English is now and then objectionable, as, at page 26,
where he speaks of

> lighted barks
> That down Syene's cataract *shoots*,

making *shoots* rhyme with flutes, below; also at page 6, and elsewhere, where the word *none* has improperly a singular, instead of a plural force. But such criticism as this is somewhat captious, for in general he is most highly polished.

At page 27, he has stolen his " woven snow" from the *ventum textilem* of Apuleius.

At page 8, he either himself has misunderstood the tenets of Epicurus, or wilfully misrepresents them through the voice of Alciphron. We incline to the former idea, however; as the philosophy of that most noble of the sophists is habitually perverted by the moderns. Nothing could be more spiritual and less sensual than the doctrines we so torture into wrong. But we have drawn out this notice at somewhat too great length, and must conclude. In truth, the exceeding beauty of "Alciphron" has bewildered and detained us. We could not point out a poem in any language which, as a whole, greatly excels it. It is far superior to Lalla Rookh. While Moore does not reach, except in rare snatches, the height of the loftiest qualities of some whom we have named, yet he has written finer poems than any, of equal length, by the greatest of his rivals. His radiance, not always as bright as some flashes from other pens, is yet a radiance of equable glow, whose total amount of light exceeds, by very much, we think, that total amount in the case of any cotemporary writer whatsoever. A vivid fancy; an epigrammatic spirit; a fine taste; vivacity, dexterity and a musical ear; have made him very easily what he is, the most popular poet now living—if not the most popular that ever lived—and, perhaps, a slight modification at birth of that which phrenologists have agreed to term *temperament*, might have made him the truest and noblest votary of the muse of any age or clime. As it is, we have only casual glimpses of that *mens divinior* which is assuredly enshrined within him.

Burton's Gentleman's Magazine, January 1840

Robert Southey

The Doctor, &c. New York: Republished by Harper and Brothers.

T HE DOCTOR has excited great attention in America as well as in England, and has given rise to every variety of conjecture and opinion, not only concerning the author's individuality, but in relation to the meaning, purpose, and character of the book itself. It is now said to be the work of one author—now of two, three, four, five—as far even as nine or ten. These writers are sometimes thought to have composed the *Doctor* conjointly—sometimes to have written each a portion. These individual portions have even been pointed out by the supremely acute, and the names of their respective fathers assigned. Supposed discrepancies of taste and manner, together with the prodigal introduction of mottoes, and other scraps of erudition (apparently beyond the compass of a single individual's reading) have given rise to this idea of a multiplicity of writers—among whom are mentioned in turn all the most witty, all the most eccentric, and especially all the most learned of Great Britain. Again—in regard to the nature of the book. It has been called an imitation of Sterne—an august and most profound exemplification, under the garb of eccentricity, of some all-important moral law—a true, under guise of a fictitious, biography—a simple jeu d'esprit—a mad farrago by a Bedlamite—and a great multiplicity of other equally fine names and hard. Undoubtedly, the best method of arriving at a decision in relation to a work of this nature, is to read it through with attention, and thus see what can be made of it. We have done so, and can make nothing of it, and are therefore clearly of opinion that the *Doctor* is precisely—nothing. We mean to say that it is nothing better than *a hoax*.

That any serious truth is meant to be inculcated by a tissue of bizarre and disjointed rhapsodies, whose *general* meaning no person can fathom, is a notion altogether untenable, unless we suppose the author a madman. But there are none of the proper evidences of madness in the book—while of mere *banter* there are instances innumerable. One half, at least, of the entire publication is taken up with palpable quizzes, reasonings in a circle, sentences, like the nonsense verses of

Du Bartas, evidently framed to mean nothing, while wearing an air of profound thought, and grotesque speculations in regard to the probable excitement to be created by the book.

It appears to have been written with the sole view (or nearly with the sole view) of exciting inquiry and comment. That this object should be fully accomplished cannot be thought very wonderful, when we consider the excessive trouble taken to accomplish it, by vivid and powerful intellect. That the *Doctor* is the offspring of such intellect, is proved sufficiently by many passages of the book, where the writer appears to have been led off from his main design. That it is written by more than one man should not be deduced either from the apparent immensity of its erudition, or from discrepancies of style. That man is a desperate mannerist who cannot vary his style *ad infinitum*; and although the book *may* have been written by a number of learned *bibliophagi*, still there is, we think, nothing to be found in the book itself at variance with the possibility of its being written by any one individual of even mediocre reading. Erudition is only certainly known in its *total* results. The mere grouping together of mottoes from the greatest multiplicity of the rarest works, or even the apparently natural inweaving into any composition, of the sentiments and manner of these works, are attainments within the reach of any well-informed, ingenious and industrious man having access to the great libraries of London. Moreover, while a single individual possessing these requisites and opportunities, might through a rabid desire of *creating a sensation*, have written, with some trouble, the Doctor, it is by no means easy to imagine that a plurality of sensible persons could be found willing to embark in such absurdity from a similar, or indeed from any imaginable inducement.

The present edition of the Harpers consists of two volumes in one. Volume one commences with a *Prelude of Mottoes* occupying two pages. Then follows a *Postscript*—then a *Table of Contents to the first volume*, occupying eighteen pages. Volume two has a similar *Prelude of Mottoes* and *Table of Contents*. The whole is subdivided into Chapters Ante-Initial, Initial and Post-Initial, with Inter-Chapters. The pages have now and then a typographical *queerity*—a monogram, a scrap of grotesque music, old English, &c. Some characters of this latter kind are printed with colored ink in the British edition, which is gotten up with great care. All these oddities are in the manner of Sterne, and some of them are exceedingly well conceived. The work professes to be a Life of one Doctor Daniel Dove and his horse Nobs—but we should put no very great faith in this biography. On the back of the book is a monogram—which appears again once or twice in the text, and whose solution is a fertile source of trouble with all readers. This monogram is a triangular pyramid; and as, in geometry, the solidity of every polyedral body may be computed by dividing the body into pyramids, the pyramid is thus considered as the base or essence of every polyedron. The author then, after his own fashion, may mean to imply that his book is the basis of all solidity or wisdom—or perhaps, since the polyedron is not only a solid, but a solid terminated by *plane faces*, that the *Doctor* is the very essence of all that spurious wisdom which will terminate in just nothing at all—in a hoax, and a consequent multiplicity of *blank visages*. The wit and humor of the *Doctor* have seldom been equalled. We cannot think Southey wrote it, but have no idea who did.

Southern Literary Messenger, July 1836

Sarah Stickney

The Poetry of Life. By Sarah Stickney, Author of "Pictures of Private Life." Philadelphia: Republished by Carey, Lea, and Blanchard.

THESE TWO volumes are subdivided as follows. Characteristics of Poetry—Why certain objects are, or are not poetical—Individual Associations—General Associations—The Poetry of Flowers—The Poetry of Trees—The Poetry of Animals—The Poetry of Evening—The Poetry of the Moon—The Poetry of Rural Life—The Poetry of Painting—The Poetry of Sound—The Poetry of Language—The Poetry of Love—The Poetry of Grief—The Poetry of Woman—The Poetry of the Bible—The Poetry of Religion—Impression—Imagination—Power—Taste—Conclusion.

In a Preface remarkable for neatness of style and precision of thought, Miss Stickney has very properly circumscribed within definite limits the design of her work—whose title, without such explanation, might have led us to expect too much at her hands. It would have been better, however, had the fair authoress, by means of a *different* title, which her habits of accurate thinking might have easily suggested, rendered this explanation unnecessary. Except in some very rare instances, where a context may be tolerated, if not altogether justified, a world, either of the pen or the pencil, should contain within itself every thing requisite for its own comprehension. "The design of the present volumes," says Miss Stickney, "is to treat of poetic feeling, rather than poetry; and this feeling I have endeavored to describe as the great connecting link between our intellects and our affections; while the customs of society, as well as the license of modern literature, afford me sufficient authority for the use of the word *life* in its widely extended sense, as comprehending all the functions, attributes, and capabilities peculiar to sentient beings."

We remember having read the "Pictures of Private Life" with interest of no common kind, and with a corresponding anxiety to know something more of the author. In them were apparent the calm enthusiasm, and the *analytical love of beauty*, which are now the distinguishing features of the volumes before us. We have perused the "Poetry of Life" with an

earnestness of attention, and a degree of real pleasure very seldom excited in our minds. It is a work giving evidence of more
profundity than discrimination—with no ordinary quantum
of either. What is said, if not always indisputable, is said with
a simplicity, and a scrupulous accuracy which leave us, not for
one moment, in doubt of what is intended, and impress us,
at the same time, with a high opinion of the author's
ability. Miss Stickney's manner is very good—her English
pure, harmonious, in every respect unexceptionable. With
a strong understanding, and withal a keen relish for the
minor forms of poetic excellence—a *strictness* of conception
which will ever prevent her from running into gross error—
she is still, we think, insufficiently alive to the *delicacies* of
the beautiful—unable fully to appreciate the *energies* of the
sublime.

We were forcibly impressed with these opinions, in looking
over, for the second time, the chapter of our fair authoress, "On
the Poetry of Language." What we have just said in relation to
her accuracy of thought and expression, and her appreciation of
the minor forms of poetic excellence, will be exemplified in the
passage we now quote, beginning at page 187, vol. i.

"There can scarcely be a more beautiful and appropriate
arrangement of words, than in the following stanza from
Childe Harold:

> The sails were filled, and fair the light winds blew,
> As glad to waft him from his native home;
> And fast the white rocks faded from his view,
> And soon were lost in circumambient foam;
> And then it may be of his wish to roam
> Repented he, but in his bosom slept
> The silent thought, nor from his lips did come
> One word of wail, whilst others sate and wept,
> And to the reckless gales unmanly moaning kept.

"Without committing a crime so heinous as that of entirely
spoiling this verse, it is easy to alter it so as to bring it down
to the level of ordinary composition; and thus we may illustrate the essential difference between poetry and mere versification.

The sails were *trimm'd* and fair the light winds blew,
As glad to *force* him from his native home,
And fast the white rocks *vanish'd* from his view,
And soon were lost *amid the circling* foam:
And then, *perchance, of his fond wish* to roam
Repented he, but in his bosom slept
The *wish*, nor from his *silent* lips did come
One *mournful word*, whilst others sat and wept,
And to *the heedless breeze their fruitless* moaning kept.

"It is impossible not to be struck with the harmony of the original words as they are placed in this stanza. The very sound is graceful, as well as musical; like the motion of the winds and waves, blended with the majestic movement of a gallant ship. 'The sails were filled' conveys no association with the work of man; but substitute the word *trimmed*, and you see the busy sailors at once. The word 'waft' follows in perfect unison with the whole of the preceding line, and maintains the invisible agency of the 'light winds;' while the word 'glad' before it, gives an idea of their power as an unseen intelligence. 'Fading' is also a happy expression, to denote the gradual obscurity and disappearing of the 'white rocks;' but the 'circumambient foam' is perhaps the most poetical expression of the whole, and such as could scarcely have proceeded from a low or ordinary mind."

All this is well—but what follows is not so. "It may be amusing"—says Miss Stickney, at page 189, "to see how a poet, and that of no mean order, can undesignedly murder his own offspring"—and she proceeds to extract, from Shelley, in illustration, some passages, of whose exquisite beauty she has evidently not the slightest comprehension. She commences with

"Music, when soft voices die
Vibrates in the memory—
Odours, when sweet violets *sicken*,
Live within the sense they quicken."

"Sicken" is here italicized; and the author of the "Poetry of Life" thinks the word so undeniably offensive as to render a farther allusion to it unnecessary. A few lines below, she quotes, in the same tone of criticism, the terrific image in the Ode to Naples.

> "Naples!—thou heart of men, which ever pantest
> Naked, beneath the lidless eye of Heaven!"

And again, on the next page, from the same author—

> "Thou art the wine whose drunkenness is all
> We can desire, O Love!"

Miss Stickney should immediately burn her copy of Shelley—it is to her capacities a sealed book.

Southern Literary Messenger, January 1836

Samuel Warren

Ten Thousand a Year. By the Author of The Diary of a London Physician. Carey and Hart: Philadelphia.

THERE ARE several circumstances connected with this book which render it an important topic for the critic. We mean its unusual length—the previous reputation of its author—the peculiarity of its subject—the apparent undercurrent of *design* which has been attributed to it—the wide difference of opinion existing in regard to its merit—and, especially, the fact of its being, if not precisely the first, yet certainly the chief of the class of *periodical* novels—the peculiar advantages and disadvantages of which it will afford a good opportunity for discussing. We much regret, therefore, that we have left ourselves no room, in the present number of the Magazine, for an extended analysis of the work. This we may possibly undertake in December; contenting ourselves, in the meantime, with a few observations at random.

It appears to us that a main source of the interest which this book possesses for the mass, is to be referred to the *pecuniary* nature of its theme. From beginning to end it is an affair of pounds, shillings, and pence—a topic which comes home at least *as* immediately to the bosoms and business of mankind, as any which could be selected. The same *character* in the choice of subject was displayed by Doctor Warren in his "Passages from the Diary of a London Physician." The *bodily health* is a point of absolutely universal interest, and was made the basis of all the excitement in that very popular but shamefully ill-written publication.

"Ten Thousand a Year" is also "shamefully ill-written." Its mere English is disgraceful to an L. L. D.—would be disgraceful to the simplest tyro in rhetoric. At every page we meet with sentences thus involved—"In order, however, to do this effectually I must go back to an earlier period in history than has yet been called to his attention. If it [*what?— attention?—history?*] shall have been unfortunate enough to attract the hasty eye of the superficial and impatient novel-reader, I make no doubt that by such a one certain portions of what has gone before, and which [*which what?*] could not fail of attracting the attention of long-headed people as being not thrown in for nothing (and therefore to be borne in mind with a view to subsequent explanation) have been entirely overlooked or forgotten." The book is full too of the grossest misusages of language—the most offensive vulgarities of speech and violations of grammar. The whole *tone* is in the last degree mawkish and inflated. What can be more ridiculous than the frequent apostrophising after this fashion— "My glorious Kate, how my heart goes forth towards you! And thou, her brother! who art of kindred spirit, who art supported by philosophy and exalted by religion, so that thy constancy cannot be shaken or overthrown by the black and ominous swell of trouble which is increasing around thee—I know that thou wilt outlive the storm—and yet it rocks thee! What indeed is to become of you all? Whither will you go? And your suffering mother, should she survive so long, is her precious form to be borne away from Yatton?" &c. &c.

There is no attempt at plot—but some of the incidents are wofully ill adapted and improbable. The moralising, throughout, is tedious in the extreme. Two-thirds of the whole novel might have been omitted with advantage. The character of Aubrey is a ridiculous piece of overdone sentimentality—and in character generally the writer fails. One of the worst features of the whole is the transparent puerile attempt to throw ridicule upon the ministerial party by dubbing them with silly names, supposed to be indicative of peculiarities of person or character. While the oppositionists, for example, rejoice in the euphonious appellations of Aubrey, Delamere, and the like, their foes are called Quirk, Gammon, Snap, Bloodsuck, Rotgut, Silly-Punctilio, and other more stupid and beastly indecencies.

Graham's Magazine, November 1841

REVIEWS OF AMERICAN
AUTHORS AND AMERICAN
LITERATURE

Contents

The American Drama

A BIOGRAPHIST of Berryer calls him *"l'homme qui, dans sa description, demande le plus grande quantité possible d'antithèse"*—but that ever recurring topic, the decline of the drama, seems to have consumed, of late, more of the material in question than would have sufficed for a dozen prime ministers—even admitting them to be French. Every trick of thought and every harlequinade of phrase have been put in operation for the purpose *"de nier ce qui est, et à expliquer ce qui n'est pas."*

Ce qui n'est pas:—for the drama has *not declined*. The facts and the philosophy of the case seem to be these. The great opponent to Progress is Conservatism. In other words—the great adversary of Invention is Imitation:—the propositions are in spirit identical. Just as an art is imitative, is it stationary. The most imitative arts are the most prone to repose—and the converse. Upon the utilitarian—upon the business arts, where Necessity impels, Invention, Necessity's well-understood offspring, is ever in attendance. And the less we see of the mother the less we behold of the child. No one complains of the decline of the art of Engineering. Here the Reason, which never retrogrades, or reposes, is called into play. But let us glance at Sculpture. We are not *worse*, here, than the ancients, let pedantry say what it may (the Venus of Canova is worth at any time two of that of Cleomenes), but it is equally certain that we have made, in general, no advances; and Sculpture, properly considered, is perhaps the *most* imitative of all arts which have a right to the title of Art at all. Looking next at Painting, we find that we have to boast of progress only in the ratio of the inferior imitativeness of Painting when compared with Sculpture. As far indeed as we have any means of judging, our improvement has been exceedingly little, and did we know anything of ancient Art in this department, we might be astonished at discovering that we had advanced even far less than we suppose. As regards Architecture, whatever progress we have made, has been precisely in those particulars which have no reference to imitation:—that is to say we have improved the utilitarian and not

the ornamental provinces of the art. Where Reason predominated, we advanced; where mere Feeling or Taste was the
guide, we remained as we were.

Coming to the Drama, we shall see that in its mechanisms
we have made progress, while in its spirituality we have done
little or nothing for centuries certainly—and, perhaps, little
or nothing for thousands of years. And this is because what
we term the spirituality of the drama is precisely its imitative
portion—is exactly that portion which distinguishes it as one
of the principal of the imitative arts.

Sculptors, painters, dramatists, are, from the very nature of
their material,—their spiritual material—imitators—conserva-
tists—prone to repose in old Feeling and in antique Taste. For
this reason—and for this reason only—the arts of Sculpture,
Painting and the Drama have not advanced—or have advanced
feebly, and inversely in the ratio of their imitativeness.

But it by no means follows that either has *declined*. All *seem*
to have declined, because they have remained stationary while
the multitudinous other arts (of reason) have flitted so rapidly
by them. In the same manner the traveler by rail-road can
imagine that the trees by the way-side are retrograding. The
trees in this case are absolutely stationary—but the Drama
has not been altogether so, although its progress has been so
slight as not to interfere with the general effect—that of
seeming retrogradation or decline.

This seeming retrogradation, however, is to all practical intents an absolute one. Whether the drama has declined, or
whether it has merely remained stationary, is a point of no
importance, so far as concerns the public encouragement of
the drama. It is unsupported, in either case, because it does
not deserve support.

But if this stagnation, or deterioration, grows out of the
very idiosyncrasy of the drama itself, as one of the principal
of the imitative arts, how is it possible that a remedy shall be
applied—since it is clearly impossible to alter the nature of
the art, and yet leave it the art which it now is?

We have already spoken of the improvements effected, in
Architecture, in all its utilitarian departments, and in the
Drama at all the points of its mechanism. "Wherever Reason
predominates we advance; where mere Feeling or Taste is the

guide, we remain as we are." We wish now to suggest that, by the engrafting of Reason upon Feeling and Taste, we shall be able, and thus alone shall be able, to force the modern Drama into the production of any profitable fruit.

At present, what is it we do? We are content if, with Feeling and Taste, a dramatist does *as other dramatists have done*. The most successful of the more immediately modern playwrights has been Sheridan Knowles and to play Sheridan Knowles seems to be the highest ambition of our writers for the stage. Now the author of "The Hunchback," possesses what we are weak enough to term the true "dramatic feeling," and this true dramatic feeling he has manifested in the most preposterous series of imitations of the Elizabethan drama, by which ever mankind were insulted and begulled. Not only did he adhere to the old plots, the old characters, the old stage conventionalities throughout; but, he went even so far as to persist in the obsolete phraseologies of the Elizabethan period—and just in proportion to his obstinacy and absurdity at all points, did we pretend to like him the better, and pretend to consider him a great dramatist.

Pretend—for every particle of it was pretence. Never was enthusiasm more utterly false than that which so many "respectable audiences" endeavored to get up for these plays—endeavored to get up, first, because there was a general desire to see the drama revive, and secondly, because we had been all along entertaining the fancy that "the decline of the drama" meant little, if anything, else than its deviation from the Elizabethan routine—and that, consequently, the return to the Elizabethan routine was, and of necessity must be, the revival of the drama.

But if the principles we have been at some trouble in explaining, are true—and most profoundly do we feel them to be so—if the spirit of imitation is, in fact, the real source of the drama's stagnation—and if it is so because of the tendency in all imitation to render Reason subservient to Feeling and to Taste—it is clear that only by deliberate counteracting of the spirit, and of the tendency of the spirit, we can hope to succeed in the drama's revival.

The first thing necessary is to burn or bury the "old models," and to forget, as quickly as possible, that ever a play has been penned. The second thing is to consider *de novo* what are the *capabilities* of the drama—not merely what hitherto have been its conventional purposes. The third and last point has reference to the composition of a play (showing to the fullest extent these capabilities), conceived and constructed with Feeling and with Taste, but with Feeling and Taste guided and controlled in every particular by the details of Reason—of Common Sense—in a word of a Natural Art.

It is obvious, in the meantime, that towards the good end in view, much may be effected by discriminative criticism on what has already been done. The field, thus stated, is of course, practically illimitable—and to Americans the American drama is the special point of interest. We propose therefore, in a series of papers, to take a somewhat deliberate survey of some few of the most noticeable American plays. We shall do this without reference either to the date of the composition, or its adaptation for the closet or the stage. We shall speak with absolute frankness both of merits and defects—our principal object being understood not as that of mere commentary on the individual play—but on the drama in general, and on the American drama in especial, of which each individual play is a constituent part. We will commence at once with

TORTESA, THE USURER

This is the third dramatic attempt of Mr. Willis, and may be regarded as particularly successful, since it has received, both on the stage and in the closet, no stinted measure of commendation. This success, as well as the high reputation of the author, will justify us in a more extended notice of the play than might, under other circumstances, be desirable.

The story runs thus:—Tortesa, an usurer of Florence, and whose character is a mingled web of good and evil feeling, gets into his possession the palace and lands of a certain Count Falcone. The usurer would wed the daughter (Isabella) of Falcone—not through love, but, in his own words,

"To please a devil that inhabits him"—

in fact to mortify the pride of the nobility, and avenge himself of their scorn. He therefore bargains with Falcone [a narrow-

souled villain] for the hand of Isabella. The deed of the Falcone property is restored to the Count, upon an agreement
that the lady shall marry the usurer—this contract being invalid should Falcone change his mind in regard to the marriage, or should the maiden demur—but valid should the wedding be prevented through any fault of Tortesa, or through
any accident not springing from the will of the father or child.
The first Scene makes us aware of this bargain, and introduces
us to Zippa, a glover's daughter, who resolves, with a view
of befriending Isabella, to feign a love for Tortesa [which, in
fact, she partially feels] hoping thus to break off the match.

The second Scene makes us acquainted with a young
painter, (Angelo) poor, but of high talents and ambition, and
with his servant, (Tomaso) an old bottle-loving rascal, entertaining no very exalted opinion of his master's abilities. Tomaso does some injury to a picture, and Angelo is about to
run him through the body, when he is interrupted by a sudden visit from the Duke of Florence, attended by Falcone.
The Duke is enraged at the murderous attempt, but admires
the paintings in the studio. Finding that the rage of the great
man will prevent his patronage if he knows the aggressor as
the artist, Angelo passes off Tomaso as himself, (Angelo)
making an exchange of names. This is a point of some importance, as it introduces the true Angelo to a job which he had
long coveted—the painting of the portrait of Isabella, of
whose beauty he had become enamored through report. The
Duke wishes the portrait painted. Falcone, however, on account of a promise to Tortesa, would have objected to admit
to his daughter's presence the handsome Angelo, but in regard to Tomaso, has no scruple. Supposing Tomaso to be
Angelo and the artist, the count writes a note to Isabella, requiring her "to admit the painter Angelo." The real Angelo is
thus admitted. He and the lady love at first sight, (much
in the manner of Romeo and Juliet,) each ignorant of the
other's attachment.

The third Scene of the second Act is occupied with a conversation between Falcone and Tortesa, during which a letter
arrives from the Duke, who, having heard of the intended
sacrifice of Isabella, offers to redeem the Count's lands and
palace, and desires him to preserve his daughter for a certain

Count Julian. But Isabella,—who, before seeing Angelo, had been willing to sacrifice herself for her father's sake, and who, since seeing him, had entertained hopes of escaping the hateful match through means of a plot entered into by herself and Zippa—Isabella, we say, is now in despair. To gain time, she at once feigns a love for the usurer, and indignantly rejects the proposal of the Duke. The hour for the wedding draws near. The lady has prepared a sleeping potion, whose effects resemble those of death. (Romeo and Juliet.) She swallows it—knowing that her supposed corpse would lie at night, pursuant to an old custom, in the sanctuary of the cathedral; and believing that Angelo—whose love for herself she has elicited, by a stratagem, from his own lips—will watch by the body, in the strength of his devotion. Her ultimate design (we may suppose, for it is not told) is to confess all to her lover, on her revival, and throw herself upon his protection— their marriage being concealed, and herself regarded as dead by the world. Zippa, who *really* loves Angelo—(her love for Tortesa, it must be understood, is a very equivocal feeling, for the fact cannot be denied that Mr. Willis makes her love both at the same time)—Zippa, who really loves Angelo—who has discovered his passion for Isabella—and who, as well as that lady, believes that the painter will watch the corpse in the cathedral,—determines, through jealousy, to prevent his so doing, and with this view informs Tortesa that she has learned it to be Angelo's design to steal the body, *for artistical purposes*,—in short as a model to be used in his studio. The usurer, in consequence, sets a guard at the doors of the cathedral. This guard does, in fact, prevent the lover from watching the corpse, but, it appears, does *not* prevent the lady, on her revival and disappointment in not seeing the one she sought, from passing unperceived from the church. Weakened by her long sleep, she wanders aimlessly through the streets, and at length finds herself, when just sinking with exhaustion, at the door of her father. She has no resource but to knock. The Count—who here, we must say, acts very much as Thimble of old—the knight, we mean, of the "scolding wife"—maintains that she is dead, and shuts the door in her face. In other words, he supposes it to be the ghost of his daughter who speaks; and so the lady is left to perish on the steps. Meantime Angelo is absent from home, attempting to get access to the cathedral; and his servant, Tomaso, takes the opportunity of absenting himself also, and of indulging his bibulous propensities while perambulating the town. He finds Isabella as we left her; and, through motives which we will leave Mr. Willis to explain, conducts her unresistingly to Angelo's residence, and— *deposits her in Angelo's bed*. The artist now returns—Tomaso is kicked out of doors—and we are not told, but left to presume, that a full explanation and perfect understanding are brought about between the lady and her lover.

We find them, next morning, in the studio, where stands, leaning against an easel, the portrait (a full length) of Isabella, with curtains adjusted before it. The stage-directions, moreover, inform us that "the back wall of the room is such as to form a natural ground for the picture." While Angelo is occupied in retouching it, he is interrupted by the arrival of Tortesa with a guard, and is accused of having stolen the corpse from the sanctuary—the lady, meanwhile, having stepped behind the curtain. The usurer insists upon seeing the painting, with a view of ascertaining whether any new touches had been put upon it, which would argue an examination, *post mortem*, of those charms of neck and bosom which the living Isabella would not have unveiled. Resistance is vain—the curtain is torn down; but, to the surprise of Angelo, the lady herself is discovered, " with her hands crossed on her breast, and her eyes fixed on the ground, standing motionless in the frame which had contained the picture." The *tableau*, we are to believe, deceives Tortesa, who steps back to contemplate what he supposes to be the portrait of his betrothed. In the meantime the guards, having searched the house, find the veil which had been thrown over the imagined corpse in the sanctuary; and, upon this evidence, the artist is carried before the duke. Here he is accused, not only of sacrilege, but of the murder of Isabella, and is about to be condemned to death, when his mistress comes forward in person; thus resigning herself to the usurer to save the life of her lover. But the nobler nature of Tortesa now breaks forth; and, smitten with admiration of the lady's conduct, as well as convinced that her love for himself was feigned, he

resigns her to Angelo—although now feeling and acknowledging for the first time that a fervent love has, in his own
bosom, assumed the place of that misanthropic ambition
which, hitherto, had alone actuated him in seeking her hand.
Moreover, he endows Isabella with the lands of her father
Falcone. The lovers are thus made happy. The usurer weds
Zippa; and the curtain drops upon the promise of the duke
to honor the double nuptials with his presence.

This story, as we have given it, hangs better together (Mr.
Willis will pardon our modesty) and is altogether more easily
comprehended, than in the words of the play itself. We have
really put the best face upon the matter, and presented the
whole in the simplest and clearest light in our power. We
mean to say that "Tortesa" (partaking largely, in this respect,
of the drama of Cervantes and Calderon) is over-clouded—
rendered misty—by a world of unnecessary and impertinent
intrigue. This folly was adopted by the Spanish comedy, and
is imitated by us, with the idea of imparting "action," "business," "vivacity." But vivacity, however desirable, can be attained in many other ways, and is dearly purchased, indeed,
when the price is intelligibility.

The truth is that *cant* has never attained a more owl-like
dignity than in the discussion of dramatic principle. A modern stage critic is nothing, if not a lofty contemner of all
things simple and direct. He delights in mystery—revels in
mystification—has transcendental notions concerning P. S.
and O. P., and talks about "stage business and stage effect,"
as if he were discussing the differential calculus. For much of
all this, we are indebted to the somewhat over-profound criticisms of Augustus William Schlegel.

But the *dicta* of common sense are of universal application,
and, touching this matter of *intrigue*, if, from its superabundance, we are compelled, even in the quiet and critical *perusal*
of a play, to pause frequently and reflect long—to re-read
passages over and over again, for the purpose of gathering
their bearing upon the whole—of maintaining in our mind a
general connection—what but fatigue can result from the exertion? How then when we come to the representation?—
when these passages—trifling, perhaps, in themselves, but
important when considered in relation to the plot,—are hur-

ried and blurred over in the stuttering enunciation of some miserable rantipole, or omitted altogether through the constitutional lapse of memory so peculiar to those lights of the age and stage, bedight (from being of no conceivable use) supernumeraries? For it must be borne in mind that these bits of *intrigue* (we use the term in the sense of the German critics) appertain generally, indeed altogether, to the after-thoughts of the drama—to the under-plots—are met with, consequently, in the mouth of the lacquies and chamber-maids—and are thus consigned to the tender mercies of the *stella minores*. Of course we get but an imperfect idea of what is going on before our eyes. Action after action ensues whose mystery we cannot unlock without the little key which these barbarians have thrown away and lost. Our weariness increases in proportion to the number of these embarrassments, and if the play escape damnation at all, it escapes *in spite* of that intrigue to which, in nine cases out of ten, the author attributes his success, and which he *will* persist in valuing exactly in proportion to the misapplied labor it has cost him.

But dramas of this kind are said, in our customary parlance, to "abound in *plot*." We have never yet met any one, however, who could tell us what precise ideas he connected with the phrase. A mere succession of incidents, even the most spirited, will no more constitute a plot, than a multiplication of zeros, even the most infinite, will result in the production of a unit. This all will admit—but few trouble themselves to think farther. The common notion seems to be in favor of mere *complexity*; but a plot, properly understood, is perfect only inasmuch as we shall find ourselves unable to detach from it *or disarrange* any single incident involved, without *destruction* to the mass. This we say is the point of perfection—a point never yet attained, but not on that account unattainable. Practically, we may consider a plot as of high excellence, when no one of its component parts shall be susceptible of *removal* without *detriment* to the whole. Here, indeed, is a vast lowering of the demand—and with less than this no writer of refined taste should content himself.

As this subject is not only in itself of great importance, but will have at all points a bearing upon what we shall say hereafter, in the examination of various plays, we shall be pardoned for quoting from the "Democratic Review" some passages (of our own) which enter more particularly into the rationale of the subject:

"All the Bridgewater treatises have failed in noticing the *great* idiosyncrasy in the Divine system of adaptation: —that idiosyncrasy which stamps the adaptation as divine, in distinction from that which is the work of merely human constructiveness. I speak of the complete *mutuality* of adaptation. For example: —in human constructions, a particular cause has a particular effect—a particular purpose brings about a particular object; but we see no reciprocity. The effect does not react upon the cause—the object does not change relations with the purpose. In Divine constructions, the object is either object or purpose as we choose to regard it, while the purpose is either purpose or object; so that we can never (abstractly—without concretion—without reference to facts of the moment) decide which is which.

"For secondary example: —In polar climates, the human frame, to maintain its animal heat, requires, for combustion in the capillary system, an abundant supply of highly azotized food, such as train oil. Again: —in polar climates nearly the sole food afforded man is the oil of abundant seals and whales. Now whether is oil at hand because imperatively demanded? or whether is it the only thing demanded because the only thing to be obtained? It is impossible to say: —there is an absolute reciprocity of adaptation for which we seek in vain among the works of man.

"The Bridgewater tractists may have avoided this point, on account of its apparent tendency to overthrow the idea of *cause* in general—consequently of a First Cause—of God. But it is more probable that they have failed to perceive what no one preceding them has, to my knowledge, perceived.

"The pleasure which we derive from any exertion of human ingenuity, is in the direct ratio of the *approach* to this species of reciprocity between cause and effect. In the construction of *plot*, for example, in fictitious literature, we should aim at so arranging the points, or incidents, that we cannot distinctly see, in respect to any one of them, whether that one depends from any one other or upholds it. In this sense, of course, perfection of plot is unattainable *in fact*—because Man is the constructor. The plots of God are perfect. The Universe is a plot of God."

The pleasure derived from the contemplation of the unity resulting from plot, is far more intense than is ordinarily supposed, and, as in Nature we meet with no such combination of *incident*, appertains to a very lofty region of the ideal. In speaking thus we have not said that plot is more than an adjunct to the drama—more than a perfectly distinct and separable source of pleasure. It is *not* an essential. In its intense artificiality it may even be conceived injurious in a certain degree (unless constructed with consummate skill) to that real *life-likeness* which is the soul of the drama of character. Good dramas have been written with very little plot—capital dramas might be written with none at all. Some plays of high merit, having plot, abound in irrelevant incident—in incident, we mean, which could be displaced or removed altogether without effect upon the plot itself, and yet are by no means objectionable as dramas; and for this reason—that the incidents are *evidently* irrelevant—*obviously* episodical. Of their digressive nature the spectator is so immediately aware, that he views them, as they arise, in the simple light of interlude, and does not fatigue his attention by attempting to establish for them a connection, or more than an illustrative connection, with the great interests of the subject. Such are the plays of Shakspeare. But all this is very different from *that* irrelevancy of intrigue which disfigures and very usually damns the work of the unskillful artist. With him the great error lies in *inconsequence*. Underplot is piled upon underplot (the very word is a paradox), and all to no purpose—*to no end*. The interposed incidents have no ultimate effect upon the main ones. They may hang upon the mass—they may even coalesce with it, or, as in some intricate cases, they may be so intimately blended as to be lost amid the chaos which they have been instrumental in bringing about—but still they have no portion in the plot, which exists, if at all, independently of their influence. Yet the *attempt* is made by the author to establish and demonstrate a dependence—an identity; and it is the *obviousness of this attempt* which is the cause of weariness in the spectator, who, of course, cannot at once see that his attention is challenged to no purpose—that intrigues so obtrusively forced upon it, are to be found, in the end, without effect upon the leading interests of the play.

"Tortesa" will afford us plentiful examples of this irrelevancy of intrigue—of this misconception of the nature and of the capacities of plot. We have said that our digest of the story is more easy of comprehension than the detail of Mr. Willis. If so, it is because we have forborne to give such portions as had no influence upon the whole. These served but to embarrass the narrative and fatigue the attention. How much was irrelevant is shown by the brevity of the space in which we have recorded, somewhat at length, all the influential incidents of a drama of five acts. There is scarcely a scene in which is not to be found the germ of an underplot—a germ, however, which seldom proceeds beyond the condition of a bud, or, if so fortunate as to swell into a flower, arrives, in no single instance, at at the dignity of fruit. Zippa, a lady altogether without character (dramatic) is the most pertinacious of all conceivable concoctors of plans never to be matured—of vast designs that terminate in nothing—of *cul-de-sac* machinations. She plots in one page and counterplots in the next. She schemes her way from P. S. to O. P., and intrigues perseveringly from the footlights to the slips. A very singular instance of the inconsequence of her manœuvres is found towards the conclusion of the play. The whole of the second scene, (occupying five pages,) in the fifth act, is obviously introduced for the purpose of giving her information, through Tomaso's means, of Angelo's arrest for the murder of Isabella. Upon learning his danger she rushes from the stage, to be present at the trial, exclaiming that her evidence can save his life. We, the audience, of course applaud, and now look with interest to her movements in the scene of the judgment hall. She, Zippa, we think, is somebody after all; she will be the means of Angelo's salvation; she will thus be the chief unraveller of the plot. All eyes are bent, therefore, upon Zippa—but alas, upon the point at issue, Zippa does not so much as open her mouth. It is scarcely too much to say that not a single action of this impertinent little busybody has any real influence upon the play:—yet she appears upon every occasion—appearing only to perplex.

Similar things abound; we should not have space even to allude to them all. The whole conclusion of the play is super-erogatory. The immensity of pure *fuss* with which it is overloaded, forces us to the reflection that all of it might have been avoided by one word of explanation to the duke—an amiable man who admires the talents of Angelo, and who, *to prevent Isabella's marrying against her will*, had *previously* offered to free Falcone of his bonds to the usurer. That he would free him *now*, and thus set all matters straight, the spectator cannot doubt for an instant, and he can conceive no better reason why explanations are *not* made, than that Mr. Willis does not think proper they should be. In fact, the whole drama is exceedingly ill *motivirt*.

We have already mentioned an inadvertence, in the fourth Act, where Isabella is made to escape from the sanctuary through the midst of guards who prevented the ingress of Angelo. Another occurs where Falcone's conscience is made to reprove him, upon the appearance of his daughter's supposed ghost, for having occasioned her death by forcing her to marry against her will. The author had forgotten that Falcone submitted to the wedding, after the duke's interposition, only upon Isabella's assurance *that she really loved the usurer*. In the third Scene, too, of the first Act, the imagination of the spectator is no doubt a little taxed, when he finds Angelo, in the first moments of his introduction to the palace of Isabella, commencing her portrait by laying on color after color, before he has made any attempt at an outline. In the last Act, moreover, Tortesa gives to Isabella a deed

> "Of the Falcone palaces and lands,
> And all the money forfeit by Falcone."

This is a terrible blunder, and the more important as upon this act of the usurer depends the development of his new-born sentiments of honor and virtue—depends, in fact, the most salient *point* of the play. Tortesa, we say, gives to Isabella the lands forfeited by Falcone; but Tortesa was surely not very generous in giving what, clearly, was not his own to give. Falcone had *not forfeited* the deed, which had been restored to him by the usurer, and which was then in his (Falcone's) possession. Hear Tortesa:

"He put it in the bond,
That if, by any humor of my own,
Or accident that came not from himself,
Or from his daughter's will, the match were marred,
His tenure stood intact."

Now Falcone is still resolute for the match; but this new generous "humor" of Tortesa induces him (Tortesa) to decline it. Falcone's tenure is then intact; he retains the deed; the usurer is giving away property not his own.

As a drama of character, "Tortesa" is by no means open to so many objections as when we view it in the light of its plot; but it is still faulty. The merits are so exceedingly negative, that it is difficult to say anything about them. The Duke is nobody; Falcone, nothing; Zippa, less than nothing. Angelo may be regarded simply as the medium through which Mr. Willis conveys to the reader his own glowing feelings—his own refined and delicate fancy—(delicate, yet bold)—his own rich voluptuousness of sentiment—a voluptuousness which would offend in almost any other language than that in which it is so skillfully appareled. Isabella is—the heroine of the Hunchback. The revolution in the character of Tortesa—or rather the final triumph of his innate virtue—is a dramatic point far older than the hills. It may be observed, too, that although the representation of no human character should be quarreled with for its inconsistency, we yet require that the inconsistencies be not absolute antagonisms to the extent of neutralization: they may be permitted to be oils and waters, but they must not be alkalies and acids. When, in the course of the *dénouement*, the usurer bursts forth into an eloquence virtue-inspired, we cannot sympathize very heartily in his fine speeches, since they proceed from the mouth of the self-same egotist who, urged by a disgusting vanity, uttered so many sotticisms (about his fine legs, &c.) in the earlier passages of the play. Tomaso is, upon the whole, the best personage. We recognize some originality in his conception, and conception was seldom more admirably carried out.

One or two observations at random. In the third Scene of the fifth Act, Tomaso, the buffoon, is made to assume pater-

nal authority over Isabella, (as usual, without sufficient purpose,) by virtue of a law which Tortesa thus expounds:

> "My gracious liege, there is a law in Florence,
>   That if a father, for no guilt or shame,
>   Disown and shut his door upon his daughter,
>   She is the child of him who succors her,
>   Who, by the shelter of a single night,
>   Becomes endowed with the authority
>   Lost by the other."

No one, of course, can be made to believe that any such
stupid law as this ever existed either in Florence or Timbuc-
too; but, on the ground *que le vrai n'est pas toujours le vrai-
semblable*, we say that even its real existence would be no justification of Mr. Willis. It has an air of the far-fetched—of
the desperate—which a fine taste will avoid as a pestilence.
Very much of the same nature is the attempt of Tortesa to
extort a second bond from Falcone. The evidence which con-
victs Angelo of murder is ridiculously frail. The idea of Isabella's assuming the place of the portrait, and so deceiving the
usurer, is not only glaringly improbable, but seems adopted
from the "Winter's Tale." But in this latter play, the deception is at least possible, for the human figure but imitates a
statue. What, however, are we to make of Mr. W.'s stage direction about the back wall's being "so arranged as to form a
natural ground for the picture?" Of course, the very slightest
movement of Tortesa (and he makes many) would have annihilated the illusion by disarranging the perspective; and in
no manner could this latter have been arranged at all for more
than one particular point of view—in other words, for more
than one particular person in the whole audience. The
"asides," moreover, are unjustifiably frequent. The prevalence
of this folly (of speaking aside) detracts as much from the
acting merit of our drama generally, as any other inartisticality. It utterly destroys verisimilitude. People are not in the
habit of soliloquizing aloud—at least, not to any positive extent; and why should an author have to be told, what the
slightest reflection would teach him, that an audience, by dint
of no imagination, can or will conceive that what is sonorous

in their own ears at the distance of fifty feet, cannot be heard by an actor at the distance of one or two?

Having spoken thus of "Tortesa"—in terms of nearly unmitigated censure—our readers may be surprised to hear us say that we think highly of the drama as a whole—and have little hesitation in ranking it before most of the dramas of Sheridan Knowles. Its leading faults are those of the modern drama generally—they are not peculiar to itself—while its great merits *are*. If in support of our opinion, we do not cite points of commendation, it is because those form the mass of the work. And were we to speak of fine passages, we should speak of the entire play. Nor by "fine passages" do we mean passages of merely fine language, embodying fine sentiment, but such as are replete with truthfulness, and teem with the loftiest qualities of the dramatic art. *Points*—capital points abound; and these have far more to do with the general excellence of a play, than a too speculative criticism has been willing to admit. Upon the whole we are proud of "Tortesa"—and here again, for the fiftieth time at least, record our warm admiration of the abilities of Mr. Willis.

We proceed now to Mr. Longfellow's

SPANISH STUDENT

The reputation of its author as a poet, and as a graceful writer of prose, is, of course, long and deservedly established—but as a dramatist he was unknown before the publication of this play. Upon its original appearance, in "Graham's Magazine," the general opinion was greatly in favor—if not exactly of "The Spanish Student"—at all events of the writer of Outre-Mer. But this general opinion is the most equivocal thing in the world. It is never self-formed. It has very seldom indeed an original development. In regard to the work of an already famous or infamous author it decides, to be sure, with a laudable promptitude; making up all the mind that it has, by reference to the reception of the author's immediately previous publication;—making up thus the ghost of a mind *pro tem.*—a species of critical shadow, that fully answers, nevertheless, all the purposes of a substance itself, until the substance itself shall be forthcoming. But, beyond this point, the general opinion can only be considered that of the public, as a man may call a book *his*, having bought it. When a *new* writer arises, the shop of the true, thoughtful, or critical opinion, is not simultaneously thrown open—is not immediately set up. Some weeks elapse; and, during this interval, the public, at a loss where to procure an opinion of the *débutant*, have necessarily no opinion of him at all, for the nonce.

The popular voice, then, which ran so much in favor of "The Spanish Student," upon its original issue, should be looked upon as merely the ghost *pro tem.*—as based upon critical decisions respecting the previous works of the author—as having reference in no manner to "The Spanish Student" itself—and thus as utterly meaningless and valueless *per se*.

The few—by which we mean those who think, in contradistinction from the many who think they think—the few who think at first hand, and thus twice before speaking at all—these received the play with a commendation somewhat less *prononcée*—somewhat more guardedly qualified—than Professor Longfellow might have desired, or may have been taught to expect. Still the composition was approved upon the whole. The few words of censure were very far, indeed, from amounting to condemnation. The chief defect insisted upon was the feebleness of the *dénouement*, and, generally, of the concluding scenes, as compared with the opening passages. We are not sure, however, that anything like detailed criticism has been attempted in the case—nor do we propose now to attempt it. Nevertheless, the work has interest, not only within itself, but as the first dramatic effort of an author who has remarkably succeeded in almost every other department of light literature than that of the drama. It may be as well, therefore, to speak of it, if not analytically, at least somewhat in detail; and we cannot, perhaps, more suitably commence than by a quotation, without comment, of some of the finer passages:

> "And, though she is a virgin outwardly,
>   Within she is a sinner; like those panels
>   Of doors and altar-pieces the old monks

Painted in convents, with the Virgin Mary
On the outside, and on the inside Venus."

                    "I believe
That woman, in her deepest degradation,
Holds something sacred, something undefiled,
Some pledge and keepsake of her higher nature,
And, like the diamond in the dark, retains
Some quenchless gleam of the celestial light."

"And we shall sit together unmolested,
And words of true love pass from tongue to tongue,
As singing birds from one bough to another."

                    "Our feelings and our thoughts
Tend ever on and rest not in the Present.
As drops of rain fall into some dark well,
And from below comes a scarce audible sound,
So fall our thoughts into the dark Hereafter,
And their mysterious echo reaches us."

"Her tender limbs are still, and, on her breast,
  The cross she prayed to, ere she fell asleep,
  Rises or falls with the soft tide of dreams,
  Like a light barge safe moored."

"Hark! how the large and ponderous mace of Time
  Knocks at the golden portals of the day!"

"The lady Violante, bathed in tears
  Of love and anger, like the maid of Colchis,
  Whom thou, another faithless Argonaut,
  Having won that golden fleece, a woman's love,
  Desertest for this Glaucé."

"I read or sit in reverie and watch
  The changing color of the waves that break
  Upon the idle sea-shore of the mind."

"I will forget her. All dear recollections
  Pressed in my heart, like flowers within a book,
  Shall be torn out and scattered to the winds."

"O yes! I see it now—
Yet rather with my heart than with mine eyes,
So faint it is. And all my thoughts sail thither,
Freighted with prayers and hopes, and forward urged
Against all stress of accident, as, in
The Eastern Tale, against the wind and tide
Great ships were drawn to the Magnetic Mountains."

"But there are brighter dreams than those of Fame,
    Which are the dreams of Love! Out of the heart
    Rises the bright ideal of these dreams,
    As from some woodland fount a spirit rises
    And sinks again into its silent deeps,
    Ere the enamored knight can touch her robe!
    'Tis this ideal that the soul of Man,
    Like the enamored knight beside the fountain,
    Waits for upon the margin of Life's stream;
    Waits to behold her rise from the dark waters,
    Clad in a mortal shape! Alas, how many
    Must wait in vain! The stream flows evermore,
    But from its silent deeps no spirit rises!
    Yet I, born under a propitious star,
    Have found the bright ideal of my dreams."

            "Yes; by the Darro's side
My childhood passed. I can remember still
The river, and the mountains capped with snow;
The villages where, yet a little child,
I told the traveler's fortune in the street;
The smuggler's horse; the brigand and the shepherd;
The march across the moor; the halt at noon;
The red fire of the evening camp, that lighted
The forest where we slept; and, farther back,
As in a dream, or in some former life,
Gardens and palace walls."

            "This path will lead us to it,
Over the wheat-fields, where the shadows sail
Across the running sea, now green, now blue,
And, like an idle mariner on the ocean,
Whistles the quail."

These extracts will be universally admired. They are grace-ful, well expressed, imaginative, and altogether replete with the true poetic feeling. We quote them *now*, at the beginning of our review, by way of justice to the poet, and because, in what follows, we are not sure that we have more than a very few words of what may be termed commendation to bestow.

The "Spanish Student" has an unfortunate beginning, in a most unpardonable, and yet, to render the matter worse, in a most indispensable "Preface:"

"The subject of the following play," says Mr. L., "is taken in part from the beautiful play of Cervantes, *La Gitanilla*. To this source, however, I am indebted for the main incident only, the love of a Spanish student for a Gipsy girl, and the name of the heroine, Preciosa. I have not followed the story in any of its details. In Spain this subject has been twice han-dled dramatically; first by Juan Perez de Montalvan, in *La Gitanilla*, and afterwards by Antonio de Solis y Rivadeneira in *La Gitanilla de Madrid*. The same subject has also been made use of by Thomas Middleton, an English dramatist of the seventeenth century. His play is called *The Spanish Gipsy*. The main plot is the same as in the Spanish pieces; but there runs through it a tragic underplot of the loves of Rodrigo and Doña Clara, which is taken from another tale of Cer-vantes, *La Fuerza de la Sangre*. The reader who is acquainted with *La Gitanilla* of Cervantes, and the plays of Montalvan, Solis, and Middleton, will perceive that my treatment of the subject differs entirely from theirs."

Now the autorial originality, properly considered, is three-fold. There is, first, the originality of the general thesis; sec-ondly, that of the several incidents, or thoughts, by which the thesis is developed; and, thirdly, that of manner, or *tone*, by which means alone, an old subject, even when developed through hackneyed incidents, or thoughts, may be made to produce a fully original *effect*—which, after all, is the end truly in view.

But originality, as it is one of the highest, is also one of the rarest of merits. In America it is especially, and very remark-ably rare:—this through causes sufficiently well understood. We are content per force, therefore, as a general thing, with either of the lower branches of originality mentioned above, and would regard with high favor indeed any author who should supply the great *desideratum* in combining the three. Still the three *should* be combined; and from whom, if not from such men as Professor Longfellow—if not from those who occupy the chief niches in our Literary Temple—shall we expect the combination? But in the present instance, what has Professor Longfellow accomplished? Is he original at any one point? Is he original in respect to the first and most important of our three divisions? "The *subject* of the following play," he says himself, "is taken *in part* from the beautiful play of Cervantes, La Gitanilla." "To this source, however, I am indebted for *the main incident only*, the love of the Spanish Student for a Gipsy Girl, and the name of the heroine, Preciosa."

The Italics are our own, and the words Italicized involve an obvious contradiction. We cannot understand how "the love of the Spanish Student for the Gipsy Girl" can be called an "incident," or even a "main incident," at all. In fact, this love—this discordant and therefore eventful or incidentful love—is the true *thesis* of the drama of Cervantes. It is this anomalous "love" which originates the incidents by means of which, itself, this "love," the thesis, is developed. Having based his play, then, upon this "love," we cannot admit his claim to originality upon our first count; nor has he any right to say that he has adopted his "subject" "in part." It is clear that he has adopted it altogether. Nor would he have been entitled to claim originality of subject, even had he based his story upon *any variety* of love arising between parties naturally separated by prejudices of *caste*—such, for example, as those which divide the Brahmin from the Pariah, the Ammonite from the African, or even the Christian from the Jew. For here in its ultimate analysis, is the real thesis of the Spaniard. But when the drama is founded, not merely upon this general thesis, but upon this general thesis in the identical application given it by Cervantes—that is to say upon the prejudice of *caste* exemplified in the case of a Catholic, and this Catholic a Spaniard, and this Spaniard a student, and this Student loving a Gipsy, and this Gipsy a dancing-girl, and this dancing-girl bearing the name Preciosa—we are not altogether prepared to be informed by Professor Longfellow that he is indebted for an "incident only" to the "beautiful Gitanilla of Cervantes."

Whether our author is original upon our second and third points—in the true incidents of his story, or in the manner and *tone* of their handling—will be more distinctly seen as we proceed.

It is to be regretted that "The Spanish Student" was not sub-entitled "A Dramatic Poem," rather than "A Play." The former title would have more fully conveyed the intention of the poet; for, of course, we shall not do Mr. Longfellow the injustice to suppose that his design has been, in any respect, *a play*, in the ordinary acceptation of the term. Whatever may be its merits in a merely poetical view, "The Spanish Student" could not be endured upon the stage.

Its plot runs thus:—Preciosa, the daughter of a Spanish gentleman, is stolen, while an infant, by Gipsies; brought up as his own daughter, and as a dancing-girl, by a Gipsy leader, Crusado; and by him betrothed to a young Gipsy, Bartolomé. At Madrid, Preciosa loves and is beloved by Victorian, a student of Alcalda, who resolves to marry her, notwithstanding her *caste*, rumors involving her purity, the dissuasions of his friends, and his betrothal to an heiress of Madrid. Preciosa is also sought by the Count of Lara, a *roué*. She rejects him. He forces his way into her chamber, and is there seen by Victorian, who, misinterpreting some words overheard, doubts the fidelity of his mistress, and leaves her in anger, after challenging the Count of Lara. In the duel, the Count receives his life at the hands of Victorian; declares his ignorance of the understanding between Victorian and Preciosa; boasts of favors received from the latter; and, to make good his words, produces a ring which she gave him, he asserts, as a pledge of her love. This ring is a duplicate of one previously given the girl by Victorian, and known to have been so given, by the Count. Victorian mistakes it for his own, believes all that has been said, and abandons the field to his rival, who, immediately afterwards, while attempting to procure access to the Gipsy, is assassinated by Bartolomé. Meantime, Victorian, wandering through the country, reaches Guadarrama. Here he receives a letter from Madrid, disclosing the treachery practised by Lara, and telling that Preciosa, rejecting his addresses, had been, through his instrumentality, hissed from the stage, and now again roamed with the Gipsies. He goes in search of her; finds her in a wood near Guadarrama; approaches her, disguising his voice; she recognizes him, pretending she does not, and unaware that he knows her innocence; a conversation of *equivoque* ensues; he sees his ring upon her finger; offers to purchase it; she refuses to part with it; a full *éclaircissement* takes place; at this juncture, a servant of Victorian's arrives with "news from court," giving the first intimation of the true parentage of Preciosa. The lovers set out, forthwith, for Madrid, to see the newly discovered father. On the route, Bartolomé dogs their steps; fires at Preciosa; misses her; the shot is returned; he falls; and "The Spanish Student" is concluded.

This plot, however, like that of "Tortesa," looks better in our naked digest than amidst the details which develop only to disfigure it. The reader of the play itself will be astonished, when he remembers the name of the author, at the inconsequence of the incidents—at the utter want of skill—of art—manifested in their conception and introduction. In dramatic writing, no principle is more clear than that nothing should be said or done which has not a tendency to develop the catastrophe, or the characters. But Mr. Longfellow's play abounds in events and conversations that have no ostensible purpose, and certainly answer no end. In what light, for example, since we cannot suppose this drama intended for the stage, are we to regard the second scene of the second act, where a long dialogue between an Archbishop and a Cardinal is wound up by a dance from Preciosa? The Pope thinks of abolishing public dances in Spain, and the priests in question have been delegated to examine, personally, the proprieties or improprieties of such exhibitions. With this view, Preciosa is summoned and required to give a specimen of her skill. Now this, in a mere spectacle, would do very well; for here all that is demanded is an occasion or an excuse for a dance; but what business has it in a pure drama? or in what regard does it further the end of a dramatic poem, intended only to be read?

In the same manner, the whole of Scene the eighth, in the same act, is occupied with six lines of stage directions, as follows:

> "*The Theatre. The orchestra plays the Cachuca. Sound of castanets behind the scenes. The curtain rises and discovers Preciosa in the attitude of commencing the dance. The Cachuca. Tumult. Hisses. Cries of Brava! and Aguera! She falters and pauses. The music stops. General confusion. Preciosa faints.*"

But the *inconsequence* of which we complain will be best exemplified by an entire scene. We take Scene the Fourth, Act the First:

> *An inn on the road to Alcalá.* BALTASAR *asleep on a bench. Enter* CHISPA.

CHISPA. And here we are, half way to Alcalá, between cocks and midnight. Body o' me! what an inn this is! The light out and the landlord asleep! Holá! ancient Baltasar!

BALTASAR (*waking*). Here I am.

CHISPA. Yes, there you are, like a one-eyed alcalde in a town without inhabitants. Bring a light, and let me have supper.

BALTASAR. Where is your master?

CHISPA. Do not trouble yourself about him. We have stopped a moment to breathe our horses; and if he chooses to walk up and down in the open air, looking into the sky as one who hears it rain, that does not satisfy my hunger, you know. But be quick, for I am in a hurry, and every one stretches his legs according to the length of his coverlet. What have we here?

BALTASAR (*setting a light on the table*). Stewed rabbit.

CHISPA (*eating*). Conscience of Portalegre! stewed kitten, you mean!

BALTASAR. And a pitcher of Pedro Ximenes, with a roasted pear in it.

CHISPA (*drinking*). Ancient Baltasar, amigo! you know how to cry wine and sell vinegar. I tell you this is nothing but vino tinto of La Mancha, with a tang of the swine-skin.

BALTASAR. I swear to you by Saint Simon and Judas, it is all as I say.

CHISPA. And I swear to you by Saint Peter and Saint Paul, that it is no such thing. Moreover, your supper is like the hidalgo's dinner—very little meat and a great deal of table-cloth.

BALTASAR. Ha! ha! ha!

CHISPA. And more noise than nuts.

BALTASAR. Ha! ha! ha! You must have your joke, Master Chispa. But shall I not ask Don Victorian in to take a draught of the Pedro Ximenes?

CHISPA. No; you might as well say, "Don't you want some?" to a dead man.

BALTASAR. Why does he go so often to Madrid?

CHISPA. For the same reason that he eats no supper. He is in love. Were you ever in love, Baltasar?

BALTASAR. I was never out of it, good Chispa. It has been the torment of my life.

CHISPA. What! are you on fire, too, old hay-stack? Why, we shall never be able to put you out.

VICTORIAN (*without*). Chispa!

CHISPA. Go to bed, Pero Grullo, for the cocks are crowing.

VICTORIAN. Ea! Chispa! Chispa!

CHISPA. Ea! Señor. Come with me, ancient Baltasar, and bring water for the horses. I will pay for the supper to-morrow.

[*Exeunt.*

Now here the question occurs—what is accomplished?—how has the subject been forwarded? We did not need to learn that Victorian was in love—that was known before; and all that we glean is that a stupid imitation of Sancho Panza drinks, in the course of two minutes, (the time occupied in the perusal of the scene) a bottle of Vino Tinto by way of Pedro Ximenes, and devours a stewed kitten in place of a rabbit.

In the beginning of the play this Chispa is the valet of Victorian; subsequently we find him the servant of another; and near the *dénouement*, he returns to his original master. No cause is assigned, and not even the shadow of an object is attained; the whole tergiversation being but another instance of the gross inconsequence which abounds in the play.

The author's deficiency of skill is especially evinced in the scene of the *éclaircissement* between Victorian and Preciosa. The former having been enlightened respecting the true character of the latter, by means *of a letter* received at Guadarrama, from a friend at Madrid (how woefully inartistical is this!) resolves to go in search of her forthwith, and forthwith, also, discovers her in a wood close at hand. Whereupon he approaches, disguising *his voice*:—yes, we are required to believe that a lover may so disguise his voice from his mistress, as even to render his person in full view, irrecognizable! He approaches, and each knowing the other, a conversation ensues under the hypothesis that each to the other is unknown—a very unoriginal and of course a very silly source of *equivoque*, fit only for the gum-elastic imagination of an infant. But what we especially complain of here, is that our poet should have taken so many and so obvious pains to bring about this position of *equivoque*, when it was impossible that it could have served any other purpose than that of injuring his intended effect! Read, for example, this passage:

VICTORIAN. I never loved a maid;
For she I loved was then a maid no more.
PRECIOSA. How know you that?
VICTORIAN. A little bird in the air
Whispered the secret.
PRECIOSA. There take back your gold!
Your hand is cold like a deceiver's hand!
There is no blessing in its charity!
Make her your wife, for you have been abused;
And you shall mend your fortunes mending hers.
VICTORIAN. How like an angel's speaks the tongue of
    woman,
When pleading in another's cause her own!

Now here it is clear that if we understood Preciosa to be really ignorant of Victorian's identity, the "pleading in another's cause her own," would create a favorable impression upon the reader, or spectator. But the advice,—"Make her your wife," &c. takes an interested and selfish turn when we remember that she knows to whom she speaks.

Again, when Victorian says,

> That is a pretty ring upon your finger.
> Pray give it me!

And when she replies:

> No, never from my hand
> Shall that be taken,

we are inclined to think her only an artful coquette, knowing, as we do, the extent of her knowledge; on the other hand, we should have applauded her constancy (as the author intended) had she been represented ignorant of Victorian's presence. The effect upon the audience, in a word, would be pleasant in place of disagreeable were the case altered as we suggest, while the effect upon Victorian would remain altogether untouched.

A still more remarkable instance of deficiency in the dramatic *tact* is to be found in the mode of bringing about the discovery of Preciosa's parentage. In the very moment of the *éclaircissement* between the lovers, Chispa arrives almost as a matter of course, and settles the point in a sentence:

> Good news from Court; Good news! Beltran Cruzado,
> The Count of the Calés is not your father,
> But your true father has returned to Spain
> Laden with wealth. You are no more a Gipsy.

Now here are three points:—first, the extreme baldness, platitude, and *independence* of the incident narrated by Chispa. The *opportune* return of the father (we are tempted to say the *excessively* opportune) stands by itself—has no relation to any other event in the play—does not appear to arise, in the way of *result*, from any incident or incidents that have arisen before. It has the air of a happy chance, of a God-send, of an ultra-accident, invented by the play-wright by way of compromise for his lack of invention. *Nec Deus intersit*, &c.—but here the God has interposed, and the knot is laughably unworthy of the God.

The second point concerns the return of the father "laden with wealth." The lover has abandoned his mistress in her poverty, and, while yet the words of his proffered reconciliation hang upon his lips, comes his own servant with the news that the mistress' father has returned "laden with wealth." Now, so far as regards the audience, who are behind the scenes and know the fidelity of the lover—so far as regards the audience, all is right; but the poet had no business to place his heroine in the sad predicament of being forced, provided she is not a fool, to suspect both the ignorance and the disinterestedness of the hero.

The third point has reference to the words—"You are now no more a Gipsy." The thesis of this drama, as we have already said, is love disregarding the prejudices of *caste*, and in the development of this thesis, the powers of the dramatist have been engaged, or should have been engaged, during the whole of the three Acts of the play. The interest excited lies in our admiration of the sacrifice, and of the love that could make it; but this interest immediately and disagreeably subsides when we find that the sacrifice has been made to no purpose. "You are no more a Gipsy" dissolves the charm, and obliterates the whole impression which the author has been at so much labor to convey. Our romantic sense of the hero's chivalry declines into a complacent satisfaction with his fate. We drop our enthusiasm, with the enthusiast, and jovially shake by the hand the mere man of good luck. But is not the latter feeling the more comfortable of the two? Perhaps so; but "comfortable" is not exactly the word Mr. Longfellow might wish applied to the end of his drama, and then why be at the trouble of building up an effect through a hundred and eighty pages, merely to knock it down at the end of the hundred and eighty-first?

We have already given, at some length, our conceptions of the nature of *plot*—and of that of "The Spanish Student," it seems almost superfluous to speak at all. It has nothing of construction about it. Indeed there is scarcely a single incident which has any necessary dependence upon any one other. Not only might we take away two-thirds of the whole without ruin—but without detriment—indeed with a positive benefit to the mass. And, even as regards the mere order of arrangement, we might with a very decided *chance* of improvement, put the scenes in a bag, give them a shake or two by way of shuffle, and tumble them out. The whole mode of collocation—not to speak of the feebleness of the incidents in themselves—evinces, on the part of the author, an utter and radical want of the adapting or constructive power which the drama so imperatively demands.

Of the unoriginality of the thesis we have already spoken; and now, to the unoriginality of the events by which the thesis is developed, we need do little more than allude. What, indeed, *could* we say of such incidents as the child stolen by gipsies—as her education as a *danseuse*—as her betrothal to a Gipsy—as her preference for a gentleman—as the rumors against her purity—as her persecution by a *roué*—as the inruption of the *roué* into her chamber—as the consequent misunderstanding between her and her lover—as the duel— as the defeat of the *roué*—as the receipt of his life from the hero—as his boasts of success with the girl—as the *ruse* of the duplicate ring—as the field, in consequence, abandoned by the lover—as the assassination of Lara while scaling the girl's bed-chamber—as the disconsolate peregrination of Victorian—as the *equivoque* scene with Preciosa—as the offering to purchase the ring and the refusal to part with it—as the "news from court" telling of the Gipsy's true parentage— what *could* we say of all these ridiculous things, except that we have met them, each and all, some two or three hundred times before, and that they have formed, in a greater or less degree, the staple material of every Hop O'My Thumb tragedy since the flood? There is not an incident, from the first page of "The Spanish Student" to the last and most satisfactory, which we would not undertake to find bodily, at ten minutes' notice, in some one of the thousand and one comedies of intrigue attributed to Calderon and Lope de Vega.

But if our poet is grossly unoriginal in his subject, and in the events which evolve it, may he not be original in his handling or *tone*? We really grieve to say that he is not, unless, indeed, we grant him the meed of originality for the peculiar manner in which he has jumbled together the quaint and stilted tone of the old English dramatists with the *dégagée* air of Cervantes. But this is a point upon which, through want

of space, we must necessarily permit the reader to judge altogether for himself. We quote, however a passage from the
Second Scene of the First Act, by way of showing how very
easy a matter it is to make a man discourse Sancho Panza:

CHISPA. Abernuncio Satanas! and a plague upon all lovers
who ramble about at night, drinking the elements, instead of
sleeping quietly in their beds. Every dead man to his ceme-
tery, say I; and every friar to his monastery. Now, here's my
master Victorian, yesterday a cow-keeper and to-day a gentleman; yesterday a student and to-day a lover; and I must be
up later than the nightingale, for as the abbot sings so must
the sacristan respond. God grant he may soon be married, for
then shall all this serenading cease. Ay, marry, marry, marry!
Mother, what does marry mean? It means to spin, to bear
children, and to weep, my daughter! And, of a truth, there is
something more in matrimony than the wedding-ring. And
now, gentlemen, Pax vobiscum! as the ass said to the cab-
bages!"

And, we might add, as an ass *only* should say.

In fact throughout "The Spanish Student," as well as
throughout other compositions of its author, there runs a
very obvious vein of *imitation*. We are perpetually reminded
of something we have seen before—some old acquaintance in
manner or matter; and even where the similarity cannot be
said to amount to plagiarism, it is still injurious to the poet
in the good opinion of him who reads.

Among the minor defects of the play, we may mention the
frequent allusion to book incidents not generally known, and
requiring each a *Note* by way of explanation. The drama demands that everything be so instantaneously evident that he
who runs may read; and the only impression effected by these
Notes to a play is that the author is desirous of showing his
reading.

We may mention, also, occasional tautologies—such as:

> "Never did I behold thee so *attired*
> And *garmented* in beauty as to-night!"

Or,

> "What we need
> Is the celestial fire to change the fruit
> Into *transparent* crystal, *bright and clear!*"

We may speak, too, of more than occasional errors of grammar. For example, p. 23:

> "Did no one see thee? None, my love, but *thou*."

Here "but" is not a conjunction, but a preposition, and governs *thee* in the objective. "None but *thee*" would be right; meaning none *except* thee, *saving* thee.

At page 27, "mayst" is somewhat incorrectly written "may'st."

At page 34 we have:

> "I have no other saint than *thou* to pray to."

Here authority and analogy are both against Mr. Longfellow. "Than" also is here a preposition governing the objective, and meaning *save*, or *except*. "I have none other God than thee," &c. See Horne Tooke. The Latin *"quam te"* is exactly equivalent.

At page 80 we read:

> "*Like thee* I am a captive, and, *like thee*,
> I have a gentle gaoler."

Here "like thee" (although grammatical of course) does not convey the idea. Mr. L. does not mean that the speaker is *like* the bird itself, but that his *condition* resembles it. The true reading would thus be:

> *As thou* I am a captive, and, *as thou*,
> I have a gentle gaoler:

That is to say, *as thou art*, and *as thou hast*.

Upon the whole, we regret that Professor Longfellow has written this work, and feel especially vexed that he has committed himself by its republication. Only when regarded as a mere poem, can it be said to have merit of any kind. For, in fact, it is only when we separate the poem from the drama, that the passages we have commended as beautiful can be understood to have beauty. We are not too sure, indeed, that a "dramatic poem" is not a flat contradiction in terms. At all events a man of true genius, (and such Mr. L. unquestionably is,) has no business with these hybrid and paradoxical compositions. Let a poem be a poem only; let a play be a play and nothing more. As for "The Spanish Student," its thesis is unoriginal; its incidents are antique; its plot is no plot; its characters have no character; in short, it is little better than a play upon words, to style it "A Play" at all.

American Whig Review, August 1845

Robert M. Bird

Sheppard Lee: written by himself. New York: Harper and Brothers.

LIKE PHILOTHEA, this novel is an original in *American* Belles Lettres at least; and these deviations, however indecisive, from the more beaten paths of imitation, look well for our future literary prospects. Thinking thus, we will be at the trouble of going though briefly, in detail, the plot and the adventures of Sheppard Lee.

The hero relates his own story. He is born "somewhere towards the close of the last century," in the State of New Jersey, in one of the oldest counties that border upon the Delaware river. His father is a farmer in good circumstances, and famous for making good sausages for the Philadelphia market. He has ten children besides Sheppard. Nine of these die, however, in six years, by a variety of odd accidents—the last expiring in a fit of laughter at seeing his brother ridden to death by a pig. Prudence, the oldest sister, survives. The mother, mourning for her children, becomes melancholy and dies insane. Sheppard is sent to good schools, and afterwards to the College at Nassau Hall, in Princeton, where he remains three years, until his father's decease. Upon this occurrence he finds himself in possession of the bulk of the property; his sister Prudence, who had recently married, receiving only a small farm in a neighboring county. After making one or two efforts to become a man of business, our hero hires an overseer to undertake the entire management of his property.

Having now nothing to do, and time hanging heavily on his hands, Sheppard Lee tries many experiments by way of killing the enemy. He turns sportsman, but has the misfortune to shoot his dog the first day, and upon the second his neighbor's cow. He breeds horses and runs them, losing more money in a single hour than his father had ever made in two years together. At the suggestion of his overseer he travels, and is robbed of his baggage and money, by an intelligent gentlemanly personage from Sing-Sing. He thinks of matrimony, and is about coming to a proposal, when his inamorata, taking offence at his backwardness, casts her eyes upon another wooer, who has made her an offer, and marries him upon the spot.

Upon attaining his twenty-eighth year, Mr. Lee discovers his overseer, Mr. Aikin Jones, to be a rogue, and himself to be ruined. Prudence, the sister, tells our hero moreover, that he has lost all the little sense he ever possessed, while her husband is so kind as to inform him that "he is wrong in the upper story." A quarrel ensues and Mr. Lee is left to bear his misfortunes alone.

In Chapter V, we have a minute description of the state of the writer's affairs at this epoch, and it must be owned that his little property of forty acres presented a sufficiently woe-begone appearance. One friend, however, remains steadfast, in the person of our hero's negro servant, Jim Jumble—an old fellow that had been the slave of his father and was left to him in the will. This is a crabbed, self-willed old rascal, who will have every thing his own way. Having some scruples of conscience about holding a slave, and thinking him of no value whatever, but, on the contrary, a great deal of trouble, our hero decides upon setting him free. The old fellow, how-ever, bursts into a passion, swears he will *not* be free, that Mr. Lee is his master and shall take care of him, and that if he dares to set him free he will have the law of him, "he will by ge-hosh!"

At length, in spite of even the services of Jim Jumble, our hero is reduced to the point of despair. His necessities have compelled him to mortgage the few miserable acres left, and ruin stares him in the face. He attempts many ingenious de-vices with a view of amending his fortune—buys lottery tick-ets which prove all blanks—purchases stock in a southern gold mining company, is forced to sell out at a bad season, and finds himself with one-fifth the sum invested—gets a new coat, and makes a declaration to a rich widow in the neigh-borhood, who makes him the laughing stock of the country for his pains—and finally turns politician, choosing the strongest party, on the principle that the majority must al-ways be right. Attending a public meeting he claps his hands and applauds the speeches with so much spirit, that he is no-ticed by some of the leaders. They encourage him to take a more prominent part in the business going on, and at the next opportunity he makes a speech. Being on the hurrah side he receives great applause, and indeed there is such a shouting and clapping that he is obliged to put an end to his discourse sooner than he had intended. He is advised to set about converting all in the neighborhood who are not of the right way of thinking, and the post office in the village is hinted at as his reward in case the county is gained. Mr. Lee sets about his task valiantly, paying his own expenses, and the hurrahs carry the day. His claim to the post-officeship is universally admitted, but, in some way or other, the appointment is bestowed upon one of the very leaders who had been foremost in commending the zeal and talents of our author, and in assuring him that the office should be his. Mr. Lee is enraged, and is upon the point of going over to the anti-hurrahs, when he is involved in a very remarkable tissue of adventure. Jim Jumble conceives that money has been buried by Captain Kid, in a certain ugly swamp, called the Owl-Roost, not many rods from an old church. The stories of the negro affect his master to such a degree that he dreams three nights in succession of finding a treasure at the foot of a beech-tree in the swamp. He resolves to dig for it in good earnest, choosing midnight, at the full of the moon, as the moment of commencing operations. On his way to the Owl-Roost at the proper time, he passes by the burial ground of the old church, and the wall having fallen down across his path, he strikes his ankle against a fragment—the pain causing him to utter a groan. To his amazement this interjection of suffering is echoed from the grave yard; a voice screaming out in awful tones, O Lord! O Lord! and, casting his eyes around, our hero beholds three or four shapes, whom he supposes to be devils incarnate, dancing about among the tomb-stones. The beech-tree, however, is finally reached in safety, and by dint of much labor a large hole excavated among the roots. But in his agitation of mind the adventurer plants an unlucky blow of the mattock among the toes of his right foot, and sinking down upon the grass, "falls straight-way into a trance."

Upon recovering from this trance, Mr. Lee finds himself in a very singular predicament. He feels exceedingly light and buoyant, with the power of moving without exertion. He sweeps along without putting his feet to the ground, and passes among shrubs and bushes without experiencing from them any hindrance to his progress. In short, he finds himself to be nothing better than a ghost. His dead body is lying quietly beside the excavation under the beech-tree. Mr. Lee is entirely overcome with horror at his unfortunate condition, and runs, or rather flies, instinctively to the nearest hut for assistance. But the dogs, at his approach, run howling among the bushes, and the only answer he receives from the terrified family is the discharge of a blunderbuss in his face. Returning in despair to the beech-tree and the pit, he finds that his body has been taken away. Its disappearance throws him into a phrenzy, and he is about to run home and summon old Jim Jumble to the rescue, when he hears a dog yelping and whining in a peculiarly doleful manner, at some little distance down in the meadow. Coming to a place in the edge of the marsh where are some willow trees, and an old worm fence, he there discovers to his extreme surprise, the body of a certain well-to-do personage, Squire Higginson. He is lying against the fence, stone dead, with his head down, and his heels resting against the rails, and looking as if, while climbing, he had fallen down and broken his neck.

Our hero pities the condition of Mr. Higginson, but being only a ghost, has no capacity to render him assistance. In this dilemma he begins to moralize upon the condition of Mr. H. and of himself. The one has no body—the other no soul. "Why might not I"—says, very reasonably, the ghost of Mr. Lee, "Why might not I—that is to say my spirit—deprived by an unhappy accident of its natural dwelling—take possession of a tenement which there remains no spirit to claim, and thus, uniting interests together, as two feeble factions unite together in the political world, become a body possessing life, strength, and usefulness? Oh, that I might be Squire Higginson!"

The words are scarcely out of his mouth, before our hero feels himself vanishing, as it were, into the dead man's nostrils, "into which his spirit rushes like a breeze," and the next moment he finds himself John Hazlewood Higginson, Esquire, to all intents and purposes—kicking the fence to pieces in a lusty effort to rise upon his feet, and feeling as if he had just tumbled over it. We must here give a couple of pages in the words of the author.

"God be thanked," I cried, dancing about as joyously as the dog, "I am now a respectable man with my pockets full of money. Farewell then, you poor miserable Sheppard Lee! you raggamuffin! you poor wretched shote! you half-starved old sand-field Jersey Kill-Deer! you vagabond! you beggar! you Dicky Dout! with the wrong place in your upper story! you are now a gentleman and a man of substance, and a happy dog into the bargain. Ha! ha! ha!" and here I fell a laughing out of pure joy; and giving my dog Ponto a buss, as if that were the most natural act in the world, and a customary way of showing my satisfaction, I began to stalk towards my old ruined house, without exactly knowing for what purpose, but having some vague idea about me, that I would set old Jim Jumble and his wife Dinah to shouting and dancing; an amusement I would willingly have seen the whole world engaged in at that moment.

I had not walked twenty yards, before a woodcock that was feeding on the edge of the marsh, started up from under my nose, when clapping my gun to my shoulder, I let fly at him, and down he came.

"Aha, Ponto," said I, "when did I ever fail to bring down a woodcock? Bring it along, Ponto, you rascal—Rum-te, ti, ti! rum-te, ti, ti!" and I went on my way singing for pure joy, without pausing to recharge or to bag my game. I reached my old house, and began to roar out, without reflecting that I was now something more than Sheppard Lee, "Hillo! Jim Jumble, you old rascal! get up and let me in."

"What you want, hah?" said old Jim, poking his head from the garret window of the kitchen, and looking as sour as a persimmon before frost. "Guess Massa Squire Higginson drunk, hah? What you want? Spose I'm gwyin to git up afo sunrise for notin, and for any body but my Massa Sheppard?"

"Why you old dog," said I, in a passion, "I am your Master Sheppard; that is, your Master John Hazlewood Higginson, Esquire; for as for Sheppard Lee, the Jersey kill-deer, I've finished him, you rascal; you'll never see him more. So get down and let me into the house, or I'll———"

"You will hah?" said Jim, "you will *what*?"

"I'll shoot you, you insolent scoundrel!" I exclaimed in a rage—as if it were the most natural thing in the world for me to be in one; and as I spoke I raised my piece; when "bow-wow-wow!" went my old dog Bull, who had not bitten a man for two years, but who now rushed from his kennel under the porch, and seized me by the leg.

"Get out Bull, you rascal," said I, but he only bit the harder; which threw me into such a fury, that I clapped the muzzle of my gun to his side, and having one charge remaining, blew him to pieces.

"Golla-matty!" said old Jim, from the window, whence he had surveyed the combat; "golla-matty!—shoot old Bull!"

And with that the black villain snatched up the half of a brick, which I suppose he kept to daunt unwelcome visiters, and taking aim at me, he cast it so well as to bring it right against my left ear, and so tumbled me to the ground. I would have blown the rascal's brains out, in requital of this assault, had there been a charge left in my piece, or had he given me time to reload; but as soon as he had cast the brick, he ran from the window, and then reappeared, holding out an old musket, that I remembered he kept to shoot wild ducks and muskrats in the neighboring marsh with. Seeing this formidable weapon, and not knowing but that the desperado would fire upon me, I was forced to beat a retreat, which I did in double quick time, being soon joined by my dog Ponto, who had fled, like a coward, at the first bow-wow of the bull-dog, and saluted in my flight by the amiable tones of Dinah, who now thrust her head from the window, beside Jim's, and abused me as long as I could hear.

Our hero finds that in assuming the body of Squire Higginson, he has invested himself with a troublesome superfluity of fat—that he has moreover a touch of the asthma—together with a whizzing, humming, and spinning in the head. One day, while gunning, these infirmities prove more than usually inconvenient, and he is upon the point of retreating to the village to get his dinner, when a crowd of men make their appearance, and setting up a great shout, begin to run towards him at full speed. Hearing them utter furious cries, and perceiving a multitude of dogs in company, he is seized with alarm and makes for the woods. He is overtaken however, charged with the murder of Sheppard Lee, and committed by Justice Parkins—a mass of evidence appearing against him, among which that of Jim Jumble is not the least important, who swears that the prisoner came to his house, shot his bull-dog, threatened to blow his brains out, and bragged that he had "just finished Mr. Lee."

In this dilemma our hero relates the whole truth to the prosecuting attorney, and is considered a madman for his pains. The body of Sheppard Lee, however, not appearing, the prisoner is set at liberty, and takes his way to Philadelphia in the charge of some new friends appertaining to him as John Hazlewood Higginson, Esquire. He finds himself a rich brewer, living in Chestnut Street, and the possessor of lands, houses, stocks, and Schuylkill coal-mines in abundance. He is troubled nevertheless with inveterate gout, and a shrew of a wife, and upon the whole he regrets his former existence as plain Sheppard Lee. Just opposite our brewer's residence is the dwelling of Mr. Periwinkle Smith, an aristocrat, wealthy or supposed to be so, although some rumors are abroad touching mortgages. He has an only daughter, and among her frequent visitors is one Isaac Dulmer Dawkins, Esq., a young dandy of the first water, tall, slim, whiskered, mustached, of pure blood, and living on his wits. This personage is often noted by our hero, upon his passage to and from the house of Mr. Smith. Suddenly his visits are discontinued—a circumstance which the brewer has soon an opportunity of explaining to his satisfaction. Going to the Schuylkill for the purpose of drowning himself, and thus putting an end at once to the gout and the assiduities of Mrs. Higginson, our hero is surprised at finding himself anticipated in his design by I. Dulmer Dawkins, Esq. who leaps into the river at the very spot selected for his own suicide. In his exertions to get Mr. D. out, he is seized with apoplexy—reviving partially from which, he discovers a crowd attempting to resuscitate the dandy.

"I could maintain," says our hero, "my equanimity no longer. In the bitterness of my heart I muttered, almost aloud, and as sincerely as I ever muttered any thing in my life, 'I would I were this addle-pate Dawkins, were it only to be lying as much like a drowned rat as he!' I had not well grumbled the last word, before a sudden fire flashed before my eyes, a loud noise like the roar of falling water passed through my head, and I lost all sensation and consciousness."

As I Dulmer Dawkins, our friend finds himself beset by the duns, whom he habitually puts off by suggestions respecting a rich uncle, of whose very existence he is sadly in doubt. Having ceased to pay attention to Miss Smith, upon hearing the rumors about the mortgages, it appears that he was jilted in turn by a Miss Betty Somebody, and thus threw himself into the river in despair. His adventures are now various and spirited, but his creditors grow importunate, and vow they will be put off no longer with the old story of the rich uncle, when an uncle, and a rich one, actually appears upon the tapis. He is an old vulgar fool, and I Dulmer Dawkins, Esquire, is in some doubts about the propriety of allowing his claim to relationship, but finally consents to introduce the old quiz, son and daughter, into fashionable society, upon considering the pecuniary advantages to himself. With this end he looks about for a house, and learns that the residence of Periwinkle Smith is for sale. Upon calling upon that gentleman however, he is treated very civilly indeed, being shown the door, after having sufficiently ascertained that the rumors about the mortgages should have been construed *in favor* of Mr. Smith—that he is a richer man than ever, and that his fair heiress is upon the point of marriage with a millionaire from Boston. He now turns his attention to his country cousin, Miss Patty Wilkins, upon finding that the uncle is to give her forty thousand dollars. At the same time, lest his designs in this quarter should fail, he makes an appointment to run off with the only daughter of a rich shaver, one Skinner. The uncle Wilkins has but little opinion of I Dulmer Dawkins, and will not harken to his suit at all. In this dilemma our hero resorts to a trick. He represents his bosom friend and ally, Mr. Tickle, as a man of fashion and property, and sets him to making love to Miss Patty, in the name of himself, I Dulmer. The uncle snaps at the bait, but the ally is instructed to proceed no farther without a definite settlement upon Miss Patty of the forty thousand dollars. The uncle makes the settlement and matters proceed to a crisis—Mr. Tickle pleasing himself with the idea of cheating his bosom friend I Dulmer, and marrying the lady himself. A farce of very pretty finesse now ensues, which terminates in Miss Patty's giving the slip to both lovers, bestowing her forty thousand dollars upon an old country sweetheart, Danny Baker, and in I Dulmer's finding, upon flying, as a dernier resort, to the broker's daughter, that she has already run away with Sammy, Miss Patty Wilkins' clodhopper brother.

Driven to desperation by his duns, our hero escapes from them by dint of hard running and takes refuge, without asking permission, in the sick chamber of old Skinner, the shaver. Finding the old gentleman dead, he takes possession of his body forthwith, leaving his own carcase on the floor.

The adventures in the person of Abram Skinner are full of interest. We have many racy details of stock-jobbing and usury. Some passages, of a different nature, are well written. The miser has two sons, and his parsimony reduces them to fearful extremity. The one involves him deeply by forgery; and the other first robs his strong box, and afterwards endeavors to murder him.

It may be supposed that the misery now weighing me to the earth was as much as could be imposed upon me; but I was destined to find before the night was over that misery is only comparative, and that there is no affliction so positively great, that greater may not be experienced. In the dead of the night, when my woes had at last been drowned in slumber, I was aroused by feeling a hand pressing upon my bosom; and starting up I saw, for there was a taper burning upon a table hard by, a man standing over me, holding a pillow in his hand, which, the moment I caught sight of him, he thrust into my face, and there endeavored to hold it, as if to suffocate me.

The horror of death endowed me with a strength not my own, and the ruffian held the pillow with a feeble and trembling arm. I dashed it aside, leaped up in the bed, and beheld in the countenance of the murderer the features of the long missing and abandoned son, Abbot Skinner.

His face was white and chalky, with livid stains around the eyes and mouth, the former of which were starting out of their orbits in a manner ghastly to behold, while his lips were drawn asunder and away from his teeth, as in the face of a mummy. He looked as if horror-struck at the act he was attempting; and yet there was something devilish and determined in his air that increased my terror to ecstacy! I sprang from the bed, threw myself on the floor, and, grasping his knees, besought him to spare my life. There seemed indeed occasion for all my supplications. His bloated and altered visage, the neglected appearance of his garments and person, and a thousand other signs, showed that the whole period of his absence had been passed in excessive toping, and the murderous and unnatural act which he meditated, manifested to what a pitch of phrenzy he had arrived by the indulgence.

As I grasped his knees, he put his hand into his bosom, and drew out a poniard, a weapon I had never before known him to carry; at the sight of which I considered myself a dead man. But the love of life still prevailing, I leaped up, and ran to a corner of the room, where I mingled adjurations and entreaties with loud screams for assistance. He stood as if rooted to the spot for a moment; then dropping his horrid weapon, he advanced a few paces, clasped his hands together, fell upon his knees, and burst into tears, and all the while without having uttered a single word. But now, my cries still continuing, he exclaimed, but with a most wild and disturbed look—"Father I won't hurt you, and pray dont hurt *me!*"

Horrors such as these induce our hero to seek a new existence. Filling his pockets with money, he sets off in search of a corpse of which to take possession. At length, when nearly exhausted, a drunken fellow, apparently dead, is found lying under a shed. Transferring the money from his own person to that of the mendicant, he utters the usual wish, once, twice, thrice—and in vain. Horribly disconcerted, and dreading lest his charm should have actually deserted him, he begins to kick the dead man with all the energy he has left. At this treatment the corpse suddenly becomes animated, knocks

our hero down with a whiskey jug, and makes off with the
contents of his pockets, being a dozen silver spoons, and four
hundred dollars in money. This accident introduces us to the
acquaintance of a genuine philanthropist, Mr. Zachariah
Longstraw, and this gentleman being at length murdered by
a worthy ex-occupant of Sing-Sing, to whom he had been
especially civil, our hero reanimates his body with excessive
pleasure at his good fortune. The result is that he finds himself cheated on all sides, is arrested for debt, and is entrapped
by a Yankee pedlar and carried off to the South as a tit-bit for
the anti-abolitionists. On the route he ascertains (by acci-
dently overhearing a conversation) that the missing body of
Sheppard Lee, which disappeared in so mysterious a manner
from the side of the pit at the Owl-Roost, was carried off by
one Dr. Feuerteufel, a German, who happened to be in search
of subjects for dissection, and whose assistants were the dancing spectres in the church yard, which so terribly disconcerted
our hero when on his way to the beech-tree. He is finally
about to be hung, when a negro who was busied in preparing
the gallows, fortunately breaks his neck in a fall, and our adventurer takes possession of his body forthwith.

In his character of Nigger Tom, Mr. Lee gives us some very
excellent chapters upon abolition and the exciting effects of
incendiary pamphlets and pictures, among our slaves in the
South. This part of the narrative closes with a spirited picture
of a negro insurrection, and with the hanging of Nigger Tom.

Our hero is revived, after execution, by the galvanic battery
of some medical students, and having, by his sudden display
of life, frightened one of them to death, he immediately possesses himself of his person. As Mr. Arthur Megrim, he passes
through a variety of adventures, and fancies himself a coffee-
pot, a puppy, a chicken, a loaded cannon, a clock, a hamper
of crockery ware, a joint stock, a Greek Demi-God and the
Emperor of France. Dr. Feuerteufel now arrives in the village
with a cargo of curiosities for exhibition—among which are
some mummies. In one of them our hero recognizes the identical long missed body of Sheppard Lee.

The sight of my body thus restored to me, and in the midst
of my sorrow and affliction, inviting me back, as it were, to

my proper home, threw me into an indescribable ferment. I stretched out my arms, I uttered a cry, and then rushing forward, to the astonishment of all present, I struck my foot against the glass case with a fury that shivered it to atoms— or at least the portion of it serving as a door, which, being dislodged by the violence of the blow, fell upon the floor and was dashed to pieces. The next instant, disregarding the cries of surprise and fear which the act occasioned, I seized upon the cold and rigid hand of the mummy, murmuring "Let me live again in my own body, and never—no! never more in another's!" Happiness of happiness! although, while I uttered the word, a boding fear was on my mind, lest the long period the body had remained inanimate, and more especially the mummifying process to which it had been subjected, might have rendered it unfit for further habitation, I had scarcely breathed the wish before I found myself in that very body, descending from the box which had so long been its prison, and stepping over the mortal frame of Mr. Arthur Megrim, now lying dead on the floor.

Indescribable was the terror produced among the spectators by this double catastrophe—the death of their townsman, and the revival of the mummy. The women fell down in fits, and the men took to their heels; and a little boy who was frightened into a paroxysm of devotion, dropped on his knees, and began fervently to exclaim

> Now I lay me down to sleep,
> I pray the Lord my soul to keep.

In short, the agitation was truly inexpressible, and fear distracted all. But on no countenance was this passion (mingled with a degree of amazement) more strikingly depicted than on that of the German Doctor, who, thus compelled to witness the object of a thousand cares, the greatest and most perfect result of his wonderful discovery, slipping off its pedestal and out of his hands, as by a stroke of enchantment, stared upon me with eyes, nose and mouth, speechless, rooted to the floor, and apparently converted into a mummy himself. As I stepped past him, however, hurrying to the door, with a vague idea that the sooner I reached it the better, his lips were unlocked, and his feelings found vent in a horrible exclama-

tion—"Der tyfel!" which I believe means the devil—"Der tyfel! I have empalm him too well!"

Sheppard Lee now makes his way home into New Jersey
(pursued however the whole way by the German Doctor,
crying "Mein Gott! Ter Tyfel! and stop mine mummy!") and
is put to bed and kindly nursed after his disaster by his sister
Prudence and her husband. It now appears (very ingeniously
indeed) that, harassed by his pecuniary distress, our hero fell
into a melancholy derangement, and upon cutting his foot
with the mattock, as related, was confined to bed, where his
wonderful transmigrations were merely the result of delirium.
At least this is the turn given to the whole story by Prudence.
Mr. Lee, however, although he partially believes her in the
right, has still a shadow of doubt upon the subject, and has
thought it better to make public his own version of the matter, with a view of letting every body decide for himself.

We must regard "Sheppard Lee," upon the whole, as a very
clever, and not altogether unoriginal, *jeu d'esprit*. Its incidents
are well conceived, and related with force, brevity, and a species of *directness* which is invaluable in certain cases of narration—while in others it should be avoided. The language is
exceedingly unaffected and (what we regard as high praise)
exceedingly well adapted to the varying subjects. Some fault
may be found with the conception of the metempsychosis
which is the basis of the narrative. There are two general
methods of telling stories such as this. One of these methods
is that adopted by the author of Sheppard Lee. He conceives
his hero endowed with some idiosyncracy beyond the common lot of human nature, and thus introduces him to a series
of adventures which, under ordinary circumstances, could occur only to a plurality of persons. The chief source of interest
in such narrative is, or should be, the contrasting of these
varied events, in their influence upon a character *unchang-
ing*—except as changed by the events themselves. This fruitful field of interest, however, is neglected in the novel before
us, where the hero, very awkwardly, partially loses, and partially does not lose, his identity, at each transmigration. The
sole object here in the various metempsychoses seem to be,
merely the depicting of seven different conditions of exis-

tence, and the enforcement of the very doubtful moral that every person should remain contented with his own. But it is clear that both these points could have been more forcibly shown, without any reference to a confused and jarring system of transmigration, by the mere narrations of seven different individuals. All deviations, especially wide ones, from nature, should be justified to the author by some specific object—the object, in the present case, might have been found, as above-mentioned, in the opportunity afforded of depicting widely-different conditions of existence actuating *one* individual.

A second peculiarity of the species of novel to which Sheppard Lee belongs, and a peculiarity which is *not* rejected by the author, is the treating the whole narrative in a jocular manner throughout (inasmuch as to say "I know I am writing nonsense, but then you must excuse me for the very reason that I know it") or the solution of the various absurdities by means of a dream, or something similar. The latter method is adopted in the present instance—and the idea is managed with unusual ingenuity. Still—having read through the whole book, and having been worried to death with incongruities (allowing such to exist) until the concluding page, it is certainly little indemnification for our sufferings to learn that, in truth, the whole matter was a dream, and that we were very wrong in being worried about it at all. The damage is done, and the apology does not remedy the grievance. For this and other reasons, we are led to prefer, in this kind of writing, the *second* general method to which we have alluded. It consists in a variety of points—principally in avoiding, as may easily be done, that *directness* of expression which we have noticed in Sheppard Lee, and thus leaving much to the imagination—in writing as if the author were firmly impressed with the truth, yet astonished at the immensity, of the wonders he relates, and for which, professedly, he neither claims nor anticipates credence—in minuteness of detail, especially upon points which have no immediate bearing upon the general story—this minuteness not being at variance with indirectness of expression—in short, by making use of the infinity of arts which give verisimilitude to a narration—and by leaving the result as a wonder not to be accounted for. It will be found that *bizzarreries* thus conducted, are usually far more effective than those otherwise managed. The attention of the author, who does not depend upon explaining away his incredibilities, is directed to giving them the character and the luminousness of truth, and thus are brought about, unwittingly, some of the most vivid creations of human intellect. The reader, too, readily perceives and falls in with the writer's humor, and suffers himself to be borne on thereby. On the other hand what difficulty, or inconvenience, or danger can there be in leaving us uninformed of the important facts that a certain hero *did not* actually discover the elixir vitæ, *could not* really make himself invisible, and *was not* either a ghost in good earnest, or a bonâ fide Wandering Jew?

Southern Literary Messenger, September 1836

John G. C. Brainard

AMONG ALL the *pioneers* of American literature, whether prose or poetical, there is *not one* whose productions have not been much over-rated by his countrymen. But this fact is more especially obvious in respect to such of these pioneers as are no longer living,—nor is it a fact of so deeply transcendental a nature as only to be accounted for by the Emersons and Alcotts. In the first place, we have but to consider that gratitude, surprise, and a species of hyper-patriotic triumph have been blended, and finally confounded, with mere admiration, or appreciation, in respect to the labors of our earlier writers; and, in the second place, that Death has thrown his customary veil of the sacred over these commingled feelings, forbidding them, in a measure, to be *now* separated or subjected to analysis. "In speaking of the deceased," says that excellent old English Moralist, James Puckle, in his "Gray Cap for a Green Head," "so fold up your discourse that their virtues may be outwardly shown, while their vices are wrapped up in silence." And with somewhat too inconsiderate a promptitude have we followed the spirit of this quaint advice. The mass of American readers have been, hitherto, in no frame of mind to view with calmness, and to discuss with discrimination, the true claims of the few who were *first* in convincing the mother country that her sons were not all brainless, as, in the plentitude of her arrogance, she, at one period, half affected and half wished to believe; and where any of these few have departed from among us, the difficulty of bringing their pretensions to the test of a proper criticism has been enhanced in a very remarkable degree. But even as concerns the living: is there any one so blind as not to see that Mr. Cooper, for example, owes much, and that Mr. Paulding, owes *all* of his reputation as a novelist, to his early occupation of the field? Is there any one so dull as not to know that fictions which neither Mr. Paulding nor Mr. Cooper *could* have written, are daily published by native authors without attracting more of commendation than can be crammed into a hack newspaper paragraph? And, again, is

there any one so prejudiced as not to acknowledge that all
this is because there is no longer either reason or wit in the
query,—"Who reads an American book?" It is not because
we lack the talent in which the days of Mr. Paulding exulted,
but because such talent has shown itself to be common. It is
not because we have *no* Mr. Coopers; but because it has been
demonstrated that we might, at any moment, have as many
Mr. Coopers as we please. In fact we are now strong in our
own resources. We have, at length, arrived at that epoch when
our literature may and must stand on its own merits, or
fall through its own defects. We have snapped asunder the
leading-strings of our British Grandmamma, and, better
still, we have survived the first hours of our novel freedom,
—the first licentious hours of a hobbledehoy braggadocio
and swagger. *At last*, then, we are in a condition to be
criticised—even more, to be neglected; and the journalist is
no longer in danger of being impeached for *lese-majesté*
of the Democratic Spirit, who shall assert, with sufficient humility, that we have committed an error in mistaking "Kettell's
Specimens" for the Pentateuch, or Joseph Rodman Drake for
Apollo.

The case of this latter gentleman is one which well illustrates what we have been saying. We believe it was some five
years ago that Mr. Dearborn republished the "Culprit Fay,"
which then, as at the period of its original issue, was belauded
by the universal American press, in a manner which must
have appeared ludicrous—not to speak *very* plainly—in the
eyes of all unprejudiced observers. With a curiosity much excited by comments at once so grandiloquent and so general,
we procured and read the poem. What we found it we ventured to express distinctly, and at some length, in the pages
of the "Southern Messenger." It is a well-versified and sufficiently fluent composition, without high merit of any kind.
Its defects are gross and superabundant. Its plot and conduct,
considered in reference to its scene, are absurd. Its originality
is none at all. Its imagination (and this was the great feature
insisted upon by its admirers,) is but a "counterfeit present-
ment,"—but the shadow of the shade of that lofty quality
which is, in fact, the soul of the Poetic Sentiment—but a
drivelling *effort to be fanciful*—an effort resulting in a species

of hop-skip-and-go-merry rhodomontade, which the uninitiated feel it a duty to call ideality, and to admire as such,
while lost in surprise at the impossibility of performing at
least the latter half of the duty with any thing like satisfaction to themselves. And all this we not only asserted, but
without difficulty *proved*. Dr. Drake has written some beautiful poems, but the "Culprit Fay," is not of them. We neither expected to hear any dissent from our opinions, nor did
we hear any. On the contrary, the approving voice of every
critic in the country whose *dictum* we had been accustomed
to respect, was to us a sufficient assurance that we had not
been very grossly in the wrong. In fact the public taste was
then *approaching* the right. The truth indeed had not, as yet,
made itself heard; but we had reached a point at which it
had but to be plainly and boldly *put*, to be, at least tacitly,
admitted.

This habit of apotheosising our literary pioneers was a most
indiscriminating one. Upon *all* who wrote, the applause was
plastered with an impartiality really refreshing. Of course, the
system favored the dunces at the expense of true merit; and,
since there existed a certain fixed standard of exaggerated
commendation to which all were adapted after the fashion of
Procrustes, it is clear that the most meritorious required *the
least stretching*,—in other words, that, although all were much
over-rated, the deserving were over-rated in a less degree than
the unworthy. Thus with Brainard:—a man of indisputable
genius, who, in any more discriminate system of panegyric,
would have been long ago bepuffed into Demi-Deism; for if
"M'Fingal," for example, is in reality what we have been told,
the commentators upon Trumbull, as a matter of the simplest
consistency, should have exalted into the seventh heaven of
poetical dominion the author of the many graceful and vigorous effusions which are now lying, in a very neat little volume, before us.*

Yet we maintain that even these effusions have been over-
praised, and materially so. It is not that Brainard has not written poems which may rank with those of any American, with
the single exception of Longfellow—but that the general

*The Poems of John G. C. Brainard. A New and Authentic Collection, with an
original Memoir of his Life. Hartford: Edward Hopkins.*

merit of our whole national Muse has been estimated too highly, and that the author of "The Connecticut River" has, individually, shared in the exaggeration. No poet among us has composed what would deserve the tithe of that amount of approbation so innocently lavished upon Brainard. But it would not suit our purpose just now, and in this department of the Magazine, to enter into any elaborate analysis of his productions. It so happens, however, that we open the book at a brief poem, an examination of which will stand us in good stead of this general analysis, since it is by this very poem that the admirers of its author are content to swear— since it is the fashion to cite it as his best—since thus, in short, it is the chief basis of his notoriety, if not the surest triumph of his fame.

We allude to "The Fall of Niagara," and shall be pardoned for quoting it in full.

> The thoughts are strange that crowd into my brain
> While I look upward to thee. It would seem
> As if God poured thee from his hollow hand,
> And hung his brow upon thine awful front,
> And spoke in that loud voice which seemed to him
> Who dwelt in Patmos for his Saviour's sake
> The "sound of many waters," and had bade
> Thy flood to chronicle the ages back
> And notch his centuries in the eternal rocks.
>
> Deep calleth unto deep. And what are we
> That hear the question of that voice sublime?
> O, what are all the notes that ever rung
> From war's vain trumpet by thy thundering side?
> Yea, what is all the riot man can make
> In his short life to thy unceasing roar?
> And yet, bold babbler, what art thou to HIM
> Who drowned a world and heaped the waters far
> Above its loftiest mountains?—a light wave
> That breaks and whispers of its Maker's might.

It is a very usual thing to hear these verses called not merely the best of their author, but the best which have been written on the subject of Niagara. Its positive merit appears to us only partial. We have been informed that the poet *had seen* the great cataract before writing the lines; but the Memoir prefixed to the present edition, denies what, for our own part, we never believed; for Brainard was truly a poet, and no poet could have looked upon Niagara, in the substance, and written thus about it. If he saw it at all, it must have been in fancy—"at a distance"—εκας—as the lying Pindar says he saw Archilocus, who died ages before the villain was born.

To the two opening verses we have no objection; but it may be well observed, in passing, that had the mind of the poet been really "crowded with strange thoughts," and not merely *engaged in an endeavor to think* he would have entered at once upon the thoughts themselves, without allusion to the state of his brain. His subject would have left him no room for self.

The third line embodies an absurd, and impossible, not to say a contemptible image. We are called upon to conceive a similarity between the *continuous* downward sweep of Niagara, and the momentary splashing of some definite and of course trifling quantity of water *from a hand*; for, although it is the hand of the Deity himself which is referred to, the mind is irresistibly led, by the words "poured from his hollow hand," to that idea which has been *customarily* attached to such phrase. It is needless to say, moreover, that the bestowing upon Deity a human form, is at best a low and most unideal conception.* In fact the poet has committed the grossest of errors in *likening* the fall to *any* material object; for the human fancy can fashion nothing which shall not be inferior in majesty to the cataract itself. Thus bathos is in-

---

*The Humanitarians held that God was to be understood as having really a human form.—See Clarke's Sermons, vol. 1, page 26, fol. edit.

"The drift of Milton's argument leads him to employ language which would appear, at first sight, to verge upon their doctrine: but it will be seen immediately that he guards himself against the charge of having adopted one of the most ignorant errors of the dark ages of the church."—Dr. Sumner's Notes on Milton's "Christian Doctrine."

The opinion could never have been very general. Andeus, a Syrian of Messopotamia, who lived in the fourth century, was condemned for the doctrine, as heretical. His few disciples were called Anthropomorphites. *See Du Pin.*

evitable; and there is no better exemplification of bathos than Mr. Brainard has here given.*

The fourth line but renders the matter worse, for here the figure is most inartistically shifted. The handful of water becomes animate; for it has a front—that is, a forehead, and upon this forehead the Deity proceeds to hang a bow, that is, a rainbow. At the same time he "speaks in that loud voice, &c;" and here it is obvious that the ideas of the writer are in a sad state of fluctuation; for he transfers the idiosyncrasy of the fall itself (that is to say its sound) to the one who pours it from his hand. But not content with all this, Mr. Brainard commands the flood to *keep a kind of tally*; for this is the low thought which the expression about "notching in the rocks" immediately and inevitably induces. The whole of this first division of the poem, embraces, we hesitate not to say, one of the most jarring, inappropriate, mean, and in every way monstrous assemblages of false imagery, which can be found out of the tragedies of Nat Lee, or the farces of Thomas Carlyle.

In the latter division, the poet recovers himself, as if ashamed of his previous bombast. His natural instinct (for Brainard was no artist) has enabled him *to feel* that *subjects which surpass in grandeur all efforts of the human imagination are well depicted only in the simplest and least metaphorical language*—a proposition as susceptible of demonstration as any in Euclid. Accordingly, we find a material sinking in tone;

*It is remarkable that Drake, of whose "Culprit Fay," we have just spoken is, perhaps, the sole poet who has employed, in the description of Niagara, imagery which does not produce a bathetic impression. In one of his minor poems he has these magnificent lines—

> How sweet 'twould be, when all the air
> *In moonlight swims*, along the river
>   To couch upon the grass and hear
> Niagara's everlasting voice
>   Far in the deep blue West away;
> That dreamy and poetic noise
>   We mark not in the glare of day—
> Oh, how unlike its torrent-cry
>   When o'er the brink the tide is driven
> *As if the vast and sheeted sky*
>   *In thunder fell from Heaven!*

although he does not at once, discard all imagery. The "Deep calleth unto deep" is nevertheless a great improvement upon his previous rhetoricianism. The personification of the waters above and below would be good in reference to any subject less august. The moral reflections which immediately follow, have at least the merit of simplicity; but the poet exhibits no very lofty imagination when he bases these reflections only upon the cataract's superiority to man *in the noise it can create*; nor is the concluding idea more spirited, where the mere difference between the quantity of water which occasioned the flood, and the quantity which Niagara precipitates, is made the measure of the Almighty Mind's superiority to that cataract which it called by a thought into existence.

But although "The Fall of Niagara" does not deserve all the unmeaning commendation it has received, there are, nevertheless, many truly beautiful poems in this collection, and even more certain evidences of poetic power. "To a Child, the Daughter of a Friend" is exceedingly graceful and terse. "To the Dead" has equal grace, with more vigor, and, moreover, a touching air of melancholy. Its melody is very rich, and in the monotonous repetition, at each stanza, of a certain rhyme, we recognise a fantastic yet true imagination. "Mr. Merry's Lament for Long Tom" would be worthy of all praise were not its unusually beautiful rhythm an imitation from Campbell, who would deserve his high poetical rank, if only for its construction. Of the merely humorous pieces we have little to say. Such things are not *poetry*. Mr. Brainard excelled in them, and they are very good in their place; but that place is not in a collection of *poems*. The prevalent notions upon this head are extremely vague; yet we see no reason why any ambiguity should exist. Humor, with an exception to be made hereafter, is directly antagonistical to that which is the soul of the Muse proper; and the omni-prevalent belief, that melancholy is inseparable from the higher manifestations of the beautiful, is not without a firm basis in nature and in reason. But it so happens that humor and that quality which we have termed the soul of the Muse (imagination) are both essentially aided in their development by the same adventitious assistance— that of rhythm and of rhyme. Thus the only bond between humorous verse and poetry, properly so called, is that they employ in common, a certain tool. But this single circumstance has been sufficient to occasion, and to maintain through long ages, a confusion of two very distinct ideas in the brain of the unthinking critic. There is, nevertheless, an individual branch of humor which blends so happily with the ideal, that from the union result some of the finest effects of legitimate poesy. We allude to what is termed *"archness"*—a trait with which popular feeling, which is unfailingly poetic, has invested, for example, the whole character of the fairy. In the volume before us there is a brief composition entitled "The Tree Toad" which will afford a fine exemplification of our idea. It seems to have been hurriedly constructed, as if its author had felt ashamed of his light labor. But that in his heart there was a secret exultation over these verses for which his reason found it difficult to account, *we know*; and there is not a really imaginative man within sound of our voice today, who, upon perusal of this little "Tree Toad" will not admit it to be one of the *truest poems* ever written by Brainard

Graham's Magazine, February 1842

William Cullen Bryant

Poems by William Cullen Bryant. Fourth Edition. New York: Harper and Brothers.

Mr. BRYANT'S poetical reputation, both at home and abroad, is greater, we presume, than that of any other American. British critics have frequently awarded him high praise; and here, the public press have been unanimous in approbation. We can call to mind no dissenting voice. Yet the nature, and, most especially the manner, of the expressed opinions in this case, should be considered as somewhat equivocal, and but too frequently must have borne to the mind of the poet, doubts and dissatisfaction. The edition now before us may be supposed to embrace all such of his poems as he deems not unworthy his name. These (amounting to about one hundred) have been "carefully revised." With the exception of some few, about which nothing could well be said, we will speak briefly of them one by one, but in such order as we may find convenient.

The Ages, a didactic piece of thirty-five Spenserian stanzas, is the first and longest in the volume. It was originally printed in 1821, with about half a dozen others now included in this collection. The design of the author in this poem is "from a survey of the past ages of the world, and of the successive advances of mankind in knowledge and virtue, to justify and confirm the hopes of the philanthropist for the future destinies of the human race." It is, indeed, an essay on the perfectibility of man, wherein, among other better arguments, some, in the very teeth of analogy, are deduced from the eternal *cycles* of physical nature, to sustain a hope of *progression* in happiness. But it is only as a poem that we wish to examine *The Ages*. Its commencement is impressive. The four initial lines arrest the attention at once by a quiet dignity of manner, an air of placid contemplation, and a versification combining the extremes of melody and force—

> When to the common rest that crowns our days,
> Called in the noon of life, the good man goes,
> Or full of years, and ripe in wisdom, lays
> His silver temples in their last repose—

The five concluding lines of the stanza, however, are not equally effective—

> When, o'er the buds of youth, the death-wind blows,
> And blights the fairest; when our bitterest tears
> Stream, as the eyes of those that love us close,
> We think on what they were, with many fears
> Lest goodness die with them, and leave the coming years.

The defects, here, are all of a metrical and of course minor nature, but are still defects. The line

> When o'er the buds of youth the death-wind blows

is impeded in its flow by the final *th* in *youth*, and especially in *death* where *w* follows. The word *tears* cannot readily be pronounced after the final *st* in *bitterest*; and its own final consonants, *rs*, in like manner render an effort necessary in the utterance of *stream* which commences the next line. In the verse

> We think on what they were, with many fears

the word *many* is, from its nature, too rapidly pronounced for the fulfilment of the *time* necessary to give weight to the foot of two syllables. All words of two syllables do not necessarily constitute a foot (we speak now of the Pentameter here employed) even although the syllables be entirely distinct, as in *many*, *very*, *often* and the like. Such as, without effort, cannot employ in their pronunciation *the time* demanded by each of the preceding and succeeding feet of the verse, and occasionally of a preceding verse, will never fail to offend. It is the perception of this fact which so frequently forces the versifier of delicate ear to employ feet exceeding what are unjustly called legitimate dimensions. For example. At page 21 of the volume before us we have the following lines—

> Lo! to the smiling Arno's classic side
> The emulous nations of the West repair!

These verses are exceedingly forcible, yet, upon scanning the latter, we find a syllable too many. We shall be told possibly that there should be an elision of the *e* in *the* at the commencement. But no—this was not intended. Both *the* and *emulous* demand a perfect accentuation. The verse commencing *Lo!*

> Lo! to the smiling Arno's classic side,

has, it will be observed, a Trochee in its first foot. As is usually the case, the whole line partakes, in consequence, of a stately and emphatic enunciation, and, to equalize the time in the verse succeeding, something more is necessary than the succession of Iambuses which constitute the ordinary English Pentameter. The equalization is therefore judiciously effected by the introduction of an additional syllable. But in the lines

> Stream, as the eyes of those that love us close,
> We think on what they were with many fears,

lines to which the preceding observations will equally apply, this additional syllable is wanting. Did the rhyme admit of the alteration, every thing necessary could be accomplished by writing

> We think on what they were with *many a* fear,
> Lest goodness die with them and leave the coming year.

These remarks may be considered hypercritical—yet it is undeniable that upon a rigid attention to minutiæ such as we have pointed out, any great degree of metrical success must altogether depend. We are more disposed, too, to dwell upon the particular point mentioned above, since, with regard to it, the American Monthly, in a late critique upon the poems of Mr. Willis, has evidently done that gentleman injustice. The reviewer has fallen into what we conceive the error of citing, *by themselves*, (that is to say insulated from the context) such verses as

> The night-wind with a *desolate* moan swept by.
> With *difficult* energy and when the rod.
> Fell through, and with the *tremulous* hand of age.
> With super*natural* whiteness loosely fell.

for the purpose of animadversion. "The license" he says "of turning such words as 'passionate' and 'delicate' into two syllables could only have been taken by a pupil of the Fantastic School." We are quite sure that Mr. Willis had no purpose of turning them into words of two syllables—nor even, as may be supposed upon a careless examination, *of pronouncing them in the same time* which would be required for two ordinary syllables. The excesses of measure are here employed (perhaps without any definite design on the part of the writer, who may have been guided solely by ear) with reference to the proper equalization, or *balancing*, if we may so term it, of time, *throughout an entire sentence*. This, we confess, is a novel idea, but, we think, perfectly tenable. Any musician will understand us. Efforts for the relief of monotone will necessarily produce fluctuations in the time of any metre, which fluctuations, if not subsequently counterbalanced, affect the ear like unresolved discords in music. The deviations then of which we have been speaking, from the strict rules of prosodial art, are but improvements upon the rigor of those rules, and are a merit, not a fault. It is the nicety of this species of equalization more than any other metrical merit, which elevates Pope as a versifier above the mere couplet-makers of his day; and, on the other hand, it is the extension of the principle to *sentences of greater length* which elevates Milton above Pope. Knowing this, it was, of course, with some surprise that we found the American Monthly (for whose opinion we still have the highest respect,) citing Pope in opposition to Mr. Willis upon the very point to which we allude. A few examples will be sufficient to show that Pope not only made free use of the license referred to, but that he used it for the reasons, and under the circumstances which we have suggested.

> Oh thou! whatever title please thine ear,
> Dean, Drapier, Bickerstaff, or Gulliver!
> Whether thou choose Cervantes' serious air,
> Or laugh and shake in *Rabelais'* easy chair.

Any person will here readily perceive that the third line

> Whether thou choose Cervantes' serious air

differs in time from the usual course of the rhythm, and requires some counterbalance in the line which succeeds. It is indeed precisely such a verse as that of Mr. Bryant's upon which we have commented,

> Stream, as the eyes of those that love us close,

and commences in the same manner with a Trochee. But again, from Pope we have—

> Hence hymning Tyburn's elegiac lines
> Hence Journals, Medleys, *Mercuries*, Magazines.

> Else all my prose and verse were much the same,
> This prose on stilts, that *poetry* fallen lame.

> And thrice he lifted high the birth-day band
> And thrice he dropped it from his *quivering* hand.

> Here stood her opium, here she nursed her owls,
> And here she planned the *imperial* seat of fools.

> Here to her chosen all her works she shows
> Prose swell'd to verse, verse *loitering* into prose.

> Rome in her Capitol saw Querno sit
> Throned on *seven* hills, the Antichrist of wit.

> And his this drum whose hoarse heroic bass
> Drowns the loud *clarion* of the braying ass.

> But such a bulk as no twelve bards could raise
> Twelve *starveling* bards of these *degenerate* days.

These are all taken at random from the first book of the *Dunciad*. In the last example it will be seen that the *two* additional syllables are employed with a view of equalizing the time with that of the verse

> But such a bulk as no twelve bards could raise—

a verse which will be perceived to labor in its progress—and which Pope, in accordance with his favorite theory of making sound accord with sense, evidently intended so to labor. It is useless to say that the words should be written with elision—*starv'ling* and *degen'rate*. Their *pronunciation* is not thereby materially effected—and, besides, granting it to be so, it may be as well to make the elision also in the case of Mr. Willis. But Pope had no such intention, nor we presume, had Mr. W. It is somewhat singular, we may remark, en passant, that the American Monthly, in a subsequent portion of the critique alluded to, quotes from Pope as a line of "sonorous grandeur" and one beyond the ability of our American poet, the well known

> Luke's iron crown and Damien's bed of steel.

Now this is indeed a line of "sonorous grandeur"—but it is rendered so principally if not altogether by that very excess of metre (in the word Damien) which the reviewer has condemned in Mr. Willis. The lines which we quote below from Mr. Bryant's poem of *The Ages* will suffice to show that the author we are now reviewing fully appreciates the force of such occasional excess, and that he has only neglected it through oversight, in the verse which suggested these observations.

> Peace to the just man's *memory*—let it grow
> Greener with years, and blossom through the flight
> Of ages: let the mimic canvass show
> His calm *benevolent* features.

> Does *prodigal* Autumn to our age deny
> The plenty that once swelled beneath his sober eye?

> Look on this *beautiful* word, and read the truth
> In her fair page.

> Will then the *merciful* one who stamped our race
> With his own image, and who gave them sway
> O'er Earth and the glad dwellers on her face,
> Now that our *flourishing* nations far away
> Are spread, where'er the moist earth drinks the day,
> Forget the ancient care that taught and nursed
> His latest offspring?

> He who has tamed the *elements* shall not live
> The slave of his own passions.

————————when Liberty awoke
New-born, amid those *beautiful* vales.

———

Oh Greece, thy *flourishing* cities were a spoil
Unto each other.

———

And thou didst drive from thy *unnatural* breast
Thy just and brave.

———

Yet her *degenerate* children sold the crown.

———

Instead of the pure heart and *innocent* hands—

———

Among thy gallant sons that guard thee well
Thou laugh'st at *enemies*. Who shall then declare—
&c.

———

Far like the comet's way thro' *infinite* space.

———

         The full region leads
  New *colonies* forth.

———

Full many a *horrible* worship that, of old,
Held o'er the *shuddering* realms unquestioned sway.

All these instances, and some others, occur in a poem of but thirty-five stanzas—yet, in only a very few cases is the license improperly used. Before quitting this subject it may be as well to cite a striking example from Wordsworth—

There was a youth whom I had loved so long,
    That when I loved him not I cannot say.
Mid the green moun*tains many and many* a song
    We two had sung like gladsome birds in May.

Another specimen, and one still more to the purpose, may be given from Milton, whose accurate ear (although he cannot justly be called the best of versifiers) included and balanced without difficulty the rhythm of the longest passages.

But say, if our *Deliverer* up to heaven
Must re-ascend, what will betide the few
His faithful, left among the unfaithful herd
The enemies of truth? who then shall guide
His people, who defend? will they not deal
More with his *followers* than with him they dealt?
Be sure they will, *said the Angel*.

The other metrical faults in *The Ages* are few. Mr. Bryant is not always successful in his Alexandrines. Too great care cannot be taken, we think, in so regulating this species of verse as to admit of the necessary pause at the end of the third foot—or at least as not to render a pause necessary elsewhere. We object, therefore, to such lines as

A palm like his, and catch from him the hallowed flame.
The truth of heaven, and kneel to Gods that heard them
   not.

That which concludes Stanza X, although correctly cadenced in the above respect, requires an accent on the monosyllable *the*, which is too unimportant to sustain it. The defect is rendered the more perceptible by the introduction of a Trochee in the first foot.

The sick untended then
Languished in *the* damp shade, and died afar from men.

We are not sure that such lines as

A boundless sea of blood and *the* wild air.
The smile of heaven, till *a* new age expands.

are in any case justifiable, and they can be easily avoided. As in the Alexandrine mentioned above, the course of the rhythm demands an accent on monosyllables too unimportant to sustain it. For this prevalent heresy in metre we are mainly indebted to Byron, who introduced it freely, with a view of imparting an abrupt energy to his verse. There are, however, many better ways of relieving a monotone.

Stanza VI is, throughout, an exquisite specimen of versification, besides embracing many beauties both of thought and expression.

> Look on this beautiful world and read the truth
> In her fair page; see every season brings
> New change, to her, of everlasting youth;
> Still the green soil with joyous living things
> Swarms; the wide air is full of joyous wings;
> And myriads, still, are happy in the sleep
> Of ocean's azure gulfs, and where he flings
> The restless surge. Eternal love doth keep
> In his complacent arms the earth, the air, the deep.

The cadences, here, at the words *page*, *swarms*, and *surge* respectively, cannot be surpassed. We shall find, upon examination, comparatively few consonants in the stanza, and by their arrangement no impediment is offered to the flow of the verse. Liquids and the most melodious vowels abound. *World*, *eternal*, *season*, *wide*, *change*, *full*, *air*, *everlasting*, *wings*, *flings*, *complacent*, *surge*, *gulfs*, *myriads*, *azure*, *ocean*, *soil*, and *joyous*, are among the softest and most sonorous sounds in the language, and the partial line after the pause at *surge*, together with the stately march of the Alexandrine which succeeds, is one of the finest imaginable of finales—

> Eternal love doth keep
> In his complacent arms, the earth, the air, the deep.

The higher beauties of the poem are not, we think, of the highest. It has unity, completeness,—a beginning, middle and end. The tone, too, of calm, hopeful, and elevated reflection, is well sustained throughout. There is an occasional quaint grace of expression, as in

> Nurse of full streams, and lifter up of proud
> Sky-mingling mountains that o'erlook the cloud—

or of antithetical and rhythmical force combined, as in

> The shock that hurled
> To dust in many fragments dashed and strown
> The throne whose roots were in another world
> And whose far-stretching shadow awed our own.

But we look in vain for something more worthy commendation. At the same time the piece is especially free from errors.

Once only we meet with an unjust metonymy, where a sheet of water is said to

> *Cradle*, in his soft *embrace*, a gay
> Young group of grassy islands.

We find little originality of thought, and less imagination. But in a poem essentially didactic, of course we cannot hope for the loftiest breathings of the Muse.

———

To the Past is a poem of fourteen quatrains—three feet and four alternately. In the second quatrain, the lines

> And glorious ages gone
> Lie deep within the shadow of thy womb

are, to us, disagreeable. Such images are common, but at best, repulsive. In the present case there is not even the merit of illustration. The womb, in any just imagery, should be spoken of with a view to things future; here it is employed, in the sense of the tomb, and with a view to things past. In Stanza XI the idea is even worse. The allegorical meaning through-out the poem, although generally well sustained, is not always so. In the quatrain

> Thine for a space are they—
> Yet shalt thou yield thy treasures up at last;
> Thy gates shall yet give way
> Thy bolts shall fall, inexorable Past!

it seems that *The Past*, as an allegorical personification, is con-founded with *Death*.

———

The Old Man's Funeral is of seven stanzas, each of six lines—four Pentameters with alternate rhymes, ending with a Pentameter and Alexandrine, rhyming. At the funeral of an old man who has lived out his full quota of years, another, as aged, reproves the company for weeping. The poem is nearly perfect in its way—the thoughts striking and natural—the versification singularly sweet. The third stanza embodies a fine idea, beautifully expressed.

Ye sigh not when the sun, his course fulfilled,
   His glorious course rejoicing earth and sky,
In the soft evening when the winds are stilled,
   Sinks where his islands of refreshment lie,
And leaves the smile of his departure spread
O'er the warm-colored heaven, and ruddy mountain head.

The technical word *chronic* should have been avoided in the fifth line of Stanza VI—

No chronic tortures racked his aged limb.

———

The Rivulet has about ninety octo-syllabic verses. They contrast the changing and perishable nature of our human frame, with the greater durability of the Rivulet. The chief merit is simplicity. We should imagine the poem to be one of the earliest pieces of Mr. Bryant, and to have undergone much correction. In the first paragraph are, however, some awkward constructions. In the verses, for example

This little rill that from the springs
Of yonder grove its current brings,
Plays on the slope awhile, and then
Goes pratling into groves again,

the reader is apt to suppose that *rill* is the nominative to *plays*, whereas it is the nominative only to *drew* in the subsequent lines,

Oft to its warbling waters drew
My little feet when life was new.

The proper verb is, of course, immediately seen upon reading these latter lines—but the ambiguity has occurred.

———

The Prairies. This is a poem, in blank Pentameter, of about one hundred and twenty-five lines, and possesses features which do not appear in any of the pieces above mentioned. Its descriptive beauty is of a high order. The peculiar points of interest in the Prairie are vividly shown forth, and as a local painting, the work is, altogether, excellent. Here are, moreover, evidences of fine imagination. For example—

> The great heavens
> Seem to *stoop down upon the scene* in love—
> A nearer vault and of a tenderer blue
> Than that which bends above the eastern hills.

> Till twilight blushed, and lovers walked and wooed
> In a forgotten language, and old tunes
> From instruments of unremembered form
> *Gave the soft winds a voice.*

> ——The bee
> Within the hollow oak. *I listen long*
> *To his domestic hum, and think I hear*
> *The sound of the advancing multitude*
> *Which soon shall fill these deserts.*

> Breezes of the south!
> Who *toss the golden and the flame-like flowers,*
> And pass the prairie-hawk that poised on high,
> Flaps his broad wings yet moves not!

There is an objectionable elipsis in the expression "I behold them for the first," meaning "first time;" and either a grammatical or typographical error of moment in the fine sentence commencing

> Fitting floor
> For this magnificent temple of the sky—
> With flowers whose glory and whose multitude
> Rival the constellations!

Earth, a poem of similar length and construction to *The Prairies*, embodies a noble conception. The poet represents himself as lying on the earth in a "midnight black with clouds," and giving ideal voices to the varied sounds of the coming tempest. The following passages remind us of some of the more beautiful portions of Young.

> On the breast of Earth
> I lie and listen to her mighty voice:
> *A voice of many tones—sent up from streams*

That wander through the gloom, from woods unseen,
Swayed by the sweeping of the tides of air,
From rocky chasms where darkness dwells all day,
And hollows of the great invisible hills,
And sands that edge the ocean stretching far
Into the night—a melancholy sound!

———

Ha! how the murmur deepens! I perceive
And tremble at its dreadful import. *Earth*
Uplifts a general cry for guilt and wrong
And Heaven is listening. The forgotten graves
Of the heart broken utter forth their plaint.
The dust of her who loved and was betrayed,
And him who died neglected in his age,
The sepulchres of those who for mankind
Labored, and earned the recompense of scorn,
Ashes of martyrs for the truth, and bones
Of those who in the strife for liberty
Were beaten down, their corses given to dogs,
Their names to infamy, all find a voice!

In this poem, and elsewhere occasionally throughout the volume, we meet with a species of grammatical construction, which, although it is to be found in writers of high merit, is a mere affectation, and of course objectionable. We mean the abrupt employment of a *direct* pronoun in place of the customary *relative*. For example—

Or haply dost thou grieve for those *that* die—
For living things *that* trod awhile thy face,
The love of thee and heaven, and how *they* sleep,
Mixed with the shapeless dust on which thy herds
Trample and graze?

The note of interrogation here, renders the affectation more perceptible.

———

The poem *To the Appenines* resembles, in metre, that entitled *The Old Man's Funeral*, except that the former has a Pentameter in place of the Alexandrine. This piece is chiefly remarkable for the force, metrical and moral, of its concluding stanza.

> In you the heart that sighs for Freedom seeks
>   Her image; there the winds no barrier know;
> Clouds come and rest, and leave your fairy peaks;
>   While even the immaterial Mind, below,
> And Thought, her winged offspring, chained by power,
> Pine silently for the redeeming hour.

The Knight's Epitaph consists of about fifty lines of blank Pentameter. This poem is well conceived and executed. Entering the Church of St. Catherine at Pisa, the poet is arrested by the image of an armed knight graven upon the lid of a sepulchre. The Epitaph consists of an imaginative portraiture of the knight, in which he is made the impersonation of the ancient Italian chivalry.

Seventy-Six has seven stanzas of a common, but musical versification, of which these lines will afford an excellent specimen.

> That death-stain on the vernal sword,
>   Hallowed to freedom all the shore—
> In fragments fell the yoke abhorred—
> The footsteps of a foreign lord
>   Profaned the soil no more.

The Living Lost has four stanzas of somewhat peculiar construction, but admirably adapted to the tone of contemplative melancholy which pervades the poem. We can call to mind few things more singularly impressive than the eight concluding verses. They combine ease with severity, and have antithetical force without effort or flippancy. The final thought has also a high ideal beauty.

> But ye who for the living lost
>   That agony in secret bear,
> Who shall with soothing words accost
>   The strength of your despair?
> Grief for your sake is scorn for them
> Whom ye lament, and all condemn,

> And o'er the world of spirits lies
> A gloom from which ye turn your eyes.

The first stanza commences with one of those affectations which we noticed in the poem "Earth."

> Matron, the children of whose love,
>   Each to his grave in youth have passed,
> And now the mould is heaped above
>   The dearest and the last.

———

The Strange Lady is of the fourteen syllable metre, answering to two lines, one of eight syllables, the other six. This rhythm is unmanageable, and requires great care in the rejection of harsh consonants. Little, however, has been taken, apparently, in the construction of the verses

> As if they loved to breast the breeze that sweeps the cool
>   clear sky.
> And thou shouldst chase the nobler game, and I bring
>   down the bird.
> Or that strange dame so gay and fair were some
>   mysterious foe.

which are not to be pronounced without labor. The story is old—of a young gentleman who going out to hunt, is inveigled into the woods and destroyed by a fiend in the guise of a fair lady. The ballad character is nevertheless well preserved, and this, we presume, is nearly every thing intended.

———

The Hunter's Vision is skilfully and sweetly told. It is the tale of a young hunter who, overcome with toil, dozes on the brink of a precipice. In this state between waking and sleeping, he fancies a spirit-land in the fogs of the valley beneath him, and sees approaching him the deceased lady of his love. Arising to meet her, he falls, with the effort, from the crag, and perishes. The state of reverie is admirably pictured in the following stanzas. The poem consists of nine such.

> All dim in haze the mountains lay
>   With dimmer vales between;

And rivers glimmered on their way
    By forests faintly seen;
While ever rose a murmuring sound
From brooks below and bees around.

He listened till he seem to hear
    A strain so soft and low
That whether in the mind or ear
    The listener scarce might know.

With such a tone, so sweet and mild
The watching mother lulls her child.

———

Catterskill Falls is a narrative somewhat similar. Here the hero is also a hunter—but of delicate frame. He is overcome with the cold at the foot of the falls, sleeps, and is near perishing—but, being found by some woodmen, is taken care of, and recovers. As in the *Hunter's Vision*, the dream of the youth is the main subject of the poem. He fancies a goblin palace in the icy network of the cascade, and peoples it in his vision with ghosts. His entry into this palace is, with rich imagination on the part of the poet, made to correspond with the time of the transition from the state of reverie to that of nearly total insensibility.

They eye him not as they pass along,
    But his hair stands up with dread,
When he feels that he moves with that phantom throng
    Till those icy turrets are over his head,
And the torrent's roar as they enter seems
Like a drowsy murmur heard in dreams.

The glittering threshold is scarcely passed
    When there gathers and wraps him round
A thick white twilight sullen and vast
    In which there is neither form nor sound;
The phantoms, the glory, vanish all
With the dying voice of the waterfall.

There are nineteen similar stanzas. The metre is formed of Iambuses and Anapests.

———

The Hunter of the Prairies (fifty-six octosyllabic verses with alternate rhymes) is a vivid picture of the life of a hunter in the desert. The poet, however, is here greatly indebted to his subject.

———

The Damsel of Peru is in the fourteen syllable metre, and has a most spirited, imaginative and musical commencement—

Where olive leaves were twinkling in every wind that blew,
There sat beneath the pleasant shade a damsel of Peru.

This is also a ballad, and a very fine one—full of action, chivalry, energy and rhythm. Some passages have even a loftier merit—that of a glowing ideality. For example—

For the noon is coming on, and the sunbeams fiercely beat,
And the silent hills and forest-tops seem reeling in the heat.

———

The Song of Pitcairn's Island is a sweet, quiet, and simple poem, of a versification differing from that of any preceding piece. We subjoin a specimen. The Tahetian maiden addresses her lover.

> Come talk of Europe's maids with me
>   Whose necks and cheeks they tell
> Outshine the beauty of the sea,
>   White foam and crimson shell.
> I'll shape like theirs my simple dress
> And bind like them each jetty tress,
>   A sight to please thee well,
> And for my dusky brow will braid
> A bonnet like an English maid.

There are seven similar stanzas.

———

Rispah is a scriptural theme from 2 Samuel, and we like it less than any poem yet mentioned. The subject, we think, derives no additional interest from its poetical dress. The metre resembling, except in the matter of rhyme, that of "Catterskill Falls," and consisting of mingled Iambuses and Anapests, is the most positively disagreeable of any which our language admits, and, having a frisky or fidgetty rhythm, is singularly ill-adapted to the lamentation of the bereaved mother. We cannot conceive how the fine ear of Mr. Bryant could admit such verses as,

> And Rispah once the loveliest of all
> That bloomed and smiled in the court of Saul,
> &c.

———

The Indian Girl's Lament and *the Arctic Lover* have nearly all the peculiarities of the *"Song of Pitcairn's Island."*

———

The Massacre at Scio is only remarkable for inaccuracy of expression in the two concluding lines—

> Till the last link of slavery's chain
> Is shivered to be worn no more.

What shall be worn no more? The chain—but the link is implied.

———

Monument Mountain is a poem of about a hundred and forty blank Pentameters, and relates the tale of an Indian maiden who loved her cousin. Such a love being deemed incestuous by the morality of her tribe, she threw herself from a precipice and perished. There is little peculiar in the story or its narration. We quote a rough verse—

> The mighty columns with which earth props heaven.

The use of the epithet *old* preceded by some other adjective, is found so frequently in this poem and elsewhere in the writings of Mr. Bryant, as to excite a smile upon each recurrence of the expression.

> In all that *proud old* world beyond the deep—
> There is a tale about these *gray old* rocks—
> The *wide old* woods resounded with her song—
> ———and the *gray old* men that passed—
> And from the *gray old* trunks that high in heaven.

We dislike too the antique use of the word *affect* in such sentences as

> ————they deemed
> Like worshippers of the elder time that God
> Doth walk on the high places and *affect*
> The earth-o'erlooking mountains.

Milton, it is true, uses it—we remember it especially in Comus—

> 'Tis most true
> That musing meditation most *affects*
> The pensive secrecy of desert cell—

but then Milton would not use it were he writing Comus *to-day*.

————

In the *Summer Wind*, our author has several successful attempts at making "the sound an echo to the sense." For example—

> For me, I lie
> *Languidly in the shade*, where the thick turf
> Yet virgin from the kisses of the sun
> Retains some freshness.

————

> All is silent, save the faint
> And interrupted murmur of the bee
> *Settling on the sick flowers*, and then again
> Instantly on the wing.

> All the green herbs
> Are stirring in his breath; a thousand flowers
> *By the road side, and the borders of the brook*
> *Nod gaily to each other.*

————

Autumn Woods. This is a poem of much sweetness and simplicity of expression, and including one or two fine thoughts, viz:

> the sweet South-west *at play*
> *Flies, rustling, where the painted leaves are strown*
> *Along the winding way.*

————

But 'neath yon crimson tree
Lover to listening maid might breathe his flame,
    Nor mark within its roseate canopy
    Her flush of maiden shame.

———

The mountains that infold
In their wide sweep the colored landscape round,
Seem *groups of giant kings in purple and gold*
    That guard the enchanted ground.

All this is beautiful—the sentences italicized especially so. Happily to endow inanimate nature with sentience and a capability of moral action, is one of the severest tests of the poet. Even the most unmusical ear will not fail to appreciate the rare beauty and strength of the extra syllable in the line

Seem groups of giant kings in *purple* and gold.

———

The *Disinterred Warrior* has a passage we do not clearly understand. Speaking of the Indian our author says—

For he was fresher from the hand
    That formed of earth the human face,
And to the elements did stand
    In nearer kindred than our race.

There are ten similar quatrains in the poem.

The Greek Boy consists of four spirited stanzas, nearly resembling, in metre, *The Living Lost*. The two concluding lines are highly ideal.

A shoot of that old vine that made
The nations silent in its shade.

———

When the Firmament Quivers with Daylight's Young Beam, belongs to a species of poetry which we cannot be brought to admire. Some natural phenomenon is observed, and the poet taxes his ingenuity to find a parallel in the moral world. In general, we may assume, that the more successful he is in sustaining the parallel, the farther he departs from the true province of the Muse. The title, here, is a specimen of the metre. This is of a kind which we have before designated as exceedingly difficult to manage.

———

To a Musquito, is droll, and has at least the merit of making, at the same time, no efforts at being sentimental. We are not inclined, however, to rank *as poems*, either this production or the article on *New England Coal*.

———

The Conjunction of Jupiter and Venus has ninety Pentameters. One of them,

> Kind influence. Lo! their orbs burn more bright,

can only be read, metrically, by drawing out *influence* into three marked syllables, shortening the long monosyllable, *Lo!* and lengthening the short one, *their*.

June is sweet and soft in its rhythm, and inexpressibly pathetic. There is an illy subdued sorrow and intense awe coming up, per force as it were, to the surface of the poet's gay sayings about his grave, which we find thrilling us to the soul.

> And what if cheerful shouts, at noon,
>   Come, from the village sent,
> Or songs of maids, beneath the moon
>   With fairy laughter blent?
> And what if, in the evening light,
> Betrothed lovers walk in sight
>   Of my low monument?
> I would the lovely scene around
> Might know no sadder sight nor sound.
> I know, I know I should not see
>   The season's glorious show,
> Nor would its brightness shine for me
>   Nor its wild music flow;
> But if, around my place of sleep,
> The friends I love should come to weep,
>   They might not haste to go.
> Soft airs, and song, and light, and bloom,
>   Should keep them lingering by my tomb.

———

Innocent Child and Snow-White Flower, is remarkable only for the deficiency of a foot in one of its verses.

White as these leaves just blown apart
Are the folds of thy own young heart,

and for the graceful repetition in its concluding quatrain—

Throw it aside in thy weary hour,
Throw to the ground the fair white flower,
Yet as thy tender years depart
Keep that white and innocent heart.

———

Of the seven original sonnets in the volume before us, it is somewhat difficult to speak. The sonnet demands, in a great degree, point, strength, unity, compression, and a species of completeness. Generally, Mr. Bryant has evinced more of the first and the last, than of the three mediate qualities. *William Tell* is feeble. No forcible line ever ended with *liberty*, and the best of the rhymes—*thee*, *me*, *free*, and the like, are destitute of the necessary vigor. But for this rhythmical defect the thought in the concluding couplet—

The bitter cup they mingled strengthened thee
For the great work to set thy country free—

would have well ended the sonnet. *Midsummer* is objectionable for the variety of its objects of allusion. Its final lines embrace a fine thought—

As if the day of fire had dawned and sent
Its deadly breath into the firmament—

but the vigor of the whole is impaired by the necessity of placing an unwonted accent on the last syllable of *firmament*. *October* has little to recommend it, but the slight epigrammatism of its conclusion—

And when my last sand twinkled in the glass,
Pass silently from men— *as thou dost pass*.

The Sonnet *to Cole*, is feeble in its final lines, and is worthy of praise only in the verses—

Paths, homes, graves, ruins, from the lowest glen
To where life shrinks from the fierce Alpine air.

Mutation, a didactic sonnet, has few either of faults or beauties. *November* is far better. The lines

> And the blue Gentian flower that, in the breeze,
> Nods lonely, of her beauteous race the last,

are very happy. A single thought pervades and gives unity to the piece. We are glad, too, to see an Alexandrine in the close. In the whole metrical construction of his sonnets, however, Mr. Bryant has very wisely declined confining himself to the laws of the Italian poem, or even to the dicta of Capel Lofft. The Alexandrine is beyond comparison the most effective finale, and we are astonished that the common Pentameter should ever be employed. The best sonnet of the seven is, we think, that *To* ——. With the exception of a harshness in the last line but one it is perfect. The finale is inimitable.

> Ay, thou art for the grave; thy glances shine
>   Too brightly to shine long; another Spring
> Shall deck her for men's eyes, but not for thine—
>   Sealed in a sleep which knows no wakening.
> The fields for thee have no medicinal leaf,
>   And the vexed ore no mineral of power;
> And they who love thee wait in anxious grief
>   Till the slow plague shall bring the fatal hour.
> Glide softly to thy rest, then; Death should come
>   Gently to one of gentle mould like thee,
> As light winds wandering through groves of bloom
>   Detach the delicate blossom from the tree.
> Close thy sweet eyes, calmly, and without pain,
> And we will trust in God to see thee yet again.

———

To a Cloud, has another instance of the affectation to which we alluded in our notice of *Earth*, and *The Living Lost*.

> Whose sons at length have heard the call that comes
>   From the old battle fields and tombs,
> And risen, and drawn the sword, and on the foe
>   Have dealt the swift and desperate blow,
> And the Othman power is cloven, and the stroke
>   Has touched its chains, and they are broke.

Of the *Translations* in the volume it is not our intention to speak in detail. *Mary Magdalen*, from the Spanish of Barto- lome Leonardo De Argensola, is the finest specimen of versi- fication in the book. *Alexis*, from the Spanish of Iglesias, is delightful in its exceeding delicacy, and general beauty. We cannot refrain from quoting it entire.

Alexis calls me cruel—
  The rifted crags that hold
The gathered ice of winter,
  He says, are not more cold.

When even the very blossoms
  Around the fountain's brim,
And forest walks, can witness
  The love I bear to him.

I would that I could utter
  My feelings without shame,
And tell him how I love him
  Nor wrong my virgin fame.

Alas! to seize the moment
  When heart inclines to heart,
And press a suit with passion
  Is not a woman's part.

If man come not to gather
  The roses where they stand,
They fade among their foliage,
  They cannot seek his hand.

The Waterfowl is very beautiful, but still not entitled to the admiration which it has occasionally elicited. There is a fidel- ity and force in the picture of the fowl as brought before the eye of the mind, and a fine sense of *effect* in throwing its figure on the back ground of the "crimson sky," amid "falling dew," "while glow the heavens with the last steps of day." But the merits which possibly have had most weight in the public estimation of the poem, are the melody and strength of its versification, (which is indeed excellent) and more particularly its *completeness*. Its rounded and didactic termination has done wonders.

> ———on my heart,
> Deeply hath sunk the lesson thou hast given
>   And shall not soon depart.
>
>   He, who, from zone to zone,
> Guides through the boundless sky thy certain flight
>   In the long way that I must tread alone
> Will lead my steps aright.

There are, however, points of more sterling merit. We fully recognize the poet in

> Thou'rt gone— *the abyss of heaven*
> *Hath swallowed up thy form.*
>
> ———
>
> There is a power whose care
> Teaches thy way along that pathless coast—
> *The desert, and illimitable air,*
> Lone, wandering, but not lost.
>
> ———

The Forest Hymn consists of about a hundred and twenty blank Pentameters, of whose great rhythmical beauty it is scarcely possible to speak too highly. With the exception of the line

> The solitude. Thou art in the soft winds,

no fault, in this respect, can be found, while excellences are frequent, of a rare order, and evincing the greatest delicacy of ear. We might, perhaps, suggest, that the two concluding verses, beautiful as they stand, would be slightly improved by transferring to the last the metrical excess of the one immediately preceding. For the appreciation of this, it is necessary to quote six or seven lines in succession.

> Oh, from these sterner aspects of thy face
> Spare me and mine, nor let us need the wrath
> Of the mad unchained elements, to teach
> Who rules them. Be it ours to meditate
> In these calm shades thy milder majesty,
> *And to the beautiful order of thy works*
> *Learn to conform the order of our lives.*

There is an excess of one syllable in the first of the lines italicized. If we discard this syllable here, and adopt it in the final line, the close will acquire strength, we think, in acquiring a fuller volume.

> Be it ours to meditate
> In these calm shades thy milder majesty,
> And to the perfect order of thy works
> Conform, if we can, the order of our lives.

Directness, boldness, and simplicity of expression, are main features in the poem.

> Oh God! when thou
> Dost *scare* the world with tempests, set on fire
> The heavens with falling thunderbolts, or fill
> With all the waters of the firmament
> The swift dark whirlwind that uproots *the* woods,
> And drowns *the* villages.

Here an ordinary writer would have preferred the word *fright* to *scare*, and omitted the definite article before *woods* and *villages*.

———

To the Evening Wind has been justly admired. It is the best specimen of that *completeness* which we have before spoken of as a characteristic feature in the poems of Mr. Bryant. It has a beginning, middle, and end, each depending upon the other, and each beautiful. Here are three lines breathing all the spirit of Shelley.

> Pleasant shall be thy way, *where meekly bows*
> *The shutting flower, and darkling waters pass,*
> *And 'twixt the o'ershadowing branches and the grass.*

The conclusion is admirable—

> Go—but the circle of eternal change,
>   Which is the life of Nature, shall restore,
> With sounds and scents from all thy mighty range,
>   Thee to thy birth-place of the deep once more;
> *Sweet odors in the sea air, sweet and strange,*
>   *Shall tell the home-sick mariner of the shore,*

And, listening to thy murmur, he shall deem
He hears the rustling leaf and running stream.

———

Thanatopsis is somewhat more than half the length of *The Forest Hymn*, and of a character precisely similar. It is, however, the finer poem. Like *The Waterfowl*, it owes much to the point, force, and general beauty of its didactic conclusion. In the commencement, the lines

> To him who, *in the love of nature*, holds
> Communion with her visible forms, &c.

belong to a class of vague phrases, which, since the days of Byron, have obtained too universal a currency. The verse

> Go forth under the open sky and list—

is sadly out of place amid the forcible and even Miltonic rhythm of such lines as

> Take the wings
> Of morning, and the Barcan desert pierce,
> Or lose thyself in the continuous woods
> Where rolls the Oregan.

But these are trivial faults indeed, and the poem embodies a great degree of the most elevated beauty. Two of its passages, passages of the purest ideality, would alone render it worthy of the general commendation it has received.

> So live, that when thy summons comes to join
> *The innumerable caravan that moves*
> *To that mysterious realm where each shall take*
> *His chamber in the silent halls of death,*
> Thou go not, like the quarry slave at night,
> Scourged to his dungeon; but, sustained and soothed
> By an unfaltering trust, approach thy grave
> *Like one who wraps the drapery of his couch*
> *About him, and lies down to pleasant dreams.*

———

> *The hills*
> *Rock-ribbed and ancient as the sun— the vales*
> *Stretching in pensive quietude between—*

> *The venerable woods—rivers that move*
> *In majesty, and the complaining brooks*
> *That make the meadows green—and, poured round all,*
> *Old Ocean's gray and melancholy waste—*
> *Are but the solemn decorations all*
> *Of the great tomb of man.*

———

Oh, Fairest of the Rural Maids! is a gem, of which we cannot sufficiently express our admiration. We quote it in full.

> *Oh, fairest of the rural maids!*
> *Thy birth was in the forest shades;*
> *Green boughs and glimpses of the sky*
> *Were all that met thine infant eye.*
>
> Thy sports, thy wanderings when a child
> Were ever in the sylvan wild;
> *And all the beauty of the place*
> *Is in thy heart and on thy face.*
>
> *The twilight of the trees and rocks*
> *Is in the light shade of thy locks,*
> Thy step is as the wind that weaves
> Its playful way among the leaves.
>
> Thine eyes are springs, in whose serene
> And silent waters Heaven is seen;
> Their lashes are the herbs that look
> On their young figures in the brook.
>
> The forest depths by foot impressed
> Are not more sinless than thy breast;
> *The holy peace that fills the air*
> *Of those calm solitudes, is there.*

A rich simplicity is a main feature in this poem—simplicity
of design and execution. This is strikingly perceptible in the
opening and concluding lines, and in *expression* throughout.
But there is a far higher and more strictly *ideal* beauty, which
it is less easy to analyze. The original conception is of the very
loftiest order of true Poesy. A maiden is born in the forest—

> *Green boughs and glimpses of the sky*
> *Are all which meet her infant eye—*

She is not merely *modelled in character* by the associations of
her childhood—this were the thought of an ordinary poet—
an idea that we meet with every day in rhyme—but she imbibes, in her physical as well as moral being, the traits, the
very features of the delicious scenery around her—*its loveliness
becomes a portion of her own*—

> The twilight of the trees and rocks
> Is in the light shade of her locks,
> And all the beauty of the place
> Is in her heart and on her face.

It would have been a highly poetical idea to imagine the
tints in the locks of the maiden deducing *a resemblance* to the
"twilight of the trees and rocks," from the constancy of her
associations—but the spirit of Ideality is immeasurably more
apparent when the "twilight" is represented as becoming
identified with the shadows of the hair.

> The twilight of the trees and rocks
> *Is in* the light shade of thy locks,
> And all the beauty of the place
> *Is in* her heart and on her face.

Feeling thus, we did not, in copying the poem, italicize the
lines, although beautiful,

> Thy step is *as* the wind that weaves
> Its playful way among the leaves,

nor those which immediately follow. The two concluding
verses, however, are again of the most elevated species of poetical merit.

> The forest depths by foot impressed
> Are not more sinless than thy breast—
> The holy peace that fills the air
> Of those calm solitudes, *is there*.

The image contained in the lines

> Thine eyes are springs in whose serene
> And silent waters Heaven is seen—

is one which, we think, for appropriateness, completeness,
and every perfect beauty of which imagery is susceptible, has

never been surpassed—but *imagery* is susceptible of *no* beauty like that we have designated in the sentences above. The latter idea, moreover, is not original with our poet.

In all the rhapsodies of Mr. Bryant, which have reference to the beauty or the majesty of nature, is a most audible and thrilling tone of love and exultation. As far as he appreciates her loveliness or her augustness, no appreciation can be more ardent, more full of heart, more replete with the glowing soul of adoration. Nor, either in the moral or physical universe coming within the periphery of his vision, does he at any time fail to perceive and designate, at once, the legitimate items of the beautiful. Therefore, could we consider (as some have considered) the mere enjoyment of the beautiful when perceived, or even this enjoyment when combined with the readiest and truest perception and discrimination in regard to beauty presented, as a sufficient test of the poetical sentiment, we could have no hesitation in according to Mr. Bryant the very highest poetical rank. But something more, we have elsewhere presumed to say, is demanded. Just above, we spoke of "objects in the moral or physical universe coming within the periphery of his vision." We now mean to say, that the relative extent of these peripheries of poetical vision must ever be a primary consideration in our classification of poets. Judging Mr. B. in this manner, and by a *general* estimate of the volume before us, we should, of course, pause long before assigning him a place with the spiritual Shelleys, or Coleridges, or Wordsworths, or with Keats, or even Tennyson, or Wilson, or with some other burning lights of our own day, to be valued in a day to come. Yet if his poems, as a whole, will not warrant us in assigning him this grade, one such poem as the last upon which we have commented, is enough to assure us that he may attain it.

The writings of our author, as we find them *here*, are characterized by an air of calm and elevated contemplation more than by any other individual feature. In their mere didactics, however, they err essentially and primitively, inasmuch as such things are the province rather of Minerva than of the Camenæ. Of imagination, we discover much—but more of its rich and certain evidences, than of its ripened fruit. In all the minor merits Mr. Bryant is pre-eminent. His *ars celare artem* is most efficient. Of his "completeness," unity, and finish of style, we have already spoken. As a versifier, we know of no writer, living or dead, who can be said greatly to surpass him. A Frenchman would assuredly call him *"un poëte des plus correctes."*

Between Cowper and Young, perhaps, (with both of whom he has many points of analogy,) would be the post assigned him by an examination at once general and superficial. Even in this view, however, he has a juster appreciation of the beautiful than the one, of the sublime than the other—a finer taste than Cowper—an equally vigorous, and far more delicate imagination than Young. In regard to his proper rank among American poets there should be no question whatever. Few—at least few who are fairly before the public, have more than very shallow claims to a rivalry with the author of *Thanatopsis*.

Southern Literary Messenger, January 1837

Complete Poetical Works of William Cullen Bryant. Illustrated edition.

MR. BRYANT'S POSITION in the poetical world is, perhaps, better settled than that of any American. There is less difference of opinion about his rank; but, as usual, the agreement is more decided in private literary circles than in what appears to be the public expression of sentiment as gleaned from the press. I may as well observe here, too, that this coincidence of opinion in private circles is in all cases very noticeable when compared with the discrepancy of the apparent public opinion. In private it is quite a rare thing to find any strongly-marked disagreement—I mean, of course, about mere autorial merit. The author accustomed to seclusion, and mingling for the first time freely with the literary people about him, is invariably startled and delighted to find that the decisions of his own unbiased judgment—decisions to which he has refrained from giving voice on account of their broad contradiction to the decision of the press—are sustained and considered quite as matters of course by almost every person with whom he converses. The fact is, that when brought face to face with each other we are constrained to a certain amount of honesty by the sheer trouble it causes us to mould the countenance to a lie. We put on paper with a grave air what we could not for our lives assert personally to a friend without either blushing or laughing outright. That the opinion of the press is not an honest opinion, that necessarily it is impossible that it should be an honest opinion, is never denied by the members of the press themselves. Individual presses, of course, are now and then honest, but I speak of the combined effect. Indeed, it would be difficult for those conversant with the *modus operandi* of public journals to deny the general falsity of impression conveyed. Let in America a book be published by an unknown, careless or uninfluential author; if he publishes it "on his own account," he will be confounded at finding that no notice of it is taken at all. If it has been entrusted to a publisher of *caste*, there will appear forthwith in each of the leading *business* papers a variously-phrased *critique* to the extent of three or four lines, and to the effect that " we have received, from the fertile press of So and So, a volume entitled This and That, which appears to be well worthy perusal, and which is 'got up' in the customary neat style of the enterprising firm of So and So." On the other hand, let our author have acquired influence, experience, or (what will stand him in good stead of either) effrontery, on the issue of his book he will obtain from his publisher a hundred copies (or more, as the case may be,) "for distribution among friends connected with the press." Armed with these, he will call personally either at the office or (if he understands his game) at the private residence of every editor within his reach, enter into conversation, compliment the journalist, interest him, as if incidentally, in the subject of the book, and finally, watching an opportunity, beg leave to hand him "a volume which, quite opportunely, is on the very matter now under discussion." If the editor seems sufficiently interested, the rest is left to fate; but if there is any lukewarmness, (usually indicated by a polite regret on the editor's part that he really has "no time to render the work that justice which its importance demands,") then our author is prepared to understand and to sympathize; has, luckily, a friend thoroughly conversant with the topic, and who (per-

haps) could be persuaded to write some account of the volume—provided that the editor would be kind enough just to
glance over the *critique* and amend it in accordance with his
own particular views. Glad to fill half a column or so of his
editorial space, and still more glad to get rid of his visitor,
the journalist assents. The author retires, consults the friend,
instructs him touching the strong points of the volume, and
insinuating in *some* shape a *quid pro quo*, gets an elaborate
critique written, (or, what is more usual and far more simple,
writes it himself,) and his business in this individual quarter
is accomplished. Nothing more than sheer impudence is requisite to accomplish it in all.

Now the effect of this system (for it has really grown to be
such) is obvious. In ninety-nine cases out of a hundred, men
of genius, too indolent and careless about worldly concerns
to bestir themselves after this fashion, have also that pride of
intellect which would prevent them, under any circumstances,
from even insinuating, by the presentation of a book to a
member of the press, a desire to have that book reviewed.
They, consequently, and their works, are utterly overwhelmed
and extinguished in the flood of the *apparent* public adulation
upon which in gilded barges are borne triumphant the ingenious toady and the diligent quack.

In general, the books of the toadies and quacks, not being
read at all, are safe from any contradiction of this self-
bestowed praise; but now and then it happens that the excess
of the laudation works out in part its own remedy. Men of
leisure, hearing one of the toady works commended, look at
it, read its preface and a few pages of its body, and throw it
aside with disgust, wondering at the ill taste of the *editors*
who extol it. But there is an iteration, and then a continuous
reiteration of the panegyric, till these men of leisure begin to
suspect themselves in the wrong, to fancy that there may
really be something good lying *perdu* in the volume. In a fit
of desperate curiosity they read it through critically, their indignation growing hotter at each succeeding page till it gets
the better even of contempt. The result is, that reviews now
appear in various quarters entirely at variance with the opinions so generally expressed, and which, but for these indig-

nation reviews, would have passed universally current as the opinion of the public. It is in this manner that those gross *seeming* discrepancies arise which so often astonish us, but which vanish instantaneously in private society.

But although it may be said, in general, that Mr. Bryant's position is *comparatively* well settled, still for some time past there has been a growing tendency to under-estimate him. The new licentious "schools" of poetry—I do not now speak of the transcendentalists, who are the merest nobodies, fatiguing even themselves—but the Tennysonian and Barrettian schools, having, in their rashness of spirit, much in accordance with the whole spirit of the age, thrown into the shade necessarily all that seems akin to the conservatism of half a century ago. The conventionalities, even the most justifiable *decora* of composition, are regarded, *per se*, with a suspicious eye. When I say *per se*, I mean that, from finding them so long in connection with conservatism of thought, we have come at last to dislike them, not merely as the outward visible signs of that conservatism, but as things evil in themselves. It is very clear that those accuracies and elegancies of style, and of general manner, which in the time of Pope were considered as *primâ facie* and indispensable indications of genius, are now conversely regarded. How few are willing to admit the possibility of reconciling genius with artistic skill! Yet this reconciliation is not only possible, but an absolute necessity. It is a mere prejudice which has hitherto prevented the union, by studiously insisting upon a natural repulsion which not only does not exist, but which is at war with all the analogies of nature. The greatest poems will not be written until this prejudice is annihilated; and I mean to express a very exalted opinion of Mr. Bryant when I say that his works in time to come will do much towards the annihilation.

I have never disbelieved in the perfect consistency, and even congeniality, of the highest genius and the profoundest art; but in the case of the author of "The Ages," I *have* fallen into the general error of undervaluing his poetic ability on account of the mere "elegances and accuracies" to which allusion has already been made. I confess that, with an absolute abstraction from all personal feelings, and with the most sincere intention to do justice, I was at one period beguiled into this popular error; there can be no difficulty, therefore, on my part, in excusing the inadvertence in others.

It will never do to claim for Bryant a genius of the loftiest order, but there has been latterly, since the days of Mr. Longfellow and Mr. Lowell, a growing disposition to deny him *genius* in *any* respect. He is now commonly spoken of as "a man of high poetical *talent*, very '*correct*,' with a warm appreciation of the beauty of nature and great descriptive powers, but rather too much of the old-school manner of Cowper, Goldsmith and Young." This is the truth, but not the whole truth. Mr. Bryant has genius, and that of a marked character, but it has been overlooked by modern schools, because deficient in those externals which have become in a measure symbolical of those schools.

Dr. Griswold, in summing up his comments on Bryant, has the following significant objections. "His genius is not versatile; he has related no history; he has not sung of the passion of love; he has not described artificial life. Still the tenderness and feeling in 'The Death of the Flowers,' 'Rizpah,' 'The Indian Girl's Lament,' and other pieces, show that he might have excelled in delineations of the gentler passions had he made them his study."

Now, in describing *no* artificial life, in relating *no* history, in *not* singing the passion of love, the poet has merely shown himself the profound artist, has merely evinced a proper consciousness that such are not the legitimate themes of poetry. That they are not, I have repeatedly shown, or attempted to show, and to go over the demonstration now would be foreign to the gossiping and desultory nature of the present article. What Dr. Griswold means by "the gentler passions" is, I presume, not very clear to himself; but it is possible that he employs the phrase in consequence of the gentle, unpassionate emotion induced by the poems of which he quotes the titles. It is precisely this "unpassionate emotion" which is the limit of the true poetical art. Passion proper and poesy are discordant. Poetry, in elevating, tranquilizes *the soul*. With *the heart* it has nothing to do. For a fuller explanation of these views I refer the reader to an analysis of a poem by Mrs. Welby—an analysis contained in an article called "Marginalia," and published about a year ago in "The Democratic Review."

The editor of "The Poets and Poetry of America" thinks the literary precocity of Bryant remarkable. "There are few recorded *more* remarkable," he says. The first edition of "The Embargo" was in 1808, and the poet was born in 1794; he was more than thirteen, then, when the satire was printed—although it is reported to have been written a year earlier. I quote a few lines.

> "Oh, might some patriot rise, the gloom dispel,
>   Chase Error's mist and break her magic spell!
>   But vain the wish; for, hark! the murmuring meed
>   Of hoarse applause from yonder shed proceed.
>   Enter and view the thronging concourse there,
>   Intent with gaping mouth and stupid stare;
>   While in the midst their supple leader stands,
>   Harangues aloud and flourishes his hands,
>   To adulation tunes his servile throat,
>   And sues successful for each blockhead's vote."

This is a fair specimen of the whole, both as regards its satirical and rhythmical power. A satire is, of course, no *poem*. I have known boys of an earlier age do better things, although the case is rare. All depends upon the course of education. Bryant's father "was familiar with the best English literature, and perceiving in his son indications of superior genius, attended carefully to his instruction, taught him the art of composition, and guided his literary taste." This being understood, the marvel of such verse as I have quoted ceases at once, even admitting it to be thoroughly the boy's own work; but it is difficult to make any such admission. The father *must* have suggested, revised, retouched.

The longest poem of Bryant is "The Ages"—thirty-five Spenserian stanzas. It is the one improper theme of its author. The design is, "from a survey of the past ages of the world, and of the successive advances of mankind in knowledge and virtue, to justify and confirm the hopes of the philanthropist for the future destinies of the human race." All this would have been more rationally, because more effectually, accomplished in prose. Dismissing it as a poem, (which in its general tendency it is not,) one might commend the force of its argumentation but for the radical error of deducing a hope of *progression* from the *cycles* of physical nature.

The sixth stanza is a specimen of noble versification (within the narrow limits of the Iambic Pentameter).

> "Look on this beautiful world and read the truth
> In her fair page; see, every season brings
> New change to her of everlasting youth;
> Still the green soil with joyous living things
> Swarms; the wide air is full of joyous wings;
> And myriads still are happy in the sleep
> Of Ocean's azure gulfs and where he flings
> The restless surge. Eternal Love doth keep
> In His complacent arms, the earth, the air, the deep."

The cadences here at *page*, *swarms* and *surge*, cannot be surpassed. There are comparatively few consonants. Liquids and the softer vowels abound, and the partial line after the pause at "surge," with the stately march of the succeeding Alexandrine, is one of the finest conceivable *finales*.

The poem, in general, has unity, completeness. Its tone of calm, elevated and hopeful contemplation, is well sustained throughout. There is an occasional quaint grace of expression, as in

> "Nurse of full streams and lifter up of proud
> Sky-mingling mountains that o'erlook the cloud!"

or of antithetical and rhythmical force combined, as in

> "The shock that hurled
> To dust, in many fragments dashed and strown,
> The throne whose roots were in another world
> And whose far-stretching shadow awed our own."

But we look in vain for anything more worthy commendation.

"Thanatopsis" is the poem by which its author is best known, but is by no means his best poem. It owes the *extent* of its celebrity to its nearly absolute freedom from *defect*, in the ordinary understanding of the term. I mean to say that its negative merit recommends it to the public attention. It is a thoughtful, well phrased, well constructed, well versified poem. The concluding thought is exceedingly noble, and has done wonders for the success of the whole composition.

"The Waterfowl" is very beautiful, but like "Thanatopsis," owes a great deal to its completeness and pointed termination.

"Oh, Fairest of the Rural Maids!" will strike every poet as the truest *poem* written by Bryant. It is richly ideal.

"June" is sweet and perfectly well modulated in its rhythm, and inexpressibly pathetic. It serves well to illustrate my previous remarks about passion in its connection with poetry. In "June" there is, very properly, nothing of the intense *passion* of grief, but the subdued sorrow which comes up, as if perforce, to the surface of the poet's gay sayings about his grave, we find thrilling us to the soul, while there is yet a spiritual *elevation* in the thrill.

> "And what if cheerful shouts at noon
>   Come, from the village sent,
> Or songs of maids beneath the moon
>   With fairy laughter blent?
> And what if, in the evening light,
> Betrothed lovers walk in sight
>   Of my low monument?
> I would the lovely scene around
> Might know no sadder sight nor sound.
> I know—I know I should not see
>   The season's glorious show,
> Nor would its brightness shine for me,
>   Nor its wild music flow;
> But if around my place of sleep
> The friends I love should come to weep,
>   They might not haste to go:—
> Soft airs, and song, and light, and bloom,
> Should keep them lingering by my tomb."

The thoughts here belong to the highest class of poetry, the imaginative-natural, and are of themselves sufficient to stamp their author a man of genius.

I copy at random a few passages of similar cast, inducing a similar conviction.

> "The great heavens
> *Seem to stoop down upon the scene in love,*
> A nearer vault and of a tenderer blue
> Than that which bends above the eastern hills."
>
> *   *   *
>
> "Till twilight blushed, and lovers walked and wooed
> In a forgotten language, and *old tunes*
> *From instruments of unremembered form,*
> *Gave the soft winds a voice.*"
>
> *   *   *
>
> "Breezes of the south,
> *That toss the golden and the flame-like flowers,*
> *And pass the prairie hawk, that, poised on high,*
> *Flaps his broad wings, yet moves not.*"
>
> *   *   *
>
> "On the breast of earth
> I lie, and listen to her mighty voice—
> *A voice of many tones sent up from streams*
> *That wander through the gloom, from woods unseen,*
> *Swayed by the sweeping of the tides of air;*
> *From rocky chasms where darkness dwells all day,*
> *And hollows of the great invisible hills,*
> *And sands that edge the ocean, stretching far*
> Into the night—a melancholy sound!"
>
> *   *   *
>
> "All the green herbs
> Are stirring in his breath; *a thousand flowers*
> *By the road side and the borders of the brook,*
> *Nod gayly to each other.*"

[There is a fine "echo of sound to sense" in "the borders of the brook," etc.; and in the same poem from which these lines are taken, ("The Summer Wind,") may be found two other equally happy examples, *e.g.*

"For me, I lie
Languidly in the shade, where the thick turf,
Yet virgin from the kisses of the sun,
Retains some freshness."

And again—

"All is silent, save the faint
And interrupted murmur of the bee
Settling on the sick flowers, and then again
Instantly on the wing."

I resume the imaginative extracts.]

"Paths, homes, graves, ruins, from the lowest glen
To where life shrinks from the fierce Alpine air."

*   *   *

"*And the blue gentian flower that in the breeze
Nods lonely, of her beauteous race the last.*"

*   *   *

"*A shoot of that old vine that made
The nations silent in the shade.*"

*   *   *

"*But 'neath yon crimson tree,
Lover to listening maid might breathe his flame,
Nor mark, within its roseate canopy,
Her flush of maiden shame.*"

*   *   *

"The mountains that infold,
In their wild sweep, the coloured landscape round,
Seem *groups of giant kings in purple and gold
That guard the enchanted ground.*"

[This latter passage is especially beautiful. Happily to
endow inanimate nature with sentience and a capability of
action, is one of the severest tests of the poet.]

*   *   *

"There is a power whose care
Teaches thy way along *that pathless coast,
The desert and illimitable air,
Lone, wandering, but not lost.*"

* * *

"Pleasant shall be thy way, *where weekly bows*
The shutting flowers and darkling waters pass,
And 'twixt the o'ershadowing branches and the grass."

* * *

"Sweet odours in the sea air, sweet and strange,
    Shall tell the home-sick mariner of the shore,
And, listening to thy murmur, he shall deem
He hears the rustling leaf and running stream."

* * *

In a "Sonnet, To ——," are some richly imaginative lines.
I quote the whole.

"Ay, thou art for the grave; thy glances shine
    Too brightly to shine long: another spring
Shall deck her for men's eyes, but not for thine,
    Sealed in a sleep which knows no waking.
The fields for thee have no medicinal leaf,
    And the vexed ore no mineral of power;
And they who love thee wait in anxious grief
    Till the slow plague shall bring the fatal hour.
Glide softly to thy rest, then: death should come
    Gently to one of gentle mould like thee,
As light winds, wandering through groves of bloom,
    Detach the delicate blossom from the tree,
Close thy sweet eyes calmly and without pain,
And we will trust in God to see thee yet again."

The happiest *finale* to these brief extracts will be the magnificent conclusion of "Thanatopsis."

"So live, that, when thy summons comes to join
The innumerable caravan that moves
To that mysterious realm where each shall take
His chamber in the silent halls of death,
Thou go not, like the quarry slave at night,
Scourged to his dungeon, but sustained and soothed
By an unfaltering trust, approach thy grave—
Like one that draws the drapery of his couch
About him and lies down to pleasant dreams."

In the minor morals of the muse Mr. Bryant excels. In versification (*as far as he goes*) he is unsurpassed in America—unless, indeed, by Mrs. Sprague. Mr. Longfellow is not so thorough a versifier within Mr. Bryant's limits, but a far better one upon the whole, on account of his greater range. Mr. B., however, is by no means always accurate—or defensible, for accurate is not the term. His lines are occasionally unpronounceable through excess of harsh consonants, as in

"As if they loved to breast the breeze that sweeps the cool
    clear sky."

Now and then he gets out of his depth in attempting anapæstic rhythm, of which he makes sad havoc, as in

"And Rizpah, once the loveliest of all
    That bloomed and smiled in the court of Saul."

Not unfrequently, too, even his pentameters are inexcusably rough, as in

"Kind influence. Lo! their orbs burn more bright."

which can only be read metrically by drawing out "influence" into three marked syllables, shortening the long monosyllable "Lo!" and lengthening the short one "their."

Mr. Bryant is not devoid of mannerisms, one of the most noticeable of which is his use of the epithet "old," preceded by some other adjective, *e.g.*—

"In all that proud old world beyond the deep;"
"There is a tale about these gray old rocks;"
"The wide old woods resounded with her song;"
"——and the gray old men that passed;"
"And from the gray old trunks that high in heaven,"

etc. etc. etc. These duplicates occur so frequently as to excite a smile upon each repetition.

Of merely grammatical errors the poet is rarely guilty. Faulty constructions are more frequently chargeable to him. In "The Massacre of Scio" we read—

"Till the last link of slavery's chain
    Is shivered to be worn no more."

What shall be worn no more? The chain, of course—but the link is implied. It will be understood that I pick these flaws only with difficulty from the poems of Bryant. He is, in the "minor morals," the most generally correct of our poets.

He is now fifty-two years of age. In height, he is, perhaps, five feet nine. His frame is rather robust. His features are large but thin. His countenance is sallow, nearly bloodless. His eyes are piercing gray, deep set, with large projecting eyebrows. His mouth is wide and massive, the expression of the smile hard, cold—even sardonic. The forehead is broad, with prominent organs of ideality; a good deal bald; the hair thin and grayish, as are also the whiskers, which he wears in a simple style. His bearing is quite distinguished, full of the aristocracy of intellect. In general, he looks in better health than before his last visit to England. He seems active—physically and morally—energetic. His dress is plain to the extreme of simplicity, although of late there is a certain degree of Anglicism about it.

In character no man stands more loftily than Bryant. The peculiarly melancholy expression of his countenance has caused him to be accused of harshness, or coldness of heart. Never was there a greater mistake. His soul is charity itself, in all respects generous and noble. His manners are undoubtedly reserved.

Of late days he has nearly, if not altogether abandoned literary pursuits, although still editing, with unabated vigour, "The New York Evening Post." He is married, (Mrs. Bryant still living,) has two daughters, (one of them Mrs. Parke Godwin,) and is residing for the present at Vice-Chancelor McCown's, near the junction of Warren and Church streets.—I have thought that these brief personal details of one of the most justly celebrated men in America, might not prove uninteresting to some of the readers of "The Lady's Book."

Godey's Lady's Book, April 1846

The Canons of Good Breeding

The Canons of Good Breeding; or, The Handbook of the Man of Fashion. By the Author of the "Laws of Etiquette." Lea and Blanchard, Philadelphia.

THIS LITTLE BOOK IS a curiosity in its way. Indeed, there is something so very singular about it that we have been led to read it through deliberately and thoughtfully, with the view of solving the mystery which envelops it. It is by the author of the "Laws of Etiquette," who is also the author of "Advice to a Young Gentleman," a volume which we commended with some warmth in a former number of the Magazine.

In regard to the "Canons of Good Breeding," the critical reader, who takes it up, will, of course, be inclined to throw it aside with contempt, upon perceiving its title. This will be his first impulse. If he proceed so far, however, as to skim over the Preface, his eye will be arrested by a certain air of *literature-ism* (we must be permitted to coin an odd word for an odd occasion) which pervades and invigorates the pages. Regarding with surprise this discrepancy between preface and title—between the apparent polish of the one, and the horribly *ad captandum* character of the other—he will be induced to finish the perusal of the book, and, we answer for it, will be thoroughly mystified before he gets well to the end. He will now find an exceeding difficulty, nearly amounting to impossibility, in making up his mind in regard to the merit or demerit of the work. If, however, he be somewhat in a hurry, there can be little doubt that he will terminate his examination with a hearty, perhaps even an enthusiastic, approval.

The truth is that the volume abounds in good things. We may safely say that, in a compass so small, we never before met with an equal radiancy of fine wit, so well commingled with scholar-like observation and profound thought— thought sometimes luminously and logically, and always elegantly, expressed. The first difficulty arising in the mind of the critic is that these good things are suspiciously *super*-abundant. He will now pass on to the observation of some inaccuracies of *adaptation*. He will then call to mind certain *niaiseries* of sentiment altogether at warfare with the prevailing tone of the book—and, finally, he will perceive, although with somewhat greater difficulty, the evidence of a radical alteration and bepatching of the language—the traces of an excessive *limae labor*. He will thus take offence at the disingenuousness which has entrapped him into momentary applause; and, while he cannot deny that the work, such as the world sees it, has merit, he will still pronounce it, without hesitation, the excessively-elaborated production of some partially-educated man, possessed with a rabid ambition for the reputation of a wit and *savant*, and who, somewhat unscrupulous in the mode of attaining such reputation, has consented to clip, cut, and most assiduously intersperse throughout his book, by wholesale, the wit, the wisdom, and the erudition, of Horace Walpole, of Bolingbroke, of Chesterfield, of Bacon, of Burton, and of Burdon,—even of Bulwer and of D'Israeli,—with occasional draughts (perhaps at second-hand) from the rich coffers of Seneca, or Machiavelli—of Montaigne, of Rochefoucault, of the author of *"La Maniere de bien penser,"* or of Bielfeld, the German who wrote in French *"Les Premiers Traits de L'Erudition Universelle."* We may be pardoned also for an allusion—which is enough—to such wealthy store-houses as the *"Lettres Edifiantes et Curieuses,"* the Literary Memoirs of Sallengré, the *"Melanges Literaires,"* of Suard and André, and the *"Pieces Interressantes et peu Connues"* of La Place.

The construction here given is the most obvious, and indeed the only one, which can be put upon the volume now before us, and upon the other efforts of the same pen. They betray the hand of the diligent adaptator of others' wit, rather than the really full mind of the educated and studious man of general letters. True erudition—by which term we here mean simply to imply much diversified reading—is certainly discoverable—is positively indicated—only in its ultimate and total *results*. The mere grouping together of fine things from the greatest multiplicity of the rarest works, or even the apparently natural inweaving into any composition, of the sentiments and manner of these works, is an attainment within the reach of every moderately-informed, ingenious, and not indolent man, having access to any ordinary collection of good books. The only available objection to what we have urged will be based upon the polish of the style. But we have already alluded to traces of the *limae labor*—and this labor has been skilfully applied. Beyond doubt, the volume has undergone a minute supervision and correction by some person whose habits and education have rendered him very thoroughly competent to the task.

We have spoken somewhat at length in regard to the *authorship* of "The Canons of Criticism," because ingenuities of this species are by no means very common. Few men are found weak enough to perpetrate them to any extent. We have said little, however, in respect to the book itself, *as it stands*—and this little has been in its favor. The publication will be read with interest, and may be read, generally speaking, with profit. Some of the *niaiseries* to which we alluded just now are sufficiently droll—being even oddly at variance with the assumed spirit of the whole work. We are told, among other things, that the writer has employed throughout his book the words "lady," and "gentleman," instead of the words " woman," and "man," which "are more correct expressions, and more usual in the best circles,"—that " when you lay down your hat in a room, or on a bench in a public place, you should put the open part downwards, so that the leather may not be seen which has been soiled by the hair,"—that "you should never present yourself at a large evening party without having your hair dressed and curled,"—and that since "the inferior classes of men, as you may see if you think fit to take notice of them, only press the rim of the hat when they speak to women of their acquaintance," you should be careful " when you salute a lady or gentleman, to take your own entirely off, and cause it to describe *a circle of at least ninety degrees*."

The effect of such fine advice can be readily conceived. It will be taken by contraries, as sure as dandies have brains. No one of that much-injured race will now venture to say "lady," or "gentleman," or have his hair curled, or place his hat upside-down upon a table, or do any other such unimaginable act, lest he should be suspected of having derived his manners from no better source than the "Canons of Good Breeding." We shall have a revolution in such matters—a revolution to be remedied only by another similar volume. As for its author—should he write it—we wish him no worse fate than to be condemned to its perpetual perusal until such time as he shall succeed in describing with his hat one of his own very funny circles—one of those circles of just ninety degrees.

Burton's Gentleman's Magazine, November 1839

William Ellery Channing

IN SPEAKING OF Mr. William Ellery Channing, who has just published a very neat little volume of poems, we feel the necessity of employing the indefinite rather than the definite article. He is *a*, and by no means *the*, William Ellery Channing. He is only *the son* of the great essayist deceased. He is just such a person, in despite of his *clarum et venerabile nomen*, as Pindar would have designated by the significant term τις. It may be said in his favor that nobody ever heard of him. Like an honest woman, he has always succeeded in keeping himself from being made the subject of gossip. His book contains about sixty-three things, which he calls poems, and which he no doubt seriously supposes so to be. They are full of all kinds of mistakes, of which the most important is that of their having been printed at all. They are not precisely English—nor will we insult a great nation by calling them Kickapoo; perhaps they are Channingese. We may convey some general idea of them by two foreign terms not in common use—the Italian *pavoneggiarsi*, "to strut like a peacock," and the German word for "sky-rocketing," *schwarmerei*. They are more preposterous, in a word, than any poems except those of the author of "Sam Patch;" for we presume we are right (are we not?) in taking it for granted that the author of "Sam Patch" is the very worst of all the wretched poets that ever existed upon earth.

In spite, however, of the customary phrase about a man's "making a fool of himself," we doubt if any one was ever a fool of his own free will and accord. A poet, therefore, should not always be taken too strictly to task. He should be treated with leniency, and, even when damned, should be damned with respect. Nobility of descent, too, should be allowed its privileges not more in social life than in letters. The son of a great author cannot be handled too tenderly by the critical Jack Ketch. Mr. Channing must be hung, that's true. He must be hung *in terrorem*—and for this there is no help under the sun; but then we shall do him all manner of justice, and observe every species of decorum, and be especially careful of his feelings, and hang him gingerly and gracefully, with a silken cord, as the Spaniards hang their grandees of the blue blood, their nobles of the *sangre azula*.

To be serious, then; as we always wish to be if possible. Mr. Channing (whom we suppose to be a *very* young man, since we are precluded from supposing him a *very* old one) appears to have been inoculated, at the same moment, with *virus* from Tennyson and from Carlyle. And here we do not wish to be misunderstood. For Tennyson, as for a man imbued with the richest and rarest poetic impulses, we have an admiration—a reverence unbounded. His "Morte D'Arthur," his "Locksley Hall," his "Sleeping Beauty," his "Lady of Shalott," his "Lotos Eaters," his "Œnone," and many other poems, are not surpassed, in all that gives to Poetry its distinctive value, by the compositions of any one living or dead. And his leading error—that error which renders him unpopular—a point, to be sure, of no particular importance—that very error, we say, is founded in truth—in a keen perception of the elements of poetic beauty. We allude to his quaintness—to what the world chooses to term his affectation. No true poet—no critic whose approbation is worth even a copy of the volume we now hold in our hand—will deny that he feels impressed, sometimes even to tears, by many of those very affectations which he is impelled by the prejudice of his education, or by the cant of his reason, to condemn. He should thus be led to examine the extent of the one, and to be wary of the deductions of the other. In fact, the profound intuition of Lord Bacon has supplied, in one of his immortal apothegmns, the whole philosophy of the point at issue. "There is no exquisite beauty," he truly says, " without some *strangeness* in its proportions." We maintain, then, that Tennyson errs, not in his occasional quaintness, but in its continual and obtrusive excess. And, in accusing Mr. Channing of having been inoculated with *virus* from Tennyson, we merely mean to say that he has adopted and exaggerated that noble poet's characteristic defect, having mistaken it for his principal merit.

Mr. Tennyson is quaint only; he is never, as some have supposed him, obscure—except, indeed, to the uneducated, whom he does not address. Mr. Carlyle, on the other hand, is obscure only; he is seldom, as some have imagined him, quaint. So far he is right; for although quaintness, employed by a man of judgment and genius, may be made auxiliary to a *poem*, whose true thesis is beauty, and beauty alone, it is grossly, and even ridiculously, out of place in a work of prose. But in his obscurity it is scarcely necessary to say that he is wrong. Either a man intends to be understood, or he does not. If he write a book which he intends *not* to be understood, we shall be very happy indeed not to understand it; but if he write a book which he means to be understood, and, in this book, be at all possible pains to prevent us from understanding it, we can only say that he is an ass—and this, to be brief, is our private opinion of Mr. Carlyle, which we now take the liberty of making public.

It seems that having deduced, from Tennyson and Carlyle, an opinion of the sublimity of every thing odd, and of the profundity of every thing meaningless, Mr. Channing has conceived the idea of setting up for himself as a poet of *unusual* depth, and *very* remarkable powers of mind. His airs and graces, in consequence, have a highly picturesque effect, and the Boston critics, who have a notion that poets are porpoises, (for they are always talking about their running in "schools,") cannot make up their minds as to what particular school he must belong. *We* say the Bobby Button school, by all means. He clearly belongs to that. And should nobody ever have heard of the Bobby Button school, that is a point of no material importance. We will answer for it, as it is one of our own. Bobby Button is a gentleman with whom, for a long time, we have had the honor of an intimate acquaintance. His personal appearance is striking. He has quite a big head. His eyes protrude and have all the air of saucers. His chin retreats. His mouth is depressed at the corners. He wears a perpetual frown of contemplation. His words are slow, emphatic, few, and oracular. His "thes," "ands," and "buts" have more meaning than other men's polysyllables. His nods would have put Burleigh's to the blush. His whole aspect, indeed, conveys the idea of a gentleman modest to a fault, and painfully overburthened with intellect. We insist, however, upon calling Mr. Channing's school of poetry the Bobby Button school, rather because Mr. Channing's poetry

is strongly suggestive of Bobby Button, than because Mr.
Button himself ever dallied, to any very great extent, with the
Muses. With the exception, indeed, of a *very* fine "Sonnet to
a Pig"—or rather the fragment of a sonnet, for he proceeded
no farther than the words "*O* piggy wiggy," with the *O* italicized for emphasis—with the exception of this, we say, we
are not aware of his having produced anything worthy of that
stupendous genius which is certainly *in* him, and only wants,
like the starling of Sterne, "to get out."

The best passage in the book before us, is to be found at
page 121, and we quote it, as a matter of simple justice, in full.

> Dear friend, in this fair atmosphere again,
> Far from the noisy echoes of the main,
> Amid the world-old mountains, and the hills
> From whose strange grouping a fine power distills
> The soothing and the calm, I seek repose,
> The city's noise forgot and hard stern woes.
> As thou once said'st, the rarest sons of earth
> Have in the dust of cities shown their worth,
> Where long collision with the human curse
> Has of great glory been the frequent nurse,
> *And only those who in sad cities dwell*
> *Are of the green trees fully sensible.*
> *To them the silver bells of tinkling streams*
> *Seem brighter than an angel's laugh in dreams.*

The four lines Italicized are highly meritorious, and the
whole extract is so far decent and intelligible, that we experienced a feeling of surprise upon meeting it amid the doggerel
which surrounds it. Not less was our astonishment upon
finding, at page 18, a fine thought so well embodied as the
following:

> *Or see the early stars, a mild sweet train,*
> *Come out to bury the diurnal sun.*

But, in the way of commendation, we have now done. We
have carefully explored the whole volume, in vain, for a single
additional line worth even the most qualified applause.

The utter *abandon*—the charming *negligé*—the perfect

looseness (to use a western phrase) of his rhythm, is one of Mr. C's. most noticeable, and certainly one of his most refreshing traits. It would be quite a pleasure to hear him read or scan, or to hear any body else read or scan, such a line as this, at page 3, for example:

Masculine almost though softly carv'd in grace,

where "masculine" has to be read as a trochee, and "almost" as an iambus; or this, at page 8:

That compels me on through wood, and fell, and moor,

where "that compels" has to be pronounced as equivalent to the iambus "me on;" or this, at page 18:

I leave thee, *the* maid spoke to *the* true youth,

where both the *"thes"* demand a strong accent to preserve the iambic rhythm; or this, at page 29:

So in our steps strides truth and honest trust,

where (to say nothing of the grammar, which *may* be Dutch but is not English) it is quite impossible to get through with the "step strides truth" without dislocating the under jaw; or this, at page 32:

The *s*erene azure *the* keen stars are now;

or this, on the same page:

Some*time* of sorrow, joy to *thy* Fu*ture*;

or this, at page 56:

Harsh action, even in repose inwardly harsh;

or this, at page 59:

Provides am*plest* enjoyment. O my brother;

or this, at page 138:

Like the swift petrel, mimicking the wave's measure;

about all of which the less we say the better.

At page 96 we read thus:

> Where the untrammelled soul on her wind pinions,
> *Fearlessly sweeping, defies my earthly foes,*
> There, there upon that infinitest sea
> *Lady thy hope, so fair a hope, summons me.*

At page 51 we have it thus:

> The river calmly flows
> Through shining banks, thro' lonely glen,
> Where the owl shrieks, tho' ne'er the cheer of men
>   Has stirred its mute repose;
> *Still if you should walk there you would go there again.*

At page 136 we read as follows:

> Tune thy clear voice to no funereal song,
> *For O Death stands to welcome thee sure.*

At page 116 he has this:

> ———These graves, you mean;
> Their histo*ry* who knows bet*ter* than I?
> For in the busy street strikes on my ear
> *Each sound, even inaudible voices*
> Lengthen the long tale my memory tells.

Just below, on the same page, he has

> I see but little difference tru*ly*;

and at page 76 he fairly puts the climax to metrical absurdity in the lines which follow:

> The spirit builds his house in *the* last flowers—
> A beautiful mansion; how the colors live,
> In*tri*cately de*li*cate!

This is to be read, of course, intrikkittly delikkit, and "intrik-kittly delikkit" it is—unless, indeed, we are very especially mistaken.

The affectations—the Tennysonisms of Mr. Channing—pervade his book at all points, and are not easily particularized. He employs, for example, the word "delight," for "delighted;" as at page 2:

> Delight to trace the mountain-brook's descent.

He uses, also, all the prepositions in a different sense from the rabble. If, for instance, he was called upon to say "on," he would n't say it by any means, but he'd say "off," and endeavor to make it answer the purpose. For "to," in the same manner, he says "from;" for " with," "of," and so on: at page 2, for example:

> Nor less in winter, mid the glittering banks
> Heaped *of* unspotted snow, the maiden roved.

For "serene," he says "*se*rene:" as at page 4:

> The influences of this *se*rene isle.

For "subdued," he says "*sub*dued:" as at page 16:

> So full of thought, so *sub*dued to bright fears.

By the way, what kind of fears *are* bright?
    For "eternal," he says "eterne:" as at page 30:

> Has risen, *and* an eterne sun now paints.

For "friendless," he substitutes "friend*less*:" as at page 31:

> Are drawn in other figures. Not friend*less*.

To "future," he prefers "fu*ture*:" as at page 32:

> Sometime of sorrow. Joy to thy fu*ture*.

To "azure," in the same way, he prefers "a*zure*:" as at page 46:

> Ye stand each separate in the a*zure*.

In place of "unheard," he writes "*un*heard:" as thus, at page 47:

> Or think, tho' *un*heard, that your sphere is dumb.

In place of "perchance," he writes "*per*chance:" as at page 71:

> When *per*chance sorrow with her icy smile.

Instead of "more infinite," he writes "infi*nit*e," with an accent on the "nit," as thus, at page 100:

> Hope's child, I summon infi*nit*er powers.

And here we might as well ask Mr. Channing, in passing, what idea he attaches to infinity, and whether he really thinks that he is at liberty to subject the adjective "infinite" to degrees of comparison. Some of these days we shall hear, no doubt, of "eternal, eternaler, and eternalest."

Our author is quite enamored of the word "sumptuous," and talks about "sumptuous trees" and "sumptuous girls," with no other object, we think, than to employ the epithet at all hazards and upon all occasions. He seems unconscious that it means nothing more than expensive, or costly; and we are not quite sure that either trees or girls are, in America, either the one or the other.

For "loved" Mr. C. prefers to say " was loving," and takes great pleasure in the law phrase "the same." Both peculiarities are examplified at page 20, where he says:

> The maid was loving this enamored same.

He is fond, also, of inversions and contractions, and employs them in a very singular manner. At page 15 he has:

> Now may I thee describe a Paradise.

At page 86 he says:

> Thou lazy river, flowing neither way
> Me figurest and yet thy banks seem gay.

At page 143 he writes:

> Men change that Heaven above not more;

meaning that men change so much that Heaven above does not change more. At page 150, he says:

> But so much soul hast thou within thy form
> Than luscious summer days thou art the more;

by which he would imply that the lady has so much soul within her form that she is more luscious than luscious summer days.

Were we to quote specimens under the general head of "utter and irredeemable nonsense," we should quote nine tenths of the book. Such nonsense, we mean, as the following, from page 11:

I hear thy solemn anthem fall,
    Of richest song, upon my ear,
That clothes thee in thy golden pall,
    As this wide sun flows on the mere.

Now let us translate this: He hears (Mr. Channing,) a solemn anthem, of richest song, fall upon his ear, and this anthem clothes the individual who sings it in that individual's golden pall, in the same manner that, or at the time when, the wide sun flows on the mere—which is all very delightful, no doubt.

At page 37, he informs us that,

——It is not living,
To a soul believing,
To change each noble joy,
Which our strength employs,
For a state half rotten
And a life of toys,

And that it is

Better to be forgotten
Than lose equipoise.

And we dare say it is, if one could only understand what kind of equipoise is intended. It is better to be forgotten, for instance, than to lose one's equipoise on the top of a shot tower.

Occupying the whole of page 88, he has the six lines which follow, and we will present any one (the author not excepted,) with a copy of the volume, if any one will tell us what they are all about:

He came and waved a little silver wand,
    He dropped the veil that hid a statue fair,
He drew a circle with that pearly hand,
    His grace confin'd that beauty in the air,
Those limbs so gentle now at rest from flight,
Those quiet eyes now musing on the night.

At page 102, he has the following:

Dry leaves with yellow ferns, they are
Fit wreath of Autumn, while a star
Still, bright, and pure, our frosty air
Shivers in twinkling points
Of thin celestial hair
And thus one side of Heaven anoints.

This we think we can explain. Let us see. Dry leaves, mixed with yellow ferns, are a wreath fit for autumn at the time when our frosty air shivers a still, bright, and pure star with twinkling points of thin celestial hair, and with this hair, or hair plaster, anoints one side of the sky. Yes—this is it—no doubt.

At page 123, we have these lines:

My sweet girl is lying still
In her lovely atmosphere;
The gentle hopes her blue veins fill
With pure silver warm and clear.

O see her hair, O mark her breast!
Would it not, *O!* comfort thee,
If thou couldst nightly go to rest
By that virgin chastity?

Yes; we think, upon the whole, it would. The eight lines are entitled a "Song," and we should like very much to hear Mr. Channing sing it.

Pages 36, 37, 38, 39, 40, and 41, are filled with short "Thoughts" in what Mr. C. supposes to be the manner of Jean Paul. One of them runs thus:

How shall I live? In earnestness.
What shall I do? Work earnestly.
What shall I give? A willingness.
What shall I gain? Tranquillity.
But do you mean a quietness
In which I act and no man bless?
Flash out in action infinite and free,
Action conjoined with deep tranquillity,
Resting upon the soul's true utterance,
And life shall flow as merry as a dance.

All our readers will be happy to hear, we are sure, that Mr. C. is going "to flash out." Elsewhere, at page 97, he expresses very similar sentiments:

> My empire is myself and I defy
> The external; yes, I rule the whole or die!

It will be observed, here, that Mr. Channing's empire is himself, (a small kingdom, however,) that he intends to defy "the external," whatever that is—perhaps he means the infernals—and that, in short, he is going to rule the whole or die; all which is very proper, indeed, and nothing more than we have to expect from Mr. C.

Again, at page 146, he is rather fierce than otherwise. He says;

> We surely were not meant to ride the sea,
>   Skimming the wave in that so prisoned small,
> Reposing our infinite faculties utterly.
>   Boom like a roaring sunlit waterfall.
> Humming to infinite abysms: speak loud, speak free!

Here Mr. Channing not only intends to "speak loud and free" himself, but advises every body else to do likewise. For his own part, he says, he is going to "*boom*"—"to hum and to boom"—to "hum like a roaring waterfall," and "boom to an infinite abysm." What, in the name of Belzebub, *is* to become of us all?

At page 39, while indulging in similar bursts of fervor and of indignation, he says:

> Thou meetest a common man
> With a delusive show of *can*,

and this passage we quote by way of instancing what we consider the only misprint in the book. Mr. Channing could never have meant to say:

> Thou meetest a common man
> With a delusive show of *can*;

for what *is* a delusive show of *can*? No doubt it should have been,

> Thou meetest a little pup
> With a delusive show of tin-cup.

A can, we believe, is a tin-cup, and the cup must have been tied to the tail of the pup. Boys *will* do such tricks, and there is no earthly way of preventing them, we believe, short of cutting off their heads—or the tails of the pups.

And this remarkable little volume is, after all, by William Ellery Channing. A great name, it has been said, is, in many cases, a great misfortune. We hear daily complaints from the George Washington Dixons, the Socrates Smiths, and the Napoleon Buonaparte Joneses, about the inconsiderate ambition of their parents and sponsors. By inducing invidious comparison, these *prænomina* get their bearers (so they say) into every variety of scrape. If George Washington Dixon, for example, does not think proper, upon compulsion, to distinguish himself as a patriot, he is considered a very singular man; and Socrates Smith is never brought up before his honor the Mayor without receiving a double allowance of thirty days; while his honor the Mayor can assign no sounder reason for his severity, than that better things than getting toddied are to be expected of Socrates. Napoleon Buonaparte Jones, on the other hand, to say nothing of being called Nota Bene Jones by all his acquaintance, is cowskinned, with perfect regularity, five times a month, merely because people *will* feel it a point of honor to cowskin a Napoleon Buonaparte.

And yet these gentlemen—the Smiths and the Joneses—are wrong *in toto*—as the Smiths and the Joneses invariably are. They are wrong, we say, in accusing their parents and sponsors. They err in attributing their misfortunes and persecutions to the *prænomina*—to the names assigned them at the baptismal font. Mr. Socrates Smith does not receive his double quantum of thirty days because he is called Socrates, but because he is called Socrates *Smith*. Mr. Napoleon Buonaparte Jones is not in the weekly receipt of a flogging on account of being Mr. Napoleon Buonaparte, but simply on account of being Mr. Napoleon Buonaparte *Jones*. Here, indeed, is a clear distinction. It is the surname which is to blame, after all. Mr. Smith must drop the Smith. Mr. Jones should discard the Jones. No one would ever think of taking

Socrates—Socrates solely—to the watch-house; and there is
not a bully living who would venture to cowskin Napoleon
Buonaparte *per se*. And the reason is plain. With nine individuals out of ten, as the world is at present happily constituted,
Mr. Socrates (without the Smith) would be taken for the veritable philosopher of whom we have heard so much, and Mr.
Napoleon Buonaparte (without the Jones) would be received
implicitly as the hero of Austerlitz. And should Mr. Napoleon
Buonaparte (without the Jones) give an opinion upon military strategy, it would be heard with the profoundest respect.
And should Mr. Socrates (without the Smith) deliver a lecture, or write a book, what critic so bold as not to pronounce
it more luminous than the logic of Emerson, and more profound than the Orphicism of Alcott. In fact, both Mr. Smith
and Mr. Jones, in the case we have imagined, would derive,
through their own ingenuity, a very material advantage. But
no such ingenuity has been needed in the case of Mr. William
Ellery Channing, who has been befriended by Fate, or the
foresight of his sponsors, and who has *no* Jones or Smith at
the end of his name.

And here, too, a question occurs. There are many people
in the world silly enough to be deceived by appearances.
There are individuals so crude in intellect—so *green*, (if we
may be permitted to employ a word which answers our purpose much better than any other in the language,) so green,
we say, as to imagine, in the absence of any indication to the
contrary, that a volume bearing upon its title-page the name
of William Ellery Channing, must necessarily be the posthumous work of that truly illustrious author, the *sole* William
Ellery Channing of whom any body in the world ever heard.
There are a vast number of uninformed young persons prowl-
ing about our book-shops, who will be raw enough to buy,
and even to read half through this pretty little book, (God
preserve and forgive them!) mistaking it for the composition
of another. But what then? Are not books made, as well as
razors, to sell? The poet's name *is* William Ellery Channing—
is it *not*? And if a man has not a right to the use of his own
name, to the use of what has he a right? And could the poet
have reconciled it to his conscience to have injured the sale of
his own volume by any uncalled-for announcement upon the

title-page, or in a preface, to the effect that he is not his father, but only his father's very intelligent son? To put the case more clearly by reference to our old friends, Mr. Smith and Mr. Jones. Is either Mr. Smith, when mistaken for Socrates, or Mr. Jones, when accosted as Napoleon, bound, by any conceivable species of honor, to inform the whole world—the one, that he is not Socrates, but only Socrates Smith; the other, that he is by no means Napoleon Buonaparte, but only Napoleon Buonaparte Jones?

Graham's Magazine, August 1843

James Fenimore Cooper

The History of the Navy of the United States of America. By J. Fenimore Cooper. Lea and Blanchard, Philadelphia.

IN APPEARING before the public with this History of our
Navy, Mr. Cooper has had two serious difficulties to surmount—one of prejudice, and one of exaggerated anticipation. It cannot be denied that, for many years past, he has
been rapidly sinking in the estimation of his countrymen, and
indeed of all right minded persons. Even his firmest friends
were becoming ashamed of the universality of his cynicism;
and his enemies, ceasing in a measure from open hostility,
have been well content to abide the apparently inevitable self-
ruin which his own unconquerable ill temper was so speedily
bringing about. A flashy succession of ill-conceived and miserably executed literary productions, each more silly than its
predecessor, and wherein the only thing noticeable was the
peevishness of the writer, the only thing amusing his self-conceit—had taught the public to suspect even a radical taint in
the intellect, an absolute and irreparable mental leprosy, rendering it a question whether he ever would or could again
accomplish any thing which should be worthy the attention
of people not positively rabid. In this state of affairs, it was
not at all wonderful that the announcement of a Naval History of the United States, by the author of the attack upon
Sir Walter Scott, was received with apathy and general distrust—with a feeling very different indeed from that which
would have agitated the whole reading world at a similar announcement during the golden days of the celebrated novelist, and once exceedingly popular man.

Among the few, on the other hand, who had better opportunities of penetrating the mystery, and fathoming the extent,
of that obstinate disease of the spleen which had so long
made the author a burden to himself, and an object of compassion to his friends—among those who knew the disorder
not altogether incurable, and who had good reason to rely
firmly upon the innate vigor and elasticity of the constitution—even among these we have noticed a want of proper
consideration in regard to the subject matter of the antici-

pated work—a misconception of the extent and capacities of the theme—which has operated to the temporary disadvantage of the historian.

Mr. Cooper's strength in sea narrative was well known, and justly appreciated; and in a work on Naval History, much was expected of a character very similar to that which had afforded its charm to the "Pilot," and rivetted attention in the "Red Rover." This expectation would have been comparatively well founded had the announcement been that of a Naval Biography. Here, an allowable minuteness of detail would have given vigor and vitality to the narration, and the personal adventures of the several heroes would have been overspread, in the simple discussion of fact with all the warm hues of the most spirit-stirring romance. In no general naval record, however, should we look too confidently for interest, beyond that grave species which is attached to the mere statement of fact. In records of our own marine, especially, we should look for little farther than this. The story of the simple events of our experience (for we are a nation of single ships) must always be deficient in that excitement which is derivable from the unity and majesty of the combined operations of fleets. Here then our sea-history labors under disadvantages not experienced by that of Europe. The tales we have to tell, of detached combat after combat, can form, at best, but a series of monotonous episode, where if the mind seeks, as it will, for connexion, this can only be established by means of a dry and barren mass of documental and statistical detail.

Notwithstanding these difficulties, however, (whose importance we have by no means adequately pointed out) Mr. Cooper has succeeded in writing a book which cannot fail to do him lasting honor, not more in a literary point of view, than as affording evidence of the final triumph of his kindlier and more manly feelings over the promptings of Satan and the spleen. The very preface is redolent of a returning good humor—of a recovered modesty—of a resuscitated common sense. Mr. Cooper is evidently Mr. Cooper once again, and as such we most cordially welcome him home to the good will, and to the affections, of his countrymen. That *he*, in preference to any one, should have written the Naval History of the United States, is a matter about which there is but little difference of opinion; and we rejoice, from the bottom of our heart, that he has arisen to the good work, from the moral death which has so long enwrapped him, while it is yet a convenient season for the undertaking—before the veteran actors in the drama have all passed away from among us— while there is yet many a tongue to tell what the eyes have seen—many a living witness to the gallant and glorious exploits which have had so much to do in the rendering us, and in the preserving us, a free people.

It is not our design, of course, to speak at length of any portion of a History which will speak so very eloquently for itself. The narrative commences with the first settlement by the English, proceeds with some details respecting the earliest achievements of the rival French and British colonies, connected with a clear and rapid survey of the condition of the maritime powers of Europe, and after discussing, in a masterly manner, every momentous event in the annals of our Navy, terminates with the contest of 1812. The war of the Revolution is brought to a close about the middle of the first volume, and the more important subsequent occurrences occupy the remainder of the publication.

The work, as a whole, has, we think, all the great requisites of a proper History—distinctness of narration, rigorous impartiality, an evident anxiety for truth, and a concise philosophical discussion of fact, rather than a shadowy speculation upon motive. Every similar book, as a matter of course, is liable to objection—to cavil—in regard to its detail; and, in the present case, we have heard occasional censures upon which we scarcely think it necessary to comment. Battles, whether by sea or land, (and battles form our staple here) are seldom witnessed by distinct authorities from the same points of observation, and this fact alone is sufficient to account for a thousand immaterial discrepancies.

In regard to style, let us hear Mr. Cooper himself.

"Some of the greatest writers of the age have impaired the dignity of their works, by permitting the peculiarities which have embellished their lighter labors to lessen the severity of manner that more properly distinguishes narratives of truth. This danger has been foreseen in the present instance, though the nature of the subject, which seldom rises to the level of

476 OF AMERICAN AUTHORS

general history, affords a constant temptation to offend. A middle course has been adopted, which, it is hoped, while some defects of execution may probably be detected, will be found on the whole to be suited to a recital of facts, in the familiar form that, in a measure, the incidents have demanded."

The mere English of our author was never, at any period, remarkable for precision of arrangement, and however easily, in a work of pure romance, such defect may be disregarded, we must own that it derogates very materially from the beauty of an otherwise excellent historic style. In the volumes before us sentences occur, by far too frequently, where positive ambiguity arises from sheer negligence in regard to the ordinary proprieties of grammar.

"Republicanism itself is brought into disrepute, in denying the just rewards of long services to officers, by attaching to it the weakness of a neglect of incentives, an ignorance on the subject of the general laws of discipline, and the odium of injustice. It is by forgetting the latter quality, more through the indifference of a divided power, than from any other cause, that republics have obtained their established character of being ungrateful."

Here is great confusion of expression. By "the latter quality" *justice* is intended, while *in*justice is implied.

"A territorial aristocracy, promotion, in both the army and the navy, is the inevitable fruit of favor, or of personal rank."

This sentence, as it stands, is utterly unintelligible, and can only be comprehended at all by placing before it the words immediately antecedent—which are "The nature of the English government is no secret." It now appears that the English government is "a territorial aristocracy." But every properly constructed sentence should have within itself the means of its own (grammatical) comprehension.

"The man who, refusing to adopt remedies that he believes unsuited to his constitution, is discreet, when he carries his system so far as to forget to look for others to supply their places, becomes careless and culpable."

This exceedingly ambiguous proposition is rendered perfectly plain by merely a different arrangement of the same words.

"The man who is discreet in refusing to adopt remedies that he believes unsuited to his constitution, becomes careless and culpable when he carries his system so far as to forget to look for others to supply their places." But upon this topic quite enough has been said.

Mr. Cooper's observations on the subject of our general marine policy are, we think, among the very best portions of his book. They are strikingly comprehensive in view, and evince a profound knowledge of the true incentives of human action. Our limits will permit us to give but a small portion of his remarks.

"A careful review of these facts and principles must satisfy all who study the subject, that the United States of America have never resorted to the means necessary to develope, or even in a limited sense, to employ their own naval resources. As a consequence, they have never yet enjoyed the advantage of possessing a powerful marine in time of war, or have felt its influence in sustaining their negotiations, and in supporting their national rights in a time of peace. As yet the ships of America have done little more than show the world what the republic might do with its energies duly directed, and its resources properly developed, by demonstrating the national aptitude for this species of warfare.

"But the probationary period of the American marine is passing away, and the body of the people are beginning to look forward to the appearance of their fleets on the ocean. It is no longer thought there is an unfitness in the republic's possessing heavy ships; and the opinion of the country in this, as in other respects, is slowly rising to the level of its wants. Still many lingering prejudices remain in the public mind, in connexion with this all important subject, and some that threaten the service with serious injury. Of these, the most prominent are, the mode in which the active vessels are employed; a neglect of the means of creating seamen for the public service; the fact that there is no force in commission on the American coast; the substitution of money for pride and self-respect, as the aim of military men; and the impairing of discipline, and lessening the deference for the justice of the state, by the denial of rank.

"Under the present system of employing the public vessels,

none of the peculiar experience that belongs to the higher objects of the profession is obtained. While ships may be likened to regiments as regards the necessity of manœuvring together, there is one important feature in which they are totally dissimilar. It may be pretty safely thought that one disciplined regiment will march as far, endure as much, and occupy its station as certainly as another, but no such calculation can be made on ships. The latter are machines, and their qualities may be improved by human ingenuity, when their imperfections have been ascertained by experiment. Intelligent comparisons are the first step in this species of improvement.

"It will be clear to the dullest mind, that the evolutions of a fleet, and, in a greater or less degree, its success, must be dependent on the qualities of its poorest vessels; since its best cannot abandon their less fortunate consorts to the enemy. The naval history of the world abounds with instances, in which the efforts of the first sea-captains have been frustrated by the defects of a portion of the ships under their command. To keep a number of vessels in compact order, to cause them to preserve their weatherly position in gales and adverse winds, and to bring them all as near as possible up to the standard that shall be formed by the most judicious and careful commander, is one of the highest aims of naval experience. On the success of such efforts depend the results of naval evolutions more frequently than on any dexterity in fighting guns. An efficient fleet can no more be formed without practice in squadrons, than an efficient army without evolutions in brigades. By not keeping ships in squadrons, there will also be less emulation, and consequently less improvement.

"Under the present system three principal stations are maintained; two in the Atlantic, and one in the Mediterranean. On neither of these stations would the presence of a vessel larger than a sloop of war be necessary, on ordinary occasions, provided a force of heavy ships could periodically and unexpectedly appear on all. It is seldom that a single ship of the line is required on any service; and it is certain that a solitary two-decked vessel could have no great influence on those important interests which it is the practice of the rest of Christendom to refer to the agency of fleets. By putting in commission six or eight two-decked ships, and by causing them to appear, from time to time, on all the more important stations this side of the two great southern capes, the country, at no material additional cost, would obtain the several objects of practice in fleets, of comparative trials of the qualities of the most important class of vessels in the navy, of a higher state of discipline, and of a vast improvement in the habits of subordination on the part of commanders, a defect that all experience shows is peculiar to the desultory mode of service now in use, and which has produced more naval disasters in the world than probably any other one cause. In a word, the principal ends of a navy can no more be obtained, by the services of single ships, than wars can be decided by armies cut up into battalions."

Burton's Gentleman's Magazine, July 1839

Wyandotté, or the Hutted Knoll. A tale, by the author of "The Pathfinder," "Deerslayer," "Last of the Mohicans," "Pioneers," "Prairie," &c., &c. Philadelphia, Lea & Blanchard.

WYANDOTTÉ, or The Hutted Knoll" is, in its general features, precisely similar to the novels enumerated in the title. It is a forest subject; and, when we say this, we give assurance that the story is a good one; for Mr. Cooper has never been known to fail, either in the forest or upon the sea. The interest, as usual, has no reference to *plot*, of which, indeed, our novelist seems altogether regardless, or incapable, but depends, first, upon the nature of the theme; secondly, upon a Robinson-Crusoe-like detail in its management; and thirdly, upon the frequently repeated portraiture of the half-civilized Indian. In saying that the interest depends, *first*, upon the nature of the theme, we mean to suggest that this theme—life in the Wilderness—is one of intrinsic and universal interest, appealing to the heart of man in all phases; a theme, like that of life upon the ocean, so unfailingly omni-prevalent in its power of arresting and absorbing attention, that while success or popularity is, with such a subject, expected as a matter of course, a failure might be properly regarded as conclusive evidence of imbecility on the part of the author. The two theses in question have been handled *usque ad nauseam*—and this through the instinctive perception of the universal interest which appertains to them. A writer, distrustful of his powers, can scarcely do better than discuss either one or the other. A man of genius will rarely, and should never, undertake either; first, because both are excessively hackneyed; and, secondly, because the reader never fails, in forming his opinion of a book, to make discount, either wittingly or unwittingly, for that intrinsic interest which is inseparable from the subject and independent of the manner in which it is treated. Very few and very dull indeed are those who do not instantaneously perceive the distinction; and thus there are two great classes of fictions,—a popular and widely circulated class, read with pleasure, but without admiration—in which the author is lost or forgotten; or remembered, if at all, with something very nearly akin to contempt; and then, a class not so popular, nor so widely diffused, in which, at every paragraph, arises a distinctive and highly pleasurable interest, springing from our perception and appreciation of the skill employed, of the genius evinced in the composition. After perusal of the one class, we think solely of the book—after reading the other, chiefly of the author. The former class leads to popularity—the latter to fame. In the former case, the books sometimes live, while the authors usually die; in the latter, even when the works perish, the man survives. Among American writers of the less generally circulated, but more worthy and more artistical fictions, we may mention Mr. Brockden Brown, Mr. John Neal, Mr. Simms, Mr. Hawthorne; at the head of the more popular division we may place Mr. Cooper.

"The Hutted Knoll," without pretending to detail facts, gives a narrative of fictitious events, similar, in nearly all respects, to occurrences which actually happened during the opening scenes of the Revolution, and at other epochs of our history. It pictures the dangers, difficulties, and distresses of a large family, living, completely insulated, in the forest. The tale commences with a description of the "region which lies in the angle formed by the junction of the Mohawk with the Hudson, extending as far south as the line of Pennsylvania, and west to the verge of that vast rolling plain which composes Western New York"—a region of which the novelist has already frequently written, and the whole of which, with a trivial exception, was a wilderness before the Revolution. Within this district, and on a creek running into the Unadilla, a certain Captain Willoughby purchases an estate, or "patent," and there retires, with his family and dependents, to pass the close of his life in agricultural pursuits. He has been an officer in the British army, but, after serving many years, has sold his commission, and purchased one for his only son, Robert, who alone does not accompany the party into the forest. This party consists of the captain himself; his wife; his daughter, Beulah; an adopted daughter, Maud Meredith; an invalid sergeant, Joyce, who had served under the captain; a Presbyterian preacher, Mr. Woods; a Scotch mason, Jamie Allen; an Irish laborer, Michael O'Hearn; a Connecticut man, Joel Strides; four negroes, Old Plin and Young Plin, Big Smash and Little Smash; eight axe-men; a house-carpenter; a millwright, &c., &c. Besides these, a Tuscarora Indian called Nick, or *Wyandotté*, accompanies the expedition. This Indian, who figures largely in the story, and gives it its title, may be considered as the principal character—the one chiefly elaborated. He is an outcast from his tribe, has been known to Captain Willoughby for thirty years, and is a compound of all the good and bad qualities which make up the character of the half-civilized Indian. He does not remain with the settlers; but appears and re-appears at intervals upon the scene.

Nearly the whole of the first volume is occupied with a detailed account of the estate purchased, (which is termed "The Hutted Knoll" from a natural mound upon which the principal house is built) and of the progressive arrangements and improvements. Toward the close of the volume the Revolution commences; and the party at the "Knoll" are besieged by a band of savages and "rebels," with whom an understanding exists, on the part of Joel Strides, the Yankee. This traitor, instigated by the hope of possessing Captain Willoughby's estate, should it be confiscated, brings about a series of defections from the party of the settlers, and finally, deserting himself, reduces the whole number to six or seven, capable of bearing arms. Captain Willoughby resolves, however, to defend his post. His son, at this juncture, pays him a clandestine visit, and, endeavoring to reconnoitre the position of the Indians, is made captive. The captain, in an attempt at rescue, is murdered by Wyandotté, whose vindictive passions had been aroused by ill-timed allusions, on the part of Willoughby, to floggings previously inflicted, by his orders, upon the Indian. Wyandotté, however, having satisfied his personal vengeance, is still the ally of the settlers. He guides Maud, who is beloved by Robert, to the hut in which the latter is confined, and effects his escape. Aroused by this escape, the Indians precipitate their attack upon the Knoll, which, through the previous treachery of Strides in ill-hanging a gate, is immediately carried. Mrs. Willoughby, Beulah, and others of the party, are killed. Maud is secreted and thus saved by Wyandotté. At the last moment, when all is apparently lost, a reinforcement appears, under command of Evert Beekman, the husband of Beulah; and the completion of the massacre is prevented. Woods, the preacher, had left the Knoll, and made his way through the enemy, to inform Beekman of the dilemma of his friends. Maud and Robert Willoughby are, of course, happily married. The concluding scene of the novel shows us Wyandotté repenting the murder of Willoughby, and converted to Christianity through the agency of Woods.

It will be at once seen that there is nothing *original* in this story. On the contrary, it is even excessively common-place. The lover, for example, rescued from captivity by the mistress; the Knoll carried through the treachery of an inmate; and the salvation of the besieged, at the very last moment, by a reinforcement arriving, in consequence of a message borne to a friend by one of the besieged, without the cognizance of the others; these, we say, are incidents which have been the common property of every novelist since the invention of letters. And as for *plot*, there has been no attempt at any thing of the kind. The tale is a mere succession of events, scarcely any one of which has any necessary dependence upon any one other. Plot, however, is, at best, an artificial effect, requiring, like music, not only a natural bias, but long cultivation of taste for its full appreciation; some of the finest narratives in the world—"Gil-Blas" and "Robinson Crusoe," for example—have been written without its employment; and "The Hutted Knoll," like all the sea and forest novels of Cooper, has been made deeply interesting, although depending upon this peculiar source of interest not at all. Thus the absence of plot can never be critically regarded as a *defect*; although its judicious use, in all cases aiding and in no case injuring other effects, must be regarded as of a very high order of merit.

There are one or two points, however, in the mere *conduct* of the story now before us, which may, perhaps, be considered as defective. For instance, there is too much *obviousness* in all that appertains to the hanging of the large gate. In more than a dozen instances, Mrs. Willoughby is made to allude to the delay in the hanging; so that the reader is too positively and pointedly forced to perceive that this delay is to result in the capture of the Knoll. As we are never in doubt of the fact, we feel diminished interest when it actually happens. A single vague allusion, well-managed, would have been in the true artistical spirit.

Again; we see too plainly, from the first, that Beekman is to marry Beulah, and that Robert Willoughby is to marry Maud. The killing of Beulah, of Mrs. Willoughby, and Jamie Allen, produces, too, a painful impression which does not properly appertain to the right fiction. Their deaths affect us as revolting and supererogatory; since the purposes of the story are not thereby furthered in any regard. To Willoughby's murder, however distressing, the reader makes no similar objection; merely because in his decease is fulfilled a species of poetical justice. We may observe here, nevertheless, that his repeated references to his flogging the Indian seem unnatural, because we have otherwise no reason to think him a fool, or a madman, and these references, under the circumstances, are absolutely insensate. We object, also, to the manner in which the general interest is dragged out, or suspended. The besieging party are kept before the Knoll so long, while so little is done, and so many opportunities of action are lost, that the reader takes it for granted that nothing of consequence will occur—that the besieged will be finally delivered. He gets so accustomed to the presence of danger that its excitement, at length, departs. The action is not sufficiently rapid. There is too much procrastination. There is too much mere talk for talk's sake. The interminable discussions between Woods and Captain Willoughby are, perhaps, the worst feature of the book, for they have not even the merit of referring to the matters on hand. In general, there is quite too much colloquy for the purpose of manifesting character, and too little for the explanation of motive. The characters of the drama would have been better made out by action; while the motives to action, the reasons for the different courses of conduct adopted by the *dramatis personæ*, might have been made to proceed more satisfactorily from their own mouths, in casual conversations, than from that of the author in person. To conclude our remarks upon the head of ill-conduct in the story, we may mention occasional incidents of the merest melodramatic absurdity: as, for example, at page 156, of the second volume, where "Willoughby had an arm round the waist of Maud, and bore her forward with a rapidity to which her own strength was entirely unequal." We may be permitted to doubt whether a young lady of sound health and limbs, exists, within the limits of Christendom, who could not run faster, on her own proper feet, for any considerable distance, than she could be carried upon *one arm* of either the Cretan Milo or of the Hercules Farnese.

On the other hand, it would be easy to designate many particulars which are admirably handled. The love of Maud Meredith for Robert Willoughby is painted with exquisite skill and truth. The incident of the tress of hair and box is naturally and effectively conceived. A fine collateral interest is thrown over the whole narrative by the connection of the theme with that of the Revolution; and, especially, there is an excellent dramatic point, at page 124 of the second volume, where Wyandotté, remembering the stripes inflicted upon him by Captain Willoughby, is about to betray him to his foes, when his purpose is arrested by a casual glimpse, through the forest, of the hut which contains Mrs. Willoughby, who had preserved the life of the Indian, by inoculation for the small-pox.

In the depicting of character, Mr. Cooper has been unusually successful in "Wyandotté." One or two of his personages, to be sure, must be regarded as little worth. Robert Willoughby, like most novel heroes, is a nobody; that is to say, there is nothing about him which may be looked upon as distinctive. Perhaps he is rather silly than otherwise; as, for instance, when he confuses all his father's arrangements for his concealment, and bursts into the room before Strides—afterward insisting upon accompanying that person to the Indian encampment, without any possible or impossible object. Woods, the parson, is a sad bore, upon the Dominie Sampson plan, and is, moreover, caricatured. Of Captain Willoughby we have already spoken—he is too often on stilts. Evert Beekman and Beulah are merely episodical. Joyce is nothing in the world but Corporal Trim—or, rather, Corporal Trim and water. Jamie Allen, with his prate about Catholicism, is insufferable. But Mrs. Willoughby, the humble, shrinking, womanly wife, whose whole existence centres in her affections, is worthy of Mr. Cooper. Maud Meredith is still better. In fact, we know no female portraiture, even in Scott, which surpasses her; and yet the world has been given to understand, by the enemies of the novelist, that he is incapable of depicting a woman. Joel Strides will be recognized by all who are conversant with his general prototypes of Connecticut. Michael O'Hearn, the County Leitrim man, is an Irishman all over, and his portraiture abounds in humor; as, for example, at page 31, of the first volume, where he has a difficulty with a skiff, not being able to account for its revolving upon its own axis, instead of moving forward! or, at page 132, where, during divine service, to exclude at least a portion of the heretical doctrine, he stops *one* of his ears with his thumb; or, at page 195, where a passage occurs so much to our purpose that we will be pardoned for quoting it in full. Captain Willoughby is drawing his son up through a window, from his enemies below. The assistants, placed at a distance from this window to avoid observation from without, are ignorant of what burthen is at the end of the rope:

"The men did as ordered, raising their load from the ground a foot or two at a time. In this manner the burthen approached, yard after yard, until it was evidently drawing near the window.

" 'It 's the captain hoisting up the big baste of a hog, for provisioning the hoose again a saige,' whispered Mike to the negroes, who grinned as they tugged; 'and, when the craitur squails, see to it, that ye do not squail yourselves.'

"At that moment, the head and shoulders of a man appeared at the window. Mike let go the rope, seized a chair, and was about to knock the intruder upon the head; but the captain arrested the blow.

" 'It 's one o' the vagabone Injins that has undermined the hog and come up in its stead,' roared Mike.

" 'It 's my son,' said the captain; 'see that you are silent and secret.' "

The negroes are, without exception, admirably drawn. The Indian, Wyandotté, however, is the great feature of the book, and is, in every respect, equal to the previous Indian creations of the author of "The Pioneer." Indeed, we think this "forest gentleman" superior to the other noted heroes of his kind— the heroes which have been immortalized by our novelist. His keen sense of the distinction, in his own character, between the chief, Wyandotté, and the drunken vagabond, Sassy Nick; his chivalrous delicacy toward Maud, in never disclosing to her that knowledge of her real feelings toward Robert Willoughby, which his own Indian intuition had discovered; his enduring animosity toward Captain Willoughby, softened, and for thirty years delayed, through his gratitude to the wife; and then, the vengeance consummated, his pity for that wife conflicting with his exultation at the deed—these, we say, are all traits of a lofty excellence indeed. Perhaps the most effective passage in the book, and that which, most distinctively, brings out the character of the Tuscarora, is to be found at pages 50, 51, 52 and 53 of the second volume, where, for some trivial misdemeanor, the captain threatens to make use of the whip. The manner in which the Indian *harps* upon the threat, returning to it again and again, in every variety of phrase, forms one of the finest pieces of mere character-painting with which we have any acquaintance.

The most obvious and most unaccountable faults of "The Hutted Knoll," are those which appertain to the *style*—to the mere grammatical construction;—for, in other and more important particulars of style, Mr. Cooper, of late days, has made a very manifest improvement. His sentences, however, are arranged with an awkwardness so remarkable as to be matter of absolute astonishment, when we consider the education of the author, and his long and continual practice with the pen. In minute descriptions of localities, any verbal inaccuracy, or confusion, becomes a source of vexation and misunderstanding, detracting very much from the pleasure of perusal; and in these inaccuracies "Wyandotté" abounds. Although, for instance, we carefully read and re-read that portion of the narrative which details the situation of the Knoll, and the construction of the buildings and walls about it, we were forced to proceed with the story without any exact or definite impressions upon the subject. Similar difficulties, from similar causes, occur *passim* throughout the book. For example: at page 41, vol. I:

"The Indian gazed at the house, with that fierce intentness which sometimes glared, in a manner that had got to be, in its ordinary aspects, dull and besotted." This it is utterly impossible to comprehend. We presume, however, the intention is to say that although the Indian's ordinary manner (of gazing) had "got to be" dull and besotted, he occasionally gazed with an intentness that glared, and that he did so in the instance in question. The "got to be" is atrocious—the whole sentence no less so.

Here, at page 9, vol. I., is something excessively vague: "Of the latter character is the face of most of that region which lies in the angle formed by the junction of the Mohawk with the Hudson," &c. &c. The Mohawk, joining the Hudson, forms *two* angles, of course,—an acute and an obtuse one; and, without farther explanation, it is difficult to say which is intended.

At page 55, vol. I., we read:—"The captain, owing to his English education, had avoided straight lines, and formal paths; giving to the little spot the improvement on nature which is a consequence of embellishing her works without destroying them. On each side of this lawn was an orchard, thrifty and young, and which *were* already beginning to show signs of putting forth their blossoms." Here we are tautologically informed that improvement is a consequence of embellishment, and supererogatorily told that the rule holds good only where the embellishment is not accompanied by destruction. Upon the "each orchard *were*" it is needless to comment.

At page 30, vol. I., is something similar, where Strides is represented as "never doing any thing that required a particle more than the exertion and strength that were absolutely nec-

essary to effect his object." Did Mr. C. ever hear of any labor
that *required* more exertion than was *necessary*? He means to
say that Strides exerted himself no farther than was necessary—that 's all.

At page 59, vol. I., we find this sentence—"He was advancing by the only road that was ever traveled by the stranger as
he approached the Hut; or, he came up the valley." This is
merely a vagueness of speech. "Or" is intended to imply "that
is to say." The whole would be clearer thus—"He was advancing by the valley—the only road traveled by a stranger
approaching the Hut." We have here sixteen words, instead
of Mr. Cooper's twenty-five.

At page 8, vol. II., is an unpardonable awkwardness, although an awkwardness strictly grammatical. "I was a favorite, I believe, with, certainly was much petted by, both."
Upon this we need make no farther observation. It speaks for
itself.

We are aware, however, that there is a certain air of unfairness, in thus quoting detached passages, for animadversion of
this kind; for, however strictly at random our quotations may
really be, we have, of course, no means of proving the fact to
our readers; and there are *no* authors, from whose works individual inaccurate sentences may not be culled. But we mean
to say that Mr. Cooper, no doubt through haste or neglect,
is *remarkably* and *especially* inaccurate, as a general rule; and,
by way of demonstrating this assertion, we will dismiss our
extracts at random, and discuss some entire page of his composition. More than this: we will endeavor to select that particular page upon which it might naturally be supposed he
would bestow the most careful attention. The reader will say
at once—"Let this be his *first* page—the first page of his
Preface." This page, then, shall be taken of course.

"The history of the borders is filled with legends of the
sufferings of isolated families, during the troubled scenes of
colonial warfare. Those which we now offer to the reader, are
distinctive in many of their leading facts, if not rigidly true in
the details. The first alone is necessary to the legitimate objects of fiction."

"*Abounds* with legends," would be better than "is filled
with legends;" for it is clear that if the history were *filled* with

legends, it would be all legend and no history. The word "of," too, occurs, in the first sentence, with an unpleasant frequency. The *"those"* commencing the second sentence, grammatically refers to the noun "scenes," immediately preceding, but is intended for "legends." The adjective *"distinctive"* is vaguely and altogether improperly employed. Mr. C. we believe means to say, merely, that although the details of his legends may not be strictly true, facts similar to his leading ones have actually occurred. By use of the word *"distinctive,"* however, he has contrived to convey a meaning nearly converse. In saying that his legend is *"distinctive"* in many of the leading facts, he has said what he, clearly, did not wish to say—viz.: that his legend contained facts which distinguished it from all other legends—in other words, facts never before discussed in other legends, and belonging peculiarly to his own. That Mr. C. *did* mean what we suppose, is rendered evident by the third sentence—"The first alone is necessary to the legitimate objects of fiction." This third sentence itself, however, is very badly constructed. "The first" can refer, grammatically, only to "facts;" but no such reference is intended. If we ask the question—what is meant by "the first?"—*what* "alone is necessary to the legitimate objects of fiction?"—the natural reply is, "that facts similar to the leading ones have actually happened." This circumstance is alone to be cared for—this consideration "alone is necessary to the legitimate objects of fiction."

"One of the misfortunes of a nation is to hear nothing besides its own praises." This is the fourth sentence, and is by no means lucid. The design is to say that individuals composing a nation, and living altogether within the national bounds, hear from each other only praises of the nation, and that this is a misfortune to the individuals, since it misleads them in regard to the actual condition of the nation. Here it will be seen that, to convey the intended idea, we have been forced to make distinction between the nation and its individual members; for it is evident that a nation is considered as such only in reference to other nations; and thus, *as a nation*, it hears *very* much "besides its own praises;" that is to say, it hears the detractions of other rival nations. In endeavoring to compel his meaning within the compass of a brief sentence, Mr. Cooper has completely sacrificed its intelligibility.

The fifth sentence runs thus:—"Although the American Revolution was probably as just an effort as was ever made by a people to resist the first inroads of oppression, the cause had its evil aspects, as well as all other human struggles."

The American Revolution is here improperly called an "effort." The effort was the cause, of which the Revolution was the result. A rebellion is an "effort" to effect a revolution. An "inroad of oppression" involves an untrue metaphor; for "inroad" appertains to *agg*ression, to attack, to active assault. "The cause had its evil aspects, as well as all other human struggles," implies that the cause had not only its evil aspects, but had, also, all other human struggles. If the words must be retained at all, they should be thus arranged—"The cause like [or as well as] all other human struggles, had its evil aspects;" or better thus—"The cause had its evil aspect, as have all human struggles." "Other" is superfluous.

The sixth sentence is thus written:—"We have been so much accustomed to hear every thing extolled, of late years, that could be dragged into the remotest connection with that great event, and the principles which led to it, that there is danger of overlooking truth in a pseudo patriotism." The "of late years," here, should follow the "accustomed," or precede the "We have been;" and the Greek "pseudo" is objectionable, since its exact equivalent is to be found in the English "false." "Spurious" would be better, perhaps, than either.

Inadvertences such as these sadly disfigure the style of "The Hutted Knoll;" and every true friend of its author must regret his inattention to the minor morals of the Muse. But these "minor morals," it may be said, are trifles at best. Perhaps so. At all events, we should never have thought of dwelling so pertinaciously upon the unessential demerits of "Wyandotté," could we have discovered any more momentous upon which to comment.

Graham's Magazine, November 1843

Rufus Dawes

As a poet," says Mr. Griswold, in his late "Poets and Poetry of America," "the standing of Mr. Dawes is as yet unsettled; there being a wide difference of opinion respecting his writings." The *width* of this difference is apparent; and, while to many it is matter for wonder, to those who have the interest of our Literature at heart, it is, more properly, a source of mortification and regret. That the author in question has long enjoyed what we term "a high poetical reputation," cannot be denied; and in no manner is this point more strikingly evinced than in the choice of his works, some two years since, by one of our most enterprising publishers, as the *initial* volume of a series, the avowed object of which was the setting forth, in the best array of paper, type and pictorial embellishment, the *élite* of the American poets. As a writer of occasional stanzas he has been long before the public; always eliciting, from a great variety of sources, *unqualified* commendation. With the exception of a solitary remark, adventured by ourselves in "A Chapter on Autography," there has been no written dissent from the universal opinion in his favor— the universal *apparent* opinion. Mr. Griswold's observation must be understood, we presume, as referring to the *conversational* opinion upon this topic; or it is not impossible that he holds in view the difference between the criticism of the newspaper paragraphs and the private comment of the educated and intelligent. Be this as it may, the rapidly growing "reputation" of our poet was much enhanced by the publication of his first compositions "of length," and attained its climax, we believe, upon the public recitation, by himself, of a tragic drama, in five acts, entitled "Athenia of Damascus," to a large assembly of admiring and applauding *friends*, gathered together for the occasion in one of the halls of the University of New York.

This popular decision, so frequent and so public, in regard to the poetical ability of Mr. Dawes, might be received as evidence of his actual merit (and by thousands it *is* so received) were it not too scandalously at variance with a species of criticism which *will not* be resisted—with the perfectly simple precepts of the very commonest common sense. The peculiarity of Mr. Griswold's observation has induced us to make inquiry into the true character of the volume to which we have before alluded, and which embraces, we believe, the chief portion of the published verse-compositions of its author.* This inquiry has but resulted in the confirmation of our previous opinion; and we now hesitate not to say, that no man in America has been more shamefully over-estimated than the one who forms the subject of this article. We say shamefully; for, though a better day is now dawning upon our literary interests, and a laudation so indiscriminate will never be sanctioned again—the laudation in this instance, as it stands upon record, must be regarded as a laughable although bitter satire upon the general zeal, accuracy and independence of that critical spirit which, but a few years ago, pervaded and degraded the land.

In what we shall say we have no intention of being profound. Here is a case in which any thing like analysis would be utterly thrown away. Our purpose (which is truth) will be more fully answered by an unvarnished exposition of fact. It appears to us, indeed, that in excessive *generalization* lies one of the leading errors of a criticism employed upon a poetical literature so immature as our own. We rhapsodize rather than discriminate; delighting more in the dictation or discussion of a principle, than in its particular and methodical application. The wildest and most erratic effusion of the Muse, not utterly worthless, will be found more or less indebted to *method* for whatever of value it embodies; and we shall discover, conversely, that, in any analysis of even this wildest effusion, we labor without method only to labor without end. There is little reason for that vagueness of comment which, of late, we so pertinaciously affect, and which has been brought into fashion, no doubt, through the proverbial facility and security of merely general remark. In regard to the leading principles of true poesy, these, we think, stand not at all in need of the elucidation hourly wasted upon them. Founded in the unerring instincts of our nature, they are enduring and immutable. In a rigid scrutiny of any number of directly conflicting opin-

*"Geraldine," "Athenia of Damascus," and Miscellaneous Poems. By Rufus Dawes. Published by Samuel Colman, New York.

ions upon a poetical topic, we will not fail to perceive that principles identical in every important point have been, in each opinion, either asserted, or intimated, or unwittingly allowed an influence. The differences of decision arose simply from those of application; and from such variety in the applied, rather than in the conceived idea, sprang, undoubtedly, the absurd distinctions of the "schools."

"Geraldine" is the title of the first and longest poem in the volume before us. It embraces some three hundred and fifty stanzas—the whole being a most servile imitation of the "Don Juan" of Lord Byron. The outrageous absurdity of the systematic *digression* in the British original, was so managed as to form not a little portion of its infinite interest and humor; and the fine discrimination of the writer pointed out to him a limit beyond which he never ventured with this tantalizing species of drollery. "Geraldine" may be regarded, however, as a simple embodiment of the whole soul of digression. It is a mere mass of irrelevancy, amid the mad *farrago* of which we detect with difficulty even the faintest vestige of a narrative, and where the continuous lapse from impertinence to impertinence is seldom justified by any shadow of appositeness or even of the commonest relation.

To afford the reader any proper conception of the *story* is of course a matter of difficulty; we must content ourselves with a mere outline of the general conduct. This we shall endeavor to give without indulgence in those feelings of risibility stirred up in us by the primitive perusal. We shall rigorously avoid every species of exaggeration, and confine ourselves, with perfect honesty, to the conveyance of a distinct image.

"Geraldine," then, opens with some four or five stanzas descriptive of a sylvan scene in America. We could, perhaps, render Mr. Dawes' poetical reputation no greater service than by the quotation of these simple verses in full.

I know a spot where poets fain would dwell,
    To gather flowers and food for after thought,
As bees draw honey from the rose's cell,
    To hive among the treasures they have wrought;
And there a cottage from a sylvan screen
Sent up a curling smoke amidst the green.

Around that hermit home of quietude
  The elm trees whispered with the summer air,
And nothing ever ventured to intrude
  But happy birds that caroled wildly there,
Or honey-laden harvesters that flew
Humming away to drink the morning dew.

Around the door the honey-suckle climbed
  And Multa-flora spread her countless roses,
And never poet sang nor minstrel rhymed
  Romantic scene where happiness reposes,
Sweeter to sense than that enchanting dell
Where home-sick memory fondly loves to dwell.

Beneath a mountain's brow the cottage stood,
  Hard by a shelving lake whose pebbled bed
Was skirted by the drapery of a wood
  That hung its festoon foliage over head,
Where wild deer came at eve unharmed, to drink,
While moonlight threw their shadows from the brink.

The green earth heaved her giant waves around,
  Where, through the mountain vista, one vast height
Towered heavenward without peer, his forehead bound
  With gorgeous clouds, at times of changeful light,
While, far below, the lake in bridal rest
Slept with his glorious picture on her breast.

Here is an air of quietude in good keeping with the theme;
the "giant waves" in the last stanza redeem it from much exception otherwise; and perhaps we need say nothing at all of
the suspicious-looking compound "mult*a*-flora." Had Mr.
Dawes always written even nearly so well, we should have
been spared to-day the painful task imposed upon us by a
stern sense of our critical duty. These passages are followed
immediately by an address or invocation to "Peerless America," including apostrophes to Allston and Claude Lorraine.
We now learn the name of the tenant of the cottage, which
is *Wilton*, and ascertain that he has an only daughter. A single
stanza quoted at this juncture will aid the reader's conception

of the queer tone of philosophical rhapsody with which the
poem teems, and some specimen of which is invariably made
to follow each little modicum of incident.

> How like the heart is to an instrument
>   A touch can wake to gladness or to wo!
> How like the circumambient element
>   The spirit with its undulating flow!
> The heart—the soul—Oh, Mother Nature, why
> This universal bond of sympathy.

After two pages much in this manner, we are told that *Geraldine* is the name of the maiden, and are informed, with
comparatively little circumlocution, of her character. She is
beautiful, and kind-hearted, and somewhat romantic, and
"some thought her reason touched"—for which we have little
disposition to blame them. There is now much about Kant
and Fichte; about Schelling, Hegel and Cousin, (which latter
is made to rhyme with *gang*;) about Milton, Byron, Homer,
Spinoza, David Hume and Mirabeau; and a good deal, too,
about the *scribendi cacoëthes*, in which an evident misunderstanding of the quantity of *cacoëthes* brings, again, into very
disagreeable suspicion the writer's cognizance of the Latin
tongue. At this point we may refer, also, to such absurdities
as

> Truth with her thousand-folded robe of error
> Close shut in her *sarcophagi* of terror—

And

> Where *candelabri* silver the white halls.

Now, no one is presupposed to be cognizant of any language
beyond his own; to be ignorant of Latin is no crime; to pretend a knowledge is beneath contempt; and the pretender will
attempt in vain to utter or to write two consecutive phrases
of a foreign idiom, without betraying his deficiency to those
who are conversant.

At page 39, there is some prospect of a progress in the
story. Here we are introduced to a Mr. Acus and his fair
daughter, Miss Alice.

> Acus had been a dashing Bond street tailor
> Some few short years before, who took his measures
> So carefully he always cut the jailor
> And filled his coffers with exhaustless treasures;
> Then with his wife, a son, and three fair daughters,
> He sunk the goose and straightway crossed the waters.

His residence is in the immediate vicinity of Wilton. The daughter, Miss Alice, who is said to be quite a belle, is enamored of one Waldron, a foreigner, a lion, and a gentleman of questionable reputation. His character (which for our life and soul we cannot comprehend) is given within the space of some forty or fifty stanzas, made to include, at the same time, an essay on motives, deduced from the text " whatever is must be," and illuminated by a long note at the end of the poem, wherein the *systime* (quere *systéme?*) *de la Nature* is sturdily attacked. Let us speak the truth: this note (and the whole of them, for there are many,) may be regarded as a glorious specimen of the concentrated essence of rigmarole, and, to say nothing of their utter absurdity *per se*, are so ludicrously uncalled-for, and grotesquely out of place, that we found it impossible to refrain, during their perusal, from a most unbecoming and uproarious guffaw. We will be pardoned for giving a specimen—selecting it for its brevity.

> Reason, he deemed, could measure every thing,
>> And reason told him that there was a law
> Of mental action which must ever fling
>> A death-bolt at all faith, and this he saw
> Was Transference. (14)

Turning to Note 14, we read thus—

"If any one has a curiosity to look into this subject, (does Mr. Dawes *really* think any one so great a fool?) and wishes to see how far the force of reasoning and analysis may carry him, independently of revelation, I would suggest (thank you, sir,) such inquiries as the following:

"Whether the first Philosophy, considered in relation to Physics, was first in time?

"How far our moral perceptions have been influenced by natural phenomena?

"How far our metaphysical notions of cause and effect are attributable to the transference of notions connected with logical language?"

And all this in a poem about Acus, a tailor!

Waldron prefers, unhappily, Geraldine to Alice, and Geraldine returns his love, exciting thus the deep indignation of the neglected fair one,

> whom love and jealousy bear up
> To mingle poison in her rival's cup.

Miss A. has among her adorers one of the genus loafer, whose appellation, not improperly, is Bore. B. is acquainted with a milliner—the milliner of the disconsolate lady.

> She made this milliner her friend, who swore,
> To work her full revenge through Mr. Bore.

And now says the poet—

> I leave your sympathetic fancies,
> To fill the outline of this pencil sketch.

This filling has been, with us at least, a matter of no little difficulty. We believe, however, that the affair is intended to run thus:—Waldron is enticed to some vile sins by Bore, and the knowledge of these, on the part of Alice, places the former gentleman in her power.

We are now introduced to a *fête champêtre* at the residence of Acus, who, by the way, has a son, Clifford, a suitor to Geraldine with the approbation of her father—that good old gentleman, for whom our sympathies were excited in the beginning of things, being influenced by the consideration that this scion of the house of the tailor will inherit a plum. The worst of the whole is, however, that the romantic Geraldine, who should have known better, and who loves Waldron, loves also the young knight of the shears. The consequence is a rencontre of the rival suitors at the *fête champêtre*; Waldron knocking his antagonist on the head, and throwing him into the lake. The murderer, as well as we can make out the narrative, now joins a piratical band, among whom he alternately cuts throats and sings songs of his own composition. In the mean time the deserted Geraldine mourns alone, till, upon a certain day,

> A shape stood by her like a thing of air—
> She started—Waldron's haggard face was there.
>
> .   .   .   .   .   .
>
> He laid her gently down, of sense bereft,
>   And sunk his picture on her bosom's snow,
> And close beside these lines in blood he left:
>   "Farewell forever, Geraldine, I go
> Another woman's victim—dare I tell?
> 'T is Alice!—curse us, Geraldine!—farewell!"

There is no possibility of denying the fact: this *is* a droll piece of business. The lover brings forth a miniature, (Mr. Dawes has a passion for miniatures,) *sinks* it in the bosom of the lady, cuts his finger, and writes with the blood an epistle, (*where* is not specified, but we presume he indites it upon the bosom as it is "close beside" the picture,) in which epistle he announces that he is "another woman's victim," giving us to understand that he himself is a woman after all, and concluding with the delicious bit of Billingsgate

> dare I tell?
> 'T is Alice!—curse us, Geraldine!—farewell!

We suppose, however, that "curse us" is a misprint; for why should Geraldine curse both herself and her lover?—it should have been "curse it!" no doubt. The whole passage, perhaps, would have read better thus—

> oh, my eye!
> 'T is Alice!—d—n it, Geraldine!—good bye!

The remainder of the narrative may be briefly summed up. Waldron returns to his professional engagements with the pirates, while Geraldine, attended by her father, goes to sea for the benefit of her health. The consequence is inevitable. The vessels of the separated lovers meet and engage in the most diabolical of conflicts. Both are blown all to pieces. In a boat from one vessel, Waldron escapes—in a boat from the other, the lady Geraldine. Now, as a second natural consequence, the parties meet again—Destiny is every thing in such cases.

Well, the parties meet again. The lady Geraldine has "that miniature" about her neck, and the circumstance proves too much for the excited state of mind of Mr. Waldron. He just seizes her ladyship, therefore, by the small of the waist and incontinently leaps with her into the sea.

However intolerably absurd this skeleton of the story may appear, a thorough perusal will convince the reader that the entire fabric is even more so. It is impossible to convey, in any such digest as we have given, a full idea of the *niaiseries* with which the narrative abounds. An utter want of *keeping* is especially manifest throughout. In the most solemnly serious passages we have, for example, incidents of the world of 1839, jumbled up with the distorted mythology of the Greeks. Our conclusion of the drama, as we just gave it, was perhaps ludicrous enough; but how much more preposterous does it appear in the grave language of the poet himself!

> And round her neck the miniature was hung
> Of him who gazed with Hell's unmingled wo;
> He saw her, kissed her cheek, and wildly flung
> His arms around her with a mad'ning throw—
> Then plunged within the cold unfathomed deep
> While sirens sang their victim to his sleep!

Only think of a group of *sirens* singing to sleep a modern "miniatured" flirt, kicking about in the water with a New York dandy in tight pantaloons!

But not even these stupidities would suffice to justify a total condemnation of the poetry of Mr. Dawes. We have known follies very similar committed by men of real ability, and have been induced to disregard them in earnest admiration of the brilliancy of the minor beauty of *style*. Simplicity, perspicuity and vigor, or a well-disciplined ornateness, of language, have done wonders for the reputation of many a writer really deficient in the higher and more essential qualities of the Muse. But upon these minor points of manner our poet has not even the shadow of a shadow to sustain him. His works, in this respect, may be regarded as a theatrical world of mere verbiage, somewhat speciously bedizzened with a tinselly meaning well adapted to the eyes of the rabble. There is not a page of any thing that he has written which will bear, for an instant, the scrutiny of a critical eye. Exceedingly fond of the glitter of metaphor, he has not the capacity to manage it, and, in the awkward attempt, jumbles together the most incongruous of ornament. Let us take any passage of "Geraldine" by way of exemplification.

> ———Thy rivers swell the sea—
> In one eternal diapason pour
> Thy cataracts the hymn of liberty,
> Teaching the clouds to thunder.

Here we have cataracts teaching clouds to thunder—and how? By means of a hymn.

> Why should chromatic discord charm the ear
> And smiles and tears stream o'er with troubled joy?

Tears may stream over, but not smiles.

> Then comes the breathing time of young Romance,
> The June of life, when summer's earliest ray
> Warms the red arteries, that bound and dance
> With soft voluptuous impulses at play,
> While the full heart sends forth as from a hive
> A thousand winged messengers alive.

Let us reduce this to a simple statement, and we have—what? The earliest ray of summer warming red arteries, which are bounding and dancing, and playing with a parcel of urchins, called voluptuous impulses, while the bee-hive of a heart attached to these dancing arteries is at the same time sending forth a swarm of its innocent little inhabitants.

> The eyes were like the sapphire of deep air,
> The garb that distance robes elysium in,
> But oh, so much of heaven lingered there
> The wayward heart forgot its blissful sin
> And worshiped all Religion well forbids
> Beneath the silken fringes of their lids.

That *distance* is *not* the cause of the sapphire of the sky, is not to our present purpose. We wish merely to call attention to the verbiage of the stanza. It is impossible to put the latter portion of it into any thing like intelligible prose. So much of heaven lingered in the lady's eyes that the wayward heart forgot its blissful sin, and worshiped every thing which religion forbids, beneath the silken fringes of the lady's eyelids. This we cannot be compelled to understand, and shall therefore say nothing further about it.

> She loved to lend Imagination wing
>   And link her heart with Juliet's in a dream,
> And feel the music of a sister string
>   That thrilled the current of her vital stream.

How delightful a picture we have here! A lady is lending one of her wings to the spirit, or genius, called Imagination, who, of course, has lost one of his own. While thus employed with one hand, with the other she is chaining her heart to the heart of the fair Juliet. At the same time she is feeling the music of a sister string, and this string is thrilling the current of the lady's vital stream. If this is downright nonsense we cannot be held responsible for its perpetration; it is but the downright nonsense of Mr. Dawes.

Again—

> Without the Palinurus of self-science
>   Byron embarked upon the stormy sea,
> To adverse breezes hurling his defiance
>   And dashing up the rainbows on his lee,
> And chasing those he made in wildest mirth,
>   Or sending back their images to earth.

This stanza we have more than once seen quoted as a fine specimen of the poetical powers of our author. His lordship, no doubt, is herein made to cut a very remarkable figure. Let us imagine him, for one moment, embarked upon a stormy sea, hurling his defiance (literally throwing his gauntlet or glove) to the adverse breezes, dashing up rainbows on his lee, laughing at them, and chasing them at the same time, and, in conclusion, "sending back their images to earth." But we have already wearied the reader with this abominable rigmarole. We shall be pardoned (after the many specimens thus given at random) for not carrying out the design we originally intended: that of commenting upon two or three successive pages of *"Geraldine,"* with a view of showing (in a spirit apparently more fair than that of particular selection) the *entireness* with which the whole poem is pervaded by unintelligibility. To every thinking mind, however, this would seem a work of supererogation. In such matters, by such understandings, the brick of the *skolastikos* will be received implicitly as a sample of the house. The writer *capable*, to any extent, of such absurdity as we have pointed out, *cannot*, by any possibility, produce a long article worth reading. We say this in the very teeth of the magnificent assembly which listened to the recital of Mr. Dawes, in the great hall of the University of New York. We shall leave "Athenia of Damascus," without comment, to the decision of those who may find time and temper for its perusal, and conclude our extracts by a quotation, from among the minor poems, of the following very respectable

ANACREONTIC

Fill again the mantling bowl
    Nor fear to meet the morning breaking!
None but slaves should bend the soul
    Beneath the chains of mortal making:
Fill your beakers to the brim,
    Bacchus soon shall lull your sorrow;
        Let delight
        But crown the night,
    And care may bring her clouds to-morrow.

Mark this cup of rosy wine
    With virgin pureness deeply blushing;
Beauty pressed it from the vine
    While Love stood by to charm its gushing;
He who dares to drain it now
    Shall drink such bliss as seldom gladdens;
        The Moslem's dream
        Would joyless seem
    To him whose brain its rapture maddens.

Pleasure sparkles on the brim—
    Lethe lies far deeper in it—
Both, enticing, wait for him
    Whose heart is warm enough to win it;

Hearts like ours, if e'er they chill
  Soon with love again must lighten.
      Skies may wear
      A darksome air
  Where sunshine most is known to brighten.

Then fill, fill high the mantling bowl!
  Nor fear to meet the morning breaking;
Care shall never cloud the soul
  While Beauty's beaming eyes are waking.
Fill your beakers to the brim,
  Bacchus soon shall lull your sorrow;
      Let delight
      But crown the night,
  And care may bring her clouds to-morrow.

Whatever shall be, hereafter, the position of Mr. Dawes in the poetical world, he will be indebted for it altogether to his shorter compositions, some of which have the merit of tenderness; others of melody and force. What seems to be the popular opinion in respect to his more voluminous effusions, has been brought about, in some measure, by a certain general *tact*, nearly amounting to taste, and more nearly the converse of talent. This tact has been especially displayed in the choice of not inelegant titles and other externals; in a peculiar imitative speciousness of manner, pervading the surface of his writings; and (here we have the anomaly of a positive benefit deduced from a radical defect) in an absolute deficiency in basis, in *stamen*, in matter, or pungency, which, if even slightly evinced, might have invited the reader to an intimate and understanding perusal, whose result would have been disgust. His poems have not been condemned, only because they have never been read. The glitter upon the surface has sufficed, with the newspaper critic, to justify his hyperboles of praise. Very few persons, we feel assured, have had sufficient nerve to wade *through* the entire volume now in question, except, as in our own case, with the single object of criticism in view. Mr. Dawes has, also, been aided to a poetical reputation by the amiability of his character as a man. How efficient such causes have before been in producing such effects, is a point but too thoroughly understood.

We have already spoken of the numerous *friends* of the poet; and we shall not here insist upon the fact, that *we* bear him no personal ill will. With those who know us, such a declaration would appear supererogatory; and by those who know us not, it would, doubtless, be received with incredulity. What we have said, however, is *not* in opposition to Mr. Dawes, nor even so much in opposition to the poems of Mr. Dawes, as in defence of the many true souls which, in Mr. Dawes' apotheosis, are aggrieved. The laudation of the unworthy is to the worthy the most bitter of all wrong. But it is unbecoming in him who merely demonstrates a truth, to offer reason or apology for the demonstration.

Graham's Magazine, October 1842

Joseph Rodman Drake—Fitz-Greene Halleck

The Culprit Fay, and other Poems, by Joseph Rodman Drake. New York: George Dearborn.
Alnwick Castle, with other Poems, by Fitz Greene Halleck. New York: George Dearborn.

B EFORE ENTERING upon the detailed notice which we propose of the volumes before us, we wish to speak a few words in regard to the present state of American criticism.

It must be visible to all who meddle with literary matters, that of late years a thorough revolution has been effected in the censorship of our press. That this revolution is infinitely for the worse we believe. There was a time, it is true, when we cringed to foreign opinion—let us even say when we paid a most servile deference to British critical dicta. That an American book could, by any possibility, be worthy perusal, was an idea by no means extensively prevalent in the land; and if we were induced to read at all the productions of our native writers, it was only after repeated assurances from England that such productions were not altogether contemptible. But there was, at all events, a shadow of excuse, and a slight basis of reason for a subserviency so grotesque. Even now, perhaps, it would not be far wrong to assert that such basis of reason may still exist. Let us grant that in many of the abstract sciences—that even in Theology, in Medicine, in Law, in Oratory, in the Mechanical Arts, we have no competitors whatever, still nothing but the most egregious national vanity would assign us a place, in the matter of Polite Literature, upon a level with the elder and riper climes of Europe, the earliest steps of whose children are among the groves of magnificently endowed Academies, and whose innumerable men of leisure, and of consequent learning, drink daily from those august fountains of inspiration which burst around them every where from out the tombs of their immortal dead, and from out their hoary and trophied monument of chivalry and song. In paying then, as a nation, a respectful and not undue deference to a supremacy rarely questioned but by prejudice or ignorance, we should, of course, be doing nothing more than acting in a rational manner. The *excess* of our subserviency was blameable—but, as we have before said, this very excess might have found a shadow of excuse in the strict justice, if properly regulated, of the principle from which it issued. Not so, however, with our present follies. We are becoming boisterous and arrogant in the pride of a too speedily assumed literary freedom. We throw off, with the most presumptuous and unmeaning hauteur, *all* deference whatever to foreign opinion—we forget, in the puerile inflation of vanity, that *the world* is the true theatre of the biblical histrio—we get up a hue and cry about the necessity of encouraging native writers of merit—we blindly fancy that we can accomplish this by indiscriminate puffing of good, bad, and indifferent, without taking the trouble to consider that what we choose to denominate encouragement is thus, by its general application, rendered precisely the reverse. In a word, so far from being ashamed of the many disgraceful literary failures to which our own inordinate vanities and misapplied patriotism have lately given birth, and so far from deeply lamenting that these daily puerilities are of home manufacture, we adhere pertinaciously to our original blindly conceived idea, and thus often find ourselves involved in the gross paradox of liking a stupid book the better, because, sure enough, its stupidity is American.*

Deeply lamenting this unjustifiable state of public feeling, it has been our constant endeavor, since assuming the Editorial duties of this Journal, to stem, with what little abilities we possess, a current so disastrously undermining the health and prosperity of our literature. We have seen our efforts applauded by men whose applauses we value. From all quarters we have received abundant private as well as public testimonials in favor of our *Critical Notices*, and, until very lately, have heard from no respectable source one word impugning their integrity or candor. In looking over, however, a number of the New York Commercial Advertiser, we meet with the following paragraph.

The last number of the Southern Literary Messenger is very readable and respectable. The contributions to the Mes-

---

*This charge of indiscriminate puffing will, of course, only apply to the *general* character of our criticism—there are some noble exceptions. We wish also especially to discriminate between those *notices* of new works which are intended merely to call public attention to them, and deliberate criticism on the works themselves.

senger are much better than the original matter. The critical department of this work—much as it would seem to boast itself of impartiality and discernment,—is in our opinion decidedly *quacky*. There is in it a great assumption of acumen, which is completely unsustained. Many a work has been slashingly condemned therein, of which the critic himself could not write a page, were he to die for it. This affectation of eccentric sternness in criticism, without the power to back one's suit withal, so far from deserving praise, as some suppose, merits the strongest reprehension.—[*Philadelphia Gazette.*

We are entirely of opinion with the Philadelphia Gazette in relation to the Southern Literary Messenger, and take this occasion to express our total dissent from the numerous and lavish encomiums we have seen bestowed upon its critical notices. Some few of them have been judicious, fair and candid; bestowing praise and censure with judgment and impartiality; but by far the greater number of those we have read, have been flippant, unjust, untenable and uncritical. The duty of the critic is to act as judge, not as enemy, of the writer whom he reviews; a distinction of which the Zoilus of the Messenger seems not to be aware. It is possible to review a book severely, without bestowing opprobrious epithets upon the writer: to condemn with courtesy, if not with kindness. The critic of the Messenger has been eulogized for his scorching and scarifying abilities, and he thinks it incumbent upon him to keep up his reputation in that line, by sneers, sarcasm, and downright abuse; by straining his vision with microscopic intensity in search of faults, and shutting his eyes, with all his might, to beauties. Moreover, we have detected him, more than once, in blunders quite as gross as those on which it was his pleasure to descant.*

*In addition to these things we observe, in the New York Mirror, what follows: "Those who have read the Notices of American books in a certain Southern Monthly, which is striving to gain notoriety by the loudness of its abuse, may find amusement in the sketch on another page, entitled 'The Successful Novel.' The Southern Literary Messenger knows ☞ *by experience* ☜ what it is to write a successless novel." We have, in this case, only to deny, flatly, the assertion of the Mirror. The Editor of the Messenger never in his life wrote or published, or attempted to publish, a novel either successful or *successless*.

In the paragraph from the Philadelphia Gazette, (which is edited by Mr. Willis Gaylord Clark, one of the Editors of the Knickerbocker) we find nothing at which we have any desire to take exception. Mr. C. has a right to think us *quacky* if he pleases, and we do not remember having assumed for a moment that we could write a single line of the works we have reviewed. But there is something equivocal, to say the least, in the remarks of Col. Stone. He acknowledges that "*some* of our notices have been judicious, fair, and candid, bestowing praise and censure with judgment and impartiality." This being the case, how can he reconcile his *total* dissent from the public verdict in our favor, with the dictates of justice? We are accused too of bestowing "opprobrious epithets" upon writers whom we review, and in the paragraph so accusing us we are called nothing less than "flippant, unjust, and uncritical."

But there is another point of which we disapprove. While in our reviews we have at all times been particularly careful *not* to deal in generalities, and have never, if we remember aright, advanced in any single instance an unsupported assertion, our accuser has forgotten to give us any better evidence of our flippancy, injustice, personality, and gross blundering, than the solitary *dictum* of Col. Stone. We call upon the Colonel for assistance in this dilemma. We wish to be shown our blunders that we may correct them—to be made aware of our flippancy, that we may avoid it hereafter—and above all to have our personalities pointed out that we may proceed forthwith with a repentant spirit, to make the *amende honorable*. In default of this aid from the Editor of the Commercial we shall take it for granted that we are neither blunderers, flippant, personal, nor unjust.

————

Who will deny that in regard to individual poems no definitive opinions can exist, so long as to Poetry in the abstract we attach no definitive idea? Yet it is a common thing to hear our critics, day after day, pronounce, with a positive air, laudatory or condemnatory sentences, *en masse*, upon metrical works of whose merits and demerits they have, in the first place, virtually confessed an utter ignorance, in confessing ignorance of all determinate principles by which to regulate a decision. Poetry has never been defined to the satisfaction of all parties. Perhaps, in the present condition of language it never will be. Words cannot hem it in. Its intangible and purely spiritual nature refuses to be bound down within the widest horizon of mere sounds. But it is not, therefore, misunderstood—at least, not by all men is it misunderstood. Very far from it. If, indeed, there be any one circle of thought distinctly and palpably marked out from amid the jarring and tumultuous chaos of human intelligence, it is that evergreen and radiant Paradise which the true poet knows, and knows alone, as the limited realm of his authority—as the circumscribed Eden of his dreams. But a definition is a thing of words—a conception of ideas. And thus while we readily believe that Poesy, the term, it will be troublesome, if not impossible to define—still, with its image vividly existing in the world, we apprehend no difficulty in so describing Poesy, the Sentiment, as to imbue even the most obtuse intellect with a comprehension of it sufficiently distinct for all the purposes of practical analysis.

To look upwards from any existence, material or immaterial, to its *design*, is, perhaps, the most direct, and the most unerring method of attaining a just notion of the nature of the existence itself. Nor is the principle at fault when we turn our eyes from Nature even to Nature's God. We find certain faculties implanted within us, and arrive at a more plausible conception of the character and attributes of those faculties, by considering, with what finite judgment we possess, the *intention* of the Deity in so implanting them within us, than by any actual investigation of their powers, or any speculative deductions from their visible and material effects. Thus, for example, we discover in all men a disposition to look with reverence upon superiority, whether real or supposititious. In some, this disposition is to be recognized with difficulty, and, in very peculiar cases, we are occasionally even led to doubt its existence altogether, until circumstances beyond the common routine bring it accidentally into development. In others again it forms a prominent and distinctive feature of character, and is rendered palpably evident in its excesses. But in all human beings it is, in a greater or less degree, finally perceptible. It has been, therefore, justly considered a primitive sentiment. Phrenologists call it Veneration. It is, indeed, the instinct given to man by God as security for his own worship.

And although, preserving its nature, it becomes perverted from its principal purpose, and although, swerving from that purpose, it serves to modify the relations of human society—the relations of father and child, of master and slave, of the ruler and the ruled—its primitive essence is nevertheless the same, and by a reference to primal causes, may at any moment be determined.

Very nearly akin to this feeling, and liable to the same analysis, is the Faculty of Ideality—which is the sentiment of Poesy. This sentiment is the sense of the beautiful, of the sublime, and of the mystical.* Thence spring immediately admiration of the fair flowers, the fairer forests, the bright valleys and rivers and mountains of the Earth—and love of the gleaming stars and other burning glories of Heaven—and, mingled up inextricably with this love and this admiration of Heaven and of Earth, the unconquerable desire— *to know*. Poesy is the sentiment of Intellectual Happiness here, and the Hope of a higher Intellectual Happiness hereafter.† Imagi-

---

*We separate the sublime and the mystical—for, despite of high authorities, we are firmly convinced that the latter *may* exist, in the most vivid degree, without giving rise to the sense of the former.

†The consciousness of this truth was possessed by no mortal more fully than by Shelley, although he has only once especially alluded to it. In his *Hymn to Intellectual Beauty* we find these lines.

> While yet a boy I sought for ghosts, and sped
>   Through many a listening chamber, cave and ruin,
>   And starlight wood, with fearful steps pursuing
> Hopes of high talk with the departed dead:
> I called on poisonous names with which our youth is fed:
>   I was not heard: I saw them not.
>   When musing deeply on the lot
> Of life at that sweet time when birds are wooing
>   All vital things that wake to bring
>   News of buds and blossoming
>   Sudden thy shadow fell on me—
> I shrieked and clasp'd my hands in ecstacy!
>
> I vow'd that I would dedicate my powers
>   To thee and thine: have I not kept the vow?
> With beating heart and streaming eyes, even now
> I call the phantoms of a thousand hours
> Each from his voiceless grave: they have in vision'd bowers
>   Of studious zeal or love's delight

nation is its Soul.* With the *passions* of mankind—although it may modify them greatly—although it may exalt, or inflame, or purify, or control them—it would require little ingenuity to prove that it has no inevitable, and indeed no necessary co-existence. We have hitherto spoken of Poetry in the abstract: we come now to speak of it in its every-day acceptation—that is to say, of the practical result arising from the sentiment we have considered.

And now it appears evident, that since Poetry, in this new sense, *is* the practical result, expressed in language, of this Poetic Sentiment in certain individuals, the only proper method of testing the merits of a poem is by measuring its capabilities of exciting the Poetic Sentiment in others. And to this end we have many aids—in observation, in experience, in ethical analysis, and in the dictates of common sense. Hence the *Poeta nascitur*, which is indisputably true if we consider the Poetic Sentiment, becomes the merest of absurdities when we regard it in reference to the practical result. We do not hesitate to say that a man highly endowed with the powers of Causality—that is to say, a man of metaphysical acumen—will, even with a very deficient share of Ideality, compose a finer poem (if we test it, as we should, by its measure of exciting the Poetic Sentiment) than one who, without such metaphysical acumen, shall be gifted, in the most extraordinary degree, with the faculty of Ideality. For a poem is not the Poetic faculty, but *the means* of exciting it in mankind. Now these means the metaphysician may discover by analysis of their effects in other cases than his own, without even conceiving the nature of these effects—thus arriving at a result

----

    Outwatch'd with me the envious night:
They know that never joy illum'd my brow,
    Unlink'd with hope that thou wouldst free,
    This world from its dark slavery,
    That thou, O awful *Loveliness*,
Wouldst give whate'er these words cannot express.

*Imagination is, possibly, in man, a lesser degree of the creative power in God. What the Deity imagines, *is*, but *was not* before. What man imagines, *is*, but *was* also. The mind of man cannot imagine what *is not*. This latter point may be demonstrated.— *See Les Premiers Traits de L'Erudition Universelle, par M. Le Baron de Bielfield, 1767.*

which the unaided Ideality of his competitor would be utterly unable, except by accident, to attain. It is more than possible that the man who, of all writers, living or dead, has been most successful in writing the purest of all poems—that is to say, poems which excite most purely, most exclusively, and most powerfully the imaginative faculties in men—owed his extraordinary and almost magical pre-eminence rather to metaphysical than poetical powers. We allude to the author of Christabel, of the Rime of the Auncient Mariner, and of Love—to Coleridge—whose head, if we mistake not its character, gave no great phrenological tokens of Ideality, while the organs of Causality and Comparison were most singularly developed.

Perhaps at this particular moment there are no American poems held in so high estimation by our countrymen, as the poems of Drake, and of Halleck. The exertions of Mr. George Dearborn have no doubt a far greater share in creating this feeling than the lovers of literature for its own sake and spiritual uses would be willing to admit. We have indeed seldom seen more beautiful volumes than the volumes now before us. But an adventitious interest of a loftier nature—the interest of the living in the memory of the beloved dead—attaches itself to the few literary remains of Drake. The poems which are now given to us with his name are nineteen in number; and whether all, or whether even the best of his writings, it is our present purpose to speak of these alone, since upon this edition his poetical reputation to all time will most probably depend.

It is only lately that we have read *The Culprit Fay*. This is a poem of six hundred and forty irregular lines, generally iambic, and divided into thirty six stanzas, of unequal length. The scene of the narrative, as we ascertain from the single line,

The moon looks down on old *Cronest*,

is principally in the vicinity of West Point on the Hudson. The plot is as follows. An Ouphe, one of the race of Fairies, has "broken his vestal vow,"

He has loved an earthly maid
And left for her his woodland shade;
He has lain upon her lip of dew,

> And sunned him in her eye of blue,
> Fann'd her cheek with his wing of air,
> Play'd with the ringlets of her hair,
> And, nestling on her snowy breast,
> Forgot the lily-king's behest—

in short, he has broken Fairy-law in becoming enamored of a mortal. The result of this misdemeanor we could not express so well as the poet, and will therefore make use of the language put into the mouth of the Fairy-King who reprimands the criminal.

> Fairy! Fairy! list and mark,
>> Thou hast broke thine elfin chain,
> Thy flame-wood lamp is quench'd and dark
>> And thy wings are dyed with a deadly stain.

The Ouphe being in this predicament, it has become necessary that his case and crime should be investigated by a jury of his fellows, and to this end the "shadowy tribes of air" are summoned by the "sentry elve" who has been awakened by the "wood-tick"—are summoned we say to the "elfin-court" at midnight to hear the doom of the *Culprit Fay*.

"Had a stain been found on the earthly fair" whose blandishments so bewildered the little Ouphe, his punishment had been severe indeed. In such case he would have been (as we learn from the Fairy judge's exposition of the criminal code,)

> Tied to the hornet's shardy wings;
> Tossed on the pricks of nettles' stings;
> Or seven long ages doomed to dwell
> With the lazy worm in the walnut shell;
> Or every night to writhe and bleed
> Beneath the tread of the centipede;
> Or bound in a cobweb dungeon dim,
> His jailer a spider huge and grim,
> Amid the carrion bodies to lie
> Of the worm and the bug and the murdered fly—

Fortunately, however, for the Culprit, his mistress is proved to be of "sinless mind" and under such redeeming circumstances the sentence is, mildly, as follows—

Thou shalt seek the beach of sand
Where the water bounds the elfin land,
Thou shalt watch the oozy brine
Till the sturgeon leaps in the bright moonshine,
Then dart the glistening arch below,
And catch a drop from his silver bow.

       *   *   *

If the spray-bead gem be won
    The stain of thy wing is washed away,
But another errand must be done
    Ere thy crime be lost for aye;
Thy flame-wood lamp is quenched and dark,
Thou must re-illume its spark.
Mount thy steed and spur him high
To the heaven's blue canopy;
And when thou seest a shooting star
Follow it fast and follow it far—
The last faint spark of its burning train
Shall light the elfin lamp again.

Upon this sin, and upon this sentence, depends the web of the narrative, which is now occupied with the elfin difficulties overcome by the Ouphe in washing away the stain of his wing, and re-illuming his flame-wood lamp. His soiled pinion having lost its power, he is under the necessity of wending his way on foot from the Elfin court upon Cronest to the river beach at its base. His path is encumbered at every step with "bog and briar," with "brook and mire," with "beds of tangled fern," with "groves of nightshade," and with the minor evils of ant and snake. Happily, however, a spotted toad coming in sight, our adventurer jumps upon her back, and "bridling her mouth with a silk-weed twist" bounds merrily along

Till the mountain's magic verge is past
And the beach of sand is reached at last.

Alighting now from his "courser-toad" the Ouphe folds his wings around his bosom, springs on a rock, breathes a prayer, throws his arms above his head,

> Then tosses a tiny curve in air
> And plunges in the waters blue.

Here, however, a host of difficulties await him by far too multitudinous to enumerate. We will content ourselves with simply stating the names of his most respectable assailants. These are the "spirits of the waves" dressed in "snail-plate armor" and aided by the "mailed shrimp," the "prickly prong," the "blood-red leech," the "stony star-fish," the "jellied quarl," the "soldier crab," and the "lancing squab." But the hopes of our hero are high, and his limbs are strong, so

> He spreads his arms like the swallow's wing
> And throws his feet with a frog-like fling.

All, however is to no purpose.

> On his thigh the leech has fixed his hold,
> The quarl's long arms are round him roll'd,
> The prickly prong has pierced his skin,
> And the squab has thrown his javelin,
> The gritty star has rubb'd him raw,
> And the crab has struck with his giant claw;
> He bawls with rage, and he shrieks with pain,
> He strikes around but his blows are vain—

So then,

> He turns him round and flies amain
> With hurry and dash to the beach again.

Arrived safely on land our Fairy friend now gathers the dew from the "sorrel-leaf and henbane-bud" and bathing therewith his wounds, finally ties them up with cobweb. Thus recruited, he

> ——treads the fatal shore
> As fresh and vigorous as before.

At length espying a "purple-muscle shell" upon the beach, he determines to use it as a boat, and thus evade the animosity of the water-spirits whose powers extend not above the wave. Making a "sculler's notch" in the stern, and providing himself with an oar of the bootle-blade, the Ouphe a second time ventures upon the deep. His perils are now diminished, but still great. The imps of the river heave the billows up before the prow of the boat, dash the surges against her side, and strike against her keel. The quarl uprears "his island-back" in her path, and the scallop, floating in the rear of the vessel, spatters it all over with water. Our adventurer however, bails it out with the colen bell (which he has luckily provided for the purpose of catching the drop from the silver bow of the sturgeon,) and keeping his little bark warily trimmed, holds on his course undiscomfited.

The object of his first adventure is at length discovered in a "brown-backed sturgeon," who

> Like the heaven-shot javelin
> Springs above the waters blue,
> And, instant as the star-fall light
> Plunges him in the deep again,
> But leaves an arch of silver bright,
> The rainbow of the moony main.

From this rainbow our Ouphe succeeds in catching, by means of his colen-bell cup, a "droplet of the sparkling dew." One half of his task is accordingly done—

> His wings are pure, for the gem is won.

On his return to land, the ripples divide before him, while the water-spirits, so rancorous before, are obsequiously attentive to his comfort. Having tarried a moment on the beach to breathe a prayer, he "spreads his wings of gilded blue" and takes his way to the elfin court—there resting until the cricket, at two in the morning, rouses him up for the second portion of his penance.

His equipments are now an "acorn helmet," a "thistle-down plume," a corslet of the " wild-bee's" skin, a cloak of the " wings of butterflies," a shield of the "shell of the lady-bug," for lance "the sting of a wasp," for sword a "blade of grass," for horse "a fire-fly," and for spurs a couple of "cockle seed." Thus accoutred,

> Away like a glance of thought he flies
> To skim the heavens and follow far
> The fiery trail of the rocket-star.

In the Heavens he has new dangers to encounter. The "shapes of air" have begun their work—a "drizzly mist" is cast around him—"storm, darkness, sleet and shade" assail him—"shadowy hands" twitch at his bridle-rein—"flame-shot tongues" play around him—"fiendish eyes" glare upon him—and

> Yells of rage and shrieks of fear
> Come screaming on his startled ear.

Still our adventurer is nothing daunted.

> He thrusts before, and he strikes behind,
> Till he pierces the cloudy bodies through
> And gashes the shadowy limbs of wind,

and the Elfin makes no stop, until he reaches the "bank of the milky way." He there checks his courser, and watches "for the glimpse of the planet shoot." While thus engaged, however, an unexpected adventure befalls him. He is approached by a company of the "sylphs of Heaven attired in sunset's crimson pall." They dance around him, and "skip before him on the plain." One receiving his "wasp-sting lance," and another taking his bridle-rein,

> With warblings wild they lead him on,
>   To where, through clouds of amber seen,
> Studded with stars resplendent shone
>   The palace of the sylphid queen.

A glowing description of the queen's beauty follows; and as the form of an earthly Fay had never been seen before in the bowers of light, she is represented as falling desperately in love at first sight with our adventurous Ouphe. He returns the compliment in some measure, of course; but, although "his heart bent fitfully," the "earthly form imprinted there" was a security against a too vivid impression. He declines, consequently, the invitation of the queen to remain with her and amuse himself by "lying within the fleecy drift," "hanging upon the rainbow's rim," having his "brow adorned with all the jewels of the sky," "sitting within the Pleiad ring," "resting upon Orion's belt," "riding upon the lightning's gleam," "dancing upon the orbed moon," and "swimming within the milky way."

> Lady, he cries, I have sworn to-night
> On the word of a fairy knight
> To do my sentence task aright.

The queen, therefore, contents herself with bidding the Fay an affectionate farewell—having first directed him carefully to that particular portion of the sky where a star is about to fall. He reaches this point in safety, and in despite of the "fiends of the cloud" who "bellow very loud," succeeds finally in catching a "glimmering spark" with which he returns triumphantly to Fairy-land. The poem closes with an Io Pæan chaunted by the elves in honor of these glorious adventures.

It is more than probable that from among ten readers of the *Culprit Fay*, nine would immediately pronounce it a poem betokening the most extraordinary powers of imagination, and of these nine, perhaps five or six, poets themselves, and fully impressed with the truth of what we have already assumed, that Ideality is indeed the soul of the Poetic Sentiment, would feel embarrassed between a half-consciousness that they *ought* to admire the production, and a wonder that they *do not*. This embarrassment would then arise from an indistinct conception of the results in which Ideality is rendered manifest. Of these results some few are seen in the *Culprit Fay*, but the greater part of it is utterly destitute of any evidence of imagination whatever. The general character of the poem will, we think, be sufficiently understood by any one who may have taken the trouble to read our foregoing compendium of the narrative. It will be there seen that what is so frequently termed the imaginative power of this story, lies especially—we should have rather said is thought to lie— in the passages we have quoted, or in others of a precisely similar nature. These passages embody, principally, mere specifications of qualities, of habiliments, of punishments, of occupations, of circumstances &c, which the poet has believed in unison with the size, firstly, and secondly with the nature of his Fairies. To all which may be added specifications of other animal existences (such as the toad, the beetle, the lance-fly, the fire-fly and the like) supposed also to be in accordance. An example will best illustrate our meaning upon this point—we take it from page 20.

> He put his acorn helmet on;
> It was plumed of the silk of the thistle down;
> The corslet plate that guarded his breast
> Was once the wild bee's golden vest;
> His cloak of a thousand mingled dyes,
> Was formed of the wings of butterflies;
> His shield was the shell of a lady-bug queen,
> Studs of gold on a ground of green;*
> And the quivering lance which he brandished bright,
> Was the sting of a wasp he had slain in fight.

We shall now be understood. Were any of the admirers of the *Culprit Fay* asked their opinion of these lines, they would most probably speak in high terms of the *imagination* they display. Yet let the most stolid and the most confessedly un-poetical of these admirers only try the experiment, and he will find, possibly to his extreme surprise, that he himself will have no difficulty whatever in substituting for the equip-ments of the Fairy, as assigned by the poet, other equipments equally comfortable, no doubt, and equally in unison with the preconceived size, character, and other qualities of the equipped. Why we could accoutre him as well ourselves—let us see.

> His blue-bell helmet, we have heard,
> Was plumed with the down of the humming-bird,
> The corslet on his bosom bold
> Was once the locust's coat of gold,
> His cloak, of a thousand mingled hues,
> Was the velvet violet, wet with dews,
> His target was the crescent shell
> Of the small sea Sidrophel,
> And a glittering beam from a maiden's eye
> Was the lance which he proudly wav'd on high.

*Chesnut color, or more slack,
  Gold upon a ground of black.
                    Ben Jonson

The truth is, that the only requisite for writing verses of this nature, *ad libitum*, is a tolerable acquaintance with the qualities of the objects to be detailed, and a very moderate endowment of the faculty of Comparison—which is the chief constituent of *Fancy* or the powers of combination. A thousand such lines may be composed without exercising in the least degree the Poetic Sentiment, which is Ideality, Imagination, or the creative ability. And, as we have before said, the greater portion of the *Culprit Fay* is occupied with these, or similar things, and upon such, depends very nearly, if not altogether, its reputation. We select another example from page 25.

> But oh! how fair the shape that lay
>   Beneath a rainbow bending bright,
> She seem'd to the entranced Fay
>   The loveliest of the forms of light;
> Her mantle was the purple rolled
>   At twilight in the west afar;
> 'Twas tied with threads of dawning gold,
>   And button'd with a sparkling star.
> Her face was like the lily roon
>   That veils the vestal planet's hue;
> Her eyes, two beamlets from the moon
>   Set floating in the welkin blue.
> Her hair is like the sunny beam,
> And the diamond gems which round it gleam
> Are the pure drops of dewy even,
> That ne'er have left their native heaven.

Here again the faculty of Comparison is alone exercised, and no mind possessing the faculty in any ordinary degree would find a difficulty in substituting for the materials employed by the poet other materials equally as good. But viewed as mere efforts of the Fancy and without reference to Ideality, the lines just quoted are much worse than those which were taken from page 20. A congruity was observable in the accoutrements of the Ouphe, and we had no trouble in forming a distinct conception of his appearance when so accoutred. But the most vivid powers of Comparison can attach no definitive idea to even "the loveliest form of light," when habited in a mantle of "rolled purple tied with threads of dawn and buttoned with a star," and sitting at the same time under a rainbow with "beamlet" eyes and a visage of "lily roon."

But if these things evince no Ideality in their author, do they not excite it in others?—if so, we must conclude, that without being himself imbued with the Poetic Sentiment, he has still succeeded in writing a fine poem—a supposition as we have before endeavored to show, not altogether paradoxical. Most assuredly we think not. In the case of a great majority of readers the only sentiment aroused by compositions of this order is a species of vague wonder at the writer's *ingenuity*, and it is this indeterminate sense of wonder which passes but too frequently current for the proper influence of the Poetic power. For our own parts we plead guilty to a predominant sense of the ludicrous while occupied in the perusal of the poem before us—a sense whose promptings we sincerely and honestly endeavored to quell, perhaps not altogether successfully, while penning our compend of the narrative. That a feeling of this nature is utterly at war with the Poetic Sentiment, will not be disputed by those who comprehend the character of the sentiment itself. This character is finely shadowed out in that popular although vague idea so prevalent throughout all time, that a species of melancholy is inseparably connected with the higher manifestations of the beautiful. But with the numerous and seriously-adduced incongruities of the Culprit Fay, we find it generally impossible to connect other ideas than those of the ridiculous. We are bidden, in the first place, and in a tone of sentiment and language adapted to the loftiest breathings of the Muse, to imagine a race of Fairies in the vicinity of West Point. We are told, with a grave air, of their camp, of their king, and especially of their sentry, who is a wood-tick. We are informed that an Ouphe of about an inch in height has committed a deadly sin in falling in love with a mortal maiden, who may, very possibly, be six feet in her stockings. The consequence to the Ouphe is—what? Why, that he has "dyed his wings," "broken his elfin chain," and "quenched his flame-wood lamp." And he is therefore sentenced to what? To catch a spark from the tail of a falling star, and a drop of water from the belly of a sturgeon. What are his equipments for the first adventure? An acorn helmet, a thistle-down plume, a butterfly cloak, a lady-bug shield, cockle-seed spurs, and a fire-fly horse. How does he ride to the second? On the back of a bull-frog. What are his opponents in the one? "Drizzly mists," "sulphur and smoke," "shadowy hands" and "flame-shot tongues." What in the other? "Mailed shrimps," "prickly prongs," "blood-red leeches," "jellied quarls," "stony star fishes," "lancing squabs" and "soldier crabs." Is that all? No—Although only an inch high he is in imminent danger of seduction from a "sylphid queen," dressed in a mantle of "rolled purple," "tied with threads of dawning gold," "buttoned with a sparkling star," and sitting under a rainbow with "beamlet eyes" and a countenance of "lily roon." In our account of all this matter we have had reference to the book—and to the book alone. It will be difficult to prove us guilty in any degree of distortion or exaggeration. Yet such are the puerilities we daily find ourselves called upon to admire, as among the loftiest efforts of the human mind, and which not to assign a rank with the proud trophies of the matured and vigorous genius of England, is to prove ourselves at once a fool, a maligner, and no patriot.*

As an instance of what may be termed the sublimely ridiculous we quote the following lines from page 17.

> With sweeping tail and quivering fin,
>   Through the wave the sturgeon flew,
> And like the heaven-shot javelin,
>   He sprung above the waters blue.
>
> Instant as the star-fall light,
>   He plunged into the deep again,
> But left an arch of silver bright
>   The rainbow of the moony main.

---

*A review of Drake's poems, emanating from one of our proudest Universities, does not scruple to make use of the following language in relation to the *Culprit Fay*. "*It is, to say the least, an elegant production, the purest specimen of Ideality we have ever met with, sustaining in each incident a most bewitching interest. Its very title is enough,*" &c. &c. We quote these expressions as a fair specimen of the general unphilosophical and adulatory tenor of our criticism.

It was a strange and lovely sight
    To see the puny goblin there;
He seemed an angel form of light
    With azure wing and sunny hair,
    Throned on a cloud of purple fair
Circled with blue and edged with white
    And sitting at the fall of even
    Beneath the bow of summer heaven.

The verses here italicized, if considered without their context, have a certain air of dignity, elegance, and chastity of thought. If however we apply the context, we are immediately overwhelmed with the grotesque. It is impossible to read without laughing, such expressions as "It was a strange and lovely sight"—"He seemed an angel form of light"—"And sitting at the fall of even, beneath the bow of summer heaven" to a Fairy—a goblin—an Ouphe—half an inch high, dressed in an acorn helmet and butterfly-cloak, and sitting on the water in a muscle-shell, with a "brown-backed sturgeon" turning somersets over his head.

In a world where evil is a mere consequence of good, and good a mere consequence of evil—in short where all of which we have any conception is good or bad only by comparison—we have never yet been fully able to appreciate the validity of that decision which would debar the critic from enforcing upon his readers the merits or demerits of a work by placing it in juxta-position with another. It seems to us that an adage based in the purest ignorance has had more to do with this popular feeling than any just reason founded upon common sense. Thinking thus, we shall have no scruple in illustrating our opinion in regard to what *is not* Ideality or the Poetic Power, by an example of what *is*.* We have already given the description of the Sylphid Queen in the *Culprit*

---

*As examples of entire poems of the purest ideality, we would cite the *Prometheus Vinctus* of Æschylus, the *Inferno* of Dante, Cervantes' *Destruction of Numantia*, the *Comus* of Milton, Pope's *Rape of the Lock*, Burns' *Tam O' Shanter*, the *Auncient Mariner*, the *Christabel*, and the *Kubla Khan* of Coleridge; and most especially the *Sensitive Plant* of Shelley, and the *Nightingale* of Keats. We have seen American poems evincing the faculty in the highest degree.

Fay. In the *Queen Mab* of Shelley a Fairy is thus introduced—

> Those who had looked upon the sight,
>   Passing all human glory,
> Saw not the yellow moon,
> Saw not the mortal scene,
> Heard not the night wind's rush,
> Heard not an earthly sound,
> Saw but the fairy pageant,
> Heard but the heavenly strains
> That filled the lonely dwelling—

and thus described—

> The Fairy's frame was slight; yon fibrous cloud
> That catches but the palest tinge of even,
> And which the straining eye can hardly seize
> When melting into eastern twilight's shadow,
> Were scarce so thin, so slight; but the fair star
> That gems the glittering coronet of morn,
> *Sheds not a light so mild, so powerful,*
> *As that which, bursting from the Fairy's form,*
> *Spread a purpureal halo round the scene,*
>   *Yet with an undulating motion,*
>   *Swayed to her outline gracefully.*

In these exquisite lines the Faculty of mere Comparison is
but little exercised—that of Ideality in a wonderful degree. It
is probable that in a similar case the poet we are now reviewing would have formed the face of the Fairy of the "fibrous
cloud," her arms of the "pale tinge of even," her eyes of the
"fair stars," and her body of the "twilight shadow." Having
so done, his admirers would have congratulated him upon his
imagination, not taking the trouble to think that they themselves could at any moment *imagine* a Fairy of materials
equally as good, and conveying an equally distinct idea. Their
mistake would be precisely analogous to that of many a
schoolboy who admires the imagination displayed in *Jack the
Giant-Killer*, and is finally rejoiced at discovering his own
imagination to surpass that of the author, since the monsters

destroyed by Jack are only about forty feet in height, and he himself has no trouble in imagining some of one hundred and forty. It will be seen that the Fairy of Shelley is not a mere compound of incongruous natural objects, inartificially put together, and unaccompanied by any *moral* sentiment—but a being, in the illustration of whose nature some physical elements are used collaterally as adjuncts, while the main conception springs immediately *or thus apparently springs*, from the brain of the poet, enveloped in the moral sentiments of grace, of color, of motion—of the beautiful, of the mystical, of the august—in short of *the ideal*.*

It is by no means our intention to deny that in the *Culprit Fay* are passages of a different order from those to which we have objected—passages evincing a degree of imagination not to be discovered in the plot, conception, or general execution of the poem. The opening stanza will afford us a tolerable example.

> 'Tis the middle watch of a summer's night—
> *The earth is dark, but the heavens are bright*
> Naught is seen in the vault on high
> But the moon, and the stars, and the cloudless sky,
> And the flood which rolls its milky hue
> A river of light on the welkin blue.
> The moon looks down on old Cronest,
> She mellows the shades of his shaggy breast,
> And seems his huge grey form to throw
> In a silver cone on the wave below;
> His sides are broken by spots of shade,
> By the walnut bough and the cedar made,
> And through their clustering branches dark
> *Glimmers and dies* the fire-fly's spark—
> Like starry twinkles that momently break
> Through the rifts of the gathering tempest rack.

There is Ideality in these lines—but except in the case of the words italicized—it is Ideality *not of a high order*. We have

---

*Among things, which not only in our opinion, but in the opinion of far wiser and better men, are to be ranked with the mere prettinesses of the Muse, are the positive similes so abundant in the writings of antiquity, and so much insisted upon by the critics of the reign of Queen Anne.

it is true, a collection of natural objects, each individually of great beauty, and, if actually seen as in nature, capable of exciting in any mind, through the means of the Poetic Sentiment more or less inherent in all, a certain sense of the beautiful. But to view such natural objects as they exist, and to behold them through the medium of words, are different things. Let us pursue the idea that such a collection as we have here will produce, of necessity, the Poetic Sentiment, and we may as well make up our minds to believe that a catalogue of such expressions as moon, sky, trees, rivers, mountains &c, shall be capable of exciting it,—it is merely an extension of the principle. But in the line "the earth is dark, *but* the heavens are bright" besides the simple mention of the "dark earth" and the "bright heaven," we have, directly, the moral sentiment of the brightness of the sky compensating for the darkness of the earth—and thus, indirectly, of the happiness of a future state compensating for the miseries of a present. All this is effected by the simple introduction of the word *but* between the "dark heaven" and the "bright earth"—this introduction, however, was prompted by the Poetic Sentiment, and by the Poetic Sentiment alone. The case is analogous in the expression "glimmers and dies," where the imagination is exalted by the moral sentiment of beauty heightened in dissolution.

In one or two shorter passages of the *Culprit Fay* the poet will recognize the purely ideal, and be able at a glance to distinguish it from that baser alloy upon which we have descanted. We give them without farther comment.

> The winds *are whist*, and the owl is still
>   The bat in the shelvy rock *is hid*
> And naught is heard on the *lonely* hill
> But the cricket's chirp and the answer *shrill*
>   Of the gauze-winged katy-did;
> And the plaint of the *wailing* whippoorwill
>   Who mourns *unseen*, and ceaseless sings
> Ever a note of wail and wo—
>
> Up to the vaulted firmament
> His path the fire-fly courser bent,

And at every gallop on the wind
He flung a glittering spark behind.

He blessed the force of the charmed line,
    And he banned the water-goblins' spite,
For he saw around *in the sweet moonshine,*
Their little wee faces above the brine,
Giggling and laughing with all their might
At the piteous hap of the Fairy wight.

The poem *"To a Friend"* consists of fourteen Spenserian stanzas. They are fine spirited verses, and probably were not supposed by their author to be more. Stanza the fourth, although beginning nobly, concludes with that very common exemplification of the bathos, the illustrating natural objects of beauty or grandeur by reference to the tinsel of artificiality.

Oh! for a seat on Appalachia's brow,
That I might scan the glorious prospects round,
Wild waving woods, and rolling floods below,
Smooth level glades and fields with grain embrowned,
High heaving hills, with tufted forests crowned,
Rearing their tall tops to the heaven's blue dome,
And emerald isles, *like banners green unwound,*
Floating along the lake, while round them roam
Bright helms of billowy blue, and plumes of dancing foam.

In the *Extracts from Leon*, are passages not often surpassed in vigor of passionate thought and expression—and which induce us to believe not only that their author would have succeeded better in prose romance than in poetry, but that his attention would have naturally fallen into the former direction, had the Destroyer only spared him a little longer.

This poem contains also lines of far greater poetic power than any to be found in the *Culprit Fay*. For example—

The stars have lit in heaven their lamps of gold,
The *viewless* dew falls lightly on the world;
The gentle air *that softly sweeps the leaves*
A strain of faint unearthly music weaves:

As when the harp of heaven *remotely* plays,
Or cygnets *wail*—or song of *sorrowing* fays
That *float amid the moonshine glimmerings pale*,
On wings of woven air in some enchanted vale.*

Niagara is objectionable in many respects, and in none more so than in its frequent inversions of language, and the artificial character of its versification. The invocation,

Roar, raging torrent! and thou, mighty river,
Pour thy white foam on the valley below!
Frown ye dark mountains, &c.

is ludicrous—and nothing more. In general, all such invocations have an air of the burlesque. In the present instance we may fancy the majestic Niagara replying, "Most assuredly I will roar, whether, worm! thou tellest me or not."

The American Flag commences with a collection of those bald conceits, which we have already shown to have no dependence whatever upon the Poetic Power—springing altogether from Comparison.

When Freedom from her mountain height
    Unfurled her standard to the air,
She tore the azure robe of night
    And set the stars of glory there.
She mingled with its gorgeous dyes
The milky baldric of the skies,
And striped its pure celestial white
With streakings of the morning light;
Then from his mansion in the sun
She called her eagle bearer down
And gave into his mighty hand
    The symbol of her chosen land.

Let us reduce all this to plain English, and we have—what? Why, a flag, consisting of the "azure robe of night," "set with stars of glory," interspersed with "streaks of morning light," relieved with a few pieces of "the milky way," and the whole

*The expression " woven air," much insisted upon by the friends of Drake, seems to be accredited to him as original. It is to be found in many English writers—and can be traced back to Apuleius who calls fine drapery *ventum textilem*.

carried by an "eagle bearer," that is to say, an eagle ensign, who bears aloft this "symbol of our chosen land" in his "mighty hand," by which we are to understand his claw. In the second stanza, the "thunder-drum of Heaven" is bathetic and grotesque in the highest degree—a commingling of the most sublime music of Heaven with the most utterly contemptible and common-place of Earth. The two concluding verses are in a better spirit, and might almost be supposed to be from a different hand. The images contained in the lines,

> When Death careering on the gale
> Sweeps darkly round the bellied sail,
> And frighted waves rush wildly back,
> Before the broadside's reeling rack,

are of the highest order of Ideality. The deficiencies of the whole poem may be best estimated by reading it in connection with "Scots wha hae," with the "Mariners of England," or with "Hohenlinden." It is indebted for its high and most undeserved reputation to our patriotism—not to our judgment.

The remaining poems in Mr. Dearborn's edition of Drake, are three Songs; Lines in an Album; Lines to a Lady; Lines on leaving New Rochelle; Hope; A Fragment; To ——; Lines; To Eva; To a Lady; To Sarah; and Bronx. These are all poems of little compass, and with the exception of Bronx and a portion of the Fragment, they have no character distinctive from the mass of our current poetical literature. Bronx, however, is in our opinion, not only the best of the writings of Drake, but altogether a lofty and beautiful poem, upon which his admirers would do better to found a hope of the writer's ultimate reputation than upon the *niaiseries* of the *Culprit Fay*. In the *Fragment* is to be found the finest individual passage in the volume before us, and we quote it as a proper finale to our Review.

> Yes! thou art lovelier now than ever;
>   How sweet 'twould be *when all the air*
> *In moonlight swims*, along thy river
>   To couch upon the grass, and hear
> Niagara's everlasting voice

> Far in the deep blue west away;
> That dreamy and poetic noise
>   We mark not in the glare of day,
> Oh! how unlike its torrent-cry,
>   When o'er the brink the tide is driven,
> *As if the vast and sheeted sky*
>   *In thunder fell from Heaven.*

Halleck's poetical powers appear to us essentially inferior, upon the whole, to those of his friend Drake. He has written nothing at all comparable to *Bronx*. By the hackneyed phrase, *sportive elegance*, we might possibly designate at once the general character of his writings and the very loftiest praise to which he is justly entitled.

Alnwick Castle is an irregular poem of one hundred and twenty-eight lines—was written, as we are informed, in October 1822—and is descriptive of a seat of the Duke of Northumberland, in Northumberlandshire, England. The effect of the first stanza is materially impaired by a defect in its grammatical arrangement. The fine lines,

> Home of the Percy's high-born race,
>   Home of their beautiful and brave,
> Alike their birth and burial place,
>   Their cradle and their grave!

are of the nature of an invocation, and thus require a continuation of the address to the "Home, &c." We are consequently disappointed when the stanza proceeds with—

> Still sternly o'er the castle gate
> *Their* house's Lion stands in state
>   As in *his* proud departed hours;
> And warriors frown in stone on high,
> And feudal banners "flout the sky"
>   Above *his* princely towers.

The objects of allusion here vary, in an awkward manner, from the castle to the Lion, and from the Lion to the towers. By writing the verses thus the difficulty would be remedied.

> Still sternly o'er the castle gate
> *Thy* house's Lion stands in state,
>   As in his proud departed hours;
> And warriors frown in stone on high,
> And feudal banners "flout the sky"
>   Above *thy* princely towers.

The second stanza, without evincing in any measure the loftier powers of a poet, has that quiet air of grace, both in thought and expression, which seems to be the prevailing feature of the Muse of Halleck.

> A gentle hill its side inclines,
>   Lovely in England's fadeless green,
> To meet the quiet stream which winds
>   Through this romantic scene
> As silently and sweetly still,
> As when, at evening, on that hill,
>   While summer's wind blew soft and low,
> Seated by gallant Hotspur's side
> His Katherine was a happy bride
>   A thousand years ago.

There are one or two brief passages in the poem evincing a degree of rich imagination not elsewhere perceptible throughout the book. For example—

> Gaze on the Abbey's ruined pile:
>   Does not the succoring Ivy keeping,
> Her watch around it seem to smile
>   As o'er a lov'd one sleeping?

and,

> One solitary turret gray
>   Still tells in melancholy glory
> The legend of the Cheviot day.

The commencement of the fourth stanza is of the highest order of Poetry, and partakes, in a happy manner, of that quaintness of expression so effective an adjunct to Ideality, when employed by the Shelleys, the Coleridges and the Tennysons, but so frequently debased, and rendered ridiculous, by the herd of brainless imitators.

> Wild roses by the Abbey towers
>   Are gay in their young bud and bloom:
>   *They were born of a race of funeral flowers,*
>   That garlanded in long-gone hours,
>   A Templar's knightly tomb.

The tone employed in the concluding portions of Alnwick Castle, is, we sincerely think, reprehensible, and unworthy of Halleck. No true poet can unite in any manner the low burlesque with the ideal, and not be conscious of incongruity and of a profanation. Such verses as

> Men in the coal and cattle line
>   From Teviot's bard and hero land,
>   From royal Berwick's beach of sand,
>   From Wooller, Morpeth, Hexham, and
>   Newcastle upon Tyne,

may lay claim to oddity—but no more. These things are the defects and not the beauties of *Don Juan*. They are totally out of keeping with the graceful and delicate manner of the initial portions of *Alnwick Castle*, and serve no better purpose than to deprive the entire poem of all unity of effect. If a poet must be farcical, let him be just that, and nothing else. To be drolly sentimental is bad enough, as we have just seen in certain passages of the *Culprit Fay*, but to be sentimentally droll is a thing intolerable to men, and Gods, and columns.

Marco Bozzaris appears to have much lyrical without any high order of *ideal* beauty. *Force* is its prevailing character—a force, however, consisting more in a well ordered and sonorous arrangement of the metre, and a judicious disposal of what may be called the circumstances of the poem, than in the true *materiel* of lyric vigor. We are introduced, first, to the Turk who dreams, at midnight, in his guarded tent,

> of the hour
>   When Greece, her knee in suppliance bent,
>   Should tremble at his power—

He is represented as revelling in the visions of ambition.

> In dreams through camp and court he bore
>   The trophies of a conqueror;

> In dreams his song of triumph heard;
> Then wore his monarch's signet ring:
> Then pressed that monarch's throne—a king;
> As wild his thoughts and gay of wing
>   As Eden's garden bird.

In direct contrast to this we have Bozzaris watchful in the forest, and ranging his band of Suliotes on the ground, and amid the memories, of Platæa. An hour elapses, and the Turk awakes from his visions of false glory—to die. But Bozzaris dies—to awake. He dies in the flush of victory to awake, in death, to an ultimate certainty of Freedom. Then follows an invocation to Death. His terrors under ordinary circumstances are contrasted with the glories of the dissolution of Bozzaris, in which the approach of the Destroyer is

>   welcome as the cry
> That told the Indian isles were nigh
>   To the world-seeking Genoese,
> When the land-wind from woods of palm,
> And orange groves and fields of balm,
>   Blew o'er the Haytian seas.

The poem closes with the poetical apotheosis of Marco Bozzaris as

> One of the few, the immortal names
>   That are not born to die.

It will be seen that these arrangements of the subject are skilfully contrived—perhaps they are a little too evident, and we are enabled too readily by the perusal of one passage, to anticipate the succeeding. The rhythm is highly artificial. The stanzas are well adapted for vigorous expression—the fifth will afford a just specimen of the versification of the whole poem.

> Come to the bridal Chamber, Death!
> Come to the mother's, when she feels
> For the first time her first born's breath;
>   Come when the blessed seals
> That close the pestilence are broke,
> And crowded cities wail its stroke;

> Come in consumption's ghastly form,
> The earthquake shock, the ocean storm;
> Come when the heart beats high and warm,
>   With banquet song, and dance, and wine;
> And thou art terrible—the tear,
> The groan, the knell, the pall, the bier;
> And all we know, or dream, or fear
>   Of agony, are thine.

Granting, however, to *Marco Bozzaris*, the minor excellences we have pointed out, we should be doing our conscience great wrong in calling it, upon the whole, any thing more than a very ordinary matter. It is surpassed, even as a lyric, by a multitude of foreign and by many American compositions of a similar character. To Ideality it has few pretensions, and the finest portion of the poem is probably to be found in the verses we have quoted elsewhere—

> Thy grasp is welcome as the hand
> Of brother in a foreign land;
> Thy summons welcome as the cry
> That told the Indian isles were nigh
>   To the world-seeking Genoese,
> When the land-wind from woods of palm
> And orange groves, and fields of balm
> Blew o'er the Haytian seas.

The verses entitled *Burns* consist of thirty eight quatrains—the three first lines of each quatrain being of four feet, the fourth of three. This poem has many of the traits of *Alnwick Castle*, and bears also a strong resemblance to some of the writings of Wordsworth. Its chief merit, and indeed the chief merit, so we think, of all the poems of Halleck is the merit of *expression*. In the brief extracts from *Burns* which follow, our readers will recognize the peculiar character of which we speak.

> Wild Rose of Alloway! my thanks:
>   Thou mind'st me of *that autumn noon*
> *When first we met upon "the banks*
>   *And braes o' bonny Doon"*—

———

Like thine, beneath the thorn-tree's bough,
    My sunny hour was glad and brief—
We've crossed the winter sea, *and thou*
    Art withered—flower and leaf.

There have been loftier themes than his,
    And longer scrolls and louder lyres
And lays lit up with Poesy's
    Purer and holier fires.

And when he breathes his master-lay
    Of Alloway's witch-haunted wall
All passions in our frames of clay
    Come thronging at his call.

Such graves as his are pilgrim-shrines,
Shrines to no code or creed confined—
The Delphian vales, the Palestines,
    The Meccas of the mind.

They linger by the Doon's low trees,
    And pastoral Nith, and wooded Ayr,
And round thy Sepulchres, Dumfries!
    The Poet's tomb is there.

Wyoming is composed of nine Spenserian stanzas. With some unusual excellences, it has some of the worst faults of Halleck. The lines which follow are of great beauty.

I then but dreamed: thou art before me now,
In life—a vision of the brain no more,
I've stood upon the wooded mountain's brow,
That beetles high thy lovely valley o'er;
And now, *where winds thy river's greenest shore,*
Within a bower of sycamores am laid;
And winds as soft and sweet as ever bore
The fragrance of wild flowers through sun and shade
Are singing in the trees, whose low boughs press my head.

The poem, however, is disfigured with the mere burlesque of some portions of Alnwick Castle—with such things as

> he would look *particularly droll*
> In his Iberian boot and Spanish plume;

and

> a girl of sweet sixteen
> Love-darting eyes and tresses like the morn
> *Without a shoe or stocking—hoeing corn,*

mingled up in a pitiable manner with images of real beauty.

The Field of the Grounded Arms contains twenty-four quatrains, without rhyme, and, we think, of a disagreeable versification. In this poem are to be observed some of the finest passages of Halleck. For example—

> Strangers! your eyes are on that valley fixed
> Intently, as we gaze on vacancy,
> *When the mind's wings o'erspread*
> *The spirit world of dreams.*

And again—

> *O'er sleepless seas of grass whose waves are flowers.*

Red-Jacket has much power of expression with little evidence of poetical ability. Its humor is very fine, and does not interfere, in any great degree, with the general tone of the poem.

A Sketch should have been omitted from the edition as altogether unworthy of its author.

The remaining pieces in the volume are *Twilight*; *Psalm* cxxxvii; *To* ****; *Love*; *Domestic Happiness*; *Magdalen*; *From the Italian*; *Woman*; *Connecticut*; *Music*; *On the Death of Lieut. William Howard Allen*; *A Poet's Daughter*; and *On the Death of Joseph Rodman Drake*. Of the majority of these we deem it unnecessary to say more than that they partake, in a more or less degree, of the general character observable in the poems of Halleck. The *Poet's Daughter* appears to us a particularly happy specimen of that general character, and we doubt whether it be not the favorite of its author. We are glad to see the vulgarity of

> I'm busy in the cotton trade
> And sugar line,

omitted in the present edition. The eleventh stanza is certainly not English as it stands—and besides it is altogether unintelligible. What is the meaning of this?

> But her who asks, though first among
> The good, the beautiful, the young,
> The birthright of a spell more strong
>   Than these have brought her.

The Lines on the Death of Joseph Rodman Drake, we prefer to any of the writings of Halleck. It has that rare merit in compositions of this kind—the union of tender sentiment and simplicity. This poem consists merely of six quatrains, and we quote them in full.

> Green be the turf above thee,
>   Friend of my better days!
> None knew thee but to love thee,
>   Nor named thee but to praise.
>
> Tears fell when thou wert dying,
>   From eyes unused to weep,
> And long, where thou art lying,
>   Will tears the cold turf steep.
>
> When hearts whose truth was proven,
>   Like thine are laid in earth,
> There should a wreath be woven
>   To tell the world their worth.
>
> And I, who woke each morrow
>   To clasp thy hand in mine,
> Who shared thy joy and sorrow,
>   Whose weal and woe were thine—
>
> It should be mine to braid it
>   Around thy faded brow,
> But I've in vain essayed it,
>   And feel I cannot now.
>
> While memory bids me weep thee,
>   Nor thoughts nor words are free,
> The grief is fixed too deeply,
>   That mourns a man like thee.

If we are to judge from the subject of these verses, they are a work of some care and reflection. Yet they abound in faults. In the line,

> Tears fell when thou wert dying;

wert is not English.

> Will tears the cold turf steep,

is an exceedingly rough verse. The metonymy involved in

> There should a wreath be woven
>   To *tell* the world their worth,

is unjust. The quatrain beginning,

> And I who woke each morrow,

is ungrammatical in its construction when viewed in connection with the quatrain which immediately follows. "Weep thee" and "deeply" are inaccurate rhymes—and the whole of the first quatrain,

> Green be the turf, &c.

although beautiful, bears too close a resemblance to the still more beautiful lines of William Wordsworth,

> She dwelt among the untrodden ways
>   Beside the springs of Dove,
> A maid whom there were none to praise
>   And very few to love.

As a versifier Halleck is by no means equal to his friend, all of whose poems evince an ear finely attuned to the delicacies of melody. We seldom meet with more inharmonious lines than those, generally, of the author of *Alnwick Castle*. At every step such verses occur as,

> And *the* monk's hymn and minstrel's song—
> True *as* the steel of *their* tried blades—
> For him the joy of *her* young years—
> Where *the* Bard-peasant first drew breath—
> And withered *my* life's leaf like thine—

in which the proper course of the rhythm would demand an accent upon syllables too unimportant to sustain it. Not unfrequently, too, we meet with lines such as this,

> Like torn branch from death's leafless tree,

in which the multiplicity of consonants renders the pronunciation of the words at all, a matter of no inconsiderable difficulty.

But we must bring our notice to a close. It will be seen that while we are willing to admire in many respects the poems before us, we feel obliged to dissent materially from that public opinion (perhaps not fairly ascertained) which would assign them a very brilliant rank in the empire of Poesy. That we have among us poets of the loftiest order we believe—but we do *not* believe that these poets are Drake and Halleck.

Southern Literary Messenger, April 1836

Theodore S. Fay

Norman Leslie. A Tale of the Present Times. New York: Published by Harper and Brothers.

WELL!—here we have it! This is *the* book—*the* book *par excellence*—the book bepuffed, beplastered, and be-*Mirrored*: the book "attributed to" Mr. Blank, and "said to be from the pen" of Mr. Asterisk: the book which has been "about to appear"—"in press"—"in progress"—"in preparation"—and "forthcoming:" the book "graphic" in anticipation—"talented" *a priori*—and God knows what *in prospectu*. For the sake of every thing puffed, puffing, and puffable, let us take a peep at its contents!

Norman Leslie, gentle reader, a Tale of the Present Times, is, after all, written by nobody in the world but Theodore S. Fay, and Theodore S. Fay is nobody in the world but "one of the Editors of the New York Mirror." The book commences with a Dedication to Colonel Herman Thorn, in which that worthy personage, whoever he may be, is held up, in about a dozen lines, to the admiration of the public, as "hospitable," "generous," "attentive," "benevolent," "kind-hearted," "liberal," "highly-esteemed," and withal "a patron of the arts." But the less we say of this matter the better.

In the Preface Mr. Fay informs us that the most important features of his story are founded on fact—that he has availed himself of certain poetical licenses—that he has transformed character, and particularly the character of a young lady, (oh fi! Mr. Fay—oh, Mr. Fay, fi!) that he has sketched certain peculiarities with a mischievous hand—and that the art of novel writing is as dignified as the art of Canova, Mozart or Raphael,—from which we are left to infer, that Mr. Fay himself is as dignified as Raphael, Mozart, and Canova—all three. Having satisfied us on this head, he goes on to say something about an humble student, with a feeble hand, throwing groupings upon a canvass, and standing behind a curtain: and then, after perpetrating all these impertinences, thinks it best "frankly to bespeak the indulgence of the solemn and sapient critics." Body of Bacchus! *we*, at least, are neither solemn nor sapient, and, therefore, do not feel ourselves bound to show him a shadow of mercy. But will any body tell us what is the object of Prefaces in general, and what is the meaning of Mr. Fay's Preface in particular?

As far as we can understand the plot of Norman Leslie, it is this. A certain family reside in Italy—"independent," "enlightened," "affectionate," "happy,"—and all that. Their villa, of course, stands upon the seashore, and their whole establishment is, we are assured, "a scene of Heaven," &c. Mr. Fay says he will not even attempt to describe it—why, therefore, should we? A daughter of this family is nineteen when she is wooed by a young Neapolitan, Rinaldo, of "mean extraction, but of great beauty and talent." The lover, being a man of suspicious character, is rejected by the parents, and a secret marriage ensues. The lady's brother pursues the bridegroom—they fight—and the former is killed. The father and mother die (it is impossible to see for what purpose they ever lived) and Rinaldo flies to Venice. Upon rejoining her husband in that city, the lady (for Mr. Fay has not thought her worth enduing with a specific appellation) discovers him, for the first time, to be a rascal. One fine day he announces his intention of leaving herself and son for an indefinite time. The lady beseeches and finally threatens. "It was the first unfolding," says she, in a letter towards the *dénouement* of the story, "of that character which neither he nor I knew belonged to my nature. It was the first uncoiling of the basilisk within me, (good Heavens, a snake in a lady's stomach!). He gazed on me incredulously, and cooly smiled. You remember that smile—I fainted!!!" Alas! Mr. Davy Crockett,—Mr. Davy Crockett, alas!—thou art beaten hollow—thou art defunct, and undone! thou hast indeed succeeded in grinning a squirrel from a tree, but it surpassed even thine extraordinary abilities to smile a lady into a fainting fit!

"When I recovered"—continues the lady—"he was gone. It was two years before I could trace him. At length I found he had sailed for America. I followed him in the depth of winter—I and my child. I knew not the name he had assumed, and I was struck mute with astonishment, in your beautiful city, on beholding, surrounded by fair ladies, the form of my husband, still beautiful, and still adored. You know the rest." But as our readers may not be as well in-

formed as the correspondent of the fair forsaken, we will enlighten them with some farther particulars.

Rinaldo, upon leaving his *cara sposa*, had taken shipping for
New York, where, assuming the name of "Count Clairmont
of the French army," he succeeds in cutting a dash, or, in
more proper parlance, in creating a sensation, among the
beaux and belles of the city of Gotham. One fair lady, and
rich heiress, Miss Flora Temple, is particularly honored by his
attentions, and the lady's mother, Mrs. T., fired with the idea
of her daughter becoming a real countess, makes no scruple
of encouraging his addresses. Matters are in this position
when the wife of the adventurer arrives in New York, and is
quite bewildered with astonishment upon beholding, one
snowy day, her beloved Rinaldo sleighing it to and fro about
the streets of New York. In the midst of her amazement she
is in danger of being run over by some horses, when a certain
personage, by name Norman Leslie, but who might, with
equal propriety, be called Sir Charles Grandison, flies to her
assistance, whisks herself and child up in the very nick of
time, and suddenly rescues them, as Mr. Fay has it, "from the
very jaws of Death"—by which we are to understand from
the very hoofs of the horses. The lady of course swoons—
then recovers—and then—is excessively grateful. Her gratitude, however, being of no service just at that moment, is
bottled up for use hereafter, and will no doubt, according to
established usage in such cases, come into play towards the
close of the second volume. But we shall see.

Having ascertained the address of Rinaldo, *alias* the Count
Clairmont, the lady, next morning, is successful in obtaining
an interview. Then follows a second edition of entreaties and
threats, but, fortunately for the nerves of Mrs. Rinaldo, the
Count, upon this occasion, is so forbearing as not to indulge
in a smile. She accuses him of a design to marry Miss Temple,
and he informs her that it is no concern of hers—that she is
not his wife, their marriage having been a feigned one. "She
would have cried him through the city for a villain," (Dust
ho!—she should have advertised him) but he swears that, in
that case, he will never sleep until he has taken the life of both
the lady and her child, which assurance puts an end to the
debate. "He then frankly confesses"—says Mrs. Rinaldo, in

the letter which we have before quoted,—"that his passion for Miss Temple was only a mask—he loved her not. *Me* he said he loved. It was his intention to fly when he could raise a large sum of money, and he declared that I should be his companion." His designs, however, upon Miss Temple fail—that lady very properly discarding the rascal. Nothing daunted at this mishap our Count proceeds to make love to a certain Miss Rosalie Romain, and with somewhat better success. He prevails upon her to fly, and to carry with her upon her person a number of diamonds which the lover hopes to find sufficient for his necessities. He manages also to engage Mrs. Rinaldo (so we must call her for want of a better name) in his schemes.

It has so happened that for some time prior to these occurrences, Clairmont and Norman Leslie, the hero of the novel, have been sworn foes. On the day fixed for Miss Romain's elopement, that young lady induces Mr. Leslie to drive her, in a gig, a short distance out of town. They are met by no less a personage than Mrs. Rinaldo herself, in another gig, and driving (*proh pudor!*) through the woods *sola*. Hereupon Miss Rosalie Romain very deliberately, and to the great astonishment, no doubt, of Mr. Leslie, gets out of that gentleman's gig, and into the gig of Mrs. Rinaldo. Here's plot! as Vapid says in the play. Our friend Norman, finding that nothing better can be done, turns his face towards New York again, where he arrives, in due time, without farther accident or adventure. Late the same evening Clairmont sends the ladies aboard a vessel bound for Naples, and which is to sail in the morning—returning himself, for the present, to his hotel in Broadway. While here he receives a horse-whipping from Mr. Leslie on account of certain insinuations in disparagement of that gentleman's character. Not relishing this treatment he determines upon revenge, and can think of no better method of accomplishing it than the directing of public suspicion against Mr. Leslie as the murderer of Miss Romain—whose disappearance has already created much excitement. He sends a message to Mrs. Rinaldo that the vessel must sail without him, and that he would, by a French ship, meet them on their landing at Naples. He then flings a hat and feathers belonging to Miss Romain upon a stream, and her handker-

chief in a wood—afterwards remaining some time in America
to avert suspicion from himself. Leslie is arrested for the murder, and the proofs are damning against him. He is, however,
to the great indignation of the populace, acquitted, Miss
Temple appearing to testify that she actually saw Miss Romain subsequently to her ride with Leslie. Our hero, however, although acquitted, is universally considered guilty, and,
through the active malice of Clairmont, is heaped with every
species of opprobrium. Miss Temple, who, it appears, is in
love with him, falls ill with grief: but is cured, after all other
means have failed, by a letter from her lover announcing a
reciprocal passion—for the young lady has hitherto supposed
him callous to her charms. Leslie himself, however, takes it
into his head, at this critical juncture, to travel; and, having
packed up his baggage, does actually forget himself so far as
to go a-Willising in foreign countries. But we have no reason
to suppose that, goose as the young gentleman is, he is silly
enough to turn travelling correspondent to any weekly paper.
In Rome, having assumed the *alias* of Montfort, he meets
with a variety of interesting adventures. All the ladies die for
him: and one in particular, Miss Antonia Torrini, the only
child of a Duke with several millions of piastres, and a palace
which Mr. Fay thinks very much like the City Hall in New
York, absolutely throws herself *sans ceremonie* into his arms,
and meets—tell it not in Gath!—with a flat and positive
refusal.

Among other persons whom he encounters is a monk Am-
brose, a painter Angelo, another painter Ducci, a Marquis
Alezzi, and a Countess D., which latter personage he is convinced of having seen at some prior period of his life. For a
page or two we are entertained with a prospect of a conspiracy, and have great hopes that the principal characters in the
plot will so far oblige us as to cut one another's throats: but
(alas for human expectations!) Mr. Fay having clapped his
hands, and cried "Presto!—vanish!" the whole matter ends in
smoke, or, as our author beautifully expresses it, is "veiled in
impenetrable mystery."

Mr. Leslie now pays a visit to the painter Ducci, and is
astonished at there beholding the portrait of the very youth
whose life he saved, together with that of his mother, from

the horses in New York. Then follows a series of interesting
ejaculations, among which we are able to remember only
"horrible suspicion!" "wonderful development!" "alack and
alas!" with some two or three others. Mr. Leslie is, however,
convinced that the portrait of the boy is, as Mr. F. gracefully
has it, "inexplicably connected with his own mysterious destiny." He pays a visit to the Countess D., and demands of her
if she was, at any time, acquainted with a gentleman called
Clairmont. The lady very properly denies all knowledge of
that character, and Mr. Leslie's "mysterious destiny" is in as
bad a predicament as ever. He is however fully convinced that
Clairmont is the origin of all evil—we do not mean to say
that he is precisely the devil—but the origin of all Mr. Leslie's evil. Therefore, and on this account, he goes to a masquerade, and, sure enough, Mr. Clairmont, (who has not
been heard of for seven or eight years,) Mr. Clairmont (we
suppose through Mr. L's "mysterious destiny") happens to
go, at precisely the same time, to precisely the same masquerade. But there are surely no bounds to Mr. Fay's excellent
invention. Miss Temple, of course, happens to be at the same
place, and Mr. Leslie is in the act of making love to her once
more, when the "inexplicable" Countess D. whispers into his
ear some ambiguous sentences in which Mr. L. is given to
understand that he must beware of all the Harlequins in the
room, one of whom is Clairmont. Upon leaving the masquerade, somebody hands him a note requesting him to meet the
unknown writer at St. Peter's. While he is busy reading the
paper he is uncivilly interrupted by Clairmont, who attempts
to assassinate him, but is finally put to flight. He hies, then,
to the rendezvous at St. Peter's, where "the unknown" tells
him St. Peter's won't answer, and that he must proceed to the
Coliseum. He goes—why should he not?—and there not
only finds the Countess D. who turns out to be Mrs. Rinaldo,
and who now uncorks her bottle of gratitude, but also Flora
Temple, Flora Temple's father, Clairmont, Kreutzner, a German friend from New York, and, last but not least, Rosalie
Romain herself; all having gone there, no doubt, at three
o'clock in the morning, under the influence of that interesting
young gentleman Norman Leslie's "most inexplicable and
mysterious destiny." Matters now come to a crisis. The hero's

innocence is established, and Miss Temple falls into his arms in consequence. Clairmont, however, thinks he can do nothing better than shoot Mr. Leslie, and is about to do so, when he is very justly and very dexterously knocked in the head by Mr. Kreutzner. Thus ends the Tale of the Present Times, and thus ends the most inestimable piece of balderdash with which the common sense of the good people of America was ever so openly or so villainously insulted.

We do not mean to say that there is positively *nothing* in Mr. Fay's novel to commend—but there is indeed very little. One incident is tolerably managed, in which, at the burning house of Mr. Temple, Clairmont anticipates Leslie in his design of rescuing Flora. A cotillon scene, too, where Morton, a simple fop, is frequently interrupted in his attempts at making love to Miss Temple, by the necessity of forward-twoing and *sachezing*, (as Mr. Fay thinks proper to call it) is by no means very bad, although savoring too much of the farcical. A duel story told by Kreutzner is really good, but unfortunately not original, there being a Tale in the *Diary of a Physician*, from which both its matter and manner are evidently borrowed. And here we are obliged to pause; for we can positively think of nothing farther worth even a qualified commendation. The plot, as will appear from the running outline we have given of it, is a monstrous piece of absurdity and incongruity. The characters *have no character*; and, with the exception of Morton, who is, (perhaps) amusing, are, one and all, vapidity itself. No attempt seems to have been made at individualization. All the good ladies and gentlemen are demi-gods and demi-goddesses, and all the bad are—the d—l. The hero, Norman Leslie, "that young and refined man with a leaning to poetry," is a great coxcomb and a great fool. What else must we think of a *bel-esprit* who, in picking up a rose just fallen from the curls of his lady fair, can hit upon no more appropriate phrase with which to make her a presentation of the same, than "Miss Temple, you have dropped your rose—allow me!"—who courts his mistress with a "Dear, dear Flora, how I love you!"—who calls a *buffet* a *bufet*, an *improvisatore* an *improvisitore*—who, before bestowing charity, is always ready with the canting question if the object be *deserving*—who is everlastingly talking of his foe "sleeping in the same red grave with himself," as if American sextons made a common practice of burying two people together—and, who having not a sous in his pocket at page 86, pulls out a handful at page 87, although he has had no opportunity of obtaining a copper in the interim?

As regards Mr. Fay's *style*, it is unworthy of a school-boy. The "Editor of the New York Mirror" has either never seen an edition of Murray's Grammar, or he has been a-Willising so long as to have forgotten his vernacular language. Let us examine one or two of his sentences at random. Page 28, vol. i. "He was doomed to wander through the *fartherest* climes alone and branded." Why not say at once *fartherertherest*? Page 150, vol. i. "Yon kindling orb should be hers; and that faint spark close to its side should teach her how dim and yet how near my soul was to her own." What is the meaning of all this? Is Mr. Leslie's soul dim to her own, as well as near to her own?—for the sentence implies as much. Suppose we say "should teach her how dim was my soul, and yet how near to her own." Page 101, vol. i. "You are both right and both wrong—you, Miss Romain, to judge so harshly of all men who are not versed in the easy elegance of the drawing room, and your father in too great lenity towards men of sense, &c." This is really something new, but we are sorry to say, something incomprehensible. Suppose we translate it. "You are both right and both wrong—you, Miss Romain, *are both right and wrong* to judge so harshly of all not versed in the elegance of the drawing-room, &c.; and your father *is both right and wrong* in too great lenity towards men of sense."—Mr. Fay, have you ever visited Ireland in your peregrinations? But the book is full to the brim of such absurdities, and it is useless to pursue the matter any farther. There is not a single page of Norman Leslie in which even a school-boy would fail to detect at least two or three gross errors in Grammar, and some two or three most egregious sins against common-sense.

We will dismiss the "Editor of the Mirror" with a few questions. When did you ever know, Mr. Fay, of any prosecuting attorney behaving so much like a bear as *your* prosecuting attorney in the novel of Norman Leslie? When did you ever hear of an American Court of Justice objecting to the testimony of a witness on the ground that the said witness *had an interest* in the cause at issue? What do you mean by informing us at page 84, vol. i, "that you *think* much faster than you write?" What do you mean by "*the wind roaring in the air?*" see page 26, vol. i. What do you mean by "an *unshadowed* Italian girl?" see page 67, vol. ii. Why are you always talking about "stamping of feet," "kindling and flashing of eyes," "plunging and parrying," "cutting and thrusting," "passes through the body," "gashes open in the cheek," "sculls cleft down," "hands cut off," and blood gushing and bubbling, and doing God knows what else—all of which pretty expressions may be found on page 88, vol. i.? What "mysterious and inexplicable destiny" compels you to the so frequent use, in all its inflections, of that euphonical dyssyllable *blister?* We will call to your recollection some few instances in which you have employed it. Page 185, vol. i. "But an arrival from the city brought the fearful intelligence in all its *blistering* and naked details." Page 193, vol. i. "What but the glaring and *blistering* truth of the charge would select him, &c." Page 39, vol. ii. "Wherever the winds of heaven wafted the English language, the *blistering* story must have been echoed." Page 150, vol. ii. "Nearly seven years had passed away, and here he found himself, as at first, still marked with the *blistering* and burning brand." Here we have a *blistering* detail, a *blistering* truth, a *blistering* story, and a *blistering* brand, to say nothing of innumerable other blisters interspersed throughout the book. But we have done with Norman Leslie,—if ever we saw as silly a thing, may we be——blistered.

Southern Literary Messenger, December 1835

Rufus W. Griswold

The Poets and Poetry of America: with a Historical Introduction. By Rufus W. Griswold. Second Edition. Philadelphia, Carey & Hart, 1842.

THAT WE are not a poetical people has been asserted so often and so roundly, both at home and abroad, that the slander, through mere dint of repetition, has come to be received as truth. Yet nothing can be farther removed from it. The mistake is but a portion, or corollary, of the old dogma, that the calculating faculties are at war with the ideal; while, in fact, it may be demonstrated that the two divisions of mental power are never to be found, in perfection, apart. The *highest* order of the imaginative intellect is always preëminently mathematical; and the converse.

The idiosyncrasy of our political position has stimulated into early action whatever practical talent we possessed. Even in our national infancy we evinced a degree of utilitarian ability which put to shame the mature skill of our forefathers. While yet in leading-strings we proved ourselves adepts in all the arts and sciences which promote the *comfort* of the animal man. But the arena of exertion, and of consequent distinction, into which our first and most obvious wants impelled us, has been regarded as the field of our deliberate choice. Our necessities have been mistaken for our propensities. Having been forced to make rail-roads, it has been deemed impossible that we should make verse. Because it suited us to construct an engine in the first instance, it has been denied that we could compose an epic in the second. Because we were not all Homers in the beginning, it has been somewhat too rashly taken for granted that we shall be all Jeremy Benthams to the end.

But this is the purest insanity. The principles of the poetic sentiment lie deep within the immortal nature of man, and have little necessary reference to the worldly circumstances which surround him. The poet in Arcady is, in Kamschadtka, the poet still. The self-same Saxon current animates the British and the American heart; nor can any social, or political, or moral, or physical conditions do more than momentarily repress the impulses which glow in our own bosoms as fervently as in those of our progenitors.

Those who have taken most careful note of our literature for the last ten or twelve years, will be most willing to admit that *we are* a poetical people; and in no respect is the fact more plainly evinced than in the eagerness with which books professing to compile or select from the productions of our native bards, are received and appreciated by the public. Such books meet with success, at least with sale, at periods when the general market for literary wares is in a state of stagnation; and even the ill taste displayed in some of them has not sufficed to condemn. The "Specimens of American Poetry," by Kettell; the "Common-place Book of American Poetry," by Cheever; a Selection by General Morris; another by Mr. Bryant; the "Poets of America," by Mr. Keese—all these have been widely disseminated and well received. In some measure, to be sure, we must regard their success as an affair of personalities. Each individual, honored with a niche in the compiler's memory, is naturally anxious to possess a copy of the book so honoring him; and this anxiety will extend, in some cases, to ten or twenty of the immediate friends of the complimented; while, on the other hand, purchasers will arise, in no small number, from among a very different class—a class animated by very different feelings. I mean the omitted—the large body of those who, supposing themselves entitled to mention, have yet been unmentioned. These buy the unfortunate book as a matter of course, for the purpose of abusing it with a clear conscience and at leisure. But holding these deductions in view, we are still warranted in believing that the demand for works of the kind in question, is to be attributed, mainly, to the general interest of the subject discussed. The public have been desirous of obtaining a more distinct view of our poetical literature than the scattered effusions of our bards and the random criticisms of our periodicals, could afford. But, hitherto, nothing has been accomplished in the way of supplying the *desideratum*. The "specimens" of Kettell were specimens of nothing but the ignorance and ill taste of the compiler. A large proportion of what he gave to the world as American poetry, to the exclusion of much that was really so, was the doggerel composition of individuals unheard of and undreamed of, except by Mr. Kettell himself.

Mr. Cheever's book did not belie its title, and was excessively "Common-place." The selection by General Morris was in so far good, that it accomplished its object to the full extent. This object looked to nothing more than single, brief extracts from the writings of every one in the country who had established even the slightest reputation as poet. The extracts, so far as our truer poets were concerned, were tastefully made; but the proverbial kind feeling of the General seduced him into the admission of an inordinate quantity of the purest twattle. It was gravely declared that we had more than *two hundred* poets in the land. The compilation of Mr. Bryant, from whom much was expected, proved a source of mortification to his friends, and of astonishment and disappointment to all; merely showing that a poet is, necessarily, neither a critical nor an unpartial judge of poetry. Mr. Keese succeeded much better. He brought to his task, if not the most rigorous impartiality, at least a fine taste, a sound judgment, and a more thorough acquaintance with our poetical literature than had distinguished either of his predecessors.

Much, however, remained to be done; and here it may be right to inquire—"What should be the aim of every compilation of the character now discussed?" The object, in general terms, may be stated, as the conveying, within moderate compass, a distinct view of our poetry and of our poets. This, in fact, is the demand of the public. A book is required, which shall not so much be the reflection of the compiler's peculiar views and opinions upon poetry in the abstract, as of the popular judgment upon such poetical works as have come immediately within its observation. It is not the author's business to insist upon his own theory, and, in its support, to rake up from the by-ways of the country the "inglorious Miltons" who may, possibly, there abound; neither, because ill according with this theory, is it his duty to dethrone and reject those who have long maintained supremacy in the estimation of the people. In this view, it will be seen that regard must be paid to the mere *quantity* of a writer's effusions. He who has published much, is not to be omitted because, in the opinion of the compiler, he has written nothing fit for publication. On the other hand, he who has extemporized a single song, which has met the eye of no one but our bibliographer, is not to be set forth among the poetical magnates, even although the one song itself be esteemed equal to the very best of Béranger.

Of the two classes of sins—the negative and the positive—those of omission and those of commission—obvious ones of the former class are, beyond doubt, the more unpardonable. It is better to introduce half a dozen "great unknowns," than to give the "cut direct" to a single individual who has been fairly acknowledged as known. The public, in short, seem to demand *such a compendium of our poetical literature as shall embrace specimens from those works alone, of our recognised poets; which, either through accident, or by dint of merit, have been most particularly the subjects of public discussion.* We wish this, that we may be put in condition to decide for ourselves upon the justice or injustice of the reputation attained. In critical opinion much diversity exists; and, although there is but one true and tenable critical opinion, there are still a thousand, upon all topics, which, being only the shadows, have all the outlines, and assume all the movements, of the substance, of truth. Thus any critic who should exclude from the compendium all which tallied not with his individual ideas of the Muse, would be found to exclude nine hundred and ninety-nine thousandths of that which the public at large, embracing *all* varieties of opinion, has been accustomed to acknowledge as poesy.

These remarks apply only to the admission or rejection of poetical specimens. The public being put fairly in possession of the matter debated, with the provisions above-mentioned, the analysis of individual claims, *so far as the specimens extend,* is not only not unbecoming in the compiler, but a thing to be expected and desired. To this department of his work he should bring analytical ability; a distinct impression of the nature, the principles, and the aims of poetry; a thorough contempt for all prejudice at war with principle; a poetic sense of the poetic; sagacity in the detection, and audacity in the exposure of demerit; in a word talent *and faith*; the lofty honor which places mere courtesy beneath its feet; the boldness to praise an enemy, and the more unusual courage to damn a friend.

It is, in fact, by the criticism of the work, that the public voice will, in the end, decide upon its merits. In proportion to the ability or incapacity here displayed, will it, sooner or later, be approved or condemned. Nevertheless, the mere *compilation* is a point, perhaps, of greater importance. With the meagre published *aids* existing previously to Mr. Griswold's book, the labor of such an undertaking must have been great; and not less great the industry and general information in respect to our literary affairs, which have enabled him so successfully to prosecute it.

The work before us is indeed so vast an improvement upon those of a similar character which have preceded it, that we do its author some wrong in classing all together. Having explained, somewhat minutely, our views of the proper mode of compilation, and of the general aims of the species of book in question, it but remains to say that these views have been very nearly fulfilled in the "Poets and Poetry of America," while altogether unsatisfied by the earlier publications.

The volume opens with a preface, which, with some little supererogation, is addressed "To the Reader;" inducing very naturally the query, whether the whole book is not addressed to the same individual. In this preface, which is remarkably well written and strictly to the purpose, the author thus evinces a just comprehension of the nature and objects of true poesy:

"He who looks on Lake George, or sees the sun rise on Mackinaw, or listens to the grand music of a storm, is divested, certainl, for a time, of a portion of the alloy of his nature. The elements of power in all sublime sights and heavenly harmonies, should live in the poet's song, to which they can be transferred only by him who possesses the creative faculty. The sense of beauty, next to the miraculous divine suasion, is the means through which the human character is purified and elevated. *The creation of beauty, the manifestation of the real by the ideal, 'in words that move in metrical array,' is poetry.*"

The italics are our own; and we quote the passage because it embodies the *sole true* definition of what has been a thousand times erroneously defined.

The earliest specimens of poetry presented in the body of the work, are from the writings of Philip Freneau, "one of

those worthies who, both with lyre and sword, aided in the
achievement of our independence." But, in a volume professing to treat, generally, of the "Poets and Poetry of America,"
some mention of those who versified before Freneau, would
of course, be considered desirable. Mr. Griswold has included, therefore, most of our earlier votaries of the Muse,
with many specimens of their powers, in an exceedingly valuable "Historical Introduction;" his design being to exhibit as
well "*the progress* as the condition of poetry in the United
States."

The basis of the compilation is formed of short biographi-
cal and critical notices, with selections from the works of
Philip Freneau, John Trumbull, Timothy Dwight, David
Humphreys, Joel Barlow, Richard Alsop, St. John Honey-
wood, William Cliffton, Robert Treat Paine, Washington
Allston, James Kirke Paulding, Levi Frisbie, John Pierpont,
Andrews Norton, Richard H. Dana, Richard Henry Wilde,
James A. Hillhouse, Charles Sprague, Hannah F. Gould, Car-
los Wilcox, Henry Ware, Jr., William Cullen Bryant, John
Neal, Joseph Rodman Drake, Maria Brooks, James Gates Per-
cival, Fitz-Green Halleck, John G. C. Brainard, Samuel Gris-
wold Goodrich, Isaac Clason, Lydia H. Sigourney, George
Washington Doane, William B. O. Peabody, Robert C.
Sands, Grenville Mellen, George Hill, James G. Brooks, Al-
bert G. Greene, William Leggett, Edward C. Pinckney, Ralph
Waldo Emerson, Sumner Lincoln Fairfield, Rufus Dawes, Ed-
mund D. Griffin, J. H. Bright, George D. Prentice, William
Croswell, Walter Colton, Charles Fenno Hoffman, Mrs. Seba
Smith, N. P. Willis, Edward Sanford, J. O. Rockwell, Thomas
Ward, John H. Bryant, Henry Wadsworth Longfellow, Wil-
liam Gilmore Simms, George Lunt, Jonathan Lawrence, Eliz-
abeth Hall, Emma C. Embury, John Greenleaf Whittier,
Oliver Wendell Holmes, Albert Pike, Park Benjamin, Willis
Gaylord Clark, William D. Gallagher, James Freeman Clarke,
Elizabeth F. Ellett, James Aldrich, Anna Peyre Dinnies, Edgar
Allan Poe, Isaac McLellan, Jr., Jones Very, Alfred B. Street,
William H. Burleigh, William Jewett Pabodie, Louis Legrand
Noble, C. P. Cranch, Henry Theodore Tuckerman, Epes Sar-
gent, Lucy Hooper, Arthur Cleveland Coxe, James Russell
Lowell, Amelia B. Welby, Lucretia and Margaret Davidson—

in all, eighty-seven, chronologically arranged. In an appendix at the end of the volume, are included specimens from the works of sixty authors, whose compositions have either been too few, or in the editor's opinion too *mediocres*, to entitle them to more particular notice. To each of these specimens are appended foot notes, conveying a brief biographical summary, without anything of critical disquisition.

Of the general plan and execution of the work we have already expressed the fullest approbation. We know no one in America who could, or *who would*, have performed the task here undertaken, at once so well in accordance with the judgment of the critical, and so much to the satisfaction of the public. The labors, the embarrassments, the great difficulties of the achievement are not easily estimated by those before the scenes.

The writer of this article, in saying that, individually, he disagrees with many of the opinions expressed by Mr. Griswold, is merely suggesting what, in itself, would have been obvious without the suggestion. It rarely happens that any two persons thoroughly agree upon any one point. It would be mere madness to imagine that any two could coincide in every point of a case where exists a multiplicity of opinions upon a multiplicity of points. There is no one who, reading the volume before us, will not in a thousand instances, be tempted to throw it aside, because its prejudices and partialities are, in a thousand instances, altogether at war with his own. But when so tempted, he should bear in mind, that had the work been that of Aristarchus himself, the discrepancies of opinion would still have startled him and vexed him as now.

We disagree then, with Mr. Griswold in *many* of his critical estimates; although in general, we are proud to find his decisions our own. He has omitted from the body of his book, some one or two whom we should have been tempted to introduce. On the other hand, he has scarcely made us amends by introducing some one or two dozen whom we should have treated with contempt. We might complain too of a prepossession, evidently unperceived by himself, for the writers of New England. We might hint also, that in two or three cases, he has rendered himself liable to the charge of personal partiality; it is often so *very* difficult a thing to keep separate in the mind's eye, our conceptions of the poetry of a friend, from our impressions of his good fellowship and our recollections of the flavor of his wine.

But having said thus much in the way of fault-finding, we have said all. The book should be regarded as *the most important addition which our literature has for many years received.* It fills a void which should have been long ago supplied. It is written with judgment, with dignity and candor. Steering with a dexterity not to be sufficiently admired, between the Scylla of Prejudice on the one hand, and the Charybdis of Conscience on the other, Mr. Griswold in the "Poets and Poetry of America," has entitled himself to the thanks of his countrymen, while showing himself a man of taste, talent, *and tact*.

Boston Miscellany, November 1842

Francis L. Hawks

Contributions to the Ecclesiastical History of the United States of America—Virginia. A Narrative of Events connected with the Rise and Progress of the Protestant Episcopal Church in Virginia. To which is added an Appendix, containing the Journals of the Conventions in Virginia, from the Commencement to the Present Time. By the Reverend Francis L. Hawks, D.D. Rector of St. Thomas's Church, New York. New York: Published by Harper and Brothers.

THIS IS a large and handsome octavo of 620 pages. The very cursory examination which we have as yet been able to give it, will not warrant us in speaking of the work in other than general terms. A word or two, however, we may say in relation to the plan, the object, and circumstances of publication, with some few observations upon points which have attracted our especial attention.

From the Preface we learn that, more than five years ago, the author, in conjunction with the Rev. Edward Rutledge, of South Carolina, first conceived the idea of gathering together such materials for the History of the Protestant Episcopal Church in the United States, as might still exist either in tradition or in the manuscripts of the earlier clergy. That these materials were abundant might rationally be supposed—still they were to be collected, if collected at all, at the expense of much patience, time, and labor, from a wide diversity of sources. Dr. Hawks and his associate, however, were stimulated to exertion by many of the bishops and clergy of the church. The plan originally proposed was merely, if we understand it, the compilation of an annalistic journal—a record of naked facts, to be subsequently arranged and shaped into narrative by the pen of the historiographer. In the prosecution of the plan thus designed, our author and his coadjutor were successful beyond expectation, and a rich variety of matter was collected. Death, at this period, deprived Dr. Hawks of his friend's assistance, and left him to pursue his labor alone. He now, very properly, determined upon attempting, himself, the execution of the work for which his Annals were intended as *materiel*. He began with Virginia—selecting it as the oldest State. The present volume is simply an experiment. Should it succeed, of which there can be no doubt whatever, we shall have other volumes in turn—and that, we suppose, speedily, for there are already on hand sufficient *data* to furnish a history of "each of the older diocesses."

For the design of this work—if even not for the manner of its execution—Dr. Hawks is entitled to the thanks of the community at large. He has taken nearly the first step (a step, too, of great decision, interest and importance) in the field of American Ecclesiastical History. To that church, especially, of which he is so worthy a member, he has rendered a service not to be lightly appreciated in the extraordinary dearth of materials for its story. In regard to Protestant Episcopalism in America it may be safely said that, prior to this publication of Dr. Hawks, there were no written memorials extant, with the exception of the Archives of the General and Diocesan Meetings, and the Journal of Bishop White. For other religious denominations the *materiel* of history is more abundant, and it would be well, if following the suggestions and example of our author, Christians of all sects would exert themselves for the collection and preservation of what is so important to the cause of our National Ecclesiastical Literature.

The History of any Religion is necessarily a very large portion of the History of the people who profess it. And regarded in this point of view the *"Narrative"* of Dr. Hawks will prove of inestimable value to Virginia. It commences with the first settlement of the colony—with the days when the first church was erected in Virginia—that very church whose hoary ruins stand so tranquilly to-day in the briar-encumbered graveyard at Jamestown—with the memorable epoch when Smith, being received into the council, partook, with his rival, the President, of the Sacrament of the Lord's Supper, and Virginia "commenced its career of civilization" with the most impressive of Christian solemnities. Bringing down the affairs of the church to the appointment of the Reverend William Meade, D.D. as Assistant Bishop of Virginia, the narration concludes with a highly gratifying account of present prosperity. The diocese is said to possess more than one hundred churches, "some of them the fruit of reviving zeal in parishes which once flourished, but have long been almost dead." Above seventy clergymen are in actual service. There is a large missionary fund, a part of which lies idle, because missionaries are not to be had. Much reliance is placed, however, upon the Seminary at Alexandria. This institution has afforded instruction, during the last three years, to sixty candidates for orders, and has given no less than thirty-six ministers to the Episcopalty.

We will mention, briefly, a few of the most striking points of the History before us. At page 48, are some remarks in reply to Burk's insinuation of a persecuting and intolerant spirit in the early colonial religion of the State—an insinuation based on no better authority than a statement in "certain ancient records of the province" concerning the trial, condemnation, and execution by fire, of a woman, for the crime of witchcraft. Dr. Hawks very justly observes, that even if the supposed execution did actually take place, it cannot sanction the inferences which are deduced from it. Evidence is wanting that the judgment was rendered by an ecclesiastical power. Witchcraft was an offence cognizable by the common courts of law, having been made a felony, without benefit of clergy, by the twelfth chapter of the first statute of James I, enacted in 1603. So that, allowing the prisoner to have suffered, her death, says our author, cannot more properly be charged to the ecclesiastical, than to the civil, authority. But in point of fact, the trial alluded to by Burk, (see Appendix xxxi,) can be no other than that of the once notorious Grace Sherwood. And this trial, we are quite certain, took place before a civil tribunal. Besides, (what is most especially to the purpose) the accused though found guilty, and condemned, was *never executed*.

Some observations of our author upon a circumstance which History has connected with the secular feelings of the colony, will be read with pleasure by all men of liberal opinions. We allude to the fact that when one of the colony's agents in England (George Sandys, we believe) took it upon himself to petition Parliament, *in the name of his constituents*, for the restoration of the old company, the colony formally disavowed the act and begged permission to remain under the royal government. Now, Burk insists that this disavowal was induced solely by attachment to the Church of England, for whose overthrow the Puritans were imagined to be particularly zealous. With Dr. Hawks we protest against the decision of the historian. It can be viewed in no other light than that of an effort (brought about, perhaps, by love of our political institutions, yet still exceedingly disingenuous) to *apologise* for the loyalty of Virginia—to apologise for our forefathers having felt what not to have felt would have required an apology indeed! By faith, by situation, by habits and by education they had been taught to be loyal—and with them, consequently, loyalty was a virtue. But if it was indeed a crime—if Virginia has committed an inexpiable offence in resisting the encroachments of the Dictator, (we shall not say of the Commonwealth) let not the Church—in the name of every thing reasonable—let not the Church be saddled with her iniquity—let not political prejudices, always too readily excited, be now enlisted against the religion we cherish, by insinuations artfully introduced, that the loyalty of the State was involved in its creed—that through faith alone it remained a slave—and that its love of monarchy was a mere necessary consequence of its attachment to the Church of England.

While upon this subject we beg leave to refer our readers to some remarks, (from the pen of Judge Beverley Tucker) which appeared under the Critical head of our Messenger before the writer of this article assumed the Editorial duties. The remarks of which we speak, are in reply to the aspersions of Mr. George Bancroft, who, in his late History of the United States, with every intention of paying Virginia a compliment, accuses her of disloyalty, immediately before, and during the Protectorate. Of such an accusation, (for Hening's suggestions, upon pages 513 and 526, of the Statutes at Large cannot be considered as such) we had never seriously dreamed prior to the publication of Mr. Bancroft's work, and that Mr. Bancroft himself should never have dreamed of it, we were sufficiently convinced by the arguments of Judge Tucker. We allude to these arguments now, with the view of apprizing such of our readers as may remember them, that the author of the History in question, in a late interview with Dr. Hawks, has "disclaimed the intention of representing Virginia as wanting in loyalty." All parties would have been better pleased with Mr. B. had he worded his disclaimer so as merely to assure us that in representing Virginia as disloyal he has found himself in error.

We will take the liberty of condensing here such of the leading points on both sides of the debated question as may either occur to us personally or be suggested by those who have written on the subject. In proof of Virginia's *disloyalty* it is said:

1. There is a deficiency of evidence to establish the fact, (a fact much insisted upon) that on the death of the governor, Matthews, in the beginning of 1659, a tumultuous assemblage resolved to throw off the government of the Protectorate, and repairing to the residence of Sir William Berkeley, then living in retirement, requested him to assume the direction of the colony. If such had been the fact, existing records would have shown it—but they do not. Moreover, these records show that Berkeley was elected precisely as the other governors had been, in Virginia, during the Protectorate.

2. After the battle of Dunbar, and the fall of Montrose, Virginia passed an act of surrender—she was therefore in favor of the Parliament.

3. The Colonial Legislature claimed the supreme power as residing within itself. In this it evinced a wish to copy the Parliament—to which it was therefore favorable.

4. Cromwell acted magnanimously towards Virginia. The terms of the article in the Treaty of Surrender by which Virginia stipulated for a trade free as that of England, were faithfully observed till the Restoration. The Protector's Navigation Act was not enforced in Virginia. Cromwell being thus lenient, Virginia must have been satisfied.

5. Virginia elected her own governors. Bennett, Digges, and Matthews, were commonwealth's men. Therefore Virginia was republican.

6. Virginia was infected with republicanism. She wished to set up for herself. Thus intent, she demands of Berkeley a distinct acknowledgement of her assembly's supremacy. His reply was "I am but the servant of the assembly." Berkeley, therefore, was republican, and his tumultuous election proves nothing but the republicanism of Virginia.

These arguments are answered in order, thus:

1. The fact of the "tumultuous assemblage," &c. might have existed without such fact appearing in the records spoken of. For these records are manifestly incomplete. Some whole documents are lost, and parts of many. Granting that Berkeley

was *elected* precisely in the usual way, it does not disprove that a multitude urged him to resume his old office. The election is all of which these records would speak. But *the call to office* might have been a popular movement—the election quite as usual. This latter was left to go on in the old mode, probably because it was well known "that those who were to make it were cavaliers."

Moreover—Beverley, Burk, Chalmers and Holmes are all direct testimony in favor of the "tumultuous assemblage."

2. The act of surrender was in self-defence, when resistance would have availed nothing. Its terms evince no acknowledgment of authority, but mere submission to force. They contain *not one word* recognizing the rightful power of Parliament, nor impeaching that of the king.

3. The "claiming the supreme power," &c. proves any thing but the fealty of the Colonial Legislature to the Commonwealth. According to Mr. Bancroft himself, Virginians in 1619 "first set the world the example of equal representation." "From that time" (we here quote the words of Judge Tucker,) "they held that the supreme power was in the hands of the Colonial Parliament, then established, and of the king as king of Virginia. Now the authority of the king being at an end, and no successor being acknowledged, it followed, as a corollary from their principles, that no power remained but that of the assembly,"—and this is precisely what they mean by claiming the supreme power as residing in the Colonial Legislature.

4. Chalmers, Beverley, Holmes, Marshall and Robertson speak, positively, of great discontents occasioned by restrictions and oppressions upon Virginian commerce; and a Memorial in behalf of the trade of the State presented to the Protector, mentions *"the poor planters' general complaints that they are the merchant's slaves,"* as a consequence of *"that Act of Navigation."*

5. It is probable that Bennett, Digges, and Matthews, (granting Bennett to have been disloyal) were forced upon the colony by Cromwell, whom Robertson (on the authority of Beverley and Chalmers,) asserts to have *named* the governors during the Protectorate. The election was possibly a mere form. The use of the equivocal word *named*, is, as Judge Tucker remarks, a proof that the historian was not speaking

at random. He does not say *appointed*. They were *named*—
with no possibility of their nomination being rejected—as the
speaker of the House of Commons was frequently named in
England. But Bennett was a staunch loyalist—a fact too well
known in Virginia to need proof.

6. The reasoning here is reasoning in a circle. Virginia is
first declared republican. From this assumed fact, deductions
are made which prove Berkeley so—and Berkeley's republicanism, thus proved, is made to establish that of Virginia. But
Berkeley's answer (from which Mr. Bancroft has extracted the
words "I am but the servant of the Assembly") runs thus.

"You desire me to do that concerning your titles and claims
to land in this northern part of America, which I am in no
capacity to do; for I am but the servant of the Assembly:
*neither do they arrogate to themselves any power farther than the
miserable distractions in England force them to*. For when God
shall be pleased to take away and dissipate the unnatural divisions of their native country, *they will immediately return to
their professed obedience*." Smith's New York. It will be seen
that Mr. Bancroft has been disingenuous in quoting only *a
portion* of this sentence. *The whole* proves incontestibly that
neither Berkeley nor the Assembly *arrogated to themselves any
power beyond what they were forced to assume by circumstances*—
in a word, it proves their loyalty. But Berkeley was loyal beyond dispute. *Norwood*, in his "Journal of a Voyage to Virginia," states that "Berkeley showed great respect to all the
royal party who made that colony their refuge. His house and
purse were open to all so qualified." The same journalist was
"sent over, at Berkeley's expense, to find out the King in Holland, and have an interview with him."

To these arguments in favor of Virginia's loyalty may be
added the following.

1. Contemporaries of Cromwell—men who were busy in
the great actions of the day—have left descendants in Virginia—descendants in whose families the loyalty of Virginia
is a cherished *tradition*.

2. The question, being one of *fact*, a mistake could hardly
have been made originally—or, if so made, could not have
been perpetuated. Now all the early historians call Virginia
loyal.

3. The cavaliers in England (as we learn from British authorities) looked upon Virginia as a place of refuge.

4. Holmes' Annals make the population of the state, at the commencement of the civil wars in England, about 20,000. Of these let us suppose only 10,000 loyal. At the Restoration the same Annals make the population 30,000. Here is an increase of 10,000, which increase consisted altogether, or nearly so, of loyalists, *for few others had reason for coming over.* The loyalists are now therefore double the republicans, and Virginia must be loyal.

5. Cromwell was always suspicious of Virginia. Of this there are many proofs. One of them may be found in the fact that when the state, sympathizing with the victims of Claiborne's oppression, (a felon employed by Cromwell to "root out popery in Maryland") afforded them a refuge, she was sternly reprimanded by the Protector, and admonished to keep a guard on her actions.

6. A pamphlet called "Virginia's Cure, an Advisive Narrative concerning Virginia," printed in 1681, speaks of the people as "men which generally bear a great love to the stated constitutions of the Church of England in her government and public worship; which gave us the advantage of liberty to use it constantly among them, after the naval force had reduced the colony under the power (*but never to the obedience*) of the usurpers."

7. John Hammond, in a book entitled "Leah and Rachell, or the two fruitful Sisters of Virginia and Maryland," printed in 1656, speaking of the State during the Protectorate, has the words *"Virginia being whole for monarchy."*

8. Immediately after the fall of Charles I, Virginia passed an Act making it *high treason* to justify his murder, or to acknowledge the Parliament. The Act is not so much as the terms of the Act.

Lastly. The distinguishing features of Virginian character at present—features of a marked nature—not elsewhere to be met with in America—and evidently akin to that chivalry which denoted the Cavalier—can be in no manner so well accounted for as by considering them the *debris* of a devoted loyalty.

At page 122 of the work before us, Dr. Hawks has entered into a somewhat detailed statement (involving much information to us entirely new) concerning the celebrated "Parson's cause"—the church's controversy with the laity on the subject of payments in money substituted for payments in tobacco. It was this controversy which first elicited the oratorical powers of Patrick Henry, and our author dwells with much emphasis, and no little candor, upon the fascinating abilities which proved so unexpectedly fatal to the clerical interest.

On page 160 are some farther highly interesting reminiscences of Mr. Henry. The opinion of Wirt is considered unfounded, that the great orator was a believer in Christianity without having a preference for any of the forms in which it is presented. We are glad to find that Mr. Wirt was in error. The Christian religion, it has been justly remarked, must assume a *distinct form of profession*—or it is worth little. An avowal of a merely general Christianity is little better than an avowal of none at all. Patrick Henry, according to Dr. Hawks, was of the Episcopalian faith. That at any period of his life he was an unbeliever is explicitly denied, on the authority of a MS. letter, in possession of our author, containing information of Mr. H. derived from his widow and descendants.

It is with no little astonishment that we have seen Dr. Hawks accused of illiberality in his few remarks upon "that noble monument of liberty," the *Act for the Establishment of Religious Freedom*. If there is any thing beyond simple justice in his observations we, for our own parts, cannot perceive it. No respect for the civil services, or the unquestionable mental powers of Jefferson shall blind us to his iniquities. That our readers may judge for themselves we quote in full the sentences which have been considered as objectionable.

"We are informed by him (Jefferson) that an amendment was proposed to the Preamble, by the insertion of the name of our Saviour before the words 'The Holy Author of our Religion.' This could at most have had no other effect upon the enacting clause, but that of granting the utmost freedom to all denominations *professing to own and worship Christ*, without affording undue preference to any; and against this, it would be unreasonable to object. Certain it is, that more than this had never been asked by any religious denomination in Virginia, in any petition presented against the Church; the public, therefore, would have been satisfied with such an amendment. The proposed alteration, however, was rejected, and it is made the subject of triumph that the law was left, in the words of its author, 'to comprehend within the mantle of its protection the Jew and the Gentile, the Christian and Mohammedan, the Hindoo, and Infidel of every denomination.' That these various classes should have been protected both in person and property, is obviously the dictate of justice, of humanity, and of enlightened policy. But it surely was not necessary, in securing to them such protection, to degrade, not the establishment, but Christianity itself to a level with the voluptuousness of Mahomet, or the worship of Juggernaut; and if it be true that there is danger in an established alliance between Christianity and the civil power, let it be remembered that there is another alliance not less fatal to the happiness and subversive of the intellectual freedom of man— it is an alliance between the civil authority and infidelity; which, whether formally recognized or not, if permitted to exert its influence, direct or indirect, will be found to be equally ruinous in its results. On this subject, Revolutionary France has once read to the world an impressive lesson, which it is to be hoped will not speedily be forgotten."

In Chapter xii, the whole history of the Glebe Law of 1802—a law the question of whose constitutionality is still undetermined—is detailed with much candor, and in a spirit of calm inquiry. A vivid picture is exhibited of some desecrations which have been consequent upon the sale.

In Chapter xiii, is an exceedingly well-written memoir of our patriarchal bishop the Right Reverend Richard Channing Moore. From this memoir we must be permitted to extract a single passage of peculiar interest.

"It was at one of his stated lectures in the church, (St. Andrew's in Staten Island) that after the usual services had concluded, and the benediction been pronounced, he sat down in his pulpit waiting for the people to retire. To his great surprise, he soon observed that not an individual present seemed disposed to leave the Church; and after the interval of a few minutes, during which a perfect silence was maintained, one of the members of the congregation arose, and respectfully requested him to address those present a second time. After singing a hymn, the bishop delivered to them a second discourse, and once more dismissed the people with the blessing. But the same state of feeling which had before kept them in their seats, still existed, and once more did they solicit the preacher to address them. Accordingly he delivered to them a third sermon, and at its close, exhausted by the labor in which he had been engaged, he informed them of the impossibility of continuing the services on his part, once more blessed them and affectionately entreated them to retire to their homes. It was within the space of six weeks, after the scene above described, that more than sixty members of the congregation became communicants; and in the course of the year more than one hundred knelt around the chancel of St. Andrew's who had never knelt there before as partakers of the sacrament of the Lord's Supper."

The historical portion of the work before us occupies about one half of its pages. The other half embraces "Journals of the Conventions of the Protestant Episcopal Church in the Diocess of Virginia—from 1785 to 1835, inclusive." It is, of course, unnecessary to dwell upon the great value to the church of such a compilation. Very few, if any, complete sets of diocesan Journals of Conventions are in existence. We will conclude our notice, by heartily recommending the entire volume, as an important addition to our Civil as well as Ecclesiastical History.

Southern Literary Messenger, March 1836

Nathaniel Hawthorne

Twice-Told Tales. By Nathaniel Hawthorne. James Munroe & Co.: Boston.

WE HAVE always regarded the *Tale* (using this word in its popular acceptation) as affording the best prose opportunity for display of the highest talent. It has peculiar advantages which the novel does not admit. It is, of course, a far finer field than the essay. It has even points of superiority over the poem. An accident has deprived us, this month, of our customary space for review; and thus nipped in the bud a design long cherished of treating this subject in detail; taking Mr. Hawthorne's volumes as a text. In May we shall endeavor to carry out our intention. At present we are forced to be brief.

With rare exception—in the case of Mr. Irving's "Tales of a Traveller" and a few other works of a like cast—we have had no American tales of high merit. We have had no skilful compositions—nothing which could bear examination as works of art. Of twattle called tale-writing we have had, perhaps, more than enough. We have had a superabundance of the Rosa-Matilda effusions—gilt-edged paper all *couleur de rose*: a full allowance of cut-and-thrust blue-blazing melodramaticisms; a nauseating surfeit of low miniature copying of low life, much in the manner, and with about half the merit, of the Dutch herrings and decayed cheeses of Van Tuyssel—of all this, *eheu jam satis!*

Mr. Hawthorne's volumes appear to us misnamed in two respects. In the first place they should not have been called "Twice-Told Tales"—for this is a title which will not bear *repetition*. If in the first collected edition they were twice-told, of course now they are thrice-told.—May we live to hear them told a hundred times! In the second place, these compositions are by no means *all* "Tales." The most of them are essays properly so called. It would have been wise in their author to have modified his title, so as to have had reference to all included. This point could have been easily arranged.

But under whatever titular blunders we receive this book, it is most cordially welcome. We have seen no prose composition by any American which can compare with *some* of these articles in the higher merits, or indeed in the lower; while there is not a single piece which would do dishonor to the best of the British essayists.

"The Rill from the Town Pump" which, through the *ad captandum* nature of its title, has attracted more of public notice than any one other of Mr. Hawthorne's compositions, is perhaps, the *least* meritorious. Among his best, we may briefly mention "The Hollow of the Three Hills;" "The Minister's Black Veil;" "Wakefield;" "Mr. Higginbotham's Catastrophe;" "Fancy's Show-Box;" "Dr. Heidegger's Experiment;" "David Swan;" "The Wedding Knell;" and "The White Old Maid." It is remarkable that all these, with one exception, are from the first volume.

The style of Mr. Hawthorne is purity itself. His *tone* is singularly effective—wild, plaintive, thoughtful, and in full accordance with his themes. We have only to object that there is insufficient diversity in these themes themselves, or rather in their character. His *originality* both of incident and of reflection is very remarkable; and this trait alone would ensure him at least *our* warmest regard and commendation. We speak here chiefly of the tales; the essays are not so markedly novel. Upon the whole we look upon him as one of the few men of indisputable genius to whom our country has as yet given birth. As such, it will be our delight to do him honor; and lest, in these undigested and cursory remarks, without proof and without explanation, we should appear to do him *more* honor than is his due, we postpone all farther comment until a more favorable opportunity.

Graham's Magazine, April 1842

Twice-Told Tales. By Nathaniel Hawthorne. Two Volumes. Boston: James Munroe and Co.

WE SAID a few hurried words about Mr. Hawthorne in our last number, with the design of speaking more fully in the present. We are still, however, pressed for room, and must necessarily discuss his volumes more briefly and more at random than their high merits deserve.

The book professes to be a collection of *tales*, yet is, in two respects, misnamed. These pieces are now in their third republication, and, of course, are thrice-told. Moreover, they are by no means *all* tales, either in the ordinary or in the legitimate understanding of the term. Many of them are pure essays, for example, "Sights from a Steeple," "Sunday at Home," "Little Annie's Ramble," "A Rill from the Town-Pump," "The Toll-Gatherer's Day," "The Haunted Mind," "The Sister Years," "Snow-Flakes," "Night Sketches," and "Foot-Prints on the Sea-Shore." We mention these matters chiefly on account of their discrepancy with that marked precision and finish by which the body of the work is distinguished.

Of the Essays just named, we must be content to speak in brief. They are each and all beautiful, without being characterised by the polish and adaptation so visible in the tales proper. A painter would at once note their leading or predominant feature, and style it *repose*. There is no attempt at effect. All is quiet, thoughtful, subdued. Yet this repose may exist simultaneously with high originality of thought; and Mr. Hawthorne has demonstrated the fact. At every turn we meet with novel combinations; yet these combinations never surpass the limits of the quiet. We are soothed as we read; and withal is a calm astonishment that ideas so apparently obvious have never occurred or been presented to us before. Herein our author differs materially from Lamb or Hunt or Hazlitt—who, with vivid originality of manner and expression, have less of the true novelty of thought than is generally supposed, and whose originality, at best, has an uneasy and meretricious quaintness, replete with startling effects unfounded in nature, and inducing trains of reflection which lead to no satisfactory result. The Essays of Hawthorne have much of the character of Irving, with more of originality, and less of finish; while, compared with the Spectator, they have a vast superiority at all points. The Spectator, Mr. Irving, and Mr. Hawthorne have in common that tranquil and subdued manner which we have chosen to denominate *repose*; but, in the case of the two former, this repose is attained rather by the absence of novel combination, or of originality, than otherwise, and consists chiefly in the calm, quiet, unostentatious expression of commonplace thoughts, in an unambitious un-adulterated Saxon. In them, by strong effort, we are made to conceive the absence of all. In the essays before us the absence of effort is too obvious to be mistaken, and a strong under-current of *suggestion* runs continuously beneath the upper stream of the tranquil thesis. In short, these effusions of Mr. Hawthorne are the product of a truly imaginative intellect, restrained, and in some measure repressed, by fastidiousness of taste, by constitutional melancholy and by indolence.

But it is of his tales that we desire principally to speak. The tale proper, in our opinion, affords unquestionably the fairest field for the exercise of the loftiest talent, which can be af-forded by the wide domains of mere prose. Were we bidden to say how the highest genius could be most advantageously employed for the best display of its own powers, we should answer, without hesitation—in the composition of a rhymed poem, not to exceed in length what might be perused in an hour. Within this limit alone can the highest order of true poetry exist. We need only here say, upon this topic, that, in almost all classes of composition, the unity of effect or impression is a point of the greatest importance. It is clear, moreover, that this unity cannot be thoroughly preserved in productions whose perusal cannot be completed at one sit-ting. We may continue the reading of a prose composition, from the very nature of prose itself, much longer than we can persevere, to any good purpose, in the perusal of a poem. This latter, if truly fulfilling the demands of the poetic senti-ment, induces an exaltation of the soul which cannot be long sustained. All high excitements are necessarily transient. Thus a long poem is a paradox. And, without unity of impression, the deepest effects cannot be brought about. Epics were the offspring of an imperfect sense of Art, and their reign is no more. A poem *too* brief may produce a vivid, but never an intense or enduring impression. Without a certain continuity of effort—without a certain duration or repetition of pur-pose—the soul is never deeply moved. There must be the dropping of the water upon the rock. De Béranger has wrought brilliant things—pungent and spirit-stirring—but, like all immassive bodies, they lack *momentum*, and thus fail to satisfy the Poetic Sentiment. They sparkle and excite, but, from want of continuity, fail deeply to impress. Extreme brevity will degenerate into epigrammatism; but the sin of extreme length is even more unpardonable. *In medio tutissimus ibis*.

Were we called upon however to designate that class of composition which, next to such a poem as we have suggested, should best fulfil the demands of high genius—should offer it the most advantageous field of exertion—we should unhesitatingly speak of the prose tale, as Mr. Hawthorne has here exemplified it. We allude to the short prose narrative, requiring from a half-hour to one or two hours in its perusal. The ordinary novel is objectionable, from its length, for reasons already stated in substance. As it cannot be read at one sitting, it deprives itself, of course, of the immense force derivable from *totality*. Worldly interests intervening during the pauses of perusal, modify, annul, or counteract, in a greater or less degree, the impressions of the book. But simple cessation in reading would, of itself, be sufficient to destroy the true unity. In the brief tale, however, the author is enabled to carry out the fulness of his intention, be it what it may. During the hour of perusal the soul of the reader is at the writer's control. There are no external or extrinsic influences—resulting from weariness or interruption.

A skilful literary artist has constructed a tale. If wise, he has not fashioned his thoughts to accommodate his incidents; but having conceived, with deliberate care, a certain unique or single *effect* to be wrought out, he then invents such incidents—he then combines such events as may best aid him in establishing this preconceived effect. If his very initial sentence tend not to the outbringing of this effect, then he has failed in his first step. In the whole composition there should be no word written, of which the tendency, direct or indirect, is not to the one pre-established design. And by such means, with such care and skill, a picture is at length painted which leaves in the mind of him who contemplates it with a kindred art, a sense of the fullest satisfaction. The idea of the tale has been presented unblemished, because undisturbed; and this is an end unattainable by the novel. Undue brevity is just as exceptionable here as in the poem; but undue length is yet more to be avoided.

We have said that the tale has a point of superiority even over the poem. In fact, while the *rhythm* of this latter is an essential aid in the development of the poem's highest idea—the idea of the Beautiful—the artificialities of this rhythm are an inseparable bar to the development of all points of thought or expression which have their basis in *Truth*. But Truth is often, and in very great degree, the aim of the tale. Some of the finest tales are tales of ratiocination. Thus the field of this species of composition, if not in so elevated a region on the mountain of Mind, is a table-land of far vaster extent than the domain of the mere poem. Its products are never so rich, but infinitely more numerous, and more appreciable by the mass of mankind. The writer of the prose tale, in short, may bring to his theme a vast variety of modes or inflections of thought and expression—(the ratiocinative, for example, the sarcastic or the humorous) which are not only antagonistical to the nature of the poem, but absolutely forbidden by one of its most peculiar and indispensable adjuncts; we allude of course, to rhythm. It may be added, here, *par parenthèse*, that the author who aims at the purely beautiful in a prose tale is laboring at great disadvantage. For Beauty can be better treated in the poem. Not so with terror, or passion, or horror, or a multitude of such other points. And here it will be seen how full of prejudice are the usual animadversions against those *tales of effect* many fine examples of which were found in the earlier numbers of Blackwood. The impressions produced were wrought in a legitimate sphere of action, and constituted a legitimate although sometimes an exaggerated interest. They were relished by every man of genius: although there were found many men of genius who condemned them without just ground. The true critic will but demand that the design intended be accomplished, to the fullest extent, by the means most advantageously applicable.

We have very few American tales of real merit—we may say, indeed, none, with the exception of "The Tales of a Traveller" of Washington Irving, and these "Twice-Told Tales" of Mr. Hawthorne. Some of the pieces of Mr. John Neal abound in vigor and originality; but in general, his compositions of this class are excessively diffuse, extravagant, and indicative of an imperfect sentiment of Art. Articles at random are, now and then, met with in our periodicals which might be advantageously compared with the best effusions of the British Magazines; but, upon the whole, we are far behind our progenitors in this department of literature.

Of Mr. Hawthorne's Tales we would say, emphatically, that they belong to the highest region of Art—an Art subservient to genius of a very lofty order. We had supposed, with good reason for so supposing, that he had been thrust into his present position by one of the impudent *cliques* which beset our literature, and whose pretensions it is our full purpose to expose at the earliest opportunity; but we have been most agreeably mistaken. We know of few compositions which the critic can more honestly commend then these "Twice-Told Tales." As Americans, we feel proud of the book.

Mr. Hawthorne's distinctive trait is invention, creation, imagination, originality—a trait which, in the literature of fiction, is positively worth all the rest. But the nature of originality, so far as regards its manifestation in letters, is but imperfectly understood. The inventive or original mind as frequently displays itself in novelty of *tone* as in novelty of matter. Mr. Hawthorne is original at *all* points.

It would be a matter of some difficulty to designate the best of these tales; we repeat that, without exception, they are beautiful. "Wakefield" is remarkable for the skill with which an old idea—a well-known incident—is worked up or discussed. A man of whims conceives the purpose of quitting his wife and residing *incognito*, for twenty years, in her immediate neighborhood. Something of this kind actually happened in London. The force of Mr. Hawthorne's tale lies in the analysis of the motives which must or might have impelled the husband to such folly, in the first instance, with the possible causes of his perseverance. Upon this thesis a sketch of singular power has been constructed.

"The Wedding Knell" is full of the boldest imagination— an imagination fully controlled by taste. The most captious critic could find no flaw in this production.

"The Minister's Black Veil" is a masterly composition of which the sole defect is that to the rabble its exquisite skill will be *caviare*. The *obvious* meaning of this article will be found to smother its insinuated one. The *moral* put into the mouth of the dying minister will be supposed to convey the *true* import of the narrative; and that a crime of dark dye, (having reference to the "young lady") has been committed, is a point which only minds congenial with that of the author will perceive.

"Mr. Higginbotham's Catastrophe" is vividly original and managed most dexterously.

"Dr. Heidegger's Experiment" is exceedingly well imagined, and executed with surpassing ability. The artist breathes in every line of it.

"The White Old Maid" is objectionable, even more than the "Minister's Black Veil," on the score of its mysticism. Even with the thoughtful and analytic, there will be much trouble in penetrating its entire import.

"The Hollow of the Three Hills" we would quote in full, had we space;—not as evincing higher talent than any of the other pieces, but as affording an excellent example of the author's peculiar ability. The subject is common-place. A witch subjects the Distant and the Past to the view of a mourner. It has been the fashion to describe, in such cases, a mirror in which the images of the absent appear; or a cloud of smoke is made to arise, and thence the figures are gradually unfolded. Mr. Hawthorne has wonderfully heightened his effect by making the ear, in place of the eye, the medium by which the fantasy is conveyed. The head of the mourner is enveloped in the cloak of the witch, and within its magic folds there arise sounds which have an all-sufficient intelligence. Throughout this article also, the artist is conspicuous—not more in positive than in negative merits. Not only is all done that should be done, but (what perhaps is an end with more difficulty attained) there is nothing done which should not be. Every word *tells*, and there is not a word which does *not* tell.

In "Howe's Masquerade" we observe something which resembles a plagiarism—but which *may be* a very flattering coincidence of thought. We quote the passage in question.

"*With a dark flush of wrath* upon his brow they saw the general *draw his sword* and *advance to meet* the figure *in the cloak* before the latter had stepped one pace upon the floor.

" '*Villain, unmuffle yourself,*' cried he, 'you pass no farther!'

"The figure, without blenching a hair's breadth from the sword which was pointed at his breast, made a solemn pause, and *lowered the cape of the cloak* from his face, yet not sufficiently for the spectators to catch a glimpse of it. But Sir William Howe had evidently seen enough. The sternness of his countenance gave place to a look of wild amazement, if not horror, while he recoiled several steps from the figure, *and let fall his sword* upon the floor."—See vol. 2, page 20.

The idea here is, that the figure in the cloak is the phantom or reduplication of Sir William Howe; but in an article called "William Wilson," one of the "Tales of the Grotesque and Arabesque," we have not only the same idea, but the same idea similarly presented in several respects. We quote two paragraphs, which our readers may compare with what has been already given. We have italicized, above, the immediate particulars of resemblance.

"The brief moment in which I averted my eyes had been sufficient to produce, apparently, a material change in the arrangement at the upper or farther end of the room. A large mirror, it appeared to me, now stood where none had been perceptible before: and as I stepped up to it in extremity of terror, mine own image, but with features all pale and dabbled in blood, *advanced* with a feeble and tottering gait to meet me.

"Thus it appeared I say, but was not. It was Wilson, who then stood before me in the agonies of dissolution. Not a line in all the marked and singular lineaments of that face which was not even identically mine own. *His mask and cloak lay where he had thrown them, upon the floor.*"—Vol. 2. p. 57.

Here it will be observed that, not only are the two general conceptions identical, but there are various *points* of similarity. In each case the figure seen is the wraith or duplication of the beholder. In each case the scene is a masquerade. In each case the figure is cloaked. In each, there is a quarrel—

that is to say, angry words pass between the parties. In each the beholder is enraged. In each the cloak and sword fall upon the floor. The "villain, unmuffle yourself," of Mr. H. is precisely paralleled by a passage at page 56 of "William Wilson."

In the way of objection we have scarcely a word to say of these tales. There is, perhaps, a somewhat too general or prevalent *tone*—a tone of melancholy and mysticism. The subjects are insufficiently varied. There is not so much of *versatility* evinced as we might well be warranted in expecting from the high powers of Mr. Hawthorne. But beyond these trivial exceptions we have really none to make. The style is purity itself. Force abounds. High imagination gleams from every page. Mr. Hawthorne is a man of the truest genius. We only regret that the limits of our Magazine will not permit us to pay him that full tribute of commendation, which, under other circumstances, we should be so eager to pay.

Graham's Magazine, May 1842

Twice-Told Tales. By Nathaniel Hawthorne. James Munroe & Co., Boston. 1842.
Mosses from an Old Manse. By Nathaniel Hawthorne. Wiley & Putnam, New York. 1846.

IN THE PREFACE to my sketches of New York Literati, while speaking of the broad distinction between the seeming public and real private opinion respecting our authors, I thus alluded to Nathaniel Hawthorne:—

"For example, Mr. Hawthorne, the author of 'Twice-Told Tales,' is scarcely recognized by the press or by the public, and when noticed at all, is noticed merely to be damned by faint praise. Now, my own opinion of him is, that although his walk is limited and he is fairly to be charged with mannerism, treating all subjects in a similar tone of dreamy *innuendo*, yet in this walk he evinces extraordinary genius, having no rival either in America or elsewhere; and this opinion I have never heard gainsaid by any one literary person in the country. That this opinion, however, is a spoken and not a written one, is referable to the facts, first, that Mr. Haw-

thorne *is* a poor man, and, secondly, that he *is not* an ubiquitous quack."

The reputation of the author of "Twice-Told Tales" has
been confined, indeed, until very lately, to literary society;
and I have not been wrong, perhaps, in citing him as *the*
example, *par excellence*, in this country, of the privately-ad-
mired and publicly-unappreciated man of genius. Within the
last year or two, it is true, an occasional critic has been urged,
by honest indignation, into very warm approval. Mr. Webber,
for instance, (than whom no one has a keener relish for that
kind of writing which Mr. Hawthorne has best illustrated,)
gave us, in a late number of "The American Review," a cordial and certainly a full tribute to his talents; and since the
issue of the "Mosses from an Old Manse," criticisms of similar tone have been by no means infrequent in our more au-
thoritative journals. I can call to mind few reviews of
Hawthorne published *before* the "Mosses." One I remember
in "Arcturus" (edited by Matthews and Duyckinck) for May,
1841; another in the "American Monthly" (edited by Hoffman
and Herbert) for March, 1838; a third in the ninety-sixth number of the "North American Review." These criticisms, however, seemed to have little effect on the popular taste—at
least, if we are to form any idea of the popular taste by reference to its expression in the newspapers, or by the sale of
the author's book. It was never the fashion (until lately) to
speak of him in any summary of our best authors. The daily
critics would say, on such occasions, "Is there not Irving and
Cooper, and Bryant and Paulding, and—Smith?" or, "Have
we not Halleck and Dana, and Longfellow and—Thompson?" or, "Can we not point triumphantly to our own
Sprague, Willis, Channing, Bancroft, Prescott and—Jenkins?"
but these unanswerable queries were never wound up by the
name of Hawthorne.

Beyond doubt, this inappreciation of him on the part of
the public arose chiefly from the two causes to which I have
referred—from the facts that he is neither a man of wealth
nor a quack;—but these are insufficient to account for the
whole effect. No small portion of it is attributable to the very
marked idiosyncrasy of Mr. Hawthorne himself. In one sense,

and in great measure, to be peculiar is to be original, and than the true originality there is no higher literary virtue. This true or commendable originality, however, implies not the uniform, but the continuous peculiarity—a peculiarity springing from ever-active vigor of fancy—better still if from ever-present force of imagination, giving its own hue, its own character to everything it touches, and, especially, *self impelled to touch everything*.

It is often said, inconsiderately, that very original writers always fail in popularity—that such and such persons are too original to be comprehended by the mass. "Too peculiar," should be the phrase, "too idiosyncratic." It is, in fact, the excitable, undisciplined and child-like popular mind which most keenly feels the original. The criticism of the conservatives, of the hackneys, of the cultivated old clergymen of the "North American Review," is precisely the criticism which condemns and alone condemns it. "It becometh not a divine," saith Lord Coke, "to be of a fiery and salamandrine spirit." Their conscience allowing them to move nothing themselves, these dignitaries have a holy horror of being moved. "Give us *quietude*," they say. Opening their mouths with proper caution, they sigh forth the word *"Repose."* And this is, indeed, the one thing they should be permitted to enjoy, if only upon the Christian principle of give and take.

The fact is, that if Mr. Hawthorne were really original, he could not fail of making himself felt by the public. But the fact is, he is *not* original in any sense. Those who speak of him as original, mean nothing more than that he differs in his manner or tone, and in his choice of subjects, from any author of their acquaintance—their acquaintance not extending to the German Tieck, whose manner, in *some* of his works, is absolutely identical with that *habitual* to Hawthorne. But it is clear that the element of the literary originality is novelty. The element of its appreciation by the reader is the reader's sense of the new. Whatever gives him a new and insomuch a pleasurable emotion, he considers original, and whoever frequently gives him such emotion, he considers an original writer. In a word, it is by the sum total of these emotions that he decides upon the writer's claim to originality. I may observe here, however, that there is clearly a point at which

even novelty itself would cease to produce the legitimate originality, if we judge this originality, as we should, by the effect
designed: this point is that at which *novelty becomes nothing
novel*; and here the artist, *to preserve his originality*, will subside
into the common-place. No one, I think, has noticed that,
merely through inattention to this matter, Moore has comparatively failed in his "Lalla Rookh." Few readers, and indeed few critics, have commended this poem for originality—
and, in fact, the effect, originality, is not produced by it—yet
no work of equal size so abounds in the happiest originalities,
individually considered. They are so excessive as, in the end,
to deaden in the reader all capacity for their appreciation.

These points properly understood, it will be seen that the
critic (unacquainted with Tieck) who reads a single tale or
essay by Hawthorne, may be justified in thinking him original; but the tone, or manner, or choice of subject, which induces in this critic the sense of the new, will—if not in a
second tale, at least in a third and all subsequent ones—not
only fail of inducing it, but bring about an exactly antagonistic impression. In concluding a volume, and more especially
in concluding all the volumes of the author, the critic will
abandon his first design of calling him "original," and content
himself with styling him "peculiar."

With the vague opinion that to be original is to be unpopular, I could, indeed, agree, were I to adopt an understanding
of originality which, to my surprise, I have known adopted
by many who have a right to be called critical. They have
limited, in a love for mere words, the literary to the metaphysical originality. They regard as original in letters, only
such combinations of thought, of incident, and so forth, as
are, in fact, absolutely novel. It is clear, however, not only
that it is the novelty of *effect* alone which is worth consideration, but that this effect is *best* wrought, for the end of all
fictitious composition, pleasure, by shunning rather than by
seeking the absolute novelty of combination. Originality, thus
understood, tasks and startles the intellect, and so brings into
undue action the faculties to which, in the lighter literature,
we least appeal. And thus understood, it cannot fail to prove
unpopular with the masses, who, seeking in this literature
amusement, are positively offended by instruction. But the

true originality—true in respect of its purposes—is that which, in bringing out the half-formed, the reluctant, or the unexpressed fancies of mankind, or in exciting the more delicate pulses of the heart's passion, or in giving birth to some universal sentiment or instinct in embryo, thus combines with the pleasurable effect of *apparent* novelty, a real egotistic delight. The reader, in the case first supposed, (that of the absolute novelty,) is excited, but embarrassed, disturbed, in some degree even pained at his own want of perception, at his own folly in not having himself hit upon the idea. In the second case, his pleasure is doubled. He is filled with an intrinsic and extrinsic delight. He feels and intensely enjoys the seeming novelty of the thought, enjoys it as really novel, as absolutely original with the writer—*and* himself. They two, he fancies, have, alone of all men, thought thus. They two have, together, created this thing. Henceforward there is a bond of sympathy between them, a sympathy which irradiates every subsequent page of the book.

There is a species of writing which, with some difficulty, may be admitted as a lower degree of what I have called the true original. In its perusal, we say to ourselves, not "how original this is!" nor "here is an idea which I and the author have alone entertained," but "here is a charmingly obvious fancy," or sometimes even, "here is a thought which I am not sure has ever occurred to myself, but which, of course, has occurred to all the rest of the world." This kind of composition (which still appertains to a high order) is usually designated as "the natural." It has little external resemblance, but strong internal affinity to the true original, if, indeed, as I have suggested, it is not of this latter an inferior degree. It is best exemplified, among English writers, in Addison, Irving and *Hawthorne*. The "ease" which is so often spoken of as its distinguishing feature, it has been the fashion to regard as ease in appearance alone, as a point of really difficult attainment. This idea, however, must be received with some reservation. The natural style is difficult only to those who should never intermeddle with it—to the unnatural. It is but the result of writing with the understanding, or with the instinct, that the *tone*, in composition, should be that which, at any given point or upon any given topic, would be the tone of the great mass of humanity. The author who, after the manner of the North Americans, is merely at *all* times *quiet*, is, of course, upon *most* occasions, merely silly or stupid, and has no more right to be thought "easy" or "natural" than has a cockney exquisite or the sleeping beauty in the wax-works.

The "peculiarity" or sameness, or monotone of Hawthorne, would, in its mere character of "peculiarity," and without reference to what *is* the peculiarity, suffice to deprive him of all chance of popular appreciation. But at his failure to be appreciated, we can, *of course*, no longer wonder, when we find him monotonous at decidedly the worst of all possible points—at that point which, having the least concern with Nature, is the farthest removed from the popular intellect, from the popular sentiment and from the popular taste. I allude to the strain of allegory which completely overwhelms the greater number of his subjects, and which in some measure interferes with the direct conduct of absolutely all.

In defence of allegory, (however, or for whatever object, employed,) there is scarcely one respectable word to be said. Its best appeals are made to the fancy—that is to say, to our sense of adaptation, not of matters proper, but of matters improper for the purpose, of the real with the unreal; having never more of intelligible connection than has something with nothing, never half so much of effective affinity as has the substance for the shadow. The deepest emotion aroused within us by the happiest allegory, *as* allegory, is a very, very imperfectly satisfied sense of the writer's ingenuity in overcoming a difficulty we should have preferred his not having attempted to overcome. The fallacy of the idea that allegory, in any of its moods, can be made to enforce a truth—that metaphor, for example, may illustrate as well as embellish an argument—could be promptly demonstrated: the converse of the supposed fact might be shown, indeed, with very little trouble—but these are topics foreign to my present purpose. One thing is clear, that if allegory ever establishes a fact, it is by dint of over-turning a fiction. Where the suggested meaning runs through the obvious one in a *very* profound undercurrent, so as never to interfere with the upper one without our own volition, so as never to show itself unless *called* to the surface, there only, for the proper uses of fictitious narrative, is it available at all. Under the best circumstances, it must always interfere with that unity of effect which, to the artist, is worth all the allegory in the world. Its vital injury, however, is rendered to the most vitally important point in fiction—that of earnestness or verisimilitude. That "The Pilgrim's Progress" is a ludicrously over-rated book, owing its seeming popularity to one or two of those accidents in critical literature which by the critical are sufficiently well understood, is a matter upon which no two thinking people disagree; but the pleasure derivable from it, in any sense, will be found in the direct ratio of the reader's capacity to smother its true purpose, in the direct ratio of his ability to keep the allegory out of sight, or of his *in*ability to comprehend it. Of allegory properly handled, judiciously subdued, seen only as a shadow or by suggestive glimpses, and making its nearest approach to truth in a not obtrusive and therefore not unpleasant *appositeness*, the "Undine" of De La Motte Fouqué is the best, and undoubtedly a very remarkable specimen.

The obvious causes, however, which have prevented Mr. Hawthorne's *popularity*, do not suffice to condemn him in the eyes of the few who belong properly to books, and to whom books, perhaps, do not quite so properly belong. These few estimate an author, not as do the public, altogether by what he does, but in great measure—indeed, even in the greatest measure—by what he evinces a capability of doing. In this view, Hawthorne stands among literary people in America much in the same light as did Coleridge in England. The few, also, through a certain warping of the taste, which long pondering upon books as books merely never fails to induce, are not in condition to view the errors of a scholar as errors altogether. At any time these gentlemen are prone to think the public not right rather than an educated author wrong. But the simple truth is, that the writer who aims at impressing the people, is *always* wrong when he fails in forcing that people to receive the impression. How far Mr. Hawthorne has addressed the people at all, is, of course, not a question for me to decide. His books afford strong internal evidence of having been written to himself and his particular friends alone.

There has long existed in literature a fatal and unfounded

prejudice, which it will be the office of this age to over-throw—the idea that the mere bulk of a work must enter largely into our estimate of its merit. I do not suppose even the weakest of the Quarterly reviewers weak enough to maintain that in a book's size or mass, abstractly considered, there is anything which especially calls for our admiration. A mountain, simply through the sensation of physical magnitude which it conveys, does, indeed, affect us with a sense of the sublime, but we cannot admit any such influence in the contemplation even of "The Columbiad." The Quarterlies themselves will not admit it. And yet, what else are we to understand by their continual prating about "sustained effort?" Granted that this sustained effort has accomplished an epic—let us then admire the effort, (if this be a thing admirable,) but certainly not the epic on the effort's account. Common sense, in the time to come, may possibly insist upon measuring a work of art rather by the object it fulfils, by the impression it makes, than by the time it took to fulfil the object, or by the extent of "sustained effort" which became necessary to produce the impression. The fact is, that perseverance is one thing and genius quite another; nor can all the transcendentalists in Heathendom confound them.

Full of its bulky ideas, the last number of the "North American Review," in what it imagines a criticism on Simms, "honestly avows that it has little opinion of the mere tale;" and the honesty of the avowal is in no slight degree guarantied by the fact that this Review has never yet been known to put forth an opinion which was *not* a very little one indeed.

The tale proper affords the fairest field which can be afforded by the wide domains of mere prose, for the exercise of the highest genius. Were I bidden to say how this genius could be most advantageously employed for the best display of its powers, I should answer, without hesitation, "in the composition of a rhymed poem not to exceed in length what might be perused in an hour." Within this limit alone can the noblest order of poetry exist. I have discussed this topic elsewhere, and need here repeat only that the phrase "a long poem" embodies a paradox. A poem must intensely excite. Excitement is its province, its essentiality. Its value is in the ratio of its (elevating) excitement. But all excitement is, from a psychal necessity, transient. It cannot be sustained through a poem of great length. In the course of an hour's reading, at most, it flags, fails; and then the poem is, in effect, no longer such. Men admire, but are wearied with the "Paradise Lost;" for platitude follows platitude, *inevitably*, at regular inter-spaces, (the depressions between the waves of excitement,) until the poem, (which, properly considered, is but a succession of brief poems,) having been brought to an end, we discover that the sums of our pleasure and of displeasure have been very nearly equal. The absolute, ultimate or aggregate effect of any epic under the sun is, for these reasons, a nullity. "The Iliad," in its form of epic, has but an imaginary existence; granting it real, however, I can only say of it that it is based on a primitive sense of Art. Of the modern epic nothing can be so well said as that it is a blindfold imitation of a "come-by-chance." By and by these propositions will be understood as self-evident, and in the meantime will not be essentially damaged as truths by being generally condemned as falsities.

A poem *too* brief, on the other hand, may produce a sharp or vivid, but never a profound or enduring impression. Without a certain continuity, without a certain duration or repetition of the cause, the soul is seldom moved to the effect. There must be the dropping of the water on the rock. There must be the pressing steadily down of the stamp upon the wax. De Béranger has wrought brilliant things, pungent and spirit-stirring, but most of them are too immassive to have *momentum*, and, as so many feathers of fancy, have been blown aloft only to be whistled down the wind. Brevity, indeed, may degenerate into epigrammatism, but this danger does not prevent extreme length from being the one unpardonable sin.

Were I called upon, however, to designate that class of composition which, next to such a poem as I have suggested, should best fulfil the demands and serve the purposes of ambitious genius, should offer it the most advantageous field of exertion, and afford it the fairest opportunity of display, I should speak at once of the brief prose tale. History, philosophy, and other matters of that kind, we leave out of the question, of course. *Of course*, I say, and in spite of the graybeards. These graver topics, to the end of time, will be best illustrated by what a discriminating world, turning up its nose at the drab pamphlets, has agreed to understand as *talent*. The ordinary novel is objectionable, from its length, for reasons analogous to those which render length objectionable in the poem. As the novel cannot be read at one sitting, it cannot avail itself of the immense benefit of *totality*. Worldly interests, intervening during the pauses of perusal, modify, counteract and annul the impressions intended. But simple cessation in reading would, of itself, be sufficient to destroy the true unity. In the brief tale, however, the author is enabled to carry out his full design without interruption. During the hour of perusal, the soul of the reader is at the writer's control.

A skillful artist has constructed a tale. He has not fashioned his thoughts to accommodate his incidents, but having deliberately conceived a certain *single effect* to be wrought, he then invents such incidents, he then combines such events, and discusses them in such tone as may best serve him in establishing this preconceived effect. If his very first sentence tend not to the outbringing of this effect, then in his very first step has he committed a blunder. In the whole composition there should be no word written of which the tendency, direct or indirect, is not to the one pre-established design. And by such means, with such care and skill, a picture is at length painted which leaves in the mind of him who contemplates it with a kindred art, a sense of the fullest satisfaction. The idea of the tale, its thesis, has been presented unblemished, because undisturbed—an end absolutely demanded, yet, in the novel, altogether unattainable.

Of skillfully-constructed tales—I speak now without reference to other points, some of them more important than construction—there are very few American specimens. I am acquainted with no better one, upon the whole, than the "Murder Will Out" of Mr. Simms, and this has some glaring defects. The "Tales of a Traveler," by Irving, are graceful and impressive narratives—"The Young Italian" is especially good—but there is not one of the series which can be commended as a whole. In many of them the interest is subdivided and frittered away, and their conclusions are insufficiently *climacic*. In the higher requisites of composition, John Neal's magazine stories excel—I mean in vigor of thought, picturesque combination of incident, and so forth—but they ramble too much, and invariably break down just before coming to an end, as if the writer had received a sudden and irresistible summons to dinner, and thought it incumbent upon him to make a finish of his story before going. One of the happiest and best-sustained tales I have seen, is "Jack Long; or, The Shot in the Eye," by Charles W. Webber, the assistant editor of Mr. Colton's "American Review." But in general skill of construction, the tales of Willis, I think, surpass those of any American writer—with the exception of Mr. Hawthorne.

I must defer to the better opportunity of a volume now in hand, a full discussion of his individual pieces, and hasten to conclude this paper with a summary of his merits and demerits.

He is peculiar and *not* original—unless in those detailed fancies and detached thoughts which his want of general originality will deprive of the appreciation due to them, in preventing them forever reaching the *public* eye. He is infinitely too fond of allegory, and can never hope for popularity so long as he persists in it. This he will not do, for allegory is at war with the whole tone of his nature, which disports itself never so well as when escaping from the mysticism of his Goodman Browns and White Old Maids into the hearty, genial, but still Indian-summer sunshine of his Wakefields and Little Annie's Rambles. Indeed, *his* spirit of "metaphor run-mad" is clearly imbibed from the phalanx and phalanstery atmosphere in which he has been so long struggling for breath. He has not half the material for the exclusiveness of authorship that he possesses for its universality. He has the purest style, the finest taste, the most available scholarship, the most delicate humor, the most touching pathos, the most radiant imagination, the most consummate ingenuity; and with these varied good qualities he has done *well* as a mystic. But is there any one of these qualities which should prevent his doing doubly as well in a career of honest, upright, sensible, prehensible and comprehensible things? Let him mend his pen, get a bottle of visible ink, come out from the Old Manse, cut Mr.

Alcott, hang (if possible) the editor of "The Dial," and throw
out of the window to the pigs all his odd numbers of "The
North American Review."

Godey's Lady's Book, November 1847

Joel T. Headley

The Sacred Mountains. By J. T. Headley,—Author of "Napoleon and his Marshals," "Washington and his Generals," etc.

THE *Reverend* Mr. HEADLEY—(why *will* he not put his full title in his title-pages?) has in his "Sacred Mountains" been reversing the facts of the old fable about the mountains that brought forth the mouse—*parturiunt montes nascitur ridiculus mus*—for in this instance it appears to be the mouse—the little *ridiculus mus*—that has been bringing forth the "Mountains," and a great litter of them, too. The epithet, funny, however, is perhaps the only one which can be considered as thoroughly applicable to the book. We say that a book is a "funny" book, and nothing else, when it spreads over two hundred pages an amount of matter which could be conveniently presented in twenty of a magazine: that a book is a "funny" book—"only this and nothing more"—when it is written in that kind of phraseology, in which John Philpot Curran, when drunk, would have made a speech at a public dinner: and, moreover, we do say, emphatically, that a book is a "funny" book, and nothing but a funny book, whenever it happens to be penned by Mr. Headley.

We should like to give some account of "The Sacred Mountains," if the thing were only possible—but we cannot conceive that it is. Mr. Headley belongs to that numerous class of authors, who must be read to be understood, and who, for that reason, very seldom are as thoroughly comprehended as they should be. Let us endeavor, however, to give some general idea of the work. "The design," says the author in his preface, "is to render more familiar and life-like some of the scenes of the Bible." Here, in the very first sentence of his preface, we suspect the Reverend Mr. Headley of fibbing: for his design, as it appears to ordinary apprehension, is merely that of making a little money by selling a little book.

The mountains described are Ararat, Moriah, Sinai, Hor, Pisgah, Horeb, Carmel, Lebanon, Zion, Tabor, Olivet, and Calvary. Taking up these, one by one, the author proceeds in his own very peculiar way to *elocutionize* about them: we really do not know how else to express what it is that Mr.

Headley does with these eminences. Perhaps if we were to say that he stood up before the reader and "made a speech" about them, one after the other, we should come still nearer the truth. By way of carrying out his design, as announced in the preface, that of rendering "more familiar and life-like some of the scenes" and so-forth, he tells not only how each mountain is, and was, but how it might have been and ought to be in his own opinion. To hear him talk, anybody would suppose that he had been at the laying of the corner-stone of Solomon's Temple—to say nothing of being born and brought up in the ark with Noah, and hail-fellow-well-met with every one of the beasts that went into it. If any person really desires to know how and why it was that the deluge took place— but especially *how*—if any person wishes to get minute and accurate information on the topic—let him read "The Sacred Mountains"—let him only listen to the Reverend Mr. Headley. He explains to us precisely how it all took place—what Noah said, and thought, while the ark was building, and what the people, who saw him building the ark, said and thought about his undertaking such a work; and how the beasts, birds, and fishes looked as they came in arm in arm; and what the dove did, and what the raven did not—in short, all the rest of it: nothing could be more beautifully posted up. What *can* Mr. Headley mean, at page 17, by the remark that "there is no one who does not lament that there is not a fuller antediluvian history?" We are quite sure that nothing that ever happened before the flood, has been omitted in the scrupulous researches of the author of "The Sacred Mountains."

He might, perhaps, wrap up the fruits of these researches in rather better English than that which he employs:

"Yet *still* the water rose around them till all through the valleys nothing but little black islands of human beings *were* seen on the surface . . . . . . The more fixed the irrevocable decree, *the heavier* he leaned on the Omnipotent arm . . . . . . And lo! a solitary cloud comes drifting along the morning sky and *catches* against the top of the mountain . . . . . . At length emboldened by their own numbers they *assembled* tumultuously *together* . . . . . . Aaron never appears *so perfect* a character as Moses . . . . . . As he advanced from rock to rock the sobbing of the multitude that *followed after*, tore his heart-strings . . . . . . Friends were *following after* whose sick Christ had healed . . . . . . The steady mountain threatened *to lift* from its base and be carried away . . . . . . Sometimes God's hatred of sin, sometimes his care for his children, sometimes the discipline of his church, *were* the motives . . . . . . Surely it was his mighty hand that *laid* on that trembling tottering mountain," &c. &c. &c.

These things are not exactly as we could wish them, perhaps:—but that a gentleman should know so much about Noah's ark and know anything about any thing else, is scarcely to be expected. We have no right to require English grammar and accurate information about Moses and Aaron at the hands of one and the same author. For our parts, now we come to think of it, if we only understood as much about Mount Sinai and other matters as Mr. Headley does, we should make a point of always writing bad English upon principle, whether we knew better or not.

It may well be made a question moreover, how far a man of genius is justified in discussing topics so serious as those handled by Mr. Headley, in any ordinary kind of *style*. One should not talk about Scriptural subjects as one would talk about the rise and fall of stocks or the proceedings of Congress. Mr. Headley has seemed to feel this and has therefore elevated his manner—a little. For example:

"The fields were smiling in verdure before his eyes; the perfumed breezes *floated by* . . . . . . The sun is *sailing* over the encampment . . . . . . That cloud was God's pavilion; the thunder was its sentinels; and the lightning the lances' points as they moved round the sacred trust . . . . . . And how could he part with his children whom he had *borne on his brave heart* for more than forty years? . . . . . . Thus everything conspired to render Zion the spell-word of the nation and on its summit the *heart of Israel seemed to lie and throb* . . . . . . The sun died in the heavens; *an earthquake thundered on* to complete the dismay," &c. &c.

Here no one can fail to perceive the beauty (in an antediluvian or at least in a Pickwickian sense) of these expressions
in general, about the floating of the breeze, the sailing of the
sun, the thundering of the earthquake, and the throbbing of
the heart as it lay on the top of the mountain.

The true artist, however, always rises as he proceeds, and
in his last page or so brings all his elocution to a climax. Only
hear Mr. Headley's *finale*. He has been describing the crucifixion and now soars into the sublime:

"How heaven regarded this disaster, and the Universe felt
at the sight, I cannot tell. I know not but tears fell like rain-
drops from angelic eyes when they saw Christ spit upon and
struck. I know not but there was silence on high for *more*
than "half an hour" when the scene of the crucifixion was
transpiring,—[a scene, as well as an event always "transpires"
with Mr. Headley]—a silence unbroken save by the solitary
sound of some harp-string on which unconsciously fell the
agitated, trembling fingers of a seraph. I know not but all the
radiant ranks on high, and even Gabriel himself, turned with
the deepest solicitude to the Father's face, to see if he was
calm and untroubled amid it all. I know not but his composed brow and serene majesty were all that restrained
Heaven from one universal shriek of horror when they heard
groans on Calvary—*dying* groans. I know not but they
thought God had given his glory to another, but one thing I
do know, [Ah, there *is* really one thing Mr. Headley
knows!]—that when they saw through the vast design, comprehended the stupendous scene, the hills of God shook to a
shout that never before rung over their bright tops, and the
crystal sea trembled to a song that had never before stirred its
bright depths, and the "Glory to God in the Highest," was a
sevenfold chorus of hallelujahs and harping symphonies."

Here we have direct evidence of Mr. Headley's accuracy
not less than of his eloquence. "I know not but that" one is
as vast as the other. The one thing that he does know he
knows to perfection: he knows not only what the chorus was
(it was one of "hallelujahs and harping symphonies") but also
how much of it there was—it was a "sevenfold chorus." Mr.

Headley is a mathematical man. Moreover he is a modest man; for he confesses (no doubt with tears in his eyes) that really there is one thing he does not know. "How Heaven regarded this disaster, and the Universe felt at the sight, I cannot tell." Only think of that! *I* cannot!—I, Headley, really cannot tell how the Universe "felt" once upon a time! This is downright bashfulness on the part of Mr. Headley. He *could* tell if he would only try. Why did he not inquire? Had he demanded of the Universe how it felt, can any one doubt that the answer would have been—"Pretty well, I thank you, my dear Headley; how do you feel yourself?"

"Quack" is a word that sounds well only in the mouth of a duck; and upon our honor we feel a scruple in using it: nevertheless the truth should be told; and the simple fact is, that the author of the "Sacred Mountains" is the Autocrat of all the Quacks. In saying this, we beg not to be misunderstood. We mean no disparagement to Mr. Headley. We admire that gentleman as much as any individual ever did except that gentleman himself. He looks remarkably well at all points—although perhaps best, EXAS—at a distance—as the lying Pindar says he saw Archilochus, who died ages before the vagabond was born:—the reader will excuse the digression; but talking of one great man is very apt to put us in mind of another. We were saying—were we not?—that Mr. Headley is by no means to be sneered at as a quack. This might be justifiable, indeed, were he only a quack in a small way—a quack doing business by retail. But the wholesale dealer is entitled to respect. Besides, the Reverend author of "Napoleon and his Marshals" was a quack to some purpose. He knows what he is about. We like perfection wherever we see it. We readily forgive a man for being a fool if he only be a *perfect* fool—and this is a particular in which we cannot put our hands upon our hearts and say that Mr. Headley is deficient. He acts upon the principle that if a thing is worth doing at all it is worth doing well:—and the thing that he "does" especially well is the public.

Southern Literary Messenger, October 1850

Henry B. Hirst

The Coming of the Mammoth—the Funeral of Time, and other Poems, by Henry B. Hirst. Boston: Philips & Sampson.

MR. HIRST is a young lawyer of Philadelphia—admitted to practice, we believe, about two years ago, and already deriving a very respectable income from his profession. Some years since, his name was frequently seen in the content-tables of our Magazines, but latterly the duties of his profession seem to have withdrawn him from literary pursuits. He has, nevertheless, done quite right in collecting his fugitive poems, and giving them to the public in a convenient and durable form. The day has happily gone by when a practitioner at the bar has anything to fear from its being understood that he is capable of inditing a *good* sonnet.

We have no hesitation in saying that Mr. Hirst has not only given indication of poetical genius, but that he has composed some *very* commendable poems. His imagination is vigorous, bold, and at the same time delicate. His sense of the true provinces of poetical art is remarkably keen and discriminating, and his versification is superior to that of any American poet. We perhaps should qualify this latter remark by observing that his knowledge of the *principles* of the metrical art is more profound and more accurate than that of any American poet—but that his knowledge too frequently leads him into the pedantry of *hyperism*. He is apt to *overdo* a good thing. He insists upon rhythmical and metrical effects until they cease to have any effect at all—or until they give to his compositions an air of mere oddity.—His other defects are, chiefly, a want of constructive ability, occasional extravagance of expression, and a far more than occasional imitativeness. This last sin, is, in poetry, never to be forgiven, and we are sorry to say that Mr. Hirst is inordinately given to it. There is not a single poem in the beautifully printed volume before us which does not remind us, instantly, of some other composition. If we except some rhythmical effects (for which the author deserves great praise) there is nothing in the book which is fairly entitled to be called original, either in its conception, execution, or manner, as a whole. Of detached thoughts, nevertheless, there are many very striking ones which are quite new, for any evidence that we have to the contrary.

As very usually happens in a case of this kind, the leading and longest poem of the collection is the least worthy of notice. It is called "The Coming of the Mammoth," and, to say nothing of its being a mere paraphrase, in all its most striking points, of Mr. Mathews' "Behemoth," is feebly and incoherently narrated—narrated, indeed, very much as a schoolboy would narrate it. In fact, we understand that it is one of the earliest compositions of the author, who began to write at a very immature age.

The story runs simply thus. The aborigines are suddenly startled from the quiet of ages, by the apparition of "myriad forms" of the mammoths. These creatures carry death and desolation every where—destroying vegetation, and animal life wherever they pass. The extravagance with which their nature is delineated, may be instanced by one stanza:

> We saw them hunt the buffalo,
>   And crush them with their tusks of steel;
> *The mountains rocking to and fro*
>   Like trees that in the tempest reel,
> When passed their herds; and lake and river
>   A draught of theirs made dry *forever*.

The aborigines themselves fall a prey and are reduced to a small band, when they bethink them of supplicating the aid of Moneddo (Manitou) who forthwith attacks the ravagers with lightning, and destroys them all but one.

> Bolt rushed on bolt till, one by one,
>   Howling in agony, they died,
> Save him, the fiercest! And alone
>   He stood—almost a God in pride—
> Then with a loud defying yell
>   Leapt, *like a shaft*, o'er hill and dell.

He flies at great speed; the lightnings and the Indians still pursuing. He reaches the Mississippi—leaps it at one bound (possibly at a point not very far from the source) and is at last brought up by the Rocky Mountains—but only for a few moments—he ascends the highest peak—throws rocks and trees "in the face of God" and fairly defies him, until at length the "mightiest spirits" are summoned to put an end to the contest:

> They heard: with one tremendous crash
>   Down on the Mammoth's forehead came
> A surging sea of withering flame.
>
> Earth trembled to its core; and weak
>   But unsubdued the Mammoth leapt
> Furiously from that lofty peak
>   To where the dark blue ocean swept.
> Down! down! The startled waters sever;
>   Then roll above him—and forever!

Our readers will agree with us that from the summit of the Rocky Mountains to the Pacific, is a tolerably long leap even for a Mammoth—although he had had some previous practice in jumping the Mississippi.

We are not extravagant in saying (are we?) that the "Coming of the Mammoth" which might as well have been called the "Coming and the *Going* of the Mammoth" is the most preposterous of all the preposterous poems ever deliberately printed by a gentleman arrived at the years of discretion. Nor has it one individual point of redeeming merit. Had Mr. Hirst written only this we should have thrown his book to the pigs without comment.

"*The Funeral of Time*" is a forcible allegory, very indistinctly made out, but well versified in some respects, and filled with majestic images—although disfigured, too often, by something even more mad than Nat Leeism.

"*Isabelle*" is the finest ballad ever written in this country, and but for its obvious and no doubt intentional imitations, might be called one of the best ever written anywhere. It is indeed exceedingly difficult to understand how the author of such trash as "The Mammoth" could be at the same time author of anything so widely different as "Isabelle." Its simplicity is exquisite—its conduct could not be improved—and its versification (within the narrow limits designed) is full of original force. We quote (unconnectedly) a few of the best quatrains:

A lustrous maid was Isabelle,
　　And quiet as a brooding bird;
She never thought of passion's spell—
　　Of love she never heard;

But in her lonely chamber sat,
　　Sighing the weary hours away
From morn till flitting of the bat
　　Around the turrets gray.

And trembling with a strange unrest—
　　A yearning for—she knew not what;
She only knew her heaving breast
　　Was heavy with its lot.

At last she passed to womanhood,
　　And sat her down on Beauty's throne,
A statue with a beating heart
　　Beneath a breast of stone.

Her lustrous eyes grew large with love;
　　Her cheeks with passion flushed and bright;
Her lips, whereon no bee might rove
　　Undrunken with delight,
Were, &c.

She felt she had not lived in vain;
　　She saw the Eden of her dreams
Close round her, and she stood again
　　Beside its silver streams.

The servants followed her with their eyes,
　　And prayed the virgin that her hours
Might ever pass under azure skies
　　And over parterres of flowers.

"Geraldine" is a far better poem than "Isabelle" and is unquestionably the best in the volume. It is, however, in manner
a palpable imitation of Tennyson. In justice to Mr. Hirst we
quote it in full:

The martins twitter round the eaves,
　　The swift adown the chimney glides,
The bees are humming 'mid the leaves
　　　　Along the garden side;

The robin whistles in the wood,
       The linnet on the vane,
       And down the alder-margined lane
The throstle sings, and by the flood
       The plover pipes again.

But ah—alas! alas! no more
   Their merry melodies delight;
No more along the river's shore
   I watch the swallow's flight:
And bees may hum and birds may sing,
       And silver streamlets shine,
       But on the rocks I sit and pine
Unheeding all; for thought will cling
       To naught but Geraldine.

Oh, Geraldine! my life, my love!
   I only wander where we met
In emerald days, when blue above
   The skies were o'er us set—
Along the glen and o'er the vale
       And by the willow tree
       I wander where at even with thee
I sang the song and told the tale
       Of olden chivalry.

I stand beneath the sombre pines
   That darken all thy father's hall,
Begirt with noisome ivy vines
   That shroud me like a pall.
Aye there!—where ruin frowns around!
       Until the cock doth crow
       I watch thy window-panes below,
Upon the sodden blackened ground
       Where nothing good will grow.

I've watched thy lattice as before
   To see the glimmer dimly pass,
(When thou wouldst open thy chamber door)
       Of lamp-light on the glass;
But none from out thy lattice peeps,
       And all within is gloom,

And silent as a vacant tomb,
Save when a bat affrighted cheeps
   In some deserted room.

Why comest thou not? Night after night,
  For many a long and weary year,
'Neath many and many a May-moon's light,
   I've waited for thee here.
Aye blackest night and wildest storm
    When frowning in the sky
    Have looked on me with lightning eye,
And charnel figures round my form
    Have gleamed and hurried by.

Why comest thou not? or wilt thou soon?
  The crimson sun doth wax and wane
Day after day; the yellow moon
    Gildeth thy casement pane
Night after night; the stars are pale
    Expecting thee; the breeze
    Rustling among the dreary trees
Sighs for thee with a woful wail
    Who art beyond the seas.

They tell me thou wilt never come—
  Alas! that thou art cold and dead,
And slumbering in the green sea-foam
    Upon some coral bed:—
That shriekingly thy ship went down
    Beneath the wailing wave,
    And none were near to hear or save—
And then they weep to see me frown—
    To hear me groan and rave.

Thou dead!—no, no!—it cannot be!
  For if thou wast, thy ghost had kept
The solemn trist thou madest with me
    When all save passion slept—
Thy ghost had come and greeted me
    And bade me be at rest;
    And long ere this upon my breast
The clod had lain; and I with thee
    Were roaming 'mid the blest.

"The Unseen River" is musical, but has the defect of being imperfectly *made out*. Few persons will understand that by the river always heard but never seen, until the traveller is overtaken by death, it is the poet's intention to typify Happiness. We quote a fine stanza of which the whole is very poetic (in the best sense) and of which the concluding line is a specimen of exquisite versification.

> From the valley—from a river
>   Which, like many a silver quiver,
>   Through the landscape stole in light:—
> From the bushes, shrubs and blossoms—
> Flowers unfolding fragrant bosoms—
>   Curled the shadows out of sight,
> Fading like a ghost in air; and ever the river rippled bright.

"The Burial of Eros" is a very effective allegorical poem—but *all* allegories are contemptible:—at least the only two which are not contemptible (The Pilgrim's Progress and The Fairy Queen) are admired in despite of themselves (as allegories) and in the direct ratio of the possibility of keeping the allegorical meaning out of sight.

"The Sea of the Mind" is another allegory, or (what is less objectionable) an allegorical enigma. It is miserably indefinite. Its only merit lies in detached thoughts, and in its admirable management of the trochaic rhythm. The metre is heptameter catalectic—consisting of seven (trochaic) feet and a final cæsura, equivalent. The trochees are finely varied, now and then, with dactyls; only the most forcible consonants are employed; the richest vowel sounds abound; and all the effects of alliteration, with other rhythmical effects less common, are skilfully introduced.—For example:

> Silvery the ocean singeth over sands of pearly glow;
> Under its surface shapes are gliding—gliding fast or sailing slow—
> Shapes of strange supernal beauty, floating through a fairy wave—
> Fairer, purer, lovelier, brighter than the streams that Iram lave.

"The Birth of a Poet" is somewhat like an imitation from John Neal's poem of the same title; the commencement, especially, is stolen.

Mr. Hirst's conception throughout is fantastical—not to say absurd. The poem, however, is redeemed by one remarkably well-managed quatrain:

> Music like what the poet hears
> When, wrapt in harmony, he wings
> His soul away through argent spheres,
> *And back their melody brings.*

The concluding anapæst here beautifully and most appropriately varies the iambic rhythm—making the sound "echo the sense."

"Everard Grey" is a superb specimen of dactylic trimeter, catalectic on one syllable—three dactyls and one equivalent cæsura. E. g.—

> Time it has passed; and the lady is pale—
> Pale as the lily that lolls on the gale:
> Weary and worn she hath waited for years
> Keeping her grief evergreen with her tears:—
> Years will she tarry—for cold is the clay
> Fettering the form of her Everard Grey.

"The Fringilla Melodia" is truly beautiful throughout, possessing a natural force and grace (without effort) which would do honor to the most noted poet in the land. We quote the first quatrain:

> Happy song-sparrow that on woodland side
> Or by the meadow sits, and ceaseless sings
> His mellow roundelay in russet pride,
> *Owning no care between his wings.*

The *"sits"* here is not ungrammatical; the sparrow is not *invoked*. The construction is nevertheless a little equivocal.

"The Coming of Autumn" is spirited—but is a little too much in the Old King Cole way.

"The Autumn Wind" has a noble beginning, and as noble an end—but as a whole is unimpressive.

"Eleanore" has no merit at all except the effect of the constantly recurring refrain, *"Eleanore!"* and this is taken from Tennyson's "Oriana."

"Mary" has some fine passages—e. g.

> He watched each motion of her rustling dress,
> Each lustrous movement of her liquid eyes—
> Envied the air its undisturbed caress
> Of her whose presence was his Paradise.

"To an Old Oak;" "To E— with a Withered Rose;" and "The Death-Song of the Nightingale" have nothing in them remarkable—"Eulalie Vere" nothing beyond the *barroques* lines,

> Cheeks where the loveliest of lustres reposes
> *On valleys of lilies and mountains of roses.*

"To the American Sky-Lark" is professedly an imitation of Bryant's "Waterfowl:" we need, therefore, say nothing about it.

"Ellena" has some glowing thoughts. For example,

> at her word
> The hushed air shook, with human passion stirred.

And again:

> a maniac tune
> Rang in mine ears, like songs sung in a swoon.

"The Coming of Night" is excellent throughout—if we except the grammatical error in the ante-penultimate line.

> Oh Blessed Night that *comes* to rich and poor.

Here are two admirable quatrains:

> Forest and field are still
> Nature seems wrapt in slumber; wholly dumb,
> Save when the frog's deep bass or beetle's hum,
> Or wailing whippoorwill,
>
> Disturb her weary ear,
> Or the far falling of the rippling rill
> That sings, while leaping down the silent hill,
> Her dreamless sleep to cheer.

"Violet" is merely an absurd imitation of Barry Cornwall's most absurd Tom-Foolery.

"A Gift" is well versified, but common-place.

"The Owl" opens with two finely imaginative stanzas:

> When twilight fades and evening falls
>   Alike on tree and tower,
> *And silence, like a pensive maid,*
>   *Walks round each slumbering bower;*
> When fragrant flowerets fold their leaves,
>   And all is still in sleep,
> The horned owl *on moonlit wing*
>   *Flies from the donjon keep.*
>
> And he calls aloud "too-whit! too-whoo!"
>   And the nightingale is still,
> And the pattering step of the hurrying hare
>   Is hushed upon the hill;
> And he crouches low in the dewy grass
>   As the lord of the night goes by,
> Not with a loudly whirring wing
>   *But like a lady's sigh.*

Every critic—at least every poetical critic—will admit that the images in these two stanzas are such as only a true poet could conceive. At the same time they are embodied with much art.

"A Song" and "Mutius Scævola" have no particular merit. "The Forsaken" ends with nerve:

> Well, go thy way! and never wake
>   The feeblest memory of me,
> To wring thy worthless heart! I break
>   Thy chains and set thee free.
> Thou to thy mirth! I to my gloom!
>   Health to the coldest of the twain!
> And mine—not thine—the iron doom
>   Of having loved in vain.

"The Lament of Adam" is chiefly remarkable for the effect of its versification—not altogether original, to be sure, but rare, and very forcible when well-managed. The rhythm is dactylic, the lines terminating with equivalent cæsuras. The metre is generally tetrameter, catalectic on one syllable (the cæsura forming the catalexis)—but the lines increase towards the closing of the stanzas, and in one instance are hexameter catalectic. We give the last stanza:

> Life hath its pleasures—but perishing they as the flowers:
> Sin hath its sorrows; and, sighing we turned from those
>   bowers:
> Bright were the angels behind with their falchions of
>   heavenly flame:
> Dark was the desolate desert before us, but darker the
>   depth of our shame.

Here the alliteration is too obvious—quite overdone, and is an instance of the hyperism to which we alluded in the beginning of our notice.

"The Statue-Love" is not very good.

"May" is a remarkably fine poem, with an exquisite close:

> ——the passionate bard
> Wanders away through sylvan lonelinesses,
> Alive with love—his heart a silver river
> On which the swan of song floats gracefully for ever.

"Dramatic Fragments" are worth nothing. "The Song of the Scald Biorne" is, to our astonishment, badly versified. How comes Mr. Hirst in an anapæstic rhythm, or in any rhythm, with such a verse as—

> My iron hand on her arm when before her I knelt?

"Summer" is quite feeble.

Twenty well-constructed sonnets conclude the volume. Among these, "Bethlehem" and "Dead Man's Island" may be cited as particularly good: but by way of *finale* to our review we quote "Astarte" as the best.

> Thy lustre, heavenly star! shines ever on me.
> I, trembling like Endymion over-bent
> By dazzling Dian, when with wonderment
> He saw her crescent light the Latmian lea:

And like a Naiad's sailing on the sea,
    Floats thy fair form before me: the azure air
    Is all ambrosial with thy hyacinth hair:
While round thy lips the moth in airy glee
Hovers, and hums in dim and dizzy dreams,
    Drunken with odorous breath: thy argent eyes
(Twin planets swimming through love's lustrous skies)
Are mirrored in my heart's serenest streams—
Such eyes saw Shakespeare, flashing, bold and bright,
When Queenly Egypt rode the Nile at night.

Broadway Journal, July 12, 1845

Joseph Holt Ingraham

Lafitte: the Pirate of the Gulf. By the author of the *South-West*. New York: Harper and Brothers.

THE "author of the *South-West*" is Professor Ingraham. We had occasion to speak favorably of that work in our Messenger for January last. *"Lafitte,"* the book now before us, may be called an historical novel. It is based, in a great degree, upon a sketch in Mr. Flint's *"Valley of the Mississippi,"* of the great Baritarian outlaw; and many of the leading incidents narrated may be found in the *"Louisiana"* of Marboi, and the *"Memoirs"* of Latour. We are not, however, to decide upon the merits of the story—which runs nearly thus—by any reference to historical truth.

An expatriated Frenchman resides upon the banks of the Kennebeck. He has two sons—twins—their mother having died in their infancy. Their names are Achille and Henri—the former proud, impetuous and ambitious—the latter of a more gentle nature. We are introduced to this little family when the boys are in their fifteenth year. At this epoch a jealousy of his brother, never felt before, and founded on the obvious preference of the father for Henri, arises in the bosom of Achille. Gertrude, now, a niece and ward of the old gentleman, becomes an inmate of the house. She is beautiful, is beloved by both the sons, but returns only the affection of Henri. Jealousy thus deepens into hatred on the part of Achille. This hatred is still farther embittered by an accident. Henri saves the life of his mistress, and, in so doing, rejects the proffered assistance of Achille. The lovers meet too by moonlight, and are overheard by the discarded brother, who in a moment of phrensy, plunges a knife in the bosom of Henri, hurries to the sea-coast, and, seizing the boat of a fisherman, pushes out immediately to sea. Upon the eve of being lost, he is picked up by a merchant vessel, and proceeds with her on a voyage to the Mediterranean. The vessel is captured by the Algerines—our hero is imprisoned—escapes by the aid of a Moorish maiden, whom he dishonors and abandons—is recaptured—escapes again in an open boat for Ceuti—is again captured by Algerines—unites with them,

and subsequently commands them—is taken by the Turks—
is promoted in their navy—turns Mussulman—becomes the
chief of an armed horde—combats in the Egyptian ranks—
becomes again a pirate—is taken by the Spaniards—is liberated and becomes a corsair again, and again. His adventures
so far, however, from the period of his attack upon Henri—
adventures occupying a period of fifteen years—are related by
the novelist in language very little more diffuse than our own.
We are now introduced, at full length to Achille, in the character of Lafitte. The scene is Jamaica, and we find the freebooter planning a descent upon the house of a wealthy
Mexican exile, Velasquez. He has a daughter, Constanza, very
beautiful, and a nephew, very much of a rascal. The nephew
is in league with the robbers, and admits them to the house
for the sake of sharing the booty. The adventure ends in the
death of the traitor by a pistol-shot from the hands of Velasquez—the death of the old man himself through agitation—
and the carrying off of the maiden, and much booty, by Lafitte. The lady however, is treated with great deference by that
noble-spirited and fine-looking young man the cut-throat,
who wears a grey cloak with a velvet collar, folds his arms,
gnashes his teeth, and has, we must admit it, a more handsomely furnished cabin than even the Red Rover himself. We
are assured that his only object in carrying the damsel off at
all, was to shield his person by means of her own, from the
shots of his pursuers. Accordingly, a merchantman, bound for
Kingston, heaving in sight, Constanza is set at liberty and put
on board of it, with an old negro wench Juana (all lips) and
a young pirate boy Theodore, (all sentiment) to attend upon
her orders and convoy her safely into port. We now have a
storm (in the usual manner) a wreck, and a capture. The dis-
masted vessel is taken by one of the galleys of Lafitte, and the
lady again falls into the clutches of the buccaneers, who carry
her to one of their rendezvous, a very romantic cavern, at the
head of the bay of Gonzares, in the island of St. Domingo.

In the meantime the lover of the fair Constanza, one Count
D'Oyley, commander of the French frigate, Le Sultan, going
to visit his mistress at her paternal residence, is made aware
of her disaster, follows immediately with his frigate's tender
in pursuit of Lafitte, and fails in meeting him, but has the

satisfaction of being taken prisoner by one of the freebooter's small vessels, and carried to the identical rendezvous in which lies the object of his search. The lovers repose in different caverns, and are totally unsuspicious of the so near presence of each other. But the maiden, of course, sings a song, made on purpose improviso, and all about love and the moon, and the lover, hearing every word of it, breaks through the wall (also of course) and—clasps her in his arms! But we are growing scurrilous. Lafitte arrives, and promises the two captives their freedom and a passage to Port-au-Prince in the morning. Count D'Oyley, however, having dreamed in succession four very ugly dreams, thinks it better to put no faith in the freebooter, and getting up in the middle of the night, makes his escape from the rendezvous with his mistress and Juana. In so doing he has only to dress his mistress as a man, and himself as a woman, to descend a precipice, to make a sentinel at the mouth of the cave drunk, and so walk over him—make another drunk in Lafitte's schooner, and so walk over him—walk over some forty or fifty of the crew on deck—and finally to walk off with the long-boat. These things are trifles with a man of genius—and an author should never let slip an opportunity of displaying his invention. D'Oyley's frigate happens just precisely at the right moment to be in the offing, and has no difficulty whatever in picking up all hands.

We are now brought to Baritaria—and some scenes follow of historical interest. An offer on the part of the British is made to Lafitte. He demands time for reflection, and proceeds to lay the pacquet of proposals before the Governor of Louisiana, demanding a free pardon for himself and associates as the reward of his information, and the price of his adherence to the States. After some trouble he succeeds in his application. He is present, and fights valiantly, at the battle of New Orleans. In the heat of the contest he is attacked pointedly and with vehemence by an individual in the uniform of a British naval officer—is wounded, and carried to the hospital. Here he discovers, as a nun, his cousin Gertrude, who after the attack by Achille upon Henri, has taken the veil, by way of atonement for her share in the disaster. Henri, she informs Lafitte, is not killed, but gone to France with his father. Our hero now, having recovered of his wound, vows to devote to penitence, among the monks of St. Bernard, the remainder of his life. His first object, however, being to restore, as far as possible, his ill-gotten wealth to the proper owners, he finds it necessary to purchase a vessel with the view of collecting his treasures. He does so, and proceeds to accomplish his purpose.

The naval officer who attacked him so fiercely on the ramparts at Orleans is now discovered to be D'Oyley, although it does seem a little singular that Lafitte, who knew D'Oyley well, should not have discovered this matter before. The Frenchman, it appears, having rescued his mistress from the cavern, as before shown, and having reached his frigate in safety, can think of no more commendable course than that of returning for the purpose of dispersing the pirates, and hanging the preserver of his own life, and of the life and honor of his mistress. With this laudable design, he drops anchor at the mouth of the cavern. In the night time, however, the poor tossed-about lady is carried off thro' a porthole, by Cudjo, an old negro, for some wise purposes of his own. Upon learning this occurrence the Count is very angry, and just then perceiving a schooner making her way out of the harbor, jumps at once to the conclusion that his lady is on board, and that Lafitte is the person who put her there. It is really distressing to see what a passion the Count is in upon this occasion. "Lafitte," says he, "thou seared and branded outlaw!—cursed of God and loathed of men!—fit compeer of hell's dark spirits!—blaster of human happiness!—destroyer of innocence! Guilty thyself, thou would'st make all like thee! Scorner of purity, thou would'st unmake and make it guilt! Like Satan, thou sowest tares of sorrow among the seeds of peace!—thou seekest good to make it evil! Renegade of mankind!—thou art a blot among thy race—the living presence of that moral pestilence which men and holy writ term *sin*!" The beauty and vigor of all this are not at all diminished by the fact that the "scorner of purity" and "renegade of mankind" was necessarily deprived of the pleasure of hearing a word of it, being otherwise busily engaged in the State of Louisiana.

The Count, having overtaken the schooner, and found out

his mistake, goes to Barataria, and thence, proceeding to New Orleans, arrives on the day of the battle. Lafitte is there discovered upon the ramparts, and the combat ensues as heretofore described. D'Oyley imagines that Lafitte is mortally wounded. In a few days, however, the newly-purchased vessel of the corsair, with the corsair on board, is pointed out to him as it is leaving the harbor, and he again starts with his frigate in pursuit. Lafitte meanwhile has proceeded to the rendezvous at which we left Constanza in the clutches of Cudjo, rescues her, and placing her safely in his vessel, determines to put her forthwith in the hands of her lover. He is met, unfortunately, by the frigate of the enraged D'Oyley. The vessels are thrown together, and the Count springs with his boarders on the deck of the schooner—turning a deaf ear to explanation. The corsair is mortally wounded by the Count. The cap of the latter falling off in the tumult, he is discovered to be Henri—the brother of Achille, or Lafitte. An old man on board, called Lafon, is at the same moment opportunely discovered to be the father. Explanations ensue. Lafitte dies—the lovers are happy—and the story terminates.

It must not be supposed that the absurdities we have here pointed out, are as obtrusive in the novel of Professor Ingraham as they appear in our naked digest. Still they are sufficiently so. *"Lafitte,"* like the "Elkswatawa" of Mr. French, is most successful, we think, in its historical details. Commodore Patterson and General Andrew Jackson are among the personages who form a portion of the story. The portrait of the President seems to us forcibly sketched. But our author is more happy in any respect than in delineations of character. Some descriptive pieces are well-drawn, and admirably colored. We may instance the several haunts of the pirates, the residence of Velasquez, the house of the council at New Orleans, and the private cabin allotted by the corsair to Constanza. The whole book possesses vigor, and a certain species of interest—and there can be little doubt of its attaining popularity. The chronological mannerism noticed in "Elkswatawa" is also observable in "Lafitte." Some other mannerisms referrible to the same sin of imitation are also to be observed. As a general rule it may be safely assumed, that the most simple, is the best, method of narration. Our author cannot be

induced to think so, and is at unnecessary pains to bring
about artificialities of construction—not so much in regard
to particular sentences, as to the introduction of his incidents.
To these he always approaches with the gait of a crab. We
have, for example, been keeping company with the buccaneers for a few pages—but now they are to make an attack
upon some old family mansion. In an instant the buccaneers
are dropped for the mansion, and the definite for the indefinite article. In place of *the* robbers proceeding in the course
wherein we have been bearing them company, and advancing
in proper order to the dwelling, they are suddenly abandoned
for a house. *A* family mansion is depicted. *A* man is sitting
within it. *A* maiden is sitting by his side, and *a* quantity of
ingots are reposing in the cellar. We are then, and not till
then, informed, that the family mansion, the man, the maiden
and the ingots, are the identical mansion, man, maiden and
ingots, of which we have already heard the buccaneers planning the attack.—Thus, at the conclusion of book the 4th,
Count D'Oyley has rescued his mistress from the cavern, and
arrived with her, in safety, upon the deck of his frigate. He
has, moreover, decided upon returning with the frigate to the
cavern for the laudable purpose, as aforesaid, of hanging his
deliverer. We naturally expect still to keep company with *the*
ship in this adventure; and turn over the page with a certainty
of finding ourselves upon her decks. But not so. She is now
merely *a* frigate which we behold at a distance— *a* stately ship
arrayed in the apparel of war, and which "sails with majestic
motion into the bay of Gonzales." Of course we are strongly
tempted to throw the book, ship and all, out of the window.

The novelist is too minutely, and by far too frequently *descriptive*. We are surfeited with unnecessary detail. Every little
figure in the picture is invested with all the dignities of light
and shadow, and chiaro 'scuro. Of mere outlines there are
none. Not a dog yelps, unsung. Not a shovel-footed negro
waddles across the stage, whether to any ostensible purpose
or not, without eliciting from the author a *vos plaudite*, with
an extended explanation of the character of his personal appearance—of his length, depth, and breadth,—and, more
particularly, of the length, depth, and breadth of his shirt-
collar, shoe-buckles and hat-band.

The English of Professor Ingraham is generally good. It possesses vigor and is very copious. Sometimes, however, we meet with a sentence without end, involving a nominative without a verb. For example,

"As the men plied their oars, and moved swiftly down the bayou, the Indian, who was the last of his name and race, with whom would expire the proud appellation, centuries before recognized among other tribes, as the synonyme for intelligence, civilization, and courage—THE NATCHEZ!—the injured, persecuted, slaughtered and unavenged Natchez—the Grecians of the aboriginal nations of North America!" See p. 125. Vol. 2.

Many odd words, too, and expressions, such as "revenge you," in place of "avenge you"—"Praxitiles," instead of "Praxiteles"—"assayed" in lieu of "essayed," and "denouément" for "dénouement"—together with such things as "frissieur," "closelier," "self-powered," "folden," and "rhodomantine" are here to be found, and, perhaps, may as well be placed at once to the account of typographical errors.

Our principal objection is to the tendency of the tale. The pirate-captain, from the author's own showing, is a weak, a vaccillating villain, a fratricide, a cowardly cut-throat, who strikes an unoffending boy under his protection, and makes nothing of hurling a man over a precipice for merely falling asleep, or shooting him down without any imaginable reason whatsoever. Yet he is never mentioned but with evident respect, or in some such sentence as the following. "I could hardly believe I was looking upon the celebrated Lafitte, when I gazed upon his elegant, even noble person and fine features, in which, in spite of their resolute expression, there is an air of frankness which assures me that *he would never be guilty of a mean action*," &c. &c. &c. In this manner, and by these means, the total result of his portraiture as depicted, leaves upon the mind of the reader no proper degree of abhorrence. The epithet "impulsive," applied so very frequently to the character of this scoundrel, as to induce a smile at every repetition of the word, seems to be regarded by the author as an all-sufficient excuse for the unnumbered legion of his iniquities. We object too—decidedly—to such expressions on the lips of a hero, as "If I cannot be the last in Heaven, I will be the first in Hell"—"Now favor me, Hell or Heaven, and I will have my revenge!"—"Back hounds, or, by the holy God, I will send one of you to breakfast in Hell," &c. &c. &c.—expressions with which the volumes before us are too plentifully besprinkled. Upon the whole, we could wish that men possessing the weight of talents and character belonging to Professor Ingraham, would either think it necessary to bestow a somewhat greater degree of labor and attention upon the composition of their novels, or otherwise, would *not* think it necessary to compose them at all.

Southern Literary Messenger, August 1836

Washington Irving

The Crayon Miscellany. By the Author of the *Sketch Book. No. 3—Containing Legends of the Conquest of Spain.* Philadelphia: Carey, Lea & Blanchard.

WE FEEL it almost an act of supererogation to speak of this book, which is long since in the hands of every American who has leisure for reading at all. The matter itself is deeply interesting, but, as usual, its chief beauty is beauty of style. The Conquest of Spain by the Saracens, an event momentous in the extreme, is yet enveloped, as regards the motives and actions of the principal *dramatis personæ* in triple doubt and confusion. To snatch from this uncertainty a few striking and picturesque legends, possessing, at the same time, some absolute portion of verity, and to adorn them in his own magical language is all that Mr. Irving has done in the present instance. But that he has done this little well it is needless to say. He does not claim for the Legends the authenticity of history properly so called—yet all are partially *facts*, and however extravagant some may appear, they will all, to use the words of the author himself, "be found in the works of sage and reverend chroniclers of yore, growing side by side with long acknowledged truths, and might be supported by learned and imposing references in the margin." Were we to instance any one of the narratives as more beautiful than the rest, it would be *The Story of the Marvellous and Portentous Tower*.

Southern Literary Messenger, December 1835

Astoria: Or, Anecdotes of an Enterprize beyond the Rocky Mountains. By Washington Irving. Philadelphia: Carey, Lea and Blanchard.

MR. IRVING'S acquaintance at Montreal, many years since, with some of the principal partners of the great North-West Fur Company, was the means of interesting him deeply in the varied concerns of trappers, hunters, and Indians, and in all the adventurous details connected with the commerce in peltries. Not long after his return from his late tour to the prairies, he held a conversation with his friend,

Mr. John Jacob Astor, of New York, in relation to an enterprize set on foot, and conducted by that gentleman, about the
year 1812,—an enterprize having for its object a participation,
on the most extensive scale, in the fur trade carried on with
the Indians in all the western and north-western regions of
North America. Finding Mr. I. fully alive to the exciting interest of this subject, Mr. Astor was induced to express a regret that the true nature and extent of the enterprize, together
with its great national character and importance, had never
been generally comprehended; and a wish that Mr. Irving
would undertake to give an account of it. To this he consented. All the papers relative to the matter were submitted
to his inspection; and the volumes now before us (two well-
sized octavos) are the result. The work has been accomplished
in a masterly manner—the modesty of the title affording no
indication of the fulness, comprehensiveness, and beauty,
with which a long and entangled series of detail, collected,
necessarily, from a mass of vague and imperfect data, has been
wrought into completeness and unity.

Supposing our readers acquainted with the main features
of the original fur trade in America, we shall not follow Mr.
Irving in his vivid account of the primitive French Canadian
Merchant, his jovial establishments and dependants—of the
licensed traders, missionaries, voyageurs, and coureurs des
bois—of the British Canadian Fur Merchant—of the rise of
the great Company of the "North-West," its constitution and
internal trade; its parliamentary hall and banquetting room;
its boatings, its huntings, its wassailings, and other magnificent feudal doings in the wilderness. It was the British Mackinaw Company, we presume,—(a Company established in
rivalry of the "North-West,") the *scene* of whose main operations first aroused the attention of our government. Its chief
factory was established at Michilimackinac, and sent forth its
perogues, by Green Bay, Fox River, and the Wisconsin, to
the Mississippi, and thence to all its tributary streams—in
this way hoping to monopolize the trade with all the Indian
tribes on the southern and western waters of our own territory, as the "North-West" had monopolized it along the waters of the North. Of course we now began to view with a
jealous eye, and to make exertions for counteracting, the in-

fluence hourly acquired over our own aborigines by these immense combinations of foreigners. In 1796, the United States sent out agents to establish rival trading houses on the frontier, and thus, by supplying the wants of the Indians, to link their interests with ours, and to divert the trade, if possible, into national channels. The enterprize failed—being, we suppose, inefficiently conducted and supported; and the design was never afterwards attempted until by the individual means and energy of Mr. Astor.

John Jacob Astor was born in Waldorf, a German village, near Heidelberg, on the banks of the Rhine. While yet a youth, he foresaw that he would arrive at great wealth, and, leaving home, took his way, alone, to London, where he found himself at the close of the American Revolution. An elder brother being in the United States, he followed him there. In January, 1784, he arrived in Hampton Roads, with some little merchandize suited to the American market. On the passage he had become acquainted with a countryman of his, a furrier, from whom he derived much information in regard to furs, and the manner of conducting the trade. Subsequently he accompanied this gentleman to New York, and, by his advice, invested the proceeds of his merchandize in peltries. With these he sailed to London, and having disposed of his adventure advantageously, he returned the same year (1784) to New York, with a view of settling in the United States, and prosecuting the business thus commenced. Mr. Astor's beginnings in this way were necessarily small—but his perseverance was indomitable, his integrity unimpeachable, and his economy of the most rigid kind. "To these," says Mr. Irving, " were added an aspiring spirit, that always looked upward; a genius bold, fertile, and expansive; a sagacity quick to grasp and convert every circumstance to its advantage, and a singular and never wavering confidence of signal success." These opinions are more than re-echoed by the whole crowd of Mr. Astor's numerous acquaintances and friends, and are most strongly insisted upon by those who have the pleasure of knowing him best.

In the United States, the fur trade was not yet sufficiently organized to form a regular line of business. Mr. A. made annual visits to Montreal for the purpose of buying peltries;

and, as no direct trade was permitted from Canada to any country but England, he shipped them, when bought, immediately to London. This difficulty being removed, however, by the treaty of 1795, he made a contract for furs with the North-West Company, and imported them from Montreal into the United States—thence shipping a portion to different parts of Europe, as well as to the principal market in China.

By the treaty just spoken of, the British possessions on our side of the Lakes were given up, and an opening made for the American fur-trader on the confines of Canada, and within the territories of the United States. Here, Mr. Astor, about the year 1807, adventured largely on his own account; his increased capital now placing him among the chief of American merchants. The influence of the Mackinaw Company, however, proved too much for him, and he was induced to consider the means of entering into successful competition. He was aware of the wish of the Government to concentrate the fur-trade within its boundaries in the hands of its own citizens; and he now offered, if national aid or protection should be afforded, "to turn the whole of the trade into American channels." He was invited to unfold his plans, and they were warmly approved, but, we believe, little more. The countenance of the Government was nevertheless of much importance, and, in 1809, he procured, from the legislature of New York, a charter, incorporating a Company, under the name of the "American Fur Company," with a capital of one million of dollars, and the privilege of increasing it to two. He himself constituted the Company, and furnished the capital. The board of directors was merely nominal, and the whole business was conducted with his own resources, and according to his own will.

We here pass over Mr. Irving's lucid, although brief account of the fur-trade in the Pacific, of Russian and American enterprize on the North-western coast, and of the discovery by Captain Gray, in 1792, of the mouth of the river Columbia. He proceeds to speak of Captain Jonathan Carver, of the British provincial army. In 1763, shortly after the acquisition of the Canadas by Great Britain, this gentleman projected a journey across the continent, between the forty-third and forty-sixth degrees of northern latitude, to the shores of the Pacific. His objects were "to ascertain the breadth of the continent at its broadest part, and to determine on some place on the shores of the Pacific, where Government might establish a post to facilitate the discovery of a north-west passage, or a communication between Hudson's Bay and the Pacific Ocean." He failed twice in individual attempts to accomplish this journey. In 1774, Richard Whitworth, a member of Parliament, came into this scheme of Captain Carver's. These two gentlemen determined to take with them fifty or sixty men, artificers and mariners, to proceed up one of the branches of the Missouri, find the source of the Oregon, (the Columbia) and sail down the river to its mouth. Here a fort was to be erected, and the vessels built necessary to carry into execution their purposed discoveries by sea. The British Government sanctioned the plan, and every thing was ready for the undertaking, when the American Revolution prevented it.

The expedition of Sir Alexander Mackenzie is well known. In 1793, he crossed the continent, and reached the Pacific Ocean in latitude 52° 20′ 48″. In latitude 52° 30′ he partially descended a river flowing to the South, and which he erroneously supposed to be the Columbia. Some years afterwards he published an account of his journey, and suggested the policy of opening an intercourse between the Atlantic and Pacific Oceans, and forming regular establishments "through the interior and at both extremes, as well as along the coasts and islands." Thus, he thought, the entire command of the fur trade of North America might be obtained from latitude 48° north to the pole, excepting that portion held by the Russians. As to the "American adventurers" along the coast, he spoke of them as entitled to but little consideration. "They would instantly disappear," he said, "before a well regulated trade." Owing to the jealousy existing between the Hudson's Bay and North-west Company, this idea of Sir Alexander Mackenzie's was never carried into execution.

The successful attempt of Messieurs Lewis and Clarke was accomplished, it will be remembered, in 1804. Their course was that proposed by Captain Carver in 1774. They passed up the Missouri to its head waters, crossed the Rocky Mountains, discovered the source of the Columbia, and followed that river down to its mouth. Here they spent the winter, and retraced their steps in the spring. Their reports declared it practicable to establish a line of communication across the continent, and first inspired Mr. Astor with the design of "grasping with his individual hands this great enterprize, which for years had been dubiously yet desirously contemplated by powerful associations and maternal governments."

His scheme was gradually matured. Its main features were as follows. A line of trading posts was to be established along the Missouri and Columbia, to the mouth of the latter, where was to be founded the chief mart. On all the tributary streams throughout this immense route were to be situated inferior posts trading directly with the Indians for their peltries. All these posts would draw upon the mart at the Columbia for their supplies of goods, and would send thither the furs collected. At this latter place also, were to be built and fitted out coasting vessels, for the purpose of trading along the Northwest coast, returning with the proceeds of their voyages to the same general rendezvous. In this manner the whole Indian trade, both of the coast and the interior, would converge to one point. To this point, in continuation of his plan, Mr. Astor proposed to despatch, every year, a ship with the necessary supplies. She would receive the peltries collected, carry them to Canton, there invest the proceeds in merchandize, and return to New York.

Another point was also to be attended to. In coasting to the North-west, the ship would be brought into contact with the Russian Fur Company's establishments in that quarter; and as a rivalry might ensue, it was politic to conciliate the good will of that body. It depended chiefly for its supplies upon transient trading vessels from the United States. The owners of these vessels, having nothing beyond their individual interests to consult, made no scruple of furnishing the natives with fire arms, and were thus productive of much injury. To this effect the Russian government had remonstrated with the United States, urging to have the traffic in arms prohibited—but, no municipal law being infringed, our government could not interfere. Still it was anxious not to offend Russia, and applied to Mr. Astor for information as to the means of remedying the evil, knowing him to be well versed in all the concerns of the trade in question. This application suggested to him the idea of paying a regular visit to the Russian settlements with his annual ship. Thus, being kept regularly in supplies, they would be independent of the casual traders, who would consequently be excluded from the coast. This whole scheme Mr. Astor communicated to President Jefferson, soliciting the countenance of Government. The cabinet "joined in warm approbation of the plan, and held out assurance of every protection that could, consistently with general policy, be afforded."

In speaking of the motives which actuated Mr. Astor in an enterprize so extensive, Mr. Irving, we are willing to believe, has done that high-minded gentleman no more than the simplest species of justice. "He was already," says our author, " wealthy beyond the ordinary desires of man, but he now aspired to that honorable fame which is awarded to men of similar scope of mind, who by their great commercial enterprizes have enriched nations, peopled wildernesses, and extended the bounds of empire. He considered his projected establishment at the mouth of the Columbia, as the emporium to an immense commerce; as a colony that would form the germ of a wide civilization; that would, in fact, carry the American population across the Rocky Mountains, and spread it along the shores of the Pacific, as it already animated the shores of the Atlantic."

A few words in relation to the North-west company. This body, following out in part the suggestion of Sir Alexander Mackenzie, had already established a few trading posts on the coast of the Pacific, in a region lying about two degrees north of the Columbia—thus throwing itself between the Russian and American territories. They would contend with Mr. Astor at an immense disadvantage, of course. They had no good post for the receipt of supplies by sea; and must get them with great risk, trouble and expense, over land. Their peltries also would have to be taken home the same way—for they were not at liberty to interfere with the East India company's monopoly, by shipping them directly to China. Mr. Astor would therefore greatly undersell them in that, the principal market. Still, as any competition would prove detrimental to both parties, Mr. A. made known his plans to the North-west company, proposing to interest them one third in his undertaking. The British company, however, had several reasons for declining the proposition—not the least forcible of which, we presume, was their secret intention to push on a party forthwith, and forestall their rival in establishing a settlement at the mouth of the Columbia.

In the meantime Mr. Astor did not remain idle. His first care was to procure proper coadjutors, and he was induced to seek them principally from among such clerks of the Northwest company, as were dissatisfied with their situation in that body—having served out their probationary term, and being still, through want of influence, without a prospect of speedy promotion. From among these (generally men of capacity and experience in their particular business), Mr. A. obtained the services of Mr. Alexander M'Kay (who had accompanied Sir Alexander Mackenzie in both of his expeditions), Mr. Donald M'Kenzie, and Mr. Duncan M'Dougal. Mr. Wilson Price Hunt, a native citizen of New Jersey, and a gentleman of great worth, was afterwards selected by Mr. Astor as his chief agent, and as the representative of himself at the contemplated establishment. In June 1810, "articles of agreement were entered into between Mr. Astor and these four gentlemen, acting for themselves, and for the several persons who had already agreed to become, or should thereafter become, associated under the firm of *"The Pacific Fur Company."* This agreement stipulated that Mr. A. was to be the head of the company, to manage its affairs at New York, and to furnish every thing requisite for the enterprize at first cost and charges, provided an advance of more than four hundred thousand dollars should not at any time be involved. The stock was to consist of a hundred shares, Mr. Astor taking fifty, the rest being divided among the other partners and their associates. A general meeting was to be held annually at Columbia river, where absent members might vote by proxy. The association was to continue twenty years—but might be dissolved within the first five years, if found unprofitable. For these five years Mr. A. agreed to bear all the loss that might be incurred. An agent, appointed for a like term, was to reside at the main establishment, and Mr. Hunt was the person first selected.

Mr. Astor determined to begin his enterprize with two expeditions—one by sea, the other by land. The former was to carry out every thing necessary for the establishment of a fortified post at the mouth of the Columbia. The latter, under the conduct of Mr. Hunt, was to proceed up the Missouri and across the Rocky Mountains to the same point. In the course of this over-land journey, the most practicable line of communication would be explored, and the best situations noted for the location of trading rendezvous. Following Mr. Irving in our brief summary of his narrative, we will now give some account of the first of these expeditions.

A ship was provided called the Tonquin, of two hundred and ninety tons, with ten guns, and twenty men. Lieutenant Jonathan Thorn of the United States navy, being on leave of absence, received the command. He was a man of courage, and had distinguished himself in the Tripolitan war. Four of the partners went in the ship—M'Kay and M'Dougal, of whom we have already spoken, and Messieurs David and Robert Stuart, new associates in the firm. M'Dougal was empowered to act as the proxy of Mr. Astor in the absence of Mr. Hunt. Twelve clerks were also of the party. These were bound to the service of the company for five years, and were to receive one hundred dollars a year, payable at the expiration of the term, with an annual equipment of clothing to the amount of forty dollars. By promises of future promotion, their interests were identified with those of Mr. Astor. Thirteen Canadian voyageurs, and several artisans, completed the ship's company. On the 8th of September, 1810, the Tonquin put to sea. Of her voyage to the mouth of the Columbia, Mr. Irving has given a somewhat ludicrous account. Thorn, the stern, straight-forward officer of the navy, having few ideas beyond those of duty and discipline, and looking with supreme contempt upon the motley "lubbers" who formed the greater part of his company, is painted with the easy yet spirited pencil of an artist indeed; while M'Dougal, the shrewd Scotch partner, bustling, yet pompous, and impressed with lofty notions of his own importance as proxy for Mr. Astor, is made as supremely ridiculous as possible, with as little apparent effort as can well be imagined;—the portraits, however, carry upon their faces the evidence of their own authenticity. The voyage is prosecuted amid a series of petty quarrels, and cross purposes, between the captain and his crew, and, occasionally, between Mr. M'Kay and Mr. M'Dougal. The contests between the two latter gentlemen were brief, it appears, although violent. "Within fifteen minutes," says Captain Thorn in a letter to Mr. Astor, "they would be caressing each other like children." The Tonquin doubled Cape Horn on Christmas day, arrived at Owhyhee on the eleventh of February, took on board fresh provisions, sailed again with twelve Sandwich islanders on the 28th, and on the 22d of March arrived at the mouth of the Columbia. In seeking a passage across the bar, a boat and nine men were lost among the breakers. On the way from Owhyhee a violent storm occurred; and the bickerings still continued between the partners and the captain—the latter, indeed, grievously suspecting the former of a design to depose him.

The Columbia for about forty miles from its mouth is, strictly speaking, an estuary, varying in breadth from three to seven miles, and indented by deep bays. Shoals and other obstructions render the navigation dangerous. Leaving this broad portion of the stream in the progress upwards, we find the mouth of the river proper—which is about half a mile wide. The entrance to the estuary from sea is bounded on the south by a long, low, and sandy beach stretching into the ocean, and called Point Adams. On the northern side of the frith is Cape Disappointment, a steep promontory. Immediately east of this cape is Baker's bay, and within this the Tonquin came to anchor.

Jealousies still continued between the captain and the worthy M'Dougal, who could come to no agreement in regard to the proper location for the contemplated establishment. On April the fifth, without troubling himself farther with the opinions of his coadjutors, Mr. Thorn landed in Baker's bay, and began operations. At this summary proceeding, the partners were, of course, in high dudgeon, and an open quarrel seemed likely to ensue, to the serious detriment of the enterprize. These difficulties, however, were at length arranged, and finally on the 12th of April, a settlement was commenced at a point of land called Point George, on the southern shore of the frith. Here was a good harbor, where vessels of two hundred tons might anchor within fifty yards of the shore. In honor of the chief partner, the new post received the title of *Astoria*. After much delay, the portion of the cargo destined for the post was landed, and the Tonquin left free to proceed on her voyage. She was to coast to the north, to trade for peltries at the different harbors, and to touch at Astoria on her return in the autumn. Mr. M'Kay went in her as supercargo, and a Mr. Lewis as ship's clerk. On the morning of the 5th of June she stood out to sea, the whole number of persons on board amounting to three and twenty. In one of the outer bays Captain Thorn procured the services of an Indian named Lamazee, who had already made two voyages along the coast, and who agreed to accompany him as interpreter. In a few days the ship arrived at Vancouver's island, and came to anchor in the harbor of Neweetee, much against the advice of the Indian, who warned Captain Thorn of the perfidious character of the natives. The result was the merciless butchery of the whole crew, with the exception of the interpreter and Mr. Lewis, the ship's clerk. The latter, finding himself mortally wounded and without companions, blew up the ship and perished with more than a hundred of the enemy. Lamazee, getting among the Indians, escaped, and was the means of bearing the news of the disaster to Astoria. In relating at length the thrilling details of this catastrophe, Mr. Irving takes occasion to comment on the headstrong, although brave and strictly honorable character of Lieutenant Thorn. The danger and folly, on the part of agents, in disobeying the matured instructions of those who deliberately plan extensive enterprizes such as that of Mr. Astor, is also justly and forcibly shown. The misfortune here spoken of, arose, altogether, from a disregard of Mr. A's often repeated advice—to admit but few Indians on board the Tonquin at one time. Her loss was a serious blow to the infant establishment at Astoria. To this post let us now return.

The natives inhabiting the borders of the estuary were divided into four tribes, of which the Chinooks were the principal. Comcomly, a one-eyed Indian, was their chief. These tribes resembled each other in nearly every respect, and were, no doubt, of a common stock. They live chiefly by fishing—the Columbia and its tributary streams abounding in fine salmon, and a variety of other fish. A trade in peltries, but to no great amount, was immediately commenced and carried on. Much disquiet was occasioned at the post by a rumor among the Indians that thirty white men had appeared on the banks of the Columbia, and were building houses at the second rapids. It was feared that these were an advance party of the North-west company endeavoring to seize upon the upper parts of the river, and thus forestall Mr. Astor in the trade of the surrounding country. Bloody feuds in this case might be anticipated, such as had prevailed between rival companies in former times. The intelligence of the Indians proved true— the "North-west" had erected a trading house on the Spokan river, which falls into the north branch of the Columbia. The Astorians could do little to oppose them in their present reduced state as to numbers. It was resolved, however, to advance a counter-check to the post on the Spokan, and Mr. David Stuart prepared to set out for this purpose with eight men and a small assortment of goods. On the fifteenth of July when this expedition was about starting, a canoe, manned with nine white men, and bearing the British flag, entered the harbor. They proved to be the party dispatched by the rival company to anticipate Mr. Astor in the settlement at the mouth of the river. Mr. David Thompson, their leader, announced himself as a partner of the "North-west"—but otherwise gave a very peaceable account of himself. It appears, however, from information subsequently derived from other sources, that he had hurried with a desperate haste across the mountains, calling at all the Indian villages in his march, presenting them with British flags, and "proclaiming formally that he took possession of the country for the North-west company, and in the name of the king of Great Britain." His plan was defeated, it seems, by the desertion of a great portion of his followers, and it was thought probable that he now merely descended the river with a view of reconnoitering. M'Dougal treated the gentlemen with great kindness, and supplied them with goods and provisions for their journey back across the mountains—this much against the wishes of Mr. David Stuart, " who did not think the object of their visit entitled them to any favor." A letter for Mr. Astor was entrusted to Thompson.

On the twenty-third of July, the party for the region of the Spokan set out, and after a voyage of much interest, succeeded in establishing the first interior trading post of the company. It was situated on a point of land about three miles long and two broad, formed by the junction of the Oakinagan with the Columbia. In the meantime the Indians near Astoria began to evince a hostile disposition, and a reason for this altered demeanor was soon after found in the report of the loss of the Tonquin. Early in August the settlers received intelligence of her fate. They now found themselves in a perilous situation, a mere handful of men, on a savage coast, and surrounded by barbarous enemies. From their dilemma they were relieved, for the present, by the ingenuity of M'Dougal. The natives had a great dread of the small-pox, which had appeared among them a few years before, sweeping off entire tribes. They believed it an evil either inflicted upon them by the Great Spirit, or brought among them by the white men. Seizing upon this latter idea, M'Dougal assembled several of the chieftains whom he believed to be inimical, and informing them that he had heard of the treachery of their northern brethren in regard to the Tonquin, produced from his pocket a small bottle. "The white men among you," said he, "are few in number, it is true, but they are mighty in medicine. See here! In this bottle I hold the small-pox safely corked up; I have but to draw the cork and let loose the pestilence, to sweep man, woman and child from the face of the earth!" The chiefs were dismayed. They represented to the "Great Small-Pox Chief" that they were the firmest friends of the white men, that they had nothing to do with the villains who murdered the crew of the Tonquin, and that it would be unjust, in uncorking the bottle, to destroy the innocent with the guilty. M'Dougal was convinced. He promised not to uncork it until some overt act should compel him to do so. In this manner tranquillity was restored to the settlement. A large house was now built, and the frame of a schooner put together. She was named the Dolly, and was the first American vessel launched on the coast. But our limits will not permit us to follow too minutely the details of the enterprize. The adventurers kept up their spirits, sending out occasional foraging parties in the Dolly, and looking forward to the arrival of Mr. Hunt. So wore away the year 1811 at the little post of Astoria. We now come to speak of the expedition by land.

This, it will be remembered, was to be conducted by Mr. Wilson Price Hunt, a native of New Jersey. He is represented as scrupulously upright, of amiable disposition, and agreeable manners. He had never been in the heart of the wilderness, but having been for some time engaged in commerce at St. Louis, furnishing Indian traders with goods, he had acquired much knowledge of the trade at second hand. Mr. Donald M'Kenzie, another partner, was associated with him. He had been ten years in the interior, in the service of the North-west Company, and had much practical experience in all Indian concerns. In July 1810, the two gentlemen repaired to Montreal, where every thing requisite to the expedition could be procured. Here they met with many difficulties—some of which were thrown in their way by their rivals. Having succeeded, however, in laying in a supply of ammunition, provisions, and Indian goods, they embarked all on board a large boat, and with a very inefficient crew, the best to be procured, took their departure from St. Ann's, near the extremity of the island of Montreal. Their course lay up the Ottawa, and along a range of small lakes and rivers. On the twenty-second of July, they arrived at Mackinaw, situated on Mackinaw island, at the confluence of Lakes Huron and Michigan. Here it was necessary to remain some time to complete the assortment of Indian goods, and engage more voyageurs. While waiting to accomplish these objects, Mr. Hunt was joined by Mr. Ramsay Crooks, a gentleman whom he had invited, by letter, to engage as a partner in the expedition. He was a native of Scotland, had served under the North-west Company, and been engaged in private trading adventures among the various tribes of the Missouri. Mr. Crooks represented, in forcible terms, the dangers to be apprehended from the Indians—especially the Blackfeet and Sioux—and it was agreed to increase the number of the party to sixty upon arriving at St. Louis. Thirty was its strength upon leaving Mackinaw. This occurred on the twelfth of August. The expedition pursued the usual route of the fur-trader—by Green bay, Fox and Wisconsin rivers, to Prairie du Chien, and thence down the Mississippi to St. Louis, where they landed

on the third of September. Here, Mr. Hunt met with some
opposition from an association called the Missouri Fur Company, and especially from its leading partner, a Mr. Manuel
Lisa. This company had a capital of about forty thousand dollars, and employed about two hundred and fifty men. Its object was to establish posts along the upper part of the river
and monopolize the trade. Mr. H. proceeded to strengthen
himself against competition. He secured to Mr. Astor the services of Mr. Joseph Miller. This gentleman had been an officer of the United States' Army, but had resigned on being
refused a furlough, and taken to trading with the Indians. He
joined the association as a partner; and, on account of his
experience and general acquirements, Mr. Hunt considered
him a valuable coadjutor. Several boatmen and hunters were
also now enlisted, but not until after a delay of several weeks.
This delay, and the previous difficulties at Montreal and
Mackinaw, had thrown Mr. H. much behind his original calculations, so that he found it would be impossible to effect
his voyage up the Missouri during the present season. There
was every likelihood that the river would be closed before the
party could reach its upper waters. To winter, however, at St.
Louis would be expensive. Mr. H. therefore, determined to
push up on his way as far as possible, to some point where
game might be found in abundance, and there take up his
quarters until spring. On the twenty-first of October he set
out. The party were distributed in three boats—two large
Schenectady barges and a keel boat. By the sixteenth of November they reached the mouth of the Nodowa, a distance of
four hundred and fifty miles, where they set up their winter
quarters. Here, Mr. Robert M'Lellan, at the invitation of Mr.
Hunt, joined the association as a partner. He was a man of
vigorous frame, of restless and impetuous temper, and had
distinguished himself as a partisan under General Wayne.
John Day also joined the company at this place—a tall and
athletic hunter from the backwoods of Virginia. Leaving the
main body at Nodowa, Mr. Hunt now returned to St. Louis
for a reinforcement. He was again impeded by the machinations of the Missouri Fur Company, but finally succeeded in
enlisting one hunter, some voyageurs, and a Sioux interpreter,
Pierre Dorion. With these, after much difficulty, he got back

to the encampment on the seventeenth of April. Soon after this period the voyage up the river was resumed. The party now consisted of nearly sixty persons—five partners, Hunt, Crooks, M'Kenzie, Miller, and M'Lellan; one clerk, John Reed; forty Canadian voyageurs; and several hunters. They embarked in four boats, one of which, of a large size, mounted a swivel and two howitzers.

We do not intend, of course, to proceed with our travellers throughout the vast series of adventure encountered in their passage through the wilderness. To the curious in these particulars we recommend the book itself. No details more intensely exciting are to be found in any work of travels within our knowledge. At times full of life and enjoying the whole luxury to be found in the career of the hunter—at times suffering every extremity of fatigue, hunger, thirst, anxiety, terror, and despair—Mr. Hunt still persisted in his journey, and finally brought it to a successful termination. A bare outline of the route pursued is all we can attempt.

Proceeding up the river, our party arrived, on the twenty-eighth of April, at the mouth of the Nebraska, or Platte, the largest tributary of the Missouri, and about six hundred miles above its junction with the Mississippi. They now halted for two days, to supply themselves with oars and poles from the tough wood of the ash, which is not to be found higher up the river. Upon the second of May, two of the hunters insisted upon abandoning the expedition, and returning to St. Louis. On the tenth, the party reached the Omaha village, and encamped in its vicinity. This village is about eight hundred and thirty miles above St. Louis, and on the west bank of the stream. Three men here deserted, but their place was luckily supplied by three others, who were prevailed upon, by liberal promises, to enlist. On the fifteenth, Mr. Hunt left Omaha, and proceeded. Not long afterwards, a canoe was descried navigated by two white men. They proved to be two adventurers who, for some years past, had been hunting and trapping near the head of the Missouri. Their names were Jones and Carson. They were now on their way to St. Louis, but readily abandoned their voyage, and turned their faces again toward the Rocky Mountains. On the twenty-third Mr. Hunt received, by a special messenger, a letter from Mr. Manuel Lisa, the leading partner of the Missouri Fur Company, and the gentleman who rendered him so many disservices at St. Louis. He had left that place, with a large party, three weeks after Mr. H., and, having heard rumors of hostile intentions on the part of the Sioux, a much dreaded tribe of Indians, made great exertions to overtake him, that they might pass through the dangerous part of the river together. Mr. H., however, was justly suspicious of the Spaniard, and pushed on. At the village of the Poncas, about a league south of the river Quicourt, he stopped only long enough to procure a supply of dried buffalo meat. On the morning of the twenty-fifth, it was discovered that Jones and Carson had deserted. They were pursued, but in vain. The next day three white men were observed, in two canoes, descending the river. They proved to be three Kentucky hunters—Edward Robinson, John Hoback, and Jacob Rezner. They also had passed several years in the upper wilderness, and were now on their way home, but willingly turned back with the expedition. Information derived from these recruits induced Mr. Hunt to alter his route. Hitherto he had intended to follow the course pursued by Messieurs Lewis and Clarke—ascending the Missouri to its forks, and thence, by land, across the mountains. He was informed, however, that, in so doing, he would have to pass through the country of the Blackfeet, a savage tribe of Indians, exasperated against the whites, on account of the death of one of their men by the hands of Captain Lewis. Robinson advised a more southerly route. This would carry them over the mountains about where the head waters of the Platte and the Yellowstone take their rise, a much more practicable pass than that of Lewis and Clarke. To this counsel Mr. Hunt agreed, and resolved to leave the Missouri at the village of the Arickaras, at which they would arrive in a few days. On the first of June, they reached "the great bend" of the river, which here winds for about thirty miles round a circular peninsula, the neck of which is not above two thousand yards across. On the morning of June the third, the party were overtaken by Lisa, much to their dissatisfaction. The meeting was, of course, far from cordial, but an outward appearance of civility was maintained for two days. On the third, a quarrel took place, which was near terminating seriously. It was, however, partially adjusted, and the rival parties coasted along opposite sides of the river, in sight of each other. On the twelfth of June, they reached the village of the Arickaras, between the forty-sixth and forty-seventh parallels of north latitude, and about fourteen hundred and thirty miles above the mouth of the Missouri. In accomplishing thus much of his journey, Mr. Hunt had not failed to meet with a crowd of difficulties, at which we have not even hinted. He was frequently in extreme peril from large bodies of the Sioux, and, at one time, it was a mere accident alone which prevented the massacre of the whole party.

At the Arickara village our adventurers were to abandon their boats, and proceed westward across the wilderness. Horses were to be purchased from the Indians; who could not, however, furnish them in sufficient numbers. In this dilemma, Lisa offered to purchase the boats, now no longer of use, and to pay for them in horses, to be obtained at a fort belonging to the Missouri Fur Company, and situated at the Mandan villages, about a hundred and fifty miles further up the river. A bargain was made, and Messieurs Lisa and Crooks went for the horses, returning with them in about a fortnight. At the Arickara village, if we understand, Mr. Hunt engaged the services of one Edward Rose. He enlisted as interpreter when the expedition should reach the country of the Upsarokas or Crow Indians, among whom he had formerly resided. On the eighteenth of July the party took up their line of march. They were still insufficiently provided with horses. The cavalcade consisted of eighty-two, most of them heavily laden with Indian goods, beaver traps, ammunition, and provisions. Each of the partners was mounted. As they took leave of Arickara, the veterans of Lisa's company, as well as Lisa himself, predicted the total destruction of our adventurers amid the innumerable perils of the wilderness.

To avoid the Blackfeet Indians, a ferocious and implacable tribe of which we have before spoken, the party kept a southwestern direction. This route took them across some of the tributary streams of the Missouri, and through immense prairies bounded only by the horizon. Their progress was at first slow, and, Mr. Crooks falling sick, it was necessary to make a

litter for him between two horses. On the twenty-third of the
month, they encamped on the banks of a little stream nicknamed Big River, where they remained several days, meeting
with a variety of adventures. Among other things they were
enabled to complete their supply of horses from a band of the
Cheyenne Indians. On the sixth of August the journey was
resumed, and they soon left the hostile region of the Sioux
behind them. About this period a plot was discovered on the
part of the interpreter, Edward Rose. This villain had been
tampering with the men, and proposed, upon arriving among
his old acquaintances the Crows, to desert to the savages with
as much booty as could be carried off. The matter was adjusted, however, and Mr. Rose, through the ingenuity of Mr.
Hunt, quietly dismissed. On the thirteenth Mr. H. varied his
course to the westward, a route which soon brought him to
a fork of the Little Missouri, and upon the skirts of the Black
Mountains. These are an extensive chain, lying about a
hundred miles east of the Rocky Mountains, stretching north-
easterly from the south fork of the river Platte to the great
north bend of the Missouri, and dividing the waters of the
Missouri from those of the Mississippi and Arkansas. The
travellers here supposed themselves to be about two hundred
and fifty miles from the village of the Arickaras. Their more
serious troubles now commenced. Hunger and thirst, with
the minor difficulties of grizzly bears, beset them at every
turn, as they attempted to force a passage through the rugged
barriers in their path. At length they emerged upon a stream
of clear water, one of the forks of Powder river, and once
more beheld wide meadows and plenty of buffalo. They ascended this stream about eighteen miles, directing their
march towards a lofty mountain which had been in sight
since the seventeenth. They reached the base of this mountain, which proved to be a spur of the Rocky chain, on the
thirtieth, having now come about four hundred miles since
leaving Arickara.

For one or two days they endeavored in vain to find a defile
in the mountains. On the third of September they made an
attempt to force a passage to the westward, but soon became
entangled among rocks and precipices, which set all their efforts at defiance. They were now too in the region of the

terrible Upsarokas, and encountered them at every step. They met also with friendly bands of Shoshonies and Flatheads. After a thousand troubles, they made some way upon their journey. On the ninth they reached Wind river, a stream which gives its name to a range of mountains consisting of three parallel chains, eighty miles long and about twenty-five broad. "One of its peaks," says our author, "is probably fifteen thousand feet above the level of the sea." For five days Mr. Hunt followed up the course of Wind river, crossing and recrossing it. He had been assured by the three hunters who advised him to strike through the wilderness, that by going on up the river, and crossing a single mountain ridge, he would come upon the head waters of the Columbia. The scarcity of game, however, determined him to pursue a different course. In the course of the day after coming to this resolve, they perceived three mountain peaks, white with snow, and which were recognized by the hunters as rising just above a fork of the Columbia. These peaks were named the Pilot Knobs by Mr. Hunt. The travellers continued their course for about forty miles to the south-west, and at length found a river flowing to the west. This proved to be a branch of the Colorado. They followed its current for fifteen miles. On the eighteenth, abandoning its main course, they took a north-westerly direction for eight miles, and reached one of its little tributaries issuing from the bosom of the mountains, and running through green meadows abounding in buffalo. Here they encamped for several days, a little repose being necessary for both men and horses. On the twenty-fourth the journey was resumed. Fifteen miles brought them to a stream about fifty feet wide, which was recognized as one of the head waters of the Columbia. They kept along it for two days, during which it gradually swelled into a river of some size. At length it was joined by another current, and both united swept off in an unimpeded stream, which from its rapidity and turbulence had received the appellation of Mad river. Down this they anticipated an uninterrupted voyage, in canoes, to the point of their ultimate destination—but their hopes were very far from being realized.

The partners held a consultation. The three hunters who had hitherto acted as guides, knew nothing of the region to the west of the Rocky Mountains. It was doubtful whether Mad river could be navigated, and they could hardly resolve to abandon their horses upon an uncertainty. The vote, nevertheless, was for embarkation, and they proceeded to build the necessary vessels. In the meantime Mr. Hunt, having now reached the head waters of the Columbia, reputed to abound in beaver, turned his thoughts to the main object of the expedition. Four men, Alexander Carson, Louis St. Michel, Pierre Detayé and Pierre Delaunay, were detached from the expedition, to remain and trap beaver by themselves in the wilderness. Having collected a sufficient quantity of peltries, they were to bring them to the depot at the mouth of the Columbia, or to some intermediate post to be established by the company. These trappers had just departed, when two Snake Indians wandered into the camp, and declared the river to be unnavigable. Scouts sent out by Mr. Hunt finally confirmed this report. On the fourth of October, therefore, the encampment was broken up, and the party proceeded to search for a post in possession of the Missouri Fur company, and said to be somewhere in the neighborhood, upon the banks of another branch of the Columbia. This post they found without much difficulty. It was deserted—and our travellers gladly took possession of the rude buildings. The stream here found was upwards of a hundred yards wide. Canoes were constructed with all despatch. In the meantime another detachment of trappers was cast loose in the wilderness. These were Robinson, Rezner, Hoback, Carr, and Mr. Joseph Miller. This latter, it will be remembered, was one of the partners—he threw up his share in the expedition, however, for a life of more perilous adventure. On the eighteenth of the month (October) fifteen canoes being completed, the voyagers embarked, leaving their horses in charge of the two Snake Indians, who were still in company.

In the course of the day the party arrived at the junction of the stream upon which they floated, with Mad river. Here Snake river commences—the scene of a thousand disasters. After proceeding about four hundred miles, by means of frequent portages, and beset with innumerable difficulties of every kind, the adventurers were brought to a halt by a series of frightful cataracts, raging, as far as the eye could reach, between stupendous ramparts of black rock, rising more than two hundred feet perpendicularly. This place they called "The Caldron Linn." Here Antoine Clappine, one of the voyageurs, perished amid the whirlpools, three of the canoes stuck immoveably among the rocks, and one was swept away with all the weapons and effects of four of the boatmen.

The situation of the party was now lamentable indeed—in the heart of an unknown wilderness, at a loss what route to take, ignorant of their distance from the place of their destination, and with no human being near them from whom counsel might be taken. Their stock of provisions was reduced to five days allowance, and famine stared them in the face. It was therefore more perilous to keep together than to separate. The goods and provisions, except a small supply for each man, were concealed in *caches* (holes dug in the earth), and the party were divided into several small detachments which started off in different directions, keeping the mouth of the Columbia in view as their ultimate point of destination. From this post they were still distant nearly a thousand miles, although this fact was unknown to them at the time.

On the twenty-first of January, after a series of almost incredible adventures, the division in which Mr. Hunt enrolled himself struck the waters of the Columbia some distance below the junction of its two great branches, Lewis and Clarke rivers, and not far from the influx of the Wallah-Wallah. Since leaving the Caldron Linn, they had toiled two hundred and forty miles through snowy wastes and precipitous mountains, and six months had now elapsed since their departure from the Arickara village on the Missouri—their whole route from that point, according to their computation, having been seventeen hundred and fifty-one miles. Some vague intelligence was now received in regard to the other divisions of the party, and also of the settlers at the mouth of the Columbia. On the thirty-first, Mr. Hunt reached the falls of the river, and encamped at the village of Wish-Ram. Here were heard tidings of the massacre on board the Tonquin. On the fifth of February, having procured canoes with much difficulty, the adventurers departed from Wish-Ram, and on the fifteenth, sweeping round an intervening cape, they came in sight of the long-desired *Astoria*. Among the first to greet them on their landing, were some of their old comrades who had parted from them at the Caldron Linn, and who had reached the settlement nearly a month before. Mr. Crooks and John Day, being unable to get on, had been left with some Indians in the wilderness—they afterwards came in. Carriere, a voyageur, who was also abandoned through the sternest necessity, was never heard of more. Jean Babtiste Prevost, likewise a voyageur, rendered frantic by famine, had been drowned in the Snake river. All parties had suffered the extremes of weariness, privation and peril. They had travelled from St. Louis, thirty-five hundred miles. Let us now return to Mr. Astor.

As yet he had received no intelligence from the Columbia, and had to proceed upon the supposition that all had gone as he desired. He accordingly fitted out a fine ship, the Beaver, of four hundred and ninety tons. Her cargo was assorted with a view to the supply of Astoria, the trade along the coast, and the wants of the Russian fur company. There embarked in her, for the settlement, a partner, five clerks, fifteen American laborers, and six Canadian voyageurs. Mr. John Clarke, the partner, was a native of the United States, although he had passed much of his life in the north-west, having been employed in the fur trade since the age of sixteen. The clerks were, chiefly, young American gentlemen of good connexions. Mr. Astor had selected this reinforcement with the design of securing an ascendancy of American influence at Astoria, and rendering the association decidedly national. This, from the peculiar circumstances of the case, he had been unable to do in the commencement of his undertaking.

Captain Sowle, the commander of the Beaver, was directed to touch at the Sandwich islands, to enquire about the fortunes of the Tonquin, and ascertain, if possible, whether the settlement had been effected at Astoria. If so, he was to enlist as many of the natives as possible and proceed. He was to use great caution in his approach to the mouth of the Columbia. If every thing was found right, however, he was to land such part of his cargo as was intended for the post, and to sail for New Archangel with the Russian supplies. Having received furs in payment, he would return to Astoria, take in the peltries there collected, and make the best of his way to Canton. These were the strict letter of his instructions—a deviation

from which was subsequently the cause of great embarrassment and loss, and contributed largely to the failure of the
whole enterprize. The Beaver sailed on the tenth of October,
1811, and, after taking in twelve natives at the Sandwich islands, reached the mouth of the Columbia, in safety, on the
ninth of May, 1812. Her arrival gave life and vigor to the establishment, and afforded means of extending the operations
of the company, and founding a number of interior trading
posts.

It now became necessary to send despatches over land to
Mr. Astor at New York, an attempt at so doing having been
frustrated some time before by the hostility of the Indians at
Wish-Ram. The task was confided to Mr. Robert Stuart,
who, though he had never been across the mountains, had
given evidence of his competency for such undertakings. He
was accompanied by Ben. Jones and John Day, Kentuckians;
Andri Vallar and Francis Le Clerc, Canadians; and two of the
partners, Messieurs M'Lellan and Crooks, who were desirous
of returning to the Atlantic states. This little party set out on
the twenty-ninth of June, and Mr. Irving accompanies them,
in detail, throughout the whole of their long and dangerous
wayfaring. As might be expected, they encountered misfortunes still more terrible than those before experienced by Mr.
Hunt and his associates. The chief features of the journey,
were the illness of Mr. Crooks, and the loss of all the horses
of the party through the villainy of the Upsarokas. This latter
circumstance was the cause of excessive trouble and great delay. On the thirtieth of April, however, the party arrived in
fine health and spirits at St. Louis, having been ten months
in performing their perilous expedition. The route taken by
Mr. Stuart coincided nearly with that of Mr. Hunt, as far as
the Wind river mountains. From this point the former struck
somewhat to the south-east, following the Nebraska to its
junction with the Missouri.

War having at length broken out between the United States
and England, Mr. Astor perceived that the harbor of New
York would be blockaded, and the departure of the annual
supply ship in the autumn prevented. In this emergency he
wrote to Captain Sowle, the commander of the Beaver, addressing him at Canton. The letter directed him to proceed to

the factory at the mouth of the Columbia, with such articles as the establishment might need, and to remain there subject to the orders of Mr. Hunt. In the meantime nothing had yet been heard from the settlement. Still, not discouraged, Mr. A. determined to send out another ship, although the risk of loss was so greatly enhanced that no insurance could be effected. The Lark was chosen—remarkable for her fast sailing. She put to sea on the sixth of March, 1813, under the command of Mr. Northrop, her mate—the officer first appointed to command her having shrunk from his engagement. Within a fortnight after her departure, Mr. A. received intelligence that the North-west company had presented a memorial to Great Britain, stating the vast scope of the contemplated operations at Astoria, expressing a fear that, unless crushed, the settlement there would effect the downfall of their own fur trade, and advising that a force be sent against the colony. In consequence, the frigate Phœbe was ordered to convoy the armed ship Isaac Todd, belonging to the North-west company, and provided with men and munitions for the formation of a new establishment. They were directed "to proceed together to the mouth of the Columbia, capture or destroy whatever American fortress they would find there, and plant the British flag on its ruins." Upon this matter's being represented to our government, the frigate Adams, Captain Crane, was detailed for the protection of Astoria; and Mr. A. proceeded to fit out a ship called the Enterprize, to sail in company with the frigate, and freighted with additional supplies. Just, however, as the two vessels were ready, a reinforcement of seamen was wanted for Lake Ontario, and the crew of the Adams were, necessarily, transferred to that service. Mr. A. was about to send off his ship alone, when a British force made its appearance off the Hook, and New York was effectually blockaded. The Enterprize therefore was unloaded and dismantled. We now return to the Beaver.

This vessel, after leaving at Astoria that portion of her cargo destined for that post, sailed for New Archangel on the fourth of August, 1812. She arrived there on the nineteenth, meeting with no incidents of moment. A long time was now expended in negotiations with the drunken Governor of the Russian fur colony—one Count Baranoff—and when they were finally completed, the month of October had arrived. Moreover, in payment for his supplies, Mr. Hunt was to receive seal-skins, and none were on the spot. It was necessary, therefore, to proceed to a seal-catching establishment belonging to the Russian company at the island of St. Paul, in the sea of Kamschatka. He set sail for this place on the fourth of October, after having wasted forty-five days at New Archangel. He arrived on the thirty-first of the month—by which time, according to his arrangement, he should have been back at Astoria. Now occurred great delay in getting the peltries on board; every pack being overhauled to prevent imposition. To make matters worse, the Beaver one night was driven off shore in a gale, and could not get back until the thirteenth of November. Having at length taken in the cargo and put to sea, Mr. Hunt was in some perplexity as to his course. The ship had been much injured in the late gale, and he thought it imprudent to attempt making the mouth of the Columbia in this boisterous time of the year. Moreover, the season was already much advanced; and should he proceed to Astoria as originally intended, he might arrive at Canton so late as to find a bad market. Unfortunately, therefore, he determined to go at once to the Sandwich islands, there await the arrival of the annual ship from New York, take passage in her to the settlement, and let the Beaver proceed on her voyage to China. It is but justice to add that he was mainly induced to this course by the timid representations of Captain Sowle. They reached Woahoo in safety, where the ship underwent the necessary repairs, and again put to sea on the first of January, 1813, leaving Mr. Hunt on the island.

At Canton, Captain Sowle found the letter of Mr. Astor, giving him information of the war, and directing him to convey the intelligence to Astoria. He wrote a reply, in which he declined complying with these orders, saying that he would wait for peace, and then return home. In the meantime Mr. Hunt waited in vain for the annual vessel. At length, about the twentieth of June, the ship Albatross, Captain Smith, arrived from China, bringing the first news of the war to the Sandwich islands. This ship Mr. H. chartered for two thousand dollars, to land him, with some supplies, at Astoria. He reached this post on the twentieth of August, where he found the affairs of the company in a perishing condition, and the partners bent upon abandoning the settlement. To this resolution Mr. Hunt was finally brought to consent. There was a large stock of furs, however, at the factory, which it was necessary to get to a market, and a ship was required for this service. The Albatross was bound to the Marquesas, and thence to the Sandwich islands; and it was resolved that Mr. H. should sail in her in quest of a vessel, returning, if possible, by the first of January, and bringing with him a supply of provisions. He departed on the twenty-sixth of August, and reached the Marquesas without accident. Commodore Porter soon afterwards arrived, bringing intelligence that the British frigate Phœbe, with a store-ship mounted with battering pieces, together with the sloops of war Cherub and Racoon, had all sailed, from Rio Janiero, on the sixth of July, bound for the mouth of the Columbia. Mr. H. after in vain attempting to purchase a whale ship from Commodore Porter, started, on the twenty-third of November, for the Sandwich islands, arriving on December the twentieth. Here he found Captain Northrop, of the Lark, which had suffered shipwreck on the coast about the middle of March. The brig Pedlar was now purchased for ten thousand dollars, and, Captain N. being put in command of her, Mr. H. sailed for Astoria on the twenty-second of January, 1814, with the view of removing the property there, as speedily as possible, to the Russian settlements in the vicinity—these were Mr. Astor's orders sent out by the Lark. On the twenty-eighth of February the brig anchored in the Columbia, when it was found that, on the twelfth of December, the British had taken possession of the post. In some negotiations carried on, just before the surrender, on the part of the North-west company and M'Dougal, that worthy personage gave full evidence that Captain Thorn was not far wrong in suspecting him to be no better than he should be. He had been for some time secretly a partner of the rival association, and shortly before the arrival of the British, took advantage of his situation as head of the post, to barter away the property of the company at less than one third of its value.

Thus failed this great enterprize of Mr. Astor. At the peace, Astoria itself, by the treaty of Ghent, reverted with the adjacent country to the United States, on the principle of *status ante bellum*. In the winter of 1815, Congress passed a law prohibiting all traffic of British traders within our territories, and Mr. A. felt anxious to seize this opportunity for the renewal of his undertaking. For good reasons, however, he could do nothing, without the direct protection of the government. This evinced much supineness in the matter; the favorable moment was suffered to pass unimproved; and, in despite of the prohibition of Congress, the British finally usurped the lucrative traffic in peltries throughout the whole of our vast territories in the North-west. A very little aid from the sources whence he had naturally a right to expect it, would have enabled Mr. Astor to direct this profitable commerce into national channels, and to render New York, what London has now long been, the great Emporium for furs.

We have already spoken of the masterly manner in which Mr. Irving has executed his task. It occurs to us that we have observed one or two slight discrepancies in the narrative. There appears to be some confusion between the names of M'Lellan, M'Lennon and M'Lennan—or do these three appellations refer to the same individual? In going up the Missouri, Mr. Hunt arrives at the Great Bend on the first of June,—the third day after which (the day on which the party is overtaken by Lisa) is said to be the third of *July*. Jones and Carson join the expedition just above the Omaha village. At page 187, vol. 1, we are told that the two men " who had joined the company at the Maha village" (meaning Omaha, we presume), deserted and were pursued, but never overtaken—at page 199, however, Carson is recognized by an Indian who is holding a parley with the party. The Lark too, only sailed from New York on the sixth of March, 1813, and on the tenth, we find her, much buffetted, somewhere in the near vicinity of the Sandwich islands. These errors are of little importance in themselves, but may as well be rectified in a future edition.

George Jones

M R. GEORGE JONES, the "American Histrion," (as he has a perfect right to style himself if he thinks proper) getting tired of sleeping at STRATFORD-ON-AVON, and other small matters of that character, and having exhausted the whole subject of Tragedy in the "Israel-Indian" drama of TECUMSEH, (whom men hitherto have accused Col. JOHNSON of murdering)—Mr. GEORGE JONES, we say, having done all this to his perfect satisfaction, has at last turned his attention to the instruction of his fellow beings on points of rather more serious importance. He has written a book, (of which only the first volume is now before us) the design of which is to demonstrate the identity of our Aborigines with the Tyrians and Israelites, and the introduction of Christianity into the Western Hemisphere by one of the twelve Apostles in person. This, to be sure, is a good deal to demonstrate, but then we have GEORGE JONES for the demonstrator. His qualifications are too well known to need comment. He has a pretty wife, a capital head of hair, and fine teeth.

When we assert, though, that, in spite of his teeth, he has contrived to compile, from a great variety of high sources, a work full of deeply interesting information—not particularly deficient in method, or even in argument—and that, by hook or by crook, he has made out his case, as well as any previous speculators on American Antiquities have made out theirs— and quite as well as any Mr. GEORGE JONES might be expected to make it—when we say all this we shall scarcely be believed by the numerous ardent admirers of this gentleman who have held their breath (and their sides) night after night, while he did OTHELLO (and them) and endangered the lives of the orchestra. How much of the book is pure George Jones, we cannot and will not pretend to say. The greater portion of it we fancy that we have seen *somewhere* in different arrangements;—a good deal of it in BRYANT—some in HUMBOLDT—some in STEPHENS—but we will not undertake to be sure that Mr. GEORGE JONES has appropriated to his own use much more than is customary with illustrious historians in all similar cases.

The style and occasional interest of the compilation may be conveyed in some measure by a quotation:

"He says (Bryant) that *where the Tyrians may have settled we may expect to hear some story or tradition about a swan or swans.* Admitting this to be truth (and he is quoted as authority upon antiquities) then there is proof that the Mexican Aborigines were Tyrians, as the following incident from acknowledged history will show. About two centuries before the Spanish Conquest, the Aztecas (Mexican proper) were oppressed by a neighbouring kingdom; the latter demanded as a tribute that the former should bring one of their celebrated floating gardens from the Lake of Mexico—this tributary present was accomplished with great labor and difficulty. The next year this demand was repeated, and with this addition—viz: that *their emblematical bird the swan,* should also be brought with it, and in the garden, sitting on her eggs—and that the present should be so timed as to its arrival, that the eggs should be hatched when the garden was presented to the King demanding tribute; this was actually accomplished, and the cygnets came forth as the imperious Monarch received the present. Now the substance of the above was recorded by the Spanish historian over three centuries since, and with no idea to establish that those aborigines were Tyrians; it may therefore be received as a record of fact,—at all events it came to the historian from the Mexicans as a 'story' of their race,—handed down from sire to son as a 'tradition' of their ancestors. In those respects alone—'story or tradition'—the proof of identity required by Bryant is completely established. 'Where the Tyrians are, you may expect to hear some story or tradition about swans.' Well, then, here is the 'story' and 'tradition' together with the historical fact—and swans form the material: but they have been dying in music for centuries yet unregarded:—they have been as a symbolical record buried in a people's sepulchre—and which the opening of a nation's tomb has alone brought to light. The classic reader will remember that Jupiter assumed the form of the bird of Canaan, when he sought and won the love of Leda!"

Mr. GEORGE JONES concludes this burst of eloquence with a note of admiration, by which he means—"See that! listen to GEORGE JONES!" The only wonder is that he did not instruct his printer to put *two* admiration notes in place of one, or have a Brobdignagian one founded on purpose. The only other noticeable point of the extract (beyond its prevalent air of innocence and slip-slop) is the writing monarch and king with a capital M and K—a fashion which Mr. JONES has very properly considered it his duty to adopt since his introduction at court. To render the compliment more pointed, we presume that, in future, he will employ only a small *g* when he is so unlucky as to have to speak of his GOD.

The true *fun* of this book, however, lies in its externals. Honestly speaking, it is one of the most magnificent things ever put forth from a press. The money to print it, perhaps *was*, and perhaps was *not* made by butchering MACBETH. However these matters may be, this great work is dedicated to His Grace the Archbishop of Canterbury, at the suggestion of an "Illustrious Prince who has honored me as his visitor and guest," and the fervor of that brotherly affection with which GEORGE JONES beseeches "the Almighty Father long to preserve the life and faculties of his Grace, that they may continue to cast their benevolent and protecting influence around the Divine Institution of Christianity"—and around GEORGE JONES and his wife and seven small children—is really a heart-rending spectacle to behold.

The *title-pages* of the book are to be cut out, we hope, and deposited in the British Museum.

First we have it thus:

"○. *An Original History of America. Founded upon the Ruins of Antiquity: The Identity of the Aborigines with the People of Tyrus and Israel: and the Introduction of Christianity by the Apostle St. Thomas. By George Jones, R.S.I., M.S.V., &c.* □ *Dedicated to his Grace the Archbishop of Canterbury. Published by Longman, Brown, Green, and Longmans, London. Harper and Brothers, New York. Alexander Duncker, Berlin, and Frederick Kliencksieck, Paris. 1843. Copyright secured in England and America.*"

And again—secondly:—"*The History of Ancient America, anterior to the time of Columbus: proving the Identity of the Ab-*

origines with the Tyrians and Israelites: and the Introduction of Christianity into the Western Hemisphere by the Apostle St. Thomas. By George Jones, M.R.S.I., F.S.V. The Tyrian Æra. Published by"—as before.

And yet once more, thirdly:—*"Volume the First, or the Tyrian Æra, in Two Books. Book I. The Ruins of Antiquity in Ancient America, Described and Analyzed; and the Original Architects Identified. ☐ Book II. The Scriptural, Political, and Commercial History of Tyrus, to the Destruction of that kingdom by Alexander of Macedon; and the Tyrian Migration to the Western Hemisphere, in the year 332 before Christ, &c."*

And still, again, fourthly, if our readers will permit us the liberty—

"The Original History of Ancient America."

And fifthly and finally, once yet again, if we can hope to be pardoned the trespass:

"The Tyrian Æra."

By the blessing of God this is all. We give them *verbatim*, first because we like a neat thing, and enough of it, and secondly because here we have discovered MILTON's allusion in his "many a winding bout of linked sweetness long drawn out." Here it is. This is it. He had reference to the title-pages of GEORGE JONES.

There is a limit, however, to the capacities of the pen. We can convey with that instrument a good deal, to be sure, (and Mr. GEORGE JONES can convey even more than ourselves,) but "Stamboul itself," the Mahometans say, "shall have an end," and there is an end even to the expression of a goose-quill. Were it not for this, we should be happy to fill up, in an adequate manner, the *hiatus* of our ☐ ☐ just above, and of our ○ a few sentences farther up. We will endeavour to aid the reader's fancy, however, in filling them up for himself.

In the ○ let him conceive the inconceivable—let him picture to himself a—a—what is it?—a person with a chin—a gentleman with a simper—a something with a scarf over its right shoulder—the throat bare—the hair well off the temples—the eyebrows well up—the whole thing looking satisfied with the existing condition of matters, so far as regards merely itself, but consumed with pity for the universe upon the whole, and exceedingly hurt and vexed, not to say mortified, that its advice was not taken in the first instance, when that sad botch of an affair was originally manufactured. This curious thing is the "Great American Histrion"—that is to say it is GEORGE JONES, and the author of the book.

In the first of our ☐ ☐, the reader is entreated to imagine a building not altogether unlike the infernal palace seen by Vathek and Nouronihar, since that was *"d'une architecture inconnue dans les annales de la terre."* We take this building to be intended either for the New York City Hall, or the Magdalen Asylum, or the Fountain in the Bowling Green—we cannot be positive that it is meant for more than *one* of these, but it is ugly enough to be all three. It is in the back-ground, floating upon the sea, (if we rightly comprehend the idea) and in the foreground is MOSES the prophet, standing guard over an assortment of kettles and pans, and holding in each hand one of the ten-commandment-tables of stone, the hardness of which he seems anxious to test upon the skull of a high priest in full pontificals, who is clearly bent upon stealing a kettle at least, and with this view brandishes an oyster-knife with which he is watching his opportunity to cut MOSES' throat— and the sooner the better, beyond doubt.

In the nethermost ☐ will the reader just oblige us by picturing to himself a NEPTUNE sitting comfortably, although a little stiffly, on a large oyster shell, with something that looks like a roll of MS. for a foot-board, and drawn by four horses with the tails of catfish, or possibly gudgeons;—one of the horses turning his head aside to take a bite, or a kiss, at a young lady who should be ashamed of herself for swimming so high out of water; above all this let there be fancied a little Cupid with knock-knees, fluttering himself into a fit, and the picture is complete; that is to say it *would* be complete, if there were only a few words printed beneath it, in the way of a hint as to what it is all about.

As matters stand, it is difficult to say whether NEPTUNE is intended for NEPTUNE in person, or for Mr. GEORGE JONES in the *character* of NEPTUNE; or whether the lady in her buff is a sea-nymph in actual fact, or only one of GEORGE JONES' supernumerary nymphs in the "Naiad Queen"; or whether the horse-headed gudgeons (or the gudgeon-tailed horses) are, or are not, merely emblematical of odd fishes in general, and by inference of GEORGE JONES in particular; or whether in fine the CUPID in a fit is a real CUPID in a *bonâ fide* fit, or only one of Mrs. GEORGE JONES' own little CUPIDS doing the heavy business in a *bene*fit.

Aristidean, March 1845

John Pendleton Kennedy

Horse-Shoe Robinson; A Tale of the Tory Ascendency. By the Author of 'Swallow Barn.' Philadelphia: Carey, Lea and Blanchard.

WE HAVE not yet forgotten, nor is it likely we shall very soon forget, the rich simplicity of diction—the manliness of tone—the admirable traits of Virginian manners, and the striking pictures of still life, to be found in Swallow Barn. The spirit of imitation was, however, visible in that book, and, in a great measure, over-clouded its rare excellence. This is by no means the case with Mr. Kennedy's new novel. If ever volumes were entitled to be called original—these are so entitled. We have read them from beginning to end with the greatest attention, and feel very little afraid of hazarding our critical reputation, when we assert that they will place Mr. Kennedy at once in the very first rank of American novelists.

Horse-Shoe Robinson (be not alarmed at the title, gentle reader!) is a tale, or more properly a succession of stirring incidents relating to the time of the Tory Ascendency in South Carolina, during the Revolution. It is well known that throughout the whole war this state evinced more disaffection to the confederated government than any other of the Union, with the exception perhaps of the neighboring state of Georgia, where the residents on the Savannah river, being nearly allied to the Carolinians in their habits and general occupations, were actuated, more or less, by the same political opinions. But we will here let the author speak for himself. "Such might be said to be the more popular sentiment of the state at the time of its subjugation by Sir Henry Clinton and Lord Cornwallis. To this common feeling there were many brilliant exceptions, and the more brilliant because they stood, as it were, apart from the preponderating mass of public judgment.   *   *   *   *   There were heroes of this mould in South Carolina, who entered with the best spirit of chivalry into the national quarrel, and brought to it hearts as bold, minds as vigorous, and arms as strong, as ever in any clime worked out a nation's redemption. These men refused submission to their conquerors, and endured exile, chains, and prison, rather than the yoke. Some few, still undiscouraged by the portents of the times, retreated into secret places, gathered their few patriot neighbors together, and contrived to keep in awe the soldier government that now professed to sway the land. They lived on the scant aliment furnished in the woods, slept in the tangled brakes and secret places of the fen, exacted contributions from the adherents of the crown, and, by rapid movements of their woodland cavalry, and brave blows, accomplished more than thrice their numbers would have done in ordinary warfare. * * * In such encounters or *frays*, as they might rather be called, from the smallness of the numbers concerned, and the hand to hand mode of fighting which they exhibited, Marion, Sumpter, Horry, Pickens, and many others had won a fame, that, in a nation of legendary or poetical associations, would have been reduplicated through a thousand channels of immortal verse. But alas! we have no ballads! and many men who as well deserve to be remembered as Percy or Douglas, as Adam Bell or Clym of the Clough, have sunk down without even a couplet epitaph upon the rude stone, that, in some unfenced and unreverenced grave yard, still marks the lap of earth whereon their heads were laid.   *   *   *   *   *

"One feature that belonged to this unhappy state of things in Carolina was the division of families. Kindred were arrayed against each other in deadly feuds, and not unfrequently brother took up arms against brother, and sons against their sires. A prevailing spirit of treachery and distrust marked the times. Strangers did not know how far they might trust to the rites of hospitality, and many a man laid his head upon his pillow, uncertain whether his fellow lodger might not invade him in the secret watches of the night, and murder him in his slumbers. All went armed, and many slept with pistols or daggers under their pillows. There are tales told of men being summoned to their doors or windows at midnight by the blaze of their farm yards, to which the incendiary torch had been applied, and shot down, in the light of the conflagration, by a concealed hand. Families were obliged to betake themselves to the shelter of the thickets and swamps, when their own homesteads were dangerous places. The enemy wore no colors, and was not to be distinguished from friends either by outward guise or speech. Nothing could be more revolting than to see the symbols of peace thus misleading the confident into the toils of war—nor is it possible to imagine a state of society characterized by a more frightful insecurity."

It will here be seen at a glance that the novelist has been peculiarly fortunate in the choice of an epoch, a scene and a subject. We sincerely think that he has done them all the fullest justice, and has worked out, with these and with other materials, a book of no ordinary character. We do not wish to attempt any analysis of the story itself—or that connecting chain which unites into one proper whole the varied events of the novel. We feel that in so doing, we should, in some measure, mar the interest by anticipation; a grievous sin too often indulged in by reviewers, and against which, should we ever be so lucky as to write a book, we would protest with all our hearts. But we may be allowed a word or two. The principal character in the novel, upon whom the chief interest of the story turns, and who, in accordance with the right usage of novel writing, should be considered the hero, and should have given a title to the book, is Brevet Major Arthur Butler of the continental army, to whose acquaintance we are first introduced about two o'clock in the afternoon of a day towards the end of July, 1780. But Mr. K. has ventured, at his own peril, to set at defiance the common ideas of propriety in this important matter, and, not having the fear of the critic before his eyes, has thought it better to call his work by the name of a very singular personage, whom all readers will agree in pronouncing worthy of the honor thus conferred upon him. The writer has also made another innovation. He has begun at the beginning. We all know this to be an unusual method of procedure. It has been too, for some time past, the custom, to delay as long as possible the main interest of a novel—no doubt with the very laudable intention of making it the more intense when it does at length arrive. Now for our own parts we can see little difference in being amused with the beginning or with the end of a book, but have a decided preference for those rare volumes which are so lucky as to amuse us throughout. And such a book is the one before us. We enter *at once* into the spirit and meaning of the author—we are introduced *at once* to the prominent characters—and we go with them *at once*, heart and hand, in the various and spirit-stirring adventures which befall them.

Horse-Shoe Robinson, who derives his nick-name of Horse-Shoe (his proper *prænomen* being Galbraith)—from the two-fold circumstance of being a blacksmith, and of living in a little nook of land hemmed in by a semi-circular bend of water, is fully entitled to the character of "an original." He is the life and soul of the drama—the bone and sinew of the book—its very breath—its every thing which gives it strength, substance, and vitality. Never was there a rarer fellow—a more laughable blacksmith—a more gallant Sancho. He is a very prince at an ambuscade, and a very devil at a fight. He is a better edition of Robin Hood—quite as sagacious—not half so much of a coxcomb—and infinitely more moral. In short, he is the man of all others we should like to have riding by our side in any very hazardous expedition.

We think Mr. K. has been particularly successful in the delineation of his female characters; and this is saying a great deal at a time when, from some unaccountable cause, almost every attempt of the kind has turned out a failure. Mildred Lindsay, in her confiding love, in her filial reverence, in her heroic espousal of the revolutionary cause, not because she approved it, but because it was her lover's, is an admirable and—need we say more?—a truly *feminine* portrait. Then the ardent, the eager, the simple-minded, the generous and the devoted Mary Musgrove! Most sincerely did we envy John Ramsay, the treasure of so pure and so exalted an affection!

With the exception of now and then a careless, or inadvertent expression, such for instance, as the word *venturesome* instead of *adventurous*, no fault whatever can be found with Mr. Kennedy's style. It varies gracefully and readily with the nature of his subject, never sinking, even in the low comedy of some parts of the book, into the insipid or the vulgar; and often, very often rising into the energetic and sublime. Its general character, as indeed the general character of all that we have seen from the same pen, is a certain unpretending simplicity, nervous, forcible, and altogether devoid of affectation. This is a style of writing above all others to be desired, and above all others difficult of attainment. Nor is it to be supposed that by simplicity we imply a rejection of ornament, or of a proper use of those advantages afforded by metaphorical illustration. A style professing to disclaim such advantages would be anything but simple—if indeed we might not be tempted to think it very silly. We have called the style of Mr. K. a style simple and forcible, and we have no hesitation in calling it, at the same time, richly figurative and poetical. We have opened the pages at random for an illustration of our meaning, and have no difficulty in finding one precisely suited to our purpose. Let us turn to vol. i. page 112.—"The path of invasion is ever a difficult road when it leads against a united people. You mistake both the disposition and the means of these republicans. They have bold partizans in the field, and eloquent leaders in their senates. The nature of the strife sorts well with their quick and earnest tempers; and by this man's play of war we breed up soldiers who delight in the game. Rebellion has long since marched beyond the middle ground, and has no thought of retreat. What was at first the mere overflow of popular passion has been hardened into principle— *like a fiery stream of lava which first rolls in a flood, and then turns into stone.*"

While we are upon the subject of style, we might as well say a word or two in regard to *punctuation*. It seems to us that the volumes before us are singularly deficient in this respect—and yet we noticed no fault of this nature in Swallow Barn. How can we reconcile these matters? Whom are we to blame in this particular, the author, or the printer? It cannot be said that the point is one of no importance—it is of very great importance. A slovenly punctuation will mar, in a greater or less degree, the brightest paragraph ever penned; and we are certain that those who have paid the most attention to this matter, will not think us hypercritical in what we say. A too frequent use of the *dash* is the besetting sin of the volumes now before us. It is lugged in upon all occasions, and invariably introduced where it has no business whatever. Even the end of a sentence is not sacred from its intrusion. Now there is no portion of a printer's fount, which can, if properly disposed, give more of strength and energy to a sentence than this same *dash*; and, for this very reason, there is none which can more effectually, if improperly arranged, disturb and distort the meaning of every thing with which it comes in contact. But not to speak of such disturbance or distortion, a fine taste will intuitively avoid, even in trifles, all that is unnecessary or superfluous, and bring nothing into use without an object or an end. We do not wish to dwell upon this thing, or to make it of more consequence than necessary. We will merely adduce an example of the punctuation to which we have alluded. Vide page 138, vol. i. "Will no lapse of time wear away this abhorred image from your memory?— Are you madly bent on bringing down misery on your head?—I do not speak of my own suffering.—Will you forever nurse a hopeless attachment for a man whom, it must be apparent to yourself, you can never meet again?—Whom, if the perils of the field, the avenging bullet of some loyal subject, do not bring him merited punishment,—the halter may reward, or, in his most fortunate destiny, disgrace, poverty, and shame pursue:—Are you forever to love that man?"—

Would not the above paragraph read equally as well thus: "Will no lapse of time wear away this abhorred image from your memory? Are you madly bent on bringing down misery on your head? I do not speak of my own suffering. Will you forever nurse a hopeless attachment for a man whom, it must be apparent to yourself, you can never meet again—whom, if the perils of the field, the avenging bullet of some loyal subject, do not bring him merited punishment, the halter may reward, or, in his more fortunate destiny, disgrace, poverty and shame pursue? Are you forever to love that man?"

The second of Mr. K's volumes is, from a naturally increasing interest taken in the fortunes of the leading characters, by far the most exciting. But we can confidently recommend them both to the lovers of the forcible, the adventurous, the stirring, and the picturesque. They will not be disappointed. A high tone of morality, healthy and masculine, breathes throughout the book, and a rigid—perhaps a too scrupulously rigid poetical justice is dealt out to the great and little villains of the story—the Tyrrells, the Wat Adairs, the Currys, and the Habershams of the drama. In conclusion, we prophecy that Horse-Shoe Robinson will be eagerly read by all classes of people, and cannot fail to place Mr. Kennedy in a high rank among the writers of this or of any other country.

We regret that the late period of receiving his book will not allow us to take that extended notice of it which we could desire.

S. Anna Lewis

The Child of the Sea and other Poems. By S. Anna Lewis, author of "Records of the Heart," etc., etc.

M RS. LEWIS HAS, in a very short space of time, attained a high poetical reputation. She is one of the youngest of our poetesses; and it is only since the publication of her "Records of the Heart," in 1844, that she can be said to have become known to the literary world:—although her "Ruins of Palenque" which appeared in the "New-World" sometime, we think, in 1840, made a most decided impression among a comparatively limited circle of readers. It was a composition of unquestionable merit, on a topic of infallible interest. In 1846, Mrs. Lewis published, in "The Democratic Review," a poem called "The Broken Heart," in three cantos, and subsequently has written many minor pieces for the "American" and "Democratic" Reviews, and for various other periodical works. In all her writings we perceive a marked idiosyncrasy—so that we might recognize her hand immediately in any of her anonymous productions. Passion, enthusiasm, and *abandon* are her prevailing traits. In these particulars she puts us more in mind of *Maria del Occidente* than of any other American poetess.

There has been lately exhibited, at the Academy of Fine Arts in New York, a portrait of Mrs. Lewis, by Elliot, which is at the same time a forcible likeness and one of the most praiseworthy pictures ever painted. In fact, we have seen nothing better from Sir Thomas Lawrence;—it alone would suffice to place Elliot at the head of his profession in this country—we mean, of course, as a painter of portraits. This picture conveys a distinct idea of the personal authoress. She is, as we have already mentioned, quite young—probably not more than 25 or 26—with dark and very expressive hazel eyes and chestnut hair, naturally curling—a poetical face, if ever one existed. Her form is finely turned—full, without being too much so, and slightly above the medium height. Her demeanour is noticeable for dignity, grace and repose. She goes little into society and resides at present in Brooklyn, N. Y. with her husband, *S. D. Lewis, Esq.*, Counsellor at Law. We have thought that these succinct personal particulars of one, who will most probably, at no very distant day, occupy a high, if not the highest, position among American poetesses, might not prove uninteresting to our readers.

The "Records of the Heart" was received with unusual favor at the period of its issue. It consists, principally, of poems of length. The leading one is "Florence," a tale of romantic passion, founded on an Italian tradition of great poetic capability and well managed by the fair authoress. It displays, however, somewhat less of polish and a good deal less of assured power than we see evinced in her "Child of the Sea." We quote a brief passage, by way, merely, of instancing the general spirit and earnest movement of the verse:

> Morn is abroad; the sun is up;
> The dew fills high each lily's cup.
> *Ten thousand flowerets springing there*
> *Diffuse their incense through the air,*
> And, smiling, hail the morning beam;
> *The fawns plunge panting in the stream,*
> Or through the vale with light foot spring:
> Insect and bird are on the wing
> And all is bright, as when in May
> Young Nature holds high holiday.

"Florence," however, is more especially noticeable for the profusion of its original imagery—as for example:

> The cypress in funereal gloom
> *Folds its dark arms above the tomb.*

"Tenel" (pronounced Thanail,) "Melpomene," (a glowing tribute to L. E. L.,) "The Last Hour of Sappho," "Laone," and "The Bride of Guayaquil," are all poems of considerable length and of rare merit in various ways. Their conduct as narratives, is, perhaps, less remarkable than their general effect as poems proper. They leave invariably on the reader's heart a sense of beauty and of sadness. In many of the shorter compositions which make up the volume of which we speak, ("Records of the Heart") we are forced to recognize the truth and perfect appositeness of the title—we are made to feel that it is here indeed *the heart* which records, rather than the fancy which invents. The passionate earnestness of the following lines will be acknowledged by every reader capable of appreciating that species of poetry of which the essentiality and inspiration is *truth*.

THE FORSAKEN

It hath been said—for all who die
    There is a tear;
Some pining, bleeding heart to sigh
    O'er every bier:—
But in that hour of pain and dread
    Who will draw near
Around my humble couch and shed
    One farewell tear?

Who watch my life's departing ray
    In deep despair
And soothe my spirit on its way
    With holy prayer?
What mourner round my bier will come
    In " weeds of wo"
And follow me to my long home
    Solemn and slow?

When lying on my clayey bed,
    In icy sleep,
Who there by pure affection led
    Will come and weep;
By the pale moon implant the rose
    Upon my breast,
And bid it cheer my dark repose—
    My lowly rest?

Could I but know when I am sleeping
    Low in the ground
One faithful heart would there be keeping
    Watch all night round,
As if some gem lay shrined beneath

> *That sod's cold gloom,*
> *'Twould mitigate the pangs of death*
> *And light the tomb.*
>
> *Yes, in that hour if I could feel*
> *From halls of glee*
> *And Beauty's presence one would steal*
> *In secresy,*
> *And come and sit and weep by me*
> *In nights' deep noon —*
> Oh! I would ask of Memory
> No other boon.
>
> But ah! a lonelier fate is mine —
> A deeper wo:
> From all I love in youth's sweet time
> I soon must go —
> *Draw round me my cold robes of white,*
> *In a dark spot,*
> To sleep through Death's long dreamless night,
> Lone and forgot.

We have read this little poem more than twenty times and always with increasing admiration. *It is inexpressibly beautiful.* No one of real feeling can peruse it without a strong inclination to tears. Its irresistible charm is its absolute *truth*—the unaffected naturalness of its thought. The sentiment which forms the basis of the composition is, perhaps, at once the most universal and the most *passionate* of sentiments. No human being exists, over the age of fifteen, who has not, in his heart of hearts, a ready echo for all here so pathetically expressed. The *essential* poetry of the ideas would only be impaired by "foreign ornament." This is a case in which we should be repelled by the mere conventionalities of the Muse. We demand, for such thoughts, the most rigorous simplicity at all points. It will be observed that, strictly speaking, there is not an attempt at "imagery" in the whole poem. All is direct, terse, penetrating. In a word nothing could be better done. The versification, while in full keeping with the general character of simplicity, has in certain passages a vigorous, trenchant euphony which would confer honor on the most accomplished masters of the art. We refer, especially to the lines:

> And follow me to my long home
> *Solemn and slow*

and to the quatrain:

> Could I but know when I am sleeping
> *Low in the ground*
> One faithful heart would there be keeping
> *Watch all night round.*

The initial trochee here, in each instance, substituted for the iambus produces, so naturally as to seem accidentally, a very effective echo of sound to sense. The thought included in the line "And *light* the tomb," should be dwelt upon to be appreciated in its full extent of beauty; and the verses which I have italicized in the last stanza are poetry—poetry in the purest sense of that much misused word. They have *power*—indisputable power; making us thrill with a sense of their weird magnificence as we read them.

In "The Child of the Sea," Mrs. Lewis has accomplished a much more comprehensive at least, if not at all points a more commendable poem than any included in her "Records of the Heart." One of its most distinguishing merits is the admirable conduct of its narrative—in which every incident has its proper position—where nothing is inconsequent or incoherent—and where, above all, the rich and vivid interest is never, for a single moment, permitted to flag. How few, even of the most accomplished and skilful of poets, are successful in the management of a *story*, when that story has to be told in verse. The difficulty is easily analyzed. In all mere narrations there are particulars of the dullest prose, which are inevitable and indispensable, but which serve no other purpose than to bind together the true interest of the incidents—in a word, *explanatory* passages which are yet to be "so done into verse" as not to *let down* the imagination from its pride of place. Absolutely to poetize these explanatory passages is beyond the reach of art, for prose, and that of the flattest kind, is their essentiality; but the *skill* of the artist should be sufficient to gloss them over so as to *seem* poetry amid the poetry by which they are surrounded. For this end a very consummate art is demanded. Here the tricks of phraseology—quaintnesses—and rhythmical effects, come opportunely into play. Of the species of skill required, Moore, in his "Alciphron," has given us, upon the whole, the happiest exemplification:—but Mrs. Lewis has very admirably succeeded in her "Child of the Sea." We are strongly tempted; by way of showing what we mean, to give here a digest of her narrative, with comments—but this would be doing the author injustice, in anticipating the interest of her work.

The poem, although widely differing in subject from any of Mrs. Lewis' prior compositions, and far superior to any of them in general vigor, artistic skill, and assured certainty of purpose, is nevertheless easily recognizable as the production of the same mind which originated "Florence" and "The Forsaken." We perceive, throughout, the same passion, the same enthusiasm, and the same seemingly reckless *abandon* of thought and manner which we have already mentioned as characterizing the writer. We should have spoken also, of a fastidious yet most sensitive and almost voluptuous sense of Beauty. These are the *general* traits of "The Child of the Sea:" but undoubtedly the chief value of the poem, to ordinary readers, will be found to lie in the aggregation of its imaginative passages—its quotable points. We give a few of these at random:—the opening lines will be at once appreciated:

> Where blooms the myrtle and *the olive flings*
> *Its aromatic breath upon the air;*
> *Where the sad bird of night forever sings*
> *Meet anthems for the Children of Despair.*

Again:

> Fresh blows the breeze on Tarick's *burnished* bay;
> The *silent* sea-mews bend them through the spray:
> *The Beauty-freighted barges bound afar*
> *To the soft music of the gay guitar.*

> ——the oblivious world of sleep—
> That rayless realm where Fancy never beams—
> *That Nothingness beyond the Land of Dreams.*

Folded his arms across his sable vest,
As if to keep the heart within his breast.
——————————he lingers by the streams,
Pondering on incommunicable themes.

Nor notes the fawn that tamely by him glides
The violets lifting up their azure eyes
Like timid virgins whom Love's steps surprise.

And all is hushed—so still—so silent there
That one might hear an angel wing the air.

Adown the groves and dewy vales afar
Tinkles the serenader's soft guitar.

——————her tender cares,
Her solemn sighs, her silent streaming tears,
Her more than woman's soft solicitude
To soothe his spirit in its frantic mood.

Now by the crags—then by each pendant bough
Steadies his steps adown the mountain's brow.

Sinks on his crimson couch, so long unsought,
And floats along the phantom stream of thought.

Ah, no! for there are times when the sick soul
Lies calm amid the storms that round it roll,
Indifferent to Fate or to what haven
By the terrific tempest it is driven.

The Dahlias, *leaning from the golden vase,*
Peer pensively upon her pallid face,
While the sweet songster o'er the oaken door
Looks through his grate and warbles "weep no more!"

——————lovely in her misery,
As jewel sparkling up through the dark sea.

Where hung the fiery moon and stars of blood,
And phantom ships rolled on the rolling flood.

My mind by grief was ripened ere its time,
And knowledge came spontaneous as a chime
That flows into the soul, unbid, unsought;
On Earth and Air and Heaven I fed my thought—
On Ocean's teachings—*Ætna's lava tears*—
Ruins and wrecks and nameless sepulchres.

Each morning brought to them untasted bliss.
No pangs—no sorrows came with varying years—
No cold distrust—no faithlessness—no tears—
But hand in hand as Eve and Adam trod
Eden, they walked beneath the smile of God.

It will be understood, of course, that we quote these brief
passages by no means as *the best*, or even as particularly excelling the rest of the poem, on an averaged estimate of merit,
but simply with a view of exemplifying some of the author's
more obvious traits—those, especially, of vigorous rhythm,
and forcible expression. In no case can the loftier qualities of
a truly great poem be conveyed through the citation of its
component portions, in detail, even when long extracts are
given—how much less, then, by such mere *points* as we have
selected. If we err not greatly, "The Child of the Sea" will
confer immortality on its author.

Southern Literary Messenger, September 1848

Francis Lieber

Reminiscences of an Intercourse with Mr. Niebuhr, the Historian, during a Residence with him in Rome, in the years 1822 and 1823. By Francis Lieber, Professor of History and Political Economy in South Carolina College. Philadelphia: Carey, Lea, and Blanchard.

M R. NIEBUHR has exercised a very powerful influence on the spirit of his age. One of the most important branches of human science has received, not only additional light, but an entirely novel interest and character from his exertions. Those historiographers of Rome who wrote before him, were either men of insufficient talents, or, possessing talents, were not practical statesmen. Niebuhr is the only writer of Roman history who unites intellect of a high order with the indispensable knowledge of what may be termed the art, in contradistinction to the science, of government. While, then, we read with avidity even common-place memorials of common-place men, (a fact strikingly characteristic of a period not inaptly denominated by the Germans "the age of wigs,") it cannot be supposed that a book like the one now before us, will fail to make a deep impression upon the mind of the public.

Beyond his *Roman History*, our acquaintance extends to only one or two of Mr. Niebuhr's publications. We remember the *Life of his Father*, of which an English translation was printed some time ago, in one of the tracts of the Library of Useful Knowledge, issued under the direction of the Society for the diffusion of Useful Knowledge—and, we have seen *The Description of the City of Rome* (one volume of it) which appeared in 1829 or '30, professedly by Bunsen and Platner, but in the getting up of which there can be no doubt of Mr. Niebuhr's having had the greater share. *The Representation of the Internal Government of Great Britain, by Baron Von Vincke*, Berlin, 1815, was also written, most probably, by Mr. N. who, however, announced himself as editor alone. "I published," says he, in the Reminiscences we are now reviewing, "I published the work on Great Britain after that unfortunate time when a foreign people ruled over us (Germans) with a cruel sword, and a heartless bureaucracy, in order to show what liberty is. Those who oppressed us called themselves all the time the harbingers of liberty, at the very moment they sucked the heart blood of our people; and we wanted to show what liberty in reality is." A translation of an *Essay on the Allegory in the first canto of Dante*, written by our historian during his perusal of the poet, and intended to be read, or perhaps actually read, in one of the learned societies of Rome, is appended to the present volume. Mr. L. copied it, by permission of the author, from the original in Italian, which was found in a copy of Dante belonging to Mr. Niebuhr. This Essay, we think, will prove of deeper interest to readers of Italian than even Mr. Lieber has anticipated. Its opinions differ singularly from those of all the commentators on Dante— the most of whom maintain that the wood (*la selva*) in this famous Allegory, should be understood as the condition of the human soul, shrouded in vice; the hill (*il colle*) encircled by light, but difficult of access, as virtue; and the furious beasts (*il fere*) which attack the poet in his attempt at ascending, as carnal sins—an interpretation, always putting us in mind of the monk in the *Gesta Romanorum*, who, speaking of the characters in the Iliad, says—"My beloved, Ulysses is Christ, and Achilles the Holy Ghost: Helen represents the Human Soul—Troy is Hell—and Paris the Devil."

Dr. Francis Lieber himself is well known to the American public as the editor of the Encyclopædia Americana, in which compilation he was assisted by Edward Wigglesworth, and T. G. Bradford, Esqrs. The first original work of our author, we believe, was called *Journal of my Residence in Greece*, and was issued at Leipzig in 1823. This book was written at the instigation of Mr. Niebuhr, who personally superintended the whole; Mr. L. reading to the historian and his wife, every morning at breakfast, what had been completed in the preceding afternoon. Since that period we have seen, from the same pen, only *The Stranger in America*, in two volumes, full of interest and extensively circulated—and the book whose title forms the heading of this article.

Not the least striking portion of this latter work, is its Preface, embracing forty-five pages. Niebuhr's noble nature is, herein, rendered hardly more apparent than the mingled simplicity and enthusiasm of his biographer. The account given

by Mr. L. of his first introduction to the Prussian minister—
of the perplexing circumstances which led to that introduction—of his invitation to dinner, and consequent embarrassment on account of his scanty nether habiliments—of his
final domestication in the house of his patron, and of the
great advantages accruing to himself therefrom—are all related without the slightest attempt at prevarication, and in a
style of irresistibly captivating *bonhommie* and *naïveté*.

Mr. Lieber went, in 1821, to Greece—led, as he himself relates, "by youthful ardor, to assist the oppressed and struggling descendants of that people, whom all civilized nations
love and admire." With a thousand others, he was disappointed in the hope of rendering any assistance to the objects
of his sympathy. He found it impossible either to fight, or to
get a dinner—either to live or to die. In 1822, therefore he
resolved, with many other Philhellenes, to return. Money,
however, was scarce, and the adventurer had sold nearly every
thing he possessed—but to remain longer was to starve. He
accordingly "bargained with a Greek," and took passage at
Missolonghi (Messalunghi) in a small vessel bound for Ancona. After a rough passage, during which the "tartan" was
forced to seek shelter in the bay of Gorzola, the wished-for
port was finally reached. Here, being altogether without
money, Mr. Lieber wrote to a friend in Rome, enclosing the
letter to an eminent artist. "My friend," says Mr. L. "happened to be at Rome, and to have money, and with the
promptness of a German student, sent me all he possessed at
the time." This assistance came very seasonably. It enabled the
Philhellenist to defray the expenses of his quarantine at Ancona. Had he failed in paying them, the Captain would have
been bound for the sum, and Mr. L. would have been obliged
finally to discharge the debt, by serving as a sailor on board
the Greek vessel.

Having, at length, obtained his *pratica*, he determined
upon visiting Rome; and the anxiety with which he appears
to have contemplated the defeat of his hopes in this respect is
strikingly characteristic of the man. His passport was in bad
order, and provisional, and he had to make his way with it
through the police office at Ancona. He was informed too,
that orders had been received from Rome forbidding the sig-

nature of passports in the possession of persons coming from
Greece, except for a direct journey home. "You are a Prussian," said the officer, "and I must direct your passport home
to Germany. I will direct it to Florence: your minister there
may direct it back to Rome. Or I will direct it to any place in
Tuscany which you may choose; for through Tuscany you
must travel in order to reach Germany." Mr. L. assures us he
never felt more wretched than on hearing this announcement.
He had made his way round Rome without seeing the Eternal City. The examination of a map of Italy, however, gave
him new hope. It pointed out to him how near the south-
western frontier line of Tuscany approaches to Rome. The
road from Ancona to Orbitello, he thought, was nearly the
same as that to the object of his desires, and he therefore
requested the officer to direct his passport to Orbitello. "Ital-
ians generally," says Mr. Lieber, "are exceedingly poor geog-
raphers." The gentleman whom he addressed, inquired of
another in the adjoining room, whether Orbitello was in Tuscany, or belonged to the Papal territory. Mr. L. pointed out
the place on the map: it was situated just within the colors
which distinguished Tuscany from the other states of Italy.
This satisfied the police, and the passport was made out.

Having hired a vetturino our traveller proceeded towards
Orbitello. A few miles beyond Nepi, at the Colonneta, the
road divides, and the coachman was desired to pursue the
path leading to Rome. A bribe silenced all objections, and
when near the city, Mr. L. jumped out of the carriage, and
entered the Porta del Populo.

But it was impossible to dwell in Rome without the sanction of the police, and this sanction could not be obtained
without a certificate from the Prussian minister that our
friend's passport was in order. Mr. Lieber therefore "hoping
that a scholar who had written the history of Rome could not
be so cruel as to drive away thence a pilgrim without allowing
him time to see and study it," resolved on disclosing his situation frankly to Mr. Niebuhr.

The Prussian minister resided at the Palazzo Orsini—he
was engaged and could not be seen—but the secretary of the
legation received the visiter kindly, and having learned his
story, retired to an inner apartment. Soon afterwards he re-

turned with a paper written in Mr. Niebuhr's own hand. It was the necessary permission to reside in Rome. A sum of money was at the same time presented to Mr. L. which the secretary assured him was part of a sum Prince Henry (brother to the reigning king,) had placed at the minister's disposal for the assistance of gentlemen who might return from Greece. Mr. L. was informed also that Niebuhr would see him on the following day. The result of the interview we must give in the words of our author.

When I went the next morning at the appointed time, as I thought, Mr. Niebuhr met me on the stairs, being on the point of going out. He received me with kindness and affability, returned with me to his room, made me relate my whole story, and appeared much pleased that I could give him some information respecting Greece, which seemed to be not void of interest to him. Our conversation lasted several hours, when he broke off, asking me to return to dinner. I hesitated in accepting the invitation, which he seemed unable to understand. He probably thought that a person in my situation ought to be glad to receive an invitation of this kind; and, in fact any one might feel gratified in being asked to dine with him, especially in Rome. When I saw that my motive for declining so flattering an invitation was not understood, I said, throwing a glance at my dress, "Really, sir, I am not in a state to dine with an excellency." He stamped with his foot, and said with some animation, "Are diplomatists always believed to be so cold-hearted! I am the same that I was in Berlin when I delivered my lectures; your remark was wrong."* No argument could be urged against such reasons.

I recollect that dinner with delight. His conversation, abounding in rich and various knowledge and striking observations; his great kindness; the acquaintance I made with Mrs. Niebuhr; his lovely children, who were so beautiful, that when, at a later period, I used to walk with them, the women would exclaim, *"Ma guardate, guardate, che angeli!"*—a good dinner (which I had not enjoyed for a long time) in a high vaulted room, the ceiling of which was painted in the style of Italian palaces; a picture by the mild Francia close by;

Das war Kleinlich were his words.

the sound of the murmuring fountain in the garden, and the refreshing beverages in coolers, which I had seen, but the day before, represented in some of the most masterly pictures of the Italian schools;—in short, my consciousness of being at dinner with Niebuhr in his house in Rome—and all this in so bold relief to my late and not unfrequently disgusting sufferings, would have rendered the moment one of almost perfect enjoyment and happiness, had it not been for an annoyance which, I have no doubt, will appear here a mere trifle. However, reality often widely differs from its description on paper. Objects of great effect for the moment become light as air, and others, shadows and vapors in reality, swell into matters of weighty consideration when subjected to the recording pen;—a truth, by the way, which applies to our daily life, as well as to transactions of powerful effect;—and it is, therefore, the sifting tact which constitutes one of the most necessary, yet difficult, requisites for a sound historian.

My dress consisted as yet of nothing better than a pair of unblacked shoes, such as are not unfrequently worn in the Levant; a pair of socks of coarse Greek wool; the brownish pantaloons frequently worn by sea-captains in the Mediterranean; and a blue frock-coat, through which two balls had passed—a fate to which the blue cloth cap had likewise been exposed. The socks were exceedingly short, hardly covering my ankles, and so indeed were the pantaloons; so that, when I was in a sitting position, they refused me the charity of meeting, with an obstinacy which reminded me of the irreconcileable temper of the two brothers in Schiller's Bride of Messina. There happened to dine with Mr. Niebuhr another lady besides Mrs. Niebuhr; and my embarrassment was not small when, towards the conclusion of the dinner, the children rose and played about on the ground, and I saw my poor extremities exposed to all the frank remarks of quick-sighted childhood; fearing as I did, at the same time, the still more trying moments after dinner, when I should be obliged to take coffee near the ladies, unprotected by the kindly shelter of the table. Mr. Niebuhr observed, perhaps, that something embarrassed me, and he redoubled, if possible, his kindness.

After dinner he proposed a walk, and asked the ladies to

accompany us. I pitied them; but as a gentleman of their acquaintance had dropped in by this time, who gladly accepted the offer to walk with us, they were spared the mortification of taking my arm. Mr. Niebuhr, probably remembering what I had said of my own appearance in the morning, put his arm under mine, and thus walked with me for a long time. After our return, when I intended to take leave, he asked me whether I wished for any thing. I said I should like to borrow his History. He had but one copy, to which he had added notes, and which he did not wish, therefore, to lend out of his house; but he said he would get a copy for me. As to his other books, he gave me the key of his library to take whatever I liked. He laughed when I returned laden with books, and dismissed me in the kindest manner.

Mr. Lieber became the constant companion of Niebuhr in his daily walks after dinner, during one of which the proposition was discussed to which we have formerly referred—that of our author's writing an account of his journey in Greece. In March 1823, the minister quitted Rome, and took Mr. Lieber with him to Naples. By way of Florence, Pisa, and Bologna, they afterwards went to the Tyrol—and in Inspruck they parted. A correspondence of the most familiar and friendly nature was, however, kept up, with little intermission, until the death of the historian in 1831.

Mr. Lieber disclaims the design of any thing like a complete record of all the interesting or important sentiments of Niebuhr during his own residence with him. He does not profess to give even all the most important facts or opinions. He observes, with great apparent justice, that he lived in too constant a state of excitement to record regularly all he saw or heard. His papers too were seized by the police—and have undergone its criticism. Some have been lost by this process, and others in a subsequent life of wandering. Still we can assure our readers that those presented to us in the present volume, are of the greatest interest. They enable us to form a more accurate idea of the truly great man to whom they relate than we have hitherto entertained, and have moreover, not unfrequently, an interest altogether their own.

Southern Literary Messenger, January 1836

Henry Wadsworth Longfellow

Hyperion, a Romance. By the author of *Outre-Mer*. Two volumes. Samuel Colman, New York.

WERE IT POSSIBLE to throw into a bag the lofty thought and manner of the "Pilgrims of the Rhine," together with the quirks and quibbles and true humor of "Tristram Shandy," not forgetting a few of the heartier drolleries of Rabelais, and one or two of the Phantasy Pieces of the Lorrainean Callôt, the whole, when well shaken up, and thrown out, would be a very tolerable imitation of "Hyperion." This may appear to be commendation, but we do not intend it as such. Works like this of Professor Longfellow, are the triumphs of Tom O'Bedlam, and the grief of all true criticism. They are potent in unsettling the popular faith in Art—a faith which, at no day more than the present, needed the support of men of letters. That such things succeed at all, is attributable to the sad fact that there exist men of genius who, now and then, unmindful of duty, indite them—that men of genius *ever* indite them is attributable to the fact that these are often the most indolent of human beings. A man of true talent who would demur at the great labor requisite for the stern demands of high art—at the unremitting toil and patient elaboration which, when soul-guided, result in the beauty of Unity, Totality, and Truth—men, we say, who would demur at such labor, make no scruple of scattering at random a profusion of rich thought in the pages of such farragos as "Hyperion." Here, indeed, there is little trouble—but even that little is most unprofitably lost. To the writers of these things we say—all Ethics lie, and all History lies, or the world shall forget ye and your *works*. We have no design of commenting, at any length, upon what Professor Longfellow has written. We are indignant that he too has been recreant to the good cause. We, therefore, dismiss his "Hyperion" in brief. We grant him high qualities, but deny him *the Future*. In the present instance, without design, without shape, without beginning, middle, or end, what earthly object has his book accomplished?—what definite impression has it left?

Burton's Gentleman's Magazine, October 1839

Voices of the Night. By Henry Wadsworth Longfellow. John Owen, Cambridge.

THE LITTLE BOOK which Professor Longfellow has entitled "The Voices of the Night," includes not only some
poems thus styled, but others composed during the collegiate
life of the writer, as well as about twenty brief translations.
Of the latter we shall say nothing. So very much of all that is
essential to the lyre—so many of its more spiritual attributes
and properties—lie *beyond* the scope of translation—so trivial, comparatively, are those mere graces which lie *within* it—
that the critic will be pardoned for declining to admit versions, of however high merit as such, into his estimate of the
poetical character of his author. Neither should any author, of
mature age, desire to have this poetical character estimated by
the productions of his mind at immaturity. We shall, therefore, confine our observations to the "Voices of the Night."

In looking over a file of newspapers, not long ago, our attention was arrested by the opening lines of a few stanzas,
headed "Hymn to the Night." We read them again and again,
and although some blemishes were readily discoverable, we
bore them away in memory, with the firm belief that a poet
of high genius had at length arisen amongst us, and with the
resolve so to express our opinion at the first opportunity
which should offer. The perusal of the entire volume now
presented to the public by the writer of this "Hymn to the
Night," has not, indeed, greatly modified our impressions in
regard to that particular poem—not greatly, even, in regard
to the genius of the poet—but very greatly in respect to his
capacity for the ultimate achievement of any well-founded
monument—any enduring reputation. Our general conclusion is one similar to that which "Hyperion" induced, and
which we stated, of late, in a concise notice of that book. The
author has, in one or two points, ability; and, in these one or
two points, that ability regards the very loftiest qualities of
the poetical soul. His imagination, for example, is vivid—and
in saying this, how much do we say! But he appears to us
singularly deficient in all those important faculties which give
artistical power, and without which never was immortality effected. He has no combining or binding force. He has absolutely nothing of unity. His brief pieces (to whose brevity he

has been led by an instinct of the deficiencies we now note) abound in high thoughts either positively insulated, or showing these same deficiencies by the recherché spirit of their connexion. And thus his productions are scintillations from the brightest poetical truth, rather than this brightest truth in itself. By truth, here, we mean that perfection which is the result only of the strictest proportion and adaptation in all the poetical requisites—these requisites being considered as each existing in the highest degree of beauty and strength.

It is by no means our design to speak of the volume before us in detail. There would be no object in such critical supererogation. The spirit of Professor Longfellow is as well determined from the shortest of these "Voices of the Night," (which are altogether his best pieces) as from all that he has written combined. We look upon the "Beleaguered City" as his finest poem. There is a certainty of purpose about it which we do not discover elsewhere; and in it, the writer's idiosyncratic excellences, which are those of expression, chiefly, and of a fitful (unsteady) imagination, are the most strikingly displayed. The "Hymn to the Night," however, will be the greatest favorite with the public, from the fact that these idiosyncratic beauties are there more evident and more glowing.

> I heard the trailing garments of the Night
>   Sweep through her marble halls!
> I saw her sable skirts all fringed with light
>   From the celestial walls!
>
> I felt her presence, by its spell of might,
>   Stoop o'er me from above;
> The calm, majestic presence of the Night,
>   As of the one I love.
>
> I heard the sounds of sorrow and delight,
>   The manifold soft chimes
> That fill the haunted chambers of the Night
>   Like some old poet's rhymes.
>
> From the cool cisterns of the midnight air
>   My spirit drank repose;
> The fountain of perpetual peace flows there—
>   From those deep cisterns flows.

O holy Night! from thee I learn to bear
    What man has borne before!
Thou layest thy finger on the lips of care,
    And they complain no more.

Peace! Peace! Orestes-like I breathe this prayer!
    Descend with broad-winged flight,
The welcome, the thrice-prayed for, the most fair,
    The best-beloved Night.

No poem ever opened with a beauty more august. The five first stanzas are nearly perfect—by which we mean that they are nearly free from fault, while embodying a supreme excellence. Had we seen nothing from the pen of the poet but these five verses, we should have formed the most exaggerated conception of his powers. Had he written always thus, we should have been tempted to speak of him not only as *our* finest poet, but as one of the noblest poets of all time. Yet even these five stanzas have their defects—defects inherent in the mind of the writer, and thence ineradicable—absolutely so. An intellect which apprehends, with full sensitiveness, the peculiar loveliness of the spirit of the *unique*—of unity—will find, in perusal here, that his fancy, in the poet's guidance, wavers disagreeably between two ideas which would have been merged by the skilful artist in one. We mean the two ideas of the absolute and of the personified Night. Even in the first stanza this difficulty occurs—enfeebling all. The words—

I heard the trailing garments of the Night
    Sweep through her *marble* halls—

convey us to a palace tenanted by the sable-draperied, by the corporate Night. But the lines

I saw her sable-skirts all fringed with light
    From the *celestial* walls—

refer us, by the single epithet *celestial*, to the natural and absolute quality or condition, to the incorporate darkness. Had the poet merely written "azure" or "heavenly" in place of marble, this conflict of thought would not have occurred, and the passage would have derived that force, from unity, which it does not at present possess. The personification, which is its main beauty, would have remained, at the same time, inviolate. A similar good effect could be produced by changing *celestial* for some word inducing the mind to receive the Night in her personified character—changing it for any term applicable to an earthly habitation.

Precisely the same fault is found in the second stanza, where the "from above" lifts the thought to the absolute night—the subsequent lines bringing it down immediately to the prosopopeia. The third stanza is in good keeping—the fourth slightly in fault as before. The fifth is correct. The sixth is again in error—and has, moreover, the great defect of not being readily intelligible. It is not every reader who will here understand the poet as invoking Peace to descend *through*, or by means of,

> The welcome, the thrice-prayed for, the most fair,
>   The best-beloved Night.

The words used are, of course, strictly grammatical; and, as the lines stand, no preposition could have been employed—Peace is invoked to descend the Night—as we say descend the stair, or ladder—but, then, the entire form of the stanza should have been altered, so as to obviate even the possibility of a misapprehension. Upon our first perusal we understood the passage as containing a double invocation—to Peace and to Night. But in regard to this single and brief poem, as a whole, (or rather when we consider it *not* as a whole, and view it through its parts) its richly ideal beauties would more than redeem a thousand inadvertences such as we point out; and we point them out at all merely as some instance of the complexion of the prevalent deficiencies of the writer.

The gross affectations which disfigure "Hyperion" in many passages, are not at all observable in this Hymn, (whose majestic simplicity is not the least of its high merits) but are wofully abundant in most of the other pieces. What can be more preposterous than such inversion as this, in the mouth of a poet of the nineteenth century?—

> *Spake full well*, in language quaint and olden
>   One who dwelleth by the castled Rhine
> When he called &c.

The titles of Professor Longfellow's books, moreover, answer no good purpose in the world. Such things as "Outre Mér," "Hyperion," "Psalms of Life" and "Voices of the Night," only lessen the perpetrator in the opinion of all reasonable men; and there was no necessity, whatever, for any "Prelude" by way of commencement to the volume now reviewed.

But we have to adduce against the poet a charge of much more serious character. One of his latest and most popular pieces runs thus—

MIDNIGHT MASS FOR THE DYING YEAR

Yes, the year is growing old,
    And his eye is pale and bleared!
Death, with frosty hand and cold,
    Plucks the old man by the beard,
        Sorely,—sorely!

The leaves are falling, falling,
    Solemnly and slow;
Caw! caw! the rooks are calling,
    It is a sound of woe,
        A sound of woe!

Through woods and mountain-passes
    The winds, like anthems, roll;
They are chanting solemn masses,
    Singing; Pray for this poor soul,
        Pray,—pray!

And the hooded clouds, like friars,
    Tell their beads in drops of rain,
And patter their doleful prayers;
    But their prayers are all in vain,
        All in vain!

There he stands in the foul weather,
    The foolish, fond Old Year,
Crowned with wild flowers and with heather,
    Like weak, despised Lear,
        A king,—a king!

Then comes the summer-like day,
   Bids the old man rejoice!
His joy! his last! O, the old man gray,
   Loveth her ever soft voice
      Gentle and low.

To the crimson woods he saith,
   And the voice, gentle and low,
Of the soft air, like a daughter's breath,
   Pray do not mock me so!
      Do not laugh at me!

And now the sweet day is dead;
   Cold in his arms it lies,
No stain from its breath is spread
   Over the glassy skies,
      No mist nor stain!

Then, too, the Old Year dieth,
   And the forests utter a moan,
Like the voice of one who crieth
   In the wilderness alone,
      Vex not his ghost!

Then comes, with an awful roar,
   Gathering and sounding on,
The storm-wind from Labrador,
   The wind Euroclydon,
      The storm-wind!

Howl! howl! and from the forest
   Sweep the red leaves away!
Would, the sins that thou abhorrest,
   O soul! could thus decay,
      And be swept away!

For there shall come a mightier blast,
   There shall be a darker day;
And the stars, from heaven down-cast,
   Like red leaves be swept away!
      Kyrie Eleyson!
      Christie Eleyson!

This piece, with many defects, has undoubtedly more beauties, and these beauties are of a high order—but in a volume of poems by Alfred Tennyson, of England, we meet with the following:

THE DEATH OF THE OLD YEAR

Full knee-deep lies the winter snow,
    And the winter winds are wearily sighing:
Toll ye the church-bell sad and slow,
And tread softly, and speak low,
    For the old year lies a-dying.
        Old year you must not die,
        You came to us so readily,
        You lived with us so steadily,
        Old year you shall not die.

He lieth still: he doth not move;
    He will not see the dawn of day.
He hath no other life above—
He gave me a friend, and a true, true love,
    And the New Year will take 'em away.
        Old year, you must not go,
        So long as you have been with us,
        Such joy as you have seen with us,
        Old year, you shall not go.

He frothed his bumpers to the brim;
    A jollier year we shall not see.
But tho' his eyes are waxing dim,
And tho' his foes speak ill of him,
    He was a friend to me.
        Old year, you shall not die;
        We did so laugh and cry with you,
        I've half a mind to die with you
        Old year, if you must die.

He was full of joke and jest,
    But all his merry quips are o'er.
To see him die, across the waste,
His son and heir doth ride post haste,
    But he'll be dead before.

> Every one for his own;
> The night is starry and cold, my friend,
> And the new year blithe and bold, my friend,
>   Comes up to take his own.

How hard he breathes! Over the snow
I heard just now the crowing cock.
The shadows flicker to and fro:
The cricket chirps: the light burns low:
    'Tis nearly one o'clock.
>   Shake hands before you die;
>   Old year we'll dearly rue for you,
>   What is it we can do for you?
>   Speak out before you die.

His face is growing sharp and thin—
    Alack! our friend is gone.
Close up his eyes: tie up his chin:
Step from the corpse and let him in
    That standeth there alone,
>   And waiteth at the door.
>   There's a new foot on the floor, my friend,
>   And a new face at the door, my friend,
>   A new face at the door.

We have no idea of commenting, at any length, upon this plagiarism; which is too palpable to be mistaken; and which belongs to the most barbarous class of literary robbery; that class in which, while the words of the wronged author are avoided, his most intangible, and therefore his least defensible and least reclaimable property, is purloined. Here, with the exception of lapses, which, however, speak volumes, (such for instance as the use of the capitalized "Old Year," the general peculiarity of the rhythm, and the absence of rhyme at the end of each stanza,) there is nothing of a visible or palpable nature by which the source of the American poem can be established. But then nearly all that is valuable in the piece of Tennyson, is the first conception of personifying the Old Year as a dying old man, with the singularly wild and fantastic *manner* in which that conception is carried out. Of this conception and of this manner he is robbed. Could he peruse to-day the "Midnight Mass" of Professor Longfellow, would he peruse it with more of indignation or of grief?

Burton's Gentleman's Magazine, February 1840

Ballads and other Poems. By Henry Wadsworth Longfellow, Author of "Voices of the Night," "Hyperion," etc: Second Edition. John Owen: Cambridge.

"IL *y a à parier,*" says Chamfort, "*que toute idée publique, toute convention recue, est une sottise, car elle a convenue au plus grand nombre.*"—One would be safe in wagering that any given public idea is erroneous, for it has been yielded to the clamor of the majority;—and this strictly philosophical, although somewhat French assertion has especial bearing upon the whole race of what are termed maxims and popular proverbs; nine-tenths of which are the quintessence of folly. One of the most deplorably false of them is the antique adage, *De gustibus non est disputandum*—there should be no disputing about taste. Here the idea designed to be conveyed is that any one person has as just right to consider his own taste *the true*, as has any one other—that taste itself, in short, is an arbitrary something, amenable to no law, and measurable by no definite rules. It must be confessed, however, that the exceedingly vague and impotent treatises which are alone extant, have much to answer for as regards confirming the general error. Not the least important service which, hereafter, mankind will owe to *Phrenology*, may perhaps, be recognised in an analysis of the real principles, and a digest of the resulting laws of taste. These principles, in fact, are as clearly traceable, and these laws as readily susceptible of system as are any whatever.

In the meantime, the inane adage above mentioned is in no respect more generally, more stupidly, and more pertinaciously quoted than by the admirers of what is termed the "good old Pope," or the "good old Goldsmith school" of poetry, in reference to the bolder, more natural, and *more ideal* compositions of such authors as Coëtlogon and Lamartine*

*We allude here chiefly to the "David" of Coëtlogon, and *only* to the "*Chûte d'un Ange*" of Lamartine.

in France; Herder, Körner, and Uhland in Germany; Brun and Baggesen in Denmark; Bellman, Tegnér, and Nyberg* in Sweden; Keats, Shelley, Coleridge, and Tennyson in England; Lowell and Longfellow in America. *"De gustibus non,"* say these "good-old-school" fellows; and we have no doubt that their mental translation of the phrase is—"We pity your taste—we pity every body's taste but our own."

It is our purpose, hereafter, when occasion shall be afforded us, to controvert in an article of some length, the popular idea that the poets just mentioned owe to novelty, to trickeries of expression,—and to other meretricious effects, their appreciation by certain readers:—to demonstrate (for the matter is susceptible of demonstration) that such poetry and *such alone* has fulfilled the legitimate office of the muse; has thoroughly satisfied an earnest and unquenchable desire existing in the heart of man. In the present number of our Magazine we have left ourselves barely room to say a few random words of welcome to these "Ballads," by Longfellow, and to tender him, and all such as he, the homage of our most earnest love and admiration.

The volume before us (in whose outward appearance the keen "taste" of genius is evinced with nearly as much precision as in its internal soul) includes, with several brief original pieces, a translation from the Swedish of Tegnér. In attempting (what never should be attempted) a literal version of both the words and the metre of this poem, Professor Longfellow has failed to do justice either to his author or himself. He has striven to do what no man ever did well and what, from the nature of language itself, never *can* be well done. Unless, for example, we shall come to have an influx of *spondees* in our English tongue, it will always be impossible to construct an English hexameter. Our spondees, or, we should say, our spondaic words, are rare. In the Swedish they are nearly as abundant as in the Latin and Greek. We have only "*compound*," "*context*," "*footfall*," and a few other similar ones. This is the difficulty; and that it *is* so will become evident upon reading "The Children of the Lord's Supper," where the sole *readable* verses are those in which we meet with the rare

*C. Julia Nyberg, author of the "Dikter von Euphrosyne."

spondaic dissyllables. We mean to say *readable as Hexameters*; for many of them will read very well as mere English Dactylics with certain irregularities.

But within the narrow compass now left us we must not indulge in anything like critical comment. Our readers will be better satisfied perhaps with a few brief extracts from the original poems of the volume—which we give for their rare excellence, without pausing now to say in what particulars this excellence exists.

> And, like the water's flow
> Under December's snow
> Came a dull voice of woe,
>   From the heart's chamber.
>
> So the loud laugh of scorn,
> Out of those lips unshorn
> From the deep drinking-horn
>   Blew the foam lightly.
>
> As with his wings aslant
> Sails the fierce cormorant
> Seeking some rocky haunt,
>   With his prey laden,
> So toward the open main,
> Beating to sea again,
> Through the wild hurricane,
>   Bore I the maiden.
>
> Down came the storm and smote amain
>   The vessel in its strength;
> She shuddered and paused like a frighted steed
>   Then leaped her cable's length.
>
>   She drifted a dreary wreck,
> And a whooping billow swept the crew
>   Like icicles from her deck.
>
> He hears the parson pray and preach,
>   He hears his daughter's voice,
> Singing in the village choir,
>   And it makes his heart rejoice.
> It sounds to him like her mother's voice

Singing in Paradise!
He needs must think of her once more
How in the grave she lies;
And with his hard rough hand he wipes
A tear out of his eyes.

Thus at the flaming forge of life
Our fortunes must be wrought;
Thus on its sounding anvil shaped
Each burning deed and thought.

The rising moon has hid the stars
Her level rays like golden bars
Lie on the landscape green
With shadows brown between.

Love lifts the boughs whose shadows deep
Are life's oblivion, the soul's sleep,
And kisses the closed eyes
Of him who slumbering lies.

Friends my soul with joy remembers!
How like quivering flames they start,
When I fan the living embers
On the hearth-stone of my heart.

Hearest thou voices on the shore,
That our ears perceive no more
Deafened by the cataract's roar?

And from the sky, serene and far,
A voice fell like a falling star.

Some of these passages cannot be fully appreciated apart from the context—but we address those who have read the book. Of the translations we have not spoken. It is but right to say, however, that "The Luck of Edenhall" is a far finer poem, in every respect, than any of the original pieces. Nor would we have our previous observations misunderstood. Much as we admire the genius of Mr. Longfellow, we are fully sensible of his many errors of affectation and imitation. His artistical skill is great, and his ideality high. But his conception of the *aims* of poesy *is all wrong*; and this we shall prove at some future day—to our own satisfaction, at least. His didactics are all *out of place*. He has written brilliant poems—by accident; that is to say when permitting his genius to get the better of his conventional habit of thinking— a habit deduced from German study. We do not mean to say that a didactic moral may not be well made the *under-current* of a poetical thesis; but that it can never be well put so obtrusively forth, as in the majority of his compositions. There is a young American who, with ideality not richer than that of Longfellow, and with less artistical knowledge, has yet composed far truer poems, merely through the greater propriety of his themes. We allude to James Russell Lowell; and in the number of this Magazine for last month, will be found a ballad entitled "Rosaline," affording an excellent exemplification of our meaning. This composition has unquestionably its defects, and the very defects which are never perceptible in Mr. Longfellow—but we sincerely think that *no American poem equals it* in the higher elements of song.

Graham's Magazine, March 1842

Ballads and Other Poems. By Henry Wadsworth Longfellow. Author of "Voices of the Night," "Hyperion," &c. Second Edition. John Owen: Cambridge.

IN OUR LAST NUMBER we had some hasty observations on these "Ballads"—observations which we now propose, in some measure, to amplify and explain.

It may be remembered that, among other points, we demurred to Mr. Longfellow's *themes*, or rather to their general character. We found fault with the too obtrusive nature of their *didacticism*. Some years ago we urged a similar objection to one or two of the longer pieces of Bryant; and neither time nor reflection has sufficed to modify, in the slightest particular, our convictions upon this topic.

We have said that Mr. Longfellow's conception of the *aims* of poesy is erroneous; and that thus, laboring at a disadvantage, he does violent wrong to his own high powers; and now the question is, what *are* his ideas of the aims of the Muse, as we gather these ideas from the *general* tendency of his poems? It will be at once evident that, imbued with the peculiar spirit of German song (a pure conventionality) he regards the inculcation of a *moral* as essential. Here we find it necessary to repeat that we have reference only to the *general* tendency of his compositions; for there are some magnificent exceptions, where, as if by accident, he has permitted his genius to get the better of his conventional prejudice. But didacticism is the prevalent *tone* of his song. His invention, his imagery, his all, is made subservient to the elucidation of some one or more points (but rarely of more than one) which he looks upon as *truth*. And that this mode of procedure will find stern defenders should never excite surprise, so long as the world is full to overflowing with cant and conventicles. There are men who will scramble on all fours through the muddiest sloughs of vice to pick up a single apple of virtue. There are things called men who, so long as the sun rolls, will greet with snuffling huzzas every figure that takes upon itself the semblance of truth, even although the figure, in itself only a "stuffed Paddy," be as much out of place as a toga on the statue of Washington, or out of season as rabbits in the days of the dog-star.

Now with as deep a reverence for "the true" as ever inspired the bosom of mortal man, we would limit, in many respects, its modes of inculcation. We would limit to enforce them. We would not render them impotent by dissipation. The demands of truth are severe. She has no sympathy with the myrtles. All that is indispensible in song is all with which she has nothing to do. To deck her in gay robes is to render her a harlot. It is but making her a flaunting paradox to wreathe her in gems and flowers. Even in stating this our present proposition, we verify our own words—we feel the necessity, in enforcing this *truth*, of descending from metaphor. Let us then be simple and distinct. To convey "the true" we are required to dismiss from the attention all inessentials. We must be perspicuous, precise, terse. We need concentration rather than expansion of mind. We must be calm, unimpassioned, unexcited—in a word, we must be in that peculiar mood which, as nearly as possible, is the exact converse of the poetical. He must be blind indeed who cannot perceive the radical and chasmal difference between the truthful and the poetical modes of inculcation. He must be grossly wedded to conventionalisms who, in spite of this difference, shall still attempt to reconcile the obstinate oils and waters of Poetry and Truth.

Dividing the world of mind into its most obvious and immediately recognisable distinctions, we have the pure intellect, taste, and the moral sense. We place *taste* between the intellect and the moral sense, because it is just this intermediate space which, in the mind, it occupies. It is the connecting link in the triple chain. It serves to sustain a mutual intelligence between the extremes. It appertains, in strict appreciation, to the former, but is distinguished from the latter by so faint a difference, that Aristotle has not hesitated to class some of its operations among the Virtues themselves. But the *offices* of the trio are broadly marked. Just as conscience, or the moral sense, recognises duty; just as the intellect deals with *truth*; so is it the part of taste alone to inform us of BEAUTY. And Poesy is the handmaiden but of Taste. Yet we would not be misunderstood. This handmaiden is not forbidden to moralise—in her own fashion. She is not forbidden to depict—but to reason and preach, of virtue. As, of this latter, conscience recognises the obligation, so intellect teaches the expediency, while taste contents herself with displaying the beauty: waging war with vice merely on the ground of its inconsistency with fitness, harmony, proportion—in a word with το χαλον.

An important condition of man's immortal nature is thus, plainly, the sense of the Beautiful. This it is which ministers to his delight in the manifold forms and colors and sounds and sentiments amid which he exists. And, just as the eyes of Amaryllis are repeated in the mirror, or the living lily in the lake, so is the mere *record* of these forms and colors and sounds and sentiments—so is their mere oral or written repetition a duplicate source of delight. But this repetition is not Poesy. He who shall merely sing with whatever rapture, in however harmonious strains, or with however vivid a truth of imitation, of the sights and sounds which greet him in common with all mankind—he, we say, has yet failed to prove his divine title. There is still a longing unsatisfied, which he has been impotent to fulfil. There is still a thirst unquenchable, which to allay he has shown us no crystal springs. This burning thirst belongs to the *immortal* essence of man's nature. It is equally a consequence and an indication of his perennial life. It is the desire of the moth for the star. It is not the mere appreciation of the beauty before us. It is a wild effort to reach the beauty above. It is a forethought of the loveliness to come. It is a passion to be satiated by no sublunary sights, or sounds, or sentiments, and the soul thus athirst strives to allay its fever in futile efforts at *creation*. Inspired with a prescient ecstasy of the beauty beyond the grave, it struggles by multiform novelty of combination among the things and thoughts of Time, to anticipate some portion of that loveliness whose very elements, perhaps, appertain solely to Eternity. And the result of such effort, on the part of souls fittingly constituted, is alone what mankind have agreed to denominate Poetry.

We say this with little fear of contradiction. Yet the spirit of our assertion must be more heeded than the letter. Mankind have *seemed* to define Poesy in a thousand, and in a thousand conflicting definitions. But the war is one only of words. Induction is as well applicable to this subject as to the most palpable and utilitarian; and by its sober processes we find that, in respect to compositions which have been really received as poems, the *imaginative*, or, more popularly, the creative portions *alone* have ensured them to be so received. Yet these works, on account of these portions, having once been so received and so named, it has happened, naturally and inevitably, that other portions totally unpoetic have not only come to be regarded by the popular voice as poetic, but have been made to serve as false standards of perfection, in the adjustment of other poetical claims. Whatever has been found in whatever has been received as a poem, has been blindly regarded as *ex statû* poetic. And this is a species of gross error which scarcely could have made its way into any less intangible topic. In fact that license which appertains to the Muse herself, it has been thought decorous, if not sagacious to indulge, in all examination of her character.

Poesy is thus seen to be a response—unsatisfactory it is true—but still in some measure a response, to a natural and irrepressible demand. Man being what he is, the time could never have been in which Poesy was not. Its first element is the thirst for supernal BEAUTY—a beauty which is not afforded the soul by any existing collocation of earth's forms—a beauty which, perhaps, *no possible* combination of these forms would fully produce. Its second element is the attempt to satisfy this thirst by *novel* combinations among those forms of beauty which already exist—or by novel combinations *of those combinations which our predecessors, toiling in chase of the same phantom, have already set in order*. We thus clearly deduce the *novelty*, the *originality*, the *invention*, the *imagination*, or lastly the *creation* of BEAUTY, (for the terms as here employed are synonimous) as the essence of all Poesy. Nor is this idea so much at variance with ordinary opinion as, at first sight, it may appear. A multitude of antique dogmas on this topic will be found, when divested of extrinsic speculation, to be easily resoluble into the definition now proposed. We do nothing more than present tangibly the vague clouds of the world's idea. We recognize the idea itself floating, unsettled, indefinite, in every attempt which has yet been made to circumscribe the conception of "Poesy" in words. A striking instance of this is observable in the fact that no definition exists, in which either "the beautiful," or some one of those qualities which we have above designated synonimously with "creation," has not been pointed out as the *chief* attribute of the Muse. "Invention," however, or "imagination," is by far more commonly insisted upon. The word ποιησις itself (creation) speaks volumes upon this point. Neither will it be amiss here to mention Count Bielfeld's definition of poetry as *"L'art d'exprimer les pensées par la fiction."* With this definition (of which the philosophy is profound to a certain extent) the German terms *Dichtkunst*, the art of fiction, and *Dichten*, to feign, which are used for "*poetry*" and "*to make verses*," are in full and remarkable accordance. It is, nevertheless, in the *combination* of the two omni-prevalent ideas that the novelty and, we believe, the force of our own proposition is to be found.

So far, we have spoken of Poesy as of an abstraction alone. As such, it is obvious that it may be applicable in various moods. The sentiment may develop itself in Sculpture, in Painting, in Music, or otherwise. But our present business is with its development in words—that development to which, in practical acceptation, the world has agreed to limit the term. And at this point there is one consideration which induces us to pause. We cannot make up our minds to admit (as some have admitted) the inessentiality of rhythm. On the contrary, the universality of its use in the earliest poetical efforts of all mankind would be sufficient to assure us, not merely of its congeniality with the Muse, or of its adaptation to her purposes, but of its elementary and indispensible importance. But here we must, perforce, content ourselves with mere suggestion; for this topic is of a character which would lead us too far. We have already spoken of Music as one of the moods of poetical development. It is in Music, perhaps, that the soul most nearly attains that end upon which we have commented—the creation of supernal beauty. It may be, indeed, that this august aim is here even partially or imperfectly attained, *in fact*. The *elements* of that beauty which is felt in sound, *may be* the mutual or common heritage of Earth and Heaven. In the soul's struggles at combination it is thus not impossible that a harp may strike notes not unfamiliar to the angels. And in this view the wonder may well be less that all attempts at defining the character or sentiment of the deeper musical impressions, has been found absolutely futile. Contenting ourselves, therefore, with the firm conviction, that music (in its modifications of rhythm and rhyme) is of so vast a moment in Poesy, as *never* to be neglected by him who is truly poetical—is of so mighty a force in furthering the great aim intended that he is mad who rejects its assistance—content with this idea we shall not pause to maintain its absolute essentiality, for the mere sake of rounding a definition. We will but add, at this point, that the highest possible development of the Poetical Sentiment is to be found in the union of song with music, in its popular sense. The old Bards and Minnesingers possessed, in the fullest perfection, the finest and truest elements of Poesy; and Thomas Moore, singing his own ballads, is but putting the final touch to their completion as poems.

To recapitulate, then, we would define in brief the Poetry of words as the *Rhythmical Creation of Beauty*. Beyond the limits of Beauty its province does not extend. Its sole arbiter is Taste. With the Intellect or with the Conscience it has only collateral relations. It has no dependence, unless incidentally, upon either Duty or *Truth*. That our definition will necessarily exclude much of what, through a supine toleration, has been hitherto ranked as poetical, is a matter which affords us not even momentary concern. We address but the thoughtful, and heed only their approval—with our own. If our suggestions are truthful, then "after many days" shall they be understood as truth, even though found in contradiction of *all* that has been hitherto so understood. If false shall we not be the first to bid them die?

We would reject, of course, all such matters as "Armstrong on Health," a revolting production; Pope's "Essay on Man," which may well be content with the title of an "Essay in Rhyme;" "Hudibras" and other merely humorous pieces. We do not gainsay the peculiar merits of either of these latter compositions—but deny them the position held. In a notice, month before last, of Brainard's Poems, we took occasion to show that the common use of a certain instrument, (rhythm) had tended, more than aught else, to confound humorous verse with poetry. The observation is now recalled to corroborate what we have just said in respect to the vast effect or force of melody in itself—an effect which could elevate into even momentary confusion with the highest efforts of mind, compositions such as are the greater number of satires or burlesques.

Of the poets who have appeared most fully instinct with the principles now developed, we may mention *Keats* as the most remarkable. He is the sole British poet who has never erred in his themes. Beauty is always his aim.

We have thus shown our ground of objection to the general *themes* of Professor Longfellow. In common with all who claim the sacred title of poet, he should limit his endeavors to the creation of novel moods of beauty, in form, in color, in sound, in sentiment; for over all this wide range has the poetry of words dominion. To what the world terms *prose* may be safely and properly left all else. The artist who doubts of his thesis, may always resolve his doubt by the single question—"might not this matter be as well or better handled in *prose*?" If it *may*, then is it no subject for the Muse. In the general acceptation of the term *Beauty* we are content to rest; being careful only to suggest that, in our peculiar views, it must be understood as inclusive of *the sublime*.

Of the pieces which constitute the present volume, there are not more than one or two thoroughly fulfilling the idea above proposed; although the volume as a whole is by no means so chargeable with didacticism as Mr. Longfellow's previous book. We would mention as poems *nearly true*, "The Village Blacksmith;" "The Wreck of the Hesperus" and especially "The Skeleton in Armor." In the first-mentioned we have the *beauty* of simple-mindedness as a genuine thesis; and this thesis is inimitably handled until the concluding stanza, where the spirit of legitimate poesy is aggrieved in the pointed antithetical deduction of a *moral* from what has gone before. In "The Wreck of the Hesperus" we have the *beauty* of child-like confidence and innocence, with that of the father's stern courage and affection. But, with slight exception, those particulars of the storm here detailed are not poetic subjects. Their thrilling *horror* belongs to prose, in which it could be far more effectively discussed, as Professor Longfellow may assure himself at any moment by experiment. There *are* points of a tempest which afford the loftiest and truest poetical themes—points in which pure beauty is found, or, better still, beauty heightened into the sublime, by terror. But when we read, among other similar things, that

> The salt sea was frozen on her breast,
> The salt tears in her eyes,

we feel, if not positive disgust, at least a chilling sense of the inappropriate. In the "Skeleton in Armor" we find a pure and perfect thesis artistically treated. We find the beauty of bold courage and self-confidence, of love and maiden devotion, of reckless adventure, and finally of life-contemning grief. Combined with all this we have numerous *points* of beauty apparently insulated, but all aiding the main effect or impression. The heart is stirred, and the mind does not lament its malinstruction. The metre is simple, sonorous, well-balanced and fully adapted to the subject. Upon the whole, there are fewer truer poems than this. It has but one defect—an important one. The prose remarks prefacing the narrative are really *nec-*

essary. But every work of art should contain within itself all that is requisite for its own comprehension. And this remark is especially true of the ballad. In poems of magnitude the mind of the reader is not, at all times, enabled to include, in one comprehensive survey, the proportions and proper adjustment of the whole. He is pleased, if at all, with particular passages; and the sum of his pleasure is compounded of the sums of the pleasurable sentiments inspired by these individual passages in the progress of perusal. But, in pieces of less extent, the pleasure is *unique*, in the proper acceptation of this term—the understanding is employed, without difficulty, in the contemplation of the picture *as a whole*; and thus its effect will depend, in great measure, upon the perfection of its finish, upon the nice adaptation of its constituent parts, and especially, upon what is rightly termed by Schlegel *the unity or totality of interest*. But the practice of prefixing explanatory passages is utterly at variance with such unity. By the prefix, we are either put in possession of the subject of the poem; or some hint, historic fact, or suggestion, is thereby afforded, not included in the body of the piece, which, without the hint, is incomprehensible. In the latter case, while perusing the poem, the reader must revert, in mind at least, to the prefix, for the necessary explanation. In the former, the poem being a mere paraphrase of the prefix, the interest is divided between the prefix and the paraphrase. In either instance the totality of effect is destroyed.

Of the other original poems in the volume before us, there is none in which the aim of instruction, or *truth*, has not been too obviously substituted for the legitimate aim, *beauty*. In our last number, we took occasion to say that a didactic moral might be happily made the *under-current* of a poetical theme, and, in "Burton's Magazine," some two years since, we treated this point at length, in a review of Moore's "Alciphron;" but the moral thus conveyed is invariably an ill effect when obtruding beyond the upper current of the thesis itself. Perhaps the worst specimen of this obtrusion is given us by our poet in "Blind Bartimeus" and the "Goblet of Life," where, it will be observed that the *sole* interest of the upper current of meaning depends upon its relation or reference to the under. What we read upon the surface would be *vox et preterea nihil* in default of the moral beneath. The Greek *finales* of "Blind Bartimeus" are an affectation altogether inexcusable. What the small, second-hand, Gibbon-ish pedantry of Byron introduced, is unworthy the imitation of Longfellow.

Of the translations we scarcely think it necessary to speak at all. We regret that our poet will persist in busying himself about such matters. *His* time might be better employed in original conception. Most of these versions are marked with the error upon which we have commented. This error is in fact, essentially Germanic. "The Luck of Edenhall," however, is a truly beautiful poem; and we say this with all that deference which the opinion of the "Democratic Review" demands. This composition appears to us *one of the very finest*. It has all the free, hearty, *obvious* movement of the true ballad-legend. The greatest force of language is combined in it with the richest imagination, acting in its most legitimate province. Upon the whole, we prefer it even to the "Sword-Song" of Körner. The pointed moral with which it terminates is so exceedingly natural—so perfectly fluent from the incidents—that we have hardly heart to pronounce it in ill taste. We may observe of this ballad, in conclusion, that its subject is more *physical* than is usual in Germany. Its images are rich rather in physical than in moral beauty. And this tendency, in Song, is the true one. It is chiefly, if we are not mistaken—it is chiefly amid forms of physical loveliness (we use the word *forms* in its widest sense as embracing modifications of sound and color) that the soul seeks the realization of its dreams of BEAUTY. It is to her demand in this sense especially, that the poet, who is wise, will most frequently and most earnestly respond.

"The Children of the Lord's Supper" is, beyond doubt, a true and most beautiful poem in great part, while, in some particulars, it is too metaphysical to have any pretension to the name. In our last number, we objected, briefly, to its metre—the ordinary Latin or Greek Hexameter—dactyls and spondees at random, with a spondee in conclusion. We maintain that the Hexameter can never be introduced into our language, from the nature of that language itself. This rhythm demands, *for English ears*, a preponderance of natural spondees. Our tongue has few. Not only does the Latin and Greek, with the Swedish, and some others, abound in them; but the Greek and Roman ear had become reconciled (why or how is unknown) to the reception of artificial spondees—that is to say, spondaic words formed partly of one word and partly of another, or from an excised part of one word. In short the ancients were content to read *as they scanned*, or nearly so. It may be safely prophesied that we shall never do this; and thus we shall never admit English Hexameters. The attempt to introduce them, after the repeated failures of Sir Philip Sidney, and others, is, perhaps, somewhat discreditable to the scholarship of Professor Longfellow. The "Democratic Review," in saying that he has triumphed over difficulties in this rhythm, has been deceived, it is evident, by the facility with which some of these verses may be read. In glancing over the poem, we do not observe a single verse which can be read, *to English ears, as a Greek Hexameter*. There are many, however, which can be well read as mere English dactylic verses; such, for example, as the well known lines of Byron, commencing

Know ye the | land where the | cypress and | myrtle.

These lines (although full of irregularities) are, in their perfection, formed of three dactyls and a cæsura—just as if we should cut short the initial verse of the Bucolics thus—

Tityre | tu patu | læ recu | bans—

The "myrtle," at the close of Byron's line, is a double rhyme, and must be understood as one syllable.

Now a great number of Professor Longfellow's Hexameters are merely these dactylic lines, *continued for two feet*. For example—

Whispered the | race of the | flowers and | merry on | balancing | branches.

In this example, also, "branches," which is a double ending, must be regarded as the cæsura, or one syllable, of which alone it has the force.

As we have already alluded, in one or two regards, to a notice of these poems which appeared in the "Democratic Review," we may as well here proceed with some few further comments upon the article in question—with whose general tenor we are happy to agree.

The Review speaks of "Maidenhood" as a poem, "not to be understood but at the expense of more time and trouble than a song can justly claim." We are scarcely less surprised at this opinion from Mr. Langtree than we were at the condemnation of "The Luck of Edenhall."

"Maidenhood" is faulty, it appears to us, only on the score of its theme, which is somewhat didactic. Its *meaning* seems simplicity itself. A maiden on the verge of womanhood, hesitating to enjoy life (for which she has a strong appetite) through a false idea of duty, is bidden to fear nothing, having purity of heart as her lion of Una.

What Mr. Langtree styles "an unfortunate peculiarity" in Mr. Longfellow, resulting from "adherence to a false system" has really been always regarded by us as one of his idiosyncratic merits. "In each poem," says the critic, "he has but *one* idea which, in the progress of his song is gradually unfolded, and at last reaches its full development in the concluding lines; this singleness of thought might lead a harsh critic to suspect intellectual barrenness." It leads *us*, individually, only to a full sense of the artistical power and knowledge of the poet. We confess that now, for the first time, we hear unity of conception objected to as a defect. But Mr. Langtree seems to have fallen into the singular error of supposing the poet to have absolutely *but one idea* in each of his ballads. Yet how "one idea" can be "gradually unfolded" without other ideas, is, to us, a mystery of mysteries. Mr. Longfellow, very properly, has but one *leading* idea which forms the basis of his poem; but to the aid and development of this one there are innumerable others, of which the rare excellence is, that all are in keeping, that none could be well omitted, that each tends to the one general effect. It is unnecessary to say another word upon this topic.

In speaking of "Excelsior," Mr. Langtree (are we wrong in attributing the notice to his very forcible pen?) seems to labor under some similar misconception. "It carries along with it," says he, "a false moral which greatly diminishes its merit in our eyes. The great merit of a picture, whether made with the pencil or pen, is its *truth*; and this merit does not belong to Mr. Longfellow's sketch. Men of genius may and probably do, meet with greater difficulties in their struggles with the world than their fellow-men who are less highly gifted; but their power of overcoming obstacles is proportionably greater, and the result of their laborious suffering is not death but immortality."

That the chief merit of a picture is its *truth*, is an assertion deplorably erroneous. Even in Painting which is, more essentially than Poetry, a mimetic art, the proposition cannot be sustained. Truth is not even *the aim*. Indeed it is curious to observe how very slight a degree of truth is sufficient to satisfy the mind, which acquiesces in the absence of numerous essentials in the thing depicted. An outline frequently stirs the spirit more pleasantly than the most elaborate picture. We need only refer to the compositions of Flaxman and of Retzsch. Here all details are omitted—nothing can be farther from *truth*. Without even color the most thrilling effects are produced. In statues we are rather pleased than disgusted with *the want of the eyeball*. The hair of the Venus de Medicis *was gilded*. Truth indeed! The grapes of Zeuxis as well as the curtain of Parrhasius were received as indisputable evidence of the truthful ability of these artists—but they were not even *classed among their pictures*. If truth is the highest aim of either Painting or Poesy, then Jan Steen was a greater artist than Angelo, and Crabbe is a more noble poet than Milton.

But we have not quoted the observation of Mr. Langtree to deny its philosophy; our design was simply to show that he has misunderstood the poet. "Excelsior" has not even a remote tendency to the interpretation assigned it by the critic. It depicts the *earnest upward impulse of the soul*—an impulse not to be subdued even in Death. Despising danger, resisting pleasure, the youth, bearing the banner inscribed *"Excelsior!"* (higher still!) struggles through all difficulties to an Alpine summit. Warned to be content with the elevation attained, his cry is still *"Excelsior!"* And, even in falling dead on the highest pinnacle, his cry is *still "Excelsior!"* There is yet an immortal height to be surmounted—an ascent in Eternity. The poet holds in view the idea of never-ending *progress*. That he is misunderstood is rather the misfortune of Mr. Langtree than the fault of Mr. Longfellow. There is an old adage about the difficulty of one's furnishing an auditor both with matter to be comprehended and brains for its comprehension.

Graham's Magazine, April 1842

Longfellow's *Waif*, with an Exchange.

OBVIOUSLY, this volume is a collection of some few of the prettiest shells that have been thrown ashore by the poetic ocean; but, looking behind this idea, we see that Mr. Longfellow's real design has been to make a book of his " waifs," and his own late compositions, conjointly; since these late compositions are not enough in number to make a book of themselves:—an ingenious thought, too, with which no one can possibly quarrel. There are fifty brief poems in all, exclusive of the Proem which is professedly by the compiler; and, of these fifty, the seventeen attributed to Anonymous (a person who writes more and better than any man living,) we take to be the work of him who composed *Outre-Mer*.

Of a book put together purposely at random, we also at random shall be forced to speak—unless we go violently out of our way to get up principles of generalization for which no one would be at the trouble of thanking us.

Let us mention—let us pronounce reverently, yet lovingly—some half dozen of the great *names* which embellish the compilation:—Shelley, Herrick, Marvel, Browning, Hood, and Horace Smith:—there are others, too, nearly, if not equally, eminent. Of course, then, we mean a compliment worth at least a bow with the hand upon the heart, when we say that the Proem is the worthiest composition in the volume. It is a *singular*—a remarkable poem, and in no particular more remarkable than in this—that its particular excellence arises from what is, generically, a gross demerit. There is no error, as a general rule, more certainly fatal to a poem than defective *rhythm*;—but in this case the cautious, skillfully planned and dexterously executed *slip-shod-iness* is so thoroughly in unison with the *nonchalant* air of the thoughts— which, again, are so capitally applicable to the thing done—

(a mere introduction of other people's fancies)—that the effect of the looseness of metre becomes palpable, and we see at once that here is a case in which to be *correct* would have been to be inartistic.

How willingly would we quote *all* the lines were it possible with our limited space—but here are three of the quatrains:

> I see the light of the village
>   Gleam through the rain and the mist,
> And a feeling of sadness comes o'er me
>   That my soul cannot resist;
>
> A feeling of sadness and longing
>   That is not akin to pain,
> And *resembles sorrow only*
>   *As the mist resembles the rain.*
>
> *   *   *
>
> And the night shall be filled with music,
>   And the cares that infest the day
> Shall fold their tents, like the Arabs,
>   *And as silently steal away.*

Now, if any man fancy that these lines are scansible, we say *no*. They are referable to no true principles of rhythm. The general idea is that of a succession of dactyls; yet, not only is this idea confounded with an idea of anapæsts, but this succession is improperly interrupted at all points—improperly, because by unequivalent feet. The partial prosaicism thus brought about, however, without any interference with the mere melody, becomes a beauty, solely through the nicety of its adaptation to the whole tone of the poem, and of this tone again to the matter in hand. In his keen sense of this adaptation (which conveys the notion of what is vaguely termed "ease") the reader so far loses sight of the rhythmical imperfection, that he can only be convinced of its existence by treating, in the same metre, a subject of different tone.

The *poetic* beauty of the passages italicised will enchant all who read. We forbear to comment on them in full, for no other reason than that we should never have done. The first quatrain of this poem, nevertheless, embodies a fault of illus-

tration which Mr. Longfellow often commits;—let us quote
the verses:

> The day is done, and the darkness
>   Falls from the wings of Night,
> As a feather is wafted downward
>   From an eagle in his flight.

The *single* feather is imperfectly illustrative of the omni-
prevalent darkness—but our more especial objection is to the
likening of the falling of one feather to the falling of another.—Night is personified as a bird, and darkness (the
feather of this bird) falls from it—how?—as another feather
falls from another bird. Why, it does this *of course*. The illustration is identical—that is to say, null. It has no more force
than an identical proposition in Logic.

We have a few words more to say of "The Waif," but we
may as well say them to-morrow—a single paragraph, however, in the meantime, about a point which is scarcely worth
mentioning, after all.

How does it happen— *not*, we trust, through affectation—
that the name of each author in this volume is carefully omitted from its proper place, at the head of his poem, to be as carefully deposited in the index?—so that the inquisitive reader,
(and *all* readers of fine compositions are profoundly inquisitive about their paternity,) is forced to spend twice or thrice
as much time in turning the leaves backward and forward, as
in perusing what is so beautifully printed upon them. We ask
this question, not by any means in the way of a sneer—a
thing which went out of date with Childe Harold—but simply and positively because we have a liking for good enigmas,
and take this to be one of the best of its species, on the
ground that the soundest nut is always the most difficult to
crack. For ourselves, we have given it up in despair.

———

LONGFELLOW'S WAIF—*A few more words for and against
it.*—By far the most vivid and vigorous, if not in all respects
the most commendable poem in this collection, is the "Bridge
of Sighs," by Hood—a man whose supremeness of fancy is
often pardonably mistaken for imagination itself. Was ever
anything on earth more full of the fantastic in pathos, the

fantastic in the picturesque, the fantastic in sublimity, and the fantastic in sarcasm, than these lines which occur in the description of a woman found drowned?

> Touch her not scornfully!
> Think of her mournfully,
>   Gently and humanly—
> *Not of the stains of her—*
> *All that remains of her*
>   *Now, is pure womanly.*
>
> Who was her father?
>   Who was her mother?
> Had she a sister?
>   Had she a brother?
> Was there a dearer one
> Still, and a nearer one
>   Yet, than all other?
>
> Alas, for the rarity
> Of Christian charity
>   Under the sun!
> O, it was pitiful!
> Near a whole city full
>   Home she had none.
>
> Where the lamps quiver
> So far in the river,
>   With many a light
> From window and casement
> From garret to basement
> She stood, *with amazement*,
>   Houseless by night!
>
> The bleak wind of March
>   Made her tremble and shiver;
> But not the dark arch
>   Or the black flowing river:
> Mad from life's history
> Glad to death's mystery
>   Swift to be hurled—
> *Anywhere, anywhere,*
>   *Out of the world!*

> In she plunged boldly—
> No matter how coldly
>   The rough river ran—
> Over the brink of it.
> *Picture it— think of it,*
>   *Dissolute man!*
> *Dive in it— drink of it*
>   *Then, if you can!*

These extracts, rich as they are, will convey a very fragmentary, and therefore a very feeble conception of the whole poem. Upon reading it, the first question occurring to an American who is himself a poet, will be—"How long has this been published?"—and if the answer be "many months," he will be lost in wonder that he has not so much as heard of it before. Our taste—our critical feelings are in sad condition indeed, when such jewels as this are fairly made part and parcel of a volume of "waifs." "The Bridge of Sighs" should have been received all over the world at once, and *with acclamation*.

From the "Hymn to the Flowers," by Horace Smith, we quote only the four noble lines which conclude it:

> Were I, O God! in churchless lands remaining,
>   Far from all teachers and from all divines,
> My soul would find, in flowers of thy ordaining,
>   Priests, sermons, shrines.

"April" (anonymous) terminates with one of those striking, yet now and then objectionable images which are the *forte* of Mr. Longfellow.

> But yet, behold! *abrupt and loud,*
>   Comes down the glittering rain—
> The farewell of a passing cloud—
>   *The fringes of her train.*

This puts us in mind of the "Night's skirts all fringed with light from the celestial walls." The "abrupt and loud" is Homeric.

We are rejoiced to find here Lovelace's *piquant* lines to Althea;—Mrs. Blackwood's "Lament of the Irish Emigrant;" and the inimitable "Kulnazatz my rein-deer."

The commencement of the "Lily of Nithsdale" is exquisite:

> She's gane to dwell in Heaven, my lassie,
>   She's gane to dwell in Heaven!
> *Ye're owre pure, quo' the voice of God,*
>   *For dwelling out o' Heaven.*

The *owre* and the *o'* of the two last verses, however, should be Anglicised. The Deity at least, should be supposed to speak so as to be understood—although we are aware that a folio has been written, to demonstrate broad Scotch as the language of Adam and Eve in Paradise.

We copy in full the "Death-Bed," by Hood, first, because of its intrinsic excellence—secondly, with the view of pointing out a parallel poem.

> We watched her breathing through the night,
>   Her breathing soft and low,
> As in her breast the wave of life
>   Kept heaving to and fro.
>
> So silently we seemed to speak,
>   So slowly moved about,
> *As we had lent her half our powers*
>   *To eke her being out.*
>
> Our very hopes belied our fears;
>   Our fears our hopes belied;
> *We thought her dying when she slept,*
>   *And sleeping when she died.*
>
> *For when the morn came dim and sad,*
>   *And chill with early showers,*
> *Her quiet eye-lids closed:—she had*
>   *Another morn than ours.*

The parallel (which we copy from Mr. Griswold's large book) runs thus:

> Her sufferings ended with the day,
>   Yet lived she at its close,
> And breathed the long long night away
>   In statue-like repose;

> But when the sun in all its state
> Illumed the eastern skies,
> She passed through Glory's morning gate,
> And walked in paradise.

Having fairly transcribed the two poems (about the respective dates of which we knew nothing) we have only to remark, as quietly as we can, that *somebody is a thief.* It is well said, however, by Leigh Hunt, that really beautiful thoughts are always sure to be spoiled in the stealing:—and if there is any spoiling in *this* case, it most assuredly is not upon the part of Mr. Hood.

We conclude our notes on the "Waif," with the observation that, although full of beauties, it is infected with a *moral taint*—or is this a mere freak of our own fancy? We shall be pleased if it be so;—but there *does* appear, in this exquisite little volume, a very careful avoidance of all American poets who may be supposed especially to interfere with the claims of Mr. Longfellow. These men Mr. Longfellow can continuously *imitate* (*is* that the word?) and yet never even incidentally commend.

———

LONGFELLOW.—We are willing to take any position to serve our friends, and if, by chance, we play the antagonist to shew another's "skill of fence" in his behalf, we trust not to be believed less his friend, after the joust is over. The criticisms on the "Waif" which lately appeared in this paper, were written in our office by an able though very critical hand, and we give the following reply to them from as able a friend of Longfellow's in Boston. We add also the *reply* to the *"reply,"* and declare the field open. We judge the poet by ourself when we presume that he prefers *rubbing* to *rust*—sure of being more brightened than fretted.

BOSTON, Jan. 15, 1845.

TO THE EDITORS OF THE EVENING MIRROR.

Your papers of January 13th and 14th contain communications on the subject of Mr. Longfellow's "Waif," in which are one or two matters deserving notice at the hands of his friends. With the literary strictures upon the poem I have nothing to do, as that is a part of the public's privilege, and every man who prints a poem must submit himself to the ordeal of criticism. It may be observed, however, in passing, that the writer does not seem to be aware of the distinction between rhythm and metre, and from not heeding that distinction, has tried the poem in question by a false standard. But he is wholly mistaken in his assertion, that the editor is responsible for the anonymous pieces, or any of them, as their author. Not one of them was written by him. But my principal concern, however, is with the sting in the tail of the second communication, in which Mr. Longfellow is charged with omitting, from discreditable motives, any extracts from American poets, though he continuously imitates some of them. This is no light accusation; and is one against which his friends feel bound to enter their most emphatic protest. Were Mr. Longfellow wholly unknown to me, my reply to such a charge would be, that the editor of such a compilation had a perfect right to select or reject, as he saw fit, and from no better reason than Corporal Nym's, that such was his humor; and that any accusation, founded upon the absence of any piece or class of pieces, was ungenerous and uncalled for. But from long and intimate knowledge of Mr. Longfellow, I pronounce the charge wholly untrue. He is remarkable, among his friends, for his warm and generous commendation of the poetical efforts of his contemporaries. He is the least fastidious and the most genial of critics. He is even too tolerant of mediocrity. If it be asked, why has he not given public demonstration of this kindness of spirit towards his poetical brethren, the answer is obvious. He is a poet himself, and addresses the public in that capacity, and not as a critic. He is not called upon to distribute praise or blame among those who are running the same race with himself, and there would be an obvious impropriety in his so doing. The charge of habitually imitating other American poets touches Mr. Longfellow in his public character as a poet, and not his personal character as a man, and therefore requires no especial reply from his friends.

H.

Post-Notes by the Critic.—If ever a man had cause to ejaculate, "Heaven preserve me from my friends!" it is Mr. Longfellow.

My 'literary strictures' on the poem consisted, generally, in the assertion, that it is the best of a collection of poems, one of which, at least, 'should have been received with acclamation.'

I defy Prof. Longfellow and his friend conjointly, to say a rational word in defence of the 'identical illustration' to which, as gently as possible, I objected.

I deny that I misconceive either rhythm or metre—call for the proofs—and assert that Prof. Longfellow knows very little about either. If the proofs are called for *here* I will give them.

Mem: it is by no means impossible, however, that on these points, I may err. I may know nothing about rhythm—for I remember (with regret) that it was precisely the *rhythm* of Mr. Longfellow in the proem, which elicited my unqualified applause.

I did not dispute Mr. L.'s *'right'* to construct his book as he thought proper. I reserve to myself the right of thinking what I choose of the construction.

I mentioned my idea that the anonymous contributions were perhaps, in general, Mr. Longfellow's, because I thought so, and because every body thought so. If they are not—what then? Does the friend, however, mean to persist in the assertion, that *not one* of them is Mr. L.'s?

As 'the charge of habitually imitating other American poets requires no especial reply'—it shall surely rest undisturbed by any reply of mine.

It seems to me that the whole state of the case may be parralleled thus:

A accosts B, with—"My dear friend, in common with all mankind, and the angels, I regard you as a demi-god. Your equal is not to be found in the country which is proud to claim you as a son. You are glorious—you are great—you are delightful; the fact is, you are transcendentally so, and therefore I lack words to express my sense of your perfection,—but, permit me! there is a very—a *very* little speck of dust on the extreme end of your nose—oblige yourself and your friends by brushing it away." "Sir," replies B, " what you have asserted is wholly untrue." [The greater part of it *was*.] "I consider you a malignant critic, and wish to have nothing further to do with you—for, know that there *are* spots upon the sun, but my proboscis is a thing without spot!"

New York Weekly Mirror, January 25, 1845

Imitation—Plagiarism—Mr. Poe's Reply to the Letter of Outis—A large account of a small matter—A voluminous history of the little Longfellow war.

IN REPLYING to the letter signed *"Outis,"* which appears in last Saturday's "Weekly Mirror", I find it advisable, for reasons which will be obvious as I proceed, to dismiss for the present the editorial " we."

For the "Evening Mirror" of January 14, before my editorial connection with the "Broadway Journal," I furnished a brief criticism on Professor Longfellow's "Waif."

In the course of my observations, I collated a poem called *"The* Death-Bed," and written by Hood, with one by Mr. Aldrich, entitled *"A* Death-Bed." The criticism ended thus:

We conclude our notes on the "Waif," with the observation that, although full of beauties, it is infected with a *moral taint*—or is this a mere freak of our own fancy? We shall be pleased if it be so;—but there *does* appear, in this little volume, a very careful avoidance of all American poets who may be supposed especially to interfere with the claims of Mr. Longfellow. These men Mr. Longfellow can continuously *imitate* (*is* that the word?) and yet never even incidentally commend.

Much discussion ensued. A friend of Mr. Longfellow's penned a defence which had at least the merit of being thoroughly impartial; for it defended Mr. L., not only from the one-tenth of very moderate disapproval in which I had indulged, but from the nine-tenths of my enthusiastic admiration into the bargain. The fact is, if I was *not* convinced that in ninety-nine hundredths of all that I had written about Mr. Longfellow I was decidedly in the wrong, at least it was no fault of Mr. Longfellow's very luminous friend.

This well-intended defence was published in the "Mirror" with a few words of preface by Mr. Willis, and of postscript by myself.

Still dissatisfied, Mr. L., through a second friend, addressed to Mr. Willis an expostulatory letter, of which the Mirror printed only the following portion:—

It has been asked, perhaps, why Lowell was neglected in this collection? Might it not as well be asked why Bryant, Dana and Halleck were neglected? The answer is obvious to any one who candidly considers the character of the collection. It professed to be, according to the Pröem, from the humbler poets; and it was intended to embrace pieces that were anonymous, or which were not easily accessible to the general reader—the *waifs* and *estrays* of literature. To put anything of Lowell's, for example, into a collection of *waifs* would be a particular liberty with pieces which are all collected and christened.

Not yet content, or misunderstanding the tenor of some of the wittily-*put* comments which accompanied the quotation, the aggrieved poet, through one of the two friends as before, or perhaps through a third, finally prevailed on the good nature of Mr. Willis to publish an explicit declaration of his disagreement with "*all* the disparagement of Longfellow" which had appeared in the criticism in question.

Now when we consider that many of the points of censure made by me in this *critique* were absolutely as plain as the nose upon Mr. Longfellow's face—that it was impossible to gainsay them—that we defied him and his coadjutors to say a syllable in reply to them—and that they held their tongues and not a syllable said—when we consider all this, I say, then the satire of the "*all*" in Mr. Willis' manifesto becomes apparent at once. Mr. Longfellow did not see it; and I presume his friends did not see it. I did. In my mind's eye it expanded itself thus;—"My dear Sir, or Sirs, what will you have? You are an insatiable set of cormorants, it is true; but if you will only let me know what you desire, I will satisfy you, if I die for it. Be quick!—merely say what it is you wish me to admit, and (for the sake of getting rid of you) I will admit it upon the spot. Come! I will grant at once that Mr. Longfellow is Jupiter Tonans, and that his three friends are the Graces, or the Furies, whichever you please. As for a fault to be found with either of you, *that* is impossible, and I say so. I disagree with *all*—with every syllable of the disparagement that ever has been whispered against you up to this date, and (not to stand upon trifles) with all that ever *shall* be whispered against you henceforward, forever and forever. May I hope at length that these assurances will be sufficient?"

But if Mr. Willis really hoped anything of the kind he was mistaken.

In the meantime Mr. Briggs in this paper—in the "Broadway Journal"—did me the honor of taking me to task for what he supposed to be my insinuations against Mr. Aldrich.

My reply (in the "Mirror") prefaced by a few words from Mr. Willis, ran as follows:

Much interest has been given in our literary circles of late to the topic of plagiarism.

About a month ago a very eminent critic connected with this paper, took occasion to point out a *parallelism* between certain lines of Thomas Hood, and certain others which appeared in the collection of American poetry edited by Mr. Griswold. Transcribing the passages, he ventured the assertion that "*somebody* is a thief." (He goes on below to speak for himself.)

The matter had been nearly forgotten, if not altogether so, when a "good-natured friend" of the American author (whose name had by us never been mentioned) considered it advisable to re-collate the passages, with the view of convincing the public (and himself) that no plagiarism is chargeable to the party of whom he thinks it chivalrous to be the "good-natured friend."

For our own part should *we* ever be guilty of an indiscretion of this kind, we deprecate all aid from our "good natured friends"—but in the mean time it is rendered necessary that once again we give publicity to the collation of poems in question. Mr. Hood's lines run thus:

We watched her breathing through the night,
    Her breathing soft and low,
As in her breast the wave of life
    Kept heaving to and fro.

So silently we seemed to speak,
    So slowly moved about,
As we had lent her half our powers
    To eke her being out.

Our very hope belied our fears;
    Our fears our hope belied;
We thought her dying when she slept,
    And sleeping when she died.

But when the morn came dim and sad,
    And chill with early showers,
Her quiet eyelids closed;—she had
    Another morn than ours.

Mr. Aldrich's thus:—

Her sufferings ended with the day,
    Yet lived she at its close,
And breathed the long, long night away
    In statue-like repose;

But when the sun in all its state
    Illumed the eastern skies,
She passed through Glory's morning gate,
    And walked in paradise.

And here, to be sure, we might well leave a decision in the
case to the verdict of common sense. But since the "Broadway
Journal" insists upon the "no resemblance," we are constrained to point out especially where our supposed similarity
lies. In the first place, then, the subject in both pieces is *death*.
In the second it is the death of a woman. In the third, it is
the death of a woman *tranquilly* dying. In the fourth, it is the
death of a woman who lies tranquilly *throughout the night*. In
the fifth it is the death of a woman whose "*breathing* soft and
low is watched through the night" in the one instance and
who "*breathed* the long long night away in statue-like repose"

in the other. In the sixth place, in both poems this woman dies just at daybreak. In the seventh place, dying just at daybreak, this woman in both cases, steps directly into Paradise. In the eighth place all these identities of circumstance are related in identical rhythms. In the ninth place these identical rhythms are arranged in identical metres; and, in the tenth place, these identical rhythms and metres are constructed into identical stanzas.

At this point the matter rested for a fortnight, when a fourth friend of Mr. Longfellow took up the cudgels for him and Mr. Aldrich conjointly, in another communication to the "Mirror." I copy it in full.

PLAGIARISM

DEAR WILLIS—Fair play is a jewel, and I hope you will let us have it. I have been much amused, by some of the efforts of your critical friend, to convict Longfellow of imitation, and Aldrich and others, of plagiarism. What *is* plagiarism? And what constitutes a good ground for the charge? Did no two men ever think alike without stealing one from the other? or, thinking alike, did no two men ever use the same, or similar words, to convey the thoughts, and that, without any communication with each other? To deny it would be absurd. It is a thing of every day occurrence.

Some years ago, a letter was written from some part of New England, describing one of those scenes, not very common during what is called "the January thaw," when the snow, mingled with rain, and freezing as it falls, forms a perfect covering of ice upon every object. The storm clears away suddenly, and the moon comes up. The letter proceeds— *"every tree and shrub, as far as the eye can reach, of pure transparent glass—a perfect garden of moving, waving, breathing chrystals.   *   *   *   Every tree is a diamond chandelier, with a whole constellation of stars clustering to every socket,"* &c. This letter was laid away where such things usually are, in a private drawer, and did not see the light for many years. But the very next autumn brought out, among the splendid annuals got up in the country, a beautiful poem from Whittier, describing the same, or rather a similar scene, in which is this line

"The trees, like chrystal chandeliers,"

was put in italics by every reviewer in the land, for the exceeding beauty of the imagery. Now *the letter* was written, probably about the same time with the *poem*, though the poem was not published till nearly a year after.—The writers were not, and never have been, acquainted with each other, and neither could possibly have seen the work of the other before writing. Now, was there any plagiarism here? Yet there are plenty of *"identities."* The author of the letter, when urged some years after, to have it published, consented very reluctantly, through fear that *he* should be charged with theft; and, very probably, the charge has been made, though I have never seen it.

May not this often occur? What is more natural? Images are not created, but suggested. And why not the same images, when the circumstances are precisely the same, to different minds? Perhaps your critic will reply, that the case is different after one of the compositions is published. How so? Does he, or you, or anybody read everything that is published? I am a great admirer, and a general reader of poetry. But, by what accident I do not know, I had never seen the beautiful lines of Hood, till your critical friend brought them to my notice in the Mirror. It is certainly possible that Aldrich had not seen them several years ago—and more than probable that Hood had not seen Aldrich's. Yet your friend affects great sympathy for both, in view of their better compunctions of conscience, for their literary piracies.

But, after all, wherein does the real resemblance between these two compositions consist? Mr. —— I had almost named him, finds nearly a dozen points of resemblance. But when he includes rhythm, metre and stanza among the dozen, he only shows a bitter resolution to make out a case, and not a disposition to do impartial justice. Surely the critic himself who is one of our finest *poets*, does not mean to deny that these mere externals are the common property of all bards. He does not feel it necessary to strike out a new stanza, or to invent new feet and measures, whenever he would clothe his "breathing thoughts in words that burn."

Again, it is not improbable that, within the period of time since these two writers, Hood and Aldrich, came on the stage, ten thousand *females* have *died*, and *died tranquilly*, and *died just at day-break*, and that *after passing a tranquil night*, and, so dying, were supposed by their friends to have passed at once to a better world, a *morning in heaven*. The poets are both describing an actual, and not an imaginary occurrence. And here—including those before-mentioned, which are common property—are *nine* of the critic's *identities*, which go to make up the evidence of plagiarism. The last six, it requires no stretch of the imagination to suppose, they might each have seen and noticed separately. The most of them, one other poet at least, *has* noticed, many years ago, in a beautiful poem on these words of the angel to the wrestling Jacob— "Let me go, for the day breaketh." Wonder if Hood ever saw that?

The few remaining "identities" are, to my mind, sufficiently disposed of by what I have already said. I confess I was not able, until the appearance of the critic's second paper, in which he brought them out specially, "marked, numbered, and labelled," to perceive the resemblance on which the grave charge of literary piracy, and moral dishonesty of the meanest kind was based. In view of all the glaring improbabilities of such a case, a critic should be very slow to make such a charge. I say *glaring improbabilities*, for it seems to me that no circumstantial evidence could be sufficient to secure a verdict of *theft* in such a case. Look at it. A man, who aspires to fame, who seeks the esteem and praise of the world, and lives upon his reputation, as his vital element, attempts to win his object—how? By stealing, in open day, the finest passages, the most beautiful thoughts (no others are worth stealing) and the rarest images of another, and claiming them as his own; and that too, when he knows that every competitor for fame, and every critical tribunal in the world, as well as the real owner, will be ready to *identify* the borrowed plumes in a moment, and cry him down as a *thief*. A madman, an idiot, if he were capable of such an achievement, might do it, but no other. A rogue may steal what he can conceal in his pocket, or his chest—but one must be utterly *non compos*, to steal a splendid shawl, or a magnificent plume, which had been admired by thousands for its singular beauty, for the purpose of sporting it in Broadway. In nine hundred and ninety-nine cases of a thousand, such charges are absurd, and indicate rather the carping littleness of the critic, than the delinquency of his victim.

Pray did you ever think the worse of Dana because your friend, John Neal, charged him with pirating upon Paul Allen, and Bryant too, in his poem of "THE DYING RAVEN?" or of yourself, because the same friend thought he had detected you in the very act of stealing from Pinckney, and Miss Francis, now Mrs. Child? Surely not. Every body knows that John Neal wishes to be supposed to have read every thing that ever was written, and never have forgotten any thing. He delights, therefore, in showing up such resemblances.

And now—for the matter of Longfellow's imitations— In what do they consist? The critic is not very specific in this charge. Of what kind are they? Are they imitations of thought? Why not call them *plagiarisms* then, and show them up? Or are they only verbal imitations of style? Perhaps *this* is one of them, in his poem on the *"Sea Weed."*

> ———"*drifting, drifting, drifting*
> On the shifting
> Currents of the restless main."

resembling, in form and collocation only, a line in a beautiful and very powerful poem of MR. EDGAR A. POE. (Write it rather EDGAR, a *Poet*, and then it is right to a T.) I have not the poem before me, and have forgotten its title. But he is describing a magnificent intellect in ruins, if I remember rightly—and, speaking of the eloquence of its better days, represents it as

> ———"*flowing, flowing, flowing*
> Like a river."

Is this what the critic means? Is it *such* imitations as this that he alludes to? If not, I am at fault, either in my reading of Longfellow, or in my general familiarity with the American

Poets. If this *be* the kind of imitation referred to, permit me to say, the charge is too paltry for any man, who valued his reputation either as a gentleman or a scholar, to make. Who, for example, would wish to be guilty of the littleness of detracting from the uncommon merit of that remarkable poem of this same Mr. Poe's, recently published in the Mirror, from the American Review, entitled "THE RAVEN," by charging *him* with the paltriness of imitation? And yet, some snarling critic, who might envy the reputation he had not the genius to secure for himself, might refer to the frequent, very forcible, but rather quaint repetition, in the last two lines of many of the stanzas, as a palpable imitation of the manner of Coleridge, in several stanzas of *the Ancient Mariner*. Let me put them together.

Mr. Poe says—

"Let me see, then, what thereat is, and this mystery explore,
    Let my heart be still a moment, and this mystery explore."

And again—

"It shall clasp a sainted maiden, whom the angels name
        Lenore—
    Clasp a rare and radiant maiden, whom the angels name
        Lenore."

Mr. Coleridge says, (running two lines into one):

"For all averred I had killed the bird, that made the breeze
        to blow.
    'Ah, wretch!' said they, 'the bird to slay, that made the
        breeze to blow.'"

And again—

"They all averred I had killed the bird, that brought the fog
        and mist.
    ' 'Twas right,' said they, 'such birds to slay, that bring the
        fog and mist.'"

I have before me an anonymous poem, which I first saw some five years ago, entitled "The Bird of the Dream." I should like to transcribe the whole—but it is too long. The author was awaked from sleep by the song of a beautiful bird, sitting on the sill of his window—the sweet notes had mingled with his dreams, and brought to his remembrance, the sweeter voice of his lost "CLARE." He says—

And thou wert in my dream—a spirit thou didst seem—
The spirit of a friend long since departed;
Oh! she was fair and bright, but she left me one dark
    night—
She left me all alone, and broken-hearted.

> *   *   *

My dream went on, and thou went a warbling too,
Mingling the harmonies of earth and heaven;
Till *away— away— away*—beyond the realms of day—
My angel CLARE to my embrace was given.

> *   *   *

Sweet bird from realms of light, oh! come again to-night,
Come to my window—perch upon my chair—
Come give me back again that deep impassioned strain
That tells me thou hast seen and loved my CLARE.

Now I shall not charge Mr. Poe with Plagiarism—for, as I have said, such charges are perfectly absurd. Ten to one, he never saw this before. But let us look at the *"identities"* that may be made out between this and "THE RAVEN." *First*, in each case, the poet is a broken-hearted lover. *Second*, that lover longs for some hereafter communion with the departed. *Third*, there is a bird. *Fourth*, the bird is at the poet's window. *Fifth*, the bird being at the poet's window, makes a noise. *Sixth*, making a noise, attracts the attention of the poet; who, *Seventh*, was half asleep, dosing, dreaming. *Eighth*, the poet invites the bird to come in. *Ninth*, a confabulation ensues. *Tenth*, the bird is supposed to be a visitor from the land of spirits. *Eleventh*, allusion is made to the departed. *Twelfth*, intimation is given that the bird knew something of the departed. *Thirteenth*, that he knew her worth and loveliness. *Fourteenth*, the bird seems willing to linger with the poet. *Fifteenth*, there is a repetition, in the second and fourth lines, of a part, and that the emphatic part, of the first and third. Here is a round baker's-dozen (and one to spare) of *identities*, to offset the dozen found between Aldrich and Hood, and that too, without a word of *rhythm*, metre or stanza, which should never form a part of such a comparison. Moreover, this same poem contains an example of that kind of repetition, which I have supposed the critic meant to charge upon Longfellow as one of his imitations—

"Away—away—away," &c.

I might pursue it further. But I will not. Such criticisms only make the *author* of them contemptible, without soiling a plume in the cap of his victim. I have selected this poem of Mr. Poe's, for illustrating my remarks, because it is recent, and must be familiar to all the lovers of true poetry hereabouts. It is remarkable for its power, beauty, and originality, (out upon the automaton owl that has presumed to croak out a miserable parody—I commend him to the tender mercies of Haynes Bayley,)* and shows more forcibly than any which I can think of, the absurdity and shallowness of this kind of criticism.

One word more,—though acquainted with Mr. Longfellow, I have never seen Mr. Aldrich, nor do I even know in what part of the country he resides; and I have no acquaintance with Mr. Poe. I have written what I have written from no personal motives, but simply because, from my earliest reading of reviews and critical notices, I have been disgusted with this wholesale mangling of victims without rhyme or reason. I scarcely remember an instance where the resemblances detected were not exceedingly far-fetched and shadowy, and only perceptible to a mind pre-disposed to suspicion, and accustomed to splitting hairs.   Outis.

What I admire in this letter is the gentlemanly grace of its manner, and the chivalry which has prompted its composition. What I do *not* admire is all the rest. In especial, I do not admire the desperation of the effort to make out a case. No gentleman should degrade himself, on any grounds, to

*"I would be a Parody, written by a ninny,
  Not worth a penny, and sold for a guinea," &c.

the paltriness of *ex-parte* argument; and I shall not insult Outis at the outset, by assuming for a moment that he (Outis) is weak enough, to suppose me (Poe) silly enough, to look upon all this abominable rigmarole as anything better than a very respectable specimen of special pleading.

As a general rule in a case of this kind, I should wish to begin with the beginning, but as I have been unable, in running my eye over Outis' remarks, to discover that they have any beginning at all, I shall be pardoned for touching them in the order which suits me best.

Outis need not have put himself to the trouble of informing his readers that he has "some acquaintance with Mr. Longfellow."

It was needless also to mention that he did not know *me*. I thank him for his many flatteries—but of their inconsistency I complain. To speak of me in one breath as a poet, and in the next to insinuate charges of "carping littleness," is simply to put forth a flat paradox.

When a plagiarism is committed and detected, the word "littleness" and other similar words are immediately brought into play. To the words themselves I have no objection whatever; but their application might occasionally be improved.

Is it altogether impossible that a critic be instigated to the exposure of a plagiarism, or still better, of plagiarism generally wherever he meets it, by a strictly honorable and even charitable motive? Let us see. A theft of this kind is committed—for the present we will admit the *possibility* that a theft of this character can be committed. The chances of course are, that an established author steals from an unknown one, rather than the converse; for in proportion to the circulation of the original, is the risk of the plagiarism's detection. The person about to commit the theft, hopes for impunity altogether on the ground of the reconditeness of the source from which he thieves. But this obvious consideration is rarely borne in mind. We read a certain passage in a certain book. We meet a passage nearly similar, in another book. The first book is not at hand, and we cannot compare dates. We decide by what we fancy the probabilities of the case. The one author is a distinguished man—our sympathies are always in favor of distinction. "It is not likely," we say in our hearts "that so distinguished a personage as A. would be guilty of plagiarism from this B. of whom nobody in the world has ever heard." We give judgment, therefore, at once against B. of whom nobody in the world has ever heard; and it is for the very reason that nobody in the world *has* ever heard of him, that, in ninety-nine cases out of the hundred, the judgment so precipitously given is erroneous. Now then the plagiarist has not merely committed a wrong in itself—a wrong whose incomparable meanness would deserve exposure on absolute grounds—but he, the guilty, the successful, the eminent, has fastened the degradation of his crime—the retribution which should have overtaken it in his own person—upon the guiltless, the toiling, the unfriended struggler up the mountainous path of Fame. Is not sympathy for the plagiarist, then, about as sagacious and about as generous as would be sympathy for the murderer whose exultant escape from the noose of the hangman should be the cause of an innocent man's being hung? And because I, for one, should wish to throttle the guilty with the view of letting the innocent go, could it be considered proper on the part of any "acquaintance of Mr. Longfellow's" who came to witness the execution—could it be thought, I say either chivalrous or decorous on the part of this "acquaintance" to get up against me a charge of "carping littleness," while we stood amicably together at the foot of the gallows?

In all this I have taken it for granted that such a sin as plagiarism exists. We are informed by Outis, however, that it does *not*. "I shall not charge Mr. Poe with plagiarism," he says, "for, as I have said, such charges are perfectly absurd." An assertion of this kind is certainly *funny* (I am aware of no other epithet which precisely applies to it); and I have much curiosity to know if Outis is prepared to swear to its truth—holding right aloft his hand, of course, and kissing the back of D'Israeli's "Curiosities," or the "*Mélanges*," of Suard and André. But if the assertion is funny (and it *is*) it is by no means an original thing. It is precisely, in fact, what all the plagiarists and all the "acquaintances" of the plagiarists since the flood, have maintained with a very praiseworthy resolution.

The attempt to *prove*, however, by reasoning *à priori*, that plagiarism cannot exist, is too good an idea on the part of Outis not to be a plagiarism in itself. Are we mistaken?—or have we seen the following words before in Joseph Miller, where that ingenious gentleman is bent upon demonstrating that a leg of mutton is and ought to be a turnip?

"A man who aspires to fame, etc. attempts to win his object—how? By stealing, *in open day*, the finest passages, the most beautiful thoughts (no others are worth stealing) and claiming them as his own; and that too when he *knows* that every competitor, etc., will be ready to cry him down as a thief."

Is it possible?—is it conceivable that Outis does not here see the begging of the whole question. Why, *of course*, if the theft had to be committed *"in open day"* it would not be committed; and if the thief *"knew"* that every one would cry him down, he would be too excessive a fool to make even a decent thief if he indulged his thieving propensities in any respect. But he thieves at night—in the dark—and *not* in the open day (if he suspects it), and he does *not* know that he will be detected at all. Of the class of wilful plagiarists nine out of ten are authors of established reputation, who plunder recondite, neglected, or forgotten books.

I pause for the present, through want of space, but will resume the subject at some length in the next "Journal," and hope to convince our friend Outis that he has made a series of very singular mistakes.

Broadway Journal, March 8, 1845

A Continuation of the voluminous History of the Little Longfellow War—Mr. Poe's farther reply to the letter of Outis.

I SHALL NOT ACCUSE Mr. Poe of plagiarism," says Outis, "for, as I have observed before, such charges are perfectly absurd"—and Outis is certainly right in dwelling on the point that he has observed this thing before. It is the one original point of his essay—for I really believe that no one else was ever silly enough to "observe it before."

Here is a gentleman who writes in certain respects as a gen-

tleman should, and who yet has the effrontery to base a defence of a friend from the charge of plagiarism, on the broad
ground that no such thing as plagiarism ever existed. I confess
that to an assertion of this nature there is no little difficulty
in getting up a reply. What in the world can a man say in a
case of this kind?—he cannot of course give utterance to the
first epithets that spring to his lips—and yet what else shall
he utter that shall not have an air of direct insult to the common sense of mankind? What could any judge on any bench
in the country do but laugh or swear at the attorney who
should begin his defence of a petty-larceny client with an oration demonstrating *à priori* that no such thing as petty larceny ever had been, or in the nature of things, ever could be
committed? And yet the attorney might make as sensible a
speech as Outis—even a more sensible one—any thing but a
less sensible one. Indeed, *mutato nomine*, he might employ
Outis' identical words. He might say—"In view, gentlemen
of the jury, of all the glaring improbabilities of such a case, a
prosecuting attorney should be very slow to make such a
charge. I say glaring improbabilities, for it seems to me that
no circumstantial evidence could be sufficient to secure a verdict of theft in such a case. Look *at* it. [Here the judge would
look at the maker of the speech.] Look at it. A man who
aspires to (the) fame (of being a beau)—who seeks the esteem and praise of all the world (of dandies) and lives upon
his reputation (for broadcloth) as his vital element, attempts
to win his object—how? By stealing in open day the finest
waist-coats, the most beautiful dress-coats (no others are
worth stealing) and the rarest pantaloons of another, and
claiming them as his own; and that too when he knows that
every competitor for (the) fame (of Brummelism) and every
fashion-plate Magazine in the world, as well as the real
owner, will be ready to identify the borrowed plumes in a
moment, and cry him down as a thief. A madman, an idiot,
if he were capable of such an achievement, might do it, gentlemen of the jury, but no other."

Now of course, no judge in the world whose sense of duty
was not overruled by a stronger sense of the facetious, would
permit the attorney to proceed with any such speech. It
would never *do* to have the time of the court occupied by this

gentleman's well-meant endeavour to show *à priori*, the impossibility of that ever happening which the clerk of this same court could show *à posteriori* had been happening by wholesale ever since there had been such a thing as a foreign count. And yet the speech of the attorney was really a very excellent speech, when we compare it with that of Outis. For the "glaring improbability" of the plagiarism, is a mere nothing by the side of the "glaring improbability" of the theft of the sky-blue dress-coat, and the yellow plaid pantaloons:—we may take it for granted, of course, that the thief was one of the upper ten thousand of thieves, and would not have put himself to the trouble of appropriating any garments that were not of indisputable *bon ton*, and patronised even by Professor Longfellow himself. The improbability of the literary theft, I say, is really a mere trifle in comparison with the broad-cloth larceny. For the plagiarist is either a man of no note or a man of note. In the first case, he is usually an ignoramus, and getting possession of a rather rare book, plunders it without scruple, on the ground that nobody has ever seen a copy of it except himself. In the second case (which is a more general one by far) he pilfers from some poverty-stricken, and therefore neglected man of genius, on the reasonable supposition that this neglected man of genius will very soon cut his throat, or die of starvation, (the sooner the better, no doubt,) and that in the mean time he will be too busy in keeping the wolf from the door to look after the purloiners of his property—and too poor, and too cowed, and for these reasons too contemptible, under any circumstances, to dare accuse of so base a thing as theft, the wealthy and triumphant gentleman of elegant leisure who has only done the vagabond too much honor in knocking him down and robbing him upon the highway.

The plagiarist, then, in either case, has very reasonable ground for expecting impunity, and at all events it is because he thinks so, that he perpetrates the plagiarism—but how is it with the count who steps into the shop of the tailor, and slips under his cloak the sky-blue dress coat, and the yellow plaid pantaloons? He, the count, would be a greater fool in these matters than a count ever was, if he did not perceive at once, that the chances were about nine hundred and ninety-nine to one, that he would be caught the next morning before

twelve o'clock, in the very first bloom and blush of his promenade down Broadway, by some one of those officious individuals who are continually on the *qui vive* to catch the
counts and take away from them their sky-blue coats and yellow plaid pantaloons. Yes, undoubtedly; the count is very well
aware of all this; but he takes into consideration, that although the nine-hundred and ninety-nine chances *are* certainly against him, the one is just as certainly in his favor—
that luck is every thing—that life is short—that the weather
is fine—and that if he can only manage to get safely through
his promenade down Broadway in the sky-blue dress coat and
the yellow plaid pantaloons, he will enjoy the high honor, for
once in his life at least, of being mistaken by fifteen ladies out
of twenty, either for Professor Longfellow, or Phœbus
Apollo. And this consideration is enough—the half of it
would have been more than enough to satisfy the count that,
in putting the garments under his cloak, he is doing a very
sagacious and very commendable thing. He steals them, then,
at once, and without scruple, and, when he is caught arrayed
in them the next morning, he is, of course, highly amused to
hear his counsel make an oration in court about the "glaring
improbability" of his having stolen them when he stole
them—by way of showing the abstract impossibility of their
ever having been stolen at all.

"What is plagiarism?" demands Outis at the outset, *avec
l'air d'un Romain qui sauve sa patrie*—" what is plagiarism and
what constitutes a good ground for the charge?"

Of course all men anticipate something unusually happy in
the way of reply to queries so cavernously propounded; but
if so, then all men have forgotten, or no man has ever known
that Outis is a Yankee. He answers the two questions by two
others—and perhaps this is quite as much as any one should
expect him to do. "Did no two men," he says, "ever think
alike without stealing one from the other?—or thinking alike,
did no two men ever use the same or similar words to convey
the thoughts, and that without any communication with each
other?—To deny it is absurd."

Of course it is—very absurd; and the only thing *more* absurd that I can call to mind at present, is the supposition
that any person ever entertained an idea of denying it. But

are we to understand the denying it, or the absurdity of denying it, or the absurdity of supposing that any person intended to deny it, as the true answer to the original queries?

But let me aid Outis to a distinct conception of his own irrelevance. I accuse his friend, specifically, of a plagiarism. This accusation Outis rebuts by asking me with a grave face—not whether the friend might not, in this individual case, and in the compass of eight short lines, have happened upon ten or twelve peculiar identities of thought and identities of expression with the author from whom I charge him with plagiarising—but simply whether I do not admit the *possibility* that once in the course of eternity some two individuals might not happen upon a single identity of thought, and give it voice in a single identity of expression.

Now, frankly, I admit the possibility in question, and would request my friends to get ready for me a strait-jacket if I did not. There can be no doubt in the world, for example, that Outis considers me a fool:—the thing is sufficiently plain: and this opinion on the part of Outis is what mankind have agreed to denominate an idea; and this idea is also entertained by Mr. Aldrich, and by Mr. Longfellow—and by Mrs. Outis and her seven children—and by Mrs. Aldrich and hers—and by Mrs. Longfellow and hers —including the grand-children and great grand-children, if any, who will be instructed to transmit the idea in unadulterated purity down an infinite vista of generations yet to come. And of this idea thus extensively entertained, it would really be a very difficult thing to vary the expression in any material degree. A remarkable similarity would be brought about, indeed, by the desire of the parties in question to put the thought into as compendious a form as possible, by way of bringing it to a focus at once and having done with it upon the spot.

Outis will perceive, therefore, that I have every desire in the world to afford him that "fair play" which he considers "a jewel," since I admit not only the possibility of the class of coincidences for which he contends, but even the impossibility of there not existing just as many of these coincidences as he may consider necessary to make out his case.

One of the species he details as follows, at some length:

Some years ago, a letter was written from some part of New England, describing one of those scenes, not very common during what is called "the January thaw," when the snow, mingled with rain, and freezing as it falls, forms a perfect covering of ice upon every object. The storm clears away suddenly, and the moon comes up. The letter proceeds— *"every tree and shrub, as far as the eye can reach, of pure transparent glass—a perfect garden of moving, waving, breathing chrystals. * * * Every tree is a diamond chandelier, with a whole constellation of stars clustering to every socket,"* &c. This letter was laid away where such things usually are, in a private drawer, and did not see the light for many years. But the very next autumn brought out, among the splendid annuals got up in the country, a beautiful poem from Whittier, describing the same, or rather a similar scene, in which the line

"The trees, like chrystal chandeliers,"

was put in italics by every reviewer in the land, for the exceeding beauty of the imagery. Now *the letter* was written, probably, about the same time with the *poem*, though the poem was not published till nearly a year after.—The writers were not, and never have been, acquainted with each other, and neither could possibly have seen the work of the other before writing. Now, was there any plagiarism here?"

After the fashion of Outis himself I shall answer his query by another. What has the question whether the chandelier friend committed a plagiarism, to do with the question whether the Death-Bed friend committed a plagiarism, or whether it is possible or impossible that plagiarism, generally, can be committed?

But, merely for courtesy's sake, I step aside from the exact matter in hand. In the case mentioned I should consider material differences in the terms of description as more remarkable than coincidences. Since the tree *really* looked like a chandelier, the true wonder would have been in likening it to anything else. Of course, nine common-place men out of ten would have maintained it to be a chandelier-looking tree. No *poet* of any pretension, however, would have committed himself so far as to put such a similitude in print. The chandelier might have been poetically likened to the chrystallized tree—but the converse is a platitude. The gorgeous unaltered handiwork of Nature is always degraded by comparison with the tawdry gew-gaws of Art—and perhaps the very ugliest thing in the world is a chandelier. If "every reviewer in the land put the passage into Italics on account of the exceeding beauty of the imagery," then every printer's devil in the land should have been flogged for not taking it out of Italics upon the spot, and putting it in the plainest Roman—which is too good for it by one half.

I put no faith in the *nil admirari*, and am apt to be amazed at every second thing which I see. One of the most amazing things I have yet seen, is the complacency with which Outis throws to the right and left his anonymous assertions, taking it for granted that because he (Nobody) asserts them, I must believe them as a matter of course. However—he is quite in the right. I am perfectly ready to admit anything that he pleases, and am prepared to put as implicit faith in his *ipse dixit* as the Bishop of Autun did in the Bible—on the ground that he knew nothing about it at all.

We will understand it, then, not merely as an anonymous assertion but as an absolute fact, that the two chandelier authors " were not and never have been acquainted with each other, and that neither could have seen the work of the other before writing." We will agree to understand all this as indisputable truth, I say, through motives of the purest charity, for the purpose of assisting a friend out of trouble, and without reference to the consideration that no third person short of Signor Blitz or Professor Rogers could in any conceivable manner have satisfied himself of the truth of the twentieth part of it. Admitting this and every thing else, to be as true as the Pentateuch, it follows that plagiarism in the case in question was a thing that could not by any possibility be—and do I rightly comprehend Outis as demonstrating the impossibility of plagiarism where it *is* possible, by adducing instances of inevitable similarity under circumstances where it is *not*?

The fact is, that through want of space and time to follow Outis through the labyrinth of impertinences in which he is scrambling about, I am constrained, much against my sense of decorum, to place him in the high-road of his argument, so that he may see where he is, and what he is doing, and what it is that he is endeavouring to demonstrate.

He wishes to show, then, that Mr. Longfellow is innocent of the imitation with which I have charged him, and that Mr. Aldrich is innocent of the plagiarism with which I have *not* charged him; and this duplicate innocence is expected to be proved by showing the possibility that a certain, or that any uncertain series of coincidences may be the result of pure accident.

Now of course I cannot be sure that Outis will regard my admission as a service or a disservice, but I admit the possibility at once; and not only this, but I would admit it as a possibility were the coincidences a billion, and each of the most definitive peculiarity that human ingenuity could conceive. But, in admitting this, I admit just nothing at all, so far as the advancement of Outis' proper argument is concerned. The affair is one of *probabilities* altogether, and can be satisfactorily settled only by reference to their Calculus.

I shall continue, if not conclude the subject in the next "Journal", and our readers may take it for granted that there will be some very "interesting developments" before I have done.

Broadway Journal, March 15, 1845

More of the Voluminous History of the Little Longfellow War—Mr. Poe's Third Chapter of Reply to the Letter of Outis.

"Pray," inquires Outis of Mr. Willis, "did you ever think the worse of Dana because your friend John Neal charged him with pirating upon Paul Allen, and Bryant, too, in his poem of THE DYING RAVEN?"

I am sincerely disposed to give Outis his due, and will not pretend to deny his happy facility in asking irrelevant questions. In the present case, we can only imagine Mr. Willis' reply:—"My dear Sir," he might say, "I certainly do not think much the worse of Mr. Dana, because Mr. Neal *charged* him with the piracy, but be so kind as not to inquire what might have been my opinion had there been any substantiation of the charge."

I quote Outis' inquiry, however, not so much to insist upon its singular luminousness, as to call attention to the argument embodied in the capital letters of "THE DYING RAVEN."

Now, were I, in any spasm of perversity, to direct Outis' catechetical artillery against himself, and demand of him explicitly *his reasons* for causing those three words to be printed in capitals, what in the world would he do for a reply? As a matter of course, for some moments, he would be profoundly embarrassed—but, being a true man, and a chivalrous one, as all defenders of Mr. Longfellow must be, he could not fail, in the end, to admit that they were so printed for the purpose of safely insinuating a charge which not even an Outis had the impudence openly to utter. Let us imagine his thoughts while carefully twice underscoring the words. Is it impossible that they ran thus?—"I am perfectly well aware, to be sure, that the only conceivable resemblance between Mr. Bryant's poem and Mr. Poe's poem, lies in their common reference to a raven; but then, what I am writing will be seen by some who have not read Mr. Bryant's poem, and by many who have never heard of Mr. Poe's, and among these classes I shall be able to do Mr. Poe a serious injustice and injury, by conveying the idea that there is really sufficient similarity to warrant that charge of plagiarism, which I, Outis, the 'acquaintance of Mr. Longfellow,' am too high-minded and too merciful to prefer."

Now, I do not pretend to be positive that any such thoughts as these ever entered the brain of Outis. Nor will I venture to designate the whole insinuation, as a specimen of "carping littleness, too paltry for any man who values his reputation as a gentleman;" for in the first place, the whole matter, as I have put it, is purely supposititious, and in the second, I should furnish ground for a new insinuation of the same character, inasmuch as I should be employing Outis' identical words.

The fact is, Outis has happened upon the idea that the most direct method of rebutting one accusation, is to get up another. By showing that *I* have committed a sin, he proposes to show that Mr. Aldrich and Mr. Longfellow have *not*. Leaving the underscored DYING RAVEN to argue its own case, he proceeds, therefore, as follows:—

"Who, for example, would wish to be guilty of the littleness of detracting from the uncommon merit of that remarkable poem of this same Mr. Poe's, recently published in the Mirror, from the American Review, entitled 'THE RAVEN,' by charging *him* with the paltriness of imitation? And yet, some snarling critic, who might envy the reputation he had not the genius to secure for himself, might refer to the frequent, very forcible, but rather quaint repetition, in the last two lines of many of the stanzas, as a palpable imitation of the manner of Coleridge, in several stanzas of the *Ancient Mariner*. Let me put them together.

Mr. Poe says—

"Let me see, then, what thereat is, and this mystery explore,
   Let my heart be still a moment, and this mystery explore."

And again—

"It shall clasp a sainted maiden whom the angels name
      Lenore—
   Clasp a rare and radiant maiden whom the angels name
      Lenore."

Mr. Coleridge says, (running two lines into one);

"For all averred I had killed the bird, that made the breeze
      to blow.
   'Ah, wretch!' said they, 'the bird to slay, that made the
      breeze to blow.'"

And again—

"They all averred I had killed the bird, that brought the fog
      and mist.
   'Twas right,' said they, 'such birds to slay, that bring the
      fog and mist.'"

The "rather quaint" is ingenious. Fully one-third of whatever effect "The Raven" has, is wrought by the quaintness in question—a point elaborately introduced, to accomplish a well-considered purpose. What idea would Outis entertain of me, were I to speak of his defence of his friends as very decent, very respectable, but rather meritorious?

In the passages collated there are two points upon which the "snarling critic" might base his insinuation—if ever so weak a "snarling critic" existed. Of these two points one is purely hypothetical—that is to say, it is disingenuously manufactured by Mr. Longfellow's acquaintance to suit his own purposes—or perhaps the purposes of the imaginary snarling critic. The argument of the second point is demolished by my not only admitting it, but insisting upon it. Perhaps the least tedious mode of refuting Outis, is to acknowledge nine tenths of every thing he may think proper to say.

But, in the present instance what am I called upon to acknowledge? I am charged with imitating the repetition of phrase in the two concluding lines of a stanza, and of imitating this from Coleridge. But why not extend the accusation, and insinuate that I imitate it from every body else? for certainly there is no poet living or dead who has not put in practice the identical effect—the well-understood effect of the *refrain*. Is Outis' argument to the end that *I* have no right to this thing for the reason that all the world has? If this is *not* his argument, will he be kind enough to inform me (at his leisure) what it *is*? Or is he prepared to confess himself so absurdly uninformed as not to know that whatever a poet claims on the score of original versification, is claimed not on account of any individual rhythmical or metrical effects (for *none* are individually original) but solely on account of the novelty of his *combinations* of old effects?

The hypothesis, or manufacture, consists in the alteration of Coleridge's metre, with the view of forcing it into a merely ocular similarity with my own, and thus of imposing upon some one or two grossly ignorant readers. I give the verses of Coleridge as they *are*:

> For all averred, I had killed the bird
> That made the breeze to blow,

> Ah wretch, said they, the bird to slay,
> That made the breeze to blow.

The verses beginning, "*They* all averred," etc., are arranged in the same manner. Now I have taken it for granted that it is Outis' design to impose the idea of similarity between my lines and those of Coleridge, upon some one or two grossly ignorant individuals: at the same time, whoever attempts such an imposition is rendered liable at least to the suspicion of very gross ignorance himself. The ignorance or the knavery are the two uncomfortable horns of his dilemma.

Let us see. Coleridge's lines are arranged in quatrains— mine in couplets. His first and third lines rhyme at the closes of the second and fourth feet—mine flow continuously, without rhyme. His metre, briefly defined, is alternately tetrameter acatalectic, and trimeter acatalectic—mine is uniformly octameter catalectic. It might be expected, however, that at least the *rhythm* would prove to be identical—but not so. Coleridge's is iambic (varied in the third foot of the first line with an anapæst)—mine is the exact converse, trochaic. The fact is, that neither in rhythm, metre, stanza, or rhyme, is there even a *single* point of *approximation* throughout; the *only* similarity being the wickedly or sillily manufactured one of Outis himself, appealing from the ears to the eyes of the most uncultivated classes of the rabble. The ingenuity and validity of the manufacture might be approached, although certainly not paralleled, by an attempt to show that blue and yellow pigments standing unmixed at separate ends of a studio, were equivalent to green. I say "not paralleled," for even the *mixing* of the pigments, in the case of Outis, would be very far, as I have shown, from producing the supposititious effect. Coleridge's lines, written together, would result in rhymed iambic heptameter acatalectic, while mine are unrhymed trochaic octameter catalectic—differing in every conceivable circumstance. A closer parallel than the one I have imagined, would be the demonstration that two are equal to four, on the ground that, possessing two dollars, a man will have four when he gets an additional couple—for that the additional couple is *somewhere*, no one, after due consideration, will deny.

If Outis will now take a seat upon one of the horns of his dilemma, I will proceed to transcribe the third variation of the charges *insinuated* through the medium of the "snarling critic."

I have before me an anonymous poem, which I first saw some five years ago, entitled "The Bird of the Dream." I should like to transcribe the whole—but it is too long. The author was awakened from sleep by the song of a beautiful bird, sitting on the sill of his window—the sweet notes had mingled with his dreams, and brought to his remembrance, the sweeter voice of his lost "CLARE." He says—

> And thou wert in my dream—a spirit thou didst seem—
> The spirit of a friend long since departed;
> Oh she was fair and bright, but she left me one dark
>   night—
> She left me all alone, and broken-hearted.
>
>   *   *   *
>
> My dream went on, and thou went a warbling too,
> Mingling the harmonies of earth and heaven;
> Till *away— away— away*—beyond the realms of day—
> My angel CLARE to my embrace was given.
>
>   *   *   *
>
> Sweet bird from realms of light, oh! come again to night,
> Come to my window—perch upon my chair—
> Give me back again that deep impassioned strain
> That tells me thou hast seen and loved my CLARE.

Now I shall not charge Mr. Poe with Plagiarism—for, as I have said, such charges are perfectly absurd. Ten to one, he never saw this before. But let us look at the *"identities"* that may be made out between this and "THE RAVEN." *First*, in each case, the poet is a broken-hearted lover. *Second*, that lover longs for some hereafter communion with the departed. *Third*, there is a bird. *Fourth*, the bird is at the poet's window. *Fifth*, the bird being at the poet's window, makes a noise. *Sixth*, making a noise attracts the attention of the poet; who, *Seventh*, was half asleep, dosing, dreaming. *Eighth*, the poet invites the bird to come in. *Ninth*, a confabulation ensues. *Tenth*, the bird is supposed to be a visitor from the land of spirits. *Eleventh*, allusion is made to the departed. *Twelfth*, intimation is given that the bird knew something of the departed. *Thirteenth*, that he knew her worth and loveliness. *Fourteenth*, the bird seems willing to linger with the poet. *Fifteenth*, there is a repetition, in the second and fourth lines, of a part, and that the emphatic part, of the first and third. Here is a round baker's dozen (and one to spare) of *identities*, to offset the dozen found between Aldrich and Hood, and that too, without a word of *rhythm*, metre or stanza, which should never form a part of such a comparison.

The first point to be attended to here is the "ten to one that I never saw it before." Ten to one that I never did—but Outis might have remembered that twenty to one I should *like* to see it. In accusing either Mr. Aldrich or Mr. Hood, I printed their poems together and in full. But an *anonymous* gentleman rebuts my accusation by telling me that there is a certain similarity between a poem of my own and an *anonymous* poem which he has before *him*, and which he would like to transcribe if it were not too long. He contents himself, therefore, with giving me, from this too long poem, three stanzas which are shown, by a series of intervening asterisks, to have been *culled*, to suit his own purposes, from different portions of the poem, but which, (again to suit his own purposes) he places before the public in consecutive connexion! The least that can be said of the whole statement is that it is deliciously frank—but, upon the whole, the poem will look quite as well before *me*, as before Outis, whose time is too much occupied to transcribe it. I, on the other hand, am entirely at leisure, and will transcribe and *print* the whole of it with the greatest pleasure in the world—provided always that it is not too long to refer to—too long to have its whereabouts pointed out—as I half suspect, from Outis' silence on the subject, that *it is*.

One thing I will take it upon myself to say, in the spirit of prophecy:—whether the poem in question is or is not in existence (and we have only Nobody's word that it is) the passages *as quoted*, are not in existence, except as quoted by Outis, who in some particulars, I maintain, has falsified the text, for the purpose of *forcing* a similarity, as in the case of the verses of Coleridge.

All this I assert in the spirit of prophecy, while we await the forthcoming of the poem. In the meantime, we will estimate the "identities" with reference to the "Raven" as collated with the passages culled by Outis—granting him every thing he is weak enough to imagine I am in duty bound to grant—admitting that the poem as a whole exists—that the words and lines are ingenuously written—that the stanzas have the connexion and sequence he gives them—and that although he has been already found guilty of chicanery in one instance, he is at least entirely innocent in this.

He has established, he says, fifteen identities, "and that, too, without a word of rhythm, metre, or stanza, which should never form a part of such comparison"—by which of course we are to understand that *with* the rhythm, metre, and stanza (omitted only because they should never form a part of such comparison) he would have succeeded in establishing eighteen. Now I insist that rhythm, metre and stanza *should* form and *must* form a part of the comparison, and I will presently demonstrate what I say. I also insist therefore, since he *could* find me guilty if he *would* upon these points, that guilty he *must* and *shall* find me upon the spot. He then, distinctly, has established eighteen identities—and I proceed to examine them one by one.

"First," he says "in each case the poet is a broken-hearted lover." Not so:—*my* poet has no indication of a broken heart. On the contrary he lives triumphantly in the expectation of meeting his Lenore in Aidenn, and is so indignant with the raven for maintaining that the meeting will never take place, as to call him a liar and order him out of the house. Not only is my lover not a broken-hearted one—but I have been at some pains to show that broken hearts and matters of that kind are improperly made the subject of poems. I refer to the last chapter of an article entitled "Marginalia" and published, in the last December number, I believe, of the "Democratic Review."

"Second," says Outis, "that lover longs for some hereafter communion with the bird." In my poem there is no expression of any such longing—the nearest approach to it is the triumphant consciousness which forms the thesis and staple of the whole. In Outis' poem the nearest approach to the "longing" is contained in the lover's request to the bird to repeat a strain that assures him (the lover) that it (the bird) has known the lost mistress.

"Third—there is a bird," says Outis. So there is. Mine however is a raven, and we may take it for granted that Outis' is either a nightingale or a cockatoo.

"Fourth, the bird is at the poet's window." As regards my poem, true; as regards Outis', not:—the poet only *requests* the bird to come to the window.

"Fifth, the bird being at the poet's window, makes a noise." The fourth specification failing, the fifth, which depends upon it, as a matter of course fails too.

"Sixth, making a noise attracts the attention of the poet." The fifth specification failing, the sixth, which depends upon it, fails likewise, and as a matter of course, as before.

"Seventh, [the poet] was half asleep, dozing, dreaming." False altogether: only *my* poet was "napping," and this in the commencement of the poem, which is occupied with realities and waking action. Outis' poet is fast asleep and dreams every thing.

"Eighth, the poet invites the bird to come in." Another palpable failure. Outis' poet indeed asked his bird in; but my raven walked in without any invitation.

"Ninth—a confabulation ensues." As regards my poem, true; but there is not a word of any confabulation in Outis'.

"Tenth—the bird is supposed to be a visiter from the land of spirits." As regards Outis' poem, this is true only if we give a wide interpretation to the phrase "realms of light." In my poem the bird is not only not from the world of spirits, but I have specifically conveyed the idea of his having escaped from "some unhappy master", of whom he had caught the word "Nevermore"—in the concluding stanza, it is true, I suddenly convert him into an allegorical emblem or personification of Mournful Remembrance, out of the shadow of which the poet is "lifted nevermore."

"Eleventh—allusion is made to the departed." Admitted.

"Twelfth—intimation is given that the bird knew something of the departed." True as regards Outis' poem only. No such intimation is given in mine.

"Thirteenth—that he knew her worth and loveliness." Again—true only as regards Outis' poem. It should be observed here that I have disproved the twelfth and thirteenth specifications purely for form's sake:—they are nothing more than disingenuous repetitions of the eleventh. The "allusion to the departed" *is* the "intimation," and the intimation *is* that "he knew her worth and loveliness."

"Fourteenth—the bird seems willing to linger with the poet." True only as regards my poem—in Outis' (as quoted) there is nothing of the kind.

"Fifteenth—there is a repetition, in the second and fourth lines, of a part, and that the emphatic part, of the first and third." What is here asserted is true only of the first stanza quoted by Outis, and of the commencement of the third. There is nothing of it in the second. In my poem there is nothing of it at all, with the exception of the repetition in the refrain, occurring at the *fifth* line of my stanza of six. I quote a stanza—by way of rendering every thing perfectly intelligible, and affording Outis his much coveted "fair play":

"Be that word our sign of parting, bird or fiend!" I shrieked, upstarting—
"Get thee back into the tempest and the Night's Plutonian shore!
  Leave no black plume as a token of that lie thy soul hath spoken!
  Leave my loneliness unbroken!—quit the bust above my door!
  Take thy beak from out my heart, and take thy form from off my door!"
                    Quoth the raven "Nevermore."

Sixteenth—concerns the rhythm. Outis' is iambic—mine the exact converse, trochaic.

Seventeenth—regards the metre. Outis' is hexameter alternating with pentameter, both acatalectic.* Mine is octameter acatalectic, alternating with heptameter catalectic repeated in the refrain of the fifth verse, and terminating with tetrameter catalectic.

Eighteenth and last has respect to the stanza—that is to say, to the general arrangement of the metre into masses. Of Outis' I need only say that it is a very common and certainly a very stupid one. My own has at least the merit of *being* my own. No writer living or dead has ever employed anything resembling it. The innumerable specific differences between it and that of Outis it would be a tedious matter to point out— but a far less difficult matter than to designate one individual point of similarity.

And now what are we to think of the eighteen identities of Outis—the fifteen that he establishes and the three that he could establish if he would—that is to say, if he could only bring himself to be so unmerciful?

Of the whole eighteen, sixteen have shown themselves to be lamentable failures—having no more substantial basis than sheer misrepresentation "too paltry for any man who values his reputation as a gentleman and a scholar," and depending altogether for effect upon the *chances* that nobody would take the trouble to investigate their falsehood or their truth.

Two—the third and the eleventh—are sustained: and these two show that in both poems there is "an allusion to the departed," and that in both poems there is "a bird."

The first idea which suggests itself at this point is, whether *not* to have a bird and *not* to have an allusion to a deceased mistress, would not be the truer features of distinctiveness after all—whether two poems which have *not* these items

*This is as accurate a description as can be given of the alternating (of the second and fourth) lines in few words. The fact is, they are indescribable without more trouble than they are worth—and seem to me either to have been written by some one ignorant of the principles of verse, or to be misquoted. The line, however,

"That tells me thou hast seen and loved my Clare,"

answers the description I have given of the alternating verses, and was no doubt the general *intention* for all of them.

might not be more rationally charged with similarity than any two poems which *have*.

But having thus disproved *all* the identities of Outis (for any one comprehending the principle of proof in such cases will admit that two *only*, are in effect just nothing at all) I am quite ready, by way again of affording him "fair play," to expunge every thing that has been said on the subject, and proceed as if every one of these eighteen identities were in the first bloom and deepest blush of a demonstration.

I might grant them as demonstrated, to be sure, on the ground which I have already touched—that to prove me or any body else an imitator is no mode of showing that Mr. Aldrich or Mr. Longfellow is *not*. But I might safely admit them on another and equally substantial consideration which seems to have been overlooked by the zeal of Outis altogether. He has clearly forgotten that the *mere* number of such coincidences proves nothing, because at any moment we can oblige it to prove too much. It is the easiest thing imaginable to suggest—and even to do that which Outis has failed in doing—to demonstrate a practically infinite series of identities between any two compositions in the world—but it by no means follows that all compositions in the world have a *similarity* one with the other, in any comprehensible sense of the term. I mean to say that regard must be had not *only* to the number of the coincidences, but to the peculiarity of each—this peculiarity growing less and less necessary, and the effect of number more and more important, in a ratio prodigiously accumulative, as the investigation progresses. And again—regard must be had not only to the number *and* peculiarity of the coincidences, but to the antagonistic differences, if any, which surround them—and very especially to *the space* over which the coincidences are spread, and the number or paucity of the events, or incidents, from among which the coincidences are selected. When Outis, for example, picks out his eighteen coincidences (which I am now granting as sustained) from a poem so long as The Raven, in collation with a poem not forthcoming, and which may therefore, for anything anybody knows to the contrary, be as long as an infinite flock of ravens, he is merely putting himself to unnecessary trouble in getting together phantoms of arguments that can have no substance wherewith to aid his demonstration, until the ascertained extent of the unknown poem from which they are culled, affords them a purpose and a palpability. Can any man doubt that between The Iliad and the Paradise Lost there might be established even a thousand very idiosyncratic identities?—and yet is any man fool enough to maintain that the Iliad is the original of the Paradise Lost?

But how is it in the case of Messieurs Aldrich and Hood? The poems here are both remarkably brief—and as I have every intention to do justice, and no other intention in the world, I shall be pardoned for collating them once again. Mr. Hood's poem runs thus:

THE DEATH-BED

We watched *her breathing through the night*,
    Her breathing soft and low,
As in her breast the wave of life
    Kept heaving to and fro.

So silently we seemed to speak,
    So slowly moved about,
As we had lent her half our powers
    To eke her being out.

Our very hope belied our fears;
    Our fears our hope belied;
We thought her dying when she slept,
    And sleeping when she died.

But when the morn came dim and sad,
    And chill with early showers,
Her quiet eyelids closed—she had
    Another morn than ours.

Mr. Aldrich's poem is as follows:

A DEATH-BED

Her sufferings ended with the day,
    Yet lived she at its close,
And breathed the long, long night away,
    In statue-like repose;

But when the sun in all its state
    Illumed the eastern skies,

> She passed through Glory's morning gate,
> And walked in Paradise.

Now, let it be understood that I am entirely uninformed as to which of these two poems was first published. And so little has the question of priority to do with my thesis, that I shall not put myself to the trouble of inquiring. What I maintain is, that there are sufficient grounds for belief that the one is plagiarised from the other:— *who* is the original and *who* is the plagiarist, are points I leave to be settled by any one who thinks the matter of sufficient consequence to give it his attention.

But the man who shall deny the plagiarism abstractly— what is it that he calls upon us to believe? First—that two poets, in remote parts of the world, conceived the idea of composing a poem on the subject of *Death*. Of course, there is nothing remarkable in this. Death is a naturally poetic theme, and suggests itself by a seeming spontaneity to every poet in the world. But had the subject chosen by the two widely separated poets, been even strikingly peculiar—had it been, for example, *a porcupine, a piece of ginger-bread*, or anything unlikely to be made the subject of a poem, still no sensible person would have insisted upon the single coincidence as any thing *beyond* a single coincidence. We have no difficulty, therefore, in believing what, so far, we are called upon to believe.

Secondly, we must credit that the two poets concluded to write not only on death, but on the death of a *woman*. Here the mind, observing the two identities, reverts to their peculiarity or non-peculiarity, and finding *no* peculiarity—admitting that the death of a woman is a naturally suggested poetic subject—has no difficulty also in admitting the two coincidences—as such and nothing beyond.

Thirdly, we are called upon to believe that the two poets not only concluded to write upon death and upon the death of a woman, but that, from the innumerable phases of death, the phase of *tranquility* was happened upon by each. Here the intellect commences a slight rebellion, but it is quieted by the admission partly of the spontaneity with which such an idea might arise, and partly of the *possibility* of the coincidences, independently of the consideration of spontaneity.

Fourthly—we are required to believe that the two poets happened not only upon death—the death of a woman—and the tranquil death of a woman—but upon the idea of representing this woman as lying tranquilly *throughout the whole night*, in spite of the infinity of different durations which might have been imagined for her trance of tranquility. At this point the reason perceives the evidence against these co-incidences, (as such and nothing more), to be increasing in geometrical ratio. It discards all idea of spontaneity, and if it yield credence at all, yields it altogether on the ground of the indisputable *possibility*.

Fifthly—we are requested to believe that our poets happened not only upon *death*—upon the death of a *woman*—upon the *tranquil* death of a woman—and upon the lying of this woman tranquilly *throughout the night*—but, also, upon the idea of selecting, from the innumerable phases which characterise a tranquil death-bed, the identical one of soft *breathing*—employing also the identical word. Here the reason gives up the endeavour to believe that one poem has not been suggested by the other:—if it be a reason accustomed to deal with the mathematical Calculus of Probabilities it has abandoned this endeavour at the preceding stage of the investigation. The evidence of suggestion has now become prodigiously accumulate. Each succeeding coincidence (however slight) is proof not merely added, but multiplied by hundreds, and hundreds of thousands.

Sixthly, we are called upon to believe not only that the two poets happened upon all this, together with the idea of the soft breathing, but also of employing the identical word *breathing*, in the same line with the identical word, *night*. This proposition the reason receives with a smile.

Seventhly, however, we are required to admit not only all that has been already found inadmissible, but in addition, that the two poets conceived the idea of representing the death of the woman as occurring precisely at the same instant, out of all the infinite instants of all time. This proposition the reason receives only with a sneer.

Eighthly—we are called upon to acquiesce in the assertion that not only all these improbabilities are probable, but that in addition again, the two poets happened upon the idea of representing the woman as stepping immediately into Paradise:—and, *ninthly*, that both should not only happen upon all this, but upon the idea of writing a peculiarly brief poem, on so admirably suggestive a thesis:—and, *tenthly*, that out of the various rhythms, that is to say variations of poetic feet, they should have both happened upon the iambus:—and, *eleventhly*, that out of the absolutely infinite metres that may be contrived from this rhythm, they should both have hit upon the tetrameter acatalectic for the first and third lines of a stanza:—and, *twelfthly*, upon the trimeter acatalectic for the second and fourth; and, *thirteenthly*, upon an absolute identity of phrase at, *fourteenthly*, an absolutely identical position, viz: upon the phrases, "But when the morn," &c., and, "But when the sun, &c.," occurring in the beginning of the first line in the last stanza of each poem:—and, *fifteenthly* and lastly, that out of the vast multitude of appropriate *titles*, they should both have happened upon one whose identity is interfered with at all, only by the difference between the definite and indefinite article.

Now the chances that these fifteen coincidences, so peculiar in character, and all occuring within the compass of eight short lines on the one part, and sixteen on the other—the chances, I say, that these coincidences are merely accidental, may be estimated, possibly, as about one to one hundred millions; and any man who reasons at all, is of course grossly insulted in being called upon to credit them as accidental.

In the next number of the Journal, I shall endeavour to bring this subject to an end.

Broadway Journal, March 22, 1845

Imitation—Plagiarism—The conclusion of Mr. Poe's reply to the letter of Outis.

I HAVE WRITTEN what I have written," says Outis, "from no personal motives, but simply because, from my earliest reading of reviews and critical notices, I have been disgusted with this wholesale mangling of victims without rhyme or reason."

I have already agreed to believe implicitly every thing asserted by the anonymous Outis, and am fully prepared to admit, even, his own contradictions, in one sentence, of what he has insisted upon in the sentence preceding. I shall assume it as indisputable, then, (since Nobody says it) that, first, he has no acquaintance with myself and "some acquaintance with Mr. Longfellow," and secondly, that he has " written what he has written from no personal motives whatever." That he has been disgusted with "the mangling of victims without rhyme or reason," is, to be sure, a little unaccountable, for the victims without rhyme or reason are precisely the victims that ought to be mangled; but that he has been disgusted "from his earliest reading" with critical notices and reviews, is credible enough if we but imagine his "earliest reading" and earliest writing to have taken place about the same epoch of time.

But to be serious; if Outis has his own private reasons for being disgusted with what he terms the " wholesale mangling of victims without rhyme or reason," there is not a man living, of common sense and common honesty, who has not better reason (if possible) to be disgusted with the insufferable cant and shameless misrepresentation practised habitually by just such persons as Outis, with the view of decrying by sheer strength of lungs—of trampling down—of rioting down—of mobbing down any man with a soul that bids him come out from among the general corruption of our public press, and take his stand upon the open ground of rectitude and honor.

The Outises who practise this species of bullyism are, as a matter of course, anonymous. They are either the "victims without rhyme or reason who have been mangled by wholesale," or they are the relatives, or the relatives *of* the relatives of the "victims without rhyme or reason who have been mangled by wholesale." Their watchwords are "carping littleness," "envious malignity," and "personal abuse." Their low artifices are insinuated calumnies, and indefatigable whispers of regret, from post to pillar, that "Mr. So-and-So, or Mr. This-and-

That *will* persist in rendering himself so dreadfully unpopular"—no one, in the meantime, being more thoroughly and
painfully aware than these very Outises, that the unpopularity
of the just critic who reasons his way, guiltless of dogmatism,
is confined altogether within the limits of the influence of the
victims without rhyme and reason who have been mangled
by wholesale. Even the manifest injustice of a Gifford is, I
grieve to say, an exceedingly popular thing; and there is *no*
literary element of popularity more absolutely and more universally effective than the pungent impartiality of a Wilson or
a Macaulay. In regard to my own course—without daring to
arrogate to myself a single other quality of either of these
eminent men than that pure contempt for mere prejudice and
conventionality which actuated them all, I will now unscrupulously call the attention of the Outises to the fact, that it
was during what they (the Outises) would insinuate to be the
unpopularity of my " wholesale mangling of the victims without rhyme and reason" that, in one year, the circulation of
the "Southern Messenger" (a five-dollar journal) extended itself from seven hundred to nearly five thousand,—and
that, in little more than twice the same time, "Graham's
Magazine" swelled its list from five to fifty-two thousand subscribers.

I make no apology for these egotisms, and I proceed with
them without hesitation—for, in myself, I am but defending
a set of principles which no honest man need be ashamed of
defending, and for whose defence no honest man will consider an apology required.

The usual watchwords of the Outises, when repelling a criticism,—their customary charges, overt or insinuated, are (as
I have already said) those of "personal abuse" and " wholesale
(or indiscriminate) mangling." In the present instance the latter solely is employed—for not even an Outis can accuse me,
with even a decent show of verisimilitude, of having ever descended, in the most condemnatory of my reviews, to that
personal abuse which, upon one or two occasions, has indeed
been levelled at myself, in the spasmodic endeavours of aggrieved authors to rebut what I have ventured to demonstrate.

I have then to refute only the accusation of mangling by

wholesale—and I refute it by the simplest reference to *fact*. What I have written remains; and is readily accessible in any of our public libraries. I have had one or two impotent enemies, and a multitude of cherished friends—and both friends and enemies have been, for the most part, literary people; yet no man can point to a single *critique*, among the very numerous ones which I have written during the last ten years, which is either wholly fault-finding or wholly in approbation; nor is there an instance to be discovered, among all that I have published, of my having set forth, either in praise or censure, a single opinion upon any critical topic of moment, without attempting, at least, to give it authority by something that wore the semblance of a reason. Now, is there a writer in the land, who, having dealt in criticism even one-fourth as much as myself, can of his own criticisms, conscientiously say the same? The fact is, that very many of the most eminent men in America whom I am proud to number among the sincerest of my friends, have been rendered so solely by their approbation of my comments upon their own works—comments in great measure directed *against* themselves as authors—belonging altogether to that very class of criticism which it is the petty policy of the Outises to cry down, with their diminutive voices, as offensive on the score of wholesale vituperation and personal abuse. If, to be brief, in what I have put forth there has been a preponderance of censure over commendation,—is there not to be imagined for this preponderance a more charitable motive than any which the Outises have been magnanimous enough to assign me—is not this preponderance, in a word, the natural and inevitable tendency of all criticism worth the name in this age of so universal an authorship, that no man in his senses will pretend to deny the vast predominance of good writers over bad?

"And now," says Outis, [and now too, say I] "for the matter of Longfellow's imitations—in what do they consist? The critic is not very specific in this charge. Of what kind are they? Are they imitations of thought? Why not call them *plagiarisms* then, and show them up? Or are they only verbal imitations of style? Perhaps *this* is one of them, in his poem on the "Sea Weed,"

> ———"*drifting, drifting, drifting,*
> On the shifting
> Currents of the restless main.*"*

resembling in form and collocation only, a line in a beautiful and very powerful poem of MR. EDGAR A. POE. (Write it rather EDGAR, a *Poet*, and then it is right to a T.) I have not the poem before me, and have forgotten its title. But he is describing a magnificent intellect in ruins, if I remember rightly—and, speaking of the eloquence of its better days, represents it as

> ———"*flowing, flowing, flowing,*
> Like a river.*"*

Is this what the critic means? Is it *such* imitations as this that he alludes to? If not, I am at fault, either in my reading of Longfellow, or in my general familiarity with the American Poets. If this *be* the kind of imitation referred to, permit me to say, the charge is too paltry for any man, who valued his reputation either as a gentleman or a scholar."

Elsewhere he says:—

Moreover, this poem contains an example of that kind of repetition which I have supposed the critic meant to charge upon Longfellow as one of his imitations—

> Away—away—away—&c.

I might pursue it farther, but I will not. Such criticisms only make the author of them contemptible, without soiling a plume in the cap of his victim.

The first point to be here observed is the complacency with which Outis *supposes* me to make a certain charge and then vituperates me for his own absurd supposition. Were I, or any man, to accuse Mr. Longfellow of imitation on the score of thrice employing a word in consecutive connexion, then I, (or any man) would only be guilty of as great a sotticism as was Outis in accusing *me* of imitation on the score of the *refrain*.

The repetition in question is assuredly not claimed by myself as original—I should therefore be wary how I charged Mr. Longfellow with imitating it from myself. It is, in fact, a musical effect, which is the common property of all mankind, and has been their common property for ages.

Nevertheless the quotation of this

"drifting, drifting, drifting"

is, on the part of Outis, a little unfortunate. Most certainly the supposed imitation had never been observed by me—nor even had I observed it, should I have considered it *individually*, as a point of any moment;—but all will admit, (since Outis himself has noticed the parallel,) that, were a second parrallel of any obviousness to be established from the same brief poem, "The Sea-Weed," this second would come in very strong corroboration of the first. Now, the sixth stanza of this very "Sea-Weed" (which was first published in "Graham's Magazine" for January 1845) commences with

"From the far off isles enchanted;"

and in a little poem of my own, addressed "To Mary," and first published at page 636 of the first volume of the "Southern Literary Messenger," will be found the lines:

"And thus thy memory is to me
Like some enchanted far off isle
In some tumultuous sea."

But to show, in general, what I mean by accusing Mr. Longfellow of imitation, I collate his "Midnight Mass for the Dying Year" with "The Death of the Old Year" of Tennyson.

MIDNIGHT MASS FOR THE DYING YEAR

Yes, the Year is growing old,
    And his eye is pale and bleared,
Death, with frosty hand and cold,
    Plucks the old man by the beard,
        Sorely,—sorely!

The leaves are falling, falling,
    Solemnly and slow;
Caw, caw, the rooks are calling;
    It is a sound of woe,
            A sound of woe!

Through woods and mountain-passes
    The winds, like anthems, roll;
They are chanting solemn masses,
    Singing, Pray for this poor soul,
            Pray,—pray!

And the hooded clouds, like friars,
    Tell their beads in drops of rain,
And patter their doleful prayers;
    But their prayers are all in vain,
            All in vain!

There he stands in the foul weather,
    The foolish, fond Old Year,
Crowned with wild flowers and with heather,
    Like weak, despised Lear,
            A king,—a king!

Then comes the summer-like day,
    Bids the old man rejoice!
His joy! his last! O, the old man gray,
    Loveth her ever soft voice
            Gentle and low.

To the crimson woods he saith—
    To the voice gentle and low,
Of the soft air like a daughter's breath,
    Pray do not mock me so!
            Do not laugh at me!

And now the sweet day is dead;
    Cold in his arms it lies;
No stain from its breath is spread
    Over the glassy skies,
            No mist nor stain!

Then, too, the Old Year dieth,
  And the forests utter a moan,
Like the voice of one who crieth
  In the wilderness alone,
        Vex not his ghost!

Then comes, with an awful roar,
  Gathering and sounding on,
The storm-wind from Labrador,
  The wind Euroclydon,
        The storm-wind!

Howl! howl! and from the forest
  Sweep the red leaves away!
Would, the sins that thou abhorrest,
  O soul! could thus decay,
        And be swept away!

For there shall come a mightier blast,
  There shall be a darker day;
And the stars, from heaven down-cast,
  Like red leaves be swept away!
        Kyrie Eleyson!
        Christie Eleyson!

THE DEATH OF THE OLD YEAR

Full knee-deep lies the winter snow,
  And the winter winds are wearily sighing;
Toll ye the church-bell sad and low,
And tread softly, and speak low,
  For the Old Year lies a-dying.
        Old Year, you must not die,
      You came to us so readily,
      You lived with us so steadily,
        Old Year, you shall not die.

He lieth still: he doth not move;
  He will not see the dawn of day;
He hath no other life above—
He gave me a friend, and a true, true love,
  And the New Year will take 'em away.

Old Year, you must not go,
So long as you have been with us,
Such joy as you have seen with us,
Old Year, you shall not go.

He frothed his bumpers to the brim;
A jollier year we shall not see;
But though his eyes are waxing dim,
And though his foes speak ill of him,
He was a friend to me.
Old Year, you shall not die;
We did so laugh and cry with you,
I've half a mind to die with you,
Old Year, if you must die.

He was full of joke and jest,
But all his merry quips are o'er;
To see him die, across the waste
His son and heir doth ride post haste,
But he'll be dead before.
Every one for his own;
The night is starry and cold, my friend,
And the New Year, blithe and bold, my friend,
Comes up to take his own.

How hard he breathes! Over the snow
I heard just now the crowing cock.
The shadows flicker to and fro:
The cricket chirps: the light burns low:
'Tis nearly one o'clock.
Shake hands before you die;
Old Year, we'll dearly rue for you,
What is it we can do for you?
Speak out before you die.

His face is growing sharp and thin—
Alack! our friend is gone!
Close up his eyes; tie up his chin;
Step from the corpse and let him in
That standeth there alone,
And waiteth at the door.
There's a new foot on the floor, my friend,

> And a new face at the door, my friend,
>   A new face at the door.

I have no idea of commenting, at any length, upon this imitation; which is too palpable to be mistaken; and which belongs to the most barbarous class of literary piracy; that class in which, while the words of the wronged author are avoided, his most intangible, and therefore his least defensible and least reclaimable property, is appropriated. Here, with the exception of lapses, which, however, speak volumes, (such for instance as the use of the capitalized "Old Year," the general peculiarity of the rhythm, and the absence of rhyme at the end of each stanza,) there is nothing of a visible or palpable nature by which the source of the American poem can be established. But then nearly all that is valuable in the piece of Tennyson, is the first conception of personifying the Old Year as a dying old man, with the singularly wild and fantastic *manner* in which that conception is carried out. Of this conception and of this manner he is robbed. What is here not taken from Tennyson, is made up mosaically, from the death scene of Cordelia, in "Lear"—to which I refer the curious reader.

In "Graham's Magazine" for February 1843, there appeared a poem, furnished by Professor Longfellow, entitled "The Good George Campbell," and purporting to be a translation from the German of O. L. B. Wolff. In "Minstrelsy Ancient and Modern by William Motherwell, published by John Wylie, Glasgow 1827," is to be found a poem partly compiled and partly written by Motherwell himself. It is entitled "The Bonnie George Campbell." I give the two side by side:

MOTHERWELL	LONGFELLOW
Hie upon Hielands	High on the Highlands,
And low upon Tay,	And deep in the day,
Bonnie George Campbell	The good George Campbell
Rade out on a day.	Rode free and away.
Saddled and bridled	All saddled, all bridled,
And gallant rade he;	Gay garments he wore;
Hame cam his gude horse,	Home came his gude steed,
But never cam he.	But he nevermore.

Out cam his auld mither
   Greeting fu' sair,
And out cam his bonnie bride
   Rivin' her hair.
Saddled and bridled
   And booted rade he;
Toom hame cam the saddle,
   But never cam he.

"My meadow lies green,
   And my corn is unshorn;
My barn is too big,
   And my baby's unborn."
Saddled and bridled
   And booted rade he;
Toom hame cam the saddle,
   But never cam he.

Out came his mother,
   Weeping so sadly;
Out came his beauteous bride
   Weeping so madly.
All saddled, all bridled,
   Strong armor he wore;
Home came the saddle,
   But he nevermore.

My meadow lies green,
   Unreaped is my corn,
My garner is empty,
   My child is unborn.
All saddled, all bridled,
   Sharp weapons he bore:
Home came the saddle,
   But he nevermore!

Professor Longfellow defends himself (I learn) from the charge of *imitation* in this case, by the assertion that he *did* translate from Wolff, but that Wolff copied from Motherwell. I am willing to believe almost anything rather than so gross a plagiarism as this seems to be—but there are difficulties which should be cleared up. In the first place how happens it that, in the transmission from the Scotch into the German, and again from the German into the English, not only the versification should have been rigidly preserved, but the *rhymes*, and *alliterations*? Again; how are we to imagine that Mr. Longfellow with his known intimate acquaintance with "Motherwell's Minstrelsy" did not at once recognize so remarkable a poem when he met it in Wolff? I have now before me a large volume of songs, ballads, etc. collected by Wolff; but there is here no such poem—and, to be sure, it should not be sought in such a collection. No collection of his *own* poems has been published, and the piece of which we are in search must be fugitive—unless, indeed, it is included in a volume of *translations* from various tongues, of which O. L. B. Wolff is also the author—but of which I am unable to obtain a copy.* It is by no means improbable that here the poem in question is to be found—but in this case it must have been

*Sammlung vorzuglicher Volkslieder der bekanntesten Nationen, grostentheils zun ersten male, metrisch in das Deutche ubertragen. Frankfurt, 1837.

plainly acknowledged as a translation, with its original designated. How, then, could Professor Longfellow have translated it as original with Wolff? These are mysteries yet to be
solved. It is observable—peculiarly so—that the Scotch
"Toom" is left untranslated in the version of Graham's Magazine. Will it be found that the same omission occurs in
Wolff's version?

In "The Spanish Student" of Mr. Longfellow, at page 80,
will be found what follows:

Scene IV.— *Preciosa's chamber. She is sitting with a book in her*
  hand near a table, on which are flowers. A bird singing in its
  cage. The Count of Lara enters behind, unperceived.
  Preciosa reads.

       All are sleeping, weary heart!
       Thou, thou only sleepless art!
Heigho! I wish Victorian were here.
I know not what it is makes me so restless! [*The bird*
    sings.
Thou little prisoner with thy motley coat,
That from thy vaulted, wiry dungeon singest,
Like thee I am a captive, and, like thee,
I have a gentle gaoler. Lack-a-day!
       All are sleeping, weary heart!
       Thou, thou only sleepless art!
       All this throbbing, all this aching,
       Evermore shall keep thee waking,
       For a heart in sorrow breaking
       Thinketh ever of its smart!
Thou speakest truly, poet! and methinks
More hearts are breaking in this world of ours
Than one would say. In distant villages
And solitudes remote, where winds have wafted
The barbed seeds of love, or birds of passage
Scattered them in their flight, do they take root,
And grow in silence, and in silence perish.
Who hears the falling of the forest leaf?
Or who takes note of every flower that dies?
Heigho! I wish Victorian would come.

Dolores! [*Turns to lay down her book, and perceives the Count.*
    Ha!
  Lara. Senora, pardon me.
  Preciosa. How's this? *Dolores!*
  Lara.   Pardon me—
  Preciosa.   *Dolores!*
  Lara. Be not alarmed; I found no one in waiting.
If I have been too bold——
  Preciosa [*turning her back upon him*]. You are too bold!
Retire! retire, and leave me!
  Lara.   My dear lady,
First hear me! I beseech you, let me speak!
'Tis for your good I come.
  Preciosa [*turning toward him with indignation*].
                    Begone! Begone!
You are the Count of Lara, but your deeds
Would make the statues of your ancestors
Blush on their tombs! Is it Castilian honor,
Is it Castilian pride, to steal in here
Upon a friendless girl, to do her wrong?
O shame! shame! shame! that you, a nobleman,
Should be so little noble in your thoughts
As to send *jewels* here to win my love,
And think to buy my honor with your gold!
I have no words to tell you how I scorn you!
Begone! The sight of you is hateful to me!
Begone, I say!

A few passages farther on in the same scene we meet the
following stage directions:— *"He tries to embrace her, she starts
back and draws a dagger from her bosom."* A little farther still
and *"Victorian enters behind."*

Compare all this with a "Scene from Politian, an Unpub-
lished Tragedy by Edgar A. Poe," to be found either at page
13, or at page 106, of the second volume of the "Southern
Literary Messenger."

The scene opens with the following stage directions:

A lady's apartment, with a window open and looking into a

garden. Lalage in deep mourning, reading at a table, on which lie some books and a hand mirror. In the back ground, JACINTA *leans carelessly on the back of a chair.*

*   *   *

Lalage reading. "It in another climate, so he said,
Bore a bright golden flower but not i' this soil.
    [*Pauses, turns over some leaves, and then resumes.*
No ling'ring winters there, nor snow, nor shower,
But ocean ever, to refresh mankind,
Breathes the shrill spirit of the western wind."
Oh, beautiful! most beautiful! how like
To what my fever'd soul doth dream of Heaven!
O happy land! [*pauses*] She died—the maiden died—
O still more happy maiden who couldst die!
Jacinta!
    [*Jacinta returns no answer, and Lalage presently resumes.*
    Again a similar tale,
Told of a beauteous dame beyond the sea!
Thus speaketh one Ferdinand i' the words of the play,
"She died full young"—one Bossola answers him
"I think not so; her infelicity
Seemed to have years too many." Ah luckless lady!
Jacinta! [*Still no answer.*] Here's a far sterner story
But like, oh very like in its despair,—
Of that Egyptian queen, winning so easily
A thousand hearts, losing at length her own.
She died. Thus endeth the history, and her maids
Lean over her and weep—two gentle maids
With gentle names, Eiros and Charmion.
Rainbow and Dove—*Jacinta!*

*   *   *

    [*Jacinta finally in a discussion about certain* jewels, *insults her mistress, who bursts into tears.*
    Lalage. Poor Lalage! and is it come to this?
Thy servant maid!——but courage!—'tis but a viper
Whom thou hast cherished to sting thee to the soul!
                    [*Taking up the mirror.*
Ha! here at least's a friend—too much a friend

In earlier days—a friend will not deceive thee.
Fair mirror and true! now tell me, for thou canst,
A tale—a pretty tale—and heed thou not
Though it be rife with woe. It answers me.
It speaks of sunken eyes, and wasted cheeks,
And beauty long deceased—remembers me
Of Joy departed—Hope, the Seraph Hope
Inurned and entombed!—now, in a tone
Low, sad, and solemn, but most audible
Whispers of early grave untimely yawning
For ruined maid. Fair mirror and true! thou liest not!
Thou hast no end to gain—no heart to break.
Castiglione lied who said he loved—
Thou true—he false!—false!—false!

    [*While she speaks a Monk enters her apartment, and*
                               approaches unobserved.

   Monk.   Refuge thou hast
Sweet daughter! in Heaven. Think of eternal things!
Give up thy soul to penitence, and pray.

   Lalage. I cannot pray!—my soul is at war with God!

                             [*Arising hurriedly.*
The frightful sounds of merriment below
Disturb my senses—go, I cannot pray!
The sweet airs from the garden worry me!
Thy presence grieves me—go!—thy priestly raiment
Fills me with dread—thy ebony crucifix
With horror and awe!

   Monk.   Think of thy precious soul!

   Lalage.   Think of my early days!—think of my father
And mother in Heaven! think of our quiet home
And the rivulet that ran before the door!
Think of my little sisters!—think of them!
And think of me!—think of my trusting love
And confidence—his vows—my ruin—think—think
Of my unspeakable misery!—*begone!*
Yet stay! yet stay! what was it thou saidst of prayer
And penitence? Didst thou not speak of faith
And vows before the throne?

   Monk.   I did.

   Lalage.   'Tis well.

There *is* a vow were fitting should be made—
A sacred vow, imperative, and urgent—
A solemn vow.
   Monk.   Daughter, this zeal is well.
   Lalage. Father! this zeal is any thing but well.
Hast thou a crucifix fit for this thing?
A crucifix whereon to register
A pious vow?   *[He hands her his own.*
            Not that—oh! no!—no! no!   *[Shuddering.*
Not that! not that! I tell thee, holy man,
Thy raiments and thy ebony cross affright me.
Stand back! I have a crucifix myself—
I have a crucifix! Methinks 'twere fitting
The deed—the vow—the symbol of the deed—
And the deed's register should tally, father!
Behold the cross wherewith a vow like mine
Is written in Heaven!
        [Draws a cross-handled dagger and raises it on high.
   Monk.   Thy words are madness, daughter!
And speak a purpose unholy—thy lips are livid—
Thine eyes are wild—tempt not the wrath divine—
Pause ere too late!—oh! be not—be not rash!
Swear not the oath—oh! swear it not!
   Lalage.   'Tis sworn!

The coincidences here are too markedly peculiar to be gain-sayed. The sitting at the table with books, etc.—the flowers on the one hand, and the garden on the other—the presence of the pert maid—the reading aloud from the book—the pausing and commenting—the plaintiveness of what is read, in accordance with the sorrow of the reader—the abstraction—the frequent calling of the maid by name—the refusal of the maid to answer—the jewels—the "begone"—the unseen entrance of a third person from behind—and the drawing of the dagger—are points sufficiently noticeable to establish at least the *imitation* beyond all doubt.

Let us now compare the concluding lines of Mr. Longfellow's "Autumn" with that of Mr. Bryant's "Thanatopsis:"
Mr. B. has it thus:

So live, that when thy summons comes to join
The innumerable caravan that moves
To that mysterious realm where each shall take
His chamber in the silent halls of Death,
Thou go not, like the quarry slave at night,
Scourged to his dungeon; but, sustained and soothed
By an unfaltering trust, approach thy grave
Like one who wraps the drapery of his couch
About him, and lies down to pleasant dreams.

Mr. L. thus:

To him the wind, aye and the yellow leaves
Shall have a voice and give him eloquent teachings.
He shall so hear the solemn hymn that Death
Has lifted up for all, that he shall go
To his long resting-place without a tear.

Again, in his "Prelude to the Voices of the Night" Mr.
Longfellow says:—

Look then into thine heart and write!

Sir Philip Sidney in the "Astrophel and Stella" has:

Foole, said my Muse to me, looke in thy heart and write!

Again—in Longfellow's "Midnight Mass" we read:

And the hooded clouds like friars.

The Lady in Milton's "Comus" says:

When the grey-hooded even
Like a sad votarist in palmer's weeds.

And again:—these lines by Professor Longfellow will be
remembered by every body:

Art is long and time is fleeting,
    And our hearts, though stout and brave,
Still like muffled drums are beating
    Funeral marches to the grave.

But if any one will turn to page 66 of John Sharpe's edition of Henry Headley's Select Beauties of Ancient English Poetry, published at London in 1810, he will there find an Exequy on the death of his wife by Henry King, Bishop of Chichester, and therein also the following lines, where the author is speaking of following his wife *to the grave*:

> But hark! *my pulse, like a soft drum,*
> *Beats* my approach—tells thee I come!
> And slow howe'er my *marches* be,
> I shall at last sit down by thee.

Were I disposed indeed, to push this subject any farther, I should have little difficulty in culling, from the works of the author of "Outre Mer," a score or two of imitations quite as palpable as any upon which I have insisted. The fact of the matter is, that the friends of Mr. Longfellow, so far from undertaking to talk about my "carping littleness" in charging Mr. Longfellow with imitation, should have given me credit, under the circumstances, for great moderation in charging him with imitation alone. Had I accused him, in loud terms, of manifest and continuous plagiarism, I should but have echoed the sentiment of every man of letters in the land beyond the immediate influence of the Longfellow *coterie*. And since I, "knowing what I know and seeing what I have seen"—submitting in my own person to accusations of plagiarism for the very sins of this gentleman against myself—since I contented myself, nevertheless, with simply setting forth the *merits* of the poet in the strongest light, whenever an opportunity was afforded me, can it be considered either decorous or equitable on the part of Professor Longfellow to beset me, upon my first adventuring an infinitesimal sentence of dispraise, with ridiculous anonymous letters from his friends, and moreover, with malice prepense, to instigate against me the pretty little witch entitled Miss Walter; advising her and instructing her to pierce me to death with the needles of innumerable epigrams, rendered unnecessarily and therefore cruelly painful to my feelings by being first carefully deprived of the point?

Broadway Journal, March 29, 1845

Plagiarism—Imitation—Postcript to Mr. Poe's Reply to the Letter of Outis.

IT SHOULD NOT BE SUPPOSED that I feel myself individually aggrieved in the letter of Outis. He has praised me even more than he has blamed. In replying to him, my design has been to place fairly and distinctly before the literary public certain principles of criticism for which I have been long contending, and which, through sheer misrepresentation, were in danger of being misunderstood.

Having brought the subject, in this view, to a close in the last Journal, I now feel at liberty to add a few words of postscript, by way of freeing myself of any suspicion of malevolence or discourtesy. The thesis of my argument, in general, has been the definition of the grounds on which a charge of plagiarism may be based, and of the species of ratiocination by which it is to be established: this is all. It will be seen by any one who shall take the trouble to read what I have written, that I make *no* charge of moral delinquency against either Mr. Longfellow, Mr. Aldrich, or Mr. Hood:—indeed, lest in the heat of argument, I may have uttered any words which may admit of being tortured into such an interpretation, I here fully disclaim them upon the spot.

In fact, the one strong point of defence for his friends has been unaccountably neglected by Outis. To attempt the rebutting of a charge of plagiarism by the broad assertion that no such thing as plagiarism exists, is a sotticism, and no more—but there would have been nothing of unreason in rebutting the charge as urged either against Mr. Longfellow, Mr. Aldrich, or Mr. Hood, by the proposition that no true poet can be guilty of a meanness—that the converse of the proposition is a contradiction in terms.

Should there be found any one willing to dispute with me this point, I would decline the disputation on the ground that my arguments are no arguments *to him*.

It appears to me that what seems to be the gross *inconsistency* of plagiarism as perpetrated by a poet, is very easily thus resolved:—the poetic sentiment (even without reference to the poetic power) implies a peculiarly, perhaps an abnormally keen appreciation of the beautiful, with a longing for its assimilation, or absorption, into the poetic identity. What the poet intensely admires, becomes thus, in very fact, although only partially, a portion of his own intellect. It has a second-ary origination within his own soul—an origination alto-gether apart, although springing, from its primary origination from without. The poet is thus possessed by another's thought, and cannot be said to take of it, possession. But, in either view, he thoroughly feels it as *his own*—and this feeling is counteracted only by the sensible presence of its true, pal-pable origin in the volume from which he has derived it—an origin which, in the long lapse of years it is almost impossible *not* to forget—for in the mean time the thought itself is for-gotten. But the frailest association will regenerate it—it springs up with all the vigor of a new birth—its absolute originality is not even a matter of suspicion—and when the poet has written it and printed it, and on its account is charged with plagiarism, there will be no one in the world more entirely astounded than himself. Now from what I have said it will be evident that the liability to accidents of this character is in the direct ratio of the poetic sentiment—of the susceptibility to the poetic impression; and in fact all literary history demonstrates that, for the most frequent and palpable plagiarisms, we must search the works of the most eminent poets.

Broadway Journal, April 5, 1845

"*Poems on Slavery*. By Henry Wadsworth Longfellow. Second edition, Cambridge: Pub-lished by John Owen. 1842." 12mo, pp. 31.
"*Voices of the Night*. By Henry Wadsworth Longfellow. Tenth edition. Cambridge: Pub-lished by John Owen. 1844." 12mo, pp. 144.
"*Ballads and other Poems*. By Henry Wadsworth Longfellow, author of 'Voices of the Night,' 'Hyperion,' &c. Eighth edition. Cambridge: Published by John Owen. 1844." 12mo, pp. 132.
"*The Waif: a collection of Poems*.
       'A waif the which by fortune came
       Upon your seas, he claimed as property;
       And yet nor his, nor his in equity, but
       Yours the waif by high prerogative.'—*The Fairie Queene*.
Second edition. Cambridge. Published by John Owen, 1845." 12mo, pp. 144.

THE POETICAL REPUTATION of Mr. LONGFELLOW is, no doubt, in some measure well-deserved; but it may be questioned whether, without the adventitious influence of his social position as Professor of Modern Languages and Belles

Lettres at HARVARD, and an access of this influence by marriage with an heiress, he would even have acquired his present
celebrity—such as it is.

We really feel no little shame in being forced, not into the
expression, but into the entertainment of opinions such as
these—the only shame we feel in respect to the matter of
their expression, is shame for others and not for ourselves—
shame that we in the infancy of our journalism, should have
been permitted to take the lead in the utterance of a thought
so long common with the *literati* of the land. In no literary
circle out of BOSTON—or, indeed, out of the small coterie of
abolitionists, transcendentalists and fanatics in general, which
is the Longfellow junto—have we heard a seriously dissenting voice on this point. It is universally, in private conversation—out of the knot of rogues and madmen aforesaid—
admitted that the poetical claims of Mr. LONGFELLOW have
been vastly overrated, and that the individual himself would
be esteemed little without the accessaries of wealth and position. It is usually said, that he has a sufficient scholarship, a
fine taste, a keen appreciation of the beautiful, a happy memory, a happier tact at imitation or transmutation, felicity of
phrase and some fancy. A few insist on his imagination—thus
proving the extent of their own—and showing themselves to
be utterly unread in the old English and modern German literature, to one or other of which, the author of "Outre Mer"
is unquestionably indebted for whatever imagination or traces
of invention his works may display. No phrenologist, indeed,
would require to be told that Mr. LONGFELLOW was not the
man of genius his friends would have us believe him—his
head giving no indication of ideality. Nor, when we speak of
phrenologists, do we mean to insist on implicit faith in the
marvels and inconsistencies of the FOWLERS *et id genus omne*.
Common observation, independently of either GALL or
SPURZHEIM, would suffice to teach all mankind that very
many of the salient points of phrenological science are undis-
putable truths—whatever falsity may be detected in the principles kindly furnished to the science by hot-headed and
asinine votaries. Now, one of these salient points, is the fact
that what men term "poetical genius," and what the phrenologists generally term the organ of ideality, are always found

co-existent in the same individual. We should as soon expect to see our old friend, SATAN, presiding at a temperance meeting, as to see a veritable poem—of his own—composed by a man whose head was flattened at the temples, like that of Professor LONGFELLOW. Holding these views, we confess that we were not a little surprised to hear Mr. POE, in a late lecture, on the Poetry of AMERICA, claim for the Professor a pre-eminence over all poets of this country on the score of the "loftiest poetical quality—imagination." There is no doubt in our minds, that an opinion so crude as this, must arise from a want of leisure or inclination to compare the works of the writer in question with the sources from which they were stolen. A defensive letter written by an unfortunate wight who called himself "OUTIS," seems to have stirred up the critic to make the proper examination, and we will make an even wager of a pound avoirdupois of nothing against LONGFELLOW's originality, that the rash opinion would not be given again. The simple truth is, that, whatever may be the talents of Professor LONGFELLOW, he is the GREAT MOGUL of the Imitators. There is, perhaps, no other country than our own, under the sun, in which it would have been possible for him to have attained his present eminence; and no other, certainly, in which, after having attained it by accident or chicanery, he would not have been hurled from it in a very brief period after its attainment.

We have now before us all the collected poems of Mr. LONG-FELLOW; and the first question which forces itself upon us as we look at them, is, how much of their success may be attributed to the luxurious manner in which, as merely physical books, they have been presented to the public. Of course we cannot pretend to answer our own question with precision; but that the *physique* has had vast influence upon the *morale*, no reflecting person of common honesty will be willing to deny.

We intend nothing in the shape of digested review; but as the subject has derived great interest of late through a discussion carried on in the pages of "The Broadway Journal," we propose to turn over these volumes, in a cursory manner, and make a few observations, in the style of the marginal note, upon each one of the poems in each.

The first volume is entitled "Poems on Slavery," and is intended for the especial use of those negrophilic old ladies of the north, who form so large a part of Mr. LONGFELLOW's friends. The first of this collection is addressed to WILLIAM ELLERY CHANNING, the great essayist, and not the very little poet of the same name. There is much force in the concluding line of the succeeding extract:—

> "Well done! thy words are great and bold;
>   At times they seem to me
> Like Luther's, in the days of old,
>   *Half-battles for the free*."

In the second poem—"The Slave's Dream"—there is also a particularly beautiful close to one of the stanzas:—

> "At night he heard the lion roar,
>   And the hyæna scream,
> And the river-horse as he crushed the reeds
>   Beside some hidden stream;
> And it passed *like a glorious roll of drums,*
>   *Through the triumph of his dream*."

This is certainly very fine; although we do do not exactly understand *what* is like the glorious roll of drums, whether it be the stream, or the various sounds aforesaid. This embarrassment in future will be prevented, if the poet will only affix a note to the next edition, declaring what he does mean, if he know himself.

The third poem—"The Good Part that shall not be taken away"—has two very effective lines:—

> "And musical as silver bells
> Their falling chains shall be."

The whole poem is in praise of a certain lady, who

> "———was rich and gave up all
>   To break the iron bands
> Of those who waited in her hall
>   And labored in her lands."

No doubt, it is a very commendable and very comfortable thing, in the Professor, to sit at ease in his library chair, and write verses instructing the southerners how to give up their all with a good grace, and abusing them if they will not; but we have a singular curiosity to know how much of his own, under a change of circumstances, the Professor himself would be willing to surrender. Advice of this character looks well only in the mouth of those who have entitled themselves to give it, by setting an example of the self-sacrifice.

The fourth is "The Slave in the Dismal Swamp." This is a shameless medley of the grossest misrepresentation. When did Professor LONGFELLOW ever *know* a slave to be hunted with bloodhounds in the DISMAL SWAMP? Because he has heard that runaway slaves are so treated in CUBA, he has certainly no right to change the locality, and by insinuating a falsehood in lieu of a fact, charge his countrymen with barbarity. What makes the matter worse, he is one of those who insist upon truth as one of the elements of poetry.

The fifth—"The Slave singing at midnight," embodies some good and novel rhymes—for example—

> "In that hour when night is *calmest*,
>   Sang he from the Hebrew *psalmist*."

"Angel" and "evangel," however, are inadmissible because identical—just as "excision" and "circumcision" would be— that is to say: the ear, instead of being gratified with a varia- tion of a sound—the principle of rhyme—is positively dis- pleased by its bare repetition. The commencement of the rhyming words, or—equally—of the rhyming portions of words, must always be different.

The sixth is "The witnesses," and is exceedingly feeble throughout. We cannot conceive how any artist could in two distinct stanzas of so brief a poem, admit such a termination as " witness *es*"—rhyming it too with "abyss."

The seventh, "The Quadroon Girl," is the old abolitionist story—worn threadbare—of a slaveholder selling his own child—a thing which may be as common in the South as in the East, is the infinitely worse crime of making matrimonial merchandise—or even less legitimate merchandise—of one's daughter.

The eighth—"The Warning," contains at least one stanza of absolute truth—as follows.

> "There is a poor, blind Sampson in this land,
>   Shorn of his strength and bound in bonds of steel,
> Who may, in some grim revel, raise his hand,
>   And shake the pillars of the common weal,
>   Till the vast temple of our Liberties,
>   A shapeless mass of wreck and rubbish lies."

One thing is certain:—if this prophecy be *not* fulfilled, it will be through no lack of incendiary doggrel on the part of Professor LONGFELLOW and his friends. We dismiss this volume with no more profound feeling than that of contempt.

The next volume we have is—"The Voices of the Night." "The Prelude," in this, is indistinct, but contains some noble passages. For example:—

> A slumberous sound—a sound that brings
>   The feelings of a dream—
> As of innumerable wings,
> As when a bell no longer swings,
> Faint the hollow murmur rings
>   O'er meadow lake and stream.

And again:

> The lids of Fancy's sleepless eyes
> Are gates unto that Paradise.

The last stanza commences with a plagiarism from Sir PHILIP SIDNEY:

> Look then into thine heart and write!

In the "Astrophel and Stella" we find it thus:—"Foole, said then my muse unto me, looke into thy heart and write!" The versification of the *Prelude* is weak, if not exactly erroneous:—we allude especially to the penultimate verse of each stanza.

The "Hymn to the Night" is one of the best of Mr. Longfellow's poems. There is a very inartistical fluctuation of thought, however, in the opening quotation:

> I heard the trailing garments of the Night
>   Sweep through her marble Halls!

> I saw her sable skirts all fringed with light
> From the celestial walls!

In the first two lines, the Night is personified as a woman in trailing garments passing through a marble palace: in the third and fourth by the use of the epithet "celestial" we are brought back to the real or unpersonified Night—and this too only in an imperfect manner, for the "sable skirts" of the personified Night are still retained. This vacillation pervades the whole poem and seriously injures its effect. Speaking of the first quatrain—what are we to understand by the notes of admiration at the closes of the second and fourth lines? They are called for by no rhetorical rules, and seem to be meant as expressive merely of the Professor's own admiration of his own magnificence. The concluding stanza is majestic, but liable to misapprehension upon a first reading. The "Peace! Peace!" of the first line will be mistaken by nine readers out of ten for an injunction of silence, rather than an invocation of the divinity, Peace. An instance occurs in this poem of Mr. LONGFELLOW's strong tendency to imitation:—so strong, indeed, that he not unfrequently imitates himself. He here speaks of "the sounds of sorrow and delight" that "fill the chambers of the Night," and just before, in the *Prelude*, he has

> "All forms of sorrow and delight
> All solemn voices of the Night."

"A Psalm of Life," is German throughout, in manner and spirit, and otherwise is chiefly remarkable for its containing one of the most palpable plagiarisms ever perpetrated by an author of equal character. We allude to the well-known lines:

> "Art is long and time is fleeting
> And our *hearts*, tho' stout and brave,
> Still like *muffled drums are beating*
> Funeral marches to the grave."

Mr. LONGFELLOW has, unfortunately, derived from these very lines, a *full half* of his poetical reputation. But they are by no means his own—the first line being an evident translation of the well-known Latin sentence—

"Ars longa, vita brêvis"—

and the remaining part pillaged from an old English writer. Mr. POE first detected this. It appears that in "HEADLEY's collection of old British Ballads," there is to be found, "An Exequy on the death of his wife, by HENRY KING, Bishop of Chichester," and in this Exequy the following verses:

> "But hark! my *pulse, like a soft drum,*
> *Beats* my approach—tells thee I come—
> And slow howe'er my *marches* be
> I shall at last sit down by thee."

Dr. KING is here speaking of soon following his wife *to the grave*. We have thus, in each poem, the identical ideas of a pulse (or heart)—of its beating like a drum—like a soft (or muffled) drum—of its beating a march; and of its beating a march to the grave:—all this identity of idea expressed in identical phraseology, and all in the compass of four lines. Now it was the seeming *originality* of this fine image which procured for it so wide a popularity in the lines of LONG-FELLOW; we presume, then, that not even the most desperate friends of his fine fortune, will attempt to defend him on the ground of this image's being one which would naturally arise in the mind of every poet—the common cant of those interested in the justification of a plagiarism. In larcenies of this kind it will always be found that an improvement is effected in externals—that is to say in point, flow of diction, etc., while there is a deterioration of the original in the higher merits of freshness, appositeness, and application of the thought to the general subject. How markedly is all this observable in the present instance!

"The Reaper and the Flowers" has nothing in it beyond common thoughts very gracefully expressed.

"The Light of Stars," opens with a very singularly silly stanza:

> "The night is come, but not too soon,
>   And, sinking silently,
>   All silently, the *little* moon
>   Drops down behind the sky."

Why *will* Mr. Longfellow persist in supposing that *ly* is a rhyme for sky?—why will he adhere to a conventionality, which has no meaning whatever? And what does he propose to himself in calling the moon *little*? The far-fetchedness of the phrase becomes at once obvious when we consider that *all* men agree in being struck with the apparent *increase* in the size of the setting moon. The first man who ever talked of its littleness under such circumstances is Professor LONG-FELLOW himself:—here at least and at last is he original.

"Footsteps of Angels." Mr. POE, in his late *exposé*, has given some very decisive instances of what he too modestly calls *imitations* on the part of Mr. LONGFELLOW from himself (Mr. Poe.) Here is one, however, which he has overlooked:

> "And, like *phantoms* grim and tall,
> *Shadows* from the fitful fire-light
> *Dance upon the parlor wall.*"

In a poem called "The Sleeper," by E. A. POE, and which we first saw a great many years ago in the "Southern Literary Messenger," we have a distinct recollection of these lines:

> "The wanton airs from the tree-top
> Laughingly through the lattice drop,
> And wave this crimson canopy
> So fitfully—so fearfully—
> Above the closed and fringéd lid
> 'Neath which thy slumbering soul lies hid,
> That o'er the floor and *down the wall*
> *Like ghosts the shadows rise and fall.*"

"Flowers"—is merely a weak amplification of the idea of a German poet, that flowers are the stars of earth. The versification is of a bad class, and of its class, bad.

"The Beleaguered City" was published in the "Southern Literary Messenger" about six weeks after the appearance in BROOKS' "Museum" (a five-dollar Baltimore Monthly) of Mr. POE's "Haunted Palace," and is a palpable imitation of the latter in matter and manner. Mr. LONGFELLOW's title is, indeed, merely a paraphrase of Mr. POE's. "The Beleaguered City" is designed to imply a mind beset with lunatic fancies; and this is, identically, the intention of "The Haunted

Palace." Mr. LONGFELLOW says, speaking of a "broad *valley*"
that in it,

> "——an army of phantoms vast and wan
>   Beleaguer the human soul,
>   Encamped beside Life's rushing *stream*
>   In Fancy's mystic light
>   *Gigantic shapes* and shadows gleam
>   Portentous through the night."

Mr. POE says:

> "And travellers, now, within that *valley*,
>   Through the red-litten windows see
>   *Vast forms*, that move fantastically
>   To a discordant melody,
>   While, *like a ghastly rapid river*
>   Through the pale door
>   A hideous throng rush out forever
>   And laugh—but smile no more."

The "Midnight Mass for the Dying Year" is a singular admixture of CORDELIA's death scene in "LEAR" and TENNY-
SON's "Death of the Old Year." A more palpable plagiarism
was never committed. At the time of the original publication
of Professor LONGFELLOW's poem, TENNYSON, was comparatively unknown, and we believe that no collection of his
works had ever been reprinted in this country. The "Midnight
Mass" concludes the later poems of the "Voices of the Night,"
which are noticeable, in general, as imitative of the German
poetry, or of poetry imbued with the German spirit. The rest
of the volume is occupied with "Earlier Poems" and "Translations." Of these the former are BRYANT, and nothing beyond. They were written in the author's youth, before his
acquaintance with German Letters—and yet it was necessary
that he should imitate something. In minds such as his, this
imitation is, indeed, as imperious a necessity as any animal
function.

"An April Day" has nothing observable *beyond* the obvious
imitation of the American model.

"Autumn" might absolutely be read *through*, in mistake for
BRYANT's "Thanatopsis." The similarity of conclusion in the

two poems is so close as to carry with it an air of parody. Mr.
BRYANT says:

> "So live, that when thy summons comes to join
> The innumerable caravan that moves
> To that mysterious realm where each shall take
> His chamber in the silent halls of Death
> Thou go not, like the quarry slave at night,
> Scourged to his dungeon; but sustained and soothed
> By an unfaltering trust, approach thy grave
> Like one who wraps the drapery of his couch
> About him, and lies down to pleasant dreams."

Mr. LONGFELLOW says:

> "To him the wind, aye and the yellow leaves
> Shall have a voice and give him eloquent teachings.
> He shall so hear the solemn hymn that Death
> Has lifted up for all, that he shall go
> To his long resting-place without a tear."

We do not like to be ill-natured; but when one gentleman's
purse is found in another gentleman's pocket, how did it
come there?

"Woods in Winter" is insipid, and totally thoughtless.

"The Hymn of the Moravian Nuns" is school-boyish in the
extreme.

"Sunrise on the Hills" is only remarkable for another instance of palpable imitation:

> "I heard the distant waters dash
> I saw the current whirl and flash,
> And richly by the blue lake's silver beach, etc."

Every body must remember the lines of the "Prisoner of
Chillon:"

> "——the wide long lake below
> And the blue Rhone in fullest flow,
> I heard the torrent leap and gush
> O'er channell'd rock and broken bush—
> I saw the white-wall 'd distant town," etc.

"The Spirit of Poetry" contains some fine thoughts—for example:

> "——where the silver brook
> From its full laver pours the white cascade,
> And, *babbling low amid the tangled woods*
> *Slips down through moss-grown stones with endless*
>   *laughter.*"

And again:

> "Groves through whose broken roof the sky looks in—
> Mountain, and shattered cliff, and sunny vale,
> The distant lake, fountains—*and mighty trees*
> *In many a lazy syllable repeating*
> *Their old poetic legends to the wind.*"

Both of these examples, however, are disfigured with that vulgar poetic solecism—the endeavour to elevate objects of natural grandeur by likening them to the mere works of man. The grove has a "broken roof"; and the brook pours the cascade from a "laver."

"Burial of the Minnisink." There is nothing about it to distinguish it from a thousand other similar things.

The Translations commence with "Coplas de Manrique" from the Spanish—and this again with the line

> "O let the soul her slumbers break!
> Let thought be quickened and awake,
> Awake to see,
> How soon," &c.

And this, we presume, is what Mr. LONGFELLOW calls original translation. We have at this moment, some verses ringing in our ears whose whereabouts we cannot call to memory—but no doubt there are many of our readers who can. They are nearly identical, however, with Mr. Longfellow's lines both in words, rhyme, metre and arrangement of stanza. They begin thus:

> "O let the soul its slumber break
> * * * * * *   and awake
> To see how soon,"
> Etc. etc.

If we are not mistaken they are quoted in some of the Notes to POPE's:

"Arise my St. JOHN, leave all meaner things."

"The Good Shepherd," from LOPE DE VEGA, has "nothing in it." In the same category is "To-morrow," from the same—"The Native Land," from FRANCISCO DE ALDANA—"The Image of GOD," from the same—and "The Brook," from the Spanish:—these pieces seem to have been translated with no other object than to show that Mr. LONGFELLOW could translate. "The Celestial Pilot"—"The Terrestrial Paradise," and "Beatrice," from DANTE, strike us as by no means equal to CARY. These pieces abound also, in sheer affectations. Were Mr. LONGFELLOW asked *why* he employed " withouten" and other words of that kind, what reasonable answer could he make?

"Spring," from the French of CHARLES D'ORLEANS, is utterly worthless as a poem:—of its merits as a translation we are not prepared to speak, never having seen the original. One thing, however, is quite certain, the versification is *not* translated. The French have no such metre or rhythm.

"The Child Asleep," from the French, is particularly French.

"The Grave," from the Anglo Saxon, is forcible—but the metre is mere prose, and, of course, should not have been retained.

"King Christian," from the Danish, has force.

"The Happiest Land," from the German, is mere common place.

"The Wave," from TIEDGE, contains one thought, but that is scarcely worth the page it occupies.

"The Dead," from KLOPSTOCK, is nothing.

"The Bird and the Ship," from MÜLLER, is pure inanity.

"Whither," from the same, is worse, if possible.

"Beware" is still worse—possible or not. We never saw a more sickening thing in a book.

"The Song of the Bell," has no business with a title which calls up the recollection of what is really meritorious.

"The Castle by the Sea," from UHLAND, should have been

rendered "The Castle *Over* the Sea." The whole dark suggestion of the poem is lost by the mis-translation. The force of the original throughout is greatly impaired by the milk and water of the version.

"The Black Knight," from the same is merely a German bugaboo story of the common kind, with no particular merit.

"The Song of the Silent Land," from SALIS, has merely the merit of a suggestive title, the repetition of which at the close of each stanza is the one good point.

The volume ends with "L'Envoi," a most affected, far-fetched, and altogether contemptible imitation, or parody, of the worst mannerisms of the Germans.

The next volume we have is—"Ballads and other Poems," which we note in the order of their succession.

"The Skeleton in Armor" is one of the best poems of LONGFELLOW; if not indeed his very best. It has the merits of directness and simplicity, and is besprinkled with vigorous thought tersely expressed. Its versification would be monotonous, did it not at points become so radically defective as to change into prose, as for example:

> "Mute did the minstrels stand
>   *To* hear my story—"
> "Like birds within their nest
>   *By* the hawk frighted—"
> "Many the hearts that bled
>   *By* our stern orders—"
> "Came a dull voice of woe
>   *For* this I sought thee."
> "Saw we old Hildebrand
>   *With* twenty horsemen—"
> "Why did they leave that night
>   *Her* nest unguarded?"
>   etc. etc. etc.

These were meant to be Dactyls—but have degenerated into such a mixture of these, with Anapests, Trochees and Iambics, as to make quite decent prose, and nothing more.

"The Wreck of the Hesperus" has some remarkably spirited

passages, but what can justify any man, to-day, in the use of daught*er*, and sail*or*?

"The Luck of Edenthall" is a capital translation of one of UHLAND's best romances.

"The Elected Knight," from the Danish, is meant to prove, we presume, the Professor's acquaintance with the literature of HARDIKNUTE.

"The Children of the Lord's Supper," from TEGNER, is remarkable for nothing but its demonstration of the Professor's ignorance of the Greek and Roman Hexameters, which he here *professes* to imitate—the "inexorable hexameter," as he calls it. It is only inexorable to those who do not comprehend its elements. Here mere pedantry will carry a man very little way—and Professor LONGFELLOW has no head for analysis. Most of his hexameters are pure prose, and, if written to the eye as such, would not be distinguished from prose by any human being. Some of them have a remarkable resemblance to the hexameters of COLERIDGE. For example: COLERIDGE says:

"Young life lowed through the meadows, the woods, and
    the echoing mountains,
  Wandered bleating in valleys and warbled on blossoming
    branches."

LONGFELLOW says:

"Clear was the Heaven and blue, and May with her cap
    crowned with roses,
  Stood in her holiday dress in the fields, and the wind and
    the brooklet
  Murmured gladness and peace, God's peace, with lips rosy-
    tinted
  Whispered the race of the flowers, and merry on balancing
    branches,"

etc. etc. etc.

"The Village Blacksmith" is a mere Hood-ism—nothing more.

"Endymion" has some well expressed common-places. For example:

> "No one is so accursed by Fate,
>   No one so utterly desolate
>   But some heart, though unknown,
>   Responds unto his own."

When we speak of expression, here, we must not be understood as commending the versification, which is wretched. We should like to hear Professor LONGFELLOW—or any one else—scan

> "But some heart, though unknown, etc."

"The Two Locks of Hair," from the German of Pfizer, should have remained in the original.

"It is not always May." The whole point of this effusion lies in the title.

"The Rainy Day." The whole point of this, lies in the repetition of "the day is dark and dreary."

"God's-Acre." Here we find one of those utterly insoluble knots of imagery which are Mr. LONGFELLOW's forte. What is any man to make of

> "Comfort to those who in the grave have sown
>   The seed that they had garnered in their hearts,
>   Their bread of life, alas! no more their own?"

Seeds (which are not seeds, but bread,) are garnered in a heart, and sown in a grave, by the persons who garnered it, and who having sown it (although it was as much bread as seed) lost possession of it thenceforward;—this is a literal rendition of the whole matter into prose—and a beautifully lucid thing it is.

"To the River Charles" is what its author calls it—"an idle song."

"Blind Bartimeus" is only *Zoe mou sas agapo* over again.

"The Goblet of Life" is terse and well versified.

"Maidenhood" is a graceful little poem, spoilt by its didacticism, and by the awkward, monotonous and grossly artificial character of its versification.

"Excelsior" has one fine thought in its conclusion:

> And from the sky, serene and far,
> *A voice fell like a falling star.*

The third volume, is called "The Spanish Student." As a poem, it is meritorious at points—as a drama it is one of the most lamentable failures. It has several sparkling passages—but little vigor—and, as a matter almost of course, not a particle of originality. Indeed it professes to be taken, *in part*, from the "Gitanilla" of CERVANTES. *In part*, also, it is taken from "Politian, a fragmentary Drama, by EDGAR A. POE," published in the second volume of the SOUTHERN LITERARY MESSENGER:—no acknowledgment, however, is made in the latter instance. The *imitation* is one of the most impudent ever known. In both cases a young and beautiful woman is sitting at table with books and flowers. In both cases there is a pert serving maid:—in both the lady reads aloud:—in both what she reads is poetry:—in both it is of a plaintive character in consonance with the sorrow of the reader:—in both the reader makes application of what is read to her own case:—in both she frequently calls on the maid:—who, in both, refuses to answer:—in both there is a quarrel about jewels:—in both a third person enters unseen behind: and lastly in both the lady reiterates the word "begone!" and draws a dagger. But the palpability of the plagiarism can be fully understood only by those who read and compare the two poems. The "Southern Literary Messenger," indeed, seems to have been the great store-house whence the Professor has derived most of his contraband goods.

The last volume to be noticed, is "The Waif." This is noticeable solely on the ground of the "Pröem," which is the only one of his acknowledged compositions it contains—but one which is, perhaps, upon the whole, the best which he has written. It is remarkably easy, graceful, and plaintive, while its versification seems to be accidentally meritorious. Nothing is more clear indeed than that *all* the merit of the Professor on this score is accidental. He knows less than nothing of the principles of verse.

Since the issue of "Ballads and other Poems" he has written several things for "Graham's Magazine," and among others "The Belfry of Bruges"—but let any person inquisitive as to Mr. LONGFELLOW's pretensions to originality, merely take the trouble to compare the lines in question with certain stanzas entitled "The Chimes of Antwerp," published in "Gra-

ham's Magazine" for April, 1841. "The Belfry of Bruges" is
the number for January, 1843.

In the "New York Mirror," Mr. POE concluded a notice of
"The Waif" in the following words:

"There does appear in this little volume a very careful
avoidance of all American poets who may be supposed especially to interfere with the claims of Mr. Longfellow. These
men Mr. Longfellow can continually *imitate* (*is* that the
word?) and yet never even incidentally commend."

To which one of the Professor's Boston friends makes answer thus:

"It has been asked, perhaps, why Lowell was neglected in
this collection. Might it not as well be asked why Bryant,
Dana, and Halleck were neglected! The answer is obvious to
any one who candidly considers the object of the collection.
It professed to be, according to the Pröem, from the humbler
poets; and it was intended to embrace pieces that were anonymous or which were not easily accessible to the general
reader—the *waifs* and *estrays* of literature."

The rejoinder to all this is obvious. If LOWELL was omitted
on these grounds why was not HORACE SMITH, omitted on
the same?—and BROWNING—and SHELLY—and A. C.
COXE—and HOOD—and MONTGOMERY—and EMERSON—
and MARVEL—and W. G. CLARK—and PIERPONT and five
or six others? The fact is, none of these gentlemen "interfered
with Mr. LONGFELLOW's claims"—but LOWELL *did*. He was
a rising poet in Mr. LONGFELLOW's own school—own manner—a Bostonian—a neighbor.

It is possible, however, that Mr. POE's allusions were not
to Mr. LOWELL, but to himself; and, if so, who shall venture
to blame him? He might have thought it no more than justice
on the part of LONGFELLOW, to give a place in "The Waif"
to that "Haunted Palace," for example, of which he had
shown so flattering an admiration as to purloin everything
that was worth purloining about it.

It is, indeed, for that whereas, Mr. LONGFELLOW has stolen so much from Mr. POE, that we have alluded so much to the *exposé* of the latter; for it appeared to us, our course was but just. The latter, driven to it by a silly letter of Mr. LONG-FELLOW's friends, has exposed the knavery of the Professor, and any one who reads the "Broadway Journal," will acknowledge he has done it well.

There are other plagiarisms of Mr. LONGFELLOW which we might easily expose; but we have said enough. There can be no reasonable doubt in the mind of any, out of the little clique, to which we at first alluded, that the author of "Outre Mer," is not only a servile imitator, but a most insolent literary thief. Commencing his literary life he began, struck with his quiet style, to imitate BRYANT. As he pored over the pages of the Spanish, and then of the great Northern writers, his imitation took a new direction. Soon, to save labor, he began to filch a little here and a little there—some straw to make his bricks, something to temper his own heavy clay. Finding he was not detected, he stole with more confidence, until stealing became habit, and so second nature. At this time we doubt whether he could write without helping himself to the ideas and style of other people. Indeed, if he were by chance to perpetrate an original idea, he would be as much astonished as the world around; and would go about cackling and "making a fuss in general," like a little bantam hen, who by a strange freak of nature, had laid a second egg on the same day.

Aristidean, April 1845

Augustus Baldwin Longstreet

Georgia Scenes, Characters, Incidents, &c. in the First Half Century of the Republic. By a Native Georgian. Augusta, Georgia.

THIS BOOK has reached us anonymously—not to say anomalously—yet it is most heartily welcome. The author, whoever he is, is a clever fellow, imbued with a spirit of the truest humor, and endowed, moreover, with an exquisitely discriminative and penetrating understanding of *character* in general, and of Southern character in particular. And we do not mean to speak of *human* character exclusively. To be sure, our Georgian is *au fait* here too—he is learned in all things appertaining to the biped without feathers. In regard, especially, to that class of southwestern mammalia who come under the generic appellation of "savagerous wild cats," he is a very Theophrastus in duodecimo. But he is not the less at home in other matters. Of geese and ganders he is the La Bruyere, and of good-for-nothing horses the Rochefoucault.

Seriously—if this book were printed in England it would make the fortune of its author. We positively mean what we say—and are quite sure of being sustained in our opinion by all proper judges who may be so fortunate as to obtain a copy of the *"Georgia Scenes,"* and who will be at the trouble of sifting their peculiar merits from amid the *gaucheries* of a Southern publication. Seldom—perhaps never in our lives—have we laughed as immoderately over any book as over the one now before us. If these *scenes* have produced such effects upon *our* cachinnatory nerves—upon *us* who are not "of the merry mood," and, moreover, have not been unused to the perusal of somewhat similar things—we are at no loss to imagine what a hubbub they would occasion in the uninitiated regions of Cockaigne. And what would Christopher North say to them?—ah, what would Christopher North say? that is the question. Certainly not a word. But we can fancy the pursing up of his lips, and the long, loud, and jovial resonnation of his wicked, and uproarious ha! ha's!

From the Preface to the Sketches before us we learn that although they are, generally, nothing more than fanciful combinations of real incidents and characters, still, in some instances, the narratives are literally true. We are told also that the publication of these pieces was commenced, rather more than a year ago, in one of the Gazettes of the State, and that they were favorably received. "For the last six months," says the author, "I have been importuned by persons from all quarters of the State to give them to the public in the present form." This speaks well for the Georgian taste. But that the publication will *succeed*, in the bookselling sense of the word, is problematical. Thanks to the long indulged literary supineness of the South, her presses are not as apt in putting forth a *saleable* book as her sons are in concocting a wise one.

From a desire of concealing the author's name, two different signatures, Baldwin and Hall, were used in the original *Sketches*, and, to save trouble, are preserved in the present volume. With the exception, however, of one scene, "The Company Drill," all the book is the production of the same pen. The first article in the list is "Georgia Theatrics." Our friend *Hall*, in this piece, represents himself as ascending, about eleven o'clock in the forenoon of a June day, "a long and gentle slope in what was called the Dark Corner of Lincoln County, Georgia." Suddenly his ears are assailed by loud, profane, and boisterous voices, proceeding, apparently, from a large company of raggamuffins, concealed in a thick covert of undergrowth about a hundred yards from the road.

"You kin, kin you?

"Yes I kin, and am able to do it! Boo-oo-oo-oo! Oh wake snakes and walk your chalks! Brimstone and fire! Dont hold me Nick Stoval! The fight's made up, and lets go at it—my soul if I dont jump down his throat, and gallop every chitterling out of him before you can say 'quit!'

"Now Nick, dont hold him! Jist let the wild cat come, and I'll tame him. Ned 'll see me a fair fight—wont you Ned?

"Oh yes; I'll see you a fair fight, my old shoes if I dont.

"That's sufficient, as Tom Haynes said when he saw the Elephant. Now let him come!" &c. &c. &c.

And now the sounds assume all the discordant intonations inseparable from a Georgia "rough and tumble" fight. Our traveller listens in dismay to the indications of a quick, violent, and deadly struggle. With the intention of acting as pacificator, he dismounts in haste, and hurries to the scene of action. Presently, through a gap in the thicket, he obtains a glimpse of one, at least, of the combatants. This one appears to have his antagonist beneath him on the ground, and to be dealing on the prostrate wretch the most unmerciful blows. Having overcome about half the space which separated him from the combatants, our friend Hall is horror-stricken at seeing "the uppermost make a heavy plunge with both his thumbs, and hearing, at the same instant, a cry in the accent of keenest torture, 'Enough! My eye's out!' "

Rushing to the rescue of the mutilated wretch the traveller is surprised at finding that all the accomplices in the hellish deed have fled at his approach—at least so he supposes, for none of them are to be seen.

"At this moment," says the narrator, "the victor saw me for the first time. He looked excessively embarrassed, and was moving off, when I called to him in a tone emboldened by the sacredness of my office, and the iniquity of his crime, 'come back, you brute! and assist me in relieving your fellow mortal, whom you have ruined forever!' My rudeness subdued his embarrassment in an instant; and with a taunting curl of the nose, he replied; you need'nt kick before you're spurred. There 'ant nobody there, nor ha'nt been nother. I was jist seein how I could 'a' *fout*! So saying, he bounded to his plow, which stood in the corner of the fence about fifty yards beyond the battle ground."

All that had been seen or heard was nothing more nor less than a Lincoln rehearsal; in which all the parts of all the characters, of a Georgian Court-House fight had been sustained by the youth of the plough *solus*. The whole anecdote is told with a raciness and vigor which would do honor to the pages of Blackwood.

The second Article is "The Dance, a Personal Adventure of the Author" in which the oddities of a back-wood reel are depicted with inimitable force, fidelity and picturesque effect. "The Horse-swap" is a vivid narration of an encounter between the wits of two Georgian horse-jockies. This is most excellent in every respect—but especially so in its delineations of Southern bravado, and the keen sense of the ludicrous evinced in the portraiture of the steeds. We think the following free and easy sketch of a *hoss* superior, in joint humor and verisimilitude, to any thing of the kind we have ever seen.

"During this harangue, little Bullet looked as if he understood it all, believed it, and was ready at any moment to verify it. He was a horse of goodly countenance, rather expressive of vigilance than fire; though an unnatural appearance of fierceness was thrown into it, by the loss of his ears, which had been cropped pretty close to his head. Nature had done but little for Bullet's head and neck, but he managed in a great measure to hide their defects by bowing perpetually. He had obviously suffered severely for corn; but if his ribs and hip bones had not disclosed the fact he never would have done it; for he was in all respects as cheerful and happy as if he commanded all the corn cribs and fodder stacks in Georgia. His height was about twelve hands; but as his shape partook somewhat of that of the giraffe his haunches stood much lower. They were short, straight, peaked, and concave. Bullet's tail, however, made amends for all his defects. All that the artist could do to beautify it had been done; and all that horse could do to compliment the artist, Bullet did. His tail was nicked in superior style, and exhibited the line of beauty in so many directions, that it could not fail to hit the most fastidious taste in some of them. From the root it dropped into a graceful festoon; then rose in a handsome curve; then resumed its first direction; and then mounted suddenly upwards like a cypress knee to a perpendicular of about two and a half inches. The whole had a careless and bewitching inclination to the right. Bullet obviously knew where his beauty lay, and took all occasions to display it to the best advantage. If a stick cracked, or if any one moved suddenly about him or coughed, or hawked, or spoke a little louder than common, up went Bullet's tail like lightning; and if the *going up* did not please, the *coming down* must of necessity, for it was as different from the other movement as was its direction. The first was a bold and rapid flight upwards usually to an angle of forty five degrees. In this position he kept his interesting appendage until he satisfied himself that nothing in particular was to be done; when he commenced dropping it by half inches, in second beats—then in triple time—then faster and shorter, and faster and shorter still, until it finally died away imperceptibly into its natural position. If I might compare sights to sounds, I should say its *settling* was more like the note of a locust than any thing else in nature."

"The character of a Native Georgian" is amusing, but not so good as the scenes which precede and succeed it. Moreover the character described (a practical humorist) is neither very original, nor appertaining exclusively to Georgia.

"The Fight" although involving some horrible and disgusting details of southern barbarity is a sketch unsurpassed in dramatic vigor, and in the vivid truth to nature of one or two of the personages introduced. *Uncle Tommy Loggins*, in particular, an oracle in "rough and tumbles," and Ransy Sniffle, a misshapen urchin "who in his earlier days had fed copiously upon red clay and blackberries," and all the pleasures of whose life concentre in a love of fisticuffs—are both forcible, accurate and original generic delineations of real existences to be found sparsely in Georgia, Mississippi and Louisiana, and very plentifully in our more remote settlements and territories. This article would positively make the fortune of any British periodical.

"The Song" is a burlesque somewhat overdone, but upon the whole a good caricature of Italian bravura singing. The following account of Miss Aurelia Emma Theodosia Augusta Crump's execution on the piano is inimitable.

"Miss Crump was educated at Philadelphia; she had been taught to sing by Madam Piggisqueaki, who was a pupil of Ma'm'selle Crokifroggietta, who had sung with Madam Catalani; and she had taken lessons on the piano, from Signor Buzzifuzzi, who had played with Paganini.

"She seated herself at the piano, rocked to the right, then to the left,—leaned forward, then backward, and began. She placed her right hand about midway the keys, and her left about two octaves below it. She now put off the right in a brisk canter up the treble notes, and the left after it. The left then led the way back, and the right pursued it in like manner. The right turned, and repeated its first movement; but the left outrun it this time, hopt over it, and flung it entirely off the track. It came in again, however, behind the left on its return, and passed it in the same style. They now became highly incensed at each other, and met furiously on the middle ground. Here a most awful conflict ensued, for about the space of ten seconds, when the right whipped off, all of a sudden, as I thought, fairly vanquished. But I was in the error, against which Jack Randolph cautions us—'It had only fallen back to a stronger position.' It mounted upon two black keys, and commenced the note of a rattle-snake. This had a wonderful effect upon the left, and placed the doctrine of snake charming beyond dispute. The left rushed furiously towards it repeatedly, but seemed invariably panic struck, when it came within six keys of it, and as invariably retired with a tremendous roaring down the bass keys. It continued its assaults, sometimes by the way of the naturals, sometimes by the way of the sharps, and sometimes by a zigzag, through both; but all its attempts to dislodge the right from its strong hold proving ineffectual, it came close up to its adversary and expired."

The *"Turn Out"* is excellent—a second edition of Miss Edgeworth's "Barring Out," and full of fine touches of the truest humor. The scene is laid in Georgia, and in the good old days of *fescues*, *abbiselfas*, and *anpersants*—terms in very common use, but whose derivation we have always been at a loss to understand. Our author thus learnedly explains the riddle.

"The *fescue* was a sharpened wire, or other instrument, used by the preceptor, to point out the letters to the children. *Abbiselfa* is a contraction of the words 'a, by itself, a.' It was usual, when either of the vowels constituted a syllable of a word, to pronounce it, and denote its independent character, by the words just mentioned, thus: 'a by itself *a*, c-o-r-n corn, *acorn*'—e by itself *e*, v-i-l vil, evil. The character which stands for the word *'and'* (&) was probably pronounced with the same accompaniment, but in terms borrowed from the Latin language, thus: '& *per se* (by itself) &.' 'Hence anpersant.' "

This whole story forms an admirable picture of school-boy democracy in the woods. The *master* refuses his pupils an Easter holiday; and upon repairing, at the usual hour of the fatal day, to his school house, "a log pen about twenty feet square," finds every avenue to his ingress fortified and barricadoed. He advances, and is assailed by a whole wilderness of sticks from the cracks. Growing desperate, he seizes a fence rail, and finally succeeds in effecting an entrance by demolishing the door. He is soundly flogged however for his pains, and the triumphant urchins suffer him to escape with his life, solely upon condition of their being allowed to do what they please as long as they shall think proper.

"*The Charming Creature as a Wife,*" is a very striking narrative of the evils attendant upon an ill-arranged marriage—but as it has nothing about it peculiarly Georgian, we pass it over without further comment.

"*The Gander Pulling*" is a gem worthy, in every respect, of the writer of "The Fight," and "The Horse Swap." What a "*Gander Pulling*" is, however, may probably not be known by a great majority of our readers. We will therefore tell them. It is a piece of unprincipled barbarity not unfrequently practised in the South and West. A circular horse path is formed of about forty or fifty yards in diameter. Over this path, and between two posts about ten feet apart, is extended a rope which, swinging loosely, vibrates in an arc of five or six feet. From the middle of this rope, lying directly over the middle of the path, a gander, whose neck and head are well greased, is suspended by the feet. The distance of the fowl from the ground is generally about ten feet—and its neck is consequently just within reach of a man on horseback. Matters being thus arranged, and the mob of vagabonds assembled, who are desirous of entering the chivalrous lists of the "Gander Pulling," a hat is handed round, into which a quarter or half dollar, as the case may be, is thrown by each competitor. The money thus collected is the prize of the victor in the game—and the game is thus conducted. The ragamuffins mounted on horseback, gallop round the circle in Indian file. At a word of command, given by the proprietor of the gander, the pulling, properly so called, commences. Each villain as he passes under the rope makes a grab at the throat of the devoted bird—the end and object of the tourney being to pull off his head. This of course is an end not easily accomplished. The fowl is obstinately bent upon retaining his caput if possible—in which determination he finds a powerful adjunct in the grease. The rope, moreover, by the efforts of the human devils, is kept in a troublesome and tantalizing state of vibration, while two assistants of the proprietor, one at each pole, are provided with a tough cowhide, for the purpose of preventing any horse from making too long a sojourn beneath the gander. Many hours, therefore, not unfrequently elapse before the contest is decided.

"*The Ball*"—a Georgia ball—is done to the life. Some passages, in a certain species of sly humor, wherein intense observation of character is disguised by simplicity of relation, put us forcibly in mind of the Spectator. For example.

"When De Bathle and I reached the ball room, a large number of gentlemen had already assembled. They all seemed cheerful and happy. Some walked in couples up and down the ball room, and talked with great volubility; but none of them understood a word that himself or his companion said.

"Ah, sir, how do you know that?

"Because the speakers showed plainly by their looks and actions, that their thoughts were running upon their own personal appearance, and upon the figure they would cut before the ladies, when they should arrive; and not upon the subject of the discourse. And furthermore, their conversation was like that of one talking in his sleep—without order, sense, or connexion. The hearer always made the speaker repeat in sentences and half sentences; often interrupting him with ' what?' before he had proceeded three words in a remark; and then laughed affectedly, as though he saw in the senseless unfinished sentence, a most excellent joke. Then would come his reply, which could not be forced into connexion with a word that he had heard; and in the course of which he was treated with precisely the civility which he had received. And yet they kept up the conversation with lively interest as long as I listened to them."

"*The Mother and her Child*," we have seen before—but read it a second time with zest. It is a laughable burlesque of the baby 'gibberish' so frequently made use of by mothers in speaking to their children. This sketch evinces, like all the rest of the Georgia scenes—a fine dramatic talent.

"The Debating Society" is the best thing in the book—and indeed one among the best things of the kind we have ever read. It has all the force and freedom of some similar articles in the Diary of a Physician—without the evident straining for effect which so disfigures that otherwise admirable series. We will need no apology for copying *The Debating Society* entire.

About three and twenty years ago, at the celebrated school in W——n, was formed a Debating Society, composed of young gentlemen between the ages of seventeen and twenty-two. Of the number were two, who, rather from an uncommon volubility, than from any superior gifts or acquirements, which they possessed over their associates, were by common consent, placed at the head of the fraternity.—At least this was true of one of them: the other certainly had higher claims to his distinction. He was a man of the highest order of intellect, who, though he has since been known throughout the Union, as one of the ablest speakers in the country, seems to me to have added but little to his powers in debate, since he passed his twenty-second year. The name of the first, was Longworth; and McDermot was the name of the last. They were congenial spirits, warm friends, and classmates, at the time of which I am speaking.

It was a rule of the Society, that every member should speak upon the subjects chosen for discussion, or pay a fine; and as all the members valued the little stock of change, with which they were furnished, more than they did their reputation for oratory, not a fine had been imposed for a breach of this rule, from the organization of the society to this time.

The subjects for discussion were proposed by the members, and selected by the President, whose prerogative it was also to arrange the speakers on either side, at his pleasure; though in selecting the subjects, he was influenced not a little by the members who gave their opinions freely of those which were offered.

It was just as the time was approaching, when most of the members were to leave the society, some for college, and some for the busy scenes of life, that McDermot went to share his classmate's bed for a night. In the course of the evening's conversation, the society came upon the tapis. "Mac," said Longworth, "would'nt we have rare sport, if we could impose a subject upon the society, which has no sense in it, and hear the members speak upon it?"

"Zounds," said McDermot, "it would be the finest fun in the world. Let's try it at all events—we can lose nothing by the experiment."

A sheet of foolscap was immediately divided between them, and they industriously commenced the difficult task of framing sentences, which should possess the *form* of a debateable question, without a particle of the *substance*.—After an hour's toil, they at length exhibited the fruits of their labor, and after some reflection, and much laughing, they selected, from about thirty subjects proposed, the following, as most likely to be received by the society:

"Whether at public elections, should the votes of faction predominate by internal suggestions or the bias of jurisprudence?"

Longworth was to propose it to the society, and McDermot was to advocate its adoption.—As they had every reason to suppose, from the practice of the past, that they would be placed at the head of the list of disputants, and on opposite sides, it was agreed between them, in case the experiment should succeed, that they would write off, and interchange their speeches, in order that each might quote literally from the other, and thus *seem* at least, to understand each other.

The day at length came for the triumph or defeat of the project; and several accidental circumstances conspired to crown it with success. The society had entirely exhausted their subjects; the discussion of the day had been protracted to an unusual length, and the horns of the several boarding-houses began to sound, just as it ended. It was at this auspicious moment, that Longworth rose, and proposed his subject. It was caught at with rapture by McDermot, as being decidedly the best that had ever been submitted; and he wondered that none of the members had ever thought of it before.

It was no sooner proposed, than several members exclaimed, that they did not understand it; and demanded an explanation from the mover. Longworth replied, that there was no time then for explanations, but that either himself or Mr. McDermot would explain it, at any other time.

Upon the credit of the *maker* and *endorser*, the subject was accepted; and under pretence of economising time, (but really to avoid a repetition of the question,) Longworth kindly offered to record it, for the Secretary. This labor ended, he announced that he was prepared for the arrangement of the disputants.

"Put yourself," said the President, "on the affirmative, and Mr. McDermot on the negative."

"The subject," said Longworth, "cannot well be resolved into an affirmative and negative. It consists more properly, of two conflicting affirmatives: I have therefore drawn out the heads, under which the speakers are to be arranged thus:
Internal Suggestions.   *Bias of Jurisprudence.*

Then put yourself Internal Suggestions—Mr. McDermot the other side, Mr. Craig on your side—Mr. Pentigall the other side," and so on.

McDermot and Longworth now determined that they would not be seen by any other member of the society during the succeeding week, except at times when explanations could not be asked, or when they were too busy to give them. Consequently, the week passed away, without any explanations; and the members were summoned to dispose of the important subject, with no other lights upon it than those which they could collect from its terms. When they assembled, there was manifest alarm on the countenances of all but two of them.

The Society was opened in due form, and Mr. Longworth was called on to open the debate. He rose and proceeded as follows:

"*Mr. President*—The subject selected for this day's discussion, is one of vast importance, pervading the profound depths of psychology, and embracing within its comprehensive range, all that is interesting in morals, government, law and politics. But, sir, I shall not follow it through all its interesting and diversified ramifications; but endeavor to deduce from it those great and fundamental principles, which have direct bearing, upon the antagonist positions of the dis-

putants; confining myself more immediately to its psychological influence when exerted, especially upon the *votes of
faction*: for here is the point upon which the question mainly
turns. In the next place, I shall consider the effects of those
'suggestions' emphatically termed *'internal'* when applied to
the same subject. And in the third place, I shall compare these
effects, with 'the bias of jurisprudence,' considered as the only
resort in times of popular excitement—for these are supposed
to exist by the very terms of the question.

"The first head of this arrangement, and indeed the whole
subject of dispute, has already been disposed of by this society. We have discussed the question, 'are there any innate
maxims?' and with that subject and this, there is such an intimate affinity, that it is impossible to disunite them, without
prostrating the vital energies of both, and introducing the
wildest disorder and confusion, where, by the very nature of
things, there exist the most harmonious coincidences, and the
most happy and euphonic congenialities. Here then might I
rest, Mr. President, upon the decision of this society, with
perfect confidence. But, sir, I am not forced to rely upon the
inseparable affinities of the two questions, for success in this
dispute, obvious as they must be to every reflecting mind. All
history, ancient and modern, furnish examples corroborative
of the views which I have taken of this deeply interesting subject. By what means did the renowned poets, philosophers,
orators and statesmen of antiquity, gain their immortality?
Whence did Milton, Shakspeare, Newton, Locke, Watts,
Paley, Burke, Chatham, Pitt, Fox, and a host of others whom
I might name, pluck their never-fading laurels? I answer
boldly, and without the fear of contradiction, that, though
they all reached the temple of fame by different routes, they
all passed through the broad vista of *'internal suggestions.'* The
same may be said of Jefferson, Madison, and many other distinguished personages of our own country.

"I challenge the gentlemen on the other side to produce
examples like these in support of their cause."

Mr. Longworth pressed these profound and logical views
to a length to which our limits will not permit us to follow
him, and which the reader's patience would hardly bear, if
they would. Perhaps, however, he will bear with us, while we

give the conclusion of Mr. Longworth's remarks: as it was here, that he put forth all his strength:

"*Mr. President*,—Let the bias of jurisprudence predominate, and how is it possible, (considering it merely as extending to those impulses which may with propriety be termed a *bias*,) how is it possible, for a government to exist, whose object is the public good? The marble hearted marauder might seize the throne of civil authority, and hurl into thraldom the votaries of rational liberty. Virtue, justice and all the nobler principles of human nature, would wither away under the pestilential breath of political faction, and an unnerved constitution be left to the sport of demagogue and parasite. Crash after crash would be heard in quick succession, as the strong pillars of the republic give way, and Despotism would shout in hellish triumph amidst the crumbling ruins—Anarchy would wave her bloody sceptre over the devoted land, and the blood-hounds of civil war, would lap the crimson gore of our most worthy citizens. The shrieks of women, and the screams of children, would be drowned amidst the clash of swords, and the cannon's peal: and Liberty, mantling her face from the horrid scene, would spread her golden-tinted pinions, and wing her flight to some far distant land, never again to re-visit our peaceful shores. In vain should we then sigh for the beatific reign of those 'suggestions' which I am proud to acknowledge as peculiarly and exclusively 'internal.' "

Mr. McDermot rose promptly at the call of the President, and proceeded as follows:

"*Mr. President*,—If I listened unmoved to the very labored appeal to the passions, which has just been made, it was not because I am insensible to the powers of eloquence; but because I happen to be blessed with the small measure of sense, which is necessary to distinguish true eloquence from the wild ravings of an unbridled imagination. Grave and solemn appeals, when ill-timed and misplaced, are apt to excite ridicule; hence it was, that I detected myself more than once, in open laughter, during the most pathetic parts of Mr. Longworth's argument, if so it can be called.* In the midst of 'crashing pillars,' 'crumbling ruins,' 'shouting despotism,' 'screaming

---

*This was extemporaneous, and well conceived; for Mr. McDermot had not played his part with becoming gravity.

women,' and 'flying Liberty,' the question was perpetually recurring to me, 'what has all this to do with the subject of
dispute?' I will not follow the example of that gentleman—It
shall be my endeavor to clear away the mist which he has
thrown around the subject, and to place it before the society,
in a clear, intelligible point of view: for I must say, that
though his speech *'bears strong marks of the pen,'* (sarcasti-
cally,) it has but few marks of sober reflection. Some of it, I
confess, is very intelligible and very plausible; but most of it,
I boldly assert, no man living can comprehend. I mention
this, for the edification of that gentleman, (who is usually
clear and forcible,) to teach him, that he is most successful
when he labors least.

"Mr. President: The gentleman, in opening the debate,
stated that the question was one of vast importance; pervading the profound depths of *psychology*, and embracing, within
its ample range, the whole circle of arts and sciences. And
really, sir, he has verified his statement; for he has extended it
over the whole moral and physical world. But, Mr. President,
I take leave to differ from the gentleman, at the very threshhold of his remarks. The subject is one which is confined
within very narrow limits. It extends no further than to the
elective franchise, and is not even commensurate with this important privilege; for it stops short at the *vote of faction*. In
this point of light, the subject comes within the grasp of the
most common intellect; it is plain, simple, natural and intelligible. Thus viewing it, Mr. President, where does the gentleman find in it, or in all nature besides, the original of the
dismal picture which he has presented to the society? It loses
all its interest, and becomes supremely ridiculous. Having
thus, Mr. President, divested the subject of all obscurity—
having reduced it to those few elements, with which we are
all familiar; I proceed to make a few deductions from the
premises, which seem to me inevitable, and decisive of the
question. Play it down as a self-evident proposition, that faction in all its forms, is hideous; and I maintain, with equal
confidence, that it never has been, nor ever will be, restrained
by those suggestions, which the gentleman *'emphatically terms
internal.'* No, sir, nothing short of the bias, and the very
strong bias too, of jurisprudence or the potent energies of the

sword, can restrain it. But, sir, I shall here, perhaps, be asked, whether there is not a very wide difference between a turbulent, lawless faction, and the *vote* of faction? Most unquestionably there is; and to this distinction I shall presently advert and demonstrably prove that it is a distinction, which makes altogether in our favor."

Thus did Mr. McDermot continue to dissect and expose his adversary's argument, in the most clear, conclusive and masterly manner, at considerable length. But we cannot deal more favorably by him, than we have dealt by Mr. Longworth. We must, therefore, dismiss him, after we shall have given the reader his concluding remarks. They were as follows:

"Let us now suppose Mr. Longworth's principles brought to the test of experiment. Let us suppose his language addressed to all mankind—We close the temples of justice as useless; we burn our codes of laws as worthless; and we substitute in their places, the more valuable restraints of *internal suggestions*. Thieves, invade not your neighbor's property: if you do, you will be arraigned before the august tribunal of *conscience*. Robbers, stay your lawless hand; or you will be visited with the tremendous penalties of *psychology*. Murderers, spare the blood of your fellow creatures; you will be exposed to the excruciating tortures of *innate maxims — when it shall be discovered that there are any*. Mr. President, could there be a broader license to crime than this? Could a better plan be devised for dissolving the bands of civil society? It requires not the gift of prophecy, to foresee the consequences of these novel and monstrous principles. The strong would tyrannize over the weak; the poor would plunder the rich; the servant would rise above the master; the drones of society would fatten upon the hard earnings of the industrious. Indeed, sir, industry would soon desert the land; for it would have neither reward nor encouragement. Commerce would cease; the arts and sciences would languish; all the sacred relations would be dissolved, and scenes of havoc, dissolution and death ensue, such as never before visited the world, and such as never will visit it, until mankind learn to repose their destinies upon 'those suggestions, *emphatically termed internal*.' From all these evils there is a secure retreat behind the brazen wall of the 'bias of jurisprudence.' "

The gentleman who was next called on to engage in the debate, was John Craig; a gentleman of good hard sense, but who was utterly incompetent to say a word upon a subject which he did not understand. He proceeded thus:

"*Mr. President*,—When this subject was proposed, I candidly confessed I did not understand it, and I was informed by Mr. Longworth and Mr. McDermot, that either of them would explain it, at any leisure moment. But, sir, they seem to have taken very good care, from that time to this, to have no leisure moment. I have inquired of both of them, repeatedly for an explanation; but they were always too busy to talk about it. Well, sir, as it was proposed by Mr. Longworth, I thought he would certainly explain it in his speech; but I understood no more of his speech than I did of the subject. Well, sir, I thought I should certainly learn something from Mr. McDermot; especially as he promised at the commencement of his speech to clear away the mist that Mr. Longworth had thrown about the subject, and to place it in a clear, intelligible point of light. But, sir, the only difference between his speech and Mr. Longworth's is, that it was not quite as flighty as Mr. Longworth's. I could n't understand head nor tail of it. At one time they seemed to argue the question, as if it were this: 'Is it better to have law or no law?' At another, as though it was, 'should factions be governed by law, or be left to their own consciences?' But most of the time they argued it, as if it were just what it seems to be—a sentence without sense or meaning. But, sir, I suppose its obscurity is owing to my dullness of apprehension, for they appeared to argue it with great earnestness and feeling, as if they understood it.

"I shall put my interpretation upon it, Mr. President, and argue it accordingly.

" '*Whether at public elections*'—that is, for members of Congress, members of the Legislature, &c. '*should the votes of faction*'—I don't know what '*faction*' has got to do with it; and therefore I shall throw it out. '*Should the votes predominate, by internal suggestions or the bias,*' I don't know what the *article* is put in here for. It seems to me, it ought to be, *be biased by* 'jurisprudence' or law. In short, Mr. President, I understand the question to be, should a man vote as he pleases, or should the law say how he should vote?"

Here Mr. Longworth rose and observed, that though Mr. Craig was on his side, he felt it due to their adversaries, to state, that this was not a true exposition of the subject. This exposition settled the question at once on his side; for nobody would, for a moment contend, that *the law* should declare how men should vote. Unless it be confined to the vote *of faction* and *the* bias of jurisprudence, it was no subject at all. To all this Mr. McDermot signified his unqualified approbation; and seemed pleased with the candor of his opponent.

"Well," said Mr. Craig, "I thought it was impossible that any one should propose such a question as that to the society; but will Mr. Longworth tell us, if it does not mean that, what does it mean? for I don't see what great change is made in it by his explanation."

Mr. Longworth replied, that if the remarks which he had just made, and his argument, had not fully explained the subject to Mr. Craig, he feared it would be out of his power to explain it.

"Then," said Mr. Craig, "I'll pay my fine, for I don't understand a word of it."

The next one summoned to the debate was Mr. Pentigall. Mr. Pentigall was one of those who would never acknowledge his ignorance of any thing, which any person else understood; and that Longworth and McDermot were both masters of the subject, was clear, both from their fluency and seriousness. He therefore determined to understand it, at all hazards. Consequently he rose at the President's command, with considerable self-confidence. I regret, however, that it is impossible to commit Mr. Pentigall's *manner* to paper, without which, his remarks lose nearly all their interest. He was a tall, handsome man; a little theatric in his manner, rapid in his delivery, and singular in his pronunciation. He gave to the *e* and *i*, of our language, the sound of *u*—at least his peculiar intonations of voice, seemed to give them that sound; and his rapidity of utterance seemed to change the termination, *"tion"* into *"ah."* With all his peculiarities, however, he was a fine fellow. If he was ambitious, he was not invidious, and he possessed an amicable disposition. He proceeded as follows:

"Mr. President,—This internal suggestion which has been so eloquently discussed by Mr. Longworth, and the bias of

jurisprudence which has been so ably advocated by Mr. McDermot—hem! Mr. President, in order to fix the line of demarkation between—ah—the internal suggestion and the bias of jurisprudence—Mr. President, I think, sir, that—ah—the subject must be confined to the *vote of faction*, and *the* bias of jurisprudence"——

Here Mr. Pentigall clapt his right hand to his forehead, as though he had that moment heard some overpowering news; and after maintaining this position for about the space of ten seconds, he slowly withdrew his hand, gave his head a slight inclination to the right, raised his eyes to the President as if just awakening from a trance, and with a voice of the most hopeless despair, concluded with "I don't understand the subject, Muster Prusidunt."

The rest of the members on both sides submitted to be fined rather than attempt the knotty subject; but by common consent, the penal rule was dispensed with. Nothing now remained to close the exercises, but the decision of the Chair.

The President, John Nuble, was a young man, not unlike Craig in his turn of mind; though he possessed an intellect a little more sprightly than Craig's. His decision was short.

"Gentlemen," said he, "I do not understand the subject. This," continued he, (pulling out his knife, and pointing to the silvered or *cross* side of it,) "is 'Internal Suggestions.' And this" (pointing to the other, or *pile* side,) "is 'Bias of Jurisprudence:' " so saying, he threw up his knife, and upon its fall, determined that "Internal Suggestions" had got it; and ordered the decision to be registered accordingly.

It is worthy of note, that in their zeal to accomplish their purpose, Longworth and McDermot forgot to destroy the lists of subjects, from which they had selected the one so often mentioned; and one of these lists containing the subject discussed, with a number more like it, was picked up by Mr. Craig, who made a public exhibition of it, threatening to arraign the conspirators before the society, for a contempt. But, as the parting hour was at hand, he overlooked it with the rest of the brotherhood, and often laughed heartily at the trick.

"The Militia Company Drill," is not by the author of the other pieces but has a strong family resemblance, and is very

well executed. Among the innumerable descriptions of Militia musters which are so rife in the land, we have met with nothing at all equal to this in the matter of broad farce.

"*The Turf*" is also capital, and bears with it a kind of dry and sarcastic morality which will recommend it to many readers.

"*An Interesting Interview*" is another specimen of exquisite dramatic talent. It consists of nothing more than a fac-simile of the speech, actions, and *thoughts* of two drunken old men—but its air of truth is perfectly inimitable.

"*The Fox-Hunt*," "*The Wax Works*," and "*A Sage Conversation*," are all good—but neither *as* good as many other articles in the book.

"*The Shooting Match*," which concludes the volume, may rank with the best of the Tales which precede it. As a portraiture of the manners of our South-Western peasantry, in especial, it is perhaps better than any.

Altogether this very humorous, and very clever book forms an æra in our reading. It has reached us per mail, and without a cover. We will have it bound forthwith, and give it a niche in our library as a sure omen of better days for the literature of the South.

Southern Literary Messenger, March 1836

William W. Lord

Poems. By William W. Lord. New York: D. Appleton & Co.

O F MR. LORD we know nothing—although we believe that he is a student at Princeton College—or perhaps a graduate, or perhaps a Professor of that Institution. Of his book, lately, we have heard a good deal—that is to say, we have heard it announced in every possible variation of phrase, as "forthcoming." For several months past, indeed, much amusement has been occasioned in the various literary coteries in New York, by the pertinacity and obviousness of an attempt made by the poet's friends to get up an anticipatory excitement in his favor. There were multitudinous dark rumors of something *in posse*—whispered insinuations that the sun had at length arisen or would certainly arise—that a book was really in press which would revolutionize the poetical world—that the MS. had been submitted to the inspection of a junto of critics, whose fiat was well understood to be Fate, (Mr. Charles King, if we remember aright, forming one of the junto)—that the work had by them been approved, and its successful reception and illimitable glorification assured.—Mr. Longfellow, in consequence, countermanding an order given his publishers (Redding & Co.,) to issue forthwith a new threepenny edition of "The Voices of the Night." Suggestions of this nature, busily circulated in private, were, in good time, insinuated through the press, until at length the public expectation was as much on tiptoe as public expectation, in America, can ever be expected to be about so small a matter as the issue of a volume of American poems. The climax of this whole effort, however, at forestalling the critical opinion, and by far the most injudicious portion of the procedure, was the publisher's announcement of the forthcoming book as "a very remarkable volume of poems."

The fact is, the only remarkable things about Mr. Lord's compositions, are their remarkable conceit, ignorance, impudence, platitude, stupidity and bombast:—we are sorry to say all this, but there is an old adage about the falling of the

Heavens. Nor must we be misunderstood. We intend to wrong neither Mr. Lord nor our own conscience, by denying him particular merits—such as they are. His book is *not* altogether contemptible—although the conduct of his friends has innoculated nine-tenths of the community with the opinion that it is—but what we wish to say, is that "remarkable" is by no means the epithet to be applied, in the way of commendation, either to anything that he has yet done or to anything that he may hereafter accomplish. In a word, while he has undoubtedly given proof of a very ordinary species of talent, no man whose opinion is entitled to the slightest respect will admit in him any indication of genius.

The "particular merits" to which, in the case of Mr. Lord, we have allusion, are merely the accidental merits of particular passages. We say *accidental*—because poetical merit which is not simply an accident, is very sure to be found, more or less, in a state of *diffusion* throughout a poem. No man is entitled to the sacred name of poet, because from 160 pages of doggrel, may be culled a few sentences of worth. Nor would the case be in any respect altered, if these few sentences, or even if a few passages of length, were of an excellence even supreme. For a poet is necessarily a man of genius, and with the spirit of true genius even its veriest common-places are intertwined and inextricably intertangled. When, therefore, amid a Sahara of platitude, we discover an occasional Oasis, we must not so far forget ourselves as to fancy any latent fertility in the sands. It is our purpose, however, to do the fullest justice to Mr. Lord, and we proceed at once to cull from his book whatever, in our opinion, will put in the fairest light his poetical pretensions.

And first we extract the *one* brief passage which aroused in us what we recognised as the Poetical Sentiment. It occurs, at page 94, in "Saint Mary's Gift," which, although excessively unoriginal at all points, is upon the whole, the least reprehensible poem of the volume. The heroine of the story having taken a sleeping draught, after the manner of Juliet, is conveyed to a vault (still in the same manner) and (still in the same manner) awakes in the presence of her lover who comes to gaze on what he supposes her corpse:

And each unto the other was a dream;
And so they gazed without a stir or breath,
Until her head into the golden stream
Of her wide tresses, loosened from their wreath,
Sank back, as she did yield again to death.

At page 3, in a composition of much general *eloquence*, there occur a few lines of which we should not hesitate to speak enthusiastically were we not perfectly well aware that Mr. Lord has no claim to their origination:

——Ye winds
That in the impalpable deep caves of air,
Moving your silent plumes, in dreams of flight,
Tumultuous lie, and from your half-stretched wings
Beat the faint zephyrs that disturb the air!

At page 6, in the same poem, we meet, also, a passage of high merit, although sadly disfigured:

Thee the bright host of Heaven,
The stars adore:—a thousand altars, fed
By pure unwearied hands, like cressets blaze
In the blue depths of night; nor all unseen
In the pale sky of day, with tempered light
Burn *radiant of thy praise.*

The disfiguration to which we allude, lies in the making a blazing altar burn merely like a blazing cresset—a simile about as forcible as would be the likening an apple to a pear, or the sea-foam to the froth on a pitcher of Burton's ale.

At page 7, still in the same poem, we find some verses which are very quotable, and will serve to make our readers understand what we mean by the eloquence of the piece:

Great Worshipper! hast thou no thought of Him
Who gave the Sun his brightness, winged the winds,
And on the everlasting deep bestowed
Its voiceless thunder—spread its fields of blue,
And made them glorious *like an inner sky*
From which the islands rise like steadfast clouds,
How beautiful! who gemmed thy zone with stars,
Around thee threw his own cerulean robe,—

And bent his coronal about thy brows,
Shaped of the seven splendors of the light—
Piled up the mountains for thy throne; and thee
The image of His beauty made and power,
And gave thee to be sharer of His state,
His majesty, His glory, and His fear!

We extract this *not* because we like it ourselves, but because we take it for granted that there are many who will, and that Mr. Lord himself would desire us to extract it as a specimen of his *power*. The "Great worshipper" is Nature. We disapprove, however, the man-milliner method in which she is tricked out, item by item. The "How beautiful!" should be understood, we fancy, as an expression of admiration on the part of Mr. Lord, for the fine idea which immediately precedes—the idea which we have italicized. It is, in fact, by no means destitute of force—but we have met it before.

At page 70, there are two stanzas addressed to "My Sister." The first of these we cite as the best thing of equal length to be found in the book. Its conclusion is particularly noble.

And shall we meet in heaven, and know and love?
Do human feelings in that world above
Unchanged survive? blest thought! but ah, I fear
That thou, dear sister, in some other sphere,
Distant from mine will (wilt) find a brighter home,
Where I, unworthy found, may never come:—
Or be so high above me glorified,
That I a meaner angel, undescried,
Seeking thine eyes, such love alone shall see
As angels give to all bestowed on me;
And when my voice upon thy ear shall fall,
Hear only such reply as angels give to all.

We give the lines as they are: their grammatical construction is faulty; and the punctuation of the ninth line renders the sense equivocal.

Of that species of composition which comes most appropriately under the head, *Drivel*, we should have no trouble in selecting as many specimens as our readers could desire. We will afflict them with one or two:

SONG

O soft is the ringdove's eye of love
When her mate returns from a weary flight;
And brightest of all the stars above
Is the one bright star that leads the night.

———

But softer thine eye than the dove's by far,
When of friendship and pity thou speakest to me;
And brighter, O brighter, than eve's one star
When of love, sweet maid, I speak to thee.

Here is another

SONG

Oh, a heart it loves, it loves thee,
    That never loved before
Oh, a heart it loves, it loves thee,
    That heart can love no more.

As the rose was in the bud, love,
    Ere it opened into sight,
As yon star in drumlie daylight
    Behind the blue was bright—

So thine image in my heart, love,
    As pure, as bright, as fair,
Thyself unseen, unheeded,
    I saw and loved it there.

Oh, a heart it loves, it loves thee
    As heart ne'er loved before;
Oh, a heart, it loves, loves, loves thee,
    That heart can love no more.

In "The Widow's Complaint" we are entertained after this fashion:

And what are these children
I once thought my own,

> What now do they seem
> But his orphans alone?

In "The New Castalia" we have it thus:

> Then a pallid beauteous maiden
> Golden ghastly robes arrayed in
> Such a wondrous strain displayed in,
> In a wondrous song of Aidenne,
> That all the gods and godd*ess*es
> Shook their golden yellow tresses,
> Parnassus' self made half afraid in.

Just above this there is something about aged beldames dreaming

> ——of white throats sweetly jagged
> With a ragged butch-knife dull,
> And of night-mares neighing, weighing,
> On a sleeper's bosom *squatting*.

But in mercy to our readers we forbear.

Mr. Lord is never elevated above the dead level of his habitual platitude, by even the happiest thesis in the world. That any man could, at one and the same time, fancy himself a poet and string together as many pitiable inanities as we see here, on so truly suggestive a thesis as that of "A Lady taking the Veil," is to our apprehension a miracle of miracles. The idea would seem to be, of itself, sufficient to elicit fire from ice— to breathe animation into the most stolid of stone. Mr. Lord winds up a dissertation on the subject by the patronizing advice—

> Ere thou, irrevocable, to that dark creed
> Art yielded, *think, Oh Lady, think again!*

the whole of which would read better if it were

> Ere thou, irrevocable, to this d—d doggrel
> Art yielded, Lord, think! think!—ah think again.

Even with the great theme, Niagara, our poet fails in his obvious effort to work himself into a fit of inspiration. One of his poems has for title "A Hymn to Niagara"—but from beginning to end it is nothing more than a very silly "Hymn to Mr. Lord." Instead of describing the fall (as well as any Mr. Lord could be supposed to describe it) he rants about what *I* feel here, and about what *I* did not feel there—till at last the figure of little Mr. Lord, in the shape of a great capital **I** gets so thoroughly in between the reader and the waterfall that not a particle of the latter is to be discovered. At one point the poet directs his soul to issue a proclamation as follows:

> Proclaim, my soul, proclaim it to the sky!
> And tell the stars, and tell the hills whose feet
> Are in the depths of earth, their peaks in heaven,
> And tell the Ocean's old familiar face
> Beheld by day and night, in calm and storm,
> That they, nor aught beside in earth or heaven,
> Like thee, tremendous torrent, have so filled
> *Its* thought of beauty, and so awed with might!

The *"Its"* has reference to the soul of Mr. Lord, who thinks it necessary to issue a proclamation to the stars and the hills and the ocean's old familiar face—lest the stars and the hills and the ocean's old familiar face should chance to be unaware of the fact that it (the soul of Mr. Lord) admitted the waterfall to be a fine thing—but whether the cataract for the compliment, or the stars for the information, are to be considered the party chiefly obliged—that, for the life of us, we cannot tell.

From the "first impression" of the cataract, he says:

> At length my soul awaked—waked not again
> To be o'erpressed, o'ermastered, and engulphed,
> But of itself possessed, o'er all without
> Felt conscious mastery!
>   And then
> Retired within, and self-withdrawn, I stood
> The two-fold centre and informing soul
> Of one vast harmony of sights and sounds,
> And from that deep abyss, that rock-built shrine,
> Though mute my own frail voice, I poured a hymn
> Of "praise and gratulation" like the noise
> Of banded angels when they shout to wake
> Empyreal echoes!

That so vast a personage as Mr. Lord should not be o'er-mastered by the cataract, but feel "conscious mastery over all without"—and over all within, too—is certainly nothing more than reasonable and proper—but then he should have left the detail of these little facts to the cataract or to some other uninterested individual—even Cicero has been held to blame for a want of modesty—and although, to be sure, Cicero was not Mr. Lord, still Mr. Lord may be in danger of blame. He may have enemies (*very* little men!) who will pretend to deny that the "hymn of praise and gratulation" (if *this* is the hymn) bears at all points more than a partial resemblance to the "noise of banded angels when they shout to wake empyreal echoes." Not that *we* intend to deny it—but *they* will:—they are *very* little people and they *will*.

We have said that the "remarkable" feature, or at least one of the "remarkable" features of this volume is its platitude—its flatness. Whenever the reader meets anything not decidedly flat, he may take it for granted at once, that it is stolen. When the poet speaks, for example, at page 148, of

Flowers, of young poets the first words—

who can fail to remember the line in the Merry Wives of Windsor.

Fairies use flowers for their charactery?

At page 10 he says:

Great oaks their heavenward lifted arms stretch forth
In suppliance!

The same thought will be found in "Pelham," where the author is describing the dead tree beneath which is committed the murder. The grossest plagiarisms, indeed, abound. We would have no trouble, even, in pointing out a score from our most unimportant self. At page 27 Mr. Lord says:

They, albeit with inward pain
Who thought to sing thy dirge, must sing thy Pæan!

In a poem called "Lenore," we have it

Avaunt! to-night my heart is light—no dirge will I upraise,
But waft the angel on her flight with a Pæan of old days.

At page 13, Mr. Lord says of certain flowers that

> Ere beheld on Earth they gardened Heaven!

We print it as printed—note of admiration and all. In a poem called "Al Aaraaf" we have it thus:

> ————————A gemmy flower,
> Inmate of highest stars, where erst it shamed
> All other loveliness:—'twas dropped from Heaven
> And fell on gardens of the unforgiven
> In Trebizond.

At page 57 Mr. Lord says:

> On the old and haunted mountain,
> There in dreams I dared to climb,
> Where the clear Castalian fountain
> (Silver fountain) ever tinkling
> All the green around it sprinkling
>   Makes perpetual rhyme—
> To my dream enchanted, golden,
> Came a vision of the olden
>   Long-forgotten time.

There are no doubt many of our friends who will remember the commencement of our "Haunted Palace."

> In the greenest of our valleys
>   By good angels tenanted,
> Once a fair and stately palace
>   (Radiant palace) reared its head.
> In the monarch Thought's dominion
>   It stood there.
> Never seraph spread a pinion
>   Over fabric half so fair.
> Banners yellow, glorious, golden,
>   On its roof did float and flow—
> This—all this—was in the olden
>   Time, long ago.

At page 60, Mr. Lord says:

> And the aged beldames napping,
> Dreamed of gently rapping, rapping,
> With a hammer gently tapping,
> Tapping on an infant's skull.

In "The Raven" we have it:

> While I pondered nearly napping,
> Suddenly there came a rapping,
> As of some one gently tapping,
> Tapping at my chamber door.

But it is folly to pursue these thefts. As to any property of our own, Mr. Lord is very cordially welcome to whatever use he can make of it. But others may not be so pacifically disposed, and the book before us might be very materially thinned and reduced in cost, by discarding from it all that belongs to Miss Barrett, Tennyson, Keats, Shelley, Proctor, Longfellow and Lowell—the very class of poets, by the way, whom Mr. William W. Lord, in his "New Castalia" the most especially effects to satirize and to contemn.

It has been rumored, we say, or rather it has been *announced* that Mr. Lord is a graduate or perhaps a Professor of Princeton College—but we have had much difficulty in believing anything of the kind. The pages before us are not only utterly devoid of that classicism of tone and manner—that better species of classicism which a liberal education never fails to impart—but they abound in the most outrageously vulgar violations of grammar—of prosody in its most extended sense.

Of versification, and all that appertains to it, Mr. Lord is ignorant in the extreme. We doubt if he can tell the difference between a dactyl and an anapæst. In the Heroic (Jambic) Pentameter he is continually introducing such verses as these:

A faint symphony to Heaven ascending—

———

No heart of love, O God, Infinite One—

———

Of a thought as weak an aspiration—

Who were the original priests of this—

Of grace, magnificence and power—

O'erwhelm me; this darkness that shuts out the sky—

Alexandrines, in the same metre, are encountered at every step—but it is very clear from the points at which they are met, and at which the cæsura is placed, that Mr. Lord has no idea of employing them as Alexandrines;—They are merely excessive that is to say defective Pentameters. In a word, judging by his rhythm, we might suppose that the poet could neither see, hear, nor make use of his fingers. We do not know, in America, a versifier so utterly wretched and contemptible.

His most extraordinary sins, however, are in point of English. Here is his dedication, embodied in the very first page of the book:—

"To Professor Albert B. Dod, These Poems, the offspring of an Earnest (if ineffectual) Desire towards the True and Beautiful, which were hardly my own by Paternity, when they became his by Adoption, are inscribed, with all Reverence and Affection, by the Author."

What is any body to make of all this? What is the meaning of a desire *toward*?—and is it the "True and Beautiful" or the "Poems" which were hardly Mr. Lord's "own by paternity before they became his [Mr. Dod's] by adoption."

At page 12, we read:

> Think heedless one, or who with wanton step
> *Tramples* the flowers.

At page 75, within the compass of eleven lines, we have three of the grossest blunders:

> Oh Thou for whom as in thyself Thou art,
> And by thyself perceived, we know no name,
> *Nor* dare *not* seek to express—but unto us,
> Adonai! who before the heavens were built
> Or Earth's foundation laid, within thyself,
> Thine own most glorious habitation *dwelt*,

> But when within the abyss,
> With sudden light illuminated,
> Thou, thine image to behold,
> Into its quickened depths
> *Looked* down with brooding eye!

At page 79, we read:

> But ah! my heart, unduteous to my will,
> Breathes only sadness; like an instrument
> From whose quick strings, when hands devoid of skill
> Solicit joy, *they* murmur and lament.

At page 86, is something even grosser than this:

> And still and rapt as pictured Saint might be
> *Like saint-like* seemed as *her* she did adore.

At page 129, there is a similar error:

> With half-closed eyes and ruffled feathers known
> As *them* that fly not with the changing year.

At page 128 we find—

> And thou didst dwell therein so truly loved
> As none have been nor shall be loved again,
> And yet *perceived* not, etc.

At page 155, we have—

> But yet it may not cannot be
> That thou at length *hath* sunk to rest.

Invariably Mr. Lord writes didst did'st; couldst could'st, etc. The fact is he is absurdly ignorant of the commonest principles of grammar—and the only excuse we can make to our readers for annoying them with specifications in this respect is that, without the specifications, we should never have been believed.

But enough of this folly. We are heartily tired of the book, and thoroughly disgusted with the impudence of the parties who have been aiding and abetting in thrusting it before the public. To the poet himself we have only to say—from any farther specimens of your stupidity, good Lord deliver us!

Broadway Journal, May 24, 1845

James Russell Lowell

Poems by James Russell Lowell. Cambridge: Published by John Owen.

THIS NEW VOLUME of poems by Mr. Lowell will place him, in the estimation of all whose opinion he will be likely to value, *at the very head* of the poets of America. For our own part, we have not the slightest hesitation in saying, that we regard the "Legend of Brittany" as by far the finest poetical work, of equal length, which the country has produced. We have only to regret, just now, that the late period at which we received the volume, and the great length to which Mr. Poe has been seduced into a notice of "Orion," will preclude an extended notice and analysis this month of Mr. Lowell's volume. This, however, we propose at some future period. For the present, we must content ourselves, perforce, with some very cursory and unconnected comments.

Mr. Lowell is, in some measure, infected with the poetical conventionalities of the day—those upon which Mr. Poe has descanted in speaking of Mr. Horne's epic. He has suffered himself to be *coteried* into conceptions of the *aims* of the muse, which his reason either now disapproves, or will disapprove hereafter, and which his keen instinct of the beautiful and proper has, long ere this, struggled to disavow. It will not be many days before he dismisses these heresies altogether; and, in his last, longest, and best work, we clearly see that he is already growing wearied with them—although the distaste may yet be scarcely perceptible to himself. We mean to say that he will soon find it wise to give every thing its due time and place. He will never the less reverence the truth—nor ever will the welfare of his race be less precious in his eyes than now—we should grieve, indeed, could we think it would—but his views of the *modes* in which these objects are to be advanced will undergo modification, and he will see distinctly, what he now but vaguely feels—that the sole legitimate object of the true poem is the *creation of beauty*.

The "Legend of Brittany" includes a hundred and eighteen of the Don Juan stanzas. Its subject is exquisitely beautiful. Whether it is original with Mr. Lowell we know not—most probably it is not—but the story itself (from whatever source derived) forms one of the truest and purest poetical theses imaginable. A Templar loves and betrays a maiden. Afterward, to conceal his guilt, he murders her, *enceinte*, concealing the corpse, temporarily, behind the altar of his church. A nameless awe prevents him from removing it. Meantime, a festival is held in the church; and, during the swell of the organ, the spirit-voice of the deceased addresses itself to the murderer. It represents that she, the murdered, cannot enjoy the heaven which she inhabits, through grief at the destiny of the unbaptized infant in her womb. She implores its baptism. The poem ends with the performance of this rite, and the death, through remorse, of the repentant lover.

The naked digest here given conveys, of course, only the most feeble idea of the rare beauty of the whole; nor of this beauty could we convey any just conception even in many pages of comment. The *sublimity* of human love was never more magnificently portrayed. We cannot refrain from quoting some passages from the words of the spirit:

> Think not in death my love could ever cease.
>   If thou wast false more need there is for me
> Still to be true; that slumber were not peace,
>   If 't were unvisited with dreams of thee:
> And thou hadst never heard such words as these,
>   Save that in heaven I must forever be
> Most comfortless and wretched, seeing this
> Our unbaptized babe shut out from bliss.

> ———

> This little spirit with imploring eyes
>   Wanders alone the dreary wild of space;
> The shadow of his pain forever lies
>   Upon my soul in this new dwelling place;
> His loneliness makes me in Paradise
>   More lonely, and unless I see his face,
> Even here for grief could I lie down and die,
> Save for my curse of immortality.

> ———

> World after world he sees around him swim,
>   Crowded with happy souls, that take no heed

Of the sad eyes that from the night's faint rim
    Gaze sick with longing on them as they speed
With golden gates that only shut out him;
    And shapes sometimes, from Hell's abysses freed,
Flap darkly by him, with enormous sweep
Of wings that roughen wide the pitchy deep.

———

I am a mother—spirits do not shake
    This much of earth from them—and I must pine
Till I can feel his little hands, and take
    His weary head upon this heart of mine;
And might it be full gladly for his sake
    Would I this solitude of bliss resign,
And be shut out of Heaven to dwell with him
Forever in that silence drear and dim.

———

I strove to hush my soul, and would not speak
    At first for thy dear sake; a woman's love
Is mighty, but a mother's heart is weak,
    And by its weakness overcomes; I strove
To smother bitter thoughts with patience meek,
    But still in the abyss my soul would rove,
Seeking my child, and drove me here to claim
The rite that gives him peace in Christ's dear name.

———

I sit and weep while blessed spirits sing;
    I can but long and pine the while they praise,
And, *leaning o'er the wall of Heaven*, I fling
    My voice to where I deem my infant strays,
Like a robbed bird that cries in vain to bring
    Her nestlings back beneath her wing's embrace;
But still he answers not, and I but know
That Heaven and Earth are both alike in wo.

The description of the swelling of the organ—immediately preceding these extracts—surpasses, in all the loftier merits, any similar passage we have seen. It is truly magnificent. For those who have the book, we instance the forty-first stanza of the second book, and the nine stanzas succeeding. We know not where to look, in all American poetry, for any thing more richly ideal, or more forcibly conveyed.

The music is suddenly interrupted by the nameless awe which indicates the presence of the unseen spirit.

> As if a lark should suddenly drop dead
>   While the blue air yet trembled with its song,
> So snapped at once that music's golden thread,
>   Struck by a nameless fear that leapt along
> From heart to heart, and like a shadow spread
>   With instantaneous shiver through the throng,
> So that some glanced behind, as half aware
> A hideous shape of dread were standing there.

The defects observable in the "Legend of Brittany" are, chiefly, consequent upon the error of *didacticism*. After every few words of narration, comes a page of morality. Not that the morality, *here*—not that the reflections deduced from the incidents, are peculiarly exceptionable, but that they are too obviously, intrusively, and artificially introduced. The story might have been rendered more *unique*, and altogether more in consonance with the true poetic sentiment, by suffering the morality to be *suggested*; as it is, for example, in the "Old Curiosity Shop," of Dickens—or in that superb *poem*, the "Undine" of De la Motte Fouqué.

The other demerits are minor ones. The versification is now and then slightly deficient—sometimes in melody—sometimes in force. The drawing out of "power," "heaven," and other similar words into two syllables, is *sure* to enfeeble the verses in which they are so drawn out. The versifier, where a doubt, however slight, exists, *never errs on the side of excess*; but this is a point we cannot argue just now. Of the positively rough lines, we quote only one:

> Earth's dust hath clotted round the soul's fresh wing.

Here the harsh consonants are excessive. But we feel ashamed of alluding to trifles such as these in the presence of beauties so numerous and so true. We extract, at random, a few of the smaller gems of the poem.

Her spirit wandered by itself and won
A golden edge from some unsetting sun.

———

For she was but a simple herdsman's child,
A lily chance-sown in the rugged wild.

———

Not the first violet on a woodland lea
Seemed a more visible gift of spring than she.

———

Low stirrings in the leaves, before the wind
    Wakes all the green strings of the forest lyre.
Faint heatings in the calyx ere the rose
Its warm, voluptuous breast doth all unclose.

———

Flooded he seemed with bright delicious pain,
As if a star had burst within his brain.

———

So, from her sky-like spirit, gentleness
    Dropt ever like a sunlit fall of rain,
And his beneath drank in the bright caress
    As thirstily as would a parched plain
That long hath watched the showers of sloping gray
Forever, ever, falling far away.

———

And when he went, his radiant memory
    Robed all his fantasies with glory fresh,
As if an angel, quitting her the while,
Left round her heart the halo of his smile.

———

Like golden ripples, hastening to the land
To wreck their freight of sunshine on the strand.

———

Hope skims o'er life as we may sometimes see
    A butterfly, whose home is in the flowers,
Blown outward far over the moaning sea,
    Remembering in vain its odorous bowers.

———

She seemed a white-browed angel sent to roll
    The heavy stone away which long had prest,
As in a living sepulchre, his soul.

In the court-yard a fountain leaped alway—
A Triton *blowing jewels thro' his shell*
Into the sunshine.

His heart went out within him like a spark
Dropt in the sea.

————as if all fäerie
Had emptied her quaint halls, or, as it were,
The illuminated marge of some old book,
While we were gazing, life and motion took.

We have left ourselves no room to speak of the other poems in detail. Those which we think best, are "The Moon," "To Perdita Singing," "Midnight," "Rosalie," "Reverie," "The Shepherd of King Admetus," and "A Dirge." These are *crowded* with excellences of the loftiest order. "Prometheus" we have not yet read so attentively as we could wish. Altogether, we intend this as merely an introduction to an extended review of all the poems of Mr. Lowell. In the mean time we repeat, that he has given evidence of at least as high poetical genius as any man in America—if not a loftier genius than any.

Graham's Magazine, March 1844

A Fable for the Critics. New-York: George P. Putnam.

W HAT HAVE we Americans accomplished in the way of Satire? "The Vision of Rubeta," by Laughton Osborn, is probably our best composition of the kind: but, in saying this, we intend no excessive commendation. Trumbull's clumsy and imitative work is scarcely worth mention—and then we have Halleck's "Croakers," local and ephemeral—but what is there besides? Park Benjamin has written a clever address, with the title "Infatuation," and Holmes has an occasional scrap, piquant enough in its way—but we can think of nothing more that can be fairly called "satire." Some matters we have produced, to be sure, which were excellent in the way of burlesque—(the Poems of William Ellery Channing, for example)—without meaning a syllable that was not utterly solemn and serious. Odes, ballads, songs, sonnets, epics and epigrams, possessed of this unintentional excellence, we should have no difficulty in designating by the dozen; but in the particular of direct and obvious satire, it cannot be denied that we are unaccountably deficient.

It has been suggested that this deficiency arises from the want of a suitable field for satirical display. In England, it is said, satire abounds, because the people there find a proper target in the aristocracy, whom they (the people) regard as a distinct race with whom they have little in common; relishing even the most virulent abuse of the upper classes with a gusto undiminished by any feeling that they (the people) have any concern in it. In Russia, or Austria, on the other hand, it is urged, satire is unknown; because there is danger in touching the aristocracy, and self-satire would be odious to the mass. In America, also, the people who write are, it is maintained, the people who read:—thus in satirizing the people we satirize only ourselves and are never in condition to sympathize with the satire.

All this is more verisimilar than true. It is forgotten that no individual considers himself as one of the mass. Each person, in his own estimate, is the pivot on which all the rest of the world spins round. We may abuse *the people* by wholesale, and yet with a clear conscience so far as regards any compunction for offending any one from among the multitude of which that "people" is composed. Every one of the crowd will cry "*Encore!*—give it to them, the vagabonds!—it serves them right." It seems to us that, in America, we have refused to encourage satire—not because what we have had touches us too nearly—but because it has been too pointless to touch us at all. Its namby-pambyism has arisen, in part, from the general want, among our men of letters, of that minute *polish*—of that skill in details—which, in combination with natural sarcastic power, satire, more than any other form of literature, so imperatively demands. In part, also, we may attribute our failure to the colonial sin of imitation. We content ourselves—at this point not less supinely than at all others—

with doing what not only has been done before, but what, however well done, has yet been done *ad nauseam*. We should not be able to endure infinite repetitions of even absolute excellence; but what is "McFingal" more than a faint echo from "Hudibras"?—and what is "The Vision of Rubeta" more than a vast gilded swill-trough overflowing with Dunciad and water? Although we are not all Archilochuses, however—although we have few pretensions to the ηχεηντες ιαμβοι—although, in short, we are no satirists ourselves—there can be no question that we answer sufficiently well as subjects for satire.

"The Vision" is bold enough—if we leave out of sight its anonymous issue—and bitter enough, and witty enough, if we forget its pitiable punning on names—and long enough (Heaven knows) and well constructed and decently versified; but it fails in the principal element of all satire—*sarcasm*—because the *intention* to be sarcastic (as in the "English Bards and Scotch Reviewers," and in all the more classical satires) is permitted to render itself manifest. The malevolence *appears*. The author is never very severe, because he is at no time particularly cool. We laugh not so much at his victims as at himself for letting them put him in such a passion. And where a deeper sentiment than mirth is excited—where it is pity or contempt that we are made to feel—the feeling is too often reflected, in its object, from the satirized to the satirist—with whom we sympathize in the discomfort of his animosity. Mr. Osborn has not many superiors in downright invective; but this is the awkward left arm of the satiric Muse. *That* satire alone is worth talking about which at least *appears* to be the genial, good humored outpouring of irrepressible merriment.

"The Fable for the Critics," just issued, has not the name of its author on the title-page; and but for some slight foreknowledge of the literary opinions, likes, dislikes, whims, prejudices and crotchets of Mr. *James Russell Lowell*, we should have had much difficulty in attributing so very *loose* a brochure to *him*. The "Fable" is essentially "loose"—ill conceived and feebly executed, as well in detail as in general. Some good hits and some sparkling witticisms do not serve to compensate us for its rambling plot (if plot it can be called) and for the want of artistic finish so particularly noticeable throughout the work—especially in its versification. In Mr. Lowell's prose efforts we have before observed a certain *disjointedness*, but never, until now, in his verse—and we confess some surprise at his putting forth so unpolished a performance. The author of "The Legend of Brittany" (which is decidedly the noblest poem, of the same length, written by an American) could not do a better thing than to take the advice of those who mean him well, in spite of his fanaticism, and leave prose, with satiric verse, to those who are better able to manage them; while he contents himself with that class of poetry for which, and for which alone, he seems to have an especial vocation—the poetry of *sentiment*. This, to be sure, is *not* the very loftiest order of verse; for it is far inferior to either that of the imagination or that of the passions—but it is the loftiest region in which Mr. Lowell can get his breath without difficulty.

Our primary objection to this "Fable for the Critics" has reference to a point which we have already touched in a general way. "The malevolence appears." We laugh not so much at the author's victims as at himself for letting them put him in such a passion. The very title of the book shows the want of a due sense in respect to the satiric essence, *sarcasm*. This "fable"—this severe lesson—is meant *"for the Critics."* "Ah!" we say to ourselves at once—" we see how it is. Mr. L. is a poor-devil poet, and some critic has been reviewing him, and making him feel very uncomfortable; whereupon, bearing in mind that Lord Byron, when similarly assailed, avenged his wrongs in a satire which he called 'English Bards and Scotch Reviewers,' he (Mr. Lowell) imitative as usual has been endeavoring to get redress in a parallel manner—by a satire with a parallel title—'A Fable for the Critics.' "

All this the reader says to himself; and all this tells *against* Mr. L. in two ways—first, by suggesting unlucky comparisons between Byron and Lowell, and, secondly, by reminding us of the various criticisms, in which we have been amused (rather ill-naturedly) at seeing Mr. Lowell "used up."

The title starts us on this train of thought and the satire sustains us in it. Every reader versed in our literary gossip, is at once put *dessous des cartes* as to the particular provocation which engendered the "Fable." Miss Margaret Fuller, some time ago, in a silly and conceited piece of Transcendentalism which she called an "Essay on American Literature," or something of that kind, had the consummate pleasantry, after *selecting* from the list of American poets, *Cornelius Mathews* and *William Ellery Channing*, for especial commendation, to speak of *Longfellow* as a booby and of *Lowell* as so wretched a poetaster "as to be disgusting even to his best friends." All this Miss Fuller *said*, if not in our precise words, still in words quite as much to the purpose. *Why* she said it, Heaven only knows—unless it was because she was Margaret Fuller, and wished to be taken for nobody else. Messrs. Longfellow and Lowell, so pointedly picked out for abuse as the *worst* of our poets, are, upon the whole, perhaps, our best—although Bryant, and one or two others are scarcely inferior. As for the two favorites, selected just as pointedly for laudation, by Miss F.—it is really difficult to think of them, in connexion with poetry, without laughing. Mr. Mathews once wrote some sonnets "On Man," and Mr. Channing some lines on "A Tin Can," or something of that kind—and if the former gentleman be not the very worst poet that ever existed on the face of the earth, it is only because he is not quite so bad as the latter. To speak algebraically:—Mr. M. is *ex*ecrable, but Mr. C. is x plus 1-ecrable.

Mr. Lowell has obviously aimed his "Fable" at Miss Fuller's head, in the first instance, with an eye to its ricochêt-ing so as to knock down Mr. Mathews in the second. Miss F. is first introduced as Miss F——, rhyming to "cooler," and afterwards as "Miranda;" while poor Mr. M. is brought in upon all occasions, head and shoulders; and now and then a sharp thing, although never very original, is said *of* them or *at* them; but all the true satiric *effect* wrought, is that produced by the satirist against himself. The reader is all the time smiling to think that so unsurpassable a—(*what* shall we call her?—we wish to be civil,) a transcendentalist as Miss Fuller, should, by *such* a criticism, have had the power to put a respectable poet in *such* a passion.

As for the plot or conduct of this Fable, the less we say of it the better. It is so weak—so flimsy—so ill put together—as to be not worth the trouble of understanding:—something, as usual, about Apollo and Daphne. Is there *no* originality on the face of the earth? Mr. Lowell's total want of it is shown at all points—very especially in his Preface of rhyming verse written without distinction by lines or initial capitals, (a hackneyed matter, originating, we believe, with Frazer's Magazine:)—very especially also, in his long continuations of some particular rhyme—a fashion introduced, if we remember aright, by Leigh Hunt, more than twenty-five years ago, in his "Feast of the Poets"—which, by the way, has been Mr. L's model in many respects.

Although ill-temper has evidently engendered this "Fable," it is by no means a satire throughout. Much of it is devoted to panegyric—but our readers would be quite puzzled to know the grounds of the author's laudations, in many cases, unless made acquainted with a fact which we think it as well they should be informed of at once. Mr. Lowell is one of the most rabid of the Abolition fanatics; and no Southerner who does not wish to be insulted, and at the same time revolted by a bigotry the most obstinately blind and deaf, should ever touch a volume by this author.* His fanaticism about slavery is a mere local outbreak of the same innate wrong-headedness which, if he owned slaves, would manifest itself in atrocious ill-treatment of them, with murder of any abolitionist who should endeavor to set them free. A fanatic of Mr. L's species, is simply a fanatic for the sake of fanaticism, and *must* be a fanatic in whatever circumstances you place him.

His prejudices on the topic of slavery break out every where in his present book. Mr. L. has not the common honesty to speak well, even in a literary sense, of any man who is not a ranting abolitionist. With the exception of Mr. Poe, (who has written some commendatory criticisms on his poems,) no Southerner is mentioned *at all* in this "Fable." It is a fashion among Mr. Lowell's set to affect a belief that there is *no such thing* as Southern Literature. Northerners— people who have really nothing to speak of as men of let-

---

*This "Fable *for the Critics*"—this *literary* satire—this benevolent *jeu d'esprit* is disgraced by such passages as the following:

> Forty fathers of Freedom, of whom twenty bred
> Their sons for the rice swamps at so much a head,
> And their daughters for—faugh!

ters,—are cited by the dozen and lauded by this candid critic without stint, while Legaré, Simms, Longstreet, and others of equal note are passed by in contemptuous silence. Mr. L. cannot carry his frail honesty of opinion even so far South as New York. All whom he praises are Bostonians. Other writers are barbarians and satirized accordingly—if mentioned at all.

To show the general *manner* of the Fable, we quote a portion of what he says about Mr. Poe:

> Here comes Poe with his Raven, like Barnaby Rudge—
> Three-fifths of him genius, and two-fifths sheer fudge;
> Who talks like a book of iambs and pentameters,
> In a way to make all men of common sense d—n metres;
> Who has written some things far the best of their kind;
> But somehow the heart seems squeezed out by the mind.*

We may observe here that *profound* ignorance on any particular topic is always sure to manifest itself by some allusion to "common sense" as an all-sufficient instructor. So far from Mr. P's talking "like a book" on the topic at issue, his chief purpose has been to demonstrate that there exists *no* book on the subject worth talking *about*; and "common sense," after all, has been the basis on which *he* relied, in contradistinction from the *un*common nonsense of Mr. L. and the small pedants.

And now let us see how far the unusual "common sense" of our satirist has availed him in the structure of his verse. First, by way of showing what his *intention* was, we quote three accidentally accurate lines:

> But a boy | he could ne | ver be right | ly defined.
> As I said | he was ne | ver precise | ly unkind.
> But as Ci | cero says | he won't say | this or that.

Here it is clearly seen that Mr. L. intends a line of four anapæsts. (An anapæst is a foot composed of two short syllables followed by a long.) With this observation, we will now simply copy a few of the lines which constitute the body of the poem; asking any of our readers to *read them if they can*;

---

*We must do Mr. L. the justice to say that his book was in press before he could have seen Mr. Poe's *"Rationale of Verse"* published in this Magazine for November and December last.

that is to say, we place the question, without argument, on the broad basis of the very commonest "common sense."

They're all from one source, monthly, weekly, diurnal . . .
Disperse all one's good and condense all one's poor
    traits . . .
The one's two-thirds Norseman, the other half Greek . . .
He has imitators in scores who omit . . .
Should suck milk, strong will-giving brave, such as
    runs . . .
Along the far rail-road the steam-snake glide white . . .
From the same runic type-fount and alphabet . . .
Earth has six truest patriots, four discoverers of ether . . .
Every cockboat that swims clears its fierce (pop) gundeck
    at him . . .
Is some of it pr—— no, 'tis not even prose . . .
O'er his principles when something else turns up
    trumps . . .
But a few silly (syllo I mean) gisms that squat 'em . . .
Nos, we don't want extra freezing in winter . . .
Plough, dig, sail, forge, build, carve, paint, make all
    things new . . .

But enough:—we have given a fair specimen of the *general* versification. It might have been better—but we are quite sure that it *could not have been worse*. So much for "common sense," in Mr. Lowell's understanding of the term. Mr. L. should not have meddled with the anapæstic rhythm: it is exceedingly awkward in the hands of one who knows nothing about it and who *will* persist in fancying that he can write it by ear. Very especially, he should have avoided this rhythm in satire, which, more than any other branch of Letters, is dependent upon seeming trifles for its effect. Two-thirds of the force of the "Dunciad" may be referred to its exquisite finish; and had "The Fable for the Critics" been, (what it is *not*,) the quintessence of the satiric spirit itself, it would nevertheless, in so slovenly a form, have failed. As it is, no failure was ever more complete or more pitiable. By the publication of a book at once so ambitious and so feeble—so malevolent in design and so harmless in execution—a work so roughly and clumsily yet so weakly constructed—so very different, in body and spirit, from anything that he has written before—Mr. Lowell has committed an irrevocable *faux pas* and lowered himself at least fifty per cent in the literary public opinion.

Southern Literary Messenger, March 1849

Cornelius Mathews

Wakondah; The Master of Life. A Poem. George L. Curry and Co.: New York.

WAKONDAH" is the composition of Mr. Cornelius Mathews, one of the editors of the Monthly Magazine,
"Arcturus." In the December number of the journal, the
poem was originally set forth by its author, very much *"avec
l'air d'un homme qui sauve sa patrie."* To be sure, it was not
what is usually termed the *leading* article of the month. It did
not occupy that post of honor which, hitherto, has been so
modestly filled by "Puffer Hopkins." But it took precedence
of some exceedingly beautiful stanzas by Professor Longfellow, and stood second only to a very serious account of a
supper which, however well it might have suited the taste of
an Ariel, would scarcely have feasted the Anakim, or satisfied
the appetite of a Grandgousier. The supper was, or might
have been, a good thing. The poem which succeeded it *is not*;
nor can we imagine what has induced Messrs. Curry & Co.
to be at the trouble of its republication. We are vexed with
these gentlemen for having thrust this affair the second time
before us. They have placed us in a predicament we dislike.
In the pages of "Arcturus" the poem did not come necessarily
under the eye of the Magazine critic. There is a tacitly-under-
stood courtesy about these matters—a courtesy upon which
we need not comment. The contributed papers in any one
journal of the class of "Arcturus" are not considered as *debateable* by any one other. General propositions, under the
editorial head, are rightly made the subject of discussion; but
in speaking of "Wakondah," for example, in the pages of our
own Magazine, we should have felt as if *making an occasion.*
Now, upon our first perusal of the poem in question, we were
both astonished and grieved that we could say, honestly, very
little in its praise:—astonished, for by some means, not just
now altogether intelligible to ourselves, we had become imbued with the idea of high poetical talent in Mr. Mathews:—
grieved, because, under the circumstances of his position as
editor of one of the *very* best journals in the country, we had
been sincerely anxious to think well of his abilities. Moreover,
we felt that to *speak ill* of them, under any circumstances

whatever, would be to subject ourselves to the charge of envy or jealousy, on the part of those who do not personally know us. We, therefore, rejoiced that "Wakondah" was not a topic we were called upon to discuss. But the poem is republished, and placed upon our table, and these very "circumstances of position," which restrained us in the first place, render it a positive duty that we speak distinctly in the second.

And *very* distinctly shall we speak. In fact this effusion is a dilemma whose horns *goad* us into frankness and candor— *"c'est un malheur,"* to use the words of Victor Hugo, *"d'où on ne pourrait se tirer par des periphrases, par des quemadmodums et des verumenimveros."* If we mention it at all, we are *forced* to employ the language of that region where, as Addison has it, "they sell the best fish and speak the plainest English." "Wakondah," then, from beginning to end, is trash. With the trivial exceptions which we shall designate, it has *no* merit whatever; while its faults, more numerous than the leaves of Valombrosa, are of that rampant class which, if any schoolboy *could* be found so uninformed as to commit them, any schoolboy should be remorselessly flogged for committing.

The story, or as the epics have it, the argument, although brief, is by no means particularly easy of comprehension. The design seems to be based upon a passage in Mr. Irving's "Astoria." He tells us that the Indians who inhabit the Chippewyan range of mountains, call it the "Crest of the World," and "think that Wakondah, or the Master of Life, as they designate the Supreme Being, has his residence among these aerial heights." Upon this hint Mr. Mathews has proceeded. He introduces us to Wakondah standing in person upon a mountain-top. He describes his appearance, and thinks that a Chinook would be frightened to behold it. He causes the "Master of Life" to make a speech, which is addressed, generally, to things at large, and particularly to the neighboring Woods, Cataracts, Rivers, Pinnacles, Steeps, and Lakes—not to mention an Earthquake. But all these (and we think, judiciously) turn a deaf ear to the oration, which, to be plain, is scarcely equal to a second-rate Piankitank stump speech. In fact, it is a bare-faced attempt at animal magnetism, and the mountains, &c., do no more than show its potency in resigning themselves to sleep, as they do.

Then shone Wakondah's dreadful eyes

—then he becomes *very* indignant, and accordingly launches forth into speech the second—with which the delinquents are afflicted, with occasional brief interruptions from the poet, in proper person, until the conclusion of the poem.

The *subject* of the two orations we shall be permitted to sum up compendiously in the one term "rigmarole." But we do not mean to say that our compendium is not an improvement, and a very considerable one, upon the speeches themselves,—which, taken altogether, are the queerest, and the most rhetorical, not to say the most miscellaneous orations we ever remember to have listened to outside of an Arkansas House of Delegates.

In saying this we mean what we say. We intend no joke. Were it possible, we would quote the whole poem in support of our opinion. But as this is *not* possible, and, moreover, as we presume Mr. Mathews has not been so negligent as to omit securing his valuable property by a copyright, we must be contented with a few extracts here and there at random, with a few comments equally so. But we have already hinted that there were really one or two words to be said of this effusion in the way of commendation, and these one or two words might as well be said now as hereafter.

The poem thus commences—

> The moon ascends the vaulted sky to-night;
> > With a slow motion full of pomp ascends,
> > But, mightier than the Moon that o'er it bends,
> A form is dwelling on the mountain height
> That boldly intercepts the struggling light
> > With darkness nobler than the planet's fire,—
> > A gloom and dreadful grandeur that aspire
> To match the cheerful Heaven's far-shining might.

If we were to shut our eyes to the repetition of "might," (which, in its various inflections, is a pet word with our author, and lugged in upon all occasions) and to the obvious imitation of Longfellow's Hymn to the Night in the second line of this stanza, we should be justified in calling it *good*. The "darkness nobler than the planet's fire" is *certainly* good.

The general conception of the colossal figure on the mountain summit, relieved against the full moon, would be unquestionably *grand* were it not for the *bullish* phraseology by which the conception is rendered, in a great measure, abortive. The moon is described as "ascending," and its "motion" is referred to, while we have the standing figure continuously intercepting its light. That the orb would soon pass from behind the figure, is a physical fact which the purpose of the poet required to be left out of sight, and which scarcely any other language than that which he has actually employed would have succeeded in forcing upon the reader's attention. With all these defects, however, the passage, especially as an opening passage, is one of high merit.

Looking carefully for something else to be commended we find at length the lines—

> Lo! where our foe up through these vales ascends,
>> Fresh from the embraces of the swelling sea,
>> A glorious, white and shining Deity.
> Upon our strength his deep blue eye he bends,
> With threatenings full of thought and steadfast ends;
>> *While desolation from his nostril breathes*
>> *His glittering rage he scornfully unsheathes*
> *And to the startled air its splendor lends.*

This again, however, is worth only qualified commendation. The first six lines preserve the personification (that of a ship) sufficiently well; but, in the seventh and eighth, the author suffers the image to slide into that of a warrior unsheathing his sword. Still there is *force* in these concluding verses, and we begin to fancy that this is saying a *very* great deal for the author of "Puffer Hopkins."

The best stanza in the poem (there are thirty-four in all) is the thirty-third.

> No cloud was on the moon, yet on His brow
>> A deepening shadow fell, and on his knees
>> *That shook like tempest-stricken mountain trees*
> *His heavy head descended sad and low*
> *Like a high city smitten by the blow*
>> *Which secret earthquakes strike and topling falls*

With all its arches, towers, and cathedrals
In swift and unconjectured overthrow.

This is, positively, not bad. The first line italicized is bold and vigorous, both in thought and expression; and the four last (although by no means original) convey a striking picture. But then the whole idea, in its general want of keeping, is preposterous. What is more absurd than the conception of a man's head descending *to his knees*, as here described—the thing could not be done by an Indian juggler or a man of gum-caoutchouc—and what is more inappropriate than the resemblance attempted to be drawn between a *single* head descending, and the *innumerable* pinnacles of a falling city? It is difficult to understand, *en passant*, why Mr. Mathews has thought proper to give "cathedrals" a quantity which does not belong to it, or to write "unconjectured" when the rhythm might have been fulfilled by "unexpected" and when "unexpected" would have fully conveyed the meaning which "unconjectured" does not.

By dint of farther microscopic survey, we are enabled to point out one, and alas, *only* one more good line in the poem.

Green dells that into silence stretch away

contains a richly poetical thought, melodiously embodied. We only refrain, however, from declaring, flatly, that the line is not the property of Mr. Mathews, because we have not at hand the volume from which we believe it to be stolen.

We quote the sixth, seventh, eighth, and ninth stanzas in full. They will serve to convey some faint idea of the general poem. The Italics are our own.

VI.
The spirit lowers and speaks: "Tremble ye wild Woods!
Ye Cataracts! your *organ-voices* sound!
Deep Crags, in earth by massy tenures bound,
Oh, Earthquake, *level flat!* The peace that broods
Above this world, and steadfastly eludes
Your power, howl Winds and break; the peace that mocks
Dismay 'mid silent streams and voiceless rocks—
Through wildernesses, cliffs, and solitudes.

VII.

"Night-shadowed Rivers—lift your dusky hands
    And clap them harshly *with a sullen roar!*
    Ye thousand Pinnacles and Steeps deplore
The glory that departs; above *you* stands,
Ye Lakes with azure waves and snowy strands,
    A Power that utters forth his loud behest
    Till mountain, lake and river shall attest,
The puissance of a Master's *large commands.*"

VIII.

So spake the Spirit with a wide-cast look
    Of bounteous power and *cheerful* majesty;
    As if he caught a sight of either sea
And all the subject realm between: then shook
His brandished arms; his stature scarce could brook
    Its confine; *swelling wide, it seemed to grow*
    As grows a cedar on a mountain's brow
By the mad air in ruffling breezes *took!*

IX.

The woods are deaf and will not be aroused—
    The mountains are asleep, they hear him not,
    Nor from deep-founded silence can be wrought,
Tho' herded bison on their steeps have browsed;
Beneath their banks in *darksome stillness* housed
    The rivers loiter like a calm-bound sea;
    In anchored nuptials to dumb apathy
Cliff, wilderness and solitude are spoused.

Let us endeavor to translate this gibberish, by way of ascertaining its import, if possible. Or, rather, let us state the stanzas, in substance. The spirit *lowers*, that is to say *grows angry*,
and speaks. He calls upon the Wild Woods to tremble, and
upon the Cataracts to sound their voices which have the tone
of an organ. He addresses, then, *an* Earthquake, or perhaps
Earthquake in general, and requests it to *level flat* all the Deep
Crags which are bound by massy tenures in earth—a request,
by the way, which any sensible Earthquake must have regarded as tautological, since it is difficult to level anything
otherwise than *flat*:—Mr. Mathews, however, is no doubt

the best judge of flatness in the abstract, and may have peculiar ideas respecting it. But to proceed with the Spirit. Turning to the Winds, he enjoins them to howl and break the peace that broods above this world and steadfastly eludes their power—the same peace that mocks a Dismay 'mid streams, rocks, et cetera. He now speaks to the night-shadowed Rivers, and commands them to lift their dusky hands, and clap them harshly *with a sullen roar*—and as *roaring* with one's *hands* is not the easiest matter in the world, we can only conclude that the Rivers here reluctantly disobeyed the injunction. Nothing daunted, however, the Spirit, addressing a thousand Pinnacles and Steeps, desires them to deplore the glory that departs, or is departing—and we can almost fancy that we see the Pinnacles deploring it upon the spot. The Lakes—at least such of them as possess azure waves and snowy strands—then come in for their share of the oration. They are called upon to observe—to take notice—that above them stands no ordinary character—no Piankitank stump orator, or anything of that sort—but a Power;—a power, in short, to use the exact words of Mr. Mathews, "that *utters forth* his loud behest, till mountain, lake and river shall attest the puissance of a Master's *large commands.*" *Utters forth* is no doubt somewhat supererogatory, since "to utter" is of itself to emit, or send forth; but as "the Power" appears to be somewhat excited he should be forgiven such mere errors of speech. We cannot, however, pass over his boast about uttering forth his loud behest *till* mountain, lake and rivers shall obey him—for the fact is that his threat is *vox et preterea nihil*, like the countryman's nightingale in Catullus; the issue showing that the mountains, lakes and rivers—all very sensible creatures—go fast asleep upon the spot, and pay no attention to his rigmarole whatever. Upon the "large commands" it is not our intention to dwell. The phrase is a singularly mercantile one to be in the mouth of "a Power." It is not impossible, however, that Mr. Mathews himself is

> —busy in the cotton trade
> And sugar line.

But to resume. We were originally told that the Spirit "lowered" and spoke, and in truth his entire speech is a scold at

Creation; yet stanza the eighth is so forgetful as to say that he spoke "with a wide-cast look of bounteous power and *cheerful* majesty." Be this point as it may, he now shakes his brandished arms, and, swelling out, seems to grow—

> As grows a cedar on a mountain's top
> By the mad air in ruffling breezes *took*

—or as swells a turkey-gobler; whose image the poet unquestionably had in his mind's eye when he penned the words about the ruffled cedar. As for *took* instead of *taken*—why not say *tuk* at once? We have heard of chaps vot vas tuk up for sheep-stealing, and we know of one or two that ought to be tuk up for murder of the Queen's English.

We shall never get on. Stanza the ninth assures us that the woods are deaf and will not be aroused, that the mountains are asleep and so forth—all which Mr. Mathews might have anticipated. But the rest he could not have foreseen. He could not have foreknown that "the rivers, housed beneath their banks in *darksome stillness*," would "loiter like a calm-bound sea," and still less could he have been aware, unless informed of the fact, that *"cliff, wilderness and solitude would be spoused in anchored nuptials to dumb apathy!"* Good Heavens—no!— nobody could have anticipated *that*! Now, Mr. Mathews, we put it to you as to a man of veracity—what *does* it all mean?

> As when in times to startle and revere.

This line, of course, is an accident on the part of our author. At the time of writing it he could not have remembered

> To haunt, to startle, and waylay.

Here is another accident of imitation; for seriously, we do not mean to *assert* that it is anything more—

> I urged the dark red hunter in his quest
> Of pard or panther with a gloomy zest;
> And while through darkling woods they swiftly fare
> *Two seeming creatures of the oak-shadowed air,*
> I sped the game and fired the follower's breast.

The line italicized we have seen quoted by some of our daily critics as beautiful; and so, barring the "oak-shadowed air," it is. In the meantime Campbell, in "Gertrude of Wyoming," has the *words*

> —the hunter and the deer a shade.

Campbell stole the idea from our own Freneau, who has the *line*

> The hunter and the deer a shade.

Between the two, Mr. Mathews' claim to originality, at this point, will, very possibly, fall to the ground.

It appears to us that the author of "Wakondah" is either very innocent or very original about matters of versification. His stanza is an ordinary one. If we are not mistaken, it is that employed by Campbell in his "Gertrude of Wyoming"—a favorite poem of our author's. At all events it is composed of pentameters whose rhymes alternate by a simple and fixed rule. But our poet's deviations from this rule are so many and so unusually picturesque, that we scarcely know what to think of them. Sometimes he introduces an Alexandrine at the close of a stanza; and here we have no right to quarrel with him. It is not *usual* in this metre; but still he *may* do it if he pleases. To put an Alexandrine in the middle, or at the beginning, of one of these stanzas is droll, to say no more. See stanza third, which commences with the verse

> Upon his brow a garland of the woods he wears,

and stanza twenty-eight, where the last line but one is

> And rivers singing all aloud tho' still unseen.

Stanza the seventh begins thus

> The Spirit lowers and speaks—tremble ye Wild Woods!

Here it must be observed that " wild woods" is not meant for a double rhyme. If scanned on the fingers (and we presume Mr. Mathews is in the practice of scanning thus) the line is a legitimate Alexandrine. Nevertheless, it cannot be *read*. It is like nothing under the sun; except, perhaps, Sir Philip Sidney's attempt at English Hexameter in his "Arcadia." Some one or two of his verses we remember. For example—

> So to the | woods Love | runs as | well as | rides to the |
> palace;
> Neither he | bears reve | rence to a | prince nor | pity to a |
> beggar,
> But like a | point in the | midst of a | circle is | still of a |
> nearness.

With the aid of an additional spondee or dactyl Mr.
Mathews' *very* odd verse might be scanned in the same manner, and would, in fact, be a legitimate Hexameter—

> The Spi | rit lowers | and speaks | tremble ye | wild woods.

Sometimes our poet takes even a higher flight and *drops* a
foot, or a half-foot, or, for the matter of that, a foot and a
half. Here, for example, is a very singular verse to be introduced in a pentameter rhythm—

> Then shone Wakondah's dreadful eyes.

Here another—

> Yon full-orbed fire shall cease to shine.

Here, again, are lines in which the rhythm demands an accent on impossible syllables.

> But ah winged *with* what agonies and pangs.
> Swiftly before me *nor* care I how vast.
> I see vi*sions* denied to mortal eyes.
> Uplifted longer *in* heaven's western glow.

But these are trifles. Mr. Mathews is young and we take it
for granted that he will improve. In the meantime what does
he mean by spelling lose, *loose*, and its (the possessive pronoun) *it's*—re-iterated instances of which fashions are to be
found *passim* in "Wakondah"? What does he mean by writing
dare, the present, for *dared* the perfect?—see stanza the
twelfth. And, as we are now in the catachetical vein, we may
as well conclude our dissertation at once with a few other
similar queries.

What do you mean, then, Mr. Mathews, by

> A sudden silence *like a tempest* fell?

What do you mean by "a quivered stream;" "a shapeless gloom;" a "habitable wish;" "natural blood;" "oak-shadowed air;" "customary peers" and "thunderous noises?"
What do you mean by

A sorrow mightier than the midnight skies?

What do you mean by

A bulk that swallows up the sea-blue sky?

Are you not aware that calling the sky as blue as the sea, is like saying of the snow that it is as white as a sheet of paper?
What do you mean, in short, by

Its feathers darker than a thousand fears?

Is not this something like "blacker than a dozen and a half of chimney-sweeps and a stack of black cats," and are not the whole of these illustrative observations of yours somewhat upon the plan of that of the witness who described a certain article stolen as being of the size and shape of a bit of chalk? What do you *mean* by them we say?

And here notwithstanding our earnest wish to satisfy the author of Wakondah, it is indispensable that we bring our notice of the poem to a close. We feel grieved that our observations have been so much at random: — but at random, after all, is it alone possible to convey either the letter or the spirit of that, which, a mere jumble of incongruous nonsense, has neither beginning, middle, nor end. We should be delighted to proceed—but how? to applaud—but what? Surely not this trumpery declamation, this maudlin sentiment, this metaphor run-mad, this twaddling verbiage, this halting and doggrel rhythm, this unintelligible rant and cant! "Slid, if these be your passados and montantes, we'll have none of them." Mr. Mathews, you have clearly mistaken your vocation, and your effusion as little deserves the title of *poem*, (oh sacred name!) as did the rocks of the royal forest of Fontainebleau that of *"mes déserts"* bestowed upon them by Francis the First. In bidding you adieu we commend to your careful consideration the remark of M. Timon *"que le Ministre de l'Instruction Publique doit lui-même savoir parler Francais."*

Graham's Magazine, February 1842

Big Abel and the Little Manhattan. Wiley & Putnam's Library of American Books, No. V. By Cornelius Mathews.

THIS IS by all means an original book, original in conception, conduct and tone. It may be called an emblematical romance of homely life. The most obvious design is to gossip, or rather give voice to under-toned comments about the condition of the Island of Manhattan, and, more especially, of the great city which oppresses its southern end. A less superficial purpose is that of contrasting the present condition with that under the aboriginal dynasty—of contrasting, apart from conventionality, the true values of the savage and civilized state. The story, on the mere face of it, runs that a houseless vagabond, the great-grandson of Henry Hudson the navigator, and the descendant from the last Indian chief of the Mannahatta, that these two being a little demented, or whimsical, or ignorant, through long desuetude of the world's usages, propose to themselves (after being armed with the proper documents) the institution of a claim, in "The Supreme Court of Judicature," to the whole island of New York. The narrative (if such it can be termed) opens with the introduction of the two claimants, who possess themselves, at the base of the white shot tower on the East river, of the papers by which the claim is to be sustained. They then proceed to a tavern, and—

"All that Lankey Fogle did, was to call out to the landlord to put more light on, which being done, he threw off his hat, turned about and looked calmly on Big Abel. There was the straight black hair, the swarthy skin, the slumberous and autumnal eye. There was no mistaking these. The Little Manhattan, beyond a doubt! And now Big Abel—where are you? A little musty scrap, out of the box, another, and still another. It seems so. In truth it does. Old Henry Hudson's lineal heir—great-grandson, it would seem. Lankey Fogle, (this was a name he got from idle boys, and not by birth,) great-grandson to that fierce old chief, who swayed with iron this island once, heading his red Manhattanese! Big Abel, great-grandson to the old navigator-trader, of brave English blood. By right of nature this city, built it who did, is the Little Manhattan's clearly, all. Big Abel claims, as first discoverer,

(Lankey Fogle glares on this;) but, better still, purchase of some old chief or other. He thinks it was the same chief that Lankey claims from; but this he can't make out so well. The oblong box is shut again; the *why* is between them, but whose, who can tell? To-morrow they will set forth, dividing it for themselves, each taking what he can, in fairness and good will. For they are friends now—perfect confidence— perfect confidence between them. The long mistrust with which they have lowered at each other through the courts is ended now, melted into a fine, twilight mist, in which each seems magnified and gentle to the other. To-bed, now, not as for many years, but hopeful of their own. Yes, these—so far apart in many things, so close together in their fortunes now—are whimsical enough to make belief that the old mer- chant-navigator and the old Indian chief are still abroad through all these streets, in spirit; that, somehow or other, as the colour of the soil shows itself in the tree, they are still out of their very graves, holding to the city as their own. Well, we shall see what came of it."

The true purpose of the book now begins. In their rovings through the city, the claimants look with appropriative eye, each to such items of house or land, or water-privilege, or what not, as seems most in accordance with the spirit (either of nature or civilization) by which he claims. The fountains, for example, and the Indian statues at the tobacco-shop doors, are turned over, without a murmur, to the Little Man- hattan. In the division which is to take place when the Su- preme Court shall have favourably decided, these (the fountains and other such matters) are to be unhesitatingly the Indian's. On the other hand, Trinity church, Delmonico's, and all the broker's offices, banks, etc., etc., with the wharves and the shipping more particularly, are as undeniably the right of the heir of Henry Hudson. The discussions carried on between the two afford opportunities for that *suggestive contrast* which may be stated, in brief, as the moral of the story. We look upon a minute account of the nooks and cor- ners of the city, most especially of that portion of it known as the East Bowery (a *terra incognita*)—we look upon this and upon an infinite variety of humourous or pathetic *obser-*

vation, as merely an underplot to the main action, an undercurrent to the upper thesis—more properly as a meaning accompaniment to the air which is the staple of the whole.

The style throughout is peculiarly the author's own. We cite a brief passage which will serve very well to exemplify it:—

"Done it was; and, out at the Mount Vernon gate again, they struck across the country.

"There is a little hill there, and rising that by winding paths, through an orchard, they got upon the road. Beyond, descending now, they come upon the sunken meadows, with little rills running, creeping rather, here and there, and glittering in the moon. About, a few late fellows, the frogs were piping, in a revel of their own; and now and then, as Lankey and Big Abel glide along, some little birds, troubled in their dreams, stirring in the bushes. In the midst of all this stillness or calm motion of the night, a figure passed them—in the very middle of the field—a figure, singing.

"It was quite clear who this was, without a question. A Poor Scholar, who had wandered out into the open country, and the clear night, to coax away certain cares that pressed at his heart; to think over a past full of gloom and sadness and hard perplexities, and to call up as he wandered on a fair shape whose shadowy hand he sought in vain, for it flew away ever as he stretched his own toward it. Pale he was, indeed, but with eyes lit as the night was with a more than common and day-time lustre. His apparel—one could see—was plain, and darkened into a better black than belonged to it in broad daylight, by the friendly night. And yet, poor and sad and sorrowful as he was, as you would suppose, he went on his way singing a cheerful song, blessing everything about him, whether it was the green earth his foot trod upon or the air that caught his fingers as he shook them in chorus to his singing, or the blue, far away sky he looked up to often as he walked.

" 'William—the Poor Scholar!' said Big Abel to the Little Manhattan, as he crossed them. 'He had a case in court once, I recollect. It was all about a book, and the judge said it was a glorious thing to write a book; and that's all he got for it.' "

The Poor Scholar here introduced, and his mistress, form the subject of an episode, by aid of which the author is enabled to bring out in truer light the main interest of his theme.

Upon the whole, Mr. Matthews has written an ingenious, an original, and altogether an excellent book—a book especially well adapted to a series which is distinctively American. Its chief defect is a very gross indefinitiveness, not of conception, but of execution. Out of ten readers nine will be totally at a loss to comprehend the meaning of the author. Of course, nothing so written can hope to be popular;—but we presume that mere popularity is by no means Mr. Matthews' intention.

Godey's Lady's Book, November 1845

Morris Mattson

Paul Ulric: Or the Adventures of an Enthusiast. New York: Published by Harper & Brothers.

THESE TWO VOLUMES are by Morris Mattson, Esq. of Philadelphia, and we presume that Mr. Mattson is a very young man. Be this as it may, when we called Norman Leslie the silliest book in the world we had certainly never seen Paul Ulric. *One* sentence in the latter, however, is worthy of our serious attention. "We want a few faithful laborers in the vineyard of literature, to root out the noxious weeds which infest it." See page 116, vol. ii.

In itself, the book before us is too purely imbecile to merit an extended critique—but as a portion of our daily literary food—as an American work published by the Harpers—as one of a class of absurdities with an inundation of which our country is grievously threatened—we shall have no hesitation, and shall spare no pains, in exposing fully before the public eye its four hundred and forty-three pages of utter folly, bombast, and inanity.

"My name," commences Mr. Mattson, "is Paul Ulric. Thus much, gentle reader, you already know of one whose history is about to be recorded for the benefit of the world. I was always an enthusiast, but of this I deem it inexpedient to say much at present. I will merely remark that I possessed by nature a wild and adventurous spirit which has led me on blindly and hurriedly, from object to object, without any definite or specific aim. My life has been one of continual excitement, and in my wild career I have tasted of joy as well as of sorrow. [Oh remarkable Mr. Ulric!] At one moment I have been elevated to the very pinnacle of human happiness, at the next I have sunk to the lowest depths of despair. Still I fancied there was always an equilibrium. This may seem a strange philosophy to some, but is it the less true? The human mind is so constituted as always to seek a level—if it is depressed it will be proportionately elevated, if elevated it will be proportionately depressed. But" says Mr. U., interrupting himself, "I am growing metaphysical!" We had thought he was only growing absurd.

He proceeds to tell us of his father who was born in Lower

Saxony—who went, when only a year old, to England—
who, being thrown upon the parish, was initiated into the
mysteries of boot cleaning—who, at the age of ten, became a
vender of newspapers in the city of London—at twelve sold
potatoes in Covent Garden—at fifteen absconded from a
soap-boiler in the Strand to whom he had been appren-
ticed—at eighteen sold old clothes—at twenty became the
proprietor of a mock auction in Cheapside—at twenty five
was owner of a house in Regent Street, and had several thousand pounds in the Funds—and before thirty was created a
Baronet, with the title of Sir John Augustus Frederick Geoffry
Ulric, Bart., for merely picking up and carrying home his
Majesty King George the Fourth, whom Mr. U. assures us
upon his word and honor, his father found lying beastly
drunk, one fine day, in some gutter, in some particular thoroughfare of London.

Our hero himself was born, we are told, on the borders of
the Thames, not far from Greenwich. When a well grown lad
he accompanies his father to the continent. In Florence he
falls in love with a Countess in her thirty-fifth year, who curls
his hair and gives him sugar-plums. The issue of the adventure with the Countess is thus told.

"You have chosen them with much taste," said the Countess; "a beautiful flower is this!" she continued, selecting one
from among the number, "its vermillion is in your cheeks, its
blue in your eyes, and for this pretty compliment I deserve a
—— you resist eh! My pretty, pretty lad, I *will!* There! Another, and you may go free. Still perverse? Oh, you stubborn
boy! How can you refuse? One—two—three! I shall *devour*
you with kisses!"

       *   *   *   *   *
        *   *   *   *   *

We have printed the passage precisely as we find it in the
book—notes of admiration—dashes—Italics—and all. Two
rows of stars wind up the matter, and stand for the catastrophe—for we hear no more of the Countess. Now if any person over curious should demand why Morris Mattson, Esq.
has mistaken notes of admiration for sense—dashes, kisses,
stars and Italics for sentiment—the answer is very simple in-

deed. The author of Vivian Grey made the same mistake before him.

Indeed we have made up our minds to forward Ben D'Israeli a copy of Paul Ulric. He will read it, and if he do not expire upon the spot, it will do him more real service than the crutch. Never was there a more laughable burlesque of any man's manner. Had Mr. Mattson only *intended it* as a burlesque we would have called him a clever fellow. But unfortunately this is not the case. No jackdaw was ever more soberly serious in fancying herself a peacock, than our author in thinking himself D'Israeli the second.

"Every day," says Paul after the kissing scene, "filled me with a new spirit of romance. I had sailed upon the winding streams of Germany; I had walked beneath the bright skies of Italy; I had clambered the majestic mountains of Switzerland." His father, however, determines upon visiting the United States, and taking his family with him. His reasons for so doing should be recorded. "His republicanism" says Paul, "had long rendered him an object of aversion to the aristocracy. He had had the hardihood to compare the *salary* of the President with the *civil list* of the king— *consequently he was threatened with an indictment for treason!* My mother suggested the propriety of immediately quitting the country."

Mr. Mattson does not give us an account of the voyage. "I have no disposition," says his hero, "to describe a trip across the Atlantic—particularly as I am not in a sentimental mood—otherwise I might turn over the poets, and make up a long chapter of extracts from Moore, Byron, and Rogers of the Old World, or Percival, Bryant, and Halleck of the New." A range of stars, accordingly, is introduced at this crisis of affairs, and we must understand them to express all the little matters which our author is too fastidious to detail. Having sufficiently admired the stars, we turn over the next leaf and "Land ho!" shouts one of the seamen on the fore-topsail yard.

Arrived in Philadelphia, Mr. Ulric (our hero's father) "is divided," so says Mr. Mattson, "between the charms of a city and country life." His family at this time, we are told, consisted of five persons; and Mr. U. Jr. takes this opportunity of formally introducing to us, his two sisters Eleanor and Rosaline. This introduction, however, is evidently to little purpose, for we hear no more, throughout the two volumes, of either the one young lady or the other. After much deliberation the family fix their residence in "Essex, a delightful country village in the interior of Pennsylvania;" and we beg our readers to bear in mind that the surprising adventures of Paul Ulric are, for the most part, perpetrated in the immediate vicinity of this village.

The young gentleman (notwithstanding his late love affair with the Countess) is now, very properly, sent to school—or rather a private tutor is engaged for him—one Lionel Wafer. A rapid proficiency in Latin, Greek, Hebrew, music, dancing, and fencing, is the result; "and with these accomplishments," says the young calf, "I believed myself fitted for the noise and bustle of the world." Accordingly, his father having given him a flogging one afternoon, he determines upon running away. In two days he "arrives in one of the Atlantic cities." Rambling about the streets he enters into conversation with a sharper, who succeeds in selling him, for forty dollars, a watch made of tinsel and put together with paste. This and subsequent adventures in the city form the best portion of the book—if *best* should be applied, in any way, to what is altogether abominable. Mr. Ulric goes to the theatre, and the play is Romeo and Juliet. The orchestra "breaks forth in full chorus" and our hero soliloquizes. We copy his soliloquy with the end of placing before our readers what we consider the finest passage in Mr. Mattson's novel. We wish to do that gentleman every possible act of justice; and when we write down the few words to which we allude, and when we say that they are not absolutely intolerable, we have done all, in the way of commendation, which lies in our power. We have not one other word of praise to throw away upon Paul Ulric.

"Oh Music!—the theme of bards from time immemorial—who can sing of thee as thou deservest? What wondrous miracles hast thou not accomplished? The war-drum beats—the clarion gives forth its piercing notes—and legions of armed men rush headlong to the fierce and devastating battle. Again, the drum is muffled, and its deep notes break heavily upon the air, while the dead warrior is borne along upon his bier, and thousands mingle their tears to his memory. The tender lute sounds upon the silvery waters, and the lover throws aside his oar, and imprints a kiss upon the lips of his beloved. The bugle rings in the mountain's recesses, and a thousand spears are uplifted for a fearful and desperate conflict. And now the organ peals, and, with its swelling notes, the soul leaps into the very presence of the Deity."

Our hero decides upon adopting the stage as a profession, and with this view takes lessons in elocution. Having perfected himself in this art, he applies to a manager, by note, for permission to display his abilities, but is informed that the nights are engaged for two months ahead, and it would be impossible for him to appear during the season. By the influence, however, of some hanger-on of the theatre, his wishes are at length gratified, and he is announced in the bills as "the celebrated Master Le Brun, the son of a distinguished English nobleman, whose success was so unprecedented in London as to have performed fifty nights in succession at the Theatre Royal, Drury Lane"—a sentence in which we are at a loss to discover whether the English nobleman, or the English nobleman's son, or the success of the English nobleman's son is the distinguished performer in question.

Our adventurer succeeds in his debût, and is in a fair way of becoming a popular performer, when his prospects are suddenly nipped in the bud. His valet one morning announces a Sir Thomas Le Brun, and Sir Thomas Le Brun proves to be that worthy gentleman Sir John Augustus Frederick Geoffry Ulric, Baronet. A scene ensues. Paul screams, and Sir John clenches his fist. The father makes a speech, and the son makes a speech and a bow. At length they fly into each other's arms, and the drama closes by the old personage taking the young personage home in his carriage. In all this balderdash about the stage, there is not one original incident or idea. The same anecdotes are told, but in infinitely better language, in every book of dramatic reminiscences since the flood.

Our author now indulges in what we suppose to be satire. The arrows of his wit are directed, with much pertinacity at least, against one Borel Bunting, by which name it strikes us that Mr. M. wishes to indicate some poor devil of an editor in bonâ fide existence—perhaps some infatuated young person who could not be prevailed upon, by love or money, to look over the MS. of Paul Ulric. If our supposition be true, we could wish Mr. Borel Bunting no better revenge than what the novelist has himself afforded by this public exposure of his imbecility. We must do our readers the favor of copying for their especial perusal, a portion of this vehement attack.

There has been much speculation as to the birth-place of Borel; (in this respect he somewhat resembled Homer) but if I have been correctly informed it was in one of the New England States. Further than this I cannot particularize. When he came to Essex he managed to procure a situation in a counting-house, which afforded him the means of support as well as leisure for study. He did not overlook these advantages, and gradually rose in public estimation until he became the editor of the Literary Herald. This gentleman was deeply read in the classics, and had also perused every novel and volume of poetry from the earliest period of English literature down to the present. Such had been his indefatigable research, that there was not a remarkable passage in the whole range of the Waverley fictions, or indeed any other fictions, to which he could not instantly turn. As to poetry, he was an oracle. He could repeat the whole of Shelley, Moore, and Wordsworth, *verbatim*. He was a very Sidrophel in his acquirements. He could tell

"How many scores a flea would jump;"

he could prove, also, "that the man in the moon's a sea Mediterranean," and

"In lyric numbers write an ode on
His mistress eating a black pudding."

He composed acrostics extempore by the dozen; we say *extempore*, though it was once remarked that he was months in bringing them to maturity. He was inimitable, moreover, in his pictures of natural scenery. When a river, or a mountain, or a waterfall was to be sketched, Borel Bunting, of all others, was the man to guide the pencil. He had the rare faculty of bringing every thing distinctly before the mind of the reader—a compliment to which a majority of his brother scribes are not entitled.

Borel Bunting possessed also a considerable degree of critical acumen. Southey was a mere doggerelist; Cooper and Irving were not men of genius: so said Borel. Pope, he declared, was the first of poets, because Lord Byron said so before him. Tom Jones, he contended, was the most perfect specimen of a novel extant. He was also willing to admit that Goldsmith had shown some talent in his Vicar of Wakefield.

In a word, Borel's wonderful acquirements secured him the favorable attention of many distinguished men; and at length (as a reward of his industry and merit) he was regularly installed in the chair editorial of the *"Literary Herald,"* an important weekly periodical, fifteen inches in diameter. His salary, it is supposed, was something less than that received by the President of the United States.

The Literary Herald, Borel (or rather, Mr. Bunting—we beg his pardon) considered the paragon of perfection. No one could ever hope to be distinguished in literature who was not a contributor to its columns. It was the only sure medium through which young Ambition could make its way to immortality. In short, (to use one of Bunting's favorite words,) it was the *"nonpareil"* of learning, literature, wit, philosophy, and science.

Mr. Bunting corresponded regularly with many distinguished individuals in Europe. I called upon him one morning, just after the arrival of a foreign mail, when he read me portions of seven letters which he had just received. One was from Lafayette, another from Charles X., a third from the author of a fashionable novel, a fourth from Miss L——, a beautiful poetess in London, a fifth from a German count, a sixth from an Italian prince, and a seventh from Stpqrstuwsptrsm, (I vouch not for the orthography, not being so well acquainted with the art of spelling as the learned Borel,) a distinguished Russian general in the service of the great "Northern Bear."

The most unfortunate charge that was ever preferred against Borel, in his editorial capacity, was that of *plagiarism*.

He had inserted an article in his paper over his acknowledged signature, entitled *"Desultory Musings,"* which some one boldly asserted was an extract from Zimmerman on Solitude; and, upon its being denied by the editor, reference was given to the identical page whence it was taken. These things boded no good to the reputation of the scribe; nevertheless, he continued his career without interruption, and, had he lived in the days of Pope, the latter might well have asked,

> "Who shames a scribbler? break one cobweb through,
> He spins the slight, self-pleasing thread anew:
> Destroy his fib or sophistry, in vain,
> The creature's at his dirty work again—
>   *   *   *   *
> Proud of a vast extent of flimsy lines."

Mr. Ulric now indulges us with another love affair, beginning as follows: "Oh thou strange and incomprehensible passion! to what canst thou be compared? At times thou art gentle as the zephyr; at others thou art mighty as the tempest. Thou canst calm the throbbing bosom, or thou canst fill it with wilder commotion. A single smile of thy benign countenance calleth new rapture to the anguished heart, and scattereth every doubt, every fear, every perplexity. But enough of this." True.

A young lady falls into a river or a ditch, (our author says she was fishing for a water lily) and Mr. Ulric is at the trouble of pulling her out. "What a charming incident!" says Mr. Mattson. Her name is Violet, and our susceptible youth falls in love with her. "Shall I ever," quoth Paul, "shall I ever forget my sensations at that period?—never!!" Among other methods of evincing his passion he writes a copy of verses "To Violet," and sends them to the *Literary Herald*. All, however, is to little purpose. The lady is no fool, and very properly does not wish a fool for a husband.

Our hero now places his affections upon the wife of a silk-dyer. He has a rival, however, in the person of the redoubted editor, Borel Bunting, and a duel ensues, in which, although the matter is a hoax, and the pistols have no load in them, Mr. Mattson assures us that the editor "in firing, lodged the *contents* of his weapon in the ground a few inches from his feet." The chapter immediately following this adventure is headed with poetical quotations occupying two-thirds of a page. One is from *Byron*—another from *All's Well that Ends Well*—and the third from *Brown's Lecture on Perpetual Motion*. The chapter itself would form not quite half a column such as we are now writing, and in it we are informed that Bunting, having discovered the perpetual motion, determines upon a tour in Europe.

The editor being thus disposed of, Mr. Mattson now enters seriously upon the business of his novel. We beg the attention of our readers while we detail a tissue of such absurdity, as we did not believe it possible, at this day, for any respectable bookseller to publish, or the very youngest of young gentlemen to indite.

Let us bear in mind that the scene of the following events is in the vicinity of Philadelphia, and the epoch, the present day. Mr. Ulric takes a stroll one May morning with his gun. "Nature seems to be at rest," &c.—"the warbling of birds," &c.—"perched among trees," &c. was all very fine, &c. "While gazing," says Paul, "upon these objects," (that is to say, the warbling of the birds) "I beheld a young and beautiful female trip lightly over the grass, and seat herself beneath a willow which stood in the middle of a park." Whereupon our adventurer throws himself into an attitude, and soliloquizes as follows.

"It seems that there is an indescribable something in the features of many women—a look, a smile, or a glance of the eye—that sends the blood thrilling to the heart, and involuntarily kindles the flame of love upon its altar. It is no wonder that sages and philosophers have worshipped with such mad devotion at the shrine of beauty! It is no wonder that the mighty Pericles knelt at the feet of his beloved Aspasia! It is no wonder that the once powerful Antony sacrificed his country to the fatal embraces of the bewitching Cleopatra! It is no wonder that the thirst for glory cooled in the heart of the philosophic Abelard, when he beheld the beauty of the exquisite Heloise! It is no wonder, indeed, that he quitted the dry maxims of Aristotle to practise the more pleasing precepts of Ovid! But this is rhapsody!" It is.

The lady is dressed in white, (probably cambric muslin,) and Mr. Mattson assures us that her features he shall not attempt to describe. He proceeds, however, to say that her "eyes are hazel, but very dark," "her complexion pure as alabaster," her lips like the lips of Canova's Venus, and her forehead like—something very fine. Mr. Ulric attempts to speak, but his embarrassment prevents him. The young lady "turns to depart," and our adventurer goes home as he came.

The next chapter commences with "How mysterious is human existence!"—which means, when translated, "How original is Mr. Mattson!" This initial paragraph concludes with a solemn assurance that we are perishable creatures, and that it is very possible we may all die—every mother's son of us. But as Mr. M. hath it—"to our story." Paul has discovered the mansion of the young lady—but can see no more of the young lady herself. He therefore stands sentinel before the door, with the purpose "of making observations." While thus engaged, he perceives a tall fellow, " with huge black whiskers and a most forbidding aspect," enter the house, in a familiar manner. Our hero is, of course, in despair. The tall gentleman could be no other than the accepted lover of the young lady. Having arrived at this conclusion, Paul espies a column of smoke in the woods, and after some trouble discovers it to proceed from "a log dwelling which stood alone, with its roof of moss, amid the silence and solitude of nature." A dog barks, and an old woman makes her appearance.

This old lady is a most portentous being. She is, however, a little given to drinking; and offers our hero a dram, of which Mr. Mattson positively assures us that gentleman did not accept.

"Can you tell me," says Paul, " who lives in the stone house?"

"Do you mean the Florence mansion," she asked.

"Very like—who is its owner?"

"A man of the same name—Richard Florence."

"Who is Richard Florence?"

"An Englishman; he came to this country a year or two ago."

"Has he a wife?"

"Not that I know of."

"Children?"

"An only daughter."

"What is her name?"

"Emily."

"Emily!—Is she beautiful?"

"Very beautiful!"

"And amiable?"

"Her like is not to be found."

"What," [exclaims our hero, perhaps starting back and running his fingers through his hair]—" what are all the fleeting and fickle pleasures of the world! what the magnificent palaces of kings, with their imperial banquetings and gorgeous processions! what, indeed, are all the treasures of the earth or the sea, in comparison with the pure, the bright, the beautiful object of our young and innocent affections!!!"

The name of the old hag is Meg Lawler, and she favors Mr. Ulric with her private history. The morality of her disclosures is questionable—but "morals, at the present day," quoth Mr. Mattson, "are rarely sought in works of fiction, and perhaps *less* rarely found." The gentleman means *more* rarely. But let us proceed. Meg Lawler relates a tale of seduction. It ends in the most approved form. "I knew," says she, "that the day of sorrow and tribulation was at hand, but alas, there was no saving power!" Here follows a double range of stars—after which, the narrative is resumed as follows.

"Dame Lawler paused, and turning upon me her glaring and blood-shot eyes exclaimed—

"Do you think there is a punishment hereafter for the evil deeds done in the body?"

"Such," I replied, "the divines have long taught us."

"Then is my destroyer writhing in the agonies of hell!!" Mr. Ulric is, of course, electrified, and the chapter closes.

Our hero, some time after this, succeeds in making the acquaintance of Miss Emily Florence. The scene of the first interview is the cottage of Meg Lawler. Mr. U. proposes a walk—the lady at first refuses, but finally consents.

"There were two paths," says our hero, "either of which we might have chosen: one led into the forest, the other towards her father's house. I struck into the latter—but she abruptly paused."

"Shall we continue our walk?" I asked, observing that she still hesitated.

"Yes," she at length answered; "but I would prefer the other path"—that is to say the path through the woods—O fi, Miss Emily Florence! During the walk, our hero arrives at the conclusion that his beloved is "some unfortunate captive" whose fears, or whose sense of dependence, might render it imprudent for her to be seen in the society of a stranger. In addition to all this, Dame Lawler has told Mr. U. that "she did not believe Emily was the daughter of Mr. Florence"—hereby filling the interesting youth with suspicions, which Mr. Mattson assures us "were materials for the most painful reflection."

On their way home our lovers meet with an adventure. Mr. Ulric happens to espy a—man. Miss Emily Florence thus explains this momentous occurrence. *"There is a band of robbers who have their retreat in the neighboring hills—and this was no doubt one of them. They are headed by a brave and reckless fellow of the name of Elmo—Captain Elmo I think they call him. They have been the terror of the inhabitants for a long time. My father went out sometime ago with an armed force in pursuit of them, but could not discover their hiding place. I have heard it said that they steal away the children of wealthy parents that they may exact a ransom."* Once more we beg our readers to remember that Mr. Mattson's novel is a Tale of the Present Times, and that its scene is in the near vicinity of the city of Brotherly Love.

Having convinced her lover that the man so portentously seen can be nobody in the world but "that brave and reckless fellow" Captain Elmo, Miss Florence proceeds to assure Mr. U. that she (Miss Florence) is neither afraid of man nor the devil—and forthwith brandishes in the eyes of our adventurer an ivory-hilted dagger, or a carving-knife, or some such murderous affair. "Scarcely knowing what I did," says our gallant friend, "I imprinted a kiss (the first—burning, passionate, and full of rapture) upon her innocent lips, and— *darted into the woods!!!"* It was impossible to stand the carving-knife.

As Mr. U. takes his way home after this memorable adventure, he is waylaid by an old woman, who turns out to be a robber in disguise. A scuffle ensues, and our hero knocks down his antagonist—what less could such a hero do? Instead however of putting an end at once to his robbership, our friend merely stands over him and requests him to recite his adventures. This the old woman does. Her name is Dingee O'Dougherty, or perhaps Dingy O'Dirty—and she proves to be one and the same personage with the little man in gray who sold Mr. U. the tinsel watch spoken of in the beginning of the history. During the catechism, however, a second robber comes up, and the odds are now against our hero. But on account of his affectionate forbearance to Dingy O'Dirty no farther molestation is offered—and the three part with an amicable understanding.

Mr. Ulric is now taken ill of a fever—and during his illness a servant of Mr. Florence having left that gentleman's service, calls upon his heroship to communicate some most astounding intelligence. Miss Florence, it appears, has been missing for some days, and her father receives a letter (purporting to be from the captain of the banditti) in which it is stated that they have carried her away, and would only return her in consideration of a ransom. Florence is requested to meet them at a certain spot and hour, when they propose to make known their conditions. Upon hearing this extraordinary news our adventurer jumps out of bed, throws himself into attitude No. 2, and swears a round oath that he will deliver Miss Emily himself. Thus ends the first volume.

Volume the second commences with spirit. Mr. U. hires "three fearless and able-bodied men to accompany and render him assistance in the event of danger. Each of them was supplied with a belt containing a brace of pistols, and a large Spanish knife." With these terrible desperadoes, our friend arrives at the spot designated by the bandit. Leaving his companions near at hand, he advances, and recognizes the redoubted Captain Elmo, who demands a thousand pounds as the ransom of Miss Emily Florence. Our hero considers this too much, and the Captain consents to take five hundred. This too Mr. U. refuses to give, and with his three friends makes an attack upon the bandit. But a posse of robbers coming to the aid of their leader, our hero is about to meet with his deserts when he is rescued by no less a personage than our old acquaintance Dingy O'Dirty, who proves to be one of the banditti. Through the intercession of this friend, Mr. U. and his trio are permitted to go home in safety—but our hero, in a private conversation with Dingy, prevails upon that gentleman to aid him in the rescue of Miss Emily. A plot is arranged between the two worthies, the most important point of which is that Mr. U. is to become one of the robber fraternity.

In a week's time, accordingly, we behold Paul Ulric, Esq. in a cavern of banditti, somewhere in the neighborhood of Philadelphia!! His doings in this cavern, as related by Mr. Mattson, we must be allowed to consider the most laughable piece of plagiarism on record—with the exception perhaps of something in this same book which we shall speak of hereafter. Our author, it appears, has read Gil Blas, Pelham, and Anne of Gierstein, and has concocted, from diverse passages in the three, a banditti scene for his own especial use, and for the readers of Paul Ulric. The *imitations* (let us be courteous!) from Pelham are not so palpable as those from the other two novels. It will be remembered that Bulwer's hero introduces himself into a nest of London rogues with the end of proving his friend's innocence of murder. Paul joins a band of robbers *near Philadelphia*, for the purpose of rescuing a mistress—the chief similarity will be found in the circumstances of the blindfold introduction, and in the slang dialect made use of by either novelist. The slang in Pelham is stupid enough—but still very natural in the mouths of the cut-throats of Cockaigne. Mr. Mattson, however, has thought proper to bring it over, will I nill I, into Pennsylvania, and to make the pickpockets of Yankeeland discourse in the most learned manner of nothing less than *"flat-catching," "velvet," "dubbing up possibles," "shelling out," "twisting French lace," "wakeful winkers," "white wool," "pig's whispers,"* and *"horses' night-caps!"*

Having introduced his adventurer *à la* Pelham, Mr. Mattson entertains him *à la* Gil Blas. The hero of Santillane finds his cavern a pleasant residence, and so does the hero of our novel. Captain Rolando is a fine fellow, and so is Captain Elmo. In Gil Blas, the robbers amuse themselves by reciting their adventures—so they do in Paul Ulric. In both the Captain tells his own history first. In the one there is a rheumatic old cook—in the other there is a rheumatic old cook. In the one there is a porter who is the main obstacle to escape—in the other ditto. In the one there is a lady in durance—in the other ditto. In the one the hero determines to release the lady—in the other ditto. In the one Gil Blas feigns illness to effect his end, in the other Mr. Ulric feigns illness for the same object. In the one, advantage is taken of the robbers' absence to escape—so in the other. The cook is sick, at the time, in both.

In regard to Anne of Gierstein the plagiarism is still more laughable. We must all remember the proceedings of the *Secret Tribunal* in Scott's novel. Mr. Mattson has evidently been ignorant that the Great Unknown's account of these proceedings was principally based on fact. He has supposed them imaginary *in toto*, and, seeing no good reason to the contrary, determined to have a Secret Tribunal of his own manufacture, and could think of no better location for it than a cavern somewhere about the suburbs of Philadelphia. We must be pardoned for giving Mr. Mattson's account of this matter in his own words.

Dingee disappeared, [this is our old friend Dingy O'Dirty] Dingee, [quoth Mr. Mattson,] disappeared—leaving me for a time alone. When he returned, he said every thing was in readiness for the ceremony, [the ceremony of Mr. Ulric's initiation as a robber.] The place appointed for this purpose was called the '*Room of Sculls*'—and thither, blindfolded, I was led.

'A candidate for our order!' said a voice, which I recognized as O'Dougherty's.

'Let him see the light!' exclaimed another in an opposite direction. The mandate was obeyed, and I was restored to sight.

I looked wildly and fearfully around—but no living object was perceptible. Before me stood an altar, hung about with red curtains, and ornamented with fringe of the same color. Above it, on a white Banner, was a painting of the human heart, with a dagger struck to the hilt, and the blood streaming from the wound. Directly under this horrible device, was written, in large letters,

The Punishment of the Unfaithful.

Around, wherever I turned my eyes, there was little else to be seen but skeletons of human bodies—with their arms uplifted, and stretching forward—suspended in every direction from the walls. One of them I involuntarily touched, and down it came with a fearful crash—its dry bones rattling upon the granite floor, until the whole cavern reverberated with the sound. I turned from this spectacle, and opposite beheld a guillotine—the fatal axe smeared with blood; and near it was a head—looking as if it had just been severed from the body—with the countenance ghastly—the lips parted—and the eyes staring wide open. There, also, was the body, covered, however, with a cloth, so that little was seen except the neck, mangled and bloody, and a small portion of the hand, hanging out from its shroud, grasping in its fingers a tablet with the following inscription:

The End of the Betrayer.

I sickened and fell. When I awoke to consciousness I found myself in the arms of O'Dougherty. He was bathing my temples with a fragrant liquor. When I had sufficiently recovered, he put his mouth close to my ear and whispered—'Where is your courage man? Do you know there is a score of eyes upon you?'

'Alas! I am unused to such scenes—I confess they have unmanned me. But now I am firm; you have only to command, and I will obey.'

'Bravo!' exclaimed O'Dougherty, 'you must now be introduced to the high priest of our order. He has taken his seat at the altar—prepared for your reception. I will retire that you may do him reverence—trusting soon to hail you as a brother.'

The curtains about the altar had been grouped up, and there, indeed, sat the high dignitary in all his splendor. He was closely masked, and reclined in a high-backed chair, with his head turned carelessly to one side, with an expression of the most singular good humor. At that moment, also, there issued from numerous recesses, which I had not hitherto observed, a number of grotesque-looking shapes, not unlike the weird sisters in Macbeth, who quietly took their stations around the apartment, and fixed upon me their fearful and startling gaze. Their garments were hanging in shreds—an emblem, perhaps, of their own desperate pursuits. Their faces were daubed with paint of various colors, which gave them a wild and fiendish aspect. Each one grasped a long knife, which he brandished furiously above his head, the blades sometimes striking heavily together. They then sprang simultaneously forward, forming themselves into a circle, while one stationed himself as the centre, around whom they slowly moved with dismal and half-suppressed groans. They continued this ceremony until some one exclaimed—

'Bring forth the dead!'

'Bring forth the dead!'—they all repeated, until the cavern rang with a thousand echoes.

The banditti now stood in a line, stretching from one end of the room to the other, and remained some time in silence. Directly a dead body—mutilated and bloody—was borne by some invisible agency into our presence. It rested upon a bier—without pall or other covering—a spectacle too horrible for description. I thought, at first, that it was some optical delusion—but, alas! it proved a fearful reality—a dread and reckless assassination, prompted by that hellish and vindictive spirit, which appeared so exclusively to govern the ruffians with whom I was voluntarily associated. The victim before me was a transgressor of their laws; and this punishment had been dealt out to him as the reward of his perfidy. Life, to all appearance, was extinct; but the sluggish and inert clay still remained, as if in mockery of all law—all humanity—all mercy.

'Behold the traitor!'—exclaimed one of the number.

'Behold the traitor!'—they all repeated in concert.

'Bear away the dead!'—commanded the priest at the altar.

'Bear away the dead! bear away the dead!'—was reiterated in succession by every tongue, until the lifeless body disappeared—and with it the fiendish revellers who had sported so terrifically in its presence.

We have only to say, that if our readers are not absolutely petrified after all this conglomeration of horrors, it is no fault either of Paul Ulric's, Morris Mattson's, or Dingy O'Dirty's.

Miss Emily Florence is at length rescued, and with her lover, is rowed down some river in a skiff by Dingy, who thus discourses on the way. We quote the passage as a specimen of exquisite morality.

"Had I the sensibility of many men, a recollection of my crimes would sink me into the dust—but as it is, I can almost fancy them to be so many virtues. I see you smile; but is it not a truth, that every thing of good and evil exists altogether in idea? The highwayman is driven by necessity to attack the traveller, and demand his purse. This is a crime—so says the law—so says society—and must be punished as our wise men have decreed. Nations go to war with each other—they plunder—burn—destroy—and murder—yet there is nothing wrong in this, because nations sanction it. But where is the difference between the highwayman, in the exercise of a profession by which he is to obtain a livelihood, and a nation, with perhaps less adequate cause, which despoils another of its treasures, and deluges it in blood? Is not this a proof that our ideas of immorality and wickedness are derived in a great measure from habit and education?" "The metaphysical outlaw," [says our hero,] "the metaphysical outlaw here concluded his discourse." [What an excessively funny idea Mr. Mattson must have of metaphysics!]

Having left the boat, taken leave of Dingy O'Dirty, and put on a pair of breeches, Miss Florence now accompanies our adventurer to a village hard by. Entering a tavern the lovers seat themselves at the breakfast table with two or three other persons. The conversation turns upon one Mr. Crawford, a great favorite in the village. In the midst of his own praises, the gentleman himself enters—"and lo!" says Mr. Ulric, "in the person of Mr. Crawford, I recognized the notorious Captain Elmo!" The hue and cry is immediately raised, but the Captain makes his escape through a window. Our hero pursues him to no purpose, and in returning from the pursuit is near being run over by a carriage and six. The carriage doors happen to be wide open, and in the vehicle Mr. Ulric discovers—oh horrible!—Miss Emily Florence in the embrace of the fellow with the big whiskers!

Having lost his sweetheart a second time, our adventurer is in despair. But despair, or indeed any thing else, is of little consequence to a hero. "It is true," says Paul, "I was sometimes melancholy; but melancholy with me is as the radiant sunlight, imparting a hue of gladness to every thing around!!" Being, therefore, in excellent spirits with his melancholy, Mr. Ulric determines upon writing a novel. The novel is written, printed, published, and puffed. Why not?—we have even seen *"Paul Ulric"* puffed. But let us hasten to the *dénouement* of our tale. The hero receives a letter from his guardian angel, Dingy O'Dirty, who, it appears, is in England. He informs Mr. U. that Miss Florence is in London, for he (Dingy O'Dirty) has seen her. Hereupon our friend takes shipping for that city. Of course he is shipwrecked—and, of course, every soul on board perishes but himself. He, indeed, is a most fortunate young man. Some person pulls him on shore, and this person proves to be the very person he was going all the way to London to look for—it was Richard Florence himself. What is more to the purpose, Mr. F. has repented of promising Miss Emily to the fellow with the big whiskers. Every thing now happens precisely as it should. Miss E. is proved to be an heiress, and no daughter of Florence's after all. Our hero leads her to the altar. Matters come rapidly to a crisis. All the good characters are made excessively happy people, and all the bad characters die sudden deaths, and go, post haste, to the devil.

Mr. Mattson is a very generous young man, and is not above patronizing a fellow-writer occasionally. Some person having sent him a MS. poem for perusal and an opinion, our author consigns the new candidate for fame to immortality at once, by heading a chapter in Paul Ulric with four entire lines from the MS., and appending the following note at the bottom of the page.

"From a MS. poem entitled '*Drusilla,*' with which we have been politely favored for perusal. It is a delightful work, and shows the writer to be a man of genius and reflection. We hope it will not be long before the lovers of poetry are favored with this production; it will win deserved celebrity for its author."

And as a farther instance of disinterestedness, see this conversation between Mr. Mattson's hero, and a young lady in London who wrote for the annuals.

"What do you think of D'Israeli's novels?"—asked she.

"Excellent! Excellent!" I replied, "especially Vivian Grey: take for example the scene in the long gallery between Vivian, and Mrs. Felix Lorraine."

"Admirable!"—returned the young lady, "but, by the way, how do you like Bulwer?"

"Well enough," I answered.

"Pray, Mr. Ulric, how many female writers of distinction have you in America? Honest old Blackwood tells us of but two or three."

"And who are they?"

"Miss Gould, Miss Sedgwick, and Mrs. Sigourney."

"He should have added another—Miss Leslie."

We fancy it is long since Miss Leslie, Miss Gould, Miss Sedgwick, Mrs. Sigourney, Lytton Bulwer, and Ben D'Israeli have been so affectionately patted on the back.

Of Mr. Mattson's *style* the less we say the better. It is quite good enough for Mr. Mattson's matter. Besides—all fine writers have pet words and phrases. Mr. Fay had his *"blisters"*—Mr. Simms had his *"coils," "hugs,"* and *"old-times"*—and Mr. M. must be allowed his *"suches"* and *"so muches."* Such is genius!—and so much for the Adventures of an Enthusiast! But we must positively say a word in regard to Mr. Mattson's *erudition*. On page 97, vol. ii, our author is discoursing of the novel which his hero is about to indite. He is speaking more particularly of *titles*. Let us see what he says.

"An ill-chosen title is sufficient to condemn the best of books. Never does an author exhibit his taste and skill more than in this particular. Just think for a moment of *the Frenchman's version of Doctor Johnson's 'Rambler' into 'Le Chevalier Errant,' and what was still more laughable, his innocently addressing the author by the appellation of Mr. Vagabond!* By the way, the modern fanatics were somewhat remarkable in the choice of their titles. Take for example the following—'The

Shop of the Spiritual Apothecary' and *'Some fine Baskets baked in the Oven of Charity, carefully conserved for the Chickens of the Church, the Sparrows of the Spirit, and the Sweet Swallows of Salvation.'* "

Having admired this specimen of deep research, let us turn to page 125, vol. ii. Mr. Ulric is here vindicating himself from some charges brought against his book. Have patience, gentle reader, while we copy what he says.

"In the first place we are accused of *vulgarity*. In this respect we certainly bear a strong resemblance to Plautus, who was censured by the satirical Horace for the same thing. Next come *Ignorance*, *Vanity*, and *Stupidity*. Of the first two, the classic reader will not forget that Aristotle (who wrote not less than four hundred volumes) was calumniated by Cicero and Plutarch, both of whom endeavored to make it appear that he was *ignorant* as well as *vain*. But what of our stupidity? Socrates himself was treated by Athenæus as *illiterate*: the divine Plato, called by some the philosopher of the Christians, by others the god of philosophers, was accused by Theopompus of *lying*, by Aristophanes of *impiety*, and by Aulus Gellius of *robbery*. The fifth charge is a *want of invention*. Pliny has alleged the same thing of Virgil—and surely it is some consolation to know that we have such excellent company. And last, though not least, is *plagiarism*. Here again Naucrates tells us that Homer pillaged some of his best thoughts from the library at Memphis. It is recorded, moreover, that Horace plundered from the minor Greek poets, and Virgil from his great prototype, Homer, as well as Nicander, and Apollonius Rhodius. Why then should we trouble ourselves about these sweeping denunciations?"

What a learned man is Morris Mattson, Esq.! He is intimately versed not only in Horace, Aristotle, Cicero, Plutarch, Virgil, Homer, Plato, Pliny, and Aristophanes—but (*credat Judæus!*) in Nicander, Aulus Gellius, Naucrates, Athenæus, Theopompus, and Apollonius Rhodius! I. D'Israeli, however, the father of Ben D'Israeli aforesaid, is (we have no hesitation in saying it,) one of the most scoundrelly plagiarists in Christendom. He has not scrupled to steal entire passages verbatim from Paul Ulric! On page 1, vol. ii, second edition, of 'The Curiosities of Literature,' in a chapter on Titles, we have all about Dr. Johnson, Le Chevalier Errant, and Mr. Vagabond, precisely in the language of Mr. Mattson. O thou abandoned robber, D'Israeli! Here is the sentence. It will be seen, that it corresponds with the first sentence italicized in the paragraph (above) beginning 'An ill-chosen title, &c.' "The Rambler was so little understood, at the time of its appearance, that a French Journalist has translated it 'Le Chevalier Errant,' and a foreigner drank Johnson's health one day, by innocently addressing him by the appellation of Mr. Vagabond!" And on page II, of the same volume, we perceive the following, which answers to the second sentence italicized in the paragraph above mentioned. "A collection of passages from the Fathers is called 'The Shop of the Spiritual Apothecary'—one of these works bears the elaborate title 'Some fine Baskets baked in the Oven of Charity, carefully conserved for the Chickens of the Church, the Sparrows of the Spirit, and the Sweet Swallows of Salvation.'" There can be no doubt whatever of D'Israeli's having pilfered this thing from Paul Ulric, for Mr. Mattson having, inadvertently we suppose, written Baskets for Biscuits, the error is adopted by the plagiarist. But we have a still more impudent piece of robbery to mention. The whole of the erudition, and two-thirds of the words in the paragraph above, beginning 'In the first place we are accused of vulgarity,' &c. is to be found on page 42, vol. i, second edition, of The 'Curiosities!' Let us transcribe some of D'Israeli's words in illustration of our remark. We refer the reader for more particular information to the book itself.

"Horace censures the coarse humor of Plautus—Aristotle (whose industry composed more than four hundred volumes) has not been less spared by the critics. Diogenes Laertius, Cicero and Plutarch have forgotten nothing that can tend to show his ignorance, his ambition, and his vanity—Socrates, considered as the wisest, and most moral of men, Cicero treated as an usurer, and the pedant Athenæus as illiterate—Plato, who has been called, by Clement of Alexandria, the Moses of Athens; the philosopher of the Christians by Arnobius, and the god of philosophers by Cicero; Athenæus accuses of envy; Theopompus of lying; Suidas of avarice; Aulus Gellius of robbery; Porphyry of incontinence, and Aristophanes of impiety—Virgil is destitute of invention, if we are to give credit to Pliny—Naucrates points out the source (of the Iliad and Odyssey,) in the library at Memphis, which, according to him, the blind bard completely pillaged—Horace has been blamed for the free use he made of the minor Greek poets. Even the author of his (Virgil's) apology, has confessed that he has stolen, from Homer, his greatest beauties, from Apollonius Rhodius many of his pathetic passages, and from Nicander hints for his Georgics."

Well, Mr. Mattson, what have you to say for yourself? Is not I. D'Israeli the most impudent thief since the days of Prometheus?

In summing up an opinion of Paul Ulric, it is by no means our intention to mince the matter at all. The book is despicable in every respect. Such are the works which bring daily discredit upon our national literature. We have no right to complain of being laughed at abroad when so villainous a compound, as the thing we now hold in our hand, of incongruous folly, plagiarism, immorality, inanity, and bombast, can command at any moment both a puff and a publisher. To Mr. Mattson himself we have only one word to say before throwing his book into the fire. Dress it up, good sir, for the nursery, and call it the "Life and Surprising Adventures of Dingy O'Dirty." Humph!—Only think of Plato, Pliny, Aristotle, Aristophanes, Nicander, Aulus Gellius, Naucrates, Athenæus, Theopompus and Apollonius Rhodius!!

Southern Literary Messenger, February 1836

Susan Rigby Morgan

The Swiss Heiress; or The Bride of Destiny—*A Tale*. Baltimore: Joseph Robinson.

T HE SWISS HEIRESS should be read by all who have nothing better to do. We are patient, and having gone
through the whole book with the most dogged determination, are now enabled to pronounce it one of the most solemn
of farces. Let us see if it be not possible to give some idea of
the plot. It is the year 1780, and "the attention of the reader
is directed, first, to a Castle whose proud battlements rise
amidst the pines and firs of the Swiss mountains, while, at its
base, roll the waters of Lake Geneva," and, second, to the sun
which is setting somewhat more slowly than usual, because
he is "unwilling to terminate the natal day of the young heiress of the Baron de Rheinswald, the wealthy proprietor of
Montargis castle, and its beautiful environs." We are thus left
to infer—putting the two sentences and circumstances in apposition—that the Montargis Castle where dwells the young
heiress of the Baron de Rheinswald, is neither more nor less
than the identical castle " with the proud battlements" et cetera, that "rises amid the pines and firs" and so forth, of the
"Swiss Mountains and the Lake of Geneva" and all that.
However this may be, the Baron de Rheinswald is a "Catholic
of high repute" who "early in life marries a lady of great
wealth, a member of his own church, actuated by ambition"—that is to say, there was either something or somebody "actuated by ambition," but we shall *not* say whether it
was a lady or a church. The lady (or perhaps now the church)
"lived but five years after the union, and at her death earnestly
and solemnly implored that her only son might be devoted to
the priesthood." The lady, or the church (let us reconcile the
difficulty by calling the thing "Mother Church") being thus
deceased, the bereaved Baron marries a second wife. She
being a protestant however, the high contracting parties sign
an instrument by which it is agreed "that the eldest child shall
be educated by the mother's direction, a protestant, the second be subject to the father's will and a catholic, and thus
alternately with all their children." This, it must be allowed is
a contrivance well adapted for effect. Only think of the inter-

esting little creatures all taking it "turn about!" What fights, too, they will have, when breeched, over their prayer-books and bread-and-butter! Our author pauses in horror at anticipated consequences, and takes this excellent opportunity of repeating what "a late writer" (a great friend of his by the bye) says in regard to "chemical combinations" and "opposite properties."

The first child is a son, and called William. The second is a daughter, Miss Laura, our heroine, the "Swiss Heiress," and the "Bride of Destiny." She is the "Swiss Heiress" in virtue of a certain "dispensation from the church of Rome, by which the estates of the Baron were to descend to his first catholic child by his second marriage" and she becomes the "Bride of Destiny" because the Baron has very properly selected for her a husband, without consulting her Heiress-ship about the matter. This intended husband is one Count Laniski, young, good-looking, noble, valiant, wise, accomplished, generous, amiable, and possessed of a thousand other good qualities— all of which, of course, are just a thousand better reasons why the Bride of Destiny, being a heroine, will have nothing to do with him. Accordingly, at eight years old, she grows melancholy and interesting, patronizes the gipsies, curses the Count Laniski, talks about "fate, fore-knowledge, and free-will," and throws aside her bread-and-butter for desperation and a guitar. In spite of all she can do, however, the narrative gets on very slowly, and we are upon the point of throwing the lady (banjo and all) into the street, when the Count himself makes his appearance at the Castle, and thereby frightens her to such a degree that, having delivered a soliloquy, she runs off with her "Brother William" to America.

"Brother William," however, is luckily killed at the siege of Yorktown, and the "Bride of Destiny" herself is recaptured by her family, the whole of whom, having nothing better to do, have set out in pursuit of her—to wit—her half brother Albert, (who is now Baron de Rheinswald, the old Baron being dead) Clermont a croaking old monk, and Madam de Montelieu a croaking old somebody else. These good people, it seems, are still determined that the "Swiss Heiress" shall be the "Bride of Destiny"—that is to say, the bride of the Count Laniski. To make matters doubly sure too on this head, the old Baron has sworn a round oath on his death-bed, leaving the "Swiss Heiress" his "eternal curse" in the event of her disobedience.

Having caught and properly secured the young lady, the new Baron de Rheinswald takes up his residence for a time "on the borders of Vermont and Canada." Some years elapse, and so forth. The "Bride of Destiny" is nearly one and twenty; and the Count Laniski makes his appearance with a view of urging his claim. The Heiress, we are forced to say, now behaves in a very unbecoming and unaccountable manner. She should have hung herself as the only rational course, and—heigho!—it would have saved us a world of trouble. But, not having forgotten her old bad habits, she persists in talking about "fate, foreknowledge, and free will," and it is not therefore to be wondered at that matters in general assume a truly distressing complexion. Just at this crisis, however, a Mr. Frederick Mortimer makes his interesting début. Never certainly was a more accomplished young man! As becomes a gentleman with such an appellation as Frederick Mortimer, he is more beautiful than Apollo, more sentimental than De Lisle, more distingué than Pelham, and, positively, more mysterious than the "mysterious lady." He sympathizes with the woes of the "Bride of Destiny," looks unutterable threats at the Count Laniski, beats even the "Swiss Heiress" at discoursing of "free will," and the author of the "Swiss Heiress" at quoting paragraphs from a "late writer." The heart of the "Bride of Destiny" is touched—sensibly touched. But Love, in romance, must have impediments, and the Loves of the "Bride of Destiny" and Mr. Frederick Mortimer have two. The first is some inexpressible mystery connected with a certain gold ring, of which the Heiress is especially careful, and the second is that rascally old Baron Rheinswald's "eternal curse." Nothing farther therefore can be done in the premises, but as we have now only reached Chapter the Sixth, and there are to be seventeen chapters in all, it is necessary to do something—and what better can be done than to talk, until Chapter the Fifteenth, about "fate, foreknowledge, and free will?" Only imagine a string of delightful sentences, such as the following, for the short space of three hundred and ninety-six pages!

"How rapidly time flies," said the Count, "I have been here weeks, and they seem but days."

"I am not surprised, my lord," said Mrs. Falkner, smiling.

"Nor I," he returned, also smiling. "This place, such society, wraps the senses in such blissful illusion that I 'take no note of time.' The clock strikes unheeded, unheard."

"Why do you smile, Miss Montargis?" asked Mrs. Falkner.

"I was just thinking," she replied, "that Count Laniski had unconsciously given a 'local habitation and a name' to the fabled region where cold is so intense as to congeal sound."

Mrs. Falkner bowed, but could not comprehend what such a region had to do with Count Laniski's compliment to the heiress.

"Take care, Mr. Mortimer," said Miss Montargis, still smiling, "you are in dangerous vicinity. Have you no fear of cold?"

"It is not sufficiently *positive*," he replied, "to destroy my belief that it exists with much *latent* warmth, which it requires but a little address to render quite *sensible*."

Mortimer spoke with mingled playfulness and seriousness, but the latter prevailed, and Miss Montargis felt it a reproof, and blushed, she scarcely knew why.

"To be sensible," she said, "it must affect others. Who ever felt its influence? not *she* at least who has painfully realized its *negativeness*."

"I am sure you speak mysteries to me," said Mrs. Falkner, laughing, " what can you mean?" &c. &c.

We would proceed, but are positively out of patience with the gross stupidity of Mrs. Falkner, who cannot understand what the other ladies and gentlemen are talking about. Now we have no doubt whatever they are discoursing of "fate, foreknowledge, and free will."

About chapter the fifteenth it appears that the Count Laniski is not the Count Laniski at all, but only Mr. Theodore Montelieu, and the son of that old rigmarole, Madam Montelieu, the housekeeper. It now appears, also, that even that Count Laniski whose appearance at Montargis Castle had such effect upon the nerves of our heroine, was not the Count Laniski at all, but only the same Mr. Theodore Montelieu, the same son of the same old rigmarole. The true Count, it seems, in his younger days, had as little partiality for the match ordained him by fate and the two fathers, as the very "Bride of Destiny" herself, and, being at college with Mr. Theodore Montelieu at the time appointed for his visit to Montargis Castle, had no scruple in allowing the latter gentleman to personate his Countship in the visit. By these means Mr. M. has an opportunity of seeing his mother, the old rigmarole, who is housekeeper, or something of that kind, at the Castle. The precious couple (that is to say the old rigmarole and her son) now get up a plot, by which it is determined that the son shall personate the Count to the end of the chapter, and so marry the heiress. It is with this end in view, that Mr. Theodore Montelieu is now playing Count at the residence of the Baron in Vermont. Mr. Frederick Mortimer, however, is sadly in his way, and torments the poor fellow grievously, by grinning at him, and sighing at him, and folding his arms at him, and looking at him asquint, and talking him to death about "fate and foreknowledge and free will." At last Mr. Mortimer tells the gentleman flatly that he knows very well who he is, leaving it to be inferred that he also knows very well who he is not. Hereupon Mr. Theodore Montelieu calls Mr. Frederick Mortimer a liar, a big liar, or something to that effect, and challenges him to a fight, with a view of either blowing out his already small modicum of brains, or having the exceedingly few blown out, which he himself (Mr. Theodore Montelieu) possesses. Mr. Mortimer, however, being a hero, declines fighting, and contents himself, for the present, with looking mysterious.

It will now be seen that matters are coming to a crisis. Mr. Mortimer is obliged to go to Philadelphia; but, lest Mr. Montelieu should whisk off the heiress in his absence, he insists upon that gentleman bearing him company. Having reached, however, the city of brotherly love, the ingenious young man gives his keeper the slip, hurries back to Vermont, and gets every thing ready for his wedding. Miss Montargis is very angry and talks about the inexplicable ring, fate, fore-knowledge and free will—but old Clermont, the Baron, and Mr. Montelieu, on the other hand, get in an absolute passion and talk about nothing less than the old Baron Rheinswald and his "eternal curse." The ceremony therefore proceeds, when just at the most proper moment, and all as it should be, in rushes—Mr. Frederick Mortimer!—it will be seen that he has come back from Philadelphia. He assures the company that the Count Laniski, (that is to say Mr. Theodore Monte-lieu,) is not the Count Laniski at all, but only Mr. Theodore Montelieu; and moreover, that he himself (Mr. Frederick Mortimer) is not only Mr. Frederick Mortimer, but the bonâ fide Count Laniski into the bargain. And more than this, it is very clearly explained how Miss Laura Montargis is not by any means Miss Laura Montargis, but only the Baroness de Thionville, and how the Baroness de Thionville is the wife of the Baron de Thionville, and how, after all, the Baron de Thionville is the Count Laniski, or else Mr. Frederick Morti-mer, or else—that is to say—how Mr. Frederick Mortimer is'nt altogether the Count Laniski, but—but only the Baron de Thionville, or else the Baro*ness* de Thionville—in short, how every body concerned in the business is not precisely what he is, and is precisely what he is not. After this horrible development, if we recollect, all the dramatis personæ faint outright, one after the other. The inquisitive reader may be assured, however, that the whole story ends judiciously, and just as it ought to do, and with a very excellent quotation from one of the very best of the "late writers."

Humph! and this is the "Swiss Heiress," to say nothing of the "Bride of Destiny." However—it is a valuable " work"— and now, in the name of "fate, fore-knowledge and free will," we solemnly consign it to the fire.

Southern Literary Messenger, October 1836

Laughton Osborn

Confessions of a Poet, 2 vols. Carey, Lea and Blanchard.

THE MOST REMARKABLE feature in this production is the bad paper on which it is printed, and the typographical ingenuity with which matter barely enough for one volume has been spread over the pages of two. The author has very few claims to the sacred name he has thought proper to assume. And indeed his own idea on this subject seem not to satisfy himself. He is in doubt, poor man, of his own qualifications, and having proclaimed himself a poet in the title page, commences his book by disavowing all pretensions to the character. We can enlighten him on this head. There is nothing of the *vates* about him. He is no poet—and most positively he is no prophet. He is a writer of notes. He is fond of annotations; and composes one upon another, putting Pelion upon Ossa. Here is an example: *"Ce n'est pas par affectation que j'aie mis en Francais ces remarques, mais pour les detourner de la connoissance du vulgaire."* Now we are very sure that none but *le vulgaire,* to speak poetically, will ever think of getting through with the confessions: thus there the matter stands. Lest his book should *not* be understood he illustrates it by notes, and then lest the notes *should* be understood, why he writes them in French. All this is very clear, and very clever to say no more. There is however some merit in this book, and not a little satisfaction. The author avers upon his word of honor that in commencing this work he loads a pistol, and places it upon the table. He farther states that, upon coming to a conclusion, it is his intention to blow out what he supposes to be his brains. Now this is excellent. But, even with so rapid a writer as the poet must undoubtedly be, there would be some little difficulty in completing the book under thirty days or thereabouts. The best of powder is apt to sustain injury by lying so long "in the load." We sincerely hope the gentleman took the precaution to examine his priming before attempting the rash act. A flash in the pan—and in such a case—were a thing to be lamented. Indeed there would be no answering for the consequences. We might even have a second series of the Confessions.

Southern Literary Messenger, April 1835

Edgar Allan Poe

Tales by Edgar A. Poe. New York: Wiley and Putnam, 161 Broadway. 1845. 18 mo. pp. 228.

THE GREAT FAULT of American and British authors is imitation of the peculiarities of thought and diction of those who have gone before them. They tread on a beaten track because it is well trodden. They follow as disciples, instead of being teachers. Hence it is that they denounce all novelty as a culpable variation from standard rules, and think all originality to be incomprehensible. To produce something which has not been produced before, in their estimation, is equal to six, at least, of the seven deadly sins—perhaps, the unpardonable sin itself—and for this crime they think the author should atone here in the purgatory of false criticism, and hereafter by the hell of oblivion. The odor of originality in a new book is "a savor of death unto death" to their productions, unless it can be destroyed. So they cry aloud—"Strange! incomprehensible! what is it about?" even though its idea may be plainly developed as the sun at noon-day. Especially, we are sorry to say, does this prevail in this country. Hence it is, that we are chained down to a wheel, which ever monotonously revolves round a fixed centre, progressing without progress.

Yet that we are beginning to emancipate ourselves from this thraldom, is seen in the book before us, and in the general appreciation of its merits, on both sides of the Atlantic. It has sold well: and the press has praised it, discriminately and yet with no stint. "The British Critic," and other English literary journals laud it most handsomely. Though, as a general rule, we do not care a fig for British criticism—conducted as it mostly is, we *do* prize a favorable review, when it is evidently wrung from the reviewer by a high admiration and a strong sense of justice—as in the case before us. And all this, as we have said, proves that we are escaping the shackles of imitation. There is just as much chance of originality at this day, as at any other—all the nonsense of the sophists to the contrary, notwithstanding. "There is nothing new under the sun," said SOLOMON. In the days of his many-wived majesty the proverb might apply—it is a dead saying now. The creative power of the mind is boundless. There is no end to the original combinations of words—nor need there be to the original combination of ideas.

The first tale in Mr. POE's book is called "The Gold Bug." If we mistake not, it was written in competition for a large premium, some years since—a premium which it obtained. It made a great noise when first issued, and was circulated to a greater extent than any American tale, before or since. The intent of the author was evidently to write a popular tale: money, and the finding of money being chosen as the most popular thesis. In this he endeavoured to carry out his idea of the perfection of the plot, which he defines as—that, in which nothing can be disarranged, or from which nothing can be removed, without ruin to the mass—as that, in which we are never able to determine whether any one point depends upon or sustains any one other. We pronounce that he has perfectly succeeded in his perfect aim. There is a marked peculiarity, by-the-by, in it, which is this. The bug, which gives title to the story, is used only in the way of mystification, having throughout a seeming and no real connection with the subject. Its purpose is to seduce the reader into the idea of supernatural machinery, and keeping him so mystified until the last moment. The ingenuity of the story cannot be surpassed. Perhaps it is the most *ingenious* story Mr. POE has written; but in the higher attributes—a great invention—an invention proper—it is not at all comparable to the "Tell-tale Heart"—and more especially to "Ligeia," the most extraordinary, of its kind, of his productions. The characters are well-drawn. The reflective qualities and steady purpose, founded on a laboriously obtained conviction of LEGRAND, is most faithfully depicted. The negro is a perfect picture. He is drawn accurately—no feature overshaded, or distorted. Most of such delineations are caricatures.*

The materials of which the "Gold Bug" is constructed are,

*We see, by-the-by, that Willis, in one of his letters, talks about the tales having to encounter an obstacle in England, because of the word "bug." This is a mere affectation—but were it not, the junction with "gold" saves it. Look at the other compounds in common English use—"*bug*bear," for instance. "Gold-bug" is peculiarly an English—not an American word.

apparently, of the simplest kind. It is the mode of grouping them around the main idea, and their absolute necessity of each to the whole—note Mr. POE's definition of plot before given—in which the perfection of their use consists. The solution of the mystery is the most curious part of the whole, and for this, which is a splendid specimen of analysis, we refer the reader to the book.

"The Black Cat" is the next tale. In our last number we found fault with this, as a reproduction of the "Tell-tale Heart." On further examination, we think ourselves in error, somewhat. It is rather an amplification of one of its phases. The *dénôuement* is a perfect printed *tableau*.

"Mesmeric Revelations," which comes next, has excited much discussion. A large number of the mesmerists, queerly enough, take it all for gospel. Some of the Swedenborgians, at PHILADELPHIA, wrote word to POE, that at first they doubted, but in the end became convinced, of its truth. This was excruciatingly and unsurpassably funny—in spite of the air of *vraisemblance* that pervades the article itself. It is evidently meant to be nothing more than the vehicle of the author's views concerning the DEITY, immateriality, spirit, &c., which he apparently believes to be true, in which belief he is joined by Professor BUSH. The matter is most rigorously condensed and simplified. It might easily have been spread over the pages of a large octavo.

"Lionizing," which PAULDING, and some others regard with great favor, has been overlooked, in general. It is an extravaganza, composed by rules—and the laws of extravaganza is as much and clearly defined as those of any other species of composition.

"The Fall of the House of Usher," was stolen by BENTLEY, who copied it in his "Miscellany," without crediting the source from whence he derived it. The thesis of this tale, is the revulsion of feeling consequent upon discovering that for a long period of time we have been mistaking sounds of agony, for those of mirth or indifference. It is an elaborate tale—surpassed only by "Ligeia," in our judgment. IRVING's view of it—and he speaks of it, in italics, as *powerful*, is correct. The *dénôuement*, where the doors open, and the figure is found standing without the door, as USHER had foretold, is grand and impressive. It appears to be better liked than the rest of Mr. Poe's productions, among literary people—though with the mass, the "Gold-bug," and "Murders in the Rue Morgue," are more popular, because of their unbroken interest, novelty of the combination of ordinary incident, and faithful minuteness of detail. "The Haunted Palace," from which we stated in our late review of his poems, LONGFELLOW had stolen, all, that was worth stealing, of his "BELEAGUERED CITY," and which is here introduced with effect, was originally sent to O'SULLIVAN, of the "Democratic Review," and by him rejected, because "he found it impossible to comprehend it." In connection with the subject of rejections, there is a good thing concerning TUCKERMAN, which would show—if it needed to show the very palpable—his utter lack of discrimination, and his supreme self-esteem. When he edited the "Boston Miscellany," POE, under the impression that the work was still conducted by HALE, sent him "The Telltale Heart," a most extraordinary, and very original composition. Whereon Master TUCKERMAN, in noting its rejection, chose to say, through his publishers, that "if Mr. POE would condescend to be more quiet, he would be a valuable contributor to the press." POE rejoined, that TUCKERMAN was the King of the Quietists, and in three months would give a quietus to the "Miscellany." The author was mistaken in time—it only took two months to finish the work. LOWELL afterwards published the "Tell-tale Heart," in the "Pioneer."

"A descent into the Maelström," is chiefly noted for the boldness of its subject—a subject never dreamed of before—and for the clearness of its descriptions.

"Monos and Una," is one of a series of *post-mortem* reveries. The style, we think, is good. Its philosophy is damnable; but this does not appear to have been a point with the author, whose purpose, doubtless, was novelty of effect—a novelty brought about by the tone of the colloquy. The reader feels as though he were listening to the talk of spirits. In the usual imaginary conversations—LANDOR's, for instance—he is permitted to see a tone of banter. He feels that the author is not in earnest. He understands that spirits have been invented for the purpose of introducing their supposed opinions.

"The man of the Crowd," is the last sketch in the work. It

is peculiar and fantastic, but contains little worthy of special note, after what has been said of others.

The three tales before the last, are "Murders in the Rue Morgue"—"Mystery of Marie Roget"—and "The Purloined Letter." They are all of the same class—a class peculiar to Mr. POE. They are inductive—tales of ratiocination—of profound and searching analysis. "The Mystery of Marie Roget"—although in this, the author appears to have been hampered by facts—reveals the whole secret of their mode of construction. It is true that there the facts were before him—so that it is not fully a parallel—but the *rationale* of the process is revealed by it. The author, as in the case of "Murders in the Rue Morgue," the first written, begins by imagining a deed committed by such a creature, or in such a manner, as would most effectually mislead inquiry. Then he applies analysis to the investigation.

There is much made of nothing in "The Purloined Letter,"—the story of which is simple; but the reasoning is remarkably clear, and directed solely to the required end. It first appeared in the "Gift," and was thence copied into CHAMBERS' "Edinburgh Journal," as a most notable production. We like it less than the others, of the same class. It has not their continuous and absorbing interest.

"The Mystery of Marie Roget" has a local, independent of any other, interest. Every one, at all familiar with the internal history of NEW YORK, for the last few years, will remember the murder of MARY ROGERS, the segar-girl. The deed baffled all attempts of the police to discover the time and mode of its commission, and the identity of the offenders. To this day, with the exception of the light afforded by the tale of Mr. POE, in which the faculty of analysis is applied to the facts, the whole matter is shrouded in complete mystery. We think, he has proven, very conclusively, that which he attempts. At all events, he has dissipated in our mind, all belief that the murder was perpetrated by more than one.

The incidents in the "Murder in the Rue Morgue" are purely imaginary. Like all the rest, it is written backwards.

We have thus noticed the entire collection—and have only to say, by way of close, that the collection embraces by no means the best of Mr. POE's productions that we have seen;

or rather is not totally so good, as might have been made, though containing some of the best.

The style of Mr. POE is clear and forcible. There is often a minuteness of detail; but on examination it will always be found that this minuteness was necessary to the developement of the plot, the effect, or the incidents. His style may be called, strictly, an earnest one. And this earnestness is one of its greatest charms. A writer must have the fullest belief in his statements, or must simulate that belief perfectly, to produce an absorbing interest in the mind of his reader. That power of simulation can only be possessed by a man of high genius. It is the result of a peculiar combination of the mental faculties. It produces earnestness, minute, not profuse detail, and fidelity of description. It is possessed by Mr. POE, in its full perfection.

The evident and most prominent aim of Mr. POE is originality, either of idea, or the combination of ideas. He appears to think it a crime to write unless he has something novel to write about, or some novel way of writing about an old thing. He rejects every word not having a tendency to develope the effect. Most writers get their subjects first, and write to develope it. The first inquiry of Mr. POE is for a novel effect—then for a subject; that is, a new arrangement of circumstance, or a new application of tone, by which the effect shall be developed. And he evidently holds whatever tends to the furtherance of the effect, to be legitimate material. Thus it is that he has produced works of the most notable character, and elevated the mere "tale," in this country, over the larger "novel"—conventionally so termed.

Aristidean, October 1845

L. H. Sigourney—H. F. Gould—E. F. Ellet

Zinzendorff, and other Poems. By Mrs. L. H. Sigourney, New York: Published by Leavitt, Lord & Co. 1836.
Poems—By Miss H. F. Gould, Third Edition. Boston: Hilliard, Gray & Co. 1835.
Poems; Translated and Original. By Mrs. E. F. Ellet. Philadelphia: Key and Biddle. 1835.

MRS. SIGOURNEY has been long known as an author. Her earliest publication was reviewed about twenty years ago, in the North American. She was then Miss Huntley. The fame which she has since acquired is extensive; and we, who so much admire her virtues and her talents, and who have so frequently expressed our admiration of both in this Journal— we, of all persons—are the least inclined to call in question the justice or the accuracy of the public opinion, by which has been adjudged to her so high a station among the *literati* of our land. Some things, however, we cannot pass over in silence. There are two kinds of popular reputation,—or rather there are two roads by which such reputation may be attained: and it appears to us an idiosyncrasy which distinguishes mere fame from most, or perhaps from *all* other human ends, that, in regarding the intrinsic value of the object, we must not fail to introduce, as a portion of our estimate, the means by which the object is acquired. To speak less abstractedly. Let us suppose two writers having a reputation apparently equal—that is to say, their names *being equally in the mouths of the people*—for we take this to be the most practicable test of what we choose to term *apparent popular reputation*. Their names then are equally in the mouths of the people. The one has written a great work—let it be either an Epic of high rank, or something which, although of seeming littleness in itself, is yet, like the Christabelle of Coleridge, entitled to be called *great* from its power of creating intense emotion in the minds of great men. And let us imagine that, by this single effort, the author has attained a certain quantum of reputation. We know it to be possible that another writer of very moderate powers may build up for himself, little by little, a reputation equally great—and this, too, merely by keeping continually in the eye, or by appealing continually with little things, to the ear, of that great, overgrown, and majestical gander, the critical and bibliographical rabble.

It would be an easy, although perhaps a somewhat disagreeable task, to point out several of the most popular writers in America—popular in the above mentioned sense—who have manufactured for themselves a celebrity by the very questionable means, and in the very questionable manner, to which we have alluded. But it must not be thought that we wish to include Mrs. Sigourney in the number. By no means. She has trod, however, upon the confines of their circle. She does not *owe* her reputation to the chicanery we mention, but it cannot be denied that it has been thereby greatly assisted. In a word—no single piece which she has written, and not even her collected works as we behold them in the present volume, and in the one published some years ago, would fairly entitle her to that exalted rank which she actually enjoys as the authoress, *time after time*, of her numerous, and, in most instances, very creditable compositions. The validity of our objections to this adventitious notoriety we must be allowed to consider unshaken, until it can be proved that any multiplication of zeros will eventuate in the production of a unit.

We have watched, too, with a species of anxiety and vexation brought about altogether by the sincere interest we take in Mrs. Sigourney, the progressive steps by which she has at length acquired the title of the "American Hemans." Mrs. S. cannot conceal from her own discernment that she has acquired this title *solely by imitation*. The very phrase "American Hemans" speaks loudly in accusation: and we are grieved that what by the over-zealous has been intended as complimentary should fall with so ill-omened a sound into the ears of the judicious. We will briefly point out those particulars in which Mrs. Sigourney stands palpably convicted of that sin which in poetry is not to be forgiven.

And first, in the *character of her subjects*. Every unprejudiced observer must be aware of the almost identity between the subjects of Mrs. Hemans and the subjects of Mrs. Sigourney. The themes of the former lady are the unobtrusive happiness, the sweet images, the cares, the sorrows, the gentle affections, of the domestic hearth—these too are the themes of the latter. The Englishwoman has dwelt upon all the "tender and true" chivalries of passion—and the American has dwelt as unequivocally upon the same. Mrs. Hemans has delighted in the radiance of a pure and humble faith—she has looked upon nature with a speculative attention—she has " watched the golden array of sunset clouds, with an eye looking beyond them to the habitations of the disembodied spirit"—she has poured all over her verses the most glorious and lofty aspirations of a redeeming Christianity, and in all this she is herself glorious and lofty. And all this too has Mrs. Sigourney not only attempted, but accomplished—yet in all this she is but, alas!—an imitator.

And secondly—in points more directly tangible than the one just mentioned, and therefore more easily appreciated by the generality of readers, is Mrs. Sigourney again open to the charge we have adduced. We mean in the structure of her versification—in the peculiar turns of her phraseology—in certain habitual expressions (principally interjectional,) such as *yea! alas!* and many others, so frequent upon the lips of Mrs. Hemans as to give an almost ludicrous air of similitude to all articles of her composition—in an invincible inclination to apostrophize every object, in both moral and physical existence—and more particularly in those mottos or quotations, sometimes of considerable extent, prefixed to nearly every poem, not as a text for discussion, nor even as an intimation of what is to follow, but as the actual subject matter itself, and of which the verses ensuing are, in most instances, merely a paraphrase. These were all, in Mrs. Hemans, mannerisms of a gross and inartificial nature; but, in Mrs. Sigourney, they are mannerisms of the most inadmissible kind—the mannerisms of imitation.

In respect to the use of the quotations, we cannot conceive how the fine taste of Mrs. Hemans could have admitted the practice, or how the good sense of Mrs. Sigourney could have thought it for a single moment worthy of her own adoption. In poems of magnitude the mind of the reader is not, at all times, enabled to include in one comprehensive survey the proportions and proper adjustment of the whole. He is pleased—if at all—with particular passages; and the sum of his pleasure is compounded of the sums of the pleasurable sensations inspired by these individual passages during the progress of perusal. But in pieces of less extent—like the poems of Mrs. Sigourney—the pleasure is *unique*, in the proper acceptation of that term—the understanding is employed, without difficulty, in the contemplation of the picture *as a whole*—and thus its effect will depend, in a very great degree, upon the perfection of its finish, upon the nice adaptation of its constituent parts, and especially upon what is rightly termed by Schlegel, the *unity or totality of interest*. Now it will readily be seen, that the practice we have mentioned as habitual with Mrs. Hemans and Mrs. Sigourney is utterly at variance with this unity. By the initial motto—often a very long one—we are either put in possession of the subject of the poem; or some hint, historic fact, or suggestion is thereby afforded, not included in the body of the article, which, without the suggestion, would be utterly incomprehensible. In the latter case, while perusing the poem, the reader must revert, in mind at least, to the motto for the necessary explanation. In the former, the poem being a mere paraphrase of the motto, the interest is divided between the motto and the paraphrase. In either instance the *totality* of effect is annihilated.

Having expressed ourselves thus far in terms of nearly unmitigated censure, it may appear in us somewhat equivocal to say that, as Americans, we are proud—very proud of the talents of Mrs. Sigourney. Yet such is the fact. The faults which we have already pointed out, and some others which we will point out hereafter, are but dust in the balance, when weighed against her very many and distinguishing excellences. Among those high qualities which give her, beyond doubt, a title to the sacred name of poet are an acute sensibility to natural loveliness—a quick and perfectly just conception of the moral and physical sublime—a calm and unostentatious vigor of thought—a mingled delicacy and strength of expression—and above all, a mind nobly and exquisitely attuned to all the gentle charities and lofty pieties of life.

The volume whose title forms the heading of this article embraces one hundred and seventy-three poems. The longest, but not the best, of these is Zinzendorff. "It owes its existence," says the author, "to a recent opportunity of personal intercourse with that sect of Christians who acknowledge Zinzendorff as their founder; and who, in their labors of self-denying benevolence, and their avoidance of the slight, yet bitter causes of controversy, have well preserved that sacred test of discipleship 'to love one another.' " Most of the other pieces were "suggested by the passing and common incidents of life,"—and we confess that we find no fault, with their "deficiency in the wonderful and wild." Not in these mountainous and stormy regions—but in the holy and quiet valley of the beautiful, must forever consent to dwell the genius of Mrs. Sigourney.

The poem of Zinzendorff includes five hundred and eighty lines. It relates, in a simple manner, some adventures of that man of God. Many passages are very noble, and breathe the truest spirit of the Muse. At page 14, for example.

> ————The high arch
> Of the *cloud-sweeping forest* proudly *cast* (casts)
> A solemn shadow, for no sound of axe
> Had taught the monarch Oak dire principles
> Of Revolution, or brought down the Pine
> Like haughty baron from his castled height.
> Thus dwelt the kings of Europe—ere the voice
> Of the crusading monk, with whirlwind tone
> Did root them from their base, with all their hosts,
> *Tossing the red-cross banner to the sky.*

Again at page 21, we have something equally beautiful, in a very different way. The passage is however much injured by the occurrence of the word 'that' at the commencement of both the sixth and seventh line.

> ————Now the infant morning raised
> Her rosy eyelids. But no soft breeze moved
> The forest lords to shake the dews of sleep
> From their green coronals. The curtaining mist
> Hung o'er the quiet river, and it seemed
> *That Nature found the summer night so sweet*
> *That 'mid the stillness of her deep repose*
> *She shunned the wakening of the king of day.*

All this is exquisite, and in Zinzendorff there are many passages of a like kind. The poem, however, is by no means free from faults. In the first paragraph we have the following:

> ————Through the *breast*
> Of that fair vale the Susquehannah roam'd,
> Wearing its *robe* of *silver* like a bride.
> Now with a noiseless current gliding slow,
> Mid the rich *velvet* of its *curtaining* banks
> It seemed to sleep.

To suppose the Susquehannah roaming through the *breast* of any thing—even of a valley—is an incongruity: and to say that such false images are common, is to say very little in their defence. But when the noble river is bedizzened out in *robes of silver*, and made to wash with its bright waters nothing better than *curtains of velvet*, we feel a very sensible and a very righteous indignation. We might have expected such language from an upholsterer, or a *marchande des modes*, but it is utterly out of place upon the lips of Mrs. Sigourney. To liken the glorious objects of natural loveliness to the trappings and tinsel of artificiality, is one of the lowest, and at the same time, one of the most ordinary exemplifications of the *bathos*. At page 21, these verses occur:

> No word was spoke,
> As when the friends of desolated Job,
> *Finding the line of language all too short*
> *To fathom woe like his*, sublimely paid
> That highest homage at the throne of grief,
> Deep silence.

The image here italicized is striking, but faulty. It is deduced not from any analogy between actual existences—between woe on the one hand, and the sea on the other—but from the *identity of epithet* (deep) frequently applied to both. We say the "deep sea," and the expression "deep woe" is certainly familiar. But in the first case the sea is actually deep; in the second, woe is but metaphorically so. Sound, therefore—not sense, is the basis of the analogy, and the image is consequently incorrect.

Some faults of a minor kind we may also discover in Zinzendorff. We dislike the use made by the poetess of antique
modes of expression—here most unequivocally out of place.
For example.

> *Where* the red council-fire
> Disturbed the trance of midnight, long they sate.

> *What time*, with hatred fierce and unsubdued,
> The woad-stained Briton, in his wattled boat,
> Quailed 'neath the glance of Rome.

The versification of Zinzendorff is particularly good—always sweet—occasionally energetic. We are enabled to point
out only one defective line in the poem, and in this the defect
has arisen from an attempt to contract *enthusiasm* into a word
of three syllables.

> He who found
> *This blest enthusiasm nerve his weary heart.*

There are, however, some errors of accentuation—for example:

> So strong in that mis*an*thrope's bosom wrought
> A frenzied malice.

Again—

> He would have made himself
> A green o*a*sis mid the strife of tongues.

We observe too that Mrs. Sigourney places the accent in *Wyoming* on the second syllable.

> 'Twas summer in Wy*o*ming. Through the breast, &c.
> ———And the lore
> Of sad Wy*o*ming's chivalry, a part
> Of classic song.

But we have no right to quarrel with her for this. The word
is so pronounced by those who should know best. Campbell,
however, places the accent on the first syllable.

> On Susquehannah's banks, fair *Wy*oming!

We will conclude our remarks upon Zinzendorff with a passage of surpassing beauty, energy, and poetic power. Why cannot Mrs. Sigourney write always thus?

> ————Not a breath
> Disturbed the tide of eloquence. So fixed
> Were that rude auditory, it would seem
> Almost as if a nation had become
> *Bronzed into statues.* Now and then a sigh,
> The unbidden messenger of thought profound,
> Parted the lip; or some barbarian brow
> Contracted closer in a haughty frown,
> As scowled the cynic, 'mid his idol fanes,
> When on Mars-Hill the inspired Apostle preached
> Jesus of Nazareth.

These lines are glowing all over with the true radiance of poetry. The image in italics is perfect. Of the versification, it is not too much to say that it reminds us of Miltonic power. The slight roughness in the line commencing "When on Mars-Hill," and the discord introduced at the word "inspired," evince an ear attuned to the *delicacies* of melody, and form an appropriate introduction to the sonorous and emphatic closing—Jesus of Nazareth.

Of the minor poems in the volume before us, we must be pardoned for speaking in a cursory manner. Of course they include many degrees of excellence. Their beauties and their faults are, generally, the beauties and the faults of Zinzendorff. We will particularize a few of each.

On page 67, in a poem entitled Female Education, occur the following lines:

> ————Break Oblivion's sleep,
> And toil with florist's art
> To plant the scenes of virtue deep
> In childhood's fruitful heart!
> To thee the babe is given,
> Fair from its glorious Sire;
> Go—nurse it for the King of Heaven,
> And *He* will *pay the hire.*

The conclusion of this is *bathetic* to a degree bordering upon the grotesque.

At page 160 is an error in metre—of course an oversight. We point it out merely because, did we write ourselves, we should like to be treated in a similar manner. For 'centred' we should probably read '*con*centred.'

> The wealth of every age
> *Thou hast center'd here,*
> The ancient tome, the classic page,
> The wit, the poet, and the sage,
> All at thy nod appear.

At page 233, line 10, the expression "Thou *wert* their friend," although many precedents may be found to justify it—is nevertheless *not English*. The same error occurs frequently in the volume.

The poem entitled *The Pholas*, at page 105, has the following introductory prose sentence: "It is a fact familiar to Conchologists, that the genus Pholas possesses the property of phosphorescence. It has been asserted that this may be restored, even when the animal is in a dried state, by the application of *water*, but is extinguished by the least quantity of *brandy*." This odd fact in Natural History is precisely what Cowley would have seized with avidity for the purpose of preaching therefrom a poetical homily on Temperance. But that Mrs. Sigourney should have thought herself justifiable in using it for such purpose, is what we cannot understand. What business has her good taste with so palpable and so ludicrous a *conceit*? Let us now turn to a more pleasing task.

In the *Friends of Man*, (a poem originally published in our own Messenger,) the versification throughout is of the first order of excellence. We select an example.

> The youth at midnight sought his bed,
>   But ere he closed his eyes,
> Two forms drew near with gentle tread,
>   In meek and saintly guise;
> One struck a lyre of wondrous power,
>   With thrilling music fraught,
> That chained the flying summer hour,

> And charmed the listener's thought—
> For still would its tender cadence be
> Follow me! follow me!
> And every morn a smile shall bring,
> Sweet as the merry lay I sing.

The lines entitled *Filial Grief*, at page 199, are worthy of high praise. Their commencement is chaste, simple, and altogether exquisite. The verse italicized contains *an unjust metaphor*, but we are forced to pardon it for the sonorous beauty of its expression.

> The love that blest our infant dream,
> That dried our earliest tear,
> The tender voice, the winning smile,
> That made our home so dear,
> The hand that urged our youthful thought
> O'er low delights to soar,
> *Whose pencil wrote upon our souls,*
> Alas, is ours no more.

We will conclude our extracts with *"Poetry"* from page 57. The burden of the song finds a ready echo in our bosoms.

> Morn on her rosy couch awoke,
> Enchantment led the hour,
> And Mirth and Music drank the dews
> That freshened Beauty's flower—
> Then from her bower of deep delight
> I heard a young girl sing,
> "Oh, speak no ill of Poetry,
> For 'tis a holy thing!"
>
> The sun in noon-day heat rose high,
> And on with heaving breast
> I saw a weary pilgrim toil,
> Unpitied and unblest—
> Yet still in trembling measures flow'd
> Forth from a broken string,
> "Oh, speak no ill of Poetry,
> For 'tis a holy thing!"

'Twas night, and Death the curtains drew,
    Mid agony severe,
While there a willing spirit went
    Home to a glorious sphere——
Yet still it sighed, even when was spread
    The waiting Angel's wing,
"Oh, speak no ill of Poetry,
    For 'tis a holy thing!"

We now bid adieu to Mrs. Sigourney—yet we trust only for a time. We shall behold her again. When that period arrives, having thrown aside the petty shackles which have hitherto enchained her, she will assume, at once, that highest station among the poets of our land which her noble talents so well qualify her for attaining.

————

The remarks which we made in the beginning of our critique on Mrs. Sigourney, will apply, in an equal degree, to Miss Gould. Her reputation has been greatly assisted by the *frequency* of her appeals to the attention of the public. The poems (one hundred and seventeen in number,) included in the volume now before us have all, we believe, appeared, from time to time, in the periodicals of the day. Yet in no other point of view, can we trace the remotest similarity between the two poetesses. We have already pointed out the prevailing characteristics of Mrs. Sigourney. In Miss Gould we recognize, first, a disposition, like that of Wordsworth, to seek beauty where it is not usually sought—in the *homelinesses* (if we may be permitted the word,) and in the most familiar realities of existence—secondly *abandon* of manner—thirdly a phraseology sparkling with antithesis, yet, strange to say, perfectly simple and unaffected.

Without Mrs. Sigourney's high reach of thought, Miss Gould surpasses her rival in the mere vehicle of thought—expression. "Words, words, words," are the true secret of her strength. *Words* are her kingdom—and in the realm of language, she rules with equal despotism and *nonchalance*. Yet we do not mean to deny her abilities of a higher order than any which a mere *logocracy* can imply. Her powers of imagination are great, and she has a faculty of inestimable worth, when considered in relation to effect — the faculty of holding ordinary ideas in so novel, and sometimes in so fantastic a light, as to give them all of the appearance, and much of the value, of originality. Miss Gould will, of course, be the favorite with the multitude — Mrs. Sigourney with the few.

We can think of no better manner of exemplifying these few observations, than by extracting part of Miss G's little poem, *The Great Refiner*.

'Tis sweet to feel that he, who tries
    The silver, takes his seat
Beside the fire that purifies;
    Lest too intense a heat,
Raised to consume the base alloy,
The precious metal too destroy.

'Tis good to think how well he knows
    The silver's power to bear
The *or*deal to which it goes;
    And that with skill and care,
He'll take it from the fire, when fit
For his own hand to polish it.

'Tis blessedness to know that he
    The piece he has begun
Will not forsake, till he can see,
    To prove the work well done,
An image by its brightness shown
The perfect likeness of his own.

The mind which could conceive the *subject* of this poem, and find poetic appropriateness in a forced analogy between a refiner of silver, over his crucible, and the Great Father of all things, occupied in the mysteries of redeeming Grace, we cannot believe a mind adapted to the loftier breathings of the lyre. On the other hand, the delicate *finish* of the illustration, the perfect fitness of one portion for another, the epigrammatic nicety and point of the language, give evidence of a taste exquisitely alive to the *prettinesses* of the Muse. It is possible that Miss Gould has been led astray in her conception of this poem by the scriptural expression, "He shall sit as a refiner and purifier of silver."

From the apparently harsh strictures we have thought it our duty to make upon the poetry of Miss Gould, must be excepted one exquisite little *morceau* at page 59 of the volume now under review. It is entitled *The Dying Storm*. We will quote it in full.

> *I am feeble, pale and weary,*
>   *And my wings are nearly furled;*
> I have caused a scene so dreary,
>   I am glad to quit the world!
> With bitterness I'm thinking
>   On the evil I have done,
> *And to my caverns sinking*
>   *From the coming of the sun.*
>
> The heart of man will sicken
>   In that pure and holy light,
> When he feels the hopes I've stricken
>   With an everlasting blight!
> For widely, in my madness,
>   Have I poured abroad my wrath,
> And changing joy to sadness,
>   Scattered ruin on my path.
>
> *Earth shuddered at my motion,*
>   And my power in silence owns;
> *But the deep and troubled ocean*
>   *O'er my deeds of horror moans!*
> I have sunk the brightest treasure—
>   I've destroyed the fairest form—
> *I have sadly filled my measure,*
>   *And am now a dying storm.*

We have much difficulty in recognizing these verses as from the pen of Miss Gould. They do not contain a single trace of her manner, and still less of the prevailing features of her thought. Setting aside the flippancy of the metre, ill adapted to the sense, we have no fault to find. All is full, forcible, and free from artificiality. The personification of the storm, in its perfect simplicity, is of a high order of

poetic excellence—the images contained in the lines italicized, all of the *very highest*.

———

Many but not all of the poems in Mrs. Ellet's volume, likewise, have been printed before—appearing, within the last
two years, in different periodicals. The whole number of
pieces now published is fifty seven. Of these thirty-nine are
original. The rest are translations from the French of Alphonse de Lamartine and Beranger—from the Spanish of
Quevedo and Yriarte—from the Italian of Ugo Foscolo, Alfieri, Fulvio Testi, Pindemonte, and Saverio Bettinelli,—
and from the German of Schiller. As evidences of the lady's
acquaintance with the modern languages, these translations
are very creditable to her. Where we have had opportunities
of testing the fidelity of her versions by reference to the originals, we have always found reason to be satisfied with her
performances. A too scrupulous adherence to the text is certainly not one of her faults—nor can we yet justly call her, in
regard to the spirit of her authors, a latitudinarian. We wish,
however, to say that, in fully developing the meaning of her
originals, she has too frequently neglected their *poetical characters*. Let us refer to the lady's translation of the *Swallows*.
We have no hesitation in saying, that not the slightest conception of Pierre Jean de Beranger, can be obtained by the perusal of the lines at page 112, of the volume now before us.

> Bring me, I pray—an exile sad—
>   Some token of that valley bright,
> Where in my sheltered childhood glad,
>   The future was a dream of light.
> Beside the gentle stream, where swell
>   Its waves beneath the lilac tree,
> Ye saw the cot I love so well—
>   And speak ye of that home to me?

We have no fault to find with these verses in themselves—
as specimens of the *manner* of the French *chansonnier*, we
have no patience with them. What we have quoted, is the
second stanza of the song. Our remarks, here, with some little

modification, would apply to the *Sepulchres* of Foscolo, especially to the passage commencing

> Yes—Pindemonte!
> The aspiring soul is fired to lofty deeds
> By great men's monuments, &c.

They would apply, also, with somewhat less force, to Lamartine's *Loss of the Anio*, in the original of which by the way, we
cannot perceive the lines answering to Mrs. E's verses

> All that obscures thy sovereign majesty
> Degrades our glory in degrading thee.

Quevedo's Sonnet *Rome in Ruins*, we happen to have by us
at this moment. The translation in this instance is faultless,
and combines, happily, a close approximation to the meaning
of the original, with its quaint air and pompous rhythm. The
Sonnet itself is a plagiarism entire, from Girolamo Preti. The
opening lines of Quevedo,

> Pilgrim! in vain thou seekest in Rome for Rome!
>   Alas! the Queen of nations is no more!
> Dust are her towers, that proudly frowned of yore,
>   And her stern hills themselves have built their tomb,

are little else than the

> Roma in Roma non è
> In se stessa cadeo morta e sepolta, &c.

of Girolamo. But this is no concern of Mrs. Ellet's.

Of the original poems, which form the greater part of
the volume, we have hardly been able to form an opinion,
during the cursory perusal we have given them. Some of
them have merit. Some we think unworthy of the talents
which their author has undoubtedly displayed. The epigram, for example, at page 102 is rather a silly joke upon a
threadbare theme, and, however well it might have suited
Mrs. Ellet's purpose to indite it, she should have had more
discretion than to give it permanency in a collection of her
poems.

> Echo was once a love sick maid
> > They say: the tale is no deceiver.
> However a woman's form might fade
> > Her voice would be the last to leave her!

The tragedy (Teresa Contarini) at the end of the volume, "is founded," says the authoress, "upon an incident well known in the history of Venice, which has formed the material for various works of fiction." Mrs. E. has availed herself of a drama of Nicolini's in part of the first scene of the first act, and in the commencement of the fifth act. The resemblance between the two plays is, however, very slight. In plot—in the spirit of the dialogue—and in the range of incidents they differ altogether. *Teresa Contarini* was received with approbation at the Park Theatre in March 1835,—Miss Philips performing the heroine. We must confine ourselves to the simple remark, that the drama appears to us better suited to the closet than the stage.

In evidence that Mrs. Ellet is a poetess of no ordinary rank, we extract, from page 51 of her volume, a little poem rich in vigorous expression, and full of solemn thought. Its chief merits, however, are condensation and energy.

> Hark—to the midnight bell!
> > The solemn peal rolls on
> That tells us, with an iron tongue,
> > Another year is gone!
> Gone with its hopes, its mockeries, and its fears,
> To the dim rest which wraps our former years.
>
> > Gray pilgrim to the past!
> > We will not bid thee stay;
> For joys of youth and passion's plaint
> > Thou bear'st alike away.
> Alike the tones of mirth, and sorrow's swell
> Gather to hymn thy parting.—Fare thee well!
>
> > Fill high the cup—and drink
> > To Time's unwearied sweep!
> He claims a parting pledge from us—
> > And let the draught be deep!
> We may not shadow moments fleet as this,
> With tales of baffled hopes, or vanished bliss.

No comrade's voice is here,
   That could not tell of grief—
Fill up!—We know that friendship's hours,
   Like their own joys—are brief.
Drink to their brightness while they yet may last,
And drown in song the memory of the past!

The winter's leafless bough
   In sunshine yet shall bloom;
And hearts that sink in sadness now
   Ere long dismiss their gloom.
Peace to the sorrowing! Let our goblets flow,
In red wine mantling, for the tears of wo!

Once more! A welcoming strain!
   A solemn sound—yet sweet!
While life is ours, Time's onward steps
   In gladness will we greet!
Fill high the cup! What prophet lips may tell
Where we shall bid another year farewell!

With this extract, we close our observations on the writings of Mrs. Ellet—of Miss Gould—and of Mrs. Sigourney. The time may never arrive again, when we shall be called upon, by the circumstances of publication, to speak of them in connexion with one another.

Southern Literary Messenger, January 1836

William Gilmore Simms

The Partisan: A Tale of the Revolution. By the author of "The Yemassee," "Guy Rivers,"
&c. New York: Published by Harper and Brothers.

MR. SIMMS has written, heretofore, "Atalantis, a Story of
the Sea"—"Martin Faber, the Story of a Criminal"—
"Guy Rivers, a Tale of Georgia," and "The Yemassee, a Romance of Carolina." Of these works, Martin Faber passed to
a second edition—"Guy Rivers," and "The Yemassee" each
to a third. With these evidences before us of our author's
long acquaintance with the Muse, we must be pardoned if, in
reviewing the volumes now upon our table, we make no allowances whatever on the score of a deficient *experience*. Mr.
Simms either writes very well, or it is high time that he
should.

"The Partisan" is *inscribed* to Richard Yeadon, Jr. Esq. of
South Carolina; and the terms in which the compliment is
conveyed, while attempting to avoid Scylla, have blundered
upon Charybdis. The cant of verbiage is bad enough—but
the cant of laconism is equally as bad. Let us transcribe the
Dedication.

TO RICHARD YEADON, JR. ESQ.
Of South Carolina.

Dear Sir,
My earliest, and, perhaps, most pleasant rambles in the
fields of literature, were taken in your company—permit me
to remind you of that period by inscribing the present volumes with your name.

THE AUTHOR.

Barnwell, South Carolina.
July 1, 1835.

This is, indeed, the quintessence of brevity. At all events it
is meant to be something better than such things usually are.
It aims at point. It affects excessive terseness, excessive appropriateness, and excessive gentility. One might almost picture
to the mind's eye the exact air and attitude of the writer as he
indited the whole thing. Probably he compressed his lips—
possibly he ran his fingers through his hair. Now a letter,

generally, we may consider as the substitute for certain oral communications which the writer of the letter would deliver in person were an opportunity afforded. Let us then imagine the author of "The Partisan" presenting a copy of that work to "Richard Yeadon, Jr. Esq. of South Carolina," and let us, from the indications afforded by the printed Dedication, endeavor to form some idea of the author's demeanor upon an occasion so highly interesting. We may suppose Mr. Yeadon, in South Carolina, at home, and in his study. By and bye with a solemn step, downcast eyes, and impressive earnestness of manner, enters the author of "The Yemassee." He advances towards Mr. Yeadon, and, without uttering a syllable, takes that gentleman affectionately, but firmly, by the hand. Mr. Y. has his suspicions, as well he may have, but says nothing. Mr. S. commences as above. *"Dear Sir,"* (here follows a pause, indicated by the comma after the word "Sir"—see Dedication. Mr. Y. very much puzzled what to make of it.) Mr. S. proceeds, *"My earliest,"* (pause the second, indicated by comma the second,) *"and,"* (pause the third, in accordance with comma the third,) *"perhaps,"* (pause the fourth, as shewn by comma the fourth. Mr. Y. exceedingly mystified,) *"most pleasant rambles in the fields of literature,"* (pause fifth) *"were taken in your company"* (pause sixth, to agree with the dash after 'company.' Mr. Y.'s hair begins to stand on end, and he looks occasionally towards the door,) *"permit me to remind you of that period by inscribing the present volumes with your name."* At the conclusion of the sentence, Mr. S. with a smile and a bow of mingled benignity and grace, turns slowly from Mr. Y. and advances to a table in the centre of the room. Pens and ink are there at his service. Drawing from the pocket of his surtout a pacquet carefully done up in silver paper, he unfolds it, and produces the two volumes of "The Partisan." With ineffable ease, and with an air of exquisite *haut ton*, he proceeds to inscribe in the title pages of each tome the name of Richard Yeadon, Jr. Esq. The scene, however, is interrupted. Mr. Y. feels it his duty to kick the author of "The Yemassee" down stairs.

Now, in this, all the actual burlesque consists in merely substituting things for words. There are many of our readers who will recognize in this imaginary interview between Mr.

Yeadon and Mr. Simms, at least a family likeness to the written Dedication of the latter. This Dedication is, nevertheless, quite as good as one half the antique and lackadaisical courtesies with which we daily see the initial leaves of our best publications disfigured.

"The Partisan," as we are informed by Mr. Simms in his Advertisement, (Preface?) was originally contemplated as one novel of a series to be devoted to our war of Independence. "With this object," says the author, "I laid the foundation more broadly and deeply than I should have done, had I purposed merely the single work. Several of the persons employed were destined to be the property of the series—that part of it at least which belonged to the locality. Three of these works were to have been devoted to South Carolina, and to comprise three distinct periods of the war of the Revolution in that State. One, and the first of these, is the story now submitted to the reader. I know not that I shall complete, or even continue the series." Upon the whole we think that he had better not.

There is very little plot or connexion in the book before us; and Mr. Simms has evidently aimed at neither. Indeed we hardly know what to think of the work at all. Perhaps, with some hesitation, we may call it an historical novel. The narrative begins in South Carolina, during the summer of 1780, and comprises the leading events of the Revolution from the fall of Charleston, to the close of that year. We have the author's own words for it that his object has been principally to give a fair picture of the province—its condition, resources, and prospects—during the struggle between Gates and Cornwallis, and the period immediately subsequent to the close of the campaign in the defeat of the Southern defending army. Mr. S. assures us that the histories of the time have been continually before him in the prosecution of this object, and that, where written records were found wanting, their places have been supplied by local chronicles and tradition. Whether the idea ever entered the mind of Mr. Simms that his very laudable design, as here detailed, might have been better carried into effect by a work of a character *purely* historical, we, of course, have no opportunity of deciding. To ourselves, every succeeding page of "The Partisan" rendered the supposition more plausible. The interweaving fact with fiction is at all times hazardous, and presupposes on the part of general readers that degree of intimate acquaintance with fact which should never be presupposed. In the present instance, the author has failed, so we think, in confining either his truth or his fable within its legitimate, individual domain. Nor do we at all wonder at his failure in performing what no novelist whatever has hitherto performed.

Some pains have been taken in the preface of "The Partisan," to bespeak the reader's favorable decision in regard to certain historical facts—or rather in regard to the coloring given them by Mr. Simms. We refer particularly to the conduct of General Gates in South Carolina. We would, generally, prefer reading an author's book, to reading his criticism upon it. But letting this matter pass, we do not think Mr. S. has erred in attributing gross negligence, headstrong obstinacy, and overweening self-conceit to the conqueror at Saratoga. These charges are sustained by the best authorities— by Lee, by Johnson, by Otho Williams, and by all the histories of the day. No apology is needed for stating the truth. In regard to the "propriety of insisting upon the faults and foibles of a man conspicuous in our history," Mr. Simms should give himself little uneasiness. It is precisely because the man *is* conspicuous in our history, that we should have no hesitation in condemning his errors.

With the events which are a portion of our chronicles, the novelist has interwoven such fictitious incidents and characters as might enable him to bind up his book in two volumes duodecimo, and call it "The Partisan." The Partisan himself, and the hero of the novel, is a Major Robert Singleton. His first introduction to the reader is as follows. "It was on a pleasant afternoon in June, that a tall, well-made youth, probably twenty-four or five years of age, rode up to the door of the "George," (in the village of Dorchester,) and throwing his bridle to a servant, entered the hotel. His person had been observed, and his appearance duly remarked upon, by several persons already assembled in the hall which he now approached. The new comer, indeed, was not one to pass unnoticed. His person was symmetry itself, and the ease with which he managed his steed, and the"———but we spare our readers any farther details in relation to either the tall, well-made youth, or his steed, which latter they may take for granted was quite as tall, and equally well made. We cut the passage short with the less hesitation, inasmuch as a perfect fac-simile of it may be found near the commencement of every fashionable novel since the flood. Singleton is a partisan in the service of Marion, whose disposition, habits, and character are well painted, and well preserved, throughout the Tale. A Mr. Walton is the uncle of Singleton, and has been induced, after the surrender of Charleston (spelt Charles-town) to accept of a British protection, the price of which is neutrality. This course he has been led to adopt, principally on account of his daughter Katharine, who would lose her all in the confiscation of her father's property—a confiscation to be avoided by no other means than those of the protection. Singleton's sister resides with Col. Walton's family, at "The Oaks," near Dorchester, where the British Col. Proctor is in command. At the instigation of Singleton, who has an eye to the daughter of Col. Walton, that gentleman is induced to tear up the disgraceful protection, and levy a troop, with which he finally reaches the army of Gates. Most of the book is occupied with the ambuscades, bush fighting, and swamp adventures of partisan warfare in South Carolina. These passages are all highly interesting—but as they have little connexion with one another, we must dismiss them *en masse*. The history of the march of Gates' army, his fool-hardiness, and consequent humiliating discomfiture by Cornwallis, are as well told as any details of a like nature can be told, in language exceedingly confused, ill-arranged, and ungrammatical. This defeat hastens the *dénouement*, or rather the leading incident, of the novel. Col. Walton is made prisoner, and condemned to be hung, as a rebel taken in arms. He is sent to Dorchester for the fulfilment of the sentence. Singleton, urged by his own affection, as well as by the passionate exhortations of his cousin Katharine, determines upon the rescue of his uncle at all hazards. A plot is arranged for this purpose. On the morning appointed for execution, a troop of horse is concealed in some underwood near the scaffold. Bella Humphries, the daughter of an avowed tory, but a whig at heart, is stationed in the belfry of the village church, and her father himself is occupied in arranging materials for setting Dorchester on fire upon a given signal. This signal (the violent ringing of the church bell by Bella) is given at the moment when Col. Walton arrives in a cart at the foot of the gallows. Great confusion ensues among those not in the secret—a confusion heightened no little by the sudden conflagration of the village. During the hubbub the troop concealed in the thicket rush upon the British guard in attendance. The latter are beaten down, and Walton is carried off in triumph by Singleton. The hand of Miss Katharine is, as a matter of course, the reward of the Major's gallantry.

Of the numerous personages who figure in the book, some are really excellent—some horrible. The historical characters are, without exception, well drawn. The portraits of Cornwallis, Gates, and Marion, are vivid realities—those of De Kalb and the Claverhouse-like Tarleton positively unsurpassed by any similar delineations within our knowledge. The fictitious existences in "The Partisan" will not bear examination. Singleton is about as much of a non-entity as most other heroes of our acquaintance. His uncle is no better. Proctor, the British Colonel, is cut out in buckram. Sergeant Hastings, the tory, is badly drawn from a bad model. Young Humphries is a braggadocio—Lance Frampton is an idiot—and Doctor Oakenburg is an ass. Goggle is another miserable addition to the list of those anomalies so swarming in fiction, who are represented as having vicious principles, for no other reason than because they have ugly faces. Of the females we can hardly speak in a more favorable manner. Bella, the innkeeper's daughter is, we suppose, very much like an innkeeper's daughter. Mrs. Blonay, Goggle's mother, is a hag worth hanging. Emily, Singleton's sister, is not what we would wish her. Too much stress is laid upon the interesting features of the consumption which destroys her; and the whole chapter of abrupt sentimentality, in which we are introduced to her sepulchre before having notice of her death, is in the very worst style of times *un peu passés*. Katharine Walton is somewhat better than either of the ladies above mentioned. In the beginning of the book, however, we are disgusted with that excessive prudishness which will not admit of a lover's hand resting for a moment upon her own—in the conclusion, we are provoked to a smile when she throws herself into the arms of the same lover, without even waiting for his consent.

One personage, a Mr. Porgy, we have not mentioned in his proper place among the *dramatis personæ*, because we think he deserves a separate paragraph of animadversion. This man is a most insufferable bore; and had we, by accident, opened the book when about to read it for the first time, at any one of his manifold absurdities, we should most probably have thrown aside "The Partisan" in disgust. Porgy is a backwoods imitation of Sir Somebody Guloseton, the epicure, in one of the Pelham novels. He is a very silly compound of gluttony, slang, belly, and balderdash philosophy, never opening his mouth for a single minute at a time, without making us feel miserable all over. The rude and unqualified oaths with which he seasons his language deserve to be seriously reprehended. There is positively neither wit nor humor in an oath of any kind—but the oaths of this Porgy are abominable. Let us see how one or two of them will look in our columns. Page 174, vol. ii—"Then there was no tricking a fellow—persuading him to put his head into a rope without showing him first how d——d strong it was." Page 169, vol. ii—"Tom, old boy, why d——n it, that fellow's bloodied your nose." Page 167, vol. ii—"I am a pacific man, and my temper is not un-gentle; but to disturb my slumbers which are so necessary to the digestive organs—stop, I say—d——n!—dont pull so!" Page 164, vol. ii—"Well, Tom, considering how d——d bad those perch were fried, I must confess I enjoyed them." Page 164, vol. ii—"Such spice is a d——d bad dish for us when lacking cayenne." Page 163, vol. ii—"Dr. Oakenburg, your d——d hatchet hip is digging into my side." Page 162, vol. ii—"The summer duck, with its glorious plumage, skims along the same muddy lake, on the edge of which the d——d bodiless crane screams and crouches." In all these handsome passages Porgy loquitur, and it will be perceived that they are all to be found within a few pages of each other—such attempts to render profanity less despicable by rendering it amusing, should be frowned down indignantly by the public. Of Porgy's philosophy we subjoin a specimen from page 89, vol. ii, "A dinner once lost is never recovered. The stomach loses a day; and regrets are not only idle to recall it, but subtract largely from the appetite the day ensuing. *Tears can only fall from a member that lacks teeth; the mouth now is never seen weeping. It is the eye only; and, as it lacks tongue, teeth, and taste alike, by Jupiter, it seems to me that tears should be its proper business.*" How Mr. Simms should ever have fallen into the error of imagining such horrible nonsense as that in Italics, to be either witty or wise, is to us a mystery of mysteries. Yet Porgy is evidently a favorite with the author.

Some two or three paragraphs above we made use of these expressions. "The history of the march of Gates' army, his fool-hardiness, &c. are as well told as any details of a like nature can be told in language exceedingly confused, ill-arranged, and ungrammatical." Mr. Simms' English is bad—shockingly bad. This is no mere assertion on our parts—we proceed to prove it. "Guilt," says our author, (see page 98, vol. i) "must always *despair its charm* in the presence of the true avenger"—what is the meaning of this sentence?—after much reflection we are unable to determine. At page 115, vol. i, we have these words. "He was under the guidance of an elderly, drinking sort of person—one of the fat, beefy class, whose worship of the belly-god has given an unhappy distension to that ambitious, though most erring member." By the 'most erring member' Mr. S. means to say *the belly*—but the sentence implies the *belly-god*. Again, at page 196, vol. i. "It was for the purpose of imparting to Col. Walton the contents of that not yet notorious proclamation of Sir Henry Clinton, with which he demanded the performance of military duty from the persons who had been paroled; and by means of which, on departing from the province, he planted the seeds of that *revolting* patriotism which finally overthrew his authority." It is unnecessary to comment on the unauthorized use here, of the word 'revolting.' In the very next sentence we see the following. "Colonel Walton received his guests with his accustomed urbanity: *he received them alone*." This language implies that Colonel Walton received those particular guests and no others, and should be read with an emphasis on the word '*them*'—but Mr. Simms' meaning is very different. He wishes to say that Col. Walton was alone when his guests were ushered into his presence. At page 136, vol. i, the hero, Singleton, concludes a soliloquy with the ungrammatical phrase, "And yet none love her like me!" At page 143, vol. i, we read—" 'That need not surprise you, Miss Walton; you remember that ours are British soldiers'—smiling, and with a bow was the response of the Colonel." We have no great difficulty here in *guessing* what Mr. Simms wishes to say—his actual words convey no meaning whatever. The present participle 'smiling' has no substantive to keep it company; and the 'bow,' as far as regards its syntactical disposition, may be referred with equal plausibility to the Colonel, to Miss Walton, to the British soldiers, or to the author of "The Partisan." At page 147, vol. i, we are told—"She breathed more freely released from his embrace, and he then gazed upon her with a *painful sort of pleasure*, her look was so clear, so dazzling, so spiritual, so *unnaturally life-like*." The attempt at paradox has here led Mr. Simms into error. The *painful sort of pleasure* we may suffer to pass; but *life* is the most natural thing in the world, and to call any object unnaturally life-like is as much a bull proper as to style it artificially natural. At page 148, we hear "that the disease had not yet *shown* upon her system." Shown is here used as a neuter verb—shown *itself* Mr. S. meant to say. We are at a loss, too, to understand what is intended, at page 149, vol. i, by "a look so pure, so bright, so fond, so becoming of heaven, yet so hopeless of earth." Becoming heaven, not *of* heaven, we presume should be the phrase—but even thus the sentence is unintelligible. At page 156, vol. i, a countryman "loves war to the knife better than degradation to the chain." This is a pitiable antithesis. In the first clause, the expression '*to the* knife' is idiomatic; in the second, the words '*to the* chain' have a literal meaning. At page 88, vol. i, we read—"The half-military eye would have studiously avoided the ridge," &c. The epithet "*half-military*" does not convey the author's meaning. At page 204, vol. i. Mrs. Blonay is represented as striding across the floor " with a rapid movement hostile to the enfeebled appearance of her frame." Here the forcing "*hostile*" to mean *not in accordance with*, is unjustifiable. At page 14, vol. ii, these words occur. "Cheerless quite, bald of home and habitation, they saw nothing throughout the melancholy waste more imposing than the plodding negro." The "*cheerless quite*" and the "*bald of home and habitation*" would refer in strict grammatical construction to the pronoun *"they"*—but the writer means them to agree with *"melancholy waste."* At page 224, vol. i, we find the following. "The moon, obscured during the early part of the night, had now sunk *westering* so far," &c. At page 194, vol. ii, we are informed that "General Gates *deigned* no general consultation." At page 13, vol. ii. "Major Singleton *bids the boy Lance Frampton in attendance"*—and at page 95, vol. ii, we have the singular phenomenon of *"an infant yet unborn adding its prayer to that of its mother for the vengeance to which he has devoted himself"*—a sentence which we defy his Satanic Majesty to translate.

Mr. Simms has one or two pet words which he never fails introducing every now and then, with or without an opportunity. One of these is *"coil"*—another, *"hug"*—another, and a still greater favorite, is the compound *"old-time."* Let us see how many instances of the latter we can discover in looking over the volumes at random. Page 7, vol. i—"And with the revival of many *old-time* feelings, I strolled through the solemn ruins." Page 18, vol. i—"The cattle graze along the clustering bricks that distinguish the *old-time* chimney places." Page 20, vol. i—"He simply cocked his hat at the *old-time* customer." Page 121, vol. i—"The Oaks was one of those *old-time* residences." Page 148, vol. i—"I only wish for mommer as we wish for an *old-time* prospect." Page 3, vol. ii—

> "Unfold—unfold—the day is going fast,
> And I would know this *old-time* history."

Page 5, vol. ii—"The Carolinian well knows these *old-time* places." Page 98, vol. ii—"Look, before we shall have gone too far to return to them, upon these *old-time* tombs of Dorchester." Here are eight *old-times* discovered in a cursory glance over "The Partisan"—we believe there are ten times as many interspersed throughout the work. The *coils* are equally abundant, and the *hugs* innumerable.

One or two other faults we are forced to find. The old affectation of beginning a chapter abruptly has been held worthy of adoption by our novelist. He has even thought himself justifiable in imitating this silly practice in its most reprehensible form—we mean the form habitual with Bulwer and D'Israeli, and which not even their undoubted and indubitable genius could render any thing but despicable—that of commencing with an *"And,"* a *"But,"* or some other conjunction—thus rendering the initial sentence of the chapter in question, a continuation of the final sentence of the chapter preceding. We have an instance of this folly at page 102, vol. ii, where Chapter XII commences as follows: "*But,* though we turn aside from the highway to plant or to pluck the flower, we may not linger there idly or long." Again, at page 50 of the same volume, Chapter VII begins—"*And* two opposing and mighty principles were at fearful strife in that chamber." This piece of frippery need only be pointed out to be despised.

Instances of bad taste—villainously bad taste—occur frequently in the book. Of these the most reprehensible are to be found in a love for that mere *physique* of the horrible which has obtained for some Parisian novelists the title of the "French convulsives." At page 97, vol. ii, we are entertained with the minutest details of a murder committed by a maniac, Frampton, on the person of Sergeant Hastings. The madman suffocates the soldier by thrusting his head in the mud of a morass—and the yells of the murderer, and the kicks of the sufferer, are dwelt upon by Mr. Simms with that species of delight with which we have seen many a ragged urchin spin a cockchafer upon a needle. At page 120, vol. i, another murder is perpetrated by the same maniac in a manner too shockingly horrible to mention. The victim in this case is a poor tory, one Clough. At page 217, vol. i, the booby Goggle receives a flogging for desertion, and Mr. S. endeavors to interest us in the screeches of the wretch—in the cries of his mother—in the cracking of the whip—in the number of the lashes—in the depth, and length, and color of the wounds. At page 105, vol. ii, our friend Porgy has caught a terrapin, and the author of "The Yemassee" luxuriates in the manner of torturing the poor reptile to death, and more particularly in the writhings and spasms of the head, which he assures us with a smile *"will gasp and jerk long after we have done eating the body."*

One or two words more. Each chapter in "The Partisan" is introduced (we suppose in accordance with the good old fashion) by a brief poetical passage. Our author, however, has been wiser than his neighbors in the art of the initial motto. While others have been at the trouble of extracting, from popular works, quotations adapted to the subject-matter of their chapters, he has manufactured his own headings. We find no fault with him for so doing. The manufactured mottos of Mr. Simms are, perhaps, quite as convenient as the extracted mottos of his cotemporaries. All, we think, are abominable. As regards the fact of the manufacture there can be no doubt. None of the verses have we ever met with before—and they are altogether too full of *coils, hugs,* and *old-times,* to have any other parent than the author of "The Yemassee."

In spite, however, of its manifest and manifold blunders and impertinences, "The Partisan" is no ordinary work. Its historical details are replete with interest. The concluding scenes are well drawn. Some passages descriptive of swamp scenery are exquisite. Mr. Simms has evidently the eye of a painter. Perhaps, in sober truth, he would succeed better in sketching a landscape than he has done in writing a novel.

Southern Literary Messenger, January 1836

Wiley & Putnam's Library of American Books. No. IV. *The Wigwam and the Cabin.* By William Gilmore Simms. First series.

M R. SIMMS, we believe, made his first, or nearly his first, appearance before an American audience with a small volume entitled "Martin Faber," an amplification of a much shorter fiction. He had some difficulty in getting it published, but the Harpers finally undertook it, and it did credit to their judgment. It was well received both by the public and the more discriminative few, although some of the critics objected that the story was an imitation of "Miserrimus," a very powerful fiction by the author of "Pickwick Abroad." The original tale, however—the germ of "Martin Faber"—was written long before the publication of "Miserrimus." But independently of this fact, there is not the slightest ground for the charge of imitation. The thesis and incidents of the two works are totally dissimilar;—the idea of resemblance arises only from the absolute identity of *effect* wrought by both.

"Martin Faber" was succeeded, at short intervals, by a great number and variety of fictions, some brief, but many of the ordinary novel size. Among these we may notice "Guy Rivers," "The Partisan," "The Yemassee," "Mellichampe," "Beauchampe," and "Richard Hurdis." The last two were issued anonymously, the author wishing to ascertain whether the success of his books (which was great) had anything to do with his mere name as the writer of previous works. The result proved that popularity, in Mr. Simms' case, arose solely from intrinsic merit, for "Beauchampe" and "Richard Hurdis" were the most popular of his fictions, and excited very general attention and curiosity. "Border Beagles" was another of his anonymous novels, published with the same end in view, and, although disfigured by some instances of bad taste, was even more successful than "Richard Hurdis."

The "bad taste" of the "Border Beagles" was more particularly apparent in "The Partisan," "The Yemassee," and one or two other of the author's earlier works, and displayed itself most offensively in a certain fondness for the purely disgusting or repulsive, where the intention was or should have been merely the horrible. The writer evinced a strange propensity for minute details of human and brute suffering, and even indulged at times in more unequivocal obscenities. His English, too, was, in his efforts, exceedingly objectionable—verbose, involute, and not unfrequently ungrammatical. He was especially given to pet words, of which we remember at present only *"hug," "coil,"* and the compound *"old-time,"* and introduced them upon all occasions. Neither was he at this period particularly dexterous in the conduct of his stories. His improvement, however, was rapid at all these points, although, on the two first counts of our indictment, there is still abundant room for improvement. But whatever may have been his early defects, or whatever are his present errors, there can be no doubt that from the very beginning he gave evidence of genius, and that of no common order. His "Martin Faber," in our opinion, is a more forcible story than its supposed prototype "Miserrimus." The difference in the American reception of the two is to be referred to the fact (we blush while recording it), that "Miserrimus" was understood to be the work of an Englishman, and "Martin Faber" was known to be the composition of an American as yet unaccredited in our Republic of Letters. The fiction of Mr. Simms gave indication, we repeat, of genius, and that of no common order. Had he been even a Yankee, this genius would have been rendered *immediately* manifest to his countrymen, but unhappily (*perhaps*) he was a southerner, and united the southern pride—the southern dislike to the making of bargains—with the southern supineness and general want of tact in all matters relating to the making of money. His book, therefore, depended entirely upon its own intrinsic value and resources, but with these it made its way in the end. The "intrinsic value" consisted first of a very vigorous imagination in the conception of the story; secondly, in artistic skill manifested in its conduct; thirdly, in general vigour, life, movement— the whole resulting in deep interest on the part of the reader. These high qualities Mr. Simms has carried with him in his subsequent books; and they are qualities which, above all others, the fresh and vigorous intellect of America should and does esteem. It may be said, upon the whole, that while there are several of our native writers who excel the author of "Martin Faber" at particular *points*, there is, nevertheless, not one who surpasses him in the aggregate of the higher excellences of fiction. We confidently expect him to do much for the lighter literature of his country.

The volume now before us has a title which may mislead the reader. "The Wigwam and the Cabin" is merely a generic phrase, intended to designate the subject matter of a series of short tales, most of which have first seen the light in the Annuals. "The material employed," says the author, " will be found to illustrate in large degree, the border history of the south. I can speak with confidence of the general truthfulness of its treatment. The life of the planter, the squatter, the Indian, the negro, the bold and hardy pioneer, and the vigorous yeoman—these are the subjects. In their delineation I have mostly drawn from living portraits, and, in frequent instances, from actual scenes and circumstances within the memories of men."

All the tales in this collection have merit, and the first has merit of a very peculiar kind. "Grayling, or Murder will Out," is the title. The story was well received in England, but on this fact no opinion can be safely based. "The Athenæum," we believe, or some other of the London weekly critical journals, having its attention called (no doubt through personal influence) to Carey & Hart's beautiful annual "The Gift," found it convenient, in the course of its notice, to speak at length of some one particular article, and "Murder Will Out" probably arrested the attention of the sub-sub-editor who was employed in so trivial a task as the patting on the head an American book—arrested his attention first from its title, (murder being a taking theme with a cockney,) and secondly, from its details of southern forest scenery. Large quotations were made, as a matter of course, and very ample commendation bestowed—the whole criticism proving nothing, in our opinion, but that the critic had not read a single syllable of the story. The *critique*, however, had at least the good effect of calling American attention to the fact that an American might possibly do a decent thing, (provided the possibility were first admitted by the British sub-editors,) and the result was first, that many persons read, and secondly, that all persons admired the "excellent story in 'The Gift' that had actually been called 'readable' by one of the English newspapers."

Now had "Murder Will Out" been a much worse story than was ever written by Professor Ingraham, still, under the circumstances, we patriotic and independent Americans would have declared it inimitable; but, by some species of odd accident, it happened to deserve all that the British sub-sub had condescended to say of it, on the strength of a guess as to what it was all about. It is really an admirable tale, nobly conceived and skilfully carried into execution—the best ghost story ever written *by an American*—for we presume that this is the ultimate extent of commendation to which we, as an humble American, dare go.

The other stories of the volume do credit to the author's abilities, and display their peculiarities in a strong light, but there is no one of them so good as "Murder Will Out."

Godey's Lady's Book, January 1846

Elizabeth Oakes Smith

The Poetical Writings of Elizabeth Oakes Smith. First complete edition. New York. J. S. Redfield.

THIS IS a very pretty little volume, neatly printed, handsomely bound, embracing some two hundred pages sixteen mo., and introduced to the public, somewhat unnecessarily, in a preface by Dr. Rufus W. Griswold. In this preface we find some few memoranda of the personal authoress, with some critical opinions in regard to her poems. The memoranda are meagre. A much more interesting account of Mrs. Smith is given by Mr. John Neal, and was included by Mr. John Keese in the introduction to a former collection of her works. The critical opinions may as well be here quoted, at least in part. Dr. Griswold says—

"Seeking expression, yet shrinking from notoriety, and with a full share of that respect for a just fame and appreciation which belongs to every high-toned mind, yet oppressed by its shadow when circumstance is the impelling motive of publication, the writings of Mrs. Smith might well be supposed to betray great inequality; still in her many contributions to the magazines, it is remarkable how few of her pieces display the usual carelessness and haste of magazine articles. As an essayist especially, while graceful and lively, she is compact and vigorous; while through poems, essays, tales and criticisms, (for her industrious pen seems equally skilful and happy in each of these departments of literature,) through all her manifold writings, indeed, there runs the same beautiful vein of philosophy, viz:—that truth and goodness of themselves impart a holy light to the mind which gives it a power far above mere intellectuality; that the highest order of human intelligence springs from the moral and not the reasoning faculties. . . . . . Mrs. Smith's most popular poem is 'The Acorn,' which, though inferior in high inspiration to 'The Sinless Child,' is by many preferred for its happy play of fancy and proper finish. Her sonnets, of which she has written many, have not yet been as much admired as the 'April Rain,' 'The Brook,' and other fugitive pieces, which we find in many popular collections."

"The Sinless Child" was originally published in the "Southern Literary Messenger," where it at once attracted much attention from the novelty of its conception and the general grace and purity of its style. Undoubtedly it is one of the most original of American poems—surpassed in this respect, we think, only by Maria del Occidente's "Bride of Seven." Of course, we speak merely of long poems. We have had in this country many brief fugitive pieces far excelling in this most important point (originality) either "The Bride of Seven" or "The Sinless Child"—far excelling, indeed, any transatlantic poems. After all, it is chiefly in works of what is absurdly termed "sustained effort" that we fall in any material respect behind our progenitors.

"The Sinless Child" is quite long, including more than two hundred stanzas, generally of eight lines. The metre throughout is iambic tetrameter, alternating with trimeter—in other words, lines of four iambuses alternate with lines of three. The variations from this order are rare. The design of the poem is very imperfectly made out. The conception is much better than the execution. "A simple cottage maiden, Eva, given to the world in the widowhood of one parent and the angelic existence of the other, ... is found from her birth to be as meek and gentle as are those pale flowers that look imploringly upon us . . . . . She is gifted with the power of interpreting the beautiful mysteries of our earth . . . . . For her the song of the bird is not merely the gushing forth of a nature too full of blessedness to be silent . . . . the humblest plant, the simplest insect is each alive with truth . . . She sees the world not merely with mortal eyes, but looks within to the pure internal life of which the outward is but a type," etc., etc. These passages are taken from the Argument prefixed to Part I. The general thesis of the poetess may, perhaps, be stated as the demonstration that the superior wisdom is moral rather than intellectual; but it may be doubted whether her subject was ever precisely apparent to herself. In a word, she seems to have vacillated between several conceptions—the only very definitive idea being that of extreme beauty and purity in a child. At one time we fancy her, for example, attempting to show that the condition of absolute sanctity is one through which mortality may know all things and hold converse with the angels; at another we suppose it her purpose to "create" (in critical language) an entirely novel being, a something that is neither angel nor mortal, nor yet fairy in the ordinary sense—in a word, an original *ens*. Besides these two prominent fancies, however, there are various others which seem continually flitting in and out of the poet's vision, so that her whole work has an indeterminate air. Of this she apparently becomes conscious towards the conclusion, and in the final stanza endeavours to remedy the difficulty by summing up her design—

> "The sinless child, with mission high,
>   Awhile to earth was given,
> To show us that our world should be
>   The vestibule of heaven.
> Did we but in the holy light
>   Of truth and goodness rise,
> We might communion hold with God
>   And spirits from the skies."

The conduct of the narrative is scarcely more determinate—if, indeed, "The Sinless Child" can be said to include a narrative at all. The poem is occupied in its first part with a description of the child, her saintly character, her lone wanderings, the lessons she deduces from all animal and vegetable things, and her communings with the angels. We have then discussions with her mother, who is made to introduce episodical tales, one of "Old Richard," another called "The Defrauded Heart," (a tale of a miser,) and another entitled "The Stepmother." Towards the end of the poem a lover, Alfred Linne, is brought upon the scene. He has been reckless and sinful, but is reclaimed by the heavenly nature of Eva. He finds her sleeping in a forest. At this point occur some of the finest and most characteristic passages of the poem.

> "Unwonted thought, unwonted calm
>   Upon his spirit fell;
> For he unwittingly had sought
>   Young Eva's hallowed dell,
> And breathed that atmosphere of love,
>   Around her path that grew;

That evil from her steps repelled
The good unto her drew."

Mem.—The last quatrain of this stanza would have been
more readily comprehended if punctuated and written thus—

"And breathed that atmosphere of love
Around her path that grew—
That evil from her steps repelled—
That good unto her drew."

We may as well observe here, too, that although neatly
printed, the volume abounds in typographical errors that very
frequently mar the sense—as at page 66, for example, where
come (near the bottom) is improperly used for *came*, and
scorching (second line from the top) is substituted for *searching*. We proceed with Alfred's discovery of Eva in the wood.

"Now Eva opes her child-like eyes
And lifts her tranquil head;
And Albert, like a guilty thing,
Had from her presence fled.
But Eva marked his troubled brow,
His sad and thoughtful eyes,
As if they sought yet shrank to hold
Their converse with the skies."

Communion with the skies—would have been far better. It
seems strange to us that any one should have overlooked the
word.

"And all her kindly nature stirred,
She prayed him to remain;
Well conscious that the pure have power,
To balm much human pain.
There mingled too, as in a dream,
About brave Albert Linne,
A real and ideal form,
Her soul had formed within."

We give the punctuation here as we find it;—it is incorrect
throughout, interfering materially with a proper understanding of the passage. There should be a comma after "And" in
the first line, a comma in place of the semicolon at the end of
the second line, no point at the end of the third line, a comma

after "mingled," and none after "form." These seeming *minu-tiæ* are of real importance; but we refer to them, in the case of "The Sinless Child," because here the aggregate of this species of minor error is unusually remarkable. Of course it is the proof-reader or editor, and not Mrs. Smith, who is to blame.

"Her trusting hand fair Eva laid
    In that of Albert Linne,
And for one trembling moment turned
    Her gentle thoughts within.
Deep tenderness was in the glance
    That rested on his face,
As if her woman-heart had found
    Its own abiding-place.

"And evermore to him it seemed
    Her voice more liquid grew—
'Dear youth, thy soul and mine are one;
    One source their being drew!
And they must mingle everymore—
    Thy thoughts of love and me
Will, as a light, thy footsteps guide
    To life and mystery.'

"There was a sadness in her tone,
    But love unfathomed deep;
As from the centre of the soul
    Where the divine may sleep;
Prophetic was the tone and look,
    And Albert's noble heart
Sank with a strange foreboding dread
    Lest Eva should depart.

"And when she bent her timid eyes
    As she beside him knelt,
The pressure of her sinless lips
    Upon his brow he felt,
And all of earth and all of sin
    Fled from her sainted side;
She, the pure virgin of the soul,
    Ordained young Albert's bride."

It would, perhaps, have been out of keeping with the more obvious plan of the poem to make Eva really the bride of Albert. She does not wed him, but dies tranquilly in bed, soon after the spiritual union in the forest, "Eva," says the Argument of Part VII, "hath fulfilled her destiny. Material things can no farther minister to the growth of her spirit. That waking of the soul to its own deep mysteries—its oneness with another—has been accomplished. A human soul is perfected." At this point the poem may be said to have its conclusion.

In looking back at its general plan, we cannot fail to see traces of high poetic capacity. The first point to be commended is the reach or aim of the poetess. She is evidently discontented with the bald routine of common-place themes, and originality has been with her a principal object. In *all* cases of fictitious composition it should be the *first* object—by which we do not mean to say that it can ever be considered as the most important. But, *ceteris paribus*, every class of fiction is the better for originality; every writer is false to his own interest if he fails to avail himself, at the outset, of the effect which is certainly and invariably derivable from the great element, *novelty*.

The execution of "The Sinless Child" is, as we have already said, inferior to its conception—that is, to its conception as it floated, rather than steadily existed, in the brain of the authoress. She enables us to see that she has very *narrowly missed* one of those happy "creations" which now and then immortalize the poet. With a good deal more of deliberate thought before putting pen to paper, with a good deal more of the constructive ability, and with more rigorous discipline in the minor merits of style, and of what is termed in the school-prospectuses, composition, Mrs. Smith would have made of "The Sinless Child" one of the best, if not the very best of American poems. While speaking of the execution, or, more properly, the conduct of the work, we may as well mention, first, the obviousness with which the stories introduced by Eva's mother are interpolated, or episodical; it is permitted every reader to see that they have no natural connection with the true theme; and, indeed, there can be no doubt that they were written long before the main narrative was projected. In the second place, we must allude to the artificiality of the *Ar-*

guments, or introductory prose passages, prefacing each Part of the poem. Mrs. Smith had no sounder reason for employing them than Milton and the rest of the epicists have employed them before. If it be said that they are necessary for the proper comprehension of a poem, we reply that this is saying nothing for *them*, but merely much against the poem which demands them as a necessity. Every work of art should contain within itself all that is required for its own comprehension. An "argument" is but another form of the "This is an ox" subjoined to the portrait of an animal with horns. But in making these objections to the management of "The Sinless Child," we must not be understood as insisting upon them as at all material, in view of the lofty merit of originality—a merit which pervades and invigorates the whole work, and which, in our opinion, at least, is far, very far more than sufficient to compensate for every inartisticality of construction. A work of art may be admirably constructed, and yet be null as regards every essentiality of that truest art which is but the happiest development of nature; but no work of art can embody within itself a proper *originality* without giving the plainest manifestations of the creative spirit, or, in more common parlance, of *genius* in its author. The originality of "The Sinless Child" would cover a multitude of greater defects than Mrs. Smith ever committed, and must forever entitle it to the admiration and respect of every competent critic.

As regards detached passages, we think that the episode of "The Stepmother" may be fairly cited as the best in the poem.

"You speak of Hobert's second wife, a lofty dame and bold;
  I like not her forbidding air, and forehead high and cold.
  The orphans have no cause for grief: she dare not give it now,
  Though nothing but a ghostly fear her heart of pride could bow.

"One night the boy his mother called; they heard him
        weeping say,
  'Sweet Mother, kiss poor Eddy's cheek and wipe his tears
    away.'
  Red grew the lady's brow with rage, and yet she feels a
    strife
  Of anger and of terror, too, at thought of that dead wife.

"Wild roars the wind; the lights burn blue; the watchdog
    howls with fear;
Loud neighs the steed from out the stall. What form is
    gliding near?
No latch is raised, no step is heard, but a phantom fills the
    space—
A sheeted spectre from the dead, with cold and leaden face.

"What boots it that no other eye beheld the shade appear?
The guilty lady's guilty soul beheld it plain and clear.
It slowly glides within the room and sadly looks around,
And, stooping, kissed her daughter's cheek with lips that
    gave no sound.

"Then softly on the step-dame's arm she laid a death-cold
    hand,
Yet it hath scorched within the flesh like to a burning
    brand;
And gliding on with noiseless foot, o'er winding stair and
    hall,
She nears the chamber where is heard her infant's trem-
    bling call.

"She smoothed the pillow where he lay, she warmly tucked
    the bed,
She wiped his tears and stroked the curls that clustered
    round his head.
The child, caressed, unknowing fear, hath nestled him to rest;
The mother folds her wings beside—the mother from the
    blest!"

The metre of this episode has been altered from its original
form, and, we think, improved by the alteration. Formerly, in
place of four lines of seven iambuses, the stanza consisted of
eight lines—a line of four iambuses alternating with one of
three—a more ordinary and artificial, therefore a less desirable arrangement. In the three last quatrains there is an awkward vacillation between the present and perfect tenses, as
in the words "beheld," "glides," "kissed," "laid," "hath
scorched," "smoothed," "wiped," "hath nestled," "folds."
These petty objections, of course, will by no means interfere

with the reader's appreciation of the episode, with his admiration of its pathos, its delicacy and its grace—we had almost forgotten to say of its pure and high imagination.

We proceed to cull from "The Sinless Child," a few brief but happy passages at random.

> "Gentle she was and full of love,
>   With voice exceeding sweet,
> *And eyes of dove-like tenderness*
>   *Where joy and sadness meet.*"

> "——with calm and tranquil eye
>   *That turned instinctively to seek*
> *The blueness of the sky.*"

> "*Bright missals from angelic throngs*
>   *In every bye-way left*—
> *How were the earth of glory shorn*
>   *Were it of flowers bereft!*"

> "And wheresoe'er the weary heart
>   Turns in its dim despair,
> *The meek-eyed blossom upward looks,*
>   *Inviting it to prayer.*"

> "The very winds were hushed to peace
>   Within the quiet dell,
> *Or murmured through the rustling bough*
>   *Like breathings of a shell.*"

> "The mystery of life;
>   Its many hopes, its many fears,
>   Its sorrow and its strife—
> A spirit to behold in all
>   To guide, admonish, cheer—
> *Forever, in all time and place,*
>   *To feel an angel near.*"

———

"I may not scorn the spirit's rights,
    For I have seen it rise,
All written o'er with thought, thought, thought,
    As with a thousand eyes!"

———

"And there are things that blight the soul
    As with a mildew blight,
And in the temple of the Lord
    Put out the blessed light."

It is in the *point* of passages such as these, in their vigour, terseness and novelty, combined with exquisite delicacy, that the more obvious merit of the poem consists. A thousand such *quotable* paragraphs are interspersed through the work, and of themselves would be sufficient to insure its popularity. But we repeat that a far loftier excellence lies *perdu* amid the minor deficiencies of "The Sinless Child."

The other poems of the volume are, as entire compositions, nearer perfection, but, in general, have less of the true poetical element. "The Acorn" is perfect as regards its construction—although, to be sure, the design is so simple that it could scarcely be marred in its execution. The idea is the old one of detailing the progress of a plant from its germ to its maturity, with the uses and general vicissitudes to which it is subjected. In this case of the acorn the vicissitudes are well imagined, and the execution is more skilfully managed—is more definite, vigorous and pronounced, than in the longer poem. The chief of the minor objections is to the rhythm, which is imperfect, vacillating awkwardly between iambuses and anapæsts, after such fashion that it is impossible to decide whether the rhythm in itself—that is, whether the general intention is anapæstical or iambic. Anapæsts introduced, for the relief of monotone, into an iambic rhythm, are not only admissible but commendable, if not absolutely demanded; but in this case they prevail to such an extent as to overpower the iambic intention, thus rendering the whole versification difficult of comprehension. We give, by way of example, a stanza with the scanning divisions and quantities—

> "They came | with gifts | that should life | bestow; |
>   The dew | and the li | ving air— |
> The bane | that should work | its dead | ly wo, |
>   The lit | tle men | had there; |
> In the gray | moss cup | was the mil | dew brought, |
>   The worm | in a rose- | leaf rolled, |
> And ma | ny things | with destruc | tion fraught |
>   That its doom | were quick | ly told." |

Here iambuses and anapæsts are so nearly balanced that the ear hesitates to receive the rhythm as either anapæstic or iambic—that is, it hesitates to receive it as anything at all. A rhythm should always be distinctly marked by its first foot—that is to say, if the design is iambic, we should commence with an unmistakeable iambus, and proceed with this foot until the ear gets fairly accustomed to it before we attempt variation; for which, indeed, there is no *necessity* unless for the relief of monotone. When the rhythm is in this manner thoroughly recognized, we may sparingly vary with anapæsts (or, if the rhythm be trochaic, with dactyls). Spondees, still more sparingly, as absolute discords, may be also introduced either in an iambic or trochaic rhythm. In common with a very large majority of American, and, indeed, of European poets, Mrs. Smith seems to be totally unacquainted with the principles of versification—by which, of course, we mean its *rationale*. Of technical *rules* on the subject there are rather more than enough in our prosodies, and from these abundant rules are deduced the abundant blunders of our poets. There is not a prosody in existence which is worth the paper on which it is printed.

Of the miscellaneous poems included in the volume before us, we greatly prefer "The Summons Answered." It has more of *power*, more of genuine imagination than anything written by its author. It is a story of three "bacchanals," who, on their way from the scene of their revelry, are arrested by the beckoning of a white hand from the partially unclosing door of a tomb. One of the party obeys the summons. It is the tomb of his wife. We quote the two concluding stanzas.

> "This restless life with its little fears,
>   Its hopes that fade so soon,
> With its yearning tenderness and tears,

· And the burning agony that sears—
  The sun gone down at noon—
The spirit crushed to its prison wall,
  Mindless of all beside—
This young Richard saw, and felt it all—
  Well might the dead abide!

"The crimson light in the east is high,
  The hoar-frost coldly gleams,
And Richard chilled to the heart well-nigh,
Hath raised his wildered and bloodshot eye
  From that long night of dreams.
He shudders to think of the reckless band
  And the fearful oath he swore—
*But most he thinks of the clay-cold hand
That opened the old tomb door.*"

With the quotation of these really noble passages—noble, because full of the truest poetic energy—we take leave of the fair authoress. She is entitled, beyond doubt, to all, and perhaps to much more than the commendation she has received. Her faults are among the peccadilloes, and her merits among the sterling excellencies of the muse.

Godey's Lady's Book, December 1845

Seba Smith

Powhatan; a Metrical Romance, in Seven Cantos. By Seba Smith. New York: Harper and Brothers.

WHAT FEW NOTICES we have seen of this poem, speak of it as the production of *Mrs.* Seba Smith. To be sure, gentlemen may be behind the scenes, and know more about the matter than we do. They may have some private reason for understanding that black is white—some reason into which we, personally, are not initiated. But, to ordinary perception, "Powhatan" is the composition of Seba Smith, *Esquire*, of Jack Downing memory, and *not* of his wife. *Seba Smith* is the name upon the title-page; and the personal pronoun which supplies the place of this well-known prænomen and cognomen in the preface, is, we are constrained to say, of the masculine gender. "The author of Powhatan,"—thus, for example, runs a portion of the prolegomena—"does not presume to claim for *his* production the merit of good and genuine poetry, nor does *he* pretend to assign it a place in the classes or forms into which poetry is divided"—in all which, by the way, he is decidedly right. But can it be that no gentleman has *read* even so far as the Preface of the book? Can it be that the critics have had no curiosity to creep into the *adyta*—into the inner mysteries of this temple? If so, they are decidedly right too.

"Powhatan" is handsomely bound. Its printing is clear beyond comparison. Its paper is magnificent, and we undertake to say (for *we have* read it through with the greatest attention) that there is not a single typographical error in it, from one end to the other. Further than this, in the way of commendation, no man with both brains and conscience should proceed. In truth, a more absurdly *flat* affair—for flat is the only epithet which applies in this case—was never before paraded to the world, with so grotesque an air of bombast and assumption.

To give some idea of the *tout ensemble* of the book—we have first a Dedication to the "Young People of the United States," in which Mr. Jack Downing lives, in "the hope that he may do some good in his day and generation, by adding something to the sources of rational enjoyment and *mental culture.*" Next, we have a Preface, occupying four pages, in which, quoting his publishers, the author tells us that poetry is a "very great bore, and won't sell"—a thing which cannot be denied in certain cases, but which Mr. Downing denies in his own. "It may be true," he says, "of endless masses of words, that are poured forth from the press, under the *name* of poetry"—but it is not true "of *genuine* poetry—of that which is worthy of the name"—in short, we presume he means to say it is not in the least little bit true of "Powhatan;" with regard to whose merits he wishes to be tried, not by the critics (we fear, in fact, that here it is the critics who will be tried), "but by the *common* taste of *common* readers"—all which ideas are common enough, to say no more.

We have next, a "Sketch of the Character of Powhatan," which is exceedingly interesting and commendable, and which is taken from Burk's "History of Virginia:"—four pages more. Then comes a *Poem*—four pages more—forty-eight lines—twelve lines to a page—in which all that we can understand, is something about the name of "Powhatan"

> "Descending to a distant age,
> Embodied forth on the deathless page"

of the author—that is to say, of Jack Downing, Esquire. We have now, one after the other, CANTOS one, two, three, four, five, six, and seven—each subdivided into PARTS, by means of Roman numerals—some of these PARTS comprehending as many as six lines—upon the principle, we presume, of packing up precious commodities in small bundles. The volume then winds up with *Notes*, in proportion of three to one, as regards the amount of text, and taken, the most of them, from Burk's Virginia, as before.

It is very difficult to keep one's countenance when reviewing such a *work* as this; but we will do our best, for the truth's sake, and put on as serious a face as the case will admit.

The leading fault of "Powhatan," then, is precisely what its author supposes to be its principal merit. "It would be difficult," he says, in that pitiable preface, in which he has so exposed himself, "to find a poem that embodies more truly the spirit of history, or indeed that follows out more faithfully many of its details." It would, indeed; and we are very sorry to say it. The truth is, Mr. Downing has never dreamed of any artistic *arrangement* of his facts. He has gone straight forward, like a blind horse, and turned neither to the one side nor to the other, for fear of stumbling. But he gets them all in—every one of them—the facts we mean. Powhatan never did anything in his life, we are sure, that Mr. Downing has not got in his poem. He begins at the beginning, and goes on steadily to the end—painting away at his story, just as a sign-painter at a sign; beginning at the left hand side of his board, and plastering through to the right. But he has omitted one very ingenious trick of the sign-painter. He has forgotten to write under his portrait—*"this is a pig,"* and thus there is some danger of mistaking it for an opossum.

But we are growing scurrilous, in spite of our promise, and must put on a sober visage once more. It *is* a hard thing, however, when we have to read and write about such doggrel as this:

> "But bravely to the river's brink
>   I led my warrior train,
>   And face to face, each glance they sent,
>   We sent it back again.
>   *Their werowance looked stern at me,*
>   *And I looked stern at him,*
>   And all my warriors clasped their bows,
>   And nerved each heart and limb.
>   I raised my heavy war-club high,
>   And swung it fiercely round,
>   And shook it towards the shallop's side,
>   Then laid it on the ground.
>   And then the lighted calumet
>   I offered to their view,
>   And thrice I drew the sacred smoke,
>   And toward the shallop blew,
>   And as the curling vapour rose
>   Soft as a spirit prayer,
>   I saw the pale-face leader wave
>   A white flag in the air.
>   Then launching out their painted skiff

They boldly came to land,
And spoke us many a kindly word,
And took us by the hand,
Presenting rich and shining gifts,
Of copper, brass, and beads,
To show that they were men like us,
And prone to generous deeds.
We held a long and friendly talk,
Inquiring whence they came,
And who the leader of their band,
And what their country's name,
And how their mighty shallop moved
Across the boundless sea,
And why they touched our great king's land
Without his liber*ty*."

It won't do. We cannot sing to this tune any longer. We greatly prefer,

"John Gilpin was a gentleman
Of credit and renown,
A train-band captain eke was he
Of famous London town."

Or—

"Old Grimes is dead, that good old man,
We ne'er shall see him more,
He used to wear an over-coat
All buttoned down before"—

or lines to that effect—we wish we could remember the words. The part, however, about

"Their werowance look'd stern at me,
And I looked stern at him"—

is not quite *original* with Mr. Downing—is it? We merely ask for information. Have we not heard something about

"An old crow sitting on a hickory limb,
Who winked at me, and I winked at him."

The simple truth is, that Mr. Downing never committed a greater mistake in his life than when he fancied himself a poet, even in the ninety-ninth degree. We doubt whether he could distinctly state the difference between an epic and an epigram. And it will not do for him to appeal from the critic to *common* readers—because we assure him his book is a very *un*common book. We never saw any one so uncommonly bad—nor one about whose parturition so uncommon a fuss has been made, so little to the satisfaction of common sense. Your poem is a curiosity, Mr. Jack Downing; your "Metrical Romance" is not worth a single half sheet of the paste-board upon which it is printed. This is our humble and honest opinion; and, although honest opinions are not very plentiful just now, you can have ours at what it is worth. But we wish, before parting, to ask you one question. What *do* you mean by that motto from Sir Philip Sidney, upon the title-page? "He cometh to you with a tale that holdeth children from play, and old men from the chimney-corner." What do you mean by it, we say. Either you cannot intend to apply it to the *"tale"* of Powhatan, or else all the "old men" in your particular neighbourhood must be *very* old men; and all the "little children" a set of dunder-headed little ignoramuses.

Graham's Magazine, July 1841

John L. Stephens

Incidents of Travel in Egypt, Arabia Petræa, and the Holy Land. By an American. New-York, Harper & Brothers. 1837. 2 vols. 12mo.

MR. STEPHENS has here given us two volumes of more than ordinary interest—written with a freshness of manner, and evincing a manliness of feeling, both worthy of high consideration. Although in some respects deficient, the work too presents some points of moment to the geographer, to the antiquarian, and more especially to the theologian. Viewed only as one of a class of writings whose direct tendency is to throw light upon the Book of Books, it has strong claims upon the attention of all who read. While the vast importance of critical and philological research in dissipating the obscurities and determining the exact sense of the Scriptures, cannot be too readily conceded, it may be doubted whether the collateral illustration derivable from records of travel be not deserving at least equal consideration. Certainly, the evidence thus afforded, exerting an enkindling influence upon the popular imagination, and so taking palpable hold upon the popular understanding, will not fail to become in time a most powerful because easily available instrument in the downfall of unbelief. Infidelity itself has often afforded unwilling and unwitting testimony to the truth. It is surprising to find with what unintentional precision both Gibbon and Volney (among others) have used, for the purpose of *description*, in their accounts of nations and countries, the identical phraseology employed by the inspired writers when foretelling the most improbable events. In this manner scepticism has been made the root of belief, and the providence of the Deity has been no less remarkable in the extent and nature of the means for bringing to light the evidence of his accomplished word, than in working the accomplishment itself.

Of late days, the immense stores of biblical elucidation derivable from the East have been rapidly accumulating in the hands of the student. When the "Observations" of Harmer were given to the public, he had access to few other works than the travels of Chardin, Pococke, Shaw, Maundrell, Pitts, and D'Arvieux, with perhaps those of Nau and Troilo, and Russell's "Natural History of Aleppo." We have now a vast accession to our knowledge of Oriental regions. Intelligent and observing men, impelled by the various motives of Christian zeal, military adventure, the love of gain, and the love of science, have made their way, often at imminent risk, into every land rendered holy by the words of revelation. Through the medium of the pencil, as well as of the pen, we are even familiarly acquainted with the territories of the Bible. Valuable books of eastern travel are abundant—of which the labours of Niebuhr, Mariti, Volney, Porter, Clarke, Chateaubriand, Burckhardt, Buckingham, Morier, Seetzen, De Lamartine, Laborde, Tournefort, Madden, Maddox, Wilkinson, Arundell, Mangles, Leigh and Hogg, besides those already mentioned, are merely the principal, or the most extensively known. As we have said, however, the work before us is not to be lightly regarded: highly agreeable, interesting, and instructive, in a general view, it also has, in the connexion now adverted to, claims to public attention possessed by no other book of its kind.

In an article prepared for this journal some months ago, we had traced the route of Mr. Stephens with a degree of minuteness not desirable now, when the work has been so long in the hands of the public. At this late day we must be content with saying, briefly, in regard to the earlier portion of the narrative, that, arriving at Alexandria in December, 1835, he thence passed up the Nile as far as the Lower Cataracts. One or two passages from this part of the tour may still be noted for observation. The annexed speculations, in regard to the present city of Alexandria, are well worth attention.

"The present city of Alexandria, even after the dreadful ravages made by the plague last year, is still supposed to contain more than 50,000 inhabitants, and is decidedly growing. It stands outside the Delta in the Libyan Desert, and, as Volney remarks, 'It is only by the canal which conducts the waters of the Nile into the reservoirs in the time of inundation, that Alexandria can be considered as connected with Egypt.' Founded by the great Alexander, to secure his conquests in the East, being the only safe harbour along the coast of Syria or Africa, and possessing peculiar commercial advantages, it soon grew into a giant city. Fifteen miles in circumference, containing a population of 300,000 citizens and as many slaves, one magnificent street 2000 feet broad ran the whole length of the city, from the Gate of the Sea to the Canopie Gate, commanding a view, at each end, of the shipping, either in the Mediterranean or in the Mareotic Lake, and another of equal length intersected it at right angles; a spacious circus without the Canopie Gate, for chariot-races, and on the east a splendid gymnasium, more than six hundred feet in length, with theatres, baths, and all that could make it a desirable residence for a luxurious people. When it fell into the hands of the Saracens, according to the report of the Saracen general to the Calif Omar, 'it was impossible to enumerate the variety of its riches and beauties;' and it is said to 'have contained four thousand palaces, four thousand baths, four hundred theatres or public edifices, twelve thousand shops, and forty thousand tributary Jews.' From that time, like every thing else which falls in the hands of the Mussulman, it has been going to ruin, and the discovery of the passage to India by the Cape of Good Hope gave the death-blow to its commercial greatness. At present it stands a phenomenon in the history of a Turkish dominion. It appears once more to be raising its head from the dust. It remains to be seen whether this rise is the legitimate and permanent effect of a wise and politic government, combined with natural advantages, or whether the pacha is not forcing it to an unnatural elevation, at the expense, if not upon the ruins, of the rest of Egypt. It is almost presumptuous, on the threshold of my entrance into Egypt, to speculate upon the future condition of this interesting country; but it is clear that the pacha is determined to build up the city of Alexandria if he can: his fleet is here, his army, his arsenal, and his forts are here; and he has forced and centred here a commerce that was before divided between several places. Rosetta has lost more than two thirds of its population. Damietta has become a mere nothing, and even Cairo the Grand has become tributary to what is called the regenerated city." *Vol.* I. pp. 21, 22.

We see no presumption in this attempt to speculate upon the future condition of Egypt. Its destinies are matter for the attentive consideration of every reader of the Bible. No words can be more definitive, more utterly free from ambiguity, than the prophecies concerning this region. No events could be more wonderful in their nature, nor more impossible to have been foreseen by the eye of man, than the events foretold concerning it. With the earliest ages of the world its line of monarchs began, and the annihilation of the entire dynasty was predicted during the zenith of that dynasty's power. One of the most lucid of the biblical commentators has justly observed that the very attempt once made by infidels to show, from the recorded number of its monarchs and the duration of their reigns, that Egypt was a kingdom previous to the Mosaic era of the deluge, places in the most striking view the extraordinary character of the prophecies regarding it. During two thousand years prior to these predictions Egypt had never been without a prince of its own; and how oppressive was its tyranny over Judea and the neighbouring nations! It, however, was distinctly foretold that this country of kings should no longer have one of its own—that it should be laid waste by the hand of strangers—that it should be a base kingdom, the basest of the base—that it should *never* again exalt itself among the nations—that it should be a desolation surrounded by desolation. Two thousand years have now afforded their testimony to the infallibility of the Divine word, and the evidence is still accumulative. "Its past and present degeneracy bears not a more remote resemblance to the former greatness and pride of its power, than the frailty of its mud-walled fabrics now bears to the stability of its imperishable pyramids." But it should be remembered that there are other prophecies concerning it which still await their fulfilment. "The whole earth shall rejoice, and Egypt *shall not be for ever base*. The Lord shall smite Egypt; he shall smite and heal it; and they shall return to the Lord, and he shall be entreated of them, and shall heal them. In that day shall Isaac be the third with Egypt and with Assyria, even a blessing in the midst of the land." Isa. xix. 19–25. In regard to the present degree of political power and importance to which the country has certainly arisen under Mohammed Aly, (an importance unknown for many centuries,) the fact, as Mr. Keith observes in his valuable Evidence of Prophecy, may possibly serve, at no distant period, to illustrate the prediction which implies, that, however base and degraded it might be throughout many generations, it would, notwithstanding, have strength sufficient to be looked to for aid or protection even at the time of the restoration of the Jews to Judea, who will seek "to strengthen themselves in the strength of Pharaoh, and trust in *the shadow of Egypt*." How emphatically her present feeble prosperity is, after all, but the *shadow* of the Egypt of the Pharaohs, we leave to the explorer of her pyramids, the wanderer among the tombs of her kings or the fragments of her Luxor and her Carnac.

At Djiddeh, formerly the capital of Upper Egypt and the largest town on the Nile, Mr. Stephens encountered two large boat-loads of slaves—probably five or six hundred—collected at Dongola and Sennaar. "In the East," he writes, "slavery exists now precisely as it did in the days of the patriarchs. The slave is received into the family of a Turk, in a relation more confidential and respectable than that of an ordinary domestic; and when liberated, which very often happens, stands upon the same footing with a freeman. The curse does not rest upon him for ever; he may sit at the same board, dip his hand in the same dish, and, if there are no other impediments, may marry his master's daughter."

Morier says, in his *Journey through Persia*—"The manners of the East, amid all the changes of government and religion, are *still the same*. They are living impressions from an original mould; and, at every step, some object, some idiom, some dress, or some custom of common life, reminds the traveller of ancient times, and confirms, above all, the beauty, the accuracy, and the propriety of the language and the history of the Bible."

Sir John Chardin, also, in the Preface to his *Travels in Persia*, employs similar language:—"And the learned, to whom I communicated my design, encouraged me very much by their commendations to proceed in it; and more especially when I informed them that it is not in Asia, as in our Europe, where there are frequent changes, more or less, in the form of things, as the habits, buildings, gardens, and the like. In the East they are constant in all things. The habits are at this day in the same manner as in the precedent ages; so that one may reasonably believe that, in that part of the world, the exterior forms of things (as their manners and customs) are the same now as they were two thousand years since, except in such changes as have been introduced by religion, which are, nevertheless, very inconsiderable."

Nor is such striking testimony unsupported. From all sources we derive evidence of the conformity, almost of the identity, of the modern with the ancient usages of the East. This steadfast resistance to innovation is a trait remarkably confined to the regions of biblical history, and (it should not be doubted) will remain in force until it shall have fulfilled all the important purposes of biblical elucidation. Hereafter, when the ends of Providence shall be thoroughly answered, it will not fail to give way before the influence of that very Word it has been instrumental in establishing; and the tide of civilization, which has hitherto flowed continuously, from the rising to the setting sun, will be driven back, with a partial ebb, into its original channels.

Returning from the Cataracts, Mr. Stephens found himself safely at Cairo, where terminated his journeyings upon the Nile. He had passed "from Migdol to Syene, even unto the borders of Ethiopia." In regard to the facilities, comforts, and minor enjoyments of the voyage, he speaks of them in a manner so favourable, that many of our young countrymen will be induced to follow his example. It is an amusement, he says, even ridiculously cheap, and attended with no degree of danger. A boat with ten men is procured for thirty or forty dollars a month, fowls for three piasters a pair, a sheep for a half or three quarters of a dollar, and eggs for the asking. "You sail under your own country's banner; and when you walk along the river, if the Arabs look particularly black and truculent, you proudly feel that there is safety in its folds."

We now approach what is by far the most interesting and the most important portion of his tour. Mr. S. had resolved to visit Mount Sinai, proceeding thence to the Holy Land. If he should return to Suez, and thus cross the desert to El Arich and Gaza, he would be subjected to a quarantine of fourteen days on account of the plague in Egypt; and this difficulty might be avoided by striking through the heart of the desert lying between Mount Sinai and the frontier of Palestine. This route was beset with danger; but, apart from the matter of avoiding quarantine, it had other strong temptations for the enterprise and enthusiasm of the traveller—temptations not to be resisted. "The route," says Mr. Stephens, "was hitherto untravelled," and moreover, it lay through a region upon which has long rested, and still rests, a remarkable curse of the Divinity, issued through the voices of his prophets. We allude to the land of Idumea—the Edom of the Scriptures. Some English friends, who first suggested this route to Mr. Stephens, referred him, for information concerning it, to Keith on the Prophecies. Mr. Keith, as our readers are aware, contends for the *literal* fulfilment of prophecy, and in the treatise in question brings forward a mass of evidence, and a world of argument, which we, at least, are constrained to consider, as a whole, irrefutable. We look upon the *literalness* of the understanding of the Bible predictions as an *essential* feature in prophecy—conceiving minuteness of detail to have been but a portion of the providential plan of the Deity for bringing more visibly to light, in after-ages, the *evidence* of the fulfilment of his word. No general meaning attached to a prediction, no general fulfilment of such prediction, could carry, to the reason of mankind, inferences so unquestionable, as its particular and minutely incidental accomplishment. General statements, except in rare instances, are susceptible of misinterpretation or misapplication: details admit no shadow of ambiguity. That, in many striking cases, the words of the prophets have been brought to pass in every particular of a series of minutiæ, whose very meaning was unintelligible before the period of fulfilment, is a truth that few are so utterly stubborn as to deny. We mean to say that, in *all* instances, the most strictly literal interpretation will apply. There is no doubt much unbelief founded upon the *obscurity* of the prophetic expression; and the question is frequently demanded—"wherein lies the use of this obscurity?—why are not the prophecies distinct?"—These words, it is said, are incoherent, unintelligible, and should be therefore regarded as untrue. That many prophecies are absolutely unintelligible should not be denied—it is a part of their essence that they should be. The obscurity, like the apparently irrelevant detail, has its object in the providence of God. Were the words of inspiration, affording insight into the events of futurity, *at all times* so pointedly clear that he who runs might read, they would in many cases, even when fulfilled, afford a rational ground for unbelief in the inspiration of their authors, and consequently in the whole truth of revelation; for it would be supposed that these distinct words, exciting union and emulation among Christians, had thus been merely the means of working out their own accomplishment. It is for this reason that the most of the predictions become intelligible only when viewed from the proper point of observation—the period of fulfilment. Perceiving this, the philosophical thinker, and the Christian, will draw no argument from the obscurity, against the verity of prophecy. Having seen palpably, incontrovertibly fulfilled, even one of these many wonderful predictions, of whose meaning, until the day of accomplishment, he could form no conception; and having thoroughly satisfied himself that no human foresight could have been equal to such amount of foreknowledge, he will await, in confident expectation, that moment certainly to come when the darkness of the veil shall be uplifted from the others.*

*We cannot do better than quote here the words of a writer in the London Quarterly Review. "Twenty years ago we read certain portions of the prophetic Scriptures with a belief that they were true, because other similar passages had in the course of ages been proved to be so; and we had an indistinct notion that all these, to us obscure and indefinite denunciations, had been—we knew not very well when or how—accomplished; but to have graphic descriptions, ground plans, and elevations showing the actual existence of all the heretofore vague and shadowy denunciations of God against Edom, does, we confess, excite our feelings, and exalt our confidence in prophecy to a height that no external evidence has hitherto done."

Many prophecies, it should be remembered, are in a state of gradual fulfilment—a chain of evidence being thus made to extend throughout a long series of ages, for the benefit of man at large, without being confined to one epoch or generation, which would be the case in a fulfilment suddenly coming to pass. Thus, some portion of the prophecies concerning Edom has reference to the year of recompenses for the controversy of Sion.

One word in regard to the work of Keith. Since penning this article we have been grieved to see, in a New-York daily paper, some strictures on this well-known treatise, which we think unnecessary, if not positively unjust; and which, indeed, are little more than a revival of the old story trumped up

Having expressed our belief in the literal fulfilment of prophecy in *all* cases,* and having suggested, as one reason for the non-prevalence of this belief, the improper point of view from which we are accustomed to regard it, it remains to be seen what were the principal predictions in respect to Idumea.

"From generation to generation it shall lie waste; *none shall pass through it* for ever and ever. But the cormorant and the bittern shall possess it; the owl also and the raven shall dwell in it; and he shall stretch out upon it the line of confusion and the stones of emptiness. They shall call the nobles thereof to the kingdom, but none shall be there, and all her princes shall be nothing. And thorns shall come up in her palaces, nettles and brambles in the fortresses thereof; and it shall be a habitation for dragons and a court for owls. The wild beasts of the desert shall also meet with the wild beasts of the island, and the satyr shall cry to his fellow; the screech-owl also shall rest there, and find for herself a place of rest. There shall the great owl make her nest, and lay and hatch, and gather under her shadow; there shall the vultures also be gathered, every

---

for purposes of its own, and in the most bitter spirit of unfairness, by the London Quarterly Review. We allude especially to the charge of plagiarism from the work of Bishop Newton. It would be quite as reasonable to accuse Dr. Webster of having stolen his Dictionary from Dr. Johnson, or any other compiler of having plundered any other. But the work of Keith, as we learn from himself, was written hastily, for the immediate service, and at the urgent solicitation, of a friend, whose faith wavered in regard to the Evidences of Prophecy, and who applied to the author to aid his unbelief with a condensed view of these Evidences. In the preface of the book thus composed, with no view to any merits of authorship, and, indeed, with none except that of immediate utility, there is found the fullest disclaimer of all pretension to originality—surely motives and circumstances such as these should have sufficed to secure Dr. Keith from the unmeaning charges of plagiarism, which have been so pertinaciously adduced! We do not mean to deny that, in the blindness of his zeal, and in the firm conviction entertained by him of the general truth of his assumptions, he frequently adopted surmises as facts, and did essential injury to his cause by carrying out his positions to an unwarrantable length. With all its inaccuracies, however, his work must still be regarded as one of the most important triumphs of faith, and, beyond doubt, as a most lucid and conclusive train of argument.

*Of course it will be understood that a proper allowance must be made for the usual hyperbolical tendency of the language of the East.

one with her mate. Seek ye out of the Book of the Lord, and read; no one of these shall fail, none shall want her mate; for my mouth it hath commanded, and his spirit it hath gathered them. And he hath cast the lot for them, and his hand hath divided it unto them by line; they shall possess it for ever and ever, from generation to generation shall they dwell therein." Isaiah: xxxiv. 5, 10–17. "Thus will I make Mount Seir most desolate, and *cut off from it him that passeth out and him that returneth*." Ezekiel: xxxv. 7.

In regard to such of the passages here quoted as are not printed in Italics, we must be content with referring to the treatise of Keith already mentioned, wherein the evidences of the fulfilment of the predictions in their most minute particulars are gathered into one view. We may as well, however, present here the substance of his observations respecting the words—"none shall pass through it for ever and ever," and "thus I will make Mount Seir desolate, and cut off from it him that passeth out and him that returneth."

He says that Volney, Burckhardt, Joliffe, Henniker, and Captains Irby and Mangles, adduce a variety of circumstances, all conspiring to prove that Idumea, which was long resorted to from every quarter, is so beset on every side with dangers to the traveller, that literally *none pass through it*; that even the Arabs of the neighbouring regions, whose home is the desert, and whose occupation is wandering, are afraid to enter it, or to conduct any within its borders. He says, too, that amid all this manifold testimony to its truth, there is not, in any single instance, the most distant allusion to the prediction—that the evidence is unsuspicious and undesigned.

A Roman road passed directly through Idumea from Jerusalem to Akaba, and another from Akaba to Moab; and when these roads were made, at a time long posterior to the date of the predictions, the conception could not have been formed, or held credible by man, that the period would ever arrive when none should pass through it. Indeed, seven hundred years after the date of the prophecy, we are informed by Strabo that the roads were actually in use. The prediction is yet more surprising, he says, when viewed in conjunction with that which implies that travellers should *pass by* Idumea—"every one that goeth by shall be astonished." The routes of the pilgrims from Damascus, and from Cairo to Mecca, the one on the east and the other towards the south of Edom, along the whole of its extent, go by it, or touch partially on its borders, *without going through it*.

Not even, he says, the cases of Seetzen and Burckhardt can be urged against the literal fulfilment, although Seetzen actually *did* pass through Idumea, and Burckhardt traversed a considerable portion of it. The former died not long after the completion of his journey; and the latter never recovered from the effects of the hardships endured on the route—dying at Cairo. "Neither of them," we have given the precise words of Mr. Keith, "lived to return to Europe. *I will cut off from Mount Seir him that passeth out and him that returneth*. Strabo mentions that there was a direct road from Petra to Jericho, of three or four days' journey. Captains Irby and Mangles were eighteen days in reaching it from Jerusalem. They did not *pass through* Idumea, and they did return. Seetzen and Burckhardt did pass through it, and they did *not* return."

"The words of the prediction," he elsewhere observes, "might well be understood as merely implying that Idumea would cease to be a thoroughfare for the commerce of the nations which adjoined it, and that its highly-frequented marts would be forsaken as centres of intercourse and traffic; and easy would have been the task of demonstrating its truth in this limited sense which scepticism itself ought not to be unwilling to authorize."

Here is, no doubt, much inaccuracy and misunderstanding; and the exact boundaries of ancient Edom are, apparently, not borne in mind by the commentator. Idumea proper was, strictly speaking, only the mountainous tract of country east of the valley of El-Ghor. The Idumeans, if we rightly apprehend, did not get possession of any portion of the south of Judea till after the exile, and consequently until after the prophecies in question. They then advanced as far as Hebron, where they were arrested by the Maccabees. That "Seetzen actually did pass through Idumea," cannot therefore be asserted; and thus much is in favour of the whole argument of Dr. Keith, while in contradiction to a branch of that argument. The traveller in question (see his own Narrative), pursuing his route on the east of the Dead Sea, proceeded no farther in this direction than to Kerek, when he retraced his way—afterwards going from Hebron to Mount Sinai, over the desert eastward of Edom. Neither is it strictly correct that he "died not long after the completion of his journey." Several years afterwards he was actively employed in Egypt, and finally died; not from constitutional injury sustained from any former adventure, but, if we remember, from the effects of poison administered by his guide in a journey from Mocha into the heart of Arabia. We see no ground either for the statement that Burckhardt owed his death to hardships endured in Idumea. Having visited Petra, and crossed the western desert of Egypt in the year 1812, we find him, four years afterwards, sufficiently well, at Mount Sinai. He did not die until the close of 1817, and then of a diarrhœa brought about by the imprudent use of cold water.

But let us dismiss these and some other instances of misstatement. It should not be a matter of surprise that, perceiving, as he no doubt did, the *object* of the circumstantiality of prophecy, clearly seeing in how many wonderful cases its minutiæ had been fulfilled, and withal being thoroughly imbued with a love of truth, and with that zeal which is becoming in a Christian, Dr. Keith should have plunged somewhat hastily or blindly into these inquiries, and pushed to an improper extent the principle for which he contended. It should be observed that the passage cited just above in regard to Seetzen and Burckhardt, is given in a foot-note, and has the appearance of an after-thought, about whose propriety its author did not feel perfectly content. It is certainly very difficult to reconcile the literal fulfilment of the prophecy with an acknowledgment militating so violently against it as we find in his own words—"Seetzen actually *did pass through* Idumea, and Burckhardt *travelled through* a considerable portion of it." And what we are told subsequently in respect to Irby and Mangles, and Seetzen and Burckhardt—that these *did not* pass through Idumea, and *did* return, while those *did* pass through and *did not* return—where a passage from Ezekiel is brought to sustain collaterally a passage from Isaiah—is certainly not in the spirit of literal investigation; partaking, indeed, somewhat of *equivoque*.

But in regard to the possibility of the actual passage through Edom, we might now consider all ambiguity at an end, could we suffer ourselves to adopt the opinion of Mr. Stephens, that he himself had at length traversed the disputed region. What we have said already, however, respecting the proper boundaries of that Idumea to which the prophecies have allusion, will assure the reader that we cannot entertain this idea. It will be clearly seen that he did not *pass through* the Edom of Ezekiel. That he might have done so, however, is sufficiently evident. The indomitable perseverance which bore him up amid the hardships and dangers of the route actually traversed, would, beyond doubt, have sufficed to ensure him a successful passage even through Idumea the proper. And this we say, maintaining still an unhesitating belief in the literal understanding of the prophecies. It is essential, however, that these prophecies be literally rendered; and it is a matter for regret as well as surprise, that Dr. Keith should have failed to determine so important a point as the exactness or falsity of the version of his text. This we will now briefly examine.

Isaiah xxiv. 10.

לָנֶצַח —"For an eternity,"

נְצָחִים — "of eternities,"

אֵין — "not,"

עֹבֵר — "moving about,"

בָּהּ : — "in it."

"For an eternity of eternities (there shall) not (be any one) moving about in it." The literal meaning of " בָּהּ " is "*in it*," not "through it." The participle " עֹבֵר " refers to one moving to and fro, or up and down, and is the same term which is rendered "*current*," as an epithet of money, in Genesis xxiii. 16. The prophet means that there shall be no marks of life in the land, no living being there, no one moving up and down in it; and are, of course, to be taken with the usual allowance for that hyperbole which is a main feature, and indeed the genius of the language.

Ezekiel xxxv. 7.

וְנָתַתִּי — "and I will give,"

אֶת־הַר — "the mountain,"

שֵׂעִיר — "Seir,"

לְשִׁמְמָה — "for a desolation,"

וּשְׁמָמָה — "and a desolation,"

וְהִכְרַתִּי — "and I will cut off,"

מִמֶּנּוּ — "from it,"

עֹבֵר — "him that goeth,"

וָשָׁב — "and him that returneth."

"And I will give mount Seir for an utter desolation, and will cut off from it him *that passeth and repasseth therein*." The reference here is the same as in the previous passage, and the inhabitants of the land are alluded to as moving about therein, and actively employed in the business of life. The meaning of "passing and repassing" is sanctioned by Gesenius, s. v. vol. 2. p. 570, Leo's Transl. Compare Zachariah vii. 14, and ix. 8. There is something analogous in the Hebrew-Greek phrase occurring in Acts ix. 28. Καὶ ἦν μετ᾽ αὐτῶν εἰσπορευόμενος καὶ ἐκπορευόμενος ἐν Ἰερουσαλημ. "And he was with them in Jerusalem coming in and going out." The Latin "versatus est" conveys the meaning precisely; which is, that Saul, the new convert, was on intimate terms with the true believers in Jerusalem, moving about among them to and fro, or in and out. It is plain, therefore, that the words of the prophets, in both cases, and when literally construed, intend only to predict the general desolation and abandonment of the land. Indeed, it should have been taken into consideration, that a strict prohibition on the part of the Deity, of an entrance into, or passage through, Idumea, would have effectually cut off from mankind all evidence of this prior sentence of desolation and abandonment; the prediction itself being thus rendered a dead letter, when viewed in regard to its ulterior and most important purpose—the dissemination of the faith.

Mr. Stephens was strongly dissuaded from his design. Almost the only person who encouraged him was Mr. Gliddon, our consul; and but for him the idea would have been abandoned. The dangers, indeed, were many, and the difficulties more. By good fortune, however, the sheik of Akaba was then at Cairo. The great yearly caravan of pilgrims for Mecca was assembling beneath the walls, and he had been summoned by the pacha to escort and protect them through the desert as far as Akaba. He was the chief of a powerful tribe of Bedouins, maintaining, in all its vigour, the independence of their race, and bidding defiance to the pacha, while they yielded him such obedience as comported with their own immediate interests.

With this potentate our traveller entered into negotiation. The precise service required of him was, to conduct Mr. Stephens from Akaba to Hebron, through the land of Edom, diverging to visit the excavated city of Petra,—a journey of about ten days. A very indefinite arrangement was at length made. Mr. Stephens, after visiting Mount Sinai, was to repair to Akaba, where he would meet the escort of the Bedouin. With a view to protection on his way from Cairo to the Holy Mountain, the latter gave him his signet, which he told him would be respected by all Arabs on the route.

The arrangements for the journey as far as Mount Sinai had been made for our traveller by Mr. Gliddon. A Bedouin was procured as guide who had been with M. Laborde to Petra, and whose faith, as well as capacity, could be depended upon. The caravan consisted of eight camels and dromedaries, with three young Arabs as drivers. The tent was the common tent of the Egyptian soldiers, bought at the government factory, being very light, easily carried and pitched. The bedding was a mattress and coverlet: provision, bread, biscuit, rice, macaroni, tea, coffee, dried apricots, oranges, a roasted leg of mutton, and two large skins containing the filtered water of the Nile. Thus equipped, the party struck immediately into the desert lying between Cairo and Suez, reaching the latter place, with but little incident, after a journey of four days. At Suez, our traveller, wearied with his experiment of the dromedary, made an attempt to hire a boat, with a view of proceeding down the Red Sea to Tor, supposed to be the Elino, or place of palm-trees mentioned in the Exodus of the Israelites, and only two days' journey from Mount Sinai. The boats, however, were all taken by pilgrims, and none could be procured—at least for so long a voyage. He accordingly sent off his camels round the head of the gulf, and crossing himself by water, met them on the Petrean side of the sea.

"I am aware," says Mr. Stephens, "that there is some dispute as to the precise spot where Moses crossed; but having no time for skepticism on such matters, I began by making up my mind that this was the place, and then looked around to see whether, according to the account given in the Bible, the face of the country and the natural landmarks did not sustain my opinion. I remember I looked up to the head of the gulf, where Suez or Kolsum now stands, and saw that almost to the very head of the gulf there was a high range of mountains which it would be necessary to cross, an undertaking which it would have been physically impossible for 600,000 people, men, women, and children, to accomplish, with a hostile army pursuing them. At Suez, Moses could not have been hemmed in as he was; he could go off into the Syrian desert, or, unless the sea has greatly changed since that time, round the head of the gulf. But here, directly opposite where I sat, was an opening in the mountains, making a clear passage from the desert to the shore of the sea. It is admitted that from the earliest history of the country, there was a caravan route from the Rameseh of the Pharaohs to this spot, and it was perfectly clear to my mind that, if the account be true at all, Moses had taken that route; that it was directly opposite me, between the two mountains, where he had come down with his multitude to the shore, and that it was there he had found himself hemmed in, in the manner described in the Bible, with the sea before him, and the army of Pharaoh in his rear; it was there he had stretched out his hand and divided the waters; and probably on the very spot where I sat the children of Israel had kneeled upon the sands to offer thanks to God for his miraculous interposition. The distance, too, was in confirmation of this opinion. It was about twenty miles across; the distance which that immense multitude, with their necessary baggage, could have passed in the space of time (a night) mentioned in the Bible. Besides my own judgment and conclusions, I had authority on the spot, in my Bedouin Toualeb, who talked of it with as much certainty as if he had seen it himself; and, by the waning light of the moon, pointed out the metes and bounds according to the tradition received from his fathers."

Mr. Stephens is here greatly in error, and has placed himself in direct opposition to all authority on the subject. It is quite evident, that since the days of the miracle, the sea *has* "greatly changed" round the head of the gulf. It is now several feet lower, as appears from the alluvial condition of several bitter lakes in the vicinity. On this topic Niebuhr, who examined the matter with his accustomed learning, acumen, and perseverance, is indisputable authority. But he merely agrees with all the most able writers on this head. The passage occurred at Suez. The chief arguments sustaining this position are deduced from the ease by which the miracle could have been wrought, on a sea so shaped, by means of a strong wind blowing from the north-east.

Resuming his journey to the southward, our traveller passed safely through a barren and mountainous region, bare of verdure, and destitute of water, in about seven days to Mount Sinai. It is to be regretted, that in his account of a country so little traversed as this peninsula, Mr. Stephens has not entered more into detail. Upon his adventures at the Holy Mountain, which are of great interest, he dwells somewhat at length.

At Akaba he met the Sheik as by agreement. A horse of the best breed of Arabia was provided, and, although suffering from ill health, he proceeded manfully through the desert to Petra and Mount Hor. The difficulties of the route proved to be chiefly those arising from the rapacity of his friend, the Sheik of Akaba, who threw a thousand impediments in his way with the purpose of magnifying the importance of the service rendered, and obtaining, in consequence, the larger allowance of *bucksheesh*.

The account given of Petra agrees in all important particulars with those rendered by the very few travellers who had previously visited it. With these accounts our readers are sufficiently acquainted. The singular character of the city, its vast antiquity, its utter loss, for more than a thousand years, to the eyes of the civilized world; and, above all, the solemn denunciations of prophecy regarding it, have combined to invest these ruins with an interest beyond that of any others in existence, and to render what has been written concerning them familiar knowledge to nearly every individual who reads.

Leaving Petra, after visiting Mount Hor, Mr. Stephens returned to the valley of El-Ghor, and fell into the caravan route for Gaza, which crosses the valley obliquely. Coming out from the ravine among the mountains to the westward, he here left the road to Gaza, and pushed immediately on to Hebron. This distance (between the Gaza route and Hebron) is, we believe, the only positively *new* route accomplished by our American tourist. We understand that, in 1826, Messieurs Strangeways and Anson passed over the ground, on the Gaza road from Petra, to the point where it deviates for Hebron. On the part of Mr. Stephens' course, which we have thus designated as new, it is well known that a great public road existed in the later days of the Roman empire, and that several cities were located immediately upon it. Mr. Stephens discovered some ruins, but his state of health, unfortunately, prevented a minute investigation. Those which he encountered are represented as forming rude and shapeless masses; there were no columns, no blocks of marble, or other large stones, indicating architectural greatness. The Pentinger Tables place Helusa in this immediate vicinity, and, but for the character of the ruins seen, we might have supposed them to be the remnants of that city.

The latter part of our author's second volume is occupied with his journeyings in the Holy Land, and, principally, with an account of his visit to Jerusalem. What relates to the Dead Sea we are induced to consider as, upon the whole, the most interesting, if not the most important portion of his book. It was his original intention to circumnavigate this lake, but the difficulty of procuring a boat proved an obstacle not to be surmounted. He traversed, nevertheless, no little extent of its shores, bathed in it, saw distinctly that the Jordan *does* mingle with its waters, and that birds floated upon it, and flew over its surface.

But it is time that we conclude. Mr. Stephens passed

through Samaria and Galilee, stopping at Nablous, the ancient Sychem; the burial-place of the patriarch Joseph; and the ruins of Sebaste; crossed the battle-plain of Jezreel; ascended Mount Tabor; visited Nazareth, the Lake of Genesareth, the cities of Tiberias and Saphet, Mount Carmel, Acre, Sour, and Sidon. At Beyroot he took passage for Alexandria, and thence, finally returned to Europe.

The volumes are written in general with a freedom, a frankness, and an utter absence of pretension, which will secure them the respect and good-will of all parties. The author professes to have compiled his narrative merely from "brief notes and recollections," admitting that he has probably fallen into errors regarding facts and impressions—errors he has been prevented from seeking out and correcting by the urgency of other occupations since his return. We have, therefore, thought it quite as well not to trouble our readers, in this cursory review, with references to parallel travels, now familiar, and whose merits and demerits are sufficiently well understood.

We take leave of Mr. Stephens with sentiments of hearty respect. We hope it is not the last time we shall hear from him. He is a traveller with whom we shall like to take other journeys. Equally free from the exaggerated sentimentality of Chateaubriand, or the sublimated, the *too French* enthusiasm of Lamartine on the one hand, and on the other from the degrading spirit of utilitarianism, which sees in mountains and waterfalls only quarries and manufacturing sites, Mr. Stephens writes like a man of good sense and sound feeling.

New York Review, October 1837

William Leete Stone

Ups and Downs in the Life of a Distressed Gentleman. By the author of *Tales and Sketches, such as they are.* New York: Leavitt, Lord & Co.

THIS BOOK is a public imposition. It is a duodecimo volume, of the usual novel size, bound in the customary muslin cover with a gilt stamp on the back, and containing 225 pages of letter press. Its price, in the bookstores, is, we believe, a dollar. Although we are in the habit of reading with great deliberation, not unfrequently perusing individual passages more than two or three times, we were occupied *little better than one hour* in getting through with the whole of the *"Ups and Downs."* A full page of the book—that is, a page in which there are no breaks in the matter occasioned by paragraphs, or otherwise, embraces precisely 150 words—an average page about 130. A full page of this our Magazine, will be found to contain 1544 words—an average page about 1600, owing to the occasional notes in a smaller type than that generally used. It follows that nearly thirteen pages of such a volume as the *"Ups and Downs"* are required to make one of our own, and that in about fourteen pages such as we are writing, (if we consider the sixteen blank half-pages at the beginning of each chapter in the *"Ups and Downs,"* with the four pages of index) the whole of the one dollar duodecimo we are now called upon to review, might be laid conveniently before the public—in other words, that we could print nearly six of them in one of our ordinary numbers, (that for March for instance) the price of which is little more than forty cents. We give the amount of six such volumes then for forty cents—of one of them for very little more than a *fi'penny bit.* And as its price is a dollar, it is clear either that the matter of which the said *"Ups and Downs"* is composed, is sixteen times as good in quality as our own matter, and that of such Magazines in general, or that the author of the *"Ups and Downs"* supposes it so to be, or that the author of the *"Ups and Downs"* is unreasonable in his exactions upon the public, and is presuming very largely upon their excessive patience, gullibility, and good nature. We will take the liberty of analyzing the narrative, with a view of letting our readers see for themselves whether the author (or publisher) is quite right in estimating it at sixteen times the value of the ordinary run of compositions.

The volume commences with a Dedication *"To all Doating Parents."* We then have four pages occupied with a content table, under the appellation of a "Bill of Lading." This is well thought of. The future man of letters might, without some assistance of this nature, meet with no little trouble in searching for any particular chapter through so dense a mass of matter as the *"Ups and Downs."* The "Introduction" fills four pages more, and in spite of the unjustifiable use of the word *"predicated,"* whose meaning is obviously misunderstood, is by much the best portion of the work—so much so, indeed, that we fancy it written by some kind, good-natured friend of the author. We now come to *Chapter I*, which proves to be Introduction the Second, and extends over seven pages farther. This is called "A Disquisition on Circles," in which we are informed that "the motion produced by the *centripetal* and *centrifugal* forces, seems to be that of nature"—that "it is very true that the *periphery* of the circles traversed by some objects is greater than that of others"—that "cast a stone into a lake or a mill-pond, and it will produce a succession of motions, circle following circle in order, and extending the radius until they disappear in the distance"—that "Time wings his flight in circles, and every year rolls round within itself"—that "the sun turns round upon his own axis, and the moon changes monthly"—that "the other celestial bodies all wheel their courses in circles around the common centre"—that "the moons of Jupiter revolve around him in circles, and he carries them along with him in his periodical circuit around the sun"—that "Saturn always moves within his rings"—that "a ship on the ocean, though apparently bounding over a plain of waters, rides in fact upon the circumference of a circle around the arch of the earth's diameter"—that "the lunar circle betokens a tempest"—that "those German principalities which are represented in the Diet are denominated circles"—and that "modern writers on pneumatics affirm every breeze that blows to be a whirlwind."

But now commences the *"Ups and Downs"* in good earnest. The hero of the narrative is Mr. Wheelwright, and the author begs leave to assure the reader that Mr. W. is no fictitious personage, that " with the single abatement that names are changed, and places not precisely designated, every essential incident that he has recorded actually occurred, much as he has related it, to a person who, if not now living, certainly was once, and most of them under his own observation."

Chapter II, treats of the birth and parentage of the hero. Mr. Daniel Wheelwright originally came from New Jersey, but resides at the opening of the story, in the beautiful valley of the Mohawk "on the banks of the river, and in a town alike celebrated for the taste of its people in architecture, and distinguished as a seat of learning." He was early instructed by his father in the "elementary principles of his trade," which was coach-making. "He was also taught in some branches of household carpentry work, which proved of no disadvantage to him in the end." "Full of good nature he was always popular with the boys," and we are told " was never so industrious as when manufacturing to their order little writing desks, fancy boxes, and other trifling articles not beyond the scope of his mechanical ingenuity." We are also assured that the young gentleman was excessively fond of oysters.

In *Chapter III*, Daniel Wheelwright "grows up a tall and stately youth." His mother "discovers a genius in him requiring only means and opportunity to wing an eagle-flight." "An arrangement therefore is effected" by which our hero is sent to school to a "man whom the mother had previously known in New Jersey, and whose occupation was that of teaching young ideas how to shoot—not grouse and woodcock—but to shoot forth into scions of learning." This is a new and excellent joke—but by no means so good as the one immediately following, where we are told that "notwithstanding the natural indolence of his character, our hero knew that he must know something before he could enter college, and that in case of a failure, he must again cultivate more acquaintance with the *felloes* of the shop than with the *fellows* of the university." He is sent to college, however, having "read *Cornelius Nepos* and three books of the Æneid, thumbed over the Greek Grammar, and gone through the Gospel of St. John."

Chapter IV, commences with two quotations from Shakspeare. Our hero is herein elected a member of the *Philo-*

Peithologicalethian Institute, commences his debates with a "Mr. President, I *are* in favor of the negative of that are question," is "read off" at the close of every quarter, "advances one grade higher" in his classic course every year, and when about to take his degree, is "announced for a poem" in the *proces verbal* of the commencement, and (one of the professors, if we comprehend, being called *Nott*) distinguishes himself by the following satirical verses—

> The warrior fights, and dies for fame—
> The empty glories of a name;—
> But we who linger round this spot,
> The warrior's guerdon covet Nott.

> Nott for the miser's glittering heap
> Within these walls is bartered sleep;
> The humble scholar's quiet lot
> With dreams of wealth is troubled Nott.

> While poring o'er the midnight lamp,
> In rooms too cold, and sometimes damp,
> O man, who land and cash hast got,
> Thy life of ease we envy Nott.

> Our troubles here are light and few;—
> An empty purse when bills fall due,
> A locker, without e'er a shot,—
> Hard recitations, or a Knot-

> Ty problem, which we can't untie—
> Our only shirt hung out to dry,—
> A chum who never pays his scot,—
> Such ills as these we value Nott.

> O, cherished ***** ! learning's home,
> Where'er the fates may bid us roam,
> Though friends and kindred be forgot,
> Be sure we shall forget thee Nott.

> For years of peaceful, calm content,
> To science and hard study lent,
> Though others thy good name may blot,
> T'were wondrous if we loved thee Nott.

For this happy effort he is admitted *ad gradum in artibus*, and thus closes chapter the fourth.

Chapter V, is also headed with two sentences from Shakspeare. The parents of Mr. W. are now inclined to make him a clergyman, being "not only conscientious people, but sincerely religious, and really desirous of doing good." This project is dismissed, however, upon our hero's giving no evidence of piety, and Daniel is "entered in the office of an eminent medical gentleman, in one of the most beautiful cities which adorn the banks of the majestic Hudson." Our author cannot be prevailed upon to state the precise place— but gives us another excellent joke by way of indemnification. "Although," says he, "like Byron, I have no fear of being taken for the hero of my own tale, yet were I to bring matters too near their homes, but too many of the real characters of my narrative might be identified. Suffice it, then, to say of the location—*Ilium fuit*." Daniel now becomes Doctor Wheelwright, reads the first chapter of *Cheselden's Anatomy*, visits New York, attends the lectures of Hosack and Post, "presses into his goblet the grapes of wisdom clustering around the tongue of Mitchill, and acquires the principles of surgery from the lips, and the skilful use of the knife from the untrembling hand, of Mott."

At the close of his second year our hero, having completed only half of Cheselden's article on Osteology, relinquishes the study of medicine in despair, and turns merchant—purchasing "the odds and ends of a fashionable fancy and jobbing concern in Albany." He is gulled however, by a confidential clerk, one John Smith, his store takes fire and burns down, and both himself and father, who indorsed for him, are ruined.

Mr. Wheelwright now retrieves his fortune by the accidental possession of a claim against government, taken by way of payment for a bad debt. But going to Washington to receive his money, he is inveigled into a lottery speculation—that is to say, he spends the whole amount of his claim in lottery-tickets—the manager fails—and our adventurer is again undone. This lottery adventure ends with the excellent joke that in regard to our hero there " were five *outs* to one *in*, viz.— *out* of money, and *out* of clothes; *out* at the heels, and *out* at the toes; *out* of credit and *in* debt!" Mr. Wheelwright now returns to New York, and is thrown into prison by Messieurs Roe and Doe. In this emergency he sends for his friend the narrator, who, of course, relieves his distresses, and opens the doors of his jail.

Chapter IX, and indeed every ensuing chapter, commences with two sentences from Shakspeare. Mr. Wheelwright now becomes agent for a steamboat company on Lake George—but fortune still frowns, and the steamboat takes fire, and is burnt up, on the eve of her first trip, thus again ruining our hero.

"What a moment!" exclaims the author, "and what a spectacle for a lover of the 'sublime and beautiful!' Could Burke have visited such a scene of mingled magnificence, and grandeur and terror, what a vivid illustration would he not have added to his inimitable treatise on that subject! The fire raged with amazing fury and power—stimulated to madness, as it were, by the pitch and tar and dried timbers, and other combustible materials used in the construction of the boat. The night-bird screamed in terror, and the beasts of prey fled in wild affright into the deep and visible darkness beyond. This is truly a gloomy place for a lone person to stand in of a dark night—particularly if he has a touch of superstition. There have been fierce conflicts on this spot—sieges and battles and fearful massacres. Here hath mailed Mars sat on his altar, up to his ears in blood, smiling grimly at the music of echoing cannons, the shrill trump, and all the rude din of arms, until like the waters of Egypt, the lake became red as the crimson flowers that blossom upon its margin!" At the word margin is the following explanatory note. "*Lobelia Cardinalis*, commonly called the *Indian Eye-bright*. It is a beautiful blossom, and is frequently met with in this region. The writer has seen large clusters of it blooming upon the margin of the 'Bloody Pond' in this neighborhood—so called from the circumstance of the slain being thrown into this pond, after the defeat of Baron Dieskau, by Sir William Johnson. The ancients would have constructed a beautiful legend from this incident, and sanctified the sanguinary flower."

In *Chapter X*, Mr. Wheelwright marries an heiress—a rich widow worth thirty thousand pound sterling in prospectu— in *Chapter XI*, sets up a *Philomathian Institute*, the whole of the chapter being occupied with his advertisement—in *Chapter XII*, his wife affronts the scholars, by "swearing by the powers she would be afther clearing them out—the spalpeens!—that's what she would, honies!" The school is broken up in consequence, and Mrs. Wheelwright herself turns out to be nothing more than "one of the unmarried wives of the lamented Captain Scarlett," the legal representatives being in secure possession of the thirty thousand pounds sterling in prospectu.

In *Chapter XIII*, Mr. Wheelwright is again in distress, and applies, of course, to the humane author of the *"Ups and Downs,"* who gives him, we are assured, "an overcoat, and a little basket of provisions." In *Chapter XIV*, the author continues his benevolence—gives a crow, (*cock-a-doodle doo!*) and concludes with "there *is* no more charitable people than those of New York!" which means when translated into good English—"there never was a more charitable man than the wise and learned author of the '*Ups and Downs.*' "

Chapter XV, is in a somewhat better vein, and embraces some tolerable incidents in relation to the pawn-brokers' shops of New York. We give an extract—believing it to be one of the best passages in the book.

To one who would study human nature, especially in its darker features, there is no better field of observation than among these pawn-brokers' shops.

In a frequented establishment, each day unfolds an ample catalogue of sorrow, misery, and guilt, developed in forms and combinations almost innumerable; and if the history of each customer could be known, the result would be such a catalogue as would scarcely be surpassed, even by the records of a police-office or a prison. Even my brief stay while arranging for the redemption of Dr. Wheelwright's personals, afforded materials, as indicated in the last chapter, for much and painful meditation.

I had scarcely made my business known, at the first of "my uncle's" establishments to which I had been directed, when a middle-aged man entered with a bundle, on which he asked a small advance, and which, on being opened, was found to contain a shawl and two or three other articles of female apparel. The man was stout and sturdy, and, as I judged from his appearance, a mechanic; but the mark of the destroyer was on his bloated countenance, and in his heavy, stupid eyes. Intemperance had marked him for his own. The pawn-broker was yet examining the offered pledge, when a woman, whose pale face and attenuated form bespoke long and intimate acquaintance with sorrow, came hastily into the shop, and with the single exclamation, "O, Robert!" darted, rather than ran, to that part of the counter where the man was standing. Words were not wanted to explain her story. Her miserable husband, not satisfied with wasting his own earnings, and leaving her to starve with her children, had descended to the meanness of plundering even her scanty wardrobe, and the pittance for the obtaining of which this robbery would furnish means, was destined to be squandered at the tippling-house. A blush of shame arose even upon his degraded face, but it quickly passed away; the brutal appetite prevailed, and the better feeling that had apparently stirred within him for the moment, soon gave way before its diseased and insatiate cravings.

"Go home," was his harsh and angry exclamation; "what brings you here, running after me with your everlasting scolding? go home, and mind your own business."

"O Robert, dear Robert!" answered the unhappy wife, "don't pawn my shawl. Our children are crying for bread, and I have none to give them. Or let me have the money; it is hard to part with that shawl, for it was my mother's gift; but I will let it go, rather than see my children starve. Give me the money, Robert, and don't leave us to perish."

I watched the face of the pawn-broker to see what effect this appeal would have upon him, but I watched in vain. He was hardened to distress, and had no sympathy to throw away. "Twelve shillings on these things," he said, tossing them back to the drunkard, with a look of perfect indifference.

"Only twelve shillings!" murmured the heart-broken wife, in a tone of despair. "O Robert, don't let them go for twelve shillings. Let me try some where else."

"Nonsense," answered the brute. "It's as much as they're worth, I suppose. Here, Mr. Crimp, give us the change."

The money was placed before him, and the bundle consigned to a drawer. The poor woman reached forth her hand toward the silver, but the movement was anticipated by her husband. "There Mary," he said, giving her half a dollar, "there, go home now, and don't make a fuss. I'm going a little way up the street, and perhaps I'll bring you something from market, when I come home."

The hopeless look of the poor woman, as she meekly turned to the door, told plainly enough how little she trusted to this ambiguous promise. They went on their way, she to her famishing children, and he to squander the dollar he had retained, at the next den of intemperance.

Chapter XVI, is entitled the "end of this eventful history." Mr. Wheelwright is rescued from the hands of the watch by the author of the *"Ups and Downs"*—turns his wife, very justly, out of doors—and finally returns to his parental occupation of coach-making.

We have given the entire pith and marrow of the book. The term *flat*, is the only general expression which would apply to it. It is written, we believe, by Col. Stone of the New York Commercial Advertiser, and should have been printed among the quack advertisements, in a spare corner of his paper.

Southern Literary Messenger, June 1836

Beverly Tucker

George Balcombe. A Novel. New York: Harper and Brothers.

THE SCENE of this novel is laid partly in Missouri, and partly in Virginia. The hero proper of the book—that is to say, the *object* of the narration—is a Mr. William Napier of Craiganet, in the Old Dominion—George Balcombe, although the most important of the dramatis personae, being merely what, in critical parlance, is termed the *machinery*.

The mother of our hero, then, was one of two daughters, the only children of Mr. Raby, a man of great wealth. This wealth, however, consisted principally of property entailed on the possessor's male descendants, with remainder to a distant English relative. There proved to be no male issue—the wife dying in giving birth to her second daughter, the mother of our hero—and the widower refusing to marry again. Moreover, through scruples of conscience, he declined taking measures for docking the entail, and even when the revolution rendered it invalid, declared his children should not profit by such invalidation. "He accordingly executed a will devising the entailed property to the remainder-man; and this will, properly attested, he transmitted to him in England." Thus matters stood until the two daughters married, and the birth, in 1799, of a grandson, our hero, excited an interest in the heart of the old gentleman. He claimed the child from its mother, and informed the father that a new will had been made, devising the whole property to be divided into two equal parts—one part for the grandson, the other to be again divided between the two daughters. This will, he added, was in the hands of a confidential friend. The name of the friend was not mentioned, and delicacy forbade inquiry.

It appears that Edward Montague, an orphan protégé of Mr. Raby's, was the depositary of this instrument. Upon the death of the old gentleman he was applied to. At first he disclaimed any knowledge of the paper; being on oath, however, he owned having once seen it, but denied that he knew what had become of it. In the meantime the devisee under the former testament brought it forward, and, none other appearing, established it. The elder Mr. Napier took no active measures to recover the lost will, and, having inherited nothing from Mr. Raby, all of whose non-entailed property was involved, died just before the ruin of his family became manifest. Upon our hero's coming of age, therefore, he finds himself penniless. The action of the novel grows out of his search for the missing will.

In the opening of the narrative we are introduced to Napier in a prairie of Missouri. He is in pursuit of Montague, with the vague hope of extorting from him, either by force or guile, some information respecting the document in question. As this beginning evinces the hand of a master, we quote it. The abruptness here is not without object. The attention is attracted at once and rivetted with skill.

At length, issuing from the wood, I entered a prairie, more beautiful than any I had yet seen. The surface, gently undulating, presented innumerable swells, on which the eye might rest with pleasure. Many of these were capped with clumps and groves of trees, thus interrupting the dull uniformity which generally wearies the traveller in these vast expanses. I gazed around for a moment with delight; but soon found leisure to observe that my road had become alarmingly indistinct. It is easy indeed, to follow the faintest trace through a prairie. The beaten track, however narrow, wears a peculiar aspect, which makes it distinguishable even at a distance. But the name of Arlington, the place of my destination, denoted at least a village; while the tedious path which I was travelling seemed more like to terminate in the midst of the prairie than to lead to a public haunt of men. I feared I had missed my way, and looked eagerly ahead for some traveller who might set me right if astray. But I looked in vain. The prairie lay before me, a wide waste without one moving object. The sun had just gone down; and as my horse, enlivened by the shade and the freshness of evening seemed to recover his mettle, I determined to push on to such termination as my path might lead to. At this moment a shout from behind reached my ear. I turned and saw a man on horseback standing between me and the sky, on the top of the east swell. Though a quarter of a mile off, his figure stood out in such distinct relief, that every limb was conspicuous and well defined on the bright back ground. He was stationary, standing erect in his stirrups, and twisted around, so that his back and his horse's head were both towards me. After repeating a shout, which I found was a call to a dog, he put his horse in motion, and advanced at a brisk trot. I was now in no hurry, and he soon overtook me.

This rencontre is of essential advantage to our hero. The stranger proves to be George Balcombe, also a protégé of old Mr. Raby's. Mr. N. accompanies him home, and discovers that he is well versed in the family affairs of the Rabys and Napiers; that he is acquainted with the matter of the will; that, with Montague, he was a witness to the instrument; and that Montague resides in the neighborhood. Balcombe believes that M. was the depositary spoken of by old Mr. Raby. Circumstances, also, induce him to think that the paper is still in existence, and in the possession of M. The train of events which have led to this conclusion—a train laid by Balcombe himself—serves admirably to develop his character.

Montague, it seems, was always, even when an open reprobate, superstitious; and, though a great liar, would at no time have sworn to a literal lie. In the interval between the death of Mr. Raby and the establishment of the first will, he became gloomy and serious, and joined the church. Balcombe, who knew his character, could thus easily conceive how the villain might have deemed "the *form* of religion and *literal* truth a sufficient salvo for wronging the dead and plundering the living by moral perjury." It was probable, he thought, that some plan had been devised, by means of which Montague had spoken the literal truth when he swore in court that "he knew not what had become of the will." The document had been handed to him by Mr. Raby in the presence of Balcombe, and a letter received by the latter from the old gentleman, and written just before his decease, a letter full of affection for his grandson, was sufficient assurance that the testament had never been revoked. At the probate of the will found, Balcombe did not appear—being absent from the country and not hearing of the death of Mr. Raby. Upon Montague's coming, however, to live near him in Missouri, and coming in evidently improved circumstances, with plenty of money, and only *affecting* to practise law, he immediately suspected the truth, and set on foot a system of observation.

One day, having need of eastern funds, he applied to a merchant for the purpose of purchasing a bill on New York. The merchant furnished one drawn by Montague on a house there, for the desired amount, one thousand dollars, and, in the course of conversation, mentioned that M. drew regularly, at the same time every year, on the same house, for the same sum. Here then was an annuity, and the question was— *unde derivatur?*

The bill was bought and sent to a correspondent in New York, with instructions to get English funds in payment. This was done, and a draft obtained upon a Liverpool house, accompanied by a letter of advice. The Liverpool correspondent was instructed in like manner to take a draft on Northumberland—this being the shire where resided the remainder-man. This latter draft was also obtained, with a letter of advice, duplicates being furnished in each instance. These several letters ran thus.

To George Balcombe, Esq.

Dear Sir,—I wrote you, under date of March tenth, that the bill remitted by you for one thousand dollars, drawn by Edward Montague, on the house of Tompkins and Todd of this city, had been paid by a draft on Bell and Brothers, of Liverpool, England. This draft I remitted, according to your directions, to my friend, John Ferguson, of the house of Ferguson and Partridge, our correspondents there, with instructions to obtain, if possible, from the same house, a draft on the county of Northumberland. In this he succeeded, by procuring a draft on Edward Raby, Esq. of that county, for a like amount.

Enclosed you have the seconds of the several bills, and duplicates of the letters of advice accompanying the same. At my request, Mr. Ferguson waited on Mr. Raby in person. The money was promptly paid, but not without a good deal of grumbling. Nothing very intelligible was said; but Mr. Ferguson could distinguish in the mutterings of Mr. Raby, such words as "harpy," "rapacious scoundrel," &c.

Your obedient servant,

JAMES LANGSTON.

New York, June 1, 1820.

To Messrs. Bell and Brothers, Merchants, Liverpool.

Gentlemen,—A draft drawn by Edward Montague, Esq. for one thousand dollars, was this day presented, and paid by us in pursuance of your standing instructions. We have accordingly drawn on you in favor of Mr. James Langston of this city, for a corresponding amount. We remain, gentlemen,

Your obedient servants,

TOMPKINS & TODD.

New York, March 9, 1820.

To Edward Raby, Esq. of Raby Hall, Northumberland.

Sir,—The draft of Messrs. Tompkins and Todd, on account of Mr. Montague's annuity, is to hand, and has been duly honored. We have this day drawn on you for the amount, in favor of Mr. John Ferguson, of this place. Hoping that it may be quite convenient for you to meet the draft, and begging a continuance of your favors, we remain, sir,

Your most obedient, humble servants,

BELL & BROTHERS.

Liverpool, April 10, 1820.

Here then Balcombe found his suspicions completely verified. Montague was in receipt of an annuity—an annuity grudgingly paid—and derived from the devisee under the primitive will. There could be little doubt that the money was granted as hush-money by the devisee, Montague still possessing the second testament, and holding it *in terrorem.* B. was about communicating with Mr. Napier upon this head, when accident threw them together in the prairie. Our hero now receives the benefit of Balcombe's energy and sagacity in many varied attempts to get possession of the will. Keizer, an original vagabond, is also a most efficient diplomatist and ally. The adventures of the trio in pursuit of the missing document, eminently display, in the author of George Balcombe, that rarest of all qualities in American novelists, and that certainly most indispensable— *invention.* With permission, we will go through these adventures one by one—doing this with the less scruple, because we intend to do it so briefly as not to interfere with the main interest of the book itself, and

because, with this object in view, we have purposely delayed
our notice until the volumes had been some time in possession of the public.

In a conversation between Balcombe and Napier, occurring
in the early part of the first volume, we learn some particulars
in regard to Mary Scott, daughter of Mr. Raby's overseer.
Both Montague and Balcombe, we have already said, were
protégés of the old gentleman, and resided at one period in
his family. Both were enamored of Mary, who was "beautiful
and intelligent—gay, sprightly and impassioned," and imbued with the spirit of romance. She, however, loved only
Montague, and seeing the necessity of arming Balcombe
against himself, frankly told him of her pre-engaged affections. The lover thus rejected, became the friend and confidant. At first, Montague would have been glad to have made
Mary his wife; but as his circumstances improved, he discovered that Scott was even poorer than he had supposed, and
his selfish heart grew chill at the supposition. A certain elderly
maiden too, of wealth, was said to look kindly on him. His
visits to Mary, therefore, grew less frequent. In one of them,
Balcombe was witness to a circumstance which led him to
suspect dishonorable intentions. Suspicion, unfortunately,
was not all; it appears that the intentions were accomplished.
Balcombe sought a private interview with the villain.

"Montague," said I, "do you love Mary Scott?"

He hesitated, muttering something about the strangeness
of the question.

"Understand me, sir," said I, "I do not ask your confidence.
I would not accept it. I demand to know the fact, for my own
purposes, and to be used at my own discretion. Mark me. I
do not ask whether you *profess* to love her. I know that you
do. I have that from her own lips. I demand to know whether
you do love her in very truth."

"Oh!" said he, in the mildest tone, "if she has made you
her confidant, I have no need to be secret. Therefore I acknowledge to you that I do love her with all my heart."

"Why, then," said I, "do you not marry her?"

He paused again.

"Speak *on*," said I, "and speak *out*."

"Why, really, Mr. Balcombe, I do not understand this peremptory tone."

"You understand it well," said I, "and you understand perfectly that I will have an answer. I want it for my own purpose, again, and to be used at my own discretion. Answer you shall. Truly or falsely, is your own concern. I hardly expect the truth, and do not care to have it. But I will know on what footing you place this thing."

"Well!" said he, "you know I have a will of old Mr. Raby's in my hands, in which I am handsomely provided for by a bequest of valuable lands. I am, therefore, careful not to offend him; and I have reason to believe this marriage would not be agreeable to him. Poor as I am, he would regard it as a duty I owe my ancestors, not to ally myself to his overseer."

"And is this," said I, "the reason you assign to her for your delay to claim her hand?"

"It is."

"Then you have told her what is false."

"How can *you* say that?" said he. "I wrote the will. You never read it."

"That is true," said I, "but I witnessed it."

"What of that?"

"Why, this, sir. It is witnessed only by us two. What can you claim under it by your own testimony? Would you, the wary, the crafty, the selfish, rapacious Edward Montague, have been content to have a will of *lands*, under which you expect to claim, so witnessed? Shame upon you, sir. Would you palm such a bare-faced lie on me, as well as on that poor, confiding, generous, true-hearted girl? I will undeceive her instantly."

I shall never forget the grim smile in which something like triumph seemed struggling to free itself from the mire of degradation into which I was trampling him.

"You will use your own pleasure about that," said he. "I mean to marry her when circumstances will permit. Before that I cannot."

"Marry her you never shall," said I.

"Will you take her off my hands?" said he, with the same incomprehensible smile. I sprung at him, I know not why. But he darted through the door, and jerked it after him. I did not pursue him.

Balcombe now sought Mary, and found her in tears. Still unsuspecting the whole truth, he revealed to her the deception practised upon her by Montague, and concluded with an offer of his own hand. Made sensible now of the value of Balcombe's affection, and alive to all the villainy of Montague, she divulges, in the first moment of her despair, the secret of her seduction. Balcombe reluctantly abandons her, and departs to the west. Scott did not long survive the ruin of his daughter's peace, and Mary, with her mother and little brother, was obliged to seek another home. Here, after the lapse of some time, Montague was seen to renew the visits which had been discontinued since the period of his interview with Balcombe. No one else visited the house—but from being steeped in poverty, the little family seemed rising above pecuniary trouble. This mystery is explained in a subsequent part of the first volume, when, shortly after the rencontre in the prairie, James, the brother of Mary, brings a letter from her to Balcombe in Missouri.

She writes that, after the departure of B. and the death of old Mr. Scott, Montague sought to renew his visits—that she refused to see him, and urged her mother to order him from the house—that Mrs. Scott was overcome, however, by his protestations, and pressed her to meet him—that, without undeceiving Mrs. S., she was unable to carry her opposition farther, and that finally, she consented. In a private interview he stated that Balcombe had misunderstood him, in supposing him to speak of *lands*, as the property bequeathed, and that no explanation had been offered before because he (Montague) had been forbidden the house by her father. He came *now*, he said, to offer reparation and marriage. She rejected the offer with scorn—and he left her, after taking measures for the comfort of Mrs. Scott, and the education of little James.

Old Mr. Raby now died, and Mary saw nothing of Montague for two months. She heard from him, indeed, and, though he did not express himself distinctly, she inferred from what he wrote that he had not been disappointed in the will. At length he called to see her, accompanying the English devisee, and requested again a private interview. She remarked a great alteration in his manner, for it was about this time that he joined the church. He professed deep contrition for his wrong to Mary—again offered marriage—offered every service in his power, and, being rejected in all offers, wound up by requesting a favor. He placed in her hand a packet as large as a dozen newspapers, and well secured with twine and seals. This he asked her to keep, and she promised to do so. He begged her to promise farther that no eye should see the contents of the packet. She did so. He mused awhile, and then added, "It is of great importance to me that that packet should never see the light." "Then why not destroy it?" said Mary. "I don't wish to destroy it," said he, "it may be of some importance hereafter. Put it away." She took it to her room and locked it up. On her return, he rose to take leave, but paused at the door, and said, hesitatingly, "Perhaps you had better destroy that packet." She replied, "I will do so." He paused again, and said, "No!—maybe better not." "As you please," she returned, "which shall I do?" "I really do not know," he said, after a thoughtful pause. "Do as you will with it. If it is in your way, throw it into the fire. If not, keep it until I call for it." He now departed, and Mary, doubting him much, determined to preserve the packet. It will be seen that the conduct of Montague in this matter was such as Balcombe had suspected, and that it enabled the conscientious rogue to swear, when summoned upon the probate, that he "could not tell what had become of the will."

Mary did not see him again for some months, and he then endeavored to get possession of the packet—first by asking for it as a matter of course—and, upon being refused, by force. He was foiled, however, in his attempt—and left the country with precipitation, after stopping the pension of Mrs. Scott. It was probable that he thought no new provocation could make matters worse. Mary proceeds, in her letter, to inform Balcombe, that thirteen years of seclusion having rendered her totally ignorant of what was going on in the world, and having no one to advise with, she had no means of conjecturing the nature of the mysterious packet. It was obvious to her, however, that its possession or destruction was an object eagerly sought by Montague, and, she doubted not, for some villainous end. Although willing to bear her own lot without murmuring, she felt it her duty to alleviate, if possible, the want she had entailed upon her mother and brother. This, her knowledge of Montague's earnest desire for the packet, would enable her to accomplish—and she felt no scruple in using such means. We give her plan in her own words.

I have just learned where he is by means of a gentleman, who, for some purpose of his own, has been endeavoring to find him out. About the same time I ascertained by mere chance, that you, my only friend, were in the same part of the country. The coincidence seemed to point out the course I should pursue. I would gladly have your counsel, and have determined to secure to myself all the benefits of it by doing nothing that you do not approve. I have accordingly directed James to find you out, and hand you this letter. He carries one also to Montague, which contains a demand of a suitable provision for my poor mother, and of such aid as may enable James to resume his studies, and qualify himself for a profession. Is this exacting too much? Of that I constitute you sole judge. If you disapprove the measure altogether, send James back as he goes. If you approve it, then I must ask that your justice and honor may preside over what is done. Your knowledge of the past, and of Montague's present condition, will make you the best judge of what it is suitable he should do. In making this demand, I do not propose to continue to hold the rod over him. It might seem too much like retaining the means of future and indefinite exaction. I have accordingly placed in James' hands a second communication, the receipt of which will enable Montague to recover the packet. This last will be delivered when you direct it, and not before; and I have to ask that you will direct it when that which is right in your judgment that Montague should do, is done, or so promised as to secure performance. . . . Do I then ask too much when I beg that you will yourself see Montague, and hand him the first letter, which James will give you; and that, when he shall have done what is right, you will direct James to deliver to him the parcel with which he is charged. You will perceive that it is not my wish that this poor boy shall understand any thing of what is done, lest by possibility he might come to the knowledge of what would drive him to acts of desperate revenge.

Montague having called upon Colonel Robinson, Balcombe's father-in-law, with the view of purchasing land, he is there encountered by our hero and Balcombe. In a conversation dexterously introduced and sustained by the latter, the rogue is led to betray himself so egregiously that no farther doubts of his guilt are entertained, or of the surety of the grounds upon which the two friends have to proceed. Keizer is engaged to prevent, by force, if necessary, his departure from the neighborhood—but this is not attempted, and Balcombe and James obtain another interview with him in the woods near a camp meeting. The letter from Mary is handed him by James. It states that she had put the packet out of the reach of his violence, and in the hands of a third person, who would deliver it only on presentation of a certain token—and that this token, together with the name of the depositary of the packet, was contained in the parcel in James' possession. Upon reading this letter Montague declares himself ready to do and submit to whatever might be required, upon the condition specified—the receipt of the parcel. Balcombe demands an advance of a thousand dollars, and ten bonds for three hundred each, payable to James Scott, at the end of each of ten successive years, with good security to each bond. To this, Montague, having no alternative, agrees—promising to deliver the money and bonds, and receive the parcel from the hands of James Scott, at the same spot, on the following Saturday evening. His real design, however, is somewhat different. Having decoyed Balcombe and James to the rendezvous, he purposes with the aid of some of his agents, to get possession of the parcel by force, before paying the money; and afterwards with a view of preventing discovery, to carry our friends across the Missouri, and leave them to perish in the wilderness. This design is easily anticipated by Balcombe, who converts it ingeniously to his own advantage. Had he possession of the token handed to James by Mary, it is clear that nothing further would be necessary in order to obtain the missing will. But James has been especially directed to deliver the parcel into no hands but those of Montague—and his scruples are not to be overcome. Neither can B. reconcile it with his conscience to pick James' pockets while asleep. He determines, therefore, to let M. get possession of his object in the manner designed. This accomplished, he, Balcombe, will have acquired the right to retake it.

Keizer, the wily agent of Balcombe, is bound to that gentleman by many ties of gratitude. Of this Montague is unaware, and having frequently tampered with him in other cases wherein B. had no concern, does not hesitate to seek his assistance in the present scheme of villainy. This also B. has anticipated, and instructs Keizer not to refuse the rogue any service required—lest he might employ other agents.

In all this scheming, however, Balcombe is somewhat overreached. Montague discovers, by accident, the league between Keizer and B.—affects to have perfect confidence in the former—and appoints as the spot of rendezvous where Balcombe is to be entrapped, a spot at some distance from the true scene of action. By these means Keizer is placed out of the way, and his interference in Balcombe's favor prevented. It must be understood that (as expected) Montague, before his suspicions of Keizer were aroused, had engaged his services with those of a couple of his Indian friends, for the robbery and abduction of Scott and B., and Balcombe's plan was to turn the villain's false allies against himself. Coming, however, with James to the rendezvous, in full assurance that Keizer and the Indians were to be the agents employed against him, B. finds himself in the power of Montague and three unknown desperadoes. Montague, getting possession of the parcel, retires, while the rest of the party hurry off our two friends in the direction of the Missouri.

In the meantime, Keizer, with his Indians, having waited an undue time at the false rendezvous appointed him by Montague, comes at length to a suspicion of the true state of affairs, starts immediately in pursuit, and overtakes the enemy in good season for a rescue. Two of the villains escape—the third, one Ramsay, is shot dead by an Indian, and his body thrown by Keizer into the river.

The time having arrived for the return of Balcombe and Scott, Napier becomes uneasy, and disclosing the matter to Colonel Robinson, they proceed together to Montague's residence—thinking there to meet with some clue for further proceedings. As they approach, the door opens, and in the darkness they can just see Montague enter. Watching him through a window they perceive him opening the identical parcel of which so much has been said. It contained a casket, and this again a broken ring and a scrap of paper. Napier taps familiarly at the door, and Montague opens it, after being seen to throw the casket hastily in a drawer. Napier approaches the drawer at once, and obtains possession of the treasure. The villain is entirely taken by surprise, and in his terror indicates the route of his agents, professing at the same time his innocence of all design to commit murder. Taking him with them, the Colonel and Napier proceed to the river, and finding blood, with other similar traces, return home in despair, supposing Balcombe to have perished, when they are agreeably disappointed by his presence, with that of Scott and Keizer and the Indians—not forgetting Montague.

The contents of the casket are found to be a fragment of a gold ring, and a slip of paper with the words "Mammy Amy, the old housekeeper at Raby Hall." Montague is dismissed with an injunction from Balcombe to be forthcoming on the Monday ensuing—an injunction which it was supposed he would be unwilling, under the circumstances, to disobey. Here, however, Balcombe reckons without his host. Although Montague has not the broken ring, yet he has read the slip of paper, and may easily persuade Mammy Amy to deliver him the will. This idea now forces itself upon Balcombe—but too late—for the arch-rogue is already far on his way to Virginia. Lest Balcombe should pursue him, he has managed, by an ingeniously laid train of circumstances, to bring about his arrest, with that of Scott and Keizer, on a charge of murdering Ramsay. This man, it will be remembered, after being shot by one of the Indians, was thrown into the river by Keizer.

The accused party, however, after much difficulty, are admitted to bail, and Keizer starts for St. Louis in pursuit of the runaway—followed the next day by Napier. About half way between St. Charles and St. Louis, our hero encounters K. on his return, attended by a party of men, and with his feet tied together under the belly of his horse. Montague finding his steps dogged by K. in St. Louis, had obtained his arrest as a party to the murder. Napier enters into conversation with one of the company, who proves to be an attorney retained especially by Montague in support of the prosecution. The statement of N. puts this gentleman in possession of the true state of the case, and as Keizer had already been arrested and discharged on bail, he is set free, by means of a *habeas corpus*, at St. Charles. Montague, however, has effected his escape, and is fairly on his way to Virginia. Nothing is now left but to write to Mary Scott, and trust to the chance of the letter's reaching her before his arrival.

In the meantime the trial comes on. This is the most interesting portion of the book—and very different is it indeed from the caricature of judicial proceeding to be met with occasionally in the novels of the day. Fiction, thus admirably managed, has all the force and essential value of truth. And here we cannot bring ourselves to mar the vivid and most ingenious details by any attempt at a digest or paraphrase. Balcombe's defence is beyond measure acute, and in every respect characteristic—the party are acquitted, however, mainly through the agency of Keizer, who, taking advantage of his bail, crosses the Missouri, and, travelling night and day in search of a material witness, arrives with him just in time for the decision.

Napier now departs for Virginia, accompanied by Balcombe and Keizer. At Cape Girardeau, the whole are arrested. This is done at Montague's instance. The affidavit being shown, it proves to be a copy of that by means of which Keizer was arrested in a similar manner at St. Louis. Balcombe, however, having taken care to get a duly authenticated record of his acquittal, the villain's efforts to delay the party are defeated, and they proceed. Just after leaving Wheeling, they are again subjected to danger through the machinations of their arch-enemy, who, on his way home, it appears, has bribed some ostlers, connected with the line of stages, to attack the one carrying our hero.

At length, reaching Craiganet in safety, Balcombe there finds a letter from Mary Scott, detailing events at home since the date of her former communication. The rapidity of Montague's journey, it appears, defeated his own object. Suspicions were entertained of him on account of James' non-appearance, and the silence of Balcombe. A few days after the former's departure for Missouri, old Mrs. Scott died of a paralytic stroke; and, about the same time, Mammy Amy, the housekeeper, was taken ill at Raby Hall. Mary became her nurse, and also (at the request of Major Swann, the steward of the English Mr. Raby) assumed her duties as housekeeper. In this new vocation she continued, the old woman never recovering her activity. Matters were thus situated when Montague made his appearance at the Hall, and entering the old woman's room, endeavored to obtain from her the packet. Mary suddenly presenting herself, however, the villain is betrayed by his confusion, and fails altogether in his design. He calls again the next day, and again the next, using every artifice to get the packet, and closing with an offer of marriage. Calling in Major Swann, as witness to this offer, Mary desires the hypocrite to repeat it in his presence. With this request, fairly caught, he complies—and having done so, is rejected with disdain. The advantage hereby derived to Mary is of much importance to herself. It entitles her to full credence in the history of her wrongs; and having given this history in full to her kind friends, the Major and his wife, she is received and cherished by them with more than parental affection. The next day Montague again appears, and with a bold face, demanding, in the name of the law, his property of Major Swann, and speaking of a search-warrant. To this the Major replies, that he himself, being a justice of the peace, will furnish him with the necessary authority, upon his calling in the morning. Montague takes the hint, and disappears. In the meantime, Mary receives the letter from Balcombe, and is put *au fait* in regard to the nature of the packet, and Montague's anxiety respecting it. She, at first, thought to hand the letter and packet to Major Swann; but it occurred to her that, by so doing, she might place him in a delicate situation, between his duty to his employer, and his duty as a man. She resolved, therefore, to let things take their course, but at the same time to use effectual measures to keep the packet from falling into Montague's hands. We here quote a passage of much interest. Mary, it will be remembered, is writing to Balcombe.

Before I gave it to Mammy Amy, I had put it into a small

toy trunk, which I locked, keeping the key myself. Near the hearth was a place where a hole had been burned in the floor, and here a short plank had been laid down. This was loose. I took it up, put down the trunk, and, with the broom handle, pushed it away to the wall. I had taken the precaution to tie a bit of tape to the handle, the end of which I left in reach, but too far under to be seen without stooping low, and putting the face to the hole. I did this while my nurse was out, so that I alone knew where it was. Having thus completed my arrangements, I patiently awaited the approach of the enemy. About noon Montague arrived. The constable was already there. Montague was a long time closeted with the Major, I supposed engaged in coining a suitable affidavit. At length they all came together to my room. The kind old gentleman apologized with the utmost courtesy and deference to my feelings, for what he was about to do, and handed me Montague's affidavit. This testified, that six years ago he had left at my mother's a packet, which he described by external marks and seals; that he had reason to believe, and did believe, that I had got possession of it, and that it was secreted somewhere in the house. The search was now commenced, and every corner of the room was ransacked. Montague took little part in it, but kept his eyes on me, and pointed out suspected places. I became at last impatient of his insolent gaze; I felt my spirit rise, and was conscious of that flash of the eye before which his always quails, even when he sees it in the face of a woman. I now kept *my* eye on *him*, and his avoided it, though he occasionally stole a furtive glance. At length, walking across the floor, he felt the loose plank move under his feet. He stooped and raised it. I felt my courage give way; and as he lifted himself up after his short and fruitless search, our eyes met, and I was conscious that mine had blenched. I felt that thick throbbing of the heart which always displays itself in the countenance, and again stole a look at him to see if he had observed me. He had replaced the plank, and looked on the protracted search with less apparent interest than before. I saw, indeed, that he was weary of its continuance, and he soon expressed himself satisfied. They now left the room—Montague last of all. There is no fastening to the door but a large bar, inconveniently heavy, and a slight latch. This caught as he closed the door after him, and I was once more alone. I listened a moment, and heard the trampling of many feet, and the sound of many voices die away along the passage. My uneasiness now took its natural course. I ran to the hole and lifted the plank. At the moment the door opened, and Montague reappeared. The sagacity of the cunning wretch had taught him to expect what I would do under the influence of my alarmed and excited feelings. He had stopped at the door while the rest went on, and came in suddenly, as soon as he had allowed time for nature to do her work. He now sprang forward, while I, powerless with alarm, sank into a chair. He stooped down, and looked eagerly along the dark hole, and finally, groping, got hold of the end of the string. He drew it out, and I heard the little trunk come grating along over the laths below. I screamed, and sprang to him. He pushed me back, drew out the trunk, crushed it with his heel, and, seizing the packet, flung it into the fire.

It was a mild October day, and there was just so much fire as an old woman needs to comfort her rheumatic limbs. I rushed to it to rescue the packet. He seized and held me back, and I struggled, still screaming. The Major, who had missed Montague, and was returning to look for him, alarmed at my cries, hurried back. As soon as I saw him, I exclaimed, "In the fire—in the fire!" He understood me, and approached the hearth. Montague flung me across the room to my bed, on which I fell half insensible. But I saw Montague rudely seize the Major around the waist, and jerk him back, when, at the moment, Charles, my foster brother, entered. He darted at Montague, and, with one blow of his fist, felled him to the floor. The Major, disengaged, rescued the package from the fire, where its surface only was scorched, and turned to confront Montague, who slowly recovered his feet.

Here Montague's over-eagerness has again thwarted him. The only result of throwing the packet in the fire is, that the seals and other external marks of identification, sworn to in the affidavit, are melted and burned off. The Major offers, however, to deliver it up upon M's. identifying *the contents*. This, of course, the rogue declines, and the packet remains in the Major's possession, who declares his intention of resigning it, unopened, to the first person who shall show a just claim to it. The scene ends by Montague's being ordered to quit the premises. Shortly afterwards he attempts to fire the house, but fails, and in escaping, receives a shot through the shoulder.

But the difficulties touching the will are not yet altogether ended. The case is laid before an attorney. As there was no doubt of the result, if the papers could be secured, he determined to take such a course as would at once put them safely into the custody of the law. A bill is drafted, to which Mr. Edward Raby in England is made defendant, setting forth the whole transaction. Major Swann is also made defendant, charged with the possession of the will, and called on to produce it. As anticipated, he disclaims the possession of any such paper, unless such a one might be concealed with the packet, and files the packet with his answer. It is necessary that the papers shall reach the court (at Fredericksburg) without having ever been in possession of Mr. Napier, and they are accordingly given in charge of James. Mr. Napier, Balcombe, and Keizer accompany him. On the road, a short distance from Fredericksburg, the party are attacked by Montague, with some of his agents, and in the struggle which ensues, M. is killed by the hand of James, who, having accidentally discovered the secret of his sister's wrong, has been long burning for revenge. In conclusion—through the instrumentality of Keizer, our friends are saved a world of legal trouble, and Mr. Napier's claims to a large inheritance are finally established.

Thus is given—and given very scantily—only the general thread of the narrative—which is really crowded with incident. We have spoken of no love adventures of our hero—but it must not be supposed that he is therefore without them. They are omitted because altogether episodical—yet they form some of the most truly interesting portions of the book, and certainly the most original. In lieu of speaking farther on this head we copy a passage of rare beauty and full of a rich and meaning philosophy. Napier loves his cousin Ann, with whom his days of childhood and boyhood were spent in unreserved communion. He has reason to think himself beloved—but friends have their own plans to arrange, and a misunderstanding of each other's true feeling, arises between the lovers. Ann thus allows herself to be plighted to another, thinking the heart of her cousin pre-occupied. Things thus situated, N. as the protector and *friend* of Ann, speaks to her of her contemplated marriage. The passage we cite occurs in a conversation between Balcombe and Napier. The latter is confiding to B. the secret of his love.

"And what answer will you give?" I said.

She hesitated, changed color, trembled, and seemed to restrain her tears with great difficulty. I continued.

"Ann, dear Ann! if you knew how deep an interest I take in this question, you would not withhold the answer. Our lives from infancy have been spent together; each, as it were, a part of the other, 'like twin cherries growing on one stalk,' and shall we separate now?"

I saw her bite her lip, and her cheek flushed a little, while her countenance assumed an expression of slight indignation.

"Would you urge me then," said she, "to accept the hand of Howard?"

"To accept Howard's hand!" exclaimed I, "to place any man on earth between you and me! Oh, Ann, who can be dearer to you than I have been? And how can I endure that any other should ever occupy that place in your heart where I have lived so long; where all I know, all I can imagine of earthly bliss is centred?"

The fervor of my manner, I suppose, more than my words, made her at length perceive my meaning. She started, drew back, and gazed at me with a countenance in which amazement and grief contended for the mastery. The latter presently prevailed, and exclaiming, "Oh William, this from *you*!" the sluices of her heart seemed to open all at once; and with a look and air of utter desolation and self-abandonment, she threw her face on the arm of the sofa and dissolved in a flood of tears. I was inexpressibly shocked and amazed. I tried to soothe her, but in vain. She wept, and wept on, speechless from sobbing, until exhausted, she sank down on the sofa, and I saw by her white lip and glazing eye that she had fainted. I screamed for help, and she was carried to her room.

I saw her no more that evening. The next morning my sister Jane handed me this note.

"What I would have said yesterday, William, could I have found utterance, I say now. My astonishment and grief at the ungenerous conduct of one I had deemed faultless; at receiving insult from my only protector, and wrong from one whose whole life had been one act of kindness, need not be expressed in words. But I owe it to myself and all concerned, to insist that the subject of yesterday's conversation shall never be resumed. I will try to forget it, and deport myself towards you as if that conversation had never taken place. Help me, dear William, to forget that you have ever for a moment thought of being any thing but a brother to   A. N."

"There is surely some strange misunderstanding here," said I. "Can I see her?"

"Not at this moment, certainly, for she keeps her bed to day. But I will know whether she thinks it right to afford you another interview, when she can sit up."

"*To afford me another interview!*" said I. "This is indeed strange. Doubtful whether it be right that I should have an *interview* with one with whom my whole life has been spent as with a sister!"

"A sister, William!" said Jane. "You forget that your strange words, yesterday, have put an end to that relation. But I will let her know of your wish."

She left me, and soon returned with this pencilled paper.

"To what purpose, William, offer explanation of what could not be misunderstood? To what purpose resume a subject on which, after all that is passed, I cannot listen with propriety, nor you speak without offence? No, William, that subject must never be named between us again. You are soon to go on a distant journey; and I tell you distinctly that nothing but a solemn promise not to renew it, shall induce me to leave my room till you are gone. Don't force me to this, dear William. It would grieve me to have my earliest and dearest friend part from me without receiving a farewell, which may be the last."

"Saw you ever any thing like that?" said I, as Balcombe sat gazing at the paper with a musing and abstracted countenance. " '*Dear* William!' 'Her earliest and dearest friend!' Are not those words there? Was ever any thing more affectionate, more tender? It had been just so all the time. And when she left her room (for of course I gave the promise) it was still the same. She was pale and sad, and I saw that she felt for me. In all things else her manner was the same as in the days of our most cordial intimacy. She had kept her room some days, and I was dreading the embarrassment of our first meeting. But she dispelled it all. She met me, indeed, with a slight tremor; I saw her lips quiver, but her eye was steady, and dwelt upon my face with an expression of holy and confiding affection. She walked directly up to me, put her arms about my neck, and kissed me as she had always done on like occasions. Her manner was graver and more tender; that was all the difference. She rested her cheek, too, a moment on my bosom, and murmured, 'Thank you, dear William, thank you for your promise.' "

"Was no one present?" said Balcombe.

"Oh yes! Jane accompanied her into the room; but that very evening she took my arm and said, 'Come, let me show you my confidence in your word. Come, take a walk with me.' "

"And did you go alone?"

"Yes; Jane moved as if to go with us, but Ann stopped her."

"And what did you talk about?"

"Of old times; of the scenes and sports of infancy and early youth; of blended thoughts; of mingled feelings; of united hearts. She led the way herself. I could but listen to the soft tones of her voice, as she poured forth her feelings in language which showed how much her heart delighted in such recollections. 'Dear, dear William,' she said in conclusion, 'my own and only brother, let it be always thus.' You may believe that my heart responded to the wish. But is it not strange that while she was thus uttering words that condemned me to despair, I was supremely happy? It was no ordinary pleasure; it was a delirium of bliss. I felt as she seemed to feel at the moment, as if all my heart had ever coveted was mine. I responded to her sentiments in a like tone of chastened and refined tenderness; our hearts overflowed in the contemplation and actual fruition of this new scheme of happiness; we revelled in all the luxury of perfect sympathy and unbounded confidence; we seemed to have found a source of enjoyment too delicate to pall, too abounding ever to fail; our spirits rose as we quaffed the nectared flow of thoughts, and sentiments, and feelings, all congenial; and we returned to the house with faces glowing with affection and happiness. Is it not strange? How can it be that this, the paramount desire of my heart, by which I know that I love her, should be reciprocated by her without a corresponding sentiment?"

"If your metaphysics can find an answer to that question," said Balcombe, "I will consent that you shall believe that she does not love you. As it is, I have no doubt that her union with any other man would be more fatal to her than to you. But I see nothing unaccountable in what you tell me. Love, disguise it as you will, is the food that satisfies the heart of love; and that her conduct was the fruit of one of those strong delusions, with which love alone can cheat us, I have no doubt. I know something, William, of the joys of mutual passion; but never have I experienced, nor can I conceive, a scene of more thrilling rapture than you have described. Such things cannot last, indeed; but then what can? Illusions are dispelled, but *realities perish*."

The misunderstanding is finally rectified, through the agency of Balcombe, and the cousins are married. Besides this love affair, there are no passages of an episodical nature— unless we choose to speak of Balcombe's account of a skirmish with Indians—a duel scene between Balcombe and Howard, Ann's rejected lover—an anecdote relating to Colonel Boon, the backwoodsman—and a vividly drawn picture of a camp-meeting. This latter we will be pardoned for giving entire.

In the bosom of a vast forest, a piece of ground nearly an acre in extent, and in form almost a square, was enclosed on three sides by a sort of shed, sloping outward, and boarded up on the outside. This was divided into something like stalls, separated from each other, and closed in front by counterpanes, blankets and sheets, disposed as curtains. Some of these were thrown up, and within we saw coarse tables, stools, and preparations for eating and sleeping, such as piles of straw, beds tied up in bundles with bed-clothes, knives and forks, plates, porringers and platters, loaves of bread, skimmed-milk cheeses, jirked meat, hams, tongues, and cold fowls. Children and dogs were nestling in the straw, and mothers sat on stools, nursing their infants. The whole centre of the area was occupied by hewn logs, placed in extended parallel lines, with the ends resting on other transverse logs, so as to form rows of rude benches. On these were seated a promiscuous multitude, of every age, sex, condition, and hue, crowded densely towards the front, and gradually thinning in the rear, where some seats were nearly vacant, or partially oc-cupied by lounging youngsters, chatting, smoking, and gig-gling, and displaying, both in dress and manner, a disposition to ape the foppery and impertinence of fashion. Of this, in-deed, they saw so little in these remote wilds, that the imita-tion was of course awkward, but none the less unequivocal.

At the open end of the area was the stand, as it is called. This was formed by raising a pen of logs to a convenient height, over which a platform of loose planks was laid, sur-mounted by a shelter to keep off the sun and rain. The plat-form was large enough for a dozen chairs, occupied by as many preachers. It was surrounded by a strong enclosure, about twenty yards square, over the whole of which a deep bed of straw was laid. This, as I understood, was intended to save the bones of those who might be unable to keep their feet, under the eloquence of the preacher, the workings of conscience, the conviction of sin, or the delirious raptures of new-born hope.

The preachers were, for the most part, men whose dress and air bespoke a low origin and narrow circumstances. Con-spicuous among them was a stout old man, whose gray hair and compressed lips, ensconced between a long nose and hooked chin, would hardly have escaped observation under any circumstances. He alone was on his feet, and moved about the platform with noiseless step, speaking in whispers to one or another of the preachers. At length he took his seat, and the officiating minister rose. He was a tall, slender youth,

whose stripling figure lost nothing of its appearance of immaturity by being dressed in clothes which he had obviously
outgrown. The bony length of naked wrist and ankle set off
to the best advantage his broad hands and splay feet, the heels
of which were turned out, as he moved forward to his place
in front of the platform. His nearly beardless face was embrowned by the sun, his features were diminutive, and only
distinguished by a full round forehead, and a hazel eye, clear,
black, and imaginative. He gave out a hymn, which was sung,
and then offered up a prayer, which, though apparently
meant to pass for extemporaneous, was obviously spoken
from memory, and made up, for the most part, of certain
forms of speech, taken from all the prayers and all the creeds
that have ever been published, and arranged to suit the taste
of the speaker, and the peculiar doctrines of his sect. Then
came another hymn, and then the sermon. It was a doctrinal
essay, a good deal after the manner of a trial sermon, in which
not a little acuteness was displayed. But the voice was un-
trained, the language ungrammatical, the style awkward, and
the pronunciation barbarous. The thing went off heavily, but
left on my mind a very favorable impression of the latent
powers of the speaker. But he was not (to use the slang of
the theatre) "a star." He was heard with decorous, but
drowsy attention, and took his seat without having excited a
shout or a groan. I could not help suspecting that the poor
young fellow, being put forward as a foil for some popular
declaimer, had had his discourse pruned of all exuberance of
language or fancy, and reduced to a mere *hortus siccus* of theological doctrine. A closing prayer by an old minister, in which
the effort of the "young brother" was complimented with a
patronizing air, was followed by another hymn, and the temporary dispersion of the assembly.   *   *   *

Now came the turn of the old minister I first described.
The audience had been wearied with a discourse not at all to
their taste. They were now refreshed and eager for some stimulus to help digestion. At first I thought they would be disappointed; for he talked for a long time in a dull prosing way,
about himself and the church; and was listened to with an air
which led me to conclude that he had established a sort of
understanding with his hearers, that whatever he might say

must be worth hearing, and taken with thankfulness. At length, however, he seemed to warm by slow degrees. His voice became louder, his utterance more rapid, his gestures more earnest; and an occasional groan from the crowd bespoke their awaking sympathy. Presently he began to catch his breath, to rant and rave and foam at the mouth, and to give all the conventional tokens of enthusiasm and eloquence. The signals were duly answered by the groans, the sobs, the cries, the shouts, the yells of the multitude. Some sprang to their feet and clapped their hands; some grasped the hands of others with smiles and tears of sympathy and mutual gratulation; some fell down and were hoisted over into the pen, where they lay tossing among the straw, and uttering the most appalling shrieks. The discourse was abruptly closed; and several of the preachers came down into the enclosure, and, kneeling among the prostrate penitents, poured forth prayer after prayer, and shouted hymn after hymn, in which the whole audience joined in one wild burst of discord broken down into harmony by the very clashing of jarring sounds. The sun went down on this tumultuous scene.

Of the *dramatis personæ* we will speak in brief. Elizabeth, the shrinking and matronly wife of Balcombe, rising suddenly into the heroine in the hour of her husband's peril, (we have not mentioned her in our outline) as a painting, is admirable—as a portrait, appears to want individuality. She is an exquisite specimen of her class, but her class is somewhat hacknied. Of Jane, Napier's sister, (neither have we yet alluded to *her*) it is sufficient now to say that she is true to herself. Upon attentively considering the character of Mary Scott, who holds the most prominent female part in the drama, it will be perceived that, although deeply interesting, it cannot be regarded as in any degree original, and that she owes her influence upon the mind of the reader mainly to the incidents with which she is enveloped. There are some most effective touches, however, in her delineation. Of Ann we have already spoken. She is our favorite, and we doubt not the favorite of the author. Her nature is barely sketched—but the sketch betrays in the artist a creative vigor of no ordinary kind. Upon the whole, no American novelist has succeeded, we think, in female character, even nearly so well as the writer of George Balcombe.

Napier himself, is, as usual with most professed heroes, a mere non-entity. James is sufficiently natural. Major Swann, although only done in outline, gives a fine idea of a decayed Virginia gentleman. Charles, a negro, old Amy's son, is drawn roughly, but to the life. Balcombe, frank, ardent, philosophical, chivalrous, sagacious—and, above all, glorying in the exercise of his sagacity—is a conception which might possibly have been entertained, but certainly could not have been executed, by a mind many degrees dissimilar from that of Balcombe himself, as depicted. Of Keizer, a character evidently much dwelt upon, and greatly labored out by the author, we have but one observation to make. It will strike every reader, not at first, but upon reflection, that George Balcombe, in John Keizer's circumstances, would have been precisely John Keizer. We find the same traits modified throughout—yet the *worldly difference* forms a distinction sufficiently marked for the purposes of the novelist. Lastly, Montague, with his low cunning, his arch-hypocrisy, his malignancy, his quibbling superstition, his moral courage and physical pusillanimity, is a character to be met with every day, and to be recognized at a glance. Nothing was ever more minutely, more forcibly, or more thoroughly painted. He is not original of course; nor must we forget that were he so, he would, necessarily, be untrue, in some measure, to nature. But we mean to say that the merit here is solely that of observation and fidelity. Original characters, so called, can only be critically praised as such, either when presenting qualities known in real life, but never before depicted, (a combination nearly impossible) or when presenting qualities (moral, or physical, or both) which, although unknown, or even known to be hypothetical, are so skilfully adapted to the circumstances which surround them, that our sense of fitness is not offended, and we find ourselves seeking a reason why those things *might not have been*, which we are still satisfied *are not*. The latter species of originality appertains to the loftier regions of the *Ideal*.

Very few objections can be urged to the *style* of George Balcombe. The general manner is that of a scholar and gentleman in the best sense of both terms—bold, vigorous, and rich—abrupt rather than diffuse—and not over scrupulous in the use of energetic vulgarisms. With the mere English, some occasional and trivial faults may be found. Perhaps it would have been better to avoid such pure technicalities as "*anasto-mozing*." Of faulty construction, we might, without trouble, pick out a few instances. For example. "Returning to dinner, a note was handed to the old gentleman, which he read and gave to Balcombe." Here it is the note which returns to dinner. "Upon his return to dinner," or something of that kind, would have rendered the sentence less equivocal. Again—"My situation is any thing but pleasant, and so impatient of it am I that I trust I do not break faith with my client when I hint to you that Mr. Balcombe will have more need of the aid of counsel than he is aware of." The meaning here is, "I am so impatient of my situation that I even warn you of Balcombe's great danger, and advise you to seek counsel for him. In so doing I trust I am not breaking faith with my client." The original sentence implies, however, that the consequence of the speaker's impatience was the speaker's trusting that he would not break faith—whereas the *advice* was the consequence. The *trust* cannot in any manner be embodied with the sentence, and must be placed in a separate one, as we have placed it.

For the occasional *philosophy* of Balcombe himself, we must not, of course, hold the author responsible. It might now and then be more exact. For example. "I am not sure that we do not purchase all our good qualities by the exercise of their opposites. How else does experience of danger make men brave? If they were not scared at first, then they were brave at first. If they were scared, then the effect of fear upon the mind has been to engender courage." As much, perhaps, as the effect of truth is to engender error, or of black paint to render a canvass white. *All* our good qualities purchased by the exercise of their opposites! Generalize this dogma, and we have, at once, virtue derivable from vice. In the particular instance here urged—that courage is engendered by fear—the quibble lies in shifting the question from "danger" to "fear," and using the two ideas as identical. But "danger" is no more "fear," than age is wisdom, than a turnip-seed is a turnip; or than any other cause is its own usual effect. In proportion, we grant, to the frequency of our "experience of danger," is our callousness to its usual effect, which is fear. But when, following Mr. Balcombe to the finale of his argument, we say that the effect of the frequent "experience of *fear*" upon the mind is to engender courage, we are merely uttering the silly paradox that we fear less in proportion as we fear more.

And again. "Value depends on demand and supply. So say the political economists, and I suppose they are right in all things but one. When truth and honor abound, they are most prized. They depreciate as they become rare." Now truth and honor form *no* exceptions to the rule of economy, that value depends upon demand and supply. The simple meaning of this rule is, that when the demand for a commodity is great, and the supply small, the value of the commodity is heightened, and the converse. Apply this to truth and honor. Let them be in demand—in esteem—and let the supply be small—that is, let there be few men true and honest; then truth and honor, as cotton and tobacco, rise in value—and, vice-versa, they fall. Mr. Balcombe's error is based upon the pre-supposition, (although this pre-supposition does not appear upon the face of his statement) that all who esteem truth and honor, are necessarily true and honest. To sustain the parallel, then, he should be prepared to admit the absurdity that the demanders of cotton and tobacco are necessarily stocked with cotton and tobacco. Let, however, the full extent of the question be seen. Truth and honor, it is asserted, are most prized where they most abound. They would be prized most of all then were no contrary qualities existing. But it is clear that were *all* men true and honest, then truth and honor, *beyond their intrinsic*, would hold no higher value, than would wine in a Paradise where all the rivers were Johannisberger, and all the duck-ponds Vin de Margaux.

We have thus spoken at length of George Balcombe, because we are induced to regard it, upon the whole, as *the best* American novel. There have been few books of its peculiar kind, we think, written in *any* country, much its superior. Its interest is intense from beginning to end. Talent of a lofty order is evinced in every page of it. Its most distinguishing features are invention, vigor, almost audacity, of thought— great variety of what the German critics term *intrigue*, and exceeding ingenuity and finish in the adaptation of its component parts. Nothing is wanting to a complete whole, and nothing is out of place, or out of time. Without being chargeable in the least degree with imitation, the novel bears a strong family resemblance to the Caleb Williams of Godwin. Thinking thus highly of George Balcombe, we still do not wish to be understood as ranking it with the more brilliant fictions of some of the living novelists of Great Britain.

In regard to the authorship of the book, some little conversation has occurred, and the matter is still considered a secret. But why so?—or rather, *how* so? The mind of the chief personage of the story, is the transcript of a mind familiar to us—an unintentional transcript, let us grant—but still one not to be mistaken. George Balcombe thinks, speaks, and acts, as no person, we are convinced, but Judge Beverly Tucker, ever precisely thought, spoke, or acted before.

Southern Literary Messenger, January 1837

Robert Walsh

Didactics—Social, Literary, and Political. By Robert Walsh. Philadelphia: Carey, Lea, and Blanchard.

HAVING READ these volumes with much attention and pleasure, we are prepared to admit that their author is one of the finest writers, one of the most accomplished scholars, and when not in too great a hurry, one of the most accurate thinkers in the country. Yet had we never seen this collection of *Didactics*, we should never have entertained these opinions. Mr. Walsh has been peculiarly an anonymous writer, and has thus been instrumental in cheating himself of a great portion of that literary renown which is most unequivocally his due. We have been not unfrequently astonished in the perusal of the book now before us, at meeting with a variety of well known and highly esteemed acquaintances, for whose paternity we had been accustomed to give credit where we now find it should not have been given. Among these we may mention in especial the very excellent Essay on the acting of Kean, entitled *"Notices of Kean's principal performances during his first season in Philadelphia,"* to be found at page 146, volume i. We have often thought of the unknown author of this Essay, as of one to whom we might speak, if occasion should at any time be granted us, with a perfect certainty of being understood. We have looked to the article itself as to a fair oasis in the general blankness and futility of our customary theatrical notices. We read it with that thrill of pleasure with which we always welcome our own long-cherished opinions, when we meet them unexpectedly in the language of another. How absolute is the necessity now daily growing, of rescuing our stage criticism from the control of illiterate mountebanks, and placing it in the hands of gentlemen and scholars!

The paper on *Collegiate Education*, beginning at page 165, volume ii, is much more than a sufficient reply to that Essay in the *Old Bachelor* of Mr. Wirt, in which the attempt is made to argue down colleges as seminaries for the young. Mr. Walsh's article does not uphold Mr. Barlow's plan of a National University—a plan which is assailed by the Attorney

General—but comments upon some errors in point of fact, and enters into a brief but comprehensive examination of the general subject. He maintains with undeniable truth, that it is illogical to deduce arguments against universities which are to exist at the present day, from the inconveniences found to be connected with institutions formed in the dark ages—institutions similar to our own in but few respects, modelled upon the principles and prejudices of the times, organized with a view to particular ecclesiastical purposes, and confined in their operations by an infinity of Gothic and perplexing regulations. He thinks, (and we believe he thinks with a great majority of our well educated fellow citizens) that in the case either of a great national institute or of State universities, nearly all the difficulties so much insisted upon will prove a series of mere chimeras—that the evils apprehended might be readily obviated, and the acknowledged benefits uninterruptedly secured. He denies, very justly, the assertion of the *Old Bachelor*—that, in the progress of society, funds for collegiate establishments will no doubt be accumulated, independently of government, when their benefits are evident, and a necessity for them felt—and that the rich who have funds will, whenever strongly impressed with the necessity of so doing, provide, either by associations or otherwise, proper seminaries for the education of their children. He shows that these assertions are contradictory to experience, and more particularly to the experience of the State of Virginia, where, notwithstanding the extent of private opulence, and the disadvantages under which the community so long labored from a want of regular and systematic instruction, it was the government which was finally compelled, and not private societies which were induced, to provide establishments for effecting the great end. He says (and therein we must all fully agree with him) that Virginia may consider herself fortunate in following the example of all the enlightened nations of modern times rather than in hearkening to the counsels of the Old Bachelor. He dissents (and who would not?) from the allegation, that "the most eminent men in Europe, particularly in England, have received their education neither at public schools or universities," and shows that the very reverse may be affirmed—that on the continent of Europe by far the greater number of its great names have been attached to the rolls of its universities—and that in England a vast majority of those minds which we have reverenced so long—the Bacons, the Newtons, the Barrows, the Clarkes, the Spencers, the Miltons, the Drydens, the Addisons, the Temples, the Hales, the Clarendons, the Mansfields, Chatham, Pitt, Fox, Wyndham, &c. were educated among the venerable cloisters of Oxford or of Cambridge. He cites the Oxford Prize Essays, so well known even in America, as direct evidence of the energetic ardor in acquiring knowledge brought about through the means of British Universities, and maintains that " when attention is given to the subsequent public stations and labors of most of the writers of these Essays, it will be found that they prove also the ultimate practical utility of the literary discipline of the colleges for the students and the nation." He argues, that were it even true that the greatest men have not been educated in public schools, the fact would have little to do with the question of their efficacy in the instruction of the mass of mankind. Great men cannot be *created*—and are usually independent of all particular schemes of education. Public seminaries are best adapted to the generality of cases. He concludes with observing that the course of study pursued at English Universities, is more liberal by far than we are willing to suppose it—that it is, demonstrably, the best, inasmuch as regards the preference given to classical and mathematical knowledge—and that upon the whole it would be an easy matter, in transferring to America the general principles of those institutions, to leave them their obvious errors, while we avail ourselves as we best may, of their still more obvious virtues and advantages.

We must take the liberty of copying an interesting paper on the subject of Oxford.

The impression made on my mind by the first aspect of Paris was scarcely more lively or profound, than that which I experienced on entering Oxford. Great towns were already familiar to my eye, but a whole city sacred to the cultivation of science, composed of edifices no less venerable for their antiquity than magnificent in their structure, was a novelty which at once delighted and overpowered my imagination.

The entire population is in some degree appended and ministerial to the colleges. They comprise nearly the whole town, and are so noble and imposing, although entirely Gothic, that I was inclined to apply to the architecture of Oxford what has been said of the schools of Athens;

"The Muse alone unequal dealt her rage,
And graced with noblest pomp her earliest stage."

Spacious gardens laid out with taste and skill are annexed to each college, and appropriated to the exercises and meditations of the students. The adjacent country is in the highest state of cultivation, and watered by a beautiful stream, which bears the name of Isis, the divinity of the Nile and the Ceres of the Egyptians. To you who know my attachment to letters, and my veneration for the great men whom this university has produced, it will not appear affectation, when I say that I was most powerfully affected by this scene, that my eyes filled with tears, that all the enthusiasm of a student burst forth.

After resting, I delivered next morning, my letter of introduction to one of the professors, Mr. V——, and who undertook to serve as my *cicerone* through the university. The whole day was consumed in wandering over the various colleges and their libraries, in discoursing on their organization, and in admiring the Gothic chapels, the splendid prospects from their domes, the collection of books, of paintings, and of statuary, and the portraits of the great men who were nursed in this seat of learning. Both here and at Cambridge, accurate likenesses of such as have by their political or literary elevation, ennobled their *alma mater*, are hung up in the great halls, in order to excite the emulation of their successors, and perpetuate the fame of the institution. I do not wish to fatigue you by making you the associate of all my wanderings and reflections, but only beg you to follow me rapidly through the picture-gallery attached to the celebrated Bodleian library. It is long indeed, and covered with a multitude of original portraits, but from them I shall merely select a few, in which your knowledge of history will lead you to take a lively interest.

I was struck with the face of Martin Luther the reformer. It was not necessary to have studied Lavater to collect from it, the character of his mind. His features were excessively harsh though regular, his eye intelligent but sullen and scowling, and the whole expression of his countenance, that of a sour, intemperate, overbearing controversialist. Near him were placed likenesses of Locke, Butler, and Charles II., painted by Sir Peter Lely; with the countenance of Locke you are well acquainted, that of Butler has nothing sportive in it—does not betray a particle of humor, but is, on the contrary, grave, solemn, and didactic in the extreme, and must have been taken in one of his splenetic moods, when brooding over the neglect of Charles, rather than in one of those moments of inspiration, as they may be styled, in which he narrated the achievements of Hudibras. The physiognomy of Charles is, I presume, familiar to you, lively but not "spiritual." Lord North is among the number of heads, and I was caught by his strong resemblance to the present king; so strong as to remind one of the scandalous chronicles of times past.

The face of Mary queen of Scots next attracted my notice. It was taken in her own time, and amply justifies what historians have written, or poets have sung, concerning her incomparable beauty. If ever there was a countenance meriting the epithet of lovely in its most comprehensive signification, it was this, which truly "vindicated the veracity of Fame," and in which I needed not the aid of imagination to trace the virtues of her heart. In reading Hume and Whitaker I have often wept over her misfortunes, and now turned with increased disgust from an original portrait of Elizabeth, her rival and assassin, which was placed immediately above, and contributed to heighten the captivations of the other by the effect of contrast. The features of Elizabeth are harsh and irregular, her eye severe, her complexion bad, her whole face, in short, just such as you would naturally attach to such a mind.

Among the curiosities of the gallery may be ranked a likeness of Sir Phillip Sydney, done with a *red hot poker*, on wood, by a person of the name of Griffith, belonging to one of the colleges. It is really a monument of human patience and ingenuity, and has the appearance of a good painting. I cannot describe to you without admiration another most extraordinary *freak* of genius exhibited here, and altogether *unique* in its kind. It is a portrait of Isaac Tuller, a celebrated painter in the reign of Charles II., executed by *himself when drunk*. Tradition represents it as an admirable likeness, and of inebriety in the abstract, there never was a more faithful or perfect delineation. This anecdote is authentic, and must amuse the fancy, if we picture to ourselves the artist completely intoxicated, inspecting his own features in a mirror, and hitting off, with complete success, not only the general character, but the peculiar stamp, which such a state must have impressed upon them. His conception was as full of humor as of originality, and well adapted to the system of manners which the reigning monarch introduced and patronized. As I am on the subject of portraits, permit me to mention three to which my attention was particularly called on my visit to the University of Dublin. They were those of Burke, Swift, and Bishop Berkeley, done by the ablest masters. The latter must have had one of the most impressive physiognomies ever given to man, *"the human face divine."* That of Burke is far inferior, but strongly marked by an indignant smile; a proper expression for the feelings by which his mind was constantly agitated towards the close of his life. The face of Swift from which you would expect every thing, is dull, heavy and unmeaning.

Portrait painting is the *forte*, as it has always been the passion of this country. Happily for the inquisitive stranger, every rich man has all his progenitors and relatives on canvass. The walls of every public institution are crowded with benefactors and pupils, and no town hall is left without the heads of the corporation, or the representatives of the borough. The same impulse that prompts us to gaze with avidity on the persons of our cotemporaries, if there be any thing prominent in their character, or peculiar in their history, leads us to turn a curious and attentive eye on the likenesses of the "mighty dead," whose souls as well as faces are thus in some degree transmitted to posterity. Next to my association with the living men of genius who render illustrious the names of Englishmen, no more sensible gratification has accrued to me from my residence in this country, than that of studying the countenances of their predecessors; no employment has tended more efficaciously to improve my acquaintance with the history of the nation, to animate research, and to quicken the spirit of competition.

I quitted Oxford with a fervent wish that such an establishment might one day grace our own country. I have uttered an ejaculation to the same effect whenever the great monuments of industry and refinement which Europe displays exclusively, have fallen under my observation. We have indeed just grounds to hope that we shall one day eclipse the old world.

> "Each rising art by just gradation moves,
>   Toil builds on toil, and age on age improves."

The only paper in the *Didactics*, to which we have any decided objection, is a tolerably long article on the subject of *Phrenology*, entitled "Memorial of the Phrenological Society of ———— to the Honorable the Congress of ———— sitting at ————." Considered as a specimen of mere burlesque the *Memorial* is well enough—but we are sorry to see the energies of a scholar and an editor (who should be, if he be not, a man of metaphysical science) so wickedly employed as in any attempt to throw ridicule upon a question, (however much maligned, or however apparently ridiculous) whose merits he has never examined, and of whose very nature, history, and assumptions, he is most evidently ignorant. Mr. Walsh is either ashamed of this article now, or he will have plentiful reason to be ashamed of it hereafter.

Southern Literary Messenger, May 1836

Robert M. Walsh

"Sketches of Conspicuous Living Characters of France." Translated by R. M. Walsh. Lea and Blanchard.

THE PUBLIC are much indebted to Mr. Walsh for this book, which is one of unusual interest and value. It is a translation from the French, of fifteen biographical and critical sketches, written, and originally published in weekly numbers at Paris, by some one who styles himself *"un homme de rien"*—the better to conceal the fact, perhaps, that he is really *un homme de beaucoup*. Whatever, unhappily, may be the case with ourselves, or in England, it is clear that in the capital of France, at least,—that hot-bed of journalism, and Paradise of journalists—nobody has any right to call himself "nobody," while wielding so vigorous and vivacious a pen as the author of these articles.

We are told in the Preface to the present translation that they met with the greatest success, upon their first appearance, and were considered by the Parisians as perfectly authentic in their statement of facts, and "as impartial in their appreciation of the different personages sketched as could be desired." "As impartial, &c." means, we presume, entirely so; for in matters of this kind an absolute impartiality, of course, is all, but still the least "that could be desired."

Mr. Walsh farther assures us that Châteaubriand wrote the author a letter "of a highly complimentary tenor" which was published, but of which the translator, "unfortunately, does not happen to have a copy in his possession." A more unfortunate circumstance is that Mr. W. should have thought it necessary to bolster a book which needs no bolstering, by the authority of any name, however great; and the most unfortunate thing of all, so far as regards the weight of the authority, is that Châteaubriand himself is belauded *ad nauseam* in those very pages to the inditer of which he sent that letter of the "complimentary tenor." When any body shall puff *us*, as this Mr. Nobody has bepuffed the author of *The Martyrs*, we will send them a letter "of a complimentary tenor" too. We do not mean to decry the general merit of the book, or the candor of him who composed it. We wish merely to observe that Châteaubriand, under the circumstances, cannot be received as evidence of the one, nor his biography as instance of the other.

These sketches of men now playing important parts in the great drama of French affairs would be interesting, if only from their subjects. We have here biographies (sufficiently full) of Thiers, Châteaubriand, Laffitte, Guizot, Lamartine, Soult, Berryer, De La Mennais, Hugo, Dupin, Bèranger, Odilion Barrot, Arago, George Sand, and the Duke De Broglie. We are most pleased with those of Thiers, Hugo, Sand, Arago, and Bèranger.

Among many good stories of Thiers, this is told. A prize had been offered by the Academy of Aix for the best eulogium on Vauvenargues. Thiers, then quite a boy, sent a M. S. It was deemed excellent; but the author being suspected, and no other candidate deserving the palm, the committee, rather than award it to a Jacobin, postponed their decision for a year. At the expiration of this time our youth's article again made its appearance, but, meanwhile, a production had arrived from Paris which was thought far better. The judges were rejoiced. They were no longer under the cruel necessity of giving the first honor to a Jacobin—but felt bound to present him with the second. The name of the Parisian victor was unsealed. It was that of Thiers—Monsieur Tonson come again. He had been at great pains to mystify the committee; (other committees of the same kind more frequently reverse affairs and mystify the public) the M. S. had been copied in a strange hand, and been sent from Aix to Paris and from Paris to Aix. Thus our little friend obtained both the main prize and the *accessit*.

An anecdote somewhat similar is related of Victor Hugo. In 1817, the Academy offered a premium for the best poem on the advantages of study. Hugo entered the lists. His piece was considered worthiest, but was rejected because a falsehood was supposed to be implied in the concluding lines, which ran thus:—

> Moi qui, toujours fuyant les cités et les cours,
> De trois lustres à peine ai vu finir le cours.

The Academy would not believe that any one under twenty-five years of age had written so fine a poem, and, supposing a mystification designed, thought to punish the author by refusing him the prize. Informed of the facts, Hugo hastened to show the certificate of his birth to the reporter, M. Raynouard; but it was too late—the premium had been awarded.

Of Laffitte many remarkable incidents are narrated evincing the noble liberality of his disposition.

In the notice of Berryer it is said that, a letter being addressed by the Dutchess of Berry to the legitimists of Paris, to inform them of her arrival, it was accompanied by a long note in cypher, the key of which she had forgotten to give. "The penetrating mind of Berryer," says our biographer, "soon discovered it. It was this phrase substituted for the twenty-four letters of the alphabet—*Le gouvernement provisoire.*"

All this is very well as an anecdote; but we cannot understand the extraordinary penetration required in the matter. The phrase *"Le gouvernement provisoire"* is French, and the note in cypher was addressed to Frenchmen. The difficulty of deciphering may well be supposed much greater had the key been in a foreign tongue; yet any one who will take the trouble may address us a note, in the same manner as here proposed, and the key-phrase may be either in French, Italian, Spanish, German, Latin or Greek, (or in any of the dialects of these languages), and we pledge ourselves for the solution of the riddle. The experiment may afford our readers some amusement—let them try it.

But we are rambling from our theme. The genius of Arago is finely painted, and the character of his quackery put in a true light. The straight-forward, plainly-written critical comments upon this philosopher, as well as upon George Sand, and that absurd antithesis-hunter, Victor Hugo, please us far more than that mere cant and rhapsody in which the biographer involves himself when speaking of Châteaubriand and Lamartine. We have observed that all great authors who fall occasionally into the sins of ranting and raving, meet with critics who think the only way to elucidate, is to out-rant and out-rave them. A beautiful confusion of thought of course ensues, which it is truly refreshing to contemplate.

The account of George Sand (Madame Dudevant) is full of piquancy and spirit. The writer, by dint of a little chicanery, obtained access, it seems, to her boudoir, with an opportunity of sketching her in dishabille. He found her in a gentleman's frock coat, smoking a cigar.

Speaking of the equivocal costume affected by this lady, Mr. Walsh, in a foot-note, comments upon a nice distinction made once by a soldier on duty at the Chamber of Deputies. Madame D., habited in male attire, was making her way into the gallery, when the man, presenting his musket before her, cried out "*Monsieur*, les *dames* ne passent pas par ici!"

But we regret that our space will not allow us to cull even a few of the good things with which the book abounds. The whole volume is exceedingly *piquant*, and replete with that racy wit which is so peculiarly French as to make us believe it a consequence of the *tournure* of the language itself. But if a Frenchman is invariably witty, he is not the less everlastingly bombastic; and these memoirs are decidedly French. What can we do but smile when we hear any one talk about Châteaubriand's *Essay upon English Poetry*, with his *Translation of Milton*! as a task which he alone was qualified to execute!— or when we read page after page in which Lamartine is discoursed of as "a noble child, with flaxen locks," "disporting upon the banks of the Seine," "picking up Grecian lyres dropped by the mild Chenier," "enriching them with Christian chords," and "ravishing the world with new melodies!" What can we do but laugh outright at such phrases as the "sympathetic swan-like cries," and the "singular lyric precocity of the crystal soul"—of such an ass as the author of Bug-Jargal?

So far as mere translation goes, the volume now before us is, in some respects, not very well done. Too little care has been taken in rendering the French idioms by English equivalents; and, because a French writer, through the impulses of his vivacity, cannot avoid telling, in the present tense, a story of the past, it does not follow that such a misusage of language is consonant with the graver genius of the Saxon. Mr. Walsh is always too literal, although sufficiently correct. He should not employ, however, even in translation, such queer words as "to legitimate," meaning "to legitimatize," or "to fulmine," meaning "to fulminate."

At page 211, the force of the compound *"l'homme-calembourg"* is not conveyed by the words *"the* punster," even when we italicize *the*. *The walking-pun*, perhaps, is an analogous phrase which might be more properly employed.

There is some odd mistake at page 274, where the translator speaks of measuring the diameter of the earth by measuring its *rays*. We presume the word in the original is *rayons*; if so we can only translate it by the Latin *radii*. No doubt a radius, literally, is a ray; but science has its own terms, and *will* employ them. We should like to see either Mr. Walsh or Monsieur Arago (or both together) trying to measure a *ray* of the earth.

The mechanical execution of the book is good, saving a thousand outrageous typographical blunders, and *that* lithograph of Thiers. We have no doubt in the world that this gentleman (who ran away during the three days and hid himself in the woods of Montmorency), is a somewhat dirty, insignificant little fellow, and so be it; but we will never be brought to believe that any individual in Christendom ever did or could look half as saucy, or as greasy, as does "Monsieur Mirabeau-mouche" in that picture.

Graham's Magazine, April 1841

Thomas Ward

THE POET now comprehended in the *cognomen* Flaccus, is by no means our ancient friend Quintus Horatius, nor even his ghost, but merely a Mr. —— Ward, of Gotham, once a contributor to the New York "American," and to the New York "Knickerbocker" Magazine. He is characterized by Mr. Griswold, in his "Poets and Poetry of America," as a gentleman of elegant leisure.

What there is in "elegant leisure" so much at war with the divine *afflatus*, it is not very difficult, but quite unnecessary, to say. The *fact* has been long apparent. Never sing the Nine so well as when penniless. The *mens divinior* is one thing, and the *otium cum dignitate* quite another.

Of course Mr. Ward is not, as a poet, altogether destitute of merit. If so, the public had been spared these paragraphs. But the sum of his deserts has been footed up by a *clique* who are in the habit of reckoning units as tens in all cases where champagne and "elegant leisure" are concerned. We do not consider him, at all points, a Pop Emmons, but, with deference to the more matured opinions of the "Knickerbocker," we may be permitted to entertain a doubt whether he is either Jupiter Tonans or Phœbus Apollo.

Justice is not, at all times, to all persons, the most desirable thing in the world, but then there is the old adage about the tumbling of the heavens, and *simple* justice is all that we propose in the case of Mr. Ward. We have *no* design to be bitter. We notice his book at all, only because it is an unusually large one of its kind, because it is here lying upon our table, and because, whether justly or unjustly, whether for good reason or for none, it has attracted some portion of the attention of the public.

The volume is entitled, somewhat affectedly, "Passaic, a Group of Poems touching that river: with Other Musings, by Flaccus," and embodies, we believe, all the previously published effusions of its author. It commences with a very pretty "Sonnet to Passaic," and from the second poem, "Introductory Musings on Rivers," we are happy in being able to quote an entire page of even remarkable beauty.

Beautiful Rivers! that a down the vale
With graceful passage journey to the deep,
Let me along your grassy marge recline
At ease, and, musing, meditate the strange
Bright history of your life; yes, from your birth
Has beauty's shadow chased your every step:
The blue sea was your mother, and the sun
Your glorious sire, clouds your voluptuous cradle,
Roofed with o'erarching rainbows; and your fall
To earth was cheered with shouts of happy birds,
With brightened faces of reviving flowers,
And meadows, while the sympathizing west
Took holiday and donn'd her richest robes.
From deep mysterious wanderings your springs
Break bubbling into beauty; where they lie
In infant helplessness awhile, but soon,
Gathering in tiny brooks, they gambol down
The steep sides of the mountain, laughing, shouting,
Teasing the wild flowers, and at every turn
Meeting new playmates still to swell their ranks;
Which, with the rich increase resistless grown,
Shed foam and thunder, that the echoing wood
Rings with the boisterous glee; while, o'er their heads,
Catching their spirit blithe, young rainbows sport,
The frolic children of the wanton sun.

Nor is your swelling prime, or green old age,
Though calm, unlovely; still, where'er ye move,
Your train is beauty; trees stand grouping by
To mark your graceful progress; giddy flowers
And vain, as beauties wont, stoop o'er the verge
To greet their faces in your flattering glass:
The thirsty herd are following at your side;
And water-birds in clustering fleets convoy
Your sea-bound tides; and jaded man, released
From worldly thraldom, here his dwelling plants—
Here pauses in your pleasant neighborhood,
Sure of repose along your tranquil shores;
And, when your end approaches, and ye blend
With the eternal ocean, ye shall fade

As placidly as when an infant dies,
And the Death-Angel shall your powers withdraw
Gently as twilight takes the parting day,
And, with a soft and gradual decline
That cheats the senses, lets it down to night.

There is nothing very *original* in all this; the general idea is, perhaps, the most absolutely trite in poetical literature; but the theme is not the less just on this account, while we must confess that it is admirably handled. The picture embodied in the whole of the concluding paragraph is perfect. The seven final lines convey not only a novel but a highly appropriate and beautiful image.

What follows, of this poem, however, is by no means worthy so fine a beginning. Instead of confining himself to the true poetical thesis, the Beauty or the Sublimity of river scenery, he descends into mere meteorology—into the uses and general philosophy of rain, &c.—matters which should be left to Mr. Espy, who knows something about them, as we are sorry to say Mr. Flaccus does *not*.

The second and chief *poem* in the volume, is entitled "The Great Descender." We emphasize the "poem" merely by way of suggesting that the "Great Descender" is any thing else. We never could understand what pleasure men of talent can take in concocting elaborate doggerel of this order. Least of all can we comprehend why, having perpetrated the atrocity, they should place it at the door of the Muse. We are at a loss to know by what right, human or divine, twattle of this character is intruded into a collection of what professes to be *Poetry*. We put it to Mr. Ward, in all earnestness, if the "Great Descender," which is a history of Sam Patch, has a single attribute, beyond that of mere versification, in common with what even Sam Patch himself would have had the hardihood to denominate a poem.

Let us call this thing a rhymed *jeu d'esprit*, a burlesque, or what not?—and, even so called, and judged by its new name, we must still regard it as a failure. Even in the loosest compositions we demand a certain degree of *keeping*. But in the "Great Descender" none is apparent. The *tone* is unsteady— fluctuating between the grave and the gay—and never being precisely either. Thus there is a failure in both. The intention being never rightly *taken*, we are, of course, never exactly in condition either to weep or to laugh.

We do not pretend to be the Oracles of Dodona, but it does really appear to us that Mr. Flaccus intended the whole matter, in the first instance, as a solemnly serious thing; and that, having composed it in a grave vein, he became apprehensive of its exciting derision, and so interwove sundry touches of the burlesque, behind whose equivocal aspect he might shelter himself at need. In no other supposition can we reconcile the *spotty* appearance of the whole with a belief in the sanity of the author. It is difficult, also, in any other view of the case, to appreciate the air of positive gravity with which he descants upon the advantages to *Science* which have accrued from a man's making a frog of himself. Mr. Ward is frequently pleased to denominate Mr. Patch "a martyr of science," and appears very doggedly in earnest in all passages such as the following:

Through the glad Heavens, which tempests now conceal,
Deep thunder-guns in quick succession peal,
As if salutes were firing from the sky,
To hail the triumph and the victory.
Shout! trump of Fame, till thy brass lungs burst out!
Shout! mortal tongues! deep-throated thunders, shout!
For lo! electric *genius*, downward hurled,
Has startled *Science* and illumed the world!

That Mr. Patch was a *genius* we do not doubt; so is Mr. Ward; but the *science* displayed in jumping down the Falls, is a point above us. There might have been some science in jumping *up*.

"The Worth of Beauty: or a Lover's Journal," is the title of the poem next in place and importance. Of this composition Mr. W. thus speaks in a Note: "The individual to whom the present poem relates, and who had suffered severely all the pains and penalties which arise from the want of those personal charms so much admired by him in others, gave the author, many years since, some fragments of a journal kept in his early days, in which he had bared his heart and set down all his thoughts and feelings. This prose journal has here been transplanted into the richer soil of verse."

The narrative of the friend of Mr. Flaccus must, originally, have been a very good thing. By "originally," we mean before it had the misfortune to be "transplanted into the richer soil of verse"—which has by no means agreed with its constitution. But, even through the dense fog of our author's rhythm, we can get an occasional glimpse of its merit. It must have been the work of a heart on fire with passion, and the utter *abandon* of the details, reminds us even of Jean Jacques. But alas for this "richer soil!" *Can* we venture to present our readers with a specimen?

> Now roses blush, and violets' eyes,
> And seas reflect the glance of skies;
> And now *that frolic pencil* streaks
> With quaintest tints the tulips' cheeks;
> Now jewels bloom in secret worth
> Like blossoms of the inner earth;
> Now painted birds are pouring round
> The beauty and the wealth of sound;
> Now sea-shells glance with quivering ray
> Too rare to seize, too fleet to stay,
> And hues out dazzling all the rest
> Are dashed profusely on the west,
> While rainbows seem to palettes changed,
> Whereon the motley tints are ranged.
> But soft the moon *that pencil* tipped
> As though, in liquid radiance dipped,
> A likeness of the sun it drew,
> But flattered him with pearlier hue;
> Which haply spilling runs astray,
> And blots with light the milky way;
> While stars besprinkle all the air
> Like spatterings of *that pencil* there.

All this by way of *exalting* the subject. The moon is made a painter and the rainbow a palette. And the moon has a pencil (*that* pencil!) which she dips, by way of a brush, in the liquid radiance, (the colors on a palette are *not* liquid,) and then *draws* (not paints) a likeness of the sun; but, in the attempt, plasters him too "pearly," puts it on too thick; the consequence of which is that some of the paint is spilt, and "runs astray" and besmears the milky way, and "spatters" the rest of the sky with stars! We can only say that a very singular picture was spoilt in the making.

The *versification* of the "Worth of Beauty" proceeds much after this fashion: we select a fair example of the whole from page 43.

> Yes! pangs have cut my soul with grief
> So keen that gushes were relief,
> And racks have rung my spirit-frame
> To which the strain of joints were tame
> And battle strife itself were nought
> Beside the inner fight I've fought. etc., etc.

Nor do we regard any portion of it (so far as rhythm is concerned) as at all comparable to some of the better ditties of William Slater. Here, for example, from his Psalms, published in 1642:

> The righteous shall his sorrow scan
>   And laugh at him, and say "behold
> What hath become of this here man
>   That on his riches was so bold."

And here, again, are lines from the edition of the same Psalms, by Archbishop Parker, which we most decidedly prefer:

> Who sticketh to God in stable trust
> As Sion's mount he stands full just,
> Which moveth no whit nor yet can reel,
> But standeth forever as stiff as steel.

"The Martyr" and the "Retreat of Seventy-Six" are merely Revolutionary incidents "done into verse," and spoilt in the doing. "The Retreat" begins with the remarkable line,

> Tramp! tramp! tramp! tramp!

which is elsewhere introduced into the poem. We look in vain, here, for any thing worth even qualified commendation.

"The Diary" is a record of events occurring to the author

during a voyage from New York to Havre. Of these events a
fit of sea-sickness is the chief. Mr. Ward, we believe, is the
first of the *genus irritabile* who has ventured to treat so delicate a subject with that grave dignity which is its due:

> Rejoice! rejoice! already on my sight
>   Bright shores, gray towers, and coming wonders reel;
> My brain grows giddy—is it with delight?
>   A swimming faintness, such as one might feel
> When stabbed and dying, gathers on my sense—
> It weighs me down—and now—help!—horror!—

But the "horror," and indeed all that ensues, we must leave
to the fancy of the poetical.

Some pieces entitled "Humorous" next succeed, and one or
two of them (for example, "The Graham System" and "The
Bachelor's Lament") are not so *very* contemptible in their
way, but the way itself is beneath even contempt.

"To an Infant in Heaven" embodies some striking
thoughts, and, although feeble as a whole, and terminating
lamely, may be cited as the best composition in the volume.
We quote two or three of the opening stanzas:

> Thou bright and star-like spirit!
>   That in my visions wild
> I see 'mid heaven's seraphic host—
>   Oh! canst thou be my child?
>
> My grief is quenched in wonder,
>   And pride arrests my sighs;
> A branch from this unworthy stock
>   Now blossoms in the skies.
>
> Our hopes of thee were lofty,
>   But have we cause to grieve?
> Oh, could our fondest, proudest wish
>   A nobler fate conceive?
>
> The little weeper tearless!
>   The sinner snatched from sin!
> The babe to more than manhood grown,
>   Ere childhood did begin!

> And I, thy earthly teacher,
>> Would blush thy powers to see:
> Thou art to me a parent now
>> And I a child to thee!

There are several other pieces in the book—but it is needless to speak of them in detail. Among them we note one or two political effusions, and one or two which are (satirically?) termed satirical. All are worthless.

Mr. Ward's *imagery*, at detached points, has occasional vigor and appropriateness; we may go so far as to say that, at times, it is strikingly beautiful—by accident of course. Let us cite a few instances. At page 53 we read—

> O! happy day!—earth, sky is fair,
> And fragrance floats along the air;
> *For all the bloomy orchards glow*
> *As with a fall of rosy snow.*

At page 91—

> How flashed the overloaded flowers
> With gems, a present from the showers!

At page 92—

> No! there is danger; all the night
> I saw her like a starry light
> More lovely in my visions lone
> Than in my day-dreams truth she shone.
> 'T is naught when on the sun we gaze
> If only dazzled by his rays,
> But when our eyes his form retain
> Some wound to vision must remain.

And again, at page 234, speaking of a slight shock of an earthquake, the earth is said to tremble

> As if some wing of passing angel, bound
> From sphere to sphere, had brushed the golden chain
> That hangs our planet to the throne of God.

This latter passage, however, is, perhaps, not altogether original with Mr. Ward. In a poem now lying before us, en-

titled "Al Aaraaf," the composition of a gentleman of Philadelphia, we find what follows:

> A dome by linkéd light from heaven let down
> Sat gently on these columns as a crown;
> A window of one circular diamond there
> Looked out above into the purple air,
> And rays from God shot down that meteor chain
> And hallow'd all the beauty twice again,
> Save when, between th' Empyrean and that ring,
> Some eager spirit flapped his dusky wing.

But if Mr. Ward's imagery is, indeed, at rare intervals,
good, it must be granted, on the other hand, that, in general,
it is atrociously inappropriate, or low. For example:

> Thou gaping chasm! whose wide devouring throat
> Swallows a river, *while the gulping note*
> *Of monstrous deglutition gurgles loud,* etc.   *Page 24.*

> Bright Beauty! child of starry birth,
> The grace, the gem, the flower of earth,
> The *damask livery* of Heaven!   *Page 44.*

Here the mind wavers between gems, and stars, and taf-
fety—between footmen and flowers. Again, at page 46—

> All thornless flowers of wit, all chaste
> And delicate essays of taste,
> All playful fancies, wingéd wiles,
> That from their pinions scatter smiles,
> All prompt resource in stress or pain,
> *Leap ready-armed* from woman's brain.

The idea of "thornless flowers," etc. leaping *"ready-armed"*
could have entered few brains except those of Mr. Ward.

Of the most ineffable *bad taste* we have instances without
number. For example—page 183—

> And, straining, fastens on her lips a kiss
> That seemed to *suck the life-blood from her heart!*

And here, very gravely, at page 25,

Again he 's rous'd, *first cramming in his cheek*
The weed, though vile, that props the nerves when weak.

Here again, at page 33,

> Full well he knew where food does not refresh
> The shrivel'd soul sinks inward with the flesh—
> That he 's best armed for danger's rash career
> *Who's crammed so full there is no room for fear.*

But we doubt if the whole world of literature, poetical or prosaic, can afford a picture more utterly *disgusting* than the following, which we quote from page 177:

> But most of all good eating cheers the brain,
>   Where other joys are rarely met—at sea—
> Unless, indeed, we lose as soon as gain—
>   Ay, there 's the rub so baffling oft to me.
> Boiled, roast, and baked— *what precious choice of dishes*
>   *My generous throat has shared among the fishes!*
>
> 'T is sweet to leave, in each forsaken spot,
>   Our foot-prints there—if only in the sand;
> 'T is sweet to feel we are not all forgot,
>   That some will weep our flight from every land;
> And sweet the knowledge, when the seas I cross,
>   *My briny messmates! ye will mourn my loss.*

This passage alone should damn the book—aye, damn a dozen such.

Of what may be termed the *niaiseries*—the sillinesses—of the volume, there is no end. Under this head we might quote two thirds of the work. For example:

> Now lightning, with convulsive spasm
> Splits heaven *in many a* fearful chasm.

> *It takes the high trees by the hair*
> And, as with *besoms*, sweeps the air.

> Now breaks the gloom and through the *chinks*
> The moon, in search of opening, *winks*—

All seriously urged, at different points of page 66. Again, on the very next page—

> Bees buzzed and wrens that throng'd the rushes
> Poured round incessant twittering gushes.

And here, at page 129—

> And now he leads her to the slippery brink
> Where ponderous tides headlong plunge down the horrid
> *chink*.

And here, page 109—

> And, like a ravenous vulture, *peck*
> The smoothness of that cheek and neck.

And here, page 111—

> While through the skin worms *wriggling* broke.

And here, page 170—

> And ride the *skittish* backs of untamed waves.

And here, page 214—

> Now clasps its mate in holy prayer
> Or *twangs* a harp of gold.

Mr. Ward, also, is constantly talking about "thunder-guns," "thunder-trumpets," and "thunder-shrieks." He has a bad habit, too, of styling an eye "a weeper," as for example, at page 208—

> Oh, curl in smiles that mouth again
> And wipe that *weeper* dry.

Somewhere else he calls two tears "two sparklers"—very much in the style of Mr. Richard Swiveller, who was fond of denominating Madeira "the rosy." "In the nick," meaning in the height, or fulness, is likewise a pet expression of the author of "The Great Descender." Speaking of American forests, at page 286, for instance, he says, "let the doubter walk through them in the nick of their glory." A phrase which may be considered as in the very nick of good taste.

We cannot pause to comment upon Mr. Ward's most extraordinary system of versification. *Is* it his own? He has quite an original way of conglomerating consonants, and seems to have been experimenting whether it were not possible to do altogether without vowels. Sometimes he strings together quite a chain of impossibilities. The line, for example, at page 51,

> Or, only such as sea-shells flash,

puts us much in mind of the schoolboy stumbling-block, beginning, "The cat ran up the ladder with a lump of raw liver in her mouth," and we defy Sam Patch himself to pronounce it twice in succession without tumbling into a blunder.

But we are fairly wearied with this absurd theme. *Who* calls Mr. Ward a poet? He is a second-rate, or a third-rate, or perhaps a ninety-ninth-rate poetaster. He is a gentleman of "elegant leisure," and gentlemen of elegant leisure are, for the most part, neither men, women, nor Harriet Martineaus. Similar opinions, we believe, were expressed by somebody else—was it Mr. Benjamin?—no very long while ago. But neither Mr. Ward nor "The Knickerbocker" would be convinced. The latter, by way of defence, went into a treatise upon Sam Patch, and Mr. Ward, "in the nick of his glory," wrote another poem against criticism in general, in which he called Mr. Benjamin "a wasp" and "an owl," and endeavored to prove him an ass. An owl is a wise bird—especially in spectacles—still, we do not look upon Mr. Benjamin as an owl. If all are owls who disbelieve in this book (which we now throw to the pigs) then the world at large cuts a pretty figure, indeed, and should be burnt up in April, as Mr. Miller desires—for it is only one immense aviary of owls.

Graham's Magazine, March 1843

Lambert A. Wilmer

The Quacks of Helicon: A Satire. By L. A. Wilmer. Philadelphia: Printed by J. W. Macclefield.

A SATIRE, professedly such, at the present day, and especially by an American writer, is a welcome novelty, indeed. We have really done very little in the line upon this side of the Atlantic—nothing, certainly, of importance—Trumbull's clumsy poem and Halleck's "Croakers" to the contrary notwithstanding. Some things we have produced, to be sure, which were excellent in the way of burlesque, without intending a syllable that was not utterly solemn and serious. Odes, ballads, songs, sonnets, epics, and epigrams, possessed of this unintentional excellence, we could have no difficulty in designating by the dozen; but, in the matter of directly-meant and genuine satire, it cannot be denied that we are sadly deficient. Although, as a literary people, however, we are not exactly Archilocuses—although we have no pretensions to the ηχεηντες ιαμβοι—although, in short, we are no satirists ourselves, there can be no question that we answer sufficiently well as subjects for satire.

We repeat, that we are glad to see this book of Mr. Wilmer's; first, because it is something new under the sun; secondly, because, in many respects, it is well executed; and, thirdly, because, in the universal corruption and rigmarole amid which we gasp for breath, it is really a pleasant thing to get even one accidental whiff of the unadulterated air of *truth*.

The "Quacks of Helicon," as a poem and otherwise, has many defects, and these we shall have no scruple in pointing out—although Mr. Wilmer is a personal friend of our own,* and we are happy and proud to say so—but it has also many remarkable merits—merits which it will be quite useless for those aggrieved by the satire—quite useless for any *clique*, or set of *cliques*, to attempt to frown down, or to affect not to see, or to feel, or to understand.

Its prevalent blemishes are referrible chiefly to the leading sin of *imitation*. Had the work been composed professedly in

*Of Mr. Poe's.

paraphrase of the whole manner of the sarcastic epistles of the times of Dryden and Pope, we should have pronounced it the most ingenious and truthful thing of the kind upon record. So close is the copy, that it extends to the most trivial points—for example to the old forms of punctuation. The turns of phraseology, the tricks of rhythm, the arrangement of the paragraphs, the general conduct of the satire—everything—all—are Dryden's. We cannot deny, it is true, that the satiric model of the days in question is insusceptible of improvement, and that the modern author who deviates therefrom, must necessarily sacrifice something of merit at the shrine of originality. Neither can we shut our eyes to the fact, that the imitation, in the present case, has conveyed, in full spirit, the higher qualities, as well as, in rigid letter, the minor elegances and general peculiarities of the author of "Absalom and Achitophel." We have here the bold, vigorous, and sonorous verse, the biting sarcasm, the pungent epigrammatism, the unscrupulous directness, as of old. Yet it will not do to forget that Mr. Wilmer has been *shown how* to accomplish these things. He is thus only entitled to the praise of a close observer, and of a thoughtful and skilful copyist. The images are, to be sure, his own. They are neither Pope's, nor Dryden's, nor Rochester's, nor Churchill's—but they are moulded in the identical mould used by these satirists.

This servility of imitation has seduced our author into errors which his better sense should have avoided. He sometimes mistakes intention; at other times he copies faults, confounding them with beauties. In the opening of the poem, for example, we find the lines—

> Against usurpers, Olney, I declare
> A righteous, just, and patriotic war.

The rhymes *war* and *declare* are here adopted from Pope, who employs them frequently; but it should have been remembered that the modern relative pronunciation of the two words differs materially from the relative pronunciation of the era of the "Dunciad."

We are also sure that the gross obscenity, the filth—we can use no gentler name—which disgraces the "Quacks of Helicon," cannot be the result of innate impurity in the mind of the writer. It is but a part of the slavish and indiscriminating imitation of the Swift and Rochester school. It has done the book an irreparable injury, both in a moral and pecuniary view, without effecting anything whatever on the score of sarcasm, vigor or wit. "Let what is to be said, be said plainly." True; but let nothing vulgar be *ever* said, or conceived.

In asserting that this satire, even in its mannerism, has imbued itself with the full spirit of the polish and of the pungency of Dryden, we have already awarded it high praise. But there remains to be mentioned the far loftier merit of speaking fearlessly the truth, at an epoch when truth is out of fashion, and under circumstances of social position which would have deterred almost any man in our community from a similar Quixotism. For the publication of the "Quacks of Helicon,"—a poem which brings under review, by name, most of our prominent *literati*, and treats them, generally, as they deserve (what treatment could be more bitter?)—for the publication of this attack, Mr. Wilmer, whose subsistence lies in his pen, has little to look for—apart from the silent respect of those at once honest and timid—but the most malignant open or covert persecution. For this reason, and because it is the truth which he has spoken, do we say to him from the bottom of our hearts, "God speed!"

We repeat it:— *it is* the truth which he has spoken, and who shall contradict us? He has said unscrupulously what every reasonable man among us has long known to be "as true as the Pentateuch"—that, as a literary people, we are one vast perambulating humbug. He has asserted that we are *clique*-ridden, and who does not smile at the obvious truism of that assertion? He maintains that chicanery is, with us, a far surer road than talent to distinction in letters. Who gainsays this? The corrupt nature of our ordinary criticism has become notorious. Its powers have been prostrated by its own arm. The intercourse between critic and publisher, as it now almost universally stands, is comprised either in the paying and pocketing of black mail, as the price of a simple forbearance, or in a direct system of petty and contemptible bribery, properly so called—a system even more injurious than the former to the true interests of the public, and more degrading to the buyers and sellers of good opinion, on ac-

count of the more positive character of the service here rendered for the consideration received. We laugh at the idea of
any denial of our assertions upon this topic; they are infa-
mously true. In the charge of general corruption there are
undoubtedly many noble exceptions to be made. There are,
indeed, some very few editors, who, maintaining an entire
independence, will receive no books from publishers at all, or
who receive them with a perfect understanding, on the part
of these latter, that an unbiassed *critique* will be given. But
these cases are insufficient to have much effect on the popular
mistrust: a mistrust heightened by late exposure of the machinations of *coteries* in New York— *coteries* which, at the bidding of leading booksellers, manufacture, as required from
time to time, a pseudo-public opinion by wholesale, for the
benefit of any little hanger on of the party, or pettifogging
protector of the firm.

We speak of these things in the bitterness of scorn. It is
unnecessary to cite instances, where one is found in almost
every issue of a book. It is needless to call to mind the desperate case of Fay—a case where the pertinacity of the effort
to gull—where the obviousness of the attempt at forestalling
a judgment—where the wofully over-done be-Mirrorment of
that man-of-straw, together with the pitiable platitude of his
production, proved a dose somewhat too potent for even the
well-prepared stomach of the mob. We say it is supererogatory to dwell upon "Norman Leslie," or other by-gone follies, when we have, before our eyes, hourly instances of the
machinations in question. To so great an extent of methodical
assurance has the *system* of puffery arrived, that publishers, of
late, have made no scruple of keeping on hand an assortment
of commendatory notices, prepared by their men of all work,
and of sending these notices around to the multitudinous papers within their influence, done up within the fly-leaves of
the book. The grossness of these base attempts, however, has
not escaped indignant rebuke from the more honorable portion of the press; and we hail these symptoms of restiveness
under the yoke of unprincipled ignorance and quackery
(strong only in combination) as the harbinger of a better era
for the interests of real merit, and of the national literature as
a whole.

It has become, indeed the plain duty of each individual connected with our periodicals, heartily to give whatever influence he possesses, to the good cause of integrity and the truth. The results thus attainable will be found worthy his closest attention and best efforts. We shall thus frown down all conspiracies to foist inanity upon the public consideration at the obvious expense of every man of talent who is not a member of a *clique* in power. We may even arrive, in time, at that desirable point from which a distinct view of our men of letters may be obtained, and their respective pretensions adjusted, by the standard of a rigorous and self-sustaining criticism alone. That their several positions are as yet properly settled; that the posts which a vast number of them now hold are maintained by any better tenure than that of the chicanery upon which we have commented, will be asserted by none but the ignorant, or the parties who have best right to feel an interest in the "good old condition of things." No two matters can be more radically different than the reputation of some of our prominent *litterateurs*, as gathered from the mouths of the people, (who glean it from the paragraphs of the papers,) and the same reputation as deduced from the private estimate of intelligent and educated men. We do not advance this fact as a new discovery. Its truth, on the contrary, is the subject, and has long been so, of every-day witticism and mirth.

Why not? Surely there can be few things more ridiculous than the general character and assumptions of the ordinary critical notices of new books! An editor, sometimes without the shadow of the commonest attainment—often without brains, always without time—does not scruple to give the world to understand that he is in the *daily* habit of critically reading and deciding upon a flood of publications one tenth of whose title-pages he may possibly have turned over, three fourths of whose contents would be Hebrew to his most desperate efforts at comprehension, and whose entire mass and amount, as might be mathematically demonstrated, would be sufficient to occupy, in the most cursory perusal, the attention of some ten or twenty readers for a month! What he wants in plausibility, however, he makes up in obsequiousness; what he lacks in time he supplies in temper. He is the most easily pleased man in the world. He admires everything, from the big Dictionary of Noah Webster to the last diamond edition of Tom Thumb. Indeed his sole difficulty is in finding tongue to express his delight. Every pamphlet is a miracle—every book in boards is an epoch in letters. His phrases, therefore, get bigger and bigger every day, and, if it were not for talking Cockney, we might call him a "regular swell."

Yet in the attempt at getting definite information in regard to any one portion of our literature, the merely general reader, or the foreigner, will turn in vain from the lighter to the heavier journals. But it is not our intention here to dwell upon the radical, antique, and systematized rigmarole of our Quarterlies. The articles here are anonymous. Who writes?— who causes to be written? Who but an ass will put faith in tirades which *may* be the result of personal hostility, or in panegyrics which nine times out of ten may be laid, directly or indirectly, to the charge of the author himself? It is in the favor of these saturnine pamphlets that they contain, now and then, a good essay *de omnibus rebus et quibusdam aliis*, which may be looked into, without decided somnolent consequences, at any period not immediately subsequent to dinner. But it is useless to expect criticism from periodicals called "Reviews" from never reviewing. Besides, all men know, or should know, that these books are sadly given to verbiage. It is a part of their nature, a condition of their being, a point of their faith. A veteran reviewer loves the safety of generalities, and is therefore rarely particular. "Words, words, words" are the secret of his strength. He has one or two ideas of his own, and is both wary and fussy in giving them out. His wit lies with his truth, in a well, and there is always a world of trouble in getting it up. He is a sworn enemy to all things simple and direct. He gives no ear to the advice of the giant Moulineau—*"Belier, mon ami, commencez au commencement."* He either jumps at once into the middle of his subject, or breaks in at a back door, or sidles up to it with the gait of a crab. No other mode of approach has an air of sufficient profundity. When fairly into it, however, he becomes dazzled with the scintillations of his own wisdom, and is seldom able to see his way out. Tired of laughing at his antics, or frightened at seeing him flounder, the reader at length shuts him up, with the book. "What song the Syrens sang," says Sir Thomas Browne, "or what name Achilles assumed when he hid himself among women, though puzzling questions, are not beyond *all* conjecture"—but it would puzzle Sir Thomas, backed by Achilles and all the Syrens in Heathendom, to say, in nine cases out of ten, *what is the object* of a thorough-going Quarterly Reviewer.

Should the opinions promulgated by our press at large be taken, in their wonderful aggregate, as an evidence of what American literature absolutely is, (and it may be said that, in general, they are really so taken,) we shall find ourselves the most enviable set of people upon the face of the earth. Our fine writers are legion. Our very atmosphere is redolent of genius; and we, the nation, are a huge, well-contented chameleon, grown pursy by inhaling it. We are *teretes et rotundi*—enwrapped in excellence. All our poets are Miltons, neither mute nor inglorious; all our poetesses are "American Hemanses;" nor will it do to deny that all our novelists are great Knowns or great Unknowns, and that every body who writes, in every possible and impossible department, is the admirable Crichton, or at least the admirable Crichton's ghost. We are thus in a glorious condition, and will remain so until forced to disgorge our ethereal honors. In truth, there is some danger that the jealousy of the Old World will interfere. It cannot long submit to that outrageous monopoly of "all the decency and all the talent" in which the gentlemen of the press give such undoubted assurance of our being so busily engaged.

But we feel angry with ourselves for the jesting tone of our observations upon this topic. The prevalence of the spirit of puffery is a subject far less for merriment than for disgust. Its truckling, yet dogmatical character—its bold, unsustained, yet self-sufficient and wholesale laudation—is becoming, more and more, an insult to the common sense of the community. Trivial as it essentially is, it has yet been made the instrument of the grossest abuse in the elevation of imbecility, to the manifest injury, to the utter ruin, of true merit. Is there any man of good feeling and of ordinary understanding—is there one single individual among all our readers—who does not feel a thrill of bitter indignation, apart from any sentiment of mirth, as he calls to mind instance after instance of the purest, of the most unadulterated quackery in letters, which has risen to a high post in the apparent popular estimation, and which still maintains it, by the sole means of a blustering arrogance, or of a busy wriggling conceit, or of the most barefaced plagiarism, or even through the simple immensity of its assumptions—assumptions not only unopposed by the press at large, but absolutely supported in proportion to the vociferous clamor with which they are made—in exact accordance with their utter baselessness and untenability? We should have no trouble in pointing out, today, some twenty or thirty so-called literary personages, who, if not idiots, as we half think them, or if not hardened to all sense of shame by a long course of disingenuousness, will now blush, in the perusal of these words, through consciousness of the shadowy nature of that purchased pedestal upon which they stand—will now tremble in thinking of the feebleness of the breath which will be adequate to the blowing it from beneath their feet. With the help of a hearty good will, even *we* may yet tumble them down.

So firm, through a long endurance, has been the hold taken upon the popular mind (at least so far as we may consider the popular mind reflected in ephemeral letters) by the laudatory system which we have deprecated, that what is, in its own essence, a vice, has become endowed with the appearance, and met with the reception of a virtue. Antiquity, as usual, has lent a certain degree of speciousness even to the absurd. So continuously have we puffed, that we have at length come to think puffing the duty, and plain speaking the dereliction. What we began in gross error, we persist in through habit. Having adopted, in the earlier days of our literature, the untenable idea that this literature, as a whole, could be advanced by an indiscriminate approbation bestowed on its every effort—having adopted this idea, we say, without attention to the obvious fact that praise of all was bitter although negative censure to the few alone deserving, and that the only result of the system, in the fostering way, would be the fostering of folly—we now continue our vile practices through the supineness of custom, even while, in our national self-conceit, we repudiate that necessity for patronage and protection in which originated our conduct. In a word, the press throughout the country has not been ashamed to make head against the very few bold attempts at independence which have, from time to time, been made in the face of the reigning order of things. And if, in one, or perhaps two, insulated cases, the spirit of severe truth, sustained by an unconquerable will, was not to be so put down, then, forthwith, were private chicaneries set in motion; then was had resort, on the part of those who considered themselves injured by the severity of criticism, (and who were so, if the just contempt of every ingenuous man is injury,) resort to arts of the most virulent indignity, to untraceable slanders, to ruthless assassination in the dark. We say these things were done, while the press in general looked on, and, with a full understanding of the wrong perpetrated, spoke not against the wrong. The idea had absolutely gone abroad—had grown up little by little into toleration—that attacks however just, upon a literary reputation however obtained, however untenable, were well retaliated by the basest and most unfounded traduction of personal fame. But is this an age—is this a day—in which it can be necessary even to advert to such considerations as that the book of the author is the property of the public, and that the issue of the book is the throwing down of the gauntlet to the reviewer—to the reviewer whose duty is the plainest; the duty not even of approbation, or of censure, or of silence, at his own will, but at the sway of those sentiments and of those opinions which are derived from the author himself, through the medium of his written and published words? True criticism is the reflection of the thing criticised upon the spirit of the critic.

But *à nos moutons*—to the "Quacks of Helicon." This satire has many faults besides those upon which we have commented. The title, for example, is not sufficiently distinctive, although otherwise good. It does not confine the subject to *American* quacks, while the work does. The two concluding lines enfeeble instead of strengthening the *finale*, which would have been exceedingly pungent without them. The individual portions of the thesis are strung together too much at random—a natural sequence is not always preserved—so that although the lights of the picture are often forcible, the whole has what, in artistical parlance, is termed an accidental and spotty appearance. In truth, the parts of the poem have evidently been composed each by each, as separate themes, and afterwards fitted into the general satire, in the best manner possible.

But a more reprehensible sin than any or than all of these is yet to be mentioned—the sin of indiscriminate censure. Even here Mr. Wilmer has erred through imitation. He has held in view the sweeping denunciations of the Dunciad, and of the later (abortive) satire of Byron. No one in his senses can deny the justice of the general charges of corruption in regard to which we have just spoken from the text of our author. But are there *no* exceptions? We should indeed blush if there were not. And is there *no* hope? Time will show. We cannot do everything in a day—*Non se gano Zamora en un ora*. Again, it cannot be gainsaid that the greater number of those who hold high places in our poetical literature are absolute nincompoops—fellows alike innocent of reason and of rhyme. But neither are we *all* brainless, nor is the devil himself so black as he is painted. Mr. Wilmer must read the chapter in Rabelais' *Gargantua, "de ce qu' est signifié par les couleurs blanc et bleu"*— for there is *some* difference after all. It will not do in a civilized land to run a-muck like a Malay. Mr. Morris *has* written good songs. Mr. Bryant is not *all* a fool. Mr. Willis is not *quite* an ass. Mr. Longfellow *will* steal, but perhaps he cannot help it, (for we have heard of such things,) and then it must not be denied that *nil tetigit quod non ornavit*.

The fact is that our author, in the rank exuberance of his zeal, seems to think as little of discrimination as the Bishop of Autun* did of the Bible. Poetical "things in general" are the windmills at which he spurs his rozinante. He as often tilts at what is true as at what is false; and thus his lines are like the mirrors of the temples of Smirna, which represent the fairest images as deformed. But the talent, the fearlessness, and especially the *design* of this book, will suffice to save it even from that dreadful damnation of "silent contempt" to which editors throughout the country, if we are not very much mistaken, will endeavor, one and all, to consign it.

*Talleyrand.

Graham's Magazine, August 1841

MAGAZINES AND CRITICISM

Contents

Supplement
(A Reply to Critics)

IN COMPLIANCE with the suggestion of many of our friends, and at the request of a majority of our contributors, we again publish a supplement consisting of *Notices of the "Messenger."* We have duly weighed the propriety and impropriety of this course, and have concluded that when we choose to adopt it, there can be no good reason why we should not. Heretofore we have made selections from the notices received—only taking care to publish what we conceived to be a fair specimen of the general character of all—and, with those who know us, no suspicion of unfairness in this selection would be entertained. Lest, however, among those who do *not* know us, any such suspicion should arise, we now publish *every* late criticism received. This supplement is, of course, not considered as a portion of the Messenger itself, being an extra expense to the publisher.

We commence with the *Newbern (North Carolina) Spectator*—a general dissenter from all favorable opinions of our Magazine.

Southern Literary Messenger.—The May number of this periodical has been on our table for some days, but our avocations have prevented us from looking into it before to-day. It is as usual, a beautiful specimen of typography, and sustains Mr. White's acknowledged mechanical taste. Its contents are various, as may be seen by referring to another column of to-day's paper, and not more various than unequal. Some of the articles are creditable to their authors, while others—indeed a majority of them—would better suit an ephemeral sheet like our own, which makes no great literary pretensions, than the pages of a magazine that assumes the high stand of a critical censor and a standard of correct taste in literature. While its pretensions were less elevated, we hailed the Messenger as an attempt, and a successful one, to call forth southern talent and to diffuse a taste for chaste and instructive reading; and had its conducters been satisfied with the useful and creditable eminence which the work attained almost immediately, the

Messenger would not only have had a more extensive circulation, but its labors would have been more beneficial to the community—the great end at which every periodical should aim. With the talent available in any particular spot in the southern country, it is out of the question, truly ridiculous, to assume the tone of a Walsh, a Blackwood or a Jeffries; and to attempt it, without the means to support the pretension, tends to accelerate the downfall of so indiscreet an attempt. We do not wish to be misunderstood in this remark. We believe, indeed we know, that the south possesses talent, and cultivated talent too, in as great abundance perhaps as any population of the same extent so situated; but the meaning which we intend to convey is, that this talent is neither sufficiently concentrated, nor sufficiently devoted to literary pursuits, to be brought forth in support of any single publication in strength adequate to establish an indisputable claim to superiority. Without these advantages, however, the Messenger has boldly put itself forth as an arbiter whose dicta are supreme; and with a severity and an indiscreetness of criticism,—especially on American works,—which few, if any, of the able and well established Reviews have ventured to exercise, has been not only unmerciful, but savage. We admit that the number before, as well as the one preceding, is more moderate; and this change encourages the hope that justness of judgment and a dignified expression of opinion will hereafter characterise the work. The May number, however, is over captious, unnecessarily devoted to faultfinding, in a few cases. In criticising "Spain Revisited," this spirit shows itself. About ninety lines are occupied in condemnation of the Author's dedication, a very unpretending one too, and one which will elevate Lieutenant Slidell in the estimation of all who prefer undoubted evidences of personal friendship to the disposition which dictates literary hyper-criticism. The errors of composition that are to be found in the work, grammatical and other, are also severely handled, we will not say ably. The following is a specimen.

"And now, too, we began"—says Spain Revisited—"to see horsemen jantily dressed in slouched hat, embroidered jacket, and worked spatterdashes, reining fiery Andalusian coursers, each having the Moorish carbine hung at hand beside him."

"Were horsemen"—says the Messenger, " 'a *generic* term,' that is, did the word allude to horsemen generally, the use of the *'slouched hat'* and *'embroidered jacket'* in the singular, would be justifiable—but it is not so in speaking of individual horsemen, where the plural is required. The participle *'reining'* probably refers to *'spatterdashes,'* although of course intended to agree with *'horsemen.'* The word 'each' also meant to refer to the *'horsemen,'* belongs, strictly speaking, to the *'coursers.'* " The whole, if construed by the rigid rules of grammar, would imply that the horsemen were dressed in spatterdashes—which spatterdashes reined the coursers—and which coursers had each a carbine."

With all deference to the Messenger, we would ask, if it never entered into the critick's mind that "slouched hat," "and embroidered jacket" are here used as generick terms? Lieutenant Slidell evidently intended that they should be so received: but that he entertained the same intention respecting "horsemen," the whole context disproves. Had the reviewer placed a comma after the word "horsemen," in the first line of the paragraph which he dissects, (the relative and verb— *who were*—being elided, there is authority for so doing,) considered as parenthetical and illustrative all that follows between that comma and the one which comes after "spatterdashes," supplied the personal relative and the proper verb, which are plainly understood before the participle "reining," we presume that this sentence, ill-constructed as it undoubtedly is, would have escaped the knife, from a conviction that there are many as bad in the Messenger itself. The only critical notice which we have had leisure to read since the reception of the number, is the one which we have named. We may resume the subject in connexion with the June number.

We are at a loss to know who is the editor of the Spectator, but have a shrewd suspicion that he is the identical gentleman who once sent us from Newbern an unfortunate copy of verses. It seems to us that he wishes to be taken notice of, and we will, for the once, oblige him with a few words— with the positive understanding, however, that it will be inconvenient to trouble ourselves hereafter with his opinions. We would respectfully suggest to him that his words, *"while its pretensions were less elevated we hailed the Messenger as a successful attempt, &c. and had its conductors been satisfied with the useful and creditable eminence, &c. we would have had no objection to it,"* &c. are a very fair and candid acknowledgment that he can find no fault with the Messenger but its success, and that to be as stupid as itself is the only sure road to the patronage of the Newbern Spectator. The paper is in error—we refer it to any decent schoolboy in Newbern—in relation to the only sentence in our Magazine upon which it has thought proper to comment specifically, viz. the sentence above (by Lieutenant Slidell) beginning "And now too we began to see horsemen jantily dressed in slouched hat, embroidered jacket, &c." The *Spectator* says, "We would ask if it never entered into the critic's mind that 'slouched hat' and 'embroidered jacket' are here used as generic terms? Lieutenant Slidell evidently intended that they should be so received; but that he entertained the same intention respecting 'horsemen,' the whole context disproves." We reply, (and the Spectator should imagine us smiling as we reply) that it is precisely because "slouched hat" and "embroidered jacket" *are* used as generic terms, while the word "horsemen" *is not*, that we have been induced to wish the sentence amended. The *Spectator* also says, "With the talent available in any particular spot in the Southern country, it is out of the question, truly ridiculous, to assume the tone of a Walsh, a Blackwood, or a Jeffries." We believe that either Walsh, or (*Blackwood?*) or alas! Jeffries, would disagree with the Newbern Spectator in its opinion of the talent of the Southern country—that is, if either Walsh or Blackwood or Jeffries could have imagined the existence of such a thing as a *Newbern Spectator*. Of the opinion of Blackwood and Jeffries, however, we cannot be positive just now. Of that of Walsh we can, having heard from him very lately with a promise of a communication for the Messenger, and compliments respecting our Editorial course, which we should really be ashamed of repeating. From *Slidell*, for whom the Spectator is for taking up the cudgels, we have yesterday heard in a similar strain and with a similar promise. From *Prof. Anthon*, ditto. *Mrs. Sigourney*, also lately reviewed, has just forwarded us her compliments and a communication. *Halleck*, since our *abuse* of his book, writes us thus: "There is no place where I shall be more desirous of seeing my humble writings than in the publication you so ably support and conduct. It is full of sound, good literature, and its frank, open, independent manliness of spirit, is characteristic of the land it hails from." *Paulding*, likewise, has sent us something for our pages, and is so kind as to say of us in a letter just received, "I should not hesitate in placing the 'Messenger' decidedly at the head of our periodicals, nor do I hesitate in expressing that opinion freely on all occasions. It is gradually growing in the public estimation, and under your conduct, and with your contributions, must soon, if it is not already, be known all over the land." Lastly, in regard to the disputed matter of Drake and Halleck, we have just received the following testimony from an individual second to no American author in the wide-spread popularity of his writings, and in their universal appreciation by men of letters, both in the United States and England. "You have given sufficient evidence on various occasions, not only of critical knowledge but of high independence; your praise is therefore of value, and your censure not to be slighted. Allow me to say that I think your article on Drake and Halleck one of the finest pieces of criticism ever published in this country."

These decisions, on the part of such men, it must be acknowledged, would be highly gratifying to our vanity, were not the decision vetoed by the poet of the *Newbern Spectator*. We wish only to add that the poet's assertion in regard to the Messenger "putting itself forth as an arbiter whose dicta are supreme," is a slight deviation from the truth. The Messenger merely expresses its particular opinions in its own particular manner. These opinions no person is bound to adopt. They are open to the comments and censures of even the most diminutive things in creation—of the very Newbern Spectators of the land. If the Editor of this little paper does not behave himself we will positively publish his verses.—*Ed. Messenger*.

Southern Literary Messenger, July 1836

Prospectus of The Penn Magazine

A MONTHLY LITERARY JOURNAL, TO BE EDITED
AND PUBLISHED IN THE CITY OF PHILADELPHIA,
BY EDGAR A. POE.

To the public.—Since resigning the conduct of The
Southern Literary Messenger, at the commencement of
its third year, I have had always in view the establishment of
a Magazine which should retain some of the chief features
of that Journal, abandoning or greatly modifying the rest. Delay, however, has been occasioned by a variety of causes, and
not until now have I found myself at liberty to attempt the
execution of the design.

I will be pardoned for speaking more directly of The Messenger. Having in it no proprietary right, my objects too
being at variance in many respects with those of its very worthy owner, I found difficulty in stamping upon its pages that
individuality which I believe essential to the full success of all
similar publications. In regard to their permanent influence,
it appears to me that a continuous, definite character, and a
marked certainty of purpose, are desiderata of vital importance, and only attainable where one mind alone has the general direction of the undertaking. Experience has rendered
obvious, what might indeed have been demonstrated *a priori*;
that in founding a Magazine of my own lies my sole chance
of carrying out to completion whatever peculiar intentions I
may have entertained.

To those who remember the early days of the Southern periodical in question it will be scarcely necessary to say that its
main feature was a somewhat overdone causticity in its department of Critical Notices of new books. The Penn Magazine will retain this trait of severity in so much only as the
calmest yet sternest sense of justice will permit. Some years
since elapsed may have mellowed down the petulance without
interfering with the rigor of the critic. Most surely they have
not yet taught him to read through the medium of a publisher's will, nor convinced him that the interests of letters are
unallied with the interests of truth. It shall be the first and
chief purpose of the Magazine now proposed to become
known as one where may be found at all times, and upon all

subjects, an honest and a fearless opinion. It shall be a leading object to assert in precept, and to maintain in practice the rights, while in effect it demonstrates the advantages, of an absolutely independent criticism—a criticism self-sustained; guiding itself only by the purest rules of Art; analyzing and urging these rules as it applies them; holding itself aloof from all personal bias; acknowledging no fear save that of outraging the right; yielding no point either to the vanity of the author, or to the assumptions of antique prejudice, or to the involute and anonymous cant of the Quarterlies, or to the arrogance of those organized *cliques* which, hanging like nightmares upon American literature, manufacture, at the nod of our principal booksellers, a pseudo-public-opinion by wholesale. These are objects of which no man need be ashamed. They are purposes, moreover, whose novelty at least will give them interest. For assurance that I will fulfil them in the best spirit and to the very letter, I appeal with confidence to the many thousands of my friends, and especially of my Southern friends, who sustained me in the Messenger, where I had but a very partial opportunity of completing my own plans.

In respect to the other features of the Penn Magazine, a few words here will suffice. It will endeavour to support the general interests of the republic of letters, without reference to particular regions; regarding the world at large as the true audience of the author. Beyond the precincts of literature, properly so called, it will leave in better hands the task of instruction upon all matters of *very* grave moment. Its aim chiefly shall be *to please*; and this through means of versatility, originality, and pungency. It may be as well here to observe that nothing said in this Prospectus should be construed into a design of sullying the Magazine with any tincture of the buffoonery, scurrility, or profanity, which are the blemish of some of the most vigorous of the European prints. In all branches of the literary department, the best aid, from the highest and purest sources, is secured.

To the mechanical execution of the work the greatest attention will be given which such a matter can require. In this respect it is proposed to surpass, by very much, the ordinary Magazine style. The form will nearly resemble that of The

Knickerbocker; the paper will be equal to that of The North American Review; the pictorial embellishments will be numerous, and by the leading artists of the country, but will be introduced only in the necessary illustration of the text.

The Penn Magazine will be published in Philadelphia, on the first of each month, and will form, half-yearly, a volume of about 500 pages. The price will be $5 per annum, payable in advance, or upon the receipt of the first number, which will be issued on the first of January, 1841. Letters addressed to the Editor and Proprietor,

EDGAR A. POE.

1840

Exordium to Critical Notices

I N COMMENCING, with the New Year, a New Volume, we shall be permitted to say a very few words by way of *exordium* to our usual chapter of Reviews, or, as we should prefer calling them, of Critical Notices. Yet we speak *not* for the sake of the *exordium*, but because we have really something to say, and know not when or where better to say it.

That the public attention, in America, has, of late days, been more than usually directed to the matter of literary criticism, is plainly apparent. Our periodicals are beginning to acknowledge the importance of the science (shall we so term it?) and to disdain the flippant *opinion* which so long has been made its substitute.

Time was when we imported our critical decisions from the mother country. For many years we enacted a perfect farce of subserviency to the *dicta* of Great Britain. At last a revulsion of feeling, with self-disgust, necessarily ensued. Urged by these, we plunged into the opposite extreme. In throwing *totally* off that "authority," whose voice had so long been so sacred, we even surpassed, and by much, our original folly. But the watchword now was, "a national literature!"—as if any true literature *could be* "national"—as if the world at large were not the only proper stage for the literary *histrio*. We became, suddenly, the merest and maddest *partizans* in letters. Our papers spoke of "tariffs" and "protection." Our Magazines had habitual passages about that "truly native novelist, Mr. Cooper," or that "staunch American genius, Mr. Paulding." Unmindful of the spirit of the axioms that "a prophet has no honor in his own land" and that "a hero is never a hero to his *valet-de-chambre*"—axioms founded in reason and in truth—our reviews urged the propriety—our booksellers the necessity, of strictly "American" themes. A foreign subject, at this epoch, was a weight more than enough to drag down into the very depths of critical damnation the finest writer owning nativity in the States; while, on the reverse, we found ourselves daily in the paradoxical dilemma of liking, or pretending to like, a stupid book the better because (sure

enough) its stupidity was of our own growth, and discussed
our own affairs.

It is, in fact, but very lately that this anomalous state of
feeling has shown any signs of subsidence. Still it *is* subsiding.
Our views of literature in general having expanded, we begin
to demand the use—to inquire into the offices and provinces
of criticism—to regard it more as an art based immoveably
in nature, less as a mere system of fluctuating and conventional dogmas. And, with the prevalence of these ideas, has
arrived a distaste even to the home-dictation of the book-
seller-*coteries*. If our editors are not as yet *all* independent of
the will of a publisher, a majority of them scruple, at least, *to
confess* a subservience, and enter into no positive combinations
against the minority who despise and discard it. And this is a
very great improvement of exceedingly late date.

Escaping these quicksands, our criticism is nevertheless in
some danger—some very little danger—of falling into the pit
of a most detestable species of cant—the cant of *generality*.
This tendency has been given it, in the first instance, by the
onward and tumultuous spirit of the age. With the increase
of the thinking-material comes the desire, if not the necessity,
of abandoning particulars for masses. Yet in our individual
case, as a nation, we seem merely to have adopted this bias
from the British Quarterly Reviews, upon which our own
Quarterlies have been slavishly and pertinaciously modelled.
In the foreign journal, the review or criticism properly so
termed, has gradually yet steadily degenerated into what we
see it at present—that is to say into anything but criticism.
Originally a "review," was not so called as *lucus a non lucendo*. Its name conveyed a just idea of its design. It reviewed, or surveyed the book whose title formed its text,
and, giving an analysis of its contents, passed judgment
upon its merits or defects. But, through the system of
anonymous contribution, this natural process lost ground
from day to day. The name of a writer being known only
to a few, it became to him an object not so much to write
well, as to write fluently, at so many guineas per sheet. The
analysis of a book is a matter of time and of mental exertion. For many classes of composition there is required a
deliberate perusal, with notes, and subsequent generaliza-

tion. An easy substitute for this labor was found in a digest or compendium of the work noticed, with copious extracts—or a still easier, in random comments upon such passages as accidentally met the eye of the critic, with the passages themselves copied at full length. The mode of reviewing most in favor, however, because carrying with it the greatest *semblance* of care, was that of diffuse essay upon the subject matter of the publication, the reviewer (?) using the facts alone which the publication supplied, and using them as material for some theory, the sole concern, bearing, and intention of which, was mere difference of opinion with the author. These came at length to be understood and habitually practised as the customary or conventional *fashions* of review; and although the nobler order of intellects did not fall into the full heresy of these fashions— we may still assert that even Macaulay's nearest approach to criticism in its legitimate sense, is to be found in his article upon Ranke's "History of the Popes"—an article in which the whole strength of the reviewer is put forth *to account* for a single fact—the progress of Romanism—which the book under discussion has established.

Now, while we do not mean to deny that a good essay is a good thing, we yet assert that these papers on general topics have nothing whatever to do with that *criticism* which their evil example has nevertheless infected *in se*. Because these dogmatising pamphlets, which *were once* "Reviews," have lapsed from their original faith, it does not follow that the faith itself is extinct—that "there shall be no more cakes and ale"—that criticism, in its old acceptation, does not exist. But we complain of a growing inclination on the part of our lighter journals to believe, on such grounds, that such is the fact—that because the British Quarterlies, through supineness, and our own, through a degrading imitation, have come to merge all varieties of vague generalization in the one title of "Review," it therefore results that criticism, being everything in the universe, is, consequently, nothing whatever in fact. For to this end, and to none other conceivable, is the tendency of such propositions, for example, as we find in a late number of that very clever monthly magazine, Arcturus.

"But *now*" (the emphasis on the *now* is our own)—"But *now*," says Mr. Mathews, in the preface to the first volume of his journal, "criticism has a wider scope and a universal interest. It dismisses errors of grammar, and hands over an imperfect rhyme or a false quantity to the proof-reader; it looks *now* to the heart of the subject and the author's design. It is a test of opinion. Its acuteness is not pedantic, but philosophical; it unravels the web of the author's mystery to interpret his meaning to others; it detects his sophistry, because sophistry is injurious to the heart and life; it promulgates his beauties with liberal, generous praise, because this is its true duty as the servant of truth. Good criticism may be well asked for, since it is the type of the literature of the day. It gives method to the universal inquisitiveness on every topic relating to life or action. A criticism, *now*, includes every form of literature, except perhaps the imaginative and the strictly dramatic. It is an essay, a sermon, an oration, a chapter in history, a philosophical speculation, a prose-poem, an art-novel, a dialogue; it admits of humor, pathos, the personal feelings of autobiography, the broadest views of statesmanship. As the ballad and the epic were the productions of the days of Homer, the review is the native characteristic growth of the nineteenth century."

We respect the talents of Mr. Mathews, but must dissent from nearly all that he here says. The species of "review" which he designates as the "characteristic growth of the nineteenth century" is only the growth of the last twenty or thirty years *in Great Britain*. The French Reviews, for example, which are *not* anonymous, are very different things, and preserve the *unique* spirit of true criticism. And what need we say of the Germans?—what of Winkelmann, of Novalis, of Schelling, of Göethe, of Augustus William, and of Frederick Schlegel?—that their magnificent *critiques raisonnées* differ from those of Kaimes, of Johnson, and of Blair, in principle not at all, (for the principles of these artists will not fail until Nature herself expires,) but solely in their more careful elaboration, their greater thoroughness, their more profound analysis and application of the principles themselves. That a criticism "*now*" should be different in spirit, as Mr. Mathews

supposes, from a criticism at any previous period, is to insinuate a charge of variability in laws that cannot vary—the laws
of man's heart and intellect—for these are the sole basis upon
which the true critical art is established. And this art *"now"*
no more than in the days of the "Dunciad," can, without neglect of its duty, "dismiss errors of grammar," or "hand over
an imperfect rhyme or a false quantity to the proof-reader."
What is meant by a "test of opinion" in the connexion here
given the words by Mr. M., we do not comprehend as clearly
as we could desire. By this phrase we are as completely enveloped in doubt as was Mirabeau in the castle of *If.* To our
imperfect appreciation it seems to form a portion of that general vagueness which is the *tone* of the whole philosophy at
this point:—but all that which our journalist describes a criticism to be, is all that which we sturdily maintain it *is not.*
Criticism is *not,* we think, an essay, nor a sermon, nor an
oration, nor a chapter in history, nor a philosophical speculation, nor a prose-poem, nor an art novel, nor a dialogue. In
fact, it *can be* nothing in the world but—a criticism. But if it
were all that Arcturus imagines, it is not very clear why it
might not be equally "imaginative" or "dramatic"—a romance or a melo-drama, or both. That it would be a farce
cannot be doubted.

It is against this frantic spirit of *generalization* that we protest. We have a word, "criticism," whose import is sufficiently
distinct, through long usage, at least; and we have an art of
high importance and clearly-ascertained limit, which this
word is quite well enough understood to represent. Of that
conglomerate science to which Mr. Mathews so eloquently
alludes, and of which we are instructed that it is anything and
everything at once—of this science we know nothing, and
really wish to know less; but we object to our contemporary's
appropriation in its behalf, of a term to which we, in common with a large majority of mankind, have been accustomed
to attach a certain and very definitive idea. Is there no word
but "criticism" which may be made to serve the purposes of
"Arcturus?" Has it any objection to Orphicism, or Dialism,
or Emersonism, or any other pregnant compound indicative
of confusion worse confounded?

Still, we must not pretend a total misapprehension of the

idea of Mr. Mathews, and we should be sorry that he misunderstood *us*. It may be granted that we differ only in terms—although the difference will yet be found not unimportant in effect. Following the highest authority, we would wish, in a word, to limit literary criticism to comment upon *Art*. A book is written—and it is only *as the book* that we subject it to review. With the opinions of the work, considered otherwise than in their relation to the work itself, the critic has really nothing to do. It is his part simply to decide upon *the mode* in which these opinions are brought to bear. Criticism is thus no "test of opinion." For this test, the work, divested of its pretensions as an *art-product*, is turned over for discussion to the world at large—and first, to that class which it especially addresses—if a history, to the historian—if a metaphysical treatise, to the moralist. In this, the only true and intelligible sense, it will be seen that criticism, the test or analysis of *Art*, (*not* of opinion,) is only properly employed upon productions which have their basis in art itself, and although the journalist (whose duties and objects are multiform) may turn aside, at pleasure, from the *mode* or vehicle of opinion to discussion of the opinion conveyed—it is still clear that he is *"critical"* only in so much as he deviates from his true province not at all.

And of the critic himself what shall we say?—for as yet we have spoken only the *proem* to the true *epopea*. What *can* we better say of him than, with Bulwer, that "he must have courage to blame boldly, magnanimity to eschew envy, genius to appreciate, learning to compare, an eye for beauty, an ear for music, and a heart for feeling." Let us add, a talent for analysis and a solemn indifference to abuse.

Graham's Magazine, January 1842

Prospectus of The Stylus

A MONTHLY JOURNAL OF GENERAL LITERATURE TO BE
EDITED BY EDGAR A. POE AND PUBLISHED IN THE
CITY OF PHILADELPHIA, BY CLARKE & POE.

> ————unbending that all men
> Of thy firm TRUTH may say—"Lo! this is writ
> With the antique *iron pen*.
>
> *Launcelot Canning.*

TO THE PUBLIC.—The Prospectus of a Monthly Journal to have been called "THE PENN MAGAZINE," has already been partially circulated. Circumstances, in which the public have no interest, induced a suspension of the project, which is now, under the best auspices, resumed, with no other modification than that of the title. "The Penn Magazine," it has been thought, was a name somewhat too local in its suggestions, and "THE STYLUS" has been finally adopted.

It has become obvious, indeed, to even the most unthinking, that the period has at length arrived when a journal of the character here proposed, is demanded and will be sustained. The late movements on the great question of International Copy-Right, are but an index of the universal *disgust* excited by what is quaintly termed the *cheap* literature of the day:—as if that which is utterly worthless in itself, can be cheap at any price under the sun.

"The Stylus" will include about one hundred royal octavo pages, in single column, per month; forming two thick volumes per year. In its mechanical appearance—in its typography, paper and binding—it will far surpass all American journals of its kind. Engravings, when used, will be in the highest style of Art, but are promised only in obvious illustration of the text, and in strict keeping with the Magazine character. Upon application to the proprietors, by any agent of repute who may desire the work, or by any other individual who may feel interested, a specimen sheet will be forwarded. As, for many reasons, it is inexpedient to commence a journal of this kind at any other period than at the beginning or middle of the year, the first number of "The Stylus" will not be regularly issued until the first of July, 1843. In the meantime,

to insure its perfect and permanent success, no means will be
left untried which long experience, untiring energy, and the
amplest capital, can supply. The price will be *Five Dollars* per
annum, or *Three Dollars* per single volume, in advance. Letters which concern only the Editorial management may be
addressed to Edgar A. Poe, individually; all others to Clarke
& Poe.

The necessity for any very rigid definition of the literary
character or aims of "The Stylus," is, in some measure, obviated by the general knowledge, on the part of the public, of
the editor's connexion, formerly, with the two most successful periodicals in the country—"The Southern Literary Messenger," and "Graham's Magazine." Having no proprietary
right, however, in either of these journals; his objects, too,
being, in many respects, at variance with those of their very
worthy owners; he found it not only impossible to effect anything, on the score of taste, for the mechanical appearance of
the works, but exceedingly difficult, also, to stamp, upon their
internal character, that *individuality* which he believes essential to the full success of all similar publications. In regard to
their extensive and permanent influence, it appears to him
that continuity, definitiveness, and a marked certainty of purpose, are requisites of vital importance; and he cannot help
thinking that these requisites are attainable, only where a single mind has at least *the general* direction of the enterprise.
Experience, in a word, has distinctly shown him—what, indeed, might have been demonstrated *à priori*—that in founding a Magazine wherein his interest should be not merely
editorial, lies his sole chance of carrying out to completion
whatever peculiar intentions he may have entertained.

In many important points, then, the new journal will differ
widely from either of those named. It will endeavor to be at
the same time more varied and more *unique*,—more vigorous, more pungent, more original, more individual, and more
independent. It will discuss not only the Belles-Lettres, but,
very thoroughly, the Fine Arts, with the Drama: and, more
in brief, will give, each month, a Retrospect of our Political
History. It will enlist the loftiest talent, but employ it not
always in the loftiest—at least not always in the most pompous or Puritanical way. It will aim at affording a fair and not

dishonorable field for the *true* intellect of the land, without reference to the mere *prestige* of celebrated names. It will support the general interests of the Republic of Letters, and insist upon regarding the world at large as the sole proper audience for the author. It will resist the dictation of Foreign Reviews. It will eschew the stilted dulness of our own Quarterlies, and while it *may*, if necessary, be no less learned, will deem it wiser to be less anonymous, and difficult to be more dishonest, than they.

An important feature of the work, and one which will be introduced in the opening number, will be a series of *Critical* and *Biographical Sketches* of *American Writers*. These sketches will be accompanied with full length and characteristic portraits; will include every person of literary note in America; and will investigate carefully, and with rigorous impartiality, the individual claims of each.

It shall, in fact, be the *chief purpose* of "The Stylus" to become known as a journal wherein may be found, at all times, upon all subjects within its legitimate reach, a sincere and a fearless opinion. It shall be a leading object to assert in precept, and to maintain in practice, the rights, while, in effect, it demonstrates the advantages, of an absolutely independent criticism;—a criticism self-sustained; guiding itself only by the purest rules of Art; analyzing and urging these rules as it applies them; holding itself aloof from all personal bias; and acknowledging no fear save that of outraging the Right.

CLARKE & POE.

N. B. Those friends of the Proprietors, throughout the country, who may feel disposed to support "The Stylus," will confer an important favor by sending in their names *at once*.

The provision in respect to payment '*in advance*,' is intended only as a general rule, and has reference to the Magazine *when established*. In the commencement, the subscription money will not be demanded untill the issue of the second number.

C. & P.

Philadelphia Saturday Museum, March 4, 1843

Some Secrets of the Magazine Prison-House

THE WANT of an International Copy-Right Law, by rendering it nearly impossible to obtain anything from the booksellers in the way of remuneration for literary labor, has had the effect of forcing many of our very best writers into the service of the Magazines and Reviews, which with a pertinacity that does them credit, keep up in a certain or uncertain degree the good old saying, that even in the thankless field of Letters the laborer is worthy of his hire. How—by dint of what dogged instinct of the honest and proper, these journals have contrived to persist in their paying practices, in the very teeth of the opposition got up by the Fosters and Leonard Scotts, who furnish for eight dollars any four of the British periodicals for a year, is a point we have had much difficulty in settling to our satisfaction, and we have been forced to settle it, at last, upon no more reasonable ground than that of a still lingering *esprit de patrie*. That Magazines can live, and not only live but thrive, and not only thrive but afford to disburse money for original contributions, are facts which can only be solved, under the circumstances, by the really fanciful but still agreeable supposition, that there is somewhere still existing an ember not altogether quenched among the fires of good feeling for letters and literary men, that once animated the American bosom.

It would *not do* (perhaps this is the idea) to let our poor devil authors absolutely starve, while we grow fat, in a literary sense, on the good things of which we unblushingly pick the pocket of all Europe: it would not be exactly the thing *comme il faut*, to permit a positive atrocity of this kind: and hence we have Magazines, and hence we have a portion of the public who subscribe to these Magazines (through sheer pity), and hence we have Magazine publishers (who sometimes take upon themselves the duplicate title of "editor *and* proprietor,")—publishers, we say, who, under certain conditions of good conduct, occasional puffs, and decent subserviency at all times, make it a point of conscience to encourage the poor devil author with a dollar or two, more or less as he behaves himself properly and abstains from the indecent habit of turning up his nose.

We hope, however, that we are not so prejudiced or so vindictive as to insinuate that what certainly does look like illiberality on the part of them (the Magazine publishers) is really an illiberality chargeable to *them*. In fact, it will be seen at once, that what we have said has a tendency directly the reverse of any such accusation. These publishers pay *something*—other publishers nothing at all. Here certainly is a difference—although a mathematician might contend that the difference might be infinitesimally small. Still, these Magazine editors and proprietors *pay* (that is the word), and with your true poor-devil author the smallest favors are sure to be thankfully received. No: the illiberality lies at the door of the demagogue-ridden public, who suffer their anointed delegates (or perhaps arointed—which is it?) to insult the common sense of them (the public) by making orations in our national halls on the beauty and conveniency of robbing the Literary Europe on the highway, and on the gross absurdity in especial of admitting so unprincipled a principle, that a man has any right and title either to his own brains or the flimsy material that he chooses to spin out of them, like a confounded caterpillar as he is. If anything of this gossamer character stands in need of protection, why we have our hands full at once with the silk-worms and the *morus multicaulis*.

But if we cannot, under the circumstances, complain of the absolute illiberality of the Magazine publishers (since pay they do), there is at least one particular in which we have against them good grounds of accusation. Why (since pay they must) do they not pay with a good grace, and *promptly*. Were we in an ill humor at this moment, we could a tale unfold which would erect the hair on the head of Shylock. A young author, struggling with Despair itself in the shape of a ghastly poverty, which has no alleviation—no sympathy from an everyday world, that cannot understand his necessities, and that would pretend not to understand them if it comprehended them ever so well—this young author is politely requested to compose an article, for which he will "be handsomely paid." Enraptured, he neglects perhaps for a month the sole employment which affords him the chance of a livelihood, and having starved through the month (he and his family) completes at length the month of starvation and the article, and despatches the latter (with a broad hint about the former) to the pursy "editor" and bottle-nosed "proprietor" who has condescended to honor him (the poor devil) with his patronage. A month (starving still), and no reply. Another month—still none. Two months more—still none. A second letter, modestly hinting that the article may not have reached its destination—still no reply. At the expiration of six additional months, personal application is made at the "editor and proprietor" 's office. Call again. The poor devil goes out, and does not fail to call again. Still call again;—and call again is the word for three or four months more. His patience exhausted, the article is demanded. No—he can't have it—(the truth is, it was too good to be given up so easily)—"it is in print," and "contributions of this character are never paid for (it is a *rule* we have) under six months after publication. Call in six months after the issue of your affair, and your money is ready for you—for we are business men, ourselves— prompt." With this the poor devil is satisfied, and makes up his mind that the "editor and proprietor" is a gentleman, and that of course he (the poor devil) will wait as requested. And it is supposable that he would have waited if he could—but Death in the meantime would not. He dies, and by the good luck of his decease (which came by starvation) the fat "editor and proprietor" is fatter henceforward and for ever to the amount of five and twenty dollars, very cleverly saved, to be spent generously in canvas-backs and champagne.

There are two things which we hope the reader will not do, as he runs over this article: first, we hope that he will not believe that we write from any personal experience of our own, for we have only the reports of actual sufferers to depend upon, and second, that he will not make any personal application of our remarks to any Magazine publisher now living, it being well known that they are all as remarkable for their generosity and urbanity, as for their intelligence, and appreciation of Genius.

Broadway Journal, February 15, 1845

About Critics and Criticism

O UR MOST ANALYTIC, if not altogether our best critic, (Mr. Whipple, perhaps, excepted,) is Mr. *William A. Jones*, author of "The Analyst." How he would write elaborate criticisms I cannot say; but his summary judgments of authors are, in general, discriminative and profound. In fact, his papers on *Emerson* and on *Macaulay*, published in "Arcturus," are better than merely "profound," if we take the word in its now desecrated sense; for they are at once pointed, lucid, and just: — as summaries, leaving nothing to be desired.

Mr. Whipple has less analysis, and far less candor, as his depreciation of "Jane Eyre" will show; but he excels Mr. Jones in sensibility to Beauty, and is thus the better critic of Poetry. I have read nothing finer in its way than his eulogy on Tennyson. I say "eulogy" — for the essay in question is unhappily little more: — and Mr. Whipple's paper on Miss Barrett, was *nothing* more. He has less discrimination than Mr. Jones, and a more obtuse sense of the critical office. In fact, he has been infected with that unmeaning and transparent heresy — the cant of critical Boswellism, by dint of which we are to shut our eyes tightly to all autorial blemishes, and open them, like owls, to all autorial merits. Papers thus composed may be good in their way, just as an impertinent *cicerone* is good in *his* way; and the way, in either case, may still be a small one.

Boccalini, in his "Advertisements from Parnassus," tells us that Zoilus once presented Apollo with a very caustic review of a very admirable poem. The god asked to be shown the beauties of the work; but the critic replied that he troubled himself only about the errors. Hereupon Apollo gave him a sack of unwinnowed wheat — bidding him pick out all the chaff for his pains.

Now this fable does very well as a hit at the critics; but I am by no means sure that the Deity was in the right. The fact is, that the limits of the strict critical duty are grossly misapprehended. We may go so far as to say that, while the critic is *permitted* to play, at times, the part of the mere commentator — while he is *allowed*, by way of merely *interesting* his readers, to put in the fairest light the merits of his author —

his *legitimate* task is still, in pointing out and analyzing defects and showing how the work might have been improved, to aid the general cause of Letters, without undue heed of the individual literary man. Beauty, to be brief, should be considered in the light of an axiom, which, to become at once evident, needs only to be distinctly *put*. It is *not* Beauty, if it require to be demonstrated as such:—and thus to point out too particularly the merits of a work, is to admit that they are *not* merits altogether.

When I say that both Mr. Jones and Mr. Whipple are, in some degree, imitators of Macaulay, I have no design that my words should be understood as disparagement. The style and general conduct of Macaulay's critical papers could scarcely be improved. To call his manner "conventional," is to do it gross injustice. The manner of Carlyle *is* conventional—with himself. The style of Emerson is conventional—with himself *and* Carlyle. The style of Miss Fuller is conventional—with herself and *Emerson* and Carlyle:—that is to say, it is a triple-distilled conventionality:—and by the word "conventionality," as here used, I mean very nearly what, as regards personal conduct, we style "affectation"—that is, an assumption of airs or *tricks* which have no basis in reason or common sense. The quips, quirks, and curt oracularities of the Emersons, Alcots and Fullers, are simply Lily's Euphuisms revived. Very different, indeed, are the *peculiarities* of Macaulay. He has his mannerisms; but we see that, by dint of them, he is enabled to accomplish the extremes of unquestionable excellences—the extreme of clearness, of vigor (dependent upon clearness) of grace, and very especially of thoroughness. For his short sentences, for his antitheses, for his modulations, for his climaxes—for every thing that he does—a very slight analysis suffices to show a distinct reason. His manner, thus, is simply the perfection of that justifiable rhetoric which has its basis in common-sense; and to say that such rhetoric is never called in to the aid of *genius*, is simply to disparage genius, and by no means to discredit the rhetoric. It is nonsense to assert that the highest genius would not be benefited by attention to its modes of manifestation—by availing itself of that Natural Art which it too frequently despises. Is it not evident that the more intrinsically valuable the rough diamond, the more gain accrues to it from polish?

Now, since it would be nearly impossible to vary the rhetoric of Macaulay, in any material degree, without deterioration in the *essential* particulars of clearness, vigor, etc., those who write *after* Macaulay have to choose between the two horns of a dilemma:—they must be weak and original, or imitative and strong:—and since imitation, in a case of this kind, is merely adherence to *Truth* and *Reason* as pointed out by one who feels their value, the author who should forego the advantages of the "imitation" for the mere sake of being erroneously original, *"n'est pas si sage qu'il croit."*

The true course to be pursued by our critics—justly sensible of Macaulay's excellences—is *not*, however, to be content with tamely following in his footsteps—but to outstrip him in his own path—a path not so much his as Nature's. We must not fall into the error of fancying that he is *perfect* merely because he excels (in point of style) all his British co-temporaries. Some such idea as this seems to have taken possession of Mr. Jones, when he says:

"Macaulay's style is admirable—full of color, perfectly clear, free from all obstructions, exactly English, and as pointedly antithetical as possible. We have marked two passages on Southey and Byron, so happy *as to defy improvement*. The one is a sharp epigrammatic paragraph on Southey's political bias:

'Government is to Mr. Southey one of the fine arts. He judges of a theory or a public measure, of a religion, a political party, a peace or a war, as men judge of a picture or a statue, by the effect produced on his imagination. A chain of associations is to him what a chain of reasoning is to other men; and what he calls his opinions are, in fact, merely his tastes.'

The other a balanced character of Lord Byron:

'In the rank of Lord Byron, in his understanding, in his character, in his very person, there was a strange union of opposite extremes. He was born to all that men covet and admire. But in every one of those eminent advantages which he possessed over others, there was mingled something of misery and debasement. He was sprung from a house, ancient, indeed, and noble, but degraded and impoverished by a series of crimes and follies, which had attained a scandalous publicity. The kinsman whom he succeeded had died poor, and but for merciful judges, would have died upon the gallows. The young peer had great intellectual powers; yet there was an unsound part in his mind. He had naturally a generous and tender heart; but his temper was wayward and irritable. He had a head which statuaries loved to copy, and a foot the deformity of which the beggars in the street mimicked.' "

Let us now look at the first of these paragraphs. The opening sentence is inaccurate at all points. The word "government" does not give the author's idea with sufficient definitiveness; for the term is *more* frequently applied to the *system* by which the affairs of a nation are regulated than to the act of regulating. "The government," we say, for example, "does so and so"—meaning those who govern. But Macaulay intends simply the act or acts called "governing," and this word should have been used, as a matter of course. The "Mr." prefixed to "Southey," is superfluous; for no sneer is designed; and, in *mistering* a well-known author, we hint that he is not entitled to that exemption which we accord to Homer, Dante, or Shakspeare. "*To* Mr Southey" would have been right, had the succeeding words been "government *seems* one of the fine arts:"—but, as the sentence stands, "*With* Mr. Southey" is demanded. "Southey," too, being the principal subject of the paragraph, should precede "government," which is mentioned only in its relation to Southey. "One of the fine arts" is pleonastic, since the phrase conveys nothing more than "a fine art" would convey.

The second sentence is quite as faulty. Here Southey loses his precedence as the subject; and thus the "He" should follow "a theory," "a public measure," etc. By "religion" is meant a "*creed*:"—this latter word should therefore be used. The conclusion of the sentence is very awkward. Southey is said to judge of a peace or war, etc., as men judge of a picture or a statue, and the words which succeed are intended to explain *how* men judge of a picture or a statue:—these words should, therefore, run thus:—"by the effect produced on *their* imaginations." "Produced," moreover, is neither so exact nor so "English" as "wrought." In saying that Southey judges of a political party, etc., as *men* judge of a picture, etc., Southey is quite excluded from the category of "men." "*Other* men," was no doubt originally written, but "other" erased, on account of the "other men" occurring in the sentence below.

Coming to this last, we find that "a chain of association*s*" is not properly paralleled by "a chain of reason*ing*." We must say either "a chain of association," to meet the "reason*ing*" or "a chain of rea*sons*," to meet the "associations." The repetition of "what" is awkward and unpleasant. The entire paragraph should be thus remodeled.

With Southey, governing is a fine art. Of a theory or a public measure—of a creed, a political party, a peace or a war—he judges by the imaginative effect; as only such things as pictures or statues are judged of by other men. What to them a chain of reasoning is, to him is a chain of association; and, as to his opinions, they are nothing but his tastes.

The blemishes in the paragraph about Byron are more negative than those in the paragraph about Southey. The first sentence needs vivacity. The adjective "opposite" is superfluous:—so is the particle "there." The second and third sentences are, properly, one. "Some" would fully supply the place of "something of." The whole phrase "which he possessed over others," is supererogatory. "Was sprung," in place of "sprang," is altogether unjustifiable. The triple repetition of "and," in the fourth sentence, is awkward. "Notorious crimes and follies," would express all that is implied in "crimes and follies which had attained a scandalous publicity." The fifth sentence might be well curtailed; and as it stands, has an unintentional and unpleasant sneer. "Intellect" would do as well as "intellectual powers;" and this (the sixth) sentence might otherwise be shortened advantageously. The whole paragraph, in my opinion, would be better thus expressed:

In Lord Byron's rank, understanding, character—even in his person—we find a strange union of extremes. Whatever men covet and admire, became his by right of birth; yet debasement and misery were mingled with each of his eminent advantages. He sprang from a house, ancient it is true, and noble, but degraded and impoverished by a series of notorious crimes. But for merciful judges, the pauper kinsman whom he succeeded would have been hanged. The young peer had an intellect great, perhaps, yet partially unsound. His heart was generous, but his temper wayward; and while statuaries copied his head, beggars mimicked the deformity of his foot.

In these remarks, my object is not so much to point out inaccuracies in the most accurate stylist of his age, as to hint that our critics might surpass him on his own ground, and yet leave themselves something to learn in the moralities of manner.

Nothing can be plainer than that our position, as a literary colony of Great Britain, leads us into wronging, indirectly, our own authors by exaggerating the merits of those across the water. Our most reliable critics extol—and extol without discrimination—such English compositions as, if written in America, would be either passed over without notice or unscrupulously condemned. Mr. Whipple, for example, whom I have mentioned in this connection with Mr. Jones, is decidedly one of our most "reliable" critics. His honesty I dispute as little as I doubt his courage or his talents—but here is an instance of the want of common discrimination into which he is occasionally hurried, by undue reverence for British intellect and British opinion. In a review of "The Drama of Exile and Other Poems" by Miss Barrett, (now Mrs. Browning,) he speaks of the following passage as "in every respect faultless—sublime."

> Hear the steep generations how they fall
> Adown the visionary stairs of Time,
> Like supernatural thunders—far yet near,
> Sowing their fiery echoes through the hills!

Now here, saying nothing of the affectation in "adown;" not alluding to the insoluble paradox of "far yet near;" not mentioning the inconsistent metaphor involved in the sowing of fiery echoes; adverting but slightly to the misusage of "like" in place of "as;" and to the impropriety of making any thing fall like *thunder*, which has never been known to fall at all; merely hinting, too, at the misapplication of "steep" to the "generations" instead of to the "stairs"—(a perversion in no degree justified by the fact that so preposterous a figure as *synecdoche* exists in the schoolbooks:)—letting these things pass, we shall still find it difficult to understand how Mrs. Browning should have been led to think the principal idea itself—the abstract idea—the idea of *tumbling down stairs*, in any shape, or under any circumstances—either a poetical or a decorous conception. And yet Mr. Whipple speaks of it as "sublime." That the lines narrowly *missed* sublimity, I grant:—that they came within a step of it, I admit; but, un-happily, the step is that *one* step which, time out of mind, has intervened between the sublime and the ridiculous. So true is this that any person—that even I—with a very partial modi-fication of the imagery—a modification that shall not inter-fere with its richly spiritual *tone*—may elevate the passage into unexceptionability. For example:

> Hear the far generations—how they crash
> From crag to crag down the precipitous Time,
> In multitudinous thunders that upstartle
> Aghast, the echoes from their cavernous lairs
> In the visionary hills!

No doubt my version has its faults; but it has at least the merit of consistency. Not only is a mountain more poetical than a pair of stairs, but echoes are more appropriately typi-fied as wild beasts than as seeds and echoes and wild beasts agree better with a mountain than does a pair of stairs with the *sowing* of seeds—even admitting that these seeds be seeds of fire, and be sown broadcast "among the hills" by a steep generation while in the act of tumbling down the stairs—that is to say, of coming down the stairs in too great a hurry to be capable of sowing the seeds as accurately as all seeds should be sown:—nor is the matter rendered any better for Mrs. Browning, even if the construction of her sentence be understood as implying that the fiery seeds were sown, not immediately by the steep generations that tumbled down the stairs, but mediately, through the intervention of the "super-natural thunders" that were *occasioned* by the steep genera-tions that were so unlucky as to tumble down the stairs.

Graham's Magazine, January 1850

A Reviewer Reviewed

BY WALTER G. BOWEN

> As we rode along the valley we saw a herd of
> *asses* on the top of one of the mountains—how
> they viewed and *reviewed* us!
> > Sterne—"Letter from France."

M R EDITOR—In a late number of your widely circulated
Magazine I had the satisfaction of reading an epigram
which appeared to me, and to your subscribers generally, if I
am not very much mistaken, to be not less well aimed and
fairly driven home to the mark, than righteously deserved. It
was in these words,

> *On P—, the Versifier, reviewing his own Verses.*
>
> When critics scourged him there was scope
> > For self-amendment and for hope;
> Reviewing his own verses, he
> > Has done the deed—*felo de se*.

I am glad to perceive that there is at least one editor of a
Magazine who is not so tied up in Mr Poe's interest as to be
afraid of expressing an honest opinion of him as a literary
man, but I do assure you that not only myself but a great
many others were astonished beyond measure at finding that
you had the courage to insert the epigram, good as it was.
Your putting it in however, has elevated you not a little in
the public opinion, and has encouraged me to hope that you
will do me the favor of publishing this Review of the Reviewer, especially as what I ask is merely in the way of perfectly fair and above board retaliation for what Mr P. upon
one or two occasions has seen fit to say of some unpretending
poems of mine, as well as of a novel by my brother-in-law.
And as for the truth and justice of what I shall write, I trust
that on that score there will be no one to offer objection, as
I do not intend to say a single word that shall not be accompanied *by the proof*. Mr Poe, to say nothing of my own case,
has done little else than "ride rough shod" over what he is in
the facetious habit of denominating the "poor devil authors"

of the land, and I presume that neither you nor any body else will think it unreasonable that, sooner or later, he should have the bitter chalice of criticism returned to his own lip—provided always and of course that the thing is done fairly, honorably, and with no trick or subterfuge—in a word, provided that the criticism be *just*.

To follow Mr Poe's own apparently frank mode of reviewing, I will begin by putting the merits of my author "in the fairest light." I shall not pretend to deny then that he has written several pieces of very considerable merit, and that some of these pieces have attracted, partly of their own accord and partly through the puffing of his friends, an unusual degree of notoriety. Among these I feel called upon to mention his Tales published by Wiley & Putnam, and especially the one called "The Murder in the Rue Morgue," which I learn has been reprinted and highly complimented in Paris, and "The Gold Bug" which Martin Farquhar Tupper justly praises, as well as the "Descent into the Maelstroom," and several other stories, all of which I am willing to admit display great power of analysis and imagination. "The Facts in the Case of Mr Valdemar" have perhaps made a greater "sensation" than anything else he has written, and has, I understand, not only gone the complete rounds of the London press, from the Morning Post down, but has been printed in pamphlet form in London, Paris and Vienna. The ingenuity and general merit of his "Raven" I do not wish to detract from, although I certainly do not think quite so highly of it as Miss Barrett or as Mr Willis professes to do; nor as Mr P himself does, if we are to judge by the laudatory criticism on it which he lately published in "Graham," a criticism which displayed, perhaps, more analysis than modesty. Some of his shorter poems are also praiseworthy, and his "Sleeper" and "Dreamland" are in my opinion better than the Raven, although in a different way. Of his criticisms I have not so much to observe in the way of commendation. They show scholarship, and the peculiar analytic talent which is the ruling feature in everything he writes. They are also remarkable for that Quixotic kind of courage which induces people of Mr P's temperament to be perpetually tilting at something—although it too often happens that the something is a windmill;

and there is one good point about them which it would be unjust to omit; and that is, they show no respect for persons. They are seldom aimed at small game. On the other hand they seem to me bitter in the extreme, captious, fault-finding, and unnecessarily severe. Mr. P. has been so often complimented for his powers of sarcasm that he thinks it incumbent upon him to keep up his reputation in that line by sneers upon all occasions and downright abuse. As for the beauties of a work, he appears to have made up his mind to neglect them altogether, or when he condescends to point one out, or to quote it, his compliments, however well they begin, are always sure to end with a point, or barb, which it is easy to mistake for satire in disguise. Real, honest, heartfelt praise is a thing not to be looked for in a criticism by Mr Poe. Even when it is his evident intention to be partial, to compliment in an extravagant manner some of his *lady* friends (for he never compliments a gentleman) there always seems to be something constrained, and shall I say malicious, at the bottom of the honey cup. These blemishes render his critical judgments of little value. They may be read for their pungency, but all the honesty they ever contain may be placed upon the point of a cambric needle.

Before proceeding with some very serious literary accusations which I have to make on my own part against Mr Poe, it may be as well, perhaps, to call his attention to something which has been said about him in the "London Literary Gazette." I wish to see if he will vouchsafe a reply to it. Mr P. has pointed out, in his late "Literati", a number of *scientific* blunders on the part of Mr. Richard Adams Locke, and perhaps the public may have some curiosity to know how he will account for his own. The "Gazette" referred to is of the date of March 14th 1846.

"*To the Editor of the Literary Gazette*—Sir, Having just read a review of Edgar Poe's Romances in the *Literary Gazette* of January p 101, allow me to advert to a curious misconception in a scientific point of view which the author has fallen into. In describing his whirling in the Maelstroom he says—'On looking out when half way down, the boat appeared *hanging* as if by magic *upon the interior surface* of a funnel of vast circumference and prodigious depth' &c. . . . 'My gaze fell instinctively *downwards* . . . . . . The smack hung on the *inclined surface of the pool which sloped at an angle* of more than forty-five degrees; so that we *seemed* to be lying on our beam ends.' &c. . . . .

Now, with all deference I would submit, first, That our only notions of *up* or *down* are derived from the direction of gravity; when therefore the direction of gravity is changed by centrifugal force, *that* direction will still *appear* to be down. 2d. That our only sense of motion is relative; when therefore all that is visible is rotating along with ourselves, we shall have no sense of motion; and in few cases do we ever *ourselves* appear to be the moving objects (witness the case of railway travelling). The only apparent motion will be the slight *difference of motion* between the various objects and ourselves. Whence it appears that the gentleman in the predicament described would, on looking about him, see a vast funnel of water apparently *laid on its side*, with its lower side horizontal, at which lower part his boat would *always appear to be lying*; the heavens appearing *at one end horizontally* and *apparently rotating*; while the chaotic abyss and foam would be at the opposite end; the waters appearing (full of local currents no doubt) stretching in a miraculous archway or tunnel, almost motionless, about and over the boat, and apparently supported by nothing; and objects nearer the entrance would appear to rotate vertically in a *slowly* retrograde direction; while objects would appear to have an opposite rotation, more and more rapid, towards the misty tumultuous end; the real velocity of the whole being unperceived, except by the contrary apparent rotation of the heavens. This would, indeed, be a wondrous spectacle, though scarcely sufficing to induce a personal experiment by your humble servant,

William Petrie."

So much for Mr Petrie, and leaving Mr Poe to reply to him, I will just here put in a point for myself, although I confess it has been suggested to me by a friend at my elbow. It is this—In accounting for his hero's escape from the Maelstrom, Mr P. quotes Archimedes *"De Incidentibus in Fluido"* lib 2. for the following fact, viz: that "a cylinder swimming in a vortex, offers more resistance to its suction and is drawn in with greater difficulty than an equally bulky body of any form whatsoever." Now the friend at my elbow asserts roundly, first, that the fact stated is no fact at all and is contrary to known laws, and secondly that there is no such passage in the second book of Archimedes as the one referred to. Thirdly he says that *no such passage, nor any resembling it, is in Archimedes at all, and that he defies Mr Poe to point it out.*

With Mr Poe's general *style* no great fault can be justly found. He has the rare merit of distinctness and simplicity, and can be forcible enough upon occasion; but as he has a most unmannerly habit of picking flaws in the grammar of other people, I feel justified in showing him that he is far from being immaculate himself. Not long ago I remember his sneering at some one for using the verb "drop" in an active sense, but at page 14 of his Tales (Wiley & Putnam edition) he commits the very same blunder—e.g—"As sure as you *drop* that beetle I'll break your neck." Again at page 18—"Was it this eye or that through which you *dropped* the beetle?" "As sure as you *let fall* that beetle" would be proper. An apple drops, but we let an apple fall. At page 34 he uses "except," with gross impropriety, for "unless"—a common error. E.g—"I found that it was impossible to retain a seat *upon* it *except* in one particular position." *"Upon"* in this sentence is also improperly employed for *"on."* This error is very usual with Mr Poe. At page 25 there are no less than five instances of it—e.g—"I doubted not that heat had been the agent in bringing to light *upon* the parchment the skull which I saw designed *upon* it." The *up* is properly used only where *action* appears. An apple, for instance, lies *on* a table; but we place an apple *up*on a table. Even in the Preface to his Poems, where we are forced to suppose him careful if ever, he is guilty of inaccurate construction. For example—"If what I have written is to circulate at all, I am naturally anxious that it should circulate as I wrote it." Now here the sentence should obviously be—"I am naturally anxious that what I have written should circulate as I wrote it, if it circulate at all." Or—"I am naturally anxious that what I have written, if it is to circulate at all, should circulate as I wrote it." But a truce with these trifles—and yet they are the very kind of *trifles* which Mr P. is so fond of exposing in other people.

The truth is, I have something more serious to speak of. The great *point* which Mr Poe has become notorious for making is that of *plagiarism*, and in his elaborate reply to *"Outis"* in the earlier numbers of the "Broadway Journal," he was at great pains to demonstrate what a plagiarism is, and by what chain of reasoning it could be established. My own purpose at present is simply to copy a few parallel passages, leaving it for the public to decide whether they do or do not come properly under the head of *wilful and deliberate literary theft*.

At page 24 of Mr P's last volume of Poems (Wiley & Putnam's edition) in a song called Eulalie, is the passage,

> Now Doubt—now Pain
> Come never again
> For her soul *gives me sigh for sigh*.

In Tom Moore's "Last Rose of Summer" we find it thus,

> No flower of her kindred,
> No rose-bud is nigh,
> To reflect back her blushes
> *Or give sigh for sigh*.

The author of the lines which follow I cannot *name* just now, but I give them because there are doubtless many of my readers who can. *Some* poet, however, is speaking of a traitor to his country and wishes him doomed

> to dwell
> Full in the sight of Paradise
> *Beholding Heaven yet feeling Hell*.

In "Al Aaraaf," at page 69 of the Poems, we read

> And there oh may my weary spirit *dwell*
> *Apart from Heaven's eternity, and yet how far from Hell!*

One of Mr Poe's most admired passages is this, forming the conclusion of the poem called "The City in the Sea," and to be found at page 22—

> And when, amid no earthly moans
>> Down, down, that town shall settle hence
>> *Hell rising from a thousand thrones*
>> *Shall do it reverence.*

But unfortunately Mrs Sigourney, in a little poem called "Musing Thoughts," first published in "The Token," for 1829, has the lines,

> *Earth slowly rising from her thousand thrones*
> *Did homage* to the Corsican.

Mr Poe has also been much praised for these lines, found at page 63 of the Poems,

> A dome by linked light from Heaven let down
> Sat gently on these columns as a crown.

Every classical scholar however must remember the Gods' Council of Homer, beginning Ἠὼς μὲν κροκόπεπλος ἐκίδνατο πᾶσαν ἐπ' αἶαν, and the lines which Pope translates (I have not the original by me)

> Let down our golden everlasting chain
> Whose strong embrace holds Heaven and Earth and Main.

That Mr Poe has in many cases obtained *help* from the more obscure classics is, I fancy, no more than a legitimate inference from so glaringly obvious an *imitation* as this, which we find at page 20.

Sonnet to Zante

> Fair isle that, from the fairest of all flowers,
>> Thy gentlest of all gentle names dost take!
> How many memories of what radiant hours
>> At sight of thee and thine at once awake!
> How many scenes of what departed bliss!
>> How many thoughts of what entombed hopes
> How many visions of a maiden that is
>> No more—no more upon thy verdant slopes!
> No more! alas that magical sad sound
>> Transforming all! Thy charms shall please no more—
> Thy memory *no more*! Accursed ground
>> Henceforth I hold thy flower-enamelled shore,

O hyacinthine isle! O purple Zante!
Isola d'oro! Fior di Levante!

Here I might safely pause; but it would not be quite proper to omit all mention of this critic's facility at *imitation!* in prose as well as verse. In his story of "Hans Phaall" published in his "Tales of the Grotesque and Arabesque," but originally appearing in the first volume of the "Southern Literary Messenger"

THE LITERARY AND
SOCIAL SCENE

Contents

Literary Small Talk

I HAVE HAD no little to do, in my day, with the trade of Aristarchus, and have even been accused of playing the Zoilus. Yet I cannot bring myself to feel any goadings of conscience for undue severity. Indeed my remorse lies somewhat the other way. How often, in commendatory reviews of books, whose purpose, whose precision, or whose piety, rendered them equivocal objects of animadversion, have I longed to close in the pregnant words of St. Austin, when speaking of the books of the Manichœans. *"Tam multi,"* says he, *"tam grandes, tam pretiosi codices"*—adding, as if aside, *"incendite omnes illas membranas."*

I have seen lately some rambling and nonsensical verses entitled "Political Squibs," in which it appeared to me the author had blundered upon a title most appropriate, and been guilty, without knowing it, of a bit of erudition. *Versus Politici*, political, that is to say, city verses, was an appellation applied by way of ridicule to the effusions of certain bards (such as Constantine Manasses, John Tzetzes, &c.) who flourished in the latter end of Rome, then so miscalled. Their verses (styled by Leo Allatius from their easiness of composition "common prostitutes") usually consisted of fifteen feet, but, like those of Peter Pindar, made laws for themselves as they went along.

Even a good Greek scholar might find himself puzzled by the following sentences. Κωνσερβετ Δεουσ ημπεριυμ βεστρυμ, βικτορ σισ σεμπερ, βηβητε Δομινι, Ημπερωτορεσ ην μουλτοσ αννοσ.

The Greeks of the Eastern empire, in the tenth century, made use of these and similar acclamations upon all occasions of public pomp. As evidence of the unlimited dominion of their emperors, the expressions were repeated in Latin, Gothic, Persian, French, and English. Constantine Porphyrogenitus, who wrote a pompous and silly volume, reducing to form and minutely detailing the ceremonies of the court, gives the above sentences as a specimen of *the Latin*. If we remember that the want of the *v* obliged the Greeks to use *b* as the nearest approach, the words, disregarding quantity, then read— *Conservet Deus imperium vestrum —victor sis semper— vivite Domini Imperatores in multos annos.* Had Constantine preserved also the words of the English acclamation, we should possibly, to-day, think them a droll specimen of our language.

———

Bulwer, in my opinion, wants the true vigor of intellect which would prompt him to seek, and enable him to seize truth upon the surface of things. He imagines her forever in the well. He is perpetually refining to no purpose upon themes which have nothing to gain, and every thing to lose in the process. He even condescends to ape the externals of a deep meaning, and will submit to be low rather than fail in appearing profound. It is this coxcombry which leads him so often into allegory and objectless personification. Does he mention "truth" in the most ordinary phrase?—she is, with a great T, Truth, the divinity. All common qualities of the mind, all immaterial or mental existences, are capitalized into persons. That he has not yet discarded this senseless mannerism, must be considered the greater wonder, as the whole head of his little imitators have already taken it up. His "Last Days of Pompeii" is ridiculously full of it. The same work, in its abundant allusions to Egyptian theology, gives also, sufficient evidence of his love of the "far-fetched." Is it indeed possible that he seriously believes one half of the abominable rigmarole put into the mouth of his philosopher Arbaces? I mean *that* rigmarole especially, which asserts the brute-worship of Egypt to have been deliberately intended as typical of certain moral and physical truths. If so, how little of the spirit of wisdom is here, with how vast a solicitude to seem wise! I remember, apropos to this subject, that in the year 1096, there thronged to the first Crusade, in the train of Peter the Hermit, and more immediately in that of the fanatic Godescal, a herd of some two hundred thousand of the most stupid, savage, drunken, and utterly worthless of the people, whose genuine leaders in the expedition were a goat and a goose. These were carried in front, and to these, *for no reason whatever, save beyond the mad whim of the mob*, was ascribed a miraculous participation in the spirit of the Deity. Had this rabble

founded an empire, we should, no doubt, have had them in-
stituting a solemn worship of goat and goose, and Mr. Bulwer, with care, might have discovered in the goat a type of
one species of deep wisdom, and in the goose a clear symbol
of another.

American Museum, January 1839

G IBBON'S "splendid and stately but artificial style," is
often discussed; yet its *details* have never, to my
knowledge, been satisfactorily pointed out. The peculiar
construction of his sentences, being since adopted by his imitators without that just reason which, perhaps, influenced the
historian, has greatly vitiated our language. For in these imitations the body is copied, without the soul, of his phraseology. It will be easy to show wherein his chief peculiarity
lies—yet this, I believe, has never been shown. In his autobiography he says—"Many experiments were made before I
could hit the middle tone between a dull chronicle, and a
rhetorical declamation." The immense theme of the decline
and fall required precisely the kind of sentence which he habitually employed. A world of essential, or at least of valuable,
information or remark, had either to be omitted altogether,
or *collaterally* introduced. In his endeavours thus to *crowd in*
his vast stores of research, much of the artificial will, of
course, be apparent; yet I cannot see that any other method
would have answered as well. For example, take a passage at
random:

"The proximity of its situation to that of Gaul, seemed to
invite their arms; the pleasing, although doubtful, intelligence of a pearl-fishery, attracted their avarice; and, as Britain was viewed in the light of a distant and insulated world,
the conquest scarcely formed any exception to the general
system of continental measures; after a war of about forty
years, undertaken by the most stupid, maintained by the
most dissolute, and terminated by the most timid of all the
emperors, the far greater part of the island submitted to the
Roman yoke."

The facts and allusions here indirectly given might have

been easily dilated into a page. It is this *indirectness* of observation, then, which forms the soul of the style of Gibbon, of which the apparently pompous phraseology is the body.

Another peculiarity, somewhat akin to this, has less reason to recommend it, and grows out of an ill-concealed admiration and imitation of Johnson, whom he styles "a bigoted, yet vigorous mind." I mean the coupling in one sentence matters that have but a very shadow of connexion. For instance—

"The Life of Julian, by the Abbé de la Breterie, first introduced me to the man and to the times, *and* I should be glad to recover my first essay on the truth of the miracle which stopped the rebuilding of the temple at Jerusalem." This laughable Gibbonism is still a great favourite with the *stellæ minores* of our literature.

In the historian's statements regarding the composition of his work, there occurs a contradiction worthy of notice. "I will add a fact"—he in one place says—"which has seldom occurred in the composition of six quartos; my rough MMS. without any intermediate copy, has been sent to press." In other passages he speaks of "frequent experiments," and states distinctly, that "three times did he compose the first chapter, twice the second and third"—and that "the fifteenth and sixteenth chapters have been reduced, by successive revisals, from a large volume to their present size;" upon every page of the work, indeed, there is most ample evidence of the *limæ labor*.

———

Voltaire betrays, on many occasions, an almost incredible ignorance of antiquity and its affairs. One of his saddest blunders is that of assigning the Canary Islands to the Roman empire.

———

There is something of *naivete*, if not much of logic, in these words of the Germans to the Ubii of Cologne, commanding them to cast off the Roman yoke. "Postulamus a vobis"—say they—"muros coloniæ, munimenta servitii, detrahatis; etiam fera animalia, si clausa teneas, virtutis obliviscuntur."

American Museum, February 1839

Letter to the Editor

IN A LATE lecture on the "Poets and Poetry of America," delivered before an audience made up chiefly of editors and their connexions, I took occasion to speak what I know to be the truth, and I endeavoured so to speak it that there should be no chance of misunderstanding what it was I intended to say. I told these gentlemen to their teeth that, with a *very* few noble exceptions, they had been engaged for many years in a system of indiscriminate laudation of American books—a system which, more than any other one thing in the world, had tended to the depression of that "American Literature" whose elevation it was designed to effect. I said this, and very much more of a similar tendency, with as thorough a distinctness as I could command. Could I, at the moment, have invented any terms *more* explicit, wherewith to express my contempt of our general editorial course of corruption and puffery, I should have employed them beyond the shadow of a doubt;—and should I think of anything more expressive *hereafter*, I will endeavour either to find or to make an opportunity for its introduction to the public.

And what, for all this, had I to anticipate? In a very few cases, the open, and, in several, the silent approval of the more chivalrous portion of the press;—but in a majority of instances, I should have been weak indeed to look for anything but abuse. To the Willises—the O'Sullivans—the Duyckincks—to the choice and magnanimous few who spoke promptly in my praise, and who have since taken my hand with a more cordial and more impressive grasp than ever—to these I return, of course, my acknowledgements, for that they have rendered me my due. To my villifiers I return also such thanks as they deserve, inasmuch as without what they have done me the honor to say, there would have been much of point wanting in the compliments of my friends. Had I, indeed, from the former, received any less equivocal tokens of disapprobation, I should at this moment have been looking about me to discover what sad blunder I had committed.

I am most sincere in what I say. I thank these, my opponents, for their good will,—manifested, of course, after their own fashion. No doubt they mean me well—if they could only be brought to believe it; and I shall expect more reasonable things from them hereafter. In the mean time, I await patiently the period when they shall have fairly made an end of what they have to say—when they shall have sufficiently exalted themselves in their own opinion—and when, especially, they shall have brought *me* over to that precise view of the question which it is their endeavor to have me adopt.

Broadway Journal, March 8, 1845

Editorial Miscellanies

FROM THE BROADWAY JOURNAL

September 20, 1845

I N A TALE called "The Broken-Hearted, a Touching Incident of Real Life, by John G. Whittier," which we find in a "Philadelphia Saturday Courier" of June 19, 18— (year torn off) there occurs the following passage:

It cannot be that earth is man's only abiding place. It cannot be that our life is a bubble, cast off by the ocean of eternity, to float a moment upon its waves, and sink into darkness and nothingness. Else why is it, that the high and glorious aspirations, which leap like angels from the temple of our hearts, are forever wandering abroad unsatisfied? Why is it that the rainbow and the cloud come over us with a beauty that is not of earth, and then pass off, and leave us to muse upon their faded loveliness? Why is it that the stars which hold their festivals around the midnight throne, are set above the grasp of our limited faculties—forever mocking us with their unapproachable glory? And why is it—that bright forms of human beauty are present to our view and then taken from us, leaving the thousand streams of our affection to flow back in an alpine torrent upon our hearts? We are born for a higher destiny than that of earth. There is a realm where the rainbow never fades—where the stars will be spread out before us, like islands that slumber on the ocean—and where the beautiful beings which here pass before us like visions, will stay in our presence forever.

The passage subjoined is also lying before us in print—but we are unable to trace its source. It is attributed to Bulwer—whether rightly or not we cannot say.

I cannot believe that earth is man's abiding place. It cannot be that life is cast upon the ocean of eternity to float for a moment upon its waves and sink into nothingness! Else why is it that the glorious aspirations which leap like angels from the temples of our hearts, are forever wandering about unsatisfied? Why is it that the rainbow and clouds come over us with a beauty that is not of earth; and then pass off and leave us to muse on their loveliness? Why is it that the stars who hold their festival around their midnight throne are set above the grasp of our limited faculties, forever mocking us with unapproachable glory? And finally, why is it that bright forms of human beauty are presented to our view and then taken from us, leaving the thousand streams of our affections to flow back in Alpine torrents upon our hearts? We are born for a higher destiny than that of earth: there is a realm where the rainbow never fades—where the stars will be spread out before us like the islands that slumber in the ocean; and where the beings that pass before us like shadows, will stay in our presence forever!

Somebody has perpetrated a gross plagiarism in the premises, but we have not the slightest idea that this somebody is Mr. Whittier. We have too high an opinion of his integrity to believe him guilty of this, the most despicable species of theft. *Most* despicable, we say. The ordinary pick-pocket filches a purse, and the matter is at an end. He neither takes honor to himself, openly, on the score of the purloined purse, nor does he subject the individual robbed to the charge of pick-pocketism in his own person; by so much the less odious is he, then, than the filcher of literary property. It is impossible, we should think, to imagine a more sickening spectacle than that of the plagiarist, who walks among mankind with an erecter step, and who feels his heart beat with a prouder impulse, on account of plaudits which he is conscious are the due of another. It is the purity, the nobility, the ethereality of just fame—it is the contrast between this ethereality and the grossness of the crime of theft, which places the sin of plagiarism in so detestable a light. We are horror-stricken to find existing in the same bosom the soul-uplifting thirst for fame, and the debasing propensity to pilfer. It is the anomaly—the discord—which so grossly offends.

We repeat, that, in the case now in question, we are quite confident of the blamelessness of Mr. Whittier—but we would wish that the true criminal be ruthlessly exposed. *Who is he?* No doubt some of our friends can tell us. We remember in one of the poems of Delta (published, perhaps in the sev-

enth volume of Blackwood) something which very remarkably resembles the passages quoted above.

ANOTHER parallel—Here are the concluding lines of
"Knowledge is Power, a Poem pronounced before the Junior
Lyceum of the City of Chicago, on the 22d of February 1813,
by William H. Bushnell."

> To each and all, may life's wide sea
> Ne'er rise before your sail—
> But may your course be ever free
> From each tempestuous gale:
> And may you pass your portals fair
> To Heaven, free and light—
> And life be mingled less with care
> Than his, who bids you now—good night.

And here are the concluding lines of "The Age; a Satire
pronounced before the New York Society of Literature at the
Second Anniversary, January 23d, 1845, by Alfred Wheeler."

> And may sweet dreams of love and truth,
>   Upon your slumbers rest,
> And cloudless hope, the joy of youth,
>   Dwell peaceful in each breast—
> And may your lives be free from care,
>   Your path be ever bright,
> Your days, more promising and fair,
>   Than mine have been— *Good night!*

PROFESSOR HORNCASTLE gave his first entertainment, in
this country, at the Society Library, last week. We were unable to attend his performance.

While glancing at his "posters" we were much struck by
the following paragraph. "The Professor thinks it right, in
consequence of the frequent mistakes, to make it generally
known that he never was on the stage. It is *a* Mr. James
Henry Horncastle, who was formerly at the theatre. If his
friends will look at the initials of the name, they will see the
mistake."

The Professor may think it right to make this announcement, but we think it extremely wrong. In the first place, of

what consequence is it, whether he was or was not upon the stage? The fact, if established, does not make him either a better singer or a better man. In the next place it would certainly have been in much better taste had he said—the party for whom I am mistaken is my brother, and not *a* Mr. James Henry Horncastle. It would have been in better taste, for the reason, that this Mr. James Henry Horncastle is very generally known in this city, not only for his talents, which are considerable and versatile, but for his gentlemanly demeanor and honorable conduct. We therefore think that the professor need not be very much shocked, even if he should be mistaken for his brother: at any rate the announcement is a gratuitous exposure of some affair with which the public has nothing to do, and which should certainly have been kept back while the party so slightingly spoken of, is absent from the country, and therefore unable to define his own position.

We have been frequently asked from what source Professor Horncastle derives his title of Professor? What Professorship does he hold? To these questions we are unable to reply, never having seen an account of Mr. Horncastle's election to a vacant chair.

———

THE MESMERIC journals, and some others, are still making a to-do about the tenability of Mr. Vankirk's doctrines as broached in a late Magazine paper of our own, entitled "Mesmeric Revelation." "The Regenerator" has some very curious comments, indeed: it says:

However accurate or inaccurate the reasons of this clairvoyant may have been, it is self-evident to me they were heterogeneous and probably were solecisms; at all events they were unintelligible in my apprehension—his "unparticled matter," i.e. "God," "God in quiescence," i.e. "mind," &c. I would fain transcribe verbatim his answers to his mesmerisers, but brevity, which is your legitimate due, forbids: therefore let the following suffice, viz.—

Question: What is God? Answer: [after a long pause,] "It is difficult to tell; he is not spirit, for he exists; nor is he matter, as you understand it—immateriality is a mere word; but there are gradations of matter, of which man knows nothing; the grosser impelling the finer, the finer pervading the grosser; the gradations of matter increase in rarity or fineness until we arrive at a matter *unparticled*;—here the law of impulsion and permeation is modified; this matter is God, and thought is this matter in motion." And lastly—"It is clear, however, that it is as fully matter as before." If this is not incoherent language, then am I no competent judge of logic. However, the argument, if sane, in reality amounts to materialism, and our clairvoyant is a materialist still, and propagating the doctrine I have maintained and held forth to the world more than thirty years, viz., that God is matter—is "all in all"—as the Christian Scriptures declare. Be that as it may, there can be no effect without a natural cause; hence I conclude Vankirk's ratiocination was the legitimate or natural effect of his former cogitations and present anxiety concerning this much harped upon theological enigma—the soul's immortality.

Now would not any one suppose, that our sentence as above given, viz.: "It is as clear, however, that it is as fully matter as before"—would not any one suppose that it immediately followed the words "matter is motion," and that the *"it"* referred to "thought?" Of course, any one would. But, as *we* wrote them, the sentences are separated by some dozen intervening paragraphs, and there is no connexion whatever.

These things, however, are of little consequence. We wait with great patience for the end of the argumentation.

————

A CORRESPONDENT of Mr. Simms' Monthly Magazine makes some odd mistakes in giving that work an account of literary people and literary doings in New York. Some *omissions* in the lists of contributors to the principal Magazines, are particularly noticeable. Many constant writers are unmentioned, and some of the occasional ones paraded forth, are no credit to the journals in question. In speaking of the "Broadway Journal," the correspondent announces, as its only contributors, Mrs. Childs and T. H. Chivers. Of the former we never heard. Dr. Chivers never contributed a line to our paper in his life. Our regular contributors would do honor to any Magazine in the land—Lowell, Simms, Benjamin, Duyckinck, Page, (the artist,) the author of the Vision of Rubeta, Tuckerman, Mrs. Osgood, Mrs. Ellett, Mrs. Hewitt, Miss Lawson, Miss Fuller, and so forth, are writers of which any journal might be proud.

EMERSON'S Arithmetic has been translated into modern Greek.

FREDERICA BREMER, the gifted Swedish novelist, will not come here, as she intended, this summer, her visit being necessarily postponed till another year, by the illness of a near friend.

A SUIT for libel has been instituted against J. Fenimore Cooper, by the Rev. Mr. Tiffany of Cooperstown.

WE CALL the attention of our readers to some beautiful six octave piano fortes, now in the store of Mr. Chambers, 385 Broadway. They are well finished, possess a beautiful quality of tone, with great power and delicacy of touch.

Let those in need of a piano forte, call and see these instruments.

THE WORK of Von Raumer, the Prussian traveller and critic, on the United States, has appeared, and its table of contents is said to be of great promise. A translation may be expected to appear shortly in this country. Mrs. Ellett, of South Carolina, will probably translate it.—*N. O. Picayune*.

The Baron's comments on American literature are particularly vapid. He seems to have not the remotest conception of the actual condition of our letters. The translation is completed. Mrs. Ellet has done only a portion—though abundantly able to have done all, and well.

We learn from Messrs. Robinson and Jones that the subscription papers for the volume of *Poems, by Lewis J. Cist*, have been very well filled, and that the work is now in press. Mr. C. has written a great deal for eastern and western magazines and papers, and has many admirers who will be pleased to possess his productions in a collected form. A number of his poems have had a very wide circulation, and given his name a place among the younger Bards of America.— *Cincinnati Gazette.*

———

MR. WILLIAM FAIRMAN, *of this city, has become, for the present, interested in the conduct of the "Broadway Journal." He is about taking a tour through some of the States, for the purpose of promoting the general interests of the work, and we commend him to the attention of our friends.*

October 4, 1845

THOMAS DUNN ENGLISH, the editor of the "Aristidean," wrote for the "New Mirror," a short time after it was established, a poem called "Ben Bolt" to which he appended his initials. From its simplicity of diction and touching truthfulness of narrative, it became popular, and being extensively copied, induced the author to acknowledge it. It runs thus:

> Don't you remember sweet Alice, Ben Bolt?
>   Sweet Alice whose hair was so brown,
> Who wept with delight when you gave her a smile,
>   And trembled with fear at your frown?
> In the old churchyard in the valley, Ben Bolt,
>   In a corner obscure and alone,
> They have fitted a slab of the granite so gray,
>   And Alice lies under the stone.
>
> Under the Hickory tree, Ben Bolt,
>   Which stood at the foot of the hill,
> Together we've lain in the noonday shade,
>   And listened to Appleton's mill.
> The mill-wheel has fallen to pieces, Ben Bolt,
>   The rafters have tumbled in,
> And a quiet which crawls round the walls as you gaze,
>   Has followed the olden din.
>
> Do you mind the cabin of logs, Ben Bolt,
>   At the edge of the pathless wood,
> And the button-ball tree with its motley limbs,
>   Which nigh by the door-step stood?

The cabin to ruin has gone, Ben Bolt,
    The tree you would seek in vain;
And where once the lords of the forest waved,
    Grow grass and the golden grain.

And don't you remember the school, Ben Bolt.
    With the master so cruel and grim,
And the shaded nook in the running brook,
    Where the children went to swim?
Grass grows on the master's grave, Ben Bolt.
    The spring of the brook is dry,
And of all the boys that were schoolmates then,
    There are only you and I.

There is change in the things I loved, Ben Bolt.
    They have changed from the old to the new;
But I feel in the core of my spirit the truth,
    There never was change in you.
Twelvemonths twenty have past, Ben Bolt.
    Since first we were friends, yet I hail
Thy presence a blessing, thy friendship a truth—
    Ben Bolt, of the salt-sea gale.

Several musical people have attempted to adapt an air to these words; and there are, in consequence, five editions of the song afloat, issued under the auspices of various publishers. In some of these a portion of the stanzas are taken—and in all there are various errors. They are such errors, however, as seem to be without intention, and bear every evidence of their accidental nature. The one before us is of a different kind. It occurs on two pages of music and words, published by Oliver & Ditsen, Washington street, Boston, with the following title:—

There's a change in the things I love. Composed and respectfully dedicated to his friend B. F. Baker, Esq., by Joseph P: Webster.

The evident intention of Mr. Webster is to claim the authorship of the words as well as the music—which latter has in it nothing remarkable. But whether this is, or is not, the intention of Mr. Webster, he has committed a most vile fraud upon Mr. English. Instead of printing the poem as given above, he gives four of the stanzas only, and in the following form—the italics, which mark the alterations and additions, being our own:—

O don't you remember sweet Alice, Ben Bolt,
 Sweet Alice with *hair so brown*;
Who wept with delight when you gave her a smile,
 And trembled with fear at your frown.
In the old church-yard in the *Abbey*, Ben Bolt,
 In a corner obscure and alone,
They have fitted a slab of the granite so gray,
 And Alice lies under the stone.

O don't you remember the wood, Ben Bolt,
 That grew on the green sunny hill;
Where oft we have played 'neath its wide-spreading shade,
 And listened to Appleton's mill.
The mill has gone to decay, Ben Bolt,
 And the rafters have *fallen* in,
And a quiet *has settled on all around,*
 In the place of the olden din.

O don't you remember the school, Ben Bolt,
 With the master so cruel and grim;
And the *quiet* nook *and* the running brook,
 Where the *school boys* went to swim.
Grass grows on the master's grave, Ben Bolt,
 And the running brook is dry:
And of all the boys *who* were schoolmates then,
 There *is* only you and I.

There's a change in the things I *love*, Ben Bolt,
 A change from the old to the new;
But I feel in the core of my *heart, Ben Bolt,*
 There never was change in you.
Twelve months—twenty have passed, Ben Bolt,
 But still with delight I hail
Thy presence a blessing, thy friendship a truth,
 Ben Bolt of the salt sea gale.

Now, in the name of the craft of authors we protest against such impudent thieving as this. The thing is growing to a nuisance. No sooner does a literary man produce anything worthy of especial note, than some lack-brained fellow—some Mr. Joseph P. Webster—takes it up, and either passes it off as his own, or mangles it shamefully in an attempt at emendation—or perhaps both. If caught, he sneaks off in silence, like a detected robber of hen-roosts—if not, he chuckles at his successful rascality, and enjoys a reputation obtained for him by alien brains.

———

MUCH HAS been said, of late, about the necessity of maintaining a proper *nationality* in American Letters; but what this nationality *is*, or what is to be gained by it, has never been distinctly understood. That an American should confine himself to American themes, or even prefer them, is rather a political than a literary idea—and at best is a questionable point. We would do well to bear in mind that "distance lends enchantment to the view." *Ceteris paribus*, a foreign theme is, in a strictly literary sense, to be preferred. After all, the world at large is the only legitimate stage for the autorial *histrio*.

But of the need of *that* nationality which defends our own literature, sustains our own men of letters, upholds our own dignity, and depends upon our own resources, there cannot be the shadow of a doubt. Yet here is the very point at which we are most supine. We complain of our want of an International Copyright, on the ground that this want justifies our publishers in inundating us with British opinion in British books; and yet when these very publishers, at their own obvious risk, and even obvious loss, do publish an American book, we turn up our noses at it with supreme contempt (this as a general thing) until it (the American book) has been dubbed "readable" by some illiterate Cockney critic. Is it too much to say that, with us, the opinion of Washington Irving—of Prescott—of Bryant—is a mere nullity in comparison with that of any anonymous sub-sub-editor of The Spectator, The Athenæum or the "London Punch"? It is *not* saying too much, to say this. It is a solemn—an absolutely awful fact. Every publisher in the country will admit it to be a fact. There is not a more disgusting spectacle under the sun than our subserviency to British criticism. It is disgusting, first, because it is truckling, servile, pusillanimous—secondly, because of its gross irrationality. We *know* the British to bear us little but ill will—we know that, in no case, do they utter unbiassed opinions of American books—we know that in the few instances in which our writers have been treated with common decency in England, these writers have either openly paid homage to English institutions, or have had lurking at the bottom of their hearts a secret principle at war with Democracy:—we *know* all this, and yet, day after day, submit our necks to the degrading yoke of the crudest opinion that emanates from the fatherland. Now if we *must* have nationality let it be a nationality that will throw off this yoke.

The chief of the rhapsodists who have ridden us to death like the Old Man of the Mountain, is the ignorant and egotistical Wilson. We use the term rhapsodists with perfect deliberation; for, Macaulay, and Dilke, and one or two others, excepted, there is not in Great Britain a critic who can be fairly considered worthy the name. The Germans and even the French are infinitely superior. As regards Wilson, no man ever penned worse criticism or better rhodomontade. That he is "egotistical" his works show to all men, running as they read. That he is "ignorant" let his absurd and continuous schoolboy blunders about Homer bear witness. Not long ago we ourselves pointed out a series of similar inanities in his review of Miss Barrett's poems—a series, we say, of gross blunders arising from sheer ignorance—and we defy him or any one to answer a single syllable of what we then advanced.

And yet this is the man whose simple *dictum* (to our shame be it spoken) has the power to make or to mar any American reputation! In the last number of Blackwood, he has a continuation of the dull "Specimens of the British Critics," and makes occasion wantonly to insult one of the noblest of our poets, Mr. Lowell. The point of the whole attack consists in the use of slang epithets and phrases of the most ineffably vulgar description. "Squabashes" is a pet term. "Faugh!" is another. "We are Scotsmen to *the spine*!" says Sawney—as if the thing were not more than self-evident. Mr. Lowell is called "a magpie," an "ape," a "Yankee cockney," and his name is intentionally mis-written *John* Russell Lowell. Now were these indecencies perpetrated by any American critic, that critic would be sent to Coventry by the whole press of the country, but since it is Wilson who insults, we, as in duty bound, not only submit to the insult, but echo it, as an excellent jest, throughout the length and breadth of the land. *Quamdiu Catilina?* We do indeed demand the nationality of self-respect. In Letters as in Government we require a Declaration of Independence. A better thing still would be a Declaration of War—and that war should be carried forthwith "into Africa."

———

A FRIEND " who knows," writing to us in reference to the Whittier and Bulwer parallel, says,

En passant the gem which you present in your last, as attributed to both Whittier and Bulwer " went the rounds," some years ago, as the property of George D. Prentice, to whom by the way, more than one of the Abolition poet's waifs have been awarded. A few years back "The Hesperian," (Gallagher's Magazine, at Columbus, Ohio,) contained a little poem "To a Lady," beginning "We are not strangers," *&c.*, over the signature of George D. Prentice, which had previously appeared in the "New England Review," then conducted by Whittier, over the initials, J. G. W. But why speak of these things?—*"de minimis non curat lex."*

———

THE UNWORTHY cabal lately entered into by some of our most "influential" citizens, to foist upon the public attention, through a concerted movement of puffs anticipatory, a collection of rather indifferent and *very* unoriginal verses by one Mr. *William W. Lord*, has met, we rejoice to find, the most signal and universal rebuke. *Tricks* of this kind will scarcely be attempted again. A *mere* trick it was. Mr. Lord had written some matters of which he had an exalted opinion. In New Jersey he had for neighbour a very gentlemanly personage connected with the press. To him application was made, and the whole scheme was immediately arranged. *Auspice Teucro* nothing was to be feared. The press as a matter of course, would be dumb—or open its mouth only to echo the *vos plaudite* of the King. Mr. Appleton is invited to dinner. Mr. Lord is invited to recite his poems; he reads them, we have been informed, with remarkable unction. It is decided in full conclave, that henceforth he shall be the "American Milton." No member of that illustrious assembly ever dreamed that there was anything farther to do—for this whole thing had, to a certain extent, been repeatedly managed before.

The result has placed Mr. Lord in a very remarkable, and certainly in a very amusing position. There is no *immediate* need, however, of his cutting his throat. The letter to Mr. Wordsworth, was the most absurd of all moves; or if a letter *was* to be sent to Mr. Wordsworth, why did Mr. Lord think it necessary to make use of Bishop Doane as an amanuensis or a catspaw? This was hardly fair play. To "one Mr. Lord" beseeching a complimentary letter about his own poems, the patriarch of the Lakes might have had no scruple in replying—"Mr. Lord, it is my honest opinion that your book is not much better than it should be"—but an answer of this kind was clearly impossible from so well-bred a man as Wordsworth, to his personal acquaintance, the Bishop of New Jersey. This letter then—or this presentation copy of the Poems—to Wordsworth—was, after all, nothing in the world but trick No. 2. The fact is, we are ashamed both of Mr. Lord and of his book. His chicaneries have done more to convince the public of his utter want of poetic (or of any other kind of) spirit, than even the bombast, egotism, and inanity of "Niagara" itself.

———

THERE IS a rumor that the plates of the Natural History Department of the Exploring Expedition book are in course of preparation either *in London or Paris*. Have we *no* artists at home—or no soul to sustain them? Perhaps the amiable "superintendent of the plates" at Washington can afford us some information about the truth or falsity of the report in question.

———

AMONG THE American books of exceeding merit which, through accident, have been nearly overlooked, we may mention "George Balcombe," a novel by Judge Beverly Tucker, of Virginia, and "The Confessions of a Poet," a very vigorous and powerful fiction by the author of "The Vision of Rubeta."

———

IN OUR LIST, last week, of contributors to "The Broadway Journal," we made some important omissions. We have pub-

lished original articles from Mrs. Osgood, Mrs. Ellet, Mrs.
Kirkland, Mrs. R. S. Nichols, Mrs. Child, Mrs. Lowell, Mrs.
Hewitt, Miss Fuller, Miss Mary Orme, Miss Colman, Miss
Lawson, Miss Wells, W. G. Simms, J. R. Lowell, H. R.
Schoolcraft, H. T. Tuckerman, Park Benjamin, E. A. Duyck-
inck, T. D. English, Wm. Page (the artist), Wm. Wallace, A.
M. Ide, Jr., Henry B. Hirst, Wm. A. Jones; the author of the
Vision of Rubeta, Henry C. Watson, Littleton Barry and
Edgar A. Poe. Our corps of anonymous correspondents is,
moreover, especially strong.

———

IN A VERY complimentary notice, by Miss Fuller, of "Tales
by Edgar A. Poe," the critic objects to the phrases "he had
many books but rarely *employed* them"—and "his results,
brought about by the very soul and essence of method, had,
in fact, the *whole air* of intuition." We bow to the well-considered opinions of Miss Fuller, whom, *of course*, we very highly
respect—but we have in vain endeavored to understand, in
these cases, the grounds of her objections. Perhaps she will
explain.

———

THE LONDON BUILDER, speaking of extraordinary mosa-
ics, mentions an exquisite specimen—a portrait of Pope Paul
V., in which the face alone consists of more than a million
and a half of fragments, each no larger than a millet seed; and
from this size up to two inches square, pieces are employed
in various ways. Another celebrated specimen is that which
Napoleon ordered to be made when his power was paramount in Italy. It was to be a mosaic copy of the celebrated
"Last Supper," by Leonardo da Vinci; and to be of the same
size of the original, viz, 24 feet by 12. The artist to whom the
task was entrusted was Glacono Raffaelle, and the men under
his direction, eight or ten in number, were engaged for eight
years on it. The mosaic cost more than seven thousand
pounds—and afterwards came into the possession of the Emperor of Austria.

———

WE ARE DELIGHTED to hear that Wiley and Putnam's "Library of American Books," is meeting with unequivocal success. We had feared that *Americans* would condescend to read

nothing less than *English*. Even of our own book, more than fifteen hundred copies have been sold here.

———

THE EDITOR of "Graham's Magazine" assures us that certainly he has paid, (according to Dr. Griswold's contract,) for Mr. William Jones' articles—but that he (Mr. Graham) has not the slightest intention of ever using them. No doubt they are at Mr. Jones' service.

———

TO CORRESPONDENTS.—Shall we not again hear from M. O.? Her many excellences are appreciated by *no one* more fully than by ourselves. A thousand thanks to W. G. for the beautiful lines without a title—also to the author of "Constance."

October 11, 1845

THE NEW-YORK MIRROR has been much enlarged, and in some respects greatly improved—although we regret the necessity of the brevier in place of the bold bourgeois—and although we miss the original and racy editorials of Willis. In newspaper not less than in theatrical management we think the * system is a bad one.

Mr. or Mrs. Asterisk honored us lately with half a column which we have been sadly at a loss to comprehend. Can any of our readers help us out?

———

POE-LEMICAL.—In the last number of the Broadway Journal, the critical and learned editor reiterates his opinion of Mr. Simms, whom he considers the "best novelist that this country has, upon the whole produced." Mr. Poe seems to have quite an original and peculiar standard of judging of the merits of men and books. *Success* is the common measure of talent, not only in regard to the productions of literary men, but in business also, in works of art or of usefulness; and in all the varied pursuits of life. It is the *victory* that confers fame on the hero, rather than brave bearing, and manly courage on the battle-field. We are too apt to look at *results* merely, and to honor and praise the successful, rather than the meritorious man. In business, the millionare, into whose lap fortune has poured her treasures, and to whose prosperity the winds of heaven have seemed subservient, gains with his wealth the reputation of being wiser and shrewder than his competitors, who may perhaps have struggled harder, and reasoned better, and yet been thwarted in their efforts beyond avoidance or control. And in literature, also, the popular man, is the great man,—the author who sells best—who is most read—and oftenest quoted,—he is the man whom the people will honor in spite of all the critics. But then one class of philosophers tell us that the judgment of the million is always wrong— that the great majority of men, blinded by passion, and swayed by prejudice, are wholly incapable of deciding in matters of taste or morals, in politics or religion. On the other hand, there are many "learned Thebans," who as strenuously maintain that the voice of the multitude is the voice of truth and God; and that in all cases it is the duty of the minority to acquiesce in the verdict of the people. Here, we take it, is the great rock on which politicians, moralists, and critics split and separate. Leaving this primal question as undecided as it is likely to remain until the "World's Convention" shall eradicate from human nature all the *causes* which lead to differences in the opinions of men, we are inclined to believe that it is above the power of any single critic—or of all the critics in the country combined, to convince the world that William Gilmore Simms is a better novelist than Cooper, or Brockden Brown. He is certainly less known and read at home and abroad. We doubt if the copy-right of all Mr. Simms' collected works would bring as good a price in America or England, as the "Norman Leslie" of Fay, or the "Sketch Book" of Irving. But our surprise at Mr. Poe's estimate is somewhat diminished, when, on turning to another article, we find him speaking of our old friend, "Christopher North," as "the *ignorant* and egotistical Wilson!" and adding, that, " with the exception of Macaulay and Dilke, and one or two others, there is not in Great Britain a critic who can be fairly considered worthy the name!" This is indeed, "bearding the lion in his den;" and as Mr. Poe is preparing to publish an edition of his "Tales" in England, (omitting the story of the Gold *Bug*, we suppose,) he can expect but little mercy from the *back*-biting reviews of the Lockharts and Fonblanques, those bull-dogs of the English press. It is, however, a matter of some pride that we have, at least, *one* critic, who is brave and Quixotic enough to attack any *wind*-mill, either in Europe or America, however formidable it may appear; and our good wishes go with our valiant neighbor.

Mr. (or Mrs.) Star suggests here first, (if we are not mistaken) that success is (or is not) the test of merit, and secondly, that it is not (or is). Are we right in this interpretation? No doubt of it.

The separation of our passage about Mr. Simms from its context, brings about a total misrepresentation of our ideas.

Mr. Simms is "better known" than Brockden Brown.

Putting the author of "Norman Leslie" by the side of the author of the "Sketch-Book," is like speaking of "The King and I"—of Pop Emmons and Homer—of a Mastodon and a mouse. If we were asked which was the most ridiculous book ever written upon the face of the earth—we should answer at once, "Norman Leslie."

We are *not* "preparing to publish" our Tales in England; we leave such manœuvres to those who are in the habit of bowing down to the Golden Calf of the British opinion. Our book, to be sure, *has been* re-published in England—long ago—but we had nothing to do with its re-publication. Should we ever think of such a thing, however, we should undoubtedly give The "Bug" a more prominent position than it even occupies at present. We should call the book "The Gold-Bug and Other Tales"—instead of "Tales," as its title stands. However highly we respect Mr. Willis' talents, we feel nothing but contempt for his affections.

But we have a curiosity to solve the anonymous of the * The star-*dust* theory is exploded—but can any one tell us which is the very smallest of all the stars to be found in the "*Milky* Way"?

October 25, 1845

WITH THIS NUMBER, it will be seen, that we assume the sole control (proprietary as well as editorial) of the "Broadway Journal." May we hope for the support of our friends?

WE HAVE been quizzing the Bostonians, and one or two of the more stupid of their editors and editresses have taken it in high dudgeon. We will attend to them all in good time.

WE MAKE room, with much pleasure, for the following explanation:

To the Editor of the Broadway Journal:

SIR—A copy of your Journal dated October 4th, was handed me this evening, containing some observations respecting alterations made in the song of Ben Bolt, to which some music was adapted by J. P. Webster. The facts were as follows. The song was in a New-Haven paper, and came into my hands as an envelope. It was without signature or reference of any kind, to the author. I was pleased with the poetry, and gave it to Mr. Webster, as he said he would compose some music for it. Before he had completed it, he lost the copy, and asked if I could give him another from memory. The words published were written down by two or three persons, as no one remembered the whole. As Mr. W. did not know the author's name, he could not of course give it. But from what I know of him, I am certain that no thoughts of claiming the authorship ever crossed his mind; and what may so appear in the publication, is the result of carelessness.

Having been (though indirectly) the cause of the censure cast upon Mr. Webster, I felt bound to make this statement, which I doubt not you will have the justice to publish. I am ready to give satisfactory reference, if you require it.

Respectfully yours,   E. S.

Derby, Conn., October 11, 1845.

TO CORRESPONDENTS.—A great pressure of business has prevented us from paying attention to several communications of value, and from cherished friends. All shall hear from us next week, or the week after.

"THE following beautiful conception," says a city paper, "is one of Samuel Lover's":

THE END OF THE ROAD.
And there, whence there's never returning,
    When we travel, as travel we must,
May the gates be all free for our journey,
    And the tears of our friends lay the dust.

This "beautiful conception" we had been hitherto mistaking for a most pitiable conceit.

November 1, 1845

WE TAKE the following paragraph from "The Sunday Times and Messenger" of October 26:

MR. POE'S POEM.—Mr. Poe was invited to deliver a poem before the Boston Lyceum, which he did to a large and distinguished audience. It was, to use the language of an intelligent hearer, "an elegant and classic production, based on the right principle; containing the essence of true poetry, mingled with a gorgeous imagination, exquisite painting, every charm of metre, and graceful delivery." And yet the papers abused him, and the audience were fidgetty—made their exit one by one, and did not at all appreciate the efforts of a man of admitted ability, whom they had invited to deliver a poem before them. The poem was called the "Messenger Star." We presume Mr. Poe will not accept another invitation to recite poetry, original or selected, in that section of the Union.

Our excellent friend Major Noah has suffered himself to be cajoled by that most beguiling of all beguiling little divinities, Miss Walters, of "The Transcript." We have been looking all over her article, with the aid of a taper, to see if we could discover a single syllable of truth in it—and really blush to acknowledge that we cannot. The adorable creature has been telling a parcel of fibs about us, by way of revenge for something that we did to Mr. Longfellow (who admires her very much) and for calling her "a pretty little witch" into the bargain.

The facts of the case seem to be these:—We *were* invited to "deliver" (stand and deliver) a poem before the Boston Lyceum. As a matter of course, we accepted the invitation. The audience *was* "large and distinguished." Mr. Cushing preceded us with a very capital discourse: he was much applauded. On arising, we were most cordially received. We occupied some fifteen minutes with an apology for not "delivering," as is usual in such cases, a didactic poem: a didactic poem, in our opinion, being precisely no poem at all. After some farther words—still of apology—for the "indefiniteness" and "general imbecility" of what we had to offer—all so unworthy a *Bostonian* audience—we commenced, and, with many interruptions of applause, concluded. Upon the whole the approbation was considerably more (the more the pity too) than that bestowed upon Mr. Cushing.

When we had made an end, the audience, of course, arose to depart—and about one-tenth of them, probably, had really departed, when Mr. Coffin, one of the managing committee, arrested those who remained, by the announcement that we had been requested to deliver "The Raven." We delivered "The Raven" forthwith—(without taking a receipt)—were very cordially applauded again—and this was the end of it—with the exception of the sad tale invented to suit her own purposes, by that amiable little enemy of ours, Miss Walters. We shall never call a woman "a pretty little witch" again, as long as we live.

We like Boston. We were born there—and perhaps it is just as well not to mention that we are heartily ashamed of the fact. The Bostonians are very well in their way. Their hotels are bad. Their pumpkin pies are delicious. Their poetry is not so good. Their common is no common thing—and the duck-pond might answer—if its answer could be heard for the frogs.

But with all these good qualities the Bostonians have no soul. They have always evinced towards us individually, the basest ingratitude for the services we rendered them in enlightening them about the originality of Mr. Longfellow. When we accepted, therefore, an invitation to "deliver" a poem in Boston—we accepted it simply and solely, because we had a curiosity to know how it felt to be publicly hissed—and because we wished to see what effect we could produce by a neat little *impromptu* speech in reply. Perhaps, however, we overrated our own importance, or the Bostonian want of common civility—which is not quite so manifest as one or two of their editors would wish the public to believe. We assure Major Noah that he is wrong. The Bostonians are well-bred—as *very* dull persons very generally are.

Still, with their vile ingratitude staring us in the eyes, it could scarcely be supposed that we would put ourselves to the trouble of composing for the Bostonians anything in the shape of an *original* poem. We did not. We had a poem (of about 500 lines) lying by us—one quite as good as new—one, at all events, that we considered would answer sufficiently well for an audience of Transcendentalists. *That* we gave them—it was the best that we had—for the price—and it *did* answer remarkably well. Its name was *not* "The Messenger-Star"—who but Miss Walters would ever think of so delicious a little bit of invention as that? We had *no* name for it at all. The poem is what is occasionally called a "juvenile poem"—but the fact is, it is anything but juvenile now, for we wrote it, printed it, and published it, in book form, before we had fairly completed our tenth year. We read it *verbatim*, from a copy now in our possession, and which we shall be happy to show at any moment to any of our inquisitive friends.

We do not, ourselves, think the poem a remarkably good one:—it is not sufficiently transcendental. Still it did well enough for the Boston audience—who evinced characteristic discrimination in understanding, and especially applauding, all those knotty passages which we ourselves have not yet been able to understand.

As regards the anger of the "Boston Times" and one or two other absurdities—as regards, we say, the wrath of Achilles—we incurred it—or rather its manifestation—by letting some of our cat out of the bag a few hours sooner than we had intended. Over a bottle of champagne, that night, we confessed to Mess. Cushing, Whipple, Hudson, Field, and a few other natives who swear not altogether by the frog-pond—we confessed, we say, the soft impeachment of the hoax. *Et hinc illae irae*. We should have waited a couple of days.

———

THE CONCORDIA (La.) Intelligencer" says:

By the bye, here is a touch from the pen of Poe the poet—
editor of the Broadway Journal. A Niagara lick like this beats
Mississippi all to *fits*.

Resolved, That the steamer Niagara will be as distinguished
in the waters of the East, as the great cataract whose name
she bears is among the waters of the West.

We are sadly puzzled to understand what all this is about.
One thing is certain:—we never made a "resolution" in our
lives. Should we ever make one, we hope it will be in better
taste than the one above.

———

IT HAS BEEN roundly asserted, of late, that "the slashing
article in the Foreign Quarterly upon American poets which
so much excited the ire of the newspapers," is ascertained, at
last, to be the work of Sir John Bell.
We happen to know better. It was written by nobody in
the world but Charles Dickens—and a very discriminating
article it was;—that is to say, discriminating so far as the
actual information of its author extended in regard to our
poetical affairs.

———

WE ARE in a fair way, at last, to obtain some accurate
knowledge of Chinese history and geography. Among other
works lately published we notice, besides Marco Polos's Travels, a "Scientific Voyage into Altay and Adjacent Countries on
the Chinese Frontier"—also "Memoirs of Father Ripa, during Thirteen Years' Residence at the Court of Pekin, &c. Selected and Translated from the Italian, by Fortunato Prandi."
Some Essays by Professor Neumann who has just returned
from Persia, demonstrate that the Chinese, from time immemorial, have *traded to Oregon and California*.

———

THE BRITISH CRITIC in a rather weak, although sufficiently complimentary review of "Tales by Edgar A. Poe,"
says, among other things—"The author seems to have
amused himself by tracing a series of references between every
minute act, and so upward to the making and dethroning of
kings [downward would have done better]. He has been as
assiduous in this scheme as an Indian who follows the trail of

a foe. He has learned from the dwellers in the American woods a marked acuteness which he has dealed out again to us, in the Tales before us."

The only objection to this theory is that we never go into the woods (for fear of the owls) and are quite sure that we never saw a live Indian in our lives.

———

IN THE HURRY of getting to press last week, there occurred one or two vexatious *errata*—the worst of which, perhaps, was the omission of a notice (prepared us by a friend) of Mr. Murdoch's Hamlet. The Greek verb which formed the motto of "The Thread-Bare," was lamentably jumbled up. In the exquisite poem entitled "Sybil" (from the pen of William Gibson, U. S. N.) the word *"raised"* at the close of the third line, being printed *"raises"*, made nonsense of the whole sentence. From the fine ballad headed "Isadore", the signature of A. M. Ide, Jr. was, also, accidentally omitted; and that of W. G. Simms should have been appended to the "Sonnet by the Poor Debtor." These errors, however, are attributable to ourselves alone.

———

MRS. SARAH JOSEPHA HALE is preparing for press a collection of her poems. Messrs. Clark & Austin will, most probably, be the publishers.

———

MESSRS. WILEY & PUTNAM will publish, in season for the holidays, "The Book of Christmas," by T. K. Hervey, the poet; La Motte Fouqué's fine romance (contrasting the Northern and Southern Chivalry) "Thiodolf the Icelander;" Mrs. Southey's (Caroline Bowles') Poetical Works, &c. &c.

———

WE HAVE BEEN glancing at an article on the Reading Room of the British Museum. The deductions are, of course, the munificence and courtesy of the English government to strangers. There is one place at least where the scholar visiting London from a foreign country is at home—the British Museum. He sits at the table and may command the books—the Royal collections and all, familiarly as he would bid his own child take down for him the esteemed volume from the single shelf at home. Here he has his privileges and dignities, a place of labor where he may "break the neck of the day" as Sir Walter used to say, over a favorite folio, and sally out among the multitudes of London with the pleasing consciousness of at least some work respectably done. Let no man undervalue this who has not felt the solitude of London, the monotony of the streets and the want of those out-of-door sympathies so freely shared in Paris.

Some of the annoyances of the Reading Room are odd— the incursions for instance of the students of the University College. "Perhaps," says the writer "it were too much to expect that each young Collegian should be at the expense of purchasing a Schrevelius' Lexicon and using it at home." Assuredly;—there were flies, it is to be presumed, in Paradise.

Another grievance is to be "fogged out" by a moist November day—the provisions of the Institution allowing no lights.

When shall we have a permanent Library in New York?— not a Circulating Library, with the volume which you want somewhere, probably, between finger and thumb in Westchester county, but a library confined to the premises, with a perpetual writ of *ne exeat*, included in the charter, against all volumes leaving the front door. It is not necessary that the library should be so large as many of the century accumulations of Europe. Fifty thousand volumes on the spot would be sufficient—gathered together scientifically, in the first instance, with proportion and completeness for the departments. Pens, ink and paper, wide chairs and wide tables, should be added; attendants for convenience and care of the books; and some formality to check mere literary loafers and all Collegians in round-a-bout jackets.

If we were autocrat for a week we should convert the Society Library buildings (after exorcising the tailors,) into just such an establishment; and we believe the Librarian and a majority of the members would be in favor of the change.

———

A COMPLETE establishment of book printing has been recently discovered and broken up in the French provinces. Upwards of 18,000 volumes were found hidden away between the inner and outer walls—the works of La Martine and Thiers' "Consulate and Empire," among the number.

MR. HUDSON, in his Shakspeare Lectures here, last winter, had the misfortune to put people unaccustomed to the operation, to the trouble of thinking—an annoyance which a certain class never forgets. There were, in his style, terseness and strength—a rude vigor. All conventionalism, pretence and affectation shrivelled in his grasp—witness his character of Jacques, in As You Like It, whom he made the type of the selfish, vain spectators in the world, men of large head and little heart who are superior in virtue to the men of action and purpose—only because they do nothing. The rigid, resolute manner of the lecturer was the index of the strength of his convictions. Perhaps his audiences were too limited to the cultivated class of readers and thinkers, for him to enjoy the highest triumphs. An assembly of *all* who attend the representation of Shakspeare at the Bowery, the Chatham and the Park, would have been impressed by his keen sarcasm upon successful evil and eloquent defence of persecuted virtue. He had that respect for the people that he would not shrink from telling them what their faint-hearted, hypocritical admirers call an unpopular truth. Mr. Hudson at the close of his lectures last winter, looked round upon his faithful audience who had kept him company through his whole course, thanked them for their kindness and attention, public and private, and remarked that *he had not yet succeeded in New-York*, but that he *would return and succeed yet*. There was a true democracy in this—a frank honesty which set aside mere cultivation and scholarship and social privileges, for an appeal to the heart of the public—that public to which he brought no letters, who would come to hear him for the sake of his subject, and not merely to keep up the appearance of a literary coterie. Mr. Hudson felt this, and had magnanimity enough to acknowledge it—and an appeal to this public was, we presume, what he meant when he said he would yet succeed in New-York.

We have not heard whether Mr. Hudson has made any arrangements to lecture in this city. Why should he not take Palmo's for a few nights and fill it as profitably as Mr. Templeton, or an interlude on the boards of the theatre itself, as well as De Meyer's piano? At any rate, he must come and give a New-York audience an opportunity of hearing his two new lectures on *Lear* and *Othello*, the composition of which, it is understood, employed him this last summer, and the first of which he has just delivered at Boston before the Lyceum. An accomplished and able critic speaks of it in "The Boston Times" of Saturday in the highest terms of commendation.

———

"THE ZOOLOGY of the English Poets, corrected by the writings of Modern Naturalists, by the Rev. R. H. Newell, pp. 8vo., with engravings on wood"—is the title of a new work about to appear in London.

———

MR. SIMMS' new collection of Miscellanies will include a miniature biography of Cortez; the Literature of the Indians; a sketch of the life of the pioneer Boone; a paper on the works of J. Fenimore Cooper, &c. It is entitled "Views and Reviews in American History, Literature and Fiction." In his capacity of Critic it will present him to the public, at the North, in a new and favorable light. His contributions to the Southern Quarterly Review are among the best papers in that periodical.

———

MR. HEADLEY has in preparation "The Alps and the Rhine," a sequel to his "Letters from Italy."

———

MR. EDWARD MATURIN, son of the author of "Bertram," is getting ready a new work—"Montezuma, the last of the Aztecs."

———

MRS. KIRKLAND's new book, with our own Poems, (including "Al Aaraaf," the one with which we quizzed the Bostonians) will be issued in about ten days by Messrs. Wiley & Putnam.

———

TO CORRESPONDENTS.—We are forced to decline "Thanatikos"—the "Lines To My Sister on Her Birth-Day"—and "Prosings on Man." "Twilight Memories" is rather *too long*.

To M. B. of Olive, we say, what you have done evinces genius, but inexperience. We cannot do you the injustice to print the communication—but hereafter shall, no doubt, be glad to publish anything you write. Persevere.

Alolo will soon appear—also "The Autumn Leaf."

November 22, 1845

WE HAVE to apologize for the insufficient variety of the present number. We were not aware of the great length of "The Spectacles" until too late to remedy the evil.

———

As WE very confidently expected, our friends in the Southern and Western country (*true* friends, and *tried,*) are taking up arms in our cause—and more especially in the cause of a national as distinguished from a sectional literature. They cannot see (it appears) any farther necessity for being ridden to death by New-England. Hear the "Charleston Patriot":

POE'S POETRY.—Mr. Edgar A. Poe is one of the most remarkable, in many respects, among our men of letters. With singular endowments of imagination, he is at the same time largely possessed of many of the qualities that go to make an admirable critic;—he is methodical, lucid, forcible;—well-read, thoughtful, and capable, at all times, of rising from the mere consideration of the individual subject, to the principles, in literature and art, by which it should be governed. Add to these qualities, as a critic, that he is not a person to be overborne and silenced by a reputation;—that mere names do not control his judgment;—that he is bold, independent, and stubbornly analytical, in the formation of his opinions. He has his defects also;—he is sometimes the victim of capricious moods;—his temper is variable—his nervous organization being such, evidently, as to subject his judgments, sometimes, to influences that may be traced to the weather and the winds.—He takes his colour from the clouds; and his sympathies are not unfrequently chilled and rendered ungenial, by the pressure of the atmosphere—the cold and the vapors of a climate affecting his moral nature, through his physical, in greater degree than is usual among literary men,—who, by the way, are generally far more susceptible to these influences, than is the case with the multitude. Such are the causes which occasionally operate to impair the value and the consistency of his judgments as a Critic.—As a Poet, Mr. Poe's imagination becomes remarkably conspicuous, and to surrender himself freely to his own moods, would be to make all his writings in verse, efforts of pure imagination only. He seems to dislike the merely practical, and to shrink from the concrete. His fancy takes the ascendant in his Poetry, and wings his thoughts to such superior elevations, as to render it too intensely spiritual for the ordinary reader. With a genius thus endowed and constituted, it was a blunder with Mr. Poe to accept the appointment, which called him to deliver himself in poetry before the Boston Lyceum. Highly imaginative men can scarcely succeed in such exhibitions. The sort of poetry called for on such occasions, is the very reverse of the spiritual, the fanciful or the metaphysical. To win the ears of a mixed audience, nothing more is required than moral or patriotic common places in rhyming heroics. The verses of Pope are just the things for such occasions. You must not pitch your flight higher than the penny-whistle elevation of

> "Know then this truth, enough for man to know,
>   Virtue alone is happiness below."

Either this, or declamatory verse,—or something patriotic, or something satirical, or something comical. At all events, you must not be mystical. You must not task the audience to study. Your song must be such as they can read running, and comprehend while munching pea-nuts. Mr. Poe is not the writer for this sort of thing. He is too original, too fanciful, too speculative, too anything in verse, for the comprehension of any but 'audience fit though few'. In obeying this call to Boston, Mr. Poe committed another mistake. He had been mercilessly exercising himself as a critic at the expense of some of their favorite writers. The swans of New England, under his delineation, had been described as mere geese, and those, too, of none of the whitest. He had been exposing the short comings and the plagiarisms of Mr. Longfellow, who is supposed, along the banks of the Penobscot, to be about the comliest bird that ever dipped his bill in Pieria. Poe had dealt with the favorites of Boston unsparingly, and they hankered after their revenges. In an evil hour, then, did he consent to commit himself, in verse to their tender mercies. It is positively amusing to see how eagerly all the little witlings of the press, in the old purlieus of the Puritan, flourish the critical tomahawk about the head of their critic. In their eagerness for retribution, one of the papers before us actually congratulates itself and readers on the (asserted) failure of the poet. The good editor himself was not present, but he hammers away not the less lustily at the victim, because his objections are to be made at second hand.—Mr. Poe committed another error in consenting to address an audience in verse, who, for three mortal hours, had been compelled to sit and hear Mr. Caleb Cushing in prose. The attempt to speak after this, in poetry, and fanciful poetry, too, was sheer madness. The most patient audience in the world, must have been utterly exhausted by the previous infliction. But it is denied that Mr. Poe failed at all. He had been summoned to recite poetry. It is asserted that he did so. The Boston Courier, one of the most thoughtful of the journals of that city, gives us a very favorable opinion of the performance which has been so harshly treated.—"The Poem," says that journal, "called 'The Messenger Star,' was an eloquent and classic production, based on the right principles, containing the essence of *true* poetry, mingled with a gorgeous imagination, exquisite painting, every charm of metre, and a graceful delivery. It strongly reminded us of Mr. Horne's 'Orion,' and resembled it in the majesty of its design, the nobleness of its incidents, and its freedom from the trammels of productions usual on these occasions. The delicious word-painting of some of its scenes brought vividly to our recollection, Keats' 'Eve of St. Agnes,' and parts of 'Paradise Lost.'

"That it was malapropos to the occasion, we take the liberty to deny. What is the use of repeating the 'mumbling farce' of having invited a poet to deliver a poem? We (too often) find a person get up and repeat a hundred or two indifferent couplets of words, with jingling rhymes and stale witticisms, with scarcely a line of *poetry* in the whole, and which will admit of no superlative to describe it. If we are to have a poem, why not have the 'true thing,' that will be recognized as such,—for poems being written for people that can appreciate them, it would be as well to cater for their tastes as for individuals who cannot distinguish between the true and the false."

The good sense of this extract should do much towards enforcing the opinion which it conveys; and it confirms our own, previously entertained and expressed, in regard to the affair in question. Mr. Poe's error was not, perhaps, in making verses, nor making them after a fashion of his own; but in delivering them before an audience of mixed elements, and just after a discourse of three mortal hours by a prosing orator. That any of his hearers should have survived the two-fold infliction, is one of those instances of good fortune which should bring every person present to his knees in profound acknowledgement to a protecting providence.

We thank our friend of "The Patriot" and agree with him fully, of course, in all points except his disparagement of Mr. Cushing, who read us a very admirable discourse. "The Patriot," it will be understood, has not yet seen our reply of week before last.

Were the question demanded of us—"What is the most exquisite of sublunary pleasures?" we should reply, without hesitation, the making a fuss, or, in the classical words of a western friend, the "kicking up a bobbery."

Never was a "bobbery" more delightful than that which we have just succeeded in "kicking up" all around about Boston Common. We never saw the Frog-Pondians so lively in our lives. They seem absolutely to be upon the point of waking up. In about nine days the puppies may get open their eyes.

That is to say they may get open their eyes to certain facts which have long been obvious to all the world except themselves—the facts that there exist other cities than Boston—other men of letters than Professor Longfellow—other vehicles of literary information than the "Down-East Review."

As regards our late poem.—Hear the "St. Louis Reveillé."

"The *Broadway Journal* is edited and owned solely by Mr. Edgar A. Poe. If he had as much tact as talent, he would make success for half a dozen papers."

So says an exchange paper. Poe, reliant upon his talent, has too much contempt for tact; he is wrong, but his error makes his career the more remarkable. He is full of eccentricity. Does he mean, by the following, that his late Boston Poem, was intended by him as a *hoax*?

"We have been quizzing the Bostonians, and one or two of the more stupid of their editors and editresses have taken it in high dudgeon. We will attend to them all in good time."

To our friend Field we thus reply: We had *tact* enough not to be "taken in and done for" by the Bostonians. *Timeo Danaos et dona ferentes*—(for *timeo* substitute *contemno* or *turn-up-our-nose-o*). We knew very well that, among a certain *clique* of the Frogpondians, there existed a predetermination to abuse us under *any* circumstances. We knew that, write what we would, they would swear it to be worthless. We knew that were we to compose for them a "Paradise Lost," they would pronounce it an indifferent poem. It would have been very weak in us, then, to put ourselves to the trouble of attempting to please these people. We preferred pleasing ourselves. We read before them a "juvenile"—a *very* "juvenile" poem— and thus the Frogpondians were *had*—were delivered up to the enemy bound hand and foot. Never were a set of people more completely demolished. They have blustered and flustered—but what have they done or said that has not made them more thoroughly ridiculous?—what, in the name of Momus, is it *possible* for them to do or to say?

We "delivered" them the "juvenile poem" and they received it with applause. This is accounted for by the fact that the *clique* (contemptible in numbers as in every thing else) were overruled by the rest of the assembly. These malignants did not *dare* to interrupt by their preconcerted hisses, the respectful and profound attention of the majority. We have been told, indeed, that as many as three or four of the personal friends of the little old lady entitled Miss Walters, did actually leave the hall during the recitation—but, upon the whole, this was the very best thing they could do. We have been told this, we say—we did not *see* them take their departure:—the fact is they belong to a class of people that we make it a point *never to see*.

The poem being thus well received, in spite of this ridiculous little cabal—the next thing to be done was to abuse it in the papers. Here, they imagined, they were sure of their game. But what have they accomplished? The poem, they say, is bad. We admit it. We insisted upon this fact in our prefatory remarks, and we insist upon it now, over and over again. It *is* bad—it is wretched—and what then? We wrote it at ten years of age—had it been worth even a pumpkin-pie undoubtedly we should not have "delivered" it to *them*.

To demonstrate its utter worthlessness, "The Boston Star" (a journal which, we presume, is to be considered as a fair representative of the Frogpondian genius) has copied the poem in full, with two or three columns of criticism (we suppose) by way of explaining that we should have been hanged for its perpetration. There is no doubt of it whatever—we should. "The Star," however, (a dull luminary) has done us more honor than it intended; it has copied our *third* edition of the poem, revised and improved. We considered this too good for the occasion by one half, and so "delivered" the *first* edition with all its imperfections on its head. It is the first— the original edition—the *delivered* edition—which we now republish in our collection of Poems.

Repelled at these points, the Frogpondian faction hire a thing they call the "Washingtonian Reformer" (or something of that kind) to insinuate that we must have been "intoxicated" to have become possessed of sufficient audacity to "deliver" such a poem to the Frogpondians.

In the first place, why cannot these miserable hypocrites say "drunk" at once and be done with it? In the second place we are perfectly willing to admit that we *were* drunk—in the face of at least eleven or twelve hundred Frogpondians who will be willing to take oath that we were *not*. We are willing to admit either that we were drunk, or that we set fire to the Frog-pond, or that once upon a time we cut the throat of our grandmother. The fact is we are perfectly ready to admit any thing at all—but what has cutting the throat of our grandmother to do with our poem, or the Frogpondian stupidity? We shall get drunk when we please. As for the editor of the "Jeffersonian Teetotaler" (or whatever it is) we advise her to get drunk, too, as soon as possible—for when sober she is a disgrace to the sex—on account of being so awfully stupid.

N. B. The "Washingtonian Teetotaler" is edited by a little old lady in a mob-cap and spectacles—at least, we presume so, for every second paper in Boston *is*.

P. S. Miss Walters (the Syren!) has seen cause, we find, to recant all the ill-natured little insinuations she has been making against us (mere white lies—she need not take them so much to heart) and is now overwhelming us with apologies—things which we have never yet been able to withstand. She defends our poem on the ground of its being "juvenile," and we think the more of her defence because she herself has been juvenile so long as to be a judge of juvenility. Well, upon the whole we must forgive her—and do. Say no more about it, you little darling! You are a delightful creature and your heart is in the right place—would to Heaven that we could always say the same thing of your wig!

In conclusion:—The Frogpondians may as well spare us their abuse. If we cared a fig for their wrath we should not first have insulted them to their teeth, and then subjected to their tender mercies a volume of our Poems:—*that*, we think, is sufficiently clear. The fact is, we despise them and defy them (the transcendental vagabonds!) and they may all go to the devil together.

———

To Correspondents.—Many thanks to W. W.—also to R. S. R.

December 13, 1845

———

THE BROADWAY JOURNAL may be obtained in the City of New York of the following agents:—Taylor, Astor House; Crosby, Exchange, William street; Graham, Tribune Buildings; Lockwood, Broadway and Grand; and Burgess & Stringer, Ann and Broadway.

———

"THE HARBINGER—Edited by The Brook-Farm Phalanx"—is, beyond doubt, the most reputable organ of the

Crazyites. We sincerely respect it—odd as this assertion may appear. It is conducted by an assemblage of well-read persons who mean no harm—and who, perhaps, can do less. Their objects are honorable, and so forth—all that anybody can understand of them—and we really believe that Mr. Albert Brisbane and one or two other ladies and gentlemen understand all about them that is necessary to be understood. But what we, individually, have done to "The Harbinger," or what we have done to "The Brook-Farm Phalanx," that "The Brook-Farm Phalanx" should stop the ordinary operations at Brook-Farm for the purpose of abusing us, is a point we are unable to comprehend. If we have done anything to affront "The Brook-Farm Phalanx" we will make an apology forthwith—provided "The Brook-Farm Phalanx" (which we have a great curiosity to see) will just step into our office, which is 304 Broadway.

In the mean time, by way of doing penance for any unintentional offence that we may have given The Phalanx, we will just copy, *verbatim*, a very severe lesson it has been lately reading to ourselves.

The Raven and other Poems. By EDGAR A. POE. *New York and London:* Wiley and Putnam, 161 Broadway; 6 Waterloo Place. pp. 91.

Mr. Poe has earned some fame by various tales and poems, which of late has become notoriety through a certain blackguard warfare which he has been waging against the poets and newspaper critics of New England, and which it would be most charitable to impute to insanity. Judging from the tone of his late articles in the Broadway Journal, he seems to think that the whole literary South and West are doing anxious battle in his person against the old time-honored tyrant of the North. But what have North or South to do with affairs only apropos to Poe? He shows himself a poet in this, at least, in the magnifying mirror of his own importance. To him facts lose their barren literality—to him a primrose is more than a primrose; and Edgar Poe, acting the constabulary part of a spy in detecting plagiarisms in favorite authors, insulting a Boston audience, inditing coarse editorials against respectable editresses, and getting singed himself the meanwhile, is nothing less than the hero of a grand mystic conflict of the elements.

The present volume is not entirely pure of this controversy, else we should ignore the late scandalous courses of the man, and speak only of the "Poems." The motive of the publication is too apparent: it contains the famous Boston poem, together with other juvenilities, which, he says, "private reasons—some of which have reference to the sin of plagiarism, and others to the date of Tennyson's first poems"—have induced him to republish. Does he mean to intimate that he is suspected of copying Tennyson? In vain have we searched the poems for a shadow of resemblance. Does he think to convict Tennyson of copying *him*? Another of those self-exaggerations which prove, we suppose, his poetic imagination.

In a sober attempt to get at the meaning and worth of these poems as poetry, we have been not a little puzzled. We must confess they have a great deal of power, a great deal of beauty, (of thought frequently, and always of rhythm and diction,) originality, and dramatic effect. But they have more of *effect* than of *expression*, to adopt a distinction from musical criticism; and if they attract you to a certain length, it is only to repulse you the more coldly at last. There is a wild unearthliness, and unheavenliness, in the tone of all his pictures, a strange unreality in all his thoughts; they seem to stand shivering, begging admission to our hearts in vain, because they look not as if they came from the heart. The ill-boding "Raven," which you meet at the threshold of his edifice, is a fit warning of the hospitality you will find inside. And yet the "Raven" has great beauty, and has won the author some renown; we were fascinated till we read it through; then we hated to look at it, or think of it again: why was that? There is something in it of the true grief of a lover, an imagination of a broken-heartedness enough to prove a lover in earnest, a power of strange, sad melody, which there is no resisting. So there is in all his poems. Mr. Poe has made a critical study of the matter of versification, and succeeded in the art rather at the expense of nature. Indeed the impression of a very *studied* effect is always uppermost after reading him. And you have to study him to understand him. This you would count no loss, if, when you had followed the man through his studies, you could find anything in them beyond the man and his most motiveless moods, which lead you nowhere; if you could find anything better at bottom than the pride of originality. What is the fancy which is merely fancy, the beauty which springs from no feeling, which neither illustrates nor promotes the great rules and purposes of life, which glimmers strangely only because it is aside from the path of human destiny? Edgar Poe does not write for Humanity; he has more of the art than the soul of poetry. He affects to despise the world while he writes for it. He certainly has struck out a remarkable course: the style and imagery of his earliest poems mark a very singular culture, a judgment most severe for a young writer, and a familiarity with the less hacknied portions of classic lore and nomenclature. He seems to have had an idea of working out his forms from pure white marble. But the poet's humility is wanting; a morbid egotism repels you. He can affect you with wonder, but rarely with the thrill of any passion, except perhaps of pride, which might be dignity, and which therefore always is interesting. We fear this writer even courts the state described by Tennyson:

A glorious devil, large in heart and brain,
That did love beauty only, (beauty seen
In all varieties of mould and mind,)
And knowledge for its beauty; or if good,
Good only for its beauty, seeing not
That Beauty, Good, and Knowledge, are three sisters
That doat upon each other, friends to man,
Living together under the same roof,
And never can be sundered without tears;
And he that shuts Love out, in turn shall be
Shut out by Love, and on her threshold lie
Howling in utter darkness.

There is something in all this which we really respect—an evident wish to be sincere, pervading the whole tone of the sermon—an anxious determination to speak the truth—at least as far as convenient. The Brook Farm Phalanx talks to us, in short, "like a Dutch uncle," and we shall reply to it, very succinctly, in the same spirit.

"Very charitable to impute to insanity." Insanity is a word

that the Brook Farm Phalanx should never be brought to mention under any circumstances whatsoever. "No more of that, Hal, an ye love me."

"The time-honored tyrant of the North." Very properly τυραννος—not βασιλευς. King Log at best. The sceptre is departed.

"Insulting a Boston audience"—very true—meant to do it—and did.

"Getting singed in return." The singeing refers, we presume, to the doubling, in five weeks, the circulation of the "Broadway Journal."

"Motive of the publication too apparent." "The Raven, etc.," was in the publishers' hands a month or six weeks before we received the invitation from the Lyceum— and we read the last proofs on the evening before that on which we "insulted the Boston audience." On these points The Brook Farm Phalanx are referred to Messrs. Wiley and Putnam.

"Discover no shade of resemblance to Tennyson." Certainly not—we never could discover any ourselves. Our foot-note (quoted by the Phalanx) has reference to an article written by Mr. Charles Dickens in the London Foreign Quarterly Review. Mr. Dickens in paying us some valued, though injudicious compliments, concluded by observing, that " we had all Tennyson's spirituality, and might be considered as the best of his imitators"—words to that effect. Our design has been merely to demonstrate (should a similar accusation again be made) that the poems in question were published before Tennyson had written at all.

"Has acquired some renown by the Raven." We cannot approve of the *"some"*—especially in the mouths of those worshippers of Truth, The Brook Farm Phalanx.

The Brook Farm Phalanx knows very well—and so do we—that no American poem gained for its author even one half *so much* "renown" in the same period of time. The renown is quite as small a thing as the poem—and we have therefore no scruple in alluding to it—although we do so only because it shocks us to hear a set of respectable Crazyites talking in so disingenuous a manner. Reform it altogether, or give up preaching about Truth.

As for the rest, we believe it is all leather and prunella—the opinion of "The Snook Farm Phalanx." We do trust that, in future, "The Snook Farm Phalanx" will never have any opinion of us at all.

———

THE MOST eminent living writer of Portugal, indeed the only one of any considerable eminence, is Senhor Almeida Garrett, a leading deputy of the ultra-liberal opposition in Lisbon, who has very high powers both as an orator and a poet; though his poetical works appear rather deficient in strength of original thought. His prose is both brilliant and powerful. His poems are of considerable extent, and not the least of their charms is that he is a good scholar and eminent for antiquarian research. He is of the blank-verse school, which in Portugal is a great misfortune. We extract the following as a favorable specimen, and the more willingly because it unfolds the beauties of a word, "Saudade," upon the exclusive possession of which the Portuguese particularly pride themselves. There is certainly no one word in any other European language which conveys the same idea. It expresses the sweet yet painful sensation created by the contemplation of a beloved object from which we are separated:—

> Oh tender yearning! bitterness of joy
> For the unhappy, thorn of absence with
> Delicious puncture piercing through the heart,
> Awakening pain that lacerates the soul.
> Yet hath it pleasure;—tender yearning grief!
> Mysterious power that canst awaken hearts,
> And make them ooze forth, drop by drop distilled,
> Not life-blood, but of soft and dewy tears
> A solacing abundance;—yearning grief;
> Beloved name, that sounds so honey-sweet
> In lips of Lucitania; sound unknown
> To the proud mouths of these Sycambrians
> Of foreign lands;—oh, tender yearning grief!
> Thou magic Power that dost transport the soul
> Of absence unto solitary friend,
> Of wandering lover to his mistress lorn,
> And even the sad and wretched exile, most

Unhappy of Earth's children, bear'st in dreams
Back to his country's bosom, dreams so sweet
That cruel 'tis the dreamer to awake.
If, on thy humid altar, tear-bedewed,
I laid my heart, which fast was throbbing still
When from my bleeding breast I plucked it forth
At Tagus' mouth beloved;—come in thy car,
By gently murmuring doves gray-pinioned drawn,
And seek my heart which, Goddess, sighs for thee!

———

MR. HUDSON, on Tuesday evening last, read to an audience of some two hundred persons, at the Society Library, his Lecture on Lear (or a portion of it) recently delivered at Boston, and much complimented in one or two of the Boston papers. We listened to the lecturer with profound attention, and (for the first time) heard him throughout. He did not favorably impress us. His good points are a happy talent for fanciful, that is to say for unexpected (too often far-fetched) *illustration*, and a certain cloudy acuteness in respect to motives of human action. His bad points are legion—want of concentration—want of consecutiveness—want of definite purpose—want of common school education—utter incapacity to comprehend a drama out of its range of mere *character*—an absurd passion for the lower species, that is to say, for the too *obvious* species of antithesis—a more absurd rage for metaphor and direct simile, without the least ability to keep them within bounds, or to render them consistent, either *per se*, or with the matter into which they are introduced—to crown all, a pitiable affectation of humility altogether unbecoming a man, an elocution that would disgrace a pig, and an odd species of gesticulation of which a baboon would have excellent reason to be ashamed.

———

THE TRIBUNE says:—"The article in the American Review of this month, entitled '*The Facts of M. Valdemar's Case*,' by EDGAR A. POE,' is of course a romance—who could have supposed it otherwise? Those who have read Mr. Poe's visit to the Maelstrom, South Pole, &c., have not been puzzled by it, yet we learn that several good matter-of-fact citizens have been, sorely. It is a pretty good specimen of Poe's style of giving an air of reality to fictions, and we utterly condemn the choice of a subject, but whoever thought it a veracious recital must have the bump of Faith large, very large indeed."

For our parts we find it difficult to understand how any dispassionate transcendentalist can doubt the facts as we state them; they are by no means so incredible as the marvels which are hourly narrated, and believed, on the topic of Mesmerism. *Why* cannot a man's death be postponed indefinitely by Mesmerism? *Why* cannot a man talk after he is dead? *Why?—why?*—that is the question; and as soon as the Tribune has answered it to our satisfaction we will talk to it farther.

———

HON. WM. C. PRESTON has been elected President of the South Carolina College at Columbia. It is understood that he will accept and commence the duties of the Presidency early in the ensuing year. In the meantime, Rev. Dr. Hooper will discharge them. Rev. Dr. Henry has been offered the Greek Professorship, and we sincerely hope that he may accept it. The accession of Mr. Preston is of course, *per se*, and without reference to the secession of Dr. Henry, a subject of congratulation to the College—but upon the whole, some injustice, we think, has been done to the late President. We shall speak more fully in our next.

———

THE MIRROR says:

The editor of the Philadelphia North American has "scared up" a feminine genius—a poetical wonder—hear him: "The greatest poet of her sex who ever lived, is Maria Brooks. She is as much above Mrs. Hemans, Miss Landon, Mrs. Norton, *et id omne genus*, as they are above the sickliest sentimentalists of the chambermaids' gazettes!!"

There is, perhaps, some exaggeration in the North American's estimate of Mrs. Brooks, but far more in the Mirror's attempt at depreciation. Mrs. Maria Brooks, author of "Zophiel, or The Bride of Seven," is fairly entitled to be called the greatest of American poetesses. Her imagination and audacity of thought and expression, are not far behind Miss Barrett. Her chief faults are bombast and extravagance.

CONNOISSEURS and amateurs of *Tea* would do well to look over the *Catalogue of Teas* on sale at the warehouse of the Pekin Tea Company, No. 75 Fulton street. See advertisement in this week's Journal. Hitherto it has been impossible to procure really good green tea at less than a dollar per pound. The Pekin Company afford an exquisite article at 75 cents—other teas at proportionate rates. We can conscientiously recommend them.

A late "Tribune" has a very just review of Longfellow. We quote a few passages:—

The portrait which adorns this volume is not merely flattered or idealized, but there is an attempt at adorning it, by expression thrown into the eyes, with just that which the original does not possess, whether in face or mind. We have often seen faces whose usually coarse and heavy lineaments were harmonized at times into beauty by the light that rises from the soul into the eyes. The intention Nature had with regard to the face and its wearer, usually eclipsed beneath bad habits or a bad education, is then disclosed and we see what hopes Death has in store for that soul. But here the enthusiasm thrown into the eyes only makes the rest of the face look more weak, and the idea suggested is the anomalous one of a Dandy Pindar.

Such is not the case with Mr. Longfellow himself. He is never a Pindar, though he is sometimes a Dandy even in the clear and ornamented streets and trim gardens of his verse. But he is still more a man of cultivated taste, delicate though not deep feeling, and some, though not much, poetic force.

Mr. Longfellow has been accused of plagiarism. We have been surprised that any one should have been anxious to fasten special charges of this kind upon him, when we had supposed it so obvious that the greater part of his mental stores were derived from the works of others. He has no style of his own growing out of his own experiences and observations of nature. Nature with him, whether human or external, is always seen through the windows of literature. There are in his poems sweet and tender passages descriptive of his personal feelings, but very few showing him as an observer, at first hand, of the passions within, or the landscape without.

This want of the free breath of nature, this perpetual borrowing of imagery, this excessive, because superficial, culture which he has derived from an acquaintance with the elegant literature of many nations and men, out of proportion to the experience of life within himself, prevent Mr. Longfellow's verses from ever being a true refreshment to ourselves. He says in one of his most graceful verses:

> From the cool cistern of the midnight air
>   My spirit drank repose;
> The fountain of perpetual peace flows there,
>   From those deep cisterns flows.

Now this is just what we cannot get from Mr. Longfellow. No solitude of the mind reveals to us the deep cisterns.

*   *   *

Yet there is a middle class, composed of men of little original poetic power, but of much poetic taste and sensibility, whom we would not wish to have silenced. They do no harm but much good, (if only their minds are not confounded with those of a higher class,) by educating in others the faculties dominant in themselves. In this class we place the writer at present before us.

We must confess a coolness toward Mr. Longfellow, in consequence of the exaggerated praises that have been bestowed upon him. When we see a person of moderate powers receive honors which should be reserved for the highest, we feel somewhat like assailing him and taking from him the crown which should be reserved for grander brows.

*   *   *

ERRATA.—Several, of a vexatious character, occurred in our last week's Journal—especially in the fine poem "Epicedium," by Mr. Rowley; among other blunders, a whole line was omitted. We have taken measures to prevent anything of this kind for the future.

———

MR. THOMAS H. LANE is the only person (besides ourself) authorized to give receipts or transact business for "The Broadway Journal."

To Correspondents.—Many thanks to the author of "The New Generation"—also to P. P. C.; we will write him fully in a few days. Our friends F. W. T. and P. B. shall also soon hear from us—if indeed they have not already quite given us up.

We are forced to decline "Remembrance" "Autumn," and the Lines to Estelle—the Sonnet may appear.

The proposition of I. R. O. is respectfully declined.

The numbers desired by our friend A. M. I. can be obtained. We thank him sincerely for his late favor.

December 27, 1845

THE BROADWAY JOURNAL may be obtained in the City of New York of the following agents: Taylor, Astor House; Crosby, Exchange, William street; Graham, Tribune Buildings; Lockwood, Broadway and Grand; and Burgess & Stringer, Ann and Broadway.

A new volume will commence on Saturday, the tenth of January next. A very few sets of the first volume are still for sale at the office, 304 Broadway.

Mr. Thomas H. Lane is the only person (beside ourself) authorized to give receipts or transact business for The Broadway Journal. For Prospectus, Terms, etc. see end of the paper.

Dr. Collyer, the eminent Mesmerist, has written to us in reference to the extraordinary case of M. Valdemar. We quote a portion of his letter:

Boston, December 16, 1815.

Dear Sir—Your account of M. Valdemar's Case has been universally copied in this city, and has created a very great sensation. It requires from me no apology, in stating, that I have not the least doubt of the *possibility* of such a phenomenon; for, I did actually restore to active animation a person who died from excessive drinking of ardent spirits. He was placed in his coffin ready for interment.

You are aware that death very often follows excessive excitement of the nervous system; this arising from the extreme prostration which follows; so that the vital powers have not sufficient energy to react.

I will give you the detailed account on your reply to this, which I require for publication, in order to put at rest the growing impression that your account is merely a *splendid creation* of your own brain, not having any truth in fact. My dear sir, I have battled the storm of public derision too long on the subject of Mesmerism, to be now found in the rear ranks—though I have not publicly lectured for more than two years, I have steadily made it a subject of deep investigation.

I sent the account to my friend Dr. Elliotson of London; also to the "Zoist,"—to which journal I have regularly contributed.

Your early reply will oblige, which I will publish, with your consent, in connection with the case I have referred to. Believe me yours, most respectfully,

ROBERT H. COLLYER.

Edgar A. Poe, Esq., New York.

We have no doubt that Mr. Collyer is perfectly correct in all that he says—and all that he desires us to say—but the truth is, there was a very small modicum of truth in the case of M. Valdemar—which, in consequence, may be called a hard case—*very* hard for M. Valdemar, for Mr. Collyer, and ourselves. If the story was not true, however, it should have been—and perhaps "The Zoist" may discover that it *is* true, after all.

———

THE TRULY beautiful poem entitled "The Mountains," and published in our last Journal, will put every reader in mind of the terseness and severe beauty of Macaulay's best ballads—while it surpasses any of them in grace and imagination. Not for years has so fine a poem been given to the American public. It is the composition of Mr. P. P. Cooke of Virginia, author of "Florence Vane," "Young Rosalie Lee," and other exquisitely graceful and delicate things. Mr. Cooke's prose, too, is nearly as meritorious as his poetry.

For the deeply interesting paper "On the Poetical Literature of Germany," (also published in our last number,) we
are indebted to *Professor T. L. Tellkampf*, of Columbia College, in this city—brother of the celebrated German poet
Adolphus Tellkampf.

————

THE DAILY NEWS—Speaking of Dickens' projected paper,
thus entitled, the correspondent of the Liverpool Chronicle says:

I told you some time ago, if I recollect aright, that a new
daily paper of ultra liberal politics was to be started, with
Charles Dickens as the editor, and his father as field marshal
or conductor. Messrs. Bradbury and Evans, the proprietors of
Punch, are the spirited men ostensibly known in the new paper—that is to be. A number of "crack" reporters, all short-
hand men, of the metropolitan journals, have been engaged,
at salaries of seven, eight and ten guineas a-week, for three
years certain. Dickens is to have two thousand a year! Jerrold,
Mark Lemon, and others of "mark" and "likelihood," are to
be among the chief writers. There is plenty of cash in bank,
and the parties are all men of undoubted honor. After a little
"hitch," the effects of which lasted only twenty-four hours,
everything has gone on cheeringly. Charles Dickens had a
dinner party the other day, composed of the principal lads
engaged; each gentleman invited had come with six names for
the future journal: after dinner these were discussed with the
champagne and claret; some of the titles were funny enough,
and your readers must lose a good laugh by my withholding
them. By general consent, "The Daily News" was adopted.
The paper is to be a rival of the old Whig Morning Chronicle.

A capital of £100,000 was required to commence operations—so great, in England, is the risk and difficulty of establishing a daily paper. The first number will be issued on the
first day of the new year. Among the collaborators is "an
American gentleman who has acquired much note as a Magazinist,"—possibly John Neal.

————

THE BOSTON POST says:

We have just learned of a most flattering compliment that

has been recently paid by a crowned head of Europe to an American writer, Mr. A. J. Downing, of Highland Gardens, New York, who published, not long since, a most charming book on landscape gardening. Mr. Henry Wikoff, who arrived yesterday in the Acadia, from Liverpool, has brought over with him an autograph letter from the Queen of Holland, together with a magnificent ruby ring encircled by three rows of fine diamonds, in acknowledgment of the pleasure she had derived from the late perusal of Mr. Downing's book. A compliment like this from a royal personage to an American author is certainly quite novel, and what enhances its value is the new mode made choice of. The gift of a jewel is the familiar form that a crowned head usually selects to express royal approbation, but it is the first instance of the kind we know of where an autograph letter was added to give a stronger emphasis to such a testimonial. We record with great pleasure this marked compliment to the talents of a fellow countryman, and congratulate Mr. Wikoff upon his honorable commission.

For our own parts we are glad that Mr. Downing has received the ring—especially as it consists of diamonds and rubies and has, therefore, much intrinsic value. We use the words "intrinsic value" not rigorously, but in distinction from the factitious value which, in the public eye, appertains to the present as that of a monarch—and which in our own sincere opinion is precisely nothing at all—unless, indeed, we are to understand that the individual monarch, in this case, is a very especial judge of the merits of a work on "Landscape Gardening." What we mean to say, is simply this:—that the value of any approbation, or any testimony of approbation, for a book, is in the ratio *not* of the worldly eminence, but in that of the judgment and good faith of the person who commends.

————

THE BOSTON COURIER says:

It is with deepest regret that we learn the death of Mrs. Maria Brooks, the authoress of "Zophiel." She died on the 11th of Nov. last, at Matanzas, in the island of Cuba, from the debility consequent upon a severe fit of sickness. Mrs. Brooks was, at the time of her decease, about fifty years old. She was born at Medford, in this state, and for a considerable period resided in this city. About fifteen years ago she visited France and England, and while there formed many friendships with distinguished persons in both countries, among others with Lafayette, Wordsworth, and Southey. Of late years she has resided principally in Matanzas.

Mrs. Brooks was one of the most remarkable women that ever lived. To great attainments in literature, she joined a powerful and original genius, and a character of singular energy and individuality. Both in England and the United States, she has been considered by all who have read her writings thoughtfully, as unmatched among poets of her sex. Southey, who superintended the publication of her "Zophiel," had the most exalted opinion of her powers, and pronounced her "the most impassioned and imaginative of all poetesses." When "Zophiel" was published, Charles Lamb wrote to a friend, that Southey was trying to pass off the poem as the production of an American woman, as if, he said, *"there ever was a woman capable of writing such a poem."* This is high praise, but it is borne out by the poem itself. It is one of the few compositions written during the present century, destined for durable fame. It is one of the most original, passionate and harmonious works of imagination ever conceived—and there breathes through the whole the vital life of genius. Though it has not been extensively circulated in the United States, there are very few American productions which shed so much glory on our literature, or which are so often quoted abroad as evidences of American genius.

That a mind of so much power and brilliancy should have departed—that one of the lights of our literature should have been quenched, we consider an occasion for the most sincere regret. But the image of that mind, stamped on her productions, will not depart. The light that illumines the records of her genius will not be quenched. Her memory will never return to the dust; her mind, even on earth, will have no grave and no tomb. Silently and surely her genius will work its way into the great public heart of the country, and her fame grow with time. And we cannot conceive of the period when an American, in reviewing the causes which have conducted to place his country in a proud intellectual position, and assisted in giving to it the immortality which springs from literature, shall cease to regard with peculiar gratitude and admiration the name of the authoress of "Zophiel."

The critic who writes this is somewhat given to excess of enthusiasm, and we certainly are very far from agreeing with him in his opinion that Mrs. Brooks was "considered by all who have read her writings thoughtfully as unmatched among poets of her sex." The author of "Zophiel" was a truly imaginative poet, but no one, " who read her writings thoughtfully," would think of comparing her with Miss Barrett—or even with Mrs. Norton. As for Lamb's pert query—" was there ever a woman capable of writing such a poem?"—it merely proves that Lamb had little understanding of the true nature of Poetry—which, appealing especially to our sense of Beauty, is, in its very essence, feminine. If the greatest poems have not been written by women, it is because, as yet, the greatest poems have not been written at all.

———

To Correspondents.—Many thanks to our friend, W. D. G. We assure him that our paper has been regularly mailed to the Gazette. Thanks, also, to A. M. F. and H. T. L.

January 3, 1846

T HE BROADWAY JOURNAL may be obtained in the City of New York of the following agents: Taylor, Astor House; Crosby, Exchange, William street; Graham, Tribune Buildings; Lockwood, Broadway and Grand; and Burgess & Stringer, Ann and Broadway.

A very few sets of the first volume are still for sale at the office, 304 Broadway.

———

VALEDICTORY.

UNEXPECTED engagements demanding my whole attention, and the objects being fulfilled, so far as regards myself personally, for which "The Broadway Journal" was established, I now, as its editor, bid farewell—as cordially to foes as to friends.

Mr. Thomas H. Lane is authorized to collect all money due the Journal.

EDGAR A. POE.

ONE of the most wonderful pieces of mechanism ever produced through mental conception is now exhibiting at Philadelphia, and will be shortly to be shown in this city. We allude to the speaking automaton of Herr Faber—an invention, after seventeen years of labor, almost perfected by the ingenious inventor. It is not a machine to labor through easy words of two syllables, indistinctly made out at that. It enunciates distinctly, at the will of the performer, any words or combinations of words; and can even sing, in perfect imitation of a man. It has excited the attention of scientific men at Philadelphia; and their investigation has led them to implicit belief in its merits as a work of art. Professor Patterson and Dr. Goddard, *savans* of note in our sister city, introduced it, a few evenings since, to the public—the latter accompanying the introduction with a brief lecture on acoustics

It is managed, externally, somewhat like a piano. There are fourteen keys, each having a simple sound; and from these and their combinations all the other sounds proceed. Mr. Faber has determined that five vowel and nine consonant sounds are sufficient for the correct enunciation of any words in the English language. The consonants are *b*, *d*, *f*, *g l*, *r*, *s*, *v* and *w*, and the vowels *a*, *e*, *i*, *o* and *u*. There are two extra keys—one for the aspirate, the other for the nasal sounds. The mechanism is so perfect that the lips of the figure move and its nostrils expand naturally, as it speaks. The performer sits at his apparent piano, and plays out the conversation of the automaton. The voice has, however, a rather dry, sepulchral sound; but, as Professor Patterson remarked, "India rubber is not flesh"—not a very original idea, to be sure, but explanatory enough.

Mr. Faber exhibited this machine—not so perfect then as now—in this city and in Philadelphia, three years since. Unknown as he was, and having no scientific men to stand as sponsors to him, the invention was pronounced to be a deceit, although reflection would have convinced all those with power to reflect that deception was out of the question. So discouraged was Faber by his ill-fortune, that he burned his machine in utter despair. We believe he was even on the point of committing suicide, when Mr. Scherr, a kind-hearted piano manufacturer of Philadelphia, struck with the merit of the invention, rendered him assistance, and encouraged him in every way to reconstruct a more perfect automaton. The result is before the public; and we venture to say, that the people of New York will flock in delighted numbers—when the opportunity is afforded them—to view this curious triumph of human ingenuity.

There remains only one achievement—a machine to think. We should say, perhaps, there *has* remained; for certain books lately printed induce us to believe that some people think by a machine. By that, if it exist, and this wonderful reproduction of Roger Bacon's brazen head, stump speakers and advocates can be provided at short notice for our political gatherings and our courts of justice.

———

N. C. BROOKS, A. M., of Baltimore, well known as a terse and vigorous writer, as well as a poet of much absolute power and refined taste, has lately been rendering substantial service to education, by preparing a series of works for the use of schools and colleges. Encouraged by the popularity of those already prepared, his publishers have issued a prospectus, which will be found in our advertising columns, for a series of Greek and Latin classics. From our knowledge of Mr. Brooks's thorough classical acquirements and nicely correct judgment, we have full confidence in the success of the undertaking, and its consequent popularity.

———

WE regret to observe that N. P. Willis and Geo. P. Morris—well known as "mi-boy and the Brigadier," as well as by their literary works, have retired from the "Evening Mirror." Mr. Fuller, however, remains, and will, no doubt, make a useful, as—we are happy to learn on good authority it is a prosperous—paper.

———

THE last picture of LEUTZE brought to this country—"The landing of the Northmen," was bought by the celebrated connoisseur, Mr. Towne, of Philadelphia, for eighteen hundred dollars. It was painted for the late E. L. Carey, but on his decease Mr. Towne, who is one of our most liberal and discerning patrons of art, obtained it.

The Literati of New York City

SOME HONEST OPINIONS AT RANDOM RESPECTING
THEIR AUTORIAL MERITS, WITH OCCASIONAL
WORDS OF PERSONALITY

IN A CRITICISM on Bryant published in the last number of this magazine, I was at some pains in pointing out the distinction between the popular "opinion" of the merits of cotemporary authors and that held and expressed of them in private literary society. The former species of "opinion" can be called "opinion" only by courtesy. It is the public's own, just as we consider a book our own when we have bought it. In general, this opinion is adopted from the journals of the day, and I have endeavoured to show that the cases are rare indeed in which these journals express any other sentiment about books than such as may be attributed directly or indirectly to the authors of the books. The most "popular," the most "successful" writers among us, (for a brief period, at least,) are, ninety-nine times out of a hundred, persons of mere address, perseverance, effrontery—in a word, busy-bodies, toadies, quacks. These people easily succeed in *boring* editors (whose attention is too often entirely engrossed by politics or other "business" matter) into the admission of favourable notices written or caused to be written by interested parties—or, at least, into the admission of *some* notice where, under ordinary circumstances, *no* notice would be given at all. In this way ephemeral "reputations" are manufactured which, for the most part, serve all the purposes designed—that is to say, the putting money into the purse of the quack and the quack's publisher; for there never was a quack who could be brought to comprehend the value of mere fame. Now, men of genius will not resort to these manœuvres, because genius involves in its very essence a scorn of chicanery; and thus for a time the quacks always get the advantage of them, both in respect to pecuniary profit and what *appears* to be public esteem.

There is another point of view, too. Your literary quacks court, in especial, the personal acquaintance of those "connected with the press." Now these latter, even when penning a voluntary, that is to say, an uninstigated notice of the book of an acquaintance, feel as if writing not so much for the eye of the public as for the eye of the acquaintance, and the notice is fashioned accordingly. The bad points of the work are slurred over and the good ones brought out into the best light, all this through a feeling akin to that which makes it unpleasant to speak ill of one to one's face. In the case of men of genius, editors, as a general rule, have no such delicacy— for the simple reason that, as a general rule, they have no acquaintance with these men of genius, a class proverbial for shunning society.

But the very editors who hesitate at saying in print an ill word of an author personally known, are usually the most frank in speaking about him privately. In literary society, they seem bent upon avenging the wrongs self-inflicted upon their own consciences. Here, accordingly, the quack is treated as he deserves—even a little more harshly than he deserves—by way of striking a balance. True merit, on the same principle, is apt to be slightly overrated; but, upon the whole, there is a close approximation to absolute honesty of opinion; and this honesty is farther secured by the mere trouble to which it puts one in conversation to model one's countenance to a falsehood. We place on paper without hesitation a tissue of flatteries, to which in society we could not give utterance, for our lives, without either blushing or laughing outright.

For these reasons there exists a very remarkable discrepancy between the apparent public opinion of any given author's merits and the opinion which is expressed of him orally by those who are best qualified to judge. For example, Mr. Hawthorne, the author of "Twice-Told Tales," is scarcely recognized by the press or by the public, and when noticed at all, is noticed merely to be damned by faint praise. Now, my own opinion of him is, that although his walk is limited and he is fairly to be charged with mannerism, treating all subjects in a similar tone of dreamy *innuendo*, yet in this walk he evinces extraordinary genius, having no rival either in America or elsewhere—and this opinion I have never heard gainsaid by any one literary person in the country. That this opinion, however, is a spoken and not a written one, is referable to the facts, first, that Mr. Hawthorne *is* a poor man, and, second, that he *is not* an ubiquitous quack.

Again, of Mr. Longfellow, who, although little quacky *per se*, has, through his social and literary position as a man of property and a professor at Harvard, a whole legion of active quacks at his control—of *him* what is the apparent popular opinion? Of course, that he is a poetical phenomenon, as entirely without fault as is the luxurious paper upon which his poems are invariably borne to the public eye. In private society he is regarded with one voice as a poet of far more than usual ability, a skillful artist and a well-read man, but as less remarkable in either capacity than as a determined imitator and a dexterous adopter of the ideas of other people. For years I have conversed with no literary person who did not entertain precisely these ideas of Professor L.; and, in fact, on all literary topics there is in society a seemingly wonderful coincidence of opinion. The author accustomed to seclusion, and mingling for the first time with those who have been associated with him only through their works, is astonished and delighted at finding common to all whom he meets conclusions which he had blindly fancied were attained by himself alone and in opposition to the judgment of mankind.

In the series of papers which I now propose, my design is, in giving my own unbiased opinion of the *literati* (male and female) of New York, to give at the same time, very closely if not with absolute accuracy, that of conversational society in literary circles. It must be expected, of course, that, in innumerable particulars, I shall differ from the voice, that is to say, from what appears to be the voice of the public—but this is a matter of no consequence whatever.

New York literature may be taken as a fair representation of that of the country at large. The city itself is the focus of American letters. Its authors include, perhaps, one-fourth of all in America, and the influence they exert on their brethren, if seemingly silent, is not the less extensive and decisive. As I shall have to speak of many individuals, my limits will not permit me to speak of them otherwise than in brief; but this brevity will be merely consistent with the design, which is that of simple *opinion*, with little of either argument or detail. With one or two exceptions I am well acquainted with every author to be introduced, and I shall avail myself of the acquaintance to convey, generally, some idea of the personal appearance of all who, in this regard, would be likely to interest the readers of the magazine. As any precise order or arrangement seems unnecessary and may be inconvenient, I shall maintain none. It will be understood that, without reference to supposed merit or demerit, each individual is introduced absolutely at random.

GEORGE BUSH

The Reverend George Bush is Professor of Hebrew in the University of New York, and has long been distinguished for the extent and variety of his attainments in oriental literature; indeed, as an oriental linguist it is probable that he has no equal among us. He has published a great deal, and his books have always the good fortune to attract attention throughout the civilized world. His "Treatise on the Millennium" is, perhaps, that of his earlier compositions by which he is most extensively as well as most favourably known. Of late days he has created a singular commotion in the realm of theology by his "Anastasis, or the Doctrine of the Resurrection: in which it is shown that the Doctrine of the Resurrection of the Body is not sanctioned by Reason or Revelation." This work has been zealously attacked, and as zealously defended by the professor and his friends. There can be no doubt that, up to this period, the Bushites have had the best of the battle. The "Anastasis" is lucidly, succinctly, vigorously and logically written, and proves, in my opinion, everything that it attempts—provided we admit the imaginary axioms from which it starts; and this is as much as can be well said of any theological disquisition under the sun. It might be hinted, too, in reference as well to Professor Bush as to his opponents, *"que la plupart des sectes ont raison dans une bonne partie de ce qu'elles avancent, mais non pas en ce qu'elles nient."* A subsequent work on "The Soul," by the author of "Anastasis," has made nearly as much noise as the "Anastasis" itself.

Taylor, who wrote so ingeniously "The Natural History of Enthusiasm," might have derived many a valuable hint from the study of Professor Bush. No man is more ardent in his theories; and these latter are neither few nor commonplace. He is a Mesmerist and a Swedenborgian—has lately been engaged in editing Swedenborg's works, publishing them in numbers. He converses with fervour, and often with eloquence. Very probably he will establish an independent church.

He is one of the most amiable men in the world, universally respected and beloved. His frank, unpretending simplicity of demeanour, is especially winning.

In person he is tall, nearly six feet, and spare, with large bones. His countenance expresses rather benevolence and profound earnestness than high intelligence. The eyes are piercing; the other features, in general, massive. The forehead, phrenologically, indicates causality and comparison, with deficient ideality—the organization which induces strict logicality from insufficient premises. He walks with a slouching gait and with an air of abstraction. His dress is exceedingly plain. In respect to the arrangement about his study, he has many of the Magliabechian habits. He is, perhaps, fifty-five years of age, and seems to enjoy good health.

George H. Colton

Mr. Colton is noted as the author of "Tecumseh," and as the originator and editor of "The American Review," a Whig magazine of the higher (that is to say, of the five dollar) class. I must not be understood as meaning any disrespect to the work. It is, in my opinion, by far the best of its order in this country, and is supported in the way of contribution by many of the very noblest intellects. Mr. Colton, if in nothing else, has shown himself a man of genius in his successful establishment of the magazine within so brief a period. It is now commencing its second year, and I can say, from my own personal knowledge, that its circulation exceeds two thousand—it is probably about two thousand five hundred. So marked and immediate a success has never been attained by any of our five dollar magazines, with the exception of "The Southern Literary Messenger," which, in the course of nineteen months, (subsequent to the seventh from its commencement,) attained a circulation of rather more than five thousand.

I cannot conscientiously call Mr. Colton a good editor, although I think that he will finally be so. He improves won-derfully with experience. His present defects are timidity and a lurking taint of partiality, amounting to positive prejudice (in the vulgar sense) for the literature of the Puritans. I do not think, however, that he is at all aware of such preposses-sion. His taste is rather unexceptionable than positively good. He has not, perhaps, sufficient fire within himself to appreci-ate it in others. Nevertheless, he endeavours to do so, and in this endeavour is not inapt to take opinions at secondhand— to adopt, I mean, the opinions of others. He is nervous, and a very trifling difficulty disconcerts him, without getting the better of a sort of dogged perseverance, which will make a thoroughly successful man of him in the end. He is (classi-cally) well educated.

As a poet he has done better things than "Tecumseh," in whose length he has committed a radical and irreparable error, sufficient in itself to destroy a far better book. Some portions of it are truly poetical; very many portions belong to a high order of eloquence; it is invariably well versified, and has no glaring defects, but, upon the whole, is insufferably tedious. Some of the author's shorter compositions, published anonymously in his magazine, have afforded indications even of genius.

Mr. Colton is marked in his personal appearance. He is probably not more than thirty, but an air of constant thought (with a pair of spectacles) causes him to seem somewhat older. He is about five feet eight or nine in height, and fairly proportioned—neither stout nor thin. His forehead is quite intellectual. His mouth has a peculiar expression difficult to describe. Hair light and generally in disorder. He converses fluently and, upon the whole, well, but grandiloquently, and with a tone half tragical half pulpital.

In character he is in the highest degree estimable, a most sincere, high-minded and altogether honourable man. He is unmarried.

N. P. WILLIS

Whatever may be thought of *Mr. Willis's* talents, there can be no doubt about the fact that, both as an author and as a man, he has made a good deal of noise in the world—at least for an American. His literary life, in especial, has been one continual *émeute*; but then his literary character is modified or impelled in a very remarkable degree by his personal one. His success (for in point of fame, if of nothing else, he has certainly been successful) is to be attributed, one-third to his mental ability and two-thirds to his physical temperament— the latter goading him into the accomplishment of what the former merely gave him the means of accomplishing.

At a very early age Mr. Willis seems to have arrived at an understanding that, in a republic such as ours, the *mere* man of letters must ever be a cipher, and endeavoured, accordingly, to unite the *éclat* of the *littérateur* with that of the man of fashion or of society. He "pushed himself," went much into the world, made friends with the gentler sex, "delivered" poetical addresses, wrote "scriptural" poems, traveled, sought the intimacy of noted women, and got into quarrels with notorious men. All these things served his purpose—if, indeed, I am right in supposing that he had any purpose at all. It is quite probable that, as before hinted, he acted only in accordance with his physical temperament; but be this as it may, his personal greatly advanced, if it did not altogether establish his literary fame. I have often carefully considered whether, without the *physique* of which I speak, there is that in the absolute *morale* of Mr. Willis which would have earned him reputation as a man of letters, and my conclusion is, that he could not have failed to become noted in *some* degree under almost any circumstances, but that about two-thirds (as above stated) of his appreciation by the public should be attributed to those *adventures* which grew immediately out of his animal constitution.

He received what is usually regarded as a "good education"—that is to say, he graduated at college; but his education, in the path he pursued, was worth to him, on account of his extraordinary *savoir faire*, fully twice as much as would have been its value in any common case. No man's knowledge is more available, no man has exhibited greater *tact* in the seemingly casual display of his wares. With *him*, at least, a little learning is *no* dangerous thing. He possessed at one time, I believe, the average quantum of American collegiate lore—"a little Latin and less Greek," a smattering of physical and metaphysical science, and (I should judge) a *very* little of the mathematics—but all this must be considered as mere *guess* on my part. Mr. Willis speaks French with some fluency, and Italian not quite so well.

Within the ordinary range of *belles lettres* authorship, he has evinced much versatility. If called on to designate him by any general literary title, I might term him a magazinist—for his compositions have invariably the species of *effect*, with the brevity which the magazine demands. We may view him as a paragraphist, an essayist, or rather "sketcher," a tale writer and a poet.

In the first capacity he fails. His points, however good when deliberately wrought, are too *recherchés* to be put hurriedly before the public eye. Mr. W. has by no means the *readiness* which the editing a newspaper demands. He composes (as did Addison, and as do many of the most brilliant and seemingly *dashing* writers of the present day,) with great labour and frequent erasure and interlineation. His MSS., in this regard, present a very singular appearance, and indicate the *vacillation* which is, perhaps, the leading trait of his character. A newspaper, too, in its longer articles—its "leaders"— very frequently demands argumentation, and here Mr. W. is remarkably out of his element. His exuberant *fancy* leads him over hedge and ditch—anywhere from the main road; and, besides, he is far too readily self-dispossessed. With time at command, however, his great *tact* stands him instead of all argumentative power, and enables him to overthrow an antagonist without permitting the latter to see how he is overthrown. A fine example of this "management" is to be found in Mr. W.'s reply to a very inconsiderate attack upon his social standing made by one of the editors of the New York "Courier and Inquirer." I have always regarded this reply as the highest evidence of its author's ability, as a masterpiece of ingenuity, if not of absolute genius. The skill of the whole lay in this—that, without troubling himself to refute the charges themselves brought against him by Mr. Raymond, he put forth his strength in rendering them null, to all intents and purposes, by obliterating, incidentally and without letting his design be perceived, all *the impression* these charges were calculated to convey. But this reply can be called a newspaper article only on the ground of its having appeared in a newspaper.

As a writer of "sketches," properly so called, Mr. Willis is unequaled. Sketches—especially of society—are his *forte*, and they are so for no other reason than that they afford him the best opportunity of introducing the personal Willis—or, more distinctly, because this species of composition is most susceptible of impression from his personal character. The *dégagé* tone of this kind of writing, too, best admits and encourages that *fancy* which Mr. W. possesses in the most extraordinary degree; it is in fancy that he reigns supreme: this, more than any one other quality, and, indeed, more than all his other *literary* qualities combined, has made him what he is.* It is this which gives him the originality, the freshness, the point, the piquancy, which appear to be the imme-

---

*As, by metaphysicians and in ordinary discourse, the word *fancy* is used with very little determinateness of meaning, I may be pardoned for repeating here what I have elsewhere said on this topic. I shall thus be saved much misapprehension in regard to the term—one which will necessarily be often employed in the course of this series.

"Fancy," says the author of "Aids to Reflection," (who aided reflection to much better purpose in his "Genevieve")—"fancy combines—imagination creates." This was intended and has been received as a distinction, but it is a distinction without a difference—without a difference even of degree. The fancy as nearly creates as the imagination, and neither at all. Novel conceptions are merely unusual combinations. The mind of man can imagine nothing which does not really exist; if it could, it would create not only ideally but substantially, as do the thoughts of God. It may be said, "We imagine a griffin, yet a griffin does not exist." Not the griffin, certainly, but its component parts. It is no more than a collation of known limbs, features, qualities. Thus with all which claims to be new, which appears to be a creation of the intellect—all is re-soluble into the old. The wildest effort of the mind cannot stand the test of this analysis.

Imagination, fancy, fantasy and humour, have in common the elements combination and novelty. The imagination is the artist of the four. From novel arrangements of old forms which present themselves to it, it selects such only as are harmonious; the result, of course, is *beauty* itself—using the word in its most extended sense and as inclusive of the sublime. The pure imagination chooses, *from either beauty or deformity*, only the most combinable things hitherto uncombined; the compound, as a general rule, partaking in character of sublimity or beauty in the ratio of the respective sublimity or beauty of the things combined, which are themselves still to be considered as atomic—that is to say, as previous combinations. But, as often analogously happens in physical chemistry, so not unfrequently does it occur in this chemistry of the intellect, that the admixture of two elements will result in a something that shall have nothing of the quality of one of them—or even nothing of the qualities of either. The range of imagination is thus unlimited.

diate, but which are, in fact, the mediate sources of his popularity.

In *tales* (written with deliberation for the magazines), he has shown greater *constructiveness* than I should have given him credit for had I not read his compositions of this order—for in this faculty all his other works indicate a singular deficiency. The chief charm even of these tales, however, is still referable to *fancy*.

As a poet, Mr. Willis is not entitled, I think, to so high a rank as he may justly claim through his prose; and this for the reason that, although fancy is not inconsistent with any of the demands of those classes of prose composition which

---

Its materials extend throughout the universe. Even out of deformities it fabricates that *beauty* which is at once its sole object and its inevitable test. But, in general, the richness of the matters combined, the facility of discovering combinable novelties worth combining, and *the absolute "chemical combination"* of the completed mass, are the particulars to be regarded in our estimate of imagination. It is this thorough harmony of an imaginative work which so often causes it to be undervalued by the undiscriminating, through the character of *obviousness* which is superinduced. We are apt to find ourselves asking *why it is that these combinations have never been imagined before*.

Now, when this question *does not occur*, when the harmony of the combination is comparatively neglected, and when, in addition to the element of novelty, there is introduced the sub-element of *unexpectedness*—when, for example, matters are brought into combination which not only have never been combined, but whose combination strikes us as a *difficulty happily overcome*, the result then appertains to the fancy, and is, to the majority of mankind, more grateful than the purely harmonious one—although, absolutely, it is less beautiful (or grand) for the reason that *it is* less harmonious.

Carrying its errors into excess—for, however enticing, they *are* errors still, or nature lies—fancy is at length found infringing upon the province of fantasy. The votaries of this latter delight not only in novelty and unexpectedness of combination, but in the *avoidance* of proportion. The result is, therefore, abnormal, and, to a healthy mind, affords less of pleasure through its novelty than of pain through its incoherence. When, proceeding a step farther, however, fancy seeks not merely disproportionate but incongruous or antagonistic elements, the effect is rendered more pleasurable by its greater positiveness; there is a merry effort of truth to shake from her that which is no property of hers, and we laugh outright in recognizing humour.

The four faculties in question seem to me all of their class; but when either fancy or humour is expressed to gain an end, is pointed at a purpose—whenever either becomes objective in place of subjective, then it becomes, also, pure wit or sarcasm, just as the purpose is benevolent or malevolent.

he has attempted, and, indeed, is a vital element of most of them, still it is at war (as will be understood from what I have said in the foot note) with that purity and perfection of *beauty* which are the soul of the poem proper. I wish to be understood as saying this *generally* of our author's poems. In some instances, seeming to *feel* the truth of my proposition, (that fancy should have no place in the loftier poesy,) he has denied it a place, as in "Melanie" and his Scriptural pieces; but, unfortunately, he has been unable to supply the void with the true imagination, and these poems consequently are deficient in vigour, in *stamen*. The Scriptural pieces are quite "correct," as the French have it, and are much admired by a certain set of readers, who judge of a poem, not by its effect on themselves, but by the effect which they imagine it *might* have upon themselves were they not unhappily soulless, and by the effect which they take it for granted it *does* have upon others. It cannot be denied, however, that these pieces are, in general, tame, or indebted for what force they possess to the Scriptural passages of which they are merely paraphrastic. I quote what, in my own opinion and in that of nearly all my friends, is really the truest poem ever written by Mr. Willis.

"UNSEEN SPIRITS.

"The shadows lay along Broadway,
　　'Twas near the twilight tide,
And slowly there a lady fair
　　Was walking in her pride—
Alone walked she, yet viewlessly
　　Walked spirits at her side.

"Peace charmed the street beneath her feet,
　　And honour charmed the air,
And all astir looked kind on her
　　And called her good as fair—
For all God ever gave to her
　　She kept with chary care.

"She kept with care her beauties rare
　　From lovers warm and true,

> For her heart was cold to all but gold,
>   And the rich came not to woo.
> Ah, honoured well are charms to sell
>   When priests the selling do!
>
> "Now, walking there was one more fair—
>   A slight girl, lily-pale,
> And she had unseen company
>   To make the spirit quail—
> 'Twixt want and scorn she walked forlorn,
>   And nothing could avail.
>
> "No mercy now can clear her brow
>   For this world's peace to pray—
> For, as love's wild prayer dissolved in air,
>   Her woman's heart gave way;
> And the sin forgiven by Christ in heaven,
>   By man is cursed alway."

There is about this little poem (evidently written in haste and through impulse) a true *imagination*. Its grace, dignity and pathos are impressive, and there is more in it of earnestness, of soul, than in anything I have seen from the pen of its author. His compositions, in general, have a taint of worldliness, of insincerity. The identical rhyme in the last stanza is very noticeable, and the whole *finale* is feeble. It would be improved by making the last two lines precede the first two of the stanza.

In classifying Mr. W.'s writings I did not think it worth while to speak of him as a dramatist, because, although he has written plays, what they have of merit is altogether in their character of poem. Of his "Bianca Visconti" I have little to say;—it deserved to fail, and did, although it abounded in *eloquent* passages. "Tortesa" abounded in the same, but had a great many dramatic *points* well calculated to tell with a conventional audience. Its characters, with the exception of Tomaso, a drunken buffoon, had no character at all, and the *plot* was a tissue of absurdities, inconsequences and inconsistencies; yet I cannot help thinking it, upon the whole, the best play ever written by an American.

Mr. Willis has made very few attempts at criticism, and those few (chiefly newspaper articles) have not impressed me with a high idea of his analytic abilities, although with a *very* high idea of his taste and discrimination.

His *style* proper may be called extravagant, *bizarre*, pointed, epigrammatic without being antithetical, (this is very rarely the case,) but, through all its whimsicalities, graceful, classic and *accurate*. He is very seldom to be caught tripping in the minor morals. His English is *correct*; his most outrageous imagery is, at all events, unmixed.

Mr. Willis's career has naturally made him enemies among the envious host of dunces whom he has outstripped in the race for fame; and these his personal manner (a little tinctured with reserve, *brusquerie*, or even haughtiness) is by no means adapted to conciliate. He has innumerable warm friends, however, and is himself a warm friend. He is impulsive, generous, bold, impetuous, vacillating, irregularly energetic—apt to be hurried into error, but incapable of deliberate wrong.

He is yet young, and, without being handsome, in the ordinary sense, is a remarkably well-looking man. In height he is, perhaps, five feet eleven, and justly proportioned. His figure is put in the best light by the ease and assured grace of his carriage. His whole person and personal demeanour bear about them the traces of "good society." His face is somewhat too full, or rather heavy, in its lower portions. Neither his nose nor his forehead can be defended; the latter would puzzle phrenology. His eyes are a dull bluish gray, and small. His hair is of a rich brown, curling naturally and luxuriantly. His mouth is well cut; the teeth fine; the expression of the smile intellectual and winning. He converses little, *well* rather than fluently, and in a subdued tone. The portrait of him published about three years ago in "Graham's Magazine," conveys by no means so true an idea of the man as does the sketch (by Lawrence) inserted as frontispiece to a late collection of his poems. He is a widower, and has one child, a daughter.

WILLIAM M. GILLESPIE

Mr. William M. Gillespie aided Mr. Park Benjamin, I believe, some years ago, in the editorial conduct of "The New

World," and has been otherwise connected with the periodical press of New York. He is more favourably known, however, as the author of a neat volume entitled "Rome as Seen by a New Yorker"—a good title to a good book. The endeavour to convey Rome only by those impressions which would naturally be made upon an American, gives the work a certain air of originality—the rarest of all qualities in descriptions of the Eternal City. The style is pure and sparkling, although occasionally flippant and *dilletantesque*. The love of remark is much in the usual way—*selon les règles*—never very exceptionable, and never very profound.

Mr. Gillespie is not unaccomplished, converses readily on many topics, has some knowledge of Italian, French, and, I believe, of the classical tongues, with such proficiency in the mathematics as has obtained for him a professorship of civil engineering at Union College, Schenectady.

In character he has much general amability, is warm-hearted, excitable, nervous. His address is somewhat awkward, but "insinuating" from its warmth and vivacity. Speaks continuously and rapidly, with a lisp which, at times, is by no means unpleasing; is fidgety, and never knows how to sit or to stand, or what to do with his hands and feet, or his hat. In the street walks irregularly, mutters to himself, and, in general, appears in a state of profound abstraction.

In person he is about five feet seven inches high, neither stout nor thin, angularly proportioned; eyes large and dark hazel, hair dark and curling, an ill-formed nose, fine teeth, and a smile of peculiar sweetness; nothing remarkable about the forehead. The general expression of the countenance when in repose is rather unprepossessing, but animation very much alters its character. He is probably thirty years of age—unmarried.

CHARLES F. BRIGGS

Mr. Briggs is better known as Harry Franco, a *nom de plume* assumed since the publication, in the "Knickerbocker Magazine," of his series of papers called "Adventures of Harry Franco." He also wrote for "The Knickerbocker" some articles entitled "The Haunted Merchant," and from time to time subsequently has been a contributor to that journal. The two productions just mentioned have some merit. They depend for their effect upon the relation in a straightforward manner, just as one would talk, of the most commonplace events—a kind of writing which, to ordinary and especially to indolent intellects, has a very observable charm. To cultivated or to active minds it is in an equal degree distasteful, even when claiming the merit of originality. Mr. Briggs' manner, however, is an obvious imitation of Smollett, and, as usual with all imitation, produces an unfavourable impression upon those conversant with the original. It is a common failing, also, with imitators, to out-Herod Herod in aping the peculiarities of the model, and too frequently the faults are more pertinaciously exaggerated than the merits. Thus, the author of "Harry Franco" carries the simplicity of Smollett to insipidity, and his picturesque low-life is made to degenerate into sheer vulgarity. A fair idea of the general tone of the work may be gathered from the following passage:—

" 'Come, colonel,' said the gentleman, slapping me on the shoulder, ' what 'll you take?'

" 'Nothing, I thank you,' I replied; 'I have taken enough already.'

" 'What! don't you liquorate?'

"I shook my head, for I did not exactly understand him.

" 'Don't drink, hey?'

" 'Sometimes,' I answered.

" 'What! temperance man?—signed a pledge?'

" 'No. I have not signed a pledge not to drink.'

" 'Then you shall take a horn—so come along.'

"And so saying he dragged me up to the bar.

" 'Now, what'll you take—julep, sling, cocktail or sherry cobbler?'

" 'Anything you choose,' I replied, for I had not the most remote idea what the drinks were composed of which he enumerated.

" 'Then give us a couple of cocktails, barkeeper,' said the gentleman; 'and let us have them as quick as you damn please, for I am as thirsty as the great desert of Sahara which old Judah Paddock traveled over.' "

If Mr. Briggs has a *forte*, it is a Flemish fidelity that omits nothing, whether agreeable or disagreeable; but I cannot call this *forte* a virtue. He has also some humour, but nothing of an original character. Occasionally he has written good things. A magazine article called "Dobbs and his Cantelope" was quite easy and clever in its way; but the way is necessarily a small one. Now and then he has attempted criticism, of which, as might be expected, he made a farce. The silliest thing of this kind ever penned, perhaps, was an elaborate attack of his on Thomas Babington Macaulay, published in "The Democratic Review;"—the force of folly could no farther go. Mr. Briggs has never composed in his life three consecutive sentences of grammatical English. He is grossly uneducated.

In connection with Mr. John Bisco he was the originator of the late "Broadway Journal"—my editorial association with that work not having commenced until the sixth or seventh number, although I wrote for it occasionally from the first. Among the principal papers contributed by Mr. B. were those discussing the paintings at the last exhibition of the Academy of Fine Arts in New York. I may be permitted to say that there was scarcely a point in his whole series of criticisms on this subject at which I did not radically disagree with him. Whatever taste he has in art is, like his taste in letters, Flemish.

Mr. Briggs's personal appearance is not prepossessing. He is about five feet six inches in height, somewhat slightly framed, with a sharp, thin face, narrow and low forehead, pert-looking nose, mouth rather pleasant in expression, eyes not so good, gray and small, although occasionally brilliant. In dress he is apt to affect the artist, priding himself especially upon his personal acquaintance with artists and his general connoisseurship. He is a member of the Art Union. He walks with a quick, nervous step. His address is quite good, frank and insinuating. His conversation has now and then the merit of humour, but he has a perfect mania for contradiction, and it is impossible to utter an uninterrupted sentence in his hearing. He has much warmth of feeling, and is not a person to be disliked, although very apt to irritate and annoy. Two of his most marked characteristics are vacillation of purpose and a passion for being mysterious. His most intimate friends seem to know nothing of his movements, and it is folly to expect from him a direct answer about anything. He has, apparently, traveled; pretends to a knowledge of French (of which he is profoundly ignorant); has been engaged in an infinite variety of employments, and now, I believe, occupies a lawyer's office in Nassau street. He is married, goes little into society, and seems about forty years of age.

WILLIAM KIRKLAND

Mr. William Kirkland—husband of the author of "A New Home"—has written much for the magazines, but has made no collection of his works. A series of "Letters from Abroad" have been among his most popular compositions. He was in Europe for some time, and is well acquainted with the French language and literature, as also with the German. He aided Dr. Turner in the late translation of Von Raumer's "America," published by the Langleys. One of his best magazine papers appeared in "The Columbian"—a review of the London Foreign Quarterly for April, 1844. The arrogance, ignorance and self-glorification of the Quarterly, with its gross injustice towards everything un-British, were severely and palpably exposed, and its narrow malignity shown to be especially *mal-à-propos* in a journal exclusively devoted to foreign concerns, and therefore presumably imbued with something of a cosmopolitan spirit. An article on "English and American Monthlies" in Godey's Magazine, and one entitled "Our English Visitors," in "The Columbian," have also been extensively read and admired. A valuable essay on "The Tyranny of Public Opinion in the United States," (published in "The Columbian" for December, 1845,) demonstrates the truth of Jefferson's assertion, that in this country, which has set the world an example of physical liberty, the inquisition of popular sentiment overrules in practice the freedom asserted in theory by the laws. "The West, the Paradise of the Poor," and "The United States' Census of 1830," the former in "The Democratic Review," the latter in "Hunt's Merchants' Magazine," with sundry essays in the daily papers, complete the list of Mr. Kirkland's works. It will be seen that he has written little, but that little is entitled to respect, for its simplicity and the evidence which it affords of scholarship and diligent research. Whatever Mr. Kirkland does is done carefully. He is occasionally very caustic, but seldom without cause. His style is vigorous, precise, and, notwithstanding his foreign acquirements, free from idiomatic peculiarities.

Mr. Kirkland is beloved by all who know him; in character mild, unassuming, benevolent, yet not without becoming energy at times; in person rather short and slight; features indistinctive; converses well and zealously, although his hearing is defective.

JOHN W. FRANCIS

Doctor Francis, although by no means a *littérateur*, cannot well be omitted in an account of the New York *literati*. In his capacity of physician and medical lecturer he is far too well known to need comment. He was the pupil, friend and partner of Hosack—the pupil of Abernethy—connected in some manner with everything that has been well said or done medicinally in America. As a medical essayist he has always commanded the highest respect and attention. Among the *points* he has made at various times, I may mention his Anatomy of Drunkenness, his views of the Asiatic Cholera, his analysis of the Avon waters of the state, his establishment of the comparative immunity of the constitution from a second attack of yellow fever, and his pathological propositions on the changes wrought in the system by specific poisons through their assimilation—propositions remarkably sustained and enforced by recent discoveries of Liebig.

In unprofessional letters Doctor Francis has also accomplished much, although necessarily in a discursive manner. His biography of Chancellor Livingston, his Horticultural Discourse, his Discourse at the opening of the new hall of the New York Lyceum of Natural History, are (each in its way) models of fine writing, just sufficiently toned down by an indomitable common sense. I had nearly forgotten to mention his admirable sketch of the personal associations of Bishop Berkeley, of Newport.

Doctor Francis is one of the old spirits of the New York Historical Society. His philanthropy, his active, untiring beneficence will forever render his name a household word among the truly Christian of heart. His professional services and his purse are always at the command of the needy; few of our wealthiest men have ever contributed to the relief of distress so bountifully—none certainly with greater readiness or with warmer sympathy.

His person and manner are richly peculiar. He is short and stout, probably five feet five in height, limbs of great muscularity and strength, the whole frame indicating prodigious vitality and energy—the latter is, in fact, the leading trait in his character. His head is large, massive—the features in keeping; complexion dark florid; eyes piercingly bright; mouth exceedingly mobile and expressive; hair gray, and worn in matted locks about the neck and shoulders—eyebrows to correspond, jagged and ponderous. His age is about fifty-eight. His general appearance is such as to arrest attention.

His address is the most genial that can be conceived, its *bonhommie* irresistible. He speaks in a loud, clear, hearty tone, dogmatically, with his head thrown back and his chest out; never waits for an introduction to anybody; slaps a perfect stranger on the back and calls him "Doctor" or "Learned Theban;" pats every lady on the head and (if she be pretty and *petite*) designates her by some such title as "My Pocket Edition of the Lives of the Saints." His conversation proper is a sort of Roman punch made up of tragedy, comedy, and the broadest of all possible farce. He has a natural, felicitous flow of talk, always overswelling its boundaries and sweeping everything before it right and left. He is very earnest, intense, emphatic; thumps the table with his fist; shocks the nerves of the ladies. His *forte*, after all, is humour, the richest conceivable—a compound of Swift, Rabelais, and the clown in the pantomime. He is married.

Anna Cora Mowatt

Mrs. Mowatt is in some respects a remarkable woman, and has undoubtedly wrought a deeper impression upon *the public* than any one of her sex in America.

She became first known through her recitations. To these she drew large and discriminating audiences in Boston, New York, and elsewhere to the north and east. Her subjects were much in the usual way of these exhibitions, including comic as well as serious pieces, chiefly in verse. In her selections she evinced no *very* refined taste, but was probably influenced by the elocutionary rather than by the literary value of her *programmes*. She read well; her voice was melodious; her youth and general appearance excited interest, but, upon the whole, she produced no great effect, and the enterprize may be termed unsuccessful, although the press, as is its wont, spoke in the most sonorous tone of her success.

It was during these recitations that her name, prefixed to occasional tales, sketches and brief poems in the magazines, first attracted an attention that, but for the recitations, it might not have attracted.

Her sketches and tales may be said to be *cleverly* written. They are lively, easy, *conventional*, scintillating with a species of sarcastic wit, which might be termed good were it in any respect original. In point of style—that is to say, of mere English, they are very respectable. One of the best of her prose papers is entitled "Ennui and its Antidote," published in "The Columbian Magazine" for June, 1845. The subject, however, is an exceedingly hackneyed one.

In looking carefully over her poems, I find no one entitled to commendation as a whole; in very few of them do I observe even noticeable passages, and I confess that I am surprised and disappointed at this result of my inquiry; nor can I make up my mind that there is not much latent poetical power in Mrs. Mowatt. From some lines addressed to Isabel M——, I copy the opening stanza as the most favourable specimen which I have seen of her verse.

> "Forever vanished from thy cheek
> Is life's unfolding rose—

> Forever quenched the flashing smile
> That conscious beauty knows!
>
> Thine orbs are lustrous with a light
> Which ne'er illumes the eye
> Till heaven is bursting on the sight
> And earth is fleeting by."

In this there is much force, and the idea in the concluding quatrain is so well *put* as to have the air of originality. Indeed, I am not sure that the thought of the last two lines is *not* original;—at all events it is exceedingly *natural* and impressive. I say "natural," because, in any imagined ascent from the orb we inhabit, when heaven should "burst on the sight"—in other words, when the attraction of the planet should be superseded by that of another sphere, then instantly would the "earth" have the appearance of "fleeting by." The versification, also, is much better here than is usual with the poetess. In general she is rough, through excess of harsh consonants. The whole poem is of higher merit than any which I can find with her name attached; but there is little of the spirit of poesy in anything she writes. She evinces more feeling than ideality.

Her first decided success was with her comedy, "Fashion," although much of this success itself is referable to the interest felt in her as a beautiful woman and an authoress.

The play is not without merit. It may be commended especially for its simplicity of plot. What the Spanish playwrights mean by dramas of *intrigue*, are the worst acting dramas in the world; the intellect of an audience can never safely be fatigued by complexity. The necessity for verbose explanation, however, on the part of Trueman, at the close of the play, is in this regard a serious defect. A *dénouement* should in all cases be taken up with *action*—with nothing else. Whatever cannot be explained by such action should be communicated at the opening of the story.

In the plot, however estimable for simplicity, there is of course not a particle of originality, of invention. Had it, indeed, been designed as a burlesque upon the arrant conventionality of stage incidents in general, it might have been received as a palpable hit. There is not an event, a character, a jest, which is not a well-understood thing, a matter of course, a stage-property time out of mind. The general tone is adopted from "The School for Scandal," to which, indeed, the whole composition bears just such an affinity as the shell of a locust to the locust that tenants it—as the spectrum of a Congreve rocket to the Congreve rocket itself. In the *management* of her imitation, nevertheless, Mrs. Mowatt has, I think, evinced a sense of theatrical effect or point which may lead her, at no very distant day, to compose an exceedingly *taking*, although it can never much aid her in composing a very meritorious drama. "Fashion," in a word, owes what it had of success to its being the work of a lovely woman who had already excited interest, and to the very commonplaceness or spirit of conventionality which rendered it readily comprehensible and appreciable by the public proper. It was much indebted, too, to the carpets, the ottomans, the chandeliers and the conservatories, which gained so decided a popularity for that despicable mass of inanity, the "London Assurance" of Bourcicault.

Since "Fashion," Mrs. Mowatt has published one or two brief novels in pamphlet form, but they have no particular merit, although they afford glimpses (I cannot help thinking) of a genius as yet unrevealed, except in her capacity of actress.

In this capacity, if she be but true to herself, she will assuredly win a very enviable distinction. She has done well, wonderfully well, both in tragedy and comedy; but if she knew her own strength she would confine herself nearly altogether to the depicting (in letters not less than on the stage) the more gentle sentiments and the most profound passions. Her sympathy with the latter is evidently intense. In the utterance of the truly generous, of the really noble, of the unaffectedly passionate, we see her bosom heave, her cheek grow pale, her limbs tremble, her lip quiver, and nature's own tear rush impetuously to the eye. It is this freshness of the heart which will provide for her the greenest laurels. It is this enthusiasm, this well of deep feeling, which should be made to prove for her an inexhaustible source of fame. As an actress, it is to her a mine of wealth worth all the dawdling *instruction* in the world. Mrs. Mowatt, on her first appearance as Pauline, was quite as able to give lessons in stage *routine* to any actor or actress in America as was any actor or actress to give lessons to her. *Now*, at least, she should throw all "support" to the winds, trust proudly to her own sense of art, her own rich and natural elocution, her beauty, which is unusual, her grace, which is queenly, and be assured that these qualities, as she *now* possesses them, are all sufficient to render her a great actress, when considered simply as the means by which the end of natural acting is to be attained, as the mere instruments by which she may effectively and unimpededly lay bare to the audience the movements of her own passionate heart.

Indeed, the great charm of her manner is its naturalness. She looks, speaks and moves with a well-controlled impulsiveness, as different as can be conceived from the customary rant and cant, the hack conventionality of the stage. Her voice is rich and voluminous, and although by no means powerful, is so well managed as to seem so. Her utterance is singularly distinct, its sole blemish being an occasional Anglicism of accent, adopted probably from her instructor, Mr. Crisp. Her reading could scarcely be improved. Her action is distinguished by an ease and self-possession which would do credit to a veteran. Her step is the perfection of grace. Often have I watched her for hours with the closest scrutiny, yet never for an instant did I observe her in an attitude of the least awkwardness or even constraint, while many of her seemingly impulsive gestures spoke in loud terms of the woman of genius, of the poet imbued with the profoundest sentiment of the beautiful in motion.

Her figure is slight, even fragile. Her face is a remarkably fine one, and of that precise character best adapted to the stage. The forehead is, perhaps, the least prepossessing feature, although it is by no means an unintellectual one. Hair light auburn, in rich profusion, and always arranged with exquisite taste. The eyes are gray, brilliant and expressive, without being full. The nose is well-formed, with the Roman curve, and indicative of energy. This quality is also shown in the somewhat excessive prominence of the chin. The mouth is large, with brilliant and even teeth and flexible lips, capable of the most instantaneous and effective variations of expression. A more radiantly beautiful smile it is quite impossible to conceive.

GEORGE B. CHEEVER

The Reverend George B. Cheever created at one time something of an excitement by the publication of a little *brochure* entitled "Deacon Giles' Distillery." He is much better known, however, as the editor of "The Commonplace Book of American Poetry," a work which has at least the merit of not belying its title, and *is* exceedingly commonplace. I am ashamed to say that for several years this compilation afforded to Europeans the only material from which it was possible to form an estimate of the poetical ability of Americans. The selections appear to me exceedingly injudicious, and have all a marked leaning to the didactic. Dr. Cheever is not without a certain sort of negative ability as critic, but works of this character should be undertaken by poets or not at all. The verses which I have seen attributed to *him* are undeniably *médiocres*.

His principal publications, in addition to those mentioned above, are "God's Hand in America," "Wanderings of a Pilgrim under the Shadow of Mont Blanc," "Wanderings of a Pilgrim under the Shadow of Jungfrau," and, lately, a "Defence of Capital Punishment." This "Defence" is at many points well reasoned, and as a clear *resumé* of all that has been already said on its own side of the question, may be considered as commendable. Its premises, however, (as well as those of all reasoners *pro* or *con* on this vexed topic,) are admitted only very partially by the world at large—a fact of which the author affects to be ignorant. Neither does he make the slightest attempt at bringing forward one novel argument. Any man of ordinary invention might have adduced and maintained a dozen.

The two series of "Wanderings" are, perhaps, the best works of their writer. They are what is called "eloquent;" a little too much in that way, perhaps, but nevertheless entertaining.

Dr. Cheever is rather small in stature, and his countenance is vivacious; in other respects there is nothing very observable about his personal appearance. He has been recently married.

CHARLES ANTHON

Doctor Charles Anthon is the well-known Jay-professor of the Greek and Latin languages in Columbia College, New York, and Rector of the Grammar School. If not absolutely the best, he is at least generally considered the best classicist in America. In England and in Europe at large, his scholastic acquirements are more sincerely respected than those of any of our countrymen. His additions to Lemprière are there justly regarded as evincing a nice perception of method and accurate as well as extensive erudition, but his "Classical Dictionary" has superseded the work of the Frenchman altogether. Most of Professor Anthon's publications have been adopted as text-books at Oxford and Cambridge—an honour to be properly understood only by those acquainted with the many high requisites for attaining it. As a commentator (if not exactly as a critic) he may rank with any of his day, and has evinced powers very unusual in men who devote their lives to classical lore. His accuracy is very remarkable; in this particular he is always to be relied upon. The trait manifests itself even in his MS., which is a model of neatness and symmetry, exceeding in these respects anything of the kind with which I am acquainted. It is somewhat *too* neat, perhaps, and *too* regular, as well as diminutive, to be called beautiful; it might be mistaken at any time, however, for very elaborate copper-plate engraving.

But his chirography, although fully in keeping so far as precision is concerned with his mental character, is, in its entire freedom from flourish or superfluity, as much *out* of keeping with his verbal style. In his notes to the Classics he is singularly Ciceronian—if, indeed, not positively Johnsonese.

An attempt was made not long ago to prepossess the public against his "Classical Dictionary," the most important of his works, by getting up a hue and cry of plagiarism—in the case of all similar books the most preposterous accusation in the world, although, from its very preposterousness, one not easily rebutted. Obviously, the design in any such compilation is, in the first place, to make a *useful school-book* or book of reference, and the scholar who should be weak enough to neglect this indispensable point for the mere purpose of winning credit with a few bookish men for originality, would deserve to be dubbed, by the public at least, a dunce. There are very few points of classical scholarship which are not the common property of "the learned" throughout the world, and in composing any book of reference recourse is unscrupulously and even necessarily had in all cases to similar books which ʜaⱱe preceded. In availing themselves of these latter, however, it is the practice of quacks to paraphrase page after page, rearranging the order of paragraphs, making a slight alteration in point of fact here and there, but preserving the spirit of the whole, its information, erudition, etc. etc., while everything is so completely *re-written* as to leave no room for a direct charge of plagiarism; and this is considered and lauded as originality. Now, he who, in availing himself of the labours of his predecessors (and it is clear that all scholars *must* avail themselves of such labours)—he who shall copy *verbatim* the passages to be desired without attempt at palming off their spirit as original with himself, is certainly no plagiarist, even if he fail to make *direct* acknowledgment of indebtedness—is unquestionably *less* of the plagiarist than the disingenuous and contemptible quack who wriggles himself, as above explained, into a reputation for originality, a reputation quite out of place in a case of this kind—the public, of course, never caring a straw whether he be original or not. These attacks upon the New York professor are to be attributed to a *clique* of pedants in and about Boston, gentlemen envious of his success, and whose own compilations are noticeable only for the singular patience and ingenuity with which their dovetailing chicanery is concealed from the *public* eye.

Doctor Anthon is, perhaps, forty-eight years of age; about five feet eight inches in height; rather stout; fair complexion; hair light and inclined to curl; forehead remarkably broad and high; eye gray, clear and penetrating; mouth well-formed, with excellent teeth—the lips having great flexibility and consequent power of expression; the smile particularly pleasing. His address in general is bold, frank, cordial, full of *bonhommie*. His whole air is *distingué* in the best understanding of the term—that is to say, he would impress any one at first sight with the idea of his being no ordinary man. He has qualities, indeed, which would have insured him eminent success in almost any pursuit; and there are times in which his friends are half disposed to regret his exclusive devotion to classical literature. He was one of the originators of the late "New York Review," his associates in the conduct and proprietorship being Doctor F. L. Hawks and Professor R. C. Henry. By far the most valuable papers, however, were those of Doctor A.

RALPH HOYT

The Reverend Ralph Hoyt is known chiefly—at least to the world of letters—by "The Chaunt of Life and other Poems, with Sketches and Essays." The publication of this work, however, was never *completed*, only a portion of the poems having appeared, and none of the essays or sketches. It is to be hoped that we shall yet have these latter.

Of the poems issued, one, entitled "Old," had so many peculiar excellences that I copied the whole of it, although quite long, in "The Broadway Journal." It will remind every reader of Durand's fine picture, "An Old Man's Recollections," although between poem and painting there is no more than a very admissible similarity.

I quote a stanza from "Old" (the opening one) by way of bringing the piece to the remembrance of any one who may have forgotten it.

> "By the wayside, on a mossy stone,
>   Sat a hoary pilgrim sadly musing;
> Oft I marked him sitting there alone,
>   All the landscape like a page perusing;
>   Poor unknown,
>   By the wayside on a mossy stone."

The quaintness aimed at here is, so far as a single stanza is concerned, to be defended as a legitimate effect, conferring high pleasure on a numerous and cultivated class of minds. Mr. Hoyt, however, in his continuous and uniform repetition of the first line in the last of each stanza of twenty-five, has by much exceeded the proper limits of the quaint and impinged upon the ludicrous. The poem, nevertheless, abounds in lofty merit, and has, in especial, some passages of rich imagination and exquisite pathos. For example—

> "Seemed it pitiful he should sit there,
>   No one sympathizing, no one heeding,
>   *None to love him for his thin gray hair.*

> "One sweet spirit broke the silent spell—
>   Ah, to me her name was always Heaven!
>   She besought him all his grief to tell—
>   (I was then thirteen and she eleven)
>   Isabel!
>   One sweet spirit broke the silent spell.

> " 'Angel,' said he, sadly, 'I am old;
>   Earthly hope no longer hath a morrow:
>   Why I sit here thou shalt soon be told'—
>   (Then his eye betrayed a pearl of sorrow—
>   Down it rolled—)
>   'Angel,' said he, sadly, *'I am old!'* "

It must be confessed that some portions of "Old" (which is by far the best of the collection) remind us forcibly of the "Old Man" of Oliver Wendell Holmes.

"Pröemus" is the concluding poem of the volume, and itself concludes with an exceedingly vigorous stanza, putting me not a little in mind of Campbell in his best days.

> "O'er all the silent sky
>   A dark and scowling frown—
>   But darker scowled each eye
>   When all resolved to die—
>   *When (night of dread renown!)*
>   *A thousand stars went down.*"

Mr. Hoyt is about forty years of age, of the medium height, pale complexion, dark hair and eyes. His countenance expresses sensibility and benevolence. He converses slowly and with perfect deliberation. He is married.

GULIAN C. VERPLANCK

Mr. Verplanck has acquired reputation—at least his literary reputation—less from what he has done than from what he has given indication of ability to do. His best, if not his principal works, have been addresses, orations and contributions to the reviews. His scholarship is more than respectable, and his taste and acumen are not to be disputed.

His legal acquirements, it is admitted, are very considerable. When in Congress he was noted as the most industrious man in that assembly, and acted as a walking register or volume of reference, ever at the service of that class of legislators who are too lofty-minded to burden their memories with mere business particulars or matters of fact. Of late years the energy of his character appears to have abated, and many of his friends go so far as to accuse him of indolence.

His family is quite influential—one of the few old Dutch ones retaining their social position.

Mr. Verplanck is short in stature, not more than five feet five inches in height, and compactly or stoutly built. The head is square, massive, and covered with thick, bushy and grizzly hair; the cheeks are ruddy; lips red and full, indicating a relish for good cheer; nose short and straight; eyebrows much arched; eyes dark blue, with what seems, to a casual glance, a sleepy expression—but they gather light and fire as we examine them.

He must be sixty, but a vigorous constitution gives promise of a ripe and healthful old age. He is active; walks firmly, with a short, quick step. His manner is affable, or (more accurately) sociable. He converses well, although with no great fluency, and has his hobbies of talk; is especially fond of old English literature. Altogether, his person, intellect, tastes and general peculiarities, bear a very striking resemblance to those of the late Nicholas Biddle.

FREEMAN HUNT

Mr. Hunt is the editor and proprietor of the well-known "Merchants' Magazine," one of the most useful of our monthly journals, and decidedly the best "property" of any work of its class. In its establishment he evinced many remarkable traits of character. He was entirely without means, and even much in debt and otherwise embarrassed, when, by one of those intuitive perceptions which belong only to genius, but which are usually attributed to "good luck," the "happy" idea entered his head of getting up a magazine devoted to the interests of the influential class of merchants. The chief happiness of this idea, however, (which no doubt had been entertained and discarded by a hundred projectors before Mr. H.,) consisted in the method by which he proposed to carry it into operation. Neglecting the hackneyed modes of advertising largely, circulating flashy prospectuses and sending out numerous "agents," who, in general, merely serve the purpose of boring people into a very temporary support of the work in whose behalf they are employed, he took the whole matter resolutely into his own hands; called personally, in the first place, upon his immediate mercantile friends; explained to them, frankly and succinctly, his object; put the value and necessity of the contemplated publication in the best light—as he well knew how to do—and in this manner obtained to head his subscription list a good many of the most eminent business men in New York. Armed with their names and with recommendatory letters from many of them, he now pushed on to the other chief cities of the Union, and thus, in less time than is taken by ordinary men to make a preparatory flourish of trumpets, succeeded in building up for himself a permanent fortune and for the public a journal of immense interest and value. In the whole proceeding he evinced a tact, a knowledge of mankind and a self-dependence which are the staple of even greater achievements than the establishment of a five dollar magazine. In the subsequent conduct of the work he gave evidence of equal ability. Having without aid put the magazine upon a satisfactory footing as regards its circulation, he also without aid undertook its editorial and business conduct—from the first germ of the conception to the present moment having kept the whole undertaking within his own hands. His subscribers and regular contributors are now among the most intelligent and influential in America; the journal is regarded as absolute authority in mercantile matters, circulates extensively not only in this country but in Europe, and even in regions more remote, affording its worthy and enterprising projector a large income, which no one knows better than himself how to put to good use.

The strong points, the marked peculiarities of Mr. Hunt could not have failed in arresting the attention of all observers of character; and Mr. Willis in especial has made him the subject of repeated comment. I copy what follows from the "New York Mirror."

"Hunt has been glorified in the 'Hong-Kong Gazette,' is regularly complimented by the English mercantile authorities, has every bank in the world for an eager subscriber, every consul, every ship-owner and navigator; is filed away as authority in every library, and thought of in half the countries of the world as early as No. 3 in their enumeration of distinguished Americans, yet who seeks to do him honour in the city he does honour to? The 'Merchants' Magazine,' though a prodigy of perseverance and industry, is not an accidental development of Hunt's energies. He has always been singularly sagacious and original in devising new works and good ones. He was the founder of the first 'Ladies' Magazine,'* of the first children's periodical; he started the 'American Magazine of Useful and Entertaining Knowledge,' compiled the best known collection of American anecdotes, and is an indefatigable writer—the author, among other things, of 'Letters About the Hudson.'

"Hunt was a playfellow of ours in round-jacket days, and we have always looked at him with a reminiscent interest. His luminous, eager eyes, as he goes along the street, keenly bent on his errand, would impress any observer with an idea of his genius and determination, and we think it quite time his earnest head was in the engraver's hand and his daily passing by

*At this point Mr. Willis is, perhaps, in error.

a mark for the *digito monstrari*. Few more worthy or more valuable citizens are among us."

Much of Mr. Hunt's character is included in what I have already said and quoted. He is "earnest," "eager," combining in a very singular manner general coolness and occasional excitability. He is a true friend, and the enemy of no man. His heart is full of the warmest sympathies and charities. No one in New York is more universally popular.

He is about five feet eight inches in height, well proportioned; complexion dark-florid; forehead capacious; chin massive and projecting, indicative (according to Lavater and general experience) of that energy which is, in fact, the chief point of his character; hair light brown, very fine, of a web-like texture, worn long and floating about the face; eyes of wonderful brilliancy and intensity of expression; the whole countenance beaming with sensibility and intelligence. He is married, and about thirty-eight years of age.

Piero Maroncelli

During his twelve years' imprisonment, *Maroncelli* composed a number of poetical works, some of which were committed to paper, others lost for the want of it. In this country he has published a volume entitled "Additions to the Memoirs of Silvio Pellico," containing numerous anecdotes of the captivity not recorded in Pellico's work, and an "Essay on the Classic and Romantic Schools," the author proposing to divide them anew and designate them by novel distinctions. There is at least some scholarship and some originality in this essay. It is also brief. Maroncelli regards it as the best of his compositions. It is strongly tinctured with transcendentalism. The volume contains, likewise, some poems, of which the "Psalm of Life" and the "Psalm of the Dawn" have never been translated into English. "Winds of the Wakened Spring," one of the pieces included, has been happily rendered by Mr. Halleck, and is the most favourable specimen that could have been selected. These "Additions" accompanied a Boston version of "My Prisons, by Silvio Pellico."

Maroncelli is now about fifty years old, and bears on his

person the marks of long suffering; he has lost a leg; his hair and beard became gray many years ago; just now he is suffering from severe illness, and from this it can scarcely be expected that he will recover.

In figure he is short and slight. His forehead is rather low, but broad. His eyes are light blue and weak. The nose and mouth are large. His features in general have all the Italian mobility; their expression is animated and full of intelligence. He speaks hurriedly and gesticulates to excess. He is irritable, frank, generous, chivalrous, warmly attached to his friends, and expecting from them equal devotion. His love of country is unbounded, and he is quite enthusiastic in his endeavours to circulate in America the literature of Italy.

LAUGHTON OSBORN

Personally, *Mr. Osborn* is little known as an author, either to the public or in literary society, but he has made a great many "sensations" anonymously or with a *nom de plume*. I am not sure that he has published anything with his own name.

One of his earliest works—if not his earliest—was "The Adventures of Jeremy Levis, by Himself," in one volume, a kind of medley of fact, fiction, satire, criticism and novel philosophy. It is a dashing, reckless *brochure*, brimful of talent and audacity. Of course it was covertly admired by the few and loudly condemned by all of the many who can fairly be said to have seen it at all. It had no great circulation. There was something wrong, I fancy, in the mode of its issue.

"Jeremy Levis" was followed by "The Dream of Alla-Ad-Deen, from the romance of 'Anastasia,' by Charles Erskine White, D.D." This is a thin pamphlet of thirty-two pages, each page containing about a hundred and forty words—the whole equal to four pages of this magazine. Alla-Ad-Deen is the son of Alladdin, of "wonderful lamp" memory, and the story is in the "Vision of Mirza" or "Rasselas" way. The design is to reconcile us to death and evil, on the somewhat unphilosophical ground that comparatively we are of little importance in the scale of creation. The author himself supposes this scale to be infinite, and thus his argument proves too much; for if evil should be regarded by man as of no consequence because, "comparatively," *he* is of none, it must be regarded as of no consequence by the angels for a similar reason—and so on in a never-ending ascent. In other words, the only thing proved is the rather bull-ish proposition that evil is no evil at all. I do not find that the "Dream" elicited any attention. It would have been more appropriately published in one of our magazines.

Next in order came, I believe, "The Confessions of a Poet, by Himself." This was in two volumes, of the ordinary novel form, but printed very openly. It made much noise in the literary world, and no little curiosity was excited in regard to its author, who was generally supposed to be John Neal. There were some grounds for this supposition, the tone and matter of the narrative bearing much resemblance to those of "Errata" and "Seventy-Six," especially in the points of boldness and vigour. The "Confessions," however, far surpassed any production of Mr. Neal's in a certain air of cultivation (if not exactly of scholarship) which pervaded it, as well as in the management of its construction—a particular in which the author of "The Battle of Niagara" invariably fails; there is no precision, no finish about anything he does—always an excessive *force* but little of refined art. Mr. N. seems to be deficient in a sense of *completeness*. He begins well, vigorously, startlingly, and proceeds by fits, quite at random, now prosing, now exciting vivid interest, but his conclusions are sure to be hurried and indistinct, so that the reader perceives a falling off, and closes the book with dissatisfaction. He has done nothing which, as a whole, is even respectable, and "The Confessions" are quite remarkable for their artistic unity and perfection. But in higher regards they are to be commended. I do not think, indeed, that a better book of its kind has been written in America. To be sure, it is not precisely the work to place in the hands of a lady, but its scenes of passion are intensely wrought, its incidents are striking and original, its sentiments audacious and suggestive at least, if not at all times tenable. In a word, it is that rare thing, a fiction of *power* without rudeness. Its spirit, in general, resembles that of "Miserrimus" and "Martin Faber."

Partly on account of what most persons would term their licentiousness, partly, also, on account of the prevalent idea that Mr. Neal (who was never very popular with the press) had written them, "The Confessions," by the newspapers, were most unscrupulously misrepresented and abused. The "Commercial Advertiser" of New York was, it appears, foremost in condemnation, and Mr. Osborn thought proper to avenge his wrongs by the publication of a bulky satirical poem, leveled at the critics in general, but more especially at Colonel Stone, the editor of the "Commercial." This satire (which was published in exquisite style as regards print and paper) was entitled "The Vision of Rubeta." Owing to the high price necessarily set upon the book, no great many copies were sold, but the few that got into circulation made quite a hubbub, and with reason, for the satire was not only bitter but personal in the last degree. It was, moreover, very censurably indecent—*filthy* is, perhaps, the more appropriate word. The press, without exception, or nearly so, condemned it in loud terms, without taking the trouble to investigate its pretensions as a literary work. But as "The Confessions of a Poet" was *one* of the best novels of its kind ever written in this country, so "The Vision of Rubeta" was decidedly *the best* satire. For its vulgarity and gross personality there is no defence, but its mordacity cannot be gainsaid. In calling it, however, the best American satire, I do not intend any excessive commendation—for it is, in fact, the *only* satire composed by an American. Trumbull's clumsy work is nothing at all, and then we have Halleck's "Croakers," which is very feeble—but what is there besides? "The Vision" is our best satire, and still a sadly deficient one. It was bold enough and bitter enough, and well constructed and decently versified, but it failed in *sarcasm* because its malignity was permitted to render itself evident. The author is never very severe because he is never sufficiently cool. We laugh not so much at the objects of his satire as we do at himself for getting into so great a passion. But, perhaps, under no circumstances is wit the *forte* of Mr. Osborn. He has few equals at downright invective.

The "Vision" was succeeded by "Arthur Carryl and other Poems," including an additional canto of the satire, and several happy although not in all cases accurate or comprehensive imitations in English of the Greek and Roman metres. "Arthur Carryl" is a fragment, in the manner of "Don Juan." I do not think it especially meritorious. It has, however, a truth-telling and discriminative preface, and its notes are well worthy perusal. Some opinions embraced in these latter on the topic of versification I have examined in an article called "Marginalia" published lately in "The Democratic Review."

I am not aware that since "Arthur Carryl" Mr. Osborn has written anything more than a "Treatise on Oil Painting," issued not long ago by Messrs. Wiley and Putnam. This work is highly spoken of by those well qualified to judge, but is, I believe, principally a compilation or compendium.

In personal character Mr. O. is one of the most remarkable men I ever yet had the pleasure of meeting. He is undoubtedly one of "Nature's own noblemen," full of generosity, courage, honour—chivalrous in every respect, but, unhappily, carrying his ideas of chivalry, or rather of independence, to the point of Quixotism, if not of absolute insanity. He has no doubt been misapprehended, and therefore wronged by the world; but he should not fail to remember that the source of the wrong lay in his own idiosyncrasy—one altogether unintelligible and unappreciable by the mass of mankind.

He is a member of one of the oldest and most influential, formerly one of the wealthiest families in New York. His acquirements and accomplishments are many and unusual. As poet, painter and musician, he has succeeded nearly equally well, and absolutely succeeded as each. His scholarship is extensive. In the French and Italian languages he is quite at home, and in everything he is thorough and accurate. His critical abilities are to be highly respected, although he is apt to swear somewhat too roundly by Johnson and Pope. Imagination is not Mr. Osborn's *forte*.

He is about thirty-two or three—certainly not more than thirty-five years of age. In person he is well made, probably five feet ten or eleven, muscular and active. Hair, eyes and complexion, rather light; fine teeth; the whole expression of the countenance manly, frank, and prepossessing in the highest degree.

Godey's Lady's Book, June 1846

Fitz-Greene Halleck

The name of *Halleck* is at least as well established in the poetical world as that of any American. Our principal poets are, perhaps, most frequently named in this order—Bryant, Halleck, Dana, Sprague, Longfellow, Willis, and so on—Halleck coming second in the series, but holding, in fact, a rank in the public opinion quite equal to that of Bryant. The accuracy of the arrangement as above made may, indeed, be questioned. For my own part, I should have it thus—Longfellow, Bryant, Halleck, Willis, Sprague, Dana; and, estimating rather the poetic capacity than the poems actually accomplished, there are three or four comparatively unknown writers whom I would place in the series between Bryant and Halleck, while there are about a dozen whom I should assign a position between Willis and Sprague. Two dozen at least might find room between Sprague and Dana—this latter, I fear, owing a very large portion of his reputation to his *quondam* editorial connection with "The North American Review." One or two poets now in my minds eye I should have no hesitation in posting above even Mr. Longfellow—still not intending this as very extravagant praise.

It is noticeable, however, that, in the arrangement which I attribute to the popular understanding, the order observed is nearly, if not exactly, that of the ages—the poetic ages—of the individual poets. Those rank first who were first known. The priority has established the strength of impression. Nor is this result to be accounted for by mere reference to the old saw—that first impressions are the strongest. Gratitude, surprise, and a species of hyper-patriotic triumph have been blended, and finally confounded with admiration or appreciation in regard to the *pioneers* of American literature, among whom there is not one whose productions have not been grossly overrated by his countrymen. Hitherto we have been in no mood to view with calmness and discuss with discrimination the real claims of the few who were *first* in convincing the mother country that her sons were not all brainless, as at one period she half affected and wholly wished to believe. Is there any one so blind as not to see that Mr. Cooper, for example, owes much, and Mr. Paulding nearly all, of his reputation as a novelist to his early occupation of the field? Is there any one so dull as not to know that fictions which neither of these gentlemen *could* have written are written daily by native authors, without attracting much more of commendation than can be included in a newspaper paragraph? And, again, is there any one so prejudiced as not to acknowledge that all this happens because there is no longer either reason or wit in the query, "Who reads an American book?"

I mean to say, of course, that Mr. Halleck, in the *apparent* public estimate, maintains a somewhat better position than that to which, on absolute grounds, he is entitled. There is something, too, in the *bonhommie* of certain of his compositions—something altogether distinct from poetic merit—which has aided to establish him; and much, also, must be admitted on the score of his personal popularity, which is deservedly great. With all these allowances, however, there will still be found a large amount of poetical fame to which he is *fairly* entitled.

He has written very little, although he began at an early age—when quite a boy, indeed. His "juvenile" works, however, have been kept very judiciously from the public eye. Attention was first called to him by his satires signed "Croaker" and "Croaker & Co.," published in "The New York Evening Post," in 1819. Of these the pieces with the signature "*Croaker & Co.*" were the joint work of Halleck and his friend Drake. The political and personal features of these *jeux d'esprit* gave them a consequence and a notoriety to which they are entitled on no other account. They are not without a species of drollery, but are loosely and no doubt carelessly written.

Neither was "Fanny," which closely followed the "Croakers," constructed with any great deliberation. "It was printed," say the ordinary memoirs, "within three weeks from its commencement;" but the truth is, that a couple of days would have been an ample allowance of time for any such composition. If we except a certain gentlemanly ease and *insouciance*, with some fancy of illustration, there is really very little about this poem to be admired. There has been no positive avowal of its authorship, although there can be no doubt of its having been written by Halleck. He, I presume, does not esteem it very highly. It is a mere extravaganza, in close imitation of "Don Juan"—a vehicle for squibs at cotemporary persons and things.

Our poet, indeed, seems to have been much impressed by "Don Juan," and attempts to engraft its farcicalities even upon the grace and delicacy of "Alnwick Castle;" as, for example, in—

> "Men in the coal and cattle line,
>   From Teviot's bard and hero land,
>   From royal Berwick's beach of sand,
>   From Wooler, Morpeth, Hexham, *and*
> Newcastle upon Tyne."

These things may lay claim to oddity, but no more. They are totally out of keeping with the tone of the sweet poem into which they are thus clumsily introduced, and serve no other purpose than to deprive it of all unity of effect. If a poet *must* be farcical, let him be just that; he can be nothing better at the same moment. To be drolly sentimental, or even sentimentally droll, is intolerable to men and gods and columns.

"Alnwick Castle" is distinguished, in general, by that air of quiet grace, both in thought and expression, which is the prevailing feature of the muse of Halleck. Its second stanza is a good specimen of this manner. The commencement of the fourth belongs to a very high order of poetry.

> "Wild roses by the Abbey towers
>   Are gay in their young bud and bloom—
> *They were born of a race of funeral flowers*
> That garlanded, in long-gone hours,
>   A Templar's knightly tomb."

This is gloriously imaginative, and the effect is singularly increased by the sudden transition from iambuses to anapæsts. The passage is, I think, the noblest to be found in Halleck, and I would be at a loss to discover its parallel in all American poetry.

"Marco Bozzaris" has much lyrical, without any great amount of *ideal* beauty. Force is its prevailing feature—force resulting rather from well-ordered metre, vigorous rhythm, and a judicious disposal of the circumstances of the poem, than from any of the truer lyric material. I should do my conscience great wrong were I to speak of "Marco Bozzaris" as it is the fashion to speak of it, at least in print. Even as a lyric or ode it is surpassed by many American and a multitude of foreign compositions of a similar character.

"Burns" has numerous passages exemplifying its author's felicity of *expression*; as, for instance—

> "Such graves as his are pilgrim shrines—
> Shrines to no code or creed confined—
> *The Delphian vales, the Palestines,*
> *The Meccas of the mind.*"

And, again—

> "There have been loftier themes than his,
> *And longer scrolls and louder lyres,*
> *And lays lit up with Poesy's*
> *Purer and holier fires.*"

But to the *sentiment* involved in this last quatrain I feel disposed to yield an assent more thorough than might be expected. Burns, indeed, was the puppet of circumstance. As a poet, no person on the face of the earth has been more extravagantly, more absurdly overrated.

"The Poet's Daughter" is one of the most characteristic works of Halleck, abounding in his most distinctive traits, grace, expression, repose, *insouciance*. The vulgarity of

> "I'm busy in the cotton trade
> And sugar line,"

has, I rejoice to see, been omitted in the late editions. The eleventh stanza is certainly not English as it stands, and, besides, is quite unintelligible. What is the meaning of this—

> "But her who asks, though first among
> The good, the beautiful, the young,
> The birthright of a spell more strong
> Than these have brought her."

The "Lines on the Death of Joseph Rodman Drake" is, as a whole, one of the best poems of its author. Its simplicity and delicacy of sentiment will recommend it to all readers. It is, however, carelessly written, and the first quatrain,

> "Green be the turf above thee,
> Friend of my better days—
> None knew thee but to love thee,
> Nor named thee but to praise,"

although beautiful, bears too close a resemblance to the still more beautiful lines of Wordsworth—

> "She dwelt among the untrodden ways
> Beside the springs of Dove,
> A maid whom there were none to praise
> And very few to love."

In versification Mr. Halleck is much as usual, although in this regard Mr. Bryant has paid him numerous compliments. "Marco Bozzaris" has certainly some vigor of rhythm, but its author, in short, writes carelessly, loosely, and, as a matter of course, seldom effectively, so far as the outworks of literature are concerned.

Of late days he has nearly given up the muses, and we recognize his existence as a poet chiefly by occasional translations from the Spanish or German.

Personally, he is a man to be admired, respected, but more especially beloved. His address has all the captivating *bonhommie* which is the leading feature of his poetry, and, indeed, of his whole moral nature. With his friends he is all ardor, enthusiasm and cordiality, but to the world at large he is reserved, shunning society, into which he is seduced only with difficulty and upon rare occasions. The love of solitude seems to have become with him a passion.

He is a good modern linguist, and an excellent *belles lettres* scholar; in general, has read a great deal, although very discursively. He is what the world calls *ultra* in most of his opinions, more particularly about literature and politics, and is fond of broaching and supporting paradoxes. He converses fluently, with animation and zeal; is choice and accurate in his language, exceedingly quick at repartee and apt at anecdote. His manners are courteous, with dignity and a little tincture of Gallicism. His age is about fifty. In height he is probably five feet seven. He *has been* stout, but may now be called well-proportioned. His forehead is a noble one, broad, massive and intellectual, a little bald about the temples; eyes dark and brilliant, but not large; nose Grecian; chin prominent; mouth finely chiseled and full of expression, although the lips are thin;—his smile is peculiarly sweet.

In "Graham's Magazine" for September, 1843, there appeared an engraving of Mr. Halleck from a painting by Inman. The likeness conveys a good general idea of the man, but is far too stout and youthful-looking for his appearance at present.

His usual pursuits have been commercial, but he is now the principal superintendent of the business of Mr. John Jacob Astor. He is unmarried.

ANN S. STEPHENS

Mrs. Stephens has made no collection of her works, but has written much for the magazines, and well. Her compositions have been brief tales with occasional poems. She made her first "sensation" in obtaining a premium of four hundred dollars, offered for "the best prose story" by some one of our journals, her "Mary Derwent" proving the successful article. The *amount* of the prize, however—a much larger one than it has been the custom to offer—had more to do with the *éclât* of the success than had the positive merit of the tale, although this is very considerable. She has subsequently written several better things—"Malina Gray," for example, "Alice Copley," and "The Two Dukes." These are on serious subjects. In comic ones she has comparatively failed. She is fond of the bold, striking, trenchant—in a word, of the melo-dramatic; has a quick appreciation of the picturesque, and is not unskillful in delineations of character. She seizes adroitly on salient incidents and presents them with vividness to the eye, but in their combinations or adaptations she is by no means so thoroughly at home—that is to say, her plots are not so good as are their individual items. Her style is what the critics usually term "powerful," but lacks real power through its verboseness and floridity. It is, in fact, generally turgid—even bombastic—involved, needlessly parenthetical, and superabundant in epithets, although these latter are frequently well chosen. Her sentences are, also, for the most part too long; we forget their commencements ere we get at their terminations. Her faults, nevertheless, both in matter and manner, belong to the effervescence of high talent, if not exactly of genius.

Of Mrs. Stephens' poetry I have seen so very little that I feel myself scarcely in condition to speak of it.

She began her literary life, I believe, by editing "The Portland Magazine," and has since been announced as editress of "The Ladies' Companion," a monthly journal published some years ago in New York, and also, at a later period, of "Graham's Magazine," and subsequently, again, of "Peterson's National Magazine." These announcements were announcements and no more; the lady had nothing to do with the editorial control of either of the three last-named works.

The portrait of Mrs. Stephens which appeared in "Graham's Magazine" for November, 1844, cannot fairly be considered a likeness at all. She is tall and slightly inclined to *embonpoint*—an English figure. Her forehead is somewhat low, but broad; the features generally massive, but full of life and intellectuality. The eyes are blue and brilliant; the hair blonde and very luxuriant.

EVERT A. DUYCKINCK

Mr. Duyckinck is one of the most influential of the New York *littérateurs*, and has done a great deal for the interests of American letters. Not the least important service rendered by him was the projection and editorship of Wiley and Putnam's "Library of Choice Reading," a series which brought to pub-

lic notice many valuable foreign works which had been suffering under neglect in this country, and at the same time
afforded unwonted encouragement to native authors by publishing their books, in good style and in good company, without trouble or risk to the authors themselves, and in the very
teeth of the disadvantages arising from the want of an international copyright law. At one period it seemed that this
happy scheme was to be overwhelmed by the competition of
rival publishers—taken, in fact, quite out of the hands of
those who, by "right of discovery," were entitled at least to
its first fruits. A great variety of "Libraries" in imitation were
set on foot, but whatever may have been the temporary success of any of these latter, the original one had already too
well established itself in the public favor to be overthrown,
and thus has not been prevented from proving of great benefit to our literature at large.

Mr. Duyckinck has slyly acquired much fame and numerous admirers under the *nom de plume* of "Felix Merry." The
various essays thus signed have attracted attention everywhere
from the judicious. The style is remarkable for its very unusual blending of purity and ease with a seemingly inconsistent
originality, force and independence.

"Felix Merry," in connection with Mr. Cornelius Matthews, was one of the editors and originators of "Arcturus,"
decidedly the very best magazine in many respects ever published in the United States. A large number of its most interesting papers were the work of Mr. D. The magazine was,
upon the whole, a little *too good* to enjoy extensive popularity—although I am here using an equivocal phrase, for a
better journal might have been far more acceptable to the
public. I must be understood, then, as employing the epithet
"good" in the sense of the literary quietists. The general taste
of "Arcturus" was, I think, *excessively tasteful*; but this character applies rather more to its external or mechanical appearance than to its essential qualities. Unhappily, magazines and
other similar publications are in the beginning judged chiefly
by externals. People saw "Arcturus" *looking* very much like
other works which had failed through notorious dullness, although admitted as *arbitri elegantiarum* in all points of what
is termed taste or decorum; and they, the people, had no

patience to examine any farther. Cæsar's wife was required not only to *be* virtuous but to seem so, and in letters it is demanded not only that we be not stupid but that we do not array ourselves in the habiliments of stupidity.

It cannot be said of "Arcturus" exactly that it wanted *force*. It was deficient in power of impression, and this deficiency is to be attributed mainly to the exceeding brevity of its articles—a brevity that degenerated into mere paragraphism, precluding dissertation or argument, and thus all permanent effect. The magazine, in fact, had some of the worst or most inconvenient features without any of the compensating advantages of a weekly literary newspaper. The mannerism to which I refer seemed to have its source in undue admiration and consequent imitation of "The Spectator."

In addition to his more obvious literary engagements, Mr. Duyckinck writes a great deal, editorially and otherwise, for "The Democratic Review," "The Morning News," and other periodicals.

In character he is remarkable, distinguished for the *bonhommie* of his manner, his simplicity and single-mindedness, his active beneficence, his hatred of wrong done even to any enemy, and especially for an almost Quixotic fidelity to his friends. He seems in perpetual good humor with all things, and I have no doubt that in his secret heart he is an optimist.

In person he is equally simple as in character—the one is a *pendent* of the other. He is about five feet eight inches high, somewhat slender. The forehead, phrenologically, is a good one; eyes and hair light; the whole expression of the face that of serenity and benevolence, contributing to give an idea of youthfulness. He is probably thirty, but does not seem to be twenty-five. His dress, also, is in full keeping with his character, scrupulously neat but plain, and conveying an instantaneous conviction of the gentleman. He is a descendant of one of the oldest and best Dutch families in the state. Married.

MARY GOVE

Mrs. Mary Gove, under the pseudonym of "Mary Orme," has written many excellent papers for the magazines. Her subjects are usually tinctured with the mysticism of the transcendentalists, but are truly imaginative. Her style is quite remarkable for its luminousness and precision—two qualities very rare with her sex. An article entitled "The Gift of Prophecy," published originally in "The Broadway Journal," is a fine specimen of her manner.

Mrs. Gove, however, has acquired less notoriety by her literary compositions than by her lectures on physiology to classes of females. These lectures are said to have been instructive and useful; they certainly elicited much attention. Mrs. G. has also given public discourses on Mesmerism, I believe, and other similar themes—matters which put to the severest test the credulity or, more properly, the faith of mankind. She is, I think, a Mesmerist, a Swedenborgian, a phrenologist, a homœopathist, and a disciple of Priesstnitz—what more I am not prepared to say.

She is rather below the medium height, somewhat thin, with dark hair and keen, intelligent black eyes. She converses well and with enthusiasm. In many respects a very interesting woman.

JAMES ALDRICH

Mr. Aldrich has written much for the magazines, etc., and at one time assisted Mr. Park Benjamin in the conduct of "The New World." He also originated, I believe, and edited a not very long-lived or successful weekly paper, called "The Literary Gazette," an imitation in its external appearance of the London journal of the same name. I am not aware that he has made any collection of his writings. His poems abound in the true poetic spirit, but they are frequently chargeable with plagiarism, or something much like it. True, I have seen but three of Mr. Aldrich's compositions in verse—the three (or perhaps there are four of them) included by Doctor Griswold in his "Poets and Poetry of America." Of these three, (or four,) however, there are two which I cannot help regarding as palpable plagiarisms. Of one of them, in especial, "*A* Death-Bed," it is impossible to say a plausible word in defence. Both in matter and manner it is nearly identical with a little piece entitled "*The* Death-Bed," by Thomas Hood.

The charge of plagiarism, nevertheless, is a purely literary one; and a plagiarism even distinctly proved by no means necessarily involves any moral delinquency. This proposition applies very especially to what appear to be *poetical* thefts. The poetic sentiment presupposes a keen appreciation of the beautiful with a longing for its assimilation into the poetic identity. What the poet intensely admires becomes, thus, in very fact, although only partially, a portion of his own soul. Within this soul it has a secondary origination; and the poet, thus possessed by another's thought, cannot be said to take of it possession. But in either view he thoroughly feels it as *his own*; and the tendency to this feeling is counteracted only by the sensible presence of the true, palpable origin of the thought in the volume whence he has derived it—an origin which, in the long lapse of years, it is impossible *not* to forget, should the thought itself, as it often is, be forgotten. But the frailest association will regenerate it; it springs up with all the vigor of a new birth; its absolute originality is not with the poet a matter even of suspicion; and when he has written it and printed it, and on its account is charged with plagiarism, there will be no one more entirely astounded than himself. Now, from what I have said, it appears that the liability to accidents of this character is in the direct ratio of the poetic sentiment, of the susceptibility to the poetic impression; and, in fact, all literary history demonstrates that, for the most frequent and palpable plagiarisms we must search the works of the most eminent poets.

Since penning the above I have found five quatrains by Mr. Aldrich, with the heading "Molly Gray." These verses are in the fullest exemplification of what I have just said of their author, evincing at once, in the most remarkable manner, both his merit as an imaginative poet and his unconquerable proneness to imitation. I quote the two concluding quatrains.

> "Pretty, fairy Molly Gray!
>   What may thy fit emblems be?
> Stream or star or bird or flower—
>   They are all too poor for thee.

> "No type to match thy beauty
>   My wandering fancy brings—
> *Not fairer than its chrysalis*
>   *Thy soul with its golden wings.*"

Here the "Pretty, fairy Molly Gray!" will put every reader in mind of Tennyson's "Airy, fairy Lillian!" by which Mr. Aldrich's whole poem has been clearly suggested; but the thought in the *finale* is, as far as I know anything about it, original, and is not more happy than happily expressed.

Mr. Aldrich is about thirty-six years of age. In regard to his person there is nothing to be especially noted.

THOMAS DUNN ENGLISH

I have seen one or two brief poems of considerable merit with the signature of *Thomas Dunn English* appended. For example—

"AZTHENE.

"A sound melodious shook the breeze
   When thy beloved name was heard:
   Such was the music in the word
   Its dainty rhythm the pulses stirred.
But passed forever joys like these.
   There is no joy, no light, no day;
   But black despair and night alway,
      And thickening gloom:
And this, Azthene, is my doom.

"Was it for this, for weary years,
   I strove among the sons of men,
   And by the magic of my pen—
   Just sorcery—walked the lion's den
Of slander void of tears and fears—
   And all for thee? For thee!—alas,
   As is the image on a glass
      So baseless seems,
Azthene, all my earthly dreams."

I must confess, however, that I do not appreciate the "dainty rhythm" of such a word as "Azthene," and, perhaps, there is a little taint of egotism in the passage about "the magic" of Mr. English's pen. Let us be charitable, however, and set all this down under the head of "pure imagination" or invention—one of the first of poetical requisites. The *inexcusable* sin of Mr. E. is imitation—if this be not too mild a term. Barry Cornwall and others of the *bizarre* school are his especial favorites. He has taken, too, most unwarrantable liberties, in the way of downright plagiarism, from a Philadelphian poet whose high merits have not been properly appreciated—*Mr. Henry B. Hirst*.

I place Mr. English, however, on my list of New York *literati*, not on account of his poetry, (which I presume he is not weak enough to estimate very highly,) but on the score of his having edited for several months, "with the aid of numerous collaborators," a monthly magazine called "The Aristidean." This work, although professedly a "monthly," was issued at irregular intervals, and was unfortunate, I fear, in not attaining at any period a very extensive circulation.

I learn that Mr. E. is not without talent; but the fate of "The Aristidean" should indicate to him the necessity of applying himself to study. No spectacle can be more pitiable than that of a man without the commonest school education busying himself in attempts to instruct mankind on topics of polite literature. The absurdity in such cases does not lie merely in the ignorance displayed by the would-be instructor, but in the transparency of the shifts by which he endeavours to keep this ignorance concealed. The editor of "The Aristidean," for example, was not laughed at so much on account of writing "lay" for "lie," etc. etc., and coupling nouns in the plural with verbs in the singular—as where he writes, above,

> "——so baseless *seems*,
> Azthene, all my earthly *dreams*—"

he was not, I say, laughed at *so much* for his excusable deficiencies in English grammar (although an editor should certainly be able to write *his own name*) as that, in the hope of disguising such deficiency, he was perpetually lamenting the "typographical blunders" that "in the most unaccountable manner" *would* creep into his work. Nobody was so stupid as to suppose for a moment that there existed in New York a single proof-reader—or even a single printer's devil—who would have permitted *such* errors to escape. By the excuses offered, therefore, the errors were only the more obviously nailed to the counter as Mr. English's own.

I make these remarks in no spirit of unkindness. Mr. E. is yet young—certainly not more than thirty-five—and might, with his talents, readily improve himself at points where he is most defective. No one of any generosity would think the worse of him for getting private instruction.

I do not personally know Mr. English. He is, I believe, from Philadelphia, where he was formerly a doctor of medicine, and subsequently took up the profession of law; more latterly he joined the Tyler party and devoted his attention to politics. About his personal appearance there is nothing very observable. I cannot say whether he is married or not.

HENRY CARY

Doctor Griswold introduces *Mr. Cary* to the appendix of "The Poets and Poetry," as Mr. Henry Car*ey*, and gives him credit for an Anacreontic song of much merit entitled, or commencing, "Old Wine to Drink." This was *not* written by Mr. C. He has composed little verse, if any, but, under the *nom de plume* of "John Waters," has acquired some note by a series of prose essays in "The New York American" and "The Knickerbocker." These essays have merit, unquestionably, but some person, in an article furnished "The Broadway Journal," before my assumption of its editorship, has gone to the extreme of toadyism in their praise. This critic (possibly Mr. Briggs) thinks that John Waters "is in some sort a Sam Rogers"—"resembles Lamb in fastidiousness of taste"—"has a finer artistic taste than the author of the 'Sketch Book' "—that his "sentences are the most perfect in the language—too perfect to be peculiar"—that "it would be a vain task to hunt through them all for a superfluous conjunction," and that " we need them (the works of John Waters!) as models of style in these days of rhodomontades and *Macaulayisms*!"

The truth seems to be that Mr. Cary is a vivacious, fanciful, entertaining essayist—a fifth or sixth rate one—with a style that, as times go—in view of such stylists as Mr. Briggs, for example—may be termed respectable, and no more. What the critic of the B. J. wishes us to understand by a style that is "too perfect," "the most perfect," etc., it is scarcely worth while to inquire, since it is generally supposed that "perfect" admits of no degrees of comparison; but if Mr. Briggs (or whoever it is) finds it "a vain task to hunt" through all Mr. John Waters' works "for a superfluous conjunction," there are few school-boys who would not prove more successful hunters than Mr. Briggs.

"It was well filled," says the essayist, on the very page containing these encomiums, "*and* yet the number of performers," etc. "We paid our visit to the incomparable ruins of the castle, *and* then proceeded to retrace our steps, and, examining our wheels at every post-house, reached," etc. "After consultation with a mechanic at Heidelberg, *and* finding that," etc. The last sentence should read, "Finding, after consultation," etc.—the "and" would thus be avoided. Those in the two sentences first quoted are obviously pleonastic. Mr. Cary, in fact, abounds *very especially* in superfluities—(as here, for example, "He seated himself at a piano *that was* near the front of the stage")—and, to speak the truth, is continually guilty of all kinds of grammatical improprieties. I repeat that, in this respect, he is decent, and no more.

Mr. Cary is what Doctor Griswold calls a "gentleman of elegant leisure." He is wealthy and much addicted to letters and *virtù*. For a long time he was President of the Phœnix Bank of New York, and the principal part of his life has been devoted to business. There is nothing remarkable about his personal appearance.

CHRISTOPHER PEASE CRANCH

The Reverend C. P. Cranch is one of the least intolerable of the school of Boston transcendentalists—and, in fact, I believe that he has at last "come out from among them," abandoned their doctrines (whatever they are) and given up their company in disgust. He was at one time one of the most noted, and undoubtedly one of the least absurd contributors to "The Dial," but has reformed his habits of thought and speech, domiciliated himself in New York, and set up the easel of an artist in one of the Gothic chambers of the University.

About two years ago a volume of "Poems by Christopher

Pease Cranch" was published by Carey & Hart. It was most unmercifully treated by the critics, and much injustice, in my opinion, was done to the poet. He seems to me to possess unusual vivacity of fancy and dexterity of expression, while his versification is remarkable for its accuracy, vigor, and even for its originality of effect. I might say, perhaps, rather more than all this, and maintain that he has imagination if he would only condescend to employ it, which he will not, or *would* not until lately—the word-compounders and quibble concoctors of Frogpondium having inoculated him with a preference for Imagination's half sister, the Cinderella, Fancy. Mr. Cranch has seldom contented himself with harmonious combinations of thought. There must always be, to afford him perfect satisfaction, a certain amount of the odd, of the whimsical, of the affected, of the *bizarre*. He is as full of absurd conceits as Cowley or Donne, with this difference, that the conceits of these latter are Euphuisms beyond redemption—flat, irremediable, self-contented nonsensicalities, and in so much are good of their kind; but the conceits of Mr. Cranch are, for the most part, conceits intentionally manufactured, for conceit's sake, out of the material for properly imaginative, harmonious, proportionate, or poetical ideas. We see every moment that he has been at uncommon *pains* to make a fool of himself.

But perhaps I am wrong in supposing that I am at all in condition to decide on the merits of Mr. C.'s poetry, which is professedly addressed to the few. "Him we will seek," says the poet—

> "Him we will seek, and none but him,
>   Whose inward sense hath not grown dim;
>   Whose soul is steeped in Nature's tinct,
>   And to the Universal linked;
>   Who loves the beauteous Infinite
>   With deep and ever new delight,
>   And carrieth where'er he goes
>   The inborn sweetness of the rose,
>   The perfume as of Paradise—
>   The talisman above all price—
>   The optic glass that wins from far
>   The meaning of the utmost star—

The key that opes the golden doors
Where earth and heaven have piled their stores—
The magic ring, the enchanter's wand—
The title-deed to Wonder-Land—
The wisdom that o'erlooketh sense,
The clairvoyance of Innocence."

This is all very well, fanciful, pretty and neatly turned—all
with the exception of the two last lines, and it is a pity they
were not left out. It is laughable to see that the transcendental
poets, if beguiled for a minute or two into respectable English
and common sense, are always sure to remember their cue
just as they get to the end of their song, which, by way of
salvo, they then round off with a bit of doggerel about "wisdom that o'erlook*eth* sense" and "the clairvoyance of Innocence." It is especially observable that, in adopting the cant of
thought, the cant of phraseology is adopted at the same instant. Can Mr. Cranch, or can anybody else, inform me why
it is that, in the really sensible opening passages of what I have
here quoted, he employs the modern, and only in the final
couplet of goosetherumfoodle makes use of the obsolete terminations of verbs in the third person singular, present tense?

One of the best of Mr. Cranch's compositions is undoubtedly his poem on *Niagara*. It has some natural thoughts, and
grand ones, suiting the subject; but then they are more than
half-divested of their nature by the attempt at adorning them
with *oddity* of expression. *Quaintness* is an admissible and important adjunct to ideality—an adjunct whose value has been
long misapprehended—but in picturing the sublime it is altogether out of place. What idea of power, of grandeur, for
example, can any human being connect even with Niagara,
when Niagara is described in language so trippingly fantastical, so palpably adapted to a purpose, as that which follows?

"I stood upon a speck of ground;
    Before me fell a stormy ocean.
  I was like a captive bound;
        And around
        A universe of sound
Troubled the heavens with ever-quivering motion.

"Down, down forever—down, down forever—
　　Something falling, falling, falling;
　Up, up forever—up, up, forever,
　　　Resting never,
　　　Boiling up forever,
Steam-clouds shot up with thunder-bursts appalling."

It is difficult to conceive anything more ludicrously out of keeping than the thoughts of these stanzas and the *petit-maître*, fidgety, hop-skip-and-jump air of the words and the Liliputian parts of the versification.

A somewhat similar metre is adopted by Mr. C. in his "Lines on Hearing Triumphant Music," but as the subject is essentially different, so the effect is by no means so displeasing. I copy one of the stanzas as the noblest individual passage which I can find among all the poems of its author.

"That glorious strain!
　　Oh, from my brain
I see the shadows flitting like scared ghosts.
　　A light—a light
　　Shines in to-night
Round the good angels trooping to their posts,
　　And the black cloud is rent in twain
　　Before the ascending strain."

Mr. Cranch is well educated, and quite accomplished. Like Mr. Osborn, he is musician, painter and poet, being in each capacity very respectably successful.

He is about thirty-three or four years of age; in height, perhaps five feet eleven; athletic; front face not unhandsome—the forehead evincing intellect, and the smile pleasant; but the profile is marred by the turning up of the nose, and, altogether is hard and disagreeable. His eyes and hair are dark brown—the latter worn short, slightly inclined to curl. Thick whiskers meeting under the chin, and much out of keeping with the shirt-collar *à la Byron*. Dresses with marked plainness. He is married.

Godey's Lady's Book, July 1846

SARAH MARGARET FULLER

Miss Fuller was at one time editor, or one of the editors of "The Dial," to which she contributed many of the most forcible, and certainly some of the most peculiar papers. She is known, too, by "Summer on the Lakes," a remarkable assemblage of sketches, issued in 1844 by Little & Brown, of Boston. More lately she has published "Woman in the Nineteenth Century," a work which has occasioned much discussion, having had the good fortune to be warmly abused and chivalrously defended. At present, she is assistant editor of "The New York Tribune," or rather a salaried contributor to that journal, for which she has furnished a great variety of matter, chiefly critical notices of new books, etc. etc., her articles being designated by an asterisk. Two of the best of them were a review of Professor Longfellow's late magnificent edition of his own works, (with a portrait,) and an appeal to the public in behalf of her friend Harro Harring. The review did her infinite credit; it was frank, candid, independent—in even ludicrous contrast to the usual mere glorifications of the day, giving honor *only* where honor was due, yet evincing the most thorough capacity to appreciate and the most sincere intention to place in the fairest light the real and idiosyncratic merits of the poet.

In my opinion it is one of the very few reviews of Longfellow's poems, ever published in America, of which the critics have not had abundant reason to be ashamed. Mr. Longfellow is entitled to a certain and very distinguished rank among the poets of his country, but that country is disgraced by the evident toadyism which would award to his social position and influence, to his fine paper and large type, to his morocco binding and gilt edges, to his flattering portrait of himself, and to the illustrations of his poems by Huntingdon, that amount of indiscriminate approbation which neither could nor would have been given to the poems themselves.

The defence of Harro Harring, or rather the Philippic against those who were doing him wrong, was one of the most eloquent and well-*put* articles I have ever yet seen in a newspaper.

"Woman in the Nineteenth Century" is a book which few women in the country could have written, and no woman in the country would have published, with the exception of Miss Fuller. In the way of independence, of unmitigated radicalism, it is one of the "Curiosities of American Literature," and Doctor Griswold should include it in his book. I need scarcely say that the essay is nervous, forcible, thoughtful, suggestive, brilliant, and to a certain extent scholar-like—for all that Miss Fuller produces is entitled to those epithets—but I must say that the conclusions reached are only in part my own. Not that they are too bold, by any means—too novel, too startling, or too dangerous in their consequences, but that in their attainment too many premises have been distorted and too many analogical inferences left altogether out of sight. I mean to say that the intention of the Deity as regards sexual differences—an intention which can be distinctly comprehended only by throwing the exterior (more sensitive) portions of the mental retina *casually* over the wide field of universal *analogy*—I mean to say that this *intention* has not been sufficiently considered. Miss Fuller has erred, too, through her own excessive objectiveness. She judges *woman* by the heart and intellect of Miss Fuller, but there are not more than one or two dozen Miss Fullers on the whole face of the earth. Holding these opinions in regard to "Woman in the Nineteenth Century," I still feel myself called upon to disavow the silly, condemnatory criticism of the work which appeared in one of the earlier numbers of "The Broadway Journal." That article was *not* written by myself, and *was* written by my associate Mr. Briggs.

The most favorable estimate of Miss Fuller's genius (for high genius she unquestionably possesses) is to be obtained, perhaps, from her contributions to "The Dial," and from her "Summer on the Lakes." Many of the *descriptions* in this volume are unrivaled for *graphicality*, (why is there not such a word?) for the force with which they convey the true by the novel or unexpected, by the introduction of touches which other artists would be sure to omit as irrelevant to the subject. This faculty, too, springs from her subjectiveness, which leads her to paint a scene less by its features than by its effects.

Here, for example, is a portion of her account of Niagara:—

"Daily these proportions widened and towered more and more upon my sight, and I got at last a proper foreground for these sublime distances. Before coming away, I think I really saw the full wonder of the scene. After awhile it *so drew me into itself as to inspire an undefined dread, such as I never knew before, such as may be felt when death is about to usher us into a new existence.* The perpetual trampling of the waters seized my senses. *I felt that no other sound, however near, could be heard, and would start and look behind me for a foe.* I realized the identity of that mood of nature in which these waters were poured down with such absorbing force, with that in which the Indian was shaped on the same soil. For continually upon my mind came, unsought and unwelcome, *images, such as had never haunted it before, of naked savages stealing behind me with uplifted tomahawks.* Again and again this illusion recurred, and even *after I had thought it over and tried to shake it off, I could not help starting and looking behind me.* What I liked best was to sit on Table Rock close to the great fall; *there all power of observing details, all separate consciousness was quite lost.*"

The truthfulness of the passages italicized will be felt by all; the feelings described are, perhaps, experienced by every (imaginative) person who visits the fall; but most persons, through predominant subjectiveness, would scarcely be conscious of the feelings, or, at best, would never think of employing them in an attempt to convey to others an impression of the scene. Hence so many desperate failures to convey it on the part of ordinary tourists. Mr. William W. Lord, to be sure, in his poem "Niagara," is sufficiently objective; he describes not the fall, but very properly the effect of the fall upon *him*. He says that it made him think of his *own* greatness, of his *own* superiority, and so forth, and so forth; and it is only when we come to think that the thought of Mr. Lord's greatness is quite idiosyncratic, confined exclusively to Mr. Lord, that we are in condition to understand how, in despite of his objectiveness, he has failed to convey an idea of anything beyond one Mr. William W. Lord.

From the essay entitled "Philip Van Artevelde," I copy a paragraph which will serve at once to exemplify Miss Fuller's more earnest (declamatory) style, and to show the tenor of her prospective speculations:—

"At Chicago I read again 'Philip Van Artevelde,' and certain passages in it will always be in my mind associated with the deep sound of the lake, as heard in the night. I used to read a short time at night, and then open the blind to look out. The moon would be full upon the lake, and the calm breath, pure light, and the deep voice, harmonized well with the thought of the Flemish hero. When will this country have such a man? It is what she needs—no thin Idealist, no coarse Realist, but a man whose eye reads the heavens while his feet step firmly on the ground and his hands are strong and dextrous in the use of human instruments. A man, religious, virtuous and—sagacious; a man of universal sympathies, but self-possessed; a man who knows the region of emotion, though he is not its slave; a man to whom this world is no mere spectacle or fleeting shadow, but a great, solemn game, to be played with good heed, for its stakes are of eternal value, yet who, if his own play be true, heeds not what he loses by the falsehood of others. A man who lives from the past, yet knows that its honey can but moderately avail him; whose comprehensive eye scans the present, neither infatuated by its golden lures nor chilled by its many ventures; who possesses prescience, as the wise man must, but not so far as to be driven mad to-day by the gift which discerns to-morrow. When there is such a man for America, the thought which urges her on will be expressed."

From what I have quoted a *general* conception of the prose style of the authoress may be gathered. Her manner, however, is infinitely varied. It is always forcible—but I am not sure that it is always anything else, unless I say picturesque. It rather indicates than evinces scholarship. Perhaps only the scholastic, or, more properly, those accustomed to look narrowly at the structure of phrases, would be willing to acquit her of ignorance of grammar—would be willing to attribute her slovenliness to disregard of the shell in anxiety for the kernel; or to waywardness, or to affectation, or to blind reverence for Carlyle—would be able to detect, in her strange and continual inaccuracies, a capacity for the accurate.

"I cannot sympathize with such an apprehension: the spectacle is *capable to* swallow *up* all such objects."

"It is fearful, too, to know, as you look, that whatever has been swallowed by the cataract, is *like* to rise suddenly to light."

"I took our *mutual* friends to see her."

"It was always obvious that they had nothing in common *between them*."

"The Indian cannot be looked at truly *except* by a poetic eye."

"McKenney's Tour to the Lakes gives some facts not to be met *with* elsewhere."

"There is that mixture of culture and rudeness in the aspect of things *as* gives a feeling of freedom," etc. etc. etc.

These are merely a few, a very few instances, taken at random from among a multitude of *wilful* murders committed by Miss Fuller on the American of President Polk. She uses, too, the word "ignore," a vulgarity adopted only of late days (and to no good purpose, since there is no necessity for it) from the barbarisms of the law, and makes no scruple of giving the Yankee interpretation to the verbs "witness" and "realize," to say nothing of "use," as in the sentence, "I used to read a short time at night." It will not do to say, in defence of such words, that in such senses they may be found in certain dictionaries—in that of Bolles', for instance;—*some* kind of "authority" may be found for *any* kind of vulgarity under the sun.

In spite of these things, however, and of her frequent unjustifiable Carlyleisms, (such as that of writing sentences which are no sentences, since, to be parsed, reference must be had to sentences preceding,) the style of Miss Fuller is one of the very best with which I am acquainted. In general effect, I know no style which surpasses it. It is singularly piquant, vivid, terse, bold, luminous—leaving details out of sight, it is everything that a style need be.

I believe that Miss Fuller has written much poetry, although she has published little. That little is tainted with the affectation of the *transcendentalists*, (I use this term, of course, in the sense which the public of late days seem resolved to give it,) but is brimful of the poetic *sentiment*. Here, for example, is something in Coleridge's manner, of which the author of "Genevieve" might have had no reason to be ashamed:—

> "A maiden sat beneath a tree;
>   Tear-bedewed her pale cheeks be,
>   And she sigheth heavily.
>
> "From forth the wood into the *light*
>   A hunter strides with carol *light*,
>   And a glance so bold and bright.
>
> "He careless stopped and eyed the maid:
>   'Why weepest thou?' he gently said;
>   'I love thee well, be not afraid.'
>
> "He takes her hand and leads her on—
>   She should have waited there alone,
>   For he was not her chosen one.
>
> "He *leans* her head upon his breast—
>   She knew 'twas not her home of rest,
>   But, ah, she had been sore distrest.
>
> "The sacred stars looked sadly down;
>   The parting moon appeared to frown,
>   To see thus dimmed the diamond crown.
>
> "Then from the thicket starts a deer—
>   The huntsman, seizing *on* his spear
>   Cries, 'Maiden, wait thou for me here.'

"She sees him vanish into night—
She starts from sleep in deep affright,
For it was not her own true knight.

"Though but in dream Gunhilda failed—
Though but a fancied ill assailed—
Though she but fancied fault bewailed—

"Yet thought of day makes dream of night;
She is not worthy of the knight;
The inmost altar burns not bright.

"If loneliness thou canst not bear—
Cannot the dragon's venom dare—
Of the pure meed thou shoulds't despair.

"Now sadder that lone maiden sighs;
Far bitterer tears profane her eyes;
Crushed in the dust her heart's flower lies."

To show the evident carelessness with which this poem was constructed, I have italicized an identical rhyme (of about the same force in versification as an identical proposition in logic) and two grammatical improprieties. *To lean* is a neuter verb, and "seizing *on*" is not properly to be called a pleonasm, merely because it is—nothing at all. The concluding line is difficult of pronunciation through excess of consonants. I should have preferred, indeed, the ante-penultimate tristich as the *finale* of the poem.

The supposition that the book of an author is a thing apart from the author's self, is, I think, ill-founded. The soul is a cypher, in the sense of a cryptograph; and the shorter a cryptograph is, the more difficulty there is in its comprehension—at a certain point of brevity it would bid defiance to an army of Champollions. And thus he who has written very little, may in that little either conceal his spirit or convey quite an erroneous idea of it—of his acquirements, talents, temper, manner, tenor and depth (or shallowness) of thought—in a word, of his character, of himself. But this is impossible with him who has written much. Of such a person we get, from his books, not merely a just, but the most just representation. Bulwer, the individual, personal man, in a green velvet waistcoat and amber gloves, is not by any means the veritable Sir Edward Lytton, who is discoverable only in "Ernest Maltravers," where his soul is deliberately and nakedly set forth. And who would ever know Dickens by looking at him or talking with him, or doing anything with him except reading his "Curiosity Shop?" What poet, in especial, but must feel at least the better portion of himself more fairly represented in even his commonest sonnet (earnestly written) than in his most elaborate or most intimate personalities?

I put all this as a general proposition, to which Miss Fuller affords a marked exception—to this extent, that her personal character and her printed book are merely one and the same thing. We get access to her soul *as* directly from the one as from the other—no *more* readily from this than from that—easily from either. Her acts are bookish, and her books are less thoughts than acts. Her literary and her conversational manner are identical. Here is a passage from her "Summer on the Lakes:"—

"The rapids enchanted me far beyond what I expected; they are so swift that they cease to *seem* so—you can think only of their *beauty*. The fountain beyond the Moss islands I discovered for myself, and thought it for some time an *accidental* beauty which it would not do to *leave*, lest I might never see it again. After I found it *permanent*, I returned many times to watch the play of its crest. In the little waterfall beyond, Nature seems, as she often does, to have made a *study* for some larger design. She delights in this—a sketch within a sketch—a dream within *a dream*. Wherever we see it, the lines of the great buttress in the fragment of stone, the hues of the waterfall, copied in the flowers that *star* its bordering mosses, we are *delighted*; for all the lineaments become *fluent*, and we mould the scene in congenial thought with its *genius*."

Now all this is precisely as Miss Fuller would *speak* it. She is perpetually saying just such things in just such words. To get the *conversational* woman in the mind's eye, all that is needed is to imagine her reciting the paragraph just quoted: but first let us have the *personal* woman. She is of the medium height; nothing remarkable about the figure; a profusion of lustrous light hair; eyes a bluish gray, full of fire; capacious forehead; the mouth when in repose indicates profound sensibility, capacity for affection, for love—when moved by a slight smile, it becomes even beautiful in the intensity of this expression; but the upper lip, as if impelled by the action of involuntary muscles, habitually uplifts itself, conveying the impression of a sneer. Imagine, now, a person of this description looking you at one moment earnestly in the face, at the next seeming to look only within her own spirit or at the wall; moving nervously every now and then in her chair; speaking in a high key, but musically, deliberately, (not hurriedly or loudly,) with a delicious distinctness of enunciation—speaking, I say, the paragraph in question, and emphasizing the words which I have italicized, not by impulsion of the breath, (as is usual,) but by drawing them out as long as possible, nearly closing her eyes the while—imagine all this, and we have both the woman and the authoress before us.

JAMES LAWSON

Mr. Lawson has himself made little effort in the field of literary labor, but is distinguished for his zeal and liberality in the good cause. He is by birth a Scotchman, but few men have more ardently at heart the welfare of American letters.

His works, so far as published in volume form, are few. I know only of "Giordano, a tragedy," and two volumes entitled "Tales and Sketches by a Cosmopolite." The former was performed some years ago, (at the Park, I believe,) and with no great success. The latter were more popular. One of them, "The Dapper Gentleman's Story," is a very clever imitation of the manner of Irving, and has "gone the rounds of the press."

Mr. Lawson is of social habits and warm sympathies. He is enthusiastic, especially in matters of art or taste; converses fluently, tells a capital story, and is generally respected and beloved.

CAROLINE M. KIRKLAND

Mrs. Kirkland's "New Home," published under the *nom de plume* of "Mary Clavers," wrought an undoubted sensation. The cause lay not so much in picturesque description, in racy humor, or in animated individual portraiture, as in *truth* and novelty. The west at the time was a field comparatively untrodden by the sketcher or the novelist. In certain works, to be sure, we had obtained brief glimpses of character strange to us sojourners in the civilized east, but to Mrs. Kirkland alone we were indebted for our acquaintance with the *home* and home-life of the backwoodsman. With a fidelity and vigor that prove her pictures to be taken from the very life, she has represented "scenes" that could have occurred only *as* and *where* she has described them. She has placed before us the veritable settlers of the forest, with all their peculiarities, national and individual; their free and fearless spirit; their homely utilitarian views; their shrewd out-looking for self-interest; their thrifty care and inventions multiform; their coarseness of manner, united with real delicacy and substantial kindness when their sympathies are called into action—in a word, with all the characteristics of the Yankee, in a region where the salient points of character are unsmoothed by contact with society. So life-like were her representations that they have been appropriated as individual portraits by many who have been disposed to plead, trumpet-tongued, against what they supposed to be "the deep damnation of their taking-off."

"Forest Life" succeeded "A New Home," and was read with equal interest. It gives us, perhaps, more of the philosophy of western life, but has the same freshness, freedom, piquancy. Of course, a truthful picture of pioneer habits could never be given in any grave history or essay so well as in the form of narration, where each character is permitted to develop itself; narration, therefore, was very properly adopted by Mrs. Kirkland in both the books just mentioned, and even more entirely in her later volume, "Western Clearings." This is the title of a collection of tales, illustrative, in general, of Western manners, customs, ideas. "The Land Fever" is a story of the wild days when the madness of speculation in land was at its height. It is a richly characteristic sketch, as is also "The Ball at Thram's Huddle." Only those who have had the fortune to visit or live in the "back settlements" can enjoy such pictures to the full. "Chances and Changes" and "Love *vs.* Aristocracy" are more regularly constructed *tales*, with the "universal passion" as the moving power, but colored with the glowing hues of the west. "The Bee Tree" exhibits a striking but too numerous class among the settlers, and explains, also, the depth of the bitterness that grows out of an unprosperous condition in that "Paradise of the Poor." "Ambuscades" and "Half-Lengths from Life" I remember as two piquant sketches to which an annual, a year or two ago, was indebted for a most unusual sale among the conscious and pen-dreading denizens of the west. "Half-Lengths" turns on the trying subject of *caste*. "The Schoolmaster's Progress" is full of truth and humor. The western pedagogue, the stiff, solitary nondescript figure in the drama of a new settlement, occupying a middle position between "our folks" and "company," and "boarding round," is irresistibly amusing, and cannot fail to be recognized as the representative of a class. The occupation, indeed, always seems to mould those engaged in it—they all soon, like Master Horner, learn to "know well what belongs to the pedagogical character, and that facial solemnity stands high on the list of indispensable qualifications." The spelling-school, also, is a "new country" feature which we owe Mrs. Kirkland many thanks for recording. The incidents of "An Embroidered Fact" are singular and picturesque, but not particularly illustrative of the "Clearings." The same may be said of "Bitter Fruits from Chance-Sown Seeds;" but this abounds in capital touches of character: all the horrors of the tale are brought about through suspicion of *pride*, an accusation as destructive at the west as that of witchcraft in olden times, or the cry of mad dog in modern.

In the way of absolute *books*, Mrs. Kirkland, I believe, has achieved nothing beyond the three volumes specified, (with another lately issued by Wiley & Putnam,) but she is a very constant contributor to the magazines. Unquestionably, she is one of our best writers, has a province of her own, and in that province has few equals. Her most noticeable trait is a certain *freshness* of style, seemingly drawn, as her subjects in general, from the west. In the second place is to be observed a species of *wit*, approximating humor, and so interspersed with pure *fun*, that " wit," after all, is nothing like a definition of it. To give an example—"Old Thoughts on the New Year" commences with a quotation from Tasso's "Aminta"—

> "Il mondo invecchia
> E invecchiando intristisce;"

and the following is given as a "free translation"—

> "The world is growing older
> And wiser day by day;
> Everybody knows beforehand
> What you're going to say.
> We used to laugh and frolic—
> Now we must behave:
> Poor old Fun is dead and buried—
> Pride dug his grave."

This, if I am not mistaken, is the only specimen of *poetry* as yet given by Mrs. Kirkland to the world. She has afforded us no means of judging in respect to her inventive powers, although fancy, and even imagination, are apparent in everything she does. Her perceptive faculties enable her to *describe* with great verisimilitude. Her mere style is admirable, lucid, terse, full of variety, faultlessly pure, and yet bold—so bold as to appear heedless of the ordinary *decora* of composition. In even her most reckless sentences, however, she betrays the woman of refinement, of accomplishment, of unusually thorough education. There are a great many points in which her general manner resembles that of Willis, whom she evidently admires. Indeed, it would not be difficult to pick out from her works an occasional Willisism, not less palpable than happy. For example—

"*Peaches were like little green velvet buttons when* George was first mistaken for Doctor Beaseley, and *before they were ripe* he," etc.

And again—

"Mr. Hammond is fortunately settled in our neighborhood, for the present at least; and he has the neatest little cottage in the world, standing, too, under a very tall oak, which bends kindly over it, looking like the Princess Glumdalclitch inclining her ear to the box which contained her pet Gulliver."

Mrs. Kirkland's personal manner is an echo of her literary one. She is frank, cordial, yet sufficiently dignified—even bold, yet especially lady-like; converses with remarkable accuracy as well as fluency; is brilliantly witty, and now and then not a little sarcastic, but a general amability prevails.

She is rather above the medium height; eyes and hair dark; features somewhat small, with no marked characteristics, but the whole countenance beams with benevolence and intellect.

Prosper M. Wetmore

General Wetmore occupied some years ago quite a conspicuous position among the *littérateurs* of New York city. His name was seen very frequently in "The Mirror" and in other similar journals, in connection with brief poems and occasional prose compositions. His only publication in volume form, I believe, is "The Battle of Lexington and other Poems," a collection of considerable merit, and one which met a very cordial reception from the press.

Much of this cordiality, however, is attributable to the personal popularity of the man, to his facility in making acquaintances and his tact in converting them into unwavering friends.

General Wetmore has an exhaustless fund of *vitality*. His energy, activity and indefatigability are proverbial, not less than his peculiar sociability. These qualities give him unusual influence among his fellow-citizens, and have constituted him (as precisely the same traits have constituted his friend General Morris) one of a standing committee for the regulation of a certain class of city affairs—such, for instance, as the getting up a complimentary benefit, or a public demonstration of respect for some deceased worthy, or a ball and dinner to Mr. Irving or Mr. Dickens.

Mr. Wetmore is not only a general, but Naval Officer of the Port of New York, Member of the Board of Trade, one of the Council of the Art Union, one of the Corresponding Committee of the Historical Society, and of more other committees than I can just now remember. His manners are *recherchés*, courteous—a little in the old school way. He is sensitive, punctilious; speaks well, roundly, fluently, plausibly, and is skilled in pouring oil upon the waters of stormy debate.

He is, perhaps, fifty years of age, but has a youthful look; is about five feet eight in height, slender, neat, with an air of military compactness; looks especially well on horseback.

EMMA C. EMBURY

Mrs. Embury is one of the most noted, and certainly one of the most meritorious of our female *littérateurs*. She has been many years before the public—her earliest compositions, I believe, having been contributed to the "New York Mirror" under the *nom de plume* "Ianthe." They attracted very general attention at the time of their appearance and materially aided the paper. They were subsequently, with some other pieces, published in volume form, with the title "Guido and other Poems." This book has been long out of print. Of late days its author has written but little poetry—that little, however, has at least indicated a poetic capacity of no common order.

Yet as a poetess she is comparatively unknown, her reputation in this regard having been quite overshadowed by that which she has acquired as a writer of tales. In this latter capacity she has, upon the whole, no equal among her sex in America—certainly no superior. She is not so vigorous as Mrs. Stephens, nor so vivacious as Miss Chubbuck, nor so caustic as Miss Leslie, nor so dignified as Miss Sedgwick, nor so graceful, fanciful and *spirituelle* as Mrs. Osgood, but is *deficient* in none of the qualities for which these ladies are noted, and in certain particulars surpasses them all. Her subjects are *fresh*, if not always vividly original, and she manages them with more skill than is usually exhibited by our magazinists. She has also much imagination and sensibility, while her style is pure, earnest, and devoid of verbiage and exaggeration. I make a point of *reading* all tales to which I see the name of Mrs. Embury appended. The story by which she has attained most reputation is "Constance Latimer, the Blind Girl."

Mrs. E. is a daughter of Doctor Manly, an eminent physician of New York city. At an early age she married a gentleman of some wealth and of education, as well as of tastes akin to her own. She is noted for her domestic virtues no less than for literary talents and acquirements.

She is about the medium height; complexion, eyes, and hair light; arched eyebrows; Grecian nose; the mouth a fine one and indicative of firmness; the whole countenance pleasing, intellectual and expressive. The portrait in "Graham's Magazine" for January, 1843, has no resemblance to her whatever.

EPES SARGENT

Mr. Sargent is well known to the public as the author of "Velasco, a Tragedy," "The Light of the Light-house, with other Poems," one or two short *nouvelettes*, and numerous contributions to the periodicals. He was also the editor of "Sargent's Magazine," a monthly work, which had the misfortune of falling between two stools, never having been able to make up its mind whether to be popular with the three or dignified with the five dollar journals. It was a "happy *medium*" between the two classes, and met the fate of all happy *media* in dying, as well through lack of foes as of friends. *In medio tutissimus ibis* is the worst advice in the world for the editor of a magazine. Its observance proved the downfall of Mr. Lowell and his really meritorious "Pioneer."

"Velasco" has received some words of commendation from the author of "Ion," and I am ashamed to say, owes most of its home appreciation to this circumstance. Mr. Talfourd's play has, itself, little truly dramatic, with much picturesque and more poetical value; its author, nevertheless, is better entitled to respect as a dramatist than as a critic of dramas. "Velasco," compared with American tragedies generally, is a good tragedy—indeed, an excellent one, but, positively considered, its merits are very inconsiderable. It has many of the traits of

Mrs. Mowatt's "Fashion," to which, in its mode of construction, its scenic effects, and several other points, it bears as close a resemblance as, in the nature of things, it could very well bear. It is by no means improbable, however, that Mrs. Mowatt received some assistance from Mr. Sargent in the composition of her comedy, or at least was guided by his advice in many particulars of technicality.

"Shells and Sea Weeds," a series of brief poems recording the incidents of a voyage to Cuba, is, I think, the best work in verse of its author, and evinces a fine fancy, with keen appreciation of the beautiful in natural scenery. Mr. Sargent is fond of sea pieces, and paints them with skill, flooding them with that warmth and geniality which are their character and their due. "A Life on the Ocean Wave" has attained great popularity, but is by no means so good as the less lyrical compositions, "A Calm," "The Gale," "Tropical Weather," and "A Night Storm at Sea."

"The Light of the Light-house" is a spirited poem, with many musical and fanciful passages, well expressed. For example—

> "But, oh, Aurora's crimson light,
>   That makes the watch-fire dim,
> Is not a more transporting sight
>   Than Ellen is to him.
> He pineth not for fields and brooks,
>   Wild flowers and singing birds,
> For summer smileth in her looks
>   And singeth in her words."

There is something of the Dibdin spirit throughout the poem, and, indeed, throughout all the sea poems of Mr. Sargent—a little *too much* of it, perhaps.

His prose is not quite so meritorious as his poetry. He writes "easily," and is apt at burlesque and sarcasm—both rather broad than original. Mr. Sargent has an excellent memory for good *hits* and no little dexterity in their application. To those who meddle little with books, some of his satirical papers must appear brilliant. In a word, he is one of the most

prominent members of a very extensive American family—
the men of industry, talent and tact.

In stature he is short—not more than five feet five—but
well proportioned. His face is a fine one; the features regular
and expressive. His demeanor is very gentlemanly. Unmarried, and about thirty years of age.

Godey's Lady's Book, August 1846

FRANCES S. OSGOOD

Mrs. Frances Sargent Osgood, for the last two or three years,
has been rapidly attaining distinction—and this, evidently,
with no effort at attaining it. She seems, in fact, to have no
object in view beyond that of giving voice to the feelings or
to the fancies of the moment. "Necessity," says the proverb,
"is the mother of Invention;" and the invention of Mrs. O.,
at least, springs plainly from necessity—from the necessity of
invention. *Not* to write poetry—not to think it, dream it, act
it, and be it, is entirely out of her power.

It may be questioned whether, with more method, more
industry, more definite purpose, more ambition, Mrs. Osgood would have made a more decided impression on the
public mind. She might, upon the whole, have written better
poems, but the chances are that she would have failed in conveying so vivid and so just an idea of her powers as poet. The
warm *abandonnement* of her style—that charm which now so
captivates—is but a portion and a consequence of her unworldly nature, of her disregard of mere fame; but it affords
us glimpses (which we could not otherwise have obtained) of
a capacity for accomplishing what she has not accomplished
and in all probability never will. But in the world of poetry
there is already more than enough of this uncongenial ambition and pretence.

Mrs. Osgood has taken no care whatever of her literary
fame. A great number of her finest compositions, both in
verse and prose, have been written anonymously, and are now
lying *perdus* about the country in out-of-the-way nooks and
corners. Many a goodly reputation has been reared upon a far
more unstable basis than her unclaimed and uncollected "fugitive pieces."

Her first volume, I believe, was published six or seven years ago, by Edward Churton, of London, during the poet's residence in that city. I have now lying before me a second edition of it, dated 1842—a most beautifully printed book, dedicated to the Reverend Hobart Caunter. It contains a number of what the Bostonians call "juvenile" poems, written when Mrs. O. (then Miss Locke) could not have been more than thirteen, and evincing a very unusual precocity. The leading piece is "Elfrida, a Dramatic Poem," but in many respects well entitled to the appellation "Drama." I allude chiefly to the passionate expression of particular portions, to delineation of character, and to occasional scenic effect; in construction, (that is to say, plot,) in general conduct and plausibility, the play fails—comparatively, of course, for the hand of genius is evinced throughout.

The story is the well-known one of Edgar, Elfrida and Earl Athelwood. The king, hearing of Elfrida's extraordinary beauty, commissions his favorite, Athelwood, to visit her and ascertain if report speaks truly of her charms. The earl, becoming himself enamored, represents the lady as anything but beautiful and agreeable, and the king is satisfied. Athelwood soon afterwards woos and weds Elfrida, giving her wealth as his reason to Edgar. The true state of the case, however, is betrayed by an enemy, and the monarch resolves to visit the earl at his castle and so judge for himself. Hearing of this resolve, Athelwood, in despair, confesses his duplicity to his wife, and entreats her to render null as far as possible the effect of her charms by dressing with unusual plainness. This the wife promises to do, but, fired with ambition and resentment at the wrong done her, arrays herself in her most magnificent and becoming costume. The king is captivated, and the result (a somewhat immoral one, although in keeping with the ordinary idea of poetical justice) is the destruction of Athelwood and the elevation of Elfrida to the throne.

These incidents are especially well adapted to dramatic purposes, and with more of that art which Mrs. Osgood does *not* possess, she might have woven them into a tragedy which the world would not have willingly let die. As it is, she has merely succeeded in showing what she might, should, and *could* have done, but unhappily did not. The character of Elfrida is the bright point of the play. Her beauty and consciousness of it, her indignation and uncompromising ambition, are depicted with power.

The English collection of which I speak was entitled "A Wreath of Wild Flowers from New England." It met with a *really* cordial reception in Great Britain—was favorably noticed by the "Literary Gazette," "Times," "Monthly Chronicle," "Atlas," and especially by the "Court Journal," the "Court and Ladies' Magazine," *"La Belle Assemblée,"* and other similar works circulating very extensively among the aristocracy. Mr. Osgood's merits as an artist had already introduced his wife into distinguished society, (she was petted in especial by Mrs. Norton and Rogers,) but her beautiful volume had at once an evidently favorable effect upon his fortunes. His pictures were all placed in a more advantageous light by her poetical and conversational grace.

As the "Wreath of Wild Flowers" has had comparatively little circulation in this country, I may be pardoned for making one or two other extracts. *"The Dying Rosebud's Lament,"* although by no means one of the best poems included, will very well serve to show the earlier and more characteristic manner of the poetess.

> "Ah me!—ah, woe is me!
>   That I should perish now,
> With the dear sunlight just let in
>   Upon my balmy brow!

> *"My leaves, instinct with glowing life,*
>   *Were quivering to unclose;*
> *My happy heart with love was rife—*
>   *I was almost a rose.*

> "Nerved by a hope, warm, rich, intense,
>   *Already I had risen*
> *Above my cage's curving fence—*
>   *My green and graceful prison.*

"*My pouting lips, by Zephyr pressed,*
    Were just prepared to part
And whisper to the wooing wind
    The rapture of my heart.

"*In new-born fancies reveling,*
    My mossy cell half riven,
Each thrilling leaflet seemed a wing
    To bear me into Heaven.

"How oft, while yet an infant flower,
    My crimson cheek I've laid
Against the green bars of my bower,
    Impatient of the shade!

"*And pressing up and peeping through*
    Its small but precious vistas,
Sighed for the lovely light and dew
    That blessed my elder sisters.

"I saw the sweet breeze rippling o'er
    Their leaves that loved the play,
Though the light thief stole all their store
    Of dew-drop gems away.

"I thought how happy I should be
    Such diamond wreaths to wear,
And frolic with a rose's glee
    With sunbeam, bird and air.

"Ah me!—ah, woe is me, that I,
    Ere yet my leaves unclose,
With all my wealth of sweets, *must die*
    Before I am a rose!"

Every true poet must here appreciate the exceeding delicacy of expression, the richness of fancy, the nice appositeness of the overt and insinuated meaning. The passages I have italicized have seldom, in their peculiar and very *graceful* way, been equaled—never surpassed.

I cannot speak of the poems of Mrs. Osgood without a strong propensity to ring the changes upon the indefinite word *"grace"* and its derivatives. It seems, indeed, the one key-phrase unlocking the cryptograph of her power—of the effect she produces. And yet the effect is scarcely more a secret than the key. *Grace*, perhaps, may be most satisfactorily defined as a term applied, in despair, to that class of the impressions of beauty which admit neither of analysis nor of comprehension. It is in this irresoluble charm—in *grace*—that Mrs. Osgood excels any poetess of her country—or, indeed, of any country under the sun. Nor is she more graceful herself than appreciative of the graceful, under whatever guise it is presented to her consideration. The sentiment, the perception, and the keenest enjoyment of grace, render themselves manifest in innumerable instances, as well throughout her prose as her poetry. A fine example is to be found in "A Letter to an Absent Friend, on seeing Celeste for the first time in the Wept-of-Wishton-Wish," included in the "Wild Flowers from New England." Celeste has been often described—the effect of her dancing, I mean—but assuredly never has she been brought so fully to the eye of the mind as in the verses which follow:—

"She comes—the spirit of the dance!
　　And but for those large, eloquent eyes,
　Where passion speaks in every glance,
　　She'd seem a wanderer from the skies.

"So light that, gazing breathless there,
　　Lest the celestial dream should go,
　You'd think the music in the air
　　Waved the fair vision to and fro!

"*Or that the melody's sweet flow*
　　Within the radiant creature played,
　And those soft wreathing arms of snow
　　And white sylph feet the music made.

"Now gliding slow with dreamy grace,
    Her eyes beneath their lashes lost,
Now motionless, with lifted face,
    And small hands on her bosom crossed.

"And now with flashing eyes she springs—
    Her whole bright figure raised in air,
As if her soul had spread its wings
    And poised her one wild instant there!

"She spoke not—but, so richly fraught
    With language are her glance and smile,
That when the curtain fell, *I thought*
    She had been talking all the while."

Messrs. Clark & Austin, of New York, have lately issued
another, but still a very imperfect collection of "Poems, by
Frances S. Osgood." In general, it embraces by no means the
best of her works, although some of her best ("The Spirit of
Poetry," for example), are included. "The Daughter of Hero-
dias," one of her longest compositions, a very noble poem—
quite as good as anything written by Mrs. Hemans—is omitted. The volume contains a number of the least meritorious
pieces in the "Wreath of Wild Flowers from New England,"
and also more than enough of a class of allegorical or emblematical verses—a kind of writing which, through an odd
perversity, the fair authoress at one time much affected, but
which no poet can admit to be poetry at all. These *jeux d'esprit* (for what else shall we call them?) afforded her, however,
a fine opportunity for the display of ingenuity and an *epigrammatism* in which she especially excels.

Of this latter quality, in its better phase—that is to say,
existing apart from the allegory—I must be permitted to give
two exquisite specimens:—

"LENORE.

"Oh, fragile and fair as the delicate chalices
    Wrought with so rare and so subtle a skill,
Bright relics that tell of the pomp of those palaces
    Venice, the sea-goddess, glories in still!

"Whose exquisite texture, transparent and tender,
    A pure blush alone from the ruby *wine* takes,
Yet, ah, if some false hand, profaning its splendor,
    Dares but to taint it with poison, it breaks.

"So when Love poured through thy pure heart his lightning,
    On thy pale cheek the soft rose-hues awoke—
So when wild Passion, that timid heart frightening,
    Poisoned the treasure, it trembled and broke!"

"TO SARAH.

"Oh, they never can know that heart of thine,
    Who dare accuse *thee* of flirtation;
They might as well say that the stars, which shine
    In the light of their joy o'er creation,
Are flirting with every wild wave in which lies
One beam of the glory that kindles the skies.

"Smile on, then, undimmed in your beauty and grace!
    Too well e'er to doubt, love, we know you;
And shed from your heaven the light of your face,
    Where the waves chase each other below you—
For none can e'er deem it *your* shame or *your* sin,
That each wave holds your star-image smiling within."

"Lenore," independently of its mere epigrammatism, well exemplifies the poet's usual turn of thought, her exactitude and facility at illustration. The versification (except in the first quatrain, which puts me in mind of Moore), is defective. The first two lines of the third are even rough. The rhythm is dactylic, but the dactyls are all false— *e.g.*:

"So when Love | poured through thy | pure heart his | lightning,
    On thy pale | cheek the soft | rose-hues a | woke."

Here the necessarily long syllables, *love*, *through*, *heart*, *pale*, *soft*, and *hues*, should be short, and the rhythm halts because they are not so. "To Sarah" is the better poem in

every respect;—the compliment in the two last lines is exqui-
sitely pointed. Both these pieces appeared originally in "The
Broadway Journal," (which has been honored by many of
Mrs. Osgood's very finest compositions;) the last, "To Sarah,"
is not included in the volume lately published by Messrs.
Clark & Austin.

What is really new in this volume shows a marked change
in the themes, in the manner, in the whole character of the
poetess. We see less of vivacity, less of fancy; more of tenderness, earnestness, even passion, and of the true imagination as
distinguished from its subordinate fancy: the one prevalent
and predominating trait, *grace*, alone distinctly remains. In
illustration of these points I feel tempted to copy some seven
or eight of the later poems, but the deep interest of my subject has already led me too far, and I am by no means writing
a review. I must refer, however, to two brief *songs* as best
exemplifying what I have said. They were quoted, about five
months ago, in a notice of the works of the poetess—a notice
by myself, published in this magazine;—the one commences,
"She loves him yet," the other, "Yes, lower to the level."
These pieces serve also to show the marked improvement of
the writer in versification. The first-named is not only rhyth-
mically perfect, but evinces much originality in its structure;
the last, although in rhythm not so novel, is more forcible,
better balanced, and more thoroughly sustained—in these respects I have seldom seen anything so good. In terse energy
of expression this poem is unsurpassed.

My extracts are already extended to a greater length than I
had designed or than comports with the plan of these papers,
yet I cannot forbear making another. Its music, simplicity and
genuine earnestness, will find their way to the hearts of all
who read it.

"A MOTHER'S PRAYER IN ILLNESS.

"Yes, take them first, my Father; let my doves
    Fold their white wings in Heaven, safe on Thy breast,
Ere I am called away! I dare not leave
    Their young hearts here—their innocent, thoughtless
        hearts!

Ah, how the shadowy train of future ills
Comes sweeping down life's vista as I gaze!
My May, my careless, ardent-tempered May,
My frank and frolic child, in whose blue eyes
Wild joy and passionate woe alternate rise;
Whose cheek the morning in her soul illumes;
Whose little loving heart a word, a glance,
Can sway to grief or glee; who leaves her play,
And puts up her sweet mouth and dimpled arms
Each moment for a kiss, and softly asks,
With her clear, flute-like voice, 'Do you love me?'
Ah, let me stay—ah, let me still be by,
To answer her and meet her warm caress!
For, I away, how oft in this rough world
That earnest question will be asked in vain!
How oft that eager, passionate, petted heart,
Will shrink abashed and chilled, to learn at length
The hateful withering lesson of distrust!
Ah, let her nestle still upon this breast,
In which each shade that dims her darling face
Is felt and answered, as the lake reflects
The clouds that cross yon smiling heaven. And thou,
My modest Ellen—tender, thoughtful, true,
Thy soul attuned to all sweet harmonies—
My pure, proud, noble Ellen, with thy gifts
Of genius, grace and loveliness, half hidden
'Neath the soft veil of innate modesty,
How will the world's wild discord reach thy heart
To startle and appal! Thy generous scorn
Of all things base and mean; thy quick, keen taste,
Dainty and delicate; thy instinctive fear
Of those unworthy of a soul so pure;
Thy rare, unchildlike dignity of mien—
All, they will all bring pain to thee, my child.
And, oh! if even their grace and goodness meet
Cold looks and careless greetings, how will all
The latent *evil* yet undisciplined
In their young, timid souls, forgiveness find—
Forgiveness and forbearance, and soft chidings,
Which I, their mother, learned of Love to give?

Ah, let me stay—albeit my heart is weary,
Weary and worn, tired of its own sad beat
That finds no echo in this busy world
Which cannot pause to answer—tired alike
Of joy and sorrow, of the day and night.
Ah, take them first, my Father, and then me!
And for their sakes—for *their* sweet sakes, my Father,
Let me find rest beside them, at thy feet!"

Mrs. Osgood has done far more in prose than in poetry, but then her prose is merely poetry in disguise. Of pure prose, of prose proper, she has, perhaps, never written a line in her life. Her usual magazine articles are a class by themselves. She begins with a desperate effort at being sedate—that is to say, sufficiently prosaic and matter-of-fact for the purpose of a legend or an essay, but in a few sentences we behold uprising the leaven of the unrighteousness of the muse; then, after some flourishes and futile attempts at repression, a scrap of verse renders itself manifest; then another and another;—then comes a poem outright, and then another and another and another, with little odd batches of prose in between, until at length the mask is thrown fairly off and far away, and the whole article—*sings*.

I shall say nothing farther, then, of Mrs. Osgood's prose.

Her character is daguerreotyped in her works—reading the one we know the other. She is ardent, sensitive, impulsive; the very soul of truth and honor; a worshiper of the beautiful, with a heart so radically artless as to seem abundant in art—universally respected, admired and beloved. In person she is about the medium height, slender even to fragility, graceful whether in action or repose; complexion usually pale; hair very black and glossy; eyes of a clear, luminous gray, large, and with a singular capacity of expression. In no respect can she be termed beautiful, (as the world understands the epithet,) but the question, "Is it really possible that she is not so?" is very frequently asked, and *most* frequently by those who most intimately know her. Her husband is still occupied with his profession. They have two children—the Ellen and May of the poem.

LYDIA M. CHILD

Mrs. Child has acquired a just celebrity by many compositions of high merit, the most noticeable of which are "Hobomok," "Philothea," and a "History of the Condition of Women." "Philothea," in especial, is written with great vigor, and, as a classical romance, is not far inferior to the "Anacharsis" of Barthelemi;—its style is a model for purity, chastity and ease. Some of her magazine papers are distinguished for graceful and brilliant *imagination*—a quality rarely noticed in our countrywomen. She continues to write a great deal for the monthlies and other journals, and invariably writes well. Poetry she has not often attempted, but I make no doubt that in this she would excel. It seems, indeed, the legitimate province of her fervid and fanciful nature. I quote one of her shorter compositions, as well to instance (from the subject) her intense appreciation of genius in others as to exemplify the force of her poetic expression:—

"MARIUS AMID THE RUINS OF CARTHAGE.

"Pillars are fallen at thy feet,
    Fanes quiver in the air,
A prostrate city is thy seat,
    And thou alone art there.

"No change comes o'er thy noble brow,
    Though ruin is around thee;
Thine eyebeam burns as proudly now
    As when the laurel crowned thee.

"It cannot bend thy lofty soul
    Though friends and fame depart—
The car of Fate may o'er thee roll
    Nor crush thy Roman heart.

"And genius hath electric power
    Which earth can never tame;
Bright suns may scorch and dark clouds lower,
    Its flash is still the same.

"The dreams we loved in early life
   May melt like mist away;
High thoughts may seem, 'mid passion's strife,
   Like Carthage in decay;

"And proud hopes in the human heart
   May be to ruin hurled,
Like mouldering monuments of art
   Heaped on a sleeping world:

"Yet there is something will not die
   Where life hath once been fair;
Some towering thoughts still rear on high,
   Some Roman lingers there."

Mrs. Child, casually observed, has nothing particularly striking in her personal appearance. One would pass her in the street a dozen times without notice. She is low in stature and slightly framed. Her complexion is florid; eyes and hair are dark; features in general diminutive. The expression of her countenance, when animated, is highly intellectual. Her dress is usually plain, not even neat—anything but fashionable. Her bearing needs excitement to impress it with life and dignity. She is of that order of beings who are themselves only on "great occasions." Her husband is still living. She has no children. I need scarcely add that she has always been distinguished for her energetic and active philanthropy.

Elizabeth Bogart

Miss Bogart has been for many years before the public as a writer of poems and tales (principally the former) for the periodicals, having made her *debût* as a contributor to the original "New York Mirror." Doctor Griswold, in a foot-note appended to one of her poems quoted in his "Poets and Poetry," speaks of the "volume" from which he quotes; but Miss Bogart has not yet collected her writings in volume form. Her fugitive pieces have usually been signed "Estelle." They are noticeable for nerve, dignity and finish. Perhaps the four stanzas entitled "He came too Late," and introduced into Doctor Griswold's compilation, are the most favorable specimen of her manner. Had he not quoted them I should have copied them here.

Miss Bogart is a member of one of the oldest families in the state. An interesting sketch of her progenitors is to be found in Thompson's "History of Long Island." She is about the medium height, straight and slender; black hair and eyes; countenance full of vivacity and intelligence. She converses with fluency and spirit, enunciates distinctly, and exhibits interest in whatever is addressed to her—a rare quality in good talkers; has a keen appreciation of genius and of natural scenery; is cheerful and fond of society.

CATHERINE M. SEDGWICK

Miss Sedgwick is not only one of our most celebrated and most meritorious writers, but attained reputation at a period when *American* reputation in letters was regarded as a phenomenon; and thus, like Irving, Cooper, Paulding, Bryant, Halleck, and one or two others, she is indebted, certainly, for *some* portion of the esteem in which she was and is held, to that patriotic pride and gratitude to which I have already alluded, and for which we must make reasonable allowance in estimating the absolute merit of our literary pioneers.

Her earliest published work of any length was "A New England Tale," designed in the first place as a religious tract, but expanding itself into a volume of considerable size. Its success—partially owing, perhaps, to the influence of the parties for whom or at whose instigation it was written—encouraged the author to attempt a novel of somewhat greater elaborateness as well as length, and "Redwood" was soon announced, establishing her at once as the first female prose writer of her country. It was reprinted in England, and translated, I believe, into French and Italian. "Hope Leslie" next appeared—also a novel—and was more favorably received even than its predecessors. Afterwards came "Clarence," not quite so successful, and then "The Linwoods," which took rank in the public esteem with "Hope Leslie." These are all of her longer prose fictions, but she has written numerous shorter ones of great merit—such as "The Rich Poor Man and the Poor Rich Man," "Live and let Live," (both in volume form,) with various articles for the magazines and annuals, to which she is still an industrious contributor. About ten years since she published a compilation of several of her fugitive prose pieces, under the title "Tales and Sketches," and a short time ago a series of "Letters from Abroad"—not the least popular or least meritorious of her compositions.

Miss Sedgwick has now and then been nicknamed "the Miss Edgeworth of America;" but she has done nothing to bring down upon her the vengeance of so equivocal a title. That she has thoroughly studied and profoundly admired Miss Edgeworth may, indeed, be gleaned from her works—but what woman has not? Of imitation there is not the slightest perceptible taint. In both authors we observe the same tone of thoughtful morality, but here all resemblance ceases. In the Englishwoman there is far more of a certain Scotch prudence, in the American more of warmth, tenderness, sympathy for the weaknesses of her sex. Miss Edgeworth is the more acute, the more inventive and the more rigid. Miss Sedgwick is the more womanly.

All her stories are full of interest. The "New England Tale" and "Hope Leslie" are especially so, but upon the whole I am best pleased with "The Linwoods." Its prevailing features are ease, purity of style, pathos, and verisimilitude. To plot it has little pretension. The scene is in America, and, as the sub-title indicates, "Sixty years since." This, by-the-by, is taken from "Waverley." The adventures of the family of a Mr. Linwood, a resident of New York, form the principal theme. The character of this gentleman is happily drawn, although there is an antagonism between the initial and concluding touches—the end has forgotten the beginning, like the government of Trinculo. Mr. L. has two children, Herbert and Isabella. Being himself a Tory, the boyish impulses of his son in favor of the revolutionists are watched with anxiety and vexation; and on the breaking out of the war, Herbert, positively refusing to drink the king's health, is expelled from home by his father— an event on which hinges the main interest of the narrative.

Isabella is the heroine proper, full of generous impulses, beautiful, intellectual, *spirituelle*—indeed, a most fascinating creature. But the family of a Widow Lee throws quite a charm over all the book—a matronly, pious and devoted mother, yielding up her son to the cause of her country—the son gallant, chivalrous, yet thoughtful; a daughter, gentle, loving, melancholy, and susceptible of light impressions. This daughter, Bessie Lee, is one of the most effective personations to be found in our fictitious literature, and may lay claims to the distinction of originality—no slight distinction where *character* is concerned. It is the old story, to be sure, of a meek and trusting heart broken by treachery and abandonment, but in the narration of Miss Sedgwick it breaks upon us with all the freshness of novel emotion. Deserted by her lover, an accomplished and aristocratical coxcomb, the spirits of the gentle girl sink gradually from trust to simple hope, from hope to anxiety, from anxiety to doubt, from doubt to melancholy, and from melancholy to madness. The gradation is depicted in a masterly manner. She escapes from her home in New England and endeavors to make her way alone to New York, with the object of restoring to him who has abandoned her, some tokens he had given her of his love—an act which her disordered fancy assures her will effect in her own person a disenthralment from passion. Her piety, her madness and her beauty, stand her in stead of the lion of Una, and she reaches the city in safety. In that portion of the narrative which embodies this journey are some passages which no mind unimbued with the purest spirit of poetry could have conceived, and they have often made me wonder why Miss Sedgwick has never written a poem.

I have already alluded to her usual excellence of style; but she has a very peculiar fault—that of discrepancy between the words and character of the speaker—the fault, indeed, more properly belongs to the depicting of character itself.

For example, at page 38, vol. 1, of "The Linwoods:"—

" 'No more of my contempt for the Yankees, Hal, an' thou lovest me,' replied Jasper. 'You remember Æsop's advice to Crœsus at the Persian court?'

" 'No, I am sure I do not. You have the most provoking

way of resting the lever by which you bring out your own knowledge, on your friend's ignorance.' "

Now all this is pointed, (although the last sentence would have been improved by letting the words "on your friend's ignorance" come immemediately after "resting,") but it is by no means the language of schoolboys—and such are the speakers.

Again, at page 226, vol. 1, of the same novel:—

" 'Now, out on you, you lazy, slavish loons!' cried Rose. 'Cannot you see these men are raised up to fight for freedom for more than themselves? If the chain be broken at one end, the links will fall apart sooner or later. When you see the sun on the mountain top, you may be sure it will shine into the deepest valleys before long.' "

Who would suppose this graceful eloquence to proceed from the mouth of a negro woman? Yet such is Rose.

Again, at page 24, vol. 1, same novel:—

" 'True, I never saw her; but I tell you, young lad, that there is such a thing as seeing the shadow of things far distant and past, and never seeing the realities, though they it be that cast the shadows.' "

Here the speaker is an old woman who, a few sentences before, has been boasting of her proficiency in "*tellin' fortins.*"

I might object, too, very decidedly to the vulgarity of such a phrase as "I put in my oar," (meaning, "I joined in the conversation,") when proceeding from the mouth of so well-bred a personage as Miss Isabella Linwood. These are, certainly, most remarkable inadvertences.

As the author of many *books*—of several absolutely bound volumes in the ordinary "novel" form of auld lang syne, Miss Sedgwick has a certain adventitious hold upon the attention of the public, a species of tenure that has nothing to do with literature proper—a very decided advantage, in short, over her more modern rivals whom fashion and the growing influence *of the want* of an international copyright law have condemned to the external insignificance of the yellow-backed pamphleteering.

We must permit, however, neither this advantage nor the more obvious one of her having been one of our *pioneers*, to bias the critical judgment as it makes estimate of her abilities in comparison with those of her *present* cotemporaries. She has neither the vigor of Mrs. Stephens nor the vivacious grace of Miss Chubbuck, nor the pure style of Mrs. Embury, nor the classic imagination of Mrs. Child, nor the naturalness of Mrs. Annan, nor the thoughtful and suggestive originality of Miss Fuller; but in many of the qualities mentioned she excels, and in no one of them is she particularly deficient. She is an author of marked talent, but by no means of such decided genius as would entitle her to that precedence among our female writers which, under the circumstances to which I have alluded, *seems* to be yielded her by the voice of the public.

Strictly speaking, Miss Sedgwick is *not* one of the *literati* of New York city, but she passes here about half or rather more than half her time. Her home is Stockbridge, Massachusetts. Her family is one of the first in America. Her father, Theodore Sedgwick the elder, was an eminent jurist and descended from one of Cromwell's major-generals. Many of her relatives have distinguished themselves in various ways.

She is about the medium height, perhaps a little below it. Her forehead is an unusually fine one; nose of a slightly Roman curve; eyes dark and piercing; mouth well-formed and remarkably pleasant in its expression. The portrait in "Graham's Magazine" is by no means a likeness, and, although the hair is represented as curled, (Miss Sedgwick at present wears a cap—at least most usually,) gives her the air of being much older than she is.

Her manners are those of a high-bred woman, but her ordinary *manner* vacillates, in a singular way, between cordiality and a reserve amounting to *hauteur*.

LEWIS GAYLORD CLARK

Mr. Clark is known principally as the twin brother of the late *Willis* Gaylord Clark, the poet, of Philadelphia, with whom he has often been confounded from similarity both of person and of name. He is known, also, within a more limited circle, as one of the editors of "The Knickerbocker Magazine," and it is in this latter capacity that I must be considered as placing him among literary people. He writes little himself, the editorial scraps which usually appear in fine type at the end of "The Knickerbocker" being the joint composition of a great variety of gentlemen (most of them possessing shrewdness and talent) connected with diverse journals about the city of New York. It is only in some such manner, as might be supposed, that so amusing and so heterogeneous a medley of chit-chat could be put together. Were a little more pains taken in elevating the *tone* of this "Editors' Table," (which its best friends are forced to admit is at present a little Boweryish,) I should have no hesitation in commending it in general as a very creditable and very entertaining specimen of what may be termed easy writing and hard reading.

It is not, of course, to be understood from anything I have here said, that Mr. Clark does not occasionally contribute editorial matter to the magazine. His compositions, however, are far from numerous, and are always to be distinguished by their style, which is more "easily to be imagined than described." It has its merit, beyond doubt, but I shall not undertake to say that either "vigor," "force" or "impressiveness" is the precise term by which that merit should be designated. Mr. Clark once did me the honor to review my poems, and ——I forgive him.

"The Knickerbocker" has been long established, and seems to have in it some important elements of success. Its title, for a merely local one, is unquestionably good. Its contributors have usually been men of eminence. Washington Irving was at one period regularly engaged. Paulding, Bryant, Neal, and several others of nearly equal note have also at various times furnished articles, although none of these gentlemen, I believe, continue their communications. In general, the contributed matter has been praiseworthy; the printing, paper, and so forth, have been excellent, and there certainly has been no lack of exertion in the way of what is termed "putting the work before the eye of the public;" still some incomprehensible *incubus* has seemed always to sit heavily upon it, and it has never succeeded in attaining *position* among intelligent or educated readers. On account of the manner in which it is

necessarily edited, the work is deficient in that absolutely indispensable element, *individuality*. As the editor has no precise character, the magazine, as a matter of course, can have
none. When I say "no precise character," I mean that Mr. C.,
as a literary man, has about him no determinateness, no distinctiveness, no saliency of point;—an apple, in fact, or a
pumpkin, has more angles. He is as smooth as oil or a sermon
from Doctor Hawks; he is noticeable for nothing in the
world except for the markedness by which he is noticeable for
nothing.

What is the precise circulation of "The Knickerbocker" at
present I am unable to say; it has been variously stated at
from eight to eighteen hundred subscribers. The former estimate is no doubt too low, and the latter, I presume, is far too
high. There are, perhaps, some fifteen hundred copies
printed.

At the period of his brother's decease, Mr. Lewis G. Clark
bore to him a striking resemblance, but within the last year
or two there has been much alteration in the person of the
editor of the "Knickerbocker." He is now, perhaps, forty-two
or three, but still good-looking. His forehead is, phrenologically, bad—round and what is termed "bullety." The mouth,
however, is much better, although the smile is too constant
and lacks expression; the teeth are white and regular. His hair
and whiskers are dark, the latter meeting voluminously beneath the chin. In height Mr. C. is about five feet ten or
eleven, and in the street might be regarded as quite a "person-
able man;" in society I have never had the pleasure of meeting
him. He is married, I believe.

ANNE C. LYNCH

Miss Anne Charlotte Lynch has written little;—her compositions are even too few to be collected in volume form. Her
prose has been, for the most part, anonymous—critical papers in "The New York Mirror" and elsewhere, with unac-
knowledged contributions to the annuals, especially "The
Gift" and "The Diadem," both of Philadelphia. Her "Diary
of a Recluse," published in the former work, is, perhaps, the
best specimen of her prose manner and ability. I remember,

also, a fair *critique* on Fanny Kemble's poems;—this appeared in "The Democratic Review."

In poetry, however, she has done better, and given evidence of at least unusual talent. Some of her compositions in this way are of merit, and one or two of excellence. In the former class I place her "Bones in the Desert," published in "The Opal" for 1846, her "Farewell to Ole Bull," first printed in "The Tribune," and one or two of her sonnets—not forgetting some graceful and touching lines on the death of Mrs. Willis. In the latter class I place two noble poems, "The Ideal" and "The Ideal Found." These should be considered as one, for each is by itself imperfect. In modulation and vigor of rhythm, in dignity and elevation of sentiment, in metaphorical appositeness and accuracy, and in energy of expression, I really do not know where to point out anything American much superior to them. Their ideality is not so manifest as their passion, but I think it an unusual indication of taste in Miss Lynch, or (more strictly) of an intuitive sense of poetry's true nature, that this passion is just sufficiently subdued to lie within the compass of the poetic art, within the limits of the beautiful. A step farther and it might have passed them. *Mere* passion, however exciting, prosaically excites; it is in its very essence homely, and delights in homeliness: but the *triumph over* passion, as so finely depicted in the two poems mentioned, is one of the purest and most idealizing manifestations of moral beauty.

In character Miss Lynch is enthusiastic, chivalric, self-sacrificing, "equal to any Fate," capable of even martyrdom in whatever should seem to her a holy cause—a most exemplary daughter. She has her hobbies, however, (of which a very indefinite idea of "duty" is one,) and is, of course, readily imposed upon by any artful person who perceives and takes advantage of this most amiable failing.

In person she is rather above the usual height, somewhat slender, with dark hair and eyes—the whole countenance at times full of intelligent expression. Her demeanor is dignified, graceful, and noticeable for repose. She goes much into literary society.

Godey's Lady's Book, September 1846

Charles Fenno Hoffman

Mr. Charles Fenno Hoffman has been long known to the public as an author. He commenced his literary career (as is usually the case in America) by writing for the newspapers— for "The New York American" especially, in the editorial conduct of which he became in some manner associated, at a very early age, with Mr. Charles King. His first *book*, I believe, was a collection (entitled "A Winter in the West") of letters published in "The American" during a tour made by their author through the "far West." This work appeared in 1834, went through several editions, was reprinted in London, was very popular, and deserved its popularity. It conveys the *natural* enthusiasm of a true *idealist*, in the proper phrenological sense, of one sensitively alive to beauty in every development. Its scenic descriptions are vivid, because fresh, genuine, unforced. There is nothing of the cant of the tourist for the sake not of nature but of *tourism*. The author writes *what* he feels and, clearly, *because* he feels it. The style, as well as that of all Mr. Hoffman's books, is easy, free from superfluities, and, although abundant in *broad* phrases, still singularly refined, gentlemanly. This ability to speak boldly without blackguardism, to use the tools of the rabble when necessary without soiling or roughening the hands with their employment, is a rare and unerring test of the natural in contradistinction from the artificial aristocrat.

Mr. H.'s next work was "Wild Scenes in the Forest and Prairie," very similar to the preceding, but more diversified with anecdote and interspersed with poetry. "Greyslaer" followed, a romance based on the well-known murder of Sharp, the Solicitor-General of Kentucky, by Beauchampe. W. Gilmore Simms (who has far more power, more passion, more movement, more skill than Mr. Hoffman) has treated the same subject more effectively in his novel "Beauchampe;" but the fact is that both gentlemen have positively failed, as might have been expected. That both books are interesting is no merit either of Mr. H. or of Mr. S. The real events were more impressive than are the fictitious ones. The *facts* of this remarkable tragedy, as arranged by actual circumstance, would put to shame the skill of the most consummate artist. Nothing was left to the novelist but the amplification of *character*, and at this point neither the author of "Greyslaer" nor of "Beauchampe" is especially *au fait*. The incidents might be better woven into a tragedy.

In the way of poetry Mr. Hoffman has also written a good deal. "The Vigil of Faith and other Poems" is the title of a volume published several years ago. The subject of the leading poem is happy—whether originally conceived by Mr. H. or based on an actual superstition, I cannot say. Two Indian chiefs are rivals in love. The accepted lover is about to be made happy, when his betrothed is murdered by the discarded suitor. The revenge taken is the careful *preservation* of the life of the assassin, under the idea that the meeting the maiden in another world is the point most desired by both the survivors. The incidents interwoven are picturesque, and there are many quotable passages; the descriptive portions are particularly good; but the author has erred, first, in narrating the story in the first person, and secondly, in putting into the mouth of the narrator language and sentiments above the nature of an Indian. I say that the narration should not have been in the first person, because, although an Indian may and does fully experience a thousand delicate shades of sentiment, (the whole idea of the story is essentially sentimental), still he has, clearly, no capacity for their various *expression*. Mr. Hoffman's hero is made to discourse very much after the manner of Rousseau. Nevertheless, "The Vigil of Faith" is, upon the whole, one of our most meritorious poems. The shorter pieces in the collection have been more popular; one or two of the *songs* particularly so—"Sparkling and Bright," for example, which is admirably adapted to song purposes, and is full of lyric feeling. It cannot be denied, however, that, in general, the whole tone, air and spirit of Mr. Hoffman's fugitive compositions are echoes of Moore. At times the very words and figures of the "British Anacreon" are unconsciously adopted. Neither can there be any doubt that this obvious similarity, if not positive imitation, is the source of the commendation bestowed upon our poet by "The Dublin University Magazine," which declares him "the best song writer in America," and does him also the honor to intimate its opinion that "he is a better fellow than the whole Yankee crew" of us taken together—after which there is very little to be said.

Whatever may be the merits of Mr. Hoffman as poet, it may be easily seen that these merits have been put in the worst possible light by the indiscriminate and lavish approbation bestowed on them by Doctor Griswold in his "Poets and Poetry of America." The compiler can find *no* blemish in Mr. H., agrees with everything and copies everything said in his praise—worse than all, gives him more space in the book than any two, or perhaps three, of our poets combined. All this is as much an insult to Mr. Hoffman as to the public, and has done the former irreparable injury—how or why, it is of course unnecessary to say. "Heaven save us from our friends!"

Mr. Hoffman was the original editor of "The Knickerbocker Magazine," and gave it while under his control a tone and character, the weight of which may be best estimated by the consideration that the work thence received an impetus which has sufficed to bear it on alive, although tottering, month after month, through even that dense region of unmitigated and unmitigable fog—that dreary realm of outer darkness, of utter and inconceivable dunderheadism, over which has so long ruled King Log the Second, in the august person of one Lewis Gaylord Clark. Mr. Hoffman subsequently owned and edited "The American Monthly Magazine," one of the best journals we have ever had. He also for one year conducted "The New York Mirror," and has always been a very constant contributor to the periodicals of the day.

He is the brother of Ogden Hoffman. Their father, whose family came to New York from Holland before the time of Peter Stuyvesant, was often brought into connection or rivalry with such men as Pinckney, Hamilton and Burr.

The character of no man is more universally esteemed and admired than that of the subject of this memoir. He has a host of friends, and it is quite impossible that he should have an enemy in the world. He is chivalric to a fault, enthusiastic, frank without discourtesy, an ardent admirer of the beautiful, a gentleman of *the best* school—a gentleman by birth, by education and by instinct. His manners are graceful and winning in the extreme—quiet, affable and dignified, yet cordial and *dégagés*. He converses much, earnestly, accurately and well. In person he is remarkably handsome. He is about five feet ten in height, somewhat stoutly made. His countenance is a noble one—a full index of the character. The features are somewhat massive but regular. The eyes are blue, or light gray, and full of fire; the mouth finely-formed, although the lips have a slight expression of voluptuousness; the forehead, to my surprise, although high, gives no indication, in the region of the temples, of that ideality (or love of the beautiful) which is the distinguishing trait of his moral nature. The hair curls, and is of a dark brown, interspersed with gray. He wears full whiskers. Is about forty years of age. Unmarried.

MARY E. HEWITT

Mrs. Hewitt has become known entirely through her contributions to our periodical literature. I am not aware that she has written any prose, but her poems have been numerous and often excellent. A collection of them was published not long ago in an exquisitely tasteful form, by Ticknor & Co., of Boston. The leading piece, entitled "Songs of Our Land," was by no means the most meritorious, although the largest in the volume. In general, these compositions evince the author's poetic fervor, classicism of taste and keen appreciation of the beautiful, in the moral as well as in the physical world. No one of them, perhaps, can be judiciously commended as a whole, but no one of them is without merit, and there are several which would do credit to any poet in the land—still even these latter are rather particularly than generally commendable. They lack unity, totality, ultimate effect, but abound in forcible passages. For example—

> "Shall I portray thee in thy glorious seeming,
> Thou that the Pharos of my darkness art?"

> *   *   *

> "Like the blue lotos on its own clear river
> Lie thy soft eyes, beloved, upon my soul."

> *   *   *

"Here, 'mid your wild and dark defile,
  O'erawed and wonder-whelmed I stand,
And ask, 'Is this the fearful vale
  That opens on the shadowy land?' "

*   *   *

"And there the slave—a slave no more—
Hung reverent up the chain he wore."

*   *   *

"Oh, friends, we would be treasured still!
  Though Time's cold hand should cast
His misty veil, in after years,
  Over the idol Past,
Yet send to us some offering thought
  O'er Memory's ocean wide—
Pure as the Hindoo's votive lamp
  On Ganga's sacred tide."

The conclusion of "The Ocean Tide to the Rivulet" puts
me in mind of the rich spirit of Horne's noble epic "Orion."

"Sadly the flowers their faded petals close
  Where on thy banks they languidly repose,
    Waiting in vain to hear thee onward press;
  And pale Narcissus by thy margin side
  Hath lingered for thy coming, drooped and died,
    Pining for thee amid the loneliness.

"Hasten, beloved!—here, 'neath th' o'erhanging rock!
  Hark! from the deep, my anxious hope to mock,
    They call me backward to my parent main.
  Brighter than Thetis thou, and, ah, more fleet!
  I hear the rushing of thy fair white feet!
    Joy, joy!—my breast receives its own again!"

The personifications here are well managed, and the idea of
the ebb-tide, conveyed in the first line italicized, is one of the
happiest imaginable; neither can anything be more fanciful or

more appropriately expressed than the "rushing of the fair white feet."

Among the most classical in spirit and altogether the best of Mrs. Hewitt's poems, I consider her three admirable sonnets entitled "Cameos." The one called "Hercules and Omphale" is noticeable for the vigor of its rhythm. Another instance of fine versification occurs in "Forgotten Heroes."

> "And the peasant mother at her door,
>> To the babe that climbed her knee,
> Sang aloud the land's heroic songs—
>> *Sang of Thermopylæ.*

> "Sang of Mycale—of Marathon—
>> Of proud Platæa's day,
> Till the wakened hills, from peak to peak,
>> Echoed the glorious lay.
> Oh, god-like name!—O, god-like deed!
>> *Song-borne afar on every breeze,*
> Ye are sounds to thrill like a battle shout—
>> *Leonidas! Miltiades!*"

I italicize what I think the effective points. In the line,

> "Sang of Thermopylæ,"

a trochee and two iambuses are employed, in very happy variation of the three preceding lines, which are formed each of an anapæst followed by three iambuses. The effect of this variation is to convey the idea of lyric or martial song. The first line of the next quatrain even more forcibly carries out this idea. Here the verse begins with an anapæst (although a faulty one, "sang" being necessarily long) and is continued in three iambuses. The variation in the last quatrain consists in an additional foot in the alternating lines, a fuller volume being thus given to the close. I must not be understood as citing these passages or giving their analysis in illustration of the rhythmical *skill* of Mrs. Hewitt, but of an occasional happiness to which she is led by a musical ear. Upon the whole, she has a keen sense of poetic excellences, and gives indication, if not direct evidence, of great ability. With more earnest endeavor she might accomplish much.

In character she is sincere, fervent, benevolent, with a heart full of the truest charity—sensitive to praise and to blame; in temperament, melancholy (although this is not precisely the term); in manner, subdued, gentle, yet with grace and dignity; converses impressively, earnestly, yet quietly and in a low tone. In person she is tall and slender, with black hair and large gray eyes; complexion also dark; the general expression of the countenance singularly interesting and agreeable.

RICHARD ADAMS LOCKE

About twelve years ago, I think, "The New York Sun," a daily paper, price one penny, was established in the city of New York by Mr. Moses Y. Beach, who engaged *Mr. Richard Adams Locke* as its editor. In a well-written prospectus, the object of the journal professed to be that of "supplying the public with the news of the day at so cheap a rate as to lie within the means of all." The consequences of the scheme, in their influence on the whole newspaper business of the country, and through this business on the interests of the country at large, are probably beyond all calculation.

Previous to "The Sun" there had been an unsuccessful attempt at publishing a penny paper in New York, and "The Sun" itself was originally projected and for a short time issued by Messrs. Day & Wisner; its *establishment*, however, is altogether due to Mr. Beach, who purchased it of its disheartened originators. The first decided *movement* of the journal, nevertheless, is to be attributed to Mr. Locke; and in so saying I by no means intend any depreciation of Mr. Beach, since in the engagement of Mr. L. he had but given one of the earliest instances of that unusual sagacity for which I am inclined to yield him credit.

At all events, "The Sun" was revolving in a comparatively narrow orbit when, one fine day, there appeared in its editorial columns a prefatory article announcing very remarkable astronomical discoveries made at the Cape of Good Hope by Sir John Herschell. The information was said to have been received by "The Sun" from an early copy of "The Edinburgh Journal of Science," in which appeared a communication from Sir John himself. This preparatory announcement took very well, (there had been no hoaxes in those days,) and was followed by full details of the reputed discoveries, which were now found to have been made chiefly in respect to the moon, and by means of a telescope to which the one lately constructed by the Earl of Rosse is a plaything. As these discoveries were gradually spread before the public, the astonishment of that public grew out of all bounds; but those who questioned the veracity of "The Sun"—the authenticity of the communication to "The Edinburgh Journal of Science"—were really very few indeed; and this I am forced to look upon as a far more wonderful thing than any "man-bat" of them all.

About six months before this occurrence the Harpers had issued an American edition of Sir John Herschell's "Treatise on Astronomy," and I had been much interested in what is there said respecting the possibility of future lunar investigations. The theme excited my fancy, and I longed to give free rein to it in depicting my day-dreams about the scenery of the moon—in short, I longed to write a story embodying these dreams. The obvious difficulty, of course, was that of accounting for the narrator's acquaintance with the satellite; and the equally obvious mode of surmounting the difficulty was the supposition of an extraordinary telescope. I saw at once that the chief interest of such a narrative must depend upon the reader's yielding his credence in some measure as to details of actual fact. At this stage of my deliberations I spoke of the design to one or two friends—to Mr. John P. Kennedy, the author of "Swallow Barn," among others—and the result of my conversations with them was that the optical difficulties of constructing such a telescope as I conceived were so rigid and so commonly understood, that it would be in vain to attempt giving due verisimilitude to any fiction having the telescope as a basis. Reluctantly, therefore, and only half convinced, (believing the public, in fact, more readily gullible than did my friends,) I gave up the idea of imparting very close verisimilitude to what I should write—that is to say, so close as really to deceive. I fell back upon a style half plausible half bantering, and resolved to give what interest I could to an actual passage from the earth to the moon, describing the lunar scenery as if surveyed and personally examined by the narrator. In this view I wrote a story which I called "Hans Phaall," publishing it about six months afterwards in "The Southern Literary Messenger," of which I was then editor.

It was three weeks after the issue of "The Messenger" containing "Hans Phaall" that the first of the "Moon-hoax" editorials made its appearance in "The Sun," and no sooner had I seen the paper than I understood the jest, which not for a moment could I doubt had been suggested by my own *jeu d'esprit*. Some of the New York journals ("The Transcript" among others) saw the matter in the same light, and published the "Moon story" side by side with "Hans Phaall," thinking that the author of the one had been detected in the author of the other. Although the details are, with some exception, very dissimilar, still I maintain that the general features of the two compositions are nearly identical. Both are *hoaxes*, (although one is in a *tone* of mere banter, the other of downright earnest;) both hoaxes are on one subject, astronomy; both on the same point of that subject, the moon; both professed to have derived exclusive information from a foreign country, and both attempt to give plausibility by minuteness of scientific detail. Add to all this that nothing of a similar nature had ever been attempted before these two hoaxes, the one of which followed immediately upon the heels of the other.

Having stated the case, however, in this form, I am bound to do Mr. Locke the justice to say that he denies having seen my article prior to the publication of his own; I am bound to add, also, that I believe him.

Immediately on the completion of the "Moon story," (it was three or four days in getting finished,) I wrote an examination of its claims to credit, showing distinctly its fictitious character, but was astonished at finding that I could obtain few listeners, so really eager were all to be deceived, so magical were the charms of a style that served as the vehicle of an exceedingly clumsy invention.

It may afford even now some amusement to see pointed

out those particulars of the hoax which should have sufficed to establish its real character. Indeed, however rich the imagination displayed in this fiction, it wanted much of the force which might have been given it by a more scrupulous attention to general analogy and to fact. That the public were misled, even for an instant, merely proves the gross ignorance which (ten or twelve years ago) was so prevalent on astronomical topics.

The moon's distance from the earth is, in round numbers, 240,000 miles. If we wish to ascertain how near, apparently, a lens would bring the satellite, (or any distant object,) we, of course, have but to divide the distance by the magnifying, or, more strictly, by the space-penetrating power of the glass. Mr. Locke gives his lens a power of 42,000 times. By this divide 240,000, (the moon's real distance,) and we have five miles and five-sevenths as the apparent distance. No animal could be seen so far, much less the minute points particularized in the story. Mr. L. speaks about Sir John Herschell's perceiving flowers (the *papaver Rheas*, etc.), and even detecting the color and the shape of the eyes of small birds. Shortly before, too, the author himself observes that the lens would not render perceptible objects less than eighteen inches in diameter; but even this, as I have said, is giving the glass far too great a power.

On page 18, (of the pamphlet edition,) speaking of "a hairy veil" over the eyes of a species of bison, Mr. L. says—"It immediately occurred to the acute mind of Doctor Herschell that this was a providential contrivance to protect the eyes of the animal from the great extremes of light and darkness to which all the inhabitants of our side of the moon are periodically subjected." But this should not be thought a very "acute" observation of the Doctor's. The inhabitants of our side of the moon have, evidently, no darkness at all; in the absence of the sun they have a light from the earth equal to that of thirteen full moons, so that there can be nothing of the extremes mentioned.

The topography throughout, even when professing to accord with Blunt's Lunar Chart, is at variance with that and all other lunar charts, and even at variance with itself. The points of the compass, too, are in sad confusion; the writer seeming to be unaware that, on a lunar map, these are not in accordance with terrestrial points—the east being to the left, and so forth.

Deceived, perhaps, by the vague titles *Mare Nubium, Mare Tranquilitatis, Mare Fæcunditatis*, etc., given by astronomers of former times to the dark patches on the moon's surface, Mr. L. has long details respecting oceans and other large bodies of water in the moon; whereas there is no astronomical point more positively ascertained than that no such bodies exist there. In examining the boundary between light and darkness in a crescent or gibbous moon, where this boundary crosses any of the dark places, the line of division is found to be jagged; but were these dark places liquid they would evidently be even.

The description of the wings of the man-bat (on page 21) is but a literal copy of Peter Wilkins' account of the wings of his flying islanders. This simple fact should at least have induced suspicion.

On page 23 we read thus—"What a prodigious influence must our thirteen times larger globe have exercised upon this satellite when an embryo in the womb of time, the passive subject of chemical affinity!" Now, this is very fine; but it should be observed that no astronomer could have made such remark, especially to any "Journal of Science," for the earth in the sense intended (that of bulk) is not only thirteen but forty-nine times *larger* than the moon. A similar objection applies to the five or six concluding pages of the pamphlet, where, by way of introduction to some discoveries in Saturn, the philosophical correspondent is made to give a minute school-boy account of that planet—an account quite supererogatory, it might be presumed, in the case of "The Edinburgh Journal of Science."

But there is one point, in especial, which should have instantly betrayed the fiction. Let us imagine the power really possessed of seeing animals on the moon's surface—what in such case would first arrest the attention of an observer from the earth? Certainly neither the shape, size, nor any other peculiarity in these animals so soon as their remarkable *position*—they would seem to be walking heels up and head down, after the fashion of flies on a ceiling. The real observer (however prepared by previous knowledge) would have commented on this odd phenomenon before proceeding to other details; the fictitious observer has not even alluded to the subject, but in the case of the man-bats speaks of seeing their entire bodies, when it is demonstrable that he could have seen little more than the apparently flat hemisphere of the head.

I may as well observe, in conclusion, that the size and especially the powers of the man-bats (for example, their ability to fly in so rare an atmosphere—if, indeed, the moon has any) with most of the other fancies in regard to animal and vegetable existence, are at variance generally with all analogical reasoning on these themes, and that analogy here will often amount to the most positive demonstration. The temperature of the moon, for instance, is rather above that of boiling water, and Mr. Locke, consequently, has committed a serious oversight in not representing his man-bats, his bisons, his game of all kinds—to say nothing of his vegetables—as each and all done to a turn.

It is, perhaps, scarcely necessary to add, that all the suggestions attributed to Brewster and Herschell in the beginning of the hoax, about the "transfusion of artificial light through the focal object of vision," etc. etc., belong to that species of figurative writing which comes most properly under the head of rigmarole. There is a real and very definite limit to optical discovery among the stars, a limit whose nature need only be stated to be understood. If, indeed, the casting of large lenses were all that is required, the ingenuity of man would ultimately prove equal to the task, and we might have them of any size demanded;* but, unhappily, in proportion to the increase of size in the lens, and consequently of space-penetrating power, is the diminution of light from the object by diffusion of the rays. And for this evil there is no remedy within human reach; for an object is seen by means of that light alone, whether direct or reflected, which proceeds from

---

*Neither of the Herschells dreamed of the possibility of a speculum six feet in diameter, and now the marvel has been triumphantly accomplished by Lord Rosse. There is, in fact, no physical *impossibility* in our casting lenses of even fifty feet diameter or more. A sufficiency of means and *skill* is all that is demanded.

the object itself. Thus the only artificial light which could avail Mr. Locke would be such as he should be able to throw, not upon "the focal object of vision," but upon *the moon*. It has been easily calculated that when the light proceeding from a heavenly body becomes so diffused as to be as weak as the natural light given out by the stars collectively in a clear, moonless night, then the heavenly body for any practical purpose is no longer visible.

The singular blunders to which I have referred being properly understood, we shall have all the better reason for wonder at the prodigious *success* of the hoax. Not one person in ten discredited it, and (strangest point of all!) the doubters were chiefly those who doubted without being able to say why—the ignorant, those uninformed in astronomy, people who *would not* believe because the thing was so novel, so entirely "out of the usual way." A grave professor of mathematics in a Virginian college told me seriously that he had *no doubt* of the truth of the whole affair! The great effect wrought upon the public mind is referable, first, to *the novelty of the idea*; secondly, to the fancy-exciting and reason-repressing character of the alleged discoveries; thirdly, to the consummate tact with which the deception was brought forth; fourthly, to the exquisite *vraisemblance* of the narration. The hoax was circulated to an immense extent, was translated into various languages—was even made the subject of (quizzical) discussion in astronomical societies; drew down upon itself the grave denunciation of Dick, and was, upon the whole, decidedly the greatest *hit* in the way of *sensation*—of merely popular sensation—ever made by any similar fiction either in America or in Europe.

Having read the Moon story to an end and found it anticipative of all the main points of my "Hans Phaall," I suffered the latter to remain unfinished. The chief design in carrying my hero to the moon was to afford him an opportunity of describing the lunar scenery, but I found that he could add very little to the minute and authentic account of Sir John Herschell. The first part of "Hans Phaall," occupying about eighteen pages of "The Messenger," embraced merely a journal of the passage between the two orbs and a few words of general observation on the most obvious features of the satellite; the second part will most probably never appear. I did not think it advisable even to bring my voyager back to his parent earth. He remains where I left him, and is still, I believe, "the man in the moon."

From the epoch of the hoax "The Sun" shone with unmitigated splendor. The start thus given the paper insured it a triumph; it has now a daily circulation of not far from fifty thousand copies, and is, therefore, probably, the most really influential journal of its kind in the world. Its success firmly established "the penny system" throughout the country, and (*through* "The Sun") consequently, we are indebted to the genius of Mr. Locke for one of the most important steps ever yet taken in the pathway of human progress.

On dissolving, about a year afterwards, his connection with Mr. Beach, Mr. Locke established a political daily paper, "The New Era," conducting it with distinguished ability. In this journal he made, very unwisely, an attempt at a second hoax, giving the *finale* of the adventures of Mungo Park in Africa—the writer pretending to have come into possession by some accident of the lost MSS. of the traveler. No one, however, seemed to be deceived, (Mr. Locke's columns were a suspected district,) and the adventures were never brought to an end. They were richly imaginative.

The next point made by their author was the getting up a book on magnetism as the *primum mobile* of the universe, in connection with Doctor Sherwood, the practitioner of magnetic remedies. The more immediate purpose of the treatise was the setting forth a new magnetic method of obtaining the longitude. The matter was brought before Congress and received with favorable attention. What definite action was had I know not. A review of the work appeared in "The Army and Navy Chronicle," and made sad havoc of the whole project. It was enabled to do this, however, by attacking in detail the accuracy of some calculations of no very radical importance. These and others Mr. Locke is now engaged in carefully revising; and my own opinion is that his theory (which he has reached more by dint of imagination than of anything else) will finally be established, although, perhaps, never thoroughly by *him*.

His prose style is noticeable for its concision, luminousness, completeness—each quality in its proper place. He has that *method* so generally characteristic of genius proper. Everything he writes is a model in its peculiar way, serving just the purposes intended and nothing to spare. He has written some poetry, which, through certain radical misapprehensions, is not very good.

Like most men of *true* imagination, Mr. Locke is a seemingly paradoxical compound of coolness and excitability.

He is about five feet seven inches in height, symmetrically formed; there is an air of distinction about his whole person—the *air noble* of genius. His face is strongly pitted by the small-pox, and, perhaps from the same cause, there is a marked obliquity in the eyes; a certain calm, clear *luminousness*, however, about these latter, amply compensates for the defect, and the forehead is truly beautiful in its intellectuality. I am acquainted with no person possessing so fine a forehead as Mr. Locke. He is married, and about forty-five years of age, although no one would suppose him to be more than thirty-eight. He is a lineal descendant from the immortal author of the "Essay on the Human Understanding."

Godey's Lady's Book, October 1846

ARTICLES AND
MARGINALIA

Contents

South-Sea Expedition

Report of the Committee on Naval Affairs, to whom was referred memorials from sundry citizens of Connecticut interested in the whale fishing, praying that an exploring expedition be fitted out to the Pacific Ocean and South Seas. March 21, 1836.

THAT A MORE ACCURATE, defined, and available knowledge than we at present possess, of the waters, islands, and continental coasts of the great Pacific and Southern Oceans, has long been desirable, no unprejudiced individual conversant with the subject, is likely to deny. A portion of the community unrivalled in activity, enterprise and perseverance, and of paramount importance both in a political and commercial point of view, has long been reaping a rich harvest of individual wealth and national honor in these vast regions. The Pacific may be termed the training ground, the gymnasium of our national navy. The hardihood and daring of that branch of our commercial marine employed in its trade and fisheries, have almost become a proverb. It is in this class we meet with the largest aggregate of that cool self-possession, courage, and enduring fortitude, which have won for us our enviable position among the great maritime powers; and it is from this class we may expect to recruit a considerable proportion of the physical strength and moral intelligence necessary to maintain and improve it. The documentary evidence upon which the report before us is based, forms an appendix to it, and is highly interesting in its character. It awakens our admiration at the energy and industry which have sustained a body of daring men, while pursuing a dangerous and arduous occupation, amid the perils and casualties of an intricate navigation, in seas imperfectly known. It enlists our sympathies in the hardships and difficulties they have combatted, places in strong relief the justice of their claims upon the nation for aid and protection, and shows the expediency of the measure which has at last resulted from their representations. The report itself is clear, manly, decided—the energetic language of men who, having examined the data submitted to them with the consideration the interests it involved seemed to require, are anxious to express their sentiments with a force and earnestness suited to their views of the urgent occasion and of the course they recommend.

It is a glorious study to contemplate the progress made by human industry, from stage to stage, when engaged in the prosecution of a laudable object. Little more than a century ago, only the crews of a few miserable open boats, too frail to venture far from land, waged a precarious warfare with the great leviathans of the deep, along the shores of Cape Cod and Nantucket—then occupied, at distant intervals, by a few inconsiderable fishing stations. The returns even of these first efforts were lucrative, and more appropriate vessels for the service were fitted out. These extended their cruises northward to Labrador, and southward to the West Indies. At length the adventurers, in vessels of yet greater capacity, strength and durability, crossed the Equator and followed their hardy calling along the Eastern Shore of the Southern Peninsula and on the Western and North Western coast of Africa. The Revolution of course operated as a temporary check to their prosperity, but shortly thereafter these dauntless mariners doubled Cape Horn, and launched their daring keels into the comparatively unknown waste beyond, in search of their gigantic prey. Since that fortunate advent, the increase in the shipping, extent, and profits of the fishery, has been unprecedented, and new sources of wealth the importance of which it is at present impossible to estimate, have been opened to us in the same quarter. The trade in skins of the sea-otter and seal, in the fur of land animals on the North West coast, &c. has been extensive in extent and avails. The last mentioned animal, besides the valuable ivory it affords, yields a coarse oil which, in the event of the whale becoming extinct before the perpetual warfare of man, would prove a valuable article of consumption. Of the magnitude of the commercial interest involved in different ways in the Pacific trade, an idea may be gathered in the following extract from the main subject of our review. Let it be borne in mind, that many of the branches of this trade are as yet in their infancy, that the natural resources to which they refer are apparently almost inexhaustible; and we shall become aware that all which is *now* in operation, is but as a dim shadow to the mighty results which may be looked for, when this vast field for national enterprise is better known and appreciated.

"No part of the commerce of this country is more important than that carried on in the Pacific Ocean. It is large in amount. Not less than $12,000,000 are invested in and actively employed by one branch of the whale fishery alone; in the whole trade there is directly and indirectly involved not less than fifty to seventy millions of property. In like manner from 170 to 200,000 tons of our shipping, and from 9 to 12000 of our seamen are employed, amounting to about one-tenth of the whole navigation of the Union. Its results are profitable. It is to a great extent not a mere exchange of commodities, but the creation of wealth by labor from the ocean. The fisheries alone produce at this time an annual income of from five to six millions of dollars; and it is not possible to look at Nantucket, New Bedford, New London, Sag Harbor and a large number of other districts upon our Northern coasts, without the deep conviction that it is an employment alike beneficial to the moral, political, and commercial interests of our fellow-citizens."

In a letter from Commodore Downes to the Honorable John Reed, which forms part of the supplement to the report, that experienced officer observes—

"During the circumnavigation of the globe, in which I crossed the equator six times, and varied my course from 40 deg. North to 57 deg. South latitude, I have never found myself beyond the limits of our commercial marine. The accounts given of the dangers and losses to which our ships are exposed by the extension of our trade into seas but little known, so far, in my opinion from being exaggerated, would admit of being placed in bolder relief, and the protection of government employed in stronger terms. I speak from practical knowledge, having myself seen the dangers and painfully felt the want of the very kind of information which our commercial interests so much need, and which, I suppose, would be the object of such an expedition as is now under consideration before the committee of Congress to give. * * *

"The commerce of our country has extended itself to remote parts of the world, is carried on around islands and reefs not laid down in the charts, among even groups of islands from ten to sixty in number, abounding in objects valuable in commerce, but of which nothing is known accurately; no not even the sketch of a harbor has been made, while of such as are inhabited our knowledge is still more imperfect."

In reading this evidence (derived from the personal observation of a judicious and experienced commander) of the vast range of our commerce in the regions alluded to, and of the imminent risks and perils to which those engaged in it are subjected, it cannot but create a feeling of surprise, that a matter of such vital importance as the adoption of means for their relief, should so long have been held in abeyance. A tabular view of the discoveries of our whaling captains in the Pacific and Southern seas, which forms part of another document, seems still further to prove the inaccuracy and almost utter worthlessness of the charts of these waters, now in use.

Enlightened liberality is the truest economy. It would not be difficult to show, that even as a matter of pecuniary policy the efficient measures at length in progress to remedy the evils complained of by this portion of our civil marine, are wise and expedient. But let us take higher ground. They were called for— *Firstly:* as a matter of public justice. Mr. Reynolds, in his comprehensive and able letter to the chairman of the committee on Naval Affairs, dated 1828, which, with many other conclusive arguments and facts furnished by that gentleman, forms the main evidence on which the late committee founded their report—observes, with reference to the Pacific;

"To look after our merchant there—to offer him every possible facility—to open new channels for his enterprise, and to keep up a respectable naval force to protect him—is only paying a debt we owe to the commerce of the country: for millions have flowed into the treasury from this source, before one cent was expended for its protection."

So far, then, we have done little as a nation to facilitate, or increase, the operations of our commerce in the quarter indicated; we have left the adventurous merchant and the hardy fisherman, to fight their way among reefs of dangerous rocks, and through the channels of undescribed Archipelagos, almost without any other guides than their own prudence and sagacity; but we have not hesitated to partake of the fruits of their unassisted toils, to appropriate to ourselves the credit, respect and consideration their enterprise has commanded, and to look to their class as the strongest support of that main prop of our national power,—a hardy, effective, and well disciplined national navy.

Secondly. Our pride as a vigorous commercial empire, should stimulate us to become our own pioneers in that vast island-studded ocean, destined, it may be, to become, not only the chief theatre of our traffic, but the arena of our future naval conflicts. Who can say, viewing the present rapid growth of our population, that the Rocky Mountains shall forever constitute the western boundary of our republic, or that it shall not stretch its dominion from sea to sea. This may not be desirable, but signs of the times render it an event by no means without the pale of possibility.

The intercourse carried on between the Pacific islands and the coast of China, is highly profitable, the immense returns of the whale fishery in the ocean which surrounds those islands, and along the continental coasts, have been already shown. Our whalers have traversed the wide expanse from Peru and Chili on the west, to the isles of Japan on the east, gathering national reverence, as well as individual emolument, in their course; and yet until the late appropriation, Congress has never yielded them any pecuniary assistance, leaving their very security to the scientific labors of countries far more distant, and infinitely less interested, than our own.

Thirdly. It is our *duty*, holding as we do a high rank in the scale of nations, to contribute a large share to that aggregate of useful knowledge, which is the common property of all. We have astronomers, mathematicians, geologists, botanists, eminent professors in every branch of physical science—we are unincumbered by the oppression of a national debt, and are free from many other drawbacks which fetter and control the measures of the trans-Atlantic governments. We possess, as a people, the mental elasticity which liberal institutions inspire, and a treasury which can afford to remunerate scientific research. Ought we not, therefore, to be foremost in the race of philanthropic discovery, in every department embraced by this comprehensive term? Our national honor and glory which, be it remembered, are to be "transmitted as well as enjoyed," are involved. In building up the fabric of our commercial prosperity, let us not filch the corner stone. Let it not be said of us, in future ages, that we ingloriously availed ourselves of a stock of scientific knowledge, to which we had not contributed our quota—that we shunned as a people to put our shoulder to the wheel—that we reaped where we had never sown. It is not to be controverted that such has been hitherto the case. We have followed in the rear of discovery, when a sense of our moral and political responsibility should have impelled us in its van. Mr. Reynolds, in a letter to which we have already referred, deprecates this servile dependence upon foreign research in the following nervous and emphatic language.

The commercial nations of the earth have done much, and much remains to be accomplished. We stand a solitary instance among those who are considered commercial, as never having put forth a particle of strength or expended a dollar of our money, to add to the accumulated stock of commercial and geographical knowledge, except in partially exploring our own territory.

When our naval commanders and hardy tars have achieved a victory on the deep, they have to seek our harbors, and conduct their prizes into port by tables and charts furnished perhaps by the very people whom they have vanquished.

Is it honorable in the United States to use, forever, the knowledge furnished by others, to teach us how to shun a rock, escape a shoal, or find a harbor; and add nothing to the great mass of information that previous ages and other nations have brought to our hands.   *   *   *   *

The exports, and, more emphatically, the imports of the United States, her receipts and expenditures, are written on every pillar erected by commerce on every sea and in every clime; but the amount of her subscription stock to erect those pillars and for the advancement of knowledge is no where to be found.

*   *   *   *   *   *

Have we not then reached a degree of mental strength, which will enable us to find our way about the globe without leading-strings? Are we forever to take the highway others have laid out for us, and fixed with mile-stones and guide boards? No: a time of enterprise and adventure must be at hand, it is already here; and its march is onward, as certain as a star approaches its zenith.

It is delightful to find that such independent statements and opinions as the above, have been approved, and acted upon by Congress, and that our President with a wisdom and promptitude which do him honor, is superintending and facilitating the execution of legislative design. We extract the following announcement from the Washington Globe.

Surveying and Exploring Expedition to the Pacific Ocean and South Seas.—We learn that the President has given orders to have the exploring vessels fitted out, with the least possible delay. The appropriation made by Congress was ample to ensure all the great objects contemplated by the expedition, and the Executive is determined that nothing shall be wanting to render the expedition in every respect worthy the character and great commercial resources of the country.

The frigate Macedonian, now undergoing thorough repairs at Norfolk, two brigs of two hundred tons each, one or more tenders, and a store ship of competent dimensions, is, we understand, the force agreed upon, and to be put in a state of immediate preparation.

Captain Thomas A. C. Jones, an officer possessing many high qualities for such a service, has been appointed to the command; and officers for the other vessels will be immediately selected.

The Macedonian has been chosen instead of a sloop of war, on account of the increased accommodations she will afford the scientific corps, a department the President has determined shall be complete in its organization, including the ablest men that can be procured, so that nothing within the whole range of every department of natural history and philosophy shall be omitted. Not only on this account has the frigate been selected, but also for the purpose of a more extended protection of our whalemen and traders; and to impress on the minds of the natives a just conception of our character, power, and policy. The frequent disturbances and massacres committed on our seamen by the natives inhabiting the islands in those distant seas, make this measure the dictate of humanity.

We understand also, that to J. N. Reynolds, Esq. the President has given the appointment of Corresponding Secretary to the expedition. Between this gentleman and Captain Jones there is the most friendly feeling and harmony of action. The cordiality they entertain for each other, we trust will be felt by all, whether citizen or officer, who shall be so fortunate as to be connected with the expedition.

Thus it will be seen, steps are being taken to remove the reproach of our country alluded to by Mr. Reynolds, and that that gentleman has been appointed to the highest civil situation in the expedition; a station which we know him to be exceedingly well qualified to fill. The liberality of the appropriation for the enterprise, the strong interest taken by our energetic chief magistrate in its organization, the experience and intelligence of the distinguished commander at its head, all promise well for its successful termination. Our most cordial good wishes will accompany the adventure, and we trust that it will prove the germ of a spirit of scientific ambition, which, fostered by legislative patronage and protection, shall build up for us a name in nautical discovery commensurate with our moral, political, and commercial position among the nations of the earth.

Southern Literary Messenger, August 1836

Address on the subject of a Surveying and Exploring Expedition to the Pacific Ocean and South Seas. Delivered in the Hall of Representatives on the Evening of April 3, 1836. By J. N. Reynolds. With Correspondence and Documents. New York: Published by Harper and Brothers.

IN the Messenger for last August we spoke briefly on this head. What we then said was embraced in the form of a Critical Notice on the "Report (March 21, 1836) of the Committee on Naval Affairs to whom was referred Memorials from sundry citizens of Connecticut interested in the Whale Fishery, praying that an exploring expedition be fitted out to the Pacific Ocean and South Seas." It is now well known to the community that this expedition, the design of which has been for ten years in agitation, has been authorized by Congress; sanctioned, and liberally provided for, by the Executive; and will almost immediately set sail. The public mind is at length thoroughly alive on the subject, and, in touching upon it now, we merely propose to give, if possible, such an outline of the history, object, and nature of the *project*, as may induce the reader to examine, for himself, the volume whose title forms the heading of this article. Therein Mr. Reynolds has embodied a precise and full account of the whole matter, with every necessary document and detail.

In beginning we must necessarily begin with Mr. Reynolds. He is the originator, the persevering and indomitable advocate, the life, the soul of the design. Whatever, of glory at least, accrue therefore from the expedition, this gentleman, whatever post he may occupy in it, or whether none, will be fairly entitled to the lion's share, and will as certainly receive it. He is a native of Ohio, where his family are highly respectable, and where he was educated and studied the law. He is known, by all who know him at all, as a man of the loftiest principles and of unblemished character. "His writings," to use the language of Mr. Hamer on the floor of the House of Representatives, "have attracted the attention of men of letters; and literary societies and institutions have conferred upon him some of the highest honors they had to bestow." For ourselves, we have frequently borne testimony to his various merits as a gentleman, a writer and a scholar.

It is now many years since Mr. R's attention was first attracted to the great national advantages derivable from an exploring expedition to the South Sea and the Pacific; time has only rendered the expediency of the undertaking more obvious. *To-day*, the argument for the design is briefly as follows. No part of the whole commerce of our country is of more importance than that carried on in the regions in question. At the lowest estimate a capital of twelve millions of dollars is actively employed by one branch of the whale fishery alone; and there is involved in the whole business, directly and collaterally, not less probably than seventy millions of property. About one tenth of the entire navigation of the United States is engaged in this service—from 9 to 12,000 seamen, and from 170 to 200,000 tons of shipping. The results of the fishery are in the highest degree profitable—it being not a mere interchange of commodities, but, in a great measure, the creation of wealth, by labor, from the ocean. It produces to the United States an annual income of from five to six millions of dollars. It is a most valuable nursery for our seamen, rearing up a race of hardy and adventurous men, eminently fit for the purposes of the navy. This fishery then is of importance—its range may be extended—at all events its interests should be protected. The scene of its operations, however, is less known and more full of peril than any other portion of the globe visited by our ships. It abounds in islands, reefs and shoals unmarked upon any chart—prudence requires that the location of these should be exactly defined. The savages in these regions have frequently evinced a murderous hostility—they should be conciliated or intimidated. The whale, and more especially all furred animals, are becoming scarce before the perpetual warfare of man—new generations will be found in the south, and the nation first to discover them will reap nearly all the rich benefits of the discovery. Our trade in ivory, in sandal-wood, in biche le-mer, in feathers, in quills, in seal-oil, in porpoise-oil, and in sea-elephant oil, may here be profitably extended. Various other sources of commerce will be met with, and may be almost exclusively appropriated. The crews, or at least some portion of the crews, of many of our vessels known to be wrecked in this vicinity, may be rescued from a life of slavery and despair. Moreover, we are degraded by the continual use of foreign charts. In matters of mere nautical or geographical science, our government has been hitherto supine, and it is due to the national character that in these respects something should be done. We have now a chance of redeeming ourselves in the Southern Sea. Here is a wide field open and nearly untouched—"a theatre peculiarly our own from position and the course of human events." Individual enterprize, even acting especially for the purpose, cannot be expected to accomplish all that should be done—dread of forfeiting insurance will prevent our whale-ships from effecting any thing of importance incidentally—and our national vessels on general service have elsewhere far more than they can efficiently attend to. In the meantime our condition is prosperous beyond example, our treasury is overflowing, a special national expedition could accomplish every thing desired, the expense of it will be comparatively little, the whole scientific world approve it, the people demand it, and thus there is a multiplicity of good reasons why it should immediately be set on foot.

Ten years ago these reasons were still in force, and Mr. Reynolds lost no opportunity of pressing them upon public attention. By a series of indefatigable exertions he at length succeeded in fully interesting the country in his scheme. Commodore Downes and Captain Jones, with nearly all the officers of our navy, gave it their unqualified approbation. Popular assemblages in all quarters spoke in its favor. Many of our commercial towns and cities petitioned for it. It was urged in Reports from the Navy and Messages from the Executive Department. The East India Marine Society of Massachusetts, all of whose members by the constitution must have personally doubled either Cape Horn, or the Cape of Good Hope, were induced to get up a memorial in its behalf; and the legislatures of eight different states—of New York, New Jersey, Rhode Island, Pennsylvania, Maryland, Ohio, North Carolina, and, we are happy to add, of Virginia, recommended the enterprize in the most earnest manner to the favorable consideration of Congress.

As early as January 1828, Mr. Reynolds submitted to the Speaker of the House of Representatives, a letter upon the subject accompanied with memorials and petitions. Among these memorials was one from Albany, dated October 19th, 1827, and signed by his Excellency Nathaniel Pitcher, lieutenant governor of the State of New York; the honorable Erastus Root, speaker of the house of delegates; and by nearly all the members of the legislature. Another, dated Charleston, South Carolina, May 31st, 1827, was signed by the mayor of the city; the president of the chamber of commerce; and by a very long list of respectable citizens. A third was dated Raleigh, North Carolina, December 24th, 1827, and contained the signatures

of his Excellency James Iredell, the governor; the honorable
B. Yancey, speaker of the senate; the honorable James Little,
speaker of the house of commons; and a large proportion of
each branch of the legislature. A fourth was dated Richmond,
Virginia, January 1st, 1828, and was sustained by a great number of the most influential inhabitants of Virginia; by the
honorable Linn Banks, speaker of the house of delegates; and
by a majority of the delegates themselves. For reference, Mr.
Reynolds handed in at the same period a preamble and resolution of the Maryland Assembly, approving in the strongest
terms the contemplated expedition. The matter was thus for
the first time, we believe, brought into a shape for the official
cognizance of the government.

The letter was referred to the committee on Naval Affairs.
That body made application to Mr. R. for a statement, in
writing, of his views. It was desired that this statement should
contain his reasons for general results, a reference to authorities for specific facts, as well as a tabular statement of the
results and facts, so far as they might be susceptible of being
stated in such form. To this application Mr. R. sent a brief
yet comprehensive reply, embracing a view of the nature and
extent of our whale-fisheries, and the several trades in the sea
otter skin, the fur seal skin, the ivory sea elephant tooth, land
animal fur, sandal wood, and feathers, together with observations on the general benefits resulting from these branches
of commerce, independent of the wealth they bring into the
country.

The Secretary of the Navy was also called upon for his
opinion. In his reply he strongly commended the design, using the main arguments we have already adduced. He stated,
moreover, that Mr. Reynolds' estimate of the value of our
commerce in the regions in question, had been much augmented, in the view of the department, through the reports,
made under its orders, of our naval officers, who had commanded vessels of war in the Pacific.

Nothing was done, however, until the next session of Congress. A bill was then proposed but did not become a law. In
consequence of its failure, the House of Representatives
passed a resolution requesting the President of the United
States "to send one of our small vessels to the Pacific Ocean

and South Seas, to examine the coasts, islands, harbors, shoals, and reefs in those seas, and to ascertain their true situation and description," and authorizing the use of such facilities as could be afforded by the Navy Department without further appropriation during the year. There was, however, no suitable national vessel in condition, at the time, to be despatched upon the service. The Peacock, therefore, was placed at the New York navy yard, to be repaired and fitted out, and an additional vessel of two hundred tons engaged, upon the agreement that Congress should be recommended to authorize the purchase—the vessel to be returned if the recommendation were not approved. These arrangements the Secretary of the Navy communicated to Congress in November, 1828. A bill now passed one house, but was finally lost.

Mr. Reynolds did not cease from his exertions. The subject of the expedition was not effectually resumed, however, until January 1835. Mr. Dickerson then transmitted to Congress, a Report by Mr. R., dated September 24th, 1828. This report had been drawn up at the request of Mr. Southard, in June, when that gentleman was called upon by the Committee on Naval Affairs. It occupies about forty pages of the volume now before us, and speaks plainly of the assiduity and energy of the reporter. He repaired, immediately, upon Mr. Southard's expressing a wish to that effect, to New-London, Stonington, New-Bedford, Edgartown, Nantucket, and other places where information might be found of the Pacific Ocean and South Seas. His desire was to avail himself of personal data, afforded by the owners and masters of the whaling vessels sailing from those ports. His main objects of inquiry were the navigation, geography and topography presented by the whole range of the seas from the Pacific to the Indian and Chinese oceans, with the extent and nature of our commerce and fisheries in those quarters. He found that "all he had before heard was confirmed by a long train of witnesses, and that every calculation he had previously made fell very far short of the truth." In February 1835, the Committee on Commerce strongly recommended Mr. Reynolds' design, and in March 1836 the Committee on Naval Affairs made a similar report. On May the 10th, a bill authorizing the expedition, but leaving nearly every thing to the discretion of the Chief

Magistrate, finally passed both houses of Congress. The friends of the bill could have desired nothing better. The President gave orders forthwith to have the exploring vessels fitted out with the least possible delay. The frigate Macedonian, now nearly ready, will be the main vessel in the enterprize. Captain Thomas Ap C. Jones will command her. She has been chosen instead of a sloop of war, on account of the increased accommodations she will afford the scientific corps, which is to be complete in its organization, including the ablest men to be procured. She will give too, extended protection to our commerce in the seas to be visited, and her imposing appearance will avail more to overawe the savages, and impress upon them a just idea of our power, than even a much larger real force distributed among vessels of less magnitude. She will be accompanied by two brigs of two hundred tons each, two tenders, and a store-ship.

In regard to the time of sailing there can be but little choice—the vessels will put to sea as soon as every thing is ready. The scientific corps, we believe, is not yet entirely filled up; nor can it be well organized until the preparations in the frigate are completed. Many gentlemen of high celebrity, however, have already offered their services. In the meantime, Lieutenant Wilkes of the Navy has been despatched to England and France, for the purpose of purchasing such instruments for the use of the expedition, as cannot readily be procured in this country. In all quarters he has met with the most gratifying reception, and with ardent wishes for the success of the contemplated enterprize.

Mr. Reynolds has received the highest civil post in the expedition—that of corresponding secretary. It is presumed that he will draw up the narrative of the voyage, (to be published under the patronage of government) embodying, possibly, and arranging in the same book, the several reports or journals of the scientific corps. How admirably well he is qualified for this task, no person can know better than ourselves. His energy, his love of polite literature, his many and various attainments, and above all, his ardent and honorable enthusiasm, point him out as the man of all men for the execution of the task. We look forward to this *finale*—to the published record of the expedition—with an intensity of eager expectation, which we cannot think we have ever experienced before.

And it has been said that envy and ill-will have been already doing their work—that the motives and character of Mr. Reynolds have been assailed. This is a matter which we fully believe. It is perfectly in unison with the history of all similar enterprizes, and of the vigorous minds which have conceived, advocated, and matured them. It is hardly necessary, however, to say a word upon this topic. We will not insult Mr. Reynolds with a defence. Gentlemen have impugned his motives—have these gentlemen ever seen him or conversed with him half an hour?

We close this notice by subjoining two interesting extracts from the eloquent Address now before us:

It is the opinion of some, as we are aware, that matters of this description are best left to individual enterprize, and that the interference of government is unnecessary. Such persons do not reflect, as they ought, that all measures of public utility which from any cause cannot be accomplished by individuals, become the legitimate objects of public care, in reference to which the government is bound to employ the means put into its hands for the general good. Indeed, while there remains a spot of untrodden earth accessible to man, no enlightened, and especially commercial and free people, should withhold its contributions for exploring it, wherever that spot may be found on the earth, from the equator to the poles!

Have we not shown that this expedition is called for by our extensive interests in those seas—interests which, from small beginnings, have increased astonishingly in the lapse of half a century, and which are every day augmenting and diffusing their beneficial results throughout the country? May we not venture on still higher grounds? Had we no commerce to be benefitted, would it not still be honorable; still worthy the patronage of Congress; still the best possible employment of a portion of our naval force?

Have we not shown, that this expedition is called for by national dignity and honor? Have we not shown, that our commanding position and rank among the commercial nations of the earth, makes it only equitable that we should take our share in exploring and surveying new islands, remote seas, and, as yet, unknown territory? Who so uninformed as to assert, that all this has been done? Who so presumptuous as to set limits to knowledge, which, by a wise law of Providence, can never cease? As long as there is mind to act upon matter, the realms of science must be enlarged; and nature and her laws be better understood, and more understandingly applied to the great purpose of life. If the nation were oppressed with debt, it might, indeed it would, still be our duty to do something, though the fact, perhaps, would operate as a reason for a delay of action. But have we any thing of this kind to allege, when the country is prosperous, without a parallel in the annals of nations?

Is not every department of industry in a state of improvement? Not only two, but a hundred blades of grass grow where one grew when we became a nation; and our manufactures have increased, not less to astonish the philosopher and patriot, than to benefit the nation; and have not agriculture and manufactures, wrought up by a capital of intelligence and enterprize, given a direct impulse to our commerce, a consequence to our navy? and if so, do they not impose new duties on every statesman?

Again, have we not shown that this expedition is demanded by public opinion, expressed in almost every form? Have not societies for the collection and diffusion of knowledge, towns and legislatures, and the commanding voice of public opinion, as seen through the public press, sanctioned and called for the enterprize? Granting, as all must, there is no dissenting voice upon the subject, that all are anxious that our country should do something for the great good of the human family, is not now the time, while the treasury, like the Nile in fruitful seasons, is overflowing its banks? If this question is settled, and I believe it is, the next is, what shall be the character of the expedition? The answer is in the minds of all— one worthy of the nation! And what would be worthy of the nation? Certainly nothing on a scale that has been attempted by any other country. If true to our national character, to the spirit of the age we live in, the first expedition sent out by this great republic must not fall short in any department— from a defective organization, or from adopting too closely the efforts of other nations as models for our own. We do, we always have done things best, when we do them in our own way. The spirit evinced by others is worthy of all imitation; but not their equipments. We must look at those seas; what we have there; what requires to be done;—and then apply the requisite means to accomplish the ends. It would not only be inglorious simply to follow a track pointed out by others, but it could never content a people proud of their fame and rejoicing in their strength! They would hurl to everlasting infamy the imbecile voyagers, who had only coasted where others had piloted. No; nothing but a goodly addition to the stock of present knowledge, would answer for those most moderate in their expectations.

But, not only to correct the errors of former navigators, and to enlarge and correct the charts of every portion of sea and land that the expedition might visit, and other duties to which we have alluded; but also to collect, preserve, and arrange every thing valuable in the whole range of natural history, from the minute madrapore to the huge spermaceti, and accurately to describe that which cannot be preserved; to secure whatever may be hoped for in natural philosophy; to examine vegetation, from the hundred mosses of the rocks, throughout all the classes of shrub, flower and tree, up to the monarch of the forest; to study man in his physical and mental powers, in his manners, habits, disposition, and social and political relations; and above all, in the philosophy of his language, in order to trace his origin from the early families of the old world; to examine the phenomena of winds and tides, of heat and cold, of light and darkness; to add geological to other surveys, when it can be done in safety; to examine the nature of soils—if not to see if they can be planted with success—yet to see if they contain any thing which may be transplanted with utility to our own country; in fine, there should be science enough to bear upon every thing that may present itself for investigation.

How, it may be asked, is all this to be effected? By an enlightened body of naval officers, joining harmoniously with a corps of scientific men, imbued with the love of science, and sufficiently learned to pursue with success the branches to which they should be designated. This body of men should be carefully selected, and made sufficiently numerous to secure the great objects of the expedition. These lights of science, and the naval officers, so far from interfering with each other's fame, would, like stars in the milky-way, shed a lustre on each other, and all on their country!

These men may be obtained, if sufficient encouragement is offered as an inducement. They should be well paid. Scholars of sufficient attainments to qualify them for such stations, do not hang loosely upon society; they must have fixed upon their professions or business in life: and what they are called to do, must be from the efforts of ripe minds; not the experiments of youthful ones to prepare them for usefulness. If we have been a by-word and a reproach among nations for pitiful remuneration of intellectual labors, this expedition will afford an excellent opportunity of wiping it away. The stimulus of fame is not a sufficient motive for a scientific man to leave his family and friends, and all the charms and duties of social life, for years together; but it must be united to the recompense of pecuniary reward, to call forth all the powers of an opulent mind. The price you pay will, in some measure, show your appreciation of such pursuits. We have no stars and ribands, no hereditary titles, to reward our men of genius for adding to the knowledge or to the comfort of mankind, and to the honor of the nation. We boast of our men of science, our philosophers, and artists, when they have paid the last tribute to envy by their death. When mouldering in their graves, they enjoy a reputation, which envy and malice and detraction may hawk at and tear, but cannot harm! Let us be more just, and stamp the value we set on science in a noble appreciation of it, and by the price we are willing to pay.

It has been justly remarked, that those who enlighten their country by their talents, strengthen it by their philosophy, enrich it by their science, and adorn it by their genius, are Atlases, who support the name and dignity of their nation, and transmit it unimpaired to future generations. Their noblest part lives and is active, when they are no more; and their names and contributions to knowledge, are legacies bequeathed to the whole world! To those who shall thus labor to enrich our country, if we would be just, we must be liberal, by giving to themselves and families an honorable support while engaged in these arduous duties!

If the objects of the expedition are noble, if the inducements to undertake it are of a high order—and we believe there can be no difference of opinion on this point—most assuredly the means to accomplish them should be adequate. No narrow views, no scanty arrangements, should enter the minds of those who have the planning and directing of the enterprize. At such a time, and in such a cause, *liberality* is *economy*, and *parsimony* is *extravagance*.

Again, if the object of the expedition were simply to attain a high southern latitude, then two small brigs or barks would be quite sufficient. If to visit a few points among the islands, a sloop of war might answer the purpose. But are these the objects? We apprehend they only form a part. From the west coast of South America, running down the longitude among the islands on both sides of the equator, though more especially south, to the very shores of Asia, is the field that lies open before us, independent of the higher latitudes south, of which we shall speak in the conclusion of our remarks. Reflecting on the picture we have sketched of our interests in that immense region, all must admit, that the armament of the expedition should be sufficient to protect our flag; to succor the unfortunate of every nation, who may be found on desolate islands, or among hordes of savages; a power that would be sufficient by the majesty of its appearance, to awe into respect and obedience the fierce and turbulent, and to give facilities to all engaged in the great purposes of the voyage. The amount of this power is a question upon which there can be but little difference of opinion, among those thoroughly acquainted with the subject; the best informed are unanimous in their opinion, that there should be a well-appointed frigate, and five other vessels—twice that number would find enough, and more than they could do. The frigate would form the *nucleus*, round which the smaller vessels should perform the labors to which we have already alluded, and which you will find pointed out in all the memorials and reports hitherto made on this subject, and which may be found among the printed documents on your tables. Some might say, and we have heard such things said, that this equipment would savor of individual pride in the commander; but they forget that the calculations of the wise are generally secured by the strength of their measure. The voyage is long—the resting places uncertain, which makes the employment of a storeship, also, a matter of prudence and economy. It would not do to be anxious about food, while the expedition was in the search of an extended harvest of knowledge.

The expectations of the people of the United States from such an expedition, most unquestionably would be great. From their education and past exertions through all the history of our national growth, the people are prepared to expect that every public functionary should discharge his duty to the utmost extent of his physical and mental powers. They will not be satisfied with any thing short of all that men can perform. The appalling weight of responsibility of those who serve their country in such an expedition, is strikingly illustrated by the instructions given to Lewis and Clarke, in 1803, by President Jefferson. The extended views and mental grasp of this distinguished philosopher no one will question, nor can any one believe that he would be unnecessarily minute.

The sage, who had conceived and matured the plan of the expedition to the far west, in his instructions to its commander under his own signature, has left us a model worthy of all imitation. With the slight variations growing out of time and place, how applicable would those instructions be for the guidance of the enterprize we have at present in view? The doubts of some politicians, that this government has no power to encourage scientific inquiry, most assuredly had no place in the mind of that great *apostle of liberty, father of democracy, and strict constructionist!* We claim no wider range than he has sanctioned; including as he does, *animate and inanimate nature, the heavens above, and all on the earth beneath!* The character and value of that paper are not sufficiently known. Among all the records of his genius, his patriotism, and his learning, to be found in our public archives, this paper deserves to take, and in time will take rank, second only to the Declaration of our Independence. The first, imbodied the spirit of our free institutions, and self-government; the latter, sanctioned those *liberal pursuits*, without a just appreciation of which, our institutions cannot be preserved, or if they can, would be scarcely worth preserving.

  * * * * * *

To complete its efficiency, individuals from other walks of life, we repeat, should be appointed to participate in its labors. No professional pique, no petty jealousies, should be allowed to defeat this object. The enterprize should be national in its object, and sustained by the national means,—belongs of right to no individual, or set of individuals, but to the country and the whole country; and he who does not view it in this light, or could not enter it with this spirit, would not be very likely to meet the public expectations were he entrusted with the entire control.

To indulge in jealousies, or feel undue solicitude about the division of honors before they are won, is the appropriate employment of carpet heroes, in whatever walk of life they may be found. The qualifications of such would fit them better to thread the mazes of the dance, or to shine in the saloon, than to venture upon an enterprize requiring men, in the most emphatic sense of the term.

There are, we know, many, very many, ardent spirits in our navy—many whom we hold among the most valued of our friends—who are tired of inglorious ease, and who would seize the opportunity thus presented to them with avidity, and enter with delight upon this new path to fame.

Our seamen are hardy and adventurous, especially those who are engaged in the seal trade and the whale fisheries; and innured as they are to the perils of navigation, are inferior to none on earth for such a service. Indeed, the enterprize, courage and perseverance of American seamen are, if not unrivalled, at least unsurpassed. What man can do, they have always felt ready to attempt,—what man has done, it is their character to feel able to do,—whether it be to grapple with an enemy on the deep, or to pursue their gigantic game under the burning line, with an intelligence and ardor that insure success, or pushing their adventurous barks into the high southern latitudes, to circle the globe within the Antarctic circle, and attain the Pole itself; yea, to cast anchor on that point where all the meridians terminate, where our eagle and star-

spangled banner may be unfurled and planted, and left to
wave on the axis of the earth itself!—where, amid the novelty, grandeur and sublimity of the scene, the vessels, instead
of sweeping a vast circuit by the diurnal movements of the
earth, would simply turn round once in twenty-four hours!

We shall not discuss, at present, the probability of this result, though its possibility might be easily demonstrated. If
this should be realized, where is the individual who does not
feel that such an achievement would add new lustre to the
annals of American philosophy, and crown with a new and
imperishable wreath the nautical glories of our country!

Southern Literary Messenger, January 1837

A Brief Account of the Discoveries and Results of the United States' Exploring Expedition.
New Haven, B. L. Hamlen.

THIS PAMPHLET, reprinted from the American Journal of
Sciences and Arts, gives a synopsis of the Reynolds Expedition of Discovery, and conveys a general idea of the material on hand for publication by the General Government.
Hitherto little has been satisfactorily known in respect to the
extent or the results of the voyage; the compendious account
furnished by Captain Charles Wilkes being, perhaps, somewhat less luminous than succinct. The general impression, deduced very naturally from the scandalous chicanery practiced
in the outfit of the Expedition, with a view to thwart the will
of the nation, as manifested in the action of Congress, and to
thrust from all participation in the enterprise the very man
who gave it origin, and who cherished it to consummation—
the general impression, we say, has very naturally been that
little or nothing was accomplished. But this opinion does injustice, not less to the scheme itself than to the many able and
respectable gentlemen who constituted the scientific corps. In
the mere point of approaching the south pole—that pole
which, in the opinion of an Honorable Secretary, formed the
sole object of the adventure—something more, indeed, might
have been performed; but so far as regards the more momentous objects, the making of surveys, the location of reefs, the
examination of harbors, the discovery and investigation of
new lands, the permanent establishment of our intercourse

with the Pacific islands, the impression produced by our vessels in remote seas, the consequent protection afforded our commerce, and, especially, so far as regards the advancement of many important branches of natural science, the results of the American Expedition have been all that could be desired.

The several vessels left the Chesapeake on August 19th, 1838, and sailed for Rio Janeiro, touching at Madeira and the Cape de Verds. From Rio they proceeded to Rio Negro— thence to Nassau Bay in Tierra del Fuego. Thence the Peacock, Porpoise, and two schooners, cruised in different directions toward the pole; the Flying Fish reaching 70° 14′— nearly the highest point attained by Cook, and almost in the same longitude. Weddell, it will be remembered, made as far as 84°. While the schooners were thus employed, the ship Relief narrowly escaped wreck, under Noir Island, in an attempt to enter a southern channel, opening from Nassau Bay into the Straits of Magellan. The Vincennes remained in the bay. In May, 1839, the Expedition rendezvoused at Valparaiso, with the exception of the Sea-Gull, which was lost in a gale. On the 6th of June they sailed for Callao, Peru, and hence the Relief, proving ill-adapted for her purposes, was sent home. On the 12th of July the squadron left the South American coast, and, proceeding westwardly, surveyed fourteen or fifteen of the Paumotu Islands, two of the Society Islands, and all the group of the Navigators. On the 28th of November they repaired to Sydney, New South Wales, and thence sailed on a second cruise in the Antarctic. The first discovery of land was in longitude 160° E. and latitude 66° 30′ S. This land was tracked by the Vincennes and Porpoise, steering to the west, along a barrier of ice, for the distance of one thousand five hundred miles. The Vincennes occasionally approached to within three fourths of a mile of the shore. At a place called Piner's Bay, soundings were obtained in thirty fathoms, and "they had hopes of soon landing on the rocks; but a storm came up suddenly which lasted for thirty-six hours, and drove the vessels far to leeward; they consequently pushed on with their explorations to the westward, hoping for some more accessible place, but were disappointed."*

*See Capt. Wilkes' Synopsis.

On the 24th of February the squadron met at Tongatabu, and were here joined by the scientific corps, who, during the Antarctic cruise, were occupied in New Holland and New Zealand. From Tongatabu our voyagers sailed to the Fejees. At the expiration of four months they proceeded thence to the Sandwich Islands, surveying several small coral islands on their way. At the Sandwich group the Vincennes spent the winter, while the Peacock and Flying Fish cruised in the equatorial regions of the Pacific; visiting, especially, the Navigators and the Kingsmill group, with others of the Caroline Archipelago. The Porpoise made charts of several of the Paumotu Islands not before surveyed, and touched again at Tahiti.

In the spring of 1841, the Vincennes and Porpoise arrived at the coast of Oregon; the Peacock and Flying Fish not reaching it until July. While attempting to enter the Columbia, the Peacock was wrecked. From the coast of Oregon several land expeditions were made into the interior; one of the most important being a journey from the Columbia, a distance of eight hundred miles, to San Francisco, in California.

Leaving California in November, 1841, the vessels touched for supplies at the Sandwich Islands, and thence sailed to Manilla; thence to Mindanao; thence, through the Sooloo Archipelago, and the Straits of Balabac, to Singapore; thence, by the Straits of Sunda, to the Cape of Good Hope; thence, by St. Helena, to New York, where they arrived in June, 1842, having been absent three years and ten months, and having sailed between eighty and ninety thousand miles.

In this memorable Expedition about two hundred and eighty islands were surveyed, beside eight hundred miles on the streams and coast of Oregon; not to speak of the fifteen hundred miles of Antarctic continent. It has been the fashion to doubt the actual discovery of this continent; but this doubt is unreasonable, and arises from a misunderstanding in relation to our dispute with the French. This dispute is not in regard to the discovery itself—but to the priority of discovery. The French have yielded their claim to this. It has been said, too, that Ross actually sailed over a portion of what Capt. Wilkes supposed to be land; but this is not so; the points sailed over were points of a discovery claimed by Bellamy and not by Capt. Wilkes. Notwithstanding all this, it must forever remain a subject for wonder, regret and mortification, that, having sailed for fifteen hundred miles along an Antartic continent, the Expedition should have been enabled to furnish no result more satisfactory than a few stones picked up from fragments of floating ice, and far more solid in themselves than as arguments of the immediate vicinity of land, or as specimens of that particular land in the neighborhood of which they happened to be found afloat.

The National Gallery at Washington contains suites of better specimens, however, from the various regions surveyed. These, of course, are of high value, and of deep interest. Among them are gems and gold and iron ores from Brazil; copper and silver ores from Peru and Chili; vast collections of shells and corals; fifty thousand plants—two hundred and four of them living; two thousand birds; and an immense variety of objects, even more important than any of these, in the numerous divisions of Natural Science.

The country will soon be put in possession of the facts of the Expedition in full. When we say "soon," we mean in a year or thereabouts. The publication will be made upon a magnificent scale, and will compare with that of the voyage of the Astrolabe. The plates alone will form several folio volumes. The mere history of the whole has been put in charge of Captain Wilkes. The purely scientific departments are in the hands of the able gentlemen who had their supervision during the voyage. Each will prepare his portion of the great work in his own manner.

To the prime mover in this important undertaking—to the active, the intelligent, the indomitable advocate of the enterprise—to him who gave it birth, and who brought it through maturity, to its triumphant result, this result can afford nothing but unmitigated pleasure. He has seen his measures adopted in the teeth of opposition, and his comprehensive views thoroughly confirmed in spite of cant, prejudice, ignorance and unbelief. For fifteen years has he contended, single-handed, in support of this good cause, against all that a jealous and miserably despicable *esprit de corps* could bring to his overthrow. He has contended, we say, single-handed, and triumphed. And well knew *we*, at least, that he would. Many years ago we maintained the impossibility of his failure. With mental powers of the highest order, his indomitable energy is precisely of that character which *will not admit* of defeat.

To him, we say—and to him in fact *solely*—does the high honor of this triumphant Expedition belong. Take from the enterprise the original impulse which *he* gave—the laborious preliminary investigation which *he* undertook—the unflinching courage and the great ability with which *he* defended it when attacked—the unwearying perseverance with which *he* urged its progress, and by which *he* finally ensured its consummation—let the Expedition have wanted all this, and what would the world have had of it but the shadow of a shade? To him, we repeat, be the glory of this important undertaking—and to those who deserve it—and who now sorely feel they deserve it—be whatever of disgrace has attached to its conduct. One thing is certain—when men, hereafter, shall come to speak of this Expedition, they will speak of it not as the American Expedition—nor even as the Poinsett Expedition, nor as the Dickerson Expedition, nor, alas! as the Wilkes Expedition—they will speak of it—if they speak at all—as "The Expedition of Mr. Reynolds."

Graham's Magazine, September 1843

Maelzel's Chess-Player

PERHAPS NO exhibition of the kind has ever elicited so general attention as the Chess-Player of Maelzel. Wherever seen it has been an object of intense curiosity, to all persons who think. Yet the question of its *modus operandi* is still undetermined. Nothing has been written on this topic which can be considered as decisive—and accordingly we find every where men of mechanical genius, of great general acuteness, and discriminative understanding, who make no scruple in pronouncing the Automaton a *pure machine*, unconnected with human agency in its movements, and consequently, beyond all comparison, the most astonishing of the inventions of mankind. And such it would undoubtedly be, were they right in their supposition. Assuming this hypothesis, it would be grossly absurd to compare with the Chess-Player, any similar thing of either modern or ancient days. Yet there have been many and wonderful automata. In Brewster's Letters on Natural Magic, we have an account of the most remarkable. Among these may be mentioned, as having beyond doubt existed, firstly, the coach invented by M. Camus for the amusement of Louis XIV. when a child. A table, about four feet square, was introduced, into the room appropriated for the exhibition. Upon this table was placed a carriage, six inches in length, made of wood, and drawn by two horses of the same material. One window being down, a lady was seen on the back seat. A coachman held the reins on the box, and a footman and page were in their places behind. M. Camus now touched a spring; whereupon the coachman smacked his whip, and the horses proceeded in a natural manner, along the edge of the table, drawing after them the carriage. Having gone as far as possible in this direction, a sudden turn was made to the left, and the vehicle was driven at right angles to its former course, and still closely along the edge of the table. In this way the coach proceeded until it arrived opposite the chair of the young prince. It then stopped, the page descended and opened the door, the lady alighted, and presented a petition to her sovereign. She then re-entered. The page put up the steps, closed the door, and resumed his station. The coachman whipped his horses, and the carriage was driven back to its original position.

The magician of M. Maillardet is also worthy of notice. We copy the following account of it from the *Letters* before mentioned of Dr. B., who derived his information principally from the Edinburgh Encyclopædia.

"One of the most popular pieces of mechanism which we have seen, is the Magician constructed by M. Maillardet, for the purpose of answering certain given questions. A figure, dressed like a magician, appears seated at the bottom of a wall, holding a wand in one hand, and a book in the other. A number of questions, ready prepared, are inscribed on oval medallions, and the spectator takes any of these he chooses, and to which he wishes an answer, and having placed it in a drawer ready to receive it, the drawer shuts with a spring till the answer is returned. The magician then arises from his seat, bows his head, describes circles with his wand, and consulting the book as if in deep thought, he lifts it towards his face. Having thus appeared to ponder over the proposed question, he raises his wand, and striking with it the wall above his head, two folding doors fly open, and display an appropriate answer to the question. The doors again close, the magician resumes his original position, and the drawer opens to return the medallion. There are twenty of these medallions, all containing different questions, to which the magician returns the most suitable and striking answers. The medallions are thin plates of brass, of an elliptical form, exactly resembling each other. Some of the medallions have a question inscribed on each side, both of which the magician answered in succession. If the drawer is shut without a medallion being put into it, the magician rises, consults his book, shakes his head, and resumes his seat. The folding doors remain shut, and the drawer is returned empty. If two medallions are put into the drawer together, an answer is returned only to the lower one. When the machinery is wound up, the movements continue about an hour, during which time about fifty questions may be answered. The inventor stated that the means by which the different medallions acted upon the machinery, so as to produce the proper answers to the questions which they contained, were extremely simple."

The duck of Vaucanson was still more remarkable. It was of the size of life, and so perfect an imitation of the living animal that all the spectators were deceived. It executed, says Brewster, all the natural movements and gestures, it ate and drank with avidity, performed all the quick motions of the head and throat which are peculiar to the duck, and like it muddled the water which it drank with its bill. It produced also the sound of quacking in the most natural manner. In the anatomical structure the artist exhibited the highest skill. Every bone in the real duck had its representative in the automaton, and its wings were anatomically exact. Every cavity, apophysis, and curvature was imitated, and each bone executed its proper movements. When corn was thrown down before it, the duck stretched out its neck to pick it up, swallowed, and digested it.*

But if these machines were ingenious, what shall we think of the calculating machine of Mr. Babbage? What shall we think of an engine of wood and metal which can not only compute astronomical and navigation tables to any given extent, but render the exactitude of its operations mathematically certain through its power of correcting its possible errors? What shall we think of a machine which can not only accomplish all this, but actually print off its elaborate results, when obtained, without the slightest intervention of the intellect of man? It will, perhaps, be said, in reply, that a machine such as we have described is altogether above comparison with the Chess-Player of Maelzel. By no means— it is altogether beneath it—that is to say provided we assume (what should never for a moment be assumed) that the Chess-Player is a *pure machine*, and performs its operations without any immediate human agency. Arithmetical or algebraical calculations are, from their very nature, fixed and determinate. Certain *data* being given, certain results necessarily and inevitably follow. These results have dependence upon nothing, and are influenced by nothing but the *data* originally given. And the question to be solved proceeds, or should proceed, to its final determination, by a succession of unerring steps liable to no change, and subject to no modifi-

*Under the head *Androides* in the Edinburgh Encyclopædia may be found a full account of the principal automata of ancient and modern times.

cation. This being the case, we can without difficulty conceive the *possibility* of so arranging a piece of mechanism, that upon starting it in accordance with the *data* of the question to be solved, it should continue its movements regularly, progressively, and undeviatingly towards the required solution, since these movements, however complex, are never imagined to be otherwise than finite and determinate. But the case is widely different with the Chess-Player. With him there is no determinate progression. No one move in chess necessarily follows upon any one other. From no particular disposition of the men at one period of a game can we predicate their disposition at a different period. Let us place the *first move* in a game of chess, in juxta-position with the *data* of an algebraical question, and their great difference will be immediately perceived. From the latter—from the *data*—the second step of the question, dependent thereupon, inevitably follows. It is modelled by the *data*. It must be *thus* and not otherwise. But from the first move in the game of chess no especial second move follows of necessity. In the algebraical question, as it proceeds towards solution, the *certainty* of its operations remains altogether unimpaired. The second step having been a consequence of the *data*, the third step is equally a consequence of the second, the fourth of the third, the fifth of the fourth, and so on, *and not possibly otherwise*, to the end. But in proportion to the progress made in a game of chess, is the *uncertainty* of each ensuing move. A few moves having been made, *no* step is certain. Different spectators of the game would advise different moves. All is then dependant upon the variable judgment of the players. Now even granting (what should not be granted) that the movements of the Automaton Chess-Player were in themselves determinate, they would be necessarily interrupted and disarranged by the indeterminate will of his antagonist. There is then no analogy whatever between the operations of the Chess-Player, and those of the calculating machine of Mr. Babbage, and if we choose to call the former a *pure machine* we must be prepared to admit that it is, beyond all comparison, the most wonderful of the inventions of mankind. Its original projector, however, Baron Kempelen, had no scruple in declaring it to be a "very ordinary piece of mechanism—a *bagatelle* whose effects appeared so marvellous only from the boldness of the conception, and the fortunate choice of the methods adopted for promoting the illusion." But it is needless to dwell upon this point. It is quite certain that the operations of the Automaton are regulated by *mind*, and by nothing else. Indeed this matter is susceptible of a mathematical demonstration, *a priori*. The only question then is of the *manner* in which human agency is brought to bear. Before entering upon this subject it would be as well to give a brief history and description of the Chess-Player for the benefit of such of our readers as may never have had an opportunity of witnessing Mr. Maelzel's exhibition.

The Automaton Chess-Player was invented in 1769, by Baron Kempelen, a nobleman of Presburg, in Hungary, who afterwards disposed of it, together with the secret of its operations, to its present possessor. Soon after its completion it was exhibited in Presburg, Paris, Vienna, and other continental cities. In 1783 and 1784, it was taken to London by Mr. Maelzel. Of late years it has visited the principal towns in the United States. Wherever seen, the most intense curiosity was excited by its appearance, and numerous have been the attempts, by men of all classes, to fathom the mystery of its evolutions. The cut above gives a tolerable representation of the figure as seen by the citizens of Richmond a few weeks ago. The right arm, however, should lie more at length upon the box, a chess-board should appear upon it, and the cushion should not be seen while the pipe is held. Some immaterial alterations have been made in the costume of the player since it came into the possession of Maelzel—the plume, for example, was not originally worn.

At the hour appointed for exhibition, a curtain is with-drawn, or folding doors are thrown open, and the machine rolled to within about twelve feet of the nearest of the spec-tators, between whom and it (the machine) a rope is stretched. A figure is seen habited as a Turk, and seated, with its legs crossed, at a large box apparently of maple wood, which serves it as a table. The exhibiter will, if requested, roll the machine to any portion of the room, suffer it to remain altogether on any designated spot, or even shift its location repeatedly during the progress of a game. The bottom of the box is elevated considerably above the floor by means of the castors or brazen rollers on which it moves, a clear view of the surface immediately beneath the Automaton being thus afforded to the spectators. The chair on which the figure sits is affixed permanently to the box. On the top of this latter is a chess-board, also permanently affixed. The right arm of the Chess-Player is extended at full length before him, at right angles with his body, and lying, in an apparently careless po-sition, by the side of the board. The back of the hand is up-wards. The board itself is eighteen inches square. The left arm of the figure is bent at the elbow, and in the left hand is a pipe. A green drapery conceals the back of the Turk, and falls partially over the front of both shoulders. To judge from the external appearance of the box, it is divided into five com-partments—three cupboards of equal dimensions, and two drawers occupying that portion of the chest lying beneath the cupboards. The foregoing observations apply to the appear-ance of the Automaton upon its first introduction into the presence of the spectators.

Maelzel now informs the company that he will disclose to their view the mechanism of the machine. Taking from his pocket a bunch of keys he unlocks with one of them, door marked 1 in the cut above, and throws the cupboard fully open to the inspection of all present. Its whole interior is ap-parently filled with wheels, pinions, levers, and other ma-chinery, crowded very closely together, so that the eye can penetrate but a little distance into the mass. Leaving this door open to its full extent, he goes now round to the back of the box, and raising the drapery of the figure, opens another door situated precisely in the rear of the one first opened. Holding a lighted candle at this door, and shifting the position of the whole machine repeatedly at the same time, a bright light is thrown entirely through the cupboard, which is now clearly seen to be full, completely full, of machinery. The spectators being satisfied of this fact, Maelzel closes the back door, locks it, takes the key from the lock, lets fall the drapery of the figure, and comes round to the front. The door marked 1, it will be remembered, is still open. The exhibiter now proceeds to open the drawer which lies beneath the cupboards at the bottom of the box—for although there are apparently two drawers, there is really only one—the two handles and two key holes being intended merely for ornament. Having opened this drawer to its full extent, a small cushion, and a set of chessmen, fixed in a frame work made to support them perpendicularly, are discovered. Leaving this drawer, as well as cupboard No. 1 open, Maelzel now unlocks door No. 2, and door No. 3, which are discovered to be folding doors, opening into one and the same compartment. To the right of this compartment, however, (that is to say the spectators' right) a small division, six inches wide, and filled with machinery, is partitioned off. The main compartment itself (in speaking of that portion of the box visible upon opening doors 2 and 3, we shall always call it the main compartment) is lined with dark cloth and contains no machinery whatever beyond two pieces of steel, quadrant-shaped, and situated one in each of the rear top corners of the compartment. A small protuberance about eight inches square, and also covered with dark cloth, lies on the floor of the compartment near the rear corner on the spectators' left hand. Leaving doors No. 2 and No. 3 open as well as the drawer, and door No. 1, the exhibiter now goes round to the back of the main compartment, and, unlocking another door there, displays clearly all the interior of the main compartment, by introducing a candle behind it and within it. The whole box being thus apparently disclosed to the scrutiny of the company, Maelzel, still leaving the doors and drawer open, rolls the Automaton entirely round, and exposes the back of the Turk by lifting up the drapery. A door about ten inches square is thrown open in the loins of the figure, and a smaller one also in the left thigh. The interior of the figure, as seen through these apertures, appears to be crowded with machinery. In general, every spectator is now thoroughly satisfied of having beheld and completely scrutinized, at one and the same time, every individual portion of the Automaton, and the idea of any person being concealed in the interior, during so complete an exhibition of that interior, if ever entertained, is immediately dismissed as preposterous in the extreme.

M. Maelzel, having rolled the machine back into its original position, now informs the company that the Automaton will play a game of chess with any one disposed to encounter him. This challenge being accepted, a small table is prepared for the antagonist, and placed close by the rope, but on the spectators' side of it, and so situated as not to prevent the company from obtaining a full view of the Automaton. From a drawer in this table is taken a set of chess-men, and Maelzel arranges them generally, but not always, with his own hands, on the chess board, which consists merely of the usual number of squares painted upon the table. The antagonist having taken his seat, the exhibiter approaches the drawer of the box, and takes therefrom the cushion, which, after removing the pipe from the hand of the Automaton, he places under its left arm as a support. Then taking also from the drawer the Automaton's set of chess-men, he arranges them upon the chess-board before the figure. He now proceeds to close the doors and to lock them—leaving the bunch of keys in door No. 1. He also closes the drawer, and, finally, winds up the machine, by applying a key to an aperture in the left end (the spectators' left) of the box. The game now commences—the Automaton taking the first move. The duration of the contest is usually limited to half an hour, but if it be not finished at the expiration of this period, and the antagonist still contend that he can beat the Automaton, M. Maelzel has seldom any objection to continue it. Not to weary the company, is the ostensible, and no doubt the real object of the limitation. It will of course be understood that when a move is made at his own table, by the antagonist, the corresponding move is made at the box of the Automaton, by Maelzel himself, who then acts as the representative of the antagonist. On the other hand, when the Turk moves, the corresponding move is made at the table of the antagonist, also by M. Maelzel, who then acts as the representative of the Automaton. In this manner it is necessary that the exhibiter should often pass from one table to the other. He also frequently goes in rear of the figure to remove the chess-men which it has taken, and which it deposits, when taken, on the box to the left (to its own left) of the board. When the Automaton hesitates in relation to its move, the exhibiter is occasionally seen to place himself very near its right side, and to lay his hand, now and then, in a careless manner upon the box. He has also a peculiar shuffle with his feet, calculated to induce suspicion of collusion with the machine in minds which are more cunning than sagacious. These peculiarities are, no doubt, mere mannerisms of M. Maelzel, or, if he is aware of them at all, he puts them in practice with a view of exciting in the spectators a false idea of the pure mechanism in the Automaton.

The Turk plays with his left hand. All the movements of the arm are at right angles. In this manner, the hand (which is gloved and bent in a natural way,) being brought directly above the piece to be moved, descends finally upon it, the fingers receiving it, in most cases, without difficulty. Occasionally, however, when the piece is not precisely in its proper situation, the Automaton fails in his attempt at seizing it. When this occurs, no second effort is made, but the arm continues its movement in the direction originally intended, precisely as if the piece were in the fingers. Having thus designated the spot whither the move should have been made, the arm returns to its cushion, and Maelzel performs the evolution which the Automaton pointed out. At every movement of the figure machinery is heard in motion. During the progress of the game, the figure now and then rolls its eyes, as if surveying the board, moves its head, and pronounces the word *echec* (check) when necessary.* If a false move be made by his antagonist, he raps briskly on the box with the fingers of his right hand, shakes his head roughly, and replacing the piece falsely moved, in its former situation, assumes the next move himself. Upon beating the game, he waves his head with an air of triumph, looks round compla-

---

*The making the Turk pronounce the word *echec*, is an improvement by M. Maelzel. When in possession of Baron Kempelen, the figure indicated a *check* by rapping on the box with his right hand.

cently upon the spectators, and drawing his left arm farther back than usual, suffers his fingers alone to rest upon the cushion. In general, the Turk is victorious—once or twice he has been beaten. The game being ended, Maelzel will again, if desired, exhibit the mechanism of the box, in the same manner as before. The machine is then rolled back, and a curtain hides it from the view of the company.

There have been many attempts at solving the mystery of the Automaton. The most general opinion in relation to it, an opinion too not unfrequently adopted by men who should have known better, was, as we have before said, that no immediate human agency was employed—in other words, that the machine was purely a machine and nothing else. Many, however maintained that the exhibiter himself regulated the movements of the figure by mechanical means operating through the feet of the box. Others again, spoke confidently of a magnet. Of the first of these opinions we shall say nothing at present more than we have already said. In relation to the second it is only necessary to repeat what we have before stated, that the machine is rolled about on castors, and will, at the request of a spectator, be moved to and fro to any portion of the room, even during the progress of a game. The supposition of the magnet is also untenable—for if a magnet were the agent, any other magnet in the pocket of a spectator would disarrange the entire mechanism. The exhibiter, however, will suffer the most powerful loadstone to remain even upon the box during the whole of the exhibition.

The first attempt at a written explanation of the secret, at least the first attempt of which we ourselves have any knowledge, was made in a large pamphlet printed at Paris in 1785. The author's hypothesis amounted to this—that a dwarf actuated the machine. This dwarf he supposed to conceal himself during the opening of the box by thrusting his legs into two hollow cylinders, which were represented to be (but which are not) among the machinery in the cupboard No. 1, while his body was out of the box entirely, and covered by the drapery of the Turk. When the doors were shut, the dwarf was enabled to bring his body within the box—the noise produced by some portion of the machinery allowing him to do so unheard, and also to close the door by which he entered. The interior of the automaton being then exhibited, and no person discovered, the spectators, says the author of this pamphlet, are satisfied that no one is within any portion of the machine. This whole hypothesis was too obviously absurd to require comment, or refutation, and accordingly we find that it attracted very little attention.

In 1789 a book was published at Dresden by M. I. F. Freyhere in which another endeavor was made to unravel the mystery. Mr. Freyhere's book was a pretty large one, and copiously illustrated by colored engravings. His supposition was that "a well-taught boy very thin and tall of his age (sufficiently so that he could be concealed in a drawer almost immediately under the chess-board") played the game of chess and effected all the evolutions of the Automaton. This idea, although even more silly than that of the Parisian author, met with a better reception, and was in some measure believed to be the true solution of the wonder, until the inventor put an end to the discussion by suffering a close examination of the top of the box.

These bizarre attempts at explanation were followed by others equally bizarre. Of late years however, an anonymous writer, by a course of reasoning exceedingly unphilosophical, has contrived to blunder upon a plausible solution—although we cannot consider it altogether the true one. His Essay was first published in a Baltimore weekly paper, was illustrated by cuts, and was entitled "An attempt to analyze the Automaton Chess-Player of M. Maelzel." This Essay we suppose to have been the original of the *pamphlet* to which Sir David Brewster alludes in his letters on Natural Magic, and which he has no hesitation in declaring a thorough and satisfactory explanation. The *results* of the analysis are undoubtedly, in the main, just; but we can only account for Brewster's pronouncing the Essay a thorough and satisfactory explanation, by supposing him to have bestowed upon it a very cursory and inattentive perusal. In the compendium of the Essay, made use of in the Letters on Natural Magic, it is quite impossible to arrive at any distinct conclusion in regard to the adequacy or inadequacy of the analysis, on account of the gross misarrangement and deficiency of the letters of reference employed. The same fault is to be found in the "Attempt &c.," as we originally saw it. The solution consists in a series of minute explanations, (accompanied by wood-cuts, the whole occupying many pages) in which the object is to show the *possibility* of *so shifting the partitions* of the box, as to allow a human being, concealed in the interior, to move portions of his body from one part of the box to another, during the exhibition of the mechanism—thus eluding the scrutiny of the spectators. There can be no doubt, as we have before observed, and as we will presently endeavor to show, that the principle, or rather the result, of this solution is the true one. Some person *is* concealed in the box during the whole time of exhibiting the interior. We object, however, to the whole verbose description of the *manner* in which the partitions are shifted, to accommodate the movements of the person concealed. We object to it as a mere theory assumed in the first place, and to which circumstances are afterwards made to adapt themselves. It was not, and could not have been, arrived at by any inductive reasoning. In whatever way the shifting is managed, it is of course concealed at every step from observation. To show that certain movements might possibly be effected in a certain way, is very far from showing that they are actually so effected. There may be an infinity of other methods by which the same results may be obtained. The probability of the one assumed proving the correct one is then as unity to infinity. But, in reality, this particular point, the shifting of the partitions, is of no consequence whatever. It was altogether unnecessary to devote seven or eight pages for the purpose of proving what no one in his senses would deny—viz: that the wonderful mechanical genius of Baron Kempelen could invent the necessary means for shutting a door or slipping aside a pannel, with a human agent too at his service in actual contact with the pannel or the door, and the whole operations carried on, as the author of the Essay himself shows, and as we shall attempt to show more fully hereafter, entirely out of reach of the observation of the spectators.

In attempting ourselves an explanation of the Automaton, we will, in the first place, endeavor to show how its operations are effected, and afterwards describe, as briefly as pos-

sible, the nature of the *observations* from which we have deduced our result.

It will be necessary for a proper understanding of the subject, that we repeat here in a few words, the routine adopted
by the exhibiter in disclosing the interior of the box—a routine from which he *never* deviates in any material particular.
In the first place he opens the door No. 1. Leaving this open,
he goes round to the rear of the box, and opens a door precisely at the back of door No. 1. To this back door he holds a
lighted candle. He then *closes the back door*, locks it, and, coming round to the front, opens the drawer to its full extent.
This done, he opens the doors No. 2 and No. 3, (the folding
doors) and displays the interior of the main compartment.
Leaving open the main compartment, the drawer, and the
front door of cupboard No. 1, he now goes to the rear again,
and throws open the back door of the main compartment. In
shutting up the box no particular order is observed, except
that the folding doors are always closed before the drawer.

Now, let us suppose that when the machine is first rolled
into the presence of the spectators, a man is already within it.
His body is situated behind the dense machinery in cupboard
No. 1, (the rear portion of which machinery is so contrived
as to slip *en masse*, from the main compartment to the cupboard No. 1, as occasion may require,) and his legs lie at full
length in the main compartment. When Maelzel opens the
door No. 1, the man within is not in any danger of discovery,
for the keenest eye cannot penetrate more than about two
inches into the darkness within. But the case is otherwise
when the back door of the cupboard No. 1, is opened. A
bright light then pervades the cupboard, and the body of the
man would be discovered if it were there. But it is not. The
putting the key in the lock of the back door was a signal on
hearing which the person concealed brought his body forward to an angle as acute as possible—throwing it altogether,
or nearly so, into the main compartment. This, however, is a
painful position, and cannot be long maintained. Accordingly
we find that Maelzel *closes the back door*. This being done,
there is no reason why the body of the man may not resume
its former situation—for the cupboard is again so dark as to
defy scrutiny. The drawer is now opened, and the legs of the

person within drop down behind it in the space it formerly occupied.* There is, consequently, now no longer any part of the man in the main compartment—his body being behind the machinery in cupboard No. 1, and his legs in the space occupied by the drawer. The exhibiter, therefore, finds himself at liberty to display the main compartment. This he does—opening both its back and front doors—and no person is discovered. The spectators are now satisfied that the whole of the box is exposed to view—and exposed too, all portions of it at one and the same time. But of course this is not the case. They neither see the space behind the drawer, nor the interior of cupboard No. 1—the front door of which latter the exhibiter virtually shuts in shutting its back door. Maelzel, having now rolled the machine around, lifted up the drapery of the Turk, opened the doors in his back and thigh, and shown his trunk to be full of machinery, brings the whole back into its original position, and closes the doors. The man within is now at liberty to move about. He gets up into the body of the Turk just so high as to bring his eyes above the level of the chess-board. It is very probable that he seats himself upon the little square block or protuberance which is seen in a corner of the main compartment when the doors are open. In this position he sees the chess-board through the bosom of the Turk which is of gauze. Bringing his right arm across his breast he actuates the little machinery necessary to guide the left arm and the fingers of the figure. This machinery is situated just beneath the left shoulder of the Turk, and is consequently easily reached by the right hand of the man concealed, if we suppose his right arm brought across the breast. The motions of the head and eyes, and of the right arm of the figure, as well as the sound *echec* are produced by other mechanism in the interior, and actuated at will by the man within. The whole of this mechanism—that is to say all the mechanism essential to the machine—is most probably

---

*Sir David Brewster supposes that there is always a large space behind this drawer even when shut—in other words that the drawer is a "false drawer," and does not extend to the back of the box. But the idea is altogether untenable. So common-place a trick would be immediately discovered—especially as the drawer is always opened to its full extent, and an opportunity thus afforded of comparing its depth with that of the box.

contained within the little cupboard (of about six inches in breadth) partitioned off at the right (the spectators' right) of the main compartment.

In this analysis of the operations of the Automaton, we have purposely avoided any allusion to the manner in which the partitions are shifted, and it will now be readily comprehended that this point is a matter of no importance, since, by mechanism within the ability of any common carpenter, it might be effected in an infinity of different ways, and since we have shown that, however performed, it is performed out of the view of the spectators. Our result is founded upon the following *observations* taken during frequent visits to the exhibition of Maelzel.*

1. The moves of the Turk are not made at regular intervals of time, but accommodate themselves to the moves of the antagonist—although this point (of regularity) so important in all kinds of mechanical contrivance, might have been readily brought about by limiting the time allowed for the moves of the antagonist. For example, if this limit were three minutes, the moves of the Automaton might be made at any given intervals longer than three minutes. The fact then of irregularity, when regularity might have been so easily attained, goes to prove that regularity is unimportant to the action of the Automaton—in other words, that the Automaton is not *a pure machine*.

2. When the Automaton is about to move a piece, a distinct motion is observable just beneath the left shoulder, and which motion agitates in a slight degree, the drapery covering the front of the left shoulder. This motion invariably precedes, by about two seconds, the movement of the arm itself—and the arm never, in any instance, moves without this preparatory motion in the shoulder. Now let the antagonist move a piece, and let the corresponding move be made by Maelzel, as usual, upon the board of the Automaton. Then let the antagonist

*Some of these *observations* are intended merely to prove that the machine must be regulated *by mind*, and it may be thought a work of supererogation to advance farther arguments in support of what has been already fully decided. But our object is to convince, in especial, certain of our friends upon whom a train of suggestive reasoning will have more influence than the most positive *a priori* demonstration.

narrowly watch the Automaton, until he detect the preparatory motion in the shoulder. Immediately upon detecting this
motion, and before the arm itself begins to move, let him
withdraw his piece, as if perceiving an error in his manœuvre.
It will then be seen that the movement of the arm, which, in
all other cases, immediately succeeds the motion in the shoulder, is withheld—is not made—although Maelzel has not yet
performed, on the board of the Automaton, any move corresponding to the withdrawal of the antagonist. In this case,
that the Automaton was about to move is evident—and that
he did not move, was an effect plainly produced by the withdrawal of the antagonist, and without any intervention of
Maelzel.

This fact fully proves, 1—that the intervention of Maelzel,
in performing the moves of the antagonist on the board of
the Automaton, is not essential to the movements of the Automaton, 2—that its movements are regulated by *mind*—by
some person who sees the board of the antagonist, 3—that
its movements are not regulated by the mind of Maelzel,
whose back was turned towards the antagonist at the withdrawal of his move.

3. The Automaton does not invariably win the game. Were
the machine a pure machine this would not be the case—it
would always win. The *principle* being discovered by which a
machine can be made to *play* a game of chess, an extension of
the same principle would enable it to *win* a game—a farther
extension would enable it to *win all* games—that is, to beat
any possible game of an antagonist. A little consideration will
convince any one that the difficulty of making a machine beat
all games, is not in the least degree greater, as regards the
principle of the operations necessary, than that of making it
beat a single game. If then we regard the Chess-Player as a
machine, we must suppose, (what is highly improbable,) that
its inventor preferred leaving it incomplete to perfecting it—
a supposition rendered still more absurd, when we reflect that
the leaving it incomplete would afford an argument against
the possibility of its being a pure machine—the very argument we now adduce.

4. When the situation of the game is difficult or complex,
we never perceive the Turk either shake his head or roll his

eyes. It is only when his next move is obvious, or when the game is so circumstanced that to a man in the Automaton's place there would be no necessity for reflection. Now these peculiar movements of the head and eyes are movements customary with persons engaged in meditation, and the ingenious Baron Kempelen would have adapted these movements (were the machine a pure machine) to occasions proper for their display—that is, to occasions of complexity. But the reverse is seen to be the case, and this reverse applies precisely to our supposition of a man in the interior. When engaged in meditation about the game he has no time to think of setting in motion the mechanism of the Automaton by which are moved the head and the eyes. When the game, however, is obvious, he has time to look about him, and, accordingly, we see the head shake and the eyes roll.

5. When the machine is rolled round to allow the spectators an examination of the back of the Turk, and when his drapery is lifted up and the doors in the trunk and thigh thrown open, the interior of the trunk is seen to be crowded with machinery. In scrutinizing this machinery while the Automaton was in motion, that is to say while the whole machine was moving on the castors, it appeared to us that certain portions of the mechanism changed their shape and position in a degree too great to be accounted for by the simple laws of perspective; and subsequent examinations convinced us that these undue alterations were attributable to mirrors in the interior of the trunk. The introduction of mirrors among the machinery could not have been intended to influence, in any degree, the machinery itself. Their operation, whatever that operation should prove to be, must necessarily have reference to the eye of the spectator. We at once concluded that these mirrors were so placed to multiply to the vision some few pieces of machinery within the trunk so as to give it the appearance of being crowded with mechanism. Now the direct inference from this is that the machine is not a pure machine. For if it were, the inventor, so far from wishing its mechanism to appear complex, and using deception for the purpose of giving it this appearance, would have been especially desirous of convincing those who witnessed his exhibition, of the

simplicity of the means by which results so wonderful were brought about.

6. The external appearance, and, especially, the deportment of the Turk, are, when we consider them as imitations of *life*, but very indifferent imitations. The countenance evinces no ingenuity, and is surpassed, in its resemblance to the human face, by the very commonest of wax-works. The eyes roll unnaturally in the head, without any corresponding motions of the lids or brows. The arm, particularly, performs its operations in an exceedingly stiff, awkward, jerking, and rectangular manner. Now, all this is the result either of inability in Maelzel to do better, or of intentional neglect—accidental neglect being out of the question, when we consider that the whole time of the ingenious proprietor is occupied in the improvement of his machines. Most assuredly we must not refer the unlife-like appearances to inability—for all the rest of Maelzel's automata are evidence of his full ability to copy the motions and peculiarities of life with the most wonderful exactitude. The rope-dancers, for example, are inimitable. When the clown laughs, his lips, his eyes, his eye-brows, and eye-lids—indeed, all the features of his countenance—are imbued with their appropriate expressions. In both him and his companion, every gesture is so entirely easy, and free from the semblance of artificiality, that, were it not for the diminutiveness of their size, and the fact of their being passed from one spectator to another previous to their exhibition on the rope, it would be difficult to convince any assemblage of persons that these wooden automata were not living creatures. We cannot, therefore, doubt Mr. Maelzel's ability, and we must necessarily suppose that he intentionally suffered his Chess-Player to remain the same artificial and unnatural figure which Baron Kempelen (no doubt also through design) originally made it. What this design was it is not difficult to conceive. Were the Automaton life-like in its motions, the spectator would be more apt to attribute its operations to their true cause, (that is, to human agency within) than he is now, when the awkward and rectangular manœuvres convey the idea of pure and unaided mechanism.

7. When, a short time previous to the commencement of the game, the Automaton is wound up by the exhibiter as

usual, an ear in any degree accustomed to the sounds produced in winding up a system of machinery, will not fail to discover, instantaneously, that the axis turned by the key in the box of the Chess-Player, cannot possibly be connected with either a weight, a spring, or any system of machinery whatever. The inference here is the same as in our last observation. The winding up is inessential to the operations of the Automaton, and is performed with the design of exciting in the spectators the false idea of mechanism.

8. When the question is demanded explicitly of Maelzel—"Is the Automaton a pure machine or not?" his reply is invariably the same—"I will say nothing about it." Now the notoriety of the Automaton, and the great curiosity it has every where excited, are owing more especially to the prevalent opinion that it *is* a pure machine, than to any other circumstance. Of course, then, it is the interest of the proprietor to represent it as a pure machine. And what more obvious, and more effectual method could there be of impressing the spectators with this desired idea, than a positive and explicit declaration to that effect? On the other hand, what more obvious and effectual method could there be of exciting a disbelief in the Automaton's being a pure machine, than by withholding such explicit declaration? For, people will naturally reason thus,—It is Maelzel's interest to represent this thing a pure machine—he refuses to do so, directly, in words, although he does not scruple, and is evidently anxious to do so, indirectly by actions—were it actually what he wishes to represent it by actions, he would gladly avail himself of the more direct testimony of words—the inference is, that a consciousness of its *not* being a pure machine, is the reason of his silence—his actions cannot implicate him in a falsehood—his words may.

9. When, in exhibiting the interior of the box, Maelzel has thrown open the door No. 1, and also the door immediately behind it, he holds a lighted candle at the back door (as mentioned above) and moves the entire machine to and fro with a view of convincing the company that the cupboard No. 1 is entirely filled with machinery. When the machine is thus moved about, it will be apparent to any careful observer, that whereas that portion of the machinery near the front door No. 1, is perfectly steady and unwavering, the portion farther

within fluctuates, in a very slight degree, with the movements of the machine. This circumstance first aroused in us the suspicion that the more remote portion of the machinery was so arranged as to be easily slipped, *en masse*, from its position when occasion should require it. This occasion we have already stated to occur when the man concealed within brings his body into an erect position upon the closing of the back door.

10. Sir David Brewster states the figure of the Turk to be of the size of life—but in fact it is far above the ordinary size. Nothing is more easy than to err in our notions of magnitude. The body of the Automaton is generally insulated, and, having no means of immediately comparing it with any human form, we suffer ourselves to consider it as of ordinary dimensions. This mistake may, however, be corrected by observing the Chess-Player when, as is sometimes the case, the exhibiter approaches it. Mr. Maelzel, to be sure, is not very tall, but upon drawing near the machine, his head will be found at least eighteen inches below the head of the Turk, although the latter, it will be remembered, is in a sitting position.

11. The box behind which the Automaton is placed, is precisely three feet six inches long, two feet four inches deep, and two feet six inches high. These dimensions are fully sufficient for the accommodation of a man very much above the common size—and the main compartment alone is capable of holding any ordinary man in the position we have mentioned as assumed by the person concealed. As these are facts, which any one who doubts them may prove by actual calculation, we deem it unnecessary to dwell upon them. We will only suggest that, although the top of the box is apparently a board of about three inches in thickness, the spectator may satisfy himself by stooping and looking up at it when the main compartment is open, that it is in reality very thin. The height of the drawer also will be misconceived by those who examine it in a cursory manner. There is a space of about three inches between the top of the drawer as seen from the exterior, and the bottom of the cupboard—a space which must be included in the height of the drawer. These contrivances to make the room within the box appear less than it

actually is, are referrible to a design on the part of the inventor, to impress the company again with a false idea, viz. that no human being can be accommodated within the box.

12. The interior of the main compartment is lined throughout with *cloth*. This cloth we suppose to have a twofold object. A portion of it may form, when tightly stretched, the only partitions which there is any necessity for removing during the changes of the man's position, viz: the partition between the rear of the main compartment and the rear of the cupboard No. 1, and the partition between the main compartment, and the space behind the drawer when open. If we imagine this to be the case, the difficulty of shifting the partitions vanishes at once, if indeed any such difficulty could be supposed under any circumstances to exist. The second object of the cloth is to deaden and render indistinct all sounds occasioned by the movements of the person within.

13. The antagonist (as we have before observed) is not suffered to play at the board of the Automaton, but is seated at some distance from the machine. The reason which, most probably, would be assigned for this circumstance, if the question were demanded, is, that were the antagonist otherwise situated, his person would intervene between the machine and the spectators, and preclude the latter from a distinct view. But this difficulty might be easily obviated, either by elevating the seats of the company, or by turning the end of the box towards them during the game. The true cause of the restriction is, perhaps, very different. Were the antagonist seated in contact with the box, the secret would be liable to discovery, by his detecting, with the aid of a quick ear, the breathings of the man concealed.

14. Although M. Maelzel, in disclosing the interior of the machine, sometimes slightly deviates from the *routine* which we have pointed out, yet *never* in any instance does he *so* deviate from it as to interfere with our solution. For example, he has been known to open, first of all, the drawer—but he never opens the main compartment without first closing the back door of cupboard No. 1—he never opens the main compartment without first pulling out the drawer—he never shuts the drawer without first shutting the main compartment—he never opens the back door of cupboard No. 1

while the main compartment is open—and the game of chess is never commenced until the whole machine is closed. Now, if it were observed that *never, in any single instance*, did M. Maelzel differ from the routine we have pointed out as necessary to our solution, it would be one of the strongest possible arguments in corroboration of it—but the argument becomes infinitely strengthened if we duly consider the circumstance that he *does occasionally* deviate from the routine, but never does *so* deviate as to falsify the solution.

15. There are six candles on the board of the Automaton during exhibition. The question naturally arises—"Why are so many employed, when a single candle, or, at farthest, two, would have been amply sufficient to afford the spectators a clear view of the board, in a room otherwise so well lit up as the exhibition room always is—when, moreover, if we suppose the machine a *pure machine*, there can be no necessity for so much light, or indeed any light at all, to enable *it* to perform its operations—and when, especially, only a single candle is placed upon the table of the antagonist?" The first and most obvious inference is, that so strong a light is requisite to enable the man within to see through the transparent material (probably fine gauze) of which the breast of the Turk is composed. But when we consider the *arrangement* of the candles, another reason immediately presents itself. There are six lights (as we have said before) in all. Three of these are on each side of the figure. Those most remote from the spectators are the longest—those in the middle are about two inches shorter—and those nearest the company about two inches shorter still—and the candles on one side differ in height from the candles respectively opposite on the other, by a ratio different from two inches—that is to say, the longest candle on one side is about three inches shorter than the longest candle on the other, and so on. Thus it will be seen that no two of the candles are of the same height, and thus also the difficulty of ascertaining the *material* of the breast of the figure (against which the light is especially directed) is greatly augmented by the dazzling effect of the complicated crossings of the rays—crossings which are brought about by placing the centres of radiation all upon different levels.

16. While the Chess-Player was in possession of Baron

Kempelen, it was more than once observed, first, that an Italian in the suite of the Baron was never visible during the playing of a game at chess by the Turk, and, secondly, that the Italian being taken seriously ill, the exhibition was suspended until his recovery. This Italian professed a *total* ignorance of the game of chess, although all others of the suite played well. Similar observations have been made since the Automaton has been purchased by Maelzel. There is a man, *Schlumberger*, who attends him wherever he goes, but who has no ostensible occupation other than that of assisting in the packing and unpacking of the automata. This man is about the medium size, and has a remarkable stoop in the shoulders. Whether he professes to play chess or not, we are not informed. It is quite certain, however, that he is never to be seen during the exhibition of the Chess-Player, although frequently visible just before and just after the exhibition. Moreover, some years ago Maelzel visited Richmond with his automata, and exhibited them, we believe, in the house now occupied by M. Bossieux as a Dancing Academy. *Schlumberger* was suddenly taken ill, and during his illness there was no exhibition of the Chess-Player. These facts are well known to many of our citizens. The reason assigned for the suspension of the Chess-Player's performances, was *not* the illness of *Schlumberger*. The inferences from all this we leave, without farther comment, to the reader.

17. The Turk plays with his *left* arm. A circumstance so remarkable cannot be accidental. Brewster takes no notice of it whatever, beyond a mere statement, we believe, that such is the fact. The early writers of treatises on the Automaton, seem not to have observed the matter at all, and have no reference to it. The author of the pamphlet alluded to by Brewster, mentions it, but acknowledges his inability to account for it. Yet it is obviously from such prominent discrepancies or incongruities as this that deductions are to be made (if made at all) which shall lead us to the truth.

The circumstance of the Automaton's playing with his left hand cannot have connexion with the operations of the machine, considered merely as such. Any mechanical arrangement which would cause the figure to move, in any given manner, the left arm—could, if reversed, cause it to move, in the same manner, the right. But these principles cannot be extended to the human organization, wherein there is a marked and radical difference in the construction, and, at all events, in the powers, of the right and left arms. Reflecting upon this latter fact, we naturally refer the incongruity notice-able in the Chess-Player to this peculiarity in the human or-ganization. If so, we must imagine some *reversion*—for the Chess-Player plays precisely as a man *would not*. These ideas, once entertained, are sufficient of themselves, to suggest the notion of a man in the interior. A few more imperceptible steps lead us, finally, to the result. The Automaton plays with his left arm, because under no other circumstances could the man within play with his right—a *desideratum* of course. Let us, for example, imagine the Automaton to play with his right arm. To reach the machinery which moves the arm, and which we have before explained to lie just beneath the shoul-der, it would be necessary for the man within either to use his right arm in an exceedingly painful and awkward position, (viz. brought up close to his body and tightly compressed between his body and the side of the Automaton,) or else to use his left arm brought across his breast. In neither case could he act with the requisite ease or precision. On the con-trary, the Automaton playing, as it actually does, with the left arm, all difficulties vanish. The right arm of the man within is brought across his breast, and his right fingers act, without any constraint, upon the machinery in the shoulder of the figure.

We do not believe that any reasonable objections can be urged against this solution of the Automaton Chess-Player.

Southern Literary Messenger, April 1836

A Few Words on Secret Writing

As WE can scarcely imagine a time when there did not exist a necessity, or at least a desire, of transmitting information from one individual to another, in such manner as to elude general comprehension; so we may well suppose the practice of writing in cipher to be of great antiquity. De La Guilletiere, therefore, who, in his "Lacedæmon Ancient and Modern," maintains that the Spartans were the inventors of Cryptography, is obviously in error. He speaks of the *scytala* as being the origin of the art; but he should only have cited it as one of its earliest instances, so far as our records extend. The *scytalæ* were two wooden cylinders, precisely similar in all respects. The general of an army, in going upon any expedition, received from the ephori one of these cylinders, while the other remained in their possession. If either party had occasion to communicate with the other, a narrow strip of parchment was so wrapped around the *scytala* that the edges of the skin fitted accurately each to each. The writing was then inscribed longitudinally, and the epistle unrolled and dispatched. If, by mischance, the messenger was intercepted, the letter proved unintelligible to his captors. If he reached his destination safely, however, the party addressed had only to involve the second cylinder in the strip to decipher the inscription. The transmission to our own times of this obvious mode of cryptography is due, probably, to the *historical* uses of the *scytala*, rather than to anything else. Similar means of secret intercommunication must have existed almost contemporaneously with the invention of letters.

It may be as well to remark, in passing, that in none of the treatises on the subject of this paper which have fallen under our cognizance, have we observed any suggestion of a method—other than those which apply alike to all ciphers—for the solution of the cipher by *scytala*. We read of instances, indeed, in which the intercepted parchments were deciphered; but we are not informed that this was ever done except accidentally. Yet a solution might be obtained with absolute certainty in this manner. The strip of skin being intercepted, let there be prepared a cone of great length comparatively—say six feet long—and whose circumference at base shall at least equal the length of the strip. Let this latter be rolled upon the cone near the base, edge to edge, as above described; then, still keeping edge to edge, and maintaining the parchment close upon the cone, let it be gradually slipped towards the apex. In this process, some of those words, syllables, or letters, whose connection is intended, will be sure to come together at that point of the cone where its diameter equals that of the *scytala* upon which the cipher was written. And as, in passing up the cone to its apex, all possible diameters are passed over, there is no chance of a failure. The circumference of the *scytala* being thus ascertained, a similar one can be made, and the cipher applied to it.

Few persons can be made to believe that it is not quite an easy thing to invent a method of secret writing which shall baffle investigation. Yet it may be roundly asserted that human ingenuity cannot concoct a cipher which human ingenuity cannot resolve. In the facility with which such writing is deciphered, however, there exist very remarkable differences in different intellects. Often, in the case of two individuals of acknowledged equality as regards ordinary mental efforts, it will be found that, while one cannot unriddle the commonest cipher, the other will scarcely be puzzled by the most abstruse. It may be observed, generally, that in such investigations the analytic ability is very forcibly called into action; and, for this reason, cryptographical solutions might with great propriety be introduced into academies, as the means of giving tone to the most important of the powers of mind.

Were two individuals, totally unpractised in cryptography, desirous of holding by letter a correspondence which should be unintelligible to all but themselves, it is most probable that they would at once think of a peculiar alphabet, to which each should have a key. At first it would, perhaps, be arranged that *a* should stand for *z*, *b* for *y*, *c* for *x*, *d* for *w*, &c. &c.; that is to say, the order of the letters would be reversed. Upon second thoughts, this arrangement appearing too obvious, a more complex mode would be adopted. The first thirteen letters might be written beneath the last thirteen, thus:

n	o	p	q	r	s	t	u	v	w	x	y	z
a	b	c	d	e	f	g	h	i	j	k	l	m;

and, so placed, *a* might stand for *n* and *n* for *a*, *o* for *b* and *b* for *o*, &c. &c. This, again, having an air of regularity which might be fathomed, the key alphabet might be constructed absolutely at random.

Thus,   a   might stand for   p
            b   "   "   "   x
            c   "   "   "   u
            d   "   "   "   o,   &c.

The correspondents, unless convinced of their error by the solution of their cipher, would no doubt be willing to rest in this latter arrangement, as affording full security. But if not, they would be likely to hit upon the plan of arbitrary marks used in place of the usual characters. For example,

        (might be employed for a
        .   "   "   " b
        :   "   "   " c
        ;   "   "   " d
)   "   "   " e, &c.

A letter composed of such characters would have an intricate appearance unquestionably. If, still, however, it did not give full satisfaction, the idea of a perpetually shifting alphabet might be conceived, and thus effected. Let two circular pieces of pasteboard be prepared, one about half an inch in diameter less than the other. Let the centre of the smaller be placed upon the centre of the larger, and secured for a moment from slipping; while *radii* are drawn from the common centre to the circumference of the smaller circle, and thus extended to the circumference of the greater. Let there be twenty-six of these *radii*, forming on each pasteboard twenty-six spaces. In each of these spaces on the under circle write one of the letters of the alphabet, so that the whole alphabet be written— if at random so much the better. Do the same with the upper circle. Now run a pin through the common centre, and let the upper circle revolve, while the under one is held fast. Now stop the revolution of the upper circle, and, while both lie still, write the epistle required; using for *a* that letter in the smaller circle which tallies with *a* in the larger, for *b* that letter in the smaller circle which tallies with *b* in the larger, &c. &c. In order that an epistle thus written may be read by the person for whom it is intended, it is only necessary that he should have in his possession circles constructed as those just described, and that he should know any two of the characters (one in the under and one in the upper circle) which were in juxta-position when his correspondent wrote the cipher. Upon this latter point he is informed by looking at the two initial letters of the document, which serve as a key. Thus, if he sees *a m* at the beginning, he concludes that, by turning his circles so as to put these characters in conjunction, he will arrive at the alphabet employed.

At a cursory glance, these various modes of constructing a cipher seem to have about them an air of inscrutable secresy. It appears almost an impossibility to unriddle what has been put together by so complex a method. And to some persons the difficulty might be great; but to others—to those skilled in deciphering—such enigmas are very simple indeed. The reader should bear in mind that the basis of the whole art of solution, as far as regards these matters, is found in the general principles of the formation of language itself, and thus is altogether independent of the particular laws which govern any cipher, or the construction of its key. The difficulty of reading a cryptographical puzzle is by no means always in accordance with the labor or ingenuity with which it has been constructed. The sole use of the key, indeed, is for those *au fait* to the cipher; in its perusal by a third party, no reference is had to it at all. The lock of the secret is picked. In the different methods of cryptography specified above, it will be observed that there is a gradually increasing complexity. But this complexity is only in shadow. It has no substance whatever. It appertains merely to the formation, and has no bearing upon the solution, of the cipher. The last mode mentioned is not in the least degree more difficult to be deciphered than the first—whatever may be the difficulty of either.

In the discussion of an analogous subject, in one of the weekly papers of this city, about eighteen months ago, the writer of this article had occasion to speak of the application of a rigorous *method* in all forms of thought—of its advantages—of the extension of its use even to what is considered the operation of pure fancy—and thus, subsequently, of the solution of cipher. He even ventured to assert that no cipher, of the character above specified, could be sent to the address of the paper, which he would not be able to resolve. This challenge excited, most unexpectedly, a very lively interest among the numerous readers of the journal. Letters were poured in upon the editor from all parts of the country; and many of the writers of these epistles were so convinced of the impenetrability of their mysteries, as to be at great pains to draw him into wagers on the subject. At the same time, they were not always scrupulous about sticking to the point. The cryptographs were, in numerous instances, altogether beyond the limits defined in the beginning. Foreign languages were employed. Words and sentences were run together without interval. Several alphabets were used in the same cipher. One gentleman, but moderately endowed with conscientiousness, inditing us a puzzle composed of pot-hooks and hangers to which the wildest typography of the office could afford nothing similar, went even so far as to jumble together no less than *seven distinct alphabets*, without intervals between the letters, *or between the lines*. Many of the cryptographs were dated in Philadelphia, and several of those which urged the subject of a bet were written by gentlemen of this city. Out of, perhaps, one hundred ciphers altogether received, there was only one which we did not immediately succeed in resolving. This one we *demonstrated* to be an imposition—that is to say, we fully proved it a jargon of random characters, having no meaning whatever. In respect to the epistle of the seven alphabets, we had the pleasure of completely *nonplus*-ing its inditer by a prompt and satisfactory translation.

The weekly paper mentioned, was, for a period of some months, greatly occupied with the hieroglyphic and cabalistic-looking solutions of the cryptographs sent us from all quarters. Yet with the exception of the writers of the ciphers, we do not believe that any individuals could have been found, among the readers of the journal, who regarded the matter in any other light than in that of a desperate humbug. We mean to say that no one really believed in the authenticity of the answers. One party averred that the mysterious figures were only inserted to give a *queer* air to the paper, for the purpose of attracting attention. Another thought it more probable that we not only solved the ciphers, but put them together ourselves for solution. This having been the state of affairs at the period when it was thought expedient to decline farther dealings in necromancy, the writer of this article avails himself of the present opportunity to maintain the truth of the journal in question—to repel the charges of rigmarole by which it was assailed—and to declare, in his own name, that the ciphers were all written in good faith, and solved in the same spirit.

A very common, and somewhat too obvious mode of secret correspondence, is the following. A card is interspersed, at irregular intervals, with oblong spaces, about the length of ordinary words of three syllables in a bourgeois type. Another card is made exactly coinciding. One is in possession of each party. When a letter is to be written, the key-card is placed upon the paper, and words conveying the true meaning inscribed in the spaces. The card is then removed and the blanks filled up, so as to make out a signification different from the real one. When the person addressed receives the cipher, he has merely to apply to it his own card, when the superfluous words are concealed, and the significant ones alone appear. The chief objection to this cryptograph is the difficulty of so filling the blanks as not to give a forced appearance to the sentences. Differences, also, in the handwriting, between the words written in the spaces, and those inscribed upon removal of the card, will always be detected by a close observer.

A pack of cards is sometimes made the vehicle of a cipher, in this manner. The parties determine, in the first place, upon certain arrangements of the pack. For example: it is agreed that, when a writing is to be commenced, a natural sequence of the spots shall be made; with spades at top, hearts next, diamonds next, and clubs last. This order being obtained, the writer proceeds to inscribe upon the top card the first letter of his epistle, upon the next the second, upon the next the third, and so on until the pack is exhausted, when, of course, he will have written fifty-two letters. He now shuffles the pack according to a preconcerted plan. For example: he takes three cards from the bottom and places them at top, then one from top, placing it at bottom, and so on, for a given number of times. This done, he again inscribes fifty-two characters as before, proceeding thus until his epistle is written. The pack being received by the correspondent, he has only to place the cards in the order agreed upon for commencement, to read, letter by letter, the first fifty-two characters as intended. He has then only to shuffle in the manner pre-arranged for the second perusal, to decipher the series of the next fifty-two letters—and so on to the end. The objection to this cryptograph lies in the nature of the missive. *A pack of cards*, sent from one party to another, would scarcely fail to excite suspicion; and it cannot be doubted that it is far better to secure ciphers from being considered as such, than to waste time in attempts at rendering them scrutiny-proof, when intercepted. Experience shows that the most cunningly constructed cryptograph, if suspected, can and will be unriddled.

An unusually secure mode of secret intercommunication might be thus devised. Let the parties each furnish themselves with a copy of the same edition of a book—the rarer the edition the better—as also the rarer the book. In the cryptograph, numbers are used altogether, and these numbers refer to the locality of letters in the volume. For example—a cipher is received commencing, 121-6-8. The party addressed refers to page 121, and looks at the sixth letter from the left of the page in the eighth line from the top. Whatever letter he there finds is the initial letter of the epistle—and so on. This method is very secure; yet it is *possible* to decipher any cryptograph written by its means—and it is greatly objectionable otherwise, on account of the time necessarily required for its solution, even with the key-volume.

It is not to be supposed that Cryptography, as a serious thing, as the means of imparting important information, has gone out of use at the present day. It is still commonly practised in diplomacy; and there are individuals, even now, holding office in the eye of various foreign governments, whose real business is that of deciphering. We have already said that a peculiar mental action is called into play in the solution of cryptographical problems, at least in those of the higher order. Good cryptographists are rare indeed; and thus their services, although seldom required, are necessarily well requited.

An instance of the modern employment of writing in cipher is mentioned in a work lately published by Messieurs Lea & Blanchard, of this city—"Sketches of Conspicuous Living Characters of France." In a notice of Berryer, it is said that a letter being addressed by the Duchess de Berri to the legitimists of Paris, to inform them of her arrival, it was accompanied by a long note in cipher, the key of which she had forgotten to give. "The penetrating mind of Berryer," says the biographer, "soon discovered it. It was this phrase substituted for the twenty-four letters of the alphabet—*Le gouvernement provisoire.*"

The assertion that Berryer "soon discovered the key-phrase," merely proves that the writer of these memoirs is entirely innocent of cryptographical knowledge. Monsieur B. no doubt ascertained the key-phrase; but it was merely to satisfy his curiosity, *after the riddle had been read*. He made no use of the key in deciphering. The lock was picked.

In our notice of the book in question (published in the April number of this Magazine) we alluded to this subject thus—

"The phrase '*Le gouvernement provisoire*' is French, and the note in cipher was addressed to Frenchmen. The difficulty of deciphering may well be supposed much greater, had the key been in a foreign tongue; yet any one who will take the trouble may address us a note, in the same manner as here proposed; and the key-phrase may be either in French, Italian, Spanish, German, Latin, or Greek, (or in any of the dialects of these languages,) and we pledge ourselves for the solution of the riddle."

This challenge has elicited but a single response, which is embraced in the following letter. The only quarrel we have with the epistle, is that its writer has declined giving us his name in full. We beg that he will take an early opportunity of doing this, and thus relieve us of the chance of that suspicion which was attached to the cryptography of the weekly journal above-mentioned—the suspicion of inditing ciphers to ourselves. The postmark of the letter is *Stonington, Conn.*

S————, Ct., April 21, 1841.

To the Editor of Graham's Magazine.

Sir:—In the April number of your magazine, while reviewing the translation by Mr. Walsh of "Sketches of Conspicuous Living Characters of France," you invite your readers to address you a note in cipher, "the key phrase to which may be either in French, Italian, Spanish, German, Latin or Greek," and pledge yourself for its solution. My attention being called, by your remarks, to this species of cipher-writing, I composed for my own amusement the following exercises, in the first part of which the key-phrase is in English—in the second in Latin. As I did not see, (by the number for May,) that any of your correspondents had availed himself of your offer, I take the liberty to send the enclosed, on which, if you should think it worth your while, you can exercise your ingenuity.

I am yours, respectfully,

S. D. L.

No. 1.

Cauhiif aud ftd sdftirf ithot tacd wdde rdchfdr tiu fuaef-shffheo fdoudf hetiusafhie tuis ied herhchriai fi aeiftdu wn sdaef it iuhfheo hiidohwid wn aen deodsf ths tiu itis hf iaf iuhoheaiin rdffhedr; aer ftd auf it ftif fdoudfin oissiehoafheo hefdiihodeod taf wdde odeduaiin fdusdr ounsfiouastn. Saen fsdohdf it fdoudf iuhfheo idud weiie fi ftd aeohdeff; fisdfhsdf, A fiacdf tdar iaf ftacdr aer ftd ouiie iuhffde isie ihft fisd her-dhwid oiiiuheo tiihr, atfdu ithot tahu wdheo sdushffdr fi ouii aoahe, hetiusafhie oiiir wd fuaefshffdr ihft ihffid raeodu ftaf rhfoicdun iiiir hefid iefhi ftd aswiiafiun dshffid fatdin udaotdr hff rdffheafhie. Ounsfiouastn tiidcdu siud suisduin dswuaodf ftifd sirdf it iuhfheo ithot aud uderdudr idohwid iein wn sdaef it fisd desiaeafiun wdn ithot sawdf weiie ftd udai fhoehthoafhie it ftd onstduf dssiindr fi hff siffdffiu.

No. 2.

Ofoiioiiaso ortsiii sov eodisoioe afduiostifoi ft iftvi si tri oistoiv oiniafetsorit ifeov rsri inotiiiiv ridiiot, irio rivvio eovit atrotfetsoria aioriti iitri tf oitovin tri aetifei ioreitit sov usttoi oioittstifo dfti afdooitior trso ifeov tri dfit otftfeov softridi ft oistoiv oriofiforiti suitteii viireiiitifoi ﬆ tri iarfoisiti, iiti trir uet otiiiotiv uitﬆi rid io tri eoviieeiiiv rfasueostr ﬆ rii dﬆrit tfoeei.

In the solution of the first of these ciphers we had little more than ordinary trouble. The second proved to be exceedingly difficult, and it was only by calling every faculty into play that we could read it at all. The first runs thus.

"Various are the methods which have been devised for transmitting secret information from one individual to another, by means of writing, illegible to any except him for whom it was originally designed; and the art of thus secretly communicating intelligence has been generally termed *cryptography*. Many species of secret writing were known to the ancients. Sometimes a slave's head was shaved, and the crown written upon with some indelible coloring fluid; after which the hair being permitted to grow again, information could be transmitted with little danger that discovery would ensue until the ambulatory epistle safely reached its destination. Cryptography, however, pure, properly embraces those modes of writing which are rendered legible only by means of some explanatory key which makes known the real signification of the ciphers employed to its possessor."

The key-phrase of this cryptograph is—"A word to the wise is sufficient."

The second is thus translated—

"Nonsensical phrases and unmeaning combinations of words, as the learned lexicographer would have confessed himself, when hidden under cryptographic ciphers, serve to *perpdex* the curious enquirer, and baffle penetration more completely than would the most profound *apothems* of learned philosophers. Abstruse disquisitions of the scholiasts, were they but presented before him in the undisguised vocabulary of his mother tongue——"

The last sentence here (as will be seen) is broken off short. The spelling we have strictly adhered to. *D*, by mistake, has been put for *l* in *perplex*.

The key-phrase is—"*Suaviter in modo, fortiter in re.*"

In the ordinary cryptograph, as will be seen in reference to most of those we have specified above, the artificial alphabet agreed upon by the correspondents, is employed, letter for letter, in place of the usual or natural one. For example:—

two parties wish to communicate secretly. It is arranged before parting that

)	shall stand	for	a
(	————	"	b
—	————	"	c
✳	————	"	d
.	————	"	e
,	————	"	f
;	————	"	g
:	————	"	h
?	————	"	i or j
!	————	"	k
&	————	"	l
0	————	"	m
'	————	"	n
†	————	"	o
‡	————	"	p
¶	————	"	q
☞	————	"	r
]	————	"	s
[	————	"	t
£	————	"	u or v
$	————	"	w
¿	————	"	x
¡	————	"	y
⌐	————	"	z

Now the following note is to be communicated—

"We must see you immediately upon a matter of great importance. Plots have been discovered, and the conspirators are in our hands. Hasten!"

These words would be written thus—

$. 0 £] [ ] . . ¡ † £ ? 0 0 . ✳ ?) [. & ¡ £
‡ † ') 0) [[. ☞ † ' ; ☞ .) [? 0 ‡ † ☞ [ )
' — . ‡ & † [ ] :) £ . (. . ' ✳ .] — † £ . ☞
. ✳) ' ✳ — † '] ‡ ? ☞) [† ☞]) ☞ . ? ' †
£ ☞ :) ' ✳] :)] [. '

This certainly has an intricate appearance, and would prove

a most difficult cipher to any one not conversant with cryptography. But it will be observed that *a*, for example, is never represented by any other character than), *b* never by any other character than (, and so on. Thus by the discovery, accidental or otherwise, of any one letter, the party intercepting the epistle would gain a permanent and decided advantage; and could apply his knowledge to all the instances in which the character in question was employed throughout the cipher.

In the cryptographs, on the other hand, which have been sent us by our correspondent at Stonington, and which are identical in conformation with the cipher resolved by Berryer, no such permanent advantage is to be obtained.

Let us refer to the second of these puzzles. Its key-phrase runs thus:

Suaviter in modo, fortiter in re.

Let us now place the alphabet beneath this phrase, letter beneath letter—

S|u|a|v|i|t|e|r|i|n|m|o|d|o|f|o|r|t|i|t|e|r| i |n|r|e
A|b|c|d|e|f|g|h|i| j | k | l |m|n|o|p|q|r|s|t|u|v|w|x|y|z

We here see that

a	stands	for	————	c
d	"	"	————	m
e	"	"	g, u and	z
f	"	"	————	o
i	"	"	e, i, s and	w
m	"	"	————	k
n	"	"	j and	x
o	"	"	l, n and	p
r	"	"	h, q, v and	y
s	"	"	————	a
t	"	"	f, r and	t
u	"	"	————	b
v	"	"	————	d

In this manner *n* stands for two letters, and *e*, *o*, and *t* for three each, while *i* and *r* represent each as many as four. Thirteen characters are made to perform the operations of the whole alphabet. The result of such a key-phrase upon the cipher, is to give it the appearance of a mere medley of the letters *e*, *o*, *t*, *r* and *i*—the latter character greatly predominating, through the accident of being employed for letters which, themselves, are inordinately prevalent in most languages—we mean *e* and *i*.

A letter thus written being intercepted, and the key-phrase unknown, the individual who should attempt to decipher it may be imagined *guessing*, or otherwise attempting to convince himself, that a certain character (*i*, for example,) represented the letter *e*. Looking throughout the cryptograph for confirmation of this idea, he would meet with nothing but a negation of it. He would see the character in situations where it could not possibly represent *e*. He might, for instance, be puzzled by four *i*'s forming of themselves a single word, without the intervention of any other character; in which case, of course, they could not be *all e*'s. It will be seen that the word *wise* might be thus constructed. We say this may be seen *now*, by us, in possession of the key-phrase; but the question will, no doubt, occur, how, *without* the key-phrase, and without cognizance of any single letter in the cipher, it would be possible for the interceptor of such a cryptograph to make any thing of such a word as *iiii*?

But again. A key-phrase might easily be constructed, in which one character would represent seven, eight, or ten letters. Let us then imagine the word *iiiiiiiii* presenting itself in a cryptograph to an individual *without* the proper key-phrase; or, if this be a supposition somewhat too perplexing, let us suppose it occurring to the person for whom the cipher is designed, and who *has* the key-phrase. What is he to do with such a word as *iiiiiiiiii*? In any of the ordinary books upon Algebra will be found a very concise *formula* (we have not the necessary type for its insertion here) for ascertaining the number of arrangements in which *m* letters may be placed, taken *n* at a time. But no doubt there are none of our readers ignorant of the innumerable combinations which may be made from these ten *i*'s. Yet, unless it occur otherwise by accident, the correspondent receiving the cipher would have to write down all these combinations before attaining the word intended; and even when he had written them, he would be inexpressibly perplexed in selecting the word designed from the vast number of other words arising in the course of the permutation.

To obviate, therefore, the exceeding difficulty of deciphering this species of cryptograph, on the part of the possessors of the key-phrase, and to confine the deep intricacy of the puzzle to those for whom the cipher was not designed, it becomes necessary that some *order* should be agreed upon by the parties corresponding—some order in reference to which those characters are to be read which represent more than one letter—and this *order* must be held in view by the writer of the cryptograph. It may be agreed, for example, that the *first* time an *i* occurs in the cipher, it is to be understood as representing that character which stands against the *first i* in the key-phrase; that the *second* time an *i* occurs it must be supposed to represent that letter which stands opposed to the *second i* in the key-phrase, &c. &c. Thus the *location* of each cipherical letter must be considered in connexion with the character itself, in order to determine its exact signification.

We say that some pre-concerted *order* of this kind is necessary, lest the cipher prove too intricate a lock to yield even to its true key. But it will be evident, upon inspection, that our correspondent at Stonington has inflicted upon us a cryptograph in which *no* order has been preserved; in which many characters, respectively, stand, at absolute random, for many others. If, therefore, in regard to the gauntlet we threw down in April, he should be half inclined to accuse us of braggadocio, he will yet admit that we have *more* than acted up to our boast. If what we then said was not said *suaviter in modo*, what we now do is at least done *fortiter in re*.

In these cursory observations we have by no means attempted to exhaust the subject of Cryptography. With such object in view, a folio might be required. We have indeed mentioned only a few of the ordinary modes of cipher. Even two thousand years ago, Æneas Tacticus detailed twenty distinct methods; and modern ingenuity has added much to the science. Our design has been chiefly suggestive; and perhaps we have already bored the readers of the Magazine. To those who desire farther information upon this topic, we may say that there are extant treatises by Trithemius, Cap. Porta, Vignere, and P. Niceron. The works of the two latter may be found, we believe, in the library of the Harvard University. If, however, there should be sought in these disquisitions— or in any— *rules for the solution* of cipher, the seeker will be disappointed. Beyond some hints in regard to the general structure of language, and some minute exercises in their practical application, he will find nothing upon record which he does not in his own intellect possess.

Graham's Magazine, July 1841

Chapter of Suggestions

IN THE LIFE of every man there occurs at least one epoch, when the spirit seems to abandon, for a brief period, the body, and, elevating itself above mortal affairs just so far as to get a comprehensive and *general* view, makes thus an estimate of its humanity, as accurate as is possible, under any circumstances, to that particular spirit. The soul here separates itself from its own idiosyncrasy, or individuality, and considers its own being, not as appertaining solely to itself, but as a portion of the universal Ens. All the important good resolutions which we keep—all startling, marked regenerations of character—are brought about at these *crises* of life. And thus it is our intense *sense of self* which debases, and which keeps us debased.

The theory of chance, or, as the mathematicians term it, the Calculus of Probabilities, has this remarkable peculiarity, that its truth in general is in direct proportion with its fallacy in particular.

We may judge of the degree of abstraction in one who meditates, by the manner in which he receives an interruption. If he is much startled, his revery was not profound; and the converse. Thus the affectation of the tribe of pretended mental-absentees, becomes transparent. These people awake from their musings with a start, and an air of bewilderment, as men naturally awake from dreams that have a close semblance of reality. But they are, clearly, ignorant that the phenomena of dreaming differ, radically, from those of reverie— of which latter the mesmeric condition is the extreme.

There are few thinkers who will not be surprised to find, upon retrospect of the world of thought, how *very* frequently the first, or intuitive, impressions have been the true ones. A poem, for example, enraptures us in our childhood. In adolescence, we perceive it to be full of fault. In the first years of manhood, we utterly despise and condemn it; and it is not until mature age has given tone to our feelings, enlarged our knowledge, and perfected our understanding, that we recur to our original sentiment, and primitive admiration, with the additional pleasure which is always deduced from knowing *how* it was that we once were pleased, and *why* it is that we still admire.

That the imagination has not been unjustly ranked as supreme among the mental faculties, appears, from the intense consciousness, on the part of the imaginative man, that the faculty in question brings his soul often to a glimpse of things supernal and eternal—to the very verge of the *great secrets*. There are moments, indeed, in which he perceives the faint perfumes, and hears the melodies of a happier world. Some of the most profound knowledge—perhaps all *very* profound knowledge—has originated from a highly stimulated imagination. Great intellects *guess* well. The laws of Kepler were, professedly, *guesses*.

An excellent Magazine paper might be written upon the subject of the progressive steps by which any great work of art—especially of literary art—attained completion. How vast a dissimilarity always exists between the germ and the fruit—between the work and its original conception! Sometimes the original conception is abandoned, or left out of sight altogether. *Most* authors sit down to write with *no* fixed design, trusting to the inspiration of the moment; it is not, therefore, to be wondered at, that *most* books are valueless. Pen should never touch paper, until at least a well-digested *general* purpose be established. In fiction, the *dénouement*— in all other composition the intended *effect*, should be definitely considered and arranged, before writing the first word; and *no* word should be then written which does not tend, or form a part of a sentence which tends, to the development of the *dénouement*, or to the strengthening of the effect. Where *plot* forms a portion of the contemplated interest, too much preconsideration cannot be had. *Plot* is very imperfectly understood, and has never been rightly defined. Many persons regard it as mere complexity of incident. In its most rigorous acceptation, it is *that from which no component atom can be removed, and in which none of the component atoms can be displaced, without ruin to the whole*; and although a sufficiently good plot may be constructed, without attention to the whole rigor of this definition, still it is the definition which the true artist should always keep in view, and always endeavor to consummate in his works. Some authors appear, however, to be totally deficient in constructiveness, and thus, even with plentiful invention, fail signally in plot. Dickens belongs to this class. His "Barnaby Rudge" shows not the least ability to *adapt*. Godwin and Bulwer are the best constructors of plot in English literature. The former has left a preface to his "Caleb Williams," in which he says that the novel was *written backwards*; the author first completing the second volume, in which the hero is involved in a maze of difficulties, and then casting about him for sufficiently probable cause of these difficulties, out of which to concoct volume the first. This mode cannot surely be recommended, but evinces the idiosyncrasy of Godwin's mind. Bulwer's "Pompeii" is an instance of admirably managed plot. His "Night and Morning," sacrifices to *mere* plot interests of far higher value.

All men of genius have their detractors; but it is merely a *non distributio medii* to argue, thence, that all men who have their detractors are men of genius. Yet, undoubtedly, of all despicable things, your habitual sneerer at real greatness, is the most despicable. What names excite, in mankind, the most unspeakable—the most insufferable disgust? The Dennises—the Frérons—the Desfontaines. Their littleness is measured by the greatness of those whom they have reviled. And yet, in the face of this well known and natural principle, there will always exist a set of *homunculi*, eager to grow notorious by the pertinacity of their yelpings at the heels of the distinguished. And this eagerness arises, less frequently from inability to appreciate genius, than from a species of cat-and-dog antipathy to it, which no suggestions of worldly prudence are adequate to quell.

That intuitive and seemingly casual perception by which we often attain knowledge, when reason herself falters and abandons the effort, appears to resemble the sudden glancing at a star, by which we see it more clearly than by a direct gaze; or the half-closing the eyes in looking at a plot of grass, the more fully to appreciate the intensity of its green.

There are few men of that peculiar sensibility which is at the root of genius, who, in early youth, have not expended much of their mental energy in *living too fast*; and, in later years, comes the unconquerable desire to goad the imagination up to that point which it would have attained, in an ordinary, normal, or well regulated life. The earnest longing for artificial excitement, which, unhappily, has characterized too many eminent men, may thus be regarded as a psychal want, or necessity,—an effort to regain the lost,—a struggle of the soul to assume the position which, under other circumstances, would have been its due.

The great variety of melodious expression which is given out from the keys of a piano, might be made, in proper hands, the basis of an excellent fairy-tale. Let the poet press his finger steadily upon each key, keeping it down, and imagine each prolonged series of undulations the history, of joy or of sorrow, related by a good or evil spirit imprisoned within. There are some of the notes which almost tell, of their own accord, true and intelligible histories.

A precise or *clear* man, in conversation or in composition, has a very important consequential advantage—more especially in matters of logic. As he proceeds with his argument, the person addressed, exactly comprehending, for that reason, and often for that reason only, agrees. Few minds, in fact, can immediately perceive the distinction between the comprehension of a proposition, and an agreement of the reason with the thing proposed. Pleased at comprehending, we often are so excited as to take it for granted that we assent. Luminous writers may thus indulge, for a long time, in pure sophistry, without being detected. Macaulay is a remarkable instance of this species of mystification. We coincide with what he says, too frequently, because we so very distinctly understand what it is that he intends to say. His essay on Bacon has been long and deservedly admired; but its concluding portions, (wherein he endeavors to depreciate the *Novum Organum*,) although logical *to a fault*, are irrational in the extreme. But not to confine myself to mere assertion. Let us refer to this great essayist's review of "Ranke's History of the Popes." His strength is here put forth to account for the progress of

Romanism, by maintaining that divinity is not a progressive science. "The enigmas," says he, in substance, " which perplex the natural theologian, are the same in all ages, while the Bible, where alone we are to seek revealed truth, has been always what it is." Here Mr. Macaulay confounds the nature of that proof from which we reason of the concerns of earth, considered as man's habitation, with the nature of that evidence from which we reason of the same earth, regarded as a unit of the universe. In the former case, the *data* being palpable, the proof is direct; in the latter it is purely *analogical*. Were the indications we derive from science, of the nature and designs of Deity, and thence, by inference, of man's destiny,—were these indications proof *direct*, it is then very true that no advance in science could strengthen them; for, as the essayist justly observes, "nothing can be added to the force of the argument which the mind finds in every beast, bird, or flower;" but, since these indications are rigidly analogical, every step in human knowledge, every astronomical discovery, in especial, throws additional light upon the august subject, *by extending the range of analogy*. That we know no more, to-day, of the nature of Deity, of its purposes, and thus of man himself, than we did even a dozen years ago, is a proposition disgracefully absurd. "If Natural Philosophy," says a greater than Macaulay, "should continue to be improved in its various branches, the bounds of moral philosophy would be enlarged also." These words of the prophetic *Newton* are felt to be true, and will be fulfilled.

The Opal, 1845

Fifty Suggestions

1.

IT IS OBSERVABLE that, while among all nations the omni-color, white, has been received as an emblem of the Pure, the no-color, black, has by no means been generally admitted as *sufficiently* typical of Impurity. There are blue devils as well as black; and when we think *very* ill of a woman, and wish to *blacken* her character, we merely call her "a *blue*-stocking" and advise her to read, in Rabelais' *"Gargantua,"* the chapter *"de ce qui est signifié par les couleurs blanc et bleu."* There is far more difference between these *"couleurs,"* in fact, than that which exists between simple *black* and white. Your "blue," when we come to talk of stockings, is black in *issimo*—*"nigrum nigrius nigro"*—like the matter from which Raymond Lully first manufactured his alcohol.

2.

Mr. ——, I perceive, has been appointed Librarian to the new——Athenæum. To him, the appointment is advantageous in many respects. Especially:—*"Mon cousin, voici une belle occasion pour apprendre à lire!"*

3.

As far as I can understand the "loving our enemies," it implies the hating our friends.

4.

In commencing our dinners with gravy soup, no doubt we have taken a hint from Horace.

> ——Da, he says, si *grave* non est,
> Quæ prima iratum ventrem placaverit isca.

5.

Of much of our cottage architecture we may safely say, I think, (admitting the good intention,) that it *would* have been Gothic if it had not felt it its duty to be Dutch.

6.

James's multitudinous novels seem to be written upon the plan of "the songs of the Bard of Schiraz," in which, we are assured by Fadladeen, "the same beautiful thought occurs again and again in every possible variety of phrase."

7.

Some of our foreign lions resemble the human brain in one very striking particular. They are without any sense themselves and yet are the centres of sensation.

8.

Mirabeau, I fancy, acquired his wonderful tact at foreseeing and meeting *contingencies*, during his residence in the stronghold of *If*.

9.

Cottle's "Reminiscences of Coleridge" is just such a book as damns its perpetrator forever in the opinion of every gentleman who reads it. More and more every day do we moderns *pavoneggiarsi* about our Christianity; yet, so far as the *spirit* of Christianity is concerned, we are immeasurably behind the ancients. Mottoes and proverbs are the indices of national character; and the Anglo-Saxons are disgraced in having no proverbial equivalent to the *"De mortuis nil nisi bonum."* Moreover—where, in all statutary Christendom, shall we find a *law* so Christian as the *"Defuncti injuriâ ne afficiantur"* of the Twelve Tables?

The simple *negative* injunction of the Latin law and proverb—the injunction *not to do ill* to the dead—seems at a first glance, scarcely susceptible of improvement in the delicate respect of its terms. I cannot help thinking, however, that the sentiment, if not the idea intended, is more forcibly conveyed in an apopthegm by one of the old English moralists, James Puckle. By an ingenious figure of speech he contrives to imbue the negation of the Roman command with a spirit of active and positive beneficence. "When speaking of the dead," he says, in his "Grey Cap for a Green Head," *"so fold up your discourse that their virtues may be outwardly shown, while their vices are wrapped up in silence."*

10.

I have no doubt that the Fourierites honestly fancy "a nasty poet fit for nothing" to be the true translation of *"poeta nascitur non fit."*

11.

There surely can *not* be "more things in Heaven and Earth than are dreamt of" (oh, Andrew Jackson Davis!) "in *your* philosophy."

12.

"It is only as the Bird of Paradise quits us in taking wing," observes, or should observe, some poet, "that we obtain a full view of the beauty of its plumage;" and it is only as the politician is about being "turned out" that—like the snake of the Irish Chronicle when touched by St. Patrick—he "awakens to a sense of his *situation.*"

13.

Newspaper editors seem to have constitutions closely similar to those of the Deities in "Walhalla," who cut each other to pieces every day, and yet got up perfectly sound and fresh every morning.

14.

As far as I can comprehend the modern cant in favor of "unadulterated Saxon," it is fast leading us to the language of that region where, as Addison has it, "they sell the best fish and speak the plainest English."

15.

The frightfully long money-pouches—"like the Cucumber called the Gigantic"—which have come in vogue among our belles—are *not* of Parisian origin, as many suppose, but are strictly indigenous here. The fact is, such a fashion would be quite out of place in Paris, where it is money *only* that women keep in a purse. The purse of an American lady, however, must be large enough to carry both her money and the soul of its owner.

16.

I can see no objection to gentlemen "standing for Congress"—provided they stand on one side—nor to their "running for Congress"—if they are in a very great hurry to get there—but it would be a blessing if some of them could be persuaded into sitting still, for Congress, after they arrive.

17.

If *Envy*, as Cyprian has it, be "the moth of the soul," whether shall we regard *Content* as its Scotch snuff or its camphor?

18.

M——, having been "used up" in the "—— Review," goes about town lauding his critic—as an epicure lauds the best London mustard—with the tears in his eyes.

19.

"Con tal que las costumbres de un autor sean puras y castas," says the Catholic Don Tomas de las Torres, in the Preface to his "Amatory Poems," *"importo muy poco qui no sean igualmente severas sus obras:"* meaning, in plain English, that, provided the personal morals of an author are pure, it matters little what those of his books are.

For so unprincipled an idea, Don Tomas, no doubt, is still having a hard time of it in Purgatory; and, by way of most pointedly manifesting their disgust at his philosophy on the topic in question, many modern theologians and divines are now busily squaring their conduct by his proposition exactly *conversed*.

20.

Children are never too tender to be whipped:—like tough beefsteaks, the more you beat them the more tender they become.

21.

Lucian, in describing the statue " with its surface of Parian marble and its interior filled with rags," must have been looking with a prophetic eye at some of our great "moneyed institutions."

22.

That poets (using the word comprehensively, as including artists in general) are a *genus irritabile*, is well understood; but the *why*, seems not to be commonly seen. An artist *is* an artist only by dint of his exquisite sense of Beauty—a sense affording him rapturous enjoyment, but at the same time implying, or involving, an equally exquisite sense of Deformity of disproportion. Thus a wrong—an injustice—done a poet who is really a poet, excites him to a degree which, to ordinary apprehension, appears disproportionate with the wrong. Poets *see* injustice— *never* where it does not exist—but very often where the unpoetical see no injustice whatever. Thus the poetical irritability has no reference to "temper" in the vulgar sense, but merely to a more than usual clear-sightedness in respect to Wrong:—this clear-sightedness being nothing more than a corollary from the vivid perception of Right—of justice—of proportion—in a word, of το χαλον.

But one thing is clear—that the man who is *not* "irritable," (to the ordinary apprehension,) is *no poet*.

23.

Let a man succeed ever so evidently—ever so demonstrably—in many different displays of *genius*, the envy of criticism will agree with the popular voice in denying him more than *talent* in any. Thus a poet who has achieved a great (by which I mean an effective) poem, should be cautious not to distinguish himself in any other walk of Letters. In especial—let him make no effort in Science—unless anonymously, or with the view of waiting patiently the judgment of posterity. Because universal or even versatile geniuses have rarely or never been known, *therefore*, thinks the world, none such can ever be. A "therefore" of this kind is, with the world, conclusive. But what is the *fact*, as taught us by analysis of mental power? Simply, that the *highest* genius—that the genius which all men instantaneously acknowledge as such—which acts upon individuals, as well as upon the mass, by a species of magnetism incomprehensible but irresistible and *never resisted*—that this genius which demonstrates itself in the simplest gesture—or even by the absence of all—this genius which speaks without a voice and flashes from the unopened eye—is but the result of generally large mental power existing in a state of *absolute proportion*—so that no one faculty has undue predominance. *That* factitious "genius"—that "genius" in the popular sense—which is but the manifestation of the abnormal predominance of some one faculty over all the others—and, of course, at the expense and to the detriment, of all the others—is a result of mental disease or rather, of organic malformation of mind:—it is this and nothing more. Not only will such "genius" fail, if turned aside from the path indicated by its predominant faculty; but, even when pursuing this path—when producing those works in which, certainly, it is *best* calculated to succeed—will give unmistakeable indications of *unsoundness*, in respect to general intellect. Hence, indeed, arises the just idea that

"Great wit to madness nearly is allied."

I say "*just* idea;" for by "great wit," in this case, the poet intends precisely the pseudo-genius to which I refer. The true genius, on the other hand, is necessarily, if not universal in its manifestations, at least capable of universality; and if, attempting all things, it succeeds in one rather better than in another, this is merely on account of a certain bias by which *Taste* leads it with more earnestness in the one direction than in the other. With equal zeal, it would succeed equally in all.

To sum up our results in respect to this very simple, but much *vexata questio*:—

What the world calls "genius" is the state of mental disease arising from the undue predominance of some one of the faculties. The works of such genius are never sound in themselves and, in especial, always betray the general mental insanity.

The *proportion* of the mental faculties, in a case where the general mental power is *not* inordinate, gives that result which we distinguish as *talent*:—and the talent is greater or less, first, as the general mental power is greater or less; and, secondly, as the proportion of the faculties is more or less absolute.

The proportion of the faculties, in a case where the mental power is inordinately great, gives that result which *is* the true *genius* (but which, on account of the proportion and seeming simplicity of its works, is seldom acknowledged to *be* so;) and the genius is greater or less, first, as the general mental power is more or less inordinately great; and, secondly, as the proportion of the faculties is more or less absolute.

An objection will be made:—that the greatest excess of mental power, however proportionate, does not seem to satisfy our idea of genius, unless we have, in addition, sensibility, passion, energy. The reply is, that the "absolute proportion" spoken of, when applied to inordinate mental power, gives, as a result, the appreciation of Beauty and horror of Deformity which we call sensibility, together with that intense vitality, which is implied when we speak of "Energy" or "Passion."

24.

"And Beauty draws us by a single hair."—Capillary attraction, of course.

25.

It is by no means clear, as regards the present revolutionary spirit of Europe, that it is a spirit which "moveth altogether if it move at all." In Great Britain it may be kept quiet for half a century yet, by placing at the head of affairs an experienced medical man. He should keep his forefinger constantly on the pulse of the patient, and exhibit *panem* in gentle doses, with as much *circenses* as the stomach can be made to retain.

26.

The taste manifested by our Transcendental poets, *is* to be treated "reverentially," beyond doubt, as one of Mr. Emerson's friends suggests—for the fact is, it is Taste on her death-bed—Taste kicking *in articulo mortis.*

27.

I should not say, of Taglioni, exactly that she dances, but that she laughs with her arms and legs, and that if she takes vengeance on her present oppressors, she will be amply justified by the *lex Talionis.*

28.

The world is infested, just now, by a new sect of philosophers, who have not yet suspected themselves of forming a sect, and who, consequently, have adopted no name. They are the *Believers in every thing Odd*. Their High Priest in the East, is Charles Fourier—in the West, Horace Greely; and high priests they are to some purpose. The only common bond among the sect, is Credulity:—let us call it Insanity at once, and be done with it. Ask any one of them *why* he believes this or that, and, if he be conscientious, (ignorant people usually are,) he will make you very much such a reply as Talleyrand made when asked why he believed in the Bible. "I believe in it first," said he, "because I am Bishop of Autun; and, secondly, *because I know nothing about it at all*." What these philosophers call "argument," is a way they have *"de nier ce qui est et d'expliquer ce qui n'est pas."**

29.

The goddess Laverna, who is a head without a body, could

*Nouvelle Héloise.

not do better, perhaps, than make advances to "La Jeune France," which, for some years to come at least, must otherwise remain a body without a head.

30.

Mr. A—— is frequently spoken of as "one of our most industrious writers;" and, in fact, when we consider how much he has written, we perceive, at once, that he *must* have been industrious, or he could never (like an honest woman as he is) have so thoroughly succeeded in keeping himself from being "talked about."

31.

H—— calls his verse a "poem," very much as Francis the First bestowed the title, *mes déserts*, upon his snug little deer-park at Fontainebleau.

32.

K——, the publisher, trying to be critical, talks about books pretty much as a washerwoman would about Niagara falls or a poulterer about a phœnix.

33.

The ingenuity of critical malice would often be laughable but for the disgust which, even in the most perverted spirits, injustice never fails to excite. A common *trick* is that of decrying, impliedly, the higher, by insisting upon the lower, merits of an author. Macaulay, for example, deeply feeling how much critical acumen is enforced by cautious attention to the mere "rhetoric" which is its vehicle, has at length become the best of modern rhetoricians. His *brother* reviewers—anonymous, of course, and likely to remain so forever—extol "the acumen of Carlyle, the analysis of Schlegel, *and* the style of Macaulay." Bancroft is a philosophical historian; but no amount of philosophy has yet taught him to despise a minute accuracy in point of fact. His *brother* historians talk of "the grace of Prescott, the erudition of Gibbon, *and* the pains-taking precision of Bancroft." Tennyson, perceiving how vividly an imaginative effect is aided, now and then, by a certain quaintness judiciously introduced, brings this latter, at times, in support of his most glorious and most delicate imagination:—whereupon his *brother* poets hasten to laud the imagination of Mr. Somebody, whom nobody imagined to have any, "*and* the somewhat affected quaintness of Tennyson."—Let the noblest poet add to his other excellences—if he dares—that of faultless versification and scrupulous attention to grammar. He is damned at once. His rivals have it in their power to discourse of "A. the true poet, *and* B. the versifier and disciple of Lindley Murray."

34.

That a cause leads to an effect, is scarcely more certain than that, so far as Morals are concerned, a repetition of effect tends to the generation of cause. Herein lies the principle of what we so vaguely term "Habit."

35.

With the exception of Tennyson's "Locksley Hall," I have never read a poem combining so much of the fiercest passion with so much of the most delicate imagination, as the "Lady Geraldine's Courtship" of Miss Barrett. I am forced to admit, however, that the latter work *is* a palpable imitation of the former, which it surpasses in thesis as much as it falls below it in a certain calm energy, lustrous and indomitable—such as we might imagine in a broad river of molten gold.

36.

What has become of the inferior planet which Decuppis, about nine years ago, declared he saw traversing the disc of the sun?

37.

"Ignorance *is* bliss"—but, that the bliss be real, the ignorance must be so profound as not to suspect itself ignorant. With this understanding, Boileau's line may be read thus:

"Le plus fou *toujours* est le plus satisfait,"

—"*toujours*" in place of "*souvent*."

38.

Bryant and Street are both, essentially, descriptive poets; and descriptive poetry, even in its happiest manifestation, is *not* of the highest order. But the distinction between Bryant and Street is very broad. While the former, in reproducing the sensible images of Nature, reproduces the sentiments with which he regards them, the latter gives us the images and nothing beyond. He never forces us to feel what we feel he must have felt.

39.

In lauding Beauty, Genius merely evinces a filial affection. To Genius Beauty gives life—reaping often a reward in Immortality.

40.

And this is the "American Drama" of ——! Well!—that "Conscience which makes cowards of us all" will permit me to say, in praise of the performance, only that it is not quite so bad as I expected it to be. But then I always expect too much.

41.

What we feel to be *Fancy* will be found fanciful still, whatever be the theme which engages it. No *subject* exalts it into Imagination. When Moore is termed "a fanciful poet," the epithet is applied with precision. He *is*. He is fanciful in "Lalla Rookh," and had he written the "Inferno," in the "Inferno" he would have contrived to be still fanciful and nothing beyond.

42.

When we speak of "a suspicious man," we may mean either one who suspects, or one to be suspected. Our language needs either the adjective "suspectful," or the adjective "suspectable."

43.

"To love," says Spencer, is

> "To fawn, to crouch, to wait, to ride, to run,
>   To speed, to give, to want, to be undone."

The philosophy, here, might be rendered more profound, by the mere omission of a comma. We all know the *willing* blindness—the *voluntary* madness of Love. We express this in thus punctuating the last line:

> To speed, to give—*to want to be undone.*

It is a case, in short, where we gain point by omitting it.

44.

Miss Edgeworth seems to have had only an approximate comprehension of "Fashion," for she says:

"If it was the fashion to burn me, and I at the stake, I hardly know ten persons of my acquaintance who would refuse to throw on a faggot."

There are *many* who, in such a case, would "refuse to throw on a faggot"—for fear of smothering out the fire.

45.

I am beginning to think with Horsely—that "the People have nothing to do with the laws but to obey them."

46.

"It is not fair to review my book without reading it," says Mr. M——, talking at the critics, and, as usual, expecting impossibilities. The man who is clever enough to *write* such a work, is clever enough to read it, no doubt; but we should not look for so much talent in the world at large. Mr. M—— will not imagine that I mean to blame *him*. The book alone is in fault, after all. The fact is, that *"er lasst sich nicht lesen"*— it will not *permit* itself to be read. Being a hobby of Mr. M——'s, and brimful of spirit, it will let nobody mount it but Mr. M——.

47.

It is only to teach his children Geography, that G—— wears a boot the picture of Italy upon the map.

48.

In his great Dictionary, Webster seems to have had an idea of being more English than the English—*"plus Arabe qu'en Arabie."**

49.

That there were once "seven wise men" is by no means, strictly speaking, an historical *fact*; and I am rather inclined to rank the idea among the Kabbala.

50.

Painting their faces to look like Macaulay, some of our critics manage to resemble him, at length, as a Massaccian does a Raffäellian Virgin; and, except that the former is feebler and

*Count Anthony Hamilton.

thinner than the other—suggesting the idea of its being the ghost of the other—not one connoisseur in ten can perceive any difference. But then, unhappily, even the street lazzaroni can feel the distinction.

Graham's Magazine, May–June 1849

Marginalia

DEMOCRATIC REVIEW, *November 1844*

IN GETTING my books, I have been always solicitous of an ample margin; this not so much through any love of the thing in itself, however agreeable, as for the facility it affords me of pencilling suggested thoughts, agreements and differences of opinion, or brief critical comments in general. Where what I have to note is too much to be included within the narrow limits of a margin, I commit it to a slip of paper, and deposit it between the leaves; taking care to secure it by an imperceptible portion of gum tragacanth paste.

All this may be whim; it may be not only a very hackneyed, but a very idle practice;—yet I persist in it still; and it affords me pleasure; which is profit, in despite of Mr. Bentham with Mr. Mill on his back.

This making of notes, however, is by no means the making of mere *memoranda*—a custom which has its disadvantages, beyond doubt. *"Ce que je mets sur papier,"* says Bernardin de St. Pierre, *"je remets de ma mémoire, et par consequence je l'oublie;"*—and, in fact, if you wish to forget anything upon the spot, make a note that this thing is to be remembered.

But the purely marginal jottings, done with no eye to the Memorandum Book, have a distinct complexion, and not only a distinct purpose, but none at all; this it is which imparts to them a value. They have a rank somewhat above the chance and desultory comments of literary chit-chat—for these latter are not unfrequently "talk for talk's sake," hurried out of the mouth; while the *marginalia* are deliberately pencilled, because the mind of the reader wishes to unburthen itself of a *thought*;—however flippant—however silly—however trivial—still a thought indeed, not merely a thing that might have been a thought in time, and under more favorable circumstances. In the *marginalia*, too, we talk only to ourselves; we therefore talk freshly—boldly—originally—with *abandonnement*—without conceit—much after the fashion of Jeremy Taylor, and Sir Thomas Browne, and Sir William Temple, and the anatomical Burton, and that most logical analogist, Butler, and some other people of the old day, who

were too full of their matter to have any room for their manner, which, being thus left out of question, was a capital manner, indeed,—a model of manners, with a richly marginalic
air.

The circumscription of space, too, in these pencillings, has
in it something more of advantage than of inconvenience. It
compels us (whatever diffuseness of idea we may clandestinely
entertain), into Montesquieu-ism, into Tacitus-ism (here I
leave out of view the concluding portion of the "Annals")—
or even into Carlyle-ism—a thing which, I have been told, is
not to be confounded with your ordinary affectation and bad
grammar. I say "bad grammar," through sheer obstinacy, because the grammarians (who should know better) insist upon
it that I should not. But then grammar is not what these
grammarians will have it; and, being merely the analysis of
language, with the result of this analysis, must be good or
bad just as the analyst is sage or silly—just as he is a Horne
Tooke or a Cobbett.

But to our sheep. During a rainy afternoon, not long ago,
being in a mood too listless for continuous study, I sought
relief from *ennui* in dipping here and there, at random,
among the volumes of my library—no very large one, certainly, but sufficiently miscellaneous; and, I flatter myself, not
a little *recherché*.

Perhaps it was what the Germans call the "brain-scattering"
humor of the moment; but, while the picturesqueness of the
numerous pencil-scratches arrested my attention, their helter-
skelter-iness of commentary amused me. I found myself at
length, forming a wish that it had been some other hand than
my own which had so bedevilled the books, and fancying
that, in such case, I might have derived no inconsiderable
pleasure from turning them over. From this the transition-
thought (as Mr. Lyell, or Mr. Murchison, or Mr. Feather-
stonhaugh would have it) was natural enough:—there might
be something even in *my* scribblings which, for the mere sake
of scribbling, would have interest for others.

The main difficulty respected the mode of transferring the
notes from the volumes—the context from the text—without
detriment to that exceedingly frail fabric of intelligibility in
which the context was imbedded. With all appliances to boot,

with the printed pages at their back, the commentaries were too often like Dodona's oracles—or those of Lycophron Tenebrosus—or the essays of the pedant's pupils, in Quintillian, which were "necessarily excellent, since even he (the pedant) found it impossible to comprehend them:"—what, then, would become of it—this context—if transferred?—if translated? Would it not rather be *traduit* (traduced) which is the French synonym, or *overzezet* (turned topsy-turvy) which is the Dutch one?

I concluded, at length, to put extensive faith in the acumen and imagination of the reader:—this as a general rule. But, in some instances, where even faith would not remove mountains, there seemed no safer plan than so to re-model the note as to convey at least the ghost of a conception as to what it was all about. Where, for such conception, the text itself was absolutely necessary, I could quote it; where the title of the book commented upon was indispensable, I could name it. In short, like a novel-hero dilemma'd, I made up my mind "to be guided by circumstances," in default of more satisfactory rules of conduct.

As for the multitudinous opinion expressed in the subjoined *farrago*—as for my present assent to all, or dissent from any portion of it—as to the possibility of my having, in some instances, altered my mind—or as to the impossibility of my not having altered it often—these are points upon which I say nothing, because upon these there can be nothing cleverly said. It may be as well to observe, however, that just as the goodness of your true pun is in the direct ratio of its intolerability, so is nonsense the essential sense of the Marginal Note.

————

Who has seen the *"Velschii Ruzname Naurus,"* of the Oriental Literature?

————

There is about the same difference between the epicyclic lines of Shelley, *et id genus*, and the epics of Hell-Fire Montgomery, as between the notes of a flute and those of the gong at Astor's. In the one class the vibrations are unequal but melodious; the other have regularity enough, but no great deal of music, and a trifle too much of the *tintamarre*.

———

The Bishop of Durham (Dr. Butler) once asked Dean Tucker whether he did not think that communities went mad *en masse*, now and then, just as individuals, individually. The thing need not have been questioned. Were not the Abderians seized, all at once, with the Euripides lunacy, during which they ran about the streets declaiming the plays of the poet? And now here is the great tweedle-dee tweedle-dum paroxysm—the uproar about Pusey. If England and America are not lunatic now—at this very moment—then I have never seen such a thing as a March hare.

———

I believe that Hannibal passed into Italy over the Pennine Alps; and if Livy were living now, I could demonstrate this fact even to him.

———

In a rail-road car, I once sat face to face with him—or, rather, προσωπον κατα προσωπον, as the Septuagint have it; for he had a tooth-ache, and three-fourths of his visage were buried in a red handkerchief. Of what remained visible, an eighth, I thought, represented his "Gaieties," and an eighth his "Gravities." The only author I ever met who looked even the fourth of his own book.

———

But for the shame of the thing, there are few of the so-called apophthegms which would not avow themselves epigrams outright. They have it in common with the fencing-school foils, that we can make no real use of any part of them but the point, while this we can never get fairly at, on account of a little flat profundity-button.

———

I make no exception, even in Dante's favor:—the only thing well said of Purgatory, is that a man may go farther and fare worse.

———

When music affects us to tears, seemingly causeless, we weep *not*, as Gravina supposes, from "excess of pleasure;" but through excess of an impatient, petulant sorrow that, as mere mortals, we are as yet in no condition to banquet upon those supernal ecstasies of which the music affords us merely a suggestive and indefinite glimpse.

———

One of the most deliberate *tricks* of Voltaire, is where he renders, by

> *Soyez justes, mortels, et ne craignez qu'un Dieu,*

the words of Phlegyas, who cries out, in Hell,

> Dicite justitiam, moniti, et non temnere *Divos.*

He gives the line this twist, by way of showing that the ancients worshipped *one* God. He is endeavoring to deny that the idea of the Unity of God originated with the Jews.

———

The theorizers on Government, who pretend always to "begin with the beginning," commence with Man in what they call his *natural* state—the savage. What right have they to suppose this his natural state? Man's chief idiosyncrasy being reason, it follows that his savage condition—his condition of action *without* reason—is his *un*natural state. The more he reasons, the nearer he approaches the position to which this chief idiosyncrasy irresistibly impels him; and not until he attains this position with exactitude—not until his reason has exhausted itself for his improvement—not until he has stepped upon the highest pinnacle of civilisation—will his *natural* state be ultimately reached, or thoroughly determined.

———

Our literature is infested with a swarm of just such little people as this—creatures who succeed in creating for themselves an absolutely positive reputation, by mere dint of the continuity and perpetuality of their appeals to the public—which is permitted, not for a single instant, to rid itself of these *Epizoæ*, or to get their pretensions out of sight.

We cannot, then, regard the microscopical works of the *animalculæ* in question, as simple nothings; for they produce, as I say, a positive effect, and no multiplication of zeros will result in unity—but as negative quantities—as less than nothings; since − into − will give +.

———

I cannot imagine why it is that Harrison Ainsworth so be-peppers his books with *his own* dog Latin and pig Greek—unless, indeed, he agrees with Encyclopædia Chambers, that nonsense sounds worse in English than in any other language.

———

These gentlemen, in attempting the dash of Carlyle, get only as far as the luminousness of Plutarch, who begins the life of Demetrius Poliorcetes with an account of his death, and informs us that the hero could not have been as tall as his father, for the simple reason that his father, after all, was only his uncle.

———

To persist in calling these places "*Magdalen* Asylums" is absurd, and worse. We have no reason to believe that Mary Magdalen ever sinned as supposed, or that she is the person alluded to in the seventh chapter of Luke. See *Macknight's "Harmony"*—p. 201—part 2.

———

Nothing, to the true taste, is so offensive as mere hyperism. In Germany *wohlgeborn* is a loftier title than *edelgeborn*; and, in Greece, the thrice-victorious at the Olympic games could claim a statue of the size of life, while he who had conquered but once was entitled *only* to a colossal.

———

The author* speaks of music like a man, and not like a fiddler. This is something—and that he has imagination is

*H. F. Chorley, author of "Conti."

more. But the philosophy of music is beyond his depth, and of its physics he, unquestionably, has no conception. By the way — of all the so-called scientific musicians, how many may we suppose cognizant of the acoustic facts and mathematical deductions? To be sure, my acquaintance with eminent composers is quite limited — but I have never met *one* who did not stare and say "yes," "no," "hum!" "ha!" "eh?" when I mentioned the mechanism of the *Siréne*, or made allusion to the oval vibrations at right angles.

———

His mind* — granting him any — is essentially at home in little statistics, twaddling gossip, and maudlin commentaries, fashioned to look profound; but the idea of his attempting original composition, is fantastic.

———

All the Bridgewater treatises have failed in noticing *the great* idiosyncrasy in the Divine system of adaptation: — that idiosyncrasy which stamps the adaptation as Divine, in distinction from that which is the work of merely human constructiveness. I speak of the complete *mutuality* of adaptation. For example: — in human constructions, a particular cause has a particular effect — a particular purpose brings about a particular object; but we see no reciprocity. The effect does not re-act upon the cause — the object does not change relations with the purpose. In Divine constructions, the object is either object or purpose, as we choose to regard it, while the purpose is either purpose or object; so that we can never (abstractedly, without concretion — without reference to facts of the moment) decide which is which. For secondary example: — In polar climates, the human frame, to maintain its due caloric, requires, for combustion in the stomach, the most highly ammoniac food, such as train oil. Again: — In polar climates, the sole food afforded man is the oil of abundant seals and whales. Now, whether is oil at hand because imperatively demanded? — or whether is it the only thing demanded because the only thing to be obtained? It is impossible to say. There is an absolute reciprocity of ad-

*Grant — author of "Walks and Wanderings."

aptation, for which we seek in vain among the works of man.

The Bridgewater tractists may have avoided this point, on account of its apparent tendency to overthrow the idea of *cause* in general—consequently of a First Cause—of God. But it is more probable that they have failed to perceive what no one preceding them, has, to my knowledge, perceived.

The pleasure which we derive from any exertion of human ingenuity, is in the direct ratio of the *approach* to this species of reciprocity between cause and effect. In the construction of *plot*, for example, in fictitious literature, we should aim at so arranging the points, or incidents, that we cannot distinctly see, in respect to any one of them, whether that one depends from any one other, or upholds it. In this sense, of course, perfection of plot is unattainable *in fact*,—because Man is the constructor. The plots of God are perfect. The Universe is a Plot of God.

———

"Who does not turn with absolute contempt from the rings, and gems, and filters, and caves, and genii of Eastern Tales, as from the trinkets of a toy-shop, and the trumpery of a raree-show?"—*Lectures on Literature, by James Montgomery.*

This is mere "pride and arrogance, and the evil way, and the froward mouth." Or, perhaps, so monstrous a proposition (querily put) springs rather from the thickness of the Montgomery skull, which is the Montgomery predominant source of error—the Eidolon of the Den wherein grovel the Montgomery curs.

———

The serious (minor) compositions of Dickens have been lost in the blaze of his comic reputation. One of the most forcible things ever written, is a short story of his, called "The Black Veil;" a strangely pathetic and richly imaginative production, replete with the loftiest tragic power.

P. S. Mr. Dickens' head must puzzle the phrenologists. The organs of ideality are small; and the conclusion of the "Curiosity-Shop" is more truly ideal (in both phrenological senses) than any composition of equal length in the English language.

———

A good book;* but, for a modern book, too abundant in faded philosophy. Here is an argument spoken of as not proving the permanency of the solar system, "because we know, from the more sure word of prophecy, that it is not destined to last for ever." Who believes—whether layman or priest—that the prophecies in question have any farther allusion than to the orb of the Earth—or, more strictly, to the crust of the orb!

———

It ranks† with "Armstrong on Health"—the "Botanic Garden"—the *"Connubia Florum."* Such works should conciliate the Utilitarians. I think I will set about a lyric on the Quadrature of Curves—or the Arithmetic of Infinites. Cotes, however, supplies me a ready-made title, in his "Harmonia Mensurarum," and there is no reason why I should not be *fluent*, at least, upon the fluents of fractional expressions.

———

In general, we should not be over-scrupulous about niceties of phrase, when the matter in hand is a dunce to be gibbeted. Speak out!—or the person may not understand you. He is to be hung? Then hang him by all means; but make no bow when you mean no obeisance, and eschew the droll delicacy of the Clown in the Play—"Be so good, sir, as to rise and be put to death."

This is the only true principle among men. Where the gentler sex is concerned, there seems but one course for the critic—speak if you can commend—be silent, if not; for a woman will never be brought to admit a non-identity between herself and her book, and "a well-bred man" says, justly, that excellent old English moralist, James Puckle, in his

*"Sacred Philosophy of the Seasons"—By the Rev. Henry Duncan—Ruthwell, Scotland.
†"Poem de Ponderibus et Mensuris," by Quintus Rhemnius Fannius Palæmon. Its conclusion:—found by Denis, in the Imperial Library, Vienna.

'Gray Cap for a Green Head,' "a well-bred man will never *give himself the liberty* to speak ill of women."

———

It* is the half-profound, half-silly, and wholly irrational composition of a very clever, very ignorant, and laughably impudent fellow—*"ingeniosus puer, sed insignis nebulo,"* as the Jesuits have well described Crébillon.

———

The Germans, just now, are afflicted with the epidemic of history-writing—the same *cacöethes* which Lucian tells us beset his countrymen upon the discomfiture of Severianus in Armenia, followed by the triumphs in Parthia.

———

The sense of high birth is a moral force whose value the democrats, albeit compact of mathematics, are never in condition to calculate. *"Pour savoir ce qu'est Dieu,"* says the Baron de Bielfeld, *"il faut être Dieu même."*

———

I have seen many computations respecting the greatest amount of erudition attainable by an individual in his lifetime; but these computations are falsely based, and fall infinitely beneath the truth. It is true that, *in general*, we retain, we remember to available purpose, scarcely one-hundredth part of what we read; yet there *are* minds which not only retain *all* receipts, but keep them at compound interest for ever. Again:—were every man supposed to read *out*, he could read, of course, very little, even in half a century; for, in such case, each individual word must be dwelt upon in some degree. But, in reading to ourselves, at the ordinary rate of what is called "light reading," we scarcely *touch* one word in ten. And, even physically considered, knowledge breeds knowledge, as gold gold; for he who reads really much, finds his capacity to read increase in geometrical ratio. The *helluo librorum* will but glance at the page which detains the ordinary

*"The Age of Reason."

reader some minutes; and the difference in the absolute *read-ing* (its uses considered), will be in favor of the *helluo*, who will have winnowed the matter of which the *tyro* mumbled both the seeds and the chaff. A deep-rooted and strictly continuous habit of reading will, with certain classes of intellect, result in an instinctive and seemingly magnetic appreciation of a thing written; and now the student reads by pages just as other men by words. Long years to come, with a careful analysis of the mental process, may even render this species of appreciation a common thing. It may be taught in the schools of our descendants of the tenth or twentieth generation. It may become the method of the mob of the eleventh or twenty-first. And should these matters come to pass—as they will—there will be in them no more legitimate cause for wonder than there is, to-day, in the marvel that, syllable by syllable, men comprehend what, letter by letter, I now trace upon this page.

———

Is it not a law that need has a tendency to engender the thing needed?

———

"The nature of the soil may indicate the countries most exposed to these formidable concussions, since they are caused by subterraneous fires, and such fires are kindled by the union and fermentation of iron and sulphur. But their times and effects appear to lie beyond the reach of human curiosity, and the philosopher will discreetly abstain from the prediction of earthquakes, till he has counted the drops of water that silently filtrate on the inflammable mineral, and measured the caverns which increase by resistance the explosion of the imprisoned air. Without assigning the cause, history will distinguish the period in which these calamitous events have been rare or frequent, and will observe, that this fever of the earth raged with uncommon violence during the reign of Justinian. Each year is marked by the repetition of earthquakes, of such duration, that Constantinople has been shaken above forty days; of such extent, that the shock has been communicated to the whole surface of the globe, or at least of the Roman Empire."

These sentences may be regarded as a full synopsis of the

style of Gibbon—a style which has been more frequently commended than almost any other in the world.

He had three hobbies which he rode to the death (stuffed puppets as they were), and which he kept in condition by the continual sacrifice of all that is valuable in language. These hobbies were *Dignity—Modulation—Laconism*.

Dignity is all very well; and history demands it for its general tone; but the being everlastingly on stilts is not only troublesome and awkward, but dangerous. He who falls *en homme ordinaire*—from the mere slipping of his feet—is usually an object of sympathy; but all men tumble now and then, and this tumbling from high sticks is sure to provoke laughter.

His modulation, however, is *always* ridiculous; for it is so uniform, so continuous, and so jauntily kept up, that we almost fancy the writer waltzing to his words.

With him, to speak lucidly was a far less merit than to speak smoothly and curtly. There is a way in which, through the nature of language itself, we may often save a few words by talking backwards; and this is, therefore, a favorite practice with Gibbon. Observe the sentence commencing—"The nature of the soil." The thought expressed could scarcely be more condensed in expression; but, for the sake of this condensation, he renders the idea difficult of comprehension, by subverting the natural order of a simple proposition, and placing a deduction before that from which it is deduced. An ordinary man would have thus written: "As these formidable concussions arise from subterranean fires kindled by the union and fermentation of iron and sulphur, we may judge of the degree in which any region is exposed to earthquake by the presence or absence of these minerals." My sentence has forty words—that of Gibbon thirty-six; but the first cannot fail of being instantly comprehended, while the latter it may be necessary to re-read.

The mere *terseness* of this historian is, however, grossly over-rated. In general, he conveys an idea (although darkly) in fewer words than others of his time; but a habit of straight thinking that rejects non-essentials, will enable any one to say, for example, what was intended above, *both* more briefly and more distinctly. He must abandon, of course, "formidable concussions" and things of that kind.

E. g.—"The sulphur and iron of any region express its liability to earthquake; their fermentation being its cause."

Here are seventeen words in place of the thirty-six; and these seventeen convey the full force of all that it was necessary to say. Such concision is, nevertheless, an error, and, so far as respects the true object of concision, is a *bull*. The most truly concise style is that which most rapidly transmits the sense. What, then, should be said of the concision of Carlyle?—that those are mad who admire a brevity which squanders our time for the purpose of economizing our printing-ink and paper.

Observe, now, the passage above quoted, commencing— "Each year is marked." What is it the historian wishes to say? Not, certainly, that every year was marked by earthquakes that shook Constantinople forty days, and extended to all regions of the earth!—yet this only is the legitimate interpretation. The earthquakes are said to be of *such* duration that Constantinople, &c., and these earthquakes (of *such* duration) were experienced every year. But this is a pure Gibbonism— an original one; no man ever so rhodomontaded before. He means to say merely that the earthquakes were of unusual duration and extent—the duration of one being so long that Constantinople shook for forty days, and the extent of another being so wide as to include the whole empire of Rome —"by which," he adds *sotto voce*—"by which insulated facts the reader may estimate that *average* duration and extent of which I speak"—a thing the reader will find it difficult to do.

A few years hence—and should any one compose a mock heroic in the manner of the "Decline and Fall," the poem will be torn to pieces by the critics, *instanter*, as an unwarrantable exaggeration of the principles of the burlesque.

———

I never knew a man, of so really decent understanding, so full of bigotry as B——d. Had he supreme power, and were he not, now and then, to meet an odd volume sufficiently silly to confirm his prejudices, there can be no doubt that he would burn every book in the world as an *auto da fe*.

It is a deeply consequential error this:—the assumption that we, being men, will, in general, be *deliberately* true. The greater amount of truth is impulsively uttered; thus the greater amount is spoken, not written. But, in examining the historic material, we leave these considerations out of sight. We dote upon records, which, in the main, lie; while we discard the *Kabbala*, which, properly interpreted, do *not*.

"The right angle of light's incidence produces a sound upon one of the Egyptian pyramids." This assertion, thus expressed, I have encountered somewhere—probably in one of the Notes to Apollonius. It is nonsense, I suppose,—but it will not do to speak hastily.

The orange ray of the spectrum and the buzz of the gnat (which never rises above the second A), affect me with nearly similar sensations. In hearing the gnat, I perceive the color. In perceiving the color, I seem to hear the gnat.

Here the vibrations of the tympanum caused by the wings of the fly, may, from within, induce abnormal vibrations of the retina, similar to those which the orange ray induces, normally, from without. By *similar*, I do not mean of equal rapidity—this would be folly;—but each millionth undulation, for example, of the retina, might accord with one of the tympanum; and I doubt whether this would not be sufficient for the effect.

How many good books suffer neglect through the inefficiency of their beginnings! It is far better that we commence irregularly—immethodically—than that we fail to arrest attention; but the two points, method and pungency, may always be combined. At all risks, let there be a few vivid sentences *imprimis*, by way of the electric bell to the telegraph.

I am far more than half serious in all that I have ever said about manuscript, as affording indication of character.

The general proposition is unquestionable—that the mental qualities will have a *tendency* to impress the MS. The difficulty lies in the comparison of this tendency, as a mathematical *force*, with the forces of the various disturbing influences of mere circumstance. But—given a man's purely physical biography, with his MS., and the moral biography may be deduced.

The actual practical extent to which these ideas are applicable, is not sufficiently understood. For my own part, I by no means shrink from acknowledging that I act, hourly, upon estimates of character derived from chirography. The estimates, however, upon which I *depend*, are chiefly negative. For example: a man may not always be a man of genius, or a man of taste, or a man of firmness, or a man of any other quality, because he writes this hand or that; but then there are MSS. which no man of firmness, or of taste, or of genius, ever did, will, or can write.

There is a certain species of hand-writing,—and a quite "elegant" one it is, too; although I hesitate to describe it, because it is written by some two or three thousand of my personal friends,—a species of hand-writing, I say, which seems to appertain, as if by prescriptive right, to the blockhead, and which has been employed by every donkey since the days of Cadmus,—has been penned by every gander since first a grey goose yielded a pen.

Now, were any one to write me a letter in this MS., requiring me to involve myself with its inditer in any enterprise of moment and of risk, it would be only on the score of the commonest civility that I would condescend to send him a reply.

———

These gentlemen may be permitted to exist yet a very little while, since it is "the darling public" who are amused, without knowing at what—

> *Mais moi, qui, dans le fond, sais bien ce que jen crois,*
> *Qui compte, tous les jours, leurs larcins par mes doigts,*
> *Je ris—etc.*

Fellows who really have no *right*—some individuals *have*—to purloin the property of their predecessors. Mere buzzards; or, in default of that, mere *pechingzies*—the species of creatures that they tell us of in the Persian Compendiums of Natural History—animals very soft and very sly, with ears of such length that, while one answers for a bed, the other is all that is necessary for a counterpane. A race of dolts—literary Cacuses, whose clumsily stolen bulls never fail of leaving behind them ample evidence of having been dragged into the thief-den by the tail.

———

In the Hebrew MS. (172 Prov. 18—22) after the word אשה, is an erasure, by which we lose some three or four letters. Could these letters have been anything but טובה? The version reads, "whoso findeth a wife, findeth a good thing;" a proposition which cannot be mathematically demonstrated. By the insertion suggested, it would be converted into "whoso findeth a *good* wife, findeth," &c.—an axiom which the most rigorous caviller for precision would make no scruple of admitting into Euclid.

———

"His imagery* is by no means destitute of merit, but is directed by an exceedingly coarse and vulgar taste."

Quite true; but the remark would have come with a better grace from almost any other lips than those of Lord Brougham and Vaux.

———

Dr. Lardner thus explains the apparent difference in size between the setting and the noon-day sun:—

"Various solutions have been proposed, and the one generally adopted by scientific minds I will now endeavor to make plain, though I fear its nature is so remarkable that I am not sure I shall make it intelligible. But here it is. If the sun, or another celestial object, be near the horizon, and I

———

*That of John Randolph.

direct my attention to it, I see between me and that object a vast number of objects upon the face of the earth, as trees, houses, mountains, the magnitudes and positions of which are familiar to me. These supply the mind with a means of estimating the size of the object at which I am looking. I know that it is much farther off than these; and yet the sun appears, perhaps, much larger than the top of the intervening mountain. I thus compare the sun, by a process of the mind so subtle and instinctive that I am unconscious of it, with the objects which I see between it and myself, and I conclude that it is much larger than those. Well, the same sun rises to the meridian; then there are no intervening objects whereby to space off the distance, as it were, and thus form a comparative estimate of its size. . . . . I am prepared to be met by the objection, that this is *an extremely learned and metaphysical reason. So it is.*"

How funny are the ideas which some persons entertain about learning, and especially about metaphysics!

Whatever may be the *foible* of Dr. Lardner's intellect, its *forte* is certainly not originality; and however ill *put* are his explanations of the phenomenon in question, he is to be blamed for them only inasmuch as he adopted them, without examination, from others. The same thing is said, very nearly in the same way, by all who have previously touched the subject. And the reasoning is not only of very partial force, but wretchedly urged. If the sun appears larger than usual merely because we compare its size with mountains and other large objects upon the earth (objects, the Doctor might have said, *beyond* all which we see the sun), how happens it that the illusion does not cease when we see the orb setting where no such objects are visible? For example, on the horizon of a smooth sea.

We appreciate *time* by events alone. For this reason we define time (somewhat improperly) as the succession of events; but the fact itself—that events are our sole means of appreciating time—tends to the engendering of the erroneous idea that events *are* time—that the more numerous the events, the longer the time; and the converse. This erroneous idea there can be no doubt that we should absolutely entertain in all cases, but for our practical means of correcting the impression—such as clocks, and the movements of the heavenly bodies—whose revolutions, after all, we only *assume* to be regular.

Space is precisely analogous with time. By objects alone we estimate space; and we might as rationally define it "the succession of objects," as time "the succession of events." But, as before.—The fact, that we have no other means of estimating space than objects afford us—tends to the false idea that objects *are* space—that the more numerous the objects the greater the space; and the converse; and this erroneous impression we should receive in all cases, but for our practical means of correcting it—such as yard measures, and other conventional measures, which resolve themselves, ultimately, into certain natural standards, such as barley-corns, which, after all, we only *assume* to be regular.

The mind can form *some* conception of the distance (however vast) between the sun and Uranus, because there are ten objects which (mentally) intervene—the planets Mercury, Venus, Earth, Mars, Ceres, Vesta, Juno, Pallas, Jupiter, and Saturn. These objects serve as stepping-stones to the mind; which, nevertheless, is utterly lost in the attempt at establishing a notion of the interval between Uranus and Sirius; *lost*— yet, clearly, not on account of the mere *distance* (for why should we not conceive the abstract idea of the distance, two miles, as readily as that of the distance, one?) but, simply, because between Uranus and Sirius we happen to know that all is void. And, from what I have already said, it follows that this vacuity—this want of intervening points—will cause *to fall short* of the truth any notion we shall endeavor to form. In fact, having once passed the limits of absolutely practical admeasurement, by means of intervening objects, our ideas of distances are *one*; they have no variation. Thus, in truth, we think of the interval between Uranus and Sirius precisely as of that between Saturn and Uranus, or of that between any one planet and its immediate neighbor. We fancy, indeed, that we form different conceptions of the different intervals; but we mistake the mathematical knowledge of the fact of the interval, for an idea of the interval itself.

It is the principle for which I contend that instinctively leads the artist, in painting what he technically calls distances, to introduce a succession of objects between the "distance" and the foreground. Here it will be said that the intention is the perspective comparison of *the size* of the objects. Several men, for example, are painted, one beyond the other, and it is the diminution of apparent size by which the idea of distance is conveyed;—this, I say, will be asserted. But here is mere confusion of the two notions of abstract and comparative distance. By this process of diminishing figures, we are, it is true, made to feel that one is at a *greater* distance than the other, but the idea we thence glean of abstract distance, is gleaned altogether from the mere succession of the figures, independently of magnitude. To prove this, let the men be painted out, and *rocks* put in their stead. A rock may be of any size. The farthest may be, for all we know, really, and not merely optically, the least. The effect of absolute distance will remain untouched, and the sole result will be confusion of idea respecting the comparative distances from rock to rock. But the thing is clear: if the artist's intention is really, as supposed, to convey the notion of great distance by perspective comparison of the *size* of men at different intervals, we must, at least, grant that he puts himself to unnecessary trouble in the multiplication of his men. *Two* would answer all the purposes of two thousand;—one in the foreground as a standard, and one in the background, of a size corresponding with the artist's conception of the distance.

In looking at the setting sun in a mountainous region, or with a city between the eye and the orb, we see it of a certain seeming magnitude, and we do not perceive that this seeming magnitude varies when we look at the same sun setting on the horizon of the ocean. In either case we have a chain of objects by which to appreciate a certain distance;—in the former case this chain is formed of mountains and towers—in the latter, of ripples, or specks of foam; but the result does not present any difference. In each case we get the same idea of the distance, and consequently of the size. This size we have in our mind when we look at the sun in his meridian place; but this distance we have *not*—for no objects intervene. That is to say, the distance falls short, while the size remains. The consequence is, that, to accord with the diminished distance, the mind instantaneously diminishes the size.

The conversed experiment gives, of course, a conversed result.

Dr. Lardner's "so it is" is amusing to say no more. In general, the mere natural philosophers have the same exaggerated notions of the perplexity of metaphysics. And, perhaps, it is this *looming* of the latter science which has brought about the vulgar derivation of its name from the supposed superiority to physics—as if μετα φυσικα had the force of *super* physicam. The fact is, that Aristotle's Treatise on Morals is next in succession to his Book on Physics, and this he supposes the rational order of study. His Ethics, therefore, commence with the words Μετα τα φυσικα—whence we take the word, Metaphysics.

That Leibnitz, who was fond of interweaving even his mathematical, with ethical speculations, making a medley rather to be wondered at than understood—that *he* made no attempt at amending the common explanation of the difference in the sun's apparent size—this, perhaps, is more really a matter for marvel than that Dr. Lardner should look upon the common explanation as only too "learned" and too "metaphysical" for an audience in Yankee-Land.

———

That "truth is stranger than fiction" is an adage for ever in the mouth of the uninformed, who quote it as they would quote any other proposition which to them seemed paradoxical—for the mere point of the paradox. People who read never quote the saying, because sheer truisms are never worth quoting. A friend of mine once read me a long poem on the planet Saturn. He was a man of genius, but his lines were a failure of course, since the realities of the planet, detailed in the most prosaic language, put to shame and quite overwhelm all the accessory fancies of the poet.

If, however, the solemn adage in question should ever stand in need of support, here is a book will support it.*

———

* *Ramaseand; or a Vocabulary of the peculiar language used by the Thugs, with an Introduction and Appendix descriptive of the System pursued by that Fraternity, and of the Measures adopted by the Supreme Government of India for its Suppression.* — *Calcutta, 1836.*

Some richly imaginative thoughts, skilfully expressed, might be culled from this poem*—which, as a whole, is nothing worth. E. g—

> And I can hear the click of that old gate,
> As once again, amid the chirping yard,
> *I see the summer rooms open and dark.*

and—

> —How calm the night moves on! and yet,
> *In the dark morrow that behind those hills*
> *Lies sleeping now, who knows what horror lurks?*

———

The great force derivable from repetition of particular vowel sounds in verse, is little understood, or quite overlooked, even by those versifiers who dwell most upon what is commonly called "alliteration." How richly melodious are these lines of Milton's "Comus!"

> May thy *brim*med waves for *this*
> Their full *tri*bute never *miss*—
> May thy *billows roll ashore*
> The beryl and the *golden ore!*

—and yet it seems especially singular that, with the full and noble volume of the long ō resounding in his ears, the poet should have written, in the last line, "beryl," when he might so well have written "onyx."

———

Moore has been noted for the number and appositeness, as well as novelty of his similes; and the renown thus acquired is indicial of his deficiency in that noble merit—the noblest of all. No poet thus distinguished was ever richly ideal. Pope and Cowper are instances. Direct similes are of too palpably artificial a character to be artistical. An artist will always contrive to weave his illustrations into the metaphorical form.

Moore has a peculiar facility in prosaically telling a poetical story. By this I mean that he preserves the tone and method

*"*The Bride of Fort Edward.*"—Anonymous.

of arrangement of a prose relation, and thus obtains great advantage, in important points, over his more stilted compeers. His is no poetical *style* (such as the French have—a distinct style for a distinct purpose) but an easy and ordinary prose manner, which rejects the licenses because it does not require them, and is merely *ornamented into poetry*. By means of this manner he is enabled to encounter, effectually, details which would baffle any other versifier of the day; and at which Lamartine would stand aghast. In "Alciphron" we see this exemplified. Here the minute and perplexed incidents of the descent into the pyramid, are detailed, in verse, with quite as much precision and intelligibility as could be attained even by the coolest prose of Mr. Jeremy Bentham.

Moore has vivacity; verbal and constructive dexterity; a musical ear not sufficiently cultivated; a vivid fancy; an epigrammatic spirit; and a fine taste—*as far as it goes*.

————

The defenders of this pitiable stuff, uphold it on the ground of its truthfulness. Taking the thesis into question, this truthfulness is the one overwhelming defect. An original idea that—to laud the accuracy with which the stone is hurled that knocks us in the head. A little less accuracy might have left us more brains. And here are critics absolutely commending the truthfulness with which only the disagreeable is conveyed! In my view, if an artist must paint decayed cheeses, is merit will lie in their looking as little like decayed cheeses as possible.

(*To be continued.*)

Marginalia

DEMOCRATIC REVIEW, *December 1844*

I AM NOT sure that Tennyson is not the greatest of poets. The uncertainty attending the public conception of the term "poet" alone prevents me from demonstrating that he *is*. Other bards produce effects which are, now and then, otherwise produced than by what we call poems; but Tennyson an effect which only a poem does. His alone are idiosyncratic poems. By the enjoyment or non-enjoyment of the "Morte D'Arthur," or of the "Ænone," I would test any one's ideal sense.

There are passages in his works which rivet a conviction I had long entertained, that the *indefinite* is an element in the true ποιησις. Why do some persons fatigue themselves in attempts to unravel such phantasy-pieces as the "Lady of Shalott?" As well unweave the *"ventum textilem."* If the author did not deliberately propose to himself a suggestive indefinitiveness of meaning, with the view of bringing about a definitiveness of vague and therefore of spiritual *effect*—this, at least, arose from the silent analytical promptings of that poetic genius which, in its supreme development, embodies all orders of intellectual capacity.

I *know* that indefinitiveness is an element of the true music—I mean of the true musical expression. Give to it any undue decision—imbue it with any very determinate tone—and you deprive it, at once, of its ethereal, its ideal, its intrinsic and essential character. You dispel its luxury of dream. You dissolve the atmosphere of the mystic upon which it floats. You exhaust it of its breath of fäery. It now becomes a tangible and easy appreciable idea—a thing of the earth, earthy. It has not, indeed, lost its power to please, but all which I consider the distinctiveness of that power. And to the uncultivated talent, or to the unimaginative apprehension, this deprivation of its most delicate grace will be, not unfrequently, a recommendation. A determinateness of expression is sought—and often by composers who should know better—is sought as a beauty rather than rejected as a blemish. Thus we have, even from high authorities, attempts at absolute *imitation* in music. Who can forget the sillinesses of the "Battle of Prague?" What man of taste but must laugh at the interminable drums, trumpets, blunderbusses, and thunder? "*Vocal* music," says L'Abbate Gravina, who would have said the same thing of instrumental, "ought to imitate the natural language of the human feelings and passions, rather than the warblings of Canary birds, which our singers, now-a-days, affect so vastly to mimic with their quaverings and boasted cadences." This is true only so far as the "rather" is concerned. If any music must imitate anything, it were assuredly better to limit the imitation as Gravina suggests.

Tennyson's shorter pieces abound in minute rhythmical lapses sufficient to assure me that—in common with all poets living or dead—he has neglected to make precise investigation of the principles of metre; but, on the other hand, so perfect is his rhythmical instinct in general, that, like the present Viscount Canterbury, he seems *to see with his ear*.

———

A man of genius, if not permitted to choose his own subject, will do worse, in letters, than if he had talents none at all. And *here* how imperatively is he controlled! To be sure, he can write to suit himself—but in the same manner his publishers print. From the nature of our Copy-Right laws, he has no individual powers. As for his free agency, it is about equal to that of the dean and chapter of the see-cathedral, in a British election of Bishops—an election held by virtue of the king's writ of *congé d'élire*, and specifying the person to be elected.

———

It may well be doubted whether a single paragraph of merit can be found either in the "Koran" of Lawrence Sterne, or in the "Lacon" of Colton, of which paragraph the origin, or at least the germ, may not be traced to Seneca, to Plutarch, (through Machiavelli) to Machiavelli himself, to Bacon, to Burdon, to Burton, to Bolinbroke, to Rochefoucault, to Balzac, the author of *"La Manière de Bien Penser,"* or to Bielfeld, the German, who wrote, in French, *"Les Premiers Traits de L'Erudition Universelle."*

———

We might give two plausible derivations of the epithet "weeping" as applied to the willow. We might say that the word has its origin in the pendulous character of the long branches, which suggest the idea of water dripping; or we might assert that the term comes from a fact in the Natural History of the tree. It has a vast insensible perspiration, which, upon sudden cold, condenses, and sometimes is precipitated in a shower. Now, one might very accurately determine the bias and value of a man's powers of causality, by observing which of these two derivations he would adopt. The former is, beyond question, the true; and, for this reason — that common or vulgar epithets are universally suggested by common or immediately obvious things, without strict regard of any exactitude in application: — but the latter would be greedily seized by nine philologists out of ten, for no better cause than its *epigrammatism* — than the pointedness with which the singular fact seems to touch the occasion.

Here, then, is a subtle source of error which Lord Bacon has neglected. It is an Idol of the Wit.

———

I believe that odors have an altogether idiosyncratic force, in affecting us through association; a force differing *essentially* from that of objects addressing the touch, the taste, the sight, or the hearing.

———

It would have been becoming, I think, in Bulwer, to have made at least a running acknowledgment of that extensive indebtedness to Arnay's "Private Life of the Romans"* which he had so little scruple about incurring, during the composition of "The Last Days of Pompeii." He acknowledges, I believe, what he owes to Sir William Gell's "Pompeiana." Why this? — why not that?

*1764.

———

La Harpe (who was no critic) has, nevertheless, done little more than strict justice to the fine taste and precise finish of Racine, in all that regards the Minor Morals of Literature. In these he as far excels Pope, as Pope the veriest dolt in his own "Dunciad."

———

"That evil predominates over good, becomes evident, when we consider that there can be found no aged person who would be willing to re-live the life he has already lived."—*Volney*.

The idea here, is not distinctly made out; for unless through the context, we cannot be sure whether the author means merely this:—that every aged person fancies he might, in a different course of life, have been happier than in the one actually lived, and, for this reason, would not be willing to live *his* life over again, *but some other life*;— or, whether the sentiment intended is this:—that if, upon the grave's brink, the choice were offered any aged person between the expected death and the re-living the old life, that person would prefer to die.

The first proposition is, perhaps, true; but the last (which is the one designed) is not only doubtful, in point of mere fact, but is of no effect, even if granted to be true, in sustaining the original proposition—that evil predominates over good.

It is assumed that the aged person will not re-live his life, because he *knows* that its evil predominated over its good. The source of error lies in the word "knows"—in the assumption that we can ever be, really, in possession of the whole knowledge to which allusion is cloudily made. But there is a *seeming*—a fictitious knowledge; and this very seeming knowledge it is, of what the life has been, which incapacitates the aged person from deciding the question upon its merits. He blindly deduces a notion of the happiness of the original real life—a notion of its preponderating evil or good—from a consideration of the secondary or supposititious one. In his estimate he merely strikes a balance between *events*, and leaves quite out of the account that elastic *Hope* which is the Harbinger and the Eos of all. Man's real life is happy, chiefly because he is ever expecting that it soon will be so. But, in regarding the supposititious life, we paint to ourselves chill certainties for warm expectations, and grievances quadrupled in being foreseen. But because we cannot avoid doing this—strain our imaginative faculties as we will—because it is so very difficult—so nearly impossible a task, to fancy the known unknown—the done unaccomplished—and because (through our inability to fancy all this) we prefer death to a secondary life—does it, in any manner, follow that the evil of the properly-considered real existence *does* predominate over the good?

In order that a just estimate be made by Mr. Volney's "aged person," and from this estimate a judicious choice:—in order, again, that from this estimate and choice, we deduce any clear comparison of good with evil in human existence, it will be necessary that we obtain the opinion, or "choice," upon this point, from an aged person who shall be in condition to appreciate, with precision, the hopes he is naturally led to leave out of question, but which reason tells us he would as strongly experience as ever, in the absolute reliving of the life. On the other hand, too, he must be in condition to dismiss from the estimate the fears which he actually feels, and which show him bodily the ills that are to happen, but which fears, again, reason assures us he would *not*, in the absolute secondary life, encounter. Now what mortal was ever in condition to make these allowances?—to perform impossibilities in giving these considerations their due weight? What mortal, then, was ever in condition to make a well-grounded choice? How, from an ill-grounded one, are we to make deductions which shall guide us aright? How out of error shall we fabricate truth?

———

A remarkable work,* and one which I find much difficulty in admitting to be the composition of a woman. Not that many good and glorious things have not been the composition of women—but, because, here, the severe precision of

*"Ellen Middleton."

style, the *thoroughness*, and the luminousness, are points never observable, in even the most admirable of their writings. Who is Lady Georgiana Fullerton? Who is that Countess of Dacre, who edited "Ellen Wareham,"—the most passionate of fictions—approached, only in some particulars of passion, by this?

The great defect of "Ellen Middleton," lies in the disgusting sternness, captiousness, and bullet-headedness of her husband. We cannot sympathize with her love for him. And the intense selfishness of the rejected lover precludes that compassion which is designed. Alice is a *creation* of true genius. The imagination, throughout, is of a lofty order, and the snatches of original verse would do honor to any poet living. But the chief merit, after all, is that of the *style*—about which it is difficult to say too much in the way of praise, although it has, now and then, an odd Gallicism—such as "she lost her head," meaning she grew crazy. There is much, in the whole manner of this book, which puts me in mind of "Caleb Williams."

———

The God-abstractions of the modern polytheism are nearly in as sad a state of perplexity and promiscuity as were the more substantial deities of the Greeks. Not a quality named that does not impinge upon some one other; and Porphyry admits that Vesta, Rhea, Ceres, Themis, Proserpina, Bacchus, Attis, Adonis, Silenus, Priapus, and the Satyrs, were merely different terms for the same thing. Even gender was never precisely settled. Servius on Virgil mentions a Venus with a beard. In Macrobius, too, Calvus talks of her as if she were a man; while Valerius Soranus expressly calls Jupiter "the Mother of the Gods."

———

Von Raumer says that Enslen, a German optician, conceived the idea of throwing a shadowy figure, by optical means, into the chair of Banquo; and that the thing was readily done. Intense effect was produced; and I do not doubt that an American audience might be electrified by the feat. But our managers not only have no invention of their own, but no energy to avail themselves of that of others.

———

It is observable that, in his brief account of the Creation, Moses employs the words, *Bara Elohim* (the *Gods* created), no less than thirty times; using the noun in the plural with the verb in the singular. Elsewhere, however—in Deuteronomy, for example—he employs the singular, *Eloah*.

———

Among the moralists who keep themselves erect by the perpetual swallowing of pokers, it is the fashion to decry the "fashionable" novels. These works have their demerits; but a vast influence which they exert for an undeniable good, has never yet been duly considered. "Ingenu*os* didicisse fideliter *libros*, emollit mores nec sinit esse feros." Now, the fashionable novels are just the books which most do circulate among the class *un*fashionable; and their effect in softening the worst callosities—in smoothing the most disgusting asperities of vulgarism, is prodigious. With the herd, to admire and to attempt imitation are the same thing. What if, in this case, the manners imitated are frippery; better frippery than brutality—and, after all, there is little danger that the intrinsic value of the sturdiest iron will be impaired by a coating of even the most diaphanous gilt.

———

The ancients had at least half an idea that we travelled on horseback to heaven. See a passage of Passeri, *"de animæ transvectione"*—quoted by Caylus. See, also, old tombs.

———

A corrupt and impious heart—a merely prurient fancy—a Saturnian brain in which invention has only the phosphorescent glimmer of rottenness.* Worthless, body and soul. A foul reproach to the nation that engendered and endures him. A fetid battener upon the garbage of thought. No man. A beast. A pig. Less scrupulous than a carrion-crow, and not very much less filthy than a Wilmer.

———

*Michel Masson, author of *"Le Cœur d'une Jeune Fille."*

In reading some books we occupy ourselves chiefly with the thoughts of the author; in perusing others, exclusively with our own. And this* is one of the "others"—a suggestive book. But there are two classes of suggestive books—the positively and the negatively suggestive. The former suggest by what they say; the latter by what they might and should have said. It makes little difference, after all. In either case the true book-purpose is answered.

———

Sallust, too. He had much the same free-and-easy idea, and Metternich himself could not have quarrelled with his *"Impune quæ libet facere, id est esse regem."*

———

The *first* periodical moral essay! Mr. Macaulay forgets the "Courtier of Baldazzar Castiglione—1528."

———

For my part I agree with Joshua Barnes:—nobody but Solomon could have written the Iliad. The catalogue of ships was the work of Robins.

———

The *à priori* reasoners upon government are, of all plausible people, the most preposterous. They only argue too cleverly to permit my thinking them silly enough to be themselves deceived by their own arguments. Yet even this is possible; for there is something in the vanity of logic which addles a man's brains. Your true logician gets, in time, to be logicalized, and then, so far as regards himself, the universe is one *word*. A thing, for him, no longer exists. He deposits upon a sheet of paper a certain assemblage of syllables, and fancies that their meaning is riveted by the act of deposition. I am serious in the opinion that some such process of thought passes through the mind of the "practised" logician, as he makes note of the thesis proposed. He is not aware that he thinks in this way—but, unwittingly, he so thinks. The syllables deposited acquire, in his view, a new character. While

*Mercier's *"L'an deux mille quatre cents quarante."*

afloat in his brain, he might have been brought to admit the possibility that these syllables were variable exponents of various phases of thought; but he will not admit this if he once gets them upon the paper.

In a single page of "Mill," I find the word "force" employed four times; and each employment varies the idea. The fact is that *à priori* argument is much worse than useless except in the mathematical sciences, where it is possible to obtain *precise* meanings. If there is any one subject in the world to which it is utterly and radically inapplicable, that subject is Government. The *identical* arguments used to sustain Mr. Bentham's positions, might, with little exercise of ingenuity, be made to overthrow them; and, by ringing small changes on the words "leg-of-mutton," and "turnip" (changes so *gradual* as to escape detection), I could *"demonstrate"* that a turnip was, is, and of right ought to be a leg-of-mutton.

———

Has any one observed the excessively close resemblance in subject, thought, general manner and particular point, which this clever composition* bears to the "Hudibras" of Butler?

———

The concord of sound-and-sense principle was never better exemplified than in these lines†:—

> "Ast amans charæ thalamum puellæ
> Deserit flens, et tibi verba dicit
> Aspera amplexu teneræ cupito a—
> —vulsus amicæ."

———

Miss Gould has much in common with Mary Howitt;—the characteristic trait of each being a sportive, quaint, epigrammatic grace, that keeps clear of the absurd by never employing itself upon very exalted topics. The verbal style of the two ladies is identical. Miss Gould has the more talent of the two, but is somewhat the less original. She has occasional flashes

*The *"Satyre Menipée."*
†By *M. Anton. Flaminius.*

of a far higher order of merit than appertains to her ordinary manner. Her "Dying Storm" might have been written by Campbell.

———

Cornelius Webbe is one of the best of that numerous school of extravaganzists who sprang from the ruins of Lamb. We must be in perfectly good humor, however, with ourselves and all the world, to be much pleased with such works as "The Man about Town," in which the harum-scarum, hyper-excursive mannerism is carried to an excess which is frequently fatiguing.

———

Nearly, if not quite the best "Essay on a Future State."* The arguments called "Deductions *from* our Reason," are, rightly enough, addressed more to the *feelings* (a vulgar term not to be done without), than *to* our reason. The arguments deduced from Revelation are (also rightly enough) brief. The pamphlet proves nothing, of course; its theorem is not to be proved.

———

Not so:—A gentleman with a pug nose is a contradiction in terms.—"Who can live idly and without manual labour, and will bear the port, charge and *countenance* of a gentleman, he alone should be called master and be taken for a gentleman."—*Sir Thomas Smith's "Commonwealth of England."*

———

It is the curse of a certain order of mind, that it can never rest satisfied with the consciousness of its ability to do a thing. Still less is it content with doing it. It must both know and show how it was done.

———

Here is something at which I find it impossible not to

———
A Sermon on a Future State, combating the opinion that "Death is an Eternal Sleep." By Gilbert Austin. London. 1794.

laugh;* and yet, I laugh without knowing why. That incongruity is the principle of all non-convulsive laughter, is to my mind as clearly demonstrated as any problem in the "Principia Mathematica;" but here I cannot trace the incongruous. It is there, I know. Still I do not see it. In the meantime let me laugh.

———

The "British Spy" of Wirt seems an imitation of the "Turkish Spy," upon which Montesquieu's "Persian Letters" are also based. Marana's work was in *Italian*—Doctor Johnson errs.

———

The style is so involute,† that one cannot help fancying it must be falsely constructed. If the use of language is to convey ideas, then it is nearly as much a demerit that our words seem to be, as that they are, indefensible. A man's grammar, like Cæsar's wife, must not only be pure, but above suspicion of impurity.

———

"It was a pile of the oyster, which yielded the precious pearls of the South, and the artist had judiciously painted some with their lips parted, and showing within the large precious fruit in the attainment of which Spanish cupidity had already proved itself capable of every peril, as well as every crime. At once true and poetical, no comment could have been more severe, &c." Mr. Simms' *"Damsel of Darien."* Body of Bacchus!—only think of poetical beauty in the countenance of a gaping oyster!

"And how natural, in an age so fanciful, to believe that the stars and starry groups beheld in the new world for the first time by the native of the old were especially assigned for its government and protection."—Now, if by the Old World be meant the East, and by the New World the West, I am at a

*Translation of the Book of Jonah into German Hexameters. By J. G. A. Müller. Contained in the *"Memorabilien" von Paulus.*
†*"Night and Morning."*

loss to know what *are* the stars seen in the one which cannot be equally seen in the other.

Mr. Simms has abundant faults—or had;—among which inaccurate English, a proneness to revolting images, and pet phrases, are the most noticeable. Nevertheless, leaving out of question Brockden Brown and Hawthorne (who are each a *genus*), he is immeasurably the best writer of fiction in America. He has more vigor, more imagination, more movement and more general capacity than all our novelists (save Cooper), combined.

———

This "species of nothingness" is quite as reasonable, at all events, as any "kind of something-ness." See Cowley's "Creation," where,

An unshaped kind of something first appeared.

———

Here is an edition,* which, so far as microscopical excellence and absolute accuracy of typography are concerned, might well be prefaced with the phrase of the Koran—"There is *no* error in this book." We cannot call a single inverted *o* an error—*can* we? But I am really as glad of having found that inverted *o*, as ever was a Columbus or an Archimedes. What, after all, are continents discovered, or silver-smiths exposed? Give us a good *o* turned upside-down, and a whole herd of bibliomanic Arguses overlooking it for years.

———

"That sweet smile and serene—that smile never seen but upon the face of the dying and the dead."—*Ernest Maltravers.* Bulwer is not the man to look a stern fact in the face. He would rather sentimentalize upon a vulgar although picturesque error. Who ever *really* saw anything but horror in the smile of the dead? We so earnestly *desire* to fancy it "sweet"—that is the source of the mistake; if, indeed, there ever was a mistake in the question.

* *Camöens — Genoa — 1798.*

This misapplication of quotations is clever, and has a capital effect when well done; but Lord Brougham has not exactly that kind of capacity which the thing requires. One of the best hits in this way is made by Tieck, and I have lately seen it appropriated, with interesting complacency, in an English Magazine. The author of the "Journey into the Blue Distance," is giving an account of some young ladies, not very beautiful, whom he caught *in mediis rebus*, at their toilet. "They were curling their monstrous heads," says he, "as Shakspeare says of the waves in a storm."

Mr. Hawthorne is one of the very few American story-tellers whom the critic can commend with the hand upon the heart. He is not always original in his entire theme—(I am not quite sure, even, that he has not borrowed an idea or two from a gentleman whom I know very well, and who is honored in the loan)—but, then, his handling is always thoroughly original. His style, although never vigorous, is purity itself. His imagination is rich. His sense of art is exquisite, and his executive ability great. He has little or no variety of tone. He handles all subjects in the same subdued, misty, dreamy, suggestive, inuendo way, and although I think him the truest genius, upon the whole, which our literature possesses, I cannot help regarding him as the most desperate mannerist of his day.

P. S. The chief—not the *leading* idea in this story "(Drowne's Wooden Image)," is precisely that of Michael Angelo's couplet, borrowed from Socrates:

> *Non ha l'ottimo artist a alcun concetto*
> *Che un marino solo in se non circunscriva.*

Here are both Dickens and Bulwer perpetually using the adverb "directly" in the sense of "as soon as." "Directly he came I did so and so"—"Directly I knew it I said this and that." But observe!—"Grammar is hardly taught" [in the United States], "being thought an unnecessary basis for other learning." I quote *"America and her Resources,"* by the British Counsellor at law, John Bristed.

————

At Ermenonville, too, there is a striking instance of the Gallic rhythm with which a Frenchman regards the English verse. There Gerardin has the following inscription to the memory of Shenstone:

> This plain stone
> To William Shenstone.
> In his writings he displayed
> A mind natural;
> At Leasowes he laid
> Arcadian greens rural.

There are few Parisians, speaking English, who would find anything *particularly* the matter with this epitaph.

————

Here is a plot which, with all its complexity, has no adaptation—no dependency;—it is involute and nothing more—having all the air of G——'s wig, or the cycles and epicycles in Ptolemy's "Almagest."

————

"Accursed be the heart that does not wildly throb, and palsied be the eye that will not weep over the woes of the wanderer of Switzerland."—*Monthly Register*, 1807.

This is "dealing damnation round the land" to some purpose;—upon the reader, and not upon the author as usual. For my part I shall be one of the damned; for I have in vain endeavored to see even a shadow of merit in anything ever written by either of the Montgomeries.

————

Strange—that I should here* find the only non-execrable

* *Forelaesninger over det Danske Sprog, eller resonneret Dansk Grammatik, ved Jacob Baden.*

barbarian attempts at imitation of the Greek and Roman measures!

———

Upon her was lavished the enthusiastic applause of the most correct taste, and of the deepest sensibility. Human triumph, in all that is most exciting and delicious, never went beyond that which she experienced—or never but in the case of Taglioni. For what are the extorted adulations that fall to the lot of the conqueror?—what even are the extensive honors of the popular author—his far-reaching fame—his high influence—or the most devout public appreciation of his works—to that rapturous approbation of the personal woman—that spontaneous, instant, present, and palpable applause—those irrepressible acclamations—those eloquent sighs and tears which the idolized Malibran at once heard, and saw, and deeply felt that she deserved? Her brief career was one gorgeous dream—for even the many sad intervals of her grief were but dust in the balance of her glory. In this book* I read much about the causes which curtailed her existence; and there seems to hang around them, as here given, an indistinctness which the fair memorialist tries in vain to illumine. She seems never to approach the full truth. She seems never to reflect that the speedy decease was but a condition of the rapturous life. No thinking person, hearing Malibran sing, could have doubted that she would die in the spring of her days. She crowded ages into hours. She left the world at twenty-five, having existed her thousands of years.

———

Were I to consign these volumes,† altogether, to the hands of any very young friend of mine, I could not, in conscience, describe them otherwise than as *"tam multi, tam grandes, tam pretiosi codices"*; and it would grieve me much to add the *"incendite omnes illas membranas."*‡

———

"Memoirs and Letters of Madame Malibran," by the Countess of Merlin.
†Voltaire.
‡St. Austin *de libris Manichæis.*

This reasoning is about as convincing as would be that of a traveller who, going from Maryland to New York without entering Pennsylvania, should advance this feat as an argument against Leibnitz' *Law of Continuity*—according to which nothing passes from one *state* to another without passing through all the intermediate states.

———

Not so:—The first number of the "Gentleman's Magazine" was published on the first of January, 1731; but long before this—in 1681—there appeared the "Monthly Recorder" with all the Magazine features.

I have a number of the "London Magazine," dated 1760;—commenced 1732, at least, but I have reason to think much earlier.

———

Stolen, body and soul (and spoilt in the stealing), from a paper *of the same title* in the "European Magazine" for December, 1817. Blunderingly done throughout, and must have cost more trouble than an original thing. This makes paragraph 33 of my *"Chapter on American Cribbage."* The beauty of these *exposés* must lie in the precision and unanswerability with which they are given—in day and date—in chapter and verse—and, above all, in an unveiling of the minute trickeries by which the thieves hope to disguise their stolen wares.

I must soon a tale unfold, and an astonishing tale it will be. The C— bears away the bell. The ladies, however, should positively not be guilty of these tricks;—for one has never the heart to unmask or deplume them.

After all, there is this advantage in purloining one's Magazine papers;—we are never forced to dispose of them under prime cost.

———

" '*Amare et sapere vix Deo conceditur,*' as the acute Seneca well observes."

However acute might be Seneca, still he was not sufficiently acute to say this. The sentence is often attributed to him, but is not to be found in his works. *"Semel insanavimus omnes,"* a phrase often quoted, is invariably placed to the account of Horace, and with equal error. It is from the *"De Honesto Amore"* of the Italian Mantuanus, who has

> *Id commune malum; semel insanavimus omnes.*

In the title, *"De Honesto Amore,"* by the way, Mantuanus misconceives the force of *honestus*—just as Dryden does in his translation of Virgil's

> *Et quocunque Deus circum caput egit honestum;*

which he renders

> On whate'er side he turns his *honest* face.

————

"Jehovah" is *not* Hebrew.

————

Macaulay, in his just admiration of Addison, over-rates Tickell, and does not seem to be aware how much the author of the "Elegy" is indebted to French models. Boileau, especially, he robbed without mercy, and without measure. A flagrant example is here. Boileau has the lines:

> *En vain contre "Le Cid" un ministre se ligue;*
> *Tout Paris pour Chimene a les yeux de Rodrigue.*

Tickell thus appropriates them:

> While the charm'd reader with thy thought complies,
> And views thy Rosamond with Henry's eyes.

————

No;—he fell by his own Fame. Like Richmann, he was blasted by the fires himself had sought, and obtained, from the Heavens.

————

I have at length attained the last page, which is a thing to thank God for; and all this may be logic, but I am sure it is nothing more. Until I get the means of refutation, however, I must be content to say, with the Jesuits, Le Sueur and

Jacquier, that "I acknowledge myself obedient to the decrees of the Pope against the motion of the Earth."

———

How overpowering a style is that of Curran! I use "overpowering" in the sense of the English exquisite. I can imagine nothing more distressing than the extent of his eloquence.

———

"With all his faults, however, this author is a man of respectable powers."

Thus discourses, of *William Godwin*, the "London Monthly Magazine:" May, 1818.

———

"Rhododaphne" is brim-full of music:—e. g.

> By living streams, in sylvan shades,
>   Where wind and wave symphonious make
> Rich melody, the youths and maids
>   No more with choral music wake
> Lone Echo from her tangled brake.

———

How thoroughly—how radically—how wonderfully has "Undine" been misunderstood! Beneath its obvious meaning there runs an under-current, simple, quite intelligible, artistically managed, and richly philosophical.

From internal evidence afforded by the book itself, I gather that the author suffered from the ills of a mal-arranged marriage—the bitter reflections thus engendered inducing the fable.

In the contrast between the artless, thoughtless, and careless character of Undine before possessing a soul, and her serious, enwrapt, and anxious yet happy condition after possessing it,—a condition which, with all its multiform disquietudes, she still feels to be preferable to her original state,—Fouqué has beautifully painted the difference between the heart unused to *love*, and the heart which has received its inspiration.

The jealousies which follow the marriage, arising from the conduct of Bertalda, are but the natural troubles of love; but the persecutions of Kuhleborn and the other water-spirits who take umbrage at Huldbrand's treatment of his wife, are meant to picture certain difficulties from the interference of relations in conjugal matters — difficulties which the author has himself experienced. The warning of Undine to Huldbrand — "Reproach me not upon the waters, or we part for ever" — is intended to embody the truth that quarrels between man and wife are seldom or never irremediable unless when taking place in the presence of third parties. The second wedding of the knight with his gradual forgetfulness of Undine, and Undine's intense grief beneath the waters — are dwelt upon so pathetically — so passionately — that there can be no doubt of the author's personal opinions on the subject of second marriages — no doubt of his deep personal interest in the question. How thrillingly are these few and simple words made to convey his belief that the mere death of a beloved wife does not imply a separation so final or so complete as to justify an union with another! — "The fisherman had loved Undine with exceeding tenderness, and it was a doubtful conclusion to his mind that the mere disappearance of his beloved child could be properly viewed as her death." — This is where the old man is endeavoring to dissuade the knight from wedding Bertalda.

I cannot say whether the novelty of the conception of "Undine," or the loftiness and purity of its ideality, or the intensity of its pathos, or the rigor of its simplicity, or the high artistical ability with which all are combined into a well-kept, well-*motivirt* whole of absolute unity of effect — is the particular chiefly to be admired.

How delicate and graceful are the transitions from subject to subject! — a point severely testing the autorial power — as, when, for the purposes of the story, it becomes necessary that the knight, with Undine and Bertalda, shall proceed down the Danube. An ordinary novelist would have here tormented both himself and his readers, in his search for a sufficient motive for the voyage. But, in a fable such as "Undine," how all-sufficient — how well in keeping — appears the simple motive assigned! — "In this grateful union of friendship and affection winter came and passed away; and spring, with its foliage of tender green, and its heaven of softest blue, succeeded to gladden the hearts of the three inmates of the castle. *What wonder, then, that its storks and swallows inspired them also with a disposition to travel?"*

How exquisitely artistic is the *management of imagination*, so visible in the passages where the brooks are water-spirits and the water-spirits brooks—neither distinctly either! What can be more ethereally ideal than the frequent indeterminate glimpses caught of Kuhleborn?—or than his wild lapses into shower and foam?—or than the evanishing of the white wagoner and his white horses into the shrieking and devouring flood?—or than the gentle melting of the passionately weeping bride into the crystal waters of the Danube? What can be more divine than the character of the soul-less Undine?—what more august than the transition into the soul-possessing wife? What can be more purely beautiful than the whole book? Fictitious literature has nothing superior, in loftiness of conception, or in felicity of execution, to those final passages which embody the uplifting of the stone from the fount by the order of Bertalda—the silent and sorrowful re-advent of Undine—and the rapturous death of Sir Huldbrand in the embraces of his spiritual wife.

These twelve Letters* are occupied, in part, with minute details of such atrocities on the part of the British, during their sojourn in Charleston, as the quizzing of Mrs. Wilkinson and the pilfering of her shoe-buckles—the remainder being made up of the indignant comments of Mrs. Wilkinson herself.

It is very true, as the Preface assures us, that "few records exist of American women either before or during the war of the Revolution, and that those perpetuated by History want the charm of personal narration,"—but then we are well delivered from such charms of personal narration as we find here. The only supposable merit in the compilation is that dogged air of truth with which the fair authoress relates the lamentable story of her misadventures. I look in vain for that

*Letters of Eliza Wilkinson, during the invasion and possession of Charleston, S. C., by the British, in the Revolutionary War. Arranged by Caroline Gilman.

"useful information" about which I have heard—unless, indeed, it is in the passage where we are told that the letter-writer "was a young and beautiful widow; that her hand-writing is clear and feminine; and that the letters were copied by herself into a blank quarto book, on which the extravagant sale-price marks one of the features of the times:"—there are other extravagant sale-prices, however, besides that;—it was seventy-five cents that I paid for these "Letters." Besides, they are silly, and I cannot conceive why Miss Gilman thought the public wished to read them. It is really too bad for her to talk at a body, in this style, about "gathering relics of past history," and "floating down streams of time."

As for Mrs. Wilkinson, I am really rejoiced that she lost her shoe-buckles.

———

A rather bold and quite unnecessary plagiarism—from a book too well known to promise impunity.

"It is now full time to begin to brush away the insects of literature, whether creeping or fluttering, which have too long crawled over and soiled the intellectual ground of this country. It is high time to shake the little sickly stems of many a puny plant, and make its fading flowerets fall."—*"Monthly Register"*—p. 243—Vol. 2—N. York, 1807.

On the other hand—"I have brushed away the insects of Literature, whether fluttering or creeping; I have shaken the little stems of many a puny plant, and the flowerets have fallen."—*Preface to the "Pursuits of Literature."*

———

Had John Bernouilli lived to have experience of G——'s occiput and sinciput, he would have abandoned, in dismay, his theory of the non-existence of hard bodies.

———

As to this last term ("high-binder") which is so confidently quoted as modern ("not in use, *certainly*, before 1819"), I can refute all that is said by referring to a journal in my own possession—"The Weekly Inspector," for December 27, 1806—published in New York:

"On Christmas Eve, a party of banditti, amounting, it is stated, to forty or fifty members of an association, calling themselves 'High-Binders,' assembled in front of St. Peter's Church, in Barclay-street, expecting that the Catholic ritual would be performed with a degree of pomp and splendor which has usually been omitted in this city. These ceremonies, however, not taking place, the High-Binders manifested great displeasure."

In a subsequent number the association are called "Hide-Binders." They were Irish.

————

Perhaps Mr. Barrow is right after all, and the dearth of genius in America *is* owing to the continual teasing of the musquitoes. See *"Voyage to Cochin-China."*

————

Mrs. *Amelia Welby* has all the imagination of *Maria del Occidente*, with more refined taste; and all the passion of Mrs. Norton, with a nicer ear, and (what is surprising) equal art. Very few American poets are at all comparable with her in the true poetic qualities. As for our *poetesses* (an absurd but necessary word), none of them approach her.

With some modifications, this little poem would do honor to any one living or dead.

> The moon within our casement beams,
>   Our blue-eyed babe hath dropped to sleep,
> And I have left it to its dreams
>   Amid the shadows deep,
> To muse beside the silver tide
> Whose waves are rippling at thy side.
>
>
> It is a still and lovely spot
>   Where they have laid thee down to rest;
> The white-rose and forget-me-not
>   Bloom sweetly on thy breast,
> And birds and streams with liquid lull
> Have made the stillness beautiful.

And softly thro' the forest bars
   Light lovely shapes, on glossy plumes,
Float ever in, like winged stars,
   Amid the purpling glooms:
Their sweet songs, borne from tree to tree,
Thrill the light leaves with melody.

Alas! the very path I trace,
   In happier hours thy footsteps made;
This spot was once thy resting-place;
   Within the silent shade
Thy white hand trained the fragrant bough
That drops its blossoms o'er me now.

'Twas here at eve we used to rove;
   'Twas here I breathed my whispered vows,
And sealed them on thy lips, my love,
   Beneath the apple-boughs.
Our hearts had melted into one,
But Death undid what Love had done.

Alas! too deep a weight of thought
   Had fill'd thy heart in youth's sweet hour;
It seem'd with love and bliss o'erfraught;
   As fleeting passion-flower
Unfolding 'neath a southern sky,
To blossom soon and soon to die.

Yet in these calm and blooming bowers,
   I seem to see thee still,
Thy breath seems floating o'er the flowers,
   Thy whisper on the hill;
The clear faint star-light and the sea
Are whispering to my heart of thee.

No more thy smiles my heart rejoice—
   Yet still I start to meet thine eye,
And call upon the low sweet voice
   That gives me no reply—
And list within my silent door
For the light feet that come no more.

In a critical mood I would speak of these stanzas thus:—
The subject has *nothing* of originality:—A widower muses by
the grave of his wife. Here then is a great demerit; for originality of theme, if not absolutely first sought, should be
sought among the first. Nothing is more clear than this proposition—although denied by the chlorine critics (the grass-
green). The desire of the new is an element of the soul. The
most exquisite pleasures grow dull in repetition. A strain of
music enchants. Heard a second time it pleases. Heard a
tenth, it does not displease. We hear it a twentieth, and ask
ourselves why we admired. At the fiftieth it enduces ennui—
at the hundredth disgust.

Mrs. Welby's theme is, therefore, radically faulty so far as
originality is concerned;—but of common themes, it is one
of the very best among the class *passionate*. True passion is
prosaic—homely. Any strong mental emotion stimulates *all*
the mental faculties; thus grief the imagination:—but in proportion as the effect is strengthened, the cause surceases. The
excited fancy triumphs—the grief is subdued—chastened—
is no longer grief. In this mood we are poetic, and it is clear
that a poem now written will be poetic in the exact ratio of
its dispassion. A passionate poem is a contradiction in terms.
When I say, then, that Mrs. Welby's stanzas are good among
the class *passionate* (using the term commonly and falsely applied), I mean that her tone is properly subdued, and is not
so much the tone of passion, as of a gentle and melancholy
regret, interwoven with a pleasant sense of the natural loveliness surrounding the lost in the tomb, and a memory of her
human beauty while alive.—Elegiac poems should either assume this character, or dwell purely on the beauty (moral or
physical) of the departed—or, better still, utter the notes of
triumph. I have endeavored to carry out this latter idea in
some verses which I have called "Lenore."

Those who object to the proposition—that poetry and passion are discordant—would, thus, cite Mrs. Welby's poem as
an instance of a passionate one. It is precisely similar to the
hundred others which have been cited for like purpose. But it
is *not* passionate; and for this reason (with others having regard to her fine genius) it *is* poetical. The critics upon this
topic display an amusing *ignoratio elenchi*.

Dismissing originality and tone, I pass to the general handling, than which nothing could be more pure, more natural, or more judicious. The perfect keeping of the various points is admirable—and the result is entire unity of impression, or effect. The time, a moonlight night; the locality of the grave; the passing thither from the cottage, and the conclusion of the theme with the return to "the silent door;" the babe left, meanwhile, "to its dreams;" the "white rose and forget-me-not" upon the breast of the entombed; the "birds and streams, with liquid lull, that make the stillness beautiful;" the birds whose songs "thrill the light leaves with melody;"—all these are appropriate and lovely conceptions:—only quite unoriginal;—and (be it observed), the higher order of genius should, and will, combine the original with that which is *natural*—not in the vulgar sense, (ordinary)—but in the artistic sense, which has reference to the *general intention of Nature.*—We have this combination well effected in the lines:

> And softly through the forest bars
>   Light lovely shapes, on glossy plumes,
> Float ever in, like winged stars,
>   Amid the purpling glooms—

which are, unquestionably, the finest in the poem.

The reflections suggested by the scene—commencing:

> Alas! the very path I trace,

are, also, something more than merely natural, and are richly ideal; especially the cause assigned for the early death; and "the fragrant bough"

> That drops its blossoms o'er me now.

The two concluding stanzas are remarkable examples of common fancies rejuvenated, and etherealised by grace of expression, and melody of rhythm.

The "light lovely shapes" in the third stanza (however beautiful in themselves), are defective, when viewed in reference to the "birds" of the stanza preceding. The topic "birds" is dismissed in the one paragraph, to be resumed in the other.

"Drops," in the last line of the fourth stanza, is improperly used in an active sense. *To drop* is a neuter verb. An apple drops; we let the apple fall.

The repetition ("seemed," "seem," "seems,") in the sixth and seventh stanzas, is ungraceful; so also that of "heart," in the last line of the seventh, and the first of the eighth. The words "breathed" and "whispered," in the second line of the fifth stanza, have a force too nearly identical. *"Neath,"* just below, is an awkward contraction. *All* contractions are awkward. It is no paradox, that the more prosaic the construction of verse, the better. *Inversions* should be dismissed. The most forcible lines are the most direct. Mrs. Welby owes three-fourths of her power (so far as style is concerned), to her freedom from these vulgar, and particularly English errors—elision and inversion. *O'er* is, however, too often used by her in place of *over*, and *'twas* for *it was*. We see instances here. The only inversions, strictly speaking, are

> The moon within our casement beams,

and—"Amid the shadows deep."

The versification throughout, is unusually good. Nothing can excel

> And birds and streams with liquid lull
> Have made the stillness beautiful;

or—

> And sealed them on thy lips, my love,
> Beneath the apple-boughs;

or the whole of the concluding stanza, if we leave out of view the unpleasant repetition of *"And,"* at the commencement of the third and fifth lines. *"Thy white hand trained"* (see stanza the fourth) involves four consonants, that unite with difficulty—*ndtr*—and the harshness is rendered more apparent, by the employment of the spondee, *"hand trained,"* in place of an iambus. *"Melody,"* is a feeble termination of the third stanza's last line. The syllable *dy* is not full enough to sustain the rhyme. All these endings, liber*ty*, proper*ty*, happi*ly*, and the like, however justified by authority, are grossly objectionable. Upon the whole, there are some poets in America (Bryant and Sprague, for example), who equal Mrs. Welby in the negative merits of that limited versification which they chiefly affect—the iambic pentameter—but none equal her in the richer and positive merits of rhythmical variety, conception—invention. They, in the old routine, rarely err. She often surprises, and always delights, by novel, rich and accurate combination of the ancient musical expressions.

———

How thoroughly comprehensive is the account of Adam, as given at the bottom of the old picture in the Vatican!—*"Adam, divinitus edoctus, primus scientiarum et literarum inventor."*

———

A ballad entitled *"Indian Serenade,"* and put into the mouth of the hero, Vasco Nunez, is, perhaps, the most really meritorious portion of Mr. Simms' "Damsel of Darien." This stanza is full of music:

> And their wild and mellow voices
>   Still to hear along the deep
> Every brooding star rejoices,
>   While the billow, on its pillow,
> Lulled to silence seems to sleep.

And also this:

> 'Tis the wail for life they waken
>   By Samana's yielding shore—
> With the tempest it is shaken;
>   The wild ocean is in motion,
> And the song is heard no more.

———

Talking of conundrums:—Why will a geologist put no faith in the Fable of the Fox that lost his tail? Because he knows that no animal remains have ever been found in trap.

———

Twenty years ago credulity was the characteristic trait of the mob, incredulity the distinctive feature of the philosophic;

now the case is conversed. The wise are wisely averse from disbelief. To be sceptical is no longer evidence either of information or of wit.

———

The title of this book* deceives us. It is by no means "talk" as men understand it—not that true talk of which Boswell has been the best historiographer. In a word it is not *gossip* which has been never better defined than by Basil, who calls it "talk for talk's sake," nor more thoroughly comprehended than by Horace Walpole and Mary Wortley Montague, who made it a profession and a purpose. Embracing all things, it has neither beginning, middle, nor end. Thus of the gossiper it was not properly said that "he commences his discourse by jumping *in medias res*." For, clearly, your gossiper commences not at all. He is begun. He is already begun. He is always begun. In the matter of end he is indeterminate. And by these extremes shall ye know him to be of the Cæsars—*porphyrogenitus*—of the right vein—of the true blood—of the blue blood—of the *sangre azula*. As for laws, he is cognizant of but one, the invariable absence of all. And for his road, were it as straight as the Appia and as broad as that " which leadeth to destruction," nevertheless would he be malcontent without a frequent hop-skip-and-jump, over the hedges, into the tempting pastures of digression beyond. Such is the gossiper, and of such alone is the true *talk*. But when Coleridge asked Lamb if he had ever heard him *preach*, the answer was quite happy—"I have never heard you do anything else." The truth is that "Table Discourse" *might* have answered as a title to this book; but its character can be fully conveyed only in "Post-Prandian Sub-Sermons," or "Three-Bottle Sermonoids."

———

Dickens is a man of higher *genius* than Bulwer. The latter is thoughtful, industrious, patient, pains-taking, educated, analytic, artistical (using the three last epithets with much mental reserve); and therefore will write the better book upon the whole:—but the former rises, at times, to an unpremeditated

*"*Coleridge's Table-Talk.*"

elevation altogether beyond the flight, and even beyond the appreciation of his cotemporary. Dickens, with care and culture, *might* have produced "The Last of the Barons," but nothing short of moral Voltaism could have spirited Bulwer into the conception of the concluding passages of the "Curiosity-Shop."

————

"Advancing briskly with a rapier, he *did the business* for him at a blow." — *Smollett*. This vulgar colloquialism had its type among the Romans. *Et ferro subitus grassatus, agit rem.* — *Juvenal*.

————

We may safely grant that the *effects* of the oratory of Demosthenes were vaster than those wrought by the eloquence of any modern, and yet not controvert the idea that the modern eloquence, itself, is superior to that of the Greek. The Greeks were an excitable, *unread* race, for they had no printed books. *Vivâ voce* exhortations carried with them, to their quick apprehensions, all the gigantic force of *the new*. They had much of that vivid interest which the first fable has upon the dawning intellect of the child — an interest which is worn away by the frequent perusal of similar things — by the frequent inception of similar fancies. The suggestions, the arguments, the incitements of the ancient rhetorician were, when compared with those of the modern, absolutely novel; possessing thus an immense adventitious force — a force which has been, oddly enough, left out of sight in all estimates of the eloquence of the two eras.

The finest Philippic of the Greek would have been hooted at in the British House of Peers, while an impromptu of Sheridan, or of Brougham, would have carried by storm all the hearts and all the intellects of Athens.

————

"The author of *"Miserrimus"* *might have been* W. G. Simms (whose *"Martin Faber"* is just such a work) — but *is* G. M. W. Reynolds, an Englishman, who wrote, also, *"Albert de Rosann,"* and "Pickwick Abroad" — both excellent things in their way.

Mr. Grattan, who, in general, writes well, has a bad habit of loitering—of toying with his subject, as a cat with a mouse, instead of grasping it firmly at once, and devouring it without ado. He takes up too much time in the ante-room. He has never done with his introductions. Sometimes one introduction is merely the vestibule to another; so that by the time he arrives at his main theme, there is none of it left. He is afflicted with a perversity common enough even among otherwise good talkers—an irrepressible desire of tantalizing by circumlocution.

If the greasy print here* exhibited is, indeed, like Mr. Grattan, then is Mr. Grattan like nobody else—for who else ever thrust forth, from beneath a wig of wire, the countenance of an over-done apple-dumpling?

———

It is said in Isaiah, respecting Idumea, that "none shall pass through thee for ever and ever." Dr. Keith here† insists, as usual, upon understanding the passage in its most strictly literal sense. He attempts to prove that neither Burckhardt nor Irby passed *through* the country—merely penetrating to Petra, and returning. And our Mr. John Stephens entered Idumea with the deliberate design of putting the question to test. He wished to see whether it was meant that Idumea should not be passed through, and "accordingly," says he, "I passed through it from one end to the other." Here is error on all sides. In the first place, he was not sufficiently informed in the Ancient Geography to know that the Idumea which he certainly did pass through, is *not* the Idumea, or Edom, intended in the prophecy—the latter lying much farther eastward. In the next place, whether he did or did not pass through the true Idumea—or whether anybody, of late days, did or did not pass through it—is a point of no consequence either to the proof or to the disproof of the literal fulfilment of the Prophecies. For it is quite a mistake on the part of Dr.

*"*High-Ways and By-Ways*"
†"Literal Fulfilment of the Prophecies."

Keith—his supposition that travelling through Idumea is prohibited at all.

The words conceived to embrace the prohibition, are found in Isaiah 34–10, and are *Lenetsach netsachim ēin over bah:* — literally—*Lenetsach*, for an eternity; *netsachim*, of eternities; *ēin*, not; *over*, moving about; *bah*, in it. That is to say; for an eternity of eternities, (there shall) not (be any one) moving about *in it*—not *through* it. The participle *over* refers to one moving to and fro, or up and down, and is the same term which is translated "current" as an epithet of money, in Genesis 23, 16. The prophet means only that there shall be no mark of life in the land—no living being there—no one moving up and down in it. He refers merely to its general abandonment and desolation.

In the same way we have received an erroneous idea of the meaning of Ezekiel 35, 7, where the same region is mentioned. The common version runs;—"Thus will I make Mount Seir most desolate, and cut off from it him that passeth out and him that returneth"—a sentence which Dr. Keith views as he does the one from Isaiah; that is, he supposes it to forbid any travelling in Idumea under penalty of death; instancing Burckhardt's death shortly after his return, as confirming this supposition, on the ground that he died in consequence of the rash attempt.

Now the words of Ezekiel are:— *Venathati eth-har Sēir leshimmamah ushemamah, vehichrati mimmennu over vasal:* — literally— *Venathati*, and I will give; *eth-har*, the mountain; *Sēir*, Seir; *leshimmamah*, for a desolation; *ushemamah*, and a desolation; *vehichrati*, and I will cut off; *mimmennu*, from it; *over*, him that goeth; *vasal*, and him that returneth:—And I will give Mount Seir for an utter desolation, and I will cut off from it him that *passeth and repasseth* therein. The reference here is as in the preceding passage; allusion is made to the inhabitants of the land, as moving about in it, and actively employed in the business of life. I am sustained in the translation of *over vasal* by Gesenius S.5—vol 2—p 570, *Leo's Trans.*: Compare, also, Zachariah 7, 14 and 9, 8. There is something analogous in the Hebrew-Greek phrase, at Acts, 9, 28—καὶ ην μετ᾽ αυτων εισπορευομενος καὶ ᾽εκπορευομενος εν ᾽Ιερουσαλημ·—And he was with them in Jerusalem, coming in and going out. The Latin *versatus est* is precisely para-phrastic. The meaning is that Saul, the new convert, was on intimate terms with the true believers in Jerusalem; moving about among them to and fro, or in and out.

———

The author of "Cromwell" does better as a writer of ballads than of prose. He has fancy, and a fine conception of rhythm. But his romantico-histories have all the effervescence of his verse, without its flavor. Nothing worse than his *tone* can be invented:—turgid sententiousness, involute, spasmodically straining after effect. And to render matters worse, he is as thorough an unistylist as Cardinal Chigi, who boasted that he wrote with the same pen for half a century.

Marginal Notes

A SEQUEL TO THE "MARGINALIA"

GODEY'S LADY'S BOOK, *August 1845*

THE MERELY mechanical style of "Athens" is far better than that of any of Bulwer's previous books. In general he is atrociously involute—this is his main defect. He wraps one sentence in another *ad infinitum*—very much in the fashion of those "nests of boxes" sold in our wooden-ware shops, or like the islands within lakes, within islands within lakes, within islands within lakes, of which we read so much in the "Periplus" of Hanno.

———

Men of genius are far more abundant than is supposed. In fact, to appreciate thoroughly the work of what we call genius, is to possess all the genius by which the work was produced. But the person appreciating may be utterly incompetent to reproduce the work, or any thing similar, and this solely through lack of what may be termed the constructive ability—a matter quite independent of what we agree to understand in the term "genius" itself. This ability is based, to be sure, in great part, upon the faculty of analysis, enabling the artist to get full view of the machinery of his proposed effect, and thus work it and regulate it at will; but a great deal depends also upon properties strictly moral—for example, upon patience, upon concentrativeness, or the power of holding the attention steadily to the one purpose, upon self-dependence and contempt for all opinion which is opinion and no more—in especial, upon energy or industry. So vitally important is this last, that it may well be doubted if any thing to which we have been accustomed to give the title of a " work of genius" was ever accomplished without it; and it is chiefly because this quality and genius are nearly incompatible, that " works of genius" are few, while mere men of genius are, as I say, abundant. The Romans, who excelled us in acuteness of *observation*, while falling below us in induction from facts observed, seem to have been so fully aware of the inseparable connection between industry and a " work of genius," as to have adopted the error that industry, in great measure, was genius itself. The highest compliment is intended by a Roman, when, of an epic, or any thing similar, he says that it is written *industriâ mirabili* or *incredibili industriâ*.

All true men must rejoice to perceive the decline of the miserable rant and cant against originality, which was so much in vogue a few years ago among a class of microscopical critics, and which at one period threatened to degrade all American literature to the level of Flemish art.

Of puns it has been said that those most dislike who are least able to utter them; but with far more of truth may it be asserted that invectives against originality proceed only from persons at once hypocritical and common-place. I say hypocritical—for the love of novelty is an indisputable element of the moral nature of man; and since to be original is merely to be novel, the dolt who professes a distaste for originality, in letters or elsewhere, proves in no degree his aversion for the thing in itself, but merely that uncomfortable hatred which ever arises in the heart of an envious man for an excellence he cannot hope to attain.

When I call to mind the preposterous "asides" and soliloquies of the drama among civilized nations, the shifts employed by the Chinese playwrights appear altogether respectable. If a general, on a Pekin or Canton stage, is ordered on an expedition, "he brandishes a whip," says Davis, "or takes in his hand the reins of a bridle, and striding three or four times around a platform, in the midst of a tremendous crash of gongs, drums and trumpets, finally stops short and tells the audience where he has arrived."

It would sometimes puzzle an European stage hero in no little degree to "tell an audience where he has arrived." Most of them seem to have a very imperfect conception of their whereabouts. In the "Mort de Cæsar," for example, Voltaire makes his populace rush to and fro, exclaiming, *"Courons au Capitole!"* Poor fellows—they are in the capitol all the time;—in his scruples about unity of place, the author has never once let them out of it.

———

It is certainly very remarkable that although destiny is the ruling idea of the Greek drama, the word Τυχη (Fortune) does not appear once in the whole Iliad.

———

"Here is a man who is a scholar and an artist, who knows precisely how every effect has been produced by every great writer, and who is resolved to reproduce them. But the heart passes by his pitfalls and traps, and carefully-planned springs, to be taken captive by some simple fellow who expected the event as little as did his prisoner."*

Perhaps I err in quoting these words as the author's own—they are in the mouth of one of his interlocutors—but whoever claims them, they are poetical and no more. The error is exactly that common one of separating practice from the theory which includes it. In all cases, if the practice fail, it is because the theory is imperfect. If Mr. Lowell's heart be not caught in the pitfall or trap, then the pitfall is ill-concealed and the trap is not properly baited or set. One who has *some artistical ability* may know how to do a thing, and even show how to do it, and yet fail in doing it after all; but the artist and the man of some artistic ability must not be confounded. He only is the former who can carry his most shadowy precepts into successful application. To say that a critic could not have written the work which he criticises, is to put forth a contradiction in terms.

The farce of this big book is equaled only by the farce of the rag-tag-and-bobtail "embassy from the whole earth" introduced by the crazy Prussian into the hall of the French National Assembly. The author is the Anacharsis Clootz of American letters.

———

Mill says that he has "demonstrated" his propositions. Just in the same way Anaxagoras demonstrated snow to be black,

*Lowell's "Conversations."

(which, perhaps, it is, if we could see the thing in the proper light,) and just in the same way the French advocate, Linguet, with Hippocrates in his hand, demonstrated bread to be a slow poison. The worst of the matter is that propositions such as these seldom *stay* demonstrated long enough to be thoroughly understood.

———

"Contempt," says an eastern proverb, "pierces even through the shell of the tortoise;" but there are some human skulls which would feel themselves insulted by a comparison, in point of impermeability, with the shell of a Gallipago turtle.

———

We might contrive a very poetical and very suggestive, although, perhaps, no very tenable philosophy, by supposing that the virtuous live while the wicked suffer annihilation, hereafter; and that the danger of the annihilation (which would be in the ratio of the sin) might be indicated nightly by slumber, and occasionally, with more distinctness, by a swoon. In proportion to the dreamlessness of the sleep, for example, would be the degree of the soul's liability to annihilation. In the same way, to swoon and awake in utter unconsciousness of any lapse of time during the syncope, would demonstrate the soul to be then in such condition that, had death occurred, annihilation would have followed. On the other hand, when the revival is attended with remembrance of visions, (as is now and then the case, in fact,) then the soul to be considered in such condition as would insure its existence after the bodily death—the bliss or wretchedness of the existence to be indicated by the character of the visions.

———

The United States' motto, *E pluribus unum*, may possibly have a sly allusion to Pythagoras' definition of beauty—the reduction of many into one.

———

Here is a book of "amusing travels," which is full enough of statistics to have been the joint composition of Messieurs Busching, Hassel, Cannabitch, Gaspari, Gutsmuth and company.

Spun out like Wollaston's wires, or the world in the Peutingerian Tables.*

————

The Swedenborgians inform me that they have discovered all that I said in a magazine article, entitled "Mesmeric Revelation," to be absolutely true, although at first they were very strongly inclined to doubt my veracity—a thing which, in that particular instance, I never dreamed of not doubting myself. The story is a pure fiction from beginning to end.

————

The drama, as the chief of the imitative arts, has a tendency to beget and keep alive in its votaries the imitative propensity. This might be supposed *à priori*, and experience confirms the supposition. Of all imitators, dramatists are the most perverse, the most unconscionable, or the most unconscious, and have been so time out of mind. Euripides and Sophocles were merely echoes of Æschylus, and not only was Terence Menander and nothing beyond, but of the sole Roman tragedies extant, (the ten attributed to Seneca,) nine are on Greek subjects. Here, then, is cause enough for the "decline of the drama," if we are to believe that the drama has declined. But it has not: on the contrary, during the last fifty years it has materially advanced. All other arts, however, have in the same interval, advanced at a far greater rate—each very nearly in the direct ratio of its non-imitativeness—painting, for example, least of all—and the effect on the drama is, of course, that of apparent retrogradation.

————

It is James Montgomery who thinks proper to style McPherson's "Ossian" a "collection of halting, dancing, lumbering, grating, nondescript paragraphs."

*"The Palais Royal," by Mancur.

———

I have never yet seen an English heroic verse on the proper model of the Greek—although there have been innumerable attempts, among which those of Coleridge are, perhaps, the most absurd, next to those of Sir Philip Sidney and Longfellow. The author of "The Vision of Rubeta" has done better, and Percival better yet; but no one has seemed to suspect that the natural preponderance of spondaic words in the Latin and Greek must, in the English, be supplied by art—that is to say, by a careful culling of the few spondaic words which the language affords—as, for example, here:

Man is a | complex, | compound, | compost, | yet is he | God-born.

This, to all intents, is a Greek hexameter, but then its spondees are spondees, and not mere trochees. The verses of Coleridge and others are dissonant, for the simple reason that there is no equality in time between a trochee and a dactyl. When Sir Philip Sidney writes,

So to the | woods Love | runnes as | well as—rides to the | palace,

he makes an heroic verse only to the eye; for " woods Love" is the only true spondee, "runs as," " well as," and "palace," have each the first syllable long and the second short—that is to say, they are all trochees, and occupy less time than the dactyls or spondee—hence the halting. Now, all this seems to be the simplest thing in the world, and the only wonder is how men professing to be scholars should attempt to engraft a verse, of which the spondee is an element, upon a stock which repels the spondee as antagonistical.

———

"The day is done, and the darkness
Falls from the wings of night,
As a feather is wafted downward
From an eagle in its flight."*

*Pröem to Longfellow's "Waif."

The *single* feather here is imperfectly illustrative of the omni-prevalent darkness; but a more especial objection is the likening of one feather to the falling of another. Night is personified as a bird, and darkness—the feather of this bird—falls from it, how?—as another feather falls from another bird. Why, it does this *of course*. The illustration is identical—that is to say, null. It has no more force than an identical proposition in logic.

Marginal Notes

GODEY'S LADY'S BOOK, *September 1845*

WORDS—printed ones especially—are murderous things. Keats did (or did not) die of a criticism, Cromwell of Titus' pamphlet "Killing no Murder," and Montfleury perished of the "Andromache." The author of the "Parnasse Réformé" makes him thus speak in Hades—*"L'homme donc qui voudrait savoir ce dont je suis mort, qu'il ne demande pas s'il fût de fievre ou de podagre ou d'autre chose, mais qu'il entende que ce fut de L'Andromache."* As for myself, I am fast dying of the *"Sartor Resartus."*

———

Since it has become fashionable to trundle houses about the streets, should there not be some remodeling of the legal definition of reality, as "that which is permanent, fixed and immoveable, that cannot be carried out of its place?" According to this, a house is by no means real estate.

———

Voltaire, in his preface to "Brutus," actually *boasts* of having introduced the Roman senate on the stage in red mantles.

———

One of the most singular pieces of literary Mosaic is Mr. Longfellow's "Midnight Mass for the Dying Year." The general idea and manner are from Tennyson's "Death of the Old Year," several of the most prominent points are from the death scene of Cordelia in "Lear," and the line about the "hooded friars" is from the "Comus" of Milton.

Some approach to this patchwork may be found in these lines from Tasso—

> "Giace l'alta Cartago: à pena i segni
> De l'alte sui ruine il lido serba:
> Muoino le città, muoino i regni;
> Copre i fasti e le pompe arena et herba:
> E l'huom d'esser mortal per che si sdegni."

This is entirely made up from Lucan and Sulspicius. The former says of Troy—

> *"Iam tota teguntur*
> *Pergama dumatis: etiam parire ruinæ."*

Sulspicius, in a letter to Cicero, says of Megara, Egina and Corinth—*"Hem! nos homunculi indignamur si quit nostrûm interiit, quorum vita brevior esse debet, cum uno loco tot oppidorum cadavera projecta jaceant."*

———

A few nuts from memory for Outis. Carey, in his "Dante," says—

> "And pilgrim newly on his road, with love
> Thrills if he hear the vesper bell from far
> That seems to mourn for the expiring day."

Gray says—

> "The curfew tolls the knell of parting day."

———

Milton says—

> "——forget thyself to marble."

Pope says—

> "I have not yet forgot myself to stone."

———

Blair says—

> "——its visits,
> Like those of angels, short and far between."

Campbell says—

> "Like angel visits, few and far between."

———

Butler says—

> "Each window a pillory appears,
>   With heads thrust through nailed by the ears."

Young says—

> "An opera, like a pillory, may be said
>   To nail our ears down and expose our head."

———

Young says—

> "Man wants but little, nor that little long."

Goldsmith says—

> "Man wants but little here below,
>   Nor wants that little long."

———

Milton says—

> "——when the scourge
> Inexorably and the torturing hour
> Call us to penance."

Gray says—

> "Thou tamer of the human breast,
>   Whose iron scourge and torturing hour
>   The bad affright."

———

Butler says—

> "This hairy meteor did announce
>   The fall of sceptres and of crowns."

Gray says—

> "Loose his beard and hoary hair
>   Streamed like a meteor to the troubled air."

———

Dryden says—

> "David for him his tuneful harp had strung,
> And heaven had wanted one immortal song."

Pope says—

> "Friend of my life, which did not you prolong,
> The world had wanted many an idle song."

———

Boileau says—

> "En vain contre 'Le Cid' un ministre se ligue,
> Tout Paris pour Chimene a les yeux de Rodrigue."

Tickell says—

> "While the charmed reader with thy thought complies,
> And views thy Rosamond with Henry's eyes."

———

Lucretius says—

> "——terras—
> Una dies dabit exitio."

Ovid says—

> "Carmine sublimis tunc sunt peritura Lucreti
> Exitio terras cum dabit una dies."

———

Freneau says—

> "The hunter and the deer a shade."

Campbell says the same identically.

———

I would have no difficulty in filling two ordinary novel volumes with just such concise parallels as these. Nevertheless, I am clearly of opinion that of one hundred plagiarisms of this character, seventy-five would be, not accidental, but unintentional. The poetic sentiment implies an abnormally keen appreciation of poetic excellence, with an unconscious assimilation of it into the poetic entity, so that an admired passage, being forgotten and afterwards reviving through an exceedingly shadowy train of association, is supposed by the plagiarizing poet to be really the coinage of his own brain. An uncharitable world, however, will never be brought to understand all this, and the poet who commits a plagiarism is, if not criminal, at least unlucky; and equally in either case does critical justice require the right of property to be traced home. Of two persons, one is to suffer—it matters not what—and there can be no question as to who should be the sufferer.

———

The question of international copyright has been overloaded with words. The right of property in a literary work is disputed merely for the sake of disputation, and no man should be at the trouble of arguing the point. Those who deny it, have made up their minds to deny every thing tending to further the law in contemplation. Nor is the question of expediency in any respect relevant. Expediency is only to be discussed where no *rights* interfere. It would no doubt be very expedient in any poor man to pick the pocket of his wealthy neighbour, (and as the poor are the majority the case is precisely parallel to the copyright case;) but what would the rich think if expediency were permitted to overrule their right?

But even the expediency is untenable, grossly so. The immediate advantage arising to the pockets of our people, in the existing condition of things, is no doubt sufficiently plain. We get more reading for less money than if the international law existed; but the remoter disadvantages are of infinitely greater weight. In brief, they are these: First, we have injury to our national literature by repressing the efforts of our men of genius; for genius, as a general rule, is poor in worldly goods and cannot write for nothing. Our genius being thus repressed, we are written *at* only by our "gentlemen of elegant leisure," and mere gentlemen of elegant leisure have been noted, time out of mind, for the insipidity of their productions. In general, too, they are obstinately conservative, and this feeling leads them into imitation of foreign, more especially of British models. This is one main source of the imitativeness with which, as a people, we have been justly charged, although the first cause is to be found in our position as a colony. Colonies have always naturally aped the mother land.

In the second place, irreparable ill is wrought by the almost exclusive dissemination among us of foreign—that is to say, of monarchical or aristocratical sentiment in foreign books; nor is this sentiment less fatal to democracy because it reaches the people themselves directly in the gilded pill of the poem or the novel.

We have next to consider the impolicy of our committing, in the national character, an open and continuous wrong on the frivolous pretext of its benefiting ourselves.

The last and by far the most important consideration of all, however, is that sense of insult and injury aroused in the whole active intellect of the world, the bitter and fatal resentment excited in the universal heart of literature—a resentment which will not and which cannot make nice distinctions between the temporary perpetrators of the wrong and that democracy in general which permits its perpetration. The autorial body is the most autocratic on the face of the earth. How, then, can those institutions even hope to be safe which systematically persist in trampling it under foot?

———

The conclusion of the Pröem in Mr. Longfellow's late "Waif" is exceedingly beautiful. The whole poem is remarkable in this, that one of its principal excellences arises from what is, generically, a demerit. No error, for example, is more certainly fatal in poetry than defective *rhythm*; but here the *slipshodiness* is so thoroughly in unison with the nonchalant air of the thoughts—which, again, are so capitally applicable to the thing done (a mere introduction of other people's fancies)—that the effect of the looseness of rhythm becomes palpable, and we see at once that here is a case in which to be *correct* would be inartistic. Here are three of the quatrains—

> "I see the lights of the village
>   Gleam through the rain and the mist,
> And a feeling of sadness comes over me
>   That my soul cannot resist—

"A feeling of sadness and longing
        That is not akin to pain,
And *resembles sorrow only*
        As the mists resemble the rain.

*   *   *   *   *   *

"And the night shall be filled with music,
        And the cares that infest the day
Shall fold their tents like the Arabs,
        And as silently steal away."

Now these lines are not to be scanned. They are referable to no true principles of rhythm. The general idea is that of a succession of anapæsts; yet not only is this idea confounded with that of dactyls, but this succession is improperly interrupted at all points—improperly, because by unequivalent feet. The partial prosaicism thus brought about, however, (without any interference with the mere melody,) becomes a beauty solely through the nicety of its adaptation to the *tone* of the poem, and of this tone, again, to the matter in hand. In his keen sense of this adaptation, (which conveys the notion of what is vaguely termed "ease,") the reader so far loses sight of the rhythmical imperfection that he can be convinced of its existence only by treating in the same rhythm (or, rather, lack of rhythm) a subject of different tone—a subject in which decision shall take the place of nonchalance.

Now, undoubtedly, I intend all this as complimentary to Mr. Longfellow; but it was for the utterance of these very opinions in the "New York Mirror" that I was accused, by some of the poet's friends, of inditing what they think proper to call "strictures" on the author of "Outre-Mer."

———

When we attend less to "authority" and more to principles, when we look *less* at merit and *more* at demerit, (instead of the converse, as some persons suggest,) we shall then be better critics than we are. We must neglect our models and study our capabilities. The mad eulogies on what occasionally has, in letters, been well done, spring from our imperfect comprehension of what it is possible for us to do better. "A man who has never seen the sun," says Calderon, "cannot be blamed for thinking that no glory can exceed that of the moon; a man who has seen neither moon nor sun, cannot be blamed for expatiating on the incomparable effulgence of the morning star." Now, it is the business of the critic so to soar that he shall *see the sun*, even although its orb be far below the ordinary horizon.

———

In the sweet "Lily of Nithsdale," we read—

> "She's gane to dwell in heaven, my lassie—
>   She's gane to dwell in heaven;—
> Ye're ow're pure, quo' the voice of God,
>   For dwelling out o' heaven."

The *owre* and the *o'* of the two last verses should be Anglicized. The Deity, at least, should be supposed to speak so as to be understood—although I am aware that a folio has been written to demonstrate broad Scotch as the language of Adam and Eve in Paradise.

———

The increase, within a few years, of the magazine literature, is by no means to be regarded as indicating what some critics would suppose it to indicate—a downward tendency in American taste or in American letters. It is but a sign of the times, an indication of an era in which men are forced upon the curt, the condensed, the well-digested in place of the voluminous—in a word, upon journalism in lieu of dissertation. We need now the light artillery rather than the peace-makers of the intellect. I will not be sure that men at present think more profoundly than half a century ago, but beyond question they think with more rapidity, with more skill, with more tact, with more of method and less of excrescence in the thought. Besides all this, they have a vast increase in the thinking material; they have more facts, more to think about. For this reason, they are disposed to put the greatest amount of thought in the smallest compass and disperse it with the utmost attainable rapidity. Hence the journalism of the age; hence, in especial, magazines. Too many we cannot have, as a general proposition; but we demand that they have sufficient merit to render them noticeable in the beginning, and that they continue in existence sufficiently long to permit us a fair estimation of their value.

———

Jack Birkenhead, *apud* Bishop Sprat, says that "a great wit's great work is to refuse." The apothegm must be swallowed *cum grano salis*. His greatest work is to originate no matter that shall require refusal.

———

Scott, in his "Presbyterian Eloquence," speaks of "that ancient fable, not much known," in which a trial of skill in singing being agreed upon between the cuckoo and the nightingale, the ass was chosen umpire. When each bird had done his best, the umpire declared that the nightingale sang extremely well, but that "for a good plain song give him the cuckoo."

The judge with the long ears, in this case, is a fine type of the tribe of critics who insist upon what they call "quietude" as the supreme literary excellence—gentlemen who rail at Tennyson and elevate Addison into apotheosis. By the way, the following passage from Sterne's "Letter from France," should be adopted at once as a motto by the "Down-East Review:" "As we rode along the valley, we saw a herd of asses on the top of one of the mountains. How they viewed and *reviewed* us!"

———

Of Berryer, somebody says "he is the man in whose description is the greatest possible consumption of antithesis." For "description" read "lectures," and the sentence would apply well to Hudson, the lecturer on Shakspeare. Antithesis is his end—he has no other. He does not employ it to enforce thought, but he gathers thought from all quarters with the sole view to its capacity for antithetical expression. His essays have thus only paragraphical effect; as wholes, they produce not the slightest impression. No man living could say what it is Mr. Hudson proposes to demonstrate; and if the question were propounded to Mr. H. himself, we can fancy how particularly embarrassed he would be for a reply. In the end, were he to answer honestly, he would say—*"Antithesis."*

As for his reading, Julius Cæsar would have said of him that he sang ill, and undoubtedly he must have "gone to the dogs" for his experience in pronouncing the *r* as if his throat were bored like a rifle-barrel.*

* *"Nec illi (Demostheni) turpe videbatur vel, optimis relictis magistris, ad canes se conferre, et ab illis e literæ vim et naturam petere, illorumque in sonando, quod satis est, morem imitari."*—Ad Meker. de vet. Pron. Ling. Græcæ.

Marginalia

GRAHAM'S MAGAZINE, *March 1846*

THE EFFECT derivable from well-managed rhyme is very imperfectly understood. Conventionally "rhyme" implies merely close similarity of sound at the ends of verse, and it is really curious to observe how long mankind have been content with their limitation of the idea. What, in rhyme, first and principally pleases, may be referred to the human sense or appreciation of *equality*—the common element, as might be easily shown, of all the gratification we derive from music in its most extended sense—very especially in its modifications of metre and rhythm. We see, for example, a crystal, and are immediately interested by the equality between the sides and angles of one of its faces—but on bringing to view a second face, in all respects similar to the first, our pleasure seems to be *squared*—on bringing to view a third, it appears to be *cubed*, and so on: I have no doubt, indeed, that the delight experienced, if measurable, would be found to have exact methematical relations, such, or nearly such, as I suggest—that is to say, as far as a certain point, beyond which there would be a decrease, in similar relations. Now here, as the ultimate result of analysis, we reach the sense of mere *equality*, or rather the human delight in this sense; and it was an instinct, rather than a clear comprehension of this delight as a principle, which, in the first instance, led the poet to attempt an increase of the effect arising from the mere similarity (that is to say equality) between two sounds—led him, I say, to attempt increasing this effect by making a secondary equalization, in placing the rhymes at equal distances—that is, at the ends of lines of equal length. In this manner, rhyme and the termination of the line grew connected in men's thoughts—grew into a conventionalism—the principle being lost sight of altogether. And it was simply because Pindaric verses had, before this epoch, existed—*i.e.* verses of unequal length—that rhymes were subsequently found at unequal distances. It was for this reason solely, I say—for none more profound—rhyme had come to be regarded as of right appertaining to the *end* of verse—and here we complain that the matter has finally rested.

But it is clear that there was much more to be considered. So far, the sense of *equality* alone, entered the effect; or, if this equality was slightly varied, it was varied only through an accident—the accident of the existence of Pindaric metres. It will be seen that the rhymes were always *anticipated*. The eye, catching the end of a verse, whether long or short, expected, for the ear, a rhyme. The great element of unexpectedness was not dreamed of—that is to say, of novelty—of originality. "But," says Lord Bacon, (how justly!) "there is no exquisite beauty without some *strangeness* in the proportions." Take away this element of strangeness—of unexpectedness—of novelty—of originality—call it what we will—and all that is *ethereal* in loveliness is lost at once. We lose—we miss the *unknown*—the vague—the uncomprehended, because offered before we have time to examine and comprehend. We lose, in short, all that assimilates the beauty of earth with what we dream of the beauty of Heaven.

Perfection of rhyme is attainable only in the combination of the two elements, Equality and Unexpectedness. But as evil cannot exist without good, so unexpectedness must arise from expectedness. We do not contend for mere *arbitrariness* of rhyme. In the first place, we must have equi-distant or regularly recurring rhymes, to form the basis, expectedness, out of which arises the element, unexpectedness, by the introduction of rhymes, not arbitrarily, but with an eye to the greatest amount of unexpectedness. We should not introduce them, for example, at such points that the entire line is a multiple of the syllables preceding the points. When, for instance, I write—

> And the silken, sad, uncertain rustling of each purple
>   curtain,

I produce more, to be sure, but not remarkably more than the ordinary effect of rhymes regularly recurring at the ends of lines; for the number of syllables in the whole verse is merely a multiple of the number of syllables preceding the rhyme introduced at the middle, and there is still left, therefore, a certain degree of expectedness. What there is of the element, unexpectedness, is addressed, in fact, to the eye only—for the ear divides the verse into two ordinary lines, thus:

> And the silken, sad, uncertain
> Rustling of each purple curtain.

I obtain, however, the whole effect of unexpectedness, when I write—

Thrilled me, *filled* me with fantastic terrors never felt before.

N. B. It is very commonly supposed that rhyme, as it now ordinarily exists, is of modern invention—but see the "Clouds" of Aristophanes. Hebrew verse, however, did *not* include it—the terminations of the lines, where most distinct, never showing any thing of the kind.

———

Talking of inscriptions—how admirable was the one circulated at Paris, for the equestrian statue of Louis XV., done by Pigal and Bouchardon—*"Statua Statuæ."*

———

In the way of original, striking, and well-sustained metaphor, we can call to mind few finer things than this—to be found in James Puckle's "Gray Cap for a Green Head:" "In speaking of the dead so fold up your discourse that their virtues may be outwardly shown, while their vices are wrapped up in silence."

———

Some Frenchman—possibly Montaigne—says: "People talk about thinking, but for my part I never think, except when I sit down to write." It is this never thinking, unless when we sit down to write, which is the cause of so much indifferent composition. But perhaps there is something more involved in the Frenchman's observation than meets the eye. It is certain that the mere act of inditing, tends, in a great degree, to the logicalization of thought. Whenever, on account of its vagueness, I am dissatisfied with a conception of the brain, I resort forthwith to the pen, for the purpose of obtaining, through its aid, the necessary form, consequence and precision.

How very commonly we hear it remarked, that such and such thoughts are beyond the compass of words! I do not believe that any thought, properly so called, is out of the reach of language. I fancy, rather, that where difficulty in expression is experienced, there is, in the intellect which experiences it, a want either of deliberateness or of method. For my own part, I have never had a thought which I could not set down in words, with even more distinctness than that with which I conceived it:—as I have before observed, the thought is logicalized by the effort at (written) expression.

There is, however, a class of fancies, of exquisite delicacy, which are *not* thoughts, and to which, *as yet*, I have found it absolutely impossible to adapt language. I use the word *fancies* at random, and merely because I must use *some* word; but the idea commonly attached to the term is not even remotely applicable to the shadows of shadows in question. They seem to me rather psychal than intellectual. They arise in the soul (alas, how rarely!) only at its epochs of most intense tranquillity—when the bodily and mental health are in perfection—and at those mere points of time where the confines of the waking world blend with those of the world of dreams. I am aware of these "fancies" only when I am upon the very brink of sleep, with the consciousness that I am so. I have satisfied myself that this condition exists but for an inappreciable *point* of time—yet it is crowded with these "shadows of shadows;" and for absolute *thought* there is demanded time's *endurance*.

These "fancies" have in them a pleasurable ecstasy as far beyond the most pleasurable of the world of wakefulness, or of dreams, as the Heaven of the Northman theology is beyond its Hell. I regard the visions, even as they arise, with an awe which, in some measure, moderates or tranquilizes the ecstasy—I so regard them, through a conviction (which seems a portion of the ecstasy itself) that this ecstasy, in itself, is of a character supernal to the Human Nature—is a glimpse of the spirit's outer world; and I arrive at this conclusion—if this term is at all applicable to instantaneous intuition—by a perception that the delight experienced has, as its element, but *the absoluteness of novelty*. I say the absoluteness—for in

these fancies—let me now term them psychal impressions—
there is really nothing even approximate in character to
impressions ordinarily received. It is as if the five senses were
supplanted by five myriad others alien to mortality.

Now, so entire is my faith in the *power of words*, that, at
times, I have believed it possible to embody even the evanes-
cence of fancies such as I have attempted to describe. In experiments with this end in view, I have proceeded so far as,
first, to control (when the bodily and mental health are good)
the existence of the condition:—that is to say, I can now
(unless when ill) be sure that the condition will supervene, if
I so wish it, at the point of time already described:—of its
supervention, until lately, I could never be certain, even under
the most favorable circumstances. I mean to say, merely, that
now I can be sure, when all circumstances are favorable, of
the supervention of the condition, and feel even the capacity
of inducing or compelling it:—the favorable circumstances,
however, are not the less rare—else had I compelled, already,
the Heaven into the Earth.

I have proceeded so far, secondly, as to prevent the lapse
from *the point* of which I speak—the point of blending between wakefulness and sleep—as to prevent at will, I say, the
lapse from this border-ground into the dominion of sleep.
Not that I can *continue* the condition—not that I can render
the point more than a point—but that I can startle myself
from the point into wakefulness— *and thus transfer the point
itself into the realm of Memory*—convey its impressions, or
more properly their recollections, to a situation where (although still for a very brief period) I can survey them with
the eye of analysis.

For these reasons—that is to say, because I have been enabled to accomplish thus much—I do not altogether despair
of embodying in words at least enough of the fancies in question to convey, to certain classes of intellect, a shadowy conception of their character.

In saying this I am not to be understood as supposing that
the fancies, or psychal impressions, to which I allude, are confined to my individual self—are not, in a word, common to
all mankind—for on this point it is quite impossible that I
should form an opinion—but nothing can be more certain

than that even a partial record of the impressions would startle the universal intellect of mankind, by the *supremeness of the novelty* of the material employed, and of its consequent suggestions. In a word—should I ever write a paper on this topic, the world will be compelled to acknowledge that, at last, I have done an original thing.

———

Mr. Hudson, among innumerable blunders, attributes to Sir Thomas Browne, the paradox of Tertullian in his *De Carne Christi*—*"Mortuus est Dei filius, credibile est quia ineptum est; et sepultus resurrexit, certum est quia impossible est."*

Bielfeld, the author of *"Les Premiers Traits de L'Erudition Universelle,"* defines poetry as *"l'art d'exprimer les pensées par la fiction."* The Germans have two words in full accordance with this definition, absurd as it is—the terms *Dichtkunst*, the art of fiction, and *Dichten*, to feign—which are generally used for poetry and to make verses.

———

Diana's Temple at Ephesus having been burnt on the night in which Alexander was born, some person observed that "it was no wonder, since, at the period of the conflagration, she was gossiping at Pella." Cicero commends this as a witty conceit—Plutarch condems it as senseless—and this is the one point in which I agree with the biographer.

———

Brown in his "Amusements," speaks of having transfused the blood of an ass into the veins of an astrological quack— and there can be no doubt that one of Hague's progenitors was the man.

Marginalia

DEMOCRATIC REVIEW, *April 1846*

IN GENERAL, our first impressions are the true ones—the chief difficulty is in making sure which *are* the first. In early youth we read a poem, for instance, and are enraptured with it. At manhood we are assured by our reason that we had no reason to be enraptured. But some years elapse, and we return to our primitive admiration, just as a matured judgment enables us precisely to see what and why we admired. Thus, as individuals, we think in cycles, and may, from the frequency or infrequency of our revolutions about the various thought-centres, form an accurate estimate of the advance of our thought toward maturity. It is really wonderful to observe how closely, in all the essentials of truth, the child-opinion coincides with that of the man proper—of the man at his best.

And as with individuals, so, perhaps, with mankind. When the world begins to return, frequently, to its first impressions, we shall then be warranted in looking for the millennium—or whatever it is:—we may safely take it for granted that we are attaining our maximum of wit, and of the happiness which is thence to ensue. The indications of such a return are, at present, like the visits of angels—but we have them now and then—in the case, for example, of *credulity*. The philosophic, of late days, are distinguished by that very facility in belief which was the characteristic of the illiterate half a century ago. Skepticism, in regard to apparent miracles, is not, as formerly, an evidence either of superior wisdom or knowledge. In a word, the wise now believe—yesterday they would not believe—and day before yesterday (in the time of Strabo for example) they believed, exclusively, anything and everything:—here, then, is one of the indicative cycles completed—indicative of the world's approach to years of discretion. I mention Strabo merely as an exception to the rule of his epoch—(just as one, in a hurry for an illustration, might describe Mr. So and So to be as witty or as amiable as Mr. This and That is *not*)—for so rarely did men reject in Strabo's time, and so much more rarely did they *err* by rejection, that the skepticism of this philosopher must be regarded as one of the most remarkable anomalies on record.

———

I cannot help believing, with Gosselin, that Hanno proceeded only so far as Cape Nun.

———

The drugging system, in medical practice, seems to me but a modification of the idea of *penance*, which has haunted the world since its infancy—the idea that the voluntary endurance of pain is atonement for sin. In this, the primary phase of the folly, there is at least a show of rationality. Man offends the Deity; thus appears to arise a necessity for retribution, or, more strictly, a desire, on the part of Deity, to punish. The *self*-infliction of punishment, then, seemed to include at once an acknowledgment of error, zeal in anticipating the will of God, and expiation of the wrong. The thought, thus stated, however absurd, is not unnatural; but the principle being gradually left out of sight, mankind at length found itself possessed of the naked idea that, in general, the suffering of mankind is grateful to the Creator:—hence the Dervishes, the Simeons, the monastic hair-cloths and shoe-peas, the present Puritanism and cant about the "mortification of the flesh." From this point the conceit makes another lapse; the fancy took root, that *in the voluntary endurance of ill there existed, in the abstract, a tendency to good*; and it was but in pursuance of this fancy, that, in sickness, remedies were selected in the ratio of their repulsiveness. How else shall we account for the fact, that in ninety-nine cases out of a hundred the articles of the Materia Medica are distasteful?

———

Mr. Henry Cary is introduced to us, in the Appendix to "The Poets and Poetry of America," as "Mr. Henry Car*ey*, author of 'Poems by John Waters,' originally printed in the 'New-York American' and the 'Knickerbocker Magazine.' " Mr. Cary's works have appeared *only* in the periodicals mentioned—that is, I believe they have not yet been collected in volume form. His poems (not so good as his prose by any means) are easily and pointedly written, neatly versified, and full of life and fancy. Doctor Griswold has made a mistake in attributing to *our* Mr. Cary the Anacreontic entitled "Old Wine to Drink," quoted in the Appendix of the "large book."

It is as an essayist that Mr. C. is best entitled to distinction. He has written some of the happiest Magazine papers, of the Spectator class, in the language. All that he does, evinces a keen relish for old English literature, and a scholastic taste. His style is pure, correct, and vigorous—a judicious mixture of the Swift and Addison manners—although he is by no means either Swift or Addison. In a well-written memoir of him furnished for "The Broadway Journal," the writer says:

"His essays are all short, as essays should be, of the Addisonian dimensions and density of expression. His sentences are the most perfect in the language; it would be a vain task to hunt through them all for a superfluous conjunction. They are too perfect to be peculiar, for writers are distinguished from each other more by their faults than their excellences. . . . . He can endure nothing that wears a slovenly aspect. His lawns must be neatly trimmed and his gardens weeded. . . . . He has not written much about flowers, but we should think that his favorite was a Camelia. He is in some sort a Sam. Rogers, but more particular . . . His descriptions have a delicacy of finish like the carvings of Grinling Gibbons. They remind you as forcibly of Nature as anything short of Nature can; but they never deceive you; you know all the while that it is not a reality that affects you."

Of course in all this there is exaggeration. The commentator seems to have had in view the twofold object of writing, himself, a John Waterish essay, and doing *full* justice to his personal friend. The only trouble is, that the justice is a little *too* full. It will not quite do to say that Mr. Cary's sentences are the "most perfect" in the language—first, because "perfect" admits of no degrees of comparison, and secondly, because the sentences in question are perfect by no means. For example—"It would be in vain," says the critic, "to hunt through them all for a superfluous conjunction"—immediately afterwards quoting from Mr. C. the following words:

"We paid our visit to the incomparable ruins of the castle, *and* then proceeded to retrace our steps, and examining our wheels at every post-house, reached the Hotel D'Angleterre. . . . . . It was well filled, *and* yet the number," etc.

Now the conjunctions which I have italicized are pleonastic. These things, however, are trifles; John Waters deserves all the spirit if not the whole letter of his friend's commendation.

————

"So violent was the state of parties in England, that I was assured by several that the Duke of Marlborough was a coward and Pope a fool."—*Voltaire*.

Both propositions have since been very seriously entertained, quite independently of all party-feeling. That Pope was a fool, indeed, seems to be an established point, at present, with the Crazy-ites—what else shall I call them?

————

Not long ago I pointed out in "The New-York Mirror," and more fully, since, in "The Broadway Journal," a very decided case of similarity between "*A* Death-Bed," by Mr. Aldrich, and "*The* Death-Bed," by Thomas Hood. The fact is, I thought, and still think, that, in this instance, Mr. A. has been guilty of plagiarism in the first degree. A short piece of his headed "Lines," is not demonstrably a plagiarism—because there seems scarcely any design of concealing the source—but I quote the poem as evidence of Mr. A's aptitude at imitation. Leaving the original out of sight, every one would admit the beauty of the parallel:

LINES.

Underneath this marble cold,
Lies a fair girl turned to mould;
One whose life was like a star,
Without toil or rest to mar
Its divinest harmony—
Its God-given serenity.

One whose form of youthful grace,
One whose eloquence of face
Matched the rarest gem of thought
By the antique sculptors wrought:
Yet her outward charms were less
Than her winning gentleness—
Her maiden purity of heart—
Which, without the aid of art,
Did in coldest hearts inspire
Love that was not all desire.
Spirit forms with starry eyes
That seem to come from Paradise—
Beings of ethereal birth—
Near us glide sometimes on Earth,
Like glimmering moonbeams dimly seen,
Glancing down through alleys green;
Of such was she who lies beneath
This silent effigy of grief.
Wo is me! when I recall
One sweet word by her let fall—
One sweet word but half expressed—
Downcast eyes told all the rest.
To think beneath this marble cold
Lies that fair girl turned to mould.

    Imitators are not, necessarily, unoriginal—except at the exact points of the imitation. Mr. Longfellow, decidedly the most audacious imitator in America, is markedly original, or, in other words, imaginative, upon the whole; and many persons have, from the latter branch of the fact, been at a loss to comprehend, and therefore, to believe, the former. Keen sensibility of appreciation—that is to say, the poetic *sentiment* (in distinction from the poetic *power*) leads almost inevitably to imitation. Thus all great poets have been gross imitators. It is, however, a mere *non distributio medii* hence to infer, that all great imitators are poets. Still—what I mean to say is, that Mr. Aldrich's *penchant* for imitation does not show him to be incapable of poetry—as some have asserted. It is my own belief that, at some future day, he will distinguish himself as a lyrist.

———

There can be no doubt, that up to this period the Bushites have had the best of the battle. The "Anastasis"* is lucidly, succinctly, vigorously, and logically written, and proves, in my opinion, everything that it attempts—provided that we admit the imaginary axioms from which it starts; and this is as much as can be well said of any theological disquisition under the sun. It might be hinted, too, in reference as well to Professor Bush, as to his opponents, *"que la plupart des sectes ont raison dans une bonne partie de ce qu'elles avancent, mais non pas en ce qu'elles nient."*

Taylor, who wrote so ingeniously the "Natural History of Enthusiasm," might have derived many a valuable hint from the study of Professor Bush.

———

A good title to a very respectable book.† The endeavor to convey Rome only by those impressions which would naturally be made upon an American, gives the work a certain air of originality—the rarest of all qualities in descriptions of the Eternal City. The style is pure and sparkling, although occasionally flippant and *dillettantesque*. The tone of remark is much in the usual way—*selon les regles*—never very exceptionable, and certainly never very profound.

———

I never read a personally abusive paragraph in the newspapers, without calling to mind the pertinent query propounded by Johnson to Goldsmith:—"My dear Doctor, what harm does it do a man to call him Holofernes?"

———

"The artist belongs to his work, not the work to the artist."—*Novalis.*‡

In nine cases out of ten it is pure waste of time to attempt

———

*"Anastasis, or The Doctrine of the Resurrection; in which it is shown that the Doctrine of the Resurrection of the Body is not sanctioned by Reason or Revelation."

†"Rome, as seen by a New-Yorker"—by William M. Gillespie.

‡The nom de plume of Von Hardenburgh.

extorting sense from a German apophthegm;—or, rather, any sense and every sense may be extorted from all of them. If, in the sentence above quoted, the intention is to assert that the artist is the slave of his theme, and must conform to it his thoughts, I have no faith in the idea, which appears to me that of an essentially prosaic intellect. In the hands of the *true* artist the theme, or "work," is but a mass of clay, of which anything (within the compass of the mass and quality of the clay) may be fashioned at will, or according to the skill of the workman. The clay is, in fact, the slave of the artist. It belongs to him. His genius, to be sure, is manifested, very distinctively, in *the choice* of the clay. It should be neither fine nor coarse, abstractly—but just so fine or so coarse—just so plastic or so rigid—as may best serve the purposes of the thing to be wrought—of the idea to be made out, or, more exactly, of the impression to be conveyed. There *are* artists, however, who fancy only the *finest* material, and who, consequently, produce only the *finest* ware. It is generally very transparent and excessively brittle.

————

I have not the slightest faith in Carlyle. In ten years—possibly in five—he will be remembered only as a butt for sarcasm. His linguistic Euphuisms might very well have been taken as *primâ facie* evidence of his philosophic ones; they were the froth which indicated, first, the shallowness, and secondly, the confusion of the waters. I would blame no man of sense for leaving the works of Carlyle unread, merely on account of these Euphuisms; for it might be shown *à priori*, that no man capable of producing a definite impression upon his age or race, could or would commit himself to such inanities and insanities. The book about "Hero-Worship"—is it possible that it ever excited a feeling beyond contempt? *No* hero-worshipper can possess anything within himself. That man is no man who stands in awe of his fellow-man. Genius regards genius with respect—with even enthusiastic admiration—but there is nothing of worship in the admiration, for it springs from a thorough cognizance of the one admired—from a perfect *sympathy*, the result of this cognizance; and it is needless to say, that sympathy and worship are antagonistic. Your hero-worshippers—your Shakspeare worshippers, for example—what do they know about Shakspeare? They worship him—rant about him—lecture about him—about *him*, *him*, and nothing else—for no other reason than that he is utterly beyond their comprehension. They have arrived at an idea of his greatness from the pertinacity with which men have called him great. As for their own opinion about him—they really have none at all. In general, the very smallest of mankind are the class of men-worshippers. *Not one* out of this class has ever accomplished anything beyond a very contemptible mediocrity.

Carlyle, however, has rendered an important service (to posterity, at least) in pushing rant and cant to that degree of excess which inevitably induces reäction. Had he not appeared, we might have gone on for yet another century, Emerson-izing in prose, Wordsworth-izing in poetry, and Fourier-izing in philosophy, Wilson-izing in criticism—Hudson-izing and Tom O'Bedlam-izing in everything. The author of the "Sartor Resartus," however, has overthrown the various arguments of his own order, by a personal *reductio ad absurdum*. Yet an Olympiad, perhaps, and the whole horde will be swept bodily from the memory of man—or be remembered only when we have occasion to talk of such fantastic tricks as, erewhile, were performed by the Abderites.

———

I cannot help thinking Doctor Cheever's* "Common-Place-Book of American Poetry" a most injudicious selection—its taste tending entirely toward the didactic. It has the merit, however, of not belying its title, and is excessively common-place. Poets are by no means, necessarily, judges of poetry, but nothing is more certain than that, to be a judge of

*The Reverend George B. Cheever, of New-York; author of "Deacon Giles' Distillery," (a *brochure* which, at the epoch of its publication, produced much excitement,) "God's Hand in America," "Travels in the East," and a "Defence of Capital Punishment." The last named has not been long published. In some respects, it is well reasoned. Its chief *data*, however, (in common with all which I have yet seen on this *vexata questio*) are the merest assumptions. Authority is obstinately insisted upon, which nine-tenths of the thinking portion of the civilized world deny, either openly or at heart, to be any authority at all.

poetry, it is necessary to have at least the poetic sentiment, if not the poetic power—the "vision," if not "the faculty divine." Dr. Cheever, very evidently, has neither. I have now before me one of the most commendable pieces of verse which I have seen from his pen, and quote from it its best quatrain, which is undeniably forcible and pointed in expression:

> A life all ease is all abused:—
>   O, precious grace that made thee wise
> To know;—affliction, rightly used,
>   Is mercy in disguise.

The greater part of the poem, however, (which consists of thirty-eight quatrains) jogs along thus:

> Those duties were love's natural *sphere*:
>   Our drooping flower I cherished *so*
> That still the more it asked my *care*
>   The dearer still it *grew*.

———

As a descriptive poet, Mr. Street is to be highly commended. He not only describes with force and fidelity—giving us a clear conception of the thing described—but never describes what, to the poet, should be nondescript. He appears, however, not at any time to have been aware that *mere* description is not poetry at all. We demand creation—ποιησις. About Mr. Street there seems to be no spirit. He is all matter—substance—what the chemists would call "simple substance"—and exceedingly simple it is.

———

As a commentator, Professor Anthon has evinced powers very unusual in men who devote their lives to the *hortus siccus* of classical lore. He has ventured to dismiss the pedant and look *en homme du monde* upon some of the most valued of the literary monuments of antiquity. The abundant Notes to his Classics will do him lasting honor among all who are qualified to give an opinion of his labors, or whose good word and will he would be likely to consider as worth having. His accuracy is extreme. I would stand by his decision, in any mere matter of classical fact, in preference to that of any man in Europe, or elsewhere. Some time ago, an attempt was made to injure his reputation by a charge of plagiarism, instituted in reference to his most important work, the Classical Dictionary; and urged against such a book, the accusation, from its mere silliness, was not easily rebutted. The Classical Dictionary is little more than a summary of *facts*, and these facts are the common property of mankind. Professor Anthon's accusers would have acted with equal wisdom in charging Legendre with robbing Euclid. The multitudinous quotations of the Classical Dictionary are made *verbatim* (unless where difference of opinion has induced alteration) without that attempt at giving the extracted matter an air of originality by merely re-writing it, which is but too common among compilers. And for this virtue he has been reviled. No doubt he would have given more satisfaction, in certain quarters, had he thought more of his own merely literary reputation, and kept his eye less steadily fixed on the true purpose of compilations such as he has undertaken—for the purpose of *making a useful book*. His talents, nevertheless, have long ago placed him in a position at which he is left free to pursue this good purpose in his own manner, without fear of injuring his character as an original writer, in the opinion of any one having sense enough to understand that there is a point at which originality ceases to be a matter for commendation.

The only noticeable demerit of Professor Anthon is diffuseness, sometimes running into Johnsonism, of style. The best specimen of his manner is to be found in an analysis of the Life and Writings of Cicero, prefacing an edition of the orator's Select Orations. This analysis occupies about forty pages of the book, and is so peculiarly Ciceronian, in point of fullness, and in other points, that I have sometimes thought it an intended imitation of the *Brutus, sive de Claris Oratoribus*.

———

With the aid of a lantern, I have been looking again at "Niagara and other Poems" (Lord only knows if that be the true title)—but "there's nothing in it:"—at least nothing of Mr. Lord's own—nothing which is not stolen—or, (more delicately,) transfused—transmitted. By the way, Newton

says a great deal about "fits of easy transmission and reflection,"* and I have no doubt that "Niagara" was put together
in one of these identical fits.

*Of the solar rays—in the "Optics."

Marginalia

DEMOCRATIC REVIEW, *July 1846*

"Génes dans ce temps achetait tout le blé de l'Europe."

FOR AN HOUR I have been endeavoring, without success, to make out the meaning of this passage—which I find in a French translation of Lady Morgan's "Letters on Italy." I could not conceive how or why all the corn of Europe should have been bought, or what corn, in any shape, had to do with the matter at issue. Procuring the original work, after some trouble, I read that "the Genoese, at this period, bought the *scorn* of all Europe by," etc., etc. Now, here the translator is by no means so much in fault as Lady Morgan, who is too prone to commit sin with the *verbum insolens*. I can see no force, here, in the unusuality of *"bought,"* as applied to scorn—(although there are cases in which the expression would be very appropriate)—and cannot condemn the Frenchman for supposing the *s* a superfluity and a misprint.

———

There is a *double entendre* in the old adage about Truth in a Well; but, taking the *profundity* of Truth as at least one of the meanings—understanding it to be implied that correct ideas on any topic are to be fished up only from great depths, and that to have common sense it is necessary to be abysmal—this being taken as the moral of the adage, I have my objections on the spot. The profundity of which so much is said, lies more frequently in the places where we seek Truth than in those where we find her. Just as the moderately-sized shop-signs are better adapted to their object than those which are Brobdignagian, so, in at least three cases out of seven, is a fact (but especially a reason) overlooked solely on account of being excessively obvious. It is almost impossible, too, to see a thing that lies immediately beneath one's nose.

I may be wrong—and no doubt I am—still it is a fancy of mine that much of what people call profundity has been fairly thrown away on that ever-recurring topic, the decline of the drama.

Were the question demanded of me—"Why has the drama

declined?" my answer should be—"It has not; it has only been left out of sight by every thing else." The dramatic art, more than any other, is essentially imitative, and thus engenders and keeps alive in its votaries the imitative propensity, as well as the imitative power. Hence one drama is apt to be fashioned too nearly after another—the dramatist of to-day is prone to step too closely in the foot-prints of the dramatist of yesterday. In a word there is less originality—less independence—less thought—less reference to principles—less effort to keep up with the general movement of the time—more supineness—more bullet-headedness—more rank and arrant conventionality in the drama than in any other single thing in existence which aspires to the dignity of Art. This spirit of imitation, developed in adherence to old, and *therefore* to uncouth models, has not, indeed, caused the drama to "decline," but has overthrown it by not permitting it to soar. While every other art* has kept pace with the thinking and improving spirit of the age, it alone has remained stationary, prating about Æschylus and the Chorus, or mouthing Euphuism because "the Old English masters" have thought proper to mouth it before. Let us imagine Bulwer to-day presenting us a novel after the model of the old novelists, or as nearly on their plan as "The Hunchback" is on the plan of "Ferrex and Porrex:"—let him write us a "Grand Cyrus," and what should we do with it, and what should we think of its inditer? And yet this "Grand Cyrus" was a very admirable work *in its day*.

The fact is, the drama is not now supported, for the simple reason that it does not deserve support. We must burn or bury the old models. We need *Art*, as Art is now beginning to be understood:—that is to say, in place of absurd conventionalities we demand *principles* founded in Nature and in common sense. The common sense even of the mob, can no longer be affronted, night after night, with impunity. If, for example, a play-wright *will* persist in making a hero deliver on the stage a soliloquy such as was soliloquized by no human being in ordinary life—ranting transcendentalism at the audience as nothing conceivable ever before ranted, short of a Piankitank candidate for Congress—splitting the ears of the

---

*Sculpture, perhaps, excepted.

house and endangering the lives of the orchestra, the while that a confidential friend who holds him by the shoulder is supposed not to hear a syllable of all that is said:—if the playwright, I say, *will* persist in perpetrating these atrocities, and a hundred worse, for no better reason than that there were people simple enough to perpetrate them five hundred years ago—if he *will* do this, and will *not* do anything else to the end of time—what right has he, I demand, to look any honest man in the face, and talk to him about what he calls "the decline of the drama?"

————

"The Alphadelphia Tocsin!"*—(Phœbus, what a name to fill the sounding trump of future fame!) and "devoted to the interest of the laboring classes!"—by which, I presume, are intended the classes who have to pronounce, every morning, the great appellation of the paper itself. Such a work should not want editors, and accordingly we are informed that it has *eight*. What on earth is the meaning of Alphadelphia? Is the "Alphadelphia Tocsin" the tocsin of the city of the double A's?—if so, the idea is too easily slipped into that of the A double S.

————

I fully agree with Simms (W. Gilmore) that the Provençal troubadour had, in his melodious vocabulary, no title more appropriate than the Cuban "Areytos" for a collection of tender or passionate songs—such as we have here.†

Passages such as this are worthy of the author of "Martin Faber:"—

> Soft, O how softly sleeping,
>   Shadowed by beauty, she lies—
> *Dreams as of rapture creeping,*
>   *Smile by smile,* over her eyes.

And this, in reference to a ship becalmed, is natural and forcible:

*Title of a new journal published at Alphadelphia, Michigan.
†"Areytos, or Songs of the South."

> A world, from all the world apart,
>   Chained idly on the sea!
> How droops the eye—how sinks the heart,
>   Vain wishing to be free!
> How dread the fear that fills the thought,
>   *That winds may never rise*
> *To waft us from this weary spot*
>   *Beneath these burning skies!*

This again is exceedingly spirited:—

> Now are the winds about us in their glee,
>   Tossing the slender tree;
> Whirling the sands about his furious car
>   March cometh from afar,
> Breaks the sealed magic of old Winter's dreams
>   And rends his glassy streams.

By the way, how happens it, in the melodious stanza which follows, (taken from an "Indian Serenade") that the sonorous *Samana* has been set aside for the far less musical and less effective *Bonita*?

> 'Tis the wail for life they waken
>   By *Bonita's silver shore*—
> With the tempest it is shaken:—
> The wide ocean is in motion,
>   And the song is heard no more.

When in the mouth of Vasco Nunez, in "The Damsel of Darien" (its author's least meritorious novel, by the bye) the line originally ran,

> By Samana's yielding shore.

Sounding shore would have been still better. Altogether I prefer this "Indian Serenade" to any of Mr. Simms' poems.

These and other imitations, however, are but the inevitable sins of the youth of genius—which invariably begins its career by imitation—an imitation, nevertheless, interspersed with vivid originality. I think I have before observed that, in letters, a copyist is, as a general rule, by no means necessarily unoriginal, except at the exact points of the copy. Mr. Simms is, beyond doubt, one of our most original writers.

————

It is really difficult to conceive what must have been the morbidity of the German intellect, or taste, when it not only tolerated but truly admired and enthusiastically applauded such an affair as "The Sorrows of Werter." The German approbation was, clearly, in good faith:—as for our own, or that of the English, it was the quintessence of affectation. Yet we did our best, as in duty bound, to work ourselves up into the fitting mood. The title, by the way, is mistranslated:— *Lieden* does not mean *Sorrows* but *Sufferings*.

————

The works of Christopher Pease Cranch are slightly tinged with the spirit of mixed Puritanism, utilitarianism, and transcendentalism, which seems to form the poetical atmosphere of Massachusetts—but, dismissing this one sin, are among the *truest* of American poetry. I know nothing finer of its kind (and that kind is a most comprehensive one) than one of his shorter pieces entitled,

MY THOUGHTS

Many are the thoughts that come to me
   In my lonely musing;
And they drift so strange and swift
   There's no time for choosing
Which to follow—for to leave
   Any seems a losing.

When they come, they come in flocks,
   As, on glancing feather,
Startled birds rise, one by one,
   In autumnal weather,
Waking one another up
   From the sheltering heather.

Some so merry that I laugh;
   Some are grave and serious;
Some so trite, their last approach

> Is enough to weary us:
> Others flit like midnight ghosts,
>   Shrouded and mysterious.
>
> There are thoughts that o'er me steal,
>   Like the day when dawning;
> Great thoughts winged with melody,
>   Common utterance scorning;
> Moving in an inward tune
>   And an inward morning.
>
> Some have dark and drooping wings,
>   Children all of sorrow;
> Some are as gay, as if to day
>   Could see no cloudy morrow—
> And yet, like light and shade, they each
>   Must from the other borrow.
>
> One by one they come to me
>   On their destined mission;
> One by one I see them fade
>   With no hopeless vision—
> For they've led me on a step
>   To their home Elysian.

There is, here, a great deal of natural fancy—I mean to say that the images are such as would naturally arise in the mind of an imaginative and educated man, seeking to describe his *"thoughts."* But the main charm of the poem is the *nice*, and at the same time, *bold* art of its rhythm. Here is no merely negative merit, but much of originality—or, if not precisely that, at least much of freshness and spirit. The opening line, barring an error to be presently mentioned, is very skilful— and, to me, the result is not less novel than happy. The general idea is merely a succession of trochees (for the long syllable, or cæsura proper, at the end of each *odd* line, is a trochee's equivalent) but, in lieu of a trochee, at the commencement of the opening verse, we have a trochee and a pyrrhic (forming the compound foot called, in Latin, *Pæon primus*, and in Greek, αστρολογος.) Here is a very bold excess

of *two* short syllables—and the result would be highly pleasurable if the reader were prepared for it—if he were prepared, my monotone, to expect variation. As it is, he is at
fault in a first attempt at perusal, and it is only on a second
or third trial, that he appreciates the effect. To be sure, he
then wonders why he did not at first catch the intention:—
but the mischief has been committed. The fact is that the line,
which would have been singularly beautiful in the body of
the poem, is in its present position, a blemish. Mr. Cranch
has violated a vital law of rhythmical art, in not permitting
his rhythm to determine itself, instantaneously, by his opening foot. A trochaic rhythm, for example, should invariably
commence with a trochee. I speak thus at length on this apparently trivial point, because I have been much interested in
the phenomenon of a marked common-place-ness of defect,
involving as marked an originality of merit.

Marginalia

GRAHAM'S MAGAZINE, *November 1846*

I HAVE just finished the "Mysteries of Paris"—a work of unquestionable power—a museum of novel and ingenious incident—a paradox of childish folly and consummate skill. It has this point in common with all the "convulsive" fictions—that the incidents are *consequential* from the premises, while the premises themselves are laughably incredible. Admitting, for instance, the possibility of such a man as Rodolphe, and of such a state of society as would tolerate his perpetual interference, we have no difficulty in agreeing to admit the possibility of his accomplishing all that is accomplished. Another point which distinguishes the Sue school, is the total want of the *ars celare artem*. In effect the writer is always saying to the reader, "Now—in one moment—you shall see what you shall see. I am about to produce on you a remarkable impression. Prepare to have your imagination, or your pity, greatly excited." The wires are not only not concealed, but displayed as things to be admired, equally with the puppets they set in motion. The result is, that in perusing, for example, a pathetic chapter in "The Mysteries of Paris" we say to ourselves, without shedding a tear—"Now, here is something which will be sure to move every reader to tears." The philosophical motives attributed to Sue are absurd in the extreme. His first, and in fact his sole object, is to make an exciting, and therefore saleable book. The cant (implied or direct) about the amelioration of society, etc., is but a very usual trick among authors, whereby they hope to add such a tone of dignity or utilitarianism to their pages as shall gild the pill of their licentiousness. The *ruse* is even more generally employed by way of engrafting a meaning upon the otherwise unintelligible. In the latter case, however, this *ruse* is an afterthought, manifested in the shape of a moral, either appended (as in Æsop) or dovetailed into the body of the work, piece by piece, with great care, but never without leaving evidence of its after-insertion.

The translation (by C. H. Town) is very imperfect, and, by a too literal rendering of idioms, contrives to destroy the whole *tone* of the original. Or, perhaps, I should say a too literal rendering of *local peculiarities of phrase*. There is one point (never yet, I believe, noticed) which, obviously, should be considered in translation. We should so render the original that *the version should impress the people for whom it is intended, just as the original impresses the people for whom it (the original) is intended.* Now, if we rigorously translate mere local idiosyncrasies of phrase (to say nothing of idioms) we inevitably distort the author's designed impression. We are sure to produce a whimsical, at least, if not always a ludicrous, effect—for novelties, in a case of this kind, are incongruities—oddities. A distinction, of course, should be observed between those peculiarities of phrase which appertain to the nation and those which belong to the author himself—for these latter will have a similar effect upon *all* nations, and should be literally translated. It is merely the general inattention to the principle here proposed, which has given rise to so much international depreciation, if not positive contempt, as regards literature. The English reviews, for example, have abundant allusions to what they call the "frivolousness" of French letters—an idea chiefly derived from the impression made by the French manner merely—this manner, again, having in it nothing *essentially* frivolous, but affecting all foreigners as such (the English especially) through that oddity of which I have already assigned the origin. The French return the compliment, complaining of the British *gaucherie* in style. The phraseology of every nation has a taint of *drollery* about it in the ears of every other nation speaking a different tongue. Now, to convey the true spirit of an author, this taint should be corrected in translation. We should pride ourselves less upon literality and more upon dexterity at paraphrase. Is it not clear that, by such dexterity, *a translation may be made to convey to a foreigner a juster conception of an original than could the original itself*?

The distinction I have made between mere idioms (which, *of course,* should never be literally rendered) and "local idiosyncrasies of *phrase*," may be exemplified by a passage at page 291 of Mr. Town's translation:

"Never mind! Go in there! You will take the cloak of Calebasse. You will wrap yourself in it," etc., etc.

These are the words of a lover to his mistress, and are meant kindly, although imperatively. They embody a local peculiarity—a *French* peculiarity of phrase, and (to French ears) convey nothing dictatorial. To our own, nevertheless, they sound like the command of a military officer to his subordinate, and thus produce an effect quite different from that intended. The translation, in such case, should be a bold paraphrase. For example:—"I must insist upon your wrapping yourself in the cloak of Calebasse."

Mr. Town's version of "The Mysteries of Paris," however, is not objectionable on the score of excessive literality alone, but abounds in misapprehensions of the author's meaning. One of the strangest errors occurs at page 368, where we read:

"From a wicked, brutal savage and riotous rascal, he has made me a kind of honest man by saying only two words to me; but these words, 'voyez vous,' were like magic."

Here "voyez vous" are made to be the two magical words spoken; but the translation should run—"these words, do you see? were like magic." The actual words described as producing the magical effect are "heart" and "honor."

Of similar character is a curious mistake at page 245.

"He is a *gueux fini* and an attack will not save him," added Nicholas. "A— yes," said the widow.

Many readers of Mr. Town's translation have no doubt been puzzled to perceive the force or relevancy of the widow's "A— yes" in this case. I have not the original before me, but take it for granted that it runs thus, or nearly so:— *"Il est un gueux fini et un assaut ne l'intimidera pas." "Un— oui!" dit la veuve.*

It must be observed that, in vivacious French colloquy, the *oui* seldom implies assent to the letter, but generally to the spirit, of a proposition. Thus a Frenchman usually says "yes" where an Englishman would say "no." The latter's reply, for example, to the sentence "An attack will not intimidate him," would be "No"—that is to say, "I grant you that it would not." The Frenchman, however, answers "Yes"—meaning, "I agree with what you say—it would not." Both replies, of course, reaching the same point, although by opposite routes. With this understanding, it will be seen that the true version of the widow's *"Un — oui!"* should be, "*One* attack, I grant you, might not," and that this *is* the version becomes apparent when we read the words immediately following—"but *every* day—*every* day it is hell!"

An instance of another class of even more reprehensible blunders, is to be found on page 297, where Bras-Rouge is made to say to a police officer—"No matter; it is not of that I complain; every trade has its *disagreements*." Here, no doubt, the French is *désagrémens*—inconveniences—disadvantages—unpleasantnesses. *Désagrémens* conveys disagreements not even so nearly as, in Latin, *religio* implies religion.

I was not a little surprised, in turning over these pages, to come upon the admirable, thrice admirable story called *"Gringalet et Coupe en Deux,"* which is related by *Pique-Vinaigre* to his companions in *La Force*. Rarely have I read any thing of which the exquisite *skill* so delighted me. For my soul I could not suggest a fault in it—except, perhaps, that the intention of telling a *very* pathetic story is a little too transparent.

But I say that I was *surprised* in coming upon this story—and I *was* so, because one of its points has been suggested to M. Sue by a tale of my own. *Coupe en Deux* has an ape remarkable for its size, strength, ferocity, and propensity to imitation. Wishing to commit a murder so cunningly that discovery would be impossible, the master of this animal teaches it to imitate the functions of a barber, and incites it to cut the throat of a child, under the idea that, when the murder is discovered, it will be considered the uninstigated deed of the ape.

On first seeing this, I felt apprehensive that some of my friends would accuse me of plagiarising from it my "Murders in the Rue Morgue." But I soon called to mind that this latter was first published in "Graham's Magazine" for April, 1841. Some years ago, "The Paris Charivari" copied my story with complimentary comments; objecting, however, to the *Rue Morgue* on the ground that no such street (to the Charivari's knowledge) existed in Paris. I do not wish, of course, to look upon M. Sue's adaptation of my property in any other light

than that of a compliment. The similarity *may* have been entirely accidental.

———

A hundred criticisms to the contrary notwithstanding, I
must regard "The Lady of Lyons" as one of the most successful dramatic efforts of modern times. It is popular, and justly
so. It could not fail to be popular so long as the people have
a heart. It abounds in sentiments which stir the soul as the
sound of a trumpet. It proceeds rapidly and consequentially;
the interest not for one moment being permitted to flag. Its
incidents are admirably conceived and skillfully wrought into
execution. Its *dramatis personæ*, throughout, have the high
merit of being natural, although, except in the case of Pauline,
there is no marked individuality. She is a creation which
would have done no dishonor to Shakspeare. She excites profound emotion. It has been sillily objected to her, that she is
weak, mercenary, and at points ignoble. She is; and what
then? We are not dealing with Clarissa Harlowe. Bulwer has
painted a woman. The chief defect of the play lies in the heroine's consenting to wed Beauseant while aware of the existence and even the continued love of Claude. As the plot
runs, there is a question in Pauline's soul between a comparatively trivial (because merely worldly) injury to her father,
and utter ruin and despair inflicted upon her husband. Here
there should not have been an instant's hesitation. The audience have no sympathy with any. Nothing on earth should
have induced the wife to give up the living Melnotte. Only
the assurance of his death could have justified her in sacrificing herself to Beauseant. As it is, we hate her for the sacrifice.
The effect is repulsive—but I must be understood as calling
this effect objectionable solely on the ground of its being at
war with the whole genius of the play.

———

One of the most singular styles in the world—certainly one
of the most loose—is that of the elder D'Israeli. For example,
he thus begins his Chapter on Bibliomania: "The preceding
article [that on Libraries] is honorable to literature." Here no
self-praise is intended. The writer means to say merely that

the facts narrated in the preceding article are honorable, etc. Three-fourths of his sentences are constructed in a similar manner. The blunders evidently arise, however, from the author's preoccupation with his subject. His thought, or rather matter, outruns his pen, and drives him upon condensation at the expense of luminousness. The manner of D'Israeli has many of the traits of Gibbon — although little of the latter's precision.

———

If need were, I should have little difficulty, perhaps, in defending a certain apparent dogmatism to which I am prone, on the topic of versification.

"What is Poetry?" notwithstanding Leigh Hunt's rigmarolic attempt at answering it, is a query that, with great care and deliberate agreement beforehand on the exact value of certain leading words, *may*, possibly, be settled to the partial satisfaction of a few analytical intellects, but which, in the existing condition of metaphysics, never *can* be settled to the satisfaction of the majority; for the question is purely metaphysical, and the whole science of metaphysics is at present a chaos, through the impossibility of fixing the meanings of the words which its very nature compels it to employ. But as regards versification, this difficulty is only partial; for although one-third of the topic may be considered metaphysical, and thus may be mooted at the fancy of this individual or of that, still the remaining two-thirds belong, undeniably, to the mathematics. The questions ordinarily discussed with so much gravity in regard to rhythm, metre, etc., are susceptible of positive adjustment by demonstration. Their laws are merely a portion of the Median laws of form and quantity — of relation. In respect, then, to any of these ordinary questions — these sillily moot points which so often arise in common criticism — the prosodist would speak as weakly in saying "this or that proposition is *probably* so and so, or *possibly* so and so," as would the mathematician in admitting that, in his humble opinion, or if he were not greatly mistaken, any two sides of a triangle were, together, greater than the third side. I must add, however, as some palliation of the discussions referred to, and of the objections so often urged with a sneer to "particular theories of versification binding no one but their inventor"—that there is really extant no such work as a Prosody *Raisonnée*. The Prosodies of the schools are merely collections of vague *laws*, with their more vague exceptions, based upon no principles whatever, but extorted in the most speculative manner from the usages of the ancients, who had *no* laws beyond those of their ears and fingers. "And these were sufficient," it will be said, "since 'The Iliad' is melodious and harmonious beyond any thing of modern times." Admit this:—but neither do we write in Greek, nor has the invention of modern times been as yet exhausted. An analysis based on the natural laws of which the bard of Scios was ignorant, would suggest multitudinous improvements to the best passages of even "The Iliad"—nor does it in any manner follow from the supposititious fact that Homer found in his ears and fingers a satisfactory system of rules (the point which I have just denied)—nor does it follow, I say, from this, that the rules which *we* deduce from the Homeric *effects* are to supersede those immutable principles of time, quantity, etc.—the mathematics, in short, of music—which must have stood to these Homeric effects in the relation of *causes*—the *mediate* causes of which these "ears and fingers" are simply the *intermedia*.

———

A book* which puzzles me beyond measure, since, while agreeing with its general conclusions, (except where it discusses *prévision*,) I invariably find fault with the reasoning through which the conclusions are attained. I think the treatise grossly illogical throughout. For example:—the origin of the work is thus stated in an introductory chapter:

"About twelve months since, I was asked by some friends to write a paper against Mesmerism—and I was furnished with materials by a highly esteemed quondam pupil, which proved incontestably that under some circumstances the operator might be duped—that hundreds of enlightened per-

———

*Human Magnetism: Its Claim to Dispassionate Inquiry. Being an Attempt to show the Utility of its Application for the Relief of Human Suffering. By W. Newnham, M. R. S. L., Author of the Reciprocal Influence of Body and Mind. Wiley & Putnam.

sons might equally be deceived—and certainly went far to show that the pretended science was wholly a delusion—a system of fraud and jugglery by which the imaginations of the credulous were held in thraldom through the arts of the designing. Perhaps in an evil hour I assented to the proposition thus made—but on reflection I found that the facts before me only led to the *direct proof* that certain phenomena might be counterfeited; and the existence of counterfeit coin is rather a proof that there is somewhere the genuine standard gold to be imitated."

The fallacy here lies in a mere variation of what is called "begging the question." Counterfeit coin is said to prove the existence of genuine:—this, of course, is no more than the truism that there can be no counterfeit where there is no genuine—just as there can be no badness where there is no goodness—the terms being purely relative. But *because* there can be no counterfeit where there is no original, does it in any manner follow that any undemonstrated original exists? In seeing a spurious coin we know it to be such by comparison with coins *admitted* to be genuine; but were *no* coin admitted to be genuine, how should we establish the counterfeit, and what right should we have to talk of counterfeits at all? Now, in the case of Mesmerism, our author is merely *begging the admission*. In saying that the existence of counterfeit proves the existence of real Mesmerism, he demands that the real *be admitted*. Either he demands this or there is no shadow of force in his proposition—for it is clear that we can *pretend to be* that which is not. A man, for instance, may feign himself a sphynx or a griffin, but it would never do to regard as thus demonstrated the actual existence of either griffins or sphynxes. A word alone—the word "counterfeit"—has been sufficient to lead Mr. Newnham astray. People cannot be properly said to "counterfeit" prévision, etc., but to *feign* these phenomena.

Dr. Newnham's argument, of course, is by no means original with *him*, although he seems to pride himself on it as if it were. Dr. More says: "That there should be so universal a fame and fear of that which never was, nor is, nor can be ever in the world, is to me the greatest miracle of all. If there had not been, at some time or other, true miracles, it had not been so easy to impose on the people by false. The alchemist would never go about to sophisticate metals, to pass them off for true gold and silver, unless that such a thing was acknowledged as true gold and silver in the world."

This is precisely the same idea as that of Dr. Newnham, and belongs to that extensive class of argumentation which is *all point*—deriving its whole effect from epigrammatism. That the belief in ghosts, or in a Deity, or in a future state, or in anything else credible or incredible—that any such belief is universal, demonstrates nothing more than that which needs no demonstration—the human unanimity—the identity of construction in the human brain—an identity of which the inevitable result must be, upon the whole, similar deductions from similar *data*.

Most especially do I disagree with the author of this book in his (implied) disparagement of the work of Chauncey Hare Townshend—a work to be valued properly only in a day to come.

Marginalia

GRAHAM'S MAGAZINE, *December 1846*

THIS BOOK* could never have been popular out of Germany. It is too simple—too direct—too obvious—too *bald*—not sufficiently complex—to be relished by any people who have *thoroughly* passed the first (or impulsive) epoch of literary civilization. The Germans have not yet passed this first epoch. It must be remembered that *during the whole of the middle ages they lived in utter ignorance of the art of writing*. From so total a darkness, of so late a date, they could not, *as a nation*, have as yet fully emerged into the second or critical epoch. Individual Germans have been critical in the best sense—but the masses are unleavened. Literary Germany thus presents the singular spectacle of the impulsive spirit surrounded by the critical, and, of course, in some measure influenced thereby. England, for example, has advanced far, and France much farther, into the critical epoch; and their effect on the German mind is seen in the wildly anomalous condition of the German literature at large. That this latter will be improved by age, however, should never be maintained. As the impulsive spirit subsides, and the critical uprises, there will appear the polished insipidity of the later England, or that ultimate *throe* of taste which has found its best exemplification in Sue. At present the German literature resembles no other on the face of the earth—for it is the result of certain conditions which, before this individual instance of their fulfillment, have never been fulfilled. And this anomalous state to which I refer is the source of our anomalous criticism upon what that state produces—is the source of the grossly conflicting opinions about German letters. For my own part, I admit the German vigor, the German directness, boldness, imagination, and some other qualities of impulse, just as I am willing to admit and admire these qualities in the first (or impulsive) epochs of British and French letters. At the German criticism, however, I cannot refrain from laughing all the more heartily, all the more seriously I hear it praised. Not

---

*"Thiodolf, the Icelander and Aslauga's Knight." No. 60 of Wiley & Putnam's Foreign Series of "The Library of Choice Reading."

that, in detail, it affects me as an absurdity—but in the adaptation of its details. It abounds in brilliant bubbles of *suggestion*, but these rise and sink and jostle each other, until the whole vortex of thought in which they originate is one indistinguishable chaos of froth. The German criticism is *unsettled*, and can only be settled by time. At present it suggests without demonstrating, or convincing, or effecting any definite purpose under the sun. We read it, rub our foreheads, and ask "What then?" I am not ashamed to say that I prefer even Voltaire to Goethe, and hold Macaulay to possess more of the true critical spirit than Augustus William and Frederick Schlegel combined.

"Thiodolf" is called by Foqué his "most *successful* work." He would not have spoken thus had he considered it his *best*. It is admirable of its kind—but its kind can *never* be appreciated by Americans. It will affect them much as would a grasp of the hand from a man of ice. Even the exquisite "Undine" is too chilly for our people, and, generally, for our epoch. We have less imagination and warmer sympathies than the age which preceded us. It would have done Foqué more ready and fuller justice than ours.

Has any one remarked the striking similarity in tone between "Undine" and the "Libussa" of Musæus?"

————

Whatever may be the merits or demerits, generally, of the Magazine Literature of America, there can be no question as to its extent or influence. The topic—Magazine Literature—is therefore an important one. In a few years its importance will be found to have increased in geometrical ratio. The whole tendency of the age is Magazine-ward. The Quarterly Reviews have *never* been popular. Not only are they too stilted, (by way of keeping up a due dignity,) but they make a point, with the same end in view, of discussing only topics which are *caviare* to the many, and which, for the most part, have only a conventional interest even with the few. Their issues, also, are at too long intervals; their subjects get cold before being served up. In a word, their ponderosity is quite out of keeping with the *rush* of the age. We now demand the light artillery of the intellect; we need the curt, the con-

densed, the pointed, the readily diffused—in place of the verbose, the detailed, the voluminous, the inaccessible. On the
other hand, the lightness of the artillery should not degenerate into popgunnery—by which term we may designate the
character of the greater portion of the newspaper press—
their sole legitimate object being the discussion of ephemeral
matters in an ephemeral manner. Whatever talent may be
brought to bear upon our daily journals, (and in many cases
this talent is very great,) still the imperative necessity of catching, *currente calamo*, each topic as it flits before the eye of the
public, must of course materially narrow the limits of their
power. The bulk and the period of issue of the monthly magazines, seem to be precisely adapted, if not to all the literary
wants of the day, at least to the largest and most imperative,
as well as the most consequential portion of them.

The chief portion of Professor Espy's theory has been anticipated by Roger Bacon.

It is a thousand pities that the puny witticisms of a few
professional objectors should have power to prevent, even for
a year, the adoption of a name for our country. At present we
have, clearly, none. There should be no hesitation about "Appalachia." In the first place, it is distinctive. "America"* is
not, and can never be made so. *We* may legislate as much as
we please, and assume for our country whatever name we
think right—but to us it will be no name, to any purpose for
which a name is needed, unless we can take it away from the
regions which employ it at present. South America is "America," and will insist upon remaining so. In the second place,
"Appalachia" is indigenous, springing from one of the most
magnificent and distinctive features of the country itself.
Thirdly, in employing this word we do honor to the Aborigines, whom, hitherto, we have at all points unmercifully de-
spoiled, assassinated and dishonored. Fourthly, the name is

*Mr. Field, in a meeting of "The New York Historical Society," proposed
that we take the name of "America," and bestow "Columbia" upon the continent.

the suggestion of, perhaps, the most deservedly eminent among all the pioneers of American literature. It is but just that Mr. Irving should name the land for which, in letters, he first established a name. The last, and by far the most truly important consideration of all, however, is the music of "Appalachia" itself; nothing could be more sonorous, more liquid, or of fuller volume, while its length is just sufficient for dignity. How the guttural "Alleghania" could ever have been preferred for a moment is difficult to conceive. I yet hope to find "Appalachia" assumed.

————

That man is not truly brave who is afraid either to seem or to be, when it suits him, a coward.

————

About the "Antigone," as about all the ancient plays, there seems to me a certain *baldness*, the result of inexperience in art, but which pedantry would force us to believe the result of a studied and supremely artistic simplicity. Simplicity, indeed, is a very important feature in all true art—but *not* the simplicity which we see in the Greek drama. That of the Greek sculpture is every thing that can be desired, because here the art in itself is simplicity in itself and in its elements. The Greek sculptor chiseled his forms from what he saw before him every day, in a beauty nearer to perfection than any work of any Cleomenes in the world. But in the drama, the direct, straight-forward, *un-German* Greek had no Nature so immediately presented from which to make copy. He did what he could—but I do not hesitate to say that that was exceedingly little worth. The profound sense of one or two tragic, or rather, melo-dramatic elements (such as the idea of inexorable Destiny)—this sense gleaming at intervals from out the darkness of the ancient stage, serves, in the very imperfection of its development, to show, not the dramatic ability, but the dramatic inability of the ancients. In a word, the simple arts spring into perfection at their origin; the complex as inevitably demand the long and painfully progressive experience of ages. To the Greeks, beyond doubt, their drama *seemed* perfection—it fully answered, to them, the dramatic end, excitement—and this fact is urged as proof of their drama's perfection in itself. It need only be said, in reply, that their art and their sense of art were, necessarily, on a level.

———

The more there are great excellences in a work, the less am I surprised at finding great demerits. When a book is said to have many faults, nothing is decided, and I cannot tell, by this, whether it is excellent or execrable. It is said of another that it is without fault; if the account be just, the work *cannot* be excellent.—*Trublet.*

The *"cannot"* here is much too positive. The opinions of Trublet are wonderfully prevalent, but they are none the less demonstrably false. It is merely the *indolence* of genius which has given them currency. The truth seems to be that genius of the highest order lives in a state of perpetual vacillation between ambition and *the scorn of it.* The ambition of a great intellect is at best negative. It struggles—it labors—it creates—not because excellence is desirable, but because to be excelled where there exists a sense of the power to excel, is unendurable. Indeed I cannot help thinking that the *greatest* intellects (since these most clearly perceive the laughable absurdity of human ambition) remain contentedly "mute and inglorious." At all events, the *vacillation* of which I speak is the prominent feature of genius. Alternately inspired and depressed, its inequalities of mood are stamped upon its labors. This is the truth, generally—but it is a truth very different from the assertion involved in the "cannot" of Trublet. Give to genius a sufficiently enduring *motive*, and the result will be harmony, proportion, beauty, perfection—all, in this case, synonymous terms. Its supposed "inevitable" irregularities shall not be found:—for it is clear that the susceptibility to impressions of beauty—that susceptibility which is the most important element of genius—implies an equally exquisite sensitiveness and aversion to deformity. The motive—the *enduring* motive—has indeed, hitherto, fallen *rarely* to the lot of genius; but I could point to several compositions which, "without any fault," are yet "excellent"—supremely so. The world, too, is on the threshold of an epoch, wherein, with the aid of a calm philosophy, such compositions shall be ordinarily the work of that genius which is *true*. One of the first and most essential steps, in overpassing this threshold, will serve to kick out of the world's way this very idea of Trublet—this untenable and paradoxical idea of the incompatibility of genius with *art*.

————

When I consider the true talent—the real force of Mr. Emerson, I am lost in amazement at finding in him little more than a respectful imitation of Carlyle. Is it possible that Mr. E. has ever seen a copy of Seneca? Scarcely—or he would long ago have abandoned his model in utter confusion at the parallel between his own worship of the author of "Sartor Resartus" and the aping of Sallust by Aruntius, as described in the 114th Epistle. In the writer of the "History of the Punic Wars" Emerson is portrayed to the life. The parallel is close; for not only is the imitation of the same character, but the things imitated are identical.

Undoubtedly it is to be said of Sallust, far more plausibly than of Carlyle, that his obscurity, his unusuality of expression, and his Laconism (which had the effect of diffuseness, since the time gained in the mere perusal of his pithiness is trebly lost in the necessity of cogitating them out)—it may be said of Sallust, more truly than of Carlyle, that these qualities bore the impress of his genius, and were but a portion of his unaffected thought.

If there is any difference between Aruntius and Emerson, this difference is clearly in favor of the former, who was in some measure excusable, on the ground that he was as great a fool as the latter *is not*.

Marginalia

GRAHAM'S MAGAZINE, *January 1848*

WE MERE MEN of the world, with no principle—a very old-fashioned and cumbersome thing—should be on our guard lest, fancying him on his last legs, we insult, or otherwise maltreat some poor devil of a genius at the very instant of his putting his foot on the top round of his ladder of triumph. It is a common trick with these fellows, when on the point of attaining some long-cherished end, to sink themselves into the deepest possible abyss of seeming despair, for no other purpose than that of increasing the space of success through which they have made up their minds immediately to soar.

———

All that the man of genius demands for his exaltation is moral matter in motion. It makes no difference *whither* tends the motion—whether for him or against him—and it is absolutely of *no* consequence "*what* is the matter."

———

In Colton's "American Review" for October, 1845, a gentleman, well known for his scholarship, has a forcible paper on "The Scotch School of Philosophy and Criticism." But although the paper is "forcible," it presents the most singular admixture of error and truth—the one dovetailed into the other, after a fashion which is novel, to say the least of it. Were I to designate in a few words what the whole article demonstrated, I should say "the folly of not beginning at the beginning—of neglecting the giant Moulineau's advice to his friend Ram." Here is a passage from the essay in question:

"The Doctors [Campbell and Johnson] both charge Pope with error and inconsistency:—error in supposing that *in English*, of metrical lines unequal in the number of syllables and pronounced in equal times, the longer suggests celerity (this being the principle of the Alexandrine:)—inconsistency, in that Pope himself uses the same contrivance to convey the contrary idea of slowness. But why in English? It is not and cannot be disputed that, in the Hexameter verse of the Greeks and Latins—which is the model in this matter—what is distinguished as the 'dactylic line' was uniformly applied to express velocity. How was it to do so? Simply from the fact of being pronounced in an equal time with, while containing a greater number of syllables or 'bars' than the ordinary or average measure; as, on the other hand, the spondaic line, composed of the minimum number, was, upon the same principle, used to indicate slowness. So, too, of the Alexandrine in English versification. No, says Campbell, there is a difference: the Alexandrine is not in fact, like the dactylic line, pronounced in the common time. But does this alter the principle? What is the rationale of Metre, whether the classical hexameter or the English heroic?"

I have written an essay on the "Rationale of Verse," in which the whole topic is surveyed *ab initio*, and with reference to general and immutable principles. To this essay (which will soon appear) I refer Mr. Bristed. In the meantime, without troubling myself to ascertain whether Doctors Johnson and Campbell are wrong, or whether Pope is wrong, or whether the reviewer is right or wrong, at this point or at that, let me succinctly state what is *the truth* on the topics at issue.

And first; the same principles, in *all* cases, govern *all* verse. What is true in English is true in Greek.

Secondly; in a series of lines, if one line contains more syllables than the law of the verse demands, and if, nevertheless, this line is pronounced in the same time, upon the whole, as the rest of the lines, then this line suggests celerity—on account of the increased rapidity of enunciation required. Thus in the Greek Hexameter the dactylic lines—those most abounding in dactyls—serve best to convey the idea of rapid motion. The spondaic lines convey that of slowness.

Thirdly; it is a gross mistake to suppose that the Greek dactylic line is "the model in this matter"—the matter of the English Alexandrine. The Greek dactylic line is of the same number of feet—bars—beats—pulsations—as the ordinary dactylic-spondaic lines among which it occurs. But the Alexandrine is longer by one foot—by one pulsation—than the pentameters among which it arises. For its pronunciation it demands *more time*, and therefore, *ceteris paribus*, it would well serve to convey the impression of length, or duration, and thus, indirectly, of slowness. I say *ceteris paribus*. But, by varying conditions, we can effect a total change in the impression conveyed. When the idea of slowness is conveyed by the Alexandrine, it is not conveyed by any slower enunciation of syllables—that is to say, it is not *directly* conveyed—but indirectly, through the idea of *length* in the whole line. Now, if we wish to convey, by means of an Alexandrine, the impression of velocity, we readily do so by giving rapidity to our enunciation of the syllables composing the several feet. To effect this, however, we must have *more* syllables, or we shall get through the whole line too quickly for the intended time. To get more syllables, all we have to do, is to use, in place of iambuses, what our prosodies call anapæsts* Thus, in the line,

Flies o'er the unbending corn and skims along the main,

the syllables *"the unbend"* form an anapæst and, demanding unusual rapidity of enunciation, in order that we may get them in the ordinary time of an iambus, serve to suggest celerity. By the elision of *e* in *the*, as is customary, the whole of the intended effect is lost; for *th'unbend* is nothing more than the usual iambus. In a word, wherever an Alexandrine expresses celerity, we shall find it to contain one or more anapæsts—the more anapæsts, the more decided the impression. But the tendency of the Alexandrine consisting merely of the usual iambuses, is to convey slowness—although it conveys this idea feebly, on account of conveying it indirectly. It follows, from what I have said, that the common pentameter, interspersed with anapæsts, would better convey celerity than the Alexandrine interspersed with them in a similar degree;—and it unquestionably does.

*I use the prosodial word "anapæst," merely because here I have no space to show what the reviewer will admit I have distinctly shown in the essay referred to—viz: that the additional syllable introduced, does *not* make the foot an anapæst, or the equivalent of an anapæst, and that, if it did, it would spoil the line. On this topic, and on all topics connected with verse, there is not a prosody in existence which is not a mere jumble of the grossest error.

———

To converse well, we need the cool tact of talent—to talk well, the glowing *abandon* of genius. Men of *very* high genius, however, talk at one time *very* well, at another *very* ill:—well, when they have full time, full scope, and a sympathetic listener:—ill, when they fear interruption and are annoyed by the impossibility of exhausting the topic during that particular talk. The partial genius is flashy—scrappy. The true genius shudders at incompleteness—imperfection—and usually prefers silence to saying the something which is not every thing that should be said. He is so filled with his theme that he is dumb, first from not knowing how to begin, where there seems eternally beginning behind beginning, and secondly from perceiving his true end at so infinite a distance. Sometimes, dashing into a subject, he blunders, hesitates, stops short, sticks fast, and, because he has been overwhelmed by the rush and multiplicity of his thoughts, his hearers sneer at his inability to think. Such a man finds his proper element in those "great occasions" which confound and prostrate the general intellect.

Nevertheless, by his conversation, the influence of the conversationist upon mankind in general, is more decided than that of the talker by his talk:—the latter invariably talks to best purpose with his pen. And good conversationists are more rare than respectable talkers. I know many of the latter; and of the former only five or six:—among whom I can call to mind, just now, Mr. Willis, Mr. J. T. S. S.—of Philadelphia, Mr. W. M. R.—of Petersburg, Va., and Mrs. S——d, formerly of New York. Most people, in conversing, force us to curse our stars that our lot was not cast among the African nation mentioned by Eudoxus—the savages who, having no mouths, never opened them, as a matter of course. And yet, if denied mouth, some persons whom I have in my eye would contrive to chatter on still—as they do now—through the nose.

———

> All in a hot and copper sky
>   The bloody sun at noon
> Just up above the mast did stand,
>   No bigger than the moon.—COLERIDGE.

Is it possible that the poet did not know the apparent diameter of the moon to be greater than that of the sun?

———

If any ambitious man have a fancy to revolutionize, at one effort, the universal world of human thought, human opinion, and human sentiment, the opportunity is his own—the road to immortal renown lies straight, open, and unencumbered before him. All that he has to do is to write and publish a very little book. Its title should be simple—a few plain words—"My Heart Laid Bare." But—this little book must be *true to its title*.

Now, is it not very singular that, with the rabid thirst for notoriety which distinguishes so many of mankind—so many, too, who care not a fig what is thought of them after death, there should not be found one man having sufficient hardihood to write this little book? To *write*, I say. There are ten thousand men who, if the book were once written, would laugh at the notion of being disturbed by its publication during their life, and who could not even conceive *why* they should object to its being published after their death. But to write it— *there* is the rub. No man dare write it. No man ever will dare write it. No man *could* write it, even if he dared. The paper would shrivel and blaze at every touch of the fiery pen.

———

For all the rhetorician's rules
Teach nothing but to name the tools.—HUDIBRAS.

What these oft-quoted lines go to show is, that a falsity in verse will travel faster and endure longer than a falsity in prose. The man who would sneer or stare at a silly proposition nakedly put, will admit that "there is a good deal in that" when *"that"* is the point of an epigram shot into the ear. The rhetorician's rules—if they *are* rules—teach him not only to name his tools, but to use his tools, the capacity of his tools—their extent—their limit; and from an examination of the nature of the tools—(an examination forced on him by their constant presence)—force him, also, into scrutiny and comprehension of the material on which the tools are employed, and thus, finally, suggest and give birth to new material for new tools.

———

Among his *eidola* of the den, the tribe, the forum, the theatre, etc., Bacon might well have placed the great *eidolon* of the parlor (or of the wit, as I have termed it in one of the previous Marginalia)—the idol whose worship blinds man to truth by dazzling him with the *apposite*. But what title could have been invented for *that* idol which has propagated, perhaps, more of gross error than all combined?—the one, I mean, which demands from its votaries that they reciprocate cause and effect—reason in a circle—lift themselves from the ground by pulling up their pantaloons—and carry themselves on their own heads, in hand-baskets, from Beersheba to Dan.

All—absolutely all the argumentation which I have seen on the nature of the soul, or of the Diety, seems to me nothing but worship of this unnameable idol. *Pour savoir ce qu'est Dieu*, says Bielfeld, although nobody listens to the solemn truth, *il faut être Dieu même*—and to reason about the reason is of all things the most unreasonable. At least, he alone is fit to discuss the topic who perceives at a glance the insanity of its discussion.

Marginalia

GRAHAM'S MAGAZINE, *February 1848*

THAT PUNCTUATION is important all agree; but how few comprehend the extent of its importance! The writer who neglects punctuation, or mis-punctuates, is liable to be misunderstood—this, according to the popular idea, is the sum of the evils arising from heedlessness or ignorance. It does not seem to be known that, even where the sense is perfectly clear, a sentence may be deprived of half its force—its spirit—its point—by improper punctuation. For the want of merely a comma, it often occurs that an axiom appears a paradox, or that a sarcasm is converted into a ser-monoid.

There is *no* treatise on the topic—and there is no topic on which a treatise is more needed. There seems to exist a vulgar notion that the subject is one of pure conventionality, and cannot be brought within the limits of intelligible and consistent *rule*. And yet, if fairly looked in the face, the whole matter is so plain that its *rationale* may be read as we run. If not anticipated, I shall, hereafter, make an attempt at a magazine paper on "The Philosophy of Point."

In the meantime let me say a word or two of *the dash*. Every writer for the press, who has any sense of the accurate, must have been frequently mortified and vexed at the distortion of his sentences by the printer's now general substitution of a semicolon, or comma, for the dash of the MS. The total or nearly total disuse of the latter point, has been brought about by the revulsion consequent upon its excessive employment about twenty years ago. The Byronic poets were *all* dash. John Neal, in his earlier novels, exaggerated its use into the grossest abuse—although his very error arose from the philosophical and self-dependent spirit which has always distinguished him, and which will even yet lead him, if I am not greatly mistaken in the man, to do something for the literature of the country which the country " will not willingly," and cannot possibly, "let die."

Without entering now into the *why*, let me observe that the printer may always ascertain when the dash of the MS. is properly and when improperly employed, by bearing in mind that this point represents *a second thought—an emendation*. In using it just above I have exemplified its use. The words "an emendation" are, speaking with reference to grammatical construction, put in *ap*position with the words "a second thought." Having written these latter words, I reflected whether it would not be possible to render their meaning more distinct by certain other words. Now, instead of erasing the phrase "a second thought," which is of *some* use—which *partially* conveys the idea intended—which advances me *a step toward* my full purpose—I suffer it to remain, and merely put a dash between it and the phrase "an emendation." The dash gives the reader a choice between two, or among three or more expressions, one of which may be more forcible than another, but all of which help out the idea. It stands, in general, for these words—*"or, to make my meaning more distinct."* This force *it has*—and this force no other point can have; since all other points have well-understood uses quite different from this. Therefore, the dash *cannot* be dispensed with.

It has its phases—its variation of the force described; but the one principle—that of second thought or emendation—will be found at the bottom of all.

In a reply to a letter signed "Outis," and defending Mr. Longfellow from certain charges supposed to have been made against him by myself, I took occasion to assert that "of the class of willful plagiarists nine out of ten are authors of established reputation who plunder recondite, neglected, or forgotten books." I came to this conclusion *à priori*; but experience has confirmed me in it. Here is a plagiarism from Channing; and as it is perpetrated by an anonymous writer in a Monthly Magazine, the theft seems at war with my assertion—until it is seen that the Magazine in question is Campbell's New Monthly for *August, 1828*. Channing, at that time, was comparatively unknown; and, besides, the plagiarism appeared in a foreign country, where there was little probability of detection.

Channing, in his essay on Bonaparte, says:

"We would observe that military talent, even of the highest order, is far from holding the first place among intellectual endowments. It is one of the lower forms of genius, for it is not conversant with the highest and richest objects of thought. . . . Still the chief work of a general is to apply physical force—to remove physical obstructions—to avail himself of physical aids and advantages—to act on matter—to overcome rivers, ramparts, mountains, and human muscles; and these are not the highest objects of mind, nor do they demand intelligence of the highest order:—and accordingly nothing is more common than to find men, eminent in this department, who are almost wholly wanting in the noblest energies of the soul—in imagination and taste—in the capacity of enjoying works of genius—in large views of human nature—in the moral sciences—in the application of analysis and generalization to the human mind and to society, and in original conceptions on the great subjects which have absorbed the most glorious understandings."

The thief in "The New Monthly," says:

"Military talent, even of the highest *grade*, is *very* far from holding the first place among intellectual endowments. It is one of the lower forms of genius, for it is *never made* conversant with the *more delicate and abstruse of mental operations*. It is used to apply physical force; to remove physical force; to remove physical obstructions; to avail itself of physical aids and advantages; and all these are not the highest objects of mind, nor do they demand intelligence of the highest *and rarest* order. Nothing is more common than to find men, eminent in the science and practice of war, *wholly* wanting in the nobler energies of the soul; in imagination, in taste, in *enlarged* views of human nature, in the moral sciences, in the application of analysis and generalization to the human mind and to society; or in original conceptions on the great subjects which have *occupied and* absorbed the most glorious *of human* understandings."

The article in "The New Monthly" is on "The State of Parties." The italics are mine.

Apparent plagiarisms frequently arise from an author's self-repetition. He finds that something he has already published has fallen dead—been overlooked—or that it is peculiarly *àpropos* to another subject now under discussion. He therefore introduces the passage; often without allusion to his having printed it before; and sometimes he introduces it into an anonymous article. An anonymous writer is thus, now and then, unjustly accused of plagiarism—when the sin is merely that of self-repetition.

In the present case, however, there has been a deliberate plagiarism of the silliest as well as meanest species. Trusting to the obscurity of his original, the plagiarist has fallen upon the idea of killing two birds with one stone—of dispensing with all disguise but that of *decoration*.

Channing says "order"—the writer in the New Monthly says "grade." The former says that this order is "far from holding," etc.—the latter says it is "*very* far from holding." The one says that military talent is "*not* conversant," and so on—the other says "it is *never made* conversant." The one speaks of "the highest and richest objects"—the other of "the more delicate and abstruse." Channing speaks of "thought"—the thief of "mental operations." Channing mentions "intelligence of the *highest* order"—the thief will have it of "the highest *and rarest*." Channing observes that military talent is often "*almost* wholly wanting," etc.—the thief maintains it to be "*wholly* wanting." Channing alludes to "*large* views of human nature"—the thief can be content with nothing less than "enlarged" ones. Finally, the American having been satisfied with a reference to "subjects which have absorbed the most glorious understandings," the Cockney puts him to shame at once by discoursing about "subjects which have *occupied and* absorbed the most glorious *of human* understandings"—as if one could be absorbed, without being occupied, by a subject—as if "*of*" were here any thing more than two superfluous letters—and as if there were any chance of the reader's supposing that the understandings in question were the understandings of frogs, or jackasses, or Johnny Bulls.

By the way, in a case of this kind, whenever there is a question as to who is the original and who the plagiarist, the point may be determined, almost invariably, by observing which passage is amplified, or exaggerated, in tone. To disguise his stolen horse, the uneducated thief cuts off the tail; but the educated thief prefers tying on a new tail at the end of the old one, and painting them both sky blue.

———

After reading all that has been written, and after thinking all that can be thought, on the topics of God and the soul, the man who has a right to say that he thinks at all, will find himself face to face with the conclusion that, on these topics, the most profound thought is that which can be the least easily distinguished from the most superficial sentiment.

Marginalia

ONE OF the happiest examples, in a small way, of the car-
rying-one's-self-in-a-hand-basket logic, is to be found in
a London weekly paper called "The Popular Record of Modern Science; a Journal of Philosophy and General Information." This work has a vast circulation, and is respected by
eminent men. Sometime in November, 1845, it copied from
the "Columbian Magazine" of New York, a rather adventurous article of mine, called "Mesmeric Revelation." It had the
impudence, also, to spoil the title by improving it to "The
Last Conversation of a Somnambule"—a phrase that is nothing at all to the purpose, since the person who "converses" is
not a somnambule. He is a sleep-waker—*not* a sleep-walker;
but I presume that "The Record" thought it was only the
difference of an *l*. What I chiefly complain of, however, is
that the London editor prefaced my paper with these
words:—"The following is an article communicated to the
Columbian Magazine, a journal of respectability and influence
in the United States, by Mr. Edgar A. Poe. *It bears internal
evidence of authenticity.*"!

There is no subject under heaven about which funnier ideas
are, in general, entertained than about this subject of internal
evidence. It is by "internal evidence," observe, that we decide
upon the mind.

But to "The Record:"—On the issue of my "Valdemar
Case," this journal copies it, as a matter of course, and (also
as a matter of course) improves the title, as in the previous
instance. But the editorial comments may as well be called
profound. Here they are:

"The following narrative appears in a recent number of *The
American Magazine*, a respectable periodical in the United
States. It comes, it will be observed, from the narrator of the
'Last Conversation of a Somnambule,' published in The Rec-
ord of the 29th of November. In extracting this case the
Morning Post of Monday last, takes what it considers the safe
side, by remarking—'For our own parts we do not believe it;

and there are several statements made, more especially with regard to the disease of which the patient died, which at once prove the case to be either a fabrication, or the work of one little acquainted with consumption. The story, however, is wonderful, and we therefore give it.' The editor, however, does not point out the especial statements which are inconsistent with what we know of the progress of consumption, and as few scientific persons would be willing to take their pathology anymore than their logic from the *Morning Post*, his caution, it is to be feared, will not have much weight. The reason assigned by the Post for publishing the account is quaint, and would apply equally to an adventure from Baron Munchausen: — 'it is wonderful and we therefore give it.' . . . The above case is obviously one that cannot be received except on the strongest testimony, and it is equally clear that the testimony by which it is at present accompanied, is not of that character. The most favorable circumstances in support of it, consist in the fact that credence is understood to be given to it at New York, within a few miles of which city the affair took place, and where consequently the most ready means must be found for its authentication or disproval. The initials of the medical men and of the young medical student must be sufficient in the immediate locality, to establish their identity, especially as M. Valdemar was well known, and had been so long ill as to render it out of the question that there should be any difficulty in ascertaining the names of the physicians by whom he had been attended. In the same way the nurses and servants under whose cognizance the case must have come during the seven months which it occupied, are of course accessible to all sorts of inquiries. It will, therefore, appear that there must have been too many parties concerned to render prolonged deception practicable. The angry excitement and various rumors which have at length rendered a public statement necessary, are also sufficient to show that *something* extraordinary must have taken place. On the other hand there is no strong point for disbelief. The circumstances are, as the Post says, ' wonderful;' but so are all circumstances that come to our knowledge for the first time — and in Mesmerism every thing is new. An objection may be made that the article has rather a Magazinish air; Mr. Poe having evidently written with a view to effect, and so as to excite rather than to subdue the vague appetite for the mysterious and the horrible which such a case, under any circumstances, is sure to awaken—but apart from this there is nothing to deter a philosophic mind from further inquiries regarding it. It is a matter entirely for testimony. [So it is.] Under this view we shall take steps to procure from some of the most intelligent and influential citizens of New York all the evidence that can be had upon the subject. No steamer will leave England for America till the 3d of February, but within a few weeks of that time we doubt not it will be possible to lay before the readers of the *Record* information which will enable them to come to a pretty accurate conclusion."

Yes; and no doubt they came to one accurate enough, in the end. But all this rigmarole is what people call testing a thing by "internal evidence." The *Record* insists upon the truth of the story because of certain facts—because "the initials of the young men *must* be sufficient to establish their identity"—because "the nurses *must* be accessible to all sorts of inquiries"—and because the "angry excitement and various rumors which at length rendered a public statement necessary, are sufficient to show that *something* extraordinary *must* have taken place."

To be sure! The story is proved by these facts—the facts about the students, the nurses, the excitement, the credence given the tale at New York. And now all we have to do is to prove these facts. Ah!—*they* are proved *by the story*.

As for the *Morning Post*, it evinces more weakness in its disbelief than the *Record* in its credulity. What the former says about doubting on account of inaccuracy in the detail of the phthisical symptoms, is a mere *fetch*, as the Cockneys have it, in order to make a very few little children believe that it, the Post, is not quite so stupid as a post proverbially is. It knows nearly as much about pathology as it does about English grammar—and I really hope it will not feel called upon to blush at the compliment. I represented the symptoms of M. Valdemar as "severe," to be sure. I put an extreme case; for it was necessary that I should leave on the reader's mind no doubt as to the certainty of death without the aid of the Mesmerist — but such symptoms *might* have appeared — the identical symptoms *have appeared*, and will be presented again and again. Had the Post been only half as honest as ignorant, it would have owned that it disbelieved for no reason more profound than that which influences all dunces in disbelieving — it would have owned that it doubted the thing merely because the thing was a " wonderful" thing, and had never yet been printed in a book.

Marginalia

SOUTHERN LITERARY MESSENGER, *April 1849*

I DO NOT BELIEVE that the whole world of Poetry can produce a more intensely energetic passage, of equal length,
than the following, from Mrs. Browning's "Drama of Exile."
The picturesque vigor of the lines italicized is much more
than Homeric:

> ——On a mountain peak
> Half sheathed in primal woods and glittering
> *In spasms of awful sunshine*, at that hour
> A Lion couched, part raised upon his paws
> With his calm massive face turned full on mine
> *And his mane listening*. When the ended curse
> Left silence in the world, right suddenly
> He sprang up rampant, and stood straight and stiff,
> *As if the new reality of Death*
> *Were dashed against his eyes*, and roared so fierce—
> (*Such thick carniverous passion in his throat*
> *Tearing a passage through the wrath and fear*)
> And roared so wild, and smote from all the hills
> Such fast keen *echoes crumbling down the vales*
> *To distant silence*—that the forest beasts,
> One after one, did mutter a response
> In savage and in sorrowful complaint
> *Which trailed along the gorges*.

There are few cases in which mere popularity should be
considered a proper test of merit; but the case of song-writing is, I think, one of the few. In speaking of song-writing,
I mean, of course, the composition of brief poems with an
eye to their adaptation for music in the vulgar sense. In this
ultimate destination of the song proper, lies its essence—its
genius. It is the strict reference to music—it is the dependence upon modulated expression—which gives to this
branch of letters a character altogether *unique*, and separates
it, in great measure and in a manner not sufficiently considered, from ordinary literature; rendering it independent of

merely ordinary proprieties; allowing it, and in fact demanding for it, a wide latitude of Law; absolutely insisting upon a certain wild license and *indefinitiveness*—an indefinitiveness recognized by every musician who is not a mere fiddler, as an important point in the philosophy of his science—as the *soul*, indeed, of the sensations derivable from its practice—sensations which bewilder while they enthral—and which would *not* so enthral if they did not so bewilder.

The sentiments deducible from the conception of sweet sound simply, are out of the reach of analysis—although referable, possibly, in their last result, to that merely mathematical recognition of *equality* which seems to be *the root of all Beauty*. Our impressions of harmony and melody in conjunction, are more readily analyzed; but one thing is certain—that the *sentimental* pleasure derivable from music, is nearly in the ratio of its indefinitiveness. Give to music any undue *decision*—imbue it with any very *determinate* tone—and you deprive it, at once, of its ethereal, its ideal, and, I sincerely believe, of its intrinsic and essential character. You dispel its dream-like luxury:—you dissolve the atmosphere of the mystic in which its whole nature is bound up:—you exhaust it of its breath of faery. It then becomes a tangible and easily appreciable thing—a conception of the earth, earthy. It will not, to be sure, lose *all* its power to please, but all that I consider the *distinctiveness* of that power. And to the *over*-cultivated talent, or to the unimaginative apprehension, this deprivation of its most delicate *nare* will be, not unfrequently, a recommendation. A *determinateness* of expression is sought—and sometimes by composers who should know better—is sought as a beauty, rather than rejected as a blemish. Thus we have, even from high authorities, attempts at absolute *imitation* in musical sounds. Who can forget, or cease to regret, the many errors of this kind into which some great minds have fallen, simply through over-estimating the triumphs of *skill*. Who can help lamenting the Battles of Pragues? What man of taste is not ready to laugh, or to weep, over their "guns, drums, trumpets, blunderbusses and thunder?" "Vocal music," says L'Abbaté Gravina, "ought to imitate the natural language of the human feelings and passions, rather than the warblings of Canary birds, which our singers, now-a-days, affect so vastly to mimic with their quaverings and boasted cadences." This is true only so far as the "rather" is concerned. If *any* music must imitate *any thing*, it were, undoubtedly, better that the imitation should be limited as Gravina suggests.

That *indefinitiveness* which is, at least, *one* of the essentials of true music, must, of course, be kept in view by the song-writer; while, by the critic, it should always be considered in his estimate of the *song*. It is, in the author, a consciousness—sometimes merely an instinctive appreciation, of this necessity for the indefinite, which imparts to all songs, rightly conceived, that free, affluent, and *hearty* manner, little scrupulous about niceties of phrase, which cannot be better expressed than by the hackneyed French word *abandonnement*, and which is so strikingly exemplified in both the serious and joyous ballads and carols of our old English progenitors. Wherever verse has been found most strictly married to music, this feature prevails. It is thus the essence of all antique song. It is the soul of Homer. It is the spirit of Anacreon. It is even the genius of Æschylus. Coming down to our own times, it is the vital principle in De Béranger. Wanting this quality, no song-writer was ever truly popular, and, for the reasons assigned, no song-writer need ever expect to be so.

These views properly understood, it will be seen how baseless are the ordinary objections to songs proper, on the score of "conceit," (to use Johnson's word,) or of hyperbole, or on various other grounds tenable enough in respect to poetry not designed for music. The "conceit," for example, which some envious rivals of *Morris* have so much objected to—

> Her heart and morning broke together
> In the storm—

this "conceit" is merely in keeping with the essential spirit of the song proper. To all reasonable persons it will be sufficient to say that the fervid, hearty, free-spoken songs of Cowley and of Donne—more especially of Cunningham, of Harrington and of Carew—abound in precisely similar things; and that they are to be met with, plentifully, in the polished pages of Moore and of Béranger, who introduce them with thought and retain them after mature deliberation.

Morris is, very decidedly, our best writer of songs—and, in saying this, I mean to assign him a high rank as *poet*. For my own part, I would much rather have written the best *song* of a nation than its noblest *epic*. One or two of Hoffman's songs have merit—but they are sad echoes of Moore, and even if this were not so (every body knows that it *is* so) they are totally deficient in the real song-essence. *"Woodman Spare that Tree"* and *"By the Lake where droops the Willow"* are compositions of which any poet, living or dead, might justly be proud. By these, if by nothing else, Morris is *immortal*. It is quite impossible to put down such things by sneers. The affectation of contemning them is of no avail—unless to render manifest the envy of those who affect the contempt. As mere *poems*, there are several of Morris's compositions equal, if not superior, to either of those just mentioned, but as *songs* I much doubt whether these latter have ever been surpassed. In quiet grace and un-affected tenderness, I know no American poem which excels the following:

> Where Hudson's wave o'er silvery sands
>   Winds through the hills afar,
> Old Crow-nest like a monarch stands,
>   Crowned with a single star.
> And there, amid the billowy swells
>   Of rock-ribbed, cloud-capped earth,
> My fair and gentle Ida dwells,
>   A nymph of mountain birth.
>
> The snow-flake that the cliff receives—
>   The diamonds of the showers—
> Spring's tender blossoms, buds and leaves—
>   The sisterhood of flowers—
> Morn's early beam—eve's balmy breeze—
>   Her purity define:—
> But Ida's dearer far than these
>   To this fond breast of mine.

My heart is on the hills; the shades
    Of night are on my brow.
Ye pleasant haunts and silent glades
    My soul is with you now.
I bless the star-crowned Highlands where
    My Ida's footsteps roam:—
Oh, for a falcon's wing to bear—
    To bear me to my home.

———

A capital book, generally speaking;* but Mr. Grattan has a bad habit—that of loitering in the road—of dallying and toying with his subjects, as a kitten with a mouse—instead of grasping it firmly at once and eating it up without more ado. He takes up too much time in the ante-room. He has never done with his introductions. Occasionally, one introduction is but the vestibule to another; so that by the time he arrives at his main incidents there is nothing more to tell. He seems afflicted with that curious yet common perversity observed in garrulous old women—the desire of tantalizing by circumlocution. Mr. G's circumlocution, however, is by no means like that which Albany Fonblanque describes as "a style of about and about and all the way round to nothing and nonsense." . . . . . If the greasy-looking lithograph here given as a frontispiece, be meant for Mr. Grattan, then is Mr. Grattan like nobody else:—for the fact is, I never yet knew an individual with a wire wig, or the countenance of an under-done apple dumpling. . . . . As a general rule, no man should put his own face in his own book. In looking at the author's countenance the reader is seldom in condition to keep his own.

———

In a "Hymn for Christmas," by Mrs. Hemans, we find the following stanza:

Oh, lovely voices of the sky
    Which hymned the Saviour's birth,
Are ye not singing still on high,
    Ye that sang "Peace on Earth"?

*"Highways and By-ways."

To us yet speak the strains
    Wherewith, in times gone by,
Ye blessed the Syrian swains,
    Oh, voices of the sky!

And at page 305 of "The Christian Keepsake and Missionary Annual for 1840"—a Philadelphian Annual—we find "A
Christmas Carol," by Richard W. Dodson:—the first stanza
running thus:

Angel voices of the sky!
    Ye that hymned Messiah's birth,
Sweetly singing from on high
    "Peace, Goodwill to all on earth!"
Oh, to us impart those strains!
    Bid our doubts and fears to cease!
Ye that cheered the Syrian swains,
    Cheer us with that song of peace!

A book* remarkable for its artistic unity. It is to be commended, also, on higher grounds. I do not think, indeed, that
a better novel of its kind has been composed by an American.
To be sure, it is not precisely the work to place in the hands
of a lady; but its incidents are striking and original, its scenes
of passion nervously wrought, and its philosophy, if not at all
times tenable, at least admirable on the important scores of
suggestiveness and audacity. In a word, it is that rare thing a
fiction of *power* without rudeness. Its spirit, in general, resembles that of Reynolds' "Miserrimus."

———

Had the "George Balcombe" of Professor Beverley Tucker
been the work of any one born North of Mason and Dixon's
line, it would have been long ago recognized as one of the
very noblest fictions ever written by an American. It is almost
as good as "Caleb Williams." The manner in which the cabal
of the "North American Review" first write all our books and
then review them, puts me in mind of the fable about the

*"Confessions of a Poet."

Lion and the Painter. It is high time that the literary South took its own interests into its own charge.

———

Here is a good idea for a Magazine paper:—let somebody "work it up:"—A flippant pretender to universal acquirement—a would-be Crichton—engrosses, for an hour or two perhaps, the attention of a large company—most of whom are profoundly impressed by his knowledge. He is very witty, in especial, at the expense of a modest young gentleman, who ventures to make no reply, and who, finally, leaves the room as if overwhelmed with confusion;—the Crichton greeting his exit with a laugh. Presently he returns, followed by a footman carrying an armfull of books. These are deposited on the table. The young gentleman, now, referring to some pencilled notes which he had been secretly taking during the Crichton's display of erudition, pins the latter to his statements, each by each, and refutes them all in turn, by reference to the very authorities cited by the egotist himself—whose ignorance at all points is thus made apparent.

———

A long time ago—twenty-three or four years at least—*Edward C. Pinckney*, of Baltimore, published an exquisite poem entitled "A Health." It was profoundly admired by the critical few, but had little circulation:—this for no better reason than that the author was born *too far South*. I quote a few lines:

> Affections are as *thoughts* to her,
>   *The measures of her hours*—
> Her feelings have the fragrancy,
>   The freshness of young *flowers*.
> To her the better elements
>   And kindlier stars have given
> *A form so fair, that, like the air,*
>   *'Tis less of Earth than Heaven.*

Now, in 1842, *Mr. George Hill* published "The Ruins of Athens and Other Poems"—and from one of the "Other Poems" I quote what follows:

And thoughts go sporting through her mind
   Like children among *flowers*;
And deeds of gentle goodness are
   The measures of her hours.
In soul or face she bears no trace
   Of one from Eden driven,
But like the rainbow seems, though born
   Of Earth, a part of Heaven.

Is this plagiarism or is it *not?*—I merely ask for information.

———

"Grace," says Horace Walpole, "will save any book, and without it none can live long." I can never read Mrs. Osgood's poetry without a strong propensity to ring the changes upon this indefinite word "grace" and its derivatives. About every thing she writes we perceive this indescribable charm; of which, perhaps, the elements are a vivid fancy and a quick sense of the proportionate. "Grace," however, may be most satisfactorily defined, at least for the present, as "a term applied, in despair, to that class of the impressions of Beauty which admit of no analysis." Mrs. O. has lately evinced a *true* imagination, with a *"movement"* (as Schlegel has it) or energy, of which I have been considering her incapable. *Beyond all question the first of American poetesses*:—and yet we must judge her less by what she has done than by what she shows ability to do. A happy refinement—an instinctive sense of the pure and delicate—is one of her most noticeable merits. She *could* accomplish much—*very* much.

———

One of our truest poets is *Thomas Buchanan Read*. His most distinctive features are, first, "tenderness," or subdued passion, and secondly, fancy. His sin is imitativeness. *At present*, although evincing high capacity, he is but a copyist of Longfellow—that is to say, but the echo of an echo. Here is a beautiful thought which is *not* the property of Mr. Read:

And, where the spring-time sun had longest shone,
A violet looked up and found itself alone.

Here again: a Spirit

> Slowly through the lake descended,
> Till from her hidden form below
> The waters took a golden glow,
> *As if the star which made her forehead bright*
> *Had burst and filled the lake with light.*

Lowell has some lines very similar, ending with

> As if a star had burst within his brain.

———

I cannot say that I ever fairly comprehended the force of the term *"insult,"* until I was given to understand, one day, by a member of the *"North American Review"* clique, that this journal was "not only willing but anxious to render me that justice which had been already rendered me by the *'Revue Francaise'* and the *'Revue des Deux Mondes'* "—but was "restrained from so doing" by my "invincible spirit of antagonism." I wish the "North American Review" to express *no* opinion of me whatever—for I have none of it. In the meantime, as I see no motto on its title-page, let me recommend it one from Sterne's "Letter from France." Here it is:—"As we rode along the valley we saw a herd of asses on the top of one of the mountains—how they viewed and *reviewed* us!"

———

I blush to see, in the — —, an invidious notice of Bayard Taylor's *"Rhymes of Travel."* What makes the matter *worse*, the *critique* is from the pen of one who, although undeservedly, holds, himself, some position as a poet:—and what makes the matter *worst*, the attack is anonymous, and (while ostensibly commending) most zealously endeavors to damn the young writer " with faint praise." In his whole life, the author of the criticism never published a poem, long or short, which could compare, either in the higher merits, or in the minor morals of the Muse, with *the worst* of Mr. Taylor's compositions.

Observe the generalizing, disingenuous, patronizing tone:—

"It is the empty charlatan, to whom all things are alike impossible, who attempts every thing. He can do one thing as well as another; for he can really do nothing. . . . . Mr. Taylor's volume, as we have intimated, is an advance upon his previous publication. We could have wished, indeed, something more of restraint in the rhetoric, *but*," &c., &c., &c.

The concluding sentence, here, is an excellent example of one of the most ingeniously malignant of critical *ruses* — that of condemning an author, in especial, for what the world, in general, *feel* to be his principal merit. In fact, the "rhetoric" of Mr. Taylor, in the sense intended by the critic, is Mr. Taylor's *distinguishing excellence*. He is, unquestionably, the most terse, glowing, and vigorous of all our poets, young or old — in point, I mean, of *expression*. His sonorous, well-balanced rhythm puts me often in mind of Campbell (in spite of our anonymous friend's *implied* sneer at "mere jingling of rhymes, brilliant and successful for the moment,") and his rhetoric in general is of the highest order: — By "rhetoric" I intend the *mode generally* in which Thought is presented. Where shall we find more magnificent passages than these?

> First queenly Asia, from the fallen thrones
>   Of twice three thousand years,
> Came *with the woe a grieving Goddess owns*
>   *Who longs for mortal tears.*
> The dust of ruin to her mantle clung
>   And dimmed her crown of gold,
> While *the majestic sorrows of her tongue*
>   *From Tyre to Indus rolled.*

> Mourn with me, sisters, in my realm of woe
>   *Whose only glory streams*
> *From its lost childhood like the Arctic glow*
>   *Which sunless winter dreams.*
> *In the red desert moulders Babylon*
>   *And the wild serpent's hiss*
> *Echoes in Petra's palaces of stone*
>   *And waste Persepolis.*

> Then from her seat, *amid the palms embowered*
> *That shade the Lion-land,*
> Swart Africa in dusky aspect towered,
> The fetters on her hand.
> Backward she saw, from out the drear eclipse,
> The mighty Theban years,
> *And the deep anguish of her mournful lips*
> *Interpreted her tears.*

I copy these passages first, because the critic in question has copied them, without the slightest appreciation of their grandeur—for they *are* grand; and secondly, to put the question of "rhetoric" at rest. No artist who reads them will deny that they are the perfection of *skill* in their way. But thirdly, I wish to call attention to the glowing *imagination* evinced in the lines italicized. My very soul revolts at *such* efforts, (as the one I refer to,) to depreciate *such* poems as Mr. Taylor's. *Is* there *no* honor—no chivalry left in the land? Are our most deserving writers to be *forever* sneered down, or hooted down, or damned down with faint praise, by a set of men who possess little other ability than that which assures temporary success to *them*, in common with Swaim's Panacea or Morrison's pills? The fact is, some person should write, at once, a Magazine paper exposing—*ruthlessly* exposing, the *dessous de cartes* of our literary affairs. He should show how and why it is that the ubiquitous quack in letters can always "succeed," while *genius*, (which implies self-respect, with a scorn of creeping and crawling,) must inevitably succumb. He should point out the "easy arts" by which any one, base enough to do it, can get himself placed at the very head of American Letters by an article in that magnanimous journal, "The —— Review." He should explain, too, how readily the same work can be induced (as in the case of Simms,) to villify, and villify *personally*, any one not a Northerner, for a trifling "consideration." In fact, our criticism needs a thorough regeneration, *and must have it.*

Marginalia

SOUTHERN LITERARY MESSENGER, *May 1849*

I F EVER MORTAL " wreaked his thoughts upon expression," it was *Shelley*. If ever poet sang—as a bird sings—earnestly—impulsively—with utter abandonment—to himself solely—and for the mere joy of his own song—that poet was the author of "The Sensitive Plant." Of Art—beyond that which is instinctive with Genius—he either had little or disdained all. He *really* disdained that Rule which is an emanation from Law, because his own soul was Law in itself. His rhapsodies are but the rough notes—the stenographic memoranda of poems—memoranda which, because they were all-sufficient for his own intelligence, he cared not to be at the trouble of writing out in full for mankind. In all his works we find no conception thoroughly wrought. For this reason he is the most fatiguing of poets. Yet he wearies in saying too little rather than too much. What, in him, seems the diffuseness of one idea, is the conglomerate concision of many: and this species of concision it is, which renders him obscure. With such a man, to imitate was out of the question. It would have served no purpose; for he spoke to his own spirit alone, which would have comprehended no alien tongue. Thus he was profoundly original. His quaintness arose from intuitive perception of that truth to which Bacon alone has given distinct utterance:—"There is no exquisite Beauty which has not some strangeness in its proportions." But whether obscure, original, or quaint, Shelley had no *affectations*. He was at all times sincere.

From his *ruins*, there sprang into existence, affronting the Heavens, a tottering and fantastic *pagoda*, in which the salient angels, tipped with mad jangling bells, were the idiosyncratic *faults* of the original—faults which cannot be considered such in view of his purposes, but which are monstrous when we regard his works as addressed to mankind. A "school" arose—if that absurd term must still be employed—a school—a system of *rules*—upon the basis of the Shelley who had none. Young men innumerable, dazzled with the glare and bewildered by the *bizarrerie* of the lightning that flickered through the clouds of "Alastor," had no trouble whatever in heaping up imitative vapors, but, for the lightning, were forced to be content with its *spectrum*, in which the *bizarrerie* appeared without the fire. Nor were mature minds unimpressed by the contemplation of a greater and more mature; and thus, gradually, into this school of all Lawlessness,—of obscurity, quaintness and exaggeration—were interwoven the out-of-place didacticism of Wordsworth, and the more anomalous metaphysicianism of Coleridge. Matters were now fast verging to their worst; and at length, in *Tennyson* poetic inconsistency attained its extreme. But it was precisely this extreme (for the greatest truth and the greatest error are scarcely two points in a circle) which, following the law of all extremes, wrought in him (Tennyson) a natural and inevitable revulsion; leading him first to contemn, and secondly to investigate, his early manner, and finally to winnow, from its magnificent elements, the truest and purest of all poetical styles. But not even yet is the process complete; and for this reason in part, but chiefly on account of the mere fortuitousness of that mental and moral combination which shall unite in one person (if *ever* it shall) the Shelleyan *abandon* and the Tennysonian poetic sense, with the most profound Art (based both in Instinct and *Analysis*) and the sternest Will properly to blend and rigorously to control all—chiefly, I say, because such combination of seeming antagonisms will be only a "happy chance"—the world has never yet seen the noblest poem which, possibly, *can* be composed.

————

In my ballad called "Lenore" I have these lines:

Avaunt! to night my heart is light. No dirge will I upraise—
But waft the angel on her flight with a Pæan of old days.

Mr. *William W. Lord*, author of "Niagara," &c., has it thus:

——They, albeit with inward pain,
Who thought to sing thy dirge, must sing thy Pæan.

The commencement of my "Haunted Palace" is as follows:

> In the greenest of our valleys
>   By good angels tenanted,
> Once a fair and stately palace
>   (Radiant palace!) reared its head.
> In the monarch Thought's dominion—
>   It stood there.
> Never seraph spread a pinion
>   Over fabric half so fair.
> Banners, yellow, glorious, golden,
>   On its roof did float and flow—
> This—all this—was in the olden
>   Time long ago.

Mr. Lord writes—

> On the old and haunted mountain—
>   (There in dreams I dared to climb,)
> Where the clear Castalian fountain
>   (Silver fountain!) ever tinkling,
>   All the green around it sprinkling,
>   Makes perpetual rhyme—
> To my dream, enchanted, golden,
> Came a vision of the olden
>   Long-forgotten time.

————

This* is a thin pamphlet of thirty-two pages; each containing about a hundred and forty words. The hero, Alla-Ad-Deen, is the son of Alladdin of wonderful lamp memory; and the story is in the "Vision of Mirza" or "Rasselas" way. The design is to reconcile us with evil on the ground that, comparatively, we are of little importance in the scale of creation. This scale, however, the author himself assumes as infinite; and thus his argument proves too much: for if evil is to be regarded by man as unimportant because, comparatively, *he*

*"*The Dream of Alla-Ad-Deen, from the Romance of 'Anastasia.' By Charles Erskine White, D. D.*" "Charles Erskine White" is *Laughton Osborn*, author of "The Vision of Rubeta," "Confessions of a Poet," "Adventures of Jeremy Levis," and several other works—among which I must not forget "Arthur Carryl."

is so, it must be regarded as unimportant by the angels for a similar reason—and so on in a never-ending ascent. In other words, nothing is proved beyond the bullish proposition that evil is no evil at all.

————

I hardly know how to account for the repeated failures of John Neal as regards the *construction* of his works. His art is great and of a high character—but it is massive and undetailed. He seems to be either deficient in a sense of completeness, or unstable in temperament; so that he becomes wearied with his work before getting it done. He always begins well—vigorously—startlingly—proceeds by fits—much at random—now prosing, now gossiping, now running away with his subject, now exciting vivid interest; but his conclusions are sure to be hurried and indistinct; so that the reader, perceiving a falling-off where he expects a climax, is pained, and, closing the book with dissatisfaction, is in no mood to give the author credit for the vivid sensations which have been aroused *during the progress* of perusal. Of all literary foibles the most fatal, perhaps, is that of defective climax. Nevertheless, I should be inclined to rank John Neal first, or at all events second, among our men of indisputable *genius*. Is it, or is it not a fact, that the air of a Democracy agrees better with mere Talent than with Genius?

————

It is not *proper*, (to use a gentle word,) nor does it seem courageous, to attack our foe by name in spirit and in effect, so that all the world shall know whom we mean, while we say to ourselves, "I have not attacked this man by name in the eye, and according to the *letter*, of the law"—yet how often are men who call themselves gentlemen, guilty of this meanness! We need reform at this point of our Literary Morality:—very sorely, too, at another—the system of anonymous reviewing. Not one respectable word can be said in defence of this most unfair—this most despicable and cowardly practice.

————

There lies a deep and sealéd well
Within yon leafy forest hid,
Whose pent and lonely waters swell
Its confines chill and drear amid.

This putting the adjective after the noun is, merely, an inex-cusable Gallicism; but the putting the preposition after the noun is alien to all language and in opposition to all its prin-ciples. Such things, in general, serve only to betray the versi-fier's poverty of resource; and, when an inversion of this kind occurs, we say to ourselves, "Here the poet lacked the skill to make out his line without distorting the natural or colloquial order of the words." Now and then, however, we must refer the error not to deficiency of skill, but to something far less defensible — to an idea that such things belong to the essence of poetry — that it needs them to distinguish it from prose — that we are poetical, in a word, very much in the ratio of our unprosaicalness at these points. Even while employing the phrase "poetic license," — a phrase which has to answer for an infinity of sins — people who think in this way seem to have an indistinct conviction that the license in question *in-volves a necessity of being adopted.* The true artist will avail himself of no "license" whatever. The very word will disgust him; for it says — "Since you seem unable to manage with-out these peccadillo advantages, you must have them, I sup-pose; and the world, half-shutting its eyes, will do its best not to see the awkwardness which they stamp upon your poem."

Few things have greater tendency than inversion, to render verse feeble and ineffective. In most cases where a line is spo-ken of as "forcible," the force may be referred to directness of expression. A vast majority of the passages which have be-come household through frequent quotation, owe their popu-larity either to this directness, or, in general, to the scorn of "poetic license." In short as regards verbal construction, *the more prosaic* a poetical style is, the better. Through this species of prosaicism, Cowper, with scarcely one of the higher poet-ical elements, came very near making his age fancy him the equal of Pope; and to the same cause are attributable three-fourths of that unusual point and force for which Thomas

Moore is distinguished. It is the *prosaicism* of these two writers to which is owing their especial *quotability*.

———

"The Reverend Arthur Coxe's 'Saul, a Mystery,' having
been condemned in no measured terms by Poe, of 'The
Broadway Journal,' and Green of 'The Emporium,' a writer
in the 'Hartford Columbian' retorts as follows:

> An entertaining history,
> Entitled 'Saul, A Mystery,'
> Has recently been published by the Reverend Arthur Coxe.
> The poem is dramatic,
> And the wit of it is attic,
> And its teachings are emphatic of the doctrines orthodox.
>
> But Mr. Poe, the poet,
> Declares he cannot go it—
> That the book is very stupid, or something of that sort:
> And Green, of the Empori-
> Um, tells a kindred story,
> And swears like any tory that it is'nt worth a groat.
>
> But maugre all the croaking
> Of the Raven and the joking
> Of the verdant little fellow of the used to be review,
> The People, in derision
> Of their impudent decision,
> Have declared, without division, that the Mystery will do."

The *truth*, of course, rather injures an epigram than otherwise; and nobody will think the worse of the one above, when
I say that, at the date of its first appearance, I had expressed
no opinion whatever of the poem to which it refers. "Give a
dog a bad name," &c. Whenever a book is abused, people
take it for granted that it is *I* who have been abusing it.

Latterly I *have* read "Saul," and agree with the epigram-
matist, that it "will do"—whoever attempts to wade through
it. It will do, also, for trunk-paper. The author is right in
calling it "A Mystery:"—for a most unfathomable mystery it
is. When I got to the end of it I found it more mysterious

than ever — and it was really a mystery how I ever did get to the end — which I half fancied that somebody had cut off, in a fit of ill-will to the critics. I have heard not a syllable about the "Mystery," of late days. "The People," seem to have forgotten it; and Mr. Coxe's friends should advertise it under the head of "Mysterious Disappearance" — that is to say, the disappearance of a Mystery.

The *pure Imagination* chooses, from *either Beauty or Deformity*, only the most combinable things hitherto uncombined; the compound, as a general rule, partaking, in character, of beauty, or sublimity, in the ratio of the respective beauty or sublimity of the things combined — which are themselves still to be considered as atomic — that is to say, as previous combinations. But, as often analogously happens in physical chemistry, so not unfrequently does it occur in this chemistry of the intellect, that the admixture of two elements results in a something that has nothing of the qualities of one of them, or even nothing of the qualities of either. . . Thus, the range of Imagination is unlimited. Its materials extend throughout the universe. Even out of deformities it fabricates that *Beauty* which is at once its sole object and its inevitable test. But, in general, the richness or force of the matters combined; the facility of discovering combinable novelties worth combining; and, especially the absolute "chemical combination" of the completed mass — are the particulars to be regarded in our estimate of Imagination. It is this thorough harmony of an imaginative work which so often causes it to be undervalued by the thoughtless, through the character of *obviousness* which is superinduced. We are apt to find ourselves asking *why* it is that these combinations have never been imagined before.

"He (Bulwer) is the most accomplished writer of the most accomplished era of English Letters; practising all styles and classes of composition, and eminent in all — novelist, dramatist, poet, historian, moral philosopher, essayist, critic, political pamphleteer; — in each superior to all others, and only rivalled in each by himself."

Ward — author of "Tremaine."

The "only rivalled in each by himself," here, puts me in mind of

None but himself can be his parallel.

But surely Mr. Ward (who, although he did write "De Vere," is by no means a fool) could never have put to paper, in his sober senses, anything so absurd as the paragraph quoted above, without stopping at every third word to hold his sides, or thrust his pocket-handkerchief into his mouth. If the serious intention be insisted upon, however, I have to remark that the opinion is the *mere* opinion of a writer remarkable for no other good trait than his facility at putting his readers to sleep according to rules Addisonian and with the least possible loss of labor and time. But as the *mere* opinion of even a Jeffrey or a Macaulay, I have an inalienable right to meet it with another.

As a novelist, then, Bulwer is far more than respectable; although *generally* inferior to Scott, Godwin, D'Israeli, Miss Burney, Sue, Dumas, Dickens, the author of "Ellen Warebam," the author of "Jane Eyre," and several others. From the list of foreign novels I could select a hundred which he could neither have written nor conceived. As a dramatist, he deserves more credit, although he receives less. His "Richelieu," "Money" and "Lady of Lyons", have done much in the way of opening the public eyes to the true value of what is superciliously termed "stage-effect" in the hands of one able to manage it. But if commendable at this point, his dramas fail egregiously in points more important; so that, upon the whole, he can be said to have written a good play, only when we think of him in connexion with the still more contemptible "old-dramatist" imitators who are his contemporaries and friends. As historian, he is sufficiently dignified, sufficiently ornate, and more than sufficiently self-sufficient. His "Athens" would have received an Etonian prize, and has all the happy air of an Etonian prize-essay re-vamped. His political pamphlets are very good as political pamphlets and very disreputable as anything else. His essays leave no doubt upon any body's mind that, with the writer, they have been essays indeed. His criticism is really beneath contempt. His moral philosophy is the most ridiculous of all the moral philosophies that ever have been imagined upon earth.

"The men of sense," says Helvetius, "those idols of the unthinking, are very far inferior to the men of passions. It is the strong passions which, rescuing us from sloth, can alone impart to us that continuous and earnest attention necessary to great intellectual efforts."

When the Swiss philosopher here speaks of "inferiority," he refers to inferiority in worldly success:—by "men of sense" he intends indolent men of genius. And Bulwer is, emphatically, one of the "men of passions" contemplated in the apophthegm. His passions, with opportunities, have made him what he is. Urged by a rabid ambition to do much, in doing nothing he would merely have proved himself an idiot. Something he has done. In aiming at Crichton, he has hit the target an inch or two above Harrison Ainsworth. Not to such intellects belong the honors of universality. His works bear about them the unmistakeable indications of mere talent—talent, I grant, of an unusual order and nurtured to its extreme of development with a very tender and elaborate care. Nevertheless, it is talent still. Genius it is not. And the proof is, that while we often fancy ourselves about to be enkindled beneath its influence, fairly enkindled we never are. That Bulwer is no *poet*, follows as a corollary from what has been already said:—for to speak of a poet without genius, is merely to put forth a flat contradiction in terms.

———

Quaintness, within reasonable limits, is not only *not* to be regarded as affectation, but has its proper uses, in aiding a fantastic effect. Miss Barret will afford me two examples. In some lines to a Dog, she says:

> Leap! thy broad tail waves a light.
> Leap thy slender feet are bright,
>   Canopied in fringes.
> Leap! those tasselled ears of thine
> Flicker strangely fair and fine
>   *Down their golden inches.*

And again—in the "Song of a Tree-Spirit."

> The Divine impulsion cleaves
> In dim movements to the leaves
> *Dropt and lifted—dropt and lifted—*
> In the sun-light greenly sifted—
> *In the sun-light and the moon-light*
> *Greenly sifted through the trees.*
> *Ever wave the Eden trees*
> *In the night-light and the moon-light,*
> With a ruffling of green branches
> *Shaded off to resonances*
> Never stirred by rain or breeze.

The thoughts here belong to a high order of poetry, but could not have been wrought into effective expression, without the aid of those repetitions—those unusual phrases—those *quaintnesses*, in a word, which it has been too long the fashion to censure, indiscriminately, under the one general head of "affectation." No poet will fail to be pleased with the two extracts I have here given; but no doubt there are some who will find it hard to reconcile the psychal impossibility of refraining from admiration, with the too-hastily attained mental conviction that, critically, there is nothing to admire.

Marginalia

SOUTHERN LITERARY MESSENGER, *June 1849*

P URE DIABOLISM is but Absolute Insanity. Lucifer was merely unfortunate in having been created without brains.

———

When a man of genius speaks of "the difficult" he means, simply, "the impossible."

———

We, of the nineteenth century, need some worker of miracles for our regeneration; but so degraded have we become that the only prophet, or preacher, who could render us much service, would be the St. Francis who converted the beasts.

———

The nose of a mob is its imagination. By this, at any time, it can be quietly led.

———

Samuel Butler, of Hudibrastic memory, must have had a prophetic eye to the American Congress when he defined a *rabble* as—"A congregation or assembly of the States-General—every one being of a several judgment concerning whatever business be under consideration". . . . "They meet only to quarrel," he adds, "and then return home full of satisfaction *and narrative.*"

———

The Romans worshipped their standards; and the Roman standard happened to be an eagle. Our standard is only one-tenth of an Eagle—a Dollar—but we make all even by adoring it with ten-fold devotion.

———

"He that is born to be a man," says Wieland in his "Peregrinus Proteus," "neither should nor can be anything nobler, greater, or better than a man." The fact is, that in efforts to soar above our nature, we invariably fall below it. Your reformist demigods are merely devils turned inside out.

———

It is only the philosophical lynxeye that, through the indignity-mist of Man's life, can still discern the dignity of Man.

———

It is by no means an irrational fancy that, in a future existence, we shall look upon what we think our present existence, as a dream.

———

In drawing a line of distinction between a people and a mob, we shall find that a people aroused to action are a mob; and that a mob, trying to think, subside into a people.

———

Tell a scoundrel, three or four times a day, that he is the pink of probity, and you make him at least the perfection of "respectability" in good earnest. On the other hand, accuse an honorable man, too pertinaciously, of being a villain, and you fill him with a perverse ambition to show you that you are not altogether in the wrong.

———

With how unaccountable an obstinacy even our best writers persist in talking about "moral courage—" as if there could be any courage that was *not* moral. The adjective is improperly applied to the subject instead of the object. The energy which overcomes fear—whether fear of evil threatening the person or threatening the impersonal circumstances amid which we exist—is, of course, simply a mental energy— is, of course, simply "moral." But, in speaking of "*moral* courage" we *imply* the existence of physical. Quite as reasonable an expression would be that of "bodily thought" or of "muscular imagination."

———

In looking at the world *as it is*, we shall find it folly to deny that, to worldly success, a surer path is Villainy than Virtue. What the Scriptures mean by the "*leaven* of unrighteousness" is that leaven by which men *rise*.

———

I have now before me a book in which the most noticeable thing is the pertinacity with which "Monarch" and "King" are printed with a capital M and a capital K. The author, it seems, has been lately presented at Court. He will employ a small *g* in future, I presume, whenever he is so unlucky as to have to speak of his God.

———

"A little learning," in the sense intended by the poet, *is*, beyond all question, "a dangerous thing:"—but, in regard to *that* learning which we call "knowledge of the world," it is *only* a little that is *not* dangerous. To be *thoroughly* conversant with Man's heart, is to take our final lesson in the iron-clasped volume of Despair.

———

Not only do I think it paradoxical to speak of a man of *genius* as personally ignoble, but I confidently maintain that the *highest* genius is but the loftiest moral nobility.

———

The phrase of which our poets, and more especially our orators, are so fond—the phrase "music of the spheres"—has arisen simply from a misconception of the Platonic word μουσικη—which, with the Athenians, included not merely the harmonies of tune and time, but *proportion* generally. In recommending the study of "music" as "the best education for the soul," Plato referred to the cultivation of the Taste, in contradistinction from that of the Pure Reason. By the "music of the spheres" is meant the agreements—the adaptations—in a word, the proportions—developed in the astronomical laws. He had *no* allusion to music in *our* understanding of the term. The word "mosaic," which we derive from μουσικη, refers, in like manner, to the proportion, or

harmony of *color*, observed—or which should be observed—
in the department of Art so entitled.

———

A pumpkin has more angles than C—, and is altogether a
cleverer thing. He is remarkable at one point only—at that
of being remarkable for nothing.

———

Not long ago, to call a man "a great wizzard," was to invoke for him fire and faggot; but now, when we wish to run
our *protégé* for President, we just dub him "a *little* magician."
The fact is, that, on account of the curious modern *bouleversement* of old opinion, one cannot be too cautious of *the
grounds* on which he lauds a friend or vituperates a foe.

———

It is laughable to observe how easily any system of Philosophy can be proved false:—but then is it not mournful to
perceive the impossibility of even fancying any particular system to be true?

———

Were I called on to define, *very* briefly, the term "Art," I
should call it "the reproduction of what the Senses perceive
in Nature through the veil of the soul." The mere imitation,
however accurate, of what *is* in Nature, entitles no man to
the sacred name of "Artist." Denner was no artist. The grapes
of Zeuxis were *in*artistic—unless in a bird's-eye view; and
not even the curtain of Parrhasius could conceal his deficiency
in point of genius. I have mentioned "the *veil* of the soul."
Something of the kind appears indispensable in Art. We can,
at any time, double the true beauty of an actual landscape by
half closing our eyes as we look at it. The naked Senses sometimes see too little—but then *always* they see too much.

———

A clever French writer of "Memoirs" is quite right in saying that "if the *Universities* had been willing to permit it, the
disgusting old *debauché* of Teos, with his eternal Batyllis,
would long ago have been buried in the darkness of oblivion."

———

"Philosophy," says Hegel, "is utterly useless and fruitless, and, *for this very reason,* is the sublimest of all pursuits, the most deserving attention, and the most worthy of our zeal." This jargon was suggested, no doubt, by Tertullian's *"Mortuus est Dei filius; credibile est quia ineptum—et sepultus resurrexit; certum est quia impossibile."*

———

I have great faith in fools:—self-confidence my friends will call it:—

> Si demain, oubliant d' éclore,
>   Le jour manquait, eh bien! demain
> Quelque fou trouverait encore
>   Un flambeau pour le genre humain.

By the way, what with the new electric light and other matters, De Béranger's idea is not so *very* extravagant.

———

I have sometimes amused myself by endeavoring to fancy what would be the fate of any individual gifted, or rather accursed, with an intellect *very* far superior to that of his race. Of course, he would be conscious of his superiority; nor could he (if otherwise constituted as man is) help manifesting his consciousness. Thus he would make himself enemies at all points. And since his opinions and speculations would widely differ from those of *all* mankind—that he would be considered a madman, is evident. How horribly painful such a condition! Hell could invent no greater torture than that of being charged with abnormal weakness on account of being abnormally strong.

In like manner, nothing can be clearer than that a *very* generous spirit—*truly* feeling what all merely profess—must inevitably find itself misconceived in every direction—its motives misinterpreted. Just as extremeness of intelligence would be thought fatuity, so excess of chivalry could not fail of being looked upon as meanness in its last degree:—and so on with other virtues. This subject is a painful one indeed. That individuals *have* so soared above the plane of their race, is scarcely to be questioned; but, in looking back through history for traces of their existence, we should pass over all biographies of "the good and the great," while we search carefully the slight records of wretches who died in prison, in Bedlam, or upon the gallows.

———

My friend, ——, can never commence what he fancies a poem, (he *is* a fanciful man, after all) without first elaborately "invoking the Muses." Like so many she-dogs of John of Nivelles, however, the more he invokes them, the more they decline obeying the invocation.

———

The German *"Schwarmerei"*—not exactly "humbug," but "sky-rocketing"—seems to be the only term by which we can conveniently designate that peculiar style of criticism which has lately come into fashion, through the influence of certain members of the *Fabian* family—people who live (upon beans) about Boston.

———

"This is right," says Epicurus, "precisely because the people are displeased with it."

"Il y a à parier," says Chamfort—one of the *Kamkars* of Mirabeau—*"que toute idée publique—toute convention reçue—est une sottise; car elle a convenue au plus grand nombre."*

"Si proficere cupis," says the great African bishop, *"primo id verum puta quod sana mens omnium hominum attestatur."*

Now,

"Who shall decide where Doctors disagree?"

To me, it appears that, in all ages, the *most* preposterous falsities have been received as truths by at least the *mens* omnium hominum. As for the *sana* mens—how are we ever to determine what that is?

———

There are moments when, even to the sober eye of Reason, the world of our sad humanity must assume the aspect of Hell; but the Imagination of Man is no Carathis, to explore with impunity its every cavern. Alas! the grim legion of sepulchral terrors can *not* be regarded as altogether fanciful; but, like the Demons in whose company Afrasiab made his voyage down the Oxus, they must sleep, or they will devour us—they must be suffered to slumber, or we perish.

————

What can be more soothing, at once to a man's Pride and to his Conscience, than the conviction that, in taking vengeance on his enemies for *in*justice done him, he has simply to do them *justice* in return?

————

Talking of puns:—"Why do they not give us quail for dinner, as usual?" demanded Count Fessis, the other day, of H—, the classicist and sportsman.

"Because at this season," replied H—, who was dozing, *"qualis sopor fessis."* (Quail is so poor, Fessis.)

————

An infinity of error makes its way into our Philosophy, through Man's habit of considering himself a citizen of a world solely—of an individual planet—instead of at least occasionally contemplating his position as cosmopolite proper—as a denizen of the universe.

————

The Carlyle-ists should adopt, as a motto, the inscription on the old bell from whose metal was cast the Great Tom, of Oxford:—"In *Thomæ* laude resono 'Bim! Bom!' sine fraude:"—and "Bim! Bom," in such case, would be a marvellous "echo of sound to sense."

————

Paulus Jovius, living in those benighted times when diamond-pointed styluses were as yet unknown, thought proper, nevertheless, to speak of his goosequill as *"aliquando ferreus, aureus aliquando*"—intending, of course, a mere figure of speech; and from the class of modern authors who use really nothing to write with but steel and gold, some, no doubt, will let their pens, *vice versâ*, descend to posterity under the designation of "anserine"—of course, intending always a mere figure of speech.

THE FISHES described by Athenæus as ἀθανάτοισι θεοισι φυὴν και ἐίδος ὀίμοιαι, were, beyond doubt, a shoal of Preserved Fish, like the one who spoke up so boldly for President Tyler.

———

The eloquence of the Honorable G— strikes me as being of that class which, *"si absit,"* as Cicero says, speaking generally of eloquence in a philosopher, *"non magnopere desideranda."*

———

In saying that "grace will save any book and without it none can live long," Horace Walpole had reference, I fancy, to that especial grace which managed to save so many books of his own—his Grace the Archbishop of Canterbury.

———

Until we analyze a religion, or a philosophy, in respect of its inducements, independently of its rationality, we shall never be in condition to estimate that religion, or that philosophy, by the mere *number* of its adherents:—unluckily,

> "No Indian Prince has to his palace
> More followers than a thief to the gallows."

———

In omitting to envelop our Gothic architecture in *foliage*, we omit, in fact, an essential point in the Gothic architecture itself. Of a Gothic *church*, especially, trees are as much a portion as the pointed arch. "Ubi *tres*, ecclesia," says Tertullian;—but no doubt he meant that "ubi ecclesia, *tres*."

———

"If, in any point," says Lord Bacon, "I have receded from what is commonly received, it hath been for the purpose of proceeding *melius* and not *in aliud*"—but the character assumed, in general, by modern "Reform" is, simply, that of Opposition.

––––––

A strong argument for the religion of Christ is this—that offences against *Charity* are about the only ones which men on their death-beds can be made—not to understand—but to *feel*—as *crime*.

––––––

That Demosthenes "turned out very badly," appears, beyond dispute, from a passage in *"Meker de vet. et rect. Pron. Ling. Græcæ,"* where we read *"Nec illi (Demostheni) turpe videbatur, optimis relictis magistris, ad canes se conferre,"* etc., etc.:— that is to say, Demosthenes was not ashamed to quit good society and *"go to the dogs."*

––––––

When —— and —— *pavoneggiarsi* about the celebrated personages whom they have "seen" in their travels, we shall not be far wrong in inferring that these celebrated personages were seen έχας—as Pindar says he "saw" Archilochus, who died ages before the former was born.

––––––

To see distinctly the machinery—the wheels and pinions— of any work of Art is, unquestionably, of itself, a pleasure, but one which we are able to enjoy only just in proportion as we do *not* enjoy the legitimate effect designed by the artist:— and, in fact, it too often happens that to reflect analytically upon Art, is to reflect after the fashion of the mirrors in the temple of Smirna, which represent the fairest images as deformed.

––––––

The modern reformist Philosophy which annihilates the individual by way of aiding the mass; and the late reformist Legislation, which prohibits pleasure with the view of advancing happiness, seem to be chips of that old block of a French feudal law which, to prevent young partridges from being disturbed, imposed penalites upon hoeing and weeding.

––––––

I cannot help thinking that romance-writers, in general, might, now and then, find their account in taking a hint from the Chinese, who, in spite of building their houses downwards, have still sense enough *to begin their books at the end*.

———

Surely M—— cannot complain of the manner in which his book has been received; for the Public, in regard to it, has given him just such an assurance as Polyphemus pacified Ulysses with, while his companions were being eaten up before his eyes. "Your book, Mr. M——," says the Public, "shall be—I pledge you my word—the very last that I devour."

———

In examining trivial details, we are apt to overlook essential generalities. Thus M——, in making a to-do about the "typographical mistakes" in his book, has permitted the printer to escape a scolding which he *did* richly deserve—a scolding for a "typographical mistake" of really vital importance—the mistake of having printed the book at all.

———

Mozart declared, on his death-bed, that he "began to see what *may* be done in music;" and it is to be hoped that DeMeyer and the rest of the spasmodists will, eventually, begin to understand what may *not* be done in this particular branch of the Fine Arts.

———

Nicholas Ferrar, were he now living, would be not a little astonished to find thoroughly established here, by our Magazine poets, that very "perpetual chant" which he so unsuccessfully struggled to establish in the village of Little Gidding.

———

In the tale proper—where there is no space for development of character or for great profusion and variety of incident—mere *construction* is, of course, far more imperatively demanded than in the novel. Defective plot, in this latter, may escape observation, but in the tale, never. Most of our tale-writers, however, neglect the distinction. They seem to begin their stories without knowing how they are to end; and their ends, generally,—like so many governments of Trinculo—appear to have forgotten their beginnings.

————

It has been well said of the French orator, Dupin, that "he spoke, as nobody else, the language of every body;" and thus his manner seems to be exactly conversed in that of the Frog-pondian Euphuists, who, on account of the familiar tone in which they lisp their *outré* phrases, may be said to speak, as every body, the language of nobody—that is to say, a language emphatically their own.

————

The *vox populi*, so much talked about to so little purpose, is, possibly, that very *vox et preterea nihil* which the country-man, in Catullus, mistook for a nightingale.

————

It is folly to assert, as some at present are fond of asserting, that the Literature of any nation or age was ever injured by plain speaking on the part of the Critics. As for American Letters, plain-speaking about *them* is, simply, the one thing needed. They are in a condition of absolute quagmire—a quagmire, to use the words of Victor Hugo, *d'ou on ne peut se tirer par des periphrases—par des quemadmodums et des verumenimveros.*

————

I believe it is Montaigne who says—"People talk about thinking, but, for my part. I never begin to think until I sit down to write." A better plan for him would have been, never to sit down to write until he had made an end of thinking.

————

There is an old German chronicle about Reynard the Fox, when crossed in love—about how he desired to turn hermit, but could find no spot in which he could be "thoroughly alone," until he came upon the desolate fortress of Malapart.

He should have taken to reading the "American Drama" of ——. I fancy he would have found himself "thoroughly alone" in that.

———

Alas! how many American critics neglect the happy suggestion of M. Timon — *"que le ministre de L'Instruction Publique doit lui-même savoir parler Français."*

———

I cannot tell how it happens, but, unless, now and then, in a case of portrait-painting, very few of our artists can justly be held guilty of the crime imputed by Apelles to Protogenes — that of "being too natural."

———

M——, as a matter of course, would rather be abused by the critics than not be noticed by them at all; but he is hardly to be blamed for growling a little, now and then, over their criticisms — just as a dog might do if pelted with bones.

———

To villify a great man is the readiest way in which a little man can himself attain greatness. The Crab might never have become a Constellation but for the courage it evinced in nibbling Hercules on the heel.

———

Our "blues" are increasing in number at a great rate; and should be decimated, at the very least. Have we no critic with nerve enough to hang a dozen or two of them, *in terrorem*? He must use a silk cord, of course — as they do, in Spain, with all grandees of the *blue* blood — of the *"sangre azula."*

———

No doubt, the association of idea is somewhat singular — but I never can hear a crowd of people singing and gesticulating, all together, at an Italian opera, without fancying myself at Athens, listening to that particular tragedy, by

Sophocles, in which he introduces a full chorus of turkeys, who set about bewailing the death of Meleager. It is noticeable in this connexion, by the way, that there is not a goose in the world who, in point of sagacity, would not feel itself insulted in being compared with a turkey. The French seem to feel this. In Paris, I am sure, no one would think of saying to Mr. F——, "What a goose you are!"—"Quel *dindon* tu es!" would be the phrase employed as equivalent.

————

They have ascertained, in China, that the abdomen is the seat of the soul; and the acute Greeks considered it a waste of words to employ more than a single term, φρενες, for the expression both of the mind and of the diaphragm.

————

Let us be charitable and account for M——'s repeated literary failures by the supposition that, like Lelius in the "Arcadia," he wishes to evince his skill rather in missing than in hitting his mark.

————

L—— is busy in attempting to prove that his Play was not fairly d——d—that it is only "scotched, not killed;" but if the poor Play could speak from the tomb, I fancy it would sing with the Opera heroine:

> "The flattering error cease to prove!
> Oh, *let* me be deceased!"

————

"What does a man learn by travelling?" demanded Doctor Johnson, one day, in a great rage—"What did Lord Charlemont learn in his travels, except that there was a snake in one of the pyramids of Egypt?"—but had Doctor Johnson lived in the days of the Silk Buckinghams, he would have seen that, so far from thinking anything of finding a snake in a pyramid, your traveller would take his oath, at a moment's notice, of having found a pyramid in a snake.

————

The next work of Carlyle will be entitled "Bow-Wow," and the title-page will have a motto from the opening chapter of the Koran: "There is *no* error in this Book."

Marginalia

SOUTHERN LITERARY MESSENGER, *September 1849*

AMONG OUR MEN of genius whom, because they *are* men of genius, we neglect, let me not fail to mention *William Wallace*, of Kentucky. Had Mr. W. been born under the wings of that ineffable buzzard, "The North American Review," his unusual merits would long ago have been blazoned to the world—as the far inferior merits of Sprague, Dana, and others of like calibre, have already been blazoned. Neither of these gentlemen has written a poem worthy to be compared with "The Chaunt of a Soul," published in "The Union Magazine" for November, 1848. It is a noble composition throughout—imaginative, eloquent, full of dignity, and well sustained. It abounds in detached images of high merit—for example:

> Your early splendor's gone
> Like stars into a cloud withdrawn—
> Like music laid asleep
> In dried up fountains.

———

> Enough, I *am*, and shall not choose to die.
> No matter *what* our future Fate may be,
> To live, is in itself a majesty.

———

> And Truth, arising from yon deep,
> Is plain *as a white statue on a tall, dark steep.*

———

> ————Then
> The Earth and Heaven were fair,
> While only less than Gods seemed all my fellow men.
> Oh, the delight—the gladness—
> *The sense, yet love, of madness—*
> The glorious choral exultations—
> The far-off sounding of the banded nations—

The wings of angels in melodious sweeps
Upon the mountain's hazy steeps—
The very dead astir within their coffined deeps—
The dreamy veil that wrapt the star and sod—
A swathe of purple, gold, and amethyst—
And, *luminous behind the billowy mist,*
Something that looked to my young eyes like God.

I admit that the defect charged, by an envious critic, upon
Bayard Taylor—the sin of excessive rhetoricianism—*is,* in
some measure, chargeable to Wallace. He, now and then, permits enthusiasm to hurry him into bombast; but at this point
he is rapidly improving; and, if not disheartened by the cowardly neglect of those who *dare* not praise a poetical aspirant
with genius and *without* influence, will soon rank as one of
the very noblest of American poets. In fact, he is so *now.*

———

"Frequently since his recent death," says the American Editor of Hood, "he has been called a great author—a phrase
used not inconsiderately or in vain." Yet, if we adopt the conventional idea of "a great author," there has lived, perhaps,
no writer of the last half century who, with equal notoriety,
was less entitled than Hood to be so called. In fact, he was a
literary merchant, whose main stock in trade was *littleness*;
for, during the larger portion of his life, he seemed to breathe
only for the purpose of perpetrating puns—things of so despicable a platitude that the man who is capable of habitually
committing them, is seldom found capable of anything else.
Whatever merit *may* be discovered in a pun, arises altogether
from *unexpectedness*. This is the pun's element and is two-fold.
First, we demand that the *combination* of the pun be unexpected; and, secondly, we require the most entire unexpectedness in the pun *per se*. A rare pun, rarely appearing, is, to a
certain extent, a pleasurable effect; but to no mind, however
debased in taste, is a continuous effort at punning otherwise
than unendurable. The man who maintains that he derives
gratification from any such chapters of punnage as Hood was
in the daily practice of committing to paper, should not be
credited upon oath.

The puns of the author of "Fair Inez," however, are to be regarded as the weak points of the man. Independently of their ill effect, in a literary view, as mere puns, they leave upon us a painful impression; for too evidently they are the hypochondriac's struggles at mirth—the grinnings of the death's head. No one can read his "Literary Reminiscences" without being convinced of his habitual despondency:—and the species of false wit in question is precisely of that character which would be adopted by an author of Hood's temperament and cast of intellect, when compelled to write at an emergency. That his heart had no interest in these *niäiseries*, is clear. I allude, of course, to his *mere* puns for the pun's sake—a class of letters by which he attained his widest renown. That he did *more* in this way than in any other, is but a corollary from what I have already said, for, generally, he was unhappy, and almost continually he wrote *invitâ Minerva*. But his true province was a very rare and ethereal *humor*, in which the mere pun was left out of sight, or took the character of the richest *grotesquerie*; impressing the imaginative reader with remarkable force, as if by a new phase of the ideal. It is in this species of brilliant, or, rather, *glowing* grotesquerie, uttered with a rushing *abandon* vastly heightening its effect, that Hood's marked originality mainly consisted:— and it is this which entitles him, at times, to the epithet "great:"—for *that* undeniably may be considered great (of whatever seeming littleness in itself) which is capable of inducing intense emotion in the minds, or hearts, of those who are themselves undeniably great.

The field in which Hood is *distinctive* is a border-land between Fancy and Fantasy. In this region he reigns supreme. Nevertheless, he has made successful and frequent incursions, although vacillatingly, into the domain of the true Imagination. I mean to say that he is never truly or purely imaginative for more than a paragraph at a time. In a word, his peculiar genius was the result of vivid *Fancy* impelled by Hypochondriasis.

Chronology

and modern languages. Finding Allan's allowance insufficient to pay expenses, resorts to gambling and loses $2,000. Allan refuses to honor debt, and Poe returns to Richmond to find that the Roysters have succeeded in quashing his engagement.

1827   Complains of Allan's lack of affection and leaves household in March, despite Frances Allan's efforts at conciliation. Sails for Boston under alias "Henri Le Rennet." In May enlists in United States Army as "Edgar A. Perry," giving his age as 22 and his occupation as "clerk," and is assigned to a coast artillery regiment at Fort Independence in Boston harbor. Persuades a young printer to publish his first book, *Tamerlane and Other Poems*, signed "by a Bostonian," a thin volume that goes unnoticed. In November Poe's unit is transferred to Fort Moultrie, South Carolina.

1828–29   After series of promotions Poe reaches highest non-commissioned rank of sergeant major and, with professional military career in mind, seeks John Allan's help in obtaining appointment to U. S. Military Academy at West Point. Mrs. Allan dies February 28, 1829, and Poe, honorably discharged from his enlistment, lives with various Poe relatives in Baltimore. While awaiting word about West Point, writes Allan for money to subsidize second volume of poems, adding "I have long given up *Byron* for a model." Allan refuses aid, but *Al Aaraaf, Tamerlane and Minor Poems* is published under Poe's own name by Hatch & Dunning of Baltimore in December 1829. Advanced sheets of the volume, which includes six new poems added to the revised *Tamerlane* poems, get a short but favorable notice from John Neal, a leading critic.

1830–31   Enters West Point, May 1830; excels in languages and is popular among cadets for his comic verses lampooning the officers. John Allan remarries in October 1830 and shortly after severs relations with Poe upon reading a letter in which Poe comments, "Mr. A. is not very often sober." Poe intentionally "disobeys orders" (absence from class, chapel, and roll-call) to obtain release from Academy, and in January 1831 is court-martialed and expelled. Goes to New York City in February. With funds donated by fellow cadets, contracts with a publisher for *Poems:*

Second Edition, dedicated to "The U.S. Corps of Cadets," and including "To Helen," "Israfel," and his first published critical statement, the prefatory "Letter to Mr. —— ——." In Baltimore, resides with paternal aunt Maria Clemm and her eight-year-old daughter Virginia; household includes Poe's brother William Henry, who dies in August, and his grandmother Elizabeth Cairnes Poe, whose small pension for her late husband's Revolutionary War services helps eke out the family's meager income. Submits five tales for a contest sponsored by Philadelphia *Saturday Courier*; none win, but all are published in the *Courier* the following year.

1832–33   Living in Clemm household; tutors cousin Virginia Clemm. Writes six stories which, along with the five *Courier* tales, he hopes to publish as "Tales of the Folio Club." Submits these tales in summer 1833 for contest announced by Baltimore *Saturday Visiter*; "MS. Found in a Bottle" wins first prize of $50, and "The Coliseum" places second in poetry competition. Both appear in the *Visiter* in October 1833.

1834–35   His tale "The Visionary" appears in January 1834 issue of *Godey's Lady's Book,* Poe's first publication in a journal of wide circulation. John Allan dies in March; though legitimate and illegitimate children are mentioned in his will, Poe is ignored. John P. Kennedy, a judge in the *Visiter* contest, recommends Poe to Thomas W. White, publisher of *Southern Literary Messenger* and, beginning in March 1835, he contributes stories, book reviews, and "Hans Phaall," his first long narrative. The same month he declines a dinner invitation from Kennedy "for reasons of the most humiliating nature in my personal appearance," and Kennedy lends him money. Grandmother Elizabeth Poe dies in July, and in August Poe goes to Richmond. Poe's trenchant reviews, which earn him the sobriquet "tomahawk man," dramatically improve the circulation and national reputation of the *Messenger*, and White hires him as editorial assistant and principal book-reviewer. When Maria Clemm hints that Virginia may move into a cousin's home, Poe asks for her hand, and in September returns to Baltimore. White writes Poe warning him that any further drinking will end his employment at the *Messenger*. In October Poe returns to Richmond with Virginia and Mrs.

Clemm, and in December White offers him the editorship
of the now prospering journal. Publishes in December
Messenger first scenes of his never-completed blank verse
tragedy *Politian*.

1836   Marries Virginia Clemm in May, shortly before her fourteenth birthday; Mrs. Clemm stays on with Poes as housekeeper. Writes over eighty reviews for the *Messenger*,
including two highly favorable ones on Dickens, and
prints or reprints his stories and poems, often with revi-
sions. Borrows money from relatives for a boarding house
to be run by Mrs. Clemm, and plans a suit against the
government to recover war loans made by his grandfather;
both schemes come to nothing. Fails to find publisher for
"Folio Club" tales, now numbering sixteen or seventeen,
despite assistance of White and James Kirke Paulding
(Harper & Brothers informs him that "Readers in this
country have a decided and strong preference for works
. . . in which a single and connected story occupies the
whole volume").

1837–38   Disputes with White over salary (approximately $10 a
week) and editorial independence lead to resignation
from *Messenger* in January 1837. Takes family to New
York to seek employment, but is unable to find editorial
post. Mrs. Clemm manages a boarding house to help
make ends meet. Publishes poems and stories, including
"Ligeia" (later singled out by Poe as "my *best* tale"); resumes work on "Arthur Gordon Pym," two installments
of which had appeared in the *Messenger*, to make it pub-
lishable as a full-length novel. Harper's brings out *The
Narrative of Arthur Gordon Pym* in July 1838. Poe moves
family to Philadelphia. Continues to free-lance but, poor
and still unable to secure editorship, considers giving up
literary work.

1839–40   In financial straits, agrees to let name appear as author of
shell-collector's manual, *The Conchologist's First Book*. Begins first series of solutions to cryptograms in *Alexander's
Weekly Messenger*. Offers editorial services to *Gentleman's
Magazine,* having first agreed to adopt policies of its founder and owner, William Burton. Contributes one signed
feature and most of the reviews each month; early contributions include "The Fall of the House of Usher" and

"William Wilson." Late in 1839 *Tales of the Grotesque and Arabesque* (2 vols.) is published by Lea and Blanchard in Philadelphia, including all twenty-five stories written up to that time. Serialization of the unsigned "Journal of Julius Rodman" begins in January 1840 *Gentleman's Magazine* but terminates in June with the long narrative unfinished when he quarrels with Burton and is discharged. Attempts to lay groundwork for *The Penn Magazine*, to be wholly under his own editorial control, and publishes a "Prospectus," but does not find financial support and postpones plans. George Graham buys *Burton's Gentleman's Magazine* in November 1840, and unites it with his *The Casket* to form *Graham's Magazine*; Poe contributes "The Man of the Crowd" for the December number.

1841–42   Becomes an editor of *Graham's Magazine* (salary of $800 with extra for literary pieces) beginning with the April 1841 issue; contributes "The Murders in the Rue Morgue," the first of what he calls his "tales of ratiocination." Subsequently, writes new stories and poems, a series of articles on cryptography and another on autography. By end of year, subscriptions to *Graham's* more than quadruple. Makes inquiries concerning a clerkship in the Tyler administration. Revives plans for *The Penn Magazine*, which he hopes Graham will support financially, and applies to Irving, Cooper, Bryant, Kennedy, and others for regular contributions. In January 1842 Virginia bursts a blood vessel while singing, almost dies, and never fully recovers. Meets Dickens. Spring contributions include "The Masque of the Red Death" and a laudatory review of Hawthorne's *Twice-Told Tales* in *Graham's*, and an article in *Saturday Evening Post* in which Poe tries to guess the solution to Dickens' *Barnaby Rudge* from the early installments (he guesses the murderer correctly but is wrong on other points). Resigns from *Graham's* in May 1842, and is succeeded by Rufus Wilmot Griswold (later Poe's literary executor). Failing to interest his Philadelphia publisher in an expanded edition of *Tales of the Grotesque and Arabesque,* works on a new, revised two-volume collection of stories to be titled *Phantasy-Pieces*. Fall publications include "The Pit and the Pendulum."

1843   Invited by James Russell Lowell to contribute regularly to his new magazine *The Pioneer*; "The Tell-Tale Heart,"

"Lenore," and an essay later titled "The Rationale of Verse" appear there, but magazine fails after three issues. Goes to Washington, D.C., to be interviewed for a minor job in the Tyler administration and to solicit subscriptions for his own journal, now called *The Stylus*. Gets drunk and ruins his chances for the job; friends have to see him onto a train for his return to Philadelphia. Resumes output of satires, poems, and reviews, but is pressed for money and tries to borrow from Griswold and Lowell. In June "The Gold-Bug" wins $100 prize in a Philadelphia *Dollar Newspaper* contest and is immediately successful; multiple reprintings of the tale and a dramatized version make Poe famous as a popular writer. First and only number of a pamphlet series, *The Prose Romances of Edgar A. Poe*, appears in July, including "The Murders in the Rue Morgue" and "The Man That Was Used Up." Becomes friends with Philadelphia gothic novelist George Lippard. Begins lecture circuit in November with "Poets and Poetry of America." Fall publications include "The Black Cat."

1844   Moves to New York City, where his successful hoax in the New York *Sun* describing a balloon journey across the Atlantic enhances his growing fame. Still planning for *The Stylus* despite past frustrations, he now envisages an audience including the "well-educated men . . . among the innumerable plantations of our vast Southern & Western Countries." Lowell requests autobiographical notes for use in a magazine article, and Poe responds, "I think that human exertion will have no appreciable effect upon humanity. Man is now only more active—not more happy—nor more wise, than he was 6000 years ago." Works on never-completed *Critical History of American Literature* and continues lectures on American poetry. In October joins staff of New York *Evening Mirror* and contributes articles on the literary marketplace, contemporary authors, the lack of international copyright law. Begins "Marginalia" series in *Democratic Review* in November.

1845   "The Raven" appears in the January *Evening Mirror* and is an enormous popular and critical success, inviting many reprints and parodies. Enters New York literary society and meets Evert Duyckinck, who selects the twelve stories published as *Tales* by Wiley and Putnam in July. The volume is well received and encourages the publishers to bring out *The Raven and Other Poems* in November. Meanwhile, begins contributing to the *Broadway Journal*, becomes its editor in July, and, soon after, on money borrowed from Griswold, Halleck, and Horace Greeley, becomes its proprietor. Reprints revised versions of most of his stories and poems there, and contributes over sixty literary essays and reviews, as well as publishing reviews in the *Messenger* and a long article on "American Drama" in the *American Whig Review*. Conducts a literary courtship in verse with the poet Frances Sargent Osgood. The "Longfellow War" (January-August), a private campaign against plagiarism with Longfellow the most eminent of those accused, brings notoriety and alienates friends such as Lowell. Lectures on "Poets and Poetry of America" in New York in May. Negative publicity from his reading "Al Aaraaf" at the Boston Lyceum in October, and the insulting jibes at Boston with which Poe responds, further damage his reputation and increase his fame. In the fall Virginia's illness becomes acute.

1846   Illness, severe nervous depression, and economic hardship force Poe to stop publication of the *Broadway Journal* after the January 3 issue. Moves family to cottage in Fordham, New York, where Virginia, a semi-invalid, is nursed by Marie Louise Shew who charitably supplies bedclothes and other necessities. Writes to Virginia, "You are my *greatest* and *only* stimulus now, to battle with this uncongenial, unsatisfactory, and ungrateful life." Poe and family are mentioned as pitiable charity cases in various papers in New York and Pennsylvania. Seriously ill most of the year, still manages to publish "The Cask of Amontillado" and "The Philosophy of Composition," place reviews in *Godey's*, and continue "Marginalia" in *Graham's* and *Democratic Review*. Begins satirical sketches of "The Literati of New York City" in *Godey's* in May. The one on Thomas Dunn English, whom Poe had known in Philadelphia, draws a vicious attack by English on Poe's morality and sanity. Poe sues the *Evening Mirror*, publisher of the piece, and collects damages the following year. Works on book-length version of "Literati" sketches to be entitled *Literary America*, hoping to incorporate in it analytic essays on versification and revised version of Hawthorne essay. Writes a young admirer, "As regards the Stylus—that is the grand purpose of my life, from which I have never swerved for a moment." Hears first rumors of nascent fame in France, where translations and a long analytic criticism of *Tales* appear.

1847   Virginia dies January 30. Poe falls gravely ill and has least productive year. Nursed back to health by devoted attentions of Mrs. Clemm and Mrs. Shew, once more seeks support for literary magazine and fails again. Completes revised versions of Hawthorne review and "The Landscape Garden," and writes two poems: one thanking Mrs. Shew ("To M. L. S—"), the other "Ulalume." Increasing interest in cosmological theories leads to preliminary notes for *Eureka*.

1848   Begins year in better health. In a letter, ascribes his past intermittent drinking to insanity caused by constant fear of Virginia's death: "My enemies referred the insanity to the drink rather than the drink to the insanity . . . it was the horrible never-ending oscillation between hope and despair which I could *not* longer have endured without total loss of reason. In the death of what was my life, then, I receive a new but—oh God! how melancholy an existence." Gives lectures and readings to raise capital for *The Stylus*. February lecture on "The Universe" in New York City surveys thematic material fully elaborated in *Eureka*, published by Putnam in June. While speaking in Lowell, Massachusetts, forms deep attachment to "Annie" (Mrs. Nancy Richmond), who becomes his confidante; subsequently, in Providence, Rhode Island, begins three-month courtship of forty-five-year-old widowed poet Sarah Helen Whitman, to whom he proposes marriage. When she delays answering because of reports of Poe's "unprincipled" character, he suffers severe anxiety and, after one trip to Providence, takes a dose of laudanum. Their brief engagement is broken off in December through influence of Mrs. Whitman's mother and friends. Reads "The Poetic Principle" as lecture in Providence. Writes "The Bells."

1849   Active as writer and lecturer; main outlet is the Boston *Flag of Our Union*, a popular weekly. In February writes to a friend, "Literature is the most noble of professions. In fact, it is about the only one fit for a man." Criticizes Lowell's "A Fable for Critics" for its omission of Southern

writers. In early summer, leaves for Richmond to seek
Southern support for *The Stylus*. Stops in Philadelphia,
sick, confused, and apparently suffering from persecution
mania; friends George Lippard and illustrator John Sartain care for him and Charles Burr pays for his train trip
to Richmond. During two-month stay in Richmond, visits sister Rosalie, joins temperance society, and becomes
engaged to boyhood sweetheart Elmira Royster Shelton,
now a widow. Possibly intending to bring Mrs. Clemm
from New York, sails for Baltimore where, a week after
arrival, he is found semi-conscious and delirious outside a
polling booth on October 3. Dies October 7 "of conges-
tion of the brain." "The Bells" and "Annabel Lee" appear
posthumously late in the year. Slanderous obituary notice
by Griswold blackens Poe's reputation for many years.

Note on the Texts

This volume provides a collection from the nearly one thousand essays, reviews, articles, columns, and critical notices by Poe that appeared in magazines, newspapers, or annuals during his lifetime or immediately after. It attempts to give as inclusive a selection as possible, while avoiding unnecessary repetition. A large number of Poe's pieces were no longer than a paragraph, and these have generally been omitted from this collection. Many of these short notices, however, were subsequently recombined—for the "Marginalia" series or the "Literati of New York" series—and they appear in this volume in their later form. Versions of many of the pieces gathered here were published in Rufus Griswold's *The Works of the Late Edgar Allan Poe* (New York, 1856), in Stedman and Woodberry's *The Works of Edgar Allan Poe* (Chicago, 1894), or in J. A. Harrison's *The Complete Works of Edgar Allan Poe* (New York, 1902). Some of the selections, however, are reprinted here for the first time since their original publication. These pieces include the reviews of *An Account of the United States' Exploring Expedition* (GM, 1843), Cooper's *History of the Navy of the United States* (BGM, 1839), *Wyandotté* (GM, 1843), and George Jones' *Ancient America* (A, 1845). Poe never collected his reviews and essays, although they would have amounted to several generous volumes. He occasionally reprinted, reworked, or excerpted his published pieces to create new columns, but he rarely revised or re-edited them with the care he gave to his poetry and tales.

The first appearance of each title has usually been selected, unless the piece was subsequently rewritten and expanded or reprinted as part of a later, more extensive article. Poe's reviews of Mathews, Simms, and Elizabeth Oakes Smith for *Godey's Lady's Book*, for example, are chosen in preference to the earlier short notices in the *Broadway Journal*, of which they are revised and expanded versions. Similarly, the "Notes upon English Verse" from *The Pioneer* has not been included because it was subsequently incorporated into the longer essay "The Rationale of Verse." In such cases of repetition, the

more complete version has been chosen. Other articles or reviews—such as Poe's review of Willis' *Tortesa* in *Burton's Gentleman's Magazine* (later incorporated into "The American
Drama"), of Lowell's *Conversations* in the New York *Weekly
Mirror* (later included in "Marginalia"), or of Sedgwick's *The
Linwoods* in the *Southern Literary Messenger* (reprinted as part
of the "Literati of New York" series)—are not reprinted separately because they appear as part of larger selections.

Many of Poe's pieces, including a number in this volume,
originally appeared unsigned. All such selections reprinted
here have been verified as his, either from information in his
correspondence, edited by John Ward Ostram (Cambridge,
1948), or by collation for content with other pieces known to
be his. William Doyle Hull's "A Canon of the Critical Works
of Edgar Allan Poe with a Study of Poe as Editor and Reviewer" (Ph.D. Diss., University of Virginia, 1941) has provided valuable assistance in assigning authorship.

Poe's editorship of or close association with most of the
magazines in which his critical writings appeared (*Southern
Literary Messenger*, *Burton's Gentleman's Magazine*, *Graham's*,
the New York *Mirror*, and the *Broadway Journal*) lends authority to the texts from these periodicals. In many cases Poe
was able to oversee the publication of his texts from manuscript through their final printed form. Other publications
that printed Poe's reviews and articles, such as *Godey's Lady's
Book*, the *Aristidean*, *The Pioneer*, the *Democratic Review*, and
the *American Whig Review*, were managed by Poe's friends or
acquaintances, and there is no evidence of substantial editorial
alteration of pieces that appeared in these magazines.

The texts in this volume (with the exception of the "Prospectus" of *The Penn Magazine* and "A Reviewer Reviewed")
have been reprinted from their original periodical appearances. Later collected editions were based upon these same
sources, and in most cases were modernized, regularized, or
otherwise differed from the original texts. A chronological
short-title catalog of the selections in this volume indicates
the original publication (with volume and page or issue) that
provides the text reprinted here. (Starred titles refer to early
notices or articles reprinted in a later version in this collection, usually as part of a longer essay or series. The last cita-

tion following the starred title is the source of the text included in this collection.)

List of Abbreviations

AM	American Museum
AWR	American Whig Review
A	Aristidean
BM	Boston Miscellany
BJ	Broadway Journal
BGM	Burton's Gentleman's Magazine
DR	United States Magazine and Democratic Review
GLB	Godey's Lady's Book
GM	Graham's Magazine
NYEM	New York Evening Mirror
NYR	New York Review
NYWM	New York Weekly Mirror
Opal	The Opal
PSM	Philadelphia Saturday Museum
P	The Pioneer
SUM	Sartain's Union Magazine
SEP	Saturday Evening Post
SLM	Southern Literary Messenger

Chronological Short-Title Catalog

Osborn, *Confessions of a Poet*	*SLM,* I (Apr. 1835), 459
Kennedy, *Horse-Shoe Robinson*	*SLM,* I (May 1835), 522–24
Euripides, *Works*	*SLM,* I (Sept. 1835), 779–80
E. S. Barrett, *The Heroine*	*SLM,* II (Dec. 1835), 41–43
Fay, *Norman Leslie*	*SLM,* II (Dec. 1835), 54–57
*Sedgwick, *The Linwoods*	*SLM,* II (Dec. 1835), 57–59
(see "The Literati of New York")	*GLB,* XXXIII (Sept. 1846), 126–33
Irving, *Crayon Miscellany*	*SLM,* II (Dec. 1835), 64–65
Godwin, *Lives of the Necromancers*	*SLM,* II (Dec. 1835), 65
L. H. Sigourney—H. F. Gould —E. F. Ellet	*SLM,* II (Jan. 1836), 112–17
Simms, *The Partisan*	*SLM,* II (Jan. 1836), 117–21
Stickney, *Poetry of Life*	*SLM,* II (Jan. 1836), 123–24
Lieber, *Reminiscences of Niebuhr*	*SLM,* II (Jan. 1836), 125–27

The "Prospectus" of *The Penn Magazine* was a privately issued promotional sheet circulated by Poe in the summer of 1840. A version of this prospectus first appeared in the *Phila-*

delphia Saturday Courier of June 13, 1840 (p. 2), but Poe revised and expanded this brief notice and printed it as a separate sheet, which he used for his correspondence. The prospectus is reprinted here from a copy in the Simon Gratz collection of the Historical Society of Pennsylvania, containing on the reverse a letter from Poe to Joseph Boyd of Cincinnati. "A Reviewer Reviewed" ("By Walter G. Bowen") was left unfinished at Poe's death. The manuscript of the article dates from the summer of 1849, and it passed to Rufus Griswold among other papers from Poe's trunk. The first complete printing of the piece was in Thomas Ollive Mabbott's *Collected Works of Edgar Allan Poe* (Cambridge: Harvard University Press, 1978), v. III, pp. 1378–86, which provides the text reprinted here. The illustration that accompanies "Maelzel's Chess-Player is reproduced from Griswold's *The Works of the Late Edgar Allan Poe* (New York: J. S. Redfield, 1855–56), IV, 350, courtesy of the New-York Historical Society.

The standards for American English continue to fluctuate, and in some ways they are conspicuously different now from what they were in earlier periods. In nineteenth-century writings, for example, a word might be spelled in more than one way, even in the same work, and such variations might be carried into print. Commas were sometimes used expressively to suggest the movements of voice, and capitals were sometimes meant to give significances to a word beyond those it might have in its uncapitalized form. Since modernization would remove such effects, this volume preserves the spelling, punctuation, capitalization, and wording of the periodical texts, which, of the available editions, appear most faithful to Poe's intentions. The present volume represents the *texts* of these editions; it does not attempt to reproduce the features of their typographic design—such as the display capitalization of chapter openings. Some changes, however, have been made. Double quotation marks have been made single where appropriate. Typographical errors have been corrected; the following is a list of those errors by page and line number: 37.18, protection; 43.11, certai; 46.31, mĕmŏry; 50.22, mānyare the; 50.32, preceeding; 52.5, Abpdos; 54.14, *crime*; 55.7, *imperfection*; 55.9, reading,; 56.19, include; 56.36, *my*,; 59.19, mŭsing;

61.11, rhythmical; 62.35, poems.; 64.22, littla; 64.27, de | ous; 64.27, meum; 64.29, fervidis; 64.31 ad | Deos; 65.11, gentle-
man; 65.19, there no; 68.20–21, frequency; 92.1–2, regret; 106.31, *naïveté*; 112.11, praised!"; 114.1, bosom; 123.38, *génie.*"; 125.18, inner; 129.29, dismis; 139.28–29, emation; 158.5, *Méchant*; 190.39, he; 196.31, sake-keeping; 197.2, on't.'; 201.32, Christendom?; 202.5–6, ourselves?; 206.16–17, *Pawnbrokers' Shops*; 211.32, Roohk; 211.33, self-dimned; 219.5, *denouement*; 219.12–13, *denouement*; 220.15, *denouement*; 224.30, O;Malley; 240.17, Notre Dâme; 242.1, he dream; 248.20, af; 258.2, tests; 272.9, critic a; 275.31, whereever; 275.35, dance.'"; 280.30, Mel-ancholy.; 318.6, ook; 318.8, detect ng; 322.33, appear; 338.6, em-barrasment; 350.8, that; 357.9, *a*'; 370.2, *any qumor*; 373.6, inval; 377.5, it not; 384.13, Gipsey; 399.34, Feurteufel; 401.30, adventure; 414.34, delilate; 415.34, chair; 421.27, alternates; 428.1, fifty six; 457.15, *niaseries*; 460.13, Æone; 460.32, no; 461.9, it,;; 461.37, of gentleman; 480.34, history,; 485.40, "At (no paragraph); 487.37, needles; 513.22, litle; 514.18, again."; 515.20, pain; 519.11, bright; 536.11, "Strangers!; 536.26, *and*; 547.10, one one; 547.19, I.; 554.4, between; 556.3, recoltions; 559.20, changed; 561.15, Montrose; 568.2, Monroe; 576.1, 'Vil-lain; 585.26, Beranger; 603.4, too; 630.16, Rizner; 631.32, Ari-cara; 639.2, Nr.; 646.1, thar; 646.11, but in; 656.28, Melpo-mene,; 656.36, "(Records; 663.32, *Berlin*; 664.23, Devil"; 665.8, *naïveté*; 683.12, Russel; 706.11, Poem; 706.13, were easily; 706.17, christened."; 711.38, madam; 714.5, "And; 717.5, in world; 730.12, "And; 731.23, purpoes; 733.7, bird,"; 742.33, acuse; 743.33, "[and; 759.25, Owon; 759.35, prerogative.' "; 764.29, peultimate; 768.24, country."; 772.1, Sea.'"; 772.10, pood; 772.24, Like; 775.23, "The; 788.12, Longworth; 789.1–2, psycological; 789.12–13, "are . . . maxims?; 799.37, Aroundt hee; 806.16, Proctor; 806.24, th-t; 816.14, construct-; 829.36, trad; 838.35, But "says; 848.19–20, day, quoth Mr. Mattson,; 849.8, captive; 857.12, America?"; 859.20, Salvation.'; 866.8, Montimer; 879.24, riends; 920.1, details.; 923.22, downfal; 971.1, 'Dear; 971.20, said.; 1002.18, thunder-shrieks."; 1043.2, imagination*s*.; 1043.11, associations."; 1049.1, My; 1061.27, Βεστουμ; 1061.27, Ημτερωτορεσ; 1064.19, press.; 1069.6, Bushnell.; 1076.30, critic,; 1077.29-30, cotinuation; 1077.30,

nBritish; 1080.8, C,; 1081.10, W,; 1083.23, re-publication,; 1090.35, pirnting; 1095.32, That; 1106.30, gazettes!!; 1109.24, COLLIER; 1115.22, wanaged; 1115.28, consonants; 1116.20 court ofs; 1116.31, podularity; 1120.31, at a; 1136.35, first; 1145.17, told"—; 1166.2, Mr. F.; 1166.35, manner; 1207.7, Old; 1219.12, alt; 1219.13, thal; 1285.20, frd; 1285.20–21-22, fuacfshffheo; 1285.21, hetmsafhie; 1285.25, ihufheo; 1285.25, aeohdəff; 1285.26, ief; 1285.28, raeoeu; 1285.30, rdffheafhil; 1285.32, desiaefiun; 1285.38, softriedi; 1286.2, tf; 1288.24, n; 1299.39, —— Review,"; 1304.40–1305.1, somethat; 1305.3, vesification; 1306.28, "is; 1342.14, apared; 1345.30, *codices*;; 1361.26, *leshimmanah*; 1386.37, *not*—; 1389.15, them?"; 1399.34, Ayretos; 1400.22 skaken; 1400.27, like; 1403.14, trival; 1420.34, "Thirdly; 1441.11, book,"; 1446.21, Shellyan; 1450.24, do.; 1457.2, Villiany; 1458.2, so so; 1461.21, coutemplating; 1464.10, *confrerre*,; 1467.17, Constellalation. Error corrected third printing: 936.20, εἰσπορευδμενος (*LOA*).

Notes

In the notes below, numbers refer to page and line of this volume (the line count includes chapter headings). No note is made for material included in a standard desk-reference book. Some queries concerning full names, authorship, and further mention of titles may be answered by checking the Index for cross-references. Notes at the foot of the page in the text are Poe's own.

THEORY OF POETRY

5.1   *Letter to B——**]   First published as the preface to *Poems* (1831) under the title "Letter to Mr. —— ——." The identity of "B" is uncertain, though the publisher of the volume, Elam Bliss, is a strong likelihood. The text here is that reprinted in the *SLM* in 1836. It is unclear whether the footnote to the title is by T. W. White, owner and at that time editor of the *Messenger*, or by Poe himself.

7.7   Aristotle]   *Poetics*, IX, 3. The phrase is taken out of context. Aristotle writes that poetry is more philosophical than history, for poetry tends to express the universal, history the particular. Poe seems to follow the lead of Wordsworth in the Preface to *Lyrical Ballads* (1800): "Aristotle, I have been told, has said, that Poetry is the most philosophic of all writings."

7.18   ceteris paribus]   "Other things being equal."

7.30–31   the devil in Melmoth]   Charles Maturin's *Melmoth the Wanderer* (1820).

8.9–10   "Trifles . . . below,"]   Slight misquotation from the Prologue (11, 25–26) of John Dryden's *All for Love* (1677). For "trifles" read "errors."

8.15–16   The ancients . . . well:]   Democritus was alleged to have said that Truth lies at the bottom of a well; see Diogenes Laertius, *Pyrrho*, IX, 72.

8.22   *de omni . . . aliis.*]   "Concerning all that can be known and certain other things."

9.11   volumes at random]   The work referred to is Wordsworth's "Essay Supplementary to the Preface" in his *Collected Poems* (1815).

9.23   *Tantæne animis?*]   Short for "Why such anger?" From Virgil, *Aeneid*, I, 11.

9.28   *"Temora"*]   One of the "Ossian" poems of James MacPherson that Wordsworth alludes to in "Essay Supplementary to the Preface."

9.35–10.3   "And now . . . Doctor!"]   From Wordsworth's "The Idiot Boy" (1798); the first two lines are reversed and two lines are omitted.

10.5–10   "The dew . . . stone."]   Wordsworth's "The Pet Lamb" (1800), with dashes added by Poe.

10.19–25   "Those who . . . title."]   From the Preface to *Lyrical Ballads*.

10.25–27   Yet let . . . turkeys.]   A series of playful allusions: Wordsworth wrote a work called "The Waggoner" (1819); the "sore toe" is a reference to *Oedipus* ("swollen foot"); Sophocles was called "the Attic Bee" (see A. W. Schlegel, *Lectures on Dramatic Art and Literature* [1808], Lecture VII) and was said by Pliny (*Natural History*, XXXVII, 40) to have used a chorus of guinea fowls to lament the death of Meleager in one of his plays.

10.30–32   "que . . . nient."]   "For the most part, most sects are right in what they advance, but not in what they deny." Quoted by Coleridge in Chapter II of the *Biographia Literaria* (1817) as from Leibnitz, *Trois Lettres à M. Remond de Mont-Mort* (1741).

11.2   Nyctanthes]   Night-blooming jasmine.

11.8   Corcyra]   Corfu, frequently renamed throughout history.

11.10   "Tres-volontiers,"]   Very willingly.

12.3–4   No . . . gallows.]   From Samuel Butler, *Hudibras*, Part II (1664), I, 272ff.

13.3–5   examination . . . backwards?]   In 1841, while Dickens' novel *Barnaby Rudge* was still appearing serially, Poe predicted who the murderer would be (see his reviews, pp. 218–44 of the present volume). Godwin's statement about writing *Caleb Williams* (1794) backwards occurs in the preface.

20.12   Aidenn]   Muslim term for paradise, *Adn* (Eden).

26.1   *The Rationale of Verse*]   This essay incorporates most of the shorter treatment, titled "Notes upon English Verse," published in *The Pioneer*, March 1843.

27.31–34   "When a . . . hypermeter."]   Goold Brown, *The Institutes of English Grammar* (1833).

28.21–28   Bacon . . . Leonicenus.]   This Bacon seems to have made an abridgment of Lindley Murray's influential *English Grammar: Comprehending the Principles and Rules of the English Language*; Alexander Miller, *A Concise Grammar of the Language* (1795); Allen Fisk, *Murray's English Grammar Simplified* (1822); Jeremiah Greenleaf, *Grammar Simplified; or, An Ocular Analysis of the English Language*, 10th ed. (1824); Charles M. Ingersoll, *Conversations on English Grammar*, 4th ed. (1824); Samuel Kirkham (for Kirkland), *English Grammar in Familiar Lectures*, 53rd ed. (1841); Joab Goldsmith Cooper, *An Abridgement of Murray's English Grammar* (1828); Abel Flint, *Murray's English Grammar Abridged* (1810); Hugh A. Pue, *A Grammar of the English Language* (1841); John Comly, *English Grammar*, 15th ed. (1826); William Lily, *Brevissima institutio, seu ratio grammatices cognoscendae, ad omnium puerorum utili-*

taten prescripta; quam solam regia majestas in omnibus scholis docendam præcipit
["in all schools by royal injunction"] (1776); Omnibonus Leonicenus, *De octo partibus orationis* (1473).

30.5–9   Fallis . . . umbram.]   From *Punica*, II, 342–46. "You are wrong if you believe he sits at table unarmed; / This lord is armed with the eternal greatness gained / From so many wars, so many slaughtered victims. / If you come close to him you will be astonished: / Cannae and Trebia will be before your eyes, the Trasimene graves / And Paulus' monstrous shade." (Translation by Anthony Kemp.)

31.20   a little ballad]   By Henry B. Hirst; see Poe's review of his *The Coming of the Mammoth*, pp. 594–605.

32.5–6   *les moutons de Panurge*]   The sheep of Panurge, a character in François Rabelais' *Gargantua and Pantagruel* (1532–52); this is a recurrent reference in Poe's criticism.

32.31–32   *Ex uno disce omnia.*]   "From one thing learn all."

37.36   Parturiunt . . . *mus*.]   "The laboring mountain gives birth to a ridiculous mouse." Horace, *Ars Poetica*, V, 139.

37.38   Litoreis . . . *sus*.]   "You will find an immense sow under the oaks of the shore." Virgil, *Aeneid*, III, 390.

42.30–33   ŏh thōu . . . chaīr.]   Alexander Pope, 1st *Dunciad* (1728), II.19–22.

47.5   Christopher Pease Cranch]   Poe consistently misspelled the name of Christopher *Pearse* Cranch (1830–92).

47.7–12   Many are . . . losing.]   "My Thoughts," printed in Rufus Wilmot Griswold, *Poets and Poetry of America* (1842) and Cranch's *Poems* (1844).

47.23–24   Coleridge . . . *system*]   In his preface to "Christabel" (1816), Coleridge explains that the meter of the poem is "founded on a new principle: namely, that of counting in each line the accents, not the syllables"; four accents per line and any number of syllables from seven to twelve.

49.24   αστρολογος]   An apparent error on Poe's part, derived from his misreading of Charles Anthon, *A System of Greek Prosody and Metre* (1842), where αστρολογος (astrologer) is used as an example of a word that scans as the foot called *pæon primus*; αστρολογος, or *astrologos*, is not a term of Greek prosody.

61.28–33   Mæcenas . . . Deos.]   Horace, *Odes*, I, 1. "Mæcenas, sprung from royal progenitors, / Oh, my protector and my dear glory, / There are those who delight in gathering / Olympic dust upon the racing-car, / Who cleared the turning-post with burning wheel. / Lords of earth, they carry to the gods / The celebrated palm." (Translation by Anthony Kemp.)

63.1–2   His sinuous . . . round.] "The Lost Hunter," printed in Griswold.

63.16   hudsonizing] A reference to Henry Norman Hudson, author of *Lectures on Shakspeare*, the second edition of which had just been published (1848).

66.21–24   Integer . . . retra.] Horace, *Odes*, I, 21. "He whose life is upright, purified / From guilt, needs no Moorish darts nor bow, / Nor quivers, Fuscus, full of / Poisonous arrows." (Translation by Anthony Kemp.)

66.25   bastard iambus] Here Poe seems to mean "bastard dactyl."

68.38   Felton . . . Frogpondian] Cornelius Conway Felton had defended Longfellow's "bastard" hexameters in the *North American Review*, 55 (1842), 114–44. "Frogpondian" is Poe's name for the Boston intelligentsia and Harvard professors, derived from the frogpond on the Boston Common, and apparently alluding to the tale of the frogs and the Log King in Aesop's *Fables*.

71.1   *The Poetic Principle*] In this essay Poe makes extensive use of his review of Longfellow's *Ballads and Other Poems* (1842). See pp. 679–96.

72.28–29   Lamartine . . . Pollock] The French poet Alphonse de Lamartine was notoriously prolix. Robert Pollock of Scotland was known for a long didactic, religious poem, *The Course of Time* (1827).

76.22–23   Pure . . . Sense.] The tripartite paradigm of Immanuel Kant, Introduction to *The Critique of Judgment* (1793).

80.23   Down] Cf. stanza 5 of the poem just quoted (79.26).

81.29   I know . . . see] In Bryant's *Poetical Works*, this line reads: "I know that no more should see."

REVIEWS OF BRITISH AND CONTINENTAL AUTHORS

104.3   "Poacher"] See Poe's review, pp. 325–28.

105.21   "What Hecuba . . . Hecuba?"] *Hamlet*, II, 2.

105.32–33   "The Ghost of Cock-Lane,"] Sensational eighteenth-century ghost (first sighted in 1762), much debated in the London newspapers, including contributions from Dr. Samuel Johnson, Horace Walpole, and Oliver Goldsmith.

116.4   Sir James Puckle] British moralist of the late seventeenth and early eighteenth centuries; Poe mentions him frequently.

118.33–35   Egyptian . . . Blitz] James Silk Buckingham was one of many who exploited popular interest in Egypt after Napoleon's armies opened it to European travel. Signor Antonio Blitz was a stage magician.

120.31   *niäiseries*]   Here and throughout, Poe uses the word in the sense of trivial or inadvertent foolishness.

127.3–4   "*spoudiotaton* . . . Aristotle."]   See note 7.7.

129.6–7   "De gustibus . . . disputand*us*;"]   "Taste is not arguable."

129.13   Ambrosianians]   An allusion to Christopher North's column, the "Noctes Ambrosianae," in *Blackwood's*, which featured esoteric satires written principally for the magazine's contributors, who wrote under various pseudonyms, like Ebony, Δ, and the Ettrick Shepherd.

133.12   Nat-Leeism]   Nathaniel Lee, eighteenth-century British playwright noted for the extravagant imagery, frenzied action, and general morbidness of his tragedies, became insane and died in Bedlam at the age of forty-two.

139.8   *skolastikos*]   A reference to the ancient scholar who demonstrated the value of his house to a prospective buyer by showing him a brick, the part absurdly representing the whole (synecdoche).

140.5–7   Lord . . . proportion."]   Francis Bacon, *Essays* (1597, 1612, 1625), No. 43, "Of Beauty," here slightly misquoted.

142.24–35   Scott . . . Smith]   Scott's title is actually *The Bride of Lammermoor* (1819). The author of *Pelham* is Bulwer. Charlotte Dacre wrote sensational novels such as *Zafloya, the Moor* (1806) and *The Libertine* (1807) under a pseudonym, which gave rise to the appellation "the Rose Matilda School" of fiction. James Kirk Paulding, a New York writer, was a friend of Poe's. The writer of *Godolphin* is Bulwer. Michael and John Banim collaborated on a series of stories of Irish life, *Tales of the O'Hara Family* (1825–29). Thomas Hope, Edward John Trelawney, Thomas Moore, and Horace Smith were British writers of prose and metrical romances.

146.25   antique.]   In the *Southern Literary Messenger* Poe introduced a long extract from the novel at this point. It is not included here.

161.26   *jurare . . . magistri*]   "To swear allegiance to a master."

163.33   vindictive . . . Lockhart.]   Literary warfare of the Scots and English magazines.

172.10–11   Wohl . . . ist!—]   "Indeed, he is gone to where there is no more snow."

174.6–16   *Corinne* . . . l'amour."]   By Mme. de Staël. "Of all my faculties, the most powerful is suffering. I am born for happiness. My character is trusting, my imagination is gay; but pain excites in me an unknown impetuosity that can disturb my reason, or lead to death. I repeat to you again, treat me with care; gaiety, mobility only serve me outwardly: but there are abysses of sadness in my soul that I cannot resist unless I preserve myself from love."

180.1   Weller]   A character in Dickens' *Pickwick Papers*.

201.17   Vapid]   Character in *The Dramatist*, a play by F. M. Reynolds.

207.9   Gin Shops.]   In the *Southern Literary Messenger* Poe introduced a
long extract from Chapter XXII of "Scenes" in *Sketches by Boz*, not printed
here.

207.34   friends.]   A long extract from Chapter XI of *The Pickwick Papers*
followed in the *Southern Literary Messenger*, again not printed here.

275.21   Meltonian]   Allusion to Melton Mowbray in Leicestershire, England, a famous hunting center.

277.1   In . . . Willis]   This review incorporates most of Poe's "American
Prose Writers No. 2—N. P. Willis" from the *Broadway Journal*, I (January 18,
1845), 37–38, omitting only the first two and the concluding paragraphs.

280.36   Ramsbottom]   "Mrs. Ramsbottom" was the name under which
Theodore Hook, editor of the *John Bull*, published his own letters to that
newspaper in 1829.

293.27–28 Fourier's dreams]   Later editions of this essay read "Cousin's
dreams."

296.13–14 *nil . . . ornavit*]   "He touched nothing he has not adorned."

REVIEWS OF AMERICAN AUTHORS AND
AMERICAN LITERATURE

357.2   Berryer]   Antoine Pierre Berryer (1790–1868), French lawyer celebrated for his solution of a linguistic riddle. See Poe's "A Few Words on
Secret Writing," pp. 1277–91.

357.2–4   *"l'homme . . . d'antithèse"*]   "A man who, in his description, demands the greatest possible quantity of antitheses."

357.9–10   *"de nier . . . pas."*]   "To deny that which is, and to explain that
which is not."

360.24   Tortesa]   Poe's review from *Burton's Gentleman's Magazine*
(August 1839) is incorporated into this essay.

364.26–27 P. S. and O. P.]   "Prompt side," i.e., the actor's right when
facing the audience, and "opposite prompt."

367.1–2   The plots . . . God.]   This passage, originally from the "Marginalia" (pp. 1315–16), is incorporated into the conclusion of *Eureka*.

387.18   Horne Tooke]   Poe called him the "greatest of philosophical
grammarians" and admired his "entirely novel theory of language."

NOTES   1499

405.19–20   "Kettell's Specimens"] *Specimens of American Poetry*, 3 vols. (Boston, 1829), compiled by Samuel Kettell (1800–55), contained selections by 189 writers from Cotton Mather to John Greenleaf Whittier.

408.36   Dr. Sumner's] Dr. Charles Richard Sumner, editor of Milton's posthumously discovered *A Treatise on Christian Doctrine (*1825).

416.14–19   Rome . . . days.] The last three extracts are from the second book of Pope's *Dunciad*.

456.16   Burdon] William Burdon, author of *Materials for Thinking* (1803–10).

456.19–20   author . . . *penser,"*] Jean-Louis Guez de Balzac.

456.23–24   *"Lettres . . . Curieuses,"*] Translated by John Lockman (1698–1771) as *Travels of the Jesuits into Various Parts of the World* (1743).

456.25   Suard and André] Actually Jean-Baptiste Antoine Suard and *Andere* (German: *others*) or *autres*.

459.1   *William Ellery Channing*] (1818–1901) The nephew, not the son, of the Unitarian minister of the same name. An abridged version of this essay was printed in the *Southern Literary Messenger* in 1850.

459.23   "Sam Patch"] The hero of the poem, "The Great Descender," by Thomas Ward ("Flaccus").

461.35–36   nods . . . Burleigh's] A "Lord Burleigh nod" is an ambiguous gesture open to any interpretation. See Richard Sheridan, *The Critic*, III, i.

495.19   *cacoëthes*] An obstinate disease; *scribendi cacoëthes* means an incurable itch to write.

544.16   a-Willising] Reference to Nathaniel Parker Willis (1806–67), New York writer, editor, and foreign correspondent.

546.19–20   *Diary . . . Physician*] *Passages from the Diary of a Late Physician,* by Samuel Warren (1807–77), serialized in *Blackwood's Magazine*, 1830–37.

559.7   Burk's] John Daly Burk (c.1775–1808), author of *The History of Virginia, from its First Settlement to the Present Time* (1804–16).

568.20   Rosa-Matilda effusions] See note 142.24–35.

588.1   "The Dial,"] The magazine of New England Transcendentalism, founded in 1840 by Theodore Parker, Bronson Alcott, Orestes Brownson, Margaret Fuller, James Freeman Clarke, and Ralph Waldo Emerson. Fuller was its editor from 1840 to 1842, and Emerson from 1842 to 1844.

596.29   Nat Leeism] See note 133.12.

610.25–26   Commodore Patterson] Daniel Todd Patterson (1786–1839), American naval officer in command of forces against the Gulf buccaneers and against the British at New Orleans.

646.7   Vathek and Nouronihar] Characters in William Beckford's Arabian romance, *Vathek* (1786).

670.1   *Longfellow*] The controversy, called by Poe "The Little Longfellow War" (in which Longfellow himself appears never to have participated directly), may be traced in the reviews and rejoinders here collected.

670.8–9   Phantasy . . . Callôt] "Phantasy Pieces" refers to the etchings of Jacques Callôt (1592–1635) of Lorraine and to the German romantic writer E. T. A. Hoffman, who titled his first collection of tales *Phantasiestücke in Callôts Manier* (1814).

685.5–7   Dividing . . . sense.] The paradigm of Immanuel Kant; see note 76.22–23.

685.26   το χαλον] "Beauty"; the discussion is Kantian rather than directly derived from Aristotle's *Ethics* or *Poetics*.

687.28   Count Bielfeld's] Baron Jacob de Bielfeld, *Les Premiers Traits de L'Erudition Universelle* (1767); translated by W. Hooper as *The Elements of Universal Erudition* (London, 1770). The work is frequently referred to by Poe.

689.12–13   "Armstrong on Health"] Dr. John Armstrong, *The Art of Preserving Health* (1744), a didactic poem.

691.15   Schlegel] A. W. Schlegel, *Lectures on Dramatic Art and Literature*.

696.5   Longfellow's *Waif*] The volume was a gift-book containing poems selected by Longfellow chiefly from forgotten sources, that is, the "waifs" and "estrays" of literature. Poe's review originally appeared in two parts in the New York *Evening Mirror*, January 13 and 14, 1845. It was reprinted in the New York *Weekly Mirror*, January 25, 1845, along with a disclaimer by N. P. Willis (the editor of both the daily and weekly), a defense of Longfellow signed "H." (George S. Hillard), and Poe's reply to the defense, titled "Post-Notes by the Critic."

696.25   Horace Smith] English writer (1779–1849) of humorous prose and verse; author of *Zillah; a Tale of the Holy City* (1828), parodied by Poe in "A Tale of Jerusalem" (1832).

698.3–14   The day . . . Logic.] Poe repeats these lines in the "Marginalia," pp. 1368–69.

700.33–34   "Night's . . . walls."] See Poe's review of *Voices of the Night*, pp. 671–79.

701.32–702.4   Her . . . paradise.] By James Aldrich, from Rufus W. Griswold's *Poets and Poetry of America*.

702.13–14   *moral taint*]   A probable reference to an article, "The Poets of America," in the British *Foreign Quarterly Review,* 32 (January 1844), which claimed that American poets, with the exception of Longfellow, were mere imitators and plagiarists. Poe was named as an imitator of Tennyson, whom he had previously charged Longfellow with imitating (see pp. 675–79). James Russell Lowell wrote to Poe (June 27, 1844) that the article was written by John Forster, "a friend of some of the Longfellow clique here."

702.21–31   LONGFELLOW . . . fretted.]   This headnote is probably by N. P. Willis, editor of the *Mirror*.

703.20   Corporal Nym's]   Character in Shakespeare's *Henry V* and *The Merry Wives of Windsor*.

703.39   H.]   George S. Hillard, a friend of Longfellow's.

704.1   POST-NOTES]   Poe's reply to "H."

705.6   Imitation—Plagiarism]   On February 15, Charles Briggs, editor of the *Broadway Journal*, published an article "Thefts of American Authors," observing (erroneously) that Aldrich's poem had been published before Hood's. Although Briggs suggested that a more precise foundation was needed for charges of plagiarism, he also referred, with ambiguous intent, to a recent charge from the *Western Literary Messenger* of Buffalo, New York, that Longfellow had stolen a Scots ballad from William Motherwell's *Minstrelsy* (1827) and misrepresented it as a "translation" from the German. Poe's response in the New York *Evening Mirror* (February 17, 1845) was reprinted in the *Weekly Mirror* (February 22, 1845), and again copied in full in the selection here, "Imitation—Plagiarism." In the meantime, there appeared in the *Evening Mirror* of March 1, 1845, an article entitled "Plagiarism," signed by "Outis" ("Nobody"). Suggestions of the true identity of "Outis" include Charles Briggs, Cornelius Conway Felton (a member of Longfellow's Cambridge circle), and, most probably, Poe himself, seeking to incite controversy to increase the circulation of the *Broadway Journal*, where he had recently joined the editorial staff. (Poe later wrote such a third-person critique of himself as a critic, entitled "A Reviewer Reviewed, by Walter G. Bowen"; see pp. 1046–53.)

709.12   in full.]   The following is a complete and accurate reprint of the letter of "Outis."

721.25–26   *avec . . . patrie*]   "With the air of a Roman defending his country."

742.7–10   Gifford . . . Wilson]   William Gifford of the *Quarterly Review*; John Wilson ("Christopher North") of *Blackwood's*.

745.26–28   Longfellow . . . Tennyson.]   See the review of *Voices of the Night,* pp. 671–79.

749.25–26   Wolff . . . Motherwell]   Poe's charge of plagiarism here was suggested by Briggs' reference to the *Western Literary Messenger*, which pointed out the parallels between the ballad "Bonnie George Campbell" and Longfellow's translation from the German. Wolff's title (given in the footnote, p. 750) makes clear that the pieces are traditional folk songs *(Volkslieder)* from various nations, rendered into German meters. Longfellow wrote *Graham's Magazine* that his source was not Wolff's collection but rather Karl Gollmickh, *Der Sängersaal; Auswahl von Geschichten zum Kompieren* (1842), which gives Wolff's version of the Scots ballad as an original composition rather than a translation into German. Gollmickh's volume also includes an error whereby the Scottish river Tay becomes the German word *Tag* (day), as in Longfellow's re-translated version—a circumstance that Longfellow felt exonerated him from the charge of misrepresentation.

751.8   "The Spanish Student"]   Reviewed by Poe in "The American Drama," pp. 372–88.

757.32   Miss Walter]   Cornelia Wells Walter, an editor of the Boston *Evening Transcript*, reprinted from the Boston *Atlas* a mocking notice of Poe's lecture "The Poets and Poetry of America," delivered at the New-York Historical Society, February 28, 1845. The Boston papers accused Poe of denigrating Boston writers in preference to those from New York.

759.37–777.26   THE POETICAL . . . day.]   Though unsigned, this article is believed by many scholars to have been partially written by Poe.

797.18   Mr. Charles King]   Editor of the *New York American* (1819–45), later associate editor of the New York *Courier and Enquirer* (1845–48), subsequently president of Columbia University.

807.16   Professor Albert B. Dod]   Professor of mathematics at Princeton College.

816.8   ηχεηντες ιαμβοι]   "Echoing iambics." The satirist Archilochus was the first to write in iambic meter.

824.10–12   *"c'est . . . verumenimveros."*]   "It is an unfortunate situation from which one can extract oneself with circumlocutions, 'quemadmodums' and 'verumenimveros.' " (The two latter words are Latin terms meaning "in what manner" and "truly to be sure.")

833.33   *"mes déserts"*]   "My wilderness."

833.35–36   *"que . . . Francais."*]   "That the Minister of Public Instruction ought to know how to speak French himself."

867.16–18   *"Ce n'est . . . vulgaire."*]   "I have not rendered these remarks in French for the sake of affectation, but to keep them from the knowledge of the vulgar."

868.4–873.29   THE GREAT . . . termed.]   This anonymous review was almost certainly written by Poe.

918.10–11   "Powhatan" . . . wife.]   Seba Smith was the husband of Elizabeth Oakes Smith. "Jack Downing" was the name he used when he contributed letters to the *Portland Courier* of Portland, Maine, from 1830 to 1861.

923.36–924.2   "Observations . . . Aleppo."]   Early travelers to the Middle East, in part cited from Chateaubriand's *Itinéraire de Paris à Jerusalem*, translated 1813.

924.11–14   Niebuhr . . . Hogg]   Later authors of accounts of travel in the Middle East.

946.17   *Ilium fuit.*]   "It was Troy."

987.8–9   *"un homme de rien"*]   "An insignificant man."

987.10   *un homme de beaucoup*]   "A considerable man."

988.37–38   Moi . . . cours.]   "I who, always fleeing the cities and the courts, / In barely fifteen years saw the course finished."

989.16–17   *Le gouvernement provisoire*]   "The provisional government."

990.13   *"Monsieur* . . . ici!"]   "Sir, ladies do not enter there!"

992.13   *mens divinior*]   "Prophetic or divine reason."

992.14   *otium cum dignitate*]   "Peace (or retirement) with honor."

1003.26   Mr. Miller]   William Miller (1782–1849), leader of the Adventist movement (the "Millerites"), believed the second coming of Christ would occur between March 1843 and March 1844.

1004.18   ηχεηντες ιαμβοι]   See note 816.8.

1009.19   *de omnibus . . . aliis*]   "Concerning all things and certain other things."

1009.33   *"Belier . . . commencement."*]   "Belier, my friend, begin at the beginning."

1013.13   *Non . . . ora.*]   "Zamora is not won in an hour."

1013.19   *"de . . . bleu"*]   "Of that which is signified by the colors white and blue." *Gargantua and Pantagruel,* Book I, ix and x.

1013.25   *nil . . . ornavit.*]   See note 296.13–14.

MAGAZINES AND CRITICISM

1019.25   Mr. White's]   T. H. White, owner of the *Southern Literary Messenger*.

1031.37   Orphicism, or Dialism,]   References to Bronson Alcott's "Orphic Sayings," and to *The Dial*, the magazine of the New England Transcendentalists.

1036.13 Fosters . . . Scotts] Theodore Foster and Leonard Scott, New York publishers who reprinted British magazines.

1037.25 *morus multicaulis*] A mulberry tree used in silkworm culture.

1041.12 *"n'est . . . croit."*] "Not as wise as he believes."

1046.1 *A Reviewer Reviewed*] The unfinished manuscript in Poe's hand-writing was found in his trunk after his death.

1046.6 Sterne . . . France."] Actually from *Tristram Shandy*, but Poe took the epigraph as quoted from *Stanley* (1838) by Horace Binney Wallace (pseud. "William Landor"); see "Marginalia," pp. 1378 and 1442.

1047.15–18 "The Murder . . . praises] Pirated adaptations of "The Murders in the Rue Morgue" by two rival French journalists led to a lawsuit between them in 1846 that helped bring Poe to the attention of the French public. His "The Gold-Bug" was widely pirated; Tupper's review, titled "American Romance," appeared in the London *Literary Gazette*, January 31, 1846.

1047.28–29 Miss Barrett . . . himself] Elizabeth Barrett wrote to Poe complimenting him on "The Raven"; Nathaniel Parker Willis praised the poem in the New York *Evening Mirror* of January 29, 1845; Poe's own "review" of the poem is in "The Philosophy of Composition."

1048.27 Mr P. . . . "Literati"] See pp. 1214–22.

1051.22–28 The author . . . *Hell.*] Also by Thomas Moore, from "The Fire-Worshippers" in *Lalla Rookh*. The lines are slightly misquoted; in Moore they read: "Just Prophet, let the damn'd one dwell / Full in sight of Paradise, / Beholding heav'n and feeling hell!"

1052.15–16 Ἠὼς . . . αἶαν] "Dawn yellow-robed spread over all the earth." *Iliad*, Book VIII, line 1. (Translation from Mabbott.)

THE LITERARY AND SOCIAL SCENE

1061.10–12 *"Tam . . . membranas."*] "So many, such great, and such costly volumes; burn all this parchment."

1065.2 lecture] Delivered at the New-York Historical Society, February 28, 1845.

1067.1 *Editorial Miscellanies*] Beginning with its first issue of January 4, 1845, the *Broadway Journal* printed a column or columns headed "Editorial Miscellany," containing short notices on "The Fine Arts," "City Chit-Chat," "Notices of New Books," etc.

1077.13 Old . . . Mountain] German mythic figure, subject of a work by Ludwig Tieck.

1078.4   *Quamdiu Catalina?*]   "How long, Cataline?"

1078.21   *"de minimis non curat lex."*]   "The law does not care about trifles."

1078.32   *Auspice Teucro*]   "Under the protection of this leader"; from Horace.

1078.34–35   *vos plaudite*]   "Applause."

1080.8   Littleton Barry]   Pseudonym used by Poe.

1081.16   brevier . . . bourgeois]   Type font sizes. The brevier is eight
points and smaller than the bourgeois.

1085.11–24   Mr. Poe . . . Noah]   The reading, on October 16, 1845, was
arranged by James Russell Lowell. Poe read "Al Aaraaf" and "The Raven,"
for which he was criticized by some of the Boston editors and reviewers,
especially by Cornelia Wells Walter in the *Evening Transcript*. In an article
titled "A Failure" (October 17, 1845), she concluded by saying that if the word
"failure" for Poe's performance were too "severe," it could be called a "suspension" of interest until the next lecture by Henry N. Hudson. (Hudson
later admitted being involved in the Walter articles against Poe.) The following day Walter "exposed" Poe's private defense of himself as having "hoaxed"
the Boston audience with a poem written before he was ten or twelve years
of age; she queried the advisability of reading a boy's poem before an audience of adults. Poe's reading was defended on October 18 by the Boston *Daily
Courier* and on October 26 by Major Mordecai M. Noah in the *Sunday Times
and Messenger*, quoted here by Poe.

1087.36–37   *Et . . . irae.*]   "And hence their wrath."

1096.15   our friend of "The Patriot"]   William Gilmore Simms.

1096.34   "Down-East Review."]   The *North American Review*.

1097.10–11   *Timeo . . . ferentes*]   "I fear the Greeks even when they bring
gifts." Virgil, *Aeneid,* II, 49.

1103.5   τυραννος—not βασιλευς]   "King by force (tyrannos), not king by
right (basileus)."

1121.30–32   *"que . . . nient."*]   See note 10.30–32.

1140.1   as Pauline]   In Bulwer's play *The Lady of Lyons*.

1176.29   Bolles']   William Bolles, *An Explanatory and Phonographic Pronouncing Dictionary* (1845).

1208.29–30   Sharp . . . Beauchampe]   These events took place in Frank-
fort, Kentucky, in 1825; Beauchampe stabbed Sharp to avenge the latter's
seduction and desertion of Anne Crowe, who subsequently married Beauchampe. Crowe committed suicide and Beauchampe was hanged. Poe makes
use of the story in his unfinished verse drama, "Politian."

1210.23   King . . . Second]   Referring to Aesop's fable of the frogs and
their King Log.

1217.38   Blunt's Lunar Chart]   Edmund March Blunt and George William
Blunt (father and son) were American hydrographers who published sea
charts and astronomical almanacs.

1218.16–17   Peter . . . islanders.]   *Peter Wilkins; or the Flying Islanders*
(1827), popular two-act stage play, by Robert Paltock (1697–1767).

1219.21   Brewster]   Sir David Brewster, physicist, also wrote *Letters on
Natural Magic.*

1222.19–20   author . . . Understanding."]   John Locke.

ARTICLES AND MARGINALIA

1255.1   Vaucanson]   French mechanical engineer (1709–82) famous for his
automatons, "The Flute Player" and "The Duck."

1297.9–10   *"de . . . bleu."*]   See note 1013.19.

1297.19–20   *"Mon . . . lire!"*]   "My cousin, here is a good chance to learn
how to read."

1297.36   Fadladeen]   The great Nazir of Aurungzebë's harem in Thomas
Moore's *Lalla Rookh.*

1298.13   *pavoneggiarsi*]   "Strut like a peacock."

1298.19–20   *"Defuncti . . . afficiantur"*]   "Expiated crimes are not to be
taken into account."

1298.35–36   *"poeta . . . fit."*]   "A poet is born, not made."

1300.40   το χαλον]   τὸ καλόν: "Beauty."

1301.37   "Great . . . allied."]   Dryden: "Great Wits are sure to Madness
near alli'd." *Absalom and Achitophel,* I, 163.

1302.38   "And Beauty . . . hair."]   Pope, *The Rape of the Lock*, II, 28.

1303.7–8   *panem . . . circenses*]   "Bread and circuses."

1303.19   *lex Talionis*]   Law of retaliation, as "an eye for an eye."

1305.30   "Le plus . . . satisfait,"]   "The most crazy are always the most
satisfied." "Ignorance is bliss" is from Thomas Gray's "Ode on a Distant
Prospect of Eton College."

1309.18–20   *"Ce . . . l'oublie;"*]   "That which I put on paper . . . I remove from my memory, and consequently I forget it."

1311.31   *Velschii Ruzname Naurus,"*]   *Commentarius in Ruzname naurus,
sive Tabulae aequinoctiales novi Persarum & Turcarum anni* (Bavaria, 1676) by

Georg Hieronymus Welsch, latinized as Georgius Hieronymus Velschius. The volume is a Persian equinoctial calendar (Ruzname naurus: calendar of "new days" or equinoxes) with Latin commentary.

1312.16   face . . . him] Horace Smith, author of *Gaities and Gravities: A Series of Essays, Comic Tales, and Fugitive Vagaries.*

1312.17   προσωπον κατα προσωπον] "Face to face."

1313.9   *Soyez . . . Dieu,*] "Be just, mortals, and fear only one God."

1313.11   Dicite . . . *Divos.*] "Be warned: do justice and do not despise the gods." Virgil, *Aeneid,* VI, 620.

1318.5   *"ingeniosus . . . nebulo,"*] "A clever child, but a notable fool." "Nebulo" is from the Greek Νεφελοκοκκυγιεύς; literally, a citizen of "Cloud-Cuckoo-Land" in Aristophanes' *The Birds.*

1318.13–14   *"Pour . . . même."*] "In order to know what God is, it is necessary to be God himself."

1323.34–36   *Mais . . . etc.*] "But myself, who at bottom well knows what I believe in, / Who counts their larcenies on my fingers every day, / I laugh—etc."

1324.8   Cacuses] Plural of Cacus, a famous robber, son of Vulcan and Medusa.

1328.8   μετα φυσικα] "Metaphysics."

1328.12   Μετα τα φυσικα] "After the physics."

1331.14   ποιησις] "A poem," literally a making.

1332.27   *congé d'élire*] "Authorization of election."

1337.10–11   "Ingenu*os* . . . feros."] "To faithfully distribute books among the people refines the manners and does not leave them wild."

1337.22–23   *"de animæ transvectione"*] "Of the soul's journey."

1338.10–11   *"Impune . . . regem."*] "To do what one wants with impunity is to be king."

1339.22–25   "Ast . . . amicæ."] "But the lover leaves weeping the bed of / His beloved, and speaks harsh words to you, / Plucked from his mistress's embrace, tender / And desired." Marcantonia Flaminio (1498–1550), *Hymnus in Auroram.* (Translation by Anthony Kemp.)

1343.8   *in mediis rebus*] "In the midst of things."

1343.28–29   *Non . . . circunscriva.*] "The greatest artist has no idea / Not inherent in the marble itself." Sonnet XV.

1345.29–31   *"tam . . . membranas."*] See note 1061.10–12.

1346.30   'Amare . . . conceditur,'] "God seldom allows one to love and to be wise."

1347.4   *Id . . . omnes.*] "It is a common evil; we will all be mad at one time."

1347.17–18   *En vain . . . Rodrique.*] "Against 'Le Cid' in vain a minister strives; / [Since] all of Paris sees Chimēne through Rodrigue's eyes."

1354.40   *ignoratio elenchi*] A logical fallacy which consists in apparently refuting an opponent while actually disproving some statement different from that advanced by him; a shifting of the argument to irrelevant grounds.

1357.8–9   *"Adam . . . inventor."*] "Adam, divinely instructed, first in learning and the inventor of letters."

1364.4–5   *industriâ . . . industriâ.*] "Marvelous industry" or "incredible diligence."

1367.3   Gutsmuth] Guts Muth. "Gutsmuth and Company" was a trademark.

1367.5–6   Peutingerian Tables] The *Tabula Peutingeriana*, road map of the Roman Empire.

1370.7–10   *"L'homme . . . L'Andromache."*] "The man who would know of what I died, let him ask not if it were of fever or gout or some other thing, but let him understand that it was of the Andromache."

1370.27–31   "Giace . . . sdegni."] "Great Carthage lies; the shore preserves, / Faintly, traces of the great ruin. / Fallen cities, fallen kingdoms: / Pride and pomp concealed in grass and sand. / And man, being mortal, also dies." *Gerusalemme Liberata*, XV, 20. (Translation by Anthony Kemp.) Poe was probably influenced by Edward Fairfax's translation of 1600, which gives the passage more resemblance to Sulpicious: "Great Carthage low in ashes cold doth lie, / Her ruins poor the herbs in height scant pass; / So cities fall, so perish kingdoms high, / Their pride and pomp lie hid in sand and grass: / Then why should mortal man repine to die, . . .?"

1371.3–4   *"Iam . . . ruinæ."*] "Now the whole citadel is covered in thorns, still bearing ruins."

1371.6–8   *"Hem! . . . jaceant."*] "Well, we little men are indignant if one is taken from among us, whose life ought to be shorter, while at the same time the ruins of whole towns lie thrown away." Servius Sulpicious Lemonia Rufus in Cicero, *Ad Familiares*, IV, 4.

1373.8–9   "En vain . . . Rodrigue."] See note 1347.17–18.

1373.14–15   "——terras . . . exitio."] "One day will bring the earth's destruction."

1373.17–18   "Carmine . . . dies."] "They are to be lost, the sublime poems of Lucretius, just as one day the world will be destroyed."

1378.21–23   "As we . . . us!"] See note 1046.6.

1379.7–9   "Nec . . . imitari."] "It did not even seem disgraceful to him (Demosthenes), abandoning the best masters, to devote himself to the dogs, and from them to seek the meaning and nature of letters, and to imitate their manner in making noise, on the ground that this was sufficient."

1385.9–10   "Mortuus . . . est."] "The son of God is dead, which is believable though absurd; and risen from the dead, which is certain though impossible."

1385.12–13   "l'art . . . fiction."] "The art of expressing thoughts by fiction."

1385.25   Hague's] Mr. Hague was a Philadelphia con artist.

1390.34   non . . . medii] "Undistributed middle."

1391.8–10   "que . . . nient."] See note 10.30–32.

1394.27   hortus siccus] "Dry garden."

1397.28   Brobdignagian] Allusion to the land of giants in the second voyage of Swift's Gulliver's Travels.

1398.23–24   "The Hunchback" . . . Cyrus,"] The Hunchback by Sheridan Knowles; Ferrex and Porrex, a sixteenth-century play now better known as Gorboduc, by Thomas Sackville, Earl of Dorset, and Thomas Norton; and Le grand Cyrus (1649–53) by Madeleine de Scúdery.

1402.36   αστρολογος] See note 49.24.

1421.17   Flies . . . main,] From Pope's "Essay on Criticism."

1422.34–37   All . . . moon.] From The Rime of the Ancient Mariner.

1424.16–18   Pour . . . même] See note 1318.13–14.

1434.1   Marginalia] The initial installment of the "Marginalia" in the Southern Literary Messenger reprinted the introductory essay from the Democratic Review of November 1844 (pages 1309.3–1311.30 of this volume). It is omitted here.

1457.11–12   "A little . . . thing:"] From Alexander Pope, "Essay on Criticism."

1458.30   Teos] Home of Anacreon; his friend's name is usually spelled Bathyllus.

1459.4–6   "Mortuus . . . impossible."] See note 1385.9–10.

1459.9–12   Si . . . humain.] "If tomorrow, forgetting the light, / One loses the day, ah well! tomorrow / Some fool will find again / A torch for the human species."

1460.21–23   "Il y . . . nombre."] "There is a contract that every public idea—every received convention—is a foolish one, since it conforms to the greatest number."

1460.24–25   "Si . . . attestatur."] "If you desire to advance, first hold that to be true which the sound reason of all men attests."—Augustine

1461.3   Carathis] A sorceress and mother of Vathek in William Beckford's *Vathek*.

1461.30–1462.1   "aliquando . . . aliquando"] "Sometimes iron, at other times gold."

1463.3–4   ἀθανάτοισι . . . ὅίμοιαι] "Of the same form and nature as the immortal gods." Athenaeus, *Deipnosophistae*, VII, 303. ὅίμοιαι is apparently a misprint for ὅμοιαι.

1463.8–10   "si . . . desideranda."] "If it is not here, it is not greatly desired."

1463.24   "Ubi *tres,* ecclesia,"] "Where there are three, there is a church"; Poe's pun translates this to "Where there is a church, there are trees."

1463.28   melius . . . in aliud] "Better" and "otherwise."

1464.9–10   "Nec . . . conferre,"] See note 1379.7–9.

1466.3   Trinculo] The jester in *The Tempest*.

1466.13   vox . . . nihil] "Voice and nothing else."

1466.20–22   d'ou . . . verumenimveros] See note 824.10–12.

1467.5–6   "que . . . Français."] See note 833.35–36.

1468.1   chorus of turkeys] See note 10.26–28.

1468.7–8   "Quel . . . es!"] "What a turkey you are!"

CATALOGING INFORMATION

Poe, Edgar Allan, 1809–1849.
  Essays and Reviews.

  (The Library of America, 20)
  "G. R. Thompson wrote the notes and selected the texts for
this volume"—Prelim. p. v.
  Includes bibliographical references and index.
  Contents: Theory of poetry—Reviews of British and Continen-
tal authors—Reviews of American authors and American litera-
ture—Magazines and criticism—The literary and social scene—
Articles and marginalia.
  I. Thompson, Gary Richard, 1937– . II. Title. III. Series.
PS2619.A1   1984   809   83–19923
ISBN 0–940450–19–4

Index

THE LIBRARY OF AMERICA SERIES

This book is set in 10 point Linotron Galliard,
a face designed for photocomposition by Matthew Carter
and based on the sixteenth-century face Granjon. The paper
is acid-free Ecusta Nyalite and meets the requirements for perma-
nence of the American National Standards Institute. The binding
material is Brillianta, a 100% woven rayon cloth made by
Van Heek-Scholco Textielfabrieken, Holland. The com-
position is by Haddon Craftsmen, Inc., and The
Clarinda Company. Printing and binding
by R. R. Donnelley & Sons Company.
Designed by Bruce Campbell.